Hands-On Unity 2021 Game Development

Second Edition

Create, customize, and optimize your own
professional games from scratch with Unity 2021

Nicolas Alejandro Borromeo

BIRMINGHAM—MUMBAI

Hands-On Unity 2021 Game Development
Second Edition

Associate Group Product Manager: Rohit Rajkumar

Associate Publishing Product Manager: Ashitosh Gupta

Senior Editor: Hayden Edwards

Content Development Editor: Aamir Ahmed

Technical Editor: Saurabh Kadave

Copy Editor: Safis Editing

Project Coordinator: Ajesh Devavaram

Proofreader: Safis Editing

Indexer: Pratik Shirodkar

Production Designer: Shankar Kalbhor

First published: July 2020

Second edition: August 2021

Production reference: 1190821

Published by Packt Publishing Ltd.

Livery Place

35 Livery Street

Birmingham

B3 2PB, UK.

ISBN 978-1-80107-148-2

www.packt.com

To Dad, who spoiled me with computers to keep learning. I miss you.
Also, to my wife, for reminding me of what I am capable of.

– Nicolas Alejandro Borromeo

Contributors

About the author

Nicolas Alejandro Borromeo works as a senior Unity developer at Product Madness, London. He was a game development career coordinator at **Universidad Argentina de la Empresa (UADE)** and has taught game development at many other Argentine universities, such as UTN, UAI, and USAL, and institutions such as Image Campus and DaVinci, since 2012. Nicolas has been a Unity Certified Instructor since 2019, teaching high-profile Unity clients all around the globe. He was an MMO client-side developer at Band of Coders in Argentina and has been a Unity freelance developer since 2012.

About the reviewers

Levent Alpsal is a senior software and game developer. In 2008, he started working on web-based projects, developing for the backend using PHP and SQL.

He started his focus on Unity and C# in 2015, working on many exciting simulation projects using Unity, VR, motion platforms, and other technologies at Sanlab Simulation. He has also developed many indie games and attended global game jams.

In 2020, he started his own company in the UK, Reenim Software LTD, providing software and Unity development services globally.

Levent likes to develop creative DIY solutions to daily real-life problems using 3D printing, thermoplastics, and K'Nex. He is the proud designer of a remote-controlled model tank. Currently, he lives in London with his lovely wife and wonderful son.

Sungkuk Park is a Berlin-based game developer. He majored in art studies at Hongik University in Seoul, Korea, but later became a software engineer in the gaming industry. He is interested in almost everything about gaming. He is now on his way to becoming a technical artist!

Here is a list of his publications:

- Authored *Seamless Society*, 21 July 2020, in collaboration with an online exhibition platform DDDD
- Authored *Wallpeckers: Breaking down the barriers between media*, an article for the Korean art magazine *Misulsegye*, in March 2019
- Authored *The Possibility of the Impossibility of the "Art Games"*, an article for the Korean art magazine *Misulsegye*, in February 2017
- Translated and edited *Game Level Generation Using Neural Networks*, a featured post of Gamasutra

Table of Contents

Section 2 – Improving Graphics and Sound

6

Materials and Effects with URP and Shader Graph

7

Visual Effects with Particle Systems and Visual Effect Graph

8

Lighting Using the Universal Render Pipeline

9

Fullscreen Effects with Postprocessing

10

Sound and Music Integration

11

User Interface Design

12

Creating a UI with the UI Toolkit

13

Creating Animations with Animator, Cinemachine, and Timeline

Section 3 – Scripting Level Interactivity with C#

14

Introduction to C# and Visual Scripting

15

Implementing Movement and Spawning

16

Physics Collisions and Health System

17

Win and Lose Condition

18

Scripting the UI, Sounds, and Graphics

19

Implementing Game AI for Building Enemies

20

Scene Performance Optimization

Section 4 – Releasing Your Game

21

Building the Project

22
Finishing Touches

23
Augmented Reality in Unity

Other Books You May Enjoy

Index

Preface

I still remember that moment of my life when I was afraid of telling my parents that I was going to study Game Development. At that time, in my region, that was considered a childish desire by most parents, and a career with no future, but I was stubborn enough not to care and to follow my dream. Today, Game Development is one of the biggest industries, generating more revenue than Film.

Of course, following my dream was more difficult than I thought. Anyone with the same dream as me sooner or later faces the fact that developing games is a difficult task that requires a deep level of knowledge in different areas. Sadly, most people give up due to this difficulty level, but I strongly believe that with the proper guidance and tools, you can make your career path easier. In my case, what helped me to flatten the learning curve was learning to use Unity.

Welcome to this book about Unity 2021. Here, you will learn how to use the most recent Unity features to create your first videogame in the simplest way possible nowadays. Unity is a tool that provides you with powerful but simple-to-use features to solve the most common problems in Game Development, such as Rendering, Animation, Physics, Sound, and Effects. We will be using all these features to create a simple but complete game, learning all the nuances needed to handle Unity.

If you have read the 2020 edition of this book, you will find that not only have the contents been updated to the latest Unity and Packages versions, but also new content has been introduced in 2021, such as coverage of UI Toolkit and Visual Scripting.

By the end of this book, you will be able to use Unity in a way that will allow you to start studying in depth the areas of Game Development that you are interested in to build your career or simply create hobby games just for the joy of doing it. Unity is a versatile tool that can be used in both Professional and Amateur projects, and is being used every day by more and more people. It is worth mentioning that Unity can be used not only for creating games but for any kind of interactive apps, from simple mobile apps to complex training or educative applications (known as Serious Gaming), using the latest technologies such as Augmented or Virtual Reality. So, even if we are creating a game here, you are starting a learning path that can end in lots of possible specializations.

Who this book is for

People with different backgrounds can take advantage of the whole book or parts of it thanks to the way it is structured. If you have basic OOP programming knowledge but have never created a game before, or have never created one in Unity, you will find the book a nice introduction to Game Development and Unity basic to advanced concepts. You can also find most parts of this book useful even if you are a seasoned Unity Developer who wants to learn how to use its latest features.

On the other side, if you don't have any programming knowledge, you can also take advantage of the book, as most of the chapters don't require programming experience to learn from them. Those chapters will give you a robust skillset to start learning coding in Unity, making the process easier than before reading them, and once you learn the basics of coding, you can take advantage of the scripting chapters of this book. Also, with the introduction of Visual Scripting, you will have an alternative language if you are more comfortable with node-based scripting.

What this book covers

Chapter 1, Designing a Game from Scratch, discusses the details of the game we are going to create in the book before even opening Unity for the first time, outlining the Unity features to use.

Chapter 2, Setting Up Unity, teaches you how to install and set up Unity on your computer, and also how to create your first project.

Chapter 3, Working with Scenes and Game Objects, teaches you the concepts of Scenes and GameObjects, the Unity way to describe what your game world is composed of.

Chapter 4, Grayboxing with Terrain and ProBuilder, is where we will be creating our first level layout, prototyping it with the Terrain and ProBuilder Unity features.

Chapter 5, Importing and Integrating Assets, teaches you how to improve your scene art by importing graphics into Unity, as Unity is not a tool for creating graphics but for displaying them.

Chapter 6, Materials and Effects with URP and Shader Graph, shows how to use one of the latest Unity Render Systems (Universal Render Pipeline) and how to create effects with the Shader Graph feature.

Chapter 7, Visual Effects with Particle Systems and Visual Effect Graph, teaches you how to create visual effects such as water and fire using the two main Unity tools for doing so, Particle Systems and VFX Graph.

Chapter 8, Lighting Using the Univeral Render Pipeline, looks at lighting, which is a concept big enough to have its own chapter. Here, we will deepen our knowledge of the Universal Render Pipeline, specifically its lighting capabilities.

Chapter 9, Fullscreen Effects with Postprocessing, teaches you how to add a layer of effects on top of your scene graphics using the Postprocessing feature of the Universal Render Pipeline to get that film effect most modern games have today.

Chapter 10, Sound and Music Integration, covers a topic that is underestimated by most beginner developers; here we will learn how to properly add sound and music to our game, taking into consideration its impact on performance.

Chapter 11, User Interface Design, looks at the **User Interface** (**UI**). Of all the graphical ways to communicate information to the user, the UI is the most direct one. We will learn how to display information in the form of text, images, and life bars using the Unity UI system.

Chapter 12, Creating a UI with the UI Toolkit, looks at UI Tookit, which, since Unity 2021, is a soon-to-be successor of Canvas, the UI system we learned about in *Chapter 11, User Interface Design*. We will explore it to get ahead and be prepared for Unity's use of this HTML-based toolkit in the future.

Chapter 13, Creating Animations with Animator, Cinemachine, and Timeline, takes us further than the static scene we have created so far. In this chapter, we will start moving our characters and creating cutscenes with the latest Unity features to do so.

Chapter 14, Introduction to C# and Visual Scripting, is the first programming chapter of the book. We will learn how to create our first script using C# in the Unity way, and then we will explore how to do the same with Visual Scripting, the new node-based coding language of Unity. The rest of the programming chapters will show how to code the game in both languages.

Chapter 15, Implementing Movement and Spawning, teaches you how to program the movement of your objects and how to spawn them. General programming knowledge is assumed from now on.

Chapter 16, Physics Collisions and Health System, teaches you how to configure the Physics settings of objects to detect when two of them collide and react to the collision, creating a Health System, in this case.

Chapter 17, Win and Lose Condition, covers how to detect when the game should end, both when the player wins and loses.

Chapter 18, Scripting the UI, Sounds, and Graphics, covers how to make the UI show the current information of the game, such as the Player's Health and Score. Also, sounds will be played when necessary, and visual effects will reflect the actions of the Player.

Chapter 19, Implementing Game AI for Building Enemies, covers creating a basic AI using several Unity features for creating challenging enemies in our game.

Chapter 20, Scene Performance Optimization, discusses how making our game perform well is no easy task, but is certainly needed to release it. Here, we will be learning how to profile our game's performance and tackle the most common performance issues.

Chapter 21, Building the Project, teaches you how to convert your Unity project into an executable format to distribute it to other people and run it without Unity installed.

Chapter 22, Finishing Touches, briefly discusses how to move forward with the development of our game after finishing this book, discussing topics such as how to iterate and release the game.

Chapter 23, Augmented Reality in Unity, teaches you how to create an AR application with Unity's AR Foundation package, one of the most recent ways to create AR applications with Unity.

To get the most out of this book

You will be developing a full project through the chapters of this book, and while you can just read the chapters, I highly recommend you practice all the steps in this project as you advance through the book, to get the experience needed to properly learn the concepts demonstrated here. The chapters are designed so you can customize the game and not create the exact game shown in the book. However, consider not deviating too much from the main idea.

The project files are split into a folder per chapter and are designed in a cumulative way, each folder having just the new files introduced by the chapter or the changed ones. This means, for example, that if a file hasn't change since *Chapter 1*, you won't find it in *Chapter 2* onward; those chapters will just use the file introduced in *Chapter 1*. This allows you to see just what we changed in each chapter, easily identifying the needed changes, and if for some reason you can't finish, for example, *Chapter 3*, you can just continue with *Chapter 4*'s steps on top of *Chapter 3*. Also note that *Chapters 15* to *19* will have two versions of the files, the C# ones and the Visual Scripting ones.

Software/Hardware covered in the book	OS requirements
Unity 2021.1	Windows, macOS X, or Linux (any)
Visual Studio 2019 Community	Windows or macOS X (any)
Xcode 12	macOS X

While we will see how to use XCode 12, is not required for most of the chapters. Also, there are alternatives to Visual Studio in Linux, like Visual Studio Code.

If you are using the digital version of this book, we advise you to type the code yourself or access the code via the GitHub repository (link available in the next section). Doing so will help you avoid any potential errors related to the copying and pasting of code.

Download the example code files

You can download the example code files for this book from GitHub at `https://github.com/PacktPublishing/-Hands-On-Unity-2021-Game-Development-Second-Edition`. If there's an update to the code, it will be updated in the GitHub repository.

We also have other code bundles from our rich catalog of books and videos available at `https://github.com/PacktPublishing/`. Check them out!

Download the color images

We also provide a PDF file that has color images of the screenshots and diagrams used in this book. You can download it here: `https://static.packt-cdn.com/downloads/9781801071482_ColorImages.pdf`.

Conventions used

There are a number of text conventions used throughout this book.

`Code in text`: Indicates code words in text, database table names, folder names, filenames, file extensions, pathnames, dummy URLs, user input, and Twitter handles. Here is an example: "Set its shader to `Universal Render Pipeline/Particles/Unlit`."

Bold: Indicates a new term, an important word, or words that you see onscreen. For example, words in menus or dialog boxes appear in the text like this. Here is an example: "Create a new empty GameObject (**GameObject | Create Empty**)."

> **Tips or important notes**
> Appear like this.

Get in touch

Feedback from our readers is always welcome.

General feedback: If you have questions about any aspect of this book, email us at customercare@packtpub.com and mention the book title in the subject of your message.

Errata: Although we have taken every care to ensure the accuracy of our content, mistakes do happen. If you have found a mistake in this book, we would be grateful if you would report this to us. Please visit www.packtpub.com/support/errata and fill in the form.

Piracy: If you come across any illegal copies of our works in any form on the internet, we would be grateful if you would provide us with the location address or website name. Please contact us at copyright@packt.com with a link to the material.

If you are interested in becoming an author: If there is a topic that you have expertise in and you are interested in either writing or contributing to a book, please visit authors.packtpub.com.

Section 1 – Our First Level

In this section, you will learn about the fundamental concepts of Unity, such as scene creation and asset management, to create your first playable prototype game level.

This section comprises the following chapters:

- *Chapter 1, Designing a Game from Scratch*
- *Chapter 2, Setting Up Unity*
- *Chapter 3, Working with Scenes and Game Objects*
- *Chapter 4, Grayboxing with Terrain and ProBuilder*
- *Chapter 5, Importing and Integrating Assets*

1

Designing a Game from Scratch

Welcome to the first chapter of the book! I am sure you are as super excited as I am to start this amazing journey into game development with Unity. We will be approaching game development in four parts. First, we will be talking about the basics of game development, looking at topics such as how to design your game before you start coding, and then we will prototype a simple first level using Unity. Then, we will dive into graphics to explore the look and feel of a good game. Later, we will learn how to get everything moving through the use of scripting. Finally, we will see how you can finish and publish your game. As you go through the chapters, you will apply every concept to a full game project, so you will end the book with a fully functional shooter game.

In this chapter, we will design our game, Super Shooter. This phase is known as pre-production, where we will create a development plan. Our game design will include all the functionality we want in our game: the player character, the non-player characters, game assets, animations, and more. We will also use screen mock-ups to document our game's design. We will look at related concepts regarding the use of Unity for our game along the way. We will be discussing which pieces of documentation are necessary for all design work we will be doing throughout this chapter.

Specifically, we will examine the following concepts in this chapter:

- Game concept
- Game characters
- Gameplay
- The difficulty balance
- Documentation

Game concept

Why not just start developing our game instead of designing it? This question is spawned from the excitement of developing games, especially with the Unity game engine. All games start with an idea. That idea is translated into a design, and that design is the basis for development and, eventually, the final game.

A game's design is like a blueprint for a house. You would not consider building a house without a blueprint, and it is an equally bad idea to develop a game without designing it first. The reason for this is to save time and frustration. For larger projects, time wasted also means unnecessary funds are expended.

Imagine that you employed a project team of 12 developers, animators, and artists. If you shared your game idea, would they have enough information to go on? Would they create a great game, but not the game you had in mind? All we are doing with our game design is documenting as much as we can in the beginning so that the development process is purposeful. Without question, you will continually modify your game's design during development, so having a strong base from which to start is critical to your success.

Our game design will serve as the foundation for the look of our game, what the player's objectives are, what the gameplay will be, supporting user actions, animations, audio, **Artificial Intelligence** (**AI**), and victory conditions. That is a lot to think about and underscores the importance of translating the game idea into the game design.

Throughout the book, we will be covering a range of components. However, in this section, we will cover those that appear in the following list:

- Game idea
- Input controls
- Winning and losing

So, let's look at each component in more detail.

Game idea

The basic concept of our Super Shooter game is that it will be a 3D game featuring a Futuristic Hero Soldier as the player character. The character must fight against Enemy Soldiers, who are intent on destroying our Hero's base and anyone that gets in their way, including our Hero.

Here is an image of what our game will look like:

Figure 1.1 – Our hero shooting bullets at enemies

Now that we have a general idea of what the game is going to be, let's talk about how the player will control the character.

Input controls

It is important to consider how players will interact with our game. Players have an expectation that the industry norms for user controls will be implemented in games, which is why, for our example, the player will control our Hero using the standard set of controls.

Our default set of user input controls, as shown in the following figure, will consist of the keyboard and mouse:

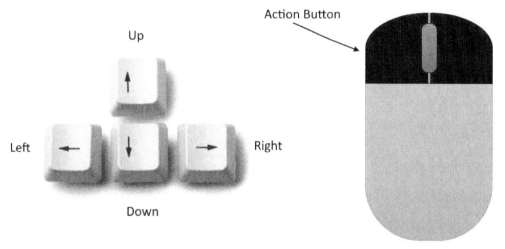

Figure 1.2 – Controls scheme

We will configure and program our game so that user input from the keyboard matches the key and action pairings shown in the following table:

Keyboard input	Action
Up arrow	Move forward
Down arrow	Move back
Left arrow	Move left
Right arrow	Move right
W	Move forward
S	Move back
A	Move left
D	Move right

Figure 1.3 – Key mapping

The mouse will also be a significant source of user input. We will implement two components using the mouse, as indicated in the following table:

Mouse input	Action
Mouse movement	Rotate character
Left mouse button	Shoot bullet

Figure 1.4 – Mouse mapping

The left mouse button will be our action button to shoot bullets, while the horizontal mouse motion will allow us to rotate our character and face the enemies. As all enemies and the player are going to be moving across a flat surface, it is not necessary to move the camera up and down.

That's how we handle input, but we also need to end the game session at some point! Let's talk about how the player will win and lose.

Winning and losing

Our winning condition will be when all the Enemy waves have been eliminated.

There will be two different ways the player can lose the game:

- The first losing condition is when the base life becomes **0**.
- The second losing condition is if the Hero's life becomes **0**.

From this short description, you can tell that there will be several things to keep track of, including the following:

- The number of remaining Waves
- The health of the Player's Base
- The health of our Hero

Now that we have defined what is called the game's **core loop** (start a level, play it, win/lose it, repeat), let's dive deeper into the specific details, starting with our characters.

Game characters

Our game will feature several objects, but only two game characters. The first game character is our Hero and will be controlled by the player. The second type of game character is the Enemies. They are non-player characters that are controlled by AI. Let's look more closely at both of these characters.

Hero

The player will play our game as the Hero, our game's protagonist. So, what can our Hero player character do? We already know we will be able to move them throughout our game environment using a combination of keyboard and mouse inputs. We also know that the left mouse button—our action button—will cause them to shoot bullets.

> **Important note**
> Because the Hero is controlled by a human player, it is referred to as the Player Character.

We will implement the following animations for the Hero:

- **Idle**: This animation will play when the character is not being moved by the player.

- **Run**: This animation will play when the character is being moved by the player.

- **Shoot**: This is an animation that will cause the Hero to shoot a bullet.

That's our player. Now, let's discuss our enemy character.

Enemies

Our game's antagonists will be Enemy Soldiers. We will control how many of them we want in our game and where they are placed. We will also control their behavior through AI. The Enemies will go straight to the base and, once there, they will start damaging it. We will determine how long it takes for our base to be completely destroyed. If during their journey to the base, the enemy encounters the player, they will prioritize shooting at them.

> **Important note:**
> Because the Enemy is controlled by AI and not a human player, it is referred to as a **Non-Player Character** (NPC).

The soldiers will share the following two animations, which the Player Character also uses, but they will be executed in different scenarios:

- **Run**: This animation will play when the Enemy's AI is moving the enemy toward the base.

- **Shoot**: This is an animation that will be played when the AI decides to shoot at the Player's Base or the Player's Character.

Careful planning and scripting will be required to create the desired Enemy behaviors; this will include decisions regarding the number and placement of the Enemies, and we will be tackling this during the designing phase and also during the development.

Now that we have defined our characters, let's discuss how the game will be played, looking at the specific details.

Gameplay

The game will start with the player in the center of the game world. The Hero, controlled by the player, will need to defend the Base from the Enemies. To fend off the Enemies, the Hero can shoot bullets. The goal is to defeat all the Enemies before the Base is completely destroyed by them.

Let's look at how we will make all this happen. The following gameplay components are covered in this section:

- Game-world layout

- Starting condition

- Ending condition

- Point system

- **Heads-Up Display (HUD)**

We will cover each of the preceding components and discuss how they change the game experience. Let's start by talking about how the game world will be designed.

Game-world layout

We will create a base environment that consists of large metallic floor tiles, walls, and doors where the enemies will spawn. The base building will be located at the opposite end of the Enemies' Spawn positions (the Doors in the following figure), where the enemies need to reach to start attacking it.

Here is a mock-up of the shape our game world will take:

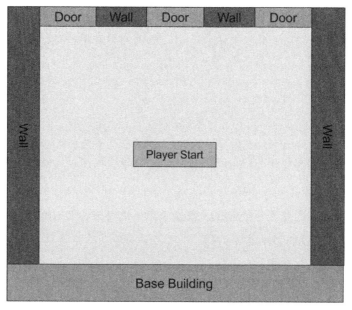

Figure 1.5 – Base layout

There are four basic things illustrated in the preceding mock-up, listed as follows:

- **Wall**: Impenetrable barriers that prevent the player from going outside the play area.
- **Door**: Impenetrable, like the walls, but will also serve as the Spawn Position of the Enemies. The Enemies will spawn behind them and can penetrate them to enter our Base Area.
- **Player Start**: This is the Hero's start position.
- **Base Building**: Our Base. The enemies must be close enough to attack it.

With our base-level design finished, let's discuss how the player will enter that world.

Starting condition

When our game is first launched, we will have several starting conditions set. Here is a list of those conditions:

- The number and placement of Enemies' Spawn Points: As you saw in our earlier mock-up, there will be several possible spawn points in the game (the doors).

- The number of Waves, the number of Enemies in each Wave, and how often the enemies will spawn: We will write a script to spawn waves of enemies, which will be used for each wave.

- Our final starting condition is the base placement: As you can see from the preceding figure, this is placed on the opposite side of the doors—so, the enemy must traverse the whole empty space between them, giving the player a chance to attack them.

We have defined the enemy spawning rules and how the player can play the game. Now, let's talk about how the game will end, looking at the exact implementation of this.

Ending condition

So far, we have established that we will track several components in the game. They are as follows:

- **Remaining Waves**: A wave is considered finished when all enemies in it die.

- **Base Health**: Damaged by the enemies.

- **Player Health**: Also damaged by the enemies.

Based on what we decided earlier regarding the end-of-game condition, we can apply the following mathematical checks to determine whether the game has ended and what the outcome is. Each end-of-game condition is listed in the following table, along with the outcome:

Condition number	End-of-game condition	Outcome
1	Remaining Waves == 0	Hero wins
2	Base Health == 0	Enemies win
3	Player Health == 0	Enemies win

Figure 1.6 – End-of-game conditions

In order to implement these three end-of-game conditions, we know we must track the number of waves, player health, and base health.

Now that we have a full game, let's think about how we can make it more rewarding, by implementing a classic point system.

Point system

Since we are tracking key information that involves numbers, it makes it easy for us to implement a point system. We could, for example, give the player 50 points each time an Enemy is exterminated, and we could also take away points each time an Enemy causes damage to the base. In our case, we will settle with just giving points when Enemies are killed, but you can feel free to expand this area if you want to.

Now, we have several systems that the player needs to be aware of, but right now, the player hasn't got any way to make informed decisions about those systems. So, let's see how we can improve that, using an HUD.

HUD

We have decided to keep track of information during gameplay that has value beyond calculating points at the end of the game. The player will want to see this information as it tends to provide motivation and adds to the fun of the game. So, we will create an HUD for the player, and dynamically update the data in the game.

> **Important note:**
> An HUD is a visual layer of information that is always present on the screen.

Here is a mock-up of what our HUD will look like in our Super Shooter game:

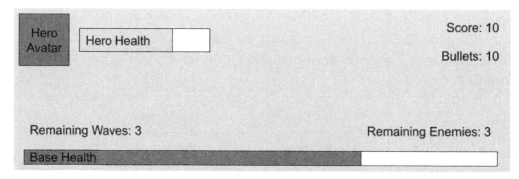

Figure 1.7 – UI layout

As you can see, there are several components to our HUD, as follows:

- **Hero Health**: A classic health bar that allows us to see the amount of life left. We choose a bar instead of a number because it is easier to see in the middle of an intense fight, instead of reading a number.

- **Hero Avatar**: An image next to the health bar just to show our Hero's face.

- **Score**: The number of points we have gathered.

- **Bullets**: The number of bullets remaining. The player must check this number frequently to avoid running out of bullets, as they are limited. Anyway, at the end of the book, you will be more than capable of creating a bullet-drop system if you want to.

- **Remaining Waves / Remaining Enemies**: Information about the current state of the wave and game, just to let the player know when the game is going to end, putting some pressure on them in the process.

- **Base Health**: Another important piece of information so the player can see the health of the Base. It's of a sufficient size to let the player notice when the base is being attacked and take action in that case.

Finally, we have a simple, yet fully fledged starter game design with lots of rules and specifications about how it will behave, and we can start creating our game right now. However, there's a good practice that is never too soon to implement: balancing the game's difficulty.

The difficulty balance

There are a lot of considerations to make when determining how difficult your game should be. If it is too difficult, players will lose interest, and if the game is too easy, it might not appeal to your intended audience. Some games include difficulty options for users to select from. Other games have multiple levels, each with increasing difficulty. There are several questions that we must contend with in order to achieve our desired difficulty balance.

In this section, we will first look at some questions relating to difficulty balance, followed by our implementation plan.

Difficulty balance questions

There are a lot of questions about our game that we need to consider in our game design. A review of the questions in this section will help us gain an appreciation of the issues that even a simple game such as ours must contend with, in order to achieve the desired difficulty balance.

The first set of questions, listed here, relates to the overall implementation of difficulty in our game:

- Should we have different levels of difficulty, selectable by the player?
- What specifically will be different with each difficulty level?
- Should we have multiple game levels, each with an increased amount of difficulty?
- What specifically will be different with each game level?

Consider the following questions regarding the Enemies in our game:

- How many Enemies should be spawned in each Wave?
- At what distance should an Enemy become aware of the Hero?
- How much damage should an Enemy inflict on the Player with each attack?
- How much damage can an Enemy endure before it dies?

The next set of questions listed here refers to our playable character, the Hero:

- How much life should the character have?
- How much damage will the character take from a single enemy attack?
- Should the character be able to outrun Enemies?

We also have the base and bullets to account for in our game. Here are a couple of questions for each of those game assets that we will implement in our game. In the case of the base, the questions are as follows:

- How many attacks should it take for an enemy to destroy a base?
- What is the ideal max number of enemies spawned in a Wave?
- Where should Doors and the Base be located in the game environment?

And now, let's talk about questions in the case of Bullets, as follows:

- At what pace should the player shoot bullets?
- At what pace should the enemy shoot bullets?
- How much damage will the bullets inflict on the Enemies?
- How much damage will the bullets inflict on the Player?

As you can see, there are several questions that we need to answer as part of our design. Some of the questions may seem redundant as they relate to more than one component in the game. Now, let's answer some of those.

Implementation plan

Based on the questions posed in the last section, we must come up with some answers. Here is a list of some of those decisions:

- We will spawn five enemies in the first wave and add two new enemies per consecutive wave.
- We will establish a pretty small vision area for the Enemies, making it easy for the Hero to sneak past them and, perhaps more importantly, outrun them.
- We will configure the Player's bullets to damage enemies so that two bullets are needed to kill them.
- We will configure the Enemies bullets to damage the player so that 10 bullets are needed to kill them.
- The Player will shoot bullets at a frequency of 2 per second.
- The Enemy will shoot 1 per second.

It's important to take into account that this is the first balance pass, and we will surely change this based on the testing we will carry out when the game is implemented. The idea is to consider this first version of the game as a Prototype, which will be tested on a small group of players to validate our ideas and iterate them. The invaluable feedback of the early players of the game could convert it completely. Usually, a Prototype is a quick version of the game, made with the most minimal features possible to quickly test and discard ideas. After a fair amount of iterations and testing sessions on the prototype, we will have solid ground to start the real development of the game (or discard it completely if we can't create a fun game).

In this book, we will skip the Prototype phase and jump directly to the development of the game due to the scope of the book, but consider doing Prototypes before starting any real project. Just remember, a prototype is a quick, cheaply done version of the project with the sole purpose of testing ideas. We will probably discard the prototype project entirely before starting the real development, so don't spend too much time doing it with clean and proper practices. Now, we can say the game design is completed… or can we? Actually, the game design never ends, even after prototyping!. It will keep evolving as the game is developed, but let's keep that for later. Now, let's talk about how we can communicate our great ideas with everyone in our team, using documentation.

Documentation

Now that we have covered all the main aspects of our game, it is important to prepare them to be shared with others. Throughout this book, you will probably work alone, but in real-life production, you will likely work with others, so sharing your vision is a crucial skill you need to learn in order to create successful games. You will not only be sharing your vision with your teammates, but also with potential investors that want to put money into your game project (if you convince them to do so). In this section, we will give recommendations about how to properly format your game information into comprehensible documents.

Game Design Document (GDD)

This document is basically the Encyclopedia of your game. It contains a breakdown of all the aspects of it, each one with detailed explanations about how the different game systems should work. Here, you will put the questions and answers we previously looked at in the Implementation Plan, and you will deep dive into those. Remember that you have an idea in your head, and making sure that others grasp that idea is complicated, so don't underestimate this important task.

Maybe you are making a game all by yourself and you think you don't need a GDD because all the ideas can fit in your head. This might be true for very small games, but any size of game and team can benefit from a GDD. It will serve as your notebook to put down your own ideas and read them. This is important because in your head everything makes sense, but once you read your own ideas and review them, you will find lots of blind spots that can easily be fixed before discovering them when coding the entire game.

Let's start by talking about how a GDD can be structured.

GDD formats

Sadly, there's no standard way of creating a GDD. Every company and team has its own way of doing this, not only in terms of which tool to use to create it but also the content of the document. This varies a lot according to the size of the team (or teams), the type of game, and the general culture of the company behind the game. As a matter of fact, some companies actually believe that there's no need to create a GDD.

A good idea when starting to create GDDs is to check out existing published GDDs of several games. There are lots of them out there, including big, well-known games (such as Doom). Most of them are, generally, Word documents with sections explaining the game systems (such as weapons, inventory, and so on) and the list of all characters, while some can be just a list of bullets explaining certain facts about the different pieces of the game. After that, you can start experimenting with different GDD formats that fit well with your project and your team.

Once you have decided on a good format, you must decide how you will actually write that format, and besides using pen and paper, a better idea is to use all those great digital tools out there. Let's look at some of them.

GDD creation tools

After reviewing existing GDDs, the next step is to pick a proper tool to write your GDD. The first matter you need to take into account is that the GDD will change… a lot… very often… all the time. In the process of creating the game, you will validate or discard ideas you wrote in the GDD, so using a dynamic tool is a good idea. This can be accomplished with any text processor you are familiar with, but there are other problems you need to tackle, so maybe text processors won't be enough.

Your GDD will be big… I mean, BIG, even for simple games. It will have lots of sections, and you will find cases where whole sections will refer to other sections, generating a big net of links between several parts of the document. A good tool for managing this instead of a text processor is using any kind of wiki, which I strongly recommend in cases like this. They allow you to break down the whole GDD into articles that can be easily edited and linked to others, and also, lots of wikis allow you to edit articles collaboratively. There are other additional features, such as comments that allow a whole conversation about a feature inside the GDD, with these recorded for future reference. The *Wikipedia* page relating to GDDs can be seen in the following screenshot:

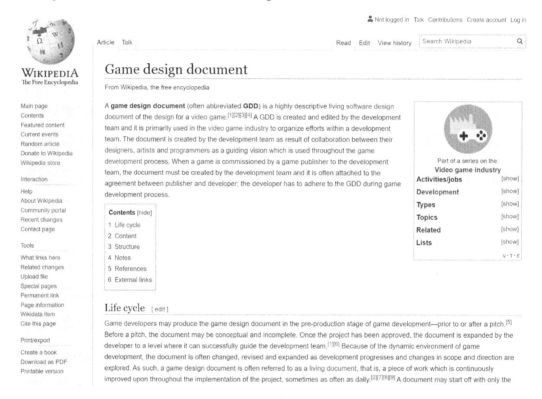

Figure 1.8 – Wikipedia site

Moreover, you can also use other tools such as Google Drive, which allows you to mix different types of documents—from regular text documents to dynamic slides—to create presentations, communicating complex aspects in a simple yet powerful medium. Also, Google Drive has lots of great collaborative tools that improve the way several people work on the GDD.

All the tools we described are generic solutions to writing documents in general, and they can work like a charm, but there are other tools specifically crafted for games (for example, Articy Draft).

Now, let's start writing our GDD. I know I said there's no standard format, but let's at least see what every GDD should have, starting with the elevator pitch.

Elevator pitch

Imagine you are riding in an elevator, and on the next floor, an important game investor gets in. They push the tenth-floor button, so you have eight floors' worth of time to convince them to throw money into your pocket to help you create a game. I know this is an improbable case, but in real life, when you are in front of an investor at a round table, you won't have lots of time to convince them. Remember that behind you there's a queue of maybe thousands of developers wanting to do the same, so you must be quick and visceral, and that's why having a good elevator pitch is so important.

An **elevator pitch** is probably the first sentence you will find in your GDD, and the most important one. It needs to describe your game in no more than two lines and convince the person reading the GDD that your game is a great idea—you need to make them want to play your game right now. Yes, it sounds super ambitious, and it is, but this can separate you from the whole crowd of developers wanting to get some funding for their game.

Again, there's no standard formula to create a successful elevator pitch (we would all be rich if such a thing existed), but here are some tips to take into account:

- You must make your pitch in no more than 10 seconds. Any longer, and you will lose the interest of the person you are trying to convince.

- You must sound like you believe in your own idea; nobody is going to invest in a game you are not sure is the next big release.

- Don't use any technical words (I'm looking at you, programmers).

- Include what differentiates your game from all the other games out there.

- Convince any person close to you to play the game, trying to test it with the most honest person you can find—a person that won't be bothered about shattering your idea into pieces (if your idea really deserves that).

- Practice your pitch over and over again, in front of a mirror, until you can say it nicely, clearly, and in one shot.

Here are some examples of an elevator pitch:

- Imagine yourself slaughtering giant Greek gods with just your arms and your strength until you become the king of Olympus. You will feel that power in [INSERT NAME OF TOTALLY NON-EXISTENT GAME HERE].

- Civilization has fallen. A horrendous infection turns people into zombies. You have the only cure, and must traverse the whole country to deliver it, or humankind will collapse.

Okay—nowadays, those pitches are not super original, but a few years ago they were. Imagine the power that those pitches had at that time; you must find something similar. I'm not saying it's easy but look how just two lines can be the start of amazing experiences, so focus first on writing those two lines, and then the rest of the game.

Now you have gained the attention of an investor, it's time to show them all the gameplay systems and the little details to hype them up further… well, no, not right now. You have just gained their attention; you haven't convinced them yet. It's time to start talking a little bit about your game, and a high concept is a good way of doing so.

High concept

A **high concept** is a series of statements that further describe your game, but again, in a simple and concise way. Even if you are not trying to convince an investor, those statements will outline the way your game will be defined.

A good high concept can include sections such as the following ones:

- **Elevator pitch**: As we explained in the previous section.

- **Genre**: Maybe you are creating something new that has never been seen before, but it will probably be inspired by several other games. Here, you will specify the type of games on which you are basing your idea, so the reader of this document can start imagining how the game will be played. Later, you will specify the differences, but it is better to put a well-known idea forward first to start constructing the concept in the mind of the reader. Also, you can specify here the point of view the player will have in the game and the setting—for example, a Top-Down, Medieval Roguelike **Role-Playing Game (RPG)**.

- **Platform** and **Demographics**: You need to be very clear about who will play your game. Creating a game for adults in North America is not the same as creating a game for Chinese teenagers, or games for business people who want to distract themselves for a few minutes on their way back home from work. Those profiles will want different experiences, with different levels of challenge and game session length. They will even use different devices to play games. Taking this into account will help you find the game mechanics and balance that best fits your target audience. It's very common to say that you are creating a game for yourself, but remember that you won't be buying that game, so also think about your wallet when creating the game—for example, casual players of mobile platforms.

- **Features**: Create a shortlist of no more than three or five features that your game will have. Select features according to the genre you have chosen—for example, you will shoot waves of enemies with a giant array of weapons, or you will level up your ship to improve its stats.

- **Unique Selling Points** (**USPs**): This is similar to the features list, but here, you will include the features that differentiate your game from the others out there (no more than three or five)—for example, you can traverse the scene using parkour-style moves, or you can craft brand new weapons using looted materials. Think about how unique those features were years ago.

Again, there's no ideal high concept. Maybe you will find some other aspects of your game that can be highlighted here and add them to the document, but try to keep this all on just one page.

Now that we have discussed what every GDD *should* have, let's talk about what a GDD *may* have.

Tips for creating GDDs

Now, it's time to define what the whole game is. We said there's no standard format for GDDs, but at least we can take into account several good practices when creating them. The following list highlights a few of them:

- **Readability**: Your GDD must be prepared to be read by anyone, including people without game development knowledge. Don't use any technical words (guess who I'm still looking at) and try to keep things simple. A good test of your GDD readability is to give it to your granny or anyone that you see as being as far from gaming as possible, and that person must be able to read it.

- **Setting and introduction**: Before you start describing the game mechanics, put the reader inside the game. Describe the world, the player character, their backstory, their motivations, and what the main problem is that the player needs to struggle with. Make the reader of the GDD interested in the setting of the game and want to keep reading, to see how they will be able to play the game and tackle all the quests the player will face in the game.

- **Gameplay sections**: These are sections that break the game into several systems and subsystems linked to each other. Some examples can be Inventory, Quests, Crafting, Battle, Movement, Shops, and so on. You will want to be super specific about every aspect of how those systems work because—remember—this document will be used by the team to craft the code and assets of your game. All the analysis we did in the previous sections of the chapter will be part of the GDD and will be further explained and analyzed.

- **Content sections**: You will also want to create content sections, such as the ones we previously designed. These can be—but are not limited to—Characters, Story, World, Levels, Aesthetics, Art Assets, Sound and Music Assets, Economics, and Input.

- **Share your idea**: Before immortalizing your ideas in the GDD and making everyone start crafting them, discuss the different GDD sections before marking them as finished. Discuss with your team, people on the internet, friends—anyone and everyone can give you valuable feedback about your idea. I'm pretty sure you are thinking that your idea will be stolen by some random person on the internet who will release the same game before you—and that can happen—but I'm not saying share the whole GDD, just some details about certain implementations you are not sure about.

- **Keep control**: Everyone in the team is a game designer—some more than others. Everyone will have ideas and things they will do differently. Listen to them—doing so will be useful, but remember you are in charge and you will have the final say. You need to be open, but set some limits and don't deviate from your original idea and concept. Prevent the famous feature creep, which consists on lots and lots of game systems unnecessarily, and know when enough is enough, especially considering the limited amount of resources we will have when beginning to create games. Again, not an easy task—you will learn this the hard way, believe me, but remember this when that happens (I told you!).

- **The game will change**: I already said that, but I like to stress this as much as I can. The game will change a lot due to many reasons you will find in the process of creating it. You may find that X mechanic is not that fun, you could have created a better way of handling Y system, or maybe test sessions with players prove that Z level needs to be completely redesigned. Be open to change and pivot your game idea when needed. If you do this the right way, your game won't be as you originally imagined but will be a better version of it.

- **Graphics**: Use graphics, diagrams, charts, and so on. Try to prevent huge text walls. Remember that a picture is worth a thousand words. You are communicating, and nobody wants to spend valuable minutes trying to understand what you want to say. Improve your visual communication skills, and you will have a focused team.

- **Paper prototypes**: You can test some ideas in your head on paper before putting them in the GDD. Even if your game is a frenetic "beat 'em up," you can have little paper characters moving around a table, seeing how they can attack the player, and which movement pattern they will have. Do some math to look at how to perfect timing, damage, health values, and so on.

- **Regular prototypes**: While your game is being developed, the GDD will constantly change based on player feedback. You must test your game, even if it's not finished, and get feedback from players as early as you can. Of course, they will tell you lots of things that you already know, but they will see lots of problems you don't see because you are creating and playing your game every day. They have the advantage of playing the game for the first time, and that is a real change.

After this, we can start creating our GDD, and remember: you will need to find out what format works best for you.

Game design and GDD creation is a complex topic that could be explored in several chapters, but there are lots of books out there that do exactly that, and game design is not the main topic of this book.

Summary

In this chapter, we fully designed our Super Shooter game, and we plan to use our design to drive our development efforts. Our game design includes gameplay, the player character, the non-player characters, game assets, animations, and more. We used screen mock-ups to help document our game's design. In addition, we planned our game's difficulty balance to help ensure the game is appropriately difficult based on user selection. We talked about what a GDD is, how we can create one, and how it and the game design will change during game production.

Remember that this is important because you want to answer all the questions you can before coding your game. If you don't do this, you will pay for it by having to recode parts of your game over and over for each unforeseen problem. You cannot prevent all possible complications, but at least a good amount will be sorted out with this analysis.

In the next chapter, you will learn how to start using Unity. You will gain knowledge of why Unity is a great option to start creating games. You will also create your first game project and analyze how it is composed.

2
Setting Up Unity

In this chapter, we will learn why Unity is a good game engine to start out with. There are lots of ways to begin a game development career, so choosing the proper tool to do so is a huge first step. Then, we will learn how to install Unity and create a project with Unity Hub, a tool that manages different Unity installations and projects.

Specifically, we will cover the following topics in this chapter:

- Why use a game engine such as Unity?
- Installing Unity
- Creating projects

Let's start by talking about why you should choose Unity to start your game development career.

Why use a game engine such as Unity?

When you want to create a game, you have several ways to do this, each with its pros and cons. So, why choose Unity? In this section, we will discuss the reasons for this while providing an overview of the previous and current industry state, and specifically look at the following concepts:

- Past and present industry insight

- Game engines

- Benefits of using Unity

Let's take a look at these concepts.

Past and present industry insight

At the beginning of the gaming industry, developers struggled with devices with limited resources but created simple game designs. As the industry evolved, the hardware became more powerful and the games became more complex than ever before. A big AAA game title requires almost 200 developers working on different areas of the game. Each role that's undertaken requires years of experience, making creating games an expensive and risky task; you never know if a game is going to be a success or a big waste of money. For these reasons, it was very difficult for a single person to make an entire game.

> **Important Note**
> AAA games are created by lots of people working in big companies, and this usually costs millions of dollars. There are also AA games, which differ from AAA games in terms of team size and budget.

In the past, a programmer needed to learn how to use lots of tools to solve different game development problems. Some tools stopped receiving support from their creators, leaving them with unresolved bugs and features. Because of that, big companies started to hire highly skilled developers to create all those tools, resulting in what is called a game engine. Let's review what this is.

Game engines

A **game engine** is a set of different pieces of software that solve game development problems such as audio, graphics, and physics issues, but are designed to work together, all operating on the same philosophy. This is important because every team and company has its own way of working. Creating a game engine from scratch is a great task, and only a few big companies can do this. The game engines that companies create are usually private, so only the company is allowed to use them. Some companies sell their engine, but the cost is very high.

But another way of getting game engines became available a couple of decades ago. You have probably heard about indie games, which are created by teams of 1 to 10 developers, but how can such a small team create games? The answer is **general-purpose game engines**. These are game engines just like the ones that companies create, but they are designed to be a good foundation for every game and provide a toolset ready to be used by anyone, for any game. These kinds of engines created a whole generation of enthusiast developers who are now able to develop their own games more easily than before. There were lots of game engine companies in the past but only a few have survived, with Unity being one of the most influential ones. But why is that? Let's discuss this further.

> **Important Note**
> Other examples of general-purpose engines are Unreal Engine, Godot, Torque, and CryEngine.

Benefits of using Unity

Well, there are lots of potential reasons why Unity is so popular. Let's discuss a few of them, as follows:

- Unity was designed with simplicity in mind, featuring a very simple and polished interface, and tools with few – but powerful – settings. This helps newcomers not immediately feel lost the very second they start the engine.

- The programming language of Unity, C#, is very well-known to both beginner and advanced programmers, and the Unity way of coding with C# is sleek and easy to understand. Unity and C# handle most of the programming problems you may encounter in other languages, decreasing your production time greatly.

- Unity was there when the mobile gaming market era started, and its creators just put all their efforts into creating all the features any mobile engine needed. In my opinion, this is one of the most important reasons why Unity became what it is today.

- With other new technologies such as **Augmented Reality** (**AR**) and **Virtual Reality** (**VR**), Unity has expanded its use not only for gaming, but also for applications, training simulations, architecture visualization, the automotive industry, films, and so on. Using Unity, you can create applications for a wide spectrum of industries, and their use out there is increasing year by year.

- Unity has a big community of developers using it, creating bibliographies and tutorials, asking and answering questions, and creating plugins for the engine. All this helps a lot when you start using Unity because the answer to your problem is just a Google search away.

- Because of its growth, there are lots of Unity jobs worldwide, more than there are for other game engines, and some of those jobs are looking for junior developers, so there are chances for newcomers to enter the industry.

Unity is not all good, though – it has its cons, and there are other engines out there (such as Unreal Engine 4 and Godot) that compete with Unity in several of those limitations, since some have better features than Unity but also their own caveats. In my opinion, picking Unity or another engine depends on what you are intending to do, and what the technologies are that you are used to using, but at the end of the day, you can do everything you need just with Unity and deal with any weaknesses with the help of their big community. Now that we know about Unity, let's learn how to install the engine.

Installing Unity

Okay; after all of that, you've decided to go with Unity – great decision! Now, where do we start? Let's start with a simple but necessary first step: installing Unity. This seems like a straightforward first step, but let's discuss the proper way to install it. In this section, we will be looking at the following concepts:

- Unity technical requirements

- Unity installs

- Installing Unity with Unity Hub

Let's start by discussing what we need to run Unity on our computers.

Unity Technical Requirements

To run Unity 2021, your computer will need to meet the following requirements:

- If you use Windows, you will need Windows 7 SP1 or higher, 8 or 10. Unity will only run on 64-bit versions of those systems; there is no 32-bit support unless you are willing to work with older versions of Unity such as 5.6, but that's outside the scope of this book.

- For Mac, you need macOS 10.13 or higher.

- For Linux, you need Ubuntu 20.04, 18.04, or CentOS 7.

- Your CPU needs to support SSE2 (most CPUs support it).

- On Windows, we need a graphics card with DirectX 10 support (most modern GPUs support it).

- On Mac, any metal-capable Intel or AMD GPU will be enough.

- On Linux, any OpenGL 3.2 or higher, or Vulkan-compatible card.

Now that we know the requirements, let's discuss the Unity installs management system.

Unity installs

In previous versions of Unity, we used to simply download the installer of a specific Unity version and hit **Next** until it was installed. But when you use Unity professionally, you need to have several versions of Unity installed because you will be working on different projects made with different versions. You may be wondering why you can't just use the latest Unity version for every project, but there are some problems with that.

In new versions of Unity, there are usually lots of changes regarding how the engine works, so you may need to rework lots of pieces of the game to upgrade it. Also, you may be using plugins that just haven't adapted to updates yet, so those will stop working. In my projects, I am used to doing project upgrades; however, for learning purposes, with a project that has a specific release date, it can take lots of time to upgrade the whole project, and that can push the release date back a lot. Maybe you need a specific feature that comes with an update that will help you a lot. In such a case, the cost of upgrading may be worthwhile, but take into account that most of the time, this doesn't happen.

Managing different projects made with different Unity versions, installing, and updating new Unity releases, and so on, used to be a huge hassle, but Unity Hub was created just to help us with this, and it has become the default way to install Unity. Let's learn more about it.

Installing Unity with Unity Hub

Unity Hub is a small piece of software you install before installing Unity. It centralizes the management of all your Unity projects and installations. You can get it from Unity's official site. The steps for downloading it change frequently, but at the time of writing this book, you need to do the following:

1. Go to unity.com.

2. Click on the **Get started** button, as shown in the following screenshot:

Figure 2.1 – Get started button on Unity site

3. Click on the **Individual** tab. Then, under the **Personal** section, click on the **Get started** button, as illustrated in the following screenshot:

Figure 2.2 – Choosing an Individual/Free license

4. Click on the **Start here** button in the **First-time Users** section, as illustrated in the following screenshot:

Figure 2.3 – Starting the download

5. Accept the terms and conditions, as illustrated in the following screenshot:

→ Have read and acknowledged Unity's Privacy Policy

Agree and download

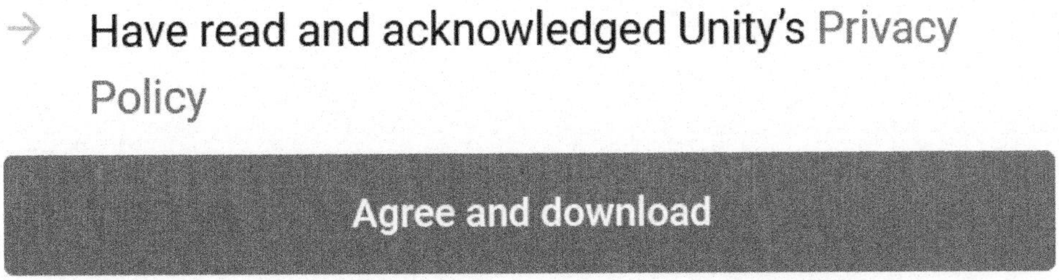

Figure 2.4 – Agreeing to the privacy policy

6. Execute the downloaded installer.

Now that we have Unity Hub installed, we must use it to install a specific Unity version. You can do this with the following steps:

1. Start **Unity Hub**.

2. Log into your account by clicking on the person icon at the top-right corner of the window and selecting **Sign in**:

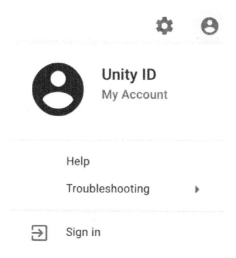

Figure 2.5 – Signing into Unity Hub – part I

Here, you also have the option to create a Unity account if you haven't already, as illustrated in the link labeled **create one**, which appears in the Unity login prompt, as shown in the following screenshot:

Figure 2.6 – Signing into Unity Hub – part II

3. Follow the steps provided by the installer. You should see the following screen:

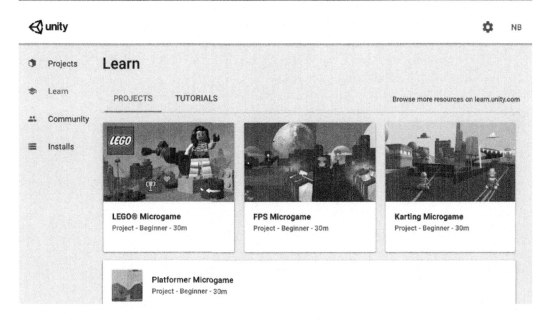

Figure 2.7 – Unity Hub window

4. Click on the **Installs** button and check if you have Unity 2021 listed there. If not, press the **ADD** button. Make sure the latest Unity 2021.1 release (in my case, Unity 2021.1.13f1) is selected, and then click on the **NEXT** button. Your screen may show a newer version than mine, so don't worry about that. This process is illustrated in the following screenshot:

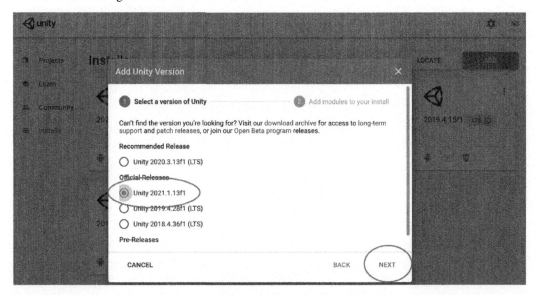

Figure 2.8 – Picking the Unity version to install

5. A feature selection window will show up. Make sure **Microsoft Visual Studio Community** is checked. At the time of writing this book, the latest version is 2019, but a newer one could work just as well. Now, click the **NEXT** button. This process is illustrated in the following screenshot:

✔ Microsoft Visual Studio Community 2019	1.4 GB	1.3 GB
Platforms		
> ☐ Android Build Support	243.1 MB	1.1 GB
☐ iOS Build Support	365.8 MB	1.6 GB
☐ tvOS Build Support	362.2 MB	1.6 GB
☐ Linux Build Support (Mono)	59.0 MB	274.7 MB
☐ Mac Build Support (Mono)	92.4 MB	480.2 MB

CANCEL   BACK   NEXT

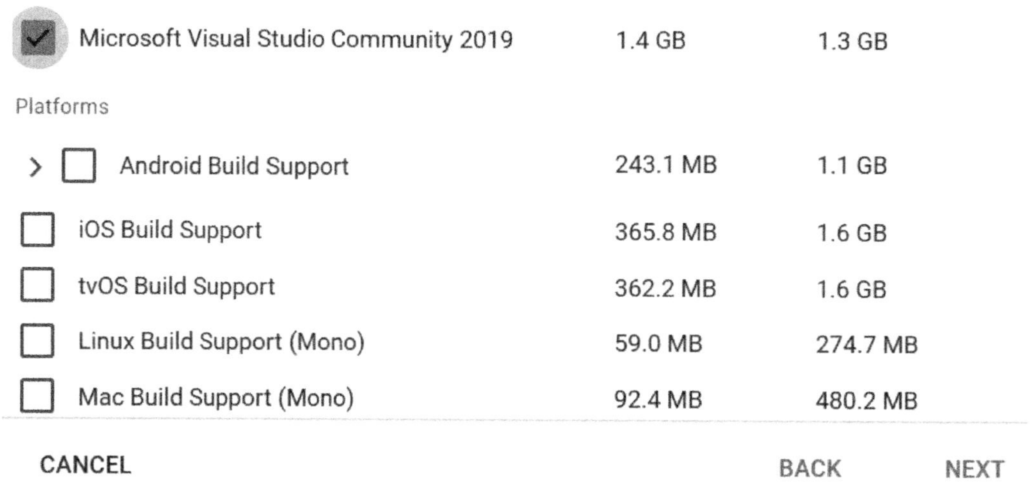

Figure 2.9 – Selecting Visual Studio

6. Accept Visual Studio's terms and conditions, as illustrated in the following screenshot:

✔ I have read and agree with the above terms and conditions

CANCEL   DONE

Figure 2.10 – Accepting Visual Studio's terms and conditions

> **Important Note**
> Visual Studio is the program we will use in *Chapter 14, Introduction to C# and Visual Scripting,* to create our code. We do not need the other Unity features right now, but you can go back later and install them if you need them.

7. You will see the selected Unity version downloading and installing in the list. Wait for this to finish. In the following screenshot, you can see that I have other Unity versions installed. However, you will only see one version, which is fine:

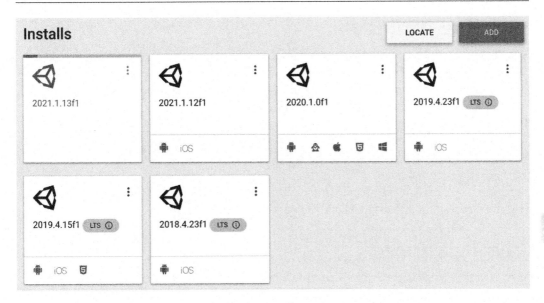

Figure 2.11 – All Unity installations I currently have on my machine

8. Once Unity has finished installing, Visual Studio Installer will automatically execute. It will download an installer that will download and install Visual Studio Community 2019, as illustrated in the following screenshot:

Figure 2.12 – Installing Visual Studio

Remember that the preceding steps may be different in new Unity versions, so just try to follow the flow that Unity designed – most of the time, it is intuitive. Now, it is time to create a project using Unity.

Creating projects

Now that we have Unity installed, we can start creating our game. To do so, we need to create a project, which is a folder containing all the files that your game will comprise. These files are called assets and there are different types, such as images, audio, 3D models, script files, and so on. In this section, we will learn how to manage a project by addressing the following concepts:

- Creating a project
- Project structure

First, let's learn how to create a blank project so that we can start developing our project.

Creating a project

As with Unity installations, we will use the Unity Hub to manage projects. We need to follow these steps to create one:

1. Open Unity Hub and click on the **Projects** button. Then, click on **NEW**, as illustrated in the following screenshot:

Figure 2.13 – Creating a new project in Unity Hub

2. Pick the **Universal Render Pipeline** template. We will be creating a 3D game with simple graphics, prepared to be run on every device Unity can execute, so the **Universal Render Pipeline** (**URP**) is the better choice for this. In *Chapter 6, Materials and Effects with URP and Shader Graph*, we will be discussing exactly why. Then, choose a **Project Name** and a **Location**, and hit **Create**. This process can be seen in the following screenshot:

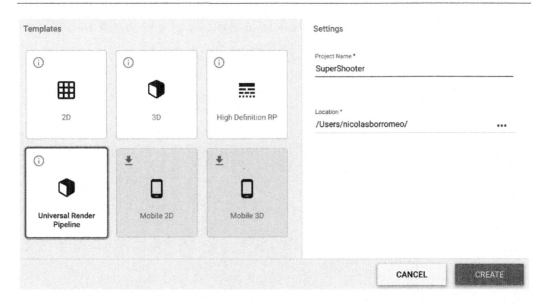

Figure 2.14 – Selecting the Universal Render Pipeline template

3. Unity will create and automatically open the project. This can take a while, but after that, you will see a screen similar to following:

Figure 2.15 – The Unity Editor window

4. Try closing the window and opening it again, then going back to Unity Hub and picking the project from the list, as follows:

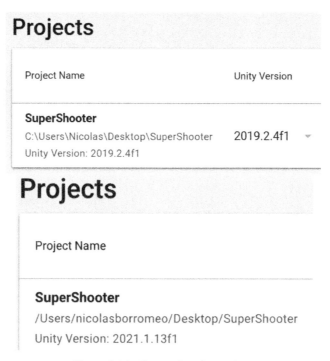

Figure 2.16 – Reopening the project

Now that we have created the project, let's explore its structure.

Project structure

We have just opened Unity, but we won't start using it until the next chapter. Now, it's time to learn how the project folder structure is composed. To do so, we need to open the folder where we created the project. If you don't remember where this is, you can do the following:

1. Right-click the Assets folder in the **Project** panel, which is located at the bottom part of the editor.

2. Click the **Show in Explorer** option (if you are using a Mac, this option is called **Reveal in Finder**). The following screenshot illustrates this:

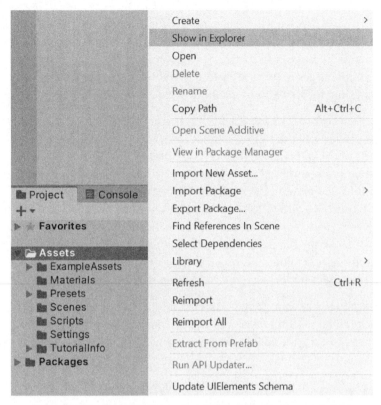

Figure 2.17 – Opening the project folder in the Explorer window

Then, you will see the following folder structure:

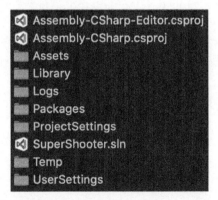

Figure 2.18 – Unity project folder's structure

If you want to move this project to another PC or send it to a colleague, you can just compress all those files and send it to them as a ZIP file. However, not all the folders are necessary all of the time. The important folders are **Assets**, **Packages**, and **ProjectSettings**. **Assets** will hold all the files we will create and use for our game, so this is a must. We will also configure different Unity systems to tailor the engine to our game; all the settings related to this can be found in the **ProjectSettings** folder. Finally, we will install different Unity modules or packages to expand its functionality, so the **Packages** folder will hold the ones we are using, for Unity to be aware of that.

It's not necessary to copy the rest of the folders if you need to move the project elsewhere, but let's at least discuss what the **Library** folder is, especially considering its usually huge size. Unity needs to convert the files we will use into its own format to operate, and an example would be audio and graphics. Unity supports **MPEG Audio Layer 3 (MP3)**, **Waveform Audio File Format (WAV)**, **Portable Network Graphics (PNG)**, and **Joint Photographic Experts Group (JPG)** files (and much more), but before using them, they need to be converted into Unity's internal formats. Those converted files will be in the **Library** folder. If you copy the project without that folder, Unity will simply take the original files in the **Assets** folder and recreate the **Library** folder entirely. This process can take time, and the bigger the project, the more time will be involved.

Take into account that you want to have all the folders Unity created while you are working on the project, so don't delete any of them while doing so. However, if you need to move an entire project, you now know exactly what you need to take with you.

Summary

In this chapter, we discussed why Unity is a great tool for creating games while comparing it to other engines on the market. This analysis was provided to help you see why you should use Unity as your first game development tool. After that, we reviewed how to install and manage different Unity versions using Unity Hub, before learning how to create and manage multiple projects with the same tool. We will use Unity Hub a lot, so it is important to know how to use it initially. Now, we are prepared to dive into the Unity Editor.

In the next chapter, we will start learning about the basic Unity tools so that we can author our first-level prototype.

3

Working with Scenes and Game Objects

Welcome to the third chapter of the book—here is where the hard work starts! In this chapter, we will develop some base knowledge of Unity in order to edit a project, and how to use several Unity Editor windows to manipulate our first scene and its objects. Also, we will learn how an object or Game Object is created and composed, and how to manage complex scenes with multiple objects using Hierarchies and Prefabs. Finally, we will review how we can properly save all our work to continue working on it later.

Specifically, we will examine the following concepts in this chapter:

- Manipulating scenes
- GameObjects and components
- Object hierarchies
- Prefabs
- Saving scenes and projects

Manipulating scenes

A **scene** is one of several kinds of files (also known as **assets**) in our project. A scene can mean different things according to the type of project or the way a company is used to working, but the most common use case is to separate your game into whole sections, the most common ones being the following:

- Main Menu
- Level 1, Level 2, Level 3, ..., Level N
- Victory Screen and Lose Screen
- Splash Screen and Loading Screen

In this section, we will cover the following concepts related to scenes:

- The purpose of a scene
- The Scene View
- Creating our first GameObject
- Navigating the Scene View
- Manipulating GameObjects

So, let's take a look at each of these concepts.

The purpose of a scene

The idea of separating your game into scenes is so that you will process and load just the data needed for the scene. Let's say you are in the Main Menu; in such cases, you will have only the textures, music, and objects that the main menu needs loaded in **Random-Access Memory (RAM)**. In that case, there's no need to have loaded the Level 10 Boss if you don't need it right now. That's why loading screens exist, just to fill the time between unloading the assets needed in one scene and loading the assets needed in another. Maybe you are thinking that open-world games such as Grand Theft Auto don't have loading screens while you roam around in the world, but they are actually loading and unloading chunks of the world in the background as you move, and those chunks are different scenes that are designed to be connected to each other.

The difference between the Main Menu and a regular level scene is the objects (also known as **GameObjects**) they have. In a menu, you will find objects such as backgrounds, music, buttons, and logos, and in a Level, you will have the player, enemies, platforms, health boxes, and so on. So, it is up to you and the GameObjects you put in the scene to decide what that scene means for your game.

But how can we create a scene? Let's start with the Scene View.

The Scene View

When you open a Unity project, you will see the Unity Editor. It will be composed of several windows or **panels**, each one helping you to change different aspects of your game. In this chapter, we will be looking at the windows that help you author scenes. The Unity Editor is shown in the following screenshot:

Figure 3.1 – Unity Editor

If you have ever programmed any kind of application before, you are probably used to having a starting function such as **Main**, where you start writing code to create several objects needed for your app, and if we are talking about games, you probably create all the objects for the scene there. The problem with this approach is that in order to ensure all objects are created properly, you will need to run the program to see the results, and if something is misplaced, you will need to manually change the coordinates of the object, which is a slow and painful process. Luckily, in Unity, we have the **Scene** View, an example of which is shown in the following screenshot:

Figure 3.2 – Scene View

This window is an implementation of the classic **WYSIWYG (What You See Is What You Get)** concept. Here, you can create objects and place them all over the scene, all through a scene previsualization where you can see how the scene will look when you hit **Play**. But before learning how to use this scene, we need to have an object in the scene, so let's create our first object.

Creating our first GameObject

The Unity **Universal Render Pipeline (URP)** template comes with a construction site test scene, but let's create our own empty scene to start exploring this new concept. To do that, you can simply use the **File | New Scene** menu to create an empty new scene, as illustrated in the following screenshot:

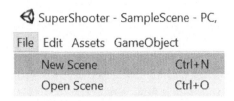

Figure 3.3 – Creating a new scene

After clicking **New Scene**, you will see a window to pick a scene template; here, select the **Basic (Built-in)** template. A template defines which objects the new scene will have, and in this case, our template came with a basic light and a camera, which will be useful for the scene we want to create. Once selected, just click the **Create** button:

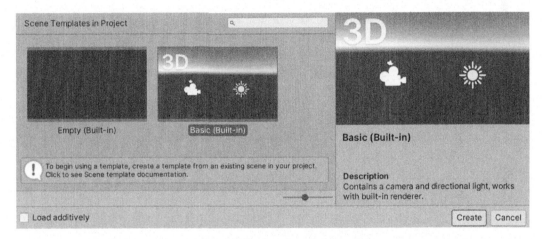

Figure 3.4 – Selecting the scene template

We will learn several ways of creating GameObjects throughout the book, but now, let's start using some basic templates that Unity provides. In order to create them, we will need to open the **GameObject** menu at the top of the Unity window, and it will show us several template categories, such as **3D Object**, **2D Object**, **Effects**, and so on, as illustrated in the following screenshot:

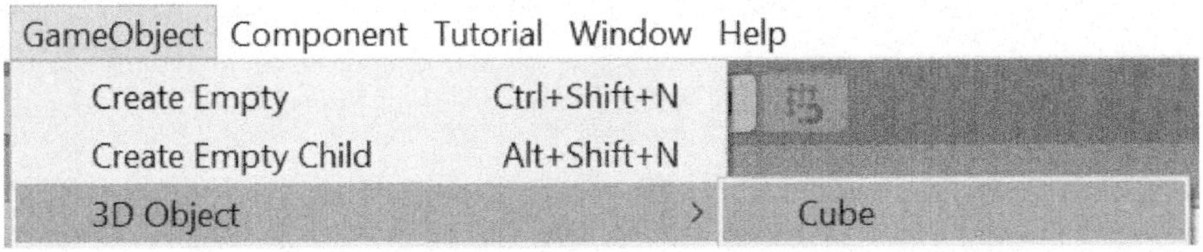

Figure 3.5 – Creating a cube

Under the **3D Object** category, we will see several 3D primitives such as **Cube**, **Sphere**, **Cylinder**, and so on, and while using them is not as exciting as using beautiful, downloaded 3D models, remember that we are only prototyping our level at the moment. This is called **gray-boxing** and means that we will use lots of prototyping primitive shapes to model our level so that we can quickly test it and see if our idea is good enough to start the complex work of converting it to a final version.

I recommend you pick the **Cube** object to start because is a versatile shape that can represent lots of objects. So, now that we have a scene with an object to edit, the first thing we need to learn to do with the Scene View is to navigate through the scene.

Navigating the Scene View

In order to manipulate a scene, we need to learn how to move through it to view the results from different perspectives. There are several ways to navigate the scene, so let's start with the most common one, the first-person view. This view allows you to move through the scene using a first-person-shooter-like navigation, using the mouse and the *W, A, S, D* keys. To navigate like this, you will need to press and hold the *right mouse button*, and while doing so, you can do the following:

- Move the mouse to rotate the camera around its current position.

- Press the *W, A, S, and D* keys to move the position of the camera, always holding the right mouse button.

- You can also press *Shift* to move faster.

- Press the *Q* and *E* keys to move up and down.

Another common way of moving is to click an object to select it (the selected object will have an orange outline), and then press the *F* key to focus on it, making the Scene View camera immediately move into a position where we can look at that object more closely. After that, we can press and hold the left *Alt* key on Windows, or *Option* on Mac, along with the left mouse click, to finally start moving the mouse and "orbit" around the object. This will allow you to see the focused object from different angles to check every part of it is properly placed, as demonstrated in the following screenshot:

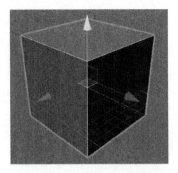

Figure 3.6 – Selecting an object

Now that we can move freely through the scene, we can start using the Scene View to manipulate GameObjects.

Manipulating GameObjects

Another use of the Scene View is to manipulate the locations of objects. In order to do so, we first need to select an object, and then click the **Transform Tool** in in the top-left corner of the Unity Editor (or press the *Y* key on the keyboard):

Figure 3.7 – The transformation tool

This will show what is called the **Transform Gizmo** over the selected object, which allows us to change the position, rotation, and scale of the object, as illustrated in the following screenshot:

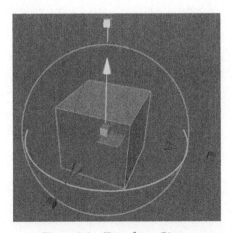

Figure 3.8 – Transform Gizmo

Let's start translating the object, which is accomplished by dragging the red, green, and blue arrows inside the Gizmo's sphere. While you do this, you will see the object moving along the selected axis. An interesting concept to explore here is the meaning of the colors of these arrows. If you pay attention to the top-right area of the Scene View, you will see an axis gizmo that serves as a reminder of those colors' meaning, as illustrated in the following screenshot:

Figure 3.9 – Axis Gizmo

Computer graphics use the classic 3D **Cartesian coordinate system** to represent objects' locations. The color red is associated with the x axis of the object, green with the y axis, and blue with the z axis. But what does each axis mean? If you come from another 3D authoring program, this could be different, but in Unity, the z axis (blue) represents the **Forward Vector**, which means that the arrow is pointing along the front of the object; the x axis is the **Right Vector**, and the y axis represents the **Up Vector**. Consider that those axes are **Local**, meaning that if you rotate the object, they will change the direction they face because the orientation of the object changes where the object is facing. Unity can show those axes in **Global Coordinates** if necessary, but for now, let's stick with local coordinates.

In order to be sure that we are working with local coordinates, make sure the **Local** mode is activated, as shown in the following screenshot:

Figure 3.10 – Switching Pivot and Local coordinates

If the right button says **Global** instead of **Local**, just click it and it will change. By the way, try to keep the left button as **Pivot**. If it says **Center**, just click it to change it.

I know—we are editing a cube, so there is no clear front or right side, but when you work with real 3D models such as cars and characters, they will certainly have those sides, and they must be properly aligned with those axes. If by any chance in the future you import a car into Unity and the front of the car is pointing along the red axis (*x*), you will need to make that model aligned along the *z* axis because the code that we will create to move our object will rely on that convention (but let's keep that for later).

Now, let's use this Transform Gizmo to rotate the object using the three colored circles around it. If you click and drag, for example, the red circle, you will rotate the object along the *x* rotation axis. If you want to rotate the object horizontally, based on the color-coding we previously discussed, you will probably pick the *x* axis—the one that is used to move horizontally—but, sadly, that's wrong. A good way to look at the rotation is like the accelerator of a bike: you need to take it and roll it. If you rotate the *x* axis like this, you will rotate the object up and down. So, in order to rotate horizontally, you would need to use the green circle or the *y* axis. The process is illustrated in the following screenshot:

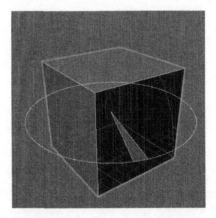

Figure 3.11 – Rotating an object

Finally, we have scaling, and we have two ways to accomplish that, one of them being through the gray cube at the center. This allows us to change the size of the object by clicking and dragging that cube. Now, as we want to prototype a simple level, sometimes we want to stretch the cube to create, for example, a column, or a flat floor, and here's where the second way comes in.

If you click and drag the colored cubes in front of the translation arrows instead of the gray one at the center, you will see how our cube is stretched over those axes, allowing you to change the shape of the object. The process is illustrated in the following screenshot:

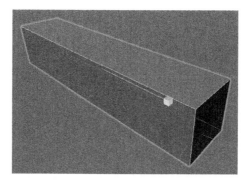

Figure 3.12 – Scaling an object

There's a slight chance that you won't see the cubes in front of the translation arrows. In such cases, you can accomplish it by using the **Scale Tool**, a separate tool specialized only in scaling the object along its axes. To enable the tool, click the fourth button in the top-left button bar (or press the *R* key):

Figure 3.13 Enabling the Scale Tool

You will notice that this gizmo looks very similar to the previous gizmo, but simpler; it has only the three arrows, one stretched along each axis, and we have only the cube-shaped arrows:

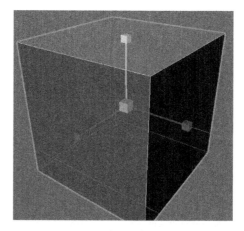

Figure 3.14 – The Scale Tool gizmo

You can also use the gray cube at the middle to scale all axes at the same time if desired, also known as Uniform Scaling, the same gray cube we had in the Transform Gizmo. Finally, something to consider here is that several objects can have the same scale values but have different sizes, given how they were originally designed. Scale is a multiplier we can apply over the original size of the object, so a building and a car with scale 1 can make perfect sense, as long as the relative size of one against the other seems correct. The main takeaway here is that scale is not size, but a way to multiply it.

Anyway, consider that scaling objects is usually a bad practice in many cases. In the final versions of your scene, you will use models with the proper size and scale, and they will be designed in a modular way so that you can plug them one next to the other. If you scale them, several bad things can happen, such as textures being stretched and becoming pixelated, and modules that no longer plug properly. There are some exceptions to this rule, such as placing lots of instances of the same tree in a forest and changing its scale slightly to simulate variation. Also, in the case of gray-boxing, it is perfectly fine to take cubes and change the scale to create floors, walls, ceilings, columns, and so on, because in the end, those cubes will be replaced with real 3D models.

Here's a challenge! Create a room composed of a floor, three regular walls, and the fourth wall with a hole for a door (three cubes). In the next screenshot, you can see what it should look like:

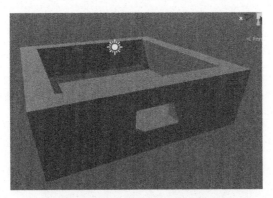

Figure 3.15 – Room task finished

Now that we can edit an object's location, let's see how we can edit all its other aspects.

GameObjects and components

We talked about our project being composed of Assets, and that a Scene (which is a specific type of Asset) is composed of GameObjects; so, how can we create an object? Through a composition of **components**.

In this section, we will cover the following concepts related to components:

- Understanding components
- Manipulating components

Let's start by discussing what a component is.

Understanding components

A **component** is one of several pieces a GameObject can be made of; each one is in charge of different features of the object. There are several components that Unity already includes that solve different tasks, such as playing a sound, rendering a mesh, applying physics, and so on; however, even though Unity has a large number of components, we will eventually need to create custom components, sooner or later.

In the next screenshot, you can see what Unity shows us when we select a GameObject.

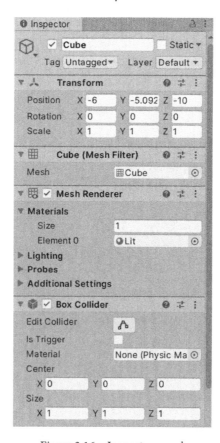

Figure 3.16 – Inspector panel

In the previous screenshot, we can see the **Inspector** panel. If we needed to guess what it does right now, we could say it shows all the properties of the selected object and allows us to configure those options to change the behavior of the object (that is, the position and rotation, whether it will project shadows or not, and so on). That is true, but we are missing a key element: those properties don't belong to the object; they belong to the components of the object. We can see some titles in bold before a group of properties, such as **Transform** and **Box Collider**, and so on. Those are the components of the object.

In this case, our object has a **Transform**, a **Mesh Filter**, a **Mesh Renderer**, and a **Box Collider** component, so let's review each one of those.

Transform just has location information, such as the position, rotation, and scale of the object, and by itself it does nothing—it's just a point in our game—but as we add components to the object, that position starts to have more meaning. That's because some components will interact with **Transform** and other components, each one affecting the other. An example of that would be the case of **Mesh Filter** and **Mesh Renderer**, both of those being in charge of rendering a 3D model. **Mesh Renderer** will render the mesh specified in the **Mesh Filter** in the position specified in the **Transform** component, so **Mesh Renderer** needs to get data from those other components and can't work without them.

Another example would be the **Box Collider**. This represents the physical shape of the object, so when the physics calculates collisions between objects, it checks whether that shape is colliding with other shapes based on the position specified in the **Transform** component.

We don't want to explore physics and rendering right now. The takeaway from this section is that a GameObject is a collection of components, each component adding a specific behavior to our object, and each one interacting with the others to accomplish the desired task. To further reinforce this, let's see how we can convert a cube into a sphere, and which falls, using physics.

Manipulating components

The tool to edit an object's components is the **Inspector**. It not only allows us to change the properties of our components but also lets us add and remove components. In this case, we want to convert a cube to a sphere, so we need to change several aspects of those components.

We can start by changing the visual shape of the object, so we need to change the rendered model or **Mesh**. The component that specifies the Mesh to be rendered is the **Mesh Filter** component. If we look at it, we can see a **Mesh** property that says **Cube**, with a little circle and a dot:

Figure 3.17 – The Mesh Filter component

> **Information box**
>
> If you don't see a particular property, such as the **Mesh** property we just mentioned, try to click the triangle to the left of the component's name. Doing this will expand and collapse all the component's properties.

If we click the button with a circle and a dot inside, the one on the right of the **Mesh** property, the **Select Mesh** window will pop up, allowing us to pick several **Mesh** options; so, in this case, select the **Sphere** component. In the future, we will add more 3D models to our project so that the window will have more options. The mesh selector is shown in the following screenshot:

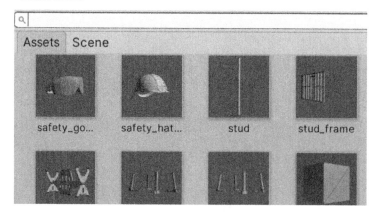

Figure 3.18 – Mesh selector

Okay—it looks like a sphere, but will it behave like a sphere? Let's find out. In order to do so, we can add a **Rigidbody** component to our sphere, which will add physics to it. In order to do so, we need to click the **Add Component** button at the bottom of the **Inspector**. It will show a **Component Selector** window with lots of categories; in this case, we need to click on the **Physics** category. The window will show all the **Physics** components, and there we can find the **Rigidbody** component. Another option would be to type **Rigidbody** in the search box at the top of the window. The following screenshot illustrates how to add a component:

Figure 3.19 – Adding components

If you click the Play button in the top-middle part of the editor, you can test your sphere physics using the Game panel. That panel will be automatically focused on when you click **Play** and will show you how the player will see the game. The playback controls are shown in the following screenshot:

Figure 3.20 – Playback controls

Here, you can just use the Transform Gizmo to rotate and position your camera in such a way that it looks at our sphere. This is important as one problem that can happen is that maybe you won't see anything playing, and that can happen if the game camera is not pointing to where our sphere is located. While you are moving, you can check the little preview in the bottom-right part of the scene window to check out the new camera perspective. Another alternative would be to select the camera in the **Hierarchy** and use the shortcut *Ctrl + Shift + F* (or *Command + Shift + F* on a Mac). The **Camera Preview** is shown in the following screenshot:

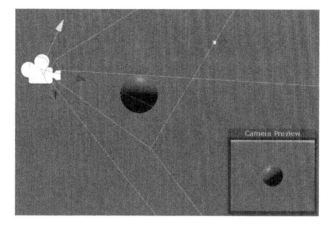

Figure 3.21 – Camera Preview

Now, to test whether Physics collisions are executing properly, let's create a cube, scale it until it has the shape of a ramp, and put that ramp below our sphere, as shown here:

Figure 3.22 – Ball and ramp objects

If you click **Play** now, you will see the sphere colliding with our ramp, but in a strange way. It looks like it's bouncing, but that's not the case. If you expand the **Box Collider** component of our sphere, you will see that even though our object looks like a sphere, the green box gizmo is showing us that our sphere is actually a box in the Physics world, as illustrated in the following screenshot:

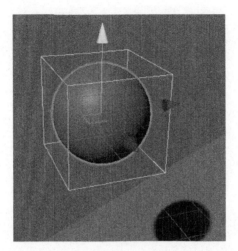

Figure 3.23 – Object with a sphere graphic and box collider

Nowadays, video cards can handle rendering highly detailed models (a high polygon count), but the Physics system is executed in the **Central Processing Unit** (**CPU**) and it needs to do complex calculations in order to detect collisions. To get decent performance in our game (at least 30 **Frames Per Second** (**FPS**)), the Physics system works using simplified collision shapes that may differ from the actual shape the player sees on the screen. That's why we have **Mesh Filter** and the different types of **Collider** components separated—one handles the visual shape and the other the physics shape.

Again, the idea of this section is not to deep dive into those Unity systems, so let's just move on for now. How can we solve this? Simple: by modifying our components! In this case, **BoxCollider** can just represent a box shape, unlike **MeshFilter**, which supports any shape. So, first, we need to remove it by right-clicking the component's title and selecting the **Remove Component** option, as illustrated in the following screenshot:

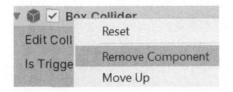

Figure 3.24 – Removing components

Now, we can again use the **Add Component** menu to select a **Physics** component, this time selecting the **Sphere Collider** component. If you look at the Physics components, you will see other types of colliders that can be used to represent other shapes, but we will look at them later in *Chapter 16, Physics Collisions and Health System*. The **Sphere Collider** component can be seen in the following screenshot:

Figure 3.25 – Adding a Sphere Collider component

So, if you click **Play** now, you will see that our sphere not only looks like a sphere but also behaves like one. Remember: the main idea of this section of the book is understanding that in Unity you can create whatever object you want just by adding, removing, and modifying components, and we will be doing a lot of this throughout the book.

Now, components are not the only thing needed in order to create objects. Complex objects may be composed of several sub-objects, so let's see how that works.

Object hierarchies

Some complex objects may need to be separated in sub-objects, each one with its own components. Those sub-objects need to be somehow attached to the main object and work together to create the necessary object behavior.

In this section, we will cover the following concepts related to components:

- Parenting objects
- Possible uses

Let's start discovering how to create a parent-child relationship between objects.

Parenting objects

Parenting consists of making an object the child of another, meaning that those objects will be related to each other. One type of relationship that happens is a **Transform relationship**, meaning that a child object will be affected by the parent's Transform. In simple terms, the child object will follow the parent, as if it is attached to it. As an example, imagine a player with a hat on their head. The hat can be a child of the player's head, making the hat follow the head while they are attached.

In order to try this, let's create a capsule that represents an enemy and a cube that represents the weapon of the enemy. Remember that in order to do so, you can use the **GameObject | 3D Object | Capsule** and **Cube** options. An example of a capsule and a cube can be seen in the following screenshot:

Figure 3.26 – A capsule and cube representing a human and a box representing a weapon

If you move the enemy object (the capsule), the weapon (the box) will keep its position, not following our enemy. So, in order to prevent that, we can simply drag the weapon to the enemy object in the **Hierarchy** window, as illustrated in the following screenshot:

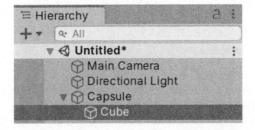

Figure 3.27 – Parenting the cube weapon to the capsule character

Now, if you move the enemy, you will see the gun moving, rotating, and being scaled along with it. So, basically, the gun transform also has the effects of the enemy transform component.

Now that we have done some basic parenting, let's explore other possible uses.

Possible uses

There are some other uses of parenting aside from creating complex objects. Another common usage for it is to organize the project hierarchy. Right now, our scene is simple, but in time it will grow, so keeping track of all the objects will become difficult. So, to prevent this, we can create empty GameObjects (in **GameObject | Create Empty**) to act as containers, putting objects into them just to organize our scene. Try to use this with caution because this has a performance cost if you abuse it. Generally, having one or two levels of parenting when organizing a scene is fine, but more than that can have a performance hit. Consider that you can—and will—have deeper parenting for the creation of complex objects; the proposed limit is just for scene organization.

To keep improving on our previous example, duplicate the enemy a couple of times all around the scene, create an empty Game Object called **Enemies**, and drag all the enemies into it so that it will act as a container. This is illustrated in the following screenshot:

Figure 3.28 – Grouping enemies in a parent object

Another common usage of parenting is to change the **pivot** (or center) of an object. Right now, if we try to rotate our gun with the Transform Gizmo, it will rotate around its center because the creator of that cube decided to put the center there. Normally, that's okay, but let's consider the case where we need to make the weapon aim at the point where our enemy is looking. In this case, we need to rotate the weapon around the weapon handle; so, in the case of this "box" weapon, it would be the closest end to the enemy. The problem here is that we cannot change the center of an object, so one solution would be to create another "weapon" 3D model or mesh with another center, which will lead to lots of duplicated versions of the weapon if we consider other possible gameplay requirements such as a rotating weapon pickup. We can fix this easily using parenting.

The idea is to create an empty GameObject and locate it where we want the new pivot of our object to be. After that, we can simply drag our weapon inside this empty GameObject, and, from now on, consider the empty object as the actual weapon. If you rotate or scale this weapon container, you will see that the weapon mesh will apply those transformations around this container, so we can say the pivot of the weapon has changed (actually, it hasn't, but our container simulates the change). The process is illustrated in the following screenshot:

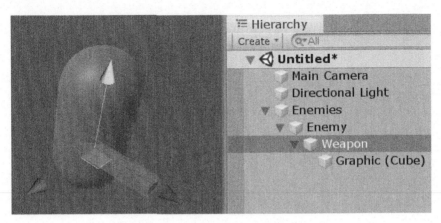

Figure 3.29 – Changing the weapon pivot

Now, let's continue seeing different ways of managing GameObjects, using Prefabs this time.

Prefabs

In the previous example, we created lots of copies of our enemy around the scene, but in doing so, we have created a new problem. Let's imagine we need to change our enemy and add a **Rigidbody** component to it, but because we have several copies of the same object, we need to take them one by one and add the same component to all of them. Maybe later we will need to change the mass of each enemy, so again, we will need to go over each one of the enemies and make the change, and here we can start to see a pattern. One solution could be to select all the enemies using the *Ctrl* key (*Command* on a Mac) and modify all of them at once, but that solution won't be of any use if we have enemy copies in other scenes. So, here is where Prefabs come in.

In this section, we will cover the following concepts related to prefabs:

- Creating Prefabs
- Prefab-instance relationships
- Prefab variants

Let's start by discussing how to create and use prefabs.

Creating Prefabs

A **prefab** is a Unity tool that allows us to convert custom-made objects, such as our enemy, into an Asset that defines how they can be created. We can use them to create new copies of our custom object easily, without needing to create its components and sub-objects all over again.

In order to create a Prefab, we can simply drag our custom object from the **Hierarchy** window to the **Project** window, and after doing that you will see a new Asset in your project files. The **Project** window is where you can navigate and explore all your project files; so, in this case, our Prefab is the first Asset we ever created. Now, you can simply drag the Prefab from the **Project** window into the Scene to easily create new Prefab copies, as illustrated in the following screenshot:

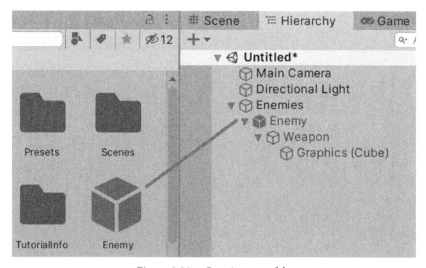

Figure 3.30 – Creating a prefab

Now, we have a little problem here. If you pay attention to the **Hierarchy** window, you will see the original prefab objects and all the new copies with their names in the color blue, while the enemies created before the prefab will have their names in black. The color blue in a name means that the object is an **instance** of a prefab, meaning that the object was created based on a Prefab. We can select those blue-named objects and click the **Select** button in the **Inspector** to select the original prefab that created that object. This is illustrated in the following screenshot:

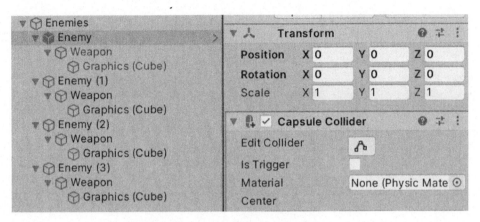

Figure 3.31 – Detecting prefabs in the hierarchy

So, the problem here is that the previous copies of the prefab are not instances of the original prefab, and sadly there's no way to make them be connected to the prefab. So, in order to make that happen, we need to simply destroy the old copies and replace them with copies created with the prefab. At first, not having all copies as instances doesn't seem to be a problem, but it will be in the next section of this chapter, where we will explore the relationship between Prefabs and their instances.

Prefab-instance relationship

An instance of a Prefab has a binding to it that helps to revert and apply changes easily between the prefab and the instance. If you take a Prefab and make some modifications to it, those changes will be automatically applied to all instances across all the scenes in the project, so we can easily create a first version of the prefab, use it all around the project, and then experiment with changes.

To practice this, let's say we want to add a **Rigidbody** component to the enemies so that they can fall. In order to do so, we can simply double-click the **Prefab** file and we will enter **Prefab Edit Mode**, where we can edit the Prefab isolated from the rest of the scene. Here, we can simply take the **Prefab** root object and add the **Rigidbody** component to it. After that, we can simply click on the **Scenes** button in the top-left part of the **Scene** window to get back to the scene we were editing, and now, we can see that all the prefab instances of the enemy have a **Rigidbody** component, as illustrated in the following screenshot:

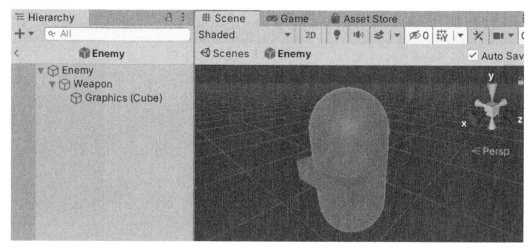

Figure 3.32 – Prefab edit mode

Now, what happens if we change a Prefab instance (the one in the scene) instead? Let's say we want one specific enemy to fly, so they won't suffer the effect of gravity. We can do that by simply selecting the specific prefab and unchecking the Use Gravity checkbox in the **Rigidbody** component. After doing that, if we play the game, we will see that only that specific instance will float. That's because changes of an instance of a Prefab become an **override**, and we can see that clearly if you see how the **Use Gravity** property of that instance becomes bold in the **Inspector** and a blue bar will be displayed on its left. Let's take another object and change its **Scale** property to make it bigger. Again, we will see how the **Scale** property becomes bold and the blue bar on its left will appear. The **Use Gravity** checkbox can be seen in the following screenshot:

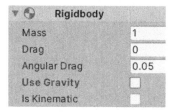

Figure 3.33 – Use Gravity being highlighted as an override

The overrides have precedence over the Prefab, so if we change the scale of the original Prefab, the one that has a scale override won't change, keeping its own version of the scale, as illustrated in the following screenshot:

Figure 3.34 – One prefab instance with a scale override

We can easily locate all overrides of an instance using the **Override** dropdown in the **Inspector**, locating all the changes our object has. It not only allows us to see all the overrides but also reverts any override we don't want and applies the ones we want. Let's say we regretted the lack of gravity of that specific prefab—no problem! We can just locate the override and revert it. The process is illustrated in the following screenshot:

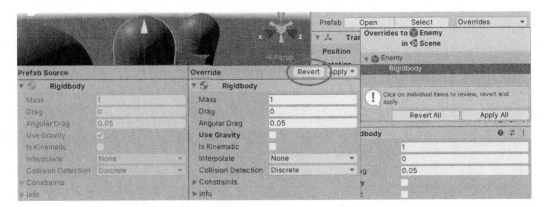

Figure 3.35 – Reverting a single override

Also, let's imagine that we really liked the new scale of that instance, so we want all instances to have that scale—great! We can simply select the specific change, click the **Apply** button, and then the **Apply to Prefab** option. Now all instances will have that scale (except the ones with an override), as illustrated in the following screenshot:

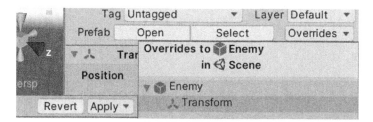

Figure 3.36 – The Apply button

Also, we have the **Revert All** and **Apply All** buttons, but use them with caution, because you can easily revert and apply changes that you are not aware of.

So, as you can see, the Prefab is a really useful Unity tool to keep track of all similar objects and apply changes to all of them, and also have specific instances with few variations. Talking about variations, there are other cases where you will want to have several instances of a Prefab with the same set of variations—for example, flying enemies and grounded enemies—but if you think about that, we will have the same problem we had when we didn't use prefabs, so we need to manually update those variated versions one by one.

Here, we have two options: one is to create a brand new prefab just to have another version with that variation. This leads to the problem that if we want all types of enemies to suffer changes, we need to manually apply the changes to each possible prefab. The second option is to create a Prefab variant. Let's review the latter.

Prefab variants

A **Prefab variant** is the result of creating a new Prefab but based on an existing one, so the new one **inherits** the features of the base Prefab. This means that our new Prefab can have differences from the base one, but the features that they have in common are still connected.

To illustrate this, let's create a variation of the enemy Prefab that can fly: the flying enemy Prefab. In order to do that, we can select an existing enemy Prefab instance in the **Hierarchy** window, name it **Flying Enemy**, and drag it again to the **Project** window, and this time we will see a prompt, asking which kind of prefab we want to create. This time, we need to choose **Prefab Variant**, as illustrated in the following screenshot:

Figure 3.37 – Creating a prefab variant

Now, we can enter the Prefab Edit Mode of the variant by double-clicking it, and then add a cube as the jet pack of our enemy, and also uncheck the **Use Gravity** property for the enemy. If we go back to the Scene, we will see the variant instance has changed, and the base enemies haven't changed. You can see this in the following screenshot:

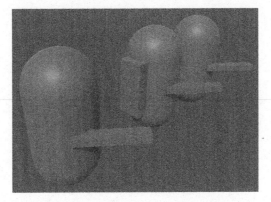

Figure 3.38 – Prefab variant instance

Now, imagine you want to add a hat to all our types of enemies. We can simply enter **Prefab Edit Mode** of the base enemy Prefab by double-clicking it and add a cube as a hat. Now, we will see that change applied to all the enemies because, remember: the **Flying Enemy** Prefab is a variant of the base enemy Prefab, meaning that it will inherit all the changes of that one.

We have created lots of content so far, but if our PC turns off for some reason, we will certainly lose it all, so let's see how we can save our progress.

Saving scenes and projects

As in any other program, we need to save our progress. The difference here is that we don't have just one giant file with all the project Assets, but several files for each Asset.

In this section, we will cover the following concepts related to saving:

- Saving our changes
- Project structure

Let's start by discussing how to save our scene.

Saving our changes

Let's start saving our progress by saving the scene, which is pretty straightforward. We can simply go to **File | Save** or press *Ctrl + S* (*Command + S* on a Mac). The first time we save our scene, a window will just ask us where we want to save our file, and you can save it wherever you want inside the Assets folder of our project, but never outside that folder. That will generate a new Asset in the **Project** window: a scene file, as illustrated in the following screenshot:

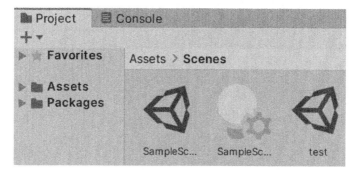

Figure 3.39 – Scene files

We can create a folder to save our scene in that dialog, or, if you already saved the scene, you can create a folder using the **Plus Icon** in the **Project** window and then click the **Folder** option. Finally, drag the created scene to that folder. Now, if you create another Scene with the **File | New Scene** menu option, you can get back to the previous scene just by double-clicking the asset in the **Project** window.

This only saved the Scene, but any changes to Prefabs and other kinds of Assets are not saved with that option. Instead, if you want to save every change to Assets other than Scenes, you can use the **File | Save Project** option. It can be a little bit confusing, but if you want to save all your changes, you need to both save the scenes and the project, as saving just the project won't save the changes to Scenes. Sometimes, the best way to be sure everything is saved is just by closing Unity, which is recommended when you try to move your project between computers or folders. Let's talk about that in the next section.

Project structure

Now that we have saved all our changes, we are ready to move the project between computers or to another folder (if you someday need to). You can close Unity to make sure everything is saved and temporary files are deleted, so you can just copy the entire project folder. If you don't remember where you saved your project, you can just right-click the `Assets` folder in the **Project** window and select **Show in Explorer** (**Reveal in Finder** on a Mac), as illustrated in the following screenshot:

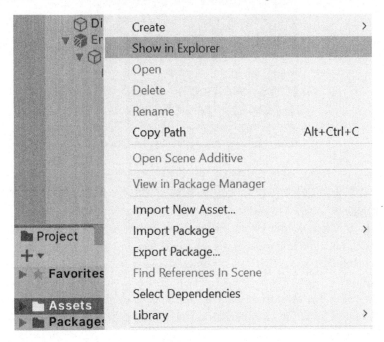

Figure 3.40 – Locating the project folder

Let's take the opportunity, now that we are in the project folder, to explore a little bit about the project folders. We will find several folders and files in a full project, but it's not necessary to copy all the files in order to move the project elsewhere. The most important folders are **Assets**, **ProjectSettings**, and **Packages**. These folders can be seen in the following screenshot:

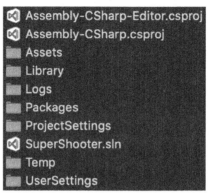

Figure 3.41 – Project folder structure

Assets is where all our scenes, prefabs, and other asset files will live, so that folder and all its content are indispensable, including those metafiles automatically created per asset. The `ProjectSettings` folder contains several configurations of different Unity systems we will fiddle with later in this book, but even if we don't change any settings, it's always a good idea to bring that folder with us. **Packages** is a Unity feature that allows you to install official and custom Unity packages or plugins that extend the engine's capabilities, this being a new, different version of what the `.unitypackage` files used to be, but let's discuss that later. So far, it's important to notice that that folder will have settings for which packages our project is using, so remember to also bring that one with you.

No other folders/files are necessary because some are them are temporary and others can be regenerated, such as **Library**, where all the converted versions of our Assets will live. By converted, we mean externally generated files, such as 3D models, images, sounds, and so on. Unity needs to convert those files to a Unity-compatible format. The original will live in **Assets** and the converted ones in **Library** so that they can be easily regenerated if necessary. Later, in *Chapter 5*, *Importing and Integrating Assets*, we will discuss integrating externally generated content.

Now, let's imagine you have compressed those three folders, copied them to a flash drive, and then decompressed the folders onto another computer. How can we open the project again? As you can see, a project doesn't have a project file or anything like that—it's just a bunch of folders. In order to open a project, the easiest way would be to find a scene file in the `Assets` folder and double-click it so that Unity will open the project in that scene. Another option would be to use the **Add** button in Unity Hub and find the project folder (the one that contains the `Assets` folder). So, we will add that project to the list of our computer projects, and later, we can just click the name in that list to open it. The following screenshot illustrates this:

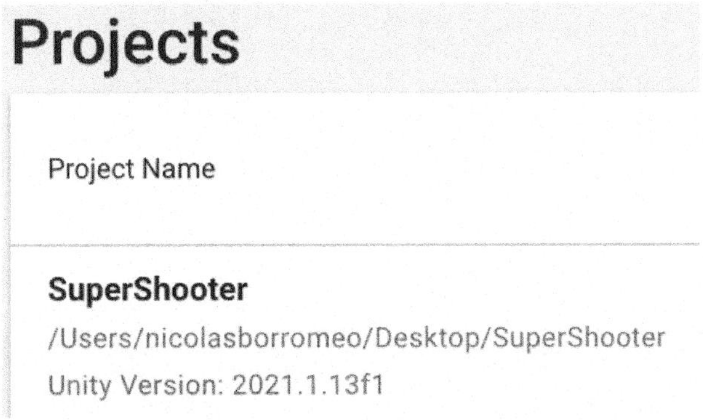

Projects

Project Name

SuperShooter
/Users/nicolasborromeo/Desktop/SuperShooter
Unity Version: 2021.1.13f1

Figure 3.42 – Reopening a project

Now, we have all the base Unity knowledge we need in order to start diving into how to use the different Unity systems so that we can start creating a real game! Let's do that in the next chapter!

Summary

In this chapter, we had a quick introduction to essential Unity concepts. We reviewed the basic Unity windows and how we can use all of them to edit a full scene, from navigating it then creating premade objects, to manipulating them to create our own types of objects using GameObjects and Components. We also discussed how to use the **Hierarchy** window to parent GameObjects to create complex object hierarchies, as well as creating Prefabs to reutilize and manipulate large amounts of the same type of objects. Finally, we discussed how we can save our progress and move the project, reviewing the structure of it and which folders are the essential ones.

In the next chapter, we will learn about different tools such as the Terrain System and ProBuilder, to create the first prototype of our game's level. This prototype will serve as a preview of where our scene will be headed – the early testing of some ideas.

4
Grayboxing with Terrain and ProBuilder

Now that we have grasped all the necessary concepts to use Unity, let's start designing our first level. The idea in this chapter is to learn how to use the Terrain tool to create the Landscape of our game and then use ProBuilder to create the 3D mesh of the base with greater detail than using cubes. At the end of the chapter, you will be able to create a prototype of any kind of scene and try out your idea before actually implementing it with final graphics.

Specifically, we will examine the following concepts in this chapter:

- Creating a Landscape with Terrain
- Creating Shapes with ProBuilder

Creating a Landscape with Terrain

So far, we have used Cubes to generate our level prototype, but we also learned that those Shapes sometimes cannot represent all possible objects we might need. Imagine something irregular, such as a full terrain with hills, canyons, and rivers. This would be a nightmare to create using cubes. Another option would be to use 3D modeling software, but the problem with that is that the generated model would be so big and so detailed that it wouldn't perform well, even on high-end PCs. In this scenario, we need to learn how to use Terrain, which we will do in this first section of this chapter.

In this section, we will cover the following concepts related to terrains:

- Discussing Height Maps
- Creating and configuring Height Maps
- Authoring Height Maps
- Adding Height Map details

Let's start by talking about Height Maps, whose textures help us define the heights of our terrain.

Discussing Height Maps

If we create a giant area of the game with Hills, canyons, craters, valleys, and rivers using regular 3D modeling tools, we will have the problem that we will use full detailed models for objects at all possible distances, thus wasting resources on details we won't see when the object is far away. We will see lots of Terrain parts from a great distance, such as mountains and rivers, so this is a serious issue.

Unity Terrain Tools uses a technique called Height Maps to generate terrain in a performant and dynamic way. Instead of generating large 3D models for the whole terrain, it uses an image called a Height Map, which looks like a top-down black and white photo of the terrain.

In the following screenshot, you can see a black and white top-down view of the heights of Scottish terrain, with white being a higher height and black being a lower height:

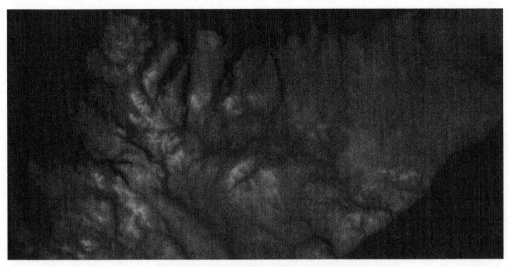

Figure 4.1 – Scottish terrain Height Map

In the preceding screenshot, you can easily spot the peaks of the mountains while looking for the whitest areas of the image. Everything below sea level is black, while anything in the middle uses gradients of gray and represents different heights between the minimum and maximum heights. The idea is that each pixel of the image determines the height of that specific area of the terrain.

Unity Terrain Tools can automatically generate a Terrain 3D mesh from that image, saving us the hard drive space of having full 3D models of that terrain. Also, Unity will create the terrain as we move, generating high-detail models for nearby areas and lower-detail models for faraway areas, making it a performant solution.

In the following screenshot, you can see the mesh that was generated for the terrain. You can appreciate that the nearer parts of the terrain have more polygons than further away parts:

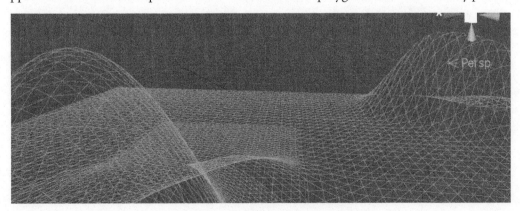

Figure 4.2 – Height Map generated mesh

Take into account that this technology also has its cons, such as the time it takes for Unity to generate those 3D models while we play and the inability to create caves, but for now, that's not a problem for us.

Now that we know what a Height Map is, let's see how we can use Unity Terrain Tools to create our own Height Maps.

Creating and configuring Height Maps

If you click on **GameObject | 3D Object | Terrain**, you will see how a giant plane appears on your scene and that a Terrain object appears in your Hierarchy window. That's our terrain, and it is plain because its Height Map starts all black, so no height whatsoever is in its initial state. In the following screenshot, you can see what a brand-new **Terrain** looks like:

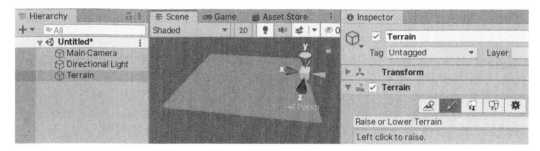

Figure 4.3 – Terrain with no heights painted yet

Before you start editing your terrain, you must configure different settings such as the size and resolution of the Terrain's Height Map, and that depends on what you are going to do with it. This is not the same as generating a whole world. Remember that our game will happen in the Player's Base, so the terrain will be small. In this case, an area that's 200 x 200 meters in size surrounded by mountains will be enough.

In order to configure our terrain for those requirements, we need to do the following:

1. Select **Terrain** from the **Hierarchy** or **Scene** window.

2. Look at the **Inspector** for the **Terrain** component and expand it if it is collapsed.

3. Click on the Wheel Icon to switch to configuration mode. In the following screenshot, you can see where that button is located:

Figure 4.4 – Terrain Settings button

4. Look for the **Mesh Resolution** section.

5. Change **Terrain Width** and **Terrain Length** to 200 in both settings. This will say that the size of our terrain is going to be 200 x 200 meters.

6. **Terrain Height** determines the maximum height possible. The white areas of our Height Map are going to be that size. We can reduce it to 500 just to limit the maximum peak of our mountains:

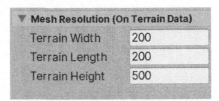

Figure 4.5 – Terrain Resolution settings

7. Look for the **Texture Resolutions** section.

8. Change **Heightmap Resolution** to **257 x 257**:

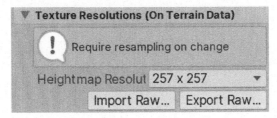

Figure 4.6 – Heightmap Resolution settings

> **Important note**
>
> Heightmap Resolution is the size of the Heightmap image that will hold the heights of the different parts of the terrain. Using a resolution of 257 x 257 in our 200 x 200-meter terrain means that each square meter in the terrain will be covered by a little bit more than 1 pixel of the Heightmap. The higher the resolution per square meter, the greater detail you can draw in that area size. Usually, terrain features are big, so having more than 1 pixel per square meter is generally a waste of resources. Find the smallest resolution you can have that allows you to create the details you need.

Another initial setting you will want to set is the initial terrain height. By default, this is 0, so you can start painting heights from the bottom part, but this way, you can't make holes in the terrain because it's already at its lowest point. Setting up a little initial height allows you to paint river paths and pits if you need them. In order to do so, do the following:

1. Select **Terrain**.

2. Click on the **Brush** button (the second button).

3. Set the dropdown to **Set Height**.

4. Set the **Height** property to 50.This will state we want all the terrain to start at 50 meters in height, allowing us to make holes with a maximum depth of 50 meters:

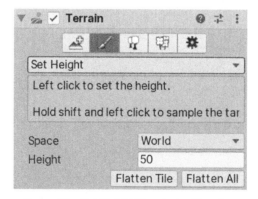

Figure 4.7 – Set Height Terrain tool location

5. Click the **Flatten All** button. You will see all the terrain has raised to the 50 meters we specified. This leaves us with 450 more meters to go up, based on the maximum of 500 meters we specified earlier.

Now that we have properly configured our Height Map, let's start editing it.

Authoring Height Maps

Remember that the Height Map is just an image with the heights, so in order to edit it, we would need to paint the heights in that image. Luckily, Unity has tools that allow us to edit the Terrain directly in the Editor and see the results of the modified heights directly. In order to do this, we must follow these steps:

1. Select **Terrain**.
2. Click the **Brush** button.
3. Set the dropdown to the **Raise or Lower Terrain** mode:

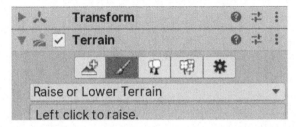

Figure 4.8 – Raise or Lower Terrain tool location

4. Select the second brush in the **Brushes** selector. This brush has blurred borders to allow us to create softer heights.
5. Set **Brush Size** to 30 so that we can create heights that span 30-meter areas. If you want to create subtler details, you can reduce this number.
6. Set **Opacity** to 10 to reduce the amount of height we paint per second or click:

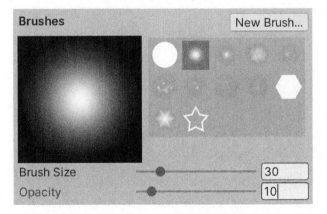

Figure 4.9 – Smooth edges brush

7. Now, if you move the mouse in the **Scene** view, you will see a little preview of the height you will paint if you click on that area. Maybe you will need to navigate closer to the terrain to see it in detail:

Figure 4.10 – Previsualization of the area to raise the terrain

> **Important note**
>
> That checker pattern you can see near the terrain allows you to see the actual size of the objects you are editing. Each cell represents a square meter area. Remember that having a reference to see the actual size of the objects you are editing is useful to prevent creating too big or too small terrain features. Maybe you can put in other kinds of references, such as a big cube with accurate sizes representing a building to get a notion of the size of the mountain or lake you are creating. Remember that the cube has a default size of 1 x 1 x 1 meter so scaling to (10,10,10) will give you a cube of 10 x 10 x 10 meters.

8. Hold, left-click, and drag the cursor over the terrain to start painting your terrain heights. Remember that you can press *Ctrl + Z (Command + Z* on Mac) to revert any undesired changes.

9. Try to paint the mountains all around the borders of our area, which will represent the background hills of our base:

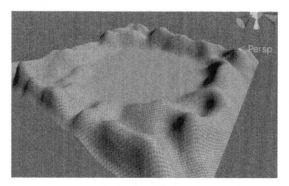

Figure 4.11 – Painted mountains around the edges of the terrain

Now, we have decent starter hills around our future base. We can also draw a river basin around our future base area. To do so, follow these steps:

1. Place a cube with a scale of (50,10,50) in the middle of the terrain. This will act as a placeholder for the base we are going to create:

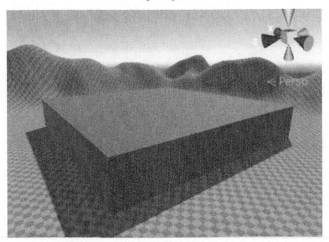

Figure 4.12 – Placeholder cube for the base area

2. Select **Terrain** and the **Brush** button once more.

3. Reduce **Brush Size** to **10**.

4. Holding the *Shift* key, left-click and drag the mouse over the terrain to paint the basin around our base placeholder. Doing this will lower the terrain instead of raising it:

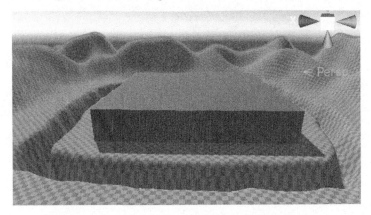

Figure 4.13 – River basin around our placeholder base

Now, we have a simple but good starter terrain that gives us a basic idea of how it will look from our base perspective. Before moving on, we will apply some finer details to make our terrain look a little bit better. In the next section, we will discuss how to simulate terrain erosion with different tools.

Adding Height Map details

In the previous section, we created a rough outline of the terrain. If you want to make it look a little bit realistic, then you need to start painting lots of tiny details here and there. Usually, this is done later in the level design process, but let's take a look now since we are exploring the Terrain Tools. Right now, our mountains look very smooth. In real life, they are sharper, so let's improve that:

1. Select **Terrain** and enable the **Brush** button.

2. Set the dropdown to the **Raise or Lower Terrain** mode.

3. Pick the fifth brush. This one has an irregular layout so that we can paint a little bit of noise here and there.

4. Set **Brush Size** to 50 so that we can cover a greater area:

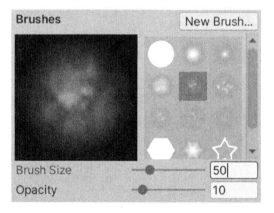

Figure 4.14 – Cloud pattern brush for randomness

5. Hold *Shift* and do small clicks over the hills of the terrain without dragging the mouse. Remember to zoom in to the areas you are applying finer details to because those can't be seen at great distances:

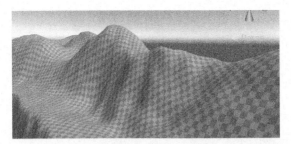

Figure 4.15 – Erosion generated with the previous brush

This has added some irregularity to our hills. Now, let's imagine we want to have a flat area on the hills to put a decorative observatory or antenna. Follow these steps to do so:

1. Select **Terrain, Brush Tool,** and **Set Height** from the dropdown.

2. Set **Height** to **60**.

3. Select the full circle brush (the first one).

4. Paint an area over the hills. You will see how the terrain will raise if it's lower than **60** meters or become lower in areas higher than **60** meters:

Figure 4.16 – Flattened hill

5. You can see that the borders have some rough corners that need to be smoothed:

Figure 4.17 – Non-smoothed terrain edges

6. Change the dropdown to the **Smooth Height** mode.

7. Select the second brush with a size of 5 and an opacity of 10:

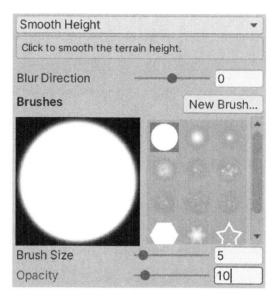

Figure 4.18 – Smooth Height brush selected

8. Click and drag over the borders of our flat area to make them smoother:

Figure 4.19 – Smoothed terrain edges

We can keep adding details here and there, but we can settle with this for now. The next step is to create our Player's Base, but this time, let's explore ProBuilder in order to generate our geometry.

Creating Shapes with ProBuilder

So far, we have created simple scenes using Cubes and primitive Shapes, and that's enough for most of the prototypes you will create, but sometimes, you will have tricky areas of the game that would be difficult to model with regular cubes, or maybe you want to have some greater detail in certain parts of your game to get a visual of how the player will feel in that area. In this case, we can use any 3D modeling tools for this, such as 3D Studio, Maya, or Blender, but those can be difficult to learn and you probably won't need all their power at this stage of your development. Luckily, Unity has a simple 3D model creator called ProBuilder, so let's explore it.

In this section, we will cover the following concepts related to ProBuilder:

- Installing ProBuilder
- Creating a shape
- Manipulating the mesh
- Adding details

Probuilder is not included by default in our Unity project, so let's start by learning how we can install it.

Installing ProBuilder

Unity is a powerful engine full of features, but having all those tools added to our project if we are not using all of them can make the engine run slower, so we need to manually specify which Unity tools we are using. To do so, we will use the Package Manager, a tool that we can use to see and select which Unity Packages we are going to need. As you may recall, earlier, we talked about the Packages folder. This is basically what the Package Manager modifies.

In order to install ProBuilder with this tool, we need to do the following:

1. Click the **Window | Package Manager** option:

Figure 4.20 – Package Manager option

2. In the window that just opened, be sure that the **Packages** mode is set to **Unity Registry** mode, by clicking on the button saying **Packages** in the top-left part of the window and selecting **Unity Registry**:

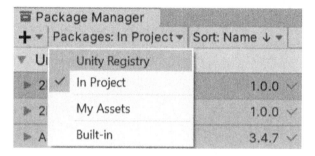

Figure 4.21 – Showing all packages

3. Wait a moment for the left list of packages to fill. Make sure you are connected to the internet to download and install the packages.

4. Look at the **ProBuilder** package in that list and select it:

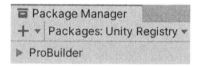

Figure 4.22 – ProBuilder in the Packages list

> **Important note**
>
> I'm using ProBuilder version 5.0.3, the newest version available at the time of writing this book. While you can use a newer version if available, consider that the steps to use it may differ. You can look at older versions using the arrow at the left of the title shown in the preceding screenshot.

5. Click on the **Install** button on the bottom right-hand side of the **Package Manager**:

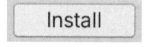

Figure 4.23 – Install button

6. Wait a moment for the package to install. You will notice the process has ended when the **Install** button has been replaced with the **Remove** label.

7. Go to **Edit | Preferences** on Windows (**Unity | Preferences** on Mac).

8. Select the **Pro Builder** option from the left list.

9. Set **Vertex Size** to 2 and **Line Size** to 1. This will help you to better visualize the 3D model we are going to create while editing its different parts.

> **Important note**
>
> The **Vertex Size** and **Line Size** values are big (2 meters and 1 meter respectively) due to the fact we are not going to edit little details of a model, but big features like walls. Consider that you might want to modify it later depending on what you are editing.

Now that we have installed ProBuilder in our project, let's use it!

Creating a Shape

We will start our base by creating a plane for our floor. We will do this by doing the following:

1. Delete the cube we placed as the base placeholder (Right-Click | **Delete** in **the Hierarchy**).

2. Open ProBuilder and go to **Tools | ProBuilder | ProBuilder Window**:

Figure 4.24 – ProBuilder Window option

3. In the window that has opened, click the **New Shape** button:

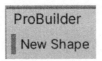

Figure 4.25 – New Shape option

4. In the **Create Shape** panel that appears in the bottom-right area of the **Scene** view, select the **Plane** icon (the first icon of the second row).

5. Expand **Shape Properties** and **Plane Settings**.

6. Set **Width Cuts** and **Height Cuts** to 2. We will need those subdivisions later.

7. Click and drag over the terrain to draw the plane. While you do that, check how the **Size** value in the **Create Shape** panel changes. Try to make it have **X** and **Z** sizes of approximately 50.

8. Release the mouse button and set the **X** and **Z** values of **Size** to 5 0:

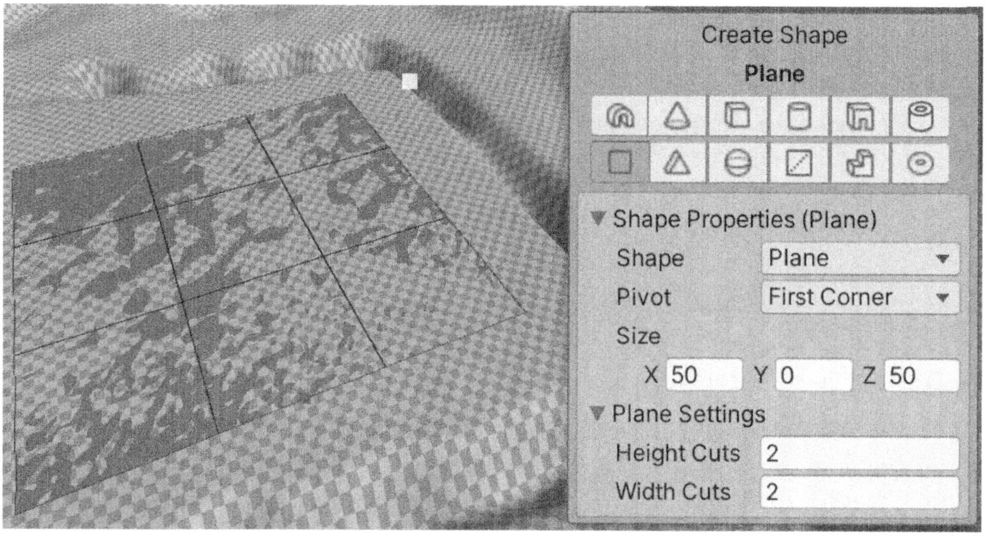

Figure 4.26 – New shape created

9. Select it in the **Hierarchy** and drag it a little bit upward using the **Transform tool**.

> **Important note**
>
> We needed to move the plane upward because it was created at the exact same height as the Terrain. That caused an effect called Z-Fighting, where the pixels that are positioned in the same position fight to determine which one will be drawn and which one will be occluded.

Now that we have created the floor, let's learn how we can manipulate its vertexes to change its shape.

Manipulating the mesh

If you select the plane, you will see that it is subdivided into a 3 x 3 grid because we set up the width and height segments to 2 (2 cuts). We did that because we will use the outer cells to create our walls, thus raising them up. The idea is to modify the size of those cells to outline the wall length and width before creating the walls. In order to do so, we will do the following:

1. Select the plane in the **Hierarchy**.

2. Click the second button (Vertex) of the four new buttons that appeared in the Scene View:

Figure 4.27 – Select the vertices tool

3. Click and drag the mouse to create a selection box that picks the four vertexes of the second row of vertexes:

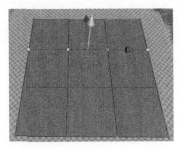

Figure 4.28 – Vertices selection

4. Click on the second button from the buttons at the top left of the Unity Editor to enable the **Move Tool**:

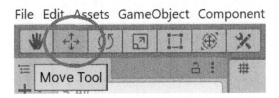

Figure 4.29 – Object Move Tool

5. Move the row of vertexes to make that subdivision of the plane thinner. You can use the checker pattern on the terrain to get a notion of the size of the wall in meters (1 meter per square in the checker):

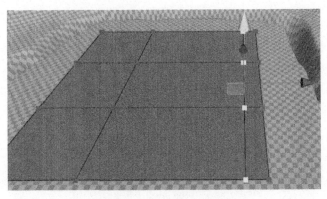

Figure 4.30 – Moved vertexes

6. Repeat *steps 3* to *5* for each row of vertexes until you get wall outlines with similar sizes:

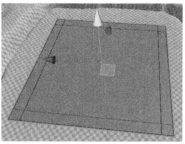

Figure 4.31 – Moved vertexes to reduce edges cell width

> **Important note**
>
> If you want the vertexes to have exact positions, I recommend that you install and explore the ProGrids Package. It is a position snapping system that works with regular Unity and ProBuilder.

Now that we have created the outline for our walls, let's add new faces to our mesh to create them. In order to use the subdivisions or "Faces" we have created to make our walls, we must pick and extrude them. Follow these steps to do so:

1. Select the plane.

2. Select the fourth button of the **ProBuilder** buttons in the Scene view:

Figure 4.32 – Select Face tool

3. While holding *Ctrl* (*Command* on Mac), click over each of the faces of the wall outlines:

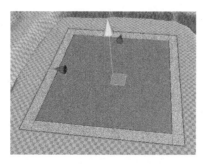

Figure 4.33 – Edge faces being selected

4. In the **ProBuilder** window, look for the plus icon (+) to the right of the **Extrude Faces** button. It will be located in the red section of the window:

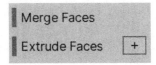

Figure 4.34 – Extrude Faces option

5. Set **Distance** to 5 in the window that appeared after we clicked the plus icon.

6. Click the **Extrude Faces** button in that window:

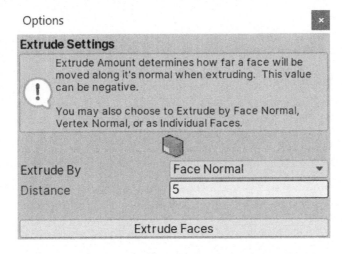

Figure 4.35 – Extrude distance option

7. Now, you should see that the outline of the walls has just raised up from the ground:

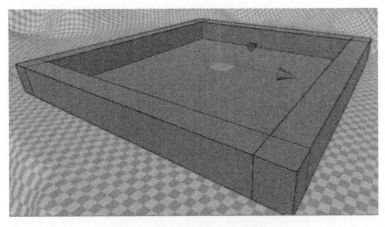

Figure 4.36 – Extruded grid edges

Now, if you pay attention to how the base floor and walls touch the Terrain, there's a little gap. We can try to move the base downward, but the floor will probably disappear because it will be buried under the terrain. A little trick we can do here is to just push the walls downward, without moving the floor, so that the walls will be buried in the Terrain but our floor will stay a little distance from it. You can see an example of how it will look in the following diagram:

Figure 4.37 – Slice of the expected result

In order to do this, we need to do the following:

1. Select the third **ProBuilder** button in the Scene view to enable edge selection:

Figure 4.38 – Select edges tool

2. While holding *Ctrl* (*Command* on Mac), select all the bottom edges of the walls.

3. If you select undesired edges, just click them again while holding *Ctrl* (*Command* on Mac) to deselect them, all while keeping the current selection:

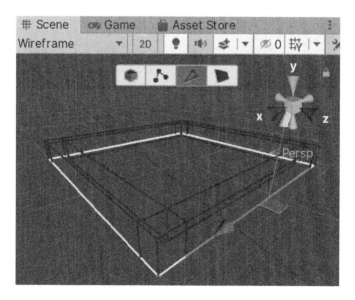

Figure 4.39 – Selecting floor edges

> **Information box**
>
> If you want to use the **Wireframe** mode in the previous screenshot, click on the **Shaded** button in the top-left part of the Scene view and select the **Wireframe** option from the drop-down menu.

4. Enable the **Move tool** by pressing the second button in the top-left part of the Unity Editor:

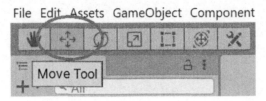

Figure 4.40 – Object Move Tool

5. Move the edges downward until they are fully buried under the terrain:

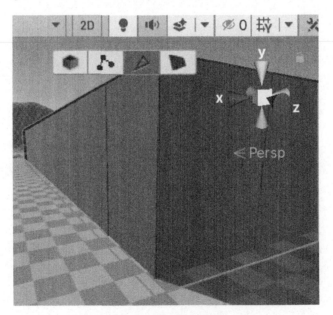

Figure 4.41 – Overlapping faces

Now that we have a base mesh, we can start adding details to it using several other ProBuilder tools.

Adding details

Let's start adding details to the base by applying a little bevel to the walls. Follow these steps:

1. Using the edge selection mode (the third button of the **ProBuilder** buttons), select the top edges of the model:

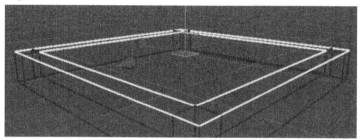

Figure 4.42 – Top wall edges being selected

2. In the **ProBuilder** window, look at the plus icon to the right of the **Bevel** button.

3. Set a distance of 0.5:

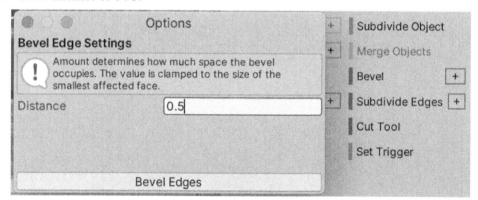

Figure 4.43 – Bevel distance to generate

4. Click on **Bevel Edges**. Now, you can see the top part of our walls with a little bevel:

Figure 4.44 – Result of the bevel process

5. Optionally, you can do that with the bottom part of the inner walls:

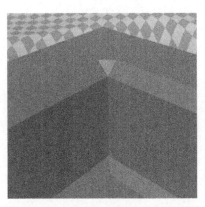

Figure 4.45 – Bevel being applied to floor-wall edges

Another detail to add could be a pit in the middle of the ground as a hazard we need to avoid falling into and to make the enemies avoid it using AI. In order to do that, follow these steps:

1. Enable the Face selection mode by clicking the fourth ProBuilder Scene view button.

2. Select the floor.

3. Click the **Subdivide faces** option in the **ProBuilder** window. You will end up with the floor split into four.

4. Click that button again to end up with a 4 x 4 grid floor:

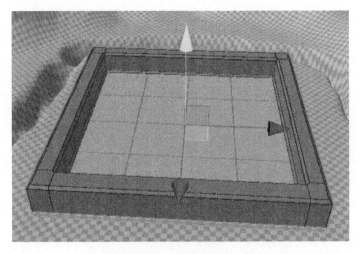

Figure 4.46 – Subidiving the floor

5. Select the four inner floor tiles using the **Select Face** tool (the third button of the ProBuilder four in the top part of the **Scene** view).

6. Enable the Scale Tool by clicking the fourth button in the top-left part of the Unity Editor:

Figure 4.47 – Scale tool

7. Using the gray cube at the center of the gizmo, scale down the center tiles:

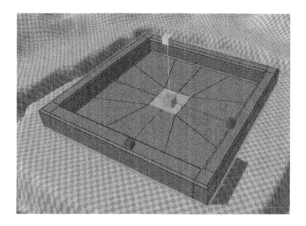

Figure 4.48 – Inner cells being scaled down

8. Click the **Extrude Faces** button in the **ProBuilder** window.

9. Push the extruded faces downward with the **Move Tool**.

10. Right-click on the **ProBuilder** window tab and select **Close Tab**. We need to get back to terrain editing and having **ProBuilder** open won't allow us to do that comfortably:

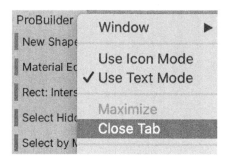

Figure 4.49 – Close Tab option

11. Select **Terrain** and lower that area of the terrain so that we can see the pit:

Figure 4.50 – Terrain being lowered for the pit to be visible

I know we didn't plan the pit in the original level layout but remember that the GDD is a document that will constantly change in the middle of game development, so sometimes, we can be bold and change it in order to improve the game. Just take care to not go too far with never-ending changes, which is a difficult-to-master art.

Summary

In this chapter, we learned how to create large Terrain meshes using Height Maps and Unity Terrain Tools such as Paint Height and Set Height to create hills and river basins. Also, we saw how to create our own 3D meshes using ProBuilder, as well as how to manipulate the vertexes, edges, and faces of a model to create a prototype base model for our game. We didn't discuss some performance optimizations we can apply to our meshes and some advanced 3D modeling concepts as that would require entire chapters and that's outside the scope of this book. Right now, our main focus is prototyping, so we are fine with our level's current status.

In the next chapter, we will learn how to download and replace these prototyping models with the final art by integrating assets (files) we created with external tools. This is the first step to improving the graphics quality of our game so that it reaches the final look, which we will finish by the end of *Part 2*.

5
Importing and Integrating Assets

In the previous chapter, we created the prototype of our level. Now, let's suppose that we have coded the game and tested it, validating the idea. With that, it's time to change the prototype art and use the real, finished art. We are going to code the game in Part 3, but for learning purposes, we'll skip that part for now. To use our final assets, we need to learn how to get them (images, 3D models, and so on), how to import them into Unity, and how to use them in our scene.

In this chapter, we will cover the following topics:

- Importing assets
- Integrating assets
- Configuring assets

Importing assets

We have different sources of assets that we can use in our project. We can simply get a file from our artist, download them from different free and paid assets sites, or we can use the Asset Store, Unity's official virtual asset store, where we can get free and paid assets ready to use within Unity. We will use a mix of downloading an asset from the internet and the Asset Store, just to get all the possible resources.

In this section, we will cover the following concepts related to importing assets:

- Importing assets from the internet
- Importing assets from the Asset Store
- Downloading and importing assets into our project from the internet

Let's get started!

Importing assets from the internet

In terms of getting art assets for our project, let's start with our terrain textures. Remember that we have our terrain painted with a grid pattern, so the idea is to replace that with grass, mud, rock, and other kinds of textures. To do that, we must get images. In this case, these kinds of images are usually top-down views of different terrain patterns, and they have the requirement of being "tileable." You can see an example of this in the following figure:

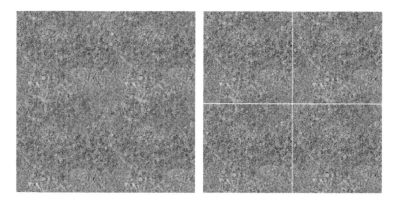

Figure 5.1 – Left – grass patch; right – the same grass patch separated to highlight the texture tiling

The grass on the left seems to be one single big image, but if you pay attention, you should be able to see some patterns repeating themselves. In this case, this grass is just a single image repeated four times in a grid, like the one on the right. This way, you can cover large areas by repeating a single small image, saving lots of RAM on your computer.

The idea is to get these kinds of images to paint our terrain. You can get them from several places, but the easiest way is to use Google Images or any image search engine. To do this, follow these steps:

1. Open your browser (Chrome, Safari, Edge, and so on).
2. Go to your preferred search engine. In this case, I will use Google.

3. Use the PATTERN, tileable, and texture keywords, replacing PATTERN with the kind of terrain you are looking for, such as grass tileable texture or mud tileable texture. In this case, I am going to type grass tileable texture and then press *Enter* to search.

4. Switch to the **Images** search mode:

Figure 5.2 – Google search for images

5. Choose any texture you find suitable for the kind of grass you need and click it. Remember that the texture must be a top-down view of the grass and must repeat.

> **Important Note**
> Try to check the image's resolution before picking it. Try to select squared images that have a resolution less than 1,024 x 1,024 for now.

6. Right-click on the opened image and select **Save image as…**:

Figure 5.3 – Save image as… option

7. Save the image in any folder you will remember.

Now that you have downloaded the image, you can add it to your project in several ways. The simplest way would be to do the following:

1. Locate your image using **File Explorer** (**Finder** on Mac).

2. Locate or create the `Textures` folder in the Project Window in Unity.

3. Put both the File Explorer and Unity Project Window next to each other.

4. Drag the file from **File Explorer** to the `Textures` folder in the Unity Project Window:

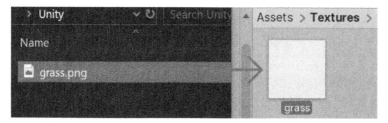

Figure 5.4 – Texture being dragged from Windows Explorer to Unity's Project Window

For simple textures like these, any search engine can be helpful, but if you want to replace the player's base geometry with detailed walls and doors or place enemies in your scene, you need to get 3D models. If you search for those in any search engine using keywords such as free, zombie, and 3D model, you will find endless free and paid 3D models sites such as TurboSquid and Mixamo. However, those sites can be problematic because those meshes are usually not prepared for being used in Unity, or even games. You will find models with very high polygons counts, incorrect sizes or orientations, unoptimized textures, and so on. To prevent those problems, we'll want to use a better source, and in this case, we will use Unity's Asset Store. So, let's explore it.

Importing assets from the Asset Store

The Asset Store is Unity's official asset marketplace where you can find lots of models, textures, sounds, and even entire Unity plugins to extend the capabilities of the engine. In this case, we will limit ourselves to downloading 3D models to replace the player's base prototype. You will want to get 3D models with a modular design, meaning that you will get several pieces, such as walls, floors, corners, and so on. You can connect them to create any kind of scenario.

To do that, you must follow these steps:

1. Click on **Window | Asset Store** in Unity, which will open a new window saying that the Asset Store has moved. In previous versions of Unity, you could see the Asset Store directly inside the editor, but now, it is recommended to open it in a regular web browser, so just click the **Search online** button, which will open `https://assetstore.unity.com/` in your preferred browser.

Figure 5.5 – The Asset Store has moved message

2. In the top menu, click on the **Assets | 3D** category to browse 3D assets:

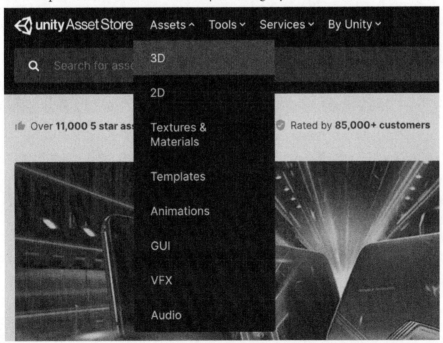

Figure 5.6 – 3D Assets menu

3. On the recently opened page, click the arrow to the right of the **3D** category in the **All Categories** panel on the right. Then, open **Environments** and check the **Sci-Fi** mark:

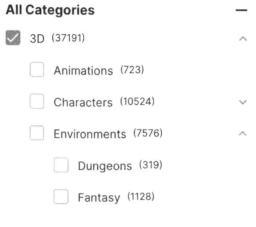

Figure 5.7 – 3D Assets menu

> **Important Note**
>
> As you can see, there are several categories for finding different types of assets, and you can pick another one if you want to. In **Environments**, you will find 3D models that can be used to generate the scenery for your game.

4. If you need to, you can pay for an asset, but let's hide the paid ones for now. You can do that by searching through the **Pricing** section on the sidebar, opening it using the plus (+) symbol on its right, and then checking the **Free Assets** checkbox:

Figure 5.8 – Free Assets option

5. In the search area, find any asset that seems to have the aesthetic you are looking for and click it. Remember to look out for outdoor assets, because most environment packs are usually interiors only. In my case, I have picked one called **Sci-Fi Styled Modular Pack** that serves both interiors and exteriors. Take into account that this package might not exist by the time you are reading this, so you might need to choose another one. If you don't find a suitable package, you can download the asset files we have provided in this book's GitHub repository:

New

ASSET STORE ORIGINALS
Snaps Prototype | Sci-Fi / In...
★★★★★ (13)
FREE

Purchased

KARBOOSX
Sci-Fi Styled Modular Pack
★★★★★ (92)
FREE

Figure 5.9 – Preview of Asset Store searched packages

> **Important Note**
> Unity offers the "Snaps" packages, which are a set of official Unity 3D models that can be used for modularly designing different kinds of environments. Some of them must be paid for, while others are free – I recommend that you try them out.

6. Now, you will see the package details in the Asset Store window. Here, you can find information regarding the package's description, videos/images, the package's contents, and the most important part, the reviews, where you can check if the package is worth buying if it's a paid one:

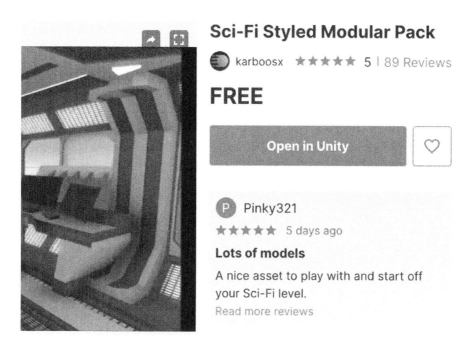

Figure 5.10 – Asset Store package details

7. If you are okay with this package, click the **Add To My Assets** button, log into Unity if requested, and click the **Open In Unity** button. You might be asked whether you meant to switch apps to open Unity; click **Yes**:

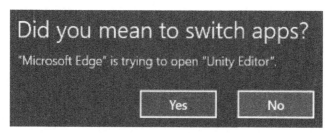

Figure 5.11 – Switching apps

8. This will open **Package Manager** again, but this time, in **My Assets**, showing a list of all the assets you have ever downloaded from the Asset Store, as well as the one you just selected, highlighted in the list:

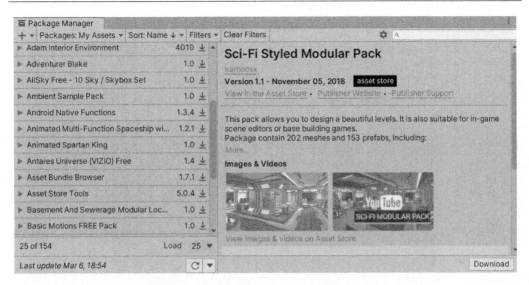

Figure 5.12 – Package Manager showing assets

9. Click on **Download** at the bottom-right corner of the window and wait for it to end. Then, hit **Import**.

10. After a while, the **Package Contents** window will appear, where you can select exactly which assets of the package you want in your project. For now, leave it as is and click **Import**:

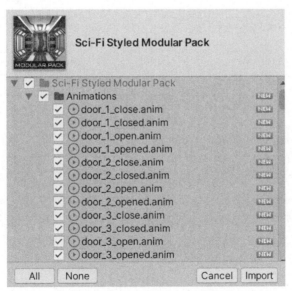

Figure 5.13 – Selecting assets to import

11. After a while, you will see all the package files in your Project window.

Take into account that importing lots of full packages will increase your project's size considerably, and that, later, you will probably want to remove the assets that you didn't use. Also, if you import assets that generate errors that prevent you from playing the scene, just delete all the .cs files that come with the package. They are usually in a folder called Scripts. These are code files that might not be compatible with your version of Unity:

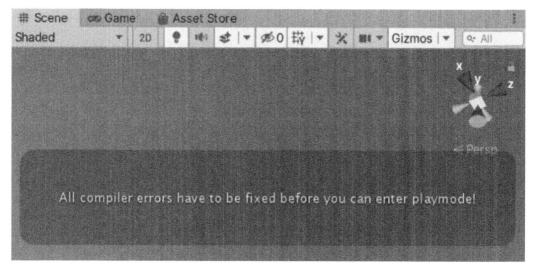

Figure 5.14 – Code error warning when hitting the play button

Important Note

The Asset Store is prone to changes, even if you are using the same Unity version I am using, so the previous steps may be changed by Unity without notice. Also, its contents change often, and you may not find the same packages that have been used in this book. If that happens, you can find another similar package, or take the files I used in the book's GitHub repository (links and instructions in the *Preface*).

Before you continue with this chapter, try to download an enemy character using the Asset Store while following the previous steps. To solve this exercise, you must complete the same steps you did previously but look in the **3D | Characters | Humanoid** category of the Asset Store.

Now that we have imported lots of art assets, let's learn how to use them in our scene.

Integrating assets

We have just imported lots of files that can be used in several ways, so the idea of this section is to see how Unity integrates those assets with the GameObjects and components that need them.

In this section, we will cover the following concepts related to importing assets:

- Integrating terrain textures
- Integrating meshes
- Integrating materials

Let's start by using the tileable textures to cover the terrain.

Integrating terrain textures

To apply textures to our terrain, do the following:

1. Select the **Terrain** object.

2. In the **Inspector** window, click the brush icon of the **Terrain** component (second button).

3. From the drop-down menu, select **Paint Texture**:

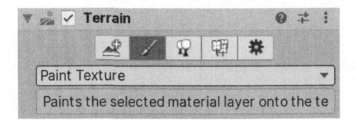

Figure 5.15 – Terrain Paint Texture option

4. Click the **Edit Terrain Layers... | Create Layer** option.

5.   Find and double-click the terrain texture you downloaded previously in the texture picker window that appears:

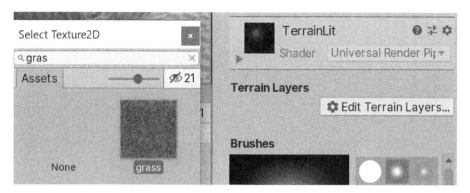

Figure 5.16 – Texture to paint picker

6.   You will see that the texture is immediately applied to the whole terrain.

7.   Repeat *steps 4* and *5* to add another texture. This time, you will see that that texture is not immediately applied.

8.   In the **Terrain Layers** section, select the new texture you have created to start painting with that. I used a mud texture.

9.   Just like when you edited the terrain, in the **Brushes** section, you can select and configure a brush to paint the terrain.

10. In the **Scene** view, paint the areas you want to have that texture applied to.

11. If your texture patterns are too obvious, open the **New Layer N** section at the top of the **Brushes** section, where N is a number that depends on the layer you have created.

> **Important Note**
>
> Each time you add a texture to the terrain, you will see that a new asset called **New Layer N** is created in the **Project** view. It holds data about the terrain layer you have created, and you can use it in other terrains if you need to. You can also rename that asset and give it a meaningful name. Finally, you can reorganize those assets in their own folder.

12. Open the section using the triangle to its left and increase the **Size** property in the **Tiling Settings** section until you find a suitable size, where the pattern is not that obvious:

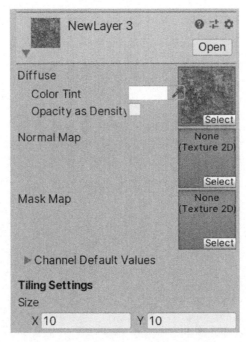

Figure 5.17 – Painting texture options

13. Repeat *steps 4* to *12* until you have applied all the textures you wanted to add to your terrain. In my case, I applied the mud texture to the river basin and used a rock texture for the hills. For the texture of the rocks, I reduced the **Opacity** property of the brush to blend it better with the grass in the mountains. You can also try to add a layer of snow at the top, just for fun:

Figure 5.18 – Results of painting our terrain with three different textures

Of course, we can improve this a lot using lots of the advanced tools provided by the system, but just let's keep things simple for now. Now, let's learn how to integrate the 3D models.

Integrating meshes

If you select one of the 3D assets we have configured previously and click the arrow to its right, one or more sub-assets will appear in the Project window. This means that FBX is not a 3D model, but a container of assets that defines the 3D model:

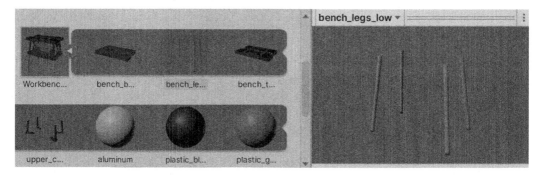

Figure 5.19 – Mesh picker

Some of those sub-assets are meshes, which are collections of triangles that define the geometry of your model. You can find at least one of those inside the file, but you can also find several, and that can happen if your model is composed of lots of pieces. For example, a car can be a single rigid mesh, but that won't allow you to rotate its wheels or open its doors; it will be just a static car, and that can be enough if the car is just a prop in the scene. However, if the player will be able to control it, you will probably need to modify it. The idea is that all the pieces of your car are different GameObjects parented to the others, in such a way that you move one and all of them will move, but you can still rotate its pieces independently.

When you drag the 3D model file to the scene, Unity will automatically create all the objects for each piece and its proper parenting based on how the artist created them. You can select the object in the **Hierarchy** window and explore all its children to see this:

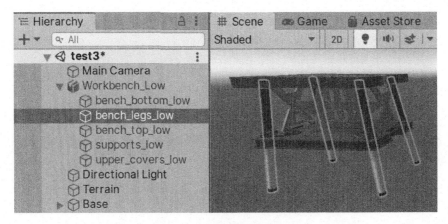

Figure 5.20 – Subobject selection

Also, you will find that each of those objects will have its own `MeshFilter` and `MeshRenderer` components, each one rendering just that piece of the car. Remember that the mesh filter is a component that provides a reference to the mesh asset to render, so the mesh filter is the one using those mesh sub-assets we talked about previously:

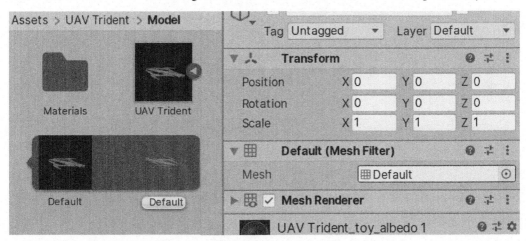

Figure 5.21 – Mesh filter – current mesh selection

Now, if you drag the 3D model file into the scene, you will get a similar result as if the model were a prefab and you were instancing it. But 3D model files are more limited than prefabs, because you can't apply changes to the model. If you've dragged the object onto the scene and edited it to have the behavior you want, I suggest that you create a prefab to get all the benefits we discussed in *Chapter 3, Working with Scenes and Game Objects*, such as applying changes to all the instances of the prefab and so on. Never create lots of instances of a model from its model file – always create them from the prefab you created based on that file.

That's the basic usage of 3D meshes. Now, let's explore the texture integration process, which will make our 3D models have more detail.

Integrating textures

Maybe your model already has the texture applied, but has a magenta color applied to all of it. In the latter case, this means the asset wasn't prepared to work with the URP template you selected when creating the project. Some assets in the Asset Store are meant to be used in older versions of Unity:

Figure 5.22 – Mesh being rendered with erroneous or no material at all

One way to fix this is by using the option in **Edit | Render Pipeline | Universal Render Pipeline | Upgrade Project Materials to UniveralRP Materials**. This will try to upgrade all your materials to the current version of Unity:

Clear All PlayerPrefs		Upgrade Project Materials to UniversalRP Materials
Render Pipeline >	Generate Shader Includes	Upgrade Selected Materials to UniversalRP Materials
Graphics Tier >	Universal Render Pipeline >	2D Renderer >

Figure 5.23 – Upgrade Project Materials to UniversalRP Materials option

The con of this method is that, sometimes, it won't upgrade the material properly. Luckily, we can fix this by reapplying the textures of the objects in this new way. Even if your assets work just fine, I suggest that you reapply your textures anyway, just to learn more about the concept of materials.

A texture is not applied directly to an object. This is because the texture is just one single configuration of all the ones that control the aspects of your model. To change the appearance of a model, you must create a material. Materials are separate assets that contain lots of settings about how Unity should render your object. You can apply such an asset to several objects that share the same graphics settings, and if you change the settings of that material, it will affect all the objects that are using it. It works like a graphics profile.

To create a material to apply the textures of your object, you need to follow these steps:

1. In the **Project** window, click the plus (+) button at the top-left part of the window.

2. Look at the **Material** option in that menu and click it.

3. Name your material. This is usually the name of the asset you are creating (for example, Car, Ship, Character, and so on).

4. Drag the material asset you created to the model instance on your scene. At the moment, if you move the mouse with the dragged asset over the object, you will be able to see a preview of how it will look with that material. You can confirm this by releasing the mouse.

5. Maybe your object has several parts. In that case, you will need to drag the material to each part of the object.

> **Important Note**
>
> Dragging the material will just change the materials property of the
> MeshRenderer component of the object you have dragged.

6. Select the material and click the circle to the left of the **Base Map** property (see *Figure 5.23*).

7. In the **Texture Selector** window, click on the texture of your model. It can be complicated to locate the texture just by looking at it. Usually, the name of the texture will match the model's name. If not, you will need to try different textures until you see one that fits your object. Also, you may find several textures with the same name as your model. Just pick the one that seems to have the proper colors instead of the ones that look black and white or light blue; we will use those later:

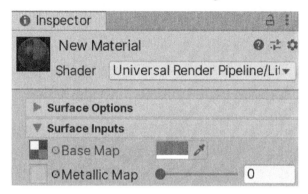

Figure 5.24 – Base Map property of the URP materials

With this, you have successfully applied the texture to the object using a material. For each object that uses the same texture, just drag the same material. Now that we have a basic understanding of how to apply the model textures, let's learn how to configure the import settings before spreading models all over the scene.

Configuring assets

As we mentioned earlier, artists are used to creating art assets outside Unity, and that can cause differences between how the asset is seen from that tool and how Unity will import it. As an example, 3D Studio can work in centimeters, inches, and so on, while Unity works in meters. We have just downloaded and used lots of assets, but we have skipped the configuration steps for solving those discrepancies, so let's take a look at this now.

In this section, we will cover the following concepts related to importing assets:

- Configuring meshes
- Configuring textures

Let's start by discussing how to configure 3D meshes.

Configuring meshes

To change the model's import settings, you need to locate the model file you have downloaded. Several file extensions contain 3D models, with the most common one being the .fbx file, but you can encounter others such as .obj, .3ds, .blender, .mb, and so on. You can identify whether the file is a 3D mesh via its extension:

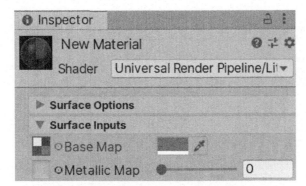

Figure 5.25 – Selected asset path extension

Also, you can click **Asset**, go to the **Inspector** window, and check the tabs, as shown in the following screenshot:

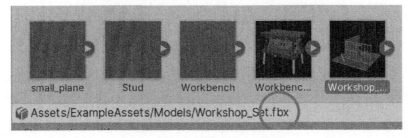

Figure 5.26– Mesh materials settings

Now that you have located the 3D mesh files, you can configure them properly. Right now, the only thing we should take into account is the proper scale of the model. Artists are used to working with different software with different setups; maybe one artist created the model using meters as its metric unit, while the other artists used inches, feet, and so on. When importing assets that have been created in different units, they will probably be unproportioned, which means we will get results such as humans being bigger than buildings.

The best solution is to just ask the artist to fix that. If all the assets were authored in your company, or if you used an external asset, you could ask the artist to fix it so that it works the way your company works, but right now, you are probably a single developer learning Unity by yourself. Luckily, Unity has a setting that allows you to rescale the original asset before using it in Unity. To change the scale factor of an object, you must do the following:

1. Locate the 3D mesh in your **Project** window.

2. Drag it onto the scene. You will see that an object will appear in your scene.

3. Create a capsule using the **GameObject | 3D Object | Capsule** option.

4. Put the capsule next to the model you dragged into the editor. See if the scale has sense. The idea is that the capsule is representing a human being (2 meters tall) so that you have a reference of its scale:

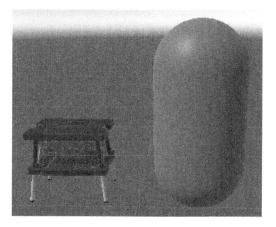

Figure 5.28 – Unproportioned asset

5. If the model is bigger or smaller than expected, select the mesh again in the **Project** window (not the GameObject instance you dragged to the editor). You will see some import settings in the **Inspector** window.

6. Look for the **Scale Factor** property and modify it, increasing it if your model is smaller than expected or reducing it in the opposite case:

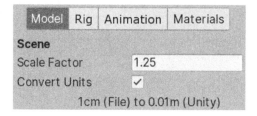

Figure 5.29 – Model mesh options

7. Click the **Apply** button at the bottom part of the **Inspector** window.

8. Repeat *steps 6* and *7* until you get the desired result.

There are plenty of other options to configure, but let's stop here for now. Now, let's discuss how to properly configure the textures of our models.

Configuring textures

Again, there are several settings to configure here, but let's focus on the texture size for now. The idea is to use the size that best fits the usage of that texture, and that depends on lots of factors. The first factor to take into account is the distance from which the object will be seen. If you are creating a first-person game, you will probably see lots of objects near enough to justify a big texture, but maybe you have lots of distant objects such as billboards at the top of buildings, which you will never be near enough to see the details of, so you can use smaller textures for that. Another thing to take into account is the importance of the object. If you are creating a racing game, you will probably have lots of 3D models that will be on the screen for a few seconds and the player will never focus on them; they will be paying attention to the road and other cars. In this case, an object such as a trash can on the street can have a smaller texture and a low polygon model and the user will never notice (unless they stop to appreciate the scenery, but that's acceptable). Finally, you can have a game with a top-down view that will never zoom in on the scene, so the same object that has a big texture in first-person games will have a less detailed texture here. In the following images, you can see that the smaller ship can use a smaller texture:

Figure 5.30 – The same model at different distances

The ideal size of the texture is relative. The usual way to find this is by changing its size, until you find the smallest possible size with a decent quality when the object is seen from the nearest position possible in the game. This is a trial-and-error method. To do this, you can do the following:

1. Locate the 3D model and put it into the scene.

2. Put the **Scene** view camera in a position that shows the object at its biggest possible in-game size. As an example, in an FPS game, it would be almost right next to the object, while in a top-down game, it would be a few meters above the object. Again, that depends on your game.

3. Find and select the texture that the object is using in the folders that were imported with the package or from the material you created previously. They usually have the .png, .jpg, or .tif extensions.

4. In the **Inspector** window, look at the **Max Size** property and reduce it, trying the next smaller value. For example, if the texture is at 2,048, try 1,024.

5. Click **Apply** and check the **Scene** view to see if the quality has decreased dramatically or if the change isn't noticeable. You will be surprised.

6. Repeat *steps 4* to *5* until you get a bad-quality result. In that case, just increase the previous resolution until you get acceptable quality. Of course, if you are targeting PC games, you can expect higher resolutions than mobile games.

Now that you have imported, integrated, and configured your objects, let's just create our player's base with those assets.

Assembling the scene

Let's start by replacing our prototype base using the environment pack we have downloaded. To do that, you must do the following:

1. In the **Environment** pack we imported previously, locate the folder that contains all the models for the different pieces of the scene and try to find a corner. You can use the search bar in the **Project** window to search for the corner keyword:

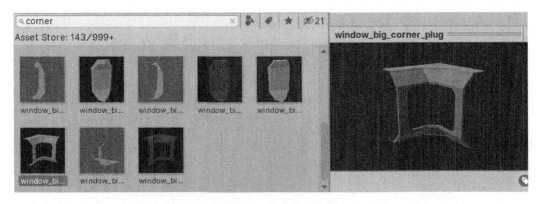

Figure 5.31 – Mesh picker

2. In my case, I have the outer and inner sides of the corner as separate models, so I need to put them together.

3. Put it in the same position as you would any corner of your prototype base:

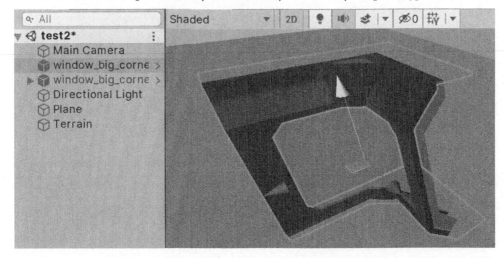

Figure 5.32– Positioning the mesh on a placeholder for replacement

4. Find the proper model that will connect with that corner to create walls. Again, you can try searching for the `wall` keyword in the **Project** window.

5.　Instance it and position it so that it's connected to the corner. Don't worry if it doesn't fit perfectly; you will go over the scene when necessary later:

> **Important Note**
>
> Press the *V* key to select a vertex of the selected object so that you can drag it to the vertex of another object. This is called vertex snapping. It allows you to connect two pieces of the scene, exactly as intended:

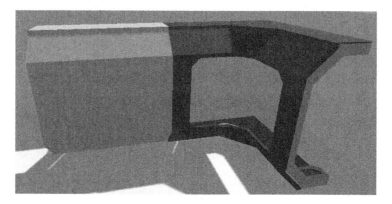

Figure 5.33 – Connecting two modules

6.　Repeat the walls until you reach the other end of the player base and position another corner. You might get a wall that's a little bit larger or smaller than the original prototype, but that's fine:

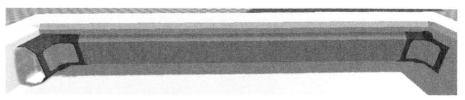

Figure 5.34 – Chain of connected modules

> **Important Note**
>
> Remember that you can move an object while pressing the *Ctrl* key (*Control* on Mac) to snap the object's position so that the clones of the wall can be easily located, right next to the others.

7.　Complete the rest of the walls and destroy the prototype. Remember that this process is slow, so you will need to be patient.

8. Add floors by looking for floor tiles and repeating them all over the surface:

Figure 5.35 – Floor modules with a hole for the pit

9. Add whatever details you want to add with other modular pieces in the package.

10. Put all those pieces in a container object called Base. Remember to create an empty object and drag the base pieces into it:

Figure 5.36 – Mesh sub-assets

After a lot of practice doing this, you will slowly gain experience with the common pitfalls and good practices of modular scene design. All the packages have different modular designs in mind, so you will need to adapt to them.

Summary

In this chapter, we learned how to import models and textures and integrate them into our scene. We discussed how to apply textures to the terrain, how to replace our prototype mesh with modular models, how to apply textures to those, and how to configure the assets, all while taking several criteria into account according to the usage of the object.

With this, we have finished *Part 1* of this book and discussed several basic Unity concepts. In *Part 2*, we will start to deep dive into several Unity systems that allow us to improve the graphics and sound quality of our game. We will start by learning how to create custom material types so that we can create interesting visual effects and animations.

Section 2 – Improving Graphics and Sound

After finishing a basic prototype, we start the production phase of the game. In this section, we will be improving the graphics quality of the game dramatically.

This section comprises the following chapters:

6

Materials and Effects with URP and Shader Graph

Welcome to the first chapter of *Part 2*! I am super excited that you have reached this part of this book because here, we will deep dive into the different graphics and audio systems of Unity to dramatically improve the look and feel of the game. We will start this part with this chapter, where we will discuss what the Shader of a material is and how to create our own shaders to achieve several custom effects that couldn't be accomplished using default Unity shaders. We will be creating a simple water animation effect to learn about this new concept.

In this chapter, we will cover the following topics:

- Introduction to shaders
- Creating shaders with Shader Graph

Introducing shaders

We created materials in the previous chapter, but we never discussed how they internally work and why their Shader properties are super important. In this section, we will explore the concept of a shader as a way to program a video card to achieve custom visual effects.

In this section, we will cover the following concepts related to shaders:

- Shader pipeline
- The render pipeline and URP
- URP's built-in shaders

Let's start by discussing how a shader modifies the shader pipeline to achieve effects.

Shader pipeline

Whenever a video card renders a 3D model, it needs several pieces of input data to process, such as meshes, textures, the transform of the object (position, rotation, and scale), and the lights that affect that object. With that data, the video card must output the pixels of the object into the back buffer, the image where the video card will be drawing our objects. That image will be shown when Unity finishes rendering all the objects (and some effects) to display the finished scene. The back buffer is the image the video card renders step by step, showing it when the drawing has finished (at that moment, it becomes the front buffer, swapping with the previous one).

That's the usual way to render an object, but what happens between the input of the data and the output of the pixels can be handled in a myriad of different ways and techniques, depending on how you want your object to look; maybe you want it to be realistic or look like a hologram, or maybe the object needs a disintegration effect or a toon effect – there are endless possibilities. The way we specify how our video card will handle rendering the object is by using a shader.

A shader is a program that's coded in specific video card languages, such as CG, HLSL, and GLSL, which configure different stages of the render process, sometimes not only configuring them but also replacing them with completely custom code to achieve the effect we want. All of the stages of rendering are what we call the shader pipeline, a chain of modifications that's applied to the input data until it's transformed into pixels.

Important Note

Sometimes, what we called the shader pipeline in this book can be also found in another bibliography as the render pipeline, and whereas the latter is also correct, in Unity, the term "render pipeline" refers to something different, so let's stick with this name.

Each stage of the pipeline is in charge of different modifications and depending on the video card's shader model, this pipeline can vary a lot. In the following diagram, you can find a simplified render pipeline, skipping advanced/optional stages that are not important right now:

Figure 6.1 – Common Shader Pipeline

Let's discuss each of the stages:

- **Input Assembler**: Here is where all the mesh data, such as vertex position, UVs, and normals, is assembled to be prepared for the next stage. You can't do much here; this process is almost always the same.

- **Vertex Shader**: In the past, this stage was limited to applying the transformation of the object, the position and perspective of the camera, and some simple but limited lighting calculations. In modern GPUs, you are in charge of doing whatever you want. This stage receives each one of the vertexes of the object to render and outputs a modified one. So, basically, you can modify the geometry of the object here. The usual code here is the same as what old video cards had, applying the transform of the object, but you can make several effects, such as inflating the object along its normals to apply an old toon effect technique or apply some distortions such as a hologram (look at the hologram effect in *Death Stranding*). There's also the opportunity to calculate data for the next stages, but we won't be going that deep for now.

- **Culling**: Most of the models you are going to render are interesting in that you will never see the backside of a model's face. Let's take a cube as an example; there's no way to look at the back or inner side of any of its sides because they will be automatically occluded by the other sides. Knowing that, rendering both sides of each face of the cube, even if the backside can't be seen, makes no sense, and luckily, this stage takes care of that. Culling will determine whether the face needs to be rendered based on the orientation of the face, saving you lots of time calculating the pixels of occluded faces. You can change this so that it behaves differently for specific cases; as an example, we can create a glass box that needs to be transparent to see all the sides of the box.

- **Rasterizer**: Now that we have the modified and visible geometry of our model calculated, it's time to convert it into pixels. The rasterizer creates all the pixels for the triangles of our mesh. Lots of things happen here, but again, we have very little control over that; the usual way to rasterize is just to create all the pixels inside the edges of the mesh triangles. We have other modes that just render the pixels on the edges so that we can see a wireframe effect, but this is usually used for debugging purposes:

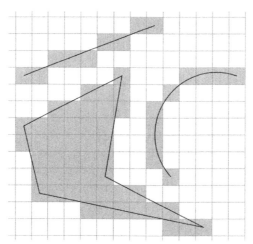

Figure 6.2 – Example of figures being rasterized

- **Fragment Shader**: This is one of the most customizable stages of all. Its purpose is simple: just determine the color of each of the fragments (pixels) that the rasterizer has generated. Here, lots of things can happen, from simply outputting a plain color, sampling a texture, to applying complex lighting calculations such as normal mapping and PBR. Also, you can use this stage to create special effects such as water animations, holograms, distortions, disintegrations, and whatever special effect that requires you to modify what the pixels look like. We will explore how we can use this stage later in this chapter.

- **Depth Testing**: Before we can say that the pixel is complete, we need to check whether the pixel can be seen. This stage checks whether the pixel's depth is behind or in front of the previously rendered pixel, guaranteeing that, regardless of the rendering order of the objects, the nearest pixels to the camera are always being drawn on top of the others. Again, usually, this stage is left in its default state, prioritizing pixels that are nearer to the camera, but some effects require different behavior. As an example, in the following screenshot, you can see an effect that allows you to see objects that are behind other objects, such as units and buildings in *Age of Empires*:

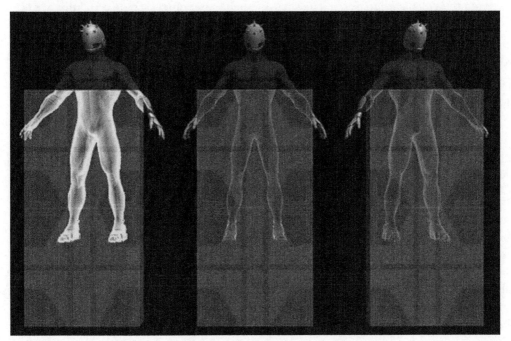

Figure 6.3 – Rendering the occluded parts of the character

- **Blending**: Once the color of the pixel has been determined and we are sure that the pixel has not been occluded by a previous pixel, the final step is to put it in the back buffer (the frame or image you are drawing). We usually do this to override whatever pixel was in that position (because our pixel is nearer to the camera), but if you think about transparent objects, we need to combine our pixel with the previous one to make the transparency effect. Transparencies have other things to take into account aside from blending, but the main idea is that blending controls exactly how the pixel will be combined with the previously rendered pixel in the back buffer.

Shader pipelines is a subject that would require an entire book, but for the scope of this book, the previous description will give you a good idea of what a shader does, as well as the possible effects that it can achieve. Now that we have discussed how a shader renders a single object, it is worth discussing how Unity renders all of the objects using render pipelines.

The Render Pipeline and URP

So far, we have covered how the video card renders an object, but Unity is in charge of asking the video card to execute its shader pipeline per object. To do so, Unity needs to do lots of preparations and calculations to determine exactly how and when each shader needs to be executed. The responsibility of doing this is what Unity calls the render pipeline.

The Render Pipeline is used to draw the objects of the scene. At first, it sounds like there should be just one simple way of doing this, such as iterating over all the objects in the scene and executing the shader pipeline with the shader specified in each object's material, but it can be more complex than that. Usually, the main difference between one render pipeline and another is how lighting and some advanced effects are calculated, but they can differ in other ways.

In previous Unity versions, there was just one single render pipeline, which is now called the built-in renderer. It was a pipeline that has all of the possible features you would need for all kinds of projects, from mobile 2D graphics and simple 3D to cutting-edge 3D, just like the ones you can find in consoles or high-end PCs. This sounds ideal, but actually, it isn't – having one single, giant renderer that needs to be highly customizable to adapt to all possible scenarios generates lots of overhead and limitations that cause more headaches than creating a custom render pipeline. Luckily, the lasts versions of Unity introduced the **Scriptable Render Pipeline** (**SRP**), a way to create render pipelines adapted for your project.

Luckily, Unity doesn't want you to create your own render pipeline per project (a complex task), so it created two custom pipelines for you that are ready to use: URP (formerly called LWRP), which stands for universal render pipeline, and HDRP, which stands for high-definition render pipeline. The idea is that you must choose one or the other based on your project's requirements (unless you really need to create your own). URP, the one we selected when creating the project for our game, is a render pipeline that's suitable for most games that don't require lots of advanced graphics features, such as mobile games or simple PC games, while HDRP is packed with lots of advanced rendering features for high-quality games.

The latter requires high-end hardware to run, while URP runs on almost every relevant target device. It is worth mentioning that you can swap between using a built-in renderer, HDRP, and URP whenever you want, including after creating the project (not recommended):

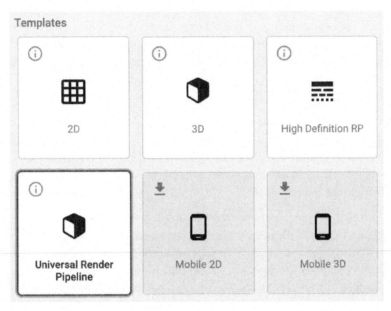

Figure 6.4 – Project wizard showing HDRP and URP templates

We could discuss how each is implemented and their differences, but again, this would fill entire chapters; right now, the idea of this section is for you to know why we picked URP when we created our project, since it has some restrictions we will encounter throughout this book that we will need to take into account. So, it is good to know why we accepted those limitations (to run our game on every relevant hardware). Also, we need to know that we have chosen URP because it provides support for Shader Graph, the Unity tool that we will be using in this chapter to create custom effects. Previous, Unity's built-in pipelines didn't provide us with such a tool (aside from third-party plugins). Finally, another reason to introduce the concept of URP is that it comes with lots of built-in shaders that we will need to know about before creating our own to prevent reinventing the wheel, as well as to adapt ourselves to those shaders. This is because if you came from previous versions of Unity, the ones you know won't work here. This is exactly what we are going to discuss in the next section of this book: the difference between URP's built-in shaders.

URP's Built-in Shaders

Now that we know the difference between URP and other pipelines, let's discuss which shaders come integrated with URP. Let's briefly describe the three most important shaders in this pipeline:

- **Lit**: This is the replacement for the old standard shader. This shader is useful for creating all kinds of realistic physics materials such as wood, rubber, metal, skin, and combinations of them (such as a character with skin and metal armor). It supports normal mapping, occlusion, metallic and specular workflows, and transparencies.

- **Simple Lit**: This is the replacement for the old mobile/diffuse shader. As its name suggests, this shader is a simpler version than Lit, meaning that its lighting calculations are simpler approximations of how light works, getting fewer features than its counterpart. When you have simple graphics without realistic lighting effects, this is the best choice.

- **Unlit**: This is the replacement for the old unlit/texture shader. Sometimes, you need objects without lighting whatsoever, and in that case, this is the shader for you. No lighting doesn't mean an absence of light or complete darkness; it means that the object has no shadows at all, and that it's fully visible without any shade. Some simplistic graphics can work with this, relying on shadowing being baked in the texture, meaning that the texture comes with the shadow. This is extremely performant, especially for low-end devices such as mobile phones. Also, you have other cases such as light tubes or screens, which are objects that can't receive shadows because they emit light, so they will be seen at their full color even in complete darkness. In the following screenshot, you can see a 3D model using an unlit shader. It looks like it's being lit, but it's just the texture of the model that has applied lighter and darker colors to different parts of the object:

Figure 6.5 – A Pod using an Unlit shader to simulate cheap lighting

Let's create an interesting disintegration effect with the simple Lit shader to demonstrate its capabilities. You must do the following:

1. Download and import a **Cloud Noise** texture from any search engine:

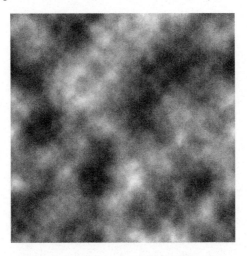

Figure 6.6 – Cloud Noise Texture

2. Select the recently imported texture in the **Project** panel.

3. In the **Inspector** window, set the **Alpha Source** property to **From Gray Scale**. This will calculate the alpha channel of the texture based on the grayscale of the image:

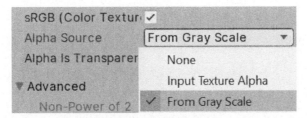

Figure 6.7 – Setting the Alpha Source property to From Gray Scale

> **Important Note**
> The alpha channel of a color is often associated with transparency, but you will notice that our object won't be transparent. The alpha channel is extra color data that can be used for several purposes when creating effects. In this case, we will use it to determine which pixels are being de-integrated first.

4. Create a material by clicking the + icon in the **Project** view and selecting **Material**:

Figure 6.8 – Material creation button

5. Create a cube with the **GameObject | 3D Object | Cube** option using the top menu of Unity:

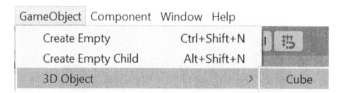

Figure 6.9 – Cube creation

6. Drag the created material from the **Project** window to the cube to apply it.

7. Click the drop-down menu to the right of the **Shader** property in the **Inspector** window and look for the **Universal Render Pipeline | Simple Lit** option. We could also work with the default shader (**Lit**), but **Simple Lit** is going to be easier on performance; besides, we won't be using the advanced features of Lit:

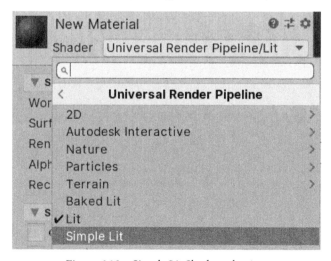

Figure 6.10 – Simple Lit Shader selection

8. Select the material. Then, in **Base Map**, select the recently downloaded cloud texture.

9. Check the **Alpha Clipping** checkbox and set the **Threshold** slider to 0.5:

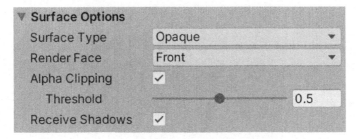

Figure 6.11 – Alpha Clipping – Threshold Material slider

10. You will see how, as you move the **Alpha Clipping** slider, the object starts to disintegrate. **Alpha Clipping** discards pixels that have less alpha intensity than the **Threshold** value:

Figure 6.12 – Disintegration effect with Alpha Clipping

11. Finally, set **Render Face** to **Both** to turn off **Culling Shader Stage** and see both sides of the cube's faces:

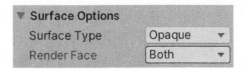

Figure 6.13 – Double-sided render face

12. Take into account that the artist that creates the texture can configure the alpha channel manually instead of calculating it from the grayscale, just to control what the disintegration effect must look like, regardless of the texture's color distribution:

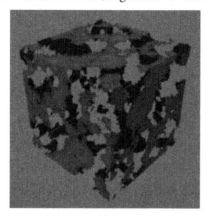

Figure 6.14 – Double-sided alpha clipping

The idea of this section is not to provide a comprehensive guide to all the properties of all URP shaders, but to give you an idea of what a shader can do when configured properly and when to use each of the integrated shaders. Sometimes, you can achieve the effect you need just by using existing shaders, which happens 99% of the time for simple games, so try to stick to them as much as you can. But if you really need to create a custom shader to create a very specific effect, the next section will teach you how to use the URP tool called Shader Graph.

Creating Shaders with Shader Graph

Now that we know how shaders work and about the existing shaders in URP, we have a basic notion of when it is necessary to create a custom shader and when it is not. If you really need to create one, then don't worry – this section will cover the basics of creating effects with Shader Graph, a tool that creates effects using a visual node-based editor. It is an easy tool to use when you are not used to coding.

In this section, we will discuss the following concepts of Shader Graph:

- Creating our first Shader Graph
- Using textures
- Combining textures
- Applying transparency
- Creating vertex effects

Let's start by learning how to create and use a Shader Graph.

Creating our first Shader Graph

Shader Graph is a tool that allows us to create custom effects using a node-based system. An effect in Shader Graph may look as follows, where you can see the nodes that are required to create a hologram effect:

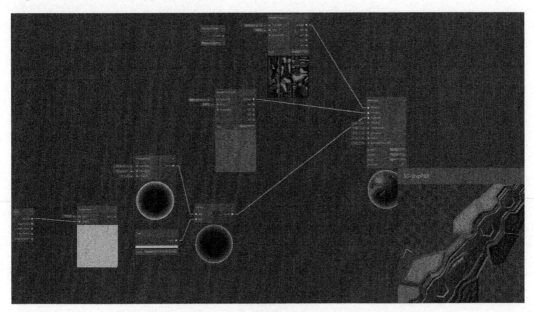

Figure 6.15 – Shader Graph with nodes to create a custom effect

We will discuss what those nodes do later while going through a step-by-step effect example, but in the preceding screenshot, you can see how the author created and connected several nodes, along with the interconnected boxes, each one going through a specific process to achieve the desired effect. The idea of creating effects with Shader Graph is to learn which specific nodes you need and how to connect them properly, to create an "algorithm" or a series of ordered steps to achieve a specific result. This is similar to the way we code the gameplay of the game, but this graph has been adapted and simplified just for effect purposes.

To create and edit our first Shader Graph, do the following:

1. In the **Project** window, click the + icon and find the **Shader | Univeral Render Pipeline | Lit Shader Graph** option. This will create a Shader Graph using PBR mode, meaning that this shader will support lighting effects (unlike unlit graphs):

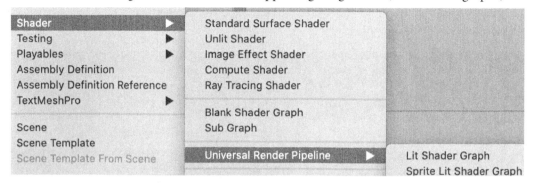

Figure 6.16 – Creating a PBR Shader Graph

2. Name it Water. If you don't rename the asset, remember that you can select the asset, right-click it, and select **Rename**:

Figure 6.17 – Shader Graph Asset

3. Create a new material called WaterMaterial and set **Shader** to **Shader Graphs/ Water**. If, for some reason, Unity doesn't allow you to do that, try right-clicking on **Water Graph** and clicking **Reimport**. As you can see, the Shader Graph we have created now appears as a shader in the material, meaning that we have already created a custom shader:

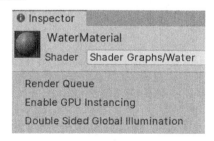

Figure 6.18 – Setting a Shader Graph as a Material Shader

4. Create a plane with the **GameObject | 3d Object | Plane** option.

5. Drag the material to the plane to apply it.

With that, you have created your first custom shader and applied it to a material. So far, it doesn't look interesting at all – it's just a gray effect. But now, it's time to edit the graph to unlock its full potential. As the name of the graph suggests, we will be creating a water effect in this chapter to illustrate several nodes of the Shader Graph toolset and how to connect them, so let's start by discussing the master node. When you open the graph by double-clicking the shader asset, you will see the following:

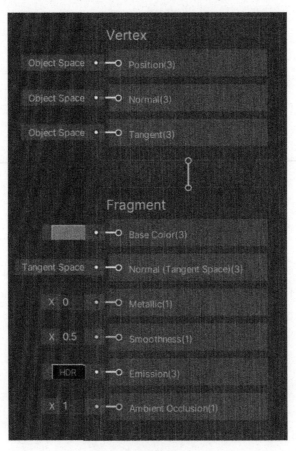

Figure 6.19 – Master node with all the properties needed to calculate the object's appearance

All nodes have input pins, which contain the data needed to work, and output pins, which are the results of its process. As an example, in a sum operation, we will have two input numbers and an output number, which is the result of the sum. In this case, you can see that the master node just has inputs, and that's because all the data that enters the master node will be used by Unity to calculate the rendering and lighting of the object – things such as the desired object color or texture (**Base Color** input pin), how smooth it is (**Smoothness** input pin), or how much metal it contains (**Metallic** input pin). There are properties that will affect how the lighting will be applied to the object. In a sense, the input of this node is the output data of the entire graph and the ones we need to fill, although this is not necessary for all of them.

Here, you can see that the master node is split between a **Vertex** section and a **Fragment** section. The first is capable of changing the mesh of the object we are modifying to deform it, animate it, and so on, while the latter will change what it will look like, which textures to use, how will be illuminated, and so on. Let's start by exploring how we can change that data of the **Fragment** section:

1. Double-click **Shader Graph** to open its editor window.

2. Click inside the gray rectangle to the left of the **Base Color** input pin:

Figure 6.20 – Base Color node input pin

3. In the color picker, select a light blue color so that it resembles water. Select the bluish part of the circle around the picker and then a shade of that color in the middle rectangle:

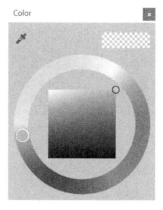

Figure 6.21 – Color picker

4. Set **Smoothness** to 0.9:

Figure 6.22 – Smoothness PBR Master node input pin

5. Click the **Save Asset** button at the top-left of the window:

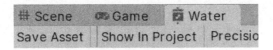

Figure 6.23 – Shader Graph saving options

6. Go back to the **Scene** view and check that the plane is light blue and with the sun reflected on it:

Figure 6.24 – Initial Shader Graph results

As you can see, the behavior of the shader varies based on the properties you set in the master node, but so far, doing this is no different than creating an unlit shader and setting up its properties; the real power of Shader Graph is when you use nodes that perform specific calculations as inputs of the master node. We will start by looking at the texturing nodes, which allow us to apply textures to our model.

Using textures

The idea of using textures is to have an image applied to the model so that we can paint different parts of the models with different colors. Remember that the model has a UV map, which allows Unity to know which part of the texture will be applied to which part of the model:

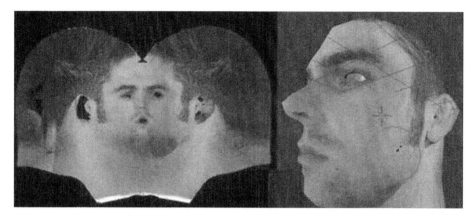

Figure 6.25 – On the left, a face texture; on the right, the same texture applied to a face mesh

We have several nodes to perform this task, with one of them being **Sample Texture 2D**, a node that has two main inputs. First, it asks us for the texture to sample or apply to the model, and then the UV. You can see this in the following screenshot:

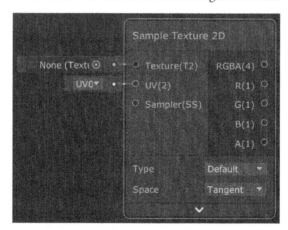

Figure 6.26 – Sample Texture node

As you can see, the default value of the **Texture** input node is **None**, so there's no texture by default, which means we need to manually specify that. For UV, the default value is **UV0**, meaning that, by default, the node will use the main UV channel of the model, and yes, a model can have several UVs set. For now, we will stick with the main one, since if you are not sure what that means, UV0 is the safest option. Let's try this node by doing the following:

1. Download and import a tileable water texture from the internet:

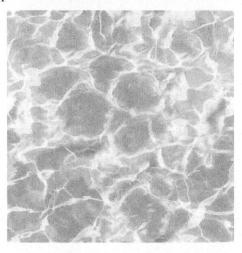

Figure 6.27 – Tileable water texture

2. Select the texture and be sure that the **Wrap Mode** property of the texture is set to **Repeat**. This will allow us to repeat the texture as we did in the terrain because the idea is to use this shader to cover large water areas:

Figure 6.28 – Texture Repeat mode

3. In **Water Shader Graph**, right-click in an empty area of **Shader Graph** and select **Create Node**:

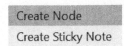

Figure 6.29 – Shader Graph – Create Node option

4.   In the search box, write `Sample texture`; all the sampler nodes will show up. Double-click **Sample Texture 2D**. If, for some reason, you can't double-click the option, right-click on it first and then try again. There is a known bug regarding this tool, and this is the workaround:

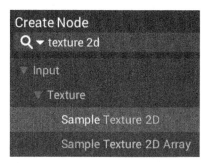

Figure 6.30 – Sample Texture node search

5.   Click in the circle to the left of the **Texture** input pin of the **Sample Texture 2D** node. This will allow us to pick a texture to sample – just select the water one. You will see that the texture can be previewed in the bottom part of the node:

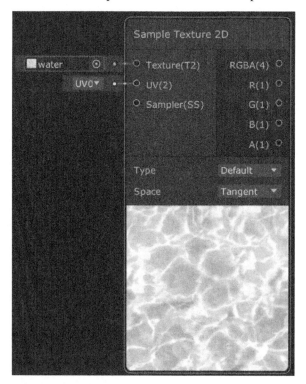

Figure 6.31 - Sample Texture node with a texture in its input pin

6. Drag the output pin, **RGBA**, from the **Sample Texture 2D** node to the **Base Color** input pin of the master node:

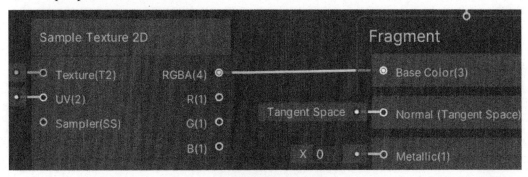

Figure 6.32 – Connecting the results of a Texture sampling with the Base Color pin of the master node

7. Click the **Save Asset** button at the top-left part of the **Shader Graph** editor and look at the changes in the **Scene** view:

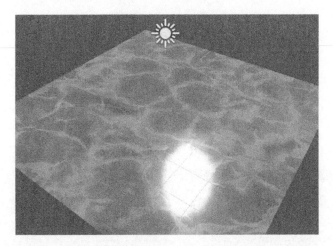

Figure 6.33 – Results of applying a Texture in our Shader Graph

As you can see, the texture has been applied to the model, but if you take into account that the default plane has a size of 10x10 meters, then the ripples of the water seem too big, so let's tile the texture! To do that, we need to change the UVs of the model, making them bigger. Having bigger UVs sounds like the texture should also get bigger. However, take into account that we are not making the object bigger; we are just modifying the UV, so the same object size will read more of the texture. This means that the bigger texture sample area will make repetitions of the texture and put them in the same object size, which will then be compressed inside the model area. To do so, follow these steps:

1. Right-click in any empty space and click **New Node** to search for the **UV** node:

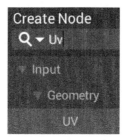

Figure 6.34 – Searching for the UV node

2. Using the same method, create a **Multiply** node.

3. Drag the **Out** pin of the UV node to the A pin of the **Multiply** node to connect them.

4. Set the B pin's input value of **Multiply** to (4,4,4,4):

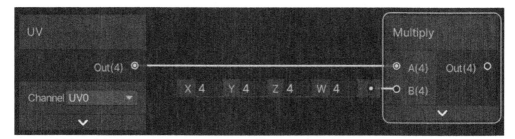

Figure 6.35 – Multiplying the UVs by 4

5. Drag the **Out** pin of the **Multiply** node to the UV of the **Sample Texture 2D** node to connect them:

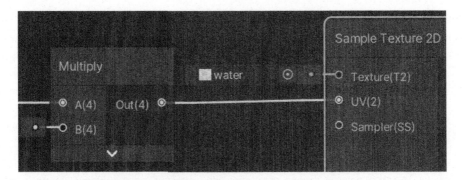

Figure 6.36 – Using the multiplied UVs to sample the Texture

6. If you save the graph and go back to the **Scene** view, you will see that the ripples are now smaller, since we have tiled the UVs of our model. You can also see this in the preview of the **Sampler Texture 2D** node:

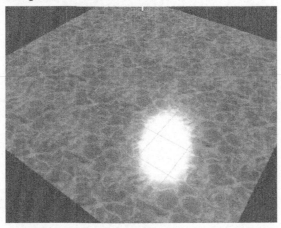

Figure 6.37 – Results of mulitplying the model's UV

Another interesting thing we can do now is apply an offset to the texture to move it. The idea is that even if the plane is not moving, we will simulate the flow of the water through it, by moving just the texture. Remember, the responsibility of determining the part of the texture to apply to each part of the model belongs to the UV, so if we add values to the UV coordinates, we will be moving them, generating a texture sliding effect. To do so, follow these steps:

1. Create an **Add** node to the right of the **UV** node.
2. Connect the **Out** pin of **UV** to the A pin of the **Add** node:

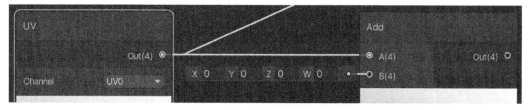

Figure 6.38 – Adding values to the UVs

3. Create a **Time** node to the left of the **Add** node.
4. Connect the **Time** node to the B pin of the **Add** node:

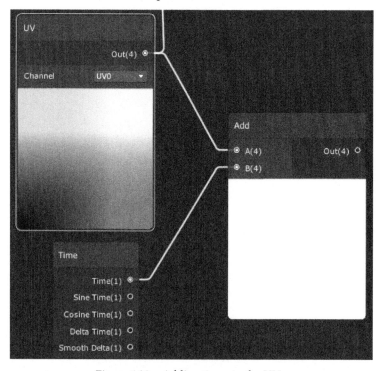

Figure 6.39 – Adding times to the UVs

5. Connect the **Out** pin of the **Add** node to the A pin of the **Multiply** node:

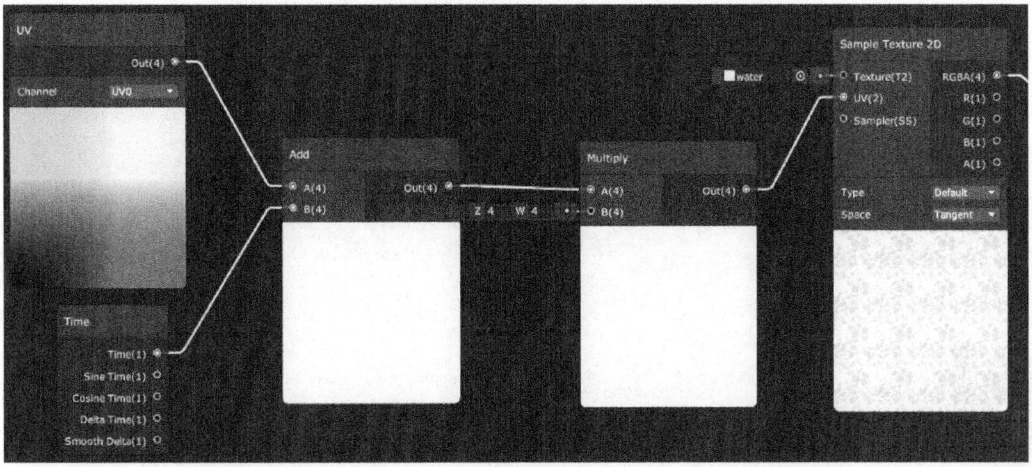

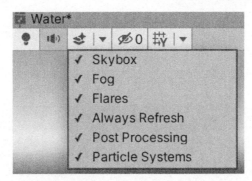

Figure 6.40 – Added and multiplied UVs as an input of our Sample Texture

6. Save and view the water moving in the **Scene** view. If you don't see it moving, click the layers icon from the top bar of the scene and check **Always Refresh**:

Figure 6.41 – Enabling Always Refresh to preview the effect

7. If you feel like the water is moving too fast, try to use the **Multiply** node to make the time a smaller value. I recommend that you try it by yourself before looking at the following screenshot, which provides the answer to this:

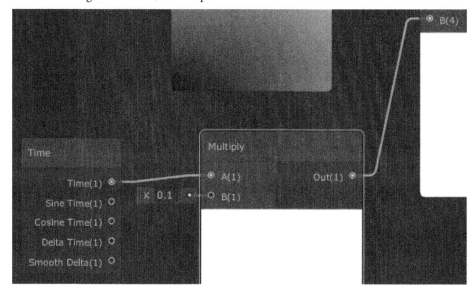

Figure 6.42 – Multiplying time to make the texture slower

8. If you feel like the graph is starting to get bigger, try to hide some of the node previews by clicking the up arrow that appears on the preview when you move the mouse over it:

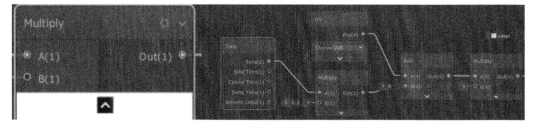

Figure 6.43 – Hiding the preview from the graph nodes

Also, you can hide unused node pins by selecting the node and clicking the arrow at the top right:

Figure 6.44 – Hiding unused pins from the graph nodes

So, to recap, first, we added the time to the UV to move it and then multiplied the result of the moved UV to make it bigger to tile the texture. It is worth mentioning that there's a tiling and offset node that does this process for us, but I wanted to show you how performing a simple multiplication to scale the UV and an add operation to move it generated a nice effect; you can't begin imagine all of the possible effects you can achieve with other simple mathematical nodes! Now, let's explore other usages of mathematical nodes so that we can combine textures.

Combining Textures

Even though we have used nodes, we haven't created anything that can't be created using regular shaders, but that's about to change. So far, we can see the water moving, but it stills look static, and that's because the ripples are always the same. We have several techniques to generate ripples, and the simplest one would be to combine two water textures moving in different directions to mix their ripples, and actually, we can simply use the same texture, just flipped, to save some memory. To combine these textures, we will sum them and then divide them by 2, so basically, we are calculating the average of the textures! Let's do that by performing the following steps:

1. Select all the nodes between **Time** and **Sampler 2D** (including them), create a selection rectangle by clicking in any empty space in the graph, hold and drag while clicking, and then release when all the target nodes have been covered:

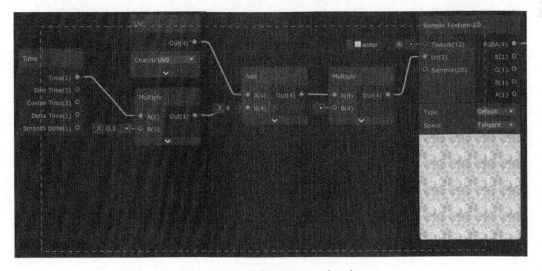

Figure 6.45 – Selecting several nodes

2. Right-click and select **Copy**, and then right-click again and select **Paste**. Alternatively, use the classic *Ctrl* + *C*, *Ctrl* + *V* commands (*Command* + *C*, *Command* + *V* on Mac), or just *Ctrl* + *D* (*Command* + *D*).

3. Move the copied nodes below the original ones:

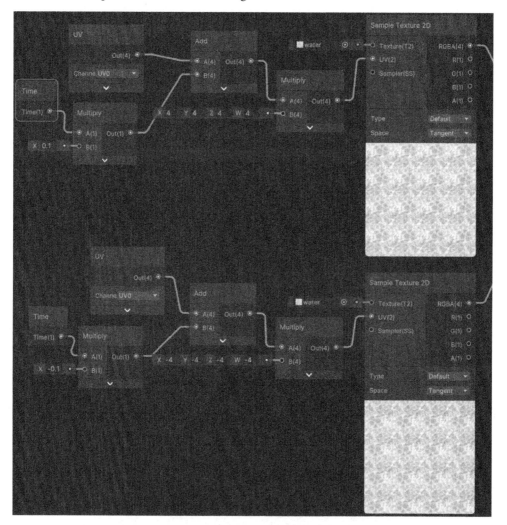

Figure 6.46 – Duplicating nodes

4. For the copied nodes, set the B pin of the **Multiply** node connected to **Sample Texture 2D** to (-4,-4,-4,-4). You will see that this flipped the texture.

5. Also, set the B pin of the **Multiply** node, which is connected to the **Time** node at -0.1:

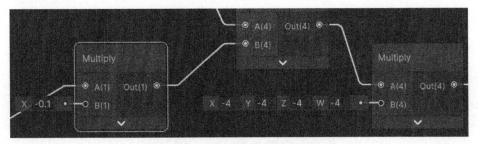

Figure 6.47 – Multiplying values

6. Create an **Add** node to the right of both **Sampler Texture 2D** nodes and connect the outputs of those nodes to the A and B input pins of the **Add** node:

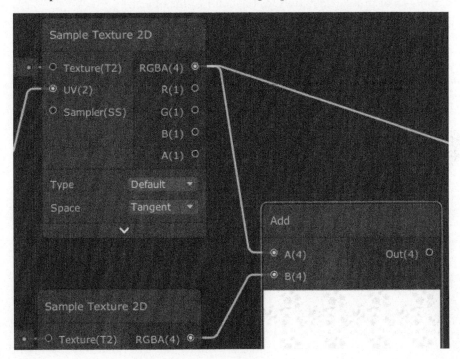

Figure 6.48 – Adding two Textures

7. Here, you can see that the resulting combination is too bright because we have summed up the intensity of both textures. So, let's fix that by multiplying the **Out** pin of the **Add** node by (0.5,0.5,0.5,0.5), which will divide each resulting color channel by 2, averaging the color:

Figure 6.49 – Dividing the sum of two textures to get the average

8. Connect the **Out** pin of the **Multiply** node to the **Base Color** pin of the master node to apply all of those calculations as the color of the object.

9. Save the asset and check the results in the **Scene** view:

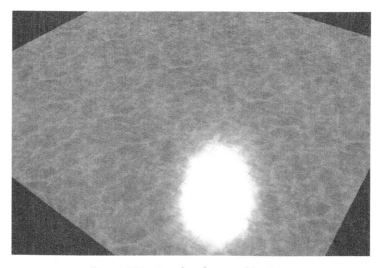

Figure 6.50 – Results of texture blending

You can keep adding nodes to make the effect more diverse, such as by using Sinus nodes to apply non-linear movements and so on, but I will let you learn that by experimenting with this by yourself. For now, we will stop here. As always, this topic deserves a full book, and this chapter intends to give you a small taste of this powerful Unity tool. I recommend that you look for other Shader Graph examples on the internet to learn about other usages for the same nodes and, of course, new nodes. One thing to consider here is that everything we just did is applied to the fragment shader stage of the shader pipeline we discussed earlier. Now, let's use the blending shader stage to apply some transparency to the water.

Applying transparency

Before declaring our effect finished, we can make the water a little bit transparent. Remember that the shader pipeline has a blending stage, which has the responsibility of blending each pixel of our model into the image being rendered on this frame. The idea is to make our Shader Graph modify that stage to apply an alpha blending, a blending that combines our model and the previous rendered models based on the alpha value of our model. To get that effect, perform the following steps:

1. Look for the **Graph Inspector** window floating around the **Shader Graph** editor.

2. Click the **Graph Settings** tab.

3. Set the **Surface** property to **Transparent**.

4. Set the **Blend** property to **Alpha**, if it isn't already at that value:

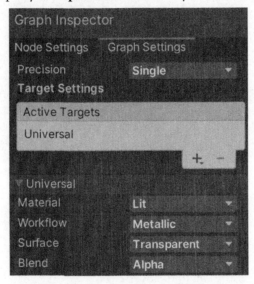

Figure 6.51 – Graph Inspector transparency settings

5. Set the **Alpha** input pin of the master node to 0.5:

Figure 6.52 – Setting the Alpha input pin of the Master node

6. Save the graph and check out the transparency that's being applied in the **Scene** view. If you can't see the effect, just put a cube in the water to make the effect more evident:

Figure 6.53 – Shadows from the water being applied to a cube

7. Here, you can see the shadows that the water is casting on our cube. That's because Unity doesn't detect that the object is transparent, so it thinks that it must cast shadows. So, let's disable them. Click on the water plane and look for the **Mesh Renderer** component in the **Inspector** window. If you don't see the shadow, click the light bulb icon at the top of the **Scene** view:

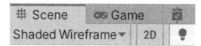

Figure 6.54 – Enabling lights in the Scene view

8. In the **Lighting** section, set **Cast Shadows** to **Off**; this will disable shadow casting from the plane on the underwater parts of the cube:

Figure 6.55 – Disabling shadow casting

Adding transparencies is a simple process but has its caveats, such as the shadow problem, and in more complex scenarios, it can have other problems, so I would suggest that you avoid using transparencies unless it is necessary. Actually, our water can live without transparencies, especially when we apply this water to the river basin around the base since we don't need to see the part under the water, but the idea is for you to know what options you have. In the following screenshot, you can see how we have put a giant plane with this effect below our base, big enough to cover the entire basin:

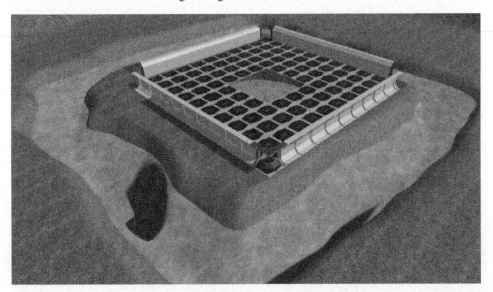

Figure 6.56 – Using our water in the main scene

Now that we modified how the object looks through the **Fragment Master Node** section, let's discuss how to use the **Vertex** section to apply a mesh animation to our water.

Creating Vertex Effects

So far, we have applied water textures to our water, but it's still a flat plane with nice textures. We can go further than this and make ripples not only via textures, but also by animating the mesh. To do so, we will apply the noise texture we used at the beginning of this chapter in the shader. However, instead of using it as another color to add to the base color of the shader, we will use it to offset the Y position of the vertexes of our plane. Due to the chaotic nature of the noise texture, the idea is that we will apply a different amount of offset to different parts of the model, so that we can emulate ripples:

Figure 6.57 – Default plane mesh subdivided in a grid of 10x10 with no offset

To accomplish something like this, you can modify the **Vertex** section of your shader so that it looks like this:

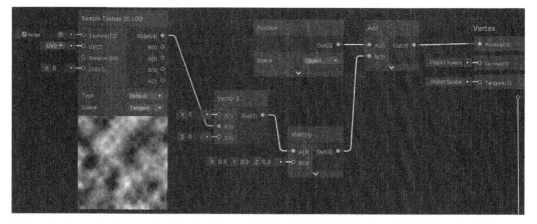

Figure 6.58 – Ripples vertex effect

In the graph, you can see how we are creating a **Vector** whose **Y** axis contains the result of the texture sampling the noise texture we downloaded from the internet at the beginning of this chapter. The idea behind this is to create a **Vector** pointing upward whose length depends on the texture. Basically, we created a Y offset based on the texture. This texture has an irregular yet smooth pattern, so it can emulate the behavior of the tide. Please notice that here, we used **Sample Texture 2D LOD** instead of **Sample Texture 2D**; the latter doesn't work in the **Vertex** section, so keep that in mind. Then, we multiplied the result by *0.3* to reduce the height of the offset to add, and then we added the result to the **Position** node, which the **Space** property has configured in **Object** with the needed position space to work with the **Vertex** section (search for `object versus world space` for more information about this). Finally, the result is connected to the **Position** node of the **Vertex** section.

If you save this, you will see something similar to the following:

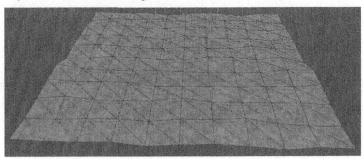

Figure 6.59 – Ripples vertex effect applied

Of course, in this case, the ripples are static because we didn't add any time offset to the UV, as we did previously. The following screenshot shows how to add that, but before looking at it, I recommend that you try to resolve this by yourself first, as a personal challenge:

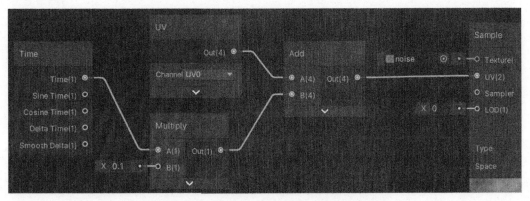

Figure 6.60 – Animated ripples vertex effect graph

As you can see, we are taking the original UV and adding the time, multiplied by any factor, so that it will slowly move, the same as we did previously with our water texture. You can keep changing what this looks like with different textures by multiplying the offset to increase or reduce the height of the ripples, applying interesting math functions such as Sine, and so much more, but for now, let's wrap this up.

Summary

In this chapter, we discussed how shaders work in GPUs and how to create our first simple shader to achieve a nice water effect. Creating shaders is a complex and interesting job, and in a team, there are usually one or more people in charge of creating all of these effects, known as technical artists. So, as you can see, this topic can expand to a whole career. Remember, this book intends to give you a small taste of all the possible roles you can take on in the industry, so if you liked this role, I suggest that you start reading shader-exclusive books. You have a long but super interesting road ahead of you.

That's enough about shaders for now! In the next chapter, we will look at how to improve our graphics and create visual effects with particle systems.

7
Visual Effects with Particle Systems and Visual Effect Graph

In this chapter, we will continue learning about visual effects we can use for our game. We will be discussing particle systems, which we can use to simulate fire, waterfalls, smoke, and all kinds of fluids. Also, we will look at the two Unity **particle systems** for creating these kinds of effects, **Shuriken** and **Visual Effect Graph**, with the latter being more powerful than the first, but requiring more hardware.

In this chapter, we will cover the following topics:

- Introduction to particle systems
- Creating fluid simulations
- Creating complex simulations with Visual Effect Graph

Introduction to particle systems

All the graphics and effects we have created so far use static meshes, 3D models that can't be skewed, bent, or deformed in any way. **Fluids** such as fire and smoke clearly can't be represented using this kind of mesh. However, we can simulate these effects with a combination of static meshes, and this is where particle systems are useful.

Particle systems are objects that emit and animate lots of **particles** or **billboards**, which are simple quad meshes that face the camera. Each particle is a static mesh, but rendering, animating, and combining lots of them can generate the illusion of a fluid. In the following figure, on the left, you can see a smoke effect using particle systems, while on the right, you can see the **Wireframe** view of the same particles. There, you can see the quads that create the illusion of smoke, which is done by applying a smoke texture to each of the particles and animating them so that they spawn at the bottom and move up in random directions:

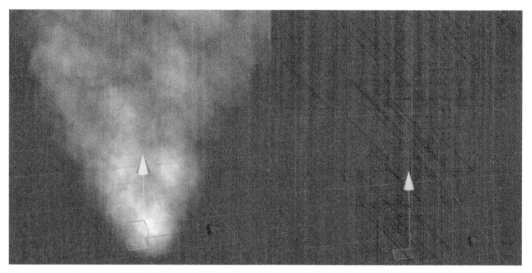

Figure 7.1 – Left, a smoke particle system; right, the wireframe of the same system

In this section, we will cover the following concepts related to particles:

- Creating a basic particle system
- Using advanced modules

Let's start by discussing how to create our very first particle system.

Creating a basic particle system

To illustrate how to create a particle system, let's create an explosion effect. The idea is to spawn lots of particles at once and spread them in all directions. Let's start by creating a particle system and configuring the basic settings it provides to change its default behavior. To do so, follow these steps:

1. Select the **GameObject | Effects | Particle System** option:

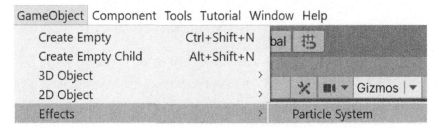

Figure 7.2 – Particle System option

2. You can see the effect in the following screenshot. The default behavior is a column of particles going up, similar to the smoke effect shown previously. Let's change that:

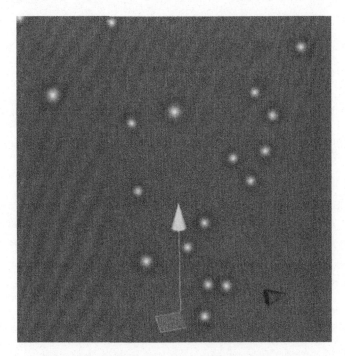

Figure 7.3 – Default appearance of the particle system

3. Click the created object in the scene and look at the **Inspector** window.

4. Open the **Shape** section by clicking on the title. Here, you can specify the particle emitter shape where the particles are going to be spawned.

5. Change the **Shape** property to **Sphere**. Now, the particles should move in all possible directions instead of following the default cone:

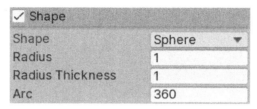

Figure 7.4 – Shape properties

6. In the particle system **module** (usually known as Main), set **Start Speed** to 10. This will make the particles move faster.

7. In the same module, set **Start Lifetime** to 0.5. This specifies how long a particle will live. In this case, we have given a lifetime of half a second. In combination with the speed (10 meters per second), this makes the particles disappear after moving 5 meters:

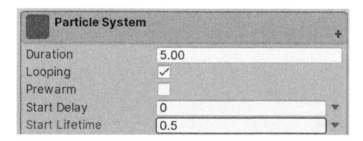

Figure 7.5 – Main Particle System module

8. Open the **Emission** module and set **Rate over Time** to 0. This property specifies how many particles will be emitted per second, but for an explosion, we need a burst of particles, so we won't emit particles constantly over time in this case.

9. In the **Bursts** list, click the + button at the bottom. Then, in the created item in the list, set the **count** column to 100:

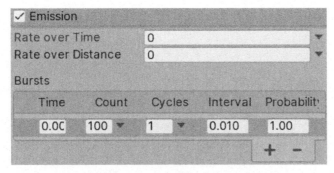

Figure 7.6 – Emission module

10. In the Main module (the one titled **Particle System**), set **Duration** to 1 and uncheck **Looping**. In our case, the explosion won't repeat constantly; we just need one explosion:

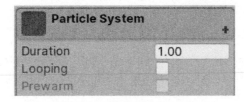

Figure 7.7 – Looping checkbox

11. Now that the particle isn't looping, you need to manually hit the **Play** button in the **Particle Effect** window, in the bottom-right part of the **Scene** view, to see the system:

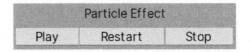

Figure 7.8 – Particle system playback controls

12. Set **Stop Action** to **Destroy**. This will destroy the object when the **Duration** time has passed. This will work when you are running the game, so you can safely use this configuration while editing your scene:

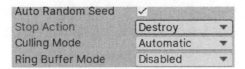

Figure 7.9 – Stop Action set to Destroy

13. Set **Start Size** of the Main module to 3. This will make the particles bigger so that they seem denser:

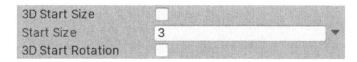

Figure 7.10 – Particle system Start Size

14. Click on the down-pointing arrow to the right of the **Start Rotation** property of the Main module and select **Random Between Two Constants**.

15. Set **Start Rotation** to 0 and 360 for the two input values that appeared after the previous step. This allows us to give the particles a random rotation when they spawn to make them look slightly different from each other:

Figure 7.11 – Random Start Rotation

16. Now, the particles behave as expected, but they don't look as expected. Let's change that. Create a new Material by clicking on the + icon in the **Project** view and selecting **Material**. Call it Explosion.

17. Set its shader to **Universal Render Pipeline/Particles/Unlit**. This is a special shader that is used to apply a texture to the Shuriken particle system:

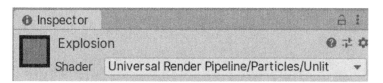

Figure 7.12 – Particle system material shader

18. Download a smoke particle texture from the internet or Unity's **Asset Store**. In this case, it is important to download one with a black background; ignore the others:

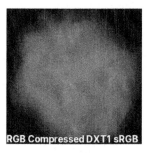

Figure 7.13 – Smoke particle texture

19. Set this texture as the Base Map of the material.

20. Set **Surface Type** to **Transparent** and **Blending Mode** to **Additive**. Doing this will make the particles blend with each other, instead of being drawn over each other, to simulate a big mass of smoke instead of individual smoke puffs. We are using **Additive** mode because our texture has a black background and because we want to create a lighting effect (the explosion will brighten the scene):

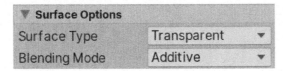

Figure 7.14 – Surface Options for particles

21. Drag your material to the **Material** property of the **Renderer** module:

Figure 7.15 – Particle material settings

22. Now, your system should look like this:

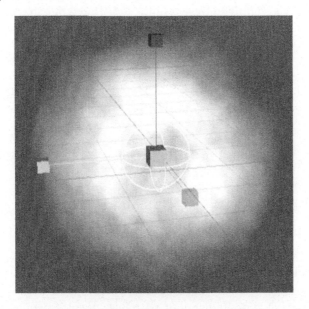

Figure 7.16 – The result of the previous settings

In the previous steps, we have changed how the particles or billboards will spawn (using the Emission module), in which direction they will move (using the **Shape** module), how fast they will move, how long they will last, how big they will be (using the **Main** module), and what they will look like (using the **Renderer** module). Creating particle systems is a simple case of configuring their different settings. Of course, doing this properly is an art on its own; it requires creativity and knowledge of how to use all the settings and configurations they provide. So, to increase our configuration toolbox, let's discuss some advanced modules.

Using advanced modules

Our system looks nice, but we can improve it a lot, so let's enable some new modules to increase its quality:

1. Check the checkbox on the left of the **Color over Lifetime** module to enable it:

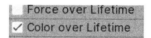

Figure 7.17 – Enabling the Color over Lifetime module

2. Open the module by clicking on the title. Then, click the white bar on the right of the **Color** property. This will open the gradient editor.

3. Click slightly to the right of the top-left white marker in the bar to create a new marker. Also, click slightly to the left of the top-right white marker to create the fourth marker. These markers will allow us to specify the transparency of the particles during its lifetime:

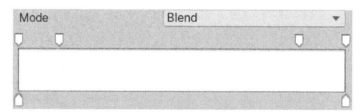

Figure 7.18 – Color over Lifetime in gradient editor

4. If you have created any unwanted markers, just drag them outside the window to remove them.

5. Click on the top-left marker (not the one we created – the one that was already there) and set the **Alpha** slider at the bottom to 0. Do the same with the top-right marker, as shown in the following screenshot. Now, you should see the particles fading away instead of popping out of existence when the explosion is finishing:

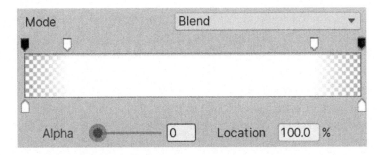

Figure 7.19 – Fading in and fading out the gradient

6. Enable the **Limit Velocity over Lifetime** module by clicking on its checkbox.

7. Set the **Dampen** setting to 0.1. This will make the particles slowly stop instead of continuing to move:

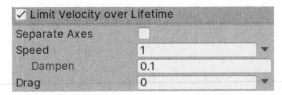

Figure 7.20 – Dampening the velocity to make the particles stop

8. Enable **Rotation over Lifetime** and set **Angular Velocity** between -90 and 90. Remember that you should set the value in **Random Between Two Constants** by clicking on the down-pointing arrow to the right of the property. Now, the particles should rotate slightly during their lifetimes to simulate more motion:

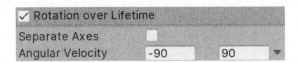

Figure 7.21 – Random rotation velocity

Some of these effects will be very subtle, given the short lifetime we set in the Main Module when we just created the particle. Feel free to increase the lifetime value to see those effects in more detail, but note that this could lead to an excessive number of particles if you spawn them frequently, thereby reducing performance. Just be wary about how they impact your performance when tweaking those values.

As you can see, there are lots of extra modules that can be enabled and disabled to add layers of behavior on top of the existing ones, so again, use them creatively to create all kinds of effects. Remember that you can create Prefabs of these systems to replicate them all over your scene. I also recommend searching for and downloading particle effects from the Asset Store to see how other people have used the same system to create amazing effects. That is the best way to learn how to create them – viewing a variety of different systems – and that is actually what we are going to do in the next section: create more systems!

Creating fluid simulations

As we mentioned previously, the best way to learn how to create particle systems is to keep looking for already-created particle systems, and then explore how people have used various system settings to create completely different simulations.

In this section, we will learn how to create the following effects using particle systems:

- A waterfall effect
- A bonfire effect

Let's start with the simplest one: the waterfall effect.

Creating a waterfall effect

In order to do this, follow these steps:

1. Create a new particle system (**GameObject | Effects | Particle System**).
2. Set **Shape** to **Edge** and its **Radius** to **5** in the **Shape** module. This will make the particles spawn along a line of emission:

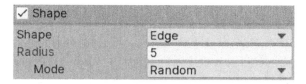

Figure 7.22 – Edge shape

3. Set **Rate over Lifetime** of the **Emission** module to 50.

4. Set **Start Size** of the Main module to 3 and **Start Lifetime** to 3:

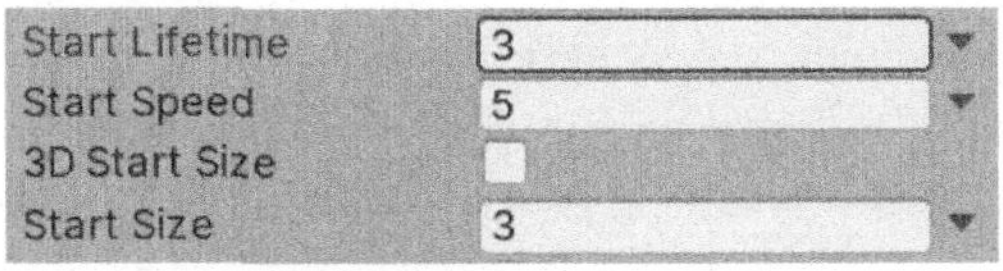

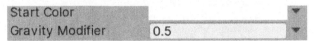

Figure 7.23 – Main module settings

5. Set **Gravity Modifier** of the Main module to 0.5. This will make the particles fall:

Figure 7.24 – Gravity Modifier in the Main module

6. Use the same **Explosion** material we created previously for this system:

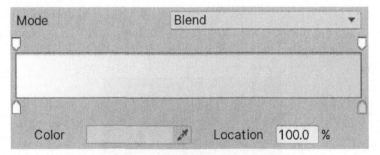

Figure 7.25 – Explosion particle material

7. Enable **Color Over Lifetime** and open the **Gradient** editor.

8. Click the bottom-right marker. This time, you should see a **Color** picker instead of an alpha slider. The top markers allow you to change the transparency over time, while the bottom ones change the color of the particles over time. Set a light blue color in this marker:

Figure 7.26 – White to light blue gradient

As a challenge, I suggest that you add a little particle system where this one ends to create some water splashes, simulating the water colliding with a lake at the bottom. Now, we can add this particle system to one of the hills of our scene to decorate it, as shown in the following screenshot. I have adjusted the system a little bit so that it looks better in this scenario. I challenge you to tweak it by yourself to make it look like this:

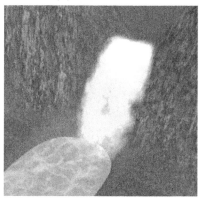

Figure 7.27 – The waterfall particle system being applied to our current scene

Now, let's create another effect: a bonfire.

Creating a bonfire effect

In order to create this, do the following:

1. Create a particle system (**GameObject | Effects | Particle System**).

2. Look for a **Fire Particle Texture Sheet** texture on the internet or the Asset Store. This kind of texture should look like a grid of different flame textures. The idea is to apply a flame animation to our particles, which swaps all those mini textures:

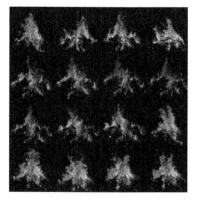

Figure 7.28 – Particles texture sprite sheet

3. Create a particle material that uses the **Univeral Render Pipeline/Particles/Unlit** shader.

4. Set the flame's sprite sheet texture as the **Base Map**.

5. Set the color to the right of the **Base Map** to white.

6. Set this material as the particle material. Remember to set **Surface Type** to **Transparent** and **Blending Mode** to **Additive**:

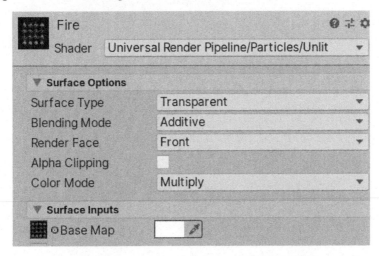

Figure 7.29 – A material with a particle sprite sheet

7. Enable the **Texture Sheet Animation** module and set the **Tiles** property according to your fire sheet. In my case, I have a grid of 4x4 sprites, so I put 4 in **X** and 4 in **Y**. After this, you should see the particles swapping textures:

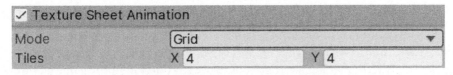

Figure 7.30 – Enabling Texture Sheet Animation

8. Set **Start Speed** to 0 and **Start Size** to 1.5 in the Main module.

9. Set **Radius** to 0.5 in **Shape**.

10. Create a second particle system and make it a child of the fire system:

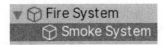

Figure 7.31 – Parenting particle systems

11. Apply the **Explosion** material from the explosion example.

12. Set **Angle** to 0 and **Radius** to 0.5 in the **Shape** module.

The system should look like this:

Figure 7.32 – Result of combining the fire and smoke particle systems

As you can see, you can combine several particle systems to create a single effect. Take care when doing this because it's easy to emit too many particles and affect the game's performance. Particles are not cheap and may cause a reduction in the game's **Frames Per Second (FPS)** if you are not cautious when using them.

So far, we have explored one of the Unity systems that you can use to create these kinds of effects, and while this system is enough for most situations, Unity recently released a new one that can generate more complex effects, called **Visual Effect Graph**. Let's learn how to use it and see how it differs from Shuriken.

Creating complex simulations with Visual Effect Graph

The particle system we have used so far is called Shuriken, and it handles all calculations in the CPU. This has pros and cons. A pro is that it can run on all possible devices that Unity supports, regardless of their capabilities (all of them have CPUs), but a con is that we can exceed CPU capabilities easily if we are not cautious regarding the number of particles we emit. Modern games require more complex particle systems to generate believable effects, and this kind of CPU-based particle system solution has started to reach its limit. This is where Visual Effect Graph comes in:

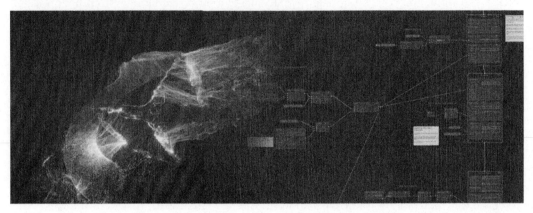

Figure 7.33 – Left, a massive particle system; right, an example of a Visual Effect Graph

Visual Effect Graph is a GPU-based particle system solution, meaning that the system is executed in the video card instead of the CPU. That's because video cards are far more efficient at executing lots and lots of little simulations, like the ones each particle of a system needs, so we can reach far higher orders of magnitude in the number of particles with the GPU than we can with the CPU. The con here is that we need a fairly modern GPU that has **compute shader** capabilities to support this system, so we will exclude certain target platforms using this system (forget about most mobile phones), so use it if your target platform supports it (mid- to high-end PCs, consoles, and some high-end phones).

In this section, we will discuss the following concepts of Visual Effect Graph:

- Installing Visual Effect Graph
- Creating and analyzing a Visual Effect Graph
- Creating a rain effect

Let's start by learning how we can add support for Visual Effect Graph in our project.

Installing Visual Effect Graph

So far, we have used lots of Unity features that were already installed in our project, but Unity can be extended with a myriad of plugins, both official and third-party ones. Visual Effect Graph is one of those features that needs to be independently installed if you are using **Universal Render Pipeline (URP)**. We can do that using Package Manager, a Unity window dedicated to managing official Unity plugins.

Something to think about when you are installing those packages is that each package or plugin has its own version, independent of the Unity version. This means that you can have Unity 2021.1 installed, but Visual Effect Graph 11.0.0 or 11.1.0, or whatever version you want, and you can update the package to a newer version without upgrading Unity. This is important because some versions of these packages require a minimum version of Unity. Moreover, some packages depend on other packages – specific versions of those packages – so we need to ensure we have the correct versions of every package to ensure we have compatibility. To be clear, the dependencies of a package are installed automatically, but sometimes, we can install them separately. So, in that scenario, we need to check the required version. It sounds complicated, but it is simpler than it sounds.

At the time of writing this book, to get Visual Effect Graph working properly, we need version 11.0.0, and also we need to have Universal RP version 11.0.0. Yes, Universal RP is another feature you can install using Package Manager, but since we created the project using the Universal RP template, it was already installed for us with the proper version. However, this may not always be true, so we must check that. With that in mind, let's install Visual Effect Graph, as follows:

1. In the top menu of Unity, go to **Window | Package Manager**:

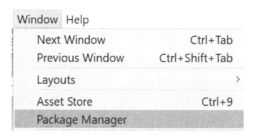

Figure 7.34 – Package Manager location

2. Remember to ensure **Package Manager** is in **Unity Registry** mode so that you can see Unity's official packages list:

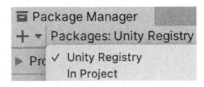

Figure 7.35 Package Manager – Unity Registry mode

3. From the left column, locate **Universal RP** and check whether it says 11.0.0 or higher to the right. If it does, jump to *step 6*. Remember, though, that a higher version may look different or have different steps you must follow to use it than the ones displayed in this chapter:

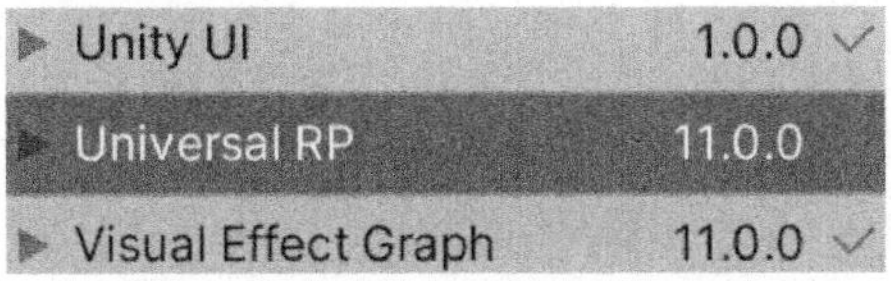

Figure 7.36 – Universal RP package

4. If you don't have version 11.0.0 or higher, click on the right-pointing arrow to the left to display a list of all possible versions to install. Locate 11.0.0 and click it. In my case, it says currently installed as I have the proper version and there are no others available for Unity 2021:

Figure 7.37 – Package version selector

5. Click on the **Update to 11.0.0** button in the bottom-right corner of the window and wait for the package to update.

6. Look for the **Visual Effect Graph** package on the left-hand side of the window. As you did with Universal RP, make sure you select version 11.0.0 or higher (whichever is closest):

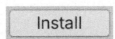

Figure 7.38 – Visual Effect Graph package

7. Click the **Install** button on the bottom right of the window and wait for the package to install:

Install

Figure 7.39 – Install button

8. Sometimes, it is recommended to restart Unity after installing these packages, so save your changes and restart Unity.

Now that we have installed Visual Effect Graph, let's create our first particle system using it.

Creating and analyzing a Visual Effect Graph

The philosophy behind creating a particle system using Visual Effect Graph is similar to the regular Particle System. We will chain and configure modules as part of the behavior of the particles, each module adding some specific behavior. However, the way we do this is very different than what we usually do with Shuriken. First, we need to create a **Visual Effect Graph**, an asset that will contain all the modules and configurations, and then make a GameObject play the graph. Let's do that by performing the following steps:

1. In the **Project** window, click on the + button and look for **Visual Effects | Visual Effect Graph**:

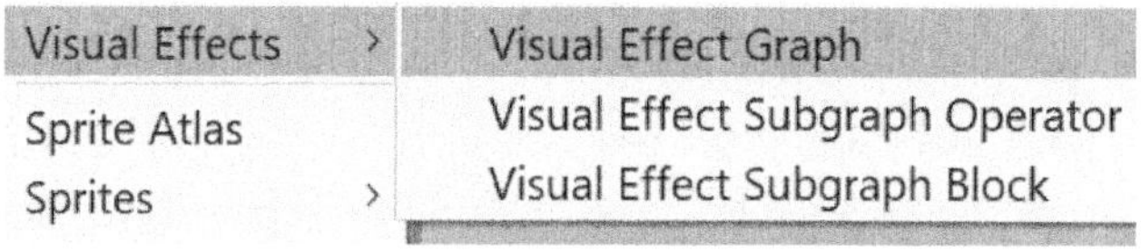

Figure 7.40 – Visual Effect Graph

2. Create an empty GameObject using the **Game Object | Create Empty** option:

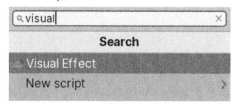

Figure 7.41 – Empty GameObject creation

3. Select the created object and look at the **Inspector** window.

4. Using the **Add Component** search bar, look for the **Visual Effect** component and click on it to add it to the object:

Figure 7.42 – Adding a component to Visual Effect Graph

5. Drag the **Visual Effect** asset we created to the **Asset Template** property of the **Visual Effect** component in our GameObject:

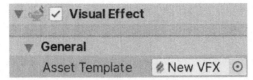

Figure 7.43 – Visual Effect using the previously created Visual Effect asset

6. You should see clock particles being emitted from our object:

Figure 7.44 – Default Visual Effect Asset results

Now that we have a base effect, let's create something that requires a lot of particles, such as dense rain. Before doing so, we will explore some core concepts of Visual Effect Graph. If you double-click the **Visual Effect** asset, you will see the following editor:

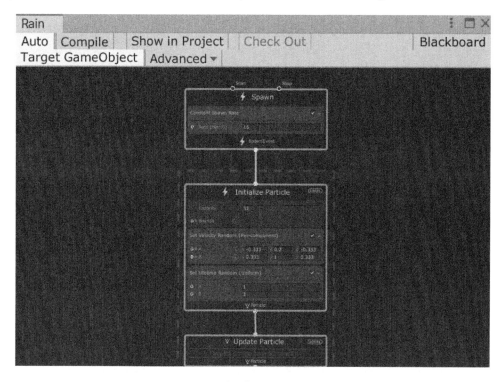

Figure 7.45 – Visual Effect Graph editor window

This window is composed of several interconnected nodes, generating a flow of actions to be executed. As with Shader Graph, you can navigate this window by holding down the *Alt* key (*Option* on Mac) and dragging over the empty areas of the graph with the mouse. At first, it seems similar to Shader Graph, but it works a little bit differently, so let's study each section of the default graph.

The first area to explore is the dotted one that contains three nodes. This is what Unity calls a **System**. A System is a set of nodes that defines how a particle will behave, and you can have as many as you want, which is the equivalent of having several particle system objects. Each System is composed of **Contexts**, the nodes inside the dotted area, and in this case, we have **Initialize Particle**, **Update Particle**, and **Output Particle Quad**. Each Context represents a different stage of the particle system's logic flow, so let's define what each context in our graph does:

- **Initialize Particle**: This defines the initial data of each emitted particle, such as position, color, speed, and size. It is similar to the **Start** properties in the Main module of the particle system we saw at the beginning of this chapter. The logic in this node will only execute when a new particle is emitted.

- **Update Particle**: Here, we can apply modifications to the data of the living particles. We can change particle data such as the current velocity or size of all the frames. This is similar to the **Over Time** nodes of the previous particle system.

- **Output Particle Quad**: This Context will be executed when the particle needs to be rendered. It will read the particle data to see where to render, how to render, which texture and color to use, and different visual settings. This is similar to the **Renderer** module of the previous particle system.

Inside each Context, apart from some base configurations, we can add **Blocks**. Each Block is an action that will be executed in the context. We have actions that can be executed in any Context and then some specific Context actions. As an example, we can use an **Add Position** Block in the **Initialize Particle** Context to move the initial particle position, but if we use the same Block in the **Update Particle** Context, it will move the particle constantly. So, basically, Contexts are different situations that occur in the life of the particle, and Blocks are actions that are executed in those situations:

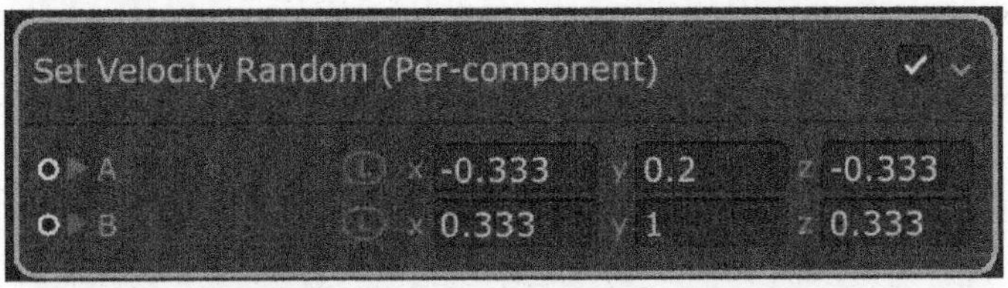

Figure 7.46 – A Set Velocity Random block inside the Initialize Particle context. This sets the initial velocity of a particle

Also, we can have **Standalone Contexts**, which are Contexts outside systems, such as **Spawn**. This Context is responsible for telling the System that a new particle needs to be created. We can add Blocks to specify when the context will tell the system to create the particle, such as at a fixed rate over time and bursts. The idea is that **Spawn** will create particles according to its blocks, while a System is responsible for initializing, updating, and rendering each of them, again, according to the blocks we set up inside each of those Contexts.

So, we can see that there are lots of similarities with Shuriken, but the way we create a system here is quite different. Let's reinforce this by creating a rain effect, which will require lots of particles. This is a nice use case for Visual Effect Graph.

Creating a rain effect

To create this effect, do the following:

1. Set the **Capacity** property of the **Initialize Particle** Context to `10000`:

Figure 7.47 – Initialize Particle context

2. Set **Rate** of **Constant Spawn Rate** of the **Spawn** context to `10000`:

Figure 7.48 – Constant Spawn Rate block

3. Set the **A** and **B** properties to (0, -50, 0) and (0, -75, 0) in the **Set Velocity Random** Block in **Initialize Particle** Contexts, respectively. This will set a random velocity pointing downward for our particles:

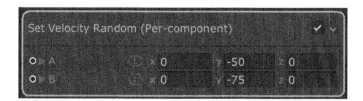

Figure 7.49 – Set Velocity Random block

4. Right-click the **Initialize Particle** title and select **Create Block**.

5. Search for the **Set Position Random** block and click on it:

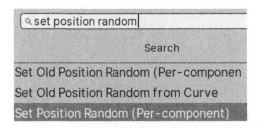

Figure 7.50 – Adding blocks

6. Set the **A** and **B** properties of the **Set Position Random** block to (-50 , 0, -50) and (50, 0, 50), respectively. This will define an initial area where we will randomly spawn the particle.

7. Click the arrow to the left of the **Bounds** property of the **Initialize Particle** Block to display its properties. Then, set **Center** and **Size** to (0, -12.5, 0) and (100, 25, 100), respectively. This will define the area where the particles should live. Particles can move outside this area, but this is important for the system to work properly (search for Frustum Culling on the internet for more information):

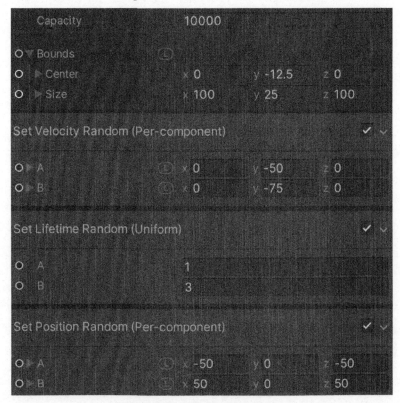

Figure 7.51 – Configuring blocks

8. Select the GameObject that is executing the system. Then, in the bottom-right window in the **Scene** view, check the **Show Bounds** checkbox to see the previously defined Bounds:

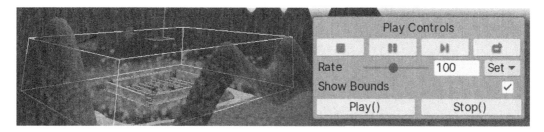

Figure 7.52 – Visual Effect Playback controls

9. Set the object's position so that it covers the whole base area. In my case, the position is (100, 37, 100). Remember that you need to change **Position** of the **Transform** component for this:

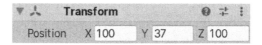

Figure 7.53 – Setting a transform position

10. Set the **A** and **B** properties of the **Set Lifetime Random** Block in **Initialize Particle** to 0.5. This will make the particles have a shorter lifetime, ensuring that they are always inside the bounds:

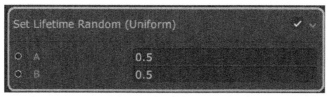

Figure 7.54 – Set Lifetime Random block

11. Change the **Main Texture** property of the **Output Particle Quad** Context to another texture. In this case, the previously downloaded smoke texture can work here, even though it's not water, because we will modify its appearance in a moment. Also, you can try to download a water droplet texture if you so wish:

Figure 7.55 – VFX Graph Main Texture

12. Set **Blend Mode** of the **Output Particle Quad** Context to **Additive**:

Figure 7.56 – Additive mode of the VFX Graph

13. If you can't see the changes being applied, click the **Compile** button in the top-left corner of the window. Also, you can save your changes using *Ctrl + S* (*Command + S* on Mac):

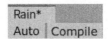

Figure 7.57 – VFX Asset Saving controls

14. We need to stretch our particles a little bit so that they look like actual raindrops instead of falling balls. Before accomplishing that, first, we need to change the orientation of our particles so that they don't point at the camera all the time. To do this, right-click on **Orient Block** in the **Output Particle Quad** Context and select **Delete** (or press *Del* on Windows or *Command + Backspace* on Mac):

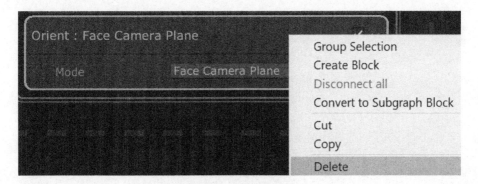

Figure 7.58 – Deleting a block

15. We want to stretch our particles according to their velocity direction. Another thing we must do before actually doing that is select the title of the **Output Particle Quad** context and hit the *space bar* to look for a block to add. In this case, we need to search for and add the **Orient Along Velocity** block (right-click on the **Output Particle Quad** title and then click on **Create Block**).

16. Add a **Set Scale** Block to the **Initialize Particle** Context and set the **Scale** property to (0.25, 1.5, 0.25). This will stretch the particles so that they look like falling drops:

Figure 7.59 – Set Scale block

17. Click the **Compile** button in the top-left window again to see the changes. Your system should look like this:

Figure 7.60 – Rain results

From here, you can experiment by adding and removing Blocks from the Contexts as you wish. Again, I recommend that you look for already-created Visual Effect Graphs to find ideas for other systems. Actually, you can get ideas for Visual Effect Graph by looking at effects made in Shuriken and using the analogous blocks. Also, I recommend that you look at the Visual Effect Graph documentation (`https://docs.unity3d.com/Packages/com.unity.visualeffectgraph@11.0/manual/index.html`) to learn more about this system. You can also access the documentation of any Unity package by clicking the **View documentation** link in **Package Manager** while the package is selected:

Figure 7.61 – Package Manager documentation link

Now, let's summarize this chapter.

Summary

In this chapter, we discussed two different ways of creating particle systems; that is, using Shuriken and Visual Effect Graph. We used them to simulate different fluid phenomena, such as fire, a waterfall, smoke, and rain. The idea is to combine particle systems with meshes to generate all the props that are needed for your scene. Also, as you can imagine, creating these kinds of effects professionally requires you to go deeper. If you want to dedicate yourself to this (another part of the job of a Technical Artist), you will need to learn how to create your own particle textures to get the exact look and feel you want, code scripts that control certain aspects of the systems, and several other aspects of particle creation. Again, that is outside the scope of this book.

Now that we have some rain in our scene, we can see that the sky and the lighting in the scene don't reflect a rainy day. We'll fix this in the next chapter!

8
Lighting Using the Universal Render Pipeline

Lighting is a complex topic and there are several possible ways to handle it, with each one having its pros and cons. In order to get the best possible quality with the best performance, you need to know exactly how your renderer handles it, and that is exactly what we are going to learn in this chapter. We will discuss how lighting is handled in Unity's **Universal Render Pipeline (URP)**, as well as how to properly configure it to adapt our scene's mood with proper lighting effects.

In this chapter, we will examine the following lighting concepts:

- Applying lighting
- Applying shadows
- Optimizing lighting

At the end of the chapter, we will have properly used the different Unity Illumination systems, such as Direct Lights and Lightmapping to reflect a cloudy and rainy night.

Applying lighting

When discussing ways to process lighting in a game, there are two main ways we can do so, known as **Forward Rendering** and **Deferred Rendering**. Both handle lighting in a different order, with different techniques, requirements, pros, and cons. Forward Rendering is usually recommended for performance, while Deferred Rendering is usually recommended for quality. The latter is used by the **High Definition Render Pipeline** of Unity, the Renderer used for high-quality graphics in high-end devices. At the time of writing this book, Unity is developing a performant version for URP. Also, in Unity, Forward Renderer comes in two flavors: **Multi-Pass Forward**, which is used in the built-in Renderer (the old Unity Renderer), and **Single-Pass Forward,** which is used in URP. Again, each has its pros and cons.

> **Important information**
> Actually, there are other options available, both official and third-party, such as **Vertex Lit**, but for now, we will focus on the three main ones – the ones you use 95% of the time.

Choosing between one or another depends on the kind of game you are creating and the target platform you need to run the game on. Your chosen option will change a lot due to the way you apply lighting to your scene, so it's crucial you understand which system you are dealing with.

In this section, we will discuss the following Realtime lighting concepts:

- Discussing lighting methods
- Configuring ambient lighting with skyboxes
- Configuring lighting in URP

Let's start by comparing the previously mentioned lighting methods.

Discussing lighting methods

To recap, we mentioned three main ways of processing lighting:

- Forward Rendering (Single-Pass)
- Forward Rendering (Multi-Pass)
- Deferred Rendering

Before we look at the differences between each, let's talk about the things they have in common. Those three renderers start drawing the scene by determining which objects can be seen by the camera; that is, the ones that fall inside the camera's frustum, and provide a giant pyramid that can be seen when you select the camera:

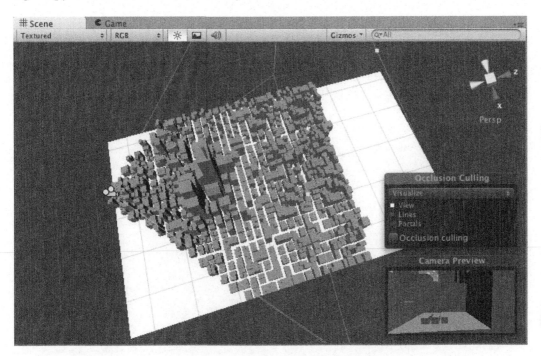

Figure 8.1 – The camera's frustum showing only the objects that can be seen by it

After that, Unity will order them from the nearest to the camera to the farthest (transparent objects are handled a little bit differently, but let's ignore that for now). It's done like this because it's more probable that objects nearer to the camera will cover most of the camera, so they will occlude others, preventing us from wasting resources calculating pixels for the occluded ones.

Finally, Unity will try to render the objects in that order. This is where differences start to arise between lighting methods, so let's start comparing the two Forward Rendering variants. For each object, Single-Pass Forward Rendering will calculate the object's appearance, including all the lights that are affecting the object, in one shot, or what we call a **Draw Call**. A Draw Call is the exact moment when Unity asks the video card to actually render the specified object. All the previous work was just preparation for this moment. In the case of the Multi-Pass Forward Renderer, by simplifying a little bit of the actual logic, Unity will render the object once for every light that affects the object. So, if the object is being lit by three lights, Unity will render the object three times, meaning that three Draw Calls will be issued, and three calls to the GPU will be made to execute the rendering process:

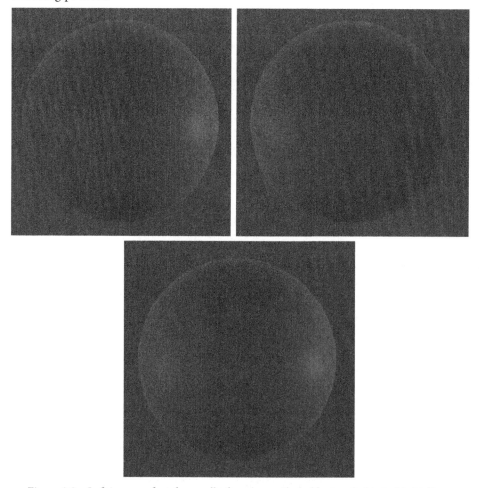

Figure 8.2 – Left image – first draw call of a sphere affected by two lights in Multi-Pass;
middle image – second draw call of the sphere; right image – the combination of both Draw Calls

Now is when you are probably thinking, *"Why should I use Multi-Pass? Single-Pass is more performant!"* And yes, you are right! Single-Pass is way more performant than Multi-Pass, and here comes the great but. A Draw Call in a GPU has a limited amount of operations that can be executed, so you have a limit to the complexity of the Draw Call. Calculating the appearance of an object and all the lights that affect it is very complex, and in order to make it fit in just one Draw Call, Single-Pass executes simplified versions of lighting calculations, meaning lower lighting quality and fewer features. They also have a limit on how many lights can be handled in one shot, which, at the time of writing this book, is eight per object (four for low-end devices). This sounds like a small number, but it's usually just enough.

On the other side, Multi-Pass can apply any number of lights you want and can execute different logic for each light. Let's say our object has four lights that are affecting it, but there are two lights that are affecting it drastically because they are nearer or have higher intensity, while the remaining ones affecting the object are just enough to be noticeable. In this scenario, we can render the first two lights with higher quality and the remaining ones with cheap calculations – no one will be able to tell the difference. In this case, Multi-Pass can calculate the first two lights using **Pixel Lighting** and the remaining ones using **Vertex Lighting**. The difference is in their names: Pixel calculates light per object pixel, while Vertex calculates lighting per object vertex and fills the pixels between these vertexes, thereby interpolating information between vertexes. You can clearly see the difference in the following screenshots:

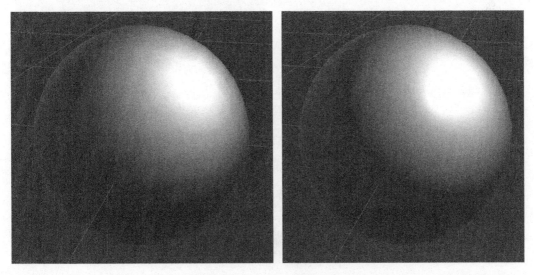

Figure 8.3 – Left image – a sphere being rendered with Vertex Lighting; right image – a sphere being rendered with Pixel Lighting

In Single-Pass, calculating everything in a single draw call forces you to use Vertex Lighting or Pixel Lighting; you cannot combine them.

So, to summarize the differences between Single- and Multi-Pass, in Single-Pass, you have better performance because each object is just drawn once, but you are limited to the number of lights that can be applied, while in Multi-Pass, you need to render the object several times, but with no limits on the number of lights, and you can specify the exact quality you want for each light. There are other things to consider, such as the actual cost of a Draw Call (one Draw Call can be more expensive than two simple ones), and special lighting effects such as toon shading, but let's keep things simple.

Finally, let's briefly discuss Deferred Rendering. Even though we are not going to use it, it's interesting to know why we are not doing that. After determining which objects fall inside the frustum and ordering them, Deferred will render the objects without any lighting, generating what is called a **G-Buffer**. A G-Buffer is a set of several images that contain different information about the objects of the scene, such as the colors of its pixels (without lighting), the direction of each pixel (known as **Normals**), and how far from the camera the pixels are. You can see a typical example of a G-Buffer in the following figure:

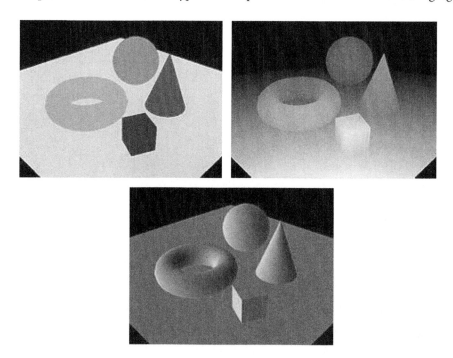

Figure 8.4 – Left image – plain colors of the object; middle image – depths of each pixel; right image – normals of the pixels

Important information

Normals are directions, and the (X,Y,Z) components of the directions are
encoded in the RGB components of the colors.

After rendering all the objects in the scene, Unity will iterate over all lights that can be
seen in the camera, thus applying a layer of lighting over the G-Buffer, taking information
from it to calculate that specific light. After all the lights have been processed, you will get
the following result:

Figure 8.5 – Combination of the three lights that were applied to the G-Buffer
shown in the previous figure

As you can see, the Deferred part of this method comes from the idea of calculating
lighting as the last stage of the rendering process. This is better because you won't waste
resources calculating lighting from objects that could potentially be occluded. If the floor
of the image is being rendered first in Forward Rendering, the pixels that the rest of the
objects are going to occlude will have been calculated in vain. Also, there's the detail that
Deferred just calculates lighting in the exact pixels that the light can reach. As an example,
if you are using a flashlight, Unity will calculate lighting only in the pixels that fall inside
the cone of the flashlight. The con here is that Deferred is not supported by some relatively
old video cards and that you can't calculate lighting with Vertex Lighting quality, so
you will need to pay the price of Pixel Lighting, which is not recommended on low-end
devices (or even necessary in simple graphics games).

So, why are we using URP with Single-Pass Forward? Because it offers the best balance
between performance, quality, and simplicity. In this game, we won't be using too many
lights, so we won't worry about the light number limitations of Single-Pass, and we won't
take advantage of the Deferred benefits too much, so it makes no sense to use more
hardware to run the game.

Now that we have a very basic notion of how URP handles lighting, let's start using it!

Configuring ambient lighting with skyboxes

There are different light sources that can affect the scene, such as the sun, torches, light bulbs, and more. Those are known as **Direct Lights**; that is, objects that emit light rays. Then, we have **Indirect Light**, light that usually represents bounces of Direct Lights. However, calculating all the bounces of all the rays emitted by all the lights is impossible if you want to get a game running at at least 30 FPS (or simply running). The problem is that not having Indirect Light will generate unrealistic results where you can observe places where the sunlight doesn't reach being completely dark because no light is bouncing from other places where light hits. In the next screenshot, you can see an example of how this could look in a wrongly configured scene:

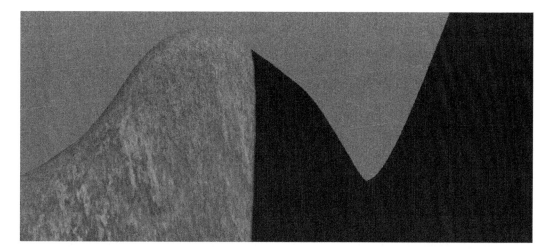

Figure 8.6 – Shadows projected onto a mountain without ambient lighting

If you ever experience this problem, the way to solve it is using approximations of those bounces. These are what we call **Ambient Light**. This represents a base layer of lighting that usually applies a little bit of light based on the color of the sky, but you can choose whatever color you want. As an example, on a clear night, we can pick a dark blue color to represent the tint from the moonlight.

If you create a new scene in Unity 2021, usually this is done automatically, but in cases where it isn't, or the scene was created through other methods, it is convenient to know how to manually trigger this process by doing the following:

1. Click on **Window | Rendering | Lighting**. This will open the **Scene Lighting Settings** window:

Figure 8.7 – Lighting settings location

2. Click the **Generate Lighting** button at the bottom of the window. If you haven't saved the scene so far, a prompt will ask you to save it, which is necessary:

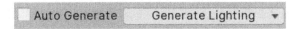

Figure 8.8 – Generate Lighting button

3. See the bottom-right part of the Unity window to find the progress calculation bar to check when the process has finished:

Figure 8.9 – Lighting generation progress bar

4. You can now see how completely dark areas now have a little effect shown on them from the light being emitted by the sky:

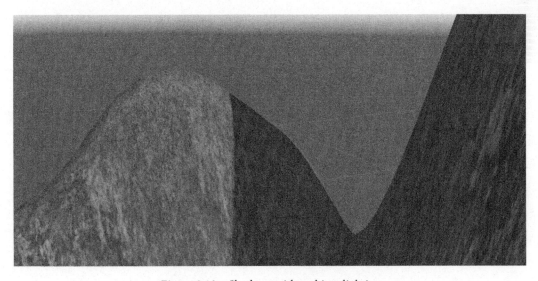

Figure 8.10 – Shadows with ambient lighting

Now, by doing this, we have better lighting, but it still looks like a sunny day. Remember, we want to have rainy weather. In order to do that, we need to change the default sky too so that it's cloudy. You can do that by downloading a **skybox**. The current sky you can see around the scene is just a big cube containing textures on each side, and those have a special projection to prevent us from detecting the edges of the cube. You can download six images for each side of the cube and apply them to have whatever sky you want, so let's do that:

1. You can download skybox textures from wherever you want, but here, I will choose the Asset Store. Open it by going to **Window | Asset Store** and going to the Asset Store website.

2. Look for **2D | Textures & Materials | Sky** in the category list on the right. Remember that you need to make that window wider if you can't see the category list:

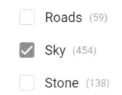

Figure 8.11 – Skybox category

3. Remember to check the **Free Assets** checkbox in the **Pricing** section:

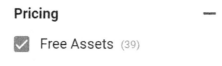

Figure 8.12 – Free Assets filtering

4. Pick any skybox you like for a rainy day. Take into account that there are different formats for skyboxes. We are using the six-image format, so check that before downloading one. In my case, I have chosen the skybox pack shown in the following screenshot. Download and import it, as we did in *Chapter 5, Importing and Integrating Assets*:

RPGWHITELOCK

AllSky Free - 10 Sky / Skybox Set

★ ★ ★ ★ ★ (13)

FREE

Figure 8.13 – Selected skybox set for this book

5. Create a new material by using the + icon in the **Project** window and selecting **Material**.

6. Set the **Shader** option of that material to **Skybox/6 Sided**. Remember that the skybox is just a cube, so we can apply a material to change how it looks. The skybox shader is prepared to apply the six textures.

7. Drag the six textures to the **Front**, **Back**, **Left**, **Right**, **Up**, and **Down** properties of the material. The six downloaded textures will have descriptive names so that you know which textures go where:

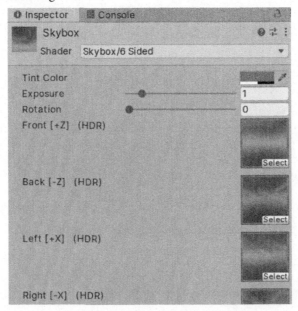

Figure 8.14 – Skybox material settings

8. Drag the material directly into the sky in the Scene View. Be sure you don't drag the material into an object because the material will be applied to it.

9. Repeat *steps 1* to *4* of the ambient light calculation steps (**Lighting Settings |
    Generate Lighting**) to recalculate it based on the new skybox. In the following
    screenshot, you can see the result of my project so far:

Figure 8.15 – Applied skybox

Important note

These lighting recalculations can take a while to complete. This is due to the
fact that the **Generate Lighting** button does more than calculate the light from
the sky. One trick to speed up the process is to uncheck the **Static** checkbox in
the **Inspector** of every object in the scene. Later, in the **Optimizing Lighting**
section of this chapter, we will talk more about that checkbox and what
it means.

Now that we have a good base layer of lighting, we can start adding light objects.

Configuring lighting in URP

We have three main types of Direct Lights we can add to our scene:

- **Directional Light**: This is a light that represents the sun. This object emits light rays in the direction it is facing, regardless of its position; the sun moving 100 meters to the right won't make a big difference. As an example, if you slowly rotate this object, you can generate a day/night cycle:

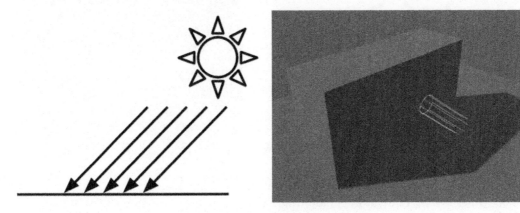

Figure 8.16 – Directional Light results

- **Point Light**: This light represents a light bulb, which emits rays in an omnidirectional way. The difference from the Directional Light is that its position matters because it's closer to our objects. Also, because it's a weaker light, the intensity of this light varies according to the distance, so its effect has a range – the further the object from the light, the weaker the received intensity:

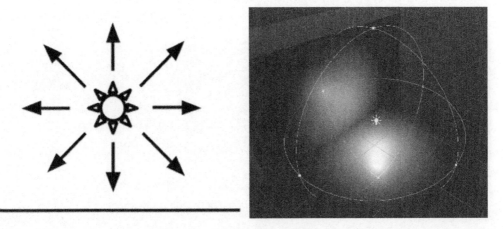

Figure 8.17 – Point Light results

- **Spotlight**: This kind of light represents a light cone, such as the one emitted by a flashlight. It behaves similarly to point lights in that its position matters and the light intensity decays over a certain distance. But here the direction it points to (hence its rotation) is also important given it will specify where to project the light:

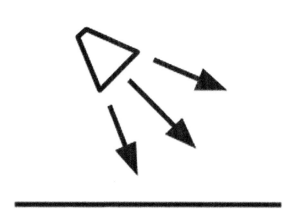 

Figure 8.18 – Spotlight results

So far, we have nice, rainy, ambient lighting, but the only Direct Light we have in the scene, the Directional Light, won't look like this, so let's change that:

1. Select the **Directional Light** object in the **Hierarchy** window and then look at the **Inspector** window.
2. Click the **Color** property to open the Color Picker.
3. Select a dark gray color to achieve sun rays partially occluded by clouds.
4. Set **Shadow Type** to **No Shadows**. Now that we have a cloudy day, the sun does not project clear shadows, but we will talk more about shadows in a moment:

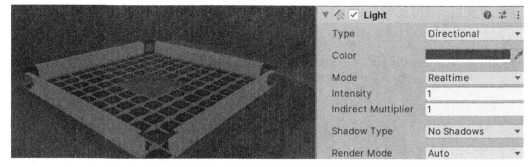

Figure 8.19 – Soft directional light with no shadows

Now that the scene is darker, we can add some lights to light up the scene, as follows:

5. Create a Spotlight by going to **GameObject | Light | Spotlight**:

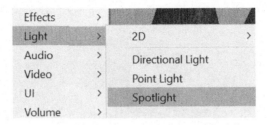

Figure 8.20 – Creating a Spotlight

6. Select it. Then, in the **Inspector** window, set **Inner / Output Spot Angle** to 90 and 120, which will increase the angle of the cone.

7. Set **Range** to 50, meaning that the light can reach up to 50 meters, decaying along the way.

8. Set **Intensity** to 1000:

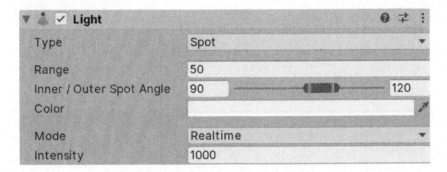

Figure 8.21 – Spotlight settings

9.   Position the light at one corner of the Base, pointing it at the center:

Figure 8.22 – Spotlight placement

10. Duplicate that light by selecting it and pressing *Ctrl + D* (*Command + D* on Mac).

11. Put it in the opposite corner of the Base:

Figure 8.23 – Two Spotlight results

You can keep adding lights to the scene but take care that you don't go too far – remember the light limits. Also, you can download some light posts to put in where the lights are located to visually justify the origin of the light. Now that we have achieved proper lighting, we can talk about shadows.

Applying shadows

Maybe you are thinking that we already have shadows in the scene, but actually, we don't. The darker areas of the object, the ones that are not facing the lights, don't have shadows – they are not being lit, and that's quite different from a shadow. In this case, we are referring to the shadows that are projected from one object to another; for example, the shadow of the player being projected on the floor, or from the mountains to other objects. Shadows can increase the quality of our scene, but they also cost a lot to calculate, so we have two options: not using shadows (recommended for low-end devices such as mobiles) or finding a balance between performance and quality according to our game and the target device. In the first case, you can skip this whole section, but if you want to achieve performant shadows (as much as possible), keep reading.

In this section, we are going to discuss the following topics about shadows:

- Understanding shadow calculations
- Configuring performant shadows

Let's start by discussing how Unity calculates shadows.

Understanding shadow calculations

In game development, it is well known that shadows are costly in terms of performance, but why? An object has a shadow when a light ray hits another object before reaching it. In that case, no lighting is applied to that pixel from that light. The problem here is the same problem we have with the light that ambient lighting simulates – it would be too costly to calculate all possible rays and their collisions. So, again, we need an approximation, and here is where Shadow Maps kick in.

A Shadow Map is an image that's rendered from the point of view of the light, but instead of drawing the full scene with all the color and lighting calculations, it will render all the objects in grayscale, where black means that the pixel is very far from the camera and whiter pixels means that the pixel is nearer to the camera. If you think about it, each pixel contains information about where a **ray** of light hits. By knowing the position and orientation of the light, you can calculate the position where each "ray" hit using the **Shadow Map**. In the following screenshot, you can see the Shadow Map of our Directional Light:

Figure 8.24 – Shadow Map generated by the Directional Light of our scene

Each type of light calculates Shadow Maps slightly differently, especially the Point Light. Since it's omnidirectional, it needs to render the scene several times in all its directions (front, back, up, down, right, and left) in order to gather information about all the rays it emits. We won't talk about this in detail here, though, as we could talk about it all day.

Now, something important to highlight here is that Shadow Maps are textures, hence they have a resolution. The higher the resolution, the more "rays" our Shadow Map calculates. You are probably wondering what a low-resolution shadow map looks like when it has only a few rays in it. Take a look at the following screenshot to see one:

Figure 8.25 – Hard Shadow rendered with a low-resolution Shadow Map

The problem here is that having fewer rays generates bigger shadow pixels, resulting in a pixelated shadow. Here, we have our first configuration to consider: what is the ideal resolution for our shadows? You will be tempted to just increase it until the shadows look smooth, but of course, that will increase how long it will take to calculate it, so it will impact the performance considerably unless your target platform can handle it (mobiles definitely can't). Here, we can use the **Soft Shadows** trick, where we can apply a blurring effect over the shadows to hide the pixelated edges, as shown in the following screenshot:

Figure 8.26 – Soft Shadows rendered with a low-resolution Shadow Map

Of course, the blurry effect is not free, but combining it with low-resolution shadow maps, if you accept its blurry result, can generate a nice balance between quality and performance.

Now, low-resolution Shadow Maps have another problem, which is called **Shadow Acne**. This is the lighting error you can see in the following screenshot:

Figure 8.27 – Shadow Acne from a low-resolution Shadow Map

A low-resolution shadow map generates false positives because it has fewer "rays" calculated. The pixels to be shaded between the rays need to interpolate information from the nearest ones. The lower the Shadow Map's resolution, the larger the gap between the rays, which means less precision and more false positives. One solution would be to increase the resolution, but again, there will be performance issues (as always). We have some clever solutions to this, such as using **depth bias**. An example of this can be seen in the following figure:

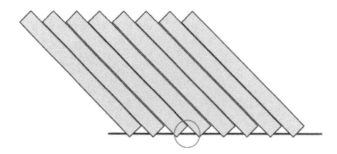

Figure 8.28 – A false positive between two far "rays." The highlighted area thinks
the ray hit an object before reaching it

The concept of **depth bias** is simple – so simple that it seems like a big cheat, and actually, it is, but game development is full of them! To prevent false positives, we "push" the rays a little bit further, just enough to make the interpolated rays reach the hitting surface:

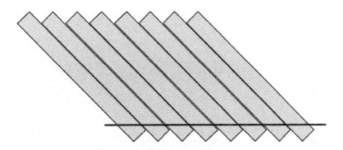

Figure 8.29 – Rays with a depth bias to eliminate false positives

Of course, as you are probably expecting, you can't solve this problem easily without having a caveat. Pushing depth generates false negatives in other areas, as shown in the following screenshot. It looks like the cube is floating, but actually, it is touching the ground – the false negatives generate the illusion that it is floating:

Figure 8.30 – False negatives due to a high depth bias

Of course, we have a counter trick to this situation known as **normal bias**. This pushes the object's mesh along the direction they are facing, not the rays. This one is a little bit tricky, so we won't go into too much detail here, but the idea is that combining a little bit of depth bias and another bit of normal bias will reduce the false positives, but not completely eliminate them. Therefore, we need to learn how to live with that and hide it by cleverly positioning objects:

Figure 8.31 – Reduced false negatives, which is the result of combining depth and normal bias

There are several other aspects that affect how a Shadow Map works, with one of them being the light range. The smaller the light range, the less area the shadows will cover. The same Shadow Map resolution can add more detail to that area, so try to reduce light ranges as much as you can.

I can imagine your face right now, and yes, lighting is complicated, and we've only just scratched the surface! But keep your spirits up! After a little trial and error fiddling with the settings, you will understand it better. We'll do that in the next section.

> **Important information**
>
> If you are really interested in learning more about the internals of the shadow system, I recommend that you look at the concept of **Shadow Cascades**, an advanced topic in Directional Light and Shadow Map generation.

Configuring performant shadows

Because we are targeting mid-end devices, we will try to achieve a good balance of quality and performance here, so let's start enabling shadows just for the spotlights. The Directional Light shadow won't be that noticeable, and actually, a rainy sky doesn't generate clear shadows, so we will use that as an excuse to not calculate those shadows. In order to do this, do the following:

1. Select both Spot Lights by clicking them in the **Hierarchy** while pressing *Ctrl* (*Command* on Mac). This will ensure that any changes made in the **Inspector** window will be applied to both:

Figure 8.32 – Selecting multiple objects

2. In the **Inspector** window, set **Shadow Type** to **Soft Shadows**. We will be using low-resolution shadow maps here and the soft mode can help to hide the pixelated resolution:

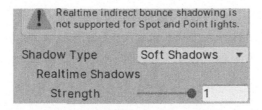

Figure 8.33 – Soft Shadows setting

3. Select **Directional light** and set **Shadow Type** to **No Shadows** to prevent it from casting shadows:

Figure 8.34 – No Shadows setting

4. Create a cube (**GameObject | 3D Object | Cube**) and place it near one of the lights, just to have an object that we can cast shadows on for testing purposes.

Now that we have a base test scenario, let's fiddle with the Shadow Maps resolution settings, preventing Shadow Acne in the process:

1. Go to **Edit | Project Settings**.

2. In the left-hand side list, look for **Graphics** and click it:

Figure 8.35 – Graphics settings

In the properties that appear after selecting this option, click in the box below **Scriptable Render Pipeline Settings** – the one that contains a name. In my case, this is **UniveralRP-HighQuality**, but yours may be different due to you having a different version of Unity:

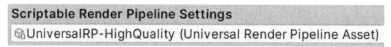

Figure 8.36 – Current render pipeline setting

3. Doing that will highlight an asset in the Project Window, so be sure that window is visible before selecting it. Select the highlighted asset:

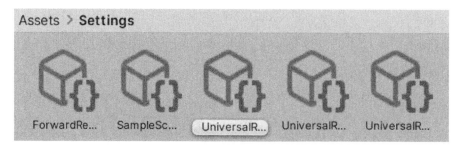

Figure 8.37 – Current pipeline highlighted

4. This asset has several graphics settings related to how URP will handle its rendering, including lighting and shadows. Expand the **Lighting** section to reveal its settings:

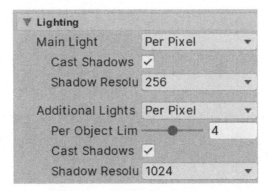

Figure 8.38 – Pipeline Lighting settings

5. The **Shadow Atlas Resolution** setting under the **Additional Lights** subsection represents the Shadow Map resolution for all the lights that aren't **Directional Light** (since it's the **Main Light**). Set it to **1024** if it's not already at that value.

6. Under the **Shadows** section, you can see the **Depth** and **Normal Bias** settings, but those will affect all **Lights**. Even if right now our Directional Light doesn't have shadows, we want only to affect **Additional Lights** bias values as they have a different Atlas Resolution compared to the **Main** one (Directional Light), so instead, select spotlights and set **Bias** to **Custom** and **Depth** and **Normal Bias** to 0.25 in order to reduce them as much as we can before we remove the Shadow Acne:

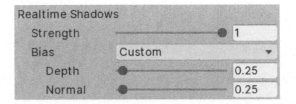

Figure 8.39 – Bias settings

7. This isn't entirely related to shadows, but in the Univeral RP settings asset, you can change the **Per Object Light** limit to increase or reduce the number of lights that can affect the object (no more than eight). For now, the default is good as is.

8. If you followed the shadow cascades tip presented earlier, you can play with the **Cascades** value a little bit to enable shadows for Directional Light to notice the effect. Remember that those shadow settings only work for the Directional Light.

9. Set both lights so that they have a 40-meter **Range**. See how the shadows improve in quality before and after this change.

Remember that those values only work in my case, so try to fiddle with the values a little bit to see how that changes the result – you may find a better setup for your scene if it was designed differently from mine. Also, remember that not having shadows is always an option, so always consider that if your game is running low on FPS (and there isn't another performance problem lurking).

You probably think that that is all we can do about performance in terms of lighting, but luckily, that's not the case! We have another resource we can use to improve it further, known as static lighting.

Optimizing lighting

We mentioned previously that not calculating lighting is good for performance, but what about not calculating lights, but still having them? Yes, it sounds too good to be true, but it is actually possible (and, of course, tricky). We can use a technique called static lighting or baking, which allows us to calculate lighting once and use the cached result.

In this section, we will cover the following concepts related to Static Lighting:

- Understanding static lighting

- Baking lightmaps

- Applying static lighting to dynamic objects

Understanding static lighting

The idea is pretty simple: just do the lighting calculations once, save the results, and then use those instead of calculating lighting all the time. You may be wondering why this isn't the default technique to use. This is because it has some limitations, with the big one being dynamic objects. **Precalculating shadows** means that they can't change once they've been calculated, but if an object that is casting a shadow is moved, the shadow will still be there, so the main thing to take into account here is that you can't use this technique with moving objects. Instead, you will need to mix **static** or **baked lighting** for static objects and **Realtime lighting** for dynamic (moving) objects. Also, consider that aside from this technique being only valid for static objects, it is also only valid for static lights. Again, if a light moves, the precalculated data becomes invalid.

Another limitation you need to take into account is that that precalculated data can have a huge impact on memory. That data occupies space in RAM, maybe hundreds of MBs, so you need to consider whether your target platform has enough space. Of course, you can reduce the precalculated lighting quality to reduce the size of that data, but you need to consider whether the loss of quality deteriorates the look and feel of your game too much. As with all options regarding optimization, you need to balance two factors: performance and quality.

We have several kinds of precalculated data in our process, but the most important one is what we call **lightmaps**. A lightmap is a texture that contains all the shadows and lighting for all the objects in the scene, so when Unity applies the precalculated or baked data, it will look at this texture to know which parts of the statics objects are lit and which aren't. You can see an example of a lightmap in the following figure:

Figure 8.40 – Left – a scene with no lighting; middle – a lightmap holding precalculated data from that scene; right – the lightmap being applied to the scene

Anyway, having lightmaps has its own benefits. The baking process is executed in Unity, before the game is shipped to users, so you can spend plenty of time calculating stuff that you can't do at runtime, such as improved accuracy, light bounces, light occlusion in corners, and light from emissive objects. However, that can also be a problem. Remember, dynamic objects still need to rely on Realtime lighting, and that lighting will look very different compared to static lighting, so we need to tweak them a lot for the user to not notice the difference.

Now that we have a basic notion of what static lighting is, let's dive into how to use it.

Baking lightmaps

To use lightmaps, we need to make some preparations regarding the 3D models. Remember that meshes have **UVs**, which contain information about which part of the texture needs to be applied to each part of the model. Sometimes, to save texture memory, you can apply the same piece of texture to different parts. For example, in a car's texture, you wouldn't have four wheels, you'd just have one, and you can apply that same piece of texture to all the wheels. The problem here is that static lighting uses textures the same way, but here, it will apply the lightmaps to light the object. In the wheel scenario, the problem would be that if one wheel receives shadows, all of them will have it, because all the wheels are sharing the same texture space. The usual solution is to have a second set of UVs in the model with no texture space being shared, just to use them for lightmapping.

Sometimes, downloaded models are already prepared for lightmapping, and sometimes, they aren't, but luckily, Unity has us covered in those scenarios. To be sure a model will calculate lightmapping properly, let's make Unity automatically generate the **Lightmapping UV** set by doing the following:

1. Select the mesh asset (FBX) in the **Project** window.

2. In the **Model** tab, look for the **Generate Lightmap UVs** checkbox at the bottom and check it.

3. Click the **Apply** button at the bottom:

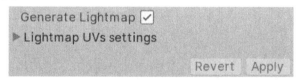

Figure 8.41 – Generate Lightmap setting

4. Repeat this process for every model. Technically, you can only do this in the models where you get artifacts and weird results after baking lightmaps, but for now, let's do this in all models, just in case.

After preparing the models for being lightmapped, the next step is to tell Unity which objects are not going to move. To do so, do the following:

1. Select the object that won't move.

2. Check the **Static** checkbox in the top-right of the **Inspector** window:

Figure 8.42 – Static checkbox

3. Repeat this for every static object (this isn't necessary for lights; we will deal with those later).

4. You can also select a container of several objects, check the **Static** checkbox and click the **Yes, All Children** button in the prompt to apply the checkbox to all child objects.

Consider that you may not want every object, even if it's static, to be lightmapped, because the more objects you lightmap, the greater texture size you will require. As an example, the terrain is too large and will consume most of the lightmapping's size. Usually, this is necessary, but in our case, the Spotlights are barely touching the terrain. Here, we have two options: leave the terrain as dynamic, or better, directly tell the Spotlights to not affect the terrain since one is only lit by ambient lighting and the Directional Light (which is not casting shadows). Remember that this is something we can do because of our type of scene; however, you may need to use other settings in other scenarios. You can exclude an object from both Realtime and Static lighting calculations by doing the following:

1. Select the object to exclude.

2. In the **Inspector** window, click the **Layer** dropdown and click on **Add Layer…**:

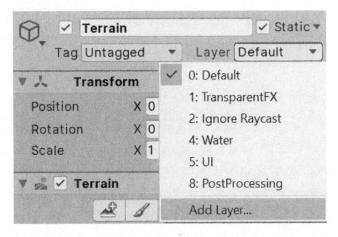

Figure 8.43 – Layer creation button

3. Here, you can create a layer, which is a group of objects that's used to identify which objects are not going to be affected by lighting. In the **Layers** list, look for an empty space and type in any name for those kinds of objects. In my case, I will only exclude the terrain, so I have just named it **Terrain**:

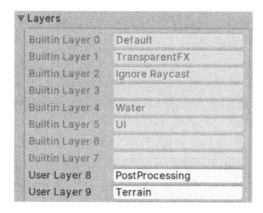

Figure 8.44 – Layers list

4. Once again, select the terrain, go to the **Layer** dropdown, and select the layer you created in the previous step. This way, you can specify that this object belongs to that group of objects:

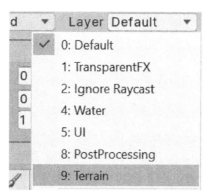

Figure 8.45 – Changing a GameObject's layer

5. Select all the Spotlights lights, look for the **Culling Mask** in the **Inspector** window, click it, and uncheck the layer you created previously. This way, you can specify that those lights won't affect that group of objects:

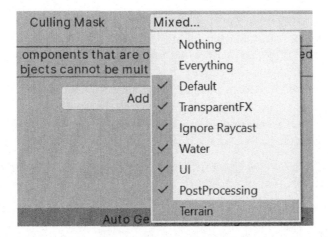

Figure 8.47 – Light Culling Mask

6. Now, you can see how those selected lights are not illuminating or applying shadows to the terrain.

Now, it's time for the lights since the **Static** checkbox won't work for them. For them, we have the following three modes:

- **Realtime**: A light in Realtime mode will affect all objects, both static and dynamic, using Realtime lighting, meaning there's no precalculation. This is useful for lights that are not static, such as the player's flashlight, a lamp that is moving due to the wind, and so on.

- **Baked**: The opposite of Realtime, this kind of light will only affect static objects with lightmaps. This means that if the player (dynamic) moves under a baked light on the street (static), the street will look lit, but the player will still be dark and won't cast any shadows on the street. The idea is to use this on lights that won't affect any dynamic objects, or on lights that are barely noticeable on them, so that we can increase performance by not calculating them.

- **Mixed**: This is the preferred mode if you are not sure which one to use. This kind of light will calculate lightmaps for static objects, but will also affect dynamic objects, combining Realtime lighting with the baked one (like Realtime lights also do).

In our case, our Directional Light will only affect the terrain, and because we don't have shadows, applying lighting to it is relatively cheap in URP, so we can leave the Directional Light in Realtime so that it won't take up any lightmap texture area. Our spotlights are affecting the Base, but actually, they are only applying lighting to them – we have no shadows because our Base is empty. In this case, it is preferable to not calculate lightmapping whatsoever, but for learning purposes, I will add a few objects as obstacles to the Base to cast some shadows and justify the use of lightmapping, as shown in the following screenshot:

Figure 8.47 – Adding objects to project light

Here, you can see how the original design of our level changes constantly during the development of the game, and that's something you can't avoid – bigger parts of the game will change in time. Now, we are ready to set up the Light Modes and execute the baking process, as follows:

1. Select **Directional Light**.
2. Set **Mode** in the **Inspector** window to **Realtime** (if it's not already in that mode).
3. Select both Spotlights.
4. Set their **Render Mode** to **Mixed**:

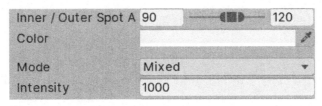

Figure 8.48 – Mixed lighting setting

5. Open the **Lighting Settings** window (**Window | Rendering | Lighting**).

6. We want to change some of the settings of the baking process. In order to enable the controls for this, click the **New Lighting Settings** button. This will create an asset with lightmapping settings that can be applied to several scenes if we want to share the same settings multiple times:

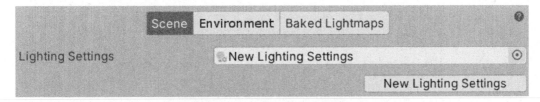

Figure 8.49 – Creating lighting settings

7. Reduce the quality of lightmapping, just to make the process go faster. Just to reiterate, the lighting can easily be reduced by using settings such as **Lightmap Resolution**, **Direct**, **Indirect**, and **Environment Samples**, all of them located under the **Lightmap Settings** category. In my case, I have those settings applied, as shown in the following screenshot. Note that even reducing those will take time; we have too many objects in the scene due to the modular level design:

▼ Lightmapping Settings	
Lightmapper	Progressive CPU
Progressive Updates	✓
Multiple Importance Sampling	✓
Direct Samples	16
Indirect Samples	256
Environment Samples	128
Light Probe Sample Multiplier	4
Max Bounces	1
Min Bounces	1
Filtering	Auto
Lightmap Resolution	20 texels per unit

Figure 8.50 – Scene lighting settings

8. Click **Generate Lighting**, which is the same button we used previously to generate ambient lighting.

9. Wait for the process to complete. You can do this by checking the progress bar at the bottom right of the Unity Editor. Note that this process could take hours in large scenes, so be patient:

Figure 8.51 – Baking progress bar

10. After the process has completed, you can check the bottom part of the **Lighting Settings** window, where you can see how many lightmaps need to be generated. We have a maximum lightmap resolution, so we probably need several of them to cover the entire scene. Also, it informs us of their size so that we can consider their impact in terms of RAM. Finally, you can check out the **Baked Lightmaps** section to see them:

Figure 8.52 – Generated lightmaps

11. Now, based on the results, you can move objects, modify light intensities, or do whatever corrections you need in order to make the scene look the way you want and recalculate the lighting every time you need to. In my case, those settings gave me good enough results, which you can see in the following screenshot:

Figure 8.53 – Lightmap result

We still have plenty of small settings to touch on, but I will leave you to discover those through trial and error or by reading the Unity documentation about lightmapping at this link: https://docs.unity3d.com/Manual/Lightmappers.html. Reading the Unity manual is a good source of knowledge and I recommend that you start using it – any good developer, no matter how experienced, should read the manual.

Applying static lighting to static objects

When marking objects as static in your scene, you probably figured out that all the objects in the scene won't move, so you probably checked the static checkbox for everyone. That's okay, but you should always put a dynamic object into the scene to really be sure that everything works okay – no games have totally static scenes. Try adding a capsule and moving it around to simulate our player, as shown in the following screenshot. If you pay attention to it, you will notice something odd – the shadows being generated by the lightmapping process are not being applied to our dynamic object:

Figure 8.54 – Dynamic object under a lightmap's precalculated shadow

You may be thinking that Mixed Light Mode was supposed to affect both dynamic and static objects, and that is exactly what it's doing. The problem here is that everything related to Static objects is precalculated in those lightmap textures, including the shadows they cast, and because our capsule is dynamic, it wasn't there when the precalculation process was executed. So, in this case, because the object that cast the shadow was static, its shadow won't affect any dynamic objects.

Here, we have several solutions. The first would be to change the Static and Realtime mixing algorithm to make everything near the camera use Realtime lighting and prevent this problem (at least near the focus of attention of the player), which would have a big impact on performance. The alternative is to use **Light Probes**. When we baked information, we only did that on lightmaps, meaning that we have information on lighting just over surfaces, not in empty spaces. Because our player is traversing the empty spaces between those surfaces, we don't know exactly how the lighting would look in those spaces, such as the middle of a corridor. Light Probes are a set of points in those empty spaces where Unity also pre-calculates information, so when some dynamic object passes through it, it will sample information from them. In the following screenshot, you can see some Light Probes that have been applied to our scene. You will notice that the ones that are inside shadows are going to be dark, while the ones exposed to light will have a greater intensity. This effect will be applied to our dynamic objects:

Figure 8.55 – Spheres representing Light Probes

If you move your object through the scene now, it will react to the shadows, as shown in the following two screenshots, where you can see a dynamic object being lit outside a baked shadow and being dark within the shadow:

Figure 8.56 – Dynamic object receiving baked lighting from Light Probes

In order to create Light Probes, do the following:

1. Create a group of **Light** Probes by going to **GameObject | Light | Light Probe Group**:

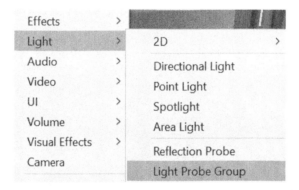

Figure 8.57 – Creating a Light Probe Group

2. Fortunately, we have some guidelines on how to locate them. It is recommended to place them where the lighting changes, such as inside and outside shadow borders. However, that is complicated. The simplest and recommended approach is to just drop a grid of Light Probes all over your playable area. To do that, you can simply copy and paste the Light Grid Group several times to cover the entire Base:

Figure 8.59 – Light Probe grid

3. Another approach would be to select one group and click the **Edit Light Probes** button to enter Light Probe edit mode:

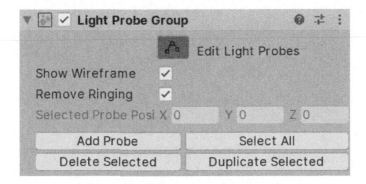

Figure 8.60 – Light Probe Group edit button

4. Click the **Select All** button and then **Duplicate Selected** to duplicate all the previously existing probes.

5. Using the translate gizmo, move them next to the previous ones, extending the grid in the process. Consider that the nearer the probes are, you will need more to cover the terrain, which will generate more data. However, Light Probes data is relatively cheap, so you can have lots of them.

6. Repeat *steps 4* to *5* until you've covered the entire area.

7. Regenerate lighting with the **Generate Lighting** button in **Lighting Settings**.

With that, you have precalculated lighting on the Light Probes affecting our dynamic objects, combining both worlds to get cohesive lighting.

Summary

In this chapter, we discussed several lighting topics, such as how Unity calculates lights and shadows, how to deal with different light sources such as direct and indirect lighting, how to configure shadows, how to bake lighting to optimize performance, and how to combine dynamic and static lighting so that the lights aren't disconnected from the world they affect. This was a long chapter, but lighting deserves that. It is a complex subject that can improve the look and feel of your scene drastically, as well as reduce your performance dramatically. It requires a lot of practice and here, we tried to summarize all the important knowledge you will need to start experimenting with it. Be patient with this topic; it is easy to get incorrect results, but you are probably just one checkbox away from solving it.

Now that we have improved all we can in the scene settings, in the next chapter, we will apply a final layer of graphic effects using the Unity Post-processing Stack, which will apply full-screen image effects – the ones that will give us that cinematic look and feel all games have nowadays.

9
Fullscreen Effects with Postprocessing

So far, we have created different objects to alter the visuals of our scene, such as meshes, particles, and lights. We can tweak the settings of those objects here and there to improve our scene's quality, but you will always feel that something is missing when you compare it with modern game scenes, and that is fullscreen or post-processing effects. In this chapter, you will learn how to apply effects to the final rendered frame, which will alter the look of the overall scene.

In this chapter, we will cover the following image effect topics:

- Using PostProcessing
- Using advanced effects

Using PostProcessing

Post Processing is a Unity feature that allows us to apply several effects (a stack of effects) one on top of the other, which will alter the final look of an image. Each one will affect the finished frame, changing the colors in it based on different criteria. In the following screenshots, you can see a scene before and after applying image effects. You will notice a dramatic difference. However, the scene hasn't changed in terms of its objects, including lights, particles, or meshes. The effects that have been applied are based on pixel analysis. Have a look at both scenes here:

Figure 9.1 – A scene without image effects (left) and the same scene with effects (right)

Something to take into account is that the previous postprocessing solution, **Post Processing Stack version 2 (PPv2)**, won't work on the **Universal Render Pipeline (URP)**; it has its own postprocessing implementation, which is the one we will cover in this chapter. Anyway, they are very similar, so even if you are using PPv2, you can still get something from this chapter.

In this section, we will discuss the following URP postprocessing concepts:

- Setting up a profile
- Using basic effects

Let's start preparing our scene to apply effects.

Setting up a profile

To start applying effects, we need to create a **profile**, an asset containing all the effects and settings we want to apply. This is a separated asset, for the same reason the material also is: because we can share the same postprocessing profile across different scenes and parts of scenes. When we refer to parts of the scenes, we are referring to volumes or areas of the game that have certain effects applied. We can define a global area that applies effects, regardless of the position of the player, or we can apply different effects – for example, when we are outdoors or indoors.

In this case, we will use a global volume, one that we will use to apply our first effect to a profile, by doing the following:

1. Create a new empty GameObject (**GameObject | Create Empty**).

2. Name it PP Volume (this stands for postprocessing volume).

3. Add the **Volume** component to it.

4. Make sure **Mode** is set to **Global**.

5. Click on the **New** button to the right of the **Profile** setting, which will generate a new profile asset with the name of our object (**PPVolume** profile). You can move this to its own folder later, which is recommended for asset organization purposes. This process is illustrated in the following screenshot:

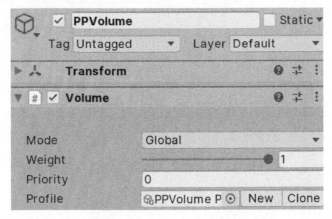

Figure 9.2 – Volume component

6. To test if the volume is working, let's add an effect. Click the **Add Override** button and select the **Post-Processing | Chromatic Aberration** option.

7. Check the **Intensity** checkbox in the **Chromatic Aberration** effect and set its intensity to 0.25, as illustrated in the following screenshot:

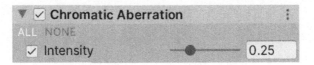

Figure 9.3 – Chromatic Aberration effect

8. Now, you will see an aberration effect being applied to the corners of the image. Remember to look at this in the **Scene** view; we will apply the effect to the **Game** view in the next step. This is illustrated in the following screenshot:

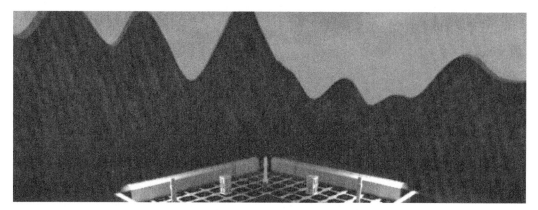

Figure 9.4 – Chromatic Aberration effect applied to the scene

9. Now, if you hit **Play** and see the game from the view of **Main Camera**, you will see that the effect is not being applied. This is because we need to check the **Post Processing** checkbox in the **Rendering** section of our **Main Camera**, as illustrated in the following screenshot:

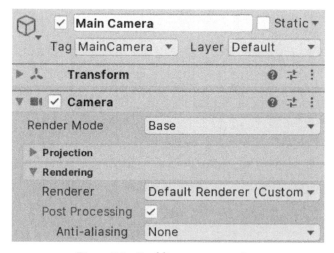

Figure 9.5 – Enabling postprocessing

Here, we have created a global volume, which will apply the effects specified as overrides to the entire scene, regardless of the player's position.

Now that we have prepared our scene to use postprocessing, we can start experimenting with different effects. We'll start with the simplest ones in the next section.

Using basic effects

Now that we have postprocessing in our scene, the only thing we need to do is to start adding effects and set them up until we have the desired look and feel. To do this, we'll explore several simple effects included in the system.

Let's start with **chromatic aberration**, the one we just used, which, as with most image effects, tries to replicate a particular real-life effect. All game engine rendering systems use a simple mathematical approximation of how eye vision works, and because of that, we don't have some effects that occur in human eyes or camera lenses. A real camera lens works by bending light rays to point them toward the camera sensors, but that bending is not perfect in some lenses (sometimes intentionally), and, hence, you can see a distortion, as shown in the following screenshot:

Figure 9.6 – Image without chromatic aberration (left) and
the same image with chromatic aberration (right)

This effect will be one of several that we will add to generate a cinematic feeling in our game, simulating the usage of real-life cameras. Of course, this effect won't look nice in every kind of game; maybe a simplistic cartoonish style won't benefit from this one, but you never know: art is subjective, so it's a matter of trial and error.

Also, we have exaggerated the intensity a little bit in the previous example to make the effect more noticeable, but I would recommend using an intensity of 0.25 in this scenario. It is usually recommended to be gentle with the intensity of the effects; it's tempting to have intense effects, but as you will be adding lots of them, after a while, the image will be bloated due to containing too many distortions. So, try to add several subtle effects instead of a few intense ones. But, again, this depends on the target style you are looking for; there are no absolute truths here (but common sense still applies).

Finally, before moving on and discussing other effects, if you are used to using other kinds of postprocessing effect frameworks, you will notice that this version of chromatic aberration has fewer settings, and that's because the URP version seeks performance, so it will be as simple as possible.

The next effect we are going to discuss is **vignette**. This is another camera lens imperfection where the image's intensity is lost at the edges of the lens. This can be applied not only to simulate older cameras but also to draw the attention of the user toward the center of the camera – for example, during cinematics. Also, if you are developing **virtual reality (VR)** applications, this can be used to reduce motion sickness by reducing the peripheral vision of the player. In the following screenshot, you can see an example of vignetting on an old camera:

Figure 9.7 – Photo taken with an old camera, with vignetting over the edges

Just to try it out, let's apply some vignetting to our scene by doing the following:

1. Select the **PP Volume** GameObject.

2. Add the **Postprocessing | Vignette** effect by clicking on the **Add Override** button.

3. Check the **Intensity** checkbox and set it to 0.3, increasing the effect.

4. Check the **Smoothness** checkbox and set it to 0.5; this will increase the spread of the effect. You can see the result in the following screenshot:

Figure 9.8 – Vignette effect

If you want, you can change the color by checking the **Color** checkbox and setting it to another value; in our case, black is okay to reinforce the rainy-day environment. Here, I invite you to check how other properties, such as **Center** and **Rounded**, work as particles. You can create nice effects just by playing with the values.

Another effect we are going to review in this basic section is **motion blur**, and again, it simulates the way the cameras work. A camera has an exposure time; that is, the time it needs to capture photons to produce each frame. When an object moves fast enough, the same object is placed in different positions during that brief exposure time, so it will appear blurred. In the following screenshot, you can see the effect being applied to our scene. In this case, we are rotating the camera up and down fast, which results in the following output:

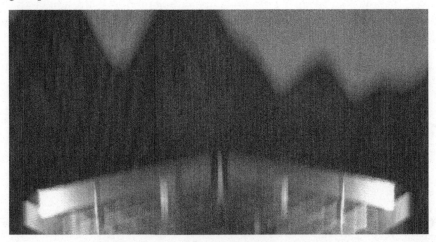

Figure 9.9 – Motion blur being applied to our scene

One thing to consider is that this blur will only be applied to the camera movement and not the movement of the objects (that is, a still camera with moving objects), since this URP doesn't support motion vectors yet.

To use this effect, follow these steps:

1. Add the **Post-processing | Motion Blur** override using the **Add override** button.

2. Check the **Intensity** checkbox and set it to 0.25.

3. Rotate the camera while in the **Game** view (not the **Scene** view). You can click and drag the **X** property of **Transform** for the camera (not the value – the **X** label), as illustrated in the following screenshot:

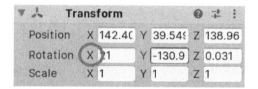

Figure 9.10 – Changing the rotation

As you can see, this effect cannot be seen in the **Scene** view, as well as other effects, so take that into account before concluding the effect is not working. Unity does this because it would be very annoying to have that effect on while you're working in the scene.

Finally, we are going to briefly discuss two final simple effects: **film grain** and **white balance**. The first is pretty simple: add it, set its intensity to 1, and you will get the famous grain effect from the old movies. You can set its **Type** with a different number of sizes to make it more subtle or obvious. White balance allows you to change the color temperature, making colors warmer or cooler depending on how you configure it. In our case, we are working in a cold, dark scene, so you can add it and set the temperature to -20 to adjust its appearance slightly and improve the look and feel of this kind of scene.

Now that we have seen a few simple effects, let's check out a few of the remaining ones that are affected by some advanced rendering features.

Using advanced effects

The effects we are going to look at in this section don't differ a lot from the previous ones; they are just a little bit trickier and you will need some background knowledge to use them. So, let's dive into them!

In this section, we are going to look at the **high dynamic range** (HDR) and depth map advanced effect concepts.

Advanced effects

Let's start by discussing some requirements for some of these effects to work properly.

HDR and Depth maps

Some effects don't just work with the rendered image – they also need additional data. First, we will discuss **depth maps**, a concept we discussed in the previous chapter. To recap, a depth map is an image that's rendered from the point of view of the camera, but instead of generating a final image of the scene, it renders the scene objects' depth, rendering the objects in shades of gray. The darker the color, the farther from the camera the pixel is, and vice versa. In the following screenshot, you can see an example of a depth map:

Figure 9.11 – Depth map of a few primitive shapes

We will see some effects such as **depth of field**, which will blur some parts of the image based on the distance of the camera, but it can be used for several purposes on custom effects (not in the base URP package).

Another concept we will discuss here that will alter how colors are treated and, hence, how some effects work is HDR. In older hardware, color channels (Red, Green, and Blue) were encoded in a 0 to 1 range, with 0 being no intensity and 1 being full intensity (per channel), so all lighting and color calculations were done in that range. That seems okay, but it doesn't reflect how light actually works. You can see full white (all channels set to 1) on a piece of paper being lit by sunlight, and you can see full white when you look directly at a light bulb, but even if both the light and paper are of the same color, the latter will, first, irritate the eye after a while, and, secondly, will have some overglow due to excess light. The problem here is that the maximum value (1) is not enough to represent the most intense color, so if you have a high-intensity light and another with even more intensity, both will generate the same color (1 in each channel) because calculations cannot go further than 1. So, that's why **HDR rendering** was created.

HDR is a way for colors to exceed the 0 to 1 range so that lighting and effects that work based on color intensity have better accuracy in this mode. It is the same idea as the new TV feature named the same, although in this case, Unity will do the calculations in HDR. However, the final image will still work using the previous color space (0 to 1, or **low dynamic range (LDR)**), so don't confuse Unity's **HDR rendering** with the display's **HDR**. To convert the HDR calculations back into LDR, Unity (and also TVs) use a concept called **tonemapping**. You can see an example of an LDR-rendered scene and tonemapping being used in an HDR scene in the following screenshots:

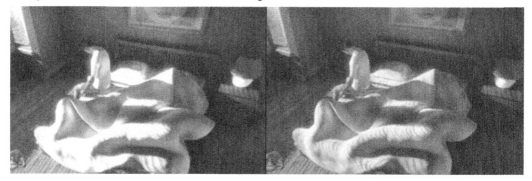

Figure 9.12 – An LDR-rendered scene (left) and an HDR scene with corrected overbrights using tonemapping (right)

Tonemapping is a way to bring colors outside the 0.1 range back to it. It uses some formulas and curves to determine how each color channel should be mapped back. You can see this in a typical darker-to-lighter scene transition, such as when you exit a building without windows to go out into a bright day. For a time, you will see everything lighter until everything goes back to normal. The idea here is that the calculations are not different when you are inside or outside the building; a white wall inside the building will have a color near the 1 intensity, while the same white wall outside will have a higher value (due to sunlight). The difference is that tonemapping will take the higher-than-1 color back to 1 when you are outside the building, and maybe it will increase the lighting of the wall inside if the scene is darker, depending on how you set it.

Even if HDR is enabled by default, let's learn how we can check this by doing the following:

1. Go to **Edit | Project Settings**.
2. Click on the **Graphics** section in the left panel.
3. Click the asset referenced under the **Scriptable Render Pipeline Settings** property.
4. Click on the highlighted asset in the **Project** panel. Ensure that this panel is visible before clicking the property in the **Graphics** settings. Alternatively, you can double-click the asset reference in the **Graphics** settings to select it.

5. Under the **Quality** section, ensure that **HDR** is checked, as illustrated in the following screenshot:

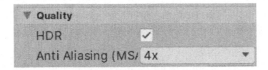

Figure 9.13 – Enabling HDR

6. Ensure that the **HDR** property of the **Camera** component in the **Main Camera** GameObject is set to **Use Pipeline Settings**, to ensure the changes that were made in the previous steps are respected.

Of course, the fact that HDR is togglable means that there are scenarios where you don't want to use it. As you can guess, not all hardware supports HDR, and using it incurs a performance overhead, so take that into account. Luckily, most effects work with both the HDR and LDR color ranges, so if you have HDR enabled but the user device doesn't support it, you won't get any errors, just different results.

Now that we are sure we have HDR enabled, let's explore some advanced effects that use this and depth mapping.

Let's look at certain effects that use the previously described techniques, starting with the commonly used: bloom. This effect, as usual, emulates the overglow that happens around a heavily lit object through a camera lens or even the human eye. In the following screenshots, you can see the difference between the default version of our scene and an exaggerated bloom version. You can observe how the effect is only applied to the brightest areas of our scene. Have a look at both effects here:

Figure 9.14 – The default scene (left) and the same scene with a high-intensity bloom (right)

This effect is very common and simple, but I consider it advanced because the results are drastically affected by HDR. This effect relies on calculating the intensity of each pixel's color to detect areas where it can be applied. In LDR, we can have a white object that isn't actually overbright, but due to the limitations in this color range, bloom may cause an overglow over it. In HDR, due to its increased color range, we can detect if an object is white or if the object is maybe light blue but just overbright, generating the illusion that it is white (such as objects near a high-intensity lamp). In the following screenshot, you can see the difference between our scene with HDR and without it. You will notice that the LDR version will have overglow in areas that are not necessarily overlit. The difference may be very subtle, but pay attention to the little details to note the difference. And remember, I exaggerated the effect here. Have a look at both scenes here:

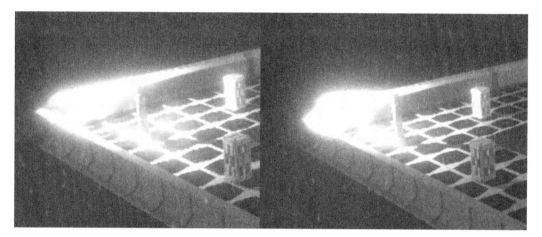

Figure 9.15 – Bloom in an LDR scene (left) and bloom in an HDR scene (right). Notice that the bloom settings were changed to try to approximate them as much as possible

For now, let's stick with the HDR version of the scene. To enable bloom, do the following:

1. Add the **Bloom** override to the profile, as usual.

2. Enable the **Intensity** checkbox by checking it and setting the value to 0.2. This controls how much overglow will be applied.

3. Enable **Threshold** and set it to 0.7. This value indicates the minimum intensity a color needs to have to be considered for overglow. In our case, our scene is somewhat dark, so we need to reduce this value in the **Bloom** effect's settings to have more pixels included. As usual, those values need to be adjusted to your specific scenario.

4. You will notice that the difference is very subtle, but again, remember that you will have several effects, so all those little differences will add up. You can see both effects in the following screenshots:

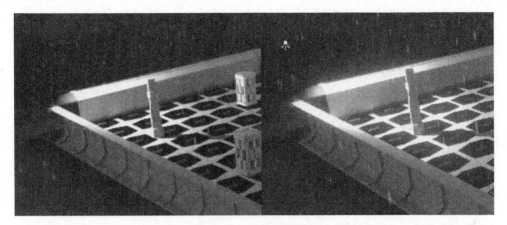

Figure 9.16 – Bloom effect

As usual, it is recommended for you to fiddle with the other values. Some interesting settings I recommend that you test are the **Dirt Texture** and **Dirt Intensity** values.

Now, let's move on and look at another common effect: **depth of field**. This one relies on the depth map we discussed earlier. It is not that obvious to the naked eye, but when you focus on an object within your sight, the surrounding objects become blurred because they are out of focus. We can use this to focus the attention of the player in key moments of the gameplay. This effect will sample the depth map to see if the object is within the focus range; if it is, no blur will be applied, and vice versa. To use it, do the following:

This effect depends on the camera positioning in your game. To test it, in this case, we will put the camera near a column to try to focus on that specific object, as illustrated in the following screenshot:

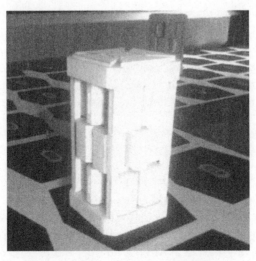

Figure 9.17 – Camera positioning

5. Add the **Depth of Field** override.

6. Enable and set the **Mode** setting to **Gaussian**. This is the simplest one to use.

7. In my case, I have set **Start** to 10 and **End** to 20, which will make the effect start at a distance behind the target object. The **End** setting will control how the blur's intensity will increase, reaching its maximum at a distance of 20 meters. Remember to tweak these values to your case.

8. If you want to exaggerate the effect a little bit, set **Max Radius** to 1.5. The result is shown in the following screenshot:

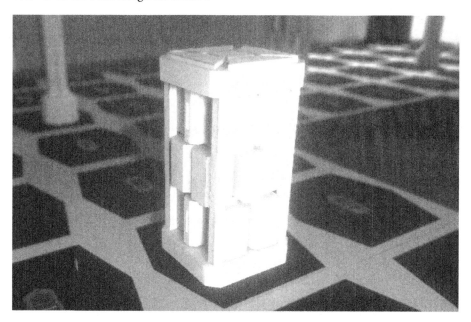

Figure 9.18 – Exaggerated effect

Something to consider here is that our particular game will have a top-down perspective, and unlike the first-person camera, where you can see distant objects, here, we will have objects near enough to not notice the effect. So, we can limit the use of this effect just to cutscenes in our scenario.

Now, most of the remaining effects provide different ways of altering the actual colors of the scene. The idea is that the real color sometimes doesn't give you the exact look and feel you are seeking. Maybe you need the dark zones to be darker to reinforce the sensation of horror ambiance, or maybe you want to do the opposite; that is, increase the dark areas to represent an open scene. Maybe you want to tint the highlights a little bit to get a neon effect if you are creating a futuristic game, or perhaps you want a sepia effect temporarily, to do a flashback. We have a myriad of ways to do this, and in this case, I will use a simple but powerful effect called **Shadow, Midtones, Highlights**.

This effect will apply different color corrections to – well – shadows, midtones, and highlights, meaning that we can modify darker, lighter, and medium areas separately. Let's try it out by doing the following:

1. Add the **Shadow, Midtones, Highlights** override.

2. Let's start by doing some testing. Check the three **Shadows**, **Midtones**, and **Highlights** checkboxes.

3. Move the **Shadow** and **Midtones** sliders all the way to the left and the one for **Highlights** to the right. This will reduce the intensity of shadows and midtones and increase the intensity of highlights. We did this so that you can see the areas that **Highlights** will alter, based on their intensity (this can also be an interesting effect in a horror game). You can do the same with the rest of the sliders to check the other two areas. You can see the result in the following screenshot:

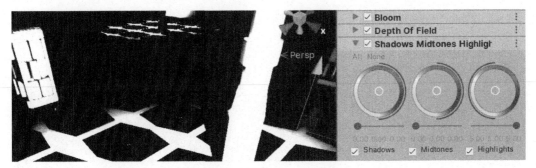

Figure 9.19 – Isolating highlights

4. Also, you can test moving the white circle at the center of the colored circle to apply a little bit of tinting to those areas. Reduce the intensity of the highlights by moving the slider a little bit to the left to make the tinting more noticeable. You can see the result in the following screenshot:

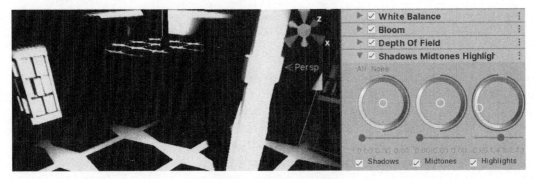

Figure 9.20 – Tinting highlights

5. By doing this, you can explore how those controls work, but of course, those extreme values are useful for some edge cases. In our scene, the settings you can see in the following screenshot worked best for me. As always, it is better to use subtler values to not distort the original result too much, as illustrated here:

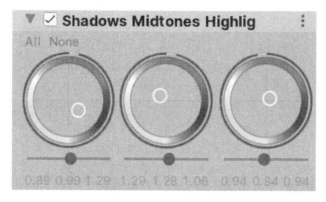

Figure 9.21 – Subtle changes

6. You can see the before and after effects in the following screenshots:

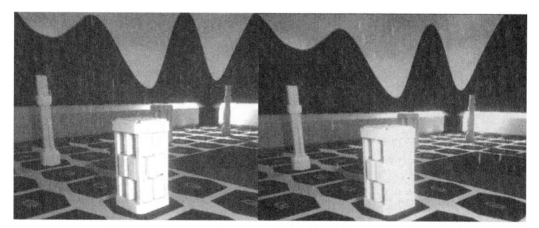

Figure 9.22 – Before and after effects

You have other simpler options as well, such as **Split Toning**, which does something similar but just with shadows and highlights, and **Color Curves**, which give you advanced control over how each color channel of the scene will be mapped, but the idea is the same – that is, to alter the actual color of the resulting scene to apply a specific color ambiance to your scene. If you remember the movie series *The Matrix*, when the characters were in the Matrix, everything had subtle green tinting and, while outside it, the tinting was blue.

Remember that the results of using HDR and not using it with these effects are important, so it is better to decide sooner rather than later whether you wish to use HDR by excluding certain target platforms (which may not be important to your target audience), or not to use it (using LDR) and have less control over your scene's lighting levels.

Also, take into account that you may need to tweak some object's settings, such as their light intensities and material properties, because sometimes, we use postprocessing to fix graphics errors that may be caused by objects that have been set incorrectly, and that's not okay. For example, increasing the ambient lighting in our scene will drastically change the output of the effects, and we can use that to increase the overall brightness instead of using an effect if we find the scene too dark.

With that, we have covered the main image effects we should use. Remember that the idea is not to use every single one but to use the ones that you feel are contributing to your scene; they are not free in terms of performance (although not that resource-intensive), so use them wisely. Also, you can check the profiles that have already been created and apply them to your game to see how little changes can make a huge difference.

Summary

In this chapter, we discussed basic and advanced fullscreen effects that we can apply to our scene, making it look more realistic in terms of camera lens effects and more stylish in terms of color distortions. We also discussed the internals of HDR and depth maps and how they are important when using those effects, which can immediately increase your game's graphics quality with minimal effort.

Now that we have covered most of the common graphics that can be found in Unity systems, in this next chapter, we will start looking at how to increase immersion in our scene by using sound.

10
Sound and Music Integration

In the previous chapter, we achieved good graphics quality, but we are missing an important part of the game's aesthetics: sound. Often relegated to being the last step in game development, sound is one of those things that if it's there, you won't notice its presence, but if you don't have it, you will feel that something is missing. It will help you reinforce the ambiance you want in your game, and it must match the graphics settings you have.

In this chapter, we will cover the following sound concepts:

- Importing audio
- Integrating and mixing audio

We will apply these concepts to our game so that we can import audio and play it in different scenarios, such as when the Player shoots. This also includes the background music. Later in this book, we will play the sounds, but for now, we will focus on how to import them into our project.

Importing audio

As with graphic assets, it is important to set up the import settings of audio assets, which can be resource-intensive if not done properly.

In this section, we will examine the following audio importing concepts:

- Audio types
- Configuring the import settings

Let's start by discussing the different kinds of audio we can use.

Audio types

There are different types of audio present in video games, as follows:

- **Music**: Music is used to enhance the player's experience according to the situation.

- **Sound effects – SFX**: These are sounds that occur as a reaction to player or NPC actions, such as clicking a button, walking, opening a door, shooting a gun, and so on.

- **Ambient sound**: A game that only has sound as reactions to events would feel empty. If you are recreating an apartment in the middle of the city, even if the player is just idle in the middle of the room doing nothing, lots of sounds should be heard, and the sources of most of them will be outside the room, such as an airplane flying overhead, a construction site two blocks away, cars in the street, and so on. Creating objects that won't be seen is a waste of resources. Instead, we can place individual sounds all over the scene to recreate the desired ambiance, but that would be resource-intensive, requiring lots of CPU and RAM to achieve believable results. Considering that these sounds are usually in the second plane of the user's attention, we can just combine them all into a single looping track and play one piece of audio. That's exactly what ambient sound is. If you want to create a café scene, you can simply go to a real café and record a few minutes of audio, and then use that as your ambient sound.

For almost all games, we will need at least one music track, one ambient track, and several SFX to start producing the audio. As always, we have different sources of audio assets, but we will be using the Asset Store here. It has three audio categories for searching for the assets we need:

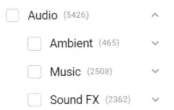

Figure 10.1 – Audio categories in the Asset Store

In my case, I also used the search bar to filter the categories even further, searching for `weather` to find a rain effect. Sometimes, you can't find the exact audio separately; in such cases, you will need to dig into **Packs and Libraries**, so have patience here. In my case, I picked the three packages you can see in the following figure. However, I only imported some of the included sounds as using all of them would weigh a lot in the project. For ambiance, I picked a rain sound file called `Ambience_Rain_Moderate_01_LOOP` in the case of this package, but it will named something different in other packages. Then, I picked **Music – Sad Hope** for music; for SFX, I picked a gun sound effect package for our future Player's Hero Character. Of course, you can pick other packages to suit your game's needs:

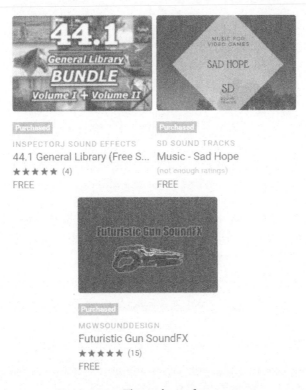

Figure 10.2 – The packages for our game

Now that we have the necessary audio packages, let's discuss how to import them.

Configuring the import settings

We have several import settings we can tweak, but the problem is that we need to consider the usage of the audio to set it up properly. So, let's look at the ideal settings for each case. To view the import settings, as always, you can select the asset and view it in the **Inspector** window, as shown in the following screenshot:

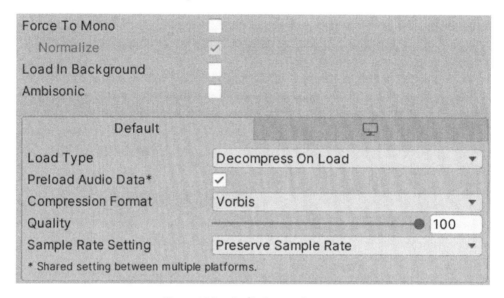

Figure 10.3 – Audio Import Settings

Let's discuss the most important ones, starting with **Force To Mono**. Some audio may come with stereo channels, meaning that we have one sound for the left ear and another one for the right ear. This means that one piece of audio can contain two different audio tracks. Stereo sound is useful for different effects and instrument spatialization in the case of music, so we want that in those scenarios, but there are other scenarios where stereo is not useful. Consider 3D sound effects such as a shooting gun or some walking-pace steps. In those cases, we need the sound to be heard in the direction of the source. So, if a gun was fired to my left, I need to hear it coming from my left. In these cases, we can convert stereo audio into mono audio by checking the **Force To Mono** checkbox in the audio import settings. This will make Unity combine the two channels into a single one, reducing the size of the audio, usually to almost half its size (sometimes more, sometimes less, depending on various aspects).

You can verify the impact of that and other settings at the bottom of the **Audio Asset** inspector, where you can see the imported audio size:

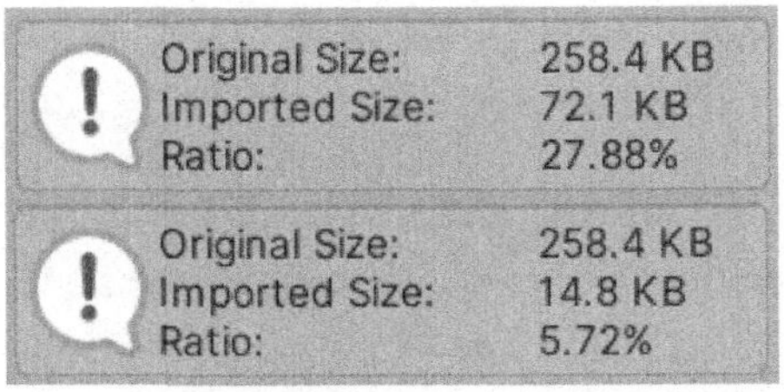

Figure 10.4 – Left: audio imported without Force To Mono; Right: same audio with Force To Mono

The next setting to discuss, and an important one at that, is **Load Type**. To play some audio, Unity needs to read the audio from disk, decompress, and then play it. **Load Type** changes the way those three processes are handled. We have the following three options here:

- **Decompress on Load**: This is the most memory-intensive option. This mode will make Unity load the audio uncompressed in memory when the scene is loaded. This means that the audio will take lots of space in RAM because we have the uncompressed version loaded. The advantage of using this mode is that playing the audio is easier because we have the raw audio data ready to play in RAM.

- **Steaming**: This is the opposite of **Decompress on Load**. This mode never loads audio in RAM. Instead, while the audio is playing, Unity reads a piece of the audio asset from disk, decompresses it, plays it, and repeats this, running this process once for each piece of audio playing in **Streaming**. This means that this mode will be CPU-intensive, but will consume almost zero bytes of RAM.

- **Compressed in Memory**: This is the middle ground. This mode will load the audio from disk when the scene is loaded but will keep it compressed in memory. When Unity needs to play the audio, it will just take a piece from RAM, decompress it, and play it. Remember that reading pieces of the audio asset from RAM is considerably faster than reading from disk.

If you are an experienced developer, you can easily determine which mode is better suited for which kind of audio, but if this is your first encounter with video games, this may sound confusing, so let's discuss the best modes for different cases:

- **Frequent Short Audio**: This could be a gun being fired or the sound of footsteps, which are sounds that last less than 1 second but can occur in several instances and play at the same time. In such cases, we can use **Decompress On Load**. Uncompressed short audio won't have a huge size difference from its compressed version. Also, since this is the most performant CPU option, having several instances won't have a huge impact on performance.

- **Infrequent Large Audio**: This includes music, ambient sound, and dialog. These kinds of audio usually have just one instance playing, and they are usually big. Those cases are better suited for the **Streaming** mode because having them compressed or decompressed in RAM can have a huge impact on low-end devices such as mobile devices (on PCs, we can sometimes use **Compressed in Memory**). A CPU can handle having two or three bits of audio playing in **Streaming** mode, but try to have no more than that.

- **Frequent Medium Audio**: This includes pre-made voice chat dialog in multiplayer games, character emotes, long explosions, or any audio that is more than 500 KB (this is not a strict rule – this number depends a lot on the target device). Having this kind of audio decompressed in RAM can have a noticeable impact on performance, but since this audio is frequently used, we can have it compressed in memory. Their relatively smaller size means they usually won't make a huge difference to our game and we will avoid wasting CPU resources when reading from disk.

There are other cases to consider, but those can be extrapolated based on the previous ones. Remember that the previous analysis was made by taking into account the requirements of a standard game, but this can vary a lot based on your game and target device. Maybe you are making a game that won't consume lots of RAM, but it is pretty intensive in terms of CPU resources, in which case you can just put everything in **Decompress on Load**. It's important to consider all aspects of your game and to balance your resources accordingly.

Finally, another thing to consider is the compression format, which will change the way Unity will encode the audio in the published game. Different compression formats will give different compression ratios in exchange for less fidelity with the original audio, or higher decompression times, and all this varies a lot based on the audio patterns and their length. We have three compression formats:

- **PCM**: This uncompressed format will give you the highest audio quality, with no noise artifacts, but will result in a bigger asset file size.

- **ADPCM**: Compressing audio this way reduces file size and yields a fast uncompressing process, but this can introduce noise artifacts that can be noticeable in certain types of audio.

- **Vorbis**: A high-quality compression format that will yield almost zero artifacts but takes longer to decompress, so playing Vorbis audio will be slightly more intensive than for other formats. It also provides a quality slider for selecting the exact amount of compression aggressiveness.

So, which one should you use? Again, that depends on the features of your audio. Short, smooth audio can use PCM, while long, noisy audio can use ADPCM; the artifacts that are introduced by this format will be hidden in the audio itself. Maybe long, smooth audio where compression artifacts are noticeable could benefit from using Vorbis. Sometimes, it's just a matter of trial and error. Maybe use Vorbis by default and when performance is reduced, try to switch to ADPCM, and if that causes glitches, just switch to PCM. Of course, the problem here is being sure that audio processing is really what's responsible for the performance issues – maybe switching all audio to ADPCM and checking whether that made a difference is a good way to detect that, but a better approach would be to use the Profiler, a performance measurement tool that we will look at later in this book.

We have other settings, such as **Sample Rate Setting**, that, again, with a little trial and error, you can use to detect the best setting.

I have set up the audio that I downloaded from the Asset Store, as shown in the following screenshots. The first one shows how I set up the music and ambient audio files (large files):

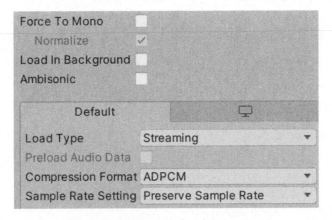

Figure 10.5 – Music and ambient settings

For stereo (**Force To Mono** unchecked), use **Streaming Load Type** because these files are large and will have just one instance playing, and **ADPCM** for **Compression Format** because Vorbis didn't result in a huge size difference.

This second screenshot shows how I set up the SFX files (small files):

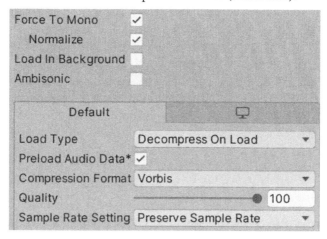

Figure 10.6 – Shooting SFX settings

This will be a 3D sound, so **Force To Mono** should be checked. It will be also short, so **Decompress on Load** works better for **Load Type**. Using Vorbis for **Compression Format** reduces the ADPCM size by more than a half.

Now that we have our pieces of audio configured, we can start using them in our scene.

Integrating and mixing audio

We can just drag our bits of audio into our scene to start using them, but we can dig a little bit further to explore the best ways to configure them for each possible scenario.

In this section, we will examine the following audio integration concepts:

- Using 2D and 3D AudioSources
- Using audio mixers

Let's start by exploring AudioSources, objects that are in charge of audio playback.

Using 2D and 3D AudioSources

AudioSources are components that can be attached to GameObjects. They are responsible for emitting sound in our game based on **AudioClips**, which are the audio assets we downloaded previously. It's important to differentiate an AudioClip from an **AudioSource**: we can have a single explosion AudioClip, but lots of AudioSources playing it, simulating several explosions. An **AudioSource** can be seen as a CD Player that can play AudioClips (our CDs, in this analogy), with the only exception that we can have several CD Players or AudioSources playing the same CD at the same time (in this example, two explosion sounds playing at the same time).

The simplest way to create an **AudioSource** is to pick an **AudioClip** (an audio asset) and drag it to the **Hierarchy** window. Try to avoid dragging the audio into an existing object; instead, drag it between objects so that Unity will create a new object with **AudioSource** instead of adding it to an existing object (sometimes, you want an existing object to have this **AudioSource**, but let's keep things simple for now):

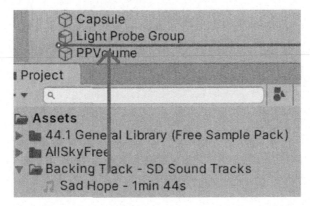

Figure 10.7 – Dragging an AudioClip to the Hierarchy window between objects

The following screenshot shows the AudioSource that was generated by dragging the music asset to the scene. You can see that the **AudioClip** field has a reference to the dragged audio:

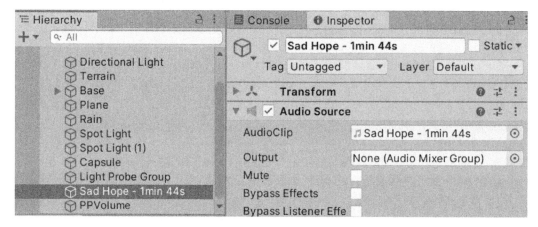

Figure 10.8 – AudioSource configured to play our music asset

As you can see, **AudioSource** has several settings, so let's review the most common ones:

- **Play on Awake**: This determines whether the audio starts playing automatically when the game starts. We can uncheck this option and play the audio via scripting, perhaps when the player shoots or jumps (more on that in *Part 3* of this book).

- **Loop**: This will make the audio repeat automatically when it finishes playing. Remember to always check this setting for the music and ambient audio clips. It is easy to forget this because those tracks are long and we may never reach the end of them in our tests.

- **Volume**: This controls the audio's intensity.

- **Pitch**: This controls the audio's velocity. This is useful for simulating effects such as slow motion or the increasing revolutions of an engine.

- **Spatial Blend**: This controls whether our audio is 2D or 3D. In 2D mode, the audio will be heard at the same volume at all distances, while 3D will make the audio's volume decrease as the distance from the camera increases.

In the case of our music track, I have configured it as shown in the following screenshot. You can drag the ambient rain sound to add it to the scene and use the same settings as these because we want the same ambient effect in all our scenes. In complex scenes, though, you can have different 3D ambient sounds scattered all over the scene to change the sound according to the current environment:

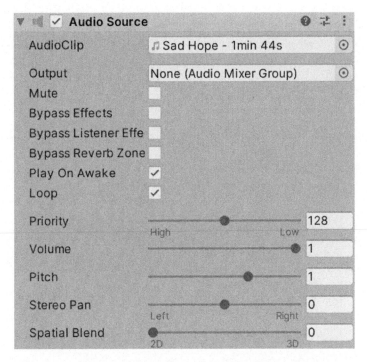

Figure 10.9 – Music and ambient settings. This will loop, is set to Play On Awake, and is 2D

Now, you can drag the shooting effect and configure it as shown in the following screenshot. As you can see, the audio, in this case, won't loop because we want the shooting effect to play once per bullet. Remember that, in our case, the bullet will be a prefab that will spawn each time we press the shoot key, so each bullet will have its own **AudioSource** that will play when the bullet is created. Also, the bullet is set to a 3D **Spatial Blend**, meaning that the effect will be transmitted through different speakers based on the position of the Audio Source and the Camera's position:

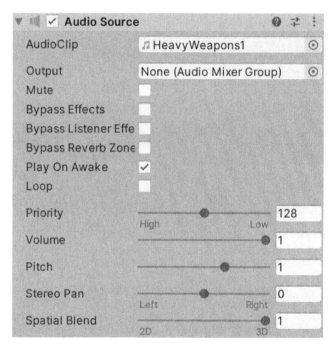

Figure 10.10 – Sound effect settings. This won't loop and is a 3D sound

Something to consider in the case of 3D sounds is the **Volume Rolloff** setting, which is inside the **3D Sound Settings** section. This setting controls how the volume decays based on its distance from the camera. By default, you can see that this setting is set to **Logarithmic Rolloff**, the way real-life sound works, but sometimes, you don't want real-life sound decay, because sounds in real life are usually heard slightly, even if the source is very far away. One option is to switch to **Linear Rolloff** and configure the exact maximum distance with the **Max Distance** setting:

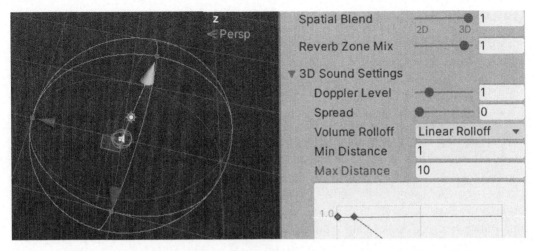

Figure 10.11– A 3D sound with a maximum distance of 10 meters, using Linear Rolloff

Considering we just discussed 3D sounds, it's worth mentioning the **AudioListener** component, which is created by default in **MainCamera**. 99% of the time, it will be there, given its usage. It serves as a way to identify which object represents the ears of the player in the world, in a way we can calculate the audio's directionality. The camera is the logical place to put it, given that it represents the eyes of the user; having the eyes and the ears of the player in different places could be confusing. There's no setting we can use regarding this, but it is important to mention that for the audio to work, we need one, and no more than one – we only have one pair of ears, after all:

Figure 10.12 – Audio Listener component in the Main Camera

Now that we know how to configure individual pieces of audio, let's learn how to apply effects to groups of audio instances using an **Audio Mixer**.

Using an Audio Mixer

We will have several audio instances playing all over our game: the footsteps of characters, shooting, bonfires, explosions, rain, and so on. Controlling exactly which sounds are supposed to sound louder or lower, depending on the use case, and applying effects to reinforce certain situations, such as being stunned due to a nearby explosion, is called audio mixing – the process of mixing several sounds in a cohesive and controlled way.

In Unity, we can create an Audio Mixer, an asset that we can use to define groups of sounds. All changes that are made to a group will affect all the sounds inside it, by raising or lowering the volume, perhaps, or by applying an effect. You can have SFX and music groups to control sounds separately – as an example, you could lower the SFX volume while in the **Pause** menu but not the music volume. Also, groups are organized in a hierarchy, where a group can also contain other groups, so changing something in a group will also apply changes to its sub-groups. In fact, every group you create will always be a child group of the master group; that is, the group that will affect every single sound in the game (that uses that mixer).

Let's create a mixer with SFX and music groups:

1. In the **Project** window, using the + button, select the **Audio Mixer** option. Name the asset as you wish; in my case, I chose the name `Main Mixer`.

2. Double-click the created asset to open the **Audio Mixer** window:

Figure 10.13 – Audio Mixer window

3. Click the + button to the right of the **Groups** label to create a child group of the master node. Name it SFX:

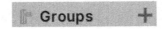

Figure 10.14 – Group creation

4. Click on the **Master** group and click again on the + button to create another master node child group called Music. Remember to select the **Master** group before clicking the + button, because if another group is selected, the new group will be a child of that one. You can rearrange a group's child-parent relationship by dragging it into the **Hierarchy** window:

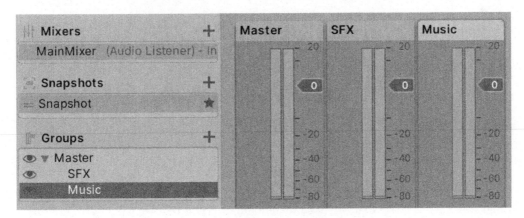

Figure 10.15 – The Master, SFX, and Music groups

5. Select the **Music** GameObject in the **Hierarchy** window and look for the **AudioSource** component in the **Inspector** window.

6. Click the circle to the right of the **Output** property and select the **Music** group in the **Audio Mixer** group selector. This will make **AudioSource** be affected by the settings on the specified Mixer group:

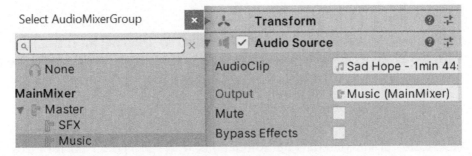

Figure 10.16 – Making an AudioSource belong to an AudioMixerGroup

7. If you play the game now, you will see how the volume meters in the Audio Mixer start to move, indicating that the music is going through the **Music** group. You will also see that the **Master** group's volume meter is also moving, indicating that the sound that is passing through the **Music** group is also passing through the **Master** group (the parent of the **Music** group) before going to the sound card of your computer:

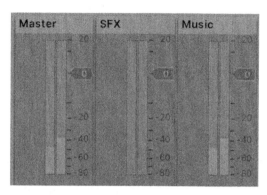

Figure 10.17 – Group volume levels

8. Repeat *steps 5* and *6* for the ambient and shooting sounds to make them belong to the **SFX** group.

Now that we have separated our sounds into groups, we can start adjusting the groups' settings. But before we do that, we need to take into account that we won't want the same settings all the time, as in the previously mentioned pause menu case, where the SFX volume should be lower. To handle those scenarios, we can create snapshots, which are presets of our mixer that can be activated via scripting during our game. We will deal with the scripting steps in *Part 3* of this book, but for now, we will create a normal snapshot for the in-game settings and a pause snapshot for the pause menu settings.

If you check the **Snapshots** list, you will see that a single snapshot has already been created – this will be our normal snapshot. So, let's create a pause snapshot by doing the following:

1. Click on the + button to the right of the **Snapshots** label and call the snapshot Pause. Remember to stop the game to edit the mixer or click the **Edit in Playmode** option to allow Unity to change the mixer during play. If you do the latter, remember that the changes will persist when you stop the game, unlike changes that are made to GameObjects. Actually, if you change other assets during play mode, those changes will also persist – only GameObject changes are reverted. There are some other cases, such as **Materials** and **Animations**, where changes are not reverted after being paused, given they are assets, but we won't discuss them right now:

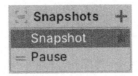

Figure 10.18 – Snapshot creation

2. Select the **Pause** snapshot and lower the volume slider of the **SFX** group:

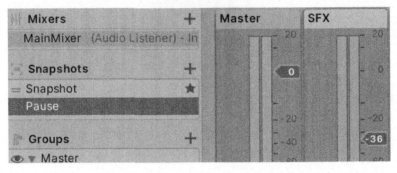

Figure 10.19 – Lowering the volume of the Pause snapshot

3. Play the game and hear how the sound is still at its normal volume. That's because the original snapshot is the default one – you can see this by looking for the star to its right. You can right-click any snapshot and make it the default one using the **Set as Start Snapshot** option.

4. Click on **Edit in Playmode** to enable **Audio Mixer** modification during runtime.

5. Click on the **Pause** snapshot to enable it and hear how the **Shooting** and **Ambient** sound volumes have decreased.

As you can see, one of the main uses of the mixer is to control group volume, especially when you can see that the intensity of a group's volume is going higher than the 0 mark, indicating that the group is too loud. However, there are other uses for the mixer, such as applying effects. If you've played any war games, you will have noticed that whenever a bomb explodes nearby, you hear the sound differently for a moment, as if the sound were located in another room. This can be accomplished by using an effect called Low Pass, which blocks high-frequency sounds, and that's exactly what happens with our ears in those scenarios: the stress of the high-volume sound that's generated by an explosion irritates our ears, making them less sensitive to high frequencies for a while.

We can add effects to any channel and configure them according to the current snapshot, just as we did for the volume, by doing the following:

1. Click on the **Add...** button at the bottom of the **Master** group and select **Lowpass Simple**:

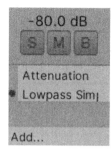

Figure 10.20 – The effects list of a channel

2. Select the normal snapshot (the one called **Snapshot**) to modify it.

3. Select the **Master** group and look at the **Inspector** window, where you will see settings for the group and its effects.

4. Set the **Cutoff freq** property of the **Lowpass Simple** setting to the possible highest value (22000). This will disable the effect.

5. Repeat *steps 3* and *4* for the **Pause** snapshot; we don't want this effect in that snapshot.

6. Create a new snapshot called **Bomb Stun** and select it to edit it.

7. Set **Cutoff freq** to 1000:

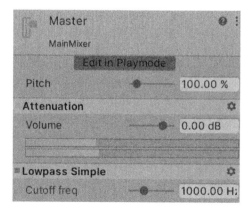

Figure 10.21 – Setting the cutoff frequency of the Lowpass Simple effect

8. Play the game and change snapshots to check out the difference.

Aside from the Low Pass filter, you can apply several other filters, such as **Echo**, to create an almost dreamy effect, or a combination of **Send, Receive**, and **Duck** to make a group lower its volume based on the intensity of another group (for instance, you may want to lower the SFX volume when there's dialog). I invite you to try those and other effects and check the results to identify potential uses.

Summary

In this chapter, we discussed how to import and integrate sounds while considering their memory impact and applied effects to generate different scenarios. Sound is a big part of achieving the desired game experience, so you should take the time to get it right.

Now that we have covered almost all the vital aesthetic aspects of our game, in the next chapter, we will create another form of visual communication: the **user interface** (UI). We will create a UI that will display the player's current score, bullets, life, and lots more.

11
User Interface Design

Everything that is shown on the screen and is transmitted through the speakers of a computer is a form of communication. In previous chapters, we used 3D models to let the user know that they are in a base in the middle of the mountains, and we reinforced that idea with the appropriate sound and music. But for our game, we need to communicate other information, such as the amount of life the user has left and the current score, and sometimes, it is difficult to express these things using the in-game graphics (some successful cases manage to do this, such as Dead Space, but let's keep things simple). To transmit this information, we need to add another layer of graphics on top of our scene, which is usually called the **User Interface (UI)** or **Heads-Up Display (HUD)**. This will contain different visual elements, such as text fields, bars, and buttons, to prepare the user to take an informed decision based on things such as fleeing to a safe place when their life is low:

Figure 11.1 – Character creation UI displays info about the character stats with numbers

In this chapter, we will visit the following topics:

- Understanding **Canvas** and **RectTransform**
- Canvas object types
- Creating a responsive UI

By the end of this chapter, you will be able to use the Unity UI system to create interfaces capable of informing the user about the state of the game and allowing them to take action by pressing buttons. Let's start by discussing the basic concepts of the Unity UI system—Canvas and RectTransform.

Understanding Canvas and RectTransform

Currently, there are three UI systems available in Unity for different purposes:

- **UI Toolkit**: A system to extend the Unity Editor with custom windows and tools. This uses several web concepts, such as stylesheets and XML-based language, to lay out your UI. In the future, it will be available to use in-game.

- **Unity UI**: A GameObject-based UI only applicable for in-game UIs (not editor extensions). You create it using GameObjects and components like any other object we have edited so far.

- **IMGUI**: A legacy code-based UI created entirely by using scripting. A long time ago, this was the only UI system used in both the editor and the in-game UI. Nowadays, it is only used to extend the editor and will soon be completely replaced by UI Elements.

In this chapter, we are only going to focus on in-game UI to communicate different information to the player regarding the state of the game, so we are going to use Unity UI. At the time of writing this book, there are plans to replace Unity UI with UI Elements, but there's no estimated date as to when this will happen. Anyway, even if Unity releases UI Elements as an in-game UI system soon, Unity UI will still be there for a while and is perfectly capable of handling all types of UI that you need to create.

If you are going to work with Unity UI, you first need to understand its two main concepts—**Canvas** and **RectTransform**. Canvas is the master object that will contain and render our UI and RectTransform is the feature in charge of positioning and adapting each UI element on our screen.

In this section, we will be performing the following tasks:

- Creating a UI with Canvas

- Positioning elements with RectTransform

Let's start by using the Canvas component to create our UI.

Creating a UI with Canvas

In Unity UI, each image, text, and element you see in the UI is a GameObject with a set of proper components, but in order for them to work, they must be a child of a master GameObject with the Canvas component. This component is responsible for triggering the UI generation and drawing iterations over each child object. We can configure this component to specify exactly how that process works and adapt it to different possible requirements.

To start, you can simply create a canvas with the **GameObject | UI | Canvas** option. After doing that, you will see a rectangle in the scene, which represents the user screen, so you can put elements inside it and preview where they will be located relative to the user's monitor. You can see an example of this rectangle in the following screenshot:

Figure 11.2 – Canvas screen rectangle

You are probably wondering two things here. First, "*why is the rectangle in the middle of the scene? I want it to always be on the screen!*". Don't worry because that will exactly be the case. When you edit the UI, you will see it as part of the level, as an object inside it, but when you play the game, it will always be projected over the screen, on top of every object. Also, you may be wondering why the rectangle is huge, and that's because one pixel of the screen maps to one meter on the scene. Again, don't worry about that; you will see all your UI elements in their proper size and position on the user's screen when you see the game in **Game** view.

Before adding elements to our UI, it's worth noting that when you created the UI, a second object is created alongside the canvas, called **EventSystem**. This object is not necessary to render a UI but is necessary if you want the UI to be interactable, which means including actions such as clicking buttons, introducing text in fields, or navigating the UI with the joystick. The **EventSystem** component is responsible for sampling the user input, such as with a keyboard, mouse, or joystick, and sending that data to the UI to react accordingly. We can change the exact buttons to interact with the UI, but the defaults are OK for now, so just know that you need this object if you want to interact with the UI. If, for some reason, you delete the object, you can recreate it again in **GameObject | UI | Event System**.

Now that we have the base objects to create our UI, let's add elements to it.

Positioning elements with RectTransform

In Unity UI, each image, text, and element you see in the UI is a GameObject with a set of proper components according to its usage, but you will see that most of them have one component in common—**RectTransform**. Each piece of the UI is essentially a rectangle filled with text or images and has different behavior, so it is important to understand how the **RectTransform** component works and how to edit it.

To experiment with this component, let's create and edit the position of a simple white box element for the UI as follows:

1. Go to **GameObject | UI | Image**. After that, you will see that a new GameObject is created within the **Canvas** element. Unity will take care of setting any new UI element as a child of Canvas; outside it, the element will not be visible:

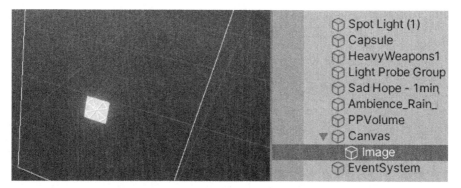

Figure 11.3 – A default image UI element—a white box

2. Click on the 2D button in the top bar of the **Scene** view. This will just change the perspective of the Scene view to one that is better suited to edit the UI (and also 2D games):

Figure 11.4 – The 2D button location

3. Double-click on the canvas in the **Hierarchy** window to make the UI fit entirely in the **Scene** view. This will allow us to edit the UI clearly. You can also navigate the UI using the mouse scroll wheel to zoom, and click and drag the scroll wheel to pan the camera:

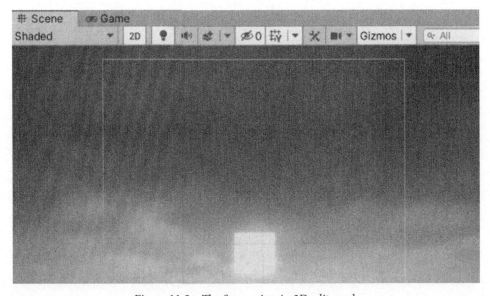

Figure 11.5 – The Scene view in 2D edit mode

4. Disable the **PPVolume** object to disable post-processing. The final UI won't have postprocessing, but the editor view still applies it. Remember to re-enable it later:

Figure 11.6 – Disabling a game object—in this case, the postprocessing volume

5. Enable (if it is not already enabled) the **RectTrasform** tool, which is the fifth button in the top-left part of the Unity Editor (or press the *T* key). That will enable the rectangle gizmo, which allows you to move, rotate, and scale 2D elements. You can use the usual transform, rotate, and scale gizmos, which were the ones we used in 3D mode, but the rectangle gizmo causes less trouble, especially with scaling:

Figure 11.7 – The rectangle gizmo button

6. Using the rectangle gizmo, drag the object to move it, use the blue dots to change its size, or locate the mouse in a tricky position near the blue dots to rotate it. Consider that resizing the object using this gizmo is not the same as scaling the object, but more on that in a moment:

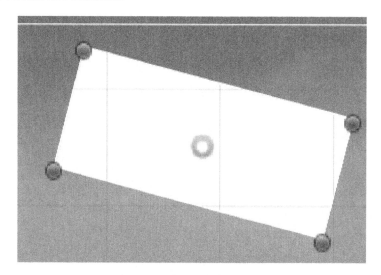

Figure 11.8 – The rectangle gizmo for editing 2D elements

7. In the **Inspector** window, notice that after changing the size of the UI element, the **Rect Transform** setting's **Scale** property is still at (1, 1, 1), but you can see how the **Width** and **Height** properties changed. **Rect Transform** is essentially a classic transform, but with **Width** and **Height** added (among other properties to explore later). You can set the exact values you want here, expressed in pixels:

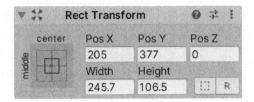

Figure 11.9 – The Rect Transform properties

Now that we know the very basics of how to position any UI object, let's explore the different types of elements you can add to Canvas.

Canvas object types

So far, we have used the simplest Canvas object type—a white box—but there are plenty of other object types we can use, such as images, buttons, and text. All of them use **RectTransform** to define their display area, but each one has its own concepts and configurations to understand.

In this section, we will explore the following Canvas object concepts:

- Integrating assets for the UI
- Creating UI controls

Let's first start exploring how we can integrate images and fonts to use in our canvas so that we can integrate them in our UI using the **Images** and **Text** UI object types.

Integrating assets for the UI

Before making our UI use nice graphics assets, we need, as always, to integrate them properly into Unity. In the following screenshot, you will find the UI design we proposed in *Chapter 1, Designing a Game from Scratch*:

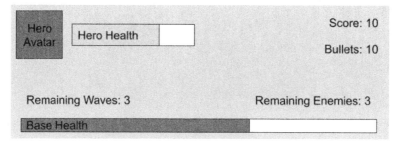

Figure 11.10 – Chapter 1's UI design

On top of that, we will add a Pause menu, which will be activated when the user presses *Esc*. It will look as in the following screenshot:

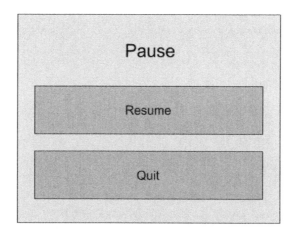

Figure 11.11 – The Pause menu design

Based on these designs, we can determine that we will need the following assets:

- The hero's avatar image
- A health bar image
- A Pause menu background image
- A Pause menu button image
- Font for the text

As always, we can find the required assets on the internet or on the **Asset Store**. In my case, I will use a mixture of both. Let's start with the simplest one—the avatar. Perform the following steps:

1. Download the avatar you want from the internet:

Figure 11.12 – Downloaded avatar asset

2. Add it into your project, either by dragging it to the **Project** window or by using the **Assets | Import New Asset** option. Add it to a `Sprites` folder.

3. Select the texture and, in the **Inspector** window, set the **Texture Type** setting to **Sprite (2D and UI)**. All textures are prepared to be used in 3D by default. This option prepares everything to be used in 2D.

For the bars, buttons, and window background, I will use Asset Store to look for a UI pack. In my case, I found the package in the following screenshot a good one for starting my UI. As usual, remember that this exact package might not be available right now. In that case, remember to look for another similar package, or pick the sprites from the GitHub repo:

PONETI
GUI Parts
★★★★★ (4)
FREE

Figure 11.13 – Selected UI pack

At first, the Package contains lots of images configured the same way as sprites, but we can further modify the import settings to achieve advanced behavior, as we will need for the buttons. The button asset comes with a fixed size, but what happens if you need a bigger button? One option is to use other button assets with different sizes, but this will lead to a lot of repetitions of the buttons and other assets, such as different-sized backgrounds for different windows, which will unnecessarily consume RAM. Another option is to use the 9 slices method, which consists of splitting an image so that the corners are separated from the other parts. This allows Unity to stretch the middle parts of the image to fit different sizes, keeping the corners at their original size, which, when combined with an image prepared for the 9 slices technique, can be used to create almost any size you need. In the following diagram, you can see a shape with nine slices in the bottom-left corner, and in the bottom-right corner of the same diagram, you can see the shape is stretched but keeps its corners at their original size. The top-right corner shows the shape stretched without slices. You can see that the non-sliced version is distorted, while the sliced version is not:

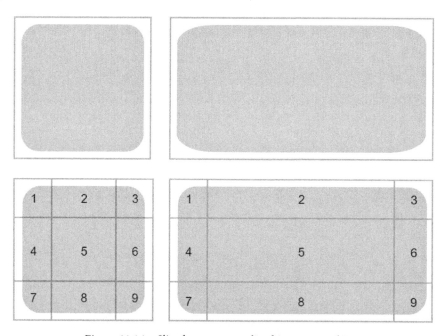

Figure 11.14 – Sliced versus non-sliced image stretching

In this case, we can apply the nine slices to the button and the panel background images to use them in different parts of our game. In order to do this, perform the following steps:

1. Open **Package Manager** using the **Window | Package Manager** option.

2. Verify that **Package Manager** is showing all the packages by setting the dropdown to the right of the + button in the top-left part of the window to Unity Registry:

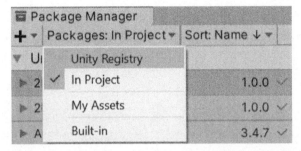

Figure 11.15 – Showing all packages in Package Manager

3. Install the **2D Sprite** package to enable the sprite editing tools (if it is not already installed):

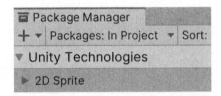

Figure 11.16 – The 2D Sprite package in Package Manager

4. Select the button sprite in the **Project** window and click on the **Sprite Editor** button in the **Inspector** window:

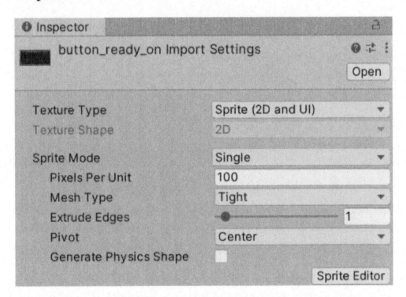

Figure 11.17 – The Sprite Editor button in the Inspector window

5. In the **Sprite Editor** window, locate and drag the green dots at the edges of the image to move the slice rulers. Try to ensure that the slices are not located in the middle of the edges of the button. One thing to notice is that in our case, we will work with three slices instead of nine because our button won't be stretched vertically.

Notice that after dragging the green dots, the Border properties (L, T, R, and B, which are Left, Top, Right, and Bottom, respectively) in the bottom-right corner changed. Those are the exact values you set moving the green dots. Feel free to change them to more round numbers to allow the 9 slices to work even. In our case, Left and Right can become a round 60, and Top and Bottom 50.

6. Click on the **Apply** button in the top-right corner of the window and close it:

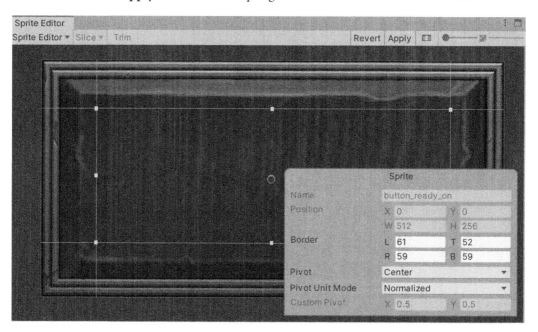

Figure 11.18 – Nine slices in the Sprite Editor window

7. Repeat *steps 4-6* for the **Background** panel image. In my case, you can see in the following screenshot that this background is not completely prepared with nine slices in mind because all the middle areas of the image can be made smaller to save memory. When displaying this image with a smaller width, the 9-slicing method will stretch the middle part and will look the same, so essentially it wasted memory. So, we can edit it with any image editing tool or just work with it as it is for now:

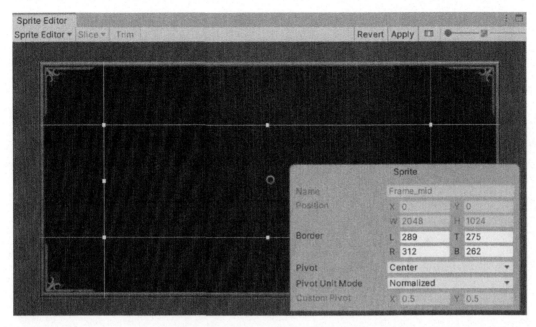

Figure 11.19 – Nine slices in the Sprite Editor window

Now that we have prepared our sprites, we can find a font to customize the text of our UI. Before discussing how to import fonts, it is worth mentioning that we will be using **TextMesh Pro**, a Unity Package (already included in the project) that provides a text rendering solution way better than the old text component. If you have never used that component before, you shouldn't worry about this detail.

You must get fonts in the `.ttf` or `.otf` formats and import them into Unity. You can find lots of good, free font websites on the internet. I am used to working with the classic `DaFont.com` site, but there are plenty of other sites that you can use. In my case, I will work with the following font:

Figure 11.20 – My chosen font from DaFont.com to use in the project

If the font download comes with more than one file, you can just drag them all into Unity and then use the one that you like the most. Also, as usual, try to put the font inside a folder called Fonts. Now, these file formats are not compatible with TextMesh Pro, our text rendering solution, so we must convert it using the **Font Asset Creator** window, as depicted in the following steps:

1. Go to **Window | Text Mesh Pro | Font Asset Creator**.

2. If this is the first time you are using Text Mesh Pro in your project, a window will appear. You must click the **Import TMP Essentials** option and wait for the import process to finish:

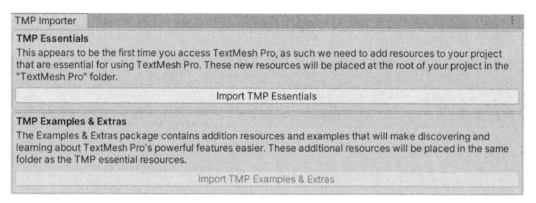

Figure 11.21 – TextMesh Pro first run initialization

3. Close the **TMP Importer** window.

4. In the **Font Asset Creator** window, drag your font from the **Project** view to **Source Font File**, or select it by clicking the **Target** button at the right (the circle with the point at the center).

5.   Click the **Generate Font Atlas** button and wait a moment:

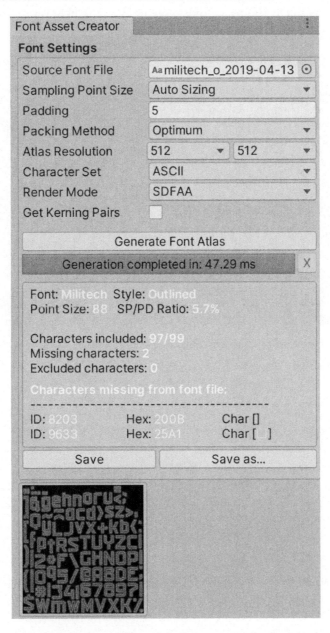

Figure 11.22 – Converting font assets to TextMesh Pro

6. Click the **Save** button and save the converted asset into the **TextMesh Pro | Resources | Fonts & Materials** folder. Saving the asset here is important, so don't forget to pick the proper folder:

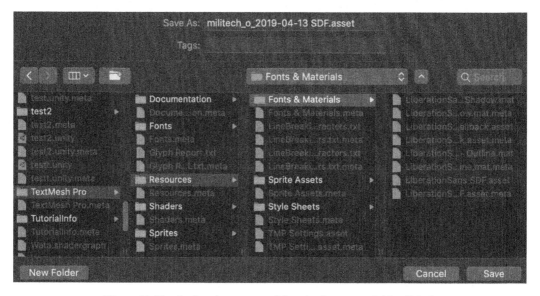

Figure 11.23 – Saving the converted font in the proper folder (Mac)

Now that we have all the required assets to create our UI, let's explore the different types of components to create all the required UI elements.

Creating UI controls

Almost every single part of the UI will be a combination of images and texts configured cleverly. In this section, we will explore the following components:

- Image
- Text
- Button

Let's start exploring Image. Actually, we already have an image in our UI—the white rectangle we created previously in this chapter. If you select it and look at the **Inspector** window, you will notice that it has an **Image** component, like the one in the following screenshot:

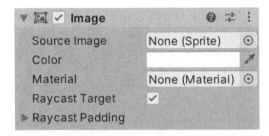

Figure 11.24 – The Image component's Inspector window

Let's start exploring the different settings of this component, starting with our hero's avatar. Perform the following steps:

1. Using the rectangle gizmo, locate the white rectangle in the top-left part of the UI:

Figure 11.25 – The white rectangle located in the top-left part of the UI

2. In the **Inspector** window, click on the circle to the right of the **Source Image** property and pick the downloaded hero avatar sprite:

Figure 11.26 – Setting the sprite of our Image component

3. We need to correct the aspect ratio of the image to prevent distortion. One way to do this is to click the **Set Native Size** button at the bottom of the **Image** component to make the image use the same size as the original sprite. However, by doing this, the image can become too big, so you can reduce the image size by pressing *Shift* to modify both the **Width** and **Height** values. Another option is to check the **Preserve Aspect** checkbox to make sure the image fits the rectangle without stretching. In my case, I will use both:

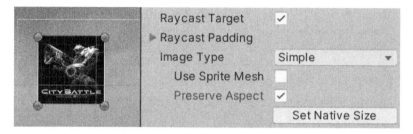

Figure 11.27 – The Preserve Aspect and Set Native Size image options

Now, let's create the life bars by doing the following:

1. Create another **Image** component using the **GameObject | UI | Image** option.

2. Set the **Source Image** property to the life bar image you downloaded:

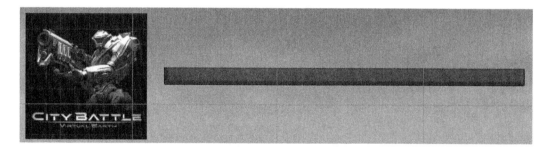

Figure 11.28 – The avatar and life bar

3. Set the **Image Type** property to **Filled**.

4. Set the **Fill Method** property to **Horizontal**.

5. Drag the **Fill Amount** slider to see how the bar is cut according to the value of the slider. We will change that value via scripting when we code the life system in *Chapter 16, Physics Collisions and Health System*, where we will be coding our own scripts:

Figure 11.29 – The Fill Amount slider, cutting the image width by 73% of its size

6. In my case, the bar image also comes with a bar frame, thereby creating another image, setting the sprite, and positioning it on top of the life bar to frame it. Bear in mind that the order the objects are in in the **Hierarchy** window determines the order in which they will be drawn. So, in my case, I need to be sure the frame GameObject is below the health bar image:

Figure 11.30 – Putting one image on top of the other to create a frame effect

7. Repeat *steps 1-6* to create the base bar at the bottom, or just copy and paste the bar and the frame and locate it at the bottom of the screen:

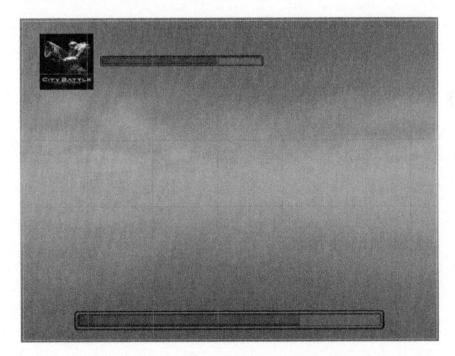

Figure 11.31 – The Player's and Player's Base health bars

8. Click on the + button in the **Project** window and select the **Sprites | Square** option. This will create a simple squared sprite. This is the same as downloading a *4 x 4* resolution full-white image and importing it into Unity.

9. Set the sprite as the base bar instead of the downloaded bar sprite. This time, we will be using a plain-white image for the bar because in my case, the original one is red, and changing the color of a red image to green is not possible. However, a white image can be easily tinted. Take into account the detail of the original bar—for example, the little shadow in my original bar won't be present here, but if you want to preserve it, you should get a white bar with that detail.

10. Select the base health bar and set the **Color** property to green:

Figure 11.32 – A bar with a squared sprite and green tint

One optional step would be to convert the bar frame image into a nine-slices image to allow us to change the original width to fit the screen.

Now, let's add the text fields for the **Score, Bullets, Remaining Waves**, and **Remaining Enemies** labels by doing the following:

1. Create a text label using the **GameObject | UI | Text - Text Mesh Pro** option (avoid the one that only says **Text**). This will be the **Score** label.

2. Position the label in the top-right part of the screen.

3. In the **Inspector** window, set the **Text Input** property to Score: 0.

4. Set the **Font Size** property to 20.

5. Apply the converted font by clicking on the circle to the right of the **Font Asset** property and select the desired font.

6. In the **Alignment** property, select the **Horizontal Right Align** icon (third button from the first row) and the **Vertical Center Align** icon (second button from the second row):

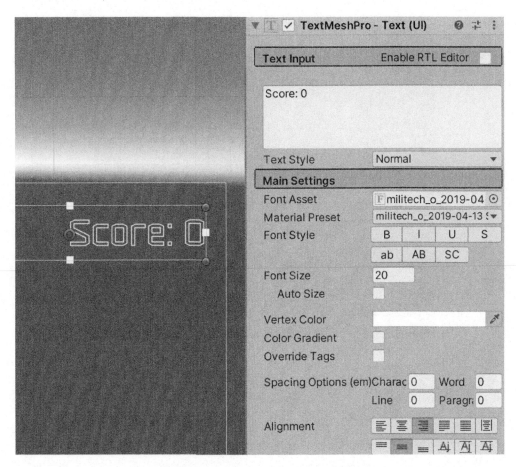

Figure 11.33 – The settings for a text label

7. Repeat *steps 1-6* to create the other three labels (or just copy and paste the score three times). For the **Remaining Waves** label, you can use the left alignment option to better match the original design:

Figure 11.34 – All the labels for our UI

8. Set the color of all the labels to white as our scene will be mainly dark.

Now that we have completed the original UI design, we can create the **Pause** menu:

1. Create an **Image** component for the menu's background (**GameObject | UI | Image**).

2. Set the **Background** panel sprite with the nine slices we made earlier.

3. Set the **Image Type** property to **Sliced** if it is not already. This mode will apply the 9-slice scaling method to prevent the corners from stretching.

4. There's a chance that the image will stretch the corners anyway, which happens because sometimes the corners are quite big compared to the **RectTransform** setting's **Size** property that you are using, so Unity has no option other than to do that. In this scenario, the correct solution is to have an artist who creates assets tailored to your game, but sometimes we don't have that option. This time, we can just increase the **Pixels Per Unit** value of the sprite, which will reduce the scale of the original image while preserving its resolution. In the following two screenshots, you can see the background image with a **Pixels Per Unit** value of 100 and again with 700. Remember to only do this for the nine-slices or tiled-image types, or if you don't have an artist to adjust it for you:

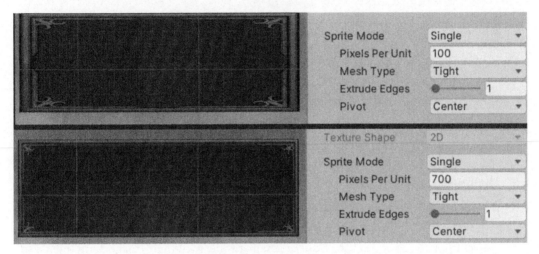

Figure 11.35 – On top, a large nine-slices image in a small RectTransform component, small enough to shrink the corners; on the bottom, the same image with Pixels Per Unit set to 700

5. Create a TextMesh Pro Text field, position it where you want the **Pause** label to be in your diagram, set it to display the **Pause** text, and set the font. Remember that you can change the text color with the **Color** property.

6. Drag the text field onto the background image. The parenting system in **Canvas** works the same—if you move the parent, the children will move with it. The idea is that if we disable the panel, it will also disable the buttons and all its content:

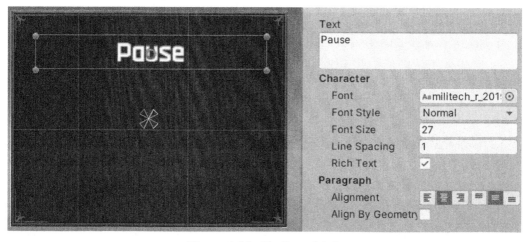

Figure 11.36 – The Pause label

7. Create two buttons by going to **GameObject | UI | Button - Text Mesh Pro** (avoid using the one that only says **Button**). Position them where you want them on the background image.

8. Set them as children of the **Pause** background image by dragging them to the **Hierarchy** window.

9. Select the buttons and set the **Source Image** property of their Image components to use the button sprite that we downloaded earlier. Remember our **Pixels Per Unit** fix from earlier if you have the same problem as before.

10. You will notice that the button is essentially an image with a child TextMesh Pro Text object. Change the font of each button and the text in each button to Resume and Quit:

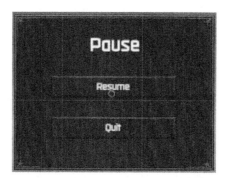

Figure 11.37 – The Pause menu implementation

11. Remember that you can hide the panel by unchecking the checkbox to the right of the name of the object in the top part of the **Inspector** window:

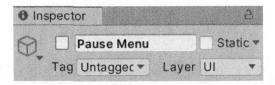

Figure 11.38 – Disabling a GameObject

As you can see, you can create almost any kind of UI just by using Image and Text components. Of course, there are more advanced components that enable you to create buttons, text fields, checkboxes, lists, and so on, but let's stick to the basic ones. One thing to notice is that we have created buttons, but they do nothing so far. Later, in *Part 3* of the book, we will see how to script them to have a function.

In this section, we discussed how to import images and fonts to be integrated through the **Image**, **Text**, and **Button** components to create a rich and informative UI. Having done that, let's discuss how to make them adapt to different devices.

Creating a responsive UI

Nowadays, it is almost impossible to design a UI in a single resolution, and our target audience display devices can vary a lot. A PC has a variety of different kinds of monitors with different resolutions (such as 1080p and 4k) and aspect ratios (such as 16:9, 16:10, and ultra-wide), and the same goes for mobile devices. We need to prepare our UI to adapt to the most common displays, and Unity UI has the tools needed to do so.

In this section, we will explore the following UI responsiveness concepts:

- Adapting object positions
- Adapting object sizes

We are going to explore how the UI elements can adapt their position and size to different screen sizes using advanced features of the **Canvas** and **RectTransform** components, such as Anchors and Scalers.

Adapting object positions

Right now, if we play our game, we will see how the UI fits nicely onto our screen. But if, for some reason, we change the **Game** view size, we will see how objects start to disappear from the screen. In the following screenshots, you can see different sized game windows and how the UI looks nice in one but bad in the others:

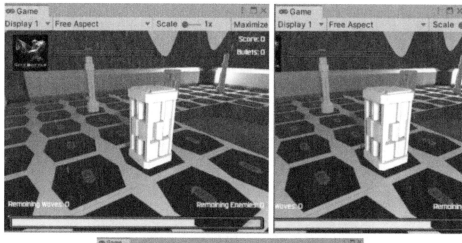

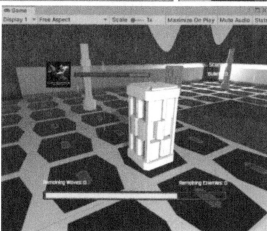

Figure 11.39 – The same UI but on different screen sizes

The problem is that we created the UI using whatever resolution we had in the editor, but as soon as we change it slightly, the UI keeps its design for the previous resolution. Also, if you look closely, you will notice that the UI is always centered, such as in the middle image, where the UI is cropped at its sides, or the third image, where extra space is visible along the borders of the screen. This happens because every single element in the UI has its own Anchor, a little cross you can see when you select an object, such as the one in the following screenshot:

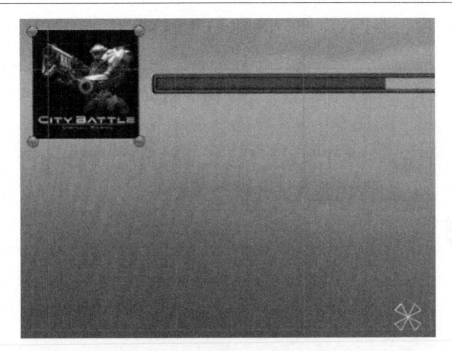

Figure 11.40 – An Anchor cross at the bottom-right part of the screen belonging to the hero avatar in the top-left part of the screen

The X and Y position of the object is measured as a distance to that Anchor, and the Anchor has a position relative to the screen, with its default position being at the center of the screen. This means that on an *800 x 600* screen, the Anchor will be placed at the *400 x 300* position, and on a *1920 x 1080* screen, the Anchor will be located at the *960 x 540* position. If the X and Y position of the element (the one in RectTransform) is 0, the object will always be at a distance of 0 from the center. In the middle screenshot of the previous three examples, the hero avatar falls outside of the screen because its distance from the center is greater than half the screen, and the current distance was calculated based on the previous, bigger screen size. So, what we can do about that? Move the Anchor!

By setting a relative position, we can position the Anchor at different parts of our screen and make that part of the screen our reference position. In the case of our hero avatar, we can place the Anchor at the top-left corner of the screen to guarantee that our avatar will be at a fixed distance from that corner. We can do that by following these steps:

1.   Select your hero avatar.

2.   Expand the **RectTranform** component in the **Inspector** window if not expanded yet in a way that you can see its properties. This will reveal **Anchors** in the **Scene** view.

3. Drag the Anchor cross with your mouse to the top-left part of the screen. If, for some reason, the Anchor breaks into pieces when you drag it, undo the change (press *Ctrl + Z* or *Command + Z* on macOS) and try to drag it by clicking in the center. We will break the Anchor later:

Figure 11.41 – An image with an Anchor at the top-left part of the screen

4. Put the Anchor of the **Health Bar** object and its frame in the same position. We want the bar to always be at the same distance from that corner so that it will move alongside the hero avatar if the screen size changes.

5. Place the Anchor at the bottom-center part of the screen for the **Boss Bar** object so that it will always be centered. Later, we will deal with adjusting its size.

6. Put the **Remaining Waves** label at the bottom-left corner and **Remaining Enemies** in the bottom-right corner:

Figure 11.42 – The Anchors for the life bar and the labels

7.   Put the **Score** and **Bullets** Anchors in the top-right corner:

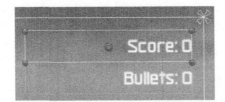

Figure 11.43 – The Anchors for the Score and Bullets labels

8.   Select any element and drag the sides of the canvas rectangle with your mouse to preview how the elements will adapt to their positions. Take into account that you must select any object that is a direct child of Canvas; the text within the buttons won't have that option:

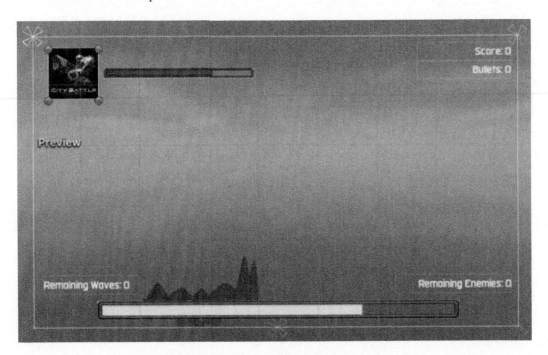

Figure 11.44 – Previewing canvas resizing

Now that our UI elements have adapted to their positions, let's consider scenarios where the object size must adapt as well.

Adapting object sizes

The first thing to consider when dealing with different aspect ratios is that our screen elements may not only move from their original design position (which we fixed in the previous section) but also, they may not fit into the original design. In our UI, we have the case of the health bar, where the bar clearly doesn't adapt to the screen width when we previewed it on a wider screen. We can fix this by breaking our Anchors.

When we break our Anchors, the position and size of our object are calculated as a distance relative to the different Anchor parts. If we split the Anchor horizontally, instead of having an **X** and **Width** property, we will have a **Left** and **Right** property, representing the distance to the left and right Anchor. We can use this in the following way:

1. Select the health bar and drag the left part of the anchor all the way to the left part of the screen, and the right part to the right part of the screen.

2. Do the same for the health bar frame:

Figure 11.45 – The splitter Anchor in the health bar

3. Check the **Rect Transform** setting's **Left** and **Right** properties in the **Inspector** window, which represent the current distance to their respective Anchors. If you want, you can add a specific value, especially if your health bars are displaying outside the screen:

Figure 11.46 – The Left and Right properties of a split anchor

This way, the object will always be at a fixed distance of a relative position on the screen—in this case, the sides of the screen. If you are working with a child object, as is the case with the Text and Image components of the buttons, the Anchors are relative to the parent. If you pay attention to the Anchors of the text, they are not only split horizontally but also vertically. This allows the text to adapt its position to the size of the button, so you won't have to change it manually:

Figure 11.47 – The split Anchors of the text of the button

Now, this solution is not suitable for all scenarios. Let's consider a case where the hero avatar is displayed in higher resolution than what it was designed for. Even if the avatar is correctly placed, it will be displayed smaller because the screen has more pixels per inch than screens with lower resolutions and the same physical size. You could consider using split Anchors, but the width and height Anchors could be scaled differently in different aspect ratio screens, so the original image becomes distorted. Instead, we can use the **Canvas Scaler** component.

The Canvas Scaler component defines what 1 pixel means in our scenario. If our UI design resolution is 1080p, but we see it in a 4k display (which is twice the resolution of 1080p), we can scale the UI so that a pixel becomes 2, adapting its size to keep the same proportional size as the original design. Basically, the idea is that if the screen is bigger, our elements should also be bigger.

We can use this component by doing the following:

1. Select the **Canvas** object and locate the **Canvas Scaler** component in the **Inspector** window.

2. Set the **UI Scale Mode** property to **Scale with Screen Size**.

3. If working with an artist, set the reference resolution to the resolution in which the artist created the UI, keeping in mind that it must be the highest target device resolution (this isn't the case for us). In our case, we are not sure which resolution the artist of the downloaded assets had in mind, so we can put 1920 x 1080, which is the full HD resolution size and is very common nowadays.

4. Set the **Match** property to **Height**. The idea of this property is that it sets which side of the resolution will be considered when carrying out the scaling calculation. In our case, if we are playing the game in 1080p resolution, 1 UI pixel equals 1 real screen pixel. However, if we are playing in 720p resolution, 1 UI pixel will be 0.6 real pixels, so the elements will be smaller on smaller resolution screens, keeping their correct size. We didn't choose a **Width** value in this case because we can have extreme widths in screens, such as ultra-wide, and if we picked that option, those screens would scale the UI unnecessarily. Another option is to set this value to 0.5 to consider the two values, but on a PC, this doesn't make too much sense. On a mobile device, you should choose this based on the orientation of the game, setting the height for landscape mode and the width for portrait mode. Try previewing a wider and higher screen and see how this setting works:

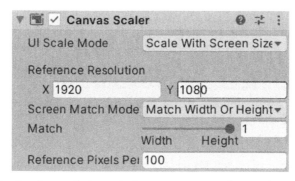

Figure 11.48 – Canvas Scaler with the correct settings for standard PC games

You will find that your UI will be smaller than your original design, which is because we should have set these properties before. Right now, the only fix is to resize everything again. Take this into account the next time you try this exercise; we only followed this order for learning purposes.

Before moving on, remember to reactivate the postprocessing volume object to show those effects again. You will notice that the UI is not affected by them in the **Game** view.

Note, if you want your UI to be affected by postprocessing effects, you can set **Canvas Render Mode** to **Screen Space – Camera**. Drag the main camera to the **Render Camera** property and set **Plane Distance** to 5. This will put the UI in the world with the rest of the objects, aligned to the camera view with a distance of 5 meters:

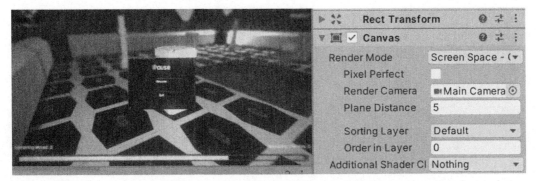

Figure 11.49 – Canvas Render Mode set to Camera mode to receive postprocessing effects

With this knowledge, you are now ready to start creating your first UIs by yourself.

Summary

In this chapter, we introduced the basics of UI design, understanding the **Canvas** and **RectTransform** components to locate objects on screen and create a UI layout. We also covered different kinds of UI elements, mainly Image and Text, to give life to our UI layout and make it appealing to the user. Finally, we discussed how to adapt UI objects to different resolutions and aspect ratios to make our UI adapt to different screen sizes, even though we cannot predict the exact monitor our user will be playing the game on. All of this allows us to create any UI we will need in our game using Canvas.

In the next chapter, we will explore how to create UIs using UI Toolkit instead, another Unity system for creating UIs, and compare both Canvas and UI Toolkit to see where it's best to use each one.

12
Creating a UI with the UI Toolkit

In the previous chapter, we discussed how to create user interfaces using **GUI** (also known as **Canvas**), one of the most common UI systems in Unity, but as we have already mentioned, this is not the only option. While, so far, UGUI has been the preferred option, Unity is working on a replacement called **UI Toolkit**, and even if it's not finished yet, we thought it would be worthwhile to cover it in this book so that you are prepared for its release.

The idea of this chapter is to create the same UI we created previously, but with UI Toolkit, so you can get a sneak peek into what creating UIs in Unity will look like soon:

Figure 12.1 – The UI created in the previous chapter

In this chapter, we will examine the following UI concepts:

- Why learn UI Toolkit?

- Creating UIs with UI Toolkit

- Making a Responsive UI with UI Toolkit

By the end of the chapter, you will know how to use UI Tookit to create basic UIs for our game, redoing the UI we did in the last chapter as a point of reference. So, let's kick off the discussion by asking, why are we using UI Tookit?

Why learn UI Toolkit?

I know this chapter might sound a little bit confusing; we just learned how to use a whole Unity system to create our UI, and now we are learning another one! Why don't we just learn this new one directly?

Well, the first part of the answer is that UI Toolkit is not ready yet, meaning that it doesn't have all the features and stability necessary to use it in real production. Even if we can create our UI without issues in this new system, it is not tested enough to guarantee that it will work well across all the different devices our game can run on (for example, several PC setups and mobile devices).

Another thing to take into account is that, even if the systems were stable enough, it's still a relatively new system, and there are still lots of games under development that were created on older Unity versions that don't support it. This means that in order to land a job in this industry, you need to get a decent amount of exposure to uGUI due to most games being created with this technology. This happens because it's neither safe nor practical to update an already tested and working game with new technologies; such changes could lead to a major rework of the game to be compatible with the new versions. Also, this could potentially introduce tons of bugs that could delay the release of new versions, not to even mention the time it will take to remake a full app in a new system.

That being said, even if the system is not yet finished, meaning that it could change radically in subsequent versions, we believe it's still worth learning its basic concepts to be prepared to use it in newer Unity versions, so let's dive into it now.

Creating UIs with UI Toolkit

In this section, we are going to learn how to create UI Documents, an asset that will define the elements our UI has. To do this, we are going to discuss the following concepts:

- Installing UI Toolkit

- Creating UI Documents

- Editing UI Documents

- Creating UI Stylesheets

Let's start by seeing how we can install UI Toolkit, as currently, it is not as straightforward as other packages.

Installing UI Toolkit

UI Toolkit can be used to create both Editor UI (custom editor windows) and In-Game UI. The tools to create Editor UI are already installed in Unity, but as we will use UI Toolkit to create In-Game UI, we need to install the **Runtime Extension**. This is essentially a package; however, the problem is that it will not appear in the Package Manager like other packages. Instead, we need to explicitly add it to the Package Manager via its URL. This is done this way due to the experimental nature of the package but, probably when it is fully released, the installation process will be easier.

In order to manually add UI Toolkit to our Package Manager, you need to do the following:

1. Open the Package Manager (**Window | Package Manager**).
2. Click the **Add** button (the plus (+) symbol at the top left).
3. Select **Add Package from git URL**:

Figure 12.2 – Adding a Package to the Package Manager

4. In the **URL** input box, write `com.unity.ui` without quotation marks:

Figure 12.3 – Adding UI Toolkit to the Package Manager

5. Click the **Add** button and wait for the package to download and install.

6. As usual, just in case, it's recommended to restart Unity after installing packages.

Now that we have installed the Runtime Extension for using UI Toolkit to create In-Game UI, let's start using it.

Creating UI Documents

When creating a UI with uGUI, we need to create GameObjects and attach components such as **Button**, **Image**, or **Text**, but with UI Toolkit, we need to create a **UI Document** instead. UI Document is a special kind of asset that will contain the definition of the elements our UI will have and its hierarchy. We will have a GameObject with a **UI Document** component (yes, it's called the same, so pay attention here) that will reference this UI document asset and render its contents. It's like a Mesh asset that contains information pertaining to the Mesh, and the `MeshRenderer` component that will render it. In this case, the elements to render are contained in an asset and we have a component that reads the asset and renders its content (UI in this case).

UI Documents are actually plain text files. You can open one with a text editor and easily see its contents. If you do that and you are familiar with HTML, you will recognize the XML-like format used to define the elements our UI will be composed of; Unity calls this format UXML. The aim of Unity with UI Toolkit is for web developers to jump easily into Unity and create UIs. In the following screenshot, you can see the typical look of a UXML document's contents:

```
<ui:UXML xmlns:ui="UnityEngine.UIElements" xmlns:uie="UnityEditor.UIElements" xsi="http://
    <ui:VisualElement name="PlayerLogo" style="position: absolute; height: 150px; width:
    <ui:Label text="Score: 100" display-tooltip-when-elided="true" style="position: absol
    <ui:VisualElement name="LifeBar" style="position: absolute; left: 113px; right: 126px;
        <ui:VisualElement name="LifeBarFilling" style="position: absolute; top: 0; left:
        <ui:VisualElement name="LifeBarBorder" style="position: absolute; height: auto;
    </ui:VisualElement>
    <ui:VisualElement name="LifeBar" style="position: absolute; height: 36px; width: 613px
        <ui:VisualElement name="LifeBarFilling" style="position: absolute; top: 0; left: 0
        <ui:VisualElement name="LifeBarBorder" style="position: absolute; height: auto; wi
    </ui:VisualElement>
</ui:UXML>
```

Figure 12.4 – Example of UI Document's internal format (UXML)

Don't worry if you don't know HTML; we will explain the core concepts in this chapter. Also, don't worry about the UXML format; later in this chapter, we will be using a Visual Editor called **UI Builder** to edit our UI without writing UXML at all, but it is worth knowing how it actually works inside.

In order to create a UI Document and add it to the scene, we need to do the following:

1. Click the **Add (+) | UI Toolkit | UI Document** option in the **Project** view to create a UI Document asset and name it GameHUD:

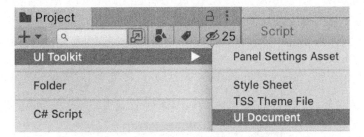

Figure 12.5 – Creating the UI Document Asset

2. Click the **Game Object | UI Tookit | UI Document** option to create a GameObject in your scene with the UI Document component, which is capable of rendering the UI Document.

3. Select and drag the **GameHUD** UI Document asset to the **Source Asset** property of the GameObject:

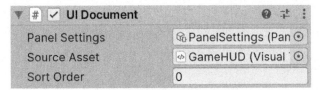

Figure 12.6 – Making the UI Document component render our UI Document asset

And that's it! Of course, we won't see anything yet on our screen as the UI Document is blank, so let's start adding elements to it.

Editing UI Documents

As our goal is to recreate the same UI we created in the last chapter, let's start with the simplest part: adding the Player Avatar to the top-left corner. One option would be to open the UI Document asset with any text editor and start writing the UXML code, but luckily, we have an easier way, which is using the **UI Builder** editor. This editor allows us to generate the UXML code visually, by dragging and dropping elements. To do that, let's first see how the **UI Builder** window works:

1. Click **Window | UI Toolkit | UI Builder** to open the tool to visually edit the **UI Document** asset.

2. Double-click the **GameHUD** asset in the **Project** view to make **UI Builder** open it:

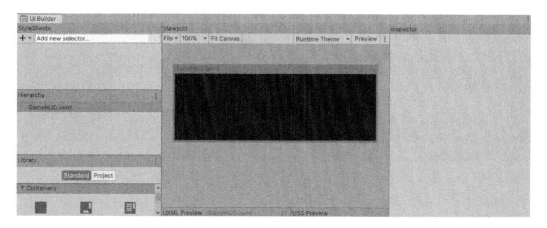

Figure 12.7 – The UI Builder editor

3. In the **Hierarchy** panel (the left part of the window) select GameHUD.uxml, which is the container element of the UI:

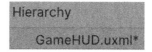

Figure 12.8 – Selecting the Asset name in Hierarchy to edit general UI settings

Look at the **Inspector** panel at the right of the **UI Builder** window (this is *not* the **Inspector** we used so far to modify GameObjects, which is anchored to the main Unity Editor window). Set the **Size** property to a **Width** of 1920 and a **Height** of 1080. This will allow us to view how our UI will look in such a resolution. You can later change this value to see how it adapts to different sizes, but more on that later:

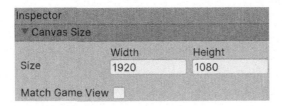

Figure 12.9 – Setting the Preview UI resolution

4. You can pan the viewport to navigate the UI by pressing the *Mouse Wheel Button* and moving the mouse. In Mac, you can press *Option + Command* and click and drag any free area of the viewport (places without our UI).

5. You can also use the *Mouse Scroll Wheel* to zoom in and out. Another option is to press *Option* on Mac (*Alt* on Windows) and click and drag horizontally. Finally, you can use the zoom percentage selection at the top-left part of the **Viewport** pane:

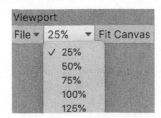

Figure 12.10 – Setting the Preview Zoom

Now that we know the basics of UI Builder, let's add our image to the UI:

1. Drag the **VisualElement** icon from the **Library** at the bottom left to the **Hierarchy** section on the left. This will create a basic UI Element capable of rendering an image and much more:

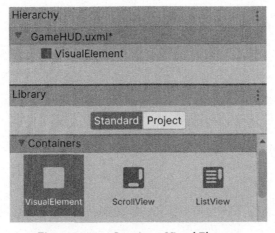

Figure 12.11 – Creating a Visual Element

2. Select **VisualElement** in **Hierarchy** (under `GameHUD.uxml`) and look at the **Inspector** at the right part of the **UI Builder** window (again, not the regular Unity Inspector panel) for the **Position** section. Expand it if not already expanded (using the arrow on the left).

3. Set **Position** to **Absolute** to allow us to move our element freely around the UI. Later in this chapter, in the *Using relative positions* section, we will explain how **Relative** mode works:

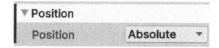

Figure 12.12 – Setting our UI Element to be freely moved around

4. In the **Viewport** pane, you can drag your element around and use the blue rectangles in the corners to change its size. Position your element at the top-left corner of the UI:

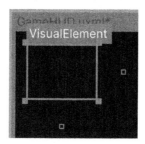

Figure 12.13 – Moving VisualElements

5. To set an exact position, you can set the **Left** and **Top** values of the **Position** section in **Inspector** to specify the exact X and Y coordinates, respectively, expressed in pixels:

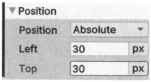

Figure 12.14 – Setting the position

6. You can also specify the exact size by changing the **Width** and **Height** of the **Size** section:

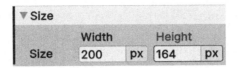

Figure 12.15 – Setting the size

7. In the Background section of **Inspector**, set the Image mode to **Sprite** using the combo box at its right. This allows us to apply a Sprite as the background of our element.

> **Important info**
>
> You can also use a regular Texture instead of a Sprite, but Sprite has better default import settings, allowing users to use Sprite Atlases and support 9 slices, among other features.

8. Drag the Sprite asset (the image) of our Player avatar we imported in *Chapter 11, User Interface Design*, from the **Project** panel to the **Image** property in order to set it. Also, you can use the target button (circle button with the dot at the middle) to select the Sprite asset from the picker window:

Figure 12.16 – Setting the Background image of the element

9. Get back to the regular Unity Editor to see the results. If you don't see any change, you can turn off and on the GameObject that renders our UI (the one we created with the UI Document).

Now that we have created the Player Avatar, we can create the Player Health bar by doing the following:

1. Repeat the previous steps to *1 to 6* to create a new element that will serve as the Player Health Bar container. It won't have any image.

2. Position it right next to the Player Avatar and set its size to be similar to the one used when we designed this UI in the previous chapter. Remember that you can do this by dragging the image and the squares at the corners, or through the **Size and Position** properties, as we did before.

3. Drag a new **VisualElement** over this element created in step 1 to make it a child of it. This will make that element position and size dependent on its parent, the same that happened when we parented Canvas objects in *Chapter 11, User Interface Design.*

4. Select the parent Visual Element and, in the **Inspector**, set the Name property to `PlayerHealth` to easily identify it. Do the same with the child element, calling it **Filling**:

Figure 12.17 – Parenting and Naming Visual Elements

5. Select the **Filling** element in the **Hierarchy** and look at **Inspector**.

6. In the **Background** section, set the **Color** property to red, clicking on the color box and using the **Color Picker**. This will fill our UI Element background with plain red instead of using an image:

Figure 12.18 – Setting a pure red background for our element

7. As usual, set **Position** to **Absolute**, and also the **Left** and **Top** properties to **0** to make the filling to be placed in the same position as its parent.

8. Set the **Width** and **Height** of **Size** to **100** and change the unit of measurement from **px** (pixels) to **%** (percentage) by clicking on the **px** button and selecting **%**. This will make the **Filling** element size to be the same as its parent (100 percent of the parent size):

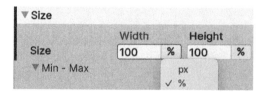

Figure 12.19 – Setting our size as the same size as our parent element

9. Add a new **VisualElement** as a child of **PlayerHealth** and call it `Border`.

10. Set **Position** and **Size**, as we did in steps *7* and *8* for the **Filling** element, but don't set the background color.

11. Set the **Border** background image to be the same border image we used in the previous chapter. Remember to set the Image mode to **Sprite** instead of texture.

12. Set the **Slice** property in the **Background** section to **15**. This applies the 9 slices technique we used in *Chapter 11, User Interface Design*, to expand an object without stretching it:

Figure 12.20 – Setting the 9 slices sizes in the element directly

> **Important info**
>
> Consider that if your image already contains the 9 slices technique (using the Sprite Editor as we did in *Chapter 11, User Interface Design*), you don't need to set the **Slice** values as we did in the previous step. We just did it here for you to be aware that the option exists. Remember that the 9 slices technique allows you to preserve the corner sizes of our image to allow resizing without distortions.

13. Now you can change the **Filling Size's Width** to simulate the **Fill Amount** property of images we used in *Chapter 11, User Interface Design*. Later, we will change **Size** to be directly proportional to the Player Health number via code:

Figure 12.21 – Health Bar result

14. Repeat steps *1 to 12* to create the bottom of the Base Health bar. Remember that the filling must be green this time. Alternatively, you can just copy and paste the **Health Bar** container, but I recommend that you repeat the steps for learning purposes.

In previous steps, we saw how to compose several UI Elements to create a complex object. We needed a parent container element to drive the size of our child's container in a way that the inner elements adapt to it, especially the filling, which requires a percentage value to represent the current player health.

Now we have our Life Bar! Well, not quite yet. Those red corners from the Filling that our border doesn't cover are pretty rough! We will improve that later in this chapter when discussing how to make our UI responsive, so for now, let's keep it as is.

Finally, let's add text elements to the UI by doing the following:

1. Drag the **Label** icon from the **Library** pane to **Hierarchy**. This will add a UI element capable of not only rendering an image in its background but also text (yes, you can add a background to the text if you want to).

2. As usual, set its **Position** and **Size**, this time putting it in the top-right corner of the screen. Remember you can simply drag the element; you don't need to put specific coordinates.

3. Change the **Text** property in the **Label** section of **Inspector** to the required text. In our case, this will be Score: 0:

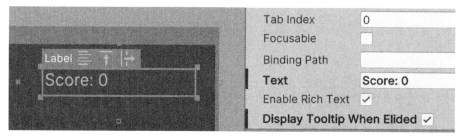

Figure 12.22 – Setting the text to display

4. Drag the Font asset we imported in *Chapter 11, User Interface Design* (the TTF or OTF file), to the **Font** property in the **Text** section of **Inspector**.

5. You will notice that your font might not work. In such a case, put the font asset in the **UI Toolkit | Resources | Fonts & Materials** folder in the **Project** panel. This will enable the font to be recognized by the system:

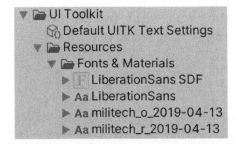

Figure 12.23 – Putting the font in the correct folder

6. Set the **Size** property of the **Text** section to any size that appears to fit:

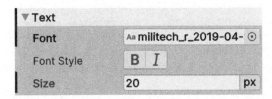

Figure 12.24 – Setting the Font and Text size of a Label

7. Repeat steps *1- 6* to add all the remaining Labels to the UI.

One last thing we need to do is save, which can be simply done by pressing *Ctrl + S* (*Command + S* on Mac) or by using the **File | Save** menu in **UI Builder**. Consider when doing this in the current state of UI Toolkit can make the Viewport to not function properly. Please close it and reopen **UI Builder** again. This will surely be fixed when the final version is released.

Now that we have created our UI, you probably noticed the need to repeat several settings to make several objects look the same, such as our Health Bars and Labels. While this is perfectly viable, we could improve our workflow greatly by reusing styles, and **Stylesheets** assets are the exact feature we need to accomplish that, so let's see them.

Creating UI Stylesheets

When creating UIs, you will find scenarios where several elements throughout the whole game will share the same style, for example, buttons with the same background, font, size, and borders. When creating the UI with uGUI, one way to not repeat configurations for each element would be to create a prefab for the button and create instances (and Prefab Variants where necessary). The problem is that here, we don't have GameObjects, hence there are no prefabs, but luckily, we have **Stylesheets**.

Stylesheets are separated assets that contains a series of styling presets for our UI elements. We can define a set of styles (for example, background, borders, font, and size) and apply them to several elements across different UI Elements. This way, if we change a style in a Stylesheet Asset, all UI Elements using that style will change, in a similar way to how Materials work.

There are several ways to create styles in a Stylesheet, with one example being the selector system. This system allows you to apply a series of rules to pick which elements should have a style applied (you guessed correctly, like CSS), but for now, let's stick with the basics, creating **Stylesheet Classes**. A **Class** is basically a style we can apply to any element via its name. For example, we can create a Class called `Button` and add that class to every button in the UI that we want to have that style. Please consider that the concept of Class here is something completely different from what a Class means in coding.

So, in this case, let's create a Class for all the labels in our UI in such a way that the appearance of all of them can be modified simply by changing the style:

1. In the **StyleSheets** pane of **UI Builder**, click the plus (+) button and click **Create New USS** (Unity Style Sheet). If that doesn't work, try restarting Unity. There is a bug in the current version of UI Toolkit that could cause this:

Figure 12.25 – Creating a Unity Style Sheet

2. Name the USS as you wish (`GameUSS` in my case) and save the file.

3. Select one of the Label elements we have in our UI Document and look at Inspector.

4. In the **StyleSheet** pane of **Inspector**, type `HUDText` in the **Style Class List** input field.

5. Click the **Extract Inlined Styles to New Class** button. This will take all the style modifications we did to our Label (position, size, font, and so on) and save it to a new style class called `HUDText`. You can observe that it was added to the list of classes applied to the element (those labels at the bottom of the **StyleSheet** section in **Inspector**):

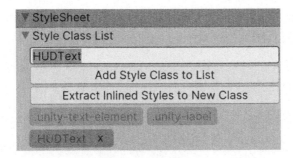

Figure 12.26 – Extracting settings into a Style Class

With these steps, we have taken a Label with the style we need to repeat and extracted its settings into a class named **HUDText**. This way, we can simply add the **HUDText** class to other elements in our UI, and we can even add the same USS Asset to other UI Documents (**Plus (+) button of StyleSheets pane | Add Existing USS**) to add this class to the elements in it.

Also, if you select the label again, you will notice how properties that previously were in bold now became normal again; that's because properties in bold represent changed properties, and we have extracted them, so the default values became whatever the style classes define:

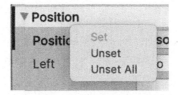

Figure 12.27 – Position is in bold, meaning it has changed. Left isn't, meaning it has the default value

Now we can start applying our style to the rest of the Labels, but before doing that, we must consider something. We have just copied every single change applied to **Label**, including **Position** and **Size**, and surely not all Labels will have the same value on those properties. We need to clean our class to have only the common changes doing the following:

1. In the **StyleSheets** section at the top-left part of **UI Builder**, select the **HUDText** class in the list. If you don't see it, try expanding the **GameUSS.uss** section:

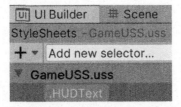

Figure 12.28 – Selecting a Style Class for modification

2. In the **Inspector** on the right, right-click on the **Left** property of the **Position** section and click **Unset**:

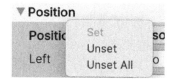

Figure 12.29 – Reverting per element changes to use the defaults in its style classes

3. Do the same for **Width**.

4. Notice that the **Position** values in **Style** are set to **Absolute**. We want to keep this in our case as all text elements in our UI are going to use this mode, but consider this is not always the case (more on that later).

5. Right-click on the **Size** section (not the property) and click **Unset**, this time to reset the entire **Size** section settings and not just specific settings thereof.

6. You will notice that our element has lost its position; you will need to relocate the element to its intended position by dragging it.

This way, we have edited our HUDText class. If other elements had this class **applied**, they would have these changes applied also. Consider that another option would be to create the Class first by typing the name in the **StyleSheets** input field and pressing enter and then applying it to elements. This way, you will avoid needing to reverse unwanted changes, but if you created the element first, it's convenient to have the option to revert:

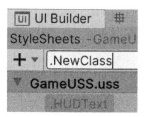

Figure 12.30 – Creating a Style Class from scratch

Now that we have our Style Class, let's apply it to other elements by doing the following:

1. Select another label of our UI.

2. Drag the **HUDText** style from the **Stylesheet** pane at the top-left part of the **UI Builder** window all the way to our element on the **Viewport** pane. You can also drag it to the **Hierarchy** element if you prefer:

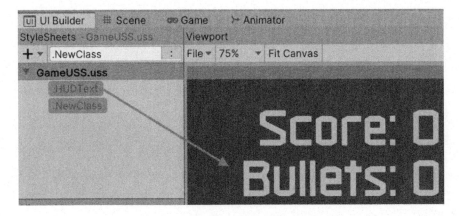

Figure 12.31 – Applying a Class to an element

3. Select the Label and check how the **HUDText** class has been added to the **StyleSheet** section on the **Inspector**.

Now, consider that even if the element now has the class applied, the element itself has changes to the text we did in previous steps, overriding the style in our class. You can easily check this by selecting the class again (in the **StyleSheets** section in the top-left corner) and changing any setting, such as the size, and seeing how not all elements have changed. This shows how the override system works; the changes in the element take precedence over the ones in the classes it has applied. If you want to remove these overrides, you can simply select the element and right-click on the overridden properties you want to take from **Class**, and unset the changes (**Right Click | Unset**). In the case of our **Label**, we can revert the entire **Text** section and probably the **Absolute** Position (as the desired values are already contained in the class).

So, with these steps, we have created a new **StyleSheet** asset and added it to the UI Document for it to use it. We have created a new Style Class in it, extracting the changes of an existing UI Element into it, and then adjusting which changes we wanted to keep. Finally, we applied that style to another element. With this, we have just scratched the surface of the real power of Style Sheets. We can start doing things such as combining different classes from different Style Sheets, or use selectors to dynamically set styles, but that's outside the scope of this chapter. Something interesting is that even if the documentation of UI Toolkit is pretty rough at the moment, all these advanced concepts can be learned by reading about CSS, the web technology that Unity based the stylesheet system on. It won't be exactly the same, but the base idea and best practices still apply.

Now, the UI looks almost exactly as in *Chapter 11*, *User Interface Design*, but it won't behave the same. If you try changing the size of the viewport (selecting **GameHUD. uxml** in the hierarchy and changing **Width** and **Height**, as we did at the beginning of the chapter), you will see that the UI won't adapt properly, so let's fix this.

Making a Responsive UI with UI Toolkit

In this section, we are going to learn how to make the UI we created previously adapt to different screen sizes. We are going to discuss the following concepts:

- Dynamic positioning
- Dynamic scaling
- Using relative positions

Let's start by discussing how we can make the position and size of our objects to adapt the screen size.

Dynamic positioning and sizing

So far, we have used the Left and Top Position attributes to specify the X and Y position of our elements with respect to the top-left corner of the screen, and then Width and Height to define the Size. While essentially, that is all that's needed to define an object position and size, it is not very useful in all cases, especially when we need to adapt to different screen sizes.

In the example, if you need to place an object in the top-right corner of the screen, knowing its size is 100x100 pixels, and the screen size is 1920x1080 pixels, we can put Left and Right position attributes as 1820x980 pixels, and this will work... only for that specific resolution, but what happens if the user runs the game at 1280x720 pixels? The object will be outside the screen! In uGUI, we used **Anchors** to solve this issue, but we don't have them here. Luckily, we have **Right** and **Bottom** to help.

As **Left** and **Top** attributes, **Right** and **Bottom** define distances to the parent element sides (if no parent, just the entire screen. Right now, we have both in **auto**, meaning that the position will be driven by **Left** and **Right** exclusively, but interesting things can happen by changing those values, so let's use them to make our **Score** and **Bullet** labels stick to the top-right corner of the screen instead by doing the following):

1. Put the cursor in the bottom part of the UI in the **Viewport** until a white bar appears.
2. Drag that bar to resize the screen and see how it adapts (or not) to the different size.
3. Do the same on the laterals to also see how it adapts to different screen widths:

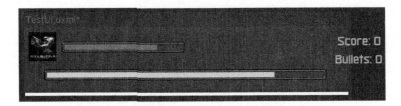

Figure 12.32 – Testing our UI under different screen sizes

4. Select the score label on the **Viewport** pane and look at **Inspector**.

5. Set the **Top** and **Right** values to 30.

6. Set the **Left** and **Bottom** values to **auto** by clicking the **px** button at the right of each attribute and selecting **auto**:

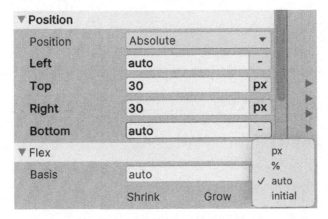

Figure 12.33 – Changing the unit type of the Position attributes to auto mode

7. Notice how the right and top golden-colored squares at the sides of the label have become filled, while the left and bottom are hollow. This means that left and bottom are in auto mode. You can also toggle **auto** mode by clicking those boxes if needed:

Figure 12.34 – Toggling auto mode of our element position attributes

8. Try changing again the size of the UI container, as we did in steps *1* and *2*, to see how our labels are always aligned to the top-right corner.

What we did with these steps was essentially make the position of the object be expressed as a distance in pixels against the Top and Right sides of the UI, or the top-right corner of the screen. We needed to set the other sides in auto mode, so they won't participate in the position calculations.

Now luckily, they aren't the only options we have to use the Position attributes. As you might imagine by now, we can start combining Left and Right and Top and Bottom if we wish. In such cases, Left and Top will take precedence in terms of defining the position, but then, what do Right and Bottom do? They define the size of the element.

For example, if we have an element with Left and Right attributes set to 100 px each and we are seeing our UI in a screen with a width of 1920 pixels, the end width of our element will be 1720 (1920 minus 100 from Left minus 100 from Right). This way, the Position attributes represent the distances of our element sides against the sides of the screen (or the parent element).

Let's see this in action by making the bottom health bar adapt to the screen width while preserving its position relative to the bottom of the screen by doing the following:

1. Select the **Bottom Health Bar** parent in **Hierarchy**. Don't select it in the **Viewport** pane as you will only be selecting the filling or the border of it.

2. Set **Left**, **Right**, and **Bottom** to 50 px.

3. Set **Top** to auto (click on the px button at the right and select auto).

4. In the **Size** section, set **Width** to **auto** also.

5. Set **Height** to 35px:

Figure 12.35 – Making the Player's Base health bar adapt to the screen width

6. Change the size of the UI to see how it adapts.

With these steps, we have defined the bar distance to the sides of the screen as 50 pixels for it to adapt to any screen width, while keeping the distance to the border and height fixed. We basically achieved the same behavior as split anchors in uGUI! Consider that we needed to set the **Width** attributes of **Size** to **auto** to let the **Left** and **Right** attributes drive the position; if you don't do that, the **Width** attributes take precedence and **Right** won't have any effect. I invite you to experiment with other combinations of px/auto.

> **Important info**
>
> Please consider the fact that the UI Builder UI preview has a bug where bottom elements are shown outside the screen, but they are actually inside. Check how the **Game** view in the main Unity Editor shows it correctly. If you don't see your UI in the **Scene** view, you can disable and enable the GameObject that renders it. It is just another bug.

One last trick we can do here is to use negative values in the **Left**, **Top**, **Right**, and **Bottom Position** attributes of the Health bar borders to make the borders slightly bigger than the container and cover the filling borders. Just set **Left**, **Top**, **Right**, and **Bottom** to -15px in this case, and remember to set both the **Size** attributes of **Width** and **Height** to auto. You might want to reduce the **Height** of the Bar container a little bit as it will now look thicker due to this change:

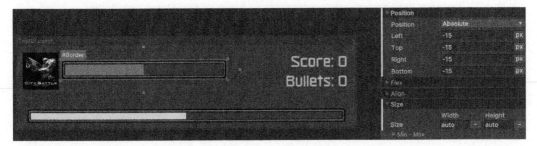

Figure 12.36 – Using negative Position attributes to cover the filling

Another mode aside from px (pixels) or auto mode is the percentage (%) mode, which allows us to represent values as percentages relative to the screen (or parent element if present) size. For example, if we set **Top** and **Bottom** to 25%, this means that our element will be vertically centered with a size of 50% of the Screen height (remember to set **Height** mode to auto here). We could achieve the same result if we set Top to 25%, **Bottom** to Auto, and **Height** to 50%. As you can see, we can achieve a clever combination of those values.

In our case, we will use percentage values in our Life Bars fillings in a way that we can express its size in percentages. We need this as later in code, we can specify the width of the bar as a percentage of the player's life (for example, a player with 25 life points and a maximum of 100 points has 25% of life). Let's try this by doing the following:

1. Select the Red filling of the Player's Health bar.

2. Set **Width** to 50% (click on px and select %).

3. You can also set **Height** to **100%** to make it adapt to the Bar container height, or also Height to **auto** instead, and set **Top** and **Bottom** to **0**:

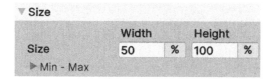

Figure 12.37 – Using percentage Sizes

4. Try changing the **Width** of the Player Health Bar Container to see how the filling changes its size proportionally to its container.

5. Do the same with the Green Filling of the Base Health Bar at the bottom.

6. Change the screen size to see how the Green Bar adapts its filling:

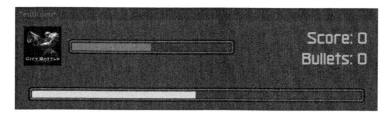

Figure 12.38 – Percentage health bars

Now, while we solved the positioning adaption to the screen size through the use of the **Left**, **Top**, **Right**, and **Bottom** properties, we still didn't solve the dynamic sizing of the elements. With sizing this time, we are referring to screens with a different number of DPI (dots per inch), so let's discuss how we can achieve that with the **Panel Settings** asset.

Dynamic Scaling

We used *1920x1080* as the UI base resolution to position and size our elements in a way that looks nice in that resolution. We also changed the UI size to see how the elements adapt their position to different screen sizes, and while that worked nicely, you can notice how the elements looked bigger or smaller while doing that.

While having a base reference resolution is good for designing our UI, we should consider the sizing on elements on different resolutions, especially in screens with high DPIs. Sometimes, you can have screens with a higher resolution, but the same physical size in centimeters. This means pixels are smaller in the ones with higher resolution, hence they have more DPIs, and so elements can be viewed smaller if not scaled properly.

In the past, we used the Canvas Scaler component of the Canvas to make the UI scale the size of its elements according to the screen resolution. We have the exact same settings here in the **Panel Settings** asset referenced in our UI Document component, so let's configure it by doing the following:

1. Look for the **Panel Settings** asset in the **Project** panel and select it. Another option would be to select the UI Document GameObject in the **Main Editor** hierarchy and click the asset referenced in the **Panel Settings** property:

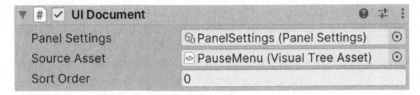

Figure 12.39 – Panel settings being referenced in the UI Document component

2. Set **Screen Match Mode** to **Match Width Or Height**.

3. Set the **Reference Resolution X** value to 1920 and **Y** to 1080.

4. Set **Match** all the way to the right, labeled **Height**:

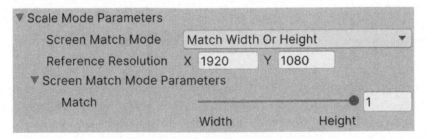

Figure 12.40 – Setting the scaling of our UI

5. Observe how changing the height of the Game panel of the Unity Editor will make the UI adapt its elements sizes accordingly (change the entire Unity Editor window height).

What we did with those changes was first to set Reference Resolution to whatever resolution we designed for our UI, in our case 1920x1080. Then we set Screen Match Mode to allow us to scale our elements according to one of the sides, Width, Height, or a combination of the two if we prefer. In our case, we chose Height, mainly because our game is targeted for PC where the screens are wide rather than tall. This means that on different screen widths, the elements will look the same size, but on different heights, the elements will be bigger or smaller.

With these settings, we can do some math to understand the values. If our screen is the same as the reference resolution (1920x1080), the element sizes will be the same as we specified in the Size of our elements in pixels, so in the case of our Player Avatar, this will be 150x150 pixels. Remember that the physical size in centimeters depends on the DPIs of the screen.

Now, imagine that we have a 4k screen, meaning a resolution of 3840x2160. As we specified that our UI matches via **Height**, we can determine that our elements will have a double size because our screen has a height that is double the reference resolution (2160 divided by 1080). Our Player Avatar will be 300x300, making the element have the same physical size on a 4k screen, double size which is achieved by double pixel density. Finally, consider an ultra-wide standard resolution of 2560×1080 (yes, very wide screens), in which case the elements will be the same size as the only change is the width, the only difference being that the elements will have more horizontal separation due to the screen size. I know these calculations can be confusing but keep experimenting with the values of the **Panel Settings** and **Game View** sizes to understand them better.

Great, now we really have the same HUD. We could start applying the concepts seen so far to do the **Options** menu, but let's take the opportunity to do it in a different way, using **Relative** positions, a way to create a flow of elements where the positions of elements depend on each other.

Using relative positions

In the HUD of our game, each element requires its own Position and Size, and the different element positions can be resized and repositioned without affecting others. We might observe the case of the Player Health Bar and the Avatar, but the changes would be trivial in this case. There are other cases where this is not that trivial, as in the cases of a **List** of elements (for example, a list of matches to join in a multiplayer game) that needs to adapt vertically or horizontally, and here is where Relative Positions helps us.

Relative Positions allow us to make the positions of the elements relative to each other, in such a way that the position of one element will depend on the position of the previous one, and that one to its previous, and so on, forming a chain or Flow. This works like Vertical and Horizontal Layouts on uGUI. In our case, we will make the **Pause** label and the **Options** and **Exit** buttons of our options menu vertically aligned and centered along its parent using those:

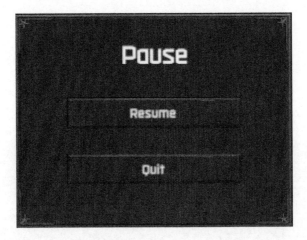

Figure 12.41 – Recap of what the options menu looks like

Let's start creating the menu by doing the following:

1. Create a new UI Document (**Plus button of Project View | UI Tookit | UI Document**) and call it `Options Menu`. We can work on the previous UI Document, but let's keep those pieces of UI separate for the purpose of easy activation and deactivation, and general asset organizing.

2. Select the root object (**OptionsMenu.uxml** in **Hierarchy**) and set the **Width** and **Height Inspector** properties to 1920x1080 pixels.

3. Create a new GameObject with the UI Document component (**GameObject | UI Toolkit | UI Document**) and drag the asset for this object to render it (as we did with the HUD created earlier in the chapter).

4. Drag a new **Visual Element** to **Hierarchy** or **Viewport** and call it `Container` (the name property in the **Inspector** in **UI Builder**).

5. Set the **Left**, **Right**, **Top**, and **Right Position** attributes to **0px**.

6. Set **Position** to **Absolute**.

7. Set **Width** and **Height** to **auto**. This will make the container fit the entire screen.

8. Drag a new **Visual Element** as a child of the container and call it **Background**.

9. Leave **Position** set to **Relative** this time.

10. Set the **Width** and **Height** of **Size** to **500px**.

11. Set **Background Image** of the **Background** object to use the same background Sprite used in the previous chapter.

12. Select the container.

13. In the **Inspector**, set **Align** Items to **center** (third button).

14. Set **Justify Content** to **Center** (second button):

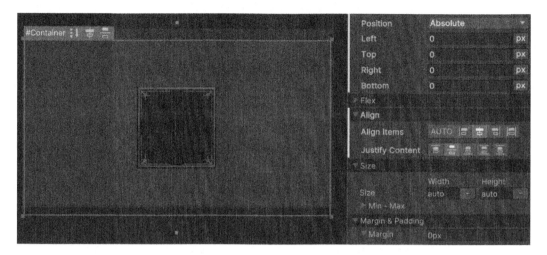

Figure 12.42 – Preparing the UI background to host elements inside

15. Change the size of the UI using the white bars at the sides to see how the background is always centered.

Even if we have only one element, we can start seeing how the relative positions work. First, we created an empty object that will always adapt to the screen size, allowing us to make the children's elements depend on the full screen size. Then we created an image element with a fixed size, but with Relative position, meaning its position will be calculated by the parent container. Finally, we told the container to make its child objects be aligned with its horizontal and vertical center, so the background immediately became centered irrespective of the screen size. When working with Absolute positions, the Align properties didn't work, so this is one of the first benefits of Absolute positioning.

But Absolute positioning becomes more powerful with multiple elements, so let's add the Label and Buttons to our Background element to explore this concept further by doing the following:

1. From the **Library** pane at the bottom-left of **UI Builder**, drag a **Label** and two **Button** elements inside the Background in **Hierarchy**:

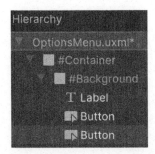

Figure 12.43 – Adding elements inside the menu background

2. Observe how, by default, the elements became vertically aligned one on top of the other due to the Relative position default settings:

Figure 12.44 – Automatic relative vertical positioning

3. Select the **Background** element and set **Justify Content** to **space-around** (fifth button). This will spread the elements along the background.

4. Set **Align Items** to **center** (third option) to center the elements horizontally:

Figure 12.45 – Automatic relative vertical positioning

> **Important info**
>
> There is a similar mode for **Justify Content** called "space-between"
> (fourth button in **Justify Content**) that will also spread the elements along
> the vertical axis but won't leave space on top of the first element nor the bottom
> of the last one. Also, Align Items have an option called "stretch" (fifth option)
> that, like center, will center elements horizontally, but also stretch them instead
> of respecting each element's width. I recommend experimenting with the
> different aligning modes to discover all opportunities.

5. Set the **Font** and **Size** attributes of the **Text** label to whatever seems to fit. In my case, I used the imported font and a size of 60px. Remember to also set **Text** to Pause.

6. Set the Buttons **Background Image** to use the same used for the button in the previous chapter.

7. Set **Font**, **Size**, and **Color** of the **Text** buttons to whatever seems appropriate to you; in my case, 50 and a gray color.

8. In the **Margin and Padding** section, set **Padding** to have some spacing between the text and the borders of the button. In my case, **30px** did the trick:

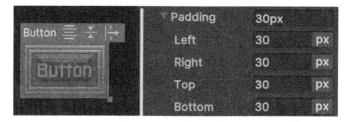

Figure 12.46 – Adding inner padding to the button contents (the text in this case)

9. Also set **Top** and **Bottom Padding** of the **Background** to allow some space between the borders of the window and its elements. In my case, the value is **40px** each:

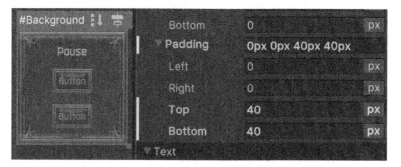

Figure 12.47 – Automatic padding to the whole menu

As you can see, we changed different settings to set the size of the elements dynamically, such as font sizes and paddings, and the Relative system, along with the Align settings, took the role of determining the position of the elements automatically. We could rearrange the order of the elements, dragging them to the Hierarchy, and they will be accommodated automatically. We could have also set the size of the elements with the **Size** property, and we can also apply some offsets if desired using the Position properties, but I will encourage you to try how these properties behave in Relative mode on your own.

One last setting I want you to explore is the **Direction** attribute of the **Flex** section. As you can imagine, this will determine the orientation that the elements will follow, vertical from top to bottom or bottom to top, and horizontally from left to right or right to left. For example, we could set **Direction** from left to right (third button) and make the background wider to have a horizontal options menu if you so wish:

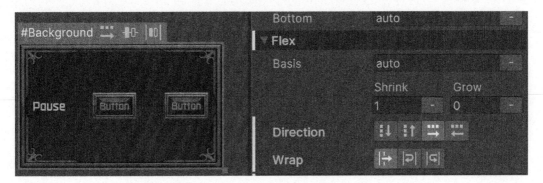

Figure 12.48 – Changing to a vertical orientation of elements

As a side note, you might notice that the images for the background and buttons will look bigger than the options menu done in the previous chapter. That's because the Pixels per Unit setting, which we changed on the Texture assets to control the scaling of the textures, won't take effect in UI Toolkit. You will need to manually change the texture file size in any Image Editor to have its proper size. The best practice here would be to always create the images with a size that will look fine in our maximum supported resolution. Usually, this is 1920x1080 on a PC, but consider the fact that 4k resolutions are becoming more popular by the day.

Summary

In this chapter, we had an introduction to the key concepts of UI Toolkit, and how to create UI Documents and Stylesheets. Regarding UI Documents, we learned how to create different elements such as images, text, and buttons, and how to position and size them using different methods, such as Absolute and Relative positioning, and pixel or percentage units. Also, we saw how to make the UI adapt to different sizes using different combinations of Position attributes. Finally, we learned how to use USS Stylesheets to share styles between different elements to easily manage our whole UI skinning.

Essentially, we learned again how to make UIs with a different system. Again, please consider the fact that this system is still in the experimental phase, and so presently, it is not recommended for real production projects. We used all these concepts to recreate the same UI created in *Chapter 11, User Interface Design*.

In the next chapter, we are going to see how to add Animations to our game to make our character move. We will also see how to create cut-scenes and dynamic cameras.

13
Creating Animations with Animator, Cinemachine, and Timeline

Regarding our game's current status, we mostly have a static Scene, but that's without considering the Shader and particle animations. In the next chapter, when we add scripting to our game, everything will start to move according to the behavior we want. But sometimes, we need to move objects in a predetermined way, such as with cutscenes, or specific characters animations, such as jumping, running, and so on. The idea of this chapter is to go over several Unity animation systems and create all the possible object movements we can get without scripting.

In this chapter, we will cover the following topics:

- Using Skinning Animations with Animator
- Creating dynamic cameras with Cinemachine
- Creating cutscenes with Timeline

By the end of this chapter, you will be able to create cutscenes to tell the history of your game or highlight specific areas of your level, as well as create dynamic cameras that are capable of giving us an accurate look at your game, regardless of the situation.

Using Skinning Animations with Animator

So far, we have used what are called static meshes, which are solid three-dimensional models that are not supposed to bend or animate in any way (aside from moving separately, like the doors of a car). We also have another kind of mesh, called skinned meshes, which are meshes that can be bent based on a skeleton, which means they can emulate the muscle movements of the human body. We are going to explore how to integrate animated humanoid characters into our project to create the enemy and player movements.

In this section, we will examine the following skeletal mesh concepts:

- Understanding skinning
- Importing skinned meshes
- Integration using Animator Controllers

First, we are going to explore the concept of skinning and how it allows you to animate characters. Then, we are going to bring animated meshes into our project so that we can apply animations to them. Let's start by discussing how to bring skeletal animations into our project.

Understanding skinning

To get an animated mesh, we need to have four pieces, starting with the mesh itself and the model that will be animated, which is created in the same way as any other mesh. Then, we need the skeleton, which is a set of bones that will match the desired mesh topology, such as the arms, fingers, feet, and so on. In *Figure 13.1*, you can see an example of a set of bones aligned with our target mesh. You will notice that these kinds of meshes are usually modeled with the *T* pose, which will facilitate the animation process:

Figure 13.1 – A ninja mesh with a skeleton matching its default pose

Once the artist has created the model and its bones, the next step is to do the skinning, which is the act of associating every vertex of the model with one or more bones. In this way, when you move a bone, the associated vertexes will move with it. This is done in this way because it is easier to animate a reduced number of bones instead of every single vertex of the model. In the following screenshot, you can see the triangles of a mesh being painted according to the color of the bone that affects it, as a way to visualize the influence of the bones. You will notice blending between colors, which means that those vertexes are affected differently by different bones to allow the vertexes near an articulation point to bend nicely. The following screenshot illustrates an example of a two-dimensional mesh being used for two-dimensional games, but the concept is the same:

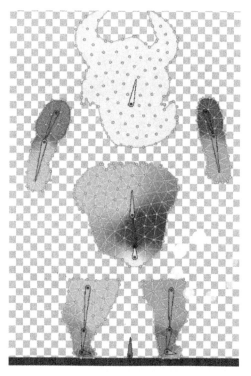

Figure 13.2 – A visual of Mesh skinning weights, represented as colors

Finally, the last piece you need is the actual animation, which will simply consist of a blend of the different poses of the meshes. The artist will create keyframes in an animation, determining which pose the model needs to have at different moments, and then the animation system will simply interpolate between them. Basically, the artist will animate the bones, and the skinning system will apply this animation to the whole mesh. You can have one or several animations, which you will later switch between based on the animation that you want to match the character's motion (such as idle, walking, falling, and so on).

To get the four parts, we need to get the proper assets containing them. The usual format in this scenario is **Filmbox (FBX)**, which is what we have used so far to import 3D models. This format can contain every piece we need – the model, the skeleton with the skinning, and the animations – but usually, we will split the parts into several files to reutilize the pieces.

Imagine a city simulator game where we have several citizen's meshes with different aspects and all of them must be animated. If we have a single FBX per citizen containing the mesh, the skinning, and the animation, it will cause each model to have its own animation, or at least a clone of the same one, repeating them. When we need to change that animation, we will need to update all the citizen's meshes, which is a time-consuming process. Instead of this, we can have one FBX per citizen, containing the mesh and the bones with the proper skinning based on that mesh, as well as a separate FBX for each animation, containing the same bones that all the citizens have with the proper animation, but without the mesh. This will allow us to mix and match the citizen FBX with the animation's FBX files. You may be wondering why both the model FBX and the animation FBX must have this mesh. This is because they need to match to make both files compatible. In the following screenshot, you can see how the files should look:

Figure 13.3 – The Animations and Model FBX files of the package we will use in our project

Also, it is worth mentioning a concept called retargeting. As we mentioned previously, to mix a model and an animation file, we need them to have the same bone structure, which means the same number of bones, hierarchy, and names. Sometimes, this is not possible, especially when we mix custom models that have been created by our artist with external animation files that you can record from an actor using motion capture techniques, or just by buying a Mocap library. In such cases, you will likely encounter different bone structures between the one in the Mocap library and your character model, so here is where retargeting kicks in. This technique allows Unity to create a generic mapping between two different humanoid-only bones structures to make them compatible. We will learn how to enable this feature shortly.

Now that we understand the basics behind skinned meshes, let's learn how to get the model's assets with bones and animations.

Importing skeletal animations

Let's start with how to import some animated models from the Asset Store, under the **3D | Characters | Humanoids** section. You can also use external sites, such as Mixamo, to download them. But for now, I will stick with the Asset Store as you will have less trouble making the assets work. In my case, I have downloaded a package, as shown in the following screenshot, that contains both Models and Animations:

VICX GAMES
SciFi Robots
★ ★ ★ ★ ☆ (14)
FREE

Figure 13.4 – Soldier models for our game

Note that sometimes, you will need to download them separately because some assets will be model- or animation-only. Also, note that the packages used in this book might not be available at the time you're reading this; in that case, you can either look for another package with similar assets (characters and animations, in this case) or download the project files from this book's GitHub repository and copy the required files from there.

In my package, I can find the animation's FBX files in the `Animations` folder and the single model FBX file in `Model`. Remember that sometimes, you won't have them separated like this, and the animations may be located in the same FBX as the model, if any animations are present at all. Now that we have the required files, let's discuss how to configure them properly.

Let's start by selecting the **Model** file and checking the **Rig** tab. Within this tab, you will find a setting called **Animation Type**, as shown in the following screenshot:

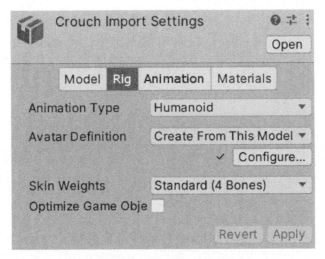

Figure 13.5 – The Rig properties

This property contains the following options:

- **None**: A mode for non-animated models; every static mesh in your game will use this mode.

- **Legacy**: The mode to be used in old Unity Projects and models; do not use this in new projects.

- **Generic**: A new animation system that can be used in all kinds of models but is commonly used in non-humanoid models, such as horses, octopuses, and so on. If you use this mode, both the model and animation FBX files must have the same bone names and structure, thereby reducing the possibility of combining animations from external sources.

- **Humanoid**: These are new animation systems designed to be used in humanoid models. It enables features such as retargeting and **Inverse Kinematics** (**IK**). This allows you to combine models with different bones than the animation because Unity will create a mapping between those structures and a generic one, called the avatar. Take into account that sometimes, automatic mapping can fail, which means you will need to correct it manually; so, if your generic model has everything you need, I recommend that you stick with the **Generic** model if that's the default configuration of the FBX.

In my case, the FBX files in my package have the modes set to **Humanoid**, so that's good, but remember, only switch to other modes if it is absolutely necessary (for example, if you need to combine different models and animations). Now that we have discussed the **Rig** settings, let's talk about the **Animation** settings.

To do this, select any animation FBX file and look for the **Animation** section of the **Inspector** window. You will find several settings, such as the **Import Animation** checkbox, which must be marked if the file contains an animation (not the model files), and the **Clips** list, where you will find all the animations in the file. In the following screenshot, you can see the **Clips** list for one of our animation files:

Clips	Start	End
HumanoidCrouchIdle	264.0	319.0
HumanoidCrouchWalk	105.0	159.0
HumanoidCrouchWalkRight	2193.0	2245.0
HumanoidCrouchWalkLeft	1542.0	1610.0
HumanoidCrouchTurnRight	1932.0	1976.0
HumanoidCrouchTurnLeft	1932.0	1976.0
HumanoidCrouchWalkRightI	1542.0	1610.0
	+	−

Figure 13.6 – A Clips list in the Animation section

An FBX file with animations usually contains a single large animation track, which can contain one or several animations. Either way, by default, Unity will create a single animation based on that track, but if that track contains several animations, you will need to split them manually. In our case, our FBX contains several animations already split by the package creator, but to learn how to do a manual split, you must perform the following steps:

1. From the **Clips** list, select any animation that you want to recreate; in my case, I will choose `HumanoidCrouchIdle`.

2. Take a look at the **Start** and **End** values below the animation timeline and remember them; we will use them to recreate this clip:

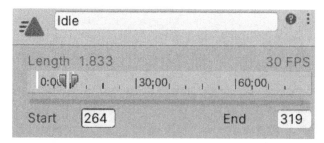

Figure 13.7 – The Clip's settings

3. Click on the minus button (-) on the bottom-right part of the **Clips** list to delete the selected clip.

4. Use the plus (+) button to create a new clip and select it.

5. Rename it to something similar to the original using the Take 001 input field. In my case, I will name it Idle.

6. Set the **End** and **Start** properties with the values we needed to remember in *step 2*. In my case, I have 319 for **End** and 264 for **Start**. This information usually comes from the artist, but you can just try the number that works best for you or simply drag the blue markers in the timeline on top of these properties.

7. Preview the clip by clicking on the bar that specifies the title of your animation (**HumanoidIdle**, in my case) at the very bottom of the **Inspector** window and click on the **Play** button. You will see the default Unity model, but you can view your own by dragging the model file to the preview window; it is important to check whether our models have been configured properly. If the animation does not play, you will need to check whether the **Animation Type** setting matches the animation file:

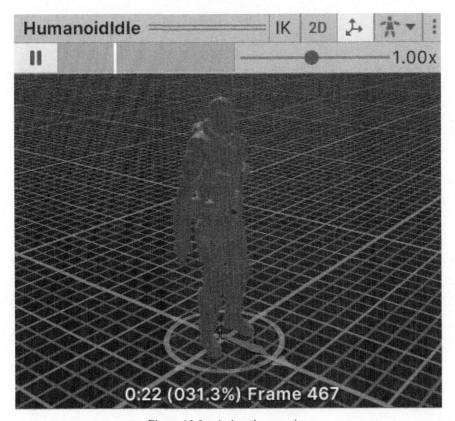

Figure 13.8 – Animation preview

8. Open the animation file, click on the down arrow, and check the sub-assets. You will see that here, there is a file for your animation, alongside the other animations in the clip list, which contains the cut clips. In a moment, we will play them. In the following screenshot, you can see the animations in our `.fbx` file:

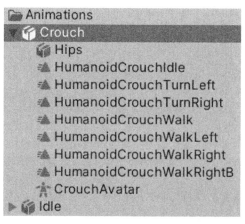

Figure 13.9 – Generated animation clips

Now that we have covered the basic configuration, let's learn how to integrate them.

Integration using Animation Controllers

When adding animations to our characters, we need to think about the flow of the animations, which means thinking about which animations must be played, when each animation must be active, and how transitions between animations should happen. In previous Unity versions, you needed to code that manually, generating complicated scripts of C# code to handle complex scenarios; but now, we have Animation Controllers.

Animation Controllers are state machine-based assets where we can diagram the transition logic between animations with a visual editor called **Animator**. The idea is that each animation is a state and that our model will have several of them. Only one state can be active at a time, so we need to create transitions to change them, which will have conditions that must be met to trigger the transition process. Conditions are comparisons of data about the character to be animated, such as its velocity, whether it's shooting or crouched, and so on.

So, basically, an Animation Controller or state machine is a set of animations with transition rules that will dictate which animation should be active. Let's create a simple Animation Controller by doing the following:

1. Click the + button under the **Project** view, click on **Animator Controller**, and call it Player. Remember to locate your asset within a folder for organization purposes; I will call mine Animators.

2. Double-click on the asset to open the **Animator** window. Don't confuse this window with the **Animation** window; the **Animation** window does something different.

3. Drag the **Idle** animation clip of your character into the **Animator** window. This will create a box in the Controller representing the animation that will be connected to the entry point of the Controller, indicating that the animation will be the default one because it is the first one that we dragged. If you don't have an **Idle** animation, I encourage you to find one. We will need at least one **Idle** animation and one walking/running animation clip:

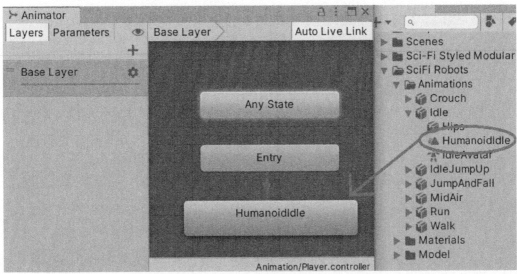

Figure 13.10 – Dragging an animation clip from an FBX asset into an Animator Controller

4. Drag the running animation in the same way.

5. Right-click on the **Idle** animation, select **Make Transition**, and left-click on the **Run** animation. This will create a transition between **Idle** and **Run**.

6. Create another transition from **Run** to **Idle** in the same way:

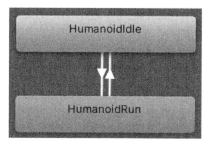

Figure 13.11 – Transitions between two animations

Transitions must have conditions to prevent animations from swapping constantly, but to create conditions, we need data to make comparisons. We will add properties to our Controller, which will represent the data that's used by the transitions. Later, in *Part 3*, we will set that data so that it matches the current state of our object. But for now, let's create the data and test how the Controller reacts with different values. In order to create conditions based on properties, do the following:

1. Click on the **Parameters** tab in the top-left part of the **Animator** window. If you don't see it, click on the crossed-eye button to display the tabs.

2. Click on the + button and select **Float** to create a number that will represent the velocity of our character, naming it `Velocity`. If you missed the renaming part, just left-click on the variable and rename it:

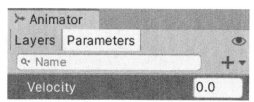

Figure 13.12 – The Parameters tab with a float Velocity property

3. Click on the **Idle** to **Run** transition (the white line with an arrow) and look at the **Conditions** property in the **Inspector** window.

4. Click on the + button at the bottom of the list, which will create a condition that will rule the transition. The default setting will take the first parameter of our animator (in this case, it is **Velocity**) and will set the default comparer, in this case, **Greater**, to a value of 0. This tells us that the transition will execute from **Idle** to **Run** if **Idle** is the current animation and the velocity of the Player is greater than 0. I recommend that you set a slightly higher value, such as 0.01, to prevent any float rounding errors (a common CPU issue). Also, remember that the actual value of **Velocity** needs to be set manually via scripting, which we will do in *Part 3*:

Figure 13.13 – Condition to check whether Velocity is greater than 0.01

5. Do the same to the **Run** to **Idle** transition, but this time, change **Greater** to **Less** and set the value to 0.01:

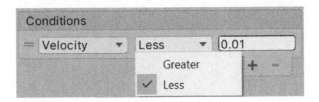

Figure 13.14 – Condition to check whether a value is less than 0.01

Now that we have our first Animator Controller set up, it's time to apply it to an object. To do that, we will need a series of components. First, when we have an animated character, rather than using a regular Mesh Renderer, we should use **Skinned Mesh Renderer**. If you drag the model of the character to the scene and explore its children, you will see a component, as shown here:

Figure 13.15 – The Skinned Mesh Renderer component

This component will be in charge of applying the bones' movements to the mesh. If you search the children of the model, you will find some bones; you can try rotating, moving, and scaling them to see their effects, as shown in the following screenshot. Consider the fact that your bone hierarchy might be different from mine if you downloaded another package from the Asset Store:

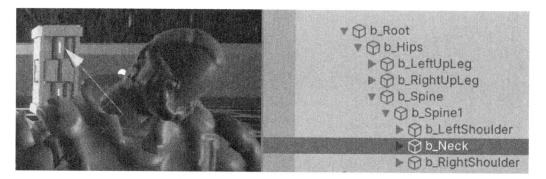

Figure 13.16 – Rotating the neckbone

The other component that we need is **Animator**, which is automatically added to skinned meshes as a root GameObject. This component will be in charge of applying the state machine that we created in the Animation Controller if the animation FBX files have been configured properly, as we mentioned earlier. To apply the Animator Controller, do the following:

1. Drag the model of the character into the Scene, if it's not already there.
2. Select it and locate the **Animator** component in the root GameObject.
3. Click on the circle to the right of the **Controller** property and select the **Player** controller we created earlier. You can also just drag it from the **Project** window.
4. Make sure that the **Avatar** property is set to the avatar inside the FBX model; this will tell the animator that we will be using that skeleton. You can identify the avatar asset by its icon of a person, as shown in the following screenshot. Usually, this property is set automatically when you drag the FBX model into the Scene:

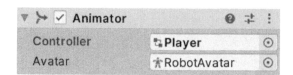

Figure 13.17 – Animator using the Player controller and RobotAvatar

5. Set the **Camera** GameObject's position so that it's looking at the player and play the game; you will see the character executing its **Idle** animation.

6. Without stopping the game, open the **Animator Controller** asset again by double-clicking it and selecting the character in the **Hierarchy** window. By doing this, you should see the current state of the animation being played by that character, using a bar to represent the current part of the animation:

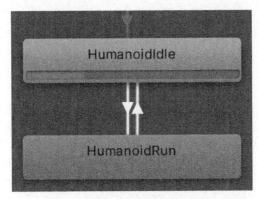

Figure 13.18 – The Animator Controller in Play mode while an object is selected, showing the current animation and its progress

7. Using the **Animator** window, change the value of **Velocity** to 1.0 and see how the transition is executed:

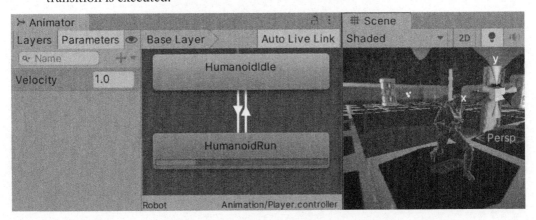

Figure 13.19 – Setting the velocity of the Controller to trigger a transition

Depending on how the **Run** animation was set, your character might start to move. This is caused by the root motion, a feature that will move the character based on the animation movement. Sometimes, this is useful, but since we will fully move our character using scripting, we want that feature to be turned off. You can do that by unchecking the **Apply Root Motion** checkbox in the **Animator** component of the **Character** object:

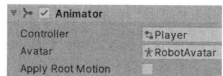

Figure 13.20 – Disabling the Apply Root Motion checkbox

8. You will also notice a delay between changing the **Velocity** value and the start of the animation's transition. That's because, by default, Unity will wait for the original animation to end before executing a transition, but in this scenario, we don't want that. We need the transition to start immediately. To do this, select each transition of the Controller and, in the **Inspector** window, uncheck the **Has Exit Time** checkbox:

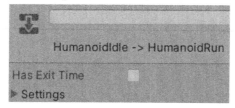

Figure 13.21 – Disabling the Has Exit Time checkbox to execute the transition immediately

You can start dragging other animations into the Controller and create complex animation logic, such as adding jump, fall, or crouched animations. I invite you to try other parameter types, such as Booleans, that use checkboxes instead of numbers. Also, as you develop your game further, your Controller will grow in terms of how many animations it has. To manage this, there are other features worth researching, such as Blend Trees and sub-state machines, but that's beyond the scope of this book.

In this section, we learned how to integrate animation clips into our character through Animator Controllers. We added all the necessary animations and created the necessary transitions between them to react to the game's circumstances, such as the character velocity changes. Now that we understand the basics of character animations in Unity, let's discuss how to create dynamic camera animations that will follow our player.

Creating dynamic cameras with Cinemachine

Cameras are a very important topic in video games. They allow the player to see their surroundings to make decisions based on what they see. The game designer usually defines how they behave to get the exact gameplay experience they want, and that's no easy task. A lot of behaviors must be layered to get the exact feeling. Also, for cutscenes, it is important to control the path that the camera will be traversing throughout, as well as where the camera is looking, to focus the action during those constantly moving scenes.

In this chapter, we will use the `Cinemachine` package to create both of the dynamic cameras that will follow the player's movements, which we will code in *Part 3*, as well as the cameras to be used during cutscenes.

In this section, we will examine the following Cinemachine concepts:

- Creating camera behaviors
- Creating dolly tracks

Let's start by discussing how to create a Cinemachine controlled camera and configure behaviors in it.

Creating camera behaviors

Cinemachine is a collection of different behaviors that can be used in the camera that, when properly combined, can generate all kinds of common camera types in video games, including following the player from behind, first-person cameras, top-down cameras, and so on. To use these behaviors, we need to understand the concept of brain and virtual cameras.

In Cinemachine, we will only keep one main camera, as we have done so far, and that camera will be controlled by virtual cameras, separated GameObjects that have the previously mentioned behaviors. We can have several virtual cameras and swap between them at will, but the active virtual camera will be the only one that will control our main camera. This is useful for switching cameras at different points of the game, such as switching between our player's first-person camera. To control the main camera with the virtual cameras, it must have a **Brain** component.

To start using Cinemachine, first, we need to install it from **Package Manager**, as we did previously with our other packages. If you don't remember how to do this, just do the following:

1. Go to **Window | Package Manager**.

2. Ensure that the **Packages** option in the top-left part of the window is set to **Unity Registry**:

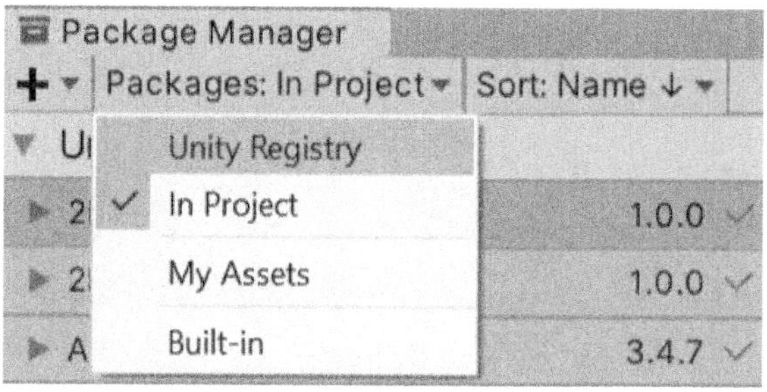

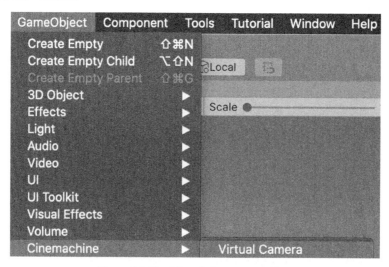

Figure 13.22 – The Packages filter mode

3. Wait a moment for the left panel to populate all the packages from the servers (an internet connection is required).

4. Look for the **Cinemachine** package from the list and select it. At the time of writing this book, the latest available version is 2.7.4, but you can use newer versions if you prefer. Ensure that the steps work as expected; if not, you can always install the closest version to ours.

5. Click the **Install** button in the bottom-right corner of the screen.

Let's start by creating a virtual camera to follow the character we animated previously, which will be our player hero. Follow these steps:

1. Click **GameObject | Cinemachine | Virtual Camera**. This will create a new object called CM vcam1:

Figure 13.23 – Virtual Camera creation

2. If you select the main camera from the **Hierarchy** window, you will also notice that a `CinemachineBrain` component has been automatically added to it, making our main camera follow the virtual camera. Try to move the created virtual camera, and you will see how the main camera follows it:

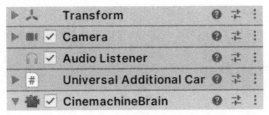

Figure 13.24 – The CinemachineBrain component

3. Select the virtual camera and drag the character to the **Follow** and **Look At** properties of the **Cinemachine** virtual camera component. This will make the movement and looking behaviors use that object to do their jobs:

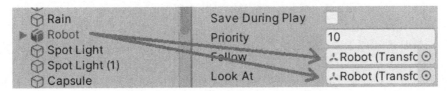

Figure 13.25 – Setting the target of our camera

4. You can see how the **Body** property of the virtual camera is set to **Transposer**, which will move the camera relative to the target that was set with the **Follow** property – in our case, the character. You can open the **Body** options (arrow to its left) and change the **Follow Offset** property and set it to the desired distance you want the camera to be from the target. In my case, I used the 0, 3, and -3 values:

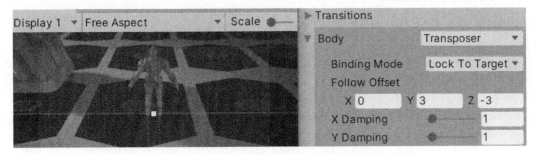

Figure 13.26 – The camera following the character from behind

5. The preceding screenshot shows the **Game** view; you can see a small, yellow rectangle indicating the target position to look at the character, and it's currently pointing at the pivot of the character – its feet. Here, we can apply an offset to the **Tracked Object Offset** property of the **Aim** section of the virtual camera. In my case, values of 0, 1.5, and 0 worked well to make the camera look at the chest instead:

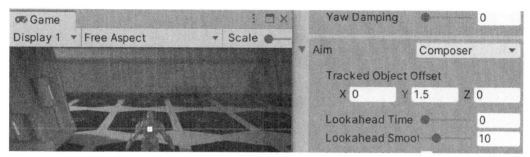

Figure 13.27 – Changing the Aim offset

As you can see, using Cinemachine is pretty simple, and in our case, the default settings were mostly enough for the kind of behavior we needed. However, if you explore the other **Body** and **Aim** modes, you will find that you can create any type of camera for any type of game. We won't cover the other modes in this book, but I strongly recommend that you look at the documentation for Cinemachine to check what the other modes do. To open the documentation, follow these steps:

1. Open **Package Manager** by going to **Window | Package Manger**.

2. Find **Cinemachine** in the left-hand side list. Wait a moment if it doesn't show up. Remember that you need an internet connection for it to work.

3. Once **Cinemachine** is selected, scroll down the right panel until you see the **View documentation** link in blue. Click on it:

Figure 13.28 – The Cinemachine documentation link

4. You can explore the documentation using the navigation menu on the left:

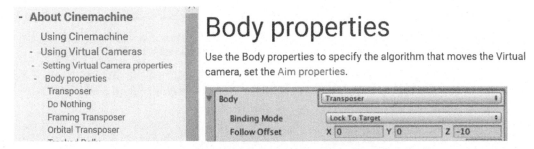

Figure 13.29 – The Cinemachine documentation

As you did with Cinemachine, you can find other packages' documentation in the same way. Now that we have achieved the basic camera behavior that we need, let's explore how we can use Cinemachine to create a camera for our introduction cutscene.

Creating dolly tracks

When the player starts the level, we want a little cutscene to play, with the camera panning over our scene and the base before the player enters the battle. This will require the camera to follow a fixed path, and that's exactly what Cinemachine's dolly camera does. It creates a path where we can attach a virtual camera so that it will follow it. We can set Cinemachine to move automatically through the track or follow a target to the closest point of the track; in our case, we will use the first option.

To create a dolly camera, follow these steps:

1. Let's start by creating the Track with a Cart, which is a little object that will move along the track. This will be the target that will follow the camera. To do this, click on **GameObject | Cinemachine | Dolly Track with Cart**:

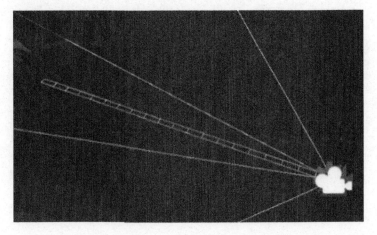

Figure 13.30 – A dolly camera with a default straight path

2. If you select the `DollyTrack1` object, you will see two circles with the numbers 0 and 1 in the **Scene** view. These are the control points of the track. Select one of them and move it as you move other objects; that is, using the arrows of the translation gizmo.

3. You can create more control points by clicking the + button at the bottom of the **Waypoints** list of the `CinemachineSmoothPath` component of the `DollyTrack1` object:

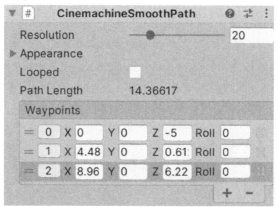

Figure 13.31 – Adding a path control point

4. Create as many waypoints as you need to create a path that will traverse the areas you want the camera to oversee in the introduction cutscene. Remember, you can move the waypoints by clicking on them and using the translation gizmo:

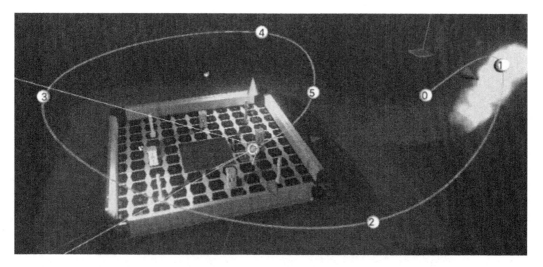

Figure 13.32 – A dolly track for our scene. It ends right behind the character

5. Create a new virtual camera. If you go to the **Game** view after creating it, you will notice that the character camera will be active. To test how the new camera looks, select it and click on the **Solo** button in the **Inspector** window:

Figure 13.33 – The Solo button, for temporarily enabling this virtual camera while editing

6. This time, set the **Follow** target to the `DollyCart1` object that we previously created with the track.

7. Set **Follow Offset** to 0, 0, and 0 to keep the camera in the same position as the cart.

8. Set **Aim** to **Same As Follow Target** to make the camera look in the same direction as the cart, which will follow the track's curves:

Figure 13.34 – Configuration to make the virtual camera follow the dolly track

9. Select the **DollyCart1** object and change its **Position** value to see how the cart moves along the track. Do this while the **Game** window is focused and **CM vcam2** is in solo mode to see how the camera will look:

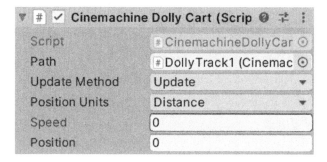

Figure 13.35 – The Cinemachine Dolly Cart component

With the dolly track set, we can create our cutscene using **Timeline** to sequence it.

Creating cutscenes with Timeline

We have our intro camera, but that's not enough to create a cutscene. A proper cutscene is a sequence of actions happening at the exact moment that they should happen, coordinating several objects to act as intended. We can have actions such as enabling and disabling objects, switching cameras, playing sounds, moving objects, and so on. To do this, Unity offers **Timeline**, which is an action sequencer that coordinates those kinds of cutscenes. We will use **Timeline** to create an intro cutscene for our scene, showing the level before starting the game.

In this section, we will examine the following Timeline concepts:

*   Creating animation clips

*   Sequencing our intro cutscene

We are going to learn how to create our own animation clips in Unity to animate our GameObjects, and then place them inside a cutscene to coordinate their activation using the Timeline sequencer tool. Let's start by creating a camera animation to use later in Timeline.

Creating animation clips

This is not a Timeline-specific feature, but rather a Unity feature that works great with Timeline. When we downloaded the character, it came with animation clips that were created using external software, but you can create custom animation clips using Unity's **Animation** window. Don't confuse it with the **Animator** window, which allows us to create animation transitions that react to the game situation. This is useful for creating small object-specific animations that you will coordinate later in Timeline with other objects' animations.

These animations can control any value of an object's component properties, such as its positions, colors, and so on. In our case, we want to animate the dolly track's **Position** property to make it go from start to finish in a given time. To do this, do the following:

1. Select the DollyCart1 object.

2. Open the **Animation** (not **Animator**) window by going to **Window | Animation | Animation**.

3. Click on the **Create** button at the center of the **Animation** window. Remember to do this while the dolly cart (not track) is selected:

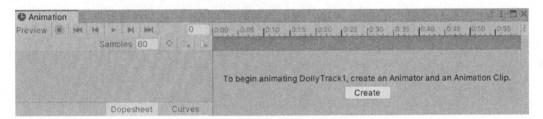

Figure 13.36 – Creating a custom animation clip

4. After doing this, you will be prompted to save the animation clip somewhere. I recommend that you create an Animations folder in the project (inside the Assets folder) and call it IntroDollyTrack.

If you pay attention, you will see that the dolly cart now has an **Animator** component with an Animator Controller inside it, which contains the animation we just created. As with any animation clip, you need to apply it to your object with an Animator Controller; custom animations are no exception. So, the **Animation** window created them for you.

Animating in this window consists of specifying the value of its properties at given moments. In our case, we want **Position** to have a value of 0 at the beginning of the animation, in the second 0 at the timeline, and have a value of 240 at the end of the animation, in second 5. I chose 240 because that's the last possible position in my cart, but that depends on the length of your dolly track. Just test which is the last possible position in yours. Also, I chose second 5 because that's what I feel is the correct length for the animation, but feel free to change it as you wish. Now, whatever happens between the animation's 0 and 5 seconds is an interpolation of the 0 and 240 values, meaning that in 2.5 seconds, the value of **Position** will be 120. Animating always consists of interpolating different states of our object at different moments.

To do this, follow these steps:

1. In the **Animation** window, click on the record button (the red circle in the top-left section). This will make Unity detect any changes in our object and save them to the animation. Remember to do this while you have selected the dolly cart.

2. Set the **Position** setting of the dolly cart to 1 and then 0. Changing this to any value and then to 0 again will create a keyframe, which is a point in the animation that says that at 0 seconds, we want the **Position** value to be 0. However, we need to set it to any other value first if the value is already at 0. You will notice that the **Position** property has been added to the animation:

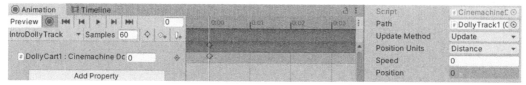

Figure 13.37 – The animation in Record mode after changing the Position value to 0

3. Using the mouse scroll wheel, zoom out the timeline to the right of the **Animation** window until you see 5 seconds in the top bar:

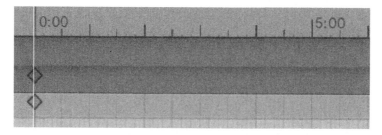

Figure 13.38 – The timeline of the Animation window showing 5 seconds

4. Click on the 5 seconds label in the top bar of the timeline to position the playback header at that moment. This will locate the next change we make at that moment.

5. Set the **Position** value of the dolly track to the highest value you can get; in my case, this is 240. Remember to have the **Animation** window in **Record** mode:

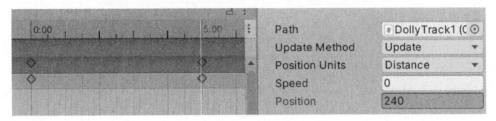

Figure 13.39 – Creating a keyframe with a value of 240, 5 seconds into the animation

6. Hit the play button in the top-left section of the **Animation** window to see the animation playing. Remember to view it in the **Game** view and while CM vcam2 is in solo mode.

Now, if we hit play, the animation will start playing, but that's something we don't want. In this scenario, the idea is to give control of the cutscene to the cutscene system, Timeline, because this animation won't be the only thing that needs to be sequenced in our cutscene. One way to prevent the **Animator** component from automatically playing the animation we created is to create an empty animation state in the Controller, and then set it as the default state. To do this, follow these steps:

1. Search for the Animator Controller that we created when we created the animation and open it. If you can't find it, just select the dolly cart and double-click on the **Controller** property of the **Animator** component of our GameObject to open the asset.

2. Right-click on an empty state in the Controller and select **Create State | Empty**. This will create a new state in the state machine as if we had created a new animation, but it is empty this time:

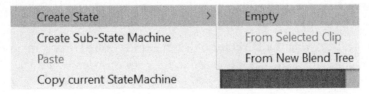

Figure 13.40 – Creating an empty state in the Animator Controller

3. Right-click on **New State** and click on **Set as Layer Default State**. The state should become orange:

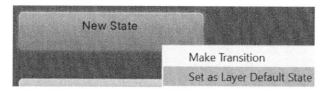

Figure 13.41 – Changing the default animation of the Controller to an empty state

4. Now, if you hit play, no animation will play as the default state of our dolly cart is empty.

Now that we have created our camera animation, let's start creating a cutscene that switches from the intro cutscene camera to the player camera by using Timeline.

Sequencing our intro cutscene

Timeline is already installed in your project, but if you go to the Package Manager window of Timeline, you may see an **Update** button so that you can get the latest version if you need some of the new features. In our case, we will keep the default version that's included in our project (1.5.2, at the time of writing this book).

The first thing we will do is create a cutscene asset and an object in the scene that's responsible for playing it. To do this, follow these steps:

1. Create an empty GameObject using the **GameObject | Create Empty** option.

2. Select the empty object and call it `Director`.

3. Go to **Window | Sequencing | Timeline** to open the **Timeline** editor.

4. Click the **Create** button in the middle of the **Timeline** window while the **Director** object is selected to convert that object into the cutscene player (or director).

5. After doing this, a window will appear, asking you to save a file. This file will be the cutscene or timeline; each cutscene will be saved in its own file. Save it in a folder called `Cutscenes` in your project (the `Assets` folder).

6. Now, you can see that the **Director** object has a **Playable Director** component with the **Intro** cutscene asset that was saved in the previous step set for the **Playable** property, meaning this cutscene will be played by the director:

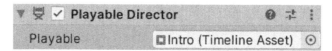

Figure 13.42 – Playable Director prepared to play Intro (Timeline Asset)

Now that we have the **Timeline** asset ready to work with, let's make it sequence actions. To start, we need to sequence two things – first, the cart position animation we created previously and then the camera swap between the dolly track camera (**CM vcam2**) and the player camera (**CM vcam1**). As we mentioned previously, a cutscene is a sequence of actions executing at given moments, and to schedule actions, you will need tracks. In Timeline, we have different kinds of tracks, each one allowing you to execute certain actions on certain objects. We will start with the animation track.

The animation track will control which animation a specific object will play; we need one track per object to animate. In our case, we want the dolly track to play the **Intro** animation that we created, so let's do that by following these steps:

1. Add an animation track by clicking the plus button (+) and then **Animation Track**:

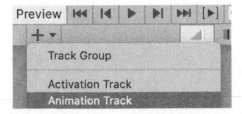

Figure 13.43 – Creating an animation track

2. Select the **Director** object and check the **Bindings** list of the **Playable Director** component in the **Inspector** window.

3. Drag the **Cart** object to specify that we want the animation track to control its animation:

Figure 13.44 – Making Animation Track control the dolly cart's animation in this director

> **Important Note**
>
> Timeline is a generic asset that can be applied to any scene, but since the tracks control specific objects, you need to manually bind them in every scene. In our case, we have an animation track that expects to control a single animator, so in every scene, if we want to apply this cutscene, we need to drag the specific animator to the control in the **Bindings** list.

4. Drag the **Intro** animation asset that we created in the animation track into the **Timeline** window. This will create a clip in the track showing when and for how long the animation will play. You can drag as many animations as possible that the cart can play into the track to sequence different animations at different moments; however, right now, we want just that one:

Figure 13.45 – Making the animator track play the Intro clip

5. You can drag the animation to change the exact moment you want it to play. Drag it to the beginning of the track.

6. Hit the **Play** button in the top-left part of the **Timeline** window to see it in action. You can also manually drag the white arrow in the **Timeline** window to view the cutscene at different moments:

Figure 13.46 – Playing a timeline and dragging the playback header

> **Important Note**
>
> Remember that you don't need to use Timeline to play animations. In this case, we did it this way to control at exactly which moment we want the animation to play. You can control animators using scripting as well.

Now, we will make our **Intro** timeline asset tell the `CinemachineBrain` component (the main camera) which camera will be active during each part of the cutscene, switching to the player camera once the camera animation is over. We will create a second track – a Cinemachine track – that specializes in making a specific `CinemachineBrain` component to switch between different virtual cameras. To do this, follow these steps:

1. Click the plus (+) button again and click on **Cinemachine Track**. Note that you can install Timeline without **Cinemachine**, but this kind of track won't show up in that case:

Figure 13.47 – Creating a new Cinemachine Track

2. In the **Playable Director** component's **Bindings** list, drag the main camera to **Cinemachine Track** to make that track control which virtual camera will be the one that controls the main camera at different moments of the cutscene:

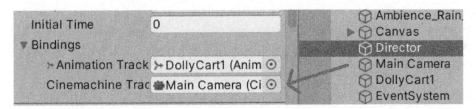

Figure 13.48 – Making Cinemachine Track control our scene's main camera

3. The next step indicates which virtual camera will be active during specific moments of the timeline. To do so, our Cinemachine track allows us to drag virtual cameras onto it, which will create virtual camera clips. Drag both **CM vcam2** and **CM vcam1**, in that order, onto the Cinemachine track:

Figure 13.49 – Dragging virtual cameras to the Cinemachine track

4. If you hit the **Play** button or just drag the **Timeline Playback** header, you will see how the active virtual camera changes when the playback header reaches the second virtual camera clip. Remember to view this in the **Game** view.

5. If you place the mouse near the ends of the clips, a resize cursor will appear. If you drag them, you can resize the clips to specify their duration. In our case, we will need to match the length of the **CM vcam2** clip with the **Cart** animation clip and then put **CM vcam1** at the end of it by dragging it, so that the camera will be active when the dolly cart's animation ends. In my case, they were already the same length, but just try to change it anyway to practice. Also, you can make the **CM vcam1** clip shorter; we just need that to play it for a few moments to execute the camera swap.

6. You can also overlap the clips a little bit to make a smooth transition between the two cameras, instead of a hard switch, which will look odd:

Figure 13.50 – Resizing and overlapping clips to interpolate them

If you wait for the full cutscene to end, you will notice how, at the very end, **CM vcam2** becomes active again. You can configure how Timeline will deal with the end of the cutscene since, by default, it does nothing. This can cause different behaviors based on the type of track; in our case, again, giving us the control to pick the virtual camera for the CinemachineBrain component, which will pick the virtual camera with the highest **Priority** value. We can change the **Priority** property of the virtual cameras to be sure that **CM vcam1** (the player camera) is always the more important one, or set **Wrap Mode** of the **Playable Director** component to **Hold**, which will keep everything as the last frame of the timeline specifies. In our case, we will use the latter option to test the Timeline-specific features:

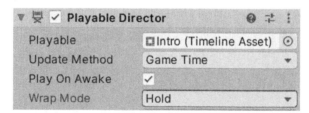

Figure 13.51 – Wrap Mode set to Hold

Most of the tracks work under the same logic; each will control a specific aspect of a specific object using clips that will execute during a set time. I encourage you to test different tracks to see what they do, such as **Activation**, which enables and disables objects during the cutscene. Remember, you can check out the documentation of the Timeline package in Package Manager.

Summary

In this chapter, we introduced the different animation systems that Unity provides for different requirements. We discussed importing character animations and controlling them with Animation Controllers. We also saw how to make cameras that can react to the game's current situation, such as the player's position, or that can be used during cutscenes. Finally, we looked at Timeline and the animation system to create an introduction cutscene for our game. These tools are useful for allowing the animators in our team work directly in Unity, without the hassle of integrating external assets (except for character animations). It also alleviates the programmer from creating repetitive scripts to create animations, wasting time in the process.

Now, you can import and create animation clips in Unity, as well as apply them to GameObjects to make them move according to the clips. Also, you can place them in the Timeline sequencer to coordinate them and create cutscenes for your game. Finally, you can create dynamic cameras to use in game or in cutscenes.

So far, we have discussed lots of Unity systems that allow us to develop different aspects of our game without coding, but sooner or later, scripting will be needed. Unity provides generic tools for generic situations, but our game's unique gameplay must usually be coded manually. In the next chapter, the first chapter of *Part 3*, we will start learning how to code in Unity using C#.

Section 3 – Scripting Level Interactivity with C#

Now that we have a fully graphically implemented prototype level, its time to add more interactivity to it by scripting with simple C# code.

This section comprises the following chapters:

14
Introduction to C# and Visual Scripting

Unity has a lot of great built-in tools to solve the most common problems in game development, such as the ones we have seen so far. Even two games of the same genre have their own little differences that make the game unique, and Unity cannot foresee that, so that's why we have scripting. Through coding, we can extend Unity's capabilities in several ways to achieve the exact behavior we need, all through a well-known language—C#. But aside from C#, Unity recently introduced **Visual Scripting**, a way to generate the scripts through a node graph tool, similar to the Shader Graphs we created in previous chapters. This means that you can create scripts without writing code but dragging **Nodes**, boxes that represent actions that can be chained:

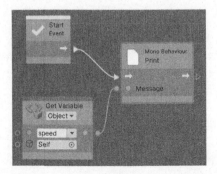

Figure 14.1 – Example of a Visual Scripting graph

While essentially both ways can achieve the same result, we can use them for different things. Usually, the core logic code of the game is written in C# due to it being usually huge and very performance-sensitive. But sometimes, using visual scripts instead allows non-programmer team members, such as Artists or Game Designers, to have more freedom to edit minor changes on the game, especially regarding balancing or visual effects. Another example would be Game Designers prototyping ideas through visual scripts that later programmers will convert to C# scripts when the idea is approved (or discarded if not). Also, C# programmers can create nodes for Visual Script programmers to use.

The ways of mixing these tools vary widely between teams, so while in the next chapters we are going to focus mainly on C#, we are going to also see the Visual Scripting equivalent version of the scripts we are going to create. This way, you will have the opportunity to experiment when is convenient to use one or the other according to your team structure.

In this chapter, we will examine the following scripting concepts:

- Creating Scripts
- Using events and instructions

We are going to create our own Unity components, learning the basic structure of a script and the way that we can execute actions and expose properties to be configured, both with C# and Visual Scripting. We are not going to create any of our actual game codes here, but just some example scripts to set the ground to start doing that in the next chapter. Let's start by discussing the basics of script creation.

Creating Scripts

The first step to creating behavior is to create Script assets. These are files that will contain the logic that our components will do. Both C# and Visual Scripting have their own type of asset to achieve that, so let's explore how to do that in both tools.

Consider that this book is intended for readers with some programming knowledge, but in this first section, we are going to discuss a basic script's structure to make sure you have a strong foundation for the behaviors that we will code in the following chapters. One thing I should point out is that even if we are going to discuss basic C# concepts, experienced programmers will learn the Unity-specific parts of the process, so even if you are familiar with C#, try to not skip this section.

In this section, we will examine the following script creation concepts:

- Initial setup
- Creating a C# script
- Adding fields
- Creating a Visual Script Graph

We are going to create our first script, which will serve to create our component, discussing the tools needed to do so and exploring how to expose our class fields to the editor. Let's start with the basics of script creation.

Initial setup

Support for Visual Scripting is added by installing the **Visual Scripting** package in the Package Manager, as we did with other packages in previous chapters, but as Unity does that automatically for us when we create the project, we don't require any further setup. That means the rest of this section will take care of setting up the tools required to work with C#.

One thing to consider before creating our first C# script is how Unity compiles the code. While coding, we are used to having an **Integrated Development Environment** (**IDE**), which is a program to create our code and compile or execute it. In Unity, we will just use an IDE as a tool to create the scripts easily with coloring and autocompletion because Unity doesn't have a custom code editor (if you have never coded before, these are valuable tools for beginners). The scripts will be created inside the Unity project and Unity will detect and compile them if any changes are made, so you won't compile in the IDE. Don't worry—you can still use breakpoints in this method.

We can use Visual Studio, Visual Studio Code, Rider, or whatever C# IDE you'd like to use, but when you install Unity, you will probably see an option to install Visual Studio automatically, which allows you to have a default IDE. This installs the free version of Visual Studio, so don't worry about the licenses here. If you don't have an IDE on your computer and didn't check the Visual Studio option while installing Unity, you can do the following:

1. Open **Unity Hub**.
2. Go to the **Installs** section.

3. Click on the three dots in the top-right area of the Unity version you are using and click on **Add Modules**:

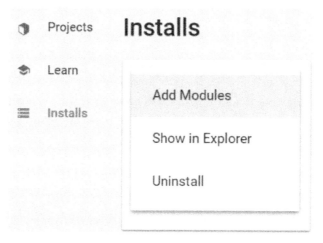

Figure 14.2 – Adding a module to the Unity installation

4. Check the option that says **Visual Studio**; the description of the option will vary depending on the version of Unity you are using.

5. Hit the **Next** button at the bottom right:

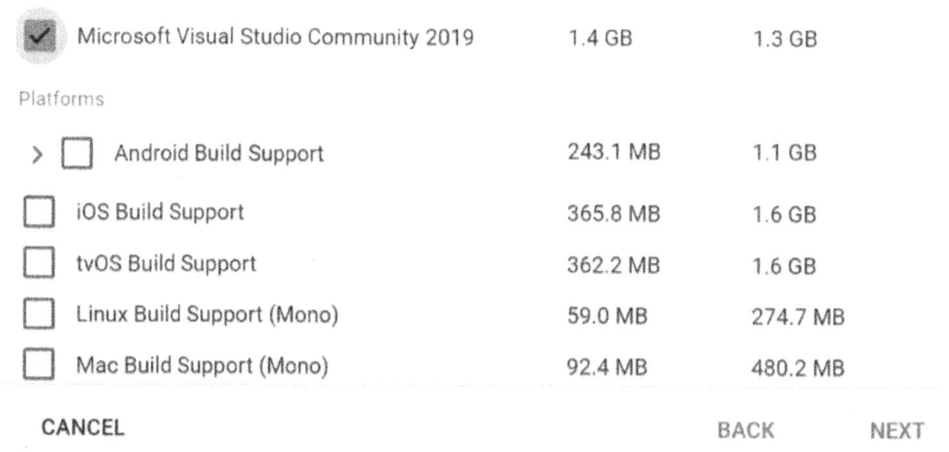

✔ Microsoft Visual Studio Community 2019	1.4 GB	1.3 GB
Platforms		
> ☐ Android Build Support	243.1 MB	1.1 GB
☐ iOS Build Support	365.8 MB	1.6 GB
☐ tvOS Build Support	362.2 MB	1.6 GB
☐ Linux Build Support (Mono)	59.0 MB	274.7 MB
☐ Mac Build Support (Mono)	92.4 MB	480.2 MB
CANCEL	BACK	NEXT

Figure 14.3 – Installing Visual Studio

6. Wait for the operation to end. This might take a few minutes.

If you have a preferred IDE, you can install it yourself and configure Unity to use it. If you can afford it or you are a teacher or a student (as it is free in these cases), I recommend Rider. It is a great IDE with lots of C# and Unity features that you will love; however, it is not vital for this exercise. To set up Unity to use a custom IDE, perform the following steps:

1. Open the project.
2. Go to **Edit | Preferences** in the top menu of the editor.
3. Select the **External Tools** menu from the left panel.
4. From the external script editor, select your preferred IDE; Unity will automatically detect the supported IDEs:

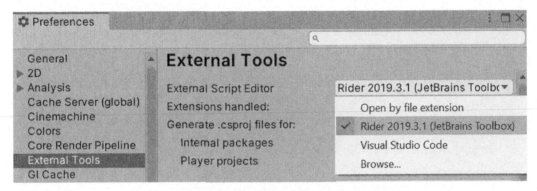

Figure 14.4 – Selecting a custom IDE

5. If you don't find your IDE in the list, you can use the **Browse…** option,

    Note that usually, IDEs that require you to use this option are not very well supported—but it's worth a shot.

Finally, some IDEs, such as Visual Studio, Visual Studio Code, and Rider, have Unity integration tools that you need to install in your project, which is optional but can be useful. Usually, Unity installs these automatically, but if you want to be sure that they are installed, follow these steps:

1. Open **Package Manager** (**Window | Package Manager**).
2. Search the list for your IDE or filter the list by using the search bar. In my case, I used Rider, and I can find a package called **JetBrains Rider Editor**:

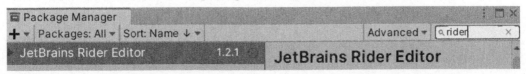

Figure 14.5 – Custom IDE editor extension installation—in this case, the Rider one

3. Check whether your IDE integration package is installed by looking at the buttons on the bottom-right part of the package manager. If you see an **Install** or **Update** button, click on it, but if it says **Installed**, everything is set up.

Now that we have an IDE configured, let's create our first script.

Creating a C# Script

C# is a heavily object-oriented language, and this is no different in Unity. Any time we want to extend Unity, we need to create our own class—a script with the instructions we want to add to Unity. If we want to create custom components, we need to create a class that inherits from MonoBehaviour, the base class of every custom component.

We can create C# script files directly within the Unity project using the editor, and you can arrange them in folders right next to other assets folders. The easiest way to create a script is by following these steps:

1. Select any game object that you want to have the component we are going to create. As we are just testing this out, select any object.

2. Click on the **Add Component** button at the bottom of the **Inspector** and look for the **New Script** option at the bottom of the list, displayed after clicking on **Add Component**:

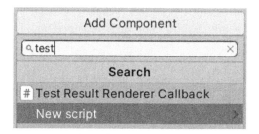

Figure 14.6 – The New script option

3. In the **Name** field, enter the desired script name. In my case, I will call it MyFirstScript, but for the scripts that you will use for your game, try to enter descriptive names, regardless of the length:

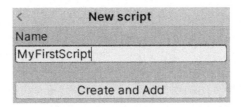

Figure 14.7 – Naming the script

> **Important note**
> It is recommended that you use Pascal case for script naming. In Pascal case, a script for the player's shooting functionality would be called `PlayerShoot`. The first letter of each word of the name is in uppercase and you can't use spaces.

4. You can check how a new asset, called the same way the script was, is created in Project View. Remember that each component has its own asset, and I suggest you put each component in a `Scripts` folder:

Figure 14.8 – Script asset

5. Now, you will also see that your Game Object has a new component in the Inspector window, which is named the same as your script. So, you have now created your first component class:

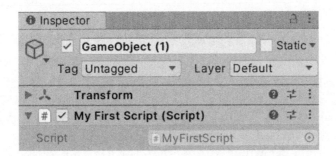

Figure 14.9 – Our script added to a game object

Now that we have created a `component` class, remember that a class is not the component itself. It is a description of what the component should be—a blueprint of how a component should work. To actually use the component, we need to instantiate it by creating a component based on the class. Each time we add a component to an object using the editor, we are instantiating it. Generally, we don't instantiate using new functions, but by using the editor or specialized functions.

Now, you can add your component as you would any other component by using the **Add Component** button in the Inspector window. Then you can look for the component in the **Scripts** category or search for it by name:

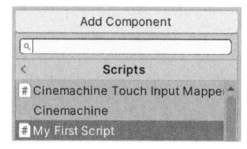

Figure 14.10 – Adding a custom component to the Scripts category

Something that you need to consider here is that we can add the same component to several game objects. We don't need to create a class for each game object that uses the component. I know this is basic programmers' knowledge, but remember that we are trying to recap the basics here.

Now that we have our component, let's explore how it looks and carry out a class structure recap by following these steps:

1. Locate the script asset in Project View and double-click on it. Remember that it should be located in the `Scripts` folder you created previously.

2. Wait for the IDE to open; this can take a while. You will know that the IDE has completed initialization when you see your script code and its keywords properly colored, which varies according to the IDE. In Rider, it looks like what is shown in the following screenshot. In my case, I knew that Rider had finished initializing because the **MonoBehaviour** type and the script name are colored the same:

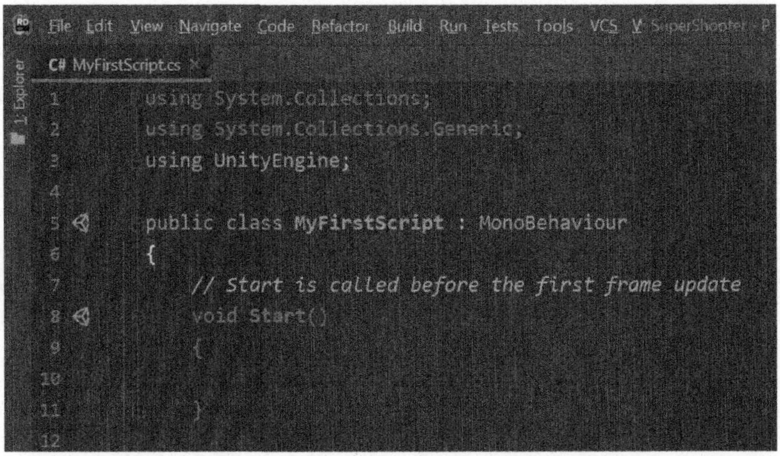

Figure 14.11 – A new script opened in the Rider IDE

The first three lines—the ones that start with the using keyword—include common namespaces. Namespaces are like code containers, which is, in this case, code created by others (such as Unity and C# creators). We will be using namespaces quite often to simplify our tasks; they already contain solved algorithms that we will use. We will be adding and removing the using component as we need; in my case, Rider is suggesting that the first two using components are not necessary because I am not using any code inside them, and so they are grayed out. But for now, keep them as you will use them in later chapters of this book. Remember, they should always be at the beginning of the class:

Figure 14.12 – The using sections

The next line, the one that starts with `public class`, is where we declare that we are creating a new class that inherits from `MonoBehaviour`, the base class of every custom component. We know this because it ends with : `MonoBehaviour`. You can see how the rest of the code is located inside brackets right below that line, meaning that the code inside them belongs to the component:

Figure 14.13 – The MyFirstScript class definition inherits from MonoBehaviour

Now that we have our C# script, let's add fields to configure it.

Adding fields

In previous chapters, when we added components as `Rigidbody` or as different kinds of colliders, adding the components wasn't enough. We needed to properly configure them to achieve the exact behavior that we need. For example, `Rigidbody` has the `Mass` property to control the object's weight, and the colliders have the `Size` property to control their shape. This way, we can reuse the same component for different scenarios, preventing the duplication of similar components. With a `Box` collider, we can represent a square or rectangular box just by changing the size properties. Our components are no exception; if we have a component that moves an object and if we want two objects to move at different speeds, we can use the same component with different configurations.

Each configuration is a **Field** or **Variable**, a specific type variable where we can hold the parameter's value. We can create class fields that can be edited in the editor in two ways:

- By marking the field as `public`, but breaking the encapsulation principle
- By making a private field and exposing it with an attribute

Now, we are going to cover both methods, but if you are not familiar with **Object-Oriented Programming (OOP)** concepts, such as encapsulation, I recommend you use the first method.

Suppose we are creating a movement script. We will add an editable number field representing the velocity using the first method—that is, by adding the `public` field. We will do this by following these steps:

1. Open the script by double-clicking it as we did before.
2. Inside the class brackets, but outside any brackets within them, add the following code:

```
public class MyFirstScript : MonoBehaviour
{
    public float speed;
```

Figure 14.14 – Creating a speed field in our component

Important note

The `public` keyword specifies that the variable can be seen and edited beyond the scope of the class. The `float` part of the code says that the variable is using the decimal number type, and speed is the name we chose for our field—this can be whatever you want. You can use other value types to represent other kinds of data, such as bool to represent checkboxes, or Booleans and strings to represent text.

---

3. To apply the changes, just save the file in the IDE (usually by pressing *Ctrl + S* or *Command + S*) and return to Unity. When you do this, you will notice a little loading wheel at the bottom-right part of the editor, indicating that Unity is compiling the code. You can't test the changes until the wheel finishes:

Figure 14.15 – The loading wheel

Remember that Unity will compile the code; don't compile it in the IDE.

4. After the compilation is finished, you can see your component in the Inspector window and the **Speed** variable should be there, allowing you to set the speed you want. Of course, right now, the variables do nothing. Unity doesn't recognize your intention according to the name of the variable; we need to set it for use in some way, but we will do that later:

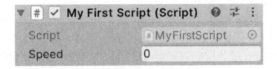

Figure 14.16 – A public field to edit data that the component will use later

5. If you don't see the **Speed** variable, please check the section at the end of this chapter called *Common beginner C# script errors*, which will give you tips about how to troubleshoot compilation errors.

6. Try adding the same component to other objects and set a different speed. This will show you how components in different game objects are independent, allowing you to change some of their behaviors via different settings.

The second way to define properties is similar, but instead of creating a `public` field, we create a `private` field, encouraging encapsulation and exposing it using the `SerializeField` attribute, as shown in the following screenshots. These screenshots show two ways of doing this—both will produce the same results; the only difference is the styling. Use the one that best fits your coding standards:

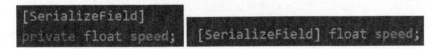

Figure 14.17 – Two ways to expose private attributes in the Inspector window

If you are not familiar with the OOP concept of encapsulation, just use the first method, which is more flexible for beginners. If you create a `private` field, it won't be accessible to other scripts because the `SerializeField` attribute only exposes the variable to the editor. Remember that Unity won't allow you to use constructors, so the only way to set initial data and inject dependencies is via serialized private fields or public fields and setting them in the editor (or using a dependency injection framework, but that is beyond the scope of this book). For simplicity, we will use the first method in most of the exercises in this book.

If you want, try to create other types of variables and check how they look in the inspector. Try replacing float for bool or string, as suggested previously. Now that we know how to configure our components through data, let's use that data to create some behavior.

Now that we have our C# script, let's see how to do the same in Visual Scripting.

Creating a Visual Script

As we need to create a Script Asset for C# scripts, we need to create the Visual Scripting equivalent called **Script Graph** and also attach it to our GameObject, although using a different approach this time. Before continuing, it is worth noticing that our objects must only have C# or the Visual Scripting version, but not both, or the behavior will be applied twice, once per version. Essentially, only perform the steps for the version you want to try or do both steps in different objects if you want to experiment.

Let's create a Visual Script by performing the following steps:

1. Select an object to add the Visual Script. You might create a new one just to test this.

2. Add the **Script Machine** component to it. This component will execute the Visual Script Graph we will be creating shortly:

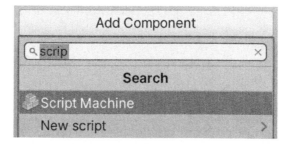

Figure 14.18 – Adding a Script Machine component

3. In the **Script Machine** component, click the **New** button and select a folder and a name to save the Visual Script Graph asset. This asset will contain the instructions of our Script, and the **Script Machine** component will execute them:

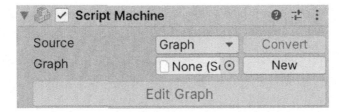

Figure 14.19 – Using the New button to create a Visual Scripting Graph asset

4. Click the **Edit Graph** button to open the Visual Script editor:

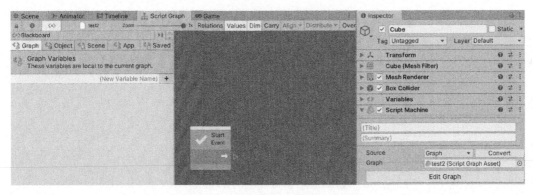

Figure 14.20 – Visual Scripting asset editor

Put the mouse in an empty area in the grid of the Visual Script editor, and while holding the middle mouse button, move the mouse to scroll through the graph. On MacBooks and Apple Magic Mouses, you can scroll using two fingers in the trackpad.

What we did is create the Visual Graph Asset that will contain the code of our script, and attached it to a GameObject through the **Script Machine** component. Unlike C# scripts, we can't attach the Graph Asset directly; that's why we need the Script Machine to run the component for us.

Regarding Fields, the ones we created in the C# scripts are contained in the script itself, but for Visual Graph, they work slightly differently. When we added the **Script Machine** component, another one was added, the **Variables** component. This will hold all the variables for all the Visual Script Graphs that a GameObject can contain. That means that all graphs we add to our object will share those variables, so consider this when modifying their values. Also remember that you will want to add several graphs to the object, given that each graph will take care of different behaviors, in a way we can mix and match them according to our needs.

In order to add a variable to our GameObject that can be used by our graph, let's do the following:

1. Select the GameObject to add the variable and look at the **Variables** component.

2. Click the input field that says **(New Variable Name)** and type the name of the variable. In my case, this is speed.

3. Click the **plus (+)** button of the **Variables** component.

4. In the **Type** dropdown, select **Float**.

5. Optionally, you can set an initial value in the **Value** field:

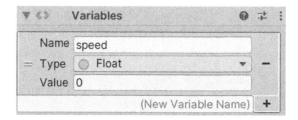

Figure 14.21 – Creating variables for the Visual Graph

We created a speed variable that we can configure in the GameObject to alter the way all Visual Scripts Graphs attached to our GameObject will work, or at least the ones that use that **Variable** value. Consider that maybe you will have different kinds of speed, such as movement and rotational speed, so in actual cases, you might want to be a little bit more specific with the variable name.

Important info

The **Variables** component used in Visual Scripting is also called Blackboard, a common programming technique. This Blackboard is a container of several values of our object, such as a memory or database, that several other components of our object will then query and use. C# scripts usually contain their own variables inside, but remember that here they are shared through the Blackboard.

With our scripts created and ready to be configured, let's see how to make both of them do something.

Using events and instructions

Now that we have a script, we are ready to do something with it. We won't implement anything useful in this chapter, but we will settle the base concepts to add interesting behavior in the scripts we are going to create in the next chapters.

In this section, we are going to cover the following concepts:

- Events and instructions in C#
- Events and instructions in Visual Scripting
- Using fields in instructions
- Common beginner C# script errors

We are going to explore the Unity event system, which will allow us to respond to different situations by executing instructions. These instructions will also be affected by the value of the editor. Finally, we are going to discuss common scripting errors and how to solve them. Let's start by introducing the concept of Unity events in C#.

Events and instructions in C#

Unity allows us to create behavior in a cause-effect fashion, which is usually called an event system. An event is a situation that Unity is monitoring—for example, when two objects collide or are destroyed, Unity tells us about this situation, allowing us to react according to our needs. As an example, we can reduce the life of a player when it collides with a bullet. Here, we will explore how to listen to these events and test them by using some simple actions.

If you are used to event systems, you will know that they usually require us to subscribe to some kind of listener or delegate, but in Unity, there is a simpler method available. For C# scripts, we just need to write a function with the exact same name as the event we want to use—and I mean *exact*. If a letter of the name doesn't have the correct casing, it won't execute, and no warning will be raised. This is the most common beginner's error that is made, so pay attention. For Visual Scripting, we will be adding a special kind of node, but will discuss that after the C# version.

There are lots of events or messages to listen to in Unity, so let's start with the most common one—Update. This event will tell you when Unity wants you to update your object, depending on the purpose of your behavior; some don't need them. The Update logic is usually something that needs to be executed constantly; to be more precise, in every frame. Remember that every game is like a movie—a sequence of images that your screen switches through fast enough to look like we have continuous motion. A common action to do in the Update event is to move objects a little bit, and by doing this, every frame will make your object constantly move.

We will learn about the sorts of things we can do with Update and other events or messages later. Now, let's focus on how to make our component at least listen to this event. Actually, the base component already comes with two Event functions that are ready to use, one being Update and the other one being in the script. If you are not familiar with the concept of functions in C#, we refer you to the code snippet in the following screenshot, which is already included in our script. Try to find it in yours:

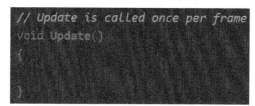

Figure 14.22 – A function called Update, which will be executed with every frame

You will notice a (usually) green line of text (depending on the IDE) above the void Update() line—this is called a comment. These are basically ignored by Unity. They are just notes that you can leave to yourself and must always begin with // to prevent Unity from trying to execute them and failing. We will use this to temporarily disable lines of code later.

Now, to test whether this actually works, let's add an instruction to be executed all the time. There is no better test function than print. This is a simple instruction that tells Unity to print a message to the console, where all kinds of messages can be seen by the developers to check whether everything is properly working. The user will never see these messages. They are similar to the classic log files that developers sometimes ask you for when something goes wrong in the game, and you are reporting an issue.

To test events in C# using functions, follow these steps:

1. Open the script by double-clicking on it.

2. To test, add `print("test");` within the `Event` function. In the following screenshot, you can see an example of how to do that in the `Update` event. Remember to write the instruction *exactly*, including the correct casing, spaces, and quotes symbols:

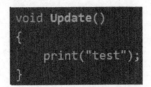

Figure 14.23 – Printing a message in all the frames

3. Save the file, go to Unity, and play the game.

> **Important note**
> Remember to save the file before switching back to Unity from the IDE. This is the only way that Unity knows your file has changed. Some IDEs, such as Rider, save the file automatically for you, but I don't recommend you use auto-save, at least in big projects (you don't want accidental recompilations of unfinished work; that takes too long in projects with lots of scripts).

4. Look for the **Console** tab and select it. This is usually found next to the **Project View** tab. If you can't find it, go to **Window | General | Console**, or press *Ctrl + Shift + C* (*Command + Shift + C* on macOS).

5. You will see lots of messages stating `"test"` printed in every frame of the **Console** tab. If you don't see this, remember to save the script file before playing the game.

6. Let's also test the Start function. Add print("test Start"); to it, save the
    file, and play the game. The full script should look as follows:

```
public class MyFirstScript : MonoBehaviour
{
    [SerializeField] float speed;

    // Start is called before the first frame update
    void Start()
    {
        print("test Start");
    }

    // Update is called once per frame
    void Update()
    {
        print("test");
    }
}
```

Figure 14.24 – The script that tests the Start and Update functions

If you check the console now and scroll all the way up, you will see a single "test
Start" message and lots of "test" messages following it. As you can guess, the Start
event tells you that the game has started and allows you to execute the code that needs to
happen just once at the beginning of the game. We will use this later in this book.

For the void Update() syntax, we will say to Unity that whatever is contained in the
brackets below this line is a function that will be executed in all the frames. It is important
to put the print instruction *inside* the Update brackets (the ones inside the brackets of
the class). Also, the print function expects to receive text inside its parentheses, called an
argument or parameter, and text in C# must be enclosed by quotation marks. Finally, all
instructions inside functions such as Update or Start *must* end with a semicolon.

Here, I challenge you to try to add another event called OnDestroy using print to
discover when it executes. A small suggestion is to play and stop the game and look at the
bottom of the console to test this one.

For advanced users, you can also use breakpoints if your IDE allows you to do that. Breakpoints allow you to freeze Unity completely before executing a specific code line to see how our field's data changes over time and to detect errors. Here, I will show you the steps to use breakpoints in Rider, but the Visual Studio version should be similar:

1. Click on the vertical bar at the left of the line where you want to add the breakpoint:

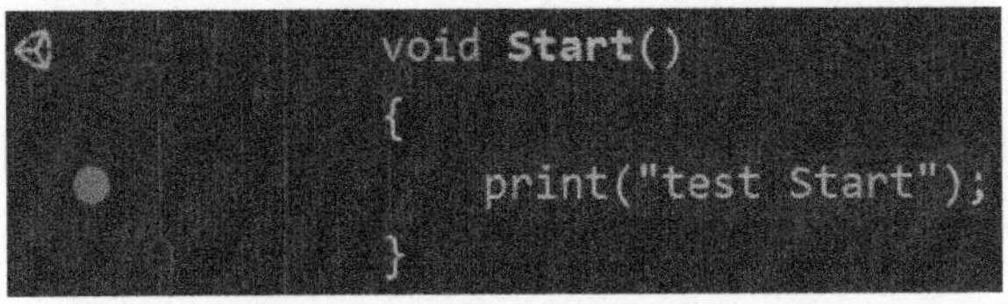

Figure 14.25 – A breakpoint in the print instruction

2. Go to **Run | Attach to Unity Process** (in Visual Studio, go to **Debug | Attach Unity Debugger**. Remember that you need the Visual Studio Unity plugin and the Visual Studio integration package of **Package Manager**):

Figure 14.26 – Attacking our IDE with a Unity process

3. From the list, look for the specific Unity instance you want to test. The list will show other opened editors or debugging builds that are executing, if any.

Stopping the debugging process won't close Unity. It will just detach the IDE from the editor.

Now, let's explore the Visual Scripting equivalent of using events and instructions.

Events and instructions in Visual Scripting

The same concept of events and instructions remains in Visual Scripting, but, of course, this will be done with nodes in the graph. Remember that a node represents an instruction of the graph, and we can connect them to chain the effects of each instruction. To add events and the print instruction to our graph, do the following:

1. Open **Visual Script Graph** (double-click the asset).

2. Right-click the **Start** and **Update** nodes that are created by default and then click **Delete**. Even if those events are the ones we need, I want you to see how to create them from scratch:

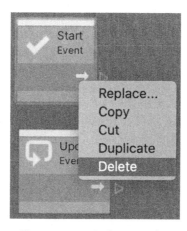

Figure 14.27 – Deleting nodes

3. Right-click in any empty space of the **Graph** and type `start` inside the **Search** box. It can take a while the first time.

4. Select the **Start** element in the list with the green checkbox to its left. In this case, I knew this was an event because I was aware of it, but usually, you will recognize that it's an event because it won't have input pins (more on that in the next steps):

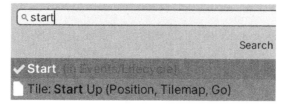

Figure 14.28 – Searching the Start event node

5. Drag the white arrow at the right of the event node, also known as the Output Flow Pin, and release the mouse button in any empty space.

6. In the **Search** box, search for the print node. Select the one that says **Mono Behaviour: Print**. This means that when the Start event happens, the connected node will be executed, in this case, **print**. This is how we start to chain instructions to events:

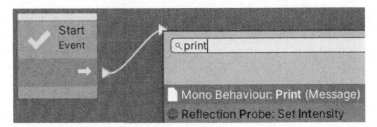

Figure 14.29 – Creating a print node connected to the event

7. Drag the empty circle at the left of the **Message** input pin of the **Print** node and release it in any empty space. This pin has a circle indicating that it is a parameter pin, data that will be used when executing the pin. The flow pins, the ones with green arrows, represent the order in which the nodes will be executed.

8. Select the **String Literal** option. This will create a node to allow us to specify the message to print:

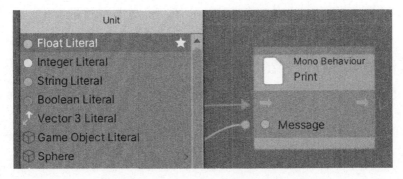

Figure 14.30 – Creating a string literal node

9. In the empty white box, write the message to be printed:

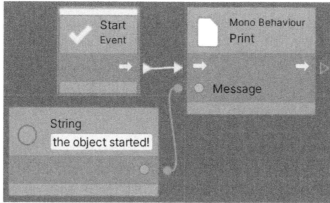

Figure 14.31 – Specifying the message to print

10. Play the game and see the message printed in the console. Be sure you have only the Visual Scripting version in the scene to avoid confusing the message in the console with the C# version. You can also use different message texts in the visual scripts to be sure which ones are actually executing.

You can chain more actions to the Start, dragging the pin at the right (Flow Output Pin) of the **Print** node, chaining new nodes, but we will do that later. Now that we have our scripts doing something, let's make the instructions use the fields we created so that the scripts use their configurations.

Using fields in instructions

We have created fields to configure our components' behavior, but we have not used them so far. We will create meaningful components in the next chapter, but one thing we will often need is to use the fields we have created to change the behavior of the object. So far, we have no real use for the speed field that we created. However, following the idea of testing whether our code is working (also known as debugging), we can learn how to use the data inside a field with a function to test whether the value is the expected one, changing the output of print in the console according to the field's value.

In our current C# script, our speed value doesn't change during runtime. However, as an example, if you are creating a life system with shield damage absorption and you want to test whether the reduced damage calculation is working properly, you might want to print the calculation values to the console and check whether they are correct. The idea here is to replace the fixed message inside the print functions with a field. When you do that, print will show the field's value in the console. So, if you set a value of 5 in speed and you print it, you will see lots of messages saying 5 in the console, and the output of the print function is governed by the field. To test this, your print message within the Update function should look as follows:

```
[SerializeField] float speed;

void Update()
{
    print(speed);
}
```

Figure 14.32 – Using a field as a print function parameter

As you can see, we just put the name of the field without quotation marks. If you use quotation marks, you will print a "speed" message. In other scenarios, you can use this speed value within some moving functions to control how fast the movement will be, or you can perhaps create a field called "fireRate" (fields use camel case instead of Pascal, with the first letter being in lowercase) to control the cool-down time between one bullet and the next:

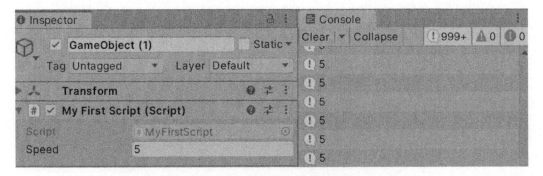

Figure 14.33 – Printing the current speed

Now, to make the Visual Script Graph print the value of the speed variable we created in the **Variables** component, perform the following steps:

1. Open the Visual Scripting graph asset (by double-clicking it).

2. In the Panel to the left, select the **Object** tab to display all the variables our object has, essentially the ones we defined in the **Variables** component previously.

3. Drag the speed variable using the two lines to the left of the variable box to any empty area of the graph. This will create a **GetVariable** node in the graph to represent the variable. Bear in mind that the drag has a bug at the moment, so you might need to try a couple of times:

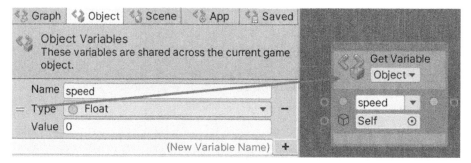

Figure 14.34 – Dragging variables to the graph to be used in the nodes

4. Drag the empty circle at the right of the **Get Variable** node to the circle at the left of the **Message** input pin of the **Print** node. This will replace the previous connection to the **String Literal** node. This node doesn't have Input or Output flow nodes (the green arrow ones), as they are data-only nodes that provide data to other nodes. In this case, when **Print** needs to execute, it will execute **Get Variable** to get the text to read:

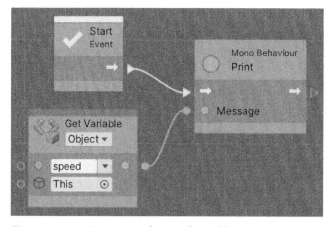

Figure 14.35 – Connecting the speed variable to the Print node

5. Right-click on the **String Literal** node and delete it.

6. Play the game and observe.

With all this, we now have the necessary tools to start creating actual components. Before moving on, let's recap some of the common errors that you will likely encounter if this is your first time creating scripts in C#.

Common beginner C# script errors

The Visual Scripting scripts are prepared in such a way that you make fewer errors, not allowing you to write incorrect syntax in the same way as C# script does. If you are an experienced programmer, I bet you are quite familiar with these errors, but let's recap the common errors that will make you lose lots of time when you are starting with C# scripting. Most of them are caused by not copying the shown code *exactly*. If you have an error in the code, Unity will show a red message in the console and won't allow you to run the game, even if you are not using the script. So, never leave anything unfinished.

Let's start with a classic error, which is a missing semicolon, which has resulted in many programmer memes and jokes. All fields and most instructions inside functions (such as print), when called, need to have a semicolon at the end. If you don't add a semicolon, Unity will show an error, such as the one in the screenshot on the left in the following figure, in the console. You will also notice that the screenshot on the right in the following figure also has an example of bad code, where the IDE is showing a red icon, suggesting something is wrong in that place:

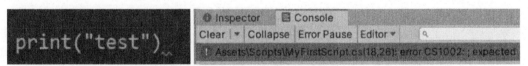

Figure 14.36 – An error in the print line hinted by the IDE and the Unity console

You will notice that the error shows the exact script (MyFirstScript.cs), the exact line of code (18, in this case), and usually, a descriptive message—in this case, ; [semicolon] expected. You can simply double-click the error and Unity will open the IDE highlighting the problematic line. You can even click on the links in the stack to jump to the line of the stack that you want.

I already mentioned why it is important to use the *exact* case for every letter of the instruction. However, based on my experience of teaching beginners, I need to stress this particular aspect more. The first scenario where this can happen is in instructions. In the following screenshots, you can see how a badly written `print` function appears—that is, the error that the console will display and how the IDE will suggest that there is something wrong. First, in the case of Rider, the instruction is colored red, saying that the instruction is not recognized (in Visual Studio, it will show a red line instead). Then, the error message says that `Print` does not exist in the current context, meaning that Unity (or C#, actually) does not recognize any instruction named `Print`. In another type of script, `Print` in uppercase may be valid, but not in regular components, which is why the in the current context clarification exists:

```
Print("test");
```

```
⓪ Assets\Scripts\MyFirstScript.cs(18,13): error CS0103: The name 'Print' does not exist in the current context
```

Figure 14.37 – Error hints when writing an instruction incorrectly

Now, if you write an event with the wrong casing, the situation is worse. You can create functions such as `Start` and `Update` with whatever name you want for other purposes. Writing `update` or `start` is perfectly valid as C# will think that you are going to use those functions not as events but as regular functions. So, no error will be shown, and your code will just not work. Try to write `update` instead of `Update` and see what happens:

```
// Update is called
void update()
{
    print("test");
}
```

Figure 14.38 – The wrong casing in the Update function will compile the function but won't execute it

Another error is to put instructions outside the function brackets, such as inside the brackets of the class or outside them. Doing this will give no hint to the function as to when it needs to execute. So, a `print` function outside an `Event` function makes no sense, and it will show an error such as the ones in the following screenshots. This time, the error is not super descriptive. The expected identifier says that C# is expecting you to create a function or a field—the kinds of structure that can be put directly inside a class:

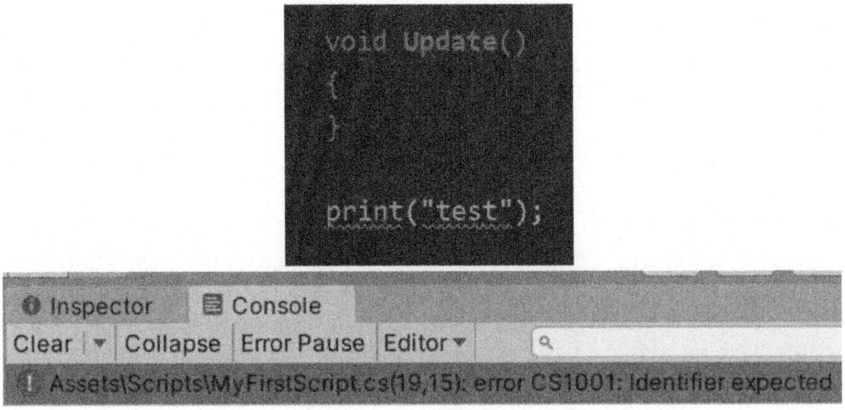

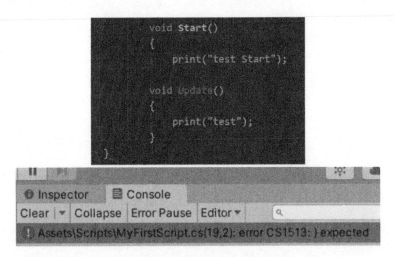

Figure 14.39 – Misplaced instruction or function call

Finally, another classic mistake is to forget to close open brackets. If you don't close a bracket, C# won't know where a function finishes and another starts or where the class function ends. This may sound redundant, but C# needs that to be perfectly defined. In the following screenshots, you can see how this would look:

Figure 14.40 – Missing closed brackets

This one is a little bit difficult to catch because the error in the code is shown way after the actual error. This is caused by the fact that C# allows you to put functions inside functions (not used often), and so C# will detect the error later, asking you to add a closing bracket. However, as we don't want to put Update inside Start, we need to fix the error before, at the end of Start. The error message will be descriptive in the console, but again, don't put the closing bracket where the message suggests you do so unless you are 100% sure that position is correct.

You will likely face lots of errors aside from these, but they all work the same. The IDE will show you a hint and the console will display a message; you will learn them with time. Just have patience as every programmer experiences this. There are other kinds of errors, such as runtime errors, code that compiles but will fail when being executed due to some misconfiguration, or the worst—logic errors, where your code compiles and executes with no error but doesn't do what you intended.

Summary

In this chapter, we explored the basic concepts that you will use while creating scripts. We discussed the concept of a script's assets and how the C# ones must inherit from **MonoBehaviour** to be accepted by Unity in order to create our own scripts. We also saw how to mix events and instructions to add behavior to an object and how to use fields in instructions to customize what they do. All of this was done using both C# and Visual Scripting.

We explored the basics of scripting to ensure that everyone is on the same page. However, from now on, we will assume that you have basic coding experience in some programming language, and you know how to use structures such as `if`, `for`, and `array`. If not, you can still read through this book and try to complement the areas you don't understand with an introductory book to C# as required.

In the next chapter, we are going to start seeing how we can use what we have learned to create movement and spawning scripts.

15
Implementing Movement and Spawning

In the previous chapter, we learned the basics of scripting, so now let's create our first behaviors for our game. We will see the basics of how to move objects through scripting using the **Transform** component, which will be applied for the movement of our Player with the keys, the constant movement of bullets, and other objects' movement. Also, we will see how to create and destroy objects during the game, such as bullets our Player and Enemy shoot and the Enemy Wave Spawners. These actions can be used in several other scenarios, so we will explore a few to reinforce the idea.

In this chapter, we will examine the following scripting concepts:

- Implementing movement
- Implementing spawning

We will start by scripting components to move our character through the keyboard, and then we will make our player shoot bullets. Something to consider is that we are going to first see the C# version and then show the Visual Scripting equivalent in each section.

Implementing movement

Almost every object in a game moves in one way or the other: the Player character with the keyboard, the Enemies through AI, the bullets simply move forward, and so on. There are several ways of moving objects in Unity, so we will start with the simplest one, that is, through the **Transform** component.

In this section, we will examine the following movement concepts:

- Moving objects through Transform
- Using Input
- Understanding Delta Time

First, we will explore how to access the **Transform** component in our script to drive the player movement, to later apply movement based on the Player's keyboard input. Then, we are going to explore the concept of Delta Time to make sure the movement speeds are consistent in every computer. We are going to start by learning about the Transform API to simplify movement.

Moving objects through Transform

Transform is the component that holds the Translation, Rotation, and Scale of the object, so every movement system, such as Physics or Pathfinding, will affect this component. Anyway, sometimes we want to move the object in a specific way according to our game by creating our own script that will handle the movement calculations we need and modify Transform to apply them.

One concept implied here is that components alter other components. The main way of coding in Unity is to create components that interact with other components. Here, the idea is to create one that accesses another and tells it to do something, in this case, to move. To create a script that tells `Transform` to move, do the following:

1. Create and add a script called `Player Movement` to our character. In this case, it would be the animated robot object we created previously. Remember to move the script to the `Scripts` folder after creation:

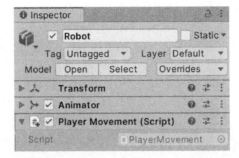

Figure 15.1 – Creating a Player Movement script in the Character

2. Double-click the created script asset to open an IDE to edit the code.

3. We are moving, and the movement is applied at every frame, so this script will only use the Update function or method, and we can remove Start (it is a good practice to remove unused functions):

```
public class PlayerMovement : MonoBehaviour
{

    void Update()
    {


    }
}
```

Figure 15.2 – A component with just the Update event function

4. To move our object along its forward axis (Z axis), add the transform. Translate(0,0,1); line to the Update function, as shown in the following screenshot:

> **Important Note**
> Every component inherits a transform field (to be specific, a getter) that is a reference to the Transform of the GameObject the component is placed in; it represents the sibling Transform of our component. Through this field, we can access the Translate function of the Transform, which will receive the offset to apply in *X*, *Y*, and *Z* local coordinates.

```
public class PlayerMovement : MonoBehaviour
{
    void Update()
    {
        transform.Translate(0, 0, 1);
    }
}
```

Figure 15.3 – A simple Move Forward script

5. Save the file and play the game to see the movement.

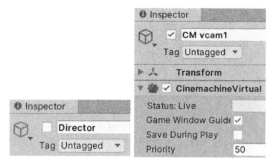

Figure 15.4 – Temporarily disabling the Director and increasing the Player Camera priority

> **Important Note**
>
> I recommend you temporarily disable the Playable Director object and increase the Priority of CM vcam1, which will disable the introduction cutscene and make the Character-Following Camera be activated by default, reducing the time needed to test the game. Another option is to create a secondary scene just to test the Player Movement, something that is actually done in real projects, but for now, let's keep things simple:

You will notice that the Player is moving too fast and that's because we are using a fixed speed of 1 meter, and because Update is executing all frames, we are moving at 1 meter per frame. In a standard 30 fps game, the player will move 30 meters per second, which is too much. We can control the Player speed by adding a speed field and using the value set in the editor instead of the fixed value of 1. You can see one way to do this in the next screenshot, but remember the other options we discussed in the previous chapter (such as using the Serialize Field attribute):

```
public float speed;

void Update()
{
    transform.Translate(0, 0, speed);
}
```

Figure 15.5 – Creating a speed field and using it as the Z speed of the movement script

Now, if you save the script to apply the changes and set the speed of the Player in the Editor, you can play the game and see the results. In my case, I used 0.1, but you might need another value (more on this later):

Figure 15.6 – Setting a speed of 0.1 meters per frame

Now, for the Visual Scripting version, first remember to not mix C# and Visual Scripting versions of our scripts, not because it is not possible, but because we want to keep things simple for now. So, you can either delete the script from the Robot object and add the Visual Scripting version or you can create two Robot objects and enable and disable them to try both versions, but it's up to you. The way I recommend tackling this is to first create the project using one of the versions and then recreate the scripts with the other, to get the full experience.

The Visual Scripting Graph of this script will look as in the following screenshot:

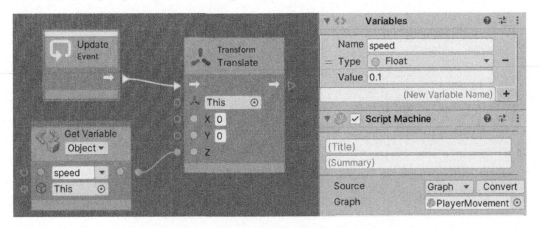

Figure 15.7 – Setting a speed of 0.1 meters per frame

As you can see, we added a **Script Machine** to our **Robot** GameObject. Then, we pressed the **New** button in the **Script Machine** component to create a new Graph called **PlayerMovement**. We also created a **Float** variable called **speed** with the value of **0.1**. In the Graph, we added the **Update** event node and attached it to the **Translate (X,Y,Z)** node of transform. Finally, we connected the **Z** parameter pin of **Translate** to the **GetVariable** node representing the speed we created in the GameObject. If you compare this Graph with the code we used in the C# version, they are essentially the same Update method and Translate function. If you don't remember how to create this Graph, you can look back to *Chapter 14, Introduction to C# and Visual Scripting*, to recap the process.

You will notice that the player will move automatically. Now let's see how to execute the movement based on Player Input such as with a keyboard and mouse.

Using Input

Unlike NPCs, we want the Player movement to be driven by the Player's Input, based on which keys they press, the mouse movement, and so on. We can recall the original key mapping we designed in *Chapter 1, Designing a Game from Scratch*, with the next two tables:

Keyboard input	Action
Up arrow	Move forward
Down arrow	Move back
Left arrow	Move left
Right arrow	Move right
W	Move forward
S	Move back
A	Move left
D	Move right

Table 15.8 – Keyboard mapping

Check out the mouse mappings in the following table:

Mouse input	Action
Mouse movement	Rotate character
Left mouse button	Shoot bullet

Table 15.9 – Mouse mapping

In C#, to know whether a certain key is pressed, such as the Up arrow, we can use the `Input.GetKey(KeyCode.W)` line, which will return a Boolean, indicating whether the key specified in the `KeyCode` enum is pressed. We can change the key to check the changing of the `KeyCode` enum value and combine the `GetKey` function with an `If` statement to make the translation execute only when that condition is met (the key is currently pressed).

Let's start implementing the keyboard movement by following these steps:

1. Make the forward movement execute only when the *W* key is pressed with the code, as shown in the next screenshot:

```csharp
void Update()
{
    if (Input.GetKey(KeyCode.W))
    {
        transform.Translate(0, 0, speed);
    }
}
```

Figure 15.10 – Conditioning the movement until the W key is pressed

2. We can add other movement directions with more `if` statements. We can use *S* to move backward and *A* and *D* to move left and right, as shown in the following screenshot. Notice how we used the minus sign to inverse the speed when we needed to move in the opposite axis direction:

```csharp
if (Input.GetKey(KeyCode.W))
    transform.Translate(0, 0, speed);

if (Input.GetKey(KeyCode.S))
    transform.Translate(0, 0, -speed);

if (Input.GetKey(KeyCode.A))
    transform.Translate(-speed, 0, 0);

if (Input.GetKey(KeyCode.D))
    transform.Translate(speed, 0, 0);
```

Figure 15.11 – Checking the W, A, S, and D keys' pressure

> **Important Note**
>
> Remember that using `if` statements without brackets means that only the line inside the `if` statement is going to be the one right next to the `if` statement, in this case, the `transform.Translate` calls. Anyway, in the final code, I recommend keeping the brackets.

3. If you also want to consider the arrow keys, you can use an OR inside `if`, as shown in the following screenshot:

```csharp
if (Input.GetKey(KeyCode.W) || Input.GetKey(KeyCode.UpArrow))
    transform.Translate(0, 0, speed);

if (Input.GetKey(KeyCode.S) || Input.GetKey(KeyCode.DownArrow))
    transform.Translate(0, 0, -speed);

if (Input.GetKey(KeyCode.A) || Input.GetKey(KeyCode.LeftArrow))
    transform.Translate(-speed, 0, 0);

if (Input.GetKey(KeyCode.D) || Input.GetKey(KeyCode.RightArrow))
    transform.Translate(speed, 0, 0);
```

Figure 15.12 – Checking the W, A, S, and D arrow keys' pressure

4. Save the changes and test the movement in Play Mode.

Something to take into account is that, first, we have another way to map several keys to a single action by configuring the Input Manager, a place where action mappings can be created, and second, at the time of writing this, Unity has released a new Input System that is more extensible than this one. For now, we will use this one because it is simple enough to make our introduction to scripting with Unity easier, but in games with complex input, controls are recommended to look for more advanced tools.

Now, for the Visual Scripting version, the graph will look like this:

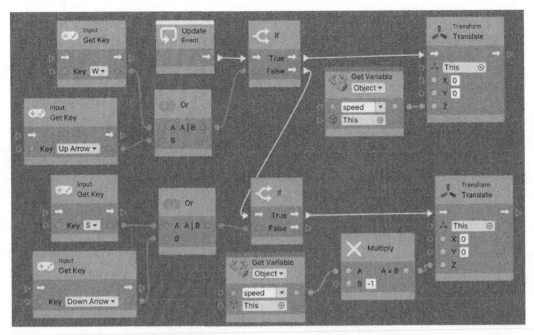

Figure 15.13 – Input movement in Visual Scripting

As you can see, the graph grows in size considerably compared to the C# version, which serves as an example of why developers prefer to code instead of using visual tools. Of course, we have several ways to split this graph into smaller chunks and make it more readable, and also consider I needed to squeeze the nodes together to be in the same image. Also, in the graph, we only see the example graph to move forward and backward, but you can easily extrapolate the needed steps for lateral movement based on this one. As usual, you can also check the GitHub repository of the project to see the completed files.

Looking at the graph, you can quickly observe all the similarities to the C# version; we chained **If** nodes to the **Update** event node, in such a way that if the first **If** node condition is true, it will execute **Translate** in the forward direction. If that condition is false, we chained the **False** output node to another **If** that checks the pressure of other keys, and in that case, we moved backward, using the **Multiply (Scalar)** node to inverse the speed. You can notice nodes such as If that have more than one Flow Output pin to branch the execution of the code.

You can also notice the usage of the **GetKey (Key)** node, the Visual Scripting version of the same GetKey function we used previously. When looking at this node in the **Search** box, you will see all the versions of the function, and in this case, we selected the **Get Key (Key)** version; the one that receives a name (string) works differently and we are not covering that one:

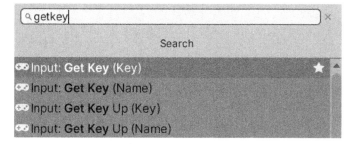

Figure 15.14 – All versions of Input GetKey

We also used the **Or** node to combine the two **Get Key (Key)** functions into one condition to give to the **If** node. These conditional operators can be found in the **Logic** category of the **Search** box:

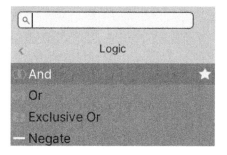

Figure 15.15 – Boolean Logic operators

One thing to highlight is the usage of the **Multiply** node to multiply the value of the speed variable by -1. We needed to create a **Float Literal** node to represent the -1 value. Finally, surely all programmers will notice a little limitation regarding how we used the If node's True and False output pins, but we will address that in a moment.

Now, let's implement the mouse controls. In this section, we will only cover rotation with mouse movement; we will shoot bullets in the next section. In the case of mouse movement, we can get a value by saying how much the mouse has moved both horizontally or vertically. This value isn't a Boolean but a number, a type of input usually known as Axis, a number that will indicate the intensity of the movement with bigger values and the direction with the sign of the number. For example, if Unity's "Mouse X" axis says 0.5, it means that the mouse moved to the right with a moderate speed, but if it says -1, it moved fast to the left, and if there is no movement, it will say 0. The same goes for sticks on gamepads; the **Horizontal** axis represents the horizontal movement of the left stick in common joysticks, so if the player pulls the stick fully to the left, it will say -1.

We can create our own axes to map other common joystick pressure-based controls, but for our game, the default ones are enough. To detect mouse movement, follow these steps:

1. Use the Input.GetAxis function inside Update, next to the movement if statements, as shown in the following screenshot, to store the value of this frame's mouse movement into a variable:

    ```
    float mouseX = Input.GetAxis("Mouse X");
    ```

    Figure 15.16 – Getting the horizontal movement of the mouse

2. Use the transform.Rotate function to rotate the character. This function receives the degrees to rotate in the *X*-, *Y*-, *Z*-axis order. In this case, we need to rotate horizontally, so we will use the mouse movement value as the *Y*-axis rotation, as shown in the next screenshot:

    ```
    float mouseX = Input.GetAxis("Mouse X");
    transform.Rotate(0, mouseX, 0);
    ```

    Figure 15.17 – Rotating the object horizontally based on mouse movement

3. If you save and test this, you will notice that the Player will rotate but very fast or slow, depending on your computer. Remember, this kind of value needs to be configurable, so let's create a rotationSpeed field to configure the speed of the player in the Editor:

    ```
    public float speed;
    public float rotationSpeed;
    ```

    Figure 15.18 – Speed and Rotation speed fields

4. Now, we need to multiply the mouse movement value by the speed, so, depending on the `rotationSpeed` value, we can increase or reduce the rotation amount. As an example, if we set a value of 0.5 in the rotation speed, multiplying that value by the mouse movement will make the object rotate at half the previous speed, as shown in the following screenshot:

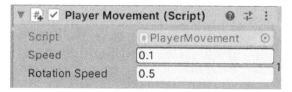

```
float mouseX = Input.GetAxis("Mouse X");
transform.Rotate(0, mouseX * rotationSpeed, 0);
```

Figure 15.19 – Multiplying the mouse movement by the rotation speed

5. Save the code and go back to the editor to set the rotation speed value. If you don't do this, the object won't rotate because the default value of the float type fields is 0:

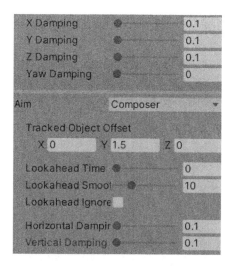

Figure 15.20 – Setting the Rotation speed

6. You might also notice that the camera controlled by Cinemachine might have a delay to adapt to the new Player position. You can adjust the interpolation speed as I did in the next screenshot to have more responsive behavior:

Figure 15.21 – Reduced damping of the body and aim sections of the character virtual camera

The Visual Scripting additions to achieve rotation will look like this:

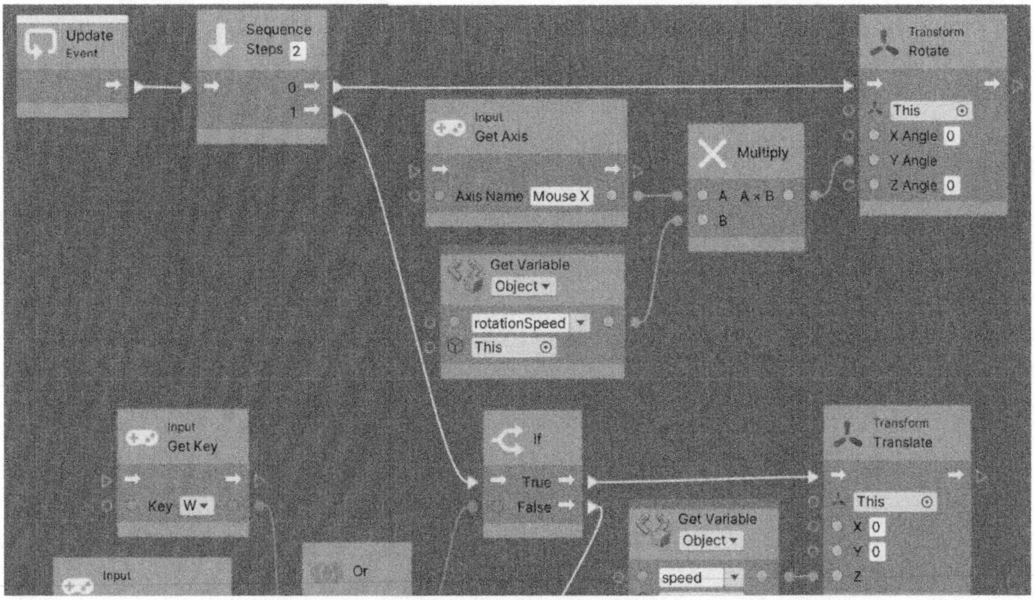

Figure 15.22 – Rotating in Visual Scripting

The first thing to notice here is the usage of the **Sequence** node. An output pin can only be attached to one another node, but in this case, **Update** needs to do two different things, to rotate and to move, each one being independent of the other. **Sequence** is a node that will execute all its output pins one after the other, regardless of the results of each one. You can specify the number of output pins in the **Step** input box; in this example, 2 is plenty.

In output pin 0, the first one, we added the rotation code, which is pretty self-explanatory given it's essentially the same as the movement with slightly different nodes (**Rotate (X, Y, Z)** and **GetAxis**). Then, to Output Pin 1, we attached the If we had originally directly attached to the Update node, in such a way that the code movement will execute after the rotation.

Regarding the limitation we mentioned before, it's basically the fact that we cannot execute both Forward and Backward rotation, given that if the forward movement keys are pressed, the first If will be true. Because the backward key rotation is checked in the false output pin, they won't be checked in such cases. Of course, in this case, it makes sense, but consider the lateral movement; if we continue the If chaining using True and False output pins, we will have a scenario where we can only move in one direction, so we cannot combine, in this example, Forward and Right to move diagonally.

A simple solution to this issue is to put the If nodes in the sequence instead of chaining them, in such a way that all the Ifs are checked, as the original C# code did. You can see an example of this in the next screenshot:

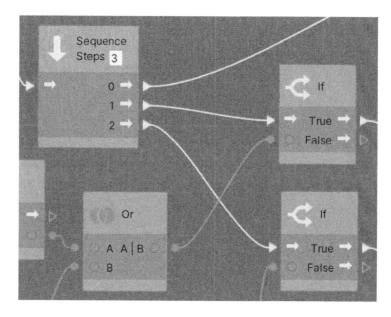

Figure 15.23 – Sequencing Ifs

Something to consider here is that the chaining of the ifs can be removed by right-clicking the line that connected them. Now that we have completed our movement script, we need to refine it to work in every machine by exploring the concept of Delta Time.

Understanding Delta Time

Unity's Update loop executes as fast as the computer can. You can specify in Unity the desired frame rate but achieving that depends exclusively on whether your computer can reach it, which depends on lots of factors, not only hardware, so you cannot expect to always have consistent FPS. You must code your scripts to handle every possible scenario. Our current script is moving at a certain speed per frame, and the *per frame* part is important here.

We have set the movement speed to 0.1, so if my computer runs the game at 120 fps, the player will move 12 meters per second. Now, what happens in a computer where the game runs at 60 fps? As you may guess, it will move only 6 meters per second, making our game have inconsistent behavior across different computers. And this is where Delta Time saves the day.

Delta Time is a value that tells us how much time has passed since the previous frame. This time depends a lot on our game's graphics, the number of entities, physics bodies, audio, and countless aspects that will dictate how fast your computer can process a frame. As an example, if your game runs at 10 fps, it means that, in a second, your computer can process the Update loop 10 times, meaning that each loop takes approximately 0.1 seconds; in that frame, Delta Time will provide that value. In the next diagram, you can see an example of four frames taking different times to process, which can happen in real-life cases:

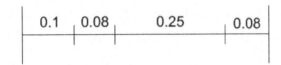

Figure 15.24 – Delta Time value varying on different frames of the game

Here, we need to code in such a way to change the *per frame* part of the movement to *per second*; we need to have consistent movement per second across different computers. A way to do that is to move proportionally to the Delta Time: the higher the Delta Time value, the longer that frame is, and the farthest the movement should be to match the real time that has passed since the last update. We can think about our speed field current value in terms of 0.1 meters per second; our Delta Time saying 0.5 means that half a second has passed, so we should move half the speed, 0.05. After two frames, 1 second has passed, and the sum of the movements of the frames (2 x 0.05) matches the target speed, 0.1. Delta Time can be interpreted as the percentage of a second that has passed.

To make the Delta Time affect our movement, we should simply multiply our speed by Delta Time every frame because Delta Time can be different every frame, so let's do that:

1. We access Delta Time using `Time.deltaTime`. We can start affecting the movement by multiplying the Delta Time in every Translate:

```
if (Input.GetKey(KeyCode.W) || Input.GetKey(KeyCode.UpArrow))
    transform.Translate(0, 0, speed * Time.deltaTime);

if (Input.GetKey(KeyCode.S) || Input.GetKey(KeyCode.DownArrow))
    transform.Translate(0, 0, -speed * Time.deltaTime);

if (Input.GetKey(KeyCode.A) || Input.GetKey(KeyCode.LeftArrow))
    transform.Translate(-speed * Time.deltaTime, 0, 0);

if (Input.GetKey(KeyCode.D) || Input.GetKey(KeyCode.RightArrow))
    transform.Translate(speed * Time.deltaTime, 0, 0);
```

Figure 15.25 – Multiplying speed by Delta Time

2.   We can do the same with the rotation speed, chaining the mouse and speed multiplications:

```
float mouseX = Input.GetAxis("Mouse X");
transform.Rotate(0, mouseX * rotationSpeed * Time.deltaTime, 0);
```

Figure 15.26 – Applying Delta Time to rotation code

3.   If you save and play the game, you will notice that the movement will be slower than before and that's because now, 0.1 is the movement per second, meaning 10 centimeters per second, which is pretty slow; try raising those values. In my case, 10 for speed and 180 for rotation speed was enough, but the rotation speed depends on the Player's preferred sensibility, which can be configurable, but let's keep that for another time.

The Visual Scripting change for rotation will look like this:

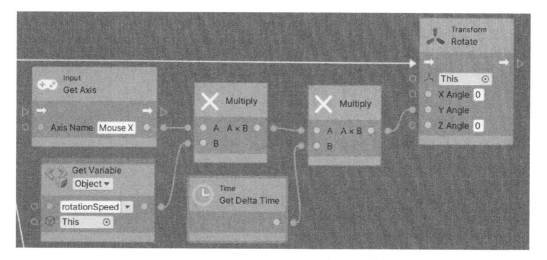

Figure 15.27 – Applying Delta Time to rotation Visual Scripting

For Movement, you can easily extrapolate from this example or remember to check the project on GitHub. We simply chained another **Multiply** node with **Get Delta Time**.

We just learned how to mix the **Input system** of Unity, which tells us about the state of the keyboard, mouse, and other input devices, with the basic Transform movement functions. This way, we can start making our game feel more dynamic.

Now that we have finished with the Player's movement, let's discuss how to make the Player shoot bullets using Instantiate functions.

Implementing spawning

We have created lots of objects in the Editor that define our level, but once the game begins, and according to the Player actions, new objects must be created to better fit the scenarios generated by Player interaction. Enemies might need to appear after a while, or bullets must be created according to the player input; even when enemies die, there's a chance of spawning some power-up. This means that we cannot create all the needed objects beforehand but should create them dynamically, and that's done through scripting.

In this section, we will examine the following spawning concepts:

- Spawning Objects
- Timing actions
- Destroying Objects

We will start by looking at the Unity `Instantiate` function, which allows us to create instances of Prefabs at runtime, such as when pressing a key, or in a time-based fashion, such as making our enemy spawn bullets after a certain amount of time. Also, we will learn how to destroy these Objects to prevent our scene from starting to perform badly due to too many Objects being processed.

Let's start with how to shoot bullets according to the Player's Input.

Spawning Objects

To spawn an Object at runtime or in Play Mode, we need a description of the Object, which components it has, and its settings and possible sub-Objects. You might be thinking about Prefabs here, and you are right; we will use an instruction that will tell Unity to create an instance of a Prefab via scripting. Remember that an instance of a Prefab is an Object created based on the Prefab, basically a clone of the original one.

We will start by shooting the Player's bullets, so first let's create the bullet Prefab by following these steps:

1. Create a sphere in **GameObject | 3D Object | Sphere**. You can replace the sphere mesh with another bullet model if you want, but we will keep the sphere in this example for now.
2. Rename the sphere `Bullet`.
3. Create a material by clicking on the + button of the Project window and choosing the **Material** option and call it `Bullet`. Remember to place it inside the `Materials` folder.

4. Check the **Emission** checkbox in the material and set the **Emission Map** and **Base Map** colors to red. Remember, the Emission color will make the bullet shine, especially with the Bloom effect in our postprocessing volume:

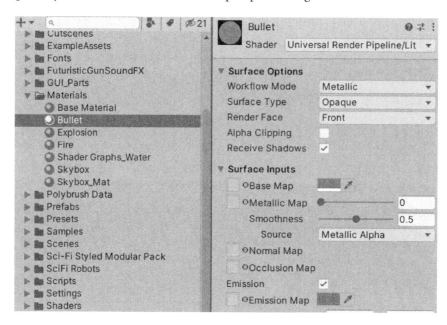

Figure 15.28 – Creating a red Bullet material with Emission Color

5. Apply the Material to the Sphere by dragging the material to it.

6. Setting the Scale to a smaller value, (0.3, 0.3, 0.3), worked in my case:

Figure 15.29 – Small red-colored bullet

7. Create a script called `ForwardMovement` to make the bullet constantly move forward at a fixed speed. You can create it with both C# and Visual Scripting, but for simplicity, we are only going to use C# in this case.

I suggest you try to solve first this by yourself and look at the screenshot in the next step with the solution later as a little challenge to recap the movement concepts we saw previously. If you don't recall how to create a script, please refer to *Chapter 14, Introduction to C# and Visual Scripting*, and check the previous section to see how to move objects.

8. The next screenshot shows you what the script should look like:

```csharp
using UnityEngine;

public class ForwardMovement : MonoBehaviour
{
    public float speed;

    void Update()
    {
        transform.Translate(0,0,speed * Time.deltaTime);
    }
}
```

Figure 15.30 – A simple Move Forward script

9. Add the script (if not already there) to the bullet and set the speed to a value you see fit. Usually, bullets are faster than the Player but that depends on the Player experience you want to get (remember the questions in *Chapter 1, Designing a Game from Scratch*). In my case, 20 worked fine. Test it by placing the bullet near the Player and playing the game:

Figure 15.31 – Forward Movement script in the bullet

10. Drag the bullet GameObject instance to the Prefabs folder to create a **Bullet** Prefab. Remember that the Prefab is an asset that has a description of the created bullet, like a blueprint of how to create a bullet:

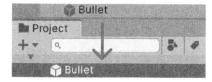

Figure 15.32 – Creating a Prefab

11. Remove the original bullet from the Scene; we will use the Prefab to create bullets when the player presses a key (if ever).

Now that we have our bullet Prefab, it is time to instantiate it (clone it) when the player presses a key. To do that, follow these steps:

1. Create and add a script to the Player's GameObject (the Robot) called PlayerShooting and open it.

    We need a way for the script to have access to the Prefab to know which Prefab to use from probably dozens we will have in our project. All of the data our script needs that depends on the desired game experience is in the form of a field, such as the speed field used so far, so in this case, we need a field of the GameObject type, a field that can reference or point to a specific Prefab, which can be set using the Editor.

2. Adding the field code would look like this:

```
using UnityEngine;

public class PlayerShooting : MonoBehaviour
{
    public GameObject prefab;
}
```

Figure 15.33 – The Prefab reference field

> **Important Note**
>
> As you might guess, we can use the GameObject type to reference not only Prefabs but also other Objects. Imagine an Enemy AI needing a reference to the Player object to get its position, using GameObject to link the two objects. The trick here is considering that Prefabs are just regular GameObjects that live outside the scene; you cannot see them, but they are in memory, ready to be copied or instantiated. You will only see them through copies or instances that are placed in the scene with scripting or via the Editor as we have done so far.

3. In the Editor, click on the circle toward the right of the property and select the Bullet Prefab. Another option is to just drag the Bullet Prefab to the property:

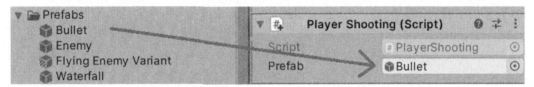

Figure 15.34 – Setting the Prefab reference to point to the bullet

This way, we tell our script that the bullet to shoot will be that one. Remember to drag the Prefab and not the bullet in the scene (which should be deleted by now).

We will shoot the bullet when the player presses the left mouse button as specified in the design document, so let's place the proper if statement to handle that in the Update event function, such as the one shown in the next screenshot:

```
void Update()
{
    if (Input.GetKeyDown(KeyCode.Mouse0))
    {

    }
}
```

Figure 15.35 – Detecting the pressure of the left mouse button

You will notice that this time, we used GetKeyDown instead of GetKey, the former being a way to detect the exact frame the pressure of the key started; this if statement will execute its code only in that frame, and until the key is released and re-pressed, it won't enter again. This is one way to prevent bullets from spawning at every frame, but just for fun, you can try using GetKey instead to check how it would behave. Also, 0 is the mouse button number that belongs to left-click, 1 the right-click, and 2 the middle-click.

We can use the `Instantiate` function to clone the Prefab, passing the reference to it as the first parameter. This will create a clone of the mentioned Prefab that will be placed in the scene:

```
if (Input.GetKeyDown(KeyCode.Mouse0))
{
    Instantiate(prefab);
}
```

Figure 15.36 – Instantiating the Prefab

If you save the script and play the game, you will notice that when you press the mouse, a bullet will be spawning, but probably not in the place you are expecting. If you don't see it, try to check the Hierarchy for new objects; it will be there. The problem here is that we didn't specify the desired spawn position, and we have two ways of setting that, which we will see in the next steps.

The first way is to use the `transform.position` and `transform.rotation` inherited fields from `MonoBehaviour`, which will tell us our current position and rotation. We can pass them as the second and third parameters of the `Instantiate` function, which will understand that this is the place we want our bullet to appear. Remember that it is important to set the rotation to make the bullet face the same direction as the Player, so it will move that way:

```
Instantiate(prefab, transform.position, transform.rotation);
```

Figure 15.37 – Instantiating the Prefab in our position and rotation

The second way, which will be longer but will give us more flexibility to change other aspects of the object, is by using the previous version of Instantiate, but saving the reference returned by the function, which will be pointing to the clone of the Prefab. Having a reference to the instantiated bullet allows us to change whatever we want from it, not only the position but also the rotation, but for now, let's limit ourselves to position and rotation. In this case, we will need the following three lines; the first will instantiate and capture the clone reference, the second will set the position of the clone, and the third will set the rotation. You will notice we will also use the `transform.position` field of the clone, but this time to change its value by using the = (assignment) operator:

```
GameObject clone = Instantiate(prefab);
clone.transform.position = transform.position;
clone.transform.rotation = transform.rotation;
```

Figure 15.38 – The longer version of instantiating a Prefab in a specific position

Use the version you like the most—both do the same. Remember that you can check the project repository to see the full, finished script. Now, you can save the file with one of the versions and try the script.

If you try the script so far, you should see the bullet spawn in the Player's position, but in our case, it will probably be the floor. The problem here is that the Robot pivot is there, and usually, every Humanoid Character has the pivot there. We have several ways to fix that, the most flexible one being to create a Shoot Point, an empty Player's child Object placed in the position we want the bullet to spawn. We can use the position of that Object instead of the Player's position by following these steps:

1. Create an empty `GameObject` in **GameObject | Create Empty**. Rename it `ShootPoint`.

2. Make it a child of the Player's Robot Character Object, and place it where you want the bullet to appear, probably a little higher and further forward than the original spawn position:

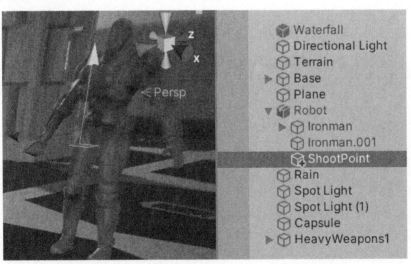

Figure 15.39 – An empty Shoot Point object placed inside the character

3. As usual, to access the data of another Object, we need a reference to it, such as the Prefab reference, but this time that one needs to point to our Shoot Point. We can create another `GameObject` type field, but this time drag `ShootPoint` instead of the Prefab. The script and the Object set would look as shown in the following screenshot:

```
public GameObject prefab;
public GameObject shootPoint;
```

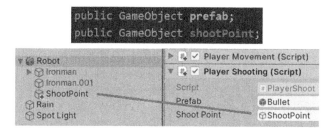

Figure 15.40 – The Prefab and Shoot Point fields and how they are set in the Editor

4. We can access the position of the `shootPoint` by using the `transform.position` field of it again, as shown in the following screenshot:

```
GameObject clone = Instantiate(prefab);
clone.transform.position = shootPoint.transform.position;
clone.transform.rotation = shootPoint.transform.rotation;
```

Figure 15.41 – The Prefab and Shoot Point fields and how they are set in the Editor

The Visual Scripting version of Forward Movement will look like this:

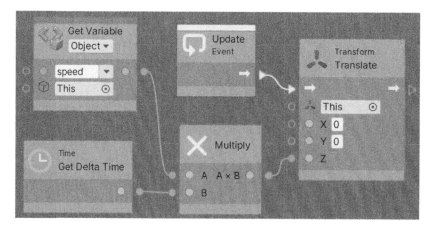

Figure 15.42 – Forward Movement with Visual Scripting

This is what it will look like for **PlayerShooting**:

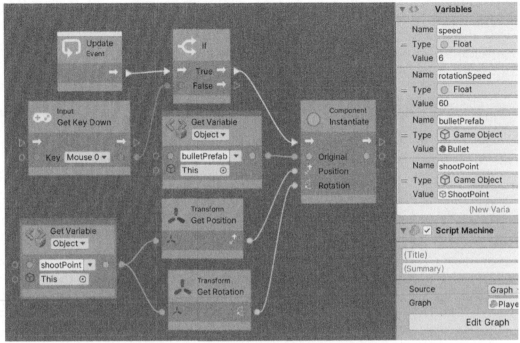

Figure 15.43 – Instantiating with Visual Scripting

As you can see, we added a second **Script Machine** component with a new Graph called **Player Shooting**. We also added a new variable called **bulletPrefab** of the **GameObject** type and dragged the **Bullet** prefab to it, and a second **GameObject** type variable called **shootPoint**, to have the reference to the bullet's spawn position. The rest of the script is essentially the counterpart of the C# version without major differences. Something to highlight here is how we connected the **Transform GetPosition** and **Transform GetRotation** nodes to the **GetVariable** node belonging to the **shootPoint**; this way, we are accessing the position and rotation of the shooting point. If you don't specify that, it will use the Player's position and rotation, which in the case of our model is in the Player's character feet.

You will notice that now, shooting and rotating with the mouse has a problem; when moving the mouse to rotate, the pointer will fall outside the Game View, and when clicking, you will accidentally click the Editor, losing the focus on the Game View, so you will need to click the Game View again to regain focus and use Input again. A way to prevent this is to disable the cursor while playing. To do this, follow these steps:

1. Add a `Start` event function to our Player Movement Script.

2. Add the two lines you can see in the following screenshot to your script. The first one will make the cursor visible, and the second one will lock it in the middle of the screen, so it will never abandon the Game View. Consider the latter; you will need to reenable the cursor when you switch back to the main menu or the pause menu, to allow the mouse to click the UI buttons:

```
void Start()
{
    Cursor.visible = false;
    Cursor.lockState = CursorLockMode.Locked;
}
```

Figure 15.44 – Disabling the mouse cursor

3. Save and test this. If you want to stop the game, you could press either *Ctrl + Shift + P* (*Command + Shift + P* on Mac) or the *Esc* key to reenable the mouse. Both only work in the Editor; in the real game, you will need to reenable it manually.

The Visual Scripting equivalent will look like this:

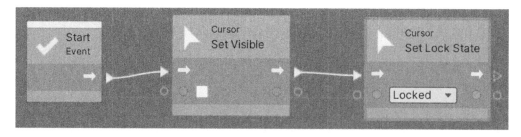

Figure 15.45 – Disabling the mouse cursor in Visual Scripting

Now that we have covered the basics of object spawning, let's see an advanced example by combining it with timers.

Timing actions

Not entirely related to spawning, but usually used together, timing actions is a common task in videogames. The idea is to schedule something to happen later; maybe we want the bullet to be destroyed after a while to prevent memory overflow, or we want to control the spawn rate of enemies or when they should spawn, and that's exactly what we are going to do in this section, starting with the second, the Enemy waves.

The idea is that we want to spawn enemies at a certain rate at different moments of the game; maybe we want to spawn enemies from second 1 to 5 at a rate of 2 per second, getting 10 enemies, and giving the Player up to 20 seconds to finish them, programming another wave starting at second 25. Of course, this depends a lot on the exact game you want, and you can start with an idea such as this one and modify it after some testing to find the exact way you want the wave system to work. In our case, we will exemplify timing with the previously mentioned logic.

First of all, we need an Enemy, and for now, we will simply use the same robot character as the Player, but adding a Forward Movement script to simply make it move forward; later in this book, we will add AI behavior to our enemies. I suggest you try to create this Prefab by yourself and look at the following steps once you have tried, to check the correct answer:

1. Drag the Robot FBX model to the scene to create another Robot character but rename it `Enemy` this time.

2. Add the `ForwardMovement` script created for the bullets but this time to `Enemy` and set it at a speed of 10 for now.

3. Drag the `Enemy` GameObject to the Project to create a Prefab based on that one; we will need to spawn it later. Remember to choose Prefab Variant, which will keep the Prefab linked with the original model to make the changes applied to the model automatically apply to the Prefab. Remember also to destroy the original Enemy from the scene.

Now, to schedule actions, we will use the Invoke functions suite, a set of functions to create timers that are basic but enough for our requirements. Let's use it by following these steps:

1. Create an Empty GameObject at one end of the Base and call it `Wave1a`.

2. Create and add a script called `WaveSpawner` to it.

3. Our spawner will need four fields: the Enemy prefab to spawn, the game time to start the wave, the `endTime` to end the wave spawning, and the spawn rate of the enemies—basically, how much time there should be between each spawn during the given spawning period. The script and the settings will look as in the following screenshot:

```
public GameObject prefab; //Prefab to spawn
public float startTime; //Time to start the wave spawning
public float endTime; //Time to end the wave spawning
public float spawnRate; //Time between each spawn
```

Figure 15.46 – The fields of the wave spawner script

We will use the `InvokeRepeating` function to schedule a custom function to repeat periodically. You will need to schedule the repetition just once; Unity will remember that, so don't do it every frame. This is a good case to use the `Start` event function instead. The first argument of the function is a string (text between quotation marks) with the name of the other function to execute periodically, and unlike Start or Update, you can name the function whatever you want. The second argument is the time to start repeating, our `startTime` field, in this case. Finally, the third argument is the repetition rate of the function, how much time needs to pass between each repetition, this being the `spawnRate` field. You can find how to call that function in the next screenshot, along with the custom `Spawn` function:

```
void Start()
{
    InvokeRepeating("Spawn", startTime, spawnRate);
}

void Spawn()
{

}
```

Figure 15.47 – Scheduling a Spawn function to repeat

4. Inside the `Spawn` function, we can put the spawning code, as we know, using the `Instantiate` function. The idea is to call this function at a certain rate to spawn one Enemy per call. This time, the spawn position will be in the same position as the spawner, so place it carefully:

```
void Spawn()
{
    Instantiate(prefab, transform.position, transform.rotation);
}
```

Figure 15.48 – Instantiating in the Spawn function

If you test this script by setting the Prefab `startTime` and `spawnRate` fields to some test values, you will notice that the enemies will start spawning but never stop, and you can see that we didn't use the `endTime` field so far. The idea is to call the `CancelInvoke` function, a function that will cancel all `InvokeRepeating` calls we made, but after a while, using the `Invoke` function, which works similarly to `InvokeRepeating`, but this one executes just once. In the next screenshot, you can see how we added an `Invoke` call to the `CancelInvoke` function in `Start`, using the `endTime` field as the time to execute `CancelInvoke`. This will execute `CancelInvoke` after a while, canceling the first `InvokeRepeating` call that spawns the prefab:

```
void Start()
{
    InvokeRepeating("Spawn", startTime, spawnRate);
    Invoke("CancelInvoke", endTime);
}
```

Figure 15.49 – Scheduling a Spawn repetition but canceling after a while with CancelInvoke

> **Important Note**
>
> This time, we used `Invoke` to delay the call to `CancelInvoke`; we didn't use a custom function because `CancelInvoke` doesn't receive arguments. If you need to schedule a function with arguments, you will need to create a parameterless wrapper function that calls the one desired and schedule that one, as we did with `Spawn`, where the only intention is to call Instantiate with specific arguments.

5. Now you can save and set some real values to our spawner. In my case, I used the ones shown in the following screenshot:

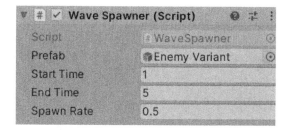

Figure 15.50 – Spawning enemies from second 1 to 5 of gameplay every 0.5 seconds, 2 per second

You should see the enemies being spawned one next to the other and because they move forward, they will form a row of enemies. This behavior will change later with AI:

Figure 15.51 – Spawning enemies

If you want, you can create several Wave Spawner objects, scheduling waves for the later stages of the game. Remember the difficulty balance we discussed in *Chapter 1, Designing a Game from Scratch*; you will need to try this with the final AI for the enemies, but the number of waves, times, and spawn rates will determine the difficulty of the game, and that's why is important to set those values properly. Also, there are plenty of methods to create waves of enemies; this is just the simplest one I could find. You may need to change it according to your game.

Now, the Visual Scripting version will look like this:

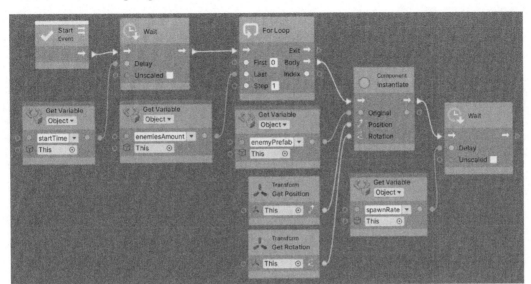

Figure 15.52 – Spawning enemies in Visual Scripting

While we could use the **InvokeRepeating** approach in Visual Scripting, here we can see some benefits of the Visual approach, given it sometimes has more flexibilities than coding. In this case, we used the Wait node at the beginning of **Start**, a node that will basically hold the execution of the flow for a couple of seconds. This will make the initial delay we had in the original script, which is why we used **startTime** as the amount of Delay.

Now, after the wait, we used a For Loop. For this example, we changed the concept of the script; we want to spawn a specific amount of enemies instead of spawning during a time. The For Loop is essentially a classic For that will repeat whatever is connected to the Body output pin a number of times specified by the Last input pin. We connected that pin to a variable to control the number of enemies we want to spawn. Then, we connected an Instantiate to the Body output pin of the For Loop to instantiate our enemies, and then a Wait, to stop the flow for a time before the loop can continue spawning enemies.

Something interesting is that if you play the game now, you will receive an error in the Console that will look like this:

[20:23:45] InvalidOperationException: Port 'enter' on 'WaitForSecondsUnit#ed5f4...' can only be triggered in a coroutine.
Unity.VisualScripting.Flow.InvokeDelegate (Unity.VisualScripting.ControlInput input) (at Library/PackageCache/com.unity

Figure 15.53 – Error when using Wait nodes

You can even get back to the graph editor and see that the conflicting node will be highlighted in red:

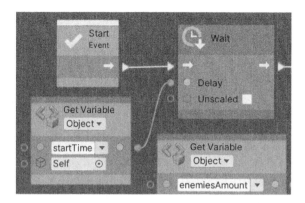

Figure 15.54 – Node causing the error

The issue here is that in order for the **Wait For Seconds** nodes to work, you need to mark the **Start** event as a **Coroutine**. This will basically allow the event to be paused for an amount of time and be resumed later. The same concept exists in C#, but as it is simpler to implement here in Visual Scripting than in C#, we decided to go with this approach here.

To solve this error, just select the **Start** event node and check the **Coroutine** checkbox in the **Graph Inspector** pane at the left of the **Script Graph** editor. If you don't see it, click the **Info** button (the circle with an i) in the top-left part of the editor:

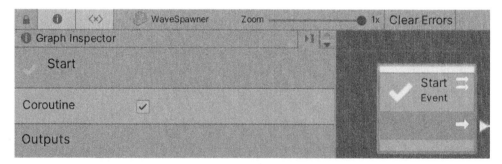

Figure 15.55 – Marking Start as a coroutine

Now that we have discussed timing and spawning, let's discuss timing and destroying to prevent our bullets from living forever in the memory.

Destroying Objects

This is going to be super short but is a widely used function, so it deserves its own section. We can use the `Destroy` function to destroy Object instances. The idea is to make the bullets have a script that schedules its own auto-destruction after a while to prevent it from living forever. We will create the script by following these steps:

1. Select the Prefab of `Bullet` and add a script called `Autodestroy` to it as you did with other Objects using the **Add Component | New Script** option. This time, the script will be added to the Prefab, and each instance of the Prefab you spawn will have it.

2. You can use the `Destroy` function as shown in the following screenshot to destroy the Object just once in `Start`.

   The `Destroy` function expects the object to destroy as the first argument, and here, we are using the `gameObject` reference, a way to point to our GameObject to destroy it. If you use the "this" pointer instead, we will be destroying only the `Autodestroy` component; remember that in Unity, you never create GameObjects but components to add to them:

```
void Start()
{
    Destroy(gameObject);
}
```

Figure 15.56 – Destroying an Object when it starts

Of course, we don't want the bullet to be destroyed as soon as it is spawned, so we need to delay the destruction. You may be thinking about using `Invoke`, but unlike most functions in Unity, `Destroy` can receive a second argument, which is the time to wait until destruction.

3. Create a delay field to use as the second argument of `Destroy`, as shown in the next screenshot:

```
public float delay;

void Start()
{
    Destroy(gameObject, delay);
}
```

Figure 15.57 – Using a field to configure the delay to destroy the Object

4. Set the `delay` field to an appropriate value; in my case, 5 was enough. Now check how the bullets de-spawn after a while by looking at them being removed from the **Hierarchy**.

The Visual Scripting equivalent will look like this:

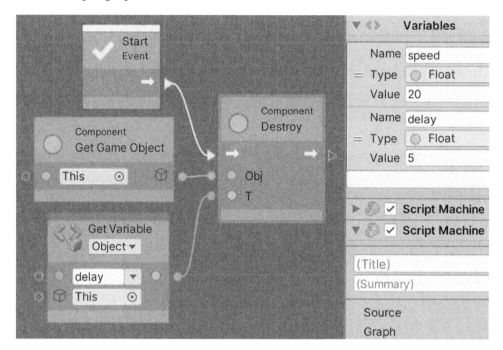

Figure 15.58 – Destroying in Visual Scripting

Regarding this version, notice how we use the **Component Destroy (Obj, T)** version of the **Destroy** node, which includes the delay time.

Now, we can create and destroy Objects at will, which is very common in Unity scripting.

> **Important Note**
> Look up the Object Pool concept; you will learn that sometimes creating and destroying Objects is not that performant.

Summary

In this chapter, we created our first real scripts, which provide useful behavior. We discussed how to instantiate Prefabs via scripting, to create Objects at will according to the game situation. Also, we saw how to schedule actions, in this case, spawning, but this can be used to schedule anything. Finally, we saw how to destroy created Objects, to prevent increasing the number of Objects to an unmanageable level. We will be using these actions to create other kinds of Objects, such as sounds and effects, later in this book.

Now you are able to create any type of movement or spawning logic your Objects will need and make sure those Objects are destroyed when needed. You might think that all games move and create shooting systems the same way, but while they are similar, being able to create your own movement and shooting scripts allows you to customize those aspects of the game to behave as intended and create the exact experience you are looking for.

In the next chapter, we will be discussing how to detect collisions to prevent the Player and bullets from passing through walls, and much more.

16
Physics Collisions and Health System

Since games try to simulate real-world behaviors, one important aspect to simulate is physics, which dictates how Objects move and how they collide with each other, such as players colliding with walls, bullets, or enemies. Physics can be difficult to control due to the myriad of reactions that can happen after a collision. So, in this chapter, we will learn how to configure this to obtain semi-accurate Physics, which will generate the desired arcade movement feeling but get collisions working – after all, sometimes, real life is not as interesting as video games.

In this chapter, we will cover the following collision concepts:

- Configuring Physics
- Detecting collisions
- Moving with Physics

First, we will learn how to properly configure Physics, a step that's needed for the collisions between Objects to be detected by our scripts, using new events we are also going to learn about. All of this is needed to detect when our bullets touch our enemies and damage them. Then, we are going to discuss the difference between moving with `Transform`, as we have done so far, and moving with `Rigidbody` and the pros and cons of each version. We will use them to experiment with different ways of moving our Player and let you decide which one you will want to use. Let's start by discussing the available Physics settings.

Configuring Physics

Unity's Physics system is prepared to cover a great range of possible gameplay applications, so configuring it properly is important to get the desired results.

In this section, we will examine the following Physics settings and concepts:

- Setting shapes
- Physics Object types
- Filtering collisions

We are going to start by learning about the different kinds of colliders that Unity offers, so that we can then learn about different ways to configure those to detect different kinds of Physics reactions (collisions and triggers). Finally, we will discuss how to ignore collisions between specific Objects to prevent situations such as the Player's bullets damaging them.

Setting shapes

At the beginning of this book, we learned that objects usually have two shapes: the visual shape, which is basically the 3D mesh, and the physical one, known as the collider, which the Physics system uses to calculate collisions. Remember that the idea of this is to allow you to have a highly detailed visual model while having a simplified Physics shape to increase performance.

Unity has several types of colliders, so here, we will recap on the common ones, starting with the primitive types; that is, **Box**, **Sphere**, and **Capsule**. These shapes are the cheapest ones (in terms of performance) for detecting collisions since the collisions between them are done via mathematical formulas, unlike other colliders, such as **Mesh Collider**, which allows you to use any mesh as the physics body of the Object, but with a higher cost and some limitations. The idea is that you should use a primitive type to represent your Objects or a combination of them. For example, a plane could be done with two Box Colliders, one for the body and the other for the wings. You can see an example of this in the following screenshot, where you can see a weapons collider made out of primitives:

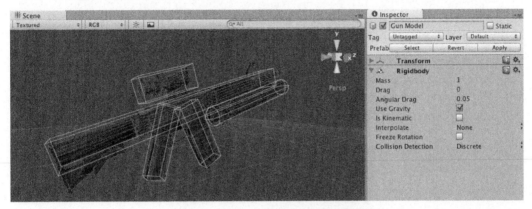

Figure 16.1 – Compound colliders

Try to avoid doing this; if we want the weapon to just fall to the ground, maybe a Box Collider covering the entire weapon can be enough, considering those kinds of collisions don't need to be accurate, thereby increasing performance. Also, some shapes cannot be represented even with a combination of primitive shapes, such as ramps or pyramids, where your only solution is to use a Mesh Collider, which asks for a 3D mesh to use for collisions. However, we won't be using them in this book; instead, we will solve all our Physics colliders with primitives.

Now, let's add the necessary colliders to our scene to prepare it to calculate collisions properly. Note that if you used an Asset Store environment package other than mine, you may already have the scene modules with colliders; I will be showing the work I needed to do in my case, but try to extrapolate the main ideas here to your scene. To add the colliders, follow these steps:

1. Select a wall in the base and check the Object and possible child Objects of the collider components; in my case, I have no colliders. If you detect a Mesh Collider, you can leave it, but I would suggest that you remove it and replace it with another option in the next step. The idea is to add the collider to it, but the problem I detected here is that, since my wall is not an instance of a Prefab, I need to add a collider to every wall.

2. One option is to create a Prefab and replace all the walls with instances of the Prefab (the recommended solution) or just select all the walls in the **Hierarchy** window (by clicking them while pressing *Ctrl* or *Cmd* on Mac) and, with them selected, use the **Add Component** button to add a collider to all of them. In my case, I will use the Box Collider component, which will adapt the size of the collider to the mesh. If this doesn't adapt, you can just change the **Size** and **Center** properties of the Box Collider so that it covers the entire wall:

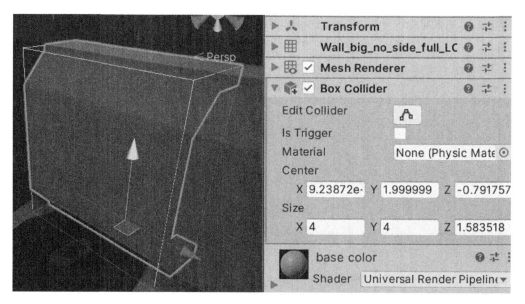

Figure 16.2 – A Box Collider added to a wall

3. Repeat *steps 1* and *2* for the corners, floor tiles, and any other obstacles that will block Player and Enemy movement.

For our Enemy and Player, we will be adding the Capsule Collider, the typical collider you use in movable characters. This is because the rounded bottom will allow the Object to smoothly climb ramps. Being horizontally rounded allows the Object to easily rotate corners without getting stuck. This is just one of the conveniences of this shape. Remember that the Enemy is a Prefab, so you will need to add the collider to the Prefab, while our Player is a simple Object in the scene, so you will need to add the collider to that one.

> **Important Note**
>
> You may be tempted to add several Box Colliders to the bones of the character to create a realistic shape for the Object, and while we can do that to apply different damage according to the part of the body where the enemies were shot, we are just creating movement colliders; the capsule is enough. In advanced damage systems, both capsule and bone colliders will coexist, one for movement and the other for damage detection; however, we will simplify this in our game.

Also, sometimes, the collider won't adapt well to the visual shape of the Object, and in my case, the Capsule Collider didn't have a nice shape for the character. I needed to fix its shape so that it matches the character by setting its values, as shown in the following screenshot:

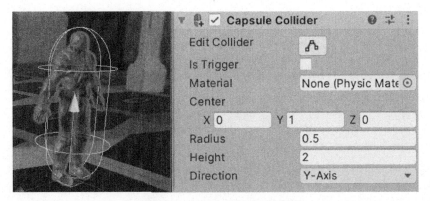

Figure 16.3 – Character collider

The bullet we created with the Sphere already had a Sphere Collider, but if you replaced the mesh of the bullet with another one, you might want to change the collider. For now, we don't need other Objects in our game. So, now that everyone has its proper collider, let's learn how to set the different Physics settings for each Object to enable proper collision detection.

Physics Object types

Now that we have added colliders to every Object by making the Objects have a presence in the Physics Simulation, it is time to configure them so that they have the exact Physics behavior we want. We have a myriad of possible combinations we can use for the settings, but we will discuss a set of common profiles that cover most situations. Remember that besides colliders, we have the `Rigidbody` component, which we looked at at the beginning of this book, which applies physics to the Object. The following profiles can be created with a combination of colliders and `Rigidbody` settings:

- **Static Collider**: As its name suggests, this kind of collider is one that is not supposed to move by any means in the game, aside from in some specific exceptions. Most of the environment Objects fall into this category, such as walls, floors, obstacles, and the Terrain. These kinds of colliders are just colliders with no `Rigidbody` component, so they have a presence in the Physics Simulation but don't have any Physics applied to them; they cannot be moved by other Objects, they won't have physics, and they will be fixed at their position, no matter what. Take into account that this has nothing to do with the static checkbox at the top-right part of the **Editor** window; those are for the previously seen systems (such as **Lighting** and others), so you can have a Static Collider with that checkbox unchecked if needed.

> **Important Note**
>
> Take into account that these Objects can be moved via scripting, but you shouldn't do this. Unity applies an optimization technique to them, and every time a Static Collider is moved, the optimization becomes invalid, needing further calculations to update it, and doing that every frame is costly.
>
> We just mentioned Terrain as an example, and if you check the Terrain's components, you will see that it has its own kind of collider, known as **Terrain Collider**. For Terrain, that's the only collider to use.

- **Physics Collider**: These are colliders with a `Rigidbody` component, as shown in the example of the falling ball we covered in the first part of this book. These are fully Physics-driven Objects that have gravity and can be moved through force; other Objects can push them and they perform every other Physics reaction you can expect. You can use this for the Player, grenade movement, falling crates, or in all Objects in heavily physics-based games such as *The Incredible Machine*.

- **Kinematic Collider**: These are colliders that have a `Rigidbody` component but have the **Is Kinematic** checkbox checked. These don't have Physics reactions, collisions, and forces as Static Colliders, but they can be moved via scripting (`transform.Translate`) with no performance penalties. Consider that since they don't have Physics, they won't have collisions either, so they can pass through walls. These can be used in Objects that need to move using animations or custom scripting movement such as moving platforms. In this case, the platform won't collide with other Objects, but the Player, which usually has a Physics Collider, will collide with them; actually, the Physics Collider is the one that will collide with every kind of collider.

- **Trigger Static Collider**: This is a regular Static Collider but with the **Is Trigger** checkbox of the Collider checked. The difference is that Kinematic and Physics Objects pass through it but by generating a `Trigger` event, an event that can be captured via scripting, that tells us that something is inside the collider. This can be used to create buttons or trigger Objects in areas of the game where the Player passes through something happening, such as a wave of enemies being spawned, a door being opened, or winning the game if that area is the goal of the Player. Consider that regular Static Colliders won't generate a trigger event when passing through this type because those aren't supposed to move.

- **Trigger Kinematic Collider**: Kinematic Colliders don't generate collisions, so they will pass through any other Object. However, they will generate Trigger events, so we can react via scripting. We can use this to create moveable power-ups that, when touched, disappear and gives us points, or bullets that move with custom scripting movement and no physics, just like our bullets, but damage other Objects they come into contact with.

We can have a Trigger Physics Collider, a collider with `Rigidbody` but with **Is Trigger** checked. Usually, it has no real use; it will be an ever-falling Object that will generate trigger events in the world but pass through everything. Of course, other profiles can exist aside from these ones to be used in some games with specific gameplay requirements, but considering all possible combinations of Physics settings is up to you to. You can always experiment with them to see whether some are useful for your case; the profiles we described here will cover 99% of cases.

To recap the previous scenarios, I leave you with the following table, which shows how the different types of colliders react to each other. You will find a row for each profile that can move; remember that static profiles aren't supposed to move. Each column represents the reaction that occurs when they collide with the other types, with "Nothing" meaning the Object will pass through with no effect, "Trigger" meaning the Object will pass through but raise trigger events, and "Collision" meaning that the Object won't be able to pass through another Object:

	Collides with Static	Collides with Dynamic	Collides with Kinematic	Collides with Trigger Static	Collides with Trigger Kinematic
Dynamic	Collision	Collision	Collision	Trigger	Trigger
Kinematic	Nothing	Nothing	Nothing	Trigger	Trigger
Trigger Kinematic	Trigger	Trigger	Trigger	Trigger	Trigger

Table 15.4 – Collision Reaction Matrix

Considering this, let's start by configuring the physics of our Scene's Objects.

The walls, corners, floor tiles, and obstacles should use the **Static Collider** Profile, so no Rigidbody components should be put on them and their colliders should have the **Is Trigger** checkbox unchecked:

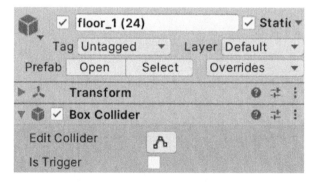

Figure 16.5 – Configuration for floor tiles; remember that the Static checkbox is for lighting only

The Player should move and generate collisions with Objects, so we need it to have a **Dynamic Profile**. This profile will generate a funny behavior with our current movement script (which I encourage you to test), especially when colliding with walls, so it won't behave as expected. We will deal with this later in this chapter:

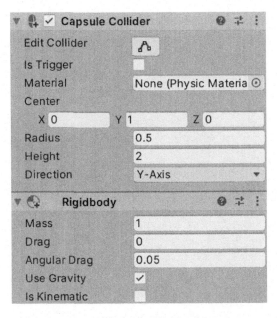

Figure 16.6 – Dynamic settings of the Player

For the `Enemy` Prefab, we will be using the **Kinematic** profile here because we will be moving this Object with Unity's AI systems later, which means we don't need Physics here. Since we want the player to collide with them, we need a Collision reaction, so there's no `Trigger` here:

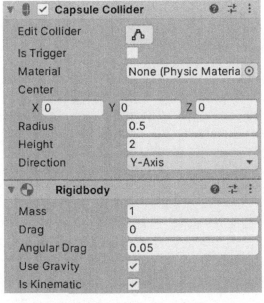

Figure 16.7 – Kinematic settings for the enemy

For the `Bullet` Prefab, it will move but with simplistic movement via scripting (just move forward), not Physics. We don't need collisions; we will code the bullet to destroy itself as soon as it touches something and will damage the collided Object (if possible), so a **Kinematic** Trigger profile is enough for this one; we will use the `Trigger` event to script the contact reactions:

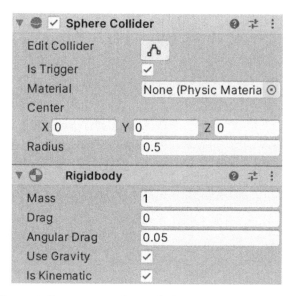

Figure 16.8 – The Kinematic Trigger setting for our bullet; Is Trigger and Is Kinematic are checked

Now that we have configured the Objects, let's learn how to filter undesired collisions between certain Object types.

Filtering collisions

After all of the hassle of configuring Objects, do we want to prevent collisions? Actually, yes – sometimes, we want certain Objects to ignore each other. As an example, the bullets that are shot by the Player shouldn't collide with the Player itself and the bullets from the enemies shouldn't hit them. We can always filter this with an `if` statement in the C# script, checking whether the hit Object is from the opposite team (or whatever filtering logic you want). However, by then, it is too late – the Physics system wasted resources by checking a collision between Objects that were never meant to collide. This is where the Layer Collision Matrix can help us.

The Layer Collision Matrix sounds scary, but it is a simple setting of the Physics system that allows us to specify which groups of Objects should collide with other groups; for example, the Player's bullets should collide with enemies, and Enemy bullets should collide with the Player. The idea is to create those groups and put our Objects inside them, and in Unity, those groups are called **layers**. We can create layers and set the layer property of the GameObject (the top part of the **Inspector** window) to assign the Object to that group or layer. Consider that you have a limited number of layers, so try to use them wisely.

Once we have created the layers and assigned the Object, we can go to the **Physics** settings and specify which layers will collide with other layers. We can achieve this by doing the following:

1. Go to **Edit | Project Settings** and look for the **Tags and Layers** option in the left pane:

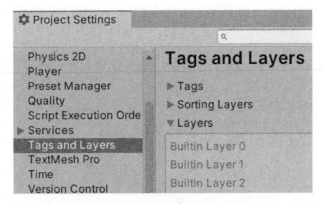

Figure 16.9 – Tags and Layers settings

2. From the **Layers** section, use the empty spaces from **Layer 10** onward to create the necessary ones. In our case, we will use this for the bullet scenario, so we need four layers called Player, Enemy, PlayerBullet, and PlayerEnemy:

User Layer 8	PostProcessing
User Layer 9	Terrain
User Layer 10	Player
User Layer 11	Enemy
User Layer 12	PlayerBullet
User Layer 13	EnemyBullet

Figure 16.10 – Creating layers

3. Select `Player` and, from the top part of the **Inspector** window, change the layer's property to `Player`. Also, change the `Enemy` Prefab so that it has the `Enemy` layer. A window will appear, asking you whether you want to change the child Objects as well; select that option:

Figure 16.11 – Changing the layers of the Player and Enemy Prefabs

In the case of the bullet, we have a problem; we have one Prefab but two layers – a Prefab can only have one layer. We have two options; that is, change the layer according to the shooter via scripting or have two bullet Prefabs with different layers. For simplicity, I will choose the latter, also taking the chance to apply another material to the Enemy bullet to make it look different.

We will be creating a Prefab Variant of the Player bullet. Remember that a Variant is a Prefab that is based on the original one, similar to how class inheritance works. When the original Prefab changes, the Variant will change, but the Variant can have differences, which will make it unique.

4. Drop a bullet prefab onto the scene to create an instance.

5. Drag the instance to the `Prefabs` folder, this time selecting the **Prefab Variant** option. Call it `Enemy Bullet`. Remember to destroy the Prefab instance in the scene.

6. Create a second material similar to the Player bullet, but yellow or whatever color you like, and put it on the `Enemy Bullet` Prefab Variant.

7. Select the Variant for the Enemy bullet, set its layer (`EnemyBullet`), and do the same for the original Prefab (`PlayerBullet`). Even if you changed the original Prefab layer, since the Variant modified it, the modified version (or override) will prevail, allowing each Prefab to have its own layer.

8. Go to **Edit | Project Settings** and look for **Physics settings** (not **Physics 2D**).

9. Scroll down until you see the Layer Collision Matrix, which is a half grid of checkboxes. You will notice that each column and row is labeled with the names of the layers, so each checkbox at the intersection of a row and column will allow us to specify whether those two should collide. In our case, we configured it like so:

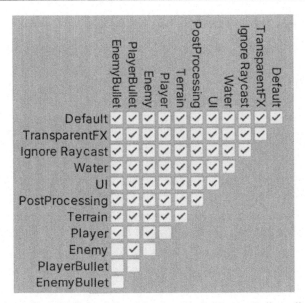

Figure 16.12 – Making PlayerBullet collide with enemies and EnemyBullet collide with the Player

It is worth noticing that sometimes, filtering logic won't be that fixed or predictable; for example, only hit Objects that have a certain amount of life or Objects that don't have an invisibility temporal buff, or conditions that can change during the game that make it difficult to generate all possible layers for all possible groups. So, in these cases, we should rely on manual filtering after the Trigger or Collision event.

Now that we have filtered the collisions, let's check whether our settings are working properly by reacting to collisions.

Detecting collisions

As you can see, proper Physics settings can be complicated and very important, but now that we have tackled that, let's do something with those settings by reacting to the contact in different ways and creating a Health System in the process.

In this section, we will examine the following collision concepts:

- Detecting Trigger events
- Modifying the other Object

First, we are going to explore the different collision and trigger events Unity offers to react to contact between two Objects through Unity's collision events. This will allow us to execute any reaction code we want to place. However, here, we are going to explore how to modify the contacted Object components using the GetComponent function.

Detecting Trigger events

If objects have been configured properly, as we previously discussed, we can get two reactions: triggers and collisions. The Collision reaction has a default effect that blocks the movement of the Objects, but we can add custom behavior on top of that using scripting. However, with triggers, unless we add custom behavior, they won't produce any noticeable effect. Either way, we can script reactions for both possible scenarios such as adding a score, reducing health, and losing the game. To do so, we can use the suite of available Physics events.

These events are split into two groups, Collision events and Trigger events, so according to your Object settings, you will need to pick the proper group. Both groups have three main events called **Enter**, **Stay**, and **Exit**, telling us when a collision or trigger began (Enter), whether they are still happening or are still in contact (Stay), and when they stopped contacting (Exit). For example, we can script a behavior such as playing a sound when two Objects start contacting each other in the Enter event, such as a friction sound, and stop it when the contact ends, in the Exit event.

Let's test this by creating our first contact behavior; that is, the bullet being destroyed when it comes into contact with something. Remember that the bullets have been configured to be triggers, so they will generate Trigger events on contact with anything. You can do this by performing the following steps:

1. Create and add a script called `ContactDestroyer` to the **Bullet Player** Prefab; since the **Bullet Enemy** Prefab is a Variant of it, it will also have the same script.

2. To detect when a trigger occurs, such as with **Start** and **Update**, create an event function named `OnTriggerEnter`.

3. Inside the event, use the `Destroy(gameObject);` line to make the bullet destroy itself when it touches something:

```
public class ContactDestroyer : MonoBehaviour
{
    void OnTriggerEnter()
    {
        Destroy(gameObject);
    }
}
```

Figure 16.13 – Auto destroying on contact with something

4. Save and shoot the bullets at the walls to see how they disappear instead of passing through them. Again, here, we don't have a collision but a trigger that destroys the bullet on contact. So, in this way, we are sure that the bullet will never pass through anything, but we are still not using Physics movement.

For now, we won't need the other Collision events, but in case you need them, they work similarly; just put OnCollisionEnter instead. Now, let's explore another version of the same function. This will not only tell us that we hit something but also what we came into contact with. We will use this to make our **Contact Destroyer** also destroy the other Object. To do this, follow these steps:

1. Replace the OnTriggerEnter method signature with the one in the following screenshot. This one receives a parameter of the Collider type, indicating the exact collider that hit us:

```
void OnTriggerEnter(Collider other)
```

Figure 16.14 – Version of the trigger event that tells us which Object we collided with

2. We can access the entire Object of that collider using the GameObject setter, so we can use this to destroy the other one as well, as shown in the following screenshot. If we just use Destroy by passing the other reference, it will only destroy the Collider component:

```
void OnTriggerEnter(Collider other)
{
    Destroy(gameObject);
    Destroy(other.gameObject);
}
```

Figure 16.15 – Destroying both Objects

3. Save and test the script. You will notice that the bullet will destroy everything it touches.

The equivalent version in Visual Scripting would look as follows:

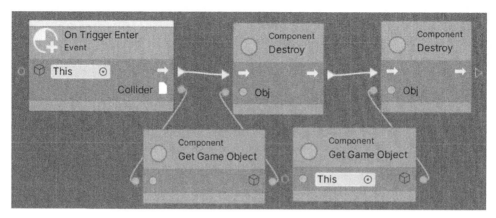

Figure 16.16 – Destroying both Objects with Visual Scripting

As you can see, we created an **On Trigger Enter** node and chained it to two **Destroy** nodes. To specify which object each **Destroy** node will destroy, we used the **Component: Get GameObject** node twice. The first one was created with no node connected to its left input pin, which means it will return the GameObject that is currently executing this script (hence the **Self** label in the node), which in this case is the bullet. For the second one, we needed to connect the **Collider** output pin to the right of the **OnTriggerEnter** node to the **Get Game Object** node. This way, we can specify we want to obtain the GameObject that contains the collider out bullet collided with.

Of course, we don't want the bullet to destroy everything on contact, just itself and the other if it complies with certain criteria, such as being the opposite team or something else, according to our game. In our case, we will move a step forward, and instead of directly destroying the Object on contact, we will make the enemies and the Player have life totals that the bullets will reduce until they reach 0.

Modifying the other Object

So far, we have used the `transform` field to access a specific component of the Object, but what happens when we need to access others? In our scenario, for the bullet to damage the collided Object, it will need to access its `Life` component to change the amount of life. Remember that Unity doesn't have all kinds of possible behaviors for games. So, in our case, the `Life` component is the one that we are going to create, just to hold a float field showing the amount of life. Every Object that has this component will be considered a damageable Object. This is where the `GetComponent` function will help us.

If you have a reference to a GameObject or Component, you can use GetComponent to access a reference of the target component if the Object contains it (if not, it will return null). Let's learn how to use this function to make the bullet lower the amount of life of the other Object if it is damaged:

1. Create and add a Life component with a public float field called amount to both the Player and enemies. Remember to set the value in the amount field for both Objects in the **Inspector** window:

```
public class Life : MonoBehaviour
{
    public float amount;
}
```

Figure 16.17 – The Life component

2. Remove the ContactDestroyer component from the Player bullet, which will also remove it from the Enemy Bullet Variant, and instead add a new one called ContactDamager; you may need the ContactDestroyer behavior later, which is why we are creating another component.

3. Add an OnTriggerEnter event that receives the other collider and add the Destroy function call, which auto destroys itself, not the one that destroyed the other Object; our script won't be responsible for destroying it, just reducing its life.

4. Add a float field called damage so that we can configure the amount of damage to inflict on the other Object. Remember to save the file and set a value before continuing.

5. Use GetComponent on the reference to the other collider to get a reference to its Life component and save it in a variable:

```
Life life = other.GetComponent<Life>();
```

Figure 16.18 – Accessing the collided Life Object component

6. Before reducing the life of the Object, we must check whether the life reference isn't null, which would happen if the other Object doesn't have the Life component, as in the case of walls and obstacles. The idea is that the bullet will destroy itself when anything collides with it, and that it will reduce the life of the other Object if it is a damageable Object that contains the Life component.

The following screenshot shows the complete script:

```
using UnityEngine;

public class ContactDamager : MonoBehaviour
{
    public float damage;

    void OnTriggerEnter(Collider other)
    {
        Destroy(gameObject);

        Life life = other.GetComponent<Life>();
        if (life != null)
        {
            life.amount -= damage;
        }
    }
}
```

Figure 16.19 – Reducing the life of the collided Object

7. Place an Enemy in the scene based on a Prefab and set the instance speed (the one in the scene) to 0 to prevent it from moving.

8. Select it before hitting **Play** and start shooting at it.

You can see how the life value reduces in the **Inspector** window. You can also press the *Esc* key to regain control of the mouse and select the Object while in **Play** mode to see the life field change at runtime in the **Editor** window.

At this point, you will notice that the life is decreasing, but that it will become negative; instead, we want the Object to destroy itself when its life goes below 0. We can do this in two ways; one is to add an Update to the Life component, which will check all of the frames for whether life is below 0, destroying itself when that happens. The second way is by encapsulating the life field and checking it inside the setter to prevent it checking all frames. I would prefer the second way, but we will implement the first one to make our scripts as simple as possible for beginners. To do this, follow these steps:

1. Add Update to the Life component.

2. Add If to check whether the amount field is below 0.

3. Add `Destroy` in case the `if` condition is true.

4. The full `Life` script will look as follows:

```
public class Life : MonoBehaviour
{
    public float amount;

    void Update()
    {
        if (amount < 0)
        {
            Destroy(gameObject);
        }
    }
}
```

Figure 16.20 – The Life component

5. Save this and see how the Object is destroyed once `life` becomes 0.

The Visual Scripting version of the `Life` component would look like this:

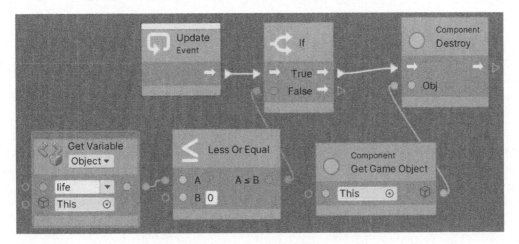

Figure 16.21 – The Life component in Visual Scripting

The script is pretty straightforward; we check if our `Life` variable is less than zero and then destroy ourselves, as we did previously. Now, let's check the `Damager` script:

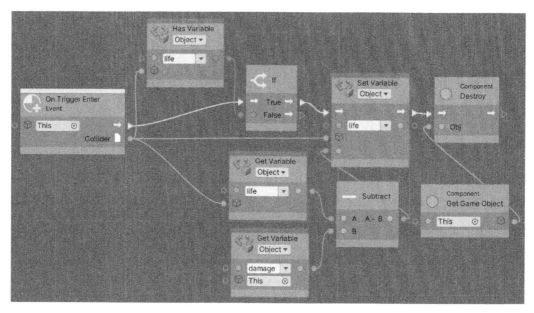

Figure 16.22 – The Damager component in Visual Scripting

This version is a little bit different from its C# counterpart. At first glance, it looks the same; we use **Get Variable**, as we did previously, to read the life, and then we use the **Subtract** node to subtract **damage** from life. The result of that calculation becomes the new value of life, using the **Set Variable** node to alter the current value of that variable.

The first difference we can see here is the absence of a **GetComponent** node. In C#, we used that instruction to get the **Life** component on the collided object to alter its **amount** variable, reducing the remaining life. But in Visual Scripting, our components don't have variables, so we don't need to access the component to read it. Instead, knowing that the enemy has a **Life** variable in its **Variables** component, we can use the **Get Variable** node and connect it to the collider we hit (the **Collider** output pin of **On Trigger Enter**), so essentially, we are reading the value of the **Life** variable of the collided object. The same goes for changing its value; we use the **Set Value** node to connect it to the collider, specifying we want to alter the value of the **Life** variable of the collider object, not ours (we don't have one). Note that this can raise an error if the collided object doesn't have the **Life** variable, and that is why we added the **Object Has Variable** node, which checks if the object actually has a variable called **Life**. If it doesn't, we just do nothing, which is useful when we collide with walls or other non-destructible objects. Finally, we make the Damager (the bullet, in this case) auto-destroy.

Optionally, you can instantiate an Object when this happens, such as a sound, a particle, or maybe a power-up. I will leave this as a challenge for you. By using a similar script, you can make a life power-up that increases the **Life** value or a speed power-up that accesses the `PlayerMovement` script and increases the speed field; from now on, use your imagination to create exciting behaviors using this.

Now that we have explored how to detect collisions and react to them, let's explore how to fix the Player falling when they hit a wall.

Moving with Physics

So far, the Player, the only Object that moves with the **Dynamic Collider** Profile and the one that will move with Physics, is moving through custom scripting using the Transform API. However, every dynamic Object should move using the Rigidbody API functions in such a way that the Physics system understands this, so here, we will explore how to move Objects, this time through the `Rigidbody` component.

In this section, we will examine the following Physics movement concepts:

- Applying forces
- Tweaking Physics

We will start by learning how to move Objects the correct physical way; that is, by using force. We will apply this concept to the movement of our player. Then, we will explore why real physics is not always fun, and how we can tweak the Physics properties of our Objects so that they have a more responsive and appealing behavior.

Applying forces

The Physically accurate way of moving an Object is through forces, which affect the Object's velocity. To apply force, we need to access `Rigidbody` instead of `Transform` and use the `AddForce` and `AddTorque` functions to move and rotate, respectively. These are functions where you can specify the amount of force to apply to each axis of position and rotation. This way of movement will have full Physics reactions; the forces will accumulate on the velocity so that it can start moving and will suffer from drag effects that will make the speed slowly decrease. The most important aspect here is that it will collide with walls, blocking the Object's way.

To get this kind of movement, we can do the following:

1. Create a `Rigidbody` field in the `PlayerMovement` script, but this time, make it `private`. This means that we do not write the `public` keyword in the field, which will make it disappear in the **Editor** window; we will get the reference another way.

    Certain coding standards specify that you need to explicitly replace the `public` keyword with the `private` keyword, but in C#, putting `private` and not putting it has the same effect, so choose what's best for you:

    ```
    private Rigidbody rb;
    ```

    Figure 16.23 – The private Rigidbody reference field

2. Using `GetComponent` in the `Start` event function, get our `Rigidbody` and save it in the field. We will use this field to cache the result of the `GetComponent` function; calling that function every frame to access `Rigidbody` is not performant. Also, note that the `GetComponent` function can be used to retrieve not only components from other Objects (as in the collision example) but also your own:

    ```
    void Start()
    {
        Cursor.visible = false;
        Cursor.lockState = CursorLockMode.Locked;

        rb = GetComponent<Rigidbody>();
    }
    ```

    Figure 16.24 – Caching the Rigidbody reference for future usage

3. Replace the `transform.Translate` calls with `rb.AddRelativeForce`. This will call the add force functions of `Rigidbody` – specifically, the relative ones, which will consider the current rotation of the Object. For example, if you specify a force in the Z-axis (the third parameter), the Object will apply its force along with its forward vector.

4. Replace the `transform.Rotate` calls with `rb.AddRelativeTorque`, which will apply rotation forces:

```
if (Input.GetKey(KeyCode.W) || Input.GetKey(KeyCode.UpArrow))
    rb.AddRelativeForce(0, 0, speed * Time.deltaTime);

if (Input.GetKey(KeyCode.S) || Input.GetKey(KeyCode.DownArrow))
    rb.AddRelativeForce(0, 0, -speed * Time.deltaTime);

if (Input.GetKey(KeyCode.A) || Input.GetKey(KeyCode.LeftArrow))
    rb.AddRelativeForce(-speed * Time.deltaTime, 0, 0);

if (Input.GetKey(KeyCode.D) || Input.GetKey(KeyCode.RightArrow))
    rb.AddRelativeForce(speed * Time.deltaTime, 0, 0);

float mouseX = Input.GetAxis("Mouse X");
rb.AddRelativeTorque(0, mouseX * rotationSpeed * Time.deltaTime, 0);
```

Figure 16.25 – Using the Rigidbody forces API

Important Note

If you are familiar with Unity, you might be thinking that I need to do this in a Fixed Update, and while that's correct, doing this in the Update won't have any noticeable effect. I prefer to use `Update` in beginners' scripts, given that using `GetKeyDown` and `GetKeyUp` in `FixedUpdate` can cause them to not work properly. This is because those functions get updated in the `Update` function and given that `FixedUpdate` could be executed more than once per frame (in low framerate cases) or can skip some frames (in high framerate cases), the behavior could be erratic.

In the Visual Script version, the change is the same: replace the **Transform** and **Rotate** nodes with the **Add Relative Force** and **Add Relative Torque** nodes. An example of **Add Relative Force** would look as follows:

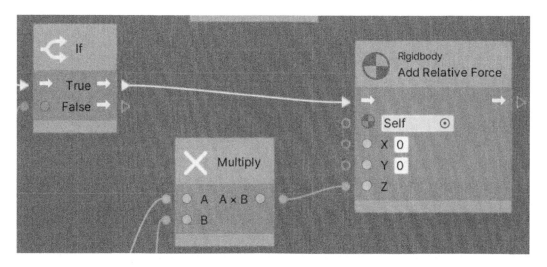

Figure 16.26 – Using the Rigidbody forces API

For rotation, this would look like this:

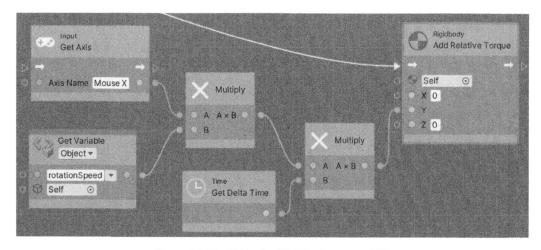

Figure 16.27 – Using the Rigidbody torque API

As you can see, we don't need to use **GetComponent** nodes here either, given that just using the **Add Relative Force** or **Torque** nodes makes Visual Scripting understand that we want to apply those actions on our own Rigidbody component (explaining again the **Self** label). If we need to call those functions on a Rigibody other than ours, we would need the **GetComponent** node there, but we'll explore that later.

Now, if you save and test the results, you will probably find that the Player is falling. That's because we are now using real physics, which provides floor friction, and due to the force being applied at the center of gravity, it will make the Object fall. Remember that, in terms of Physics, you are a Capsule; you don't have legs to move, and this is where standard physics is not suitable for our game. The solution is to tweak the Physics to emulate the kind of behavior we need.

Tweaking Physics

To make our Player move as if they were in a regular platformer game, we will need to freeze certain axes to prevent the Object from falling. Remove the friction from the ground and increase the air friction (drag) to make the Player reduce speed automatically when releasing the keys. To do this, follow these steps:

1. In the Rigidbody component, look at the **Constraints** section at the bottom and check the **X** and **Z** axes of the **Freeze Rotation** property:

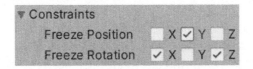

Figure 16.28 – Freezing rotation axes

This will prevent the Object from falling sideways but will allow the Object to rotate horizontally. You can also freeze the Y-axis of the **Freeze Position** property if you don't want the Player to jump, preventing some undesired vertical movement on collisions.

2. You will probably need to change the speed values because you changed from a meters-per-second value to newtons per second, which is the expected value of the **Add Force** and **Add Torque** functions. Using 1000 for speed and 160 for rotation speed was enough for me.

3. Now, you will probably notice that the speed will increase a lot over time, as will the rotation. Remember that you are using forces, which affect your velocity. When you stop applying forces, the velocity is preserved, and that's why the player kill keeps rotating, even if you are not moving the mouse. To fix this, increase **Drag** and **Angular Drag**, which emulate air friction and will reduce the movement and rotation, respectively, when no force is applied. Experiment with values that you think will be suitable; in my case, I used 2 for **Drag** and 10 for **Angular Drag**, but I needed to increase **Rotation Speed** to 150 to compensate for the drag increase:

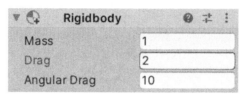

Figure 16.29 – Setting air friction for rotation and movement

4. Now, if you move while touching the wall, instead of sliding, like most games, your Player will stick to the obstacles due to contact friction. We can remove this by creating a **Physics Material**, an asset that can be assigned to the colliders to control how they react in those scenarios.

5. Start creating one by clicking on the + button in the **Project** window and selecting **Physics Material** (not the 2D version). Call it Player and remember to put it in a folder for those kinds of assets.

6. Select it and set **Static Friction** and **Dynamic Friction** to 0, and **Friction Combine** to Minimum, which will make the Physics system pick the minimum friction of the two colliding Objects, which will always be the minimum – in our case, zero:

Figure 16.30 – Creating a Physics Material

7. Select the Player and drag this asset to the **Material** property of **Capsule Collider**:

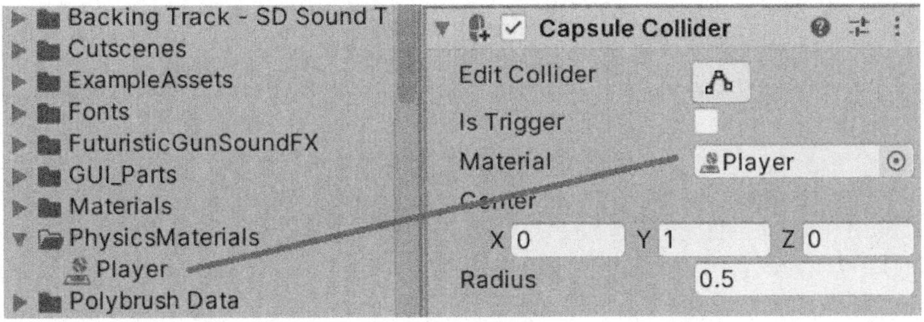

Figure 16.31 – Setting the Physics material of the Player

8. If you play the game now, you may notice that the Player will move faster than before because we don't have any kind of friction on the floor; you may need to reduce the movement force.

9. A little error you might find here is that the motion blur effect that's applied by the camera PostProcessing on the Player has some hiccups, such as frames where the Object is moving and others where it's not. The problem is that Physics is not executed in every frame due to performance and determinism (by default, it is executed 50 times per frame), but the rendering does, and that is affecting the postprocessing. You can set the **Interpolate** property of Rigidbody to the **Interpolate** value to make Rigidbody calculate Physics at its own rate but interpolate the position every frame to simulate fluidness:

Figure 16.32 – Making Rigidbody interpolate its position

As you can see, we needed to bend the Physics rules to allow responsive player movement. You can get more responsiveness by increasing drags and forces, so the speeds are applied faster and reduced faster, but that depends, again, on the experience you want your game to have. Some games want an immediate response with no velocity interpolation, going from 0 to full speed and vice versa from one frame to the other. In these cases, you can override the velocity and rotation vectors of the Player directly at your will or even use other systems instead of Physics, such as the **Character Controller** component, which has special physics for platformer characters. However, let's keep things simple for now.

Summary

Every game has physics, one way or the other, for movement, collision detection, or both. In this chapter, we learned how to use Unity's Physics system for both and learned about how to use its settings to make the system work properly, in terms of reacting to collisions to generate gameplay systems and moving the Player in such a way that they collide with obstacles, keeping its physically inaccurate movement. We used these concepts to create our Player and bullet movement and make our bullets damage the Enemies, but we can reuse this knowledge to create a myriad of other possible gameplay requirements, so I suggest that you play a little bit with the physics concepts we showed here; you can discover a lot of interesting use cases.

In the next chapter, we will be discussing how to program the visual aspects of the game, such as effects, and make the UI react to the input.

17
Win and Lose Condition

Now that we have a basic gameplay experience, it's time to make the game end sometime, when the player wins or loses. One common way to implement this is through separated components with the responsibility of overseeing a set of Objects to detect certain situations that need to happen, such as the Player life becoming 0 or all of the waves being cleared. We will implement this through the concept of Managers, components that will manage several Objects, monitoring them.

In this chapter, we will examine the following Manager concepts:

- Creating Object Managers
- Creating Game Modes
- Improving our code with events

With this knowledge, you will not only be able to create the victory and losing conditions of the game but also be able to do so in a properly structured way using design patterns such as Singleton and Event Listeners. These skills are not just useful for creating the winning and losing code of the game but for any code in general.

Creating Object Managers

Not every Object in a scene should be something that can be seen, heard, or collided with. Some Objects can also exist with a conceptual meaning, not something tangible. Imagine you need to keep a count of the number of enemies; where do you save that? You also need someplace to save the current score of the Player, and you may be thinking it could be on the Player itself, but what happens if the Player dies and respawns? The data would be lost! In such scenarios, the concept of a Manager can be a useful way of solving this in our first games, so let's explore it.

In this chapter, we are going to look at the following Object Manager concepts:

- Sharing Variables with the Singleton design pattern
- Sharing Variables in Visual Scripting
- Creating Managers

We will start by discussing what the Singleton design pattern is and how it helps us to simplify the communication of Objects. With it we will create Manager Objects, which will allow us to centralize information of a group of Objects, among other things. Let's start by discussing the Singleton design pattern.

Sharing Variables with the Singleton design pattern

Design patterns are usually described as common solutions to common problems. There are several coding design decisions you will have to make while you code your game, but luckily, the ways to tackle the most common situations are well-known and well-documented. In this section, we are going to discuss one of the most common design patterns, the Singleton, a very controversial but convenient pattern to implement in simple projects.

A Singleton pattern is used when we need a single instance of an Object, meaning that there shouldn't be more than one instance of a class and that we want it to be easily accessible (not necessary, but useful in our scenario). We have plenty of cases in our game where this can be applied, for example, `ScoreManager`, a component that will hold the current score. In this case, we will never have more than one score, so we can take advantage of the benefits of the Singleton Manager here.

One benefit is being sure that we won't have duplicated scores, which makes our code less error-prone. Also, so far, we have needed to create public references and drag Objects via the Editor to connect two Objects or look for them using `GetComponent`, but with this pattern, we will have global access to our Singleton component, meaning you can just write the name of the component and you will access it. In the end, there's just one `ScoreManager` component, so specifying which one via the Editor is redundant. This is similar to `Time.deltaTime`, the class responsible for managing time—we have just one time.

> **Important Note**
>
> If you are an advanced programmer, you may be thinking about code testing and dependency injection now, and you are right, but remember, we are trying to write simple code at the moment, so we will stick to this simple solution.

Let's create a Score Manager Object, responsible for handling the score, to show an example of a Singleton by doing the following:

1. Create an empty GameObject (**GameObject | Create Empty**) and call it `ScoreManager`; usually, Managers are put in empty Objects, separated from the rest of the scene Objects.

2. Add a script called `ScoreManager` to this Object with an `int` field called `amount` that will hold the current score.

3. Add a field of the `ScoreManager` type called `instance`, but add the `static` keyword to it; this will make the variable global, meaning it can be accessed anywhere by just writing its name:

```
using UnityEngine;

public class ScoreManager : MonoBehaviour
{
    public static ScoreManager instance;

    public int amount;
}
```

Figure 17.1 – A static field that can be accessed anywhere in the code

4. In `Awake`, check whether the `instance` field is not null, and in that case, set this `ScoreManager` instance as the instance reference using the `this` reference.

5. In the else clause of the null-checking `if` statement, print a message indicating that there's a second `ScoreManager` instance that must be destroyed:

```
void Awake()
{
    if (instance == null)
    {
        instance = this;
    }
    else
    {
        print("Duplicated ScoreManager, ignoring this one");
    }
}
```

Figure 17.2 – Checking whether there's only one Singleton instance

The idea is to save the reference to the only `ScoreManager` instance in the instance static field, but if by mistake the user creates two objects with the `ScoreManager` component, this `if` statement will detect it and inform the user of the error, asking them to take action. In this scenario, the first `ScoreManager` instance to execute `Awake` will find that there's no instance set (the field is null) so it will set itself as the current instance, while the second `ScoreManager` instance will find the instance is already set and will print the message. Remember that `instance` is a static field, one shared between all classes, unlike regular reference fields, where each component will have its own reference; so in this case, we have two `ScoreManager` instances added to the scene, and both will share the same instance field.

To improve the example a little bit, it would be ideal to have a simple way to find the second `ScoreManager` in the game. It will be hidden somewhere in the Hierarchy and it will be difficult to find. We can replace `print` with `Debug.Log`, which is basically the same but allows us to pass a second argument to the function, which is an Object, to highlight when the message is clicked in the console. In this case, we will pass the `gameObject` reference to allow the console to highlight the duplicated Object:

```
Debug.Log("Duplicated ScoreManager, ignoring this one", gameObject);
```

Figure 17.3 – Printing messages in the console with Debug.Log

6. After clicking the log message, this GameObject must be highlighted in the Hierarchy:

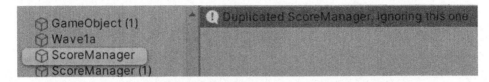

Figure 17.4 – The highlighted Object after clicking the message

7. Finally, a little improvement can be made here by replacing `Debug.Log` with `Debug.LogError`, which will also print the message but with an error icon. In a real game, you will have lots of messages in the console, and highlighting the errors in information messages will help us to identify them quickly:

```
Debug.LogError("Duplicated ScoreManager, ignoring this one", gameObject);
```

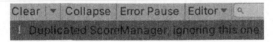

Figure 17.5 – Using LogError to print an error message

8. Try the code and observe the error message in the console:

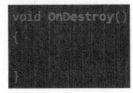

Figure 17.6 – An error message in the console

The next step would be to use this Singleton somewhere, so in this case, we will make the enemies give points when they are killed by doing the following:

1. Add a script to the `Enemy` Prefab called `ScoreOnDeath` with an `int` field called `amount`, which will indicate the number of points the Enemy will give when killed. Remember to set the value to something other than 0 in the Editor for the Prefab.
2. Create the `OnDestroy` event function, which will be automatically called by Unity when this Object, in our case, the Enemy, is destroyed:

```
void OnDestroy()
{

}
```

Figure 17.7 – The OnDestroy event function

> **Important note**
>
> Note that the `OnDestroy` function is also called when we change scenes or the game is quitting, so in this scenario, we may get points when changing scenes, which is not correct. At the moment, this is not a problem in our case, but later in this chapter, we will see a way to prevent this.

3. Access the Singleton reference in the `OnDestroy` function by writing `ScoreManager.instance`, and add the `amount` field of our script to the `amount` field of the Singleton to increase the score when an Enemy is killed:

```
public int amount;

void OnDestroy()
{
    ScoreManager.instance.amount += amount;
}
```

Figure 17.8 – Full ScoreOnDeath component class contents

4. Select the `ScoreManager` in the hierarchy, hit play, and kill some enemies to see the score raise with every kill. Remember to set the amount field of the `ScoreOnDeath` component of the Prefab.

As you can see, the Singleton simplified the way to access `ScoreManager` a lot and prevented us from having two versions of the same Object, which will help us to reduce errors in our code. Something to take into account is that now you may be tempted to just make everything a Singleton, such as the Player life or Player bullets, or to make your life easier to create gameplay such as power-ups, and while that will totally work, remember that your game will change, and I mean change a lot; any real project will suffer that. Maybe today the game has just one Player, but in the future, you may want to add a second Player or an AI companion, and you may want the power-ups to affect them too; so if you abuse the Singleton pattern, you will have trouble handling those scenarios. Maybe the companion will try to get the pickup but the main Player will be healed instead!

The point here is to try to use the pattern as few times as you can and only if you don't have any other way to solve the problem. To be honest, there are always ways to solve problems without Singleton, but they are a little bit more difficult to implement for beginners, so I prefer to simplify your life a little bit to keep you motivated. With enough practice, you will reach a point where you will be ready to improve your coding standards.

Now, let's discuss how to achieve this in Visual Scripting, which deserves its own section given it will be a little bit different. You can skip the following section if you are not interested in the Visual Scripting side of these scripts.

Sharing Variables with Visual Scripting

Visual Scripting has a mechanism that replaces Singleton as a holder of variables to be shared between objects, the **Scene Variables**. If you check the left panel in the **Script Graph** editor (the window where we edit the nodes of a script) under the Blackboard Panel (the panel that shows the variables of our object), you will notice it has many tabs: **Graph**, **Object**, **Scene**, **App**, and **Saved**. If you don't see it, click the third button from the left in the top-left part of the window, the button to the right of the **i** (information) button:

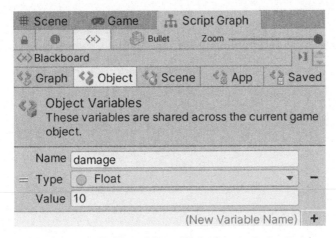

Figure 17.9 – Blackboard (variables) editor in Script Graph

So far, when we have created a variable in the **Variables** component of any object, we were actually creating **Object Variables**, variables that belong to an object and are shared between all Visual Scripts in that one, but that's not the only scope a variable can have. Here's a list of the remaining scopes:

- **Graph**: Variables that can only be accessed by our current graph. No other script can read or write that variable. Useful to save the internal state, such as private variables in C#.

- **Scene**: Variables that can be accessed by all objects in the current Scene. When we change the scene, those variables are lost.

- **App**: Variables that can be accessed in any part of the game at any time. Useful to move values from one scene to the other. For example, you can increase the score in one level and keep increasing it in the next, instead of resetting the score to 0.

- **Saved**: Variables whose values are kept between game runs. You can save persistent data such as the Player Level or Inventory to continue the quest, or simpler things such as the sound volume that the user can change in the Options menu (if you created one).

In this case, the Scene scope is the one we want, as the Score we intend to increase will be accessed by several objects in the scene (more on that later) and we don't want it to persist if we reset the level to play again; it will need to be set again to 0 in each run of the level and game.

To create Scene Variables, you can simply select the **Scene** tab in the **Blackboard** pane of the **Script Graph** editor, while you are editing any **Script Graph**, or you can also use the Scene Variables GameObject that is created automatically when you start editing any graph. That object is the one that really holds the variables and must not be deleted. You will notice it will have a **Variables** component as we have done before, but it will also have the Scene **Variables** component, indicating those variables are Scene variables.

In the next screenshot, you can see how we have simply added the score variable to the Scene Variables tab to make it accessible in any of our Script Graphs:

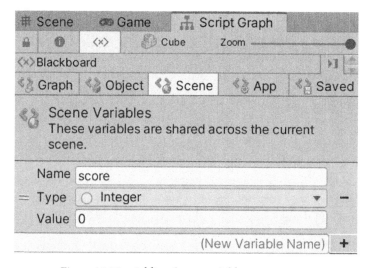

Figure 17.10 – Adding Scene variables to our game

Finally, for the score-increasing behavior, we can add the following graph to our Enemy. Remember, as usual, to use the C# or the Visual Scripting version of the scripts, not both:

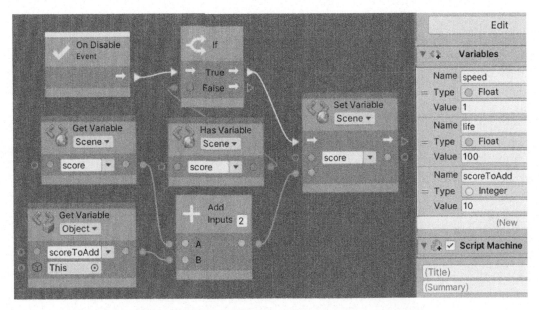

Figure 17.11 – Adding the score when an object is destroyed

At first, this script seems pretty similar to our C# version. We add the `scoreToAdd` variable of our object (Object scope), and then we add it to the whole Scene's `score` variable, as specified in the node. The main difference you can see is that here we are using the **OnDisable** event instead of **OnDestroy**. Actually, **OnDestroy** is the correct one, but in the current version of Visual Scripting, there is a bug that prevents it from working properly, so I replaced it for now. The problem with **OnDisable** is that it executes whenever the object is disabled, and while the object is disabled before it's destroyed, it can also be disabled in other circumstances (for example, using **Object Pooling**, a way to recycle objects instead of destroying and instantiating them constantly), but at the moment, this for us is enough. Please consider using **OnDestroy** first when you try this graph to see whether it runs properly in your Unity or Visual Scripting package version.

Something to highlight is the usage of the **Has Variable** node to check whether the **score** variable exists. This is done because **OnDisable** can be executed either at the moment the enemy is destroyed or when the scene changes, which we will do later in this chapter to the lose/win screens. If we try to get a scene variable at that moment, we risk getting an error if the Scene Variables object is destroyed before the GameMode object, given the change of scene involves destroying every object in the scene first.

As you may have noticed by now, even if Visual Scripting is most of the time extremely similar to C#, one has concepts to solve certain scenarios that the other doesn't. Now that we know how to share variables, let's look at some other Managers that we will need later in the game.

Creating Managers

Sometimes, we need a place to put together information about a group of similar Objects, for example, an Enemy Manager to check the number of enemies and potentially access an array of them to iterate over them and do something, or maybe `MissionManager`, to have access to all of the active missions in our game. Again, these cases can be considered Singletons, single Objects that won't be repeated (in our current game design), so let's create the ones we will need in our game, that is, `EnemyManager` and `WaveManager`.

In our game, `EnemyManager` and `WaveManager` will just be places to save an array of references to the existing enemies and waves in our game, just as a way to know the current amount of them. There are ways to search all Objects of a certain type to calculate the count of them, but those functions are expensive and not recommended to use unless you really know what you are doing. So, having a Singleton with a separate updated list of references to the target Object type will require more code but will perform better. Also, as the game features increase, these Managers will have more functionality and helper functions to interact with these Objects.

Let's start with the enemies Manager by doing the following:

1. Add a script called `Enemy` to the Enemy Prefab; this will be the script that will connect this Object with `EnemyManager` in a moment.

2. Create an empty `GameObject` called `EnemyManager` and add a script to it called `EnemiesManager`.

3. Create a `public` static field of the `EnemiesManager` type called `instance` inside the script and set the Singleton repetition check to `Awake` as we did in `ScoreManager`.

4. Create a public field of the `List<Enemy>` type called `enemies`:

```
public List<Enemy> enemies;
```

Figure 17.12 – List of Enemy components

A list in C# represents a dynamic array, an array capable of adding and removing Objects. You will see that you can add and remove elements to this list in the Editor, but keep the list empty; we will add enemies another way. Take into account that `List` is in the `System.Collections.Generic` namespace; you will find the `using` sentence at the beginning of our script. Also, consider that you can make the list private and expose it to the code via a getter instead of making it a public field; but as usual, we will make our code as simple as possible for now.

> **Important note**
>
> Note that `List` is a class type, so it must be instantiated, but as this type has exposing support in the Editor, Unity will automatically instantiate it. You must use the new keyword to instantiate it in cases where you want a non-Editor-exposed list, such as a private one or a list in a regular non-component C# class.
>
> A C# list is internally implemented as an array. If you need a linked list, look at the `LinkedList` collection type.

5. In the `Start` function of the `Enemy` script, access the `EnemyManager` Singleton and, using the `Add` function of the enemies list, add this Object to the list. This will "register" this Enemy as active in the Manager, so other Objects can access the Manager and check for the current enemies. The `Start` function is called after all of the `Awake` function calls, and this is important because we need to be sure that the `Awake` function of the Manager is executed prior to the `Start` function of the Enemy to ensure that there is a Manager set as the instance.

> **Important note**
>
> The problem we solved with the `Start` function is called a race condition, which is when two pieces of code are not guaranteed to be executed in the same order, whereas the `Awake` execution order can change due to different reasons. There are plenty of situations in code where this will happen, so pay attention to the possible race conditions in your code. Also, you might consider using more advanced solutions such as lazy initialization here, which can give you better stability, but again, for the sake of simplicity and exploring the Unity API, we will use the `Start` function approach for now.

6. In the `OnDestroy` function, remove the Enemy from the list to keep the list updated with just the active ones:

```
public class Enemy : MonoBehaviour
{
    void Start()
    {
        EnemyManager.instance.enemies.Add(this);
    }

    void OnDestroy()
    {
        EnemyManager.instance.enemies.Remove(this);
    }
}
```

Figure 17.13 – The Enemy script to register ourselves as an active Enemy

With this, we now have a centralized place to access all of the active enemies in a simple but efficient way. I challenge you to do the same with the waves, using `WaveManager`, which will have the collection of all active Waves to later check whether all waves finished their work to consider the game as won. Take some time to solve this; you will find the solution in the following screenshots, starting with `WavesManager`:

```
using System.Collections.Generic;
using UnityEngine;

public class WavesManager : MonoBehaviour
{
    public static WavesManager instance;

    public List<WaveSpawner> waves;

    void Awake()
    {
        if (instance == null)
            instance = this;
        else
            Debug.LogError("Duplicated WavesManager", gameObject);
    }
}
```

Figure 17.14 – The full WavesManager script

You will also need the `WavesSpawner` script:

```csharp
using UnityEngine;

public class WaveSpawner : MonoBehaviour
{
    public GameObject prefab;
    public float startTime;
    public float endTime;
    public float spawnRate;

    void Start()
    {
        WavesManager.instance.waves.Add(this);
        InvokeRepeating("Spawn", startTime, spawnRate);
        Invoke("EndSpawner", endTime);
    }

    void Spawn()
    {
        Instantiate(prefab, transform.position, transform.rotation);
    }

    void EndSpawner()
    {
        WavesManager.instance.waves.Remove(this);
        CancelInvoke();
    }
}
```

Figure 17.15 – The modified WaveSpawner script to support WaveManager

As you can see, WaveManager is created the same way EnemyManager was, just a Singleton with a list of WaveSpawner references, but WaveSpawner is different. We execute the Add function of the list in the Start event of WaveSpawner to register the wave as an active one, but the Remove function needs more work.

The idea is to deregister the wave from the active waves list when it finishes spawning all enemies when the spawner finishes its work. Before this modification, we used `Invoke` to call the `CancelInvoke` function after a while to stop the spawning, but now we need to do more after the end time. Instead of calling `CancelInvoke` after the specified wave end time, we will call a custom function called `EndSpawner`, which will call `CancelInvoke` to stop the spawner, `InvokeRepeating`, but will also call the remove from `WavesManager` list function to make sure the removing from the list is called exactly when `WaveSpawner` finishes its work.

Regarding the Visual Scripting version, we can add two Lists of GameObject to the Scene Variables to hold the references to the existing Waves and Enemies so we can keep track of them. In this case, the Lists contain only GameObjects given that the Visual Scripting versions of **WaveSpawner** and Enemy scripts are not types we can reference like C# ones. If you carried out both C# and Visual Scripting versions of these, you would see that you can reference the C# versions, but for now, we are not going to mix C# and Visual Scripting, so ignore this. Anyway, given how the **Variables** system of Visual Scripting works, we can still access variables inside them if needed using the **GetVariable** node. Remember the variables are not in the Visual Scripts but in the Variables node:

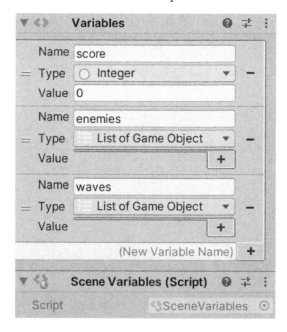

Figure 17.16 – Adding lists to the Scene Variables

Then, we can add the following to the **WaveSpawner** graph:

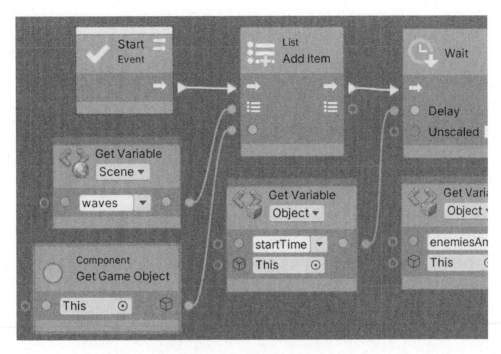

Figure 17.17 – Adding elements to List

We used the **Add List Item** node to add our GameObject to the **waves** variable. We added this as the first thing to do in the **Start** event node before anything. To remove that wave from the active ones, you will need to make the following change:

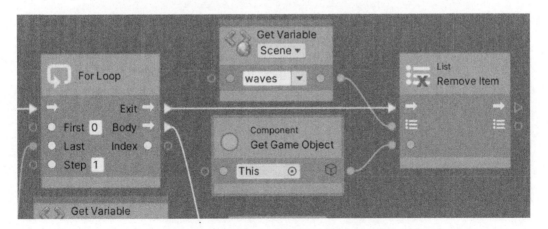

Figure 17.18 – Removing elements from the List

We remove this spawner from the list using the **Exit** flow output pin of **For Loop**, which is executed when the for loop finishes iterating.

Finally, regarding the **Enemy**, you will need to create a new Enemy Script graph that will look similar to the following:

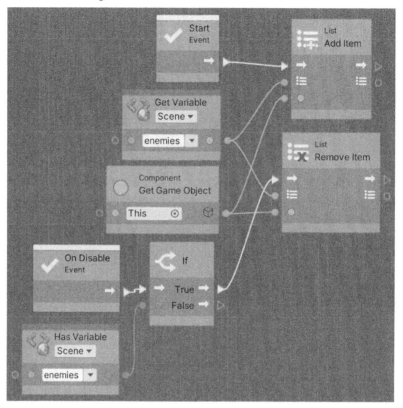

Figure 17.19 – Enemy adding and removing itself from the lists

As you can see, we simply add the enemy on **Start** and remove it in **OnDisable**. Remember to first try to use **OnDestroy** instead of **OnDisable** due to the bug we mentioned previously. You can check these changes by playing the game while having the Scene Variables GameObject selected and seeing how its value changes. Also, remember the need to use the **Has Variable** node if we are changing scenes.

Using Object Managers, we have now centralized information about a group of Objects, and we can add all sorts of Object group logic here. We created EnemiesManager, WavesManager, and ScoreManager as centralized places to store some game system information, such as the enemies and waves present in the scene, and the score as well. We also saw the Visual Scripting version of those centralizing that data in the Scene Variables object, so all Visual Scripts can read that data. But besides having this information for updating the UI (which we will do in the next chapter), we can use this information to detect whether the Victory and Lose conditions of our game are met, creating a Game Mode Object to detect that.

Creating Game Modes

We have created Objects to simulate lots of gameplay aspects of our game, but the game needs to end sometime, whether we win or lose. As always, the question is where to put this logic, and that leads us to further questions. The main questions would be, will we always win or lose the game the same way? Will we have a special level with different criteria that kill all of the waves, such as a timed survival? Only you know the answer to those questions, but if right now the answer is no, it doesn't mean that it won't change later, so it is advisable to prepare our code to adapt seamlessly to changes.

> **Important note**
>
> To be honest, preparing our code to adapt seamlessly to changes is almost impossible; there's no way to have perfect code that will consider every possible case, and we will always need to rewrite some code sooner or later. We will try to make the code as adaptable as possible to changes; always doing that doesn't consume lots of developing time and it's sometimes preferable to write simple code quickly than complex code that might not necessarily be slow, and so balance your time budget wisely.

To do this, we will separate the Victory and Lose conditions' logic into its own Object, which I like to call the "Game Mode" (not necessarily an industry-standard term). This will be a component that will oversee the game, checking conditions that need to be met in order to consider the game over. It will be like the referee of our game. The Game Mode will constantly check the information in the Object Managers and maybe other sources of information to detect the needed conditions. Having this Object separated from other Objects allows us to create different levels with different Game Modes; just use another Game Mode script in that level and that's all.

In our case, we will have a single Game Mode for now, which will check whether the number of waves and enemies becomes 0, meaning that we have killed all of the possible enemies and the game is won. Also, it will check whether the life of the Player reaches 0, considering the game as lost in that situation. Let's create it by doing the following:

1. Create a `GameMode` empty Object and add a `WavesGameMode` script to it. As you can see, we called the script with a descriptive name considering that we can add other game modes.

2. In its `Update` function, check whether the number of enemies and waves reached 0 by using the Enemy and Wave Managers; in that case, just `print` a message in the console for now. All lists have a `Count` property, which will tell you the number of elements stored inside.

3. Add a `public` field of the `Life` type called `PlayerLife` and drag the Player to it; the idea is to also detect the lose condition here.

4. In `Update`, add another check to detect whether the life amount of the `PlayerLife` reference reached `0`, and in that case, `print` a lose message in the console:

```
[SerializeField] Life playerLife;

void Update()
{
    if (EnemyManager.instance.enemies.Count <= 0 && WavesManager.instance.waves.Count <= 0)
    {
        print("You win!");
    }

    if (playerLife.amount <= 0)
    {
        print("You lose!");
    }
}
```

Figure 17.20 – Win and lose condition checks in WavesGameMode

5. Play the game and test both cases, whether the Player life reaches 0 or whether you have killed all enemies and waves.

> **Important note**
>
> Consider that we don't want two instances of this Object, so we can also make it a Singleton, but as this Object won't be accessed by others, that might be redundant; I will leave this up to you. Anyway, note that this won't prevent you from having two different `GameModes` instantiated; for doing so, you can create a `GameMode` base class, with the Singleton functionality ready to prevent two `GameModes` in the same scene.

Now, it is time to replace the messages with something more interesting. For now, we will just change the current scene to a Win scene and Lose scene, which will just have a UI with a win and lose message and a button to play again. In the future, you can add a Main Menu scene and have an option to get back to it. Let's do that by doing the following:

1. Create a new scene (**File | New Scene**) and save it, calling it `WinScreen`.

2. Add a UI Text and center it with the text **You won!**.

3. Add a UI Button right below the text and change its text to **Play Again**:

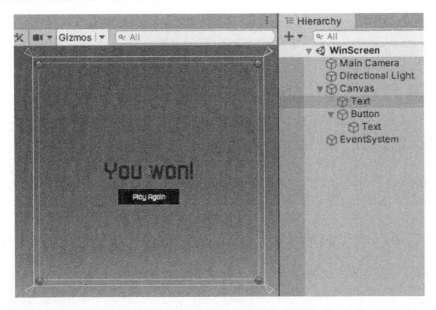

Figure 17.21 – WinScreen

4. Select the Scene in the Project View and press *Ctrl + D (Cmd + D* on Mac) to duplicate the scene. Rename it `LoseScreen`.

5. Double-click the `LoseScreen` scene to open it and just change the **You won!** text to **You lose!**.

6. Go to **File | Build Settings** to open the Scenes in the Build list inside this window.

    The idea is that Unity needs you to explicitly declare all scenes that must be included in the game. You might have test scenes or scenes that you don't want to release yet, so that's why we need to do this. In our case, our game will have `WinScreen`, `LoseScreen`, and the scene we have created so far with the game scenario, which I called "Game," so just drag those scenes from the Project View to the list of the Build Settings window; we will need this to make the Game Mode script change the scenes properly. Also, consider that the first scene in this list will be the first scene to be opened when we play the game in its final version (known as the build), so you may want to rearrange the list according to that:

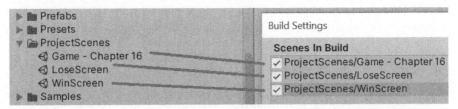

Figure 17.22 – Registering the scenes to be included in the build of the game

7. In `WavesGameMode`, add a using statement for the `UnityEngine.`
    `SceneManagement` namespace to enable the scene-changing functions
    in this script.

8. Replace the console `print` messages with calls to the `SceneManager.`
    `LoadScene` function, which will receive a string with the name of the scene to
    load; in this case, it would be `WinScreen` and `LoseScreen`. You just need the
    scene name, not the entire path to the file.

    If you want to chain different levels, you can create a `public` string field to allow
    you to specify via the Editor which scenes to load. Remember to have the scenes
    added to the Build Settings; if not, you will receive an error message in the console
    when you try to change the scenes:

```csharp
using UnityEngine;
using UnityEngine.SceneManagement;

public class WavesGameMode : MonoBehaviour
{

    [SerializeField] Life playerLife;

    void Update()
    {
        if (EnemyManager.instance.enemies.Count <= 0 && WavesManager.instance.waves.Count <= 0)
        {
            SceneManager.LoadScene("WinScreen");
        }

        if (playerLife.amount <= 0)
        {
            SceneManager.LoadScene("LoseScreen");
        }
    }
}
```

Figure 17.23 – Changing scenes with SceneManager

9. Play the game and check whether the scenes change properly.

> **Important note**
>
> Right now, we picked the simplest way to show that we lost or won, but maybe
> in the future you will want something gentler than a sudden change of the
> scene, such as waiting a few moments with Invoke to delay that change or
> directly show the winning message inside the game without changing the
> scenes. Consider that when testing the game with people and checking whether
> they understood what happens while they play, game feedback is important to
> keep the Player aware of what is happening and is not an easy task to tackle.

Regarding the Visual Scripting version, we added a new Script Graph to a separated object. Let's examine it piece by piece to see it clearly. Let's start with the win condition:

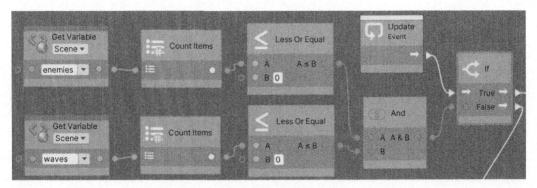

Figure 17.24 – Win condition in Visual Scripting

Here, we are getting the Enemies list from the Scene context (the **Get Variable** node), and knowing that it contains a List, we are using the **Count Items** node to check how many enemies are remaining in this List. Remember we have a script that adds the enemy to the list when it's spawned and removes it when is destroyed. We do the same for the waves, combining the conditions with an and connecting it with an **If** to then do something (more on that in a moment).

Now let's examine the Lose condition:

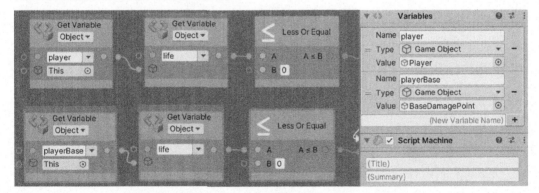

Figure 17.25 – Lose condition in Visual Scripting

As the Player's life is not in the Scene context (and shouldn't be), and the Player is a separated GameObject from this one (we created a GameObject called GameMode for this script), we need a variable of the GameObject type called player to reference it. As you can see, we dragged our Player to it in the **Variables** component. Finally, we used **Get Variable** to access our Player reference in the Graph, and then another **Get Variable** to extract the life from it. We accomplished that by connecting the player reference to the **Get Variable** node of the life variable. Then, we repeated this for the Player's base.

Finally, we load scenes by doing the following:

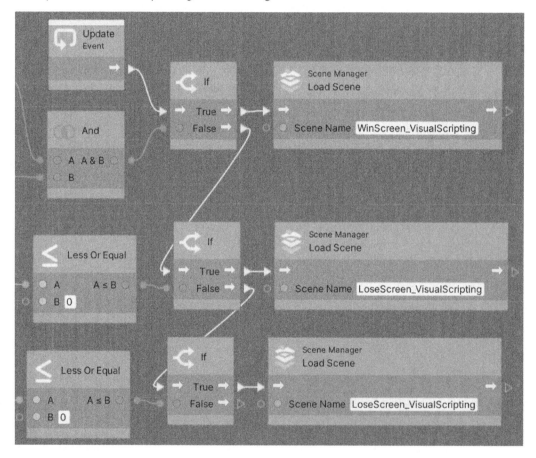

Figure 17.26 – Loading scenes in Visual Scripting

Now we have a fully functional simple game, with mechanics and win and lose conditions, and while this is enough to start developing other aspects of our game, I want to discuss some issues with our current Manager approach and how to solve them with events.

Improving our code with events

So far, we have used Unity event functions to detect situations that can happen in the game, such as `Awake` and `Update`. These functions are ways for Unity to communicate two components, as in the case of `OnTriggerEnter`, which is a way for the Rigidbody to inform other components in the GameObject that a collision has happened. In our case, we are using `if` statements inside Updates to detect changes on other components, such as `GameMode` checking whether the number of enemies reached 0. But we can improve this if we are informed by the Enemy Manager when something has changed, and just do the check in that moment, such as with the Rigidbody telling us the collisions instead of checking collisions every frame.

Also, sometimes, we rely on Unity events to execute logic, such as the score being given in the `OnDestroy` event, which informs us when the Object is destroyed, but due to the nature of the event, it can be called in situations where we don't want to add the score, such as when the scene is changed or the game is closed. Objects are destroyed in those cases, but not because the Player killed the Enemy, leading to the score being raised when it shouldn't. In this case, it would be great to have an event that tells us that the number of lives reached 0 to execute this logic, instead of relying on the general-purpose destroy event.

The idea of events is to improve the model of communication between our Objects, being sure that at the exact moment something happens, the interested parts in that situation are notified to react accordingly. Unity has lots of events, but we can create ones specific to our gameplay logic. Let's start by seeing this applied in the Score scenario we discussed earlier; the idea is to make the `Life` component have an event to communicate to other components that the Object was destroyed because the number of lives reached 0.

There are several ways to implement this, and we will use a little bit of a different approach than the Awake and Update methods; we will use the `UnityEvent` field type. This is a field type capable of holding references to functions to be executed when we want to, such as C# delegates, but with other benefits, such as better Unity Editor integration. To implement this, do the following:

1. In the `Life` component, create a `public` field of the `UnityEvent` type called `onDeath`. This field will represent an event where other classes can subscribe to it to be aware of when Life reaches 0:

```
public class Life : MonoBehaviour
{
    public float amount;
    public UnityEvent onDeath;
```

Figure 17.27 – Creating a custom event field

2. If you save the script and go to the Editor, you can see the event in the Inspector. Unity Events support subscribing methods to them in the Editor so we can connect two Objects together. We will use this in the UI scripting chapter, so let's just ignore this for now:

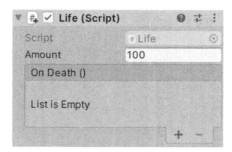

Figure 17.28 – UnityEvents showing up in the Inspector

> **Important note**
>
> You can use the generic delegate action or a custom delegate to create events instead of using `UnityEvent`, and aside from certain performance aspects, the only noticeable difference is that `UnityEvent` will show up in the Editor, as demonstrated in *step 2*.

3. When the number of lives reaches 0, call the `Invoke` function of the event, and this way, we will be telling anyone interested in the event that it has happened:

```
public float amount;
public UnityEvent onDeath;

void Update()
{
    if (amount <= 0)
    {
        onDeath.Invoke();
        Destroy(gameObject);
    }
}
```

Figure 17.29 – Executing the event

4. In `ScoreOnDeath`, rename the `OnDestroy` function `GivePoints` or whatever name you prefer; the idea here is to stop giving points in the `OnDestroy` event.

5. In the `Awake` function of the `ScoreOnDeath` script, get the `Life` component using `GetComponent` and save it in a local variable.

6. Call the `AddListener` function of the `onDeath` field of the Life reference and pass the `GivePoints` function as the first argument. The idea is to tell `Life` to execute `GivePoints` when the `onDeath` event is invoked. This way, `Life` informs us about that situation. Remember that you don't need to call `GivePoints`, but just pass the function as a field:

```
void Awake()
{
    var life = GetComponent<Life>();
    life.onDeath.AddListener(GivePoints);
}

void GivePoints()
{
    ScoreManager.instance.amount += amount;
}
```

Figure 17.30 – Subscribing to the OnDeath event to give points in that scenario

> **Important note**
>
> Consider calling `RemoveListener` in `OnDestroy`; as usual, it is convenient to unsubscribe listeners when possible to prevent any memory leak (reference preventing the GC to deallocate memory). In this scenario, it is not entirely necessary because both the `Life` and `ScoreOnDeath` components will be destroyed at the same time, but try to get used to that good practice.

7. Save, select `ScoreManager` in the Editor, and hit play to test this. Try deleting an Enemy from the Hierarchy while in Play Mode to see how the score doesn't rise because the Enemy was destroyed for any other reason than the number of lives becoming 0; you must destroy an Enemy by shooting at them to see the score being raised.

Now that `Life` has an `onDeath` event, we can also replace the Player's Life check from the Waves Game Mode to use the event by doing the following.

8. Create an `OnLifeChanged` function on the `WavesGameMode` script and move the life-checking condition from `Update` to this function.

9. In `Awake`, subscribe to this new function to the `onDeath` event of the Player's Life component reference:

```
void Awake()
{
    playerLife.onDeath.AddListener(OnPlayerLifeChanged);
}

void OnPlayerLifeChanged()
{
    if (playerLife.amount <= 0)
    {
        SceneManager.LoadScene("LoseScreen");
    }
}
```

Figure 17.31 – Checking the lose condition with events

As you can see, creating custom events allows you to detect more specific situations other than the defaults in Unity, and keeps your code clean, without needing to constantly ask conditions in the Update function, which is not necessarily bad, but the event approach generates clearer code.

Remember that we can also lose our game by the Player's Base Life reaching 0; we will explore the concept of the Player's base later in this book, but for now, let's create a cube that represents the Object that Enemies will attack to reduce the Base Life, like the Base Core. Taking this into account, I challenge you to add this other lose condition to our script. When you finish, you can check the solution in the following screenshot:

```
[SerializeField] Life playerLife;
[SerializeField] Life playerBaseLife;

void Start()
{
    playerLife.onDeath.AddListener(OnPlayerLifeChanged);
    playerBaseLife.onDeath.AddListener(OnPlayerBaseLifeChanged);
}

void OnPlayerLifeChanged()
{
    if (playerLife.amount <= 0)
    {
        SceneManager.LoadScene("LoseScreen");
    }
}

void OnPlayerBaseLifeChanged()
{
    if (playerBaseLife.amount <= 0)
    {
        SceneManager.LoadScene("LoseScreen");
    }
}
```

Figure 17.32 – Complete Waves Game Mode lose condition

As you can see, we just repeated the life event subscription; remember to create an Object to represent the Player's Base damage point, add a `Life` script to it, and drag that one as the Player Base Life reference of the Waves Game Mode.

Now, let's keep illustrating this concept by applying it in the Managers to prevent the Game Mode from checking conditions at every frame:

1. Add a `UnityEvent` field to `EnemyManager` called `onChanged`. This event will be executed whenever an Enemy is added or removed from the list.

2. Create two functions, `AddEnemy` and `RemoveEnemy`, both receiving a parameter of the `Enemy` type. The idea is that instead of `Enemy` adding and removing itself from the list directly, it should use these functions.

3. Inside these two functions, invoke the onChanged event to inform others that the enemies list has been updated. The idea is that anyone who wants to add or remove enemies from the list needs to use these functions:

```
public UnityEvent onChanged;

public void AddEnemy(Enemy enemy)
{
    enemies.Add(enemy);
    onChanged.Invoke();
}

public void RemoveEnemy(Enemy enemy)
{
    enemies.Remove(enemy);
    onChanged.Invoke();
}
```

Figure 17.33 – Calling events when enemies are added or removed

> **Important note**
>
> Here, we have the problem that nothing stops us from bypassing those two functions and using the list directly. You can solve that by making the list private and exposing it using the IReadOnlyList interface. Remember that this way, the list won't be visible in the Editor for debugging purposes.

4. Change the Enemy script to use these functions:

```
public class Enemy : MonoBehaviour
{
    void Start()
    {
        EnemyManager.instance.AddEnemy(this);
    }

    void OnDestroy()
    {
        EnemyManager.instance.RemoveEnemy(this);
    }
}
```

Figure 17.34 – Making the Enemy use the add and remove functions

5. Repeat the same process for `WaveManager` and `WaveSpawner`, create an `onChanged` event, and create the `AddWave` and `RemoveWave` functions and call them in `WaveSpawner` instead of directly accessing the list. This way, we are sure the event is called when necessary as we did with `EnemyManager`. Try to solve this step by yourself and then check the solution in the following screenshot, starting with `WavesManager`:

```csharp
public class WavesManager : MonoBehaviour
{
    public static WavesManager instance;

    public List<WaveSpawner> waves;
    public UnityEvent onChanged;

    public void AddWave(WaveSpawner wave)
    {
        waves.Add(wave);
        onChanged.Invoke();
    }

    public void RemoveWave(WaveSpawner wave)
    {
        waves.Remove(wave);
        onChanged.Invoke();
    }


    void Awake()
    {
        if (instance == null)
            instance = this;
        else
            Debug.LogError("Duplicated WavesManager", gameObject);
    }
}
```

Figure 17.35 – WavesManager onChanged event implementation

Also, `WavesSpawner` needed changes:

```
public class WaveSpawner : MonoBehaviour
{
    public GameObject prefab;
    public float startTime;
    public float endTime;
    public float spawnRate;

    void Start()
    {
        WavesManager.instance.AddWave(this);
        InvokeRepeating("Spawn", startTime, spawnRate);
        Invoke("EndSpawner", endTime);
    }

    void Spawn()
    {
        Instantiate(prefab, transform.position, transform.rotation);
    }

    void EndSpawner()
    {
        WavesManager.instance.RemoveWave(this);
        CancelInvoke();
    }
}
```

Figure 17.36 – Implementing Add and Remove Wave functions

6. In `WavesGameMode`, rename `Update` to `CheckWinCondition` and subscribe this function to the `onChanged` event of `EnemyManager` and the `onChanged` event of `WavesManager`. The idea is to check for the number of enemies and waves being changed just when it is necessary. Remember to do the subscription to the events in the `Start` function due to the Singletons being initialized in `Awake`:

```
void Start()
{
    playerLife.onDeath.AddListener(OnPlayerLifeChanged);
    playerBaseLife.onDeath.AddListener(OnPlayerBaseLifeChanged);
    EnemyManager.instance.onChanged.AddListener(CheckWinCondition);
    WavesManager.instance.onChanged.AddListener(CheckWinCondition);
}

void CheckWinCondition()
{
    if (EnemyManager.instance.enemies.Count <= 0 && WavesManager.instance.waves.Count <= 0)
    {
        SceneManager.LoadScene("WinScreen");
    }
}
```

Figure 17.37 – Checking the win condition when the enemies or waves amount is changed

Regarding the Visual Scripting version, let's start checking the Lose condition with events, checking first some changes needed in the Life Script Graph:

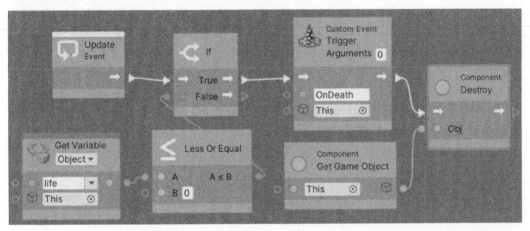

Figure 17.38 – Triggering a Custom Event in our Life graph

First, after destroying the object when the number of lives reaches 0, we use the **Trigger Custom Event** node, specifying the name of our event as OnDeath. This will tell anyone listening for us to execute the OnDeath event that we did. Remember this is our Life Script Graph. Be sure to call destroy after triggering the event, while most of the time the order doesn't matter given the Destroy doesn't actually happen until the end of the frame. Sometimes it can cause issues, so it's better to be safe here. In this case, Game Mode should listen to the Player's OnDeath event, so let's make the following change in our Game Mode Graph:

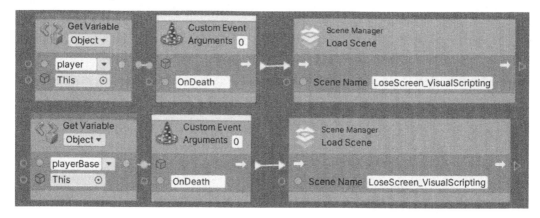

Figure 17.39 – Listening to the OnDeath event of the Player in Visual Scripting

We used the **CustomEvent** node, connecting it to the player reference of our GameMode. This way, we are specifying that if that Player executes that event, we will execute the **Load Scene** node. Remember that the player reference is crucial to specify for whom we want to execute the OnDeath event and that the Life Visual Graph will also be present in the enemies and we are not interested in them here. Also remember to remove the If and the conditions we used previously to detect this; the only If our GameMode will have is the one for the Win condition.

Essentially, we set it so any object with the Life script has an OnDeath event, and we made the GameMode listen to the OnDeath event of the player specifically.

We could also create events for the Enemies and Waves, but that would complicate our Graphs a little bit, given we don't have WaveManager or EnemyManager in the Visual Scripting versions. We could certainly create those to accomplish this but sometimes the point of using Visual Scripting is to create simple logic, and these kinds of changes tend to make a graph grow pretty much. Another possible solution is to make the Enemy and the Wave inform the Game Mode directly.

We could use **Trigger Custom Event** in the Enemies and Waves, connecting that node to the Game Mode, to finally let the Game Mode have a Custom Event node to listen to. The issue is that this would violate the correct dependencies between our objects; lower-level objects such as Enemy and Waves shouldn't communicate with higher-level object such as Game Mode. At the end, Game Mode was supposed to be an overseer. If we do that, we won't be able to have an Enemy in another scene or game without having a Game Mode. So, for simplicity and code decoupling, let's keep the other conditions as they are. At the end, more complex logic such as this will probably be handled in C# in full production projects.

Yes, by using events we have to write more code than before, and in terms of functionality, we didn't obtain anything new, but in bigger projects, managing conditions through Update checks will lead to different kinds of problems, as previously discussed, such as race conditions and performance issues. Having a scalable code base sometimes requires more code, and this is one of those cases.

Before we finish, something to consider is that Unity Events are not the only way to create this kind of event communication in Unity; you will find a similar approach called **Action**, the native C# version of events, which I recommend you look up if you want to see all of the options out there.

Summary

In this chapter, we finished an important part of the game, the ending, both by victory or by defeat. We discussed a simple but powerful way to separate the different layers of responsibilities by using Managers created through Singletons to guarantee that there's no more than one instance of every kind of manager and simplifying the connections between them through static access (something to consider when you discover code testing). Also, we encountered the concept of events to streamline the communication between Objects to prevent problems and create more meaningful communication between Objects.

With this knowledge, you are now able not only to detect the victory and lose conditions of a game but also to do that in a better-structured way. These patterns can be useful to improve our game code in general, and I recommend you try to apply them in other relevant scenarios.

In the next chapter, we are going to explore how to create visual and audio feedback to respond to our gameplay, combining scripting and the assets we integrated in *Part 2* of this book.

18
Scripting the UI, Sounds, and Graphics

In a game, even if the player sees the game through the camera, there is important information that is not visible in plain sight, such as the exact number of bullets remaining, their health, the enemies, whether there's an enemy behind them, and so on. We have already discussed how to tackle those issues with the UI, sounds, and visual effects (VFX), but as we start to move on with scripting in our game, those elements also need to adapt to the game. The idea of this chapter is to make our UI, sounds, and VFX react to the game situation through scripting, reflecting what is happening in the world.

In this chapter, we will examine the following feedback scripting concepts:

- Scripting the UI
- Scripting feedback

By the end of this chapter, you will be able to make the UI react to the game situation, showing relevant information in the form of text and bars, and also be able to make the game react to interactions with the UI, such as with buttons. Also, you will be able to make the game inform the user of this information through other mediums, such as sound and particle graphics, which can be as effective as the UI, but more appealing.

Scripting the UI

We previously created a UI layout with elements including bars, text, and buttons, but so far, they are static. We need to make them adapt to the game's actual state. In this chapter, we are going to discuss the following UI scripting concepts:

- Showing information in the UI
- Programming the Pause menu

We will start by seeing how to display information on our UI using scripts that modify the text and images that are displayed with Canvas elements. After that, we will create the Pause functionality, which will be used throughout the UI.

Showing information in the UI

As discussed earlier, we will use the UI to display information to the user to allow them to make informed decisions, so let's start by seeing how we can make the player's health bar react to the amount of life they have left in the `Life` script we created earlier:

1. Add a new script called **Life Bar** to the **HealthBar** Canvas child object, which is the UI `Image` component we created earlier to represent the life bar:

Figure 18.1 – The Life Bar component in the player's HealthBar Canvas

2. In the `LifeBar` script, add a `Life` type field. This way, our script will ask the editor which `Life` component we will be monitoring. Save the script:

```
public class LifeBar : MonoBehaviour
{
    public Life targetLife;
}
```

Figure 18.2 – Editor-configurable reference to a Life component

3. In the Editor, drag the `Player` GameObject from the **Hierarchy** window to the `targetlife` property to make the life bar reference the player's life, and remember to have the `HealthBar` object selected before dragging **Player**.

    This way, we are telling our `LifeBar` script which `Life` component to check to see how much life the player has remaining. Something interesting here is that the enemies have the same `Life` component, so we can easily use this component to create life bars for every other object that has lives in our game:

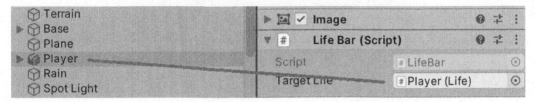

Figure 18.3 – Dragging Player to reference its life component

4. Add the `using UnityEngine.UI;` line right after the `using` statements in the first few lines of the script. This will tell C# that we will be interacting with the UI scripts:

```
using System;
using System.Collections;
using System.Collections.Generic;
using UnityEngine;
using UnityEngine.UI;
```

Figure 18.4 – All the using statements in our script. We are not going to use them all, but let's keep them for now

5. Create a `private` field (without the `public` keyword) of the `Image` type. We will save the reference to the component here in a moment:

```
Image image;
public Life targetLife;
```

Figure 18.5 – Private reference to an image

6. Using GetComponent in Awake, access the reference to the Image component in our GameObject (HealthBar) and save it in the image field. As usual, the idea is to get this reference just once and save it for later use in the Update function. Of course, this will always work when you put this component in an object with an Image component. If not, the other option would be to create a public field of the Image type and drag the image component into it:

```
void Awake()
{
    image = GetComponent<Image>();
}
```

Figure 18.6 – Saving the reference to the Image component in this object

7. Create an Update event function in the LifeBar script. We will use this to constantly update the life bar according to the player's life.

8. In the Update event, divide the amount of life by 100 to have our current life percentage expressed in the 0 to 1 range (assuming our maximum life is 100), and set the result in the fillAmount field of the Image component as in the following screenshot. Remember that fillAmount expects a value between 0 and 1, with 0 signaling that the bar is empty, and 1 that the bar is at its full capacity:

```
void Update()
{
    image.fillAmount = targetLife.amount / 100;
}
```

Figure 18.7 – Updating the fill amount of the LifeBar script's Image component
according to the Life component

> **Important note**
>
> Remember that putting 100 within the code is considered hardcoding (it is also known as a magic number), meaning later changes to that value would require us to look through the code for that value, which is a complicated task in big projects. That's why it is considered bad practice. It would be better to have a Maximum Life field in the Life component, or at least have a constant with this value.

9. Save the script and, in the editor, select the player and play the game. During **Play** mode, press *Esc* to regain access to the mouse and change the player's health in the Inspector window to see how the life bar updates accordingly. You can also test this by making the player receive damage somehow, such as by making enemies spawn bullets (more on enemies later):

```csharp
using UnityEngine;
using UnityEngine.UI;

public class LifeBar : MonoBehaviour
{
    Image image;
    public Life targetLife;

    void Awake()
    {
        image = GetComponent<Image>();
    }

    void Update()
    {
        image.fillAmount = targetLife.amount / 100;
    }
}
```

Figure 18.8 – Full LifeBar script

Important note

In the previous chapter, we explored the concept of events to detect changes in the state of other objects. The life bar is another example of using an event as we can change the fill amount of the image when the life actually changes. I challenge you to try to create an event when the life changes and implement this script using the one we looked at in the previous chapter.

You may be thinking that this UI behavior could be directly coded within the `Life` component, and that's completely possible, but the idea here is to create simple scripts with little pressure to keep our code separate. Each script should have just one reason to be modified, and mixing UI behavior and gameplay behavior in a single script would give the script two responsibilities, which results in two possible reasons to change our script. With this approach, we can also set the player's base life bar at the bottom by just adding the same script to its life bar, but dragging the **Base Damage** object, which we created in the previous chapter, as the target life this time.

Regarding the Visual Scripting version, here is what you need to add to your health bar image Game Object:

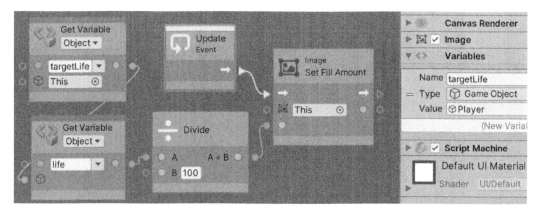

Figure 18.9 – Full LifeBar Visual Graph

First, we added a `targetLife` variable of the `GameObject` type to the **Variables** component of our life bar Image. Then we dragged our `Player` GameObject (called Robot so far) to this variable in such a way that the Life Bar now has a reference to the object from which we want to display its life. Then, we added a **LifeBar** Visual Graph that, in the **Update** node, calls the **Set Fill Amount** node in order to update the fill amount of the image. Remember that in this case, just calling the **Set Fill Amount** node will understand we are referring to the Image component where this Visual Graph is located, so there is no need to use **GetComponent** here. In order to calculate the fill amount, we get the **targetLife** GameObject reference, and using a second **Get Variable** node, we extract the life variable of that object. Finally, we divide it by 100 (we needed to create a Float Literal node in order to represent the value 100) and pass it to the **Set Fill Amount** node. As usual, you can check the complete version on the GitHub repository.

Important note

The single object responsibility principle we just mentioned is one of the five object-oriented programming principles known as SOLID. If you don't know what SOLID is, I strongly recommend you look it up to improve your programming best practices.

Now that we have sorted out the player's life bar, let's make the `Bullets` label update according to the player's remaining bullets. Something to consider here is that our current Player Shooting script has unlimited bullets, so let's change that by following these steps:

1. Add a public `int` type field to the Player Shooting script called `bulletsAmount`.

2. In the `if` statement that checks the pressure of the left mouse button, add a condition to check whether the number of bullets is greater than `0`.

3. Inside the `if` statement, reduce the number of bullets by `1`:

```
void Update()
{
    if (Input.GetKeyDown(KeyCode.Mouse0) && bulletsAmount > 0)
    {
        bulletsAmount--;

        GameObject clone = Instantiate(prefab);
        clone.transform.position = shootPoint.transform.position;
        clone.transform.rotation = shootPoint.transform.rotation;
    }
}
```

Figure 18.10 – Limiting the number of bullets to shoot

The Visual Scripting version, the modified shooting condition of the **PlayerShooting** visual graph, will look like this:

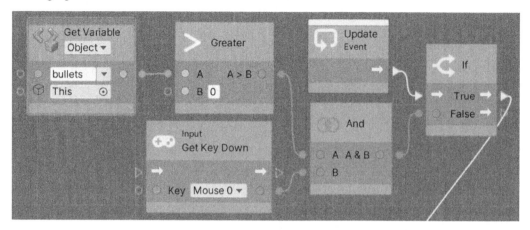

Figure 18.11 – Shooting only if bullets available in Visual Graph

As you can see, we simply check whether the number of bullets is greater than zero and then use an **And** node to combine that condition with the previously existing **Get Key Down** condition. Consider bullets was a variable we needed to create in the Variables component of our `Player` GameObject. Regarding the bullets decrement, it will look like this:

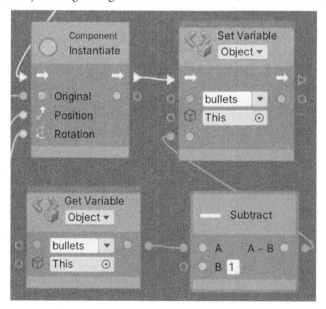

Figure 18.12 – Decrementing bullet count in Visual Graph

We simply subtract one from the bullets variable and set bullets again with this value.

Now that we have a field indicating the number of remaining bullets, we can create a script to display that number in the UI by doing the following:

1. Add a `PlayerBulletsUI` script to the bullet's `Text` GameObject. In my case, I called it `Bullets Label`.

2. Add the `using UnityEngine.UI` statement and add a private field of the `Text` type, saving it in the reference to our own `Text` component in `Awake`:

```csharp
using UnityEngine;
using UnityEngine.UI;

public class PlayerBulletsUI : MonoBehaviour
{
    Text text;

    void Awake()
    {
        text = GetComponent<Text>();
    }
}
```

Figure 18.13 – Caching the reference to our own Text component

3. Create a `public` field of the `PlayerShooting` type called `targetShooting` and drag `Player` to this property in the Editor. As was the case for the life bar component, the idea is that our UI script will access the script that has the remaining bullets to update the text, bridging the two scripts (`Text` and `PlayerShooting`) to keep their responsibilities separate.

4. Create an `Update` statement and inside it, set the `text` field of the text reference (I know, confusing) with a concatenation of `"Bullets: "` and the `bulletsAmount` field of the `targetShooting` reference. This way, we will replace the text of the label according to the current number of bullets:

```csharp
void Update()
{
    text.text = "Bullets: " + targetShooting.bulletsAmount;
}
```

Figure 18.14 – Updating the bullet's text label

> **Important note**
>
> Remember that concatenating strings allocates memory, so again, I urge you to only do this when necessary, using events.

Regarding Visual Scripting, before actually setting the text, we need to add support for TextMeshPro in Visual Scripting. Visual Scripting requires manual specification of the Unity systems and Packages we are going to use, and as TextMeshPro is not strictly a core Unity feature, this is not included by default. We can add support for TextMeshPro in Visual Scripting by doing the following:

1. Go to **Edit | Project Settings** and select the **Visual Scripting** category.
2. Expand the **Node Library** option using the arrow at its left.
3. Use the **plus (+) button** at the bottom of the list to add a new library.
4. Click where it says **(No Assembly)** and search for **Unity.TextMeshPro**.
5. Click the **Regenerate Units** button and wait:

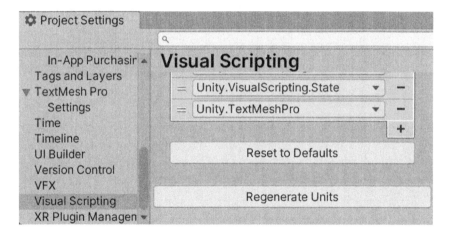

Figure 18.15 – Adding TextMeshPro support to Visual Scripting

After setting that, this is what the Visual Graph to add to the Bullets text GameObject will look like:

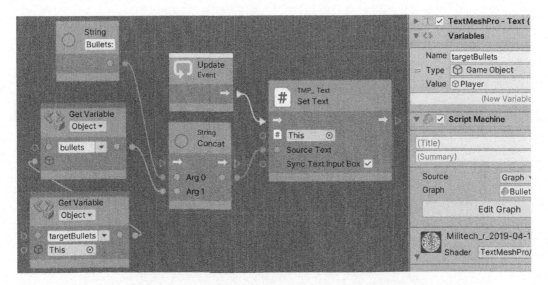

Figure 18.16 – Updating the bullet's text label in Visual Scripting

As usual, we need a reference to the Player to check its bullets, so we created a targetBullets variable of the GameObject type and dragged the player there. Then, we use a **Get Variable** node to extract the bullet amount from that reference and concatenate the string "Bullets: ", using the **String Literal** node, with the number of bullets using the **Concat** node. That node will do the same as when we added two strings together using the + operator in C#. Finally, we use the **Set Text (Source Text, Sync Text InputBox)** node to update the text of our text field.

If you look at the two scripts, you will find a pattern. You can access the UI and Gameplay components and update the UI component accordingly, and most UI scripts will behave in the same way. Keeping this in mind, I challenge you to create the necessary scripts to make the **Score**, **Enemies**, and **Waves** counters work. Remember to add using UnityEngine.UI to use the Text component. After finishing this, you can compare your solution with the one in the following screenshot, starting with ScoreUI:

```
using UnityEngine;
using UnityEngine.UI;

public class ScoreUI : MonoBehaviour
{
    Text text;

    void Awake()
    {
        text = GetComponent<Text>();
    }

    void Update()
    {
        text.text = "Score: " + ScoreManager.instance.amount;
    }
}
```

Figure 18.17 – The ScoreUI script

Also, we need the WavesUI component:

```
using UnityEngine;
using UnityEngine.UI;

public class WavesUI : MonoBehaviour
{
    Text text;

    void Start()
    {
        text = GetComponent<Text>();
        WavesManager.instance.onChanged.AddListener(RefreshText);
    }

    void RefreshText()
    {
        text.text = "Remaining Waves: " + WavesManager.instance.waves.Count;
    }
}
```

Figure 18.18 – The WavesUI script

Finally, we need EnemiesUI:

```
using UnityEngine;
using UnityEngine.UI;

public class EnemiesUI : MonoBehaviour
{
    Text text;

    void Start()
    {
        text = GetComponent<Text>();
        EnemyManager.instance.onChanged.AddListener(RefreshText);
    }

    void RefreshText()
    {
        text.text = "Remaining Enemies: " + EnemyManager.instance.enemies.Count;
    }
}
```

Figure 18.19 – The EnemiesUI script

Regarding Visual Scripting, we have the **Score UI**:

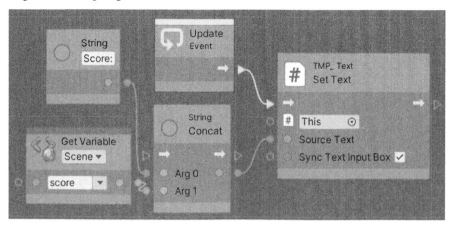

Figure 18.20 – The ScoreUI Visual script

Then, we have the Waves UI:

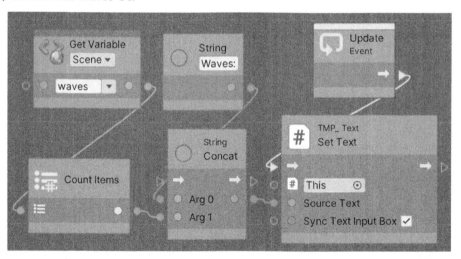

Figure 18.21 – The Waves UI Visual script

And finally, we have the Enemies UI:

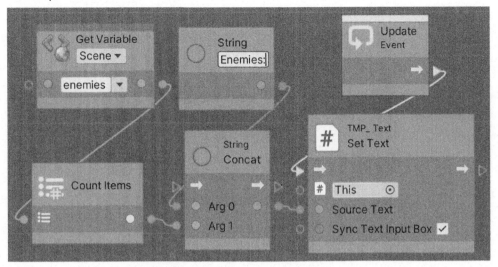

Figure 18.22 – The Enemies UI Visual script

As you can see, we have used the events already coded in the managers to change the UI only when necessary. Now that we have coded the UI labels and bars, let's code the Pause menu.

Programming the Pause menu

Recall how we created a Pause menu in a previous chapter, but it is currently disabled, so let's make it work. First, we need to code Pause, which can be quite complicated. So again, we will use a simple approach for pausing most behaviors, which is stopping the time! Remember that most of our movement scripts use time functionality, such as **Delta Time**, as a way to calculate the amount of movement to apply, and there's a way to simulate time going slower or faster, which is by setting timeScale. This field will affect Unity's time system's speed, and we can set it to 0 to simulate that time has stopped, which will pause animations, stop particles, and reduce **Delta Time** to 0, making our movements stop. So, let's do it:

1. Create a script called Pause and add it to a new object in the scene, also called Pause.

2. In `Update`, detect when the *Esc* key is pressed, and in that scenario, set `Time.timeScale` to `0`:

```
public class Pause : MonoBehaviour
{
    void Update()
    {
        if (Input.GetKeyDown(KeyCode.Escape))
        {
            Time.timeScale = 0;
        }
    }
}
```

Figure 18.23 – Stopping time to simulate a pause

3. Save and test this.

You will notice that almost everything will stop, but you can see how the shoot functionality still works. That's because the Player Shooting script is not time-dependent. One solution here could be to simply check whether `Time.timeScale` is greater than `0` to prevent this:

```
if (Input.GetKeyDown(KeyCode.Mouse0) && bulletsAmount > 0 && Time.timeScale > 0)
{
    bulletsAmount--;
```

Figure 18.24 – Checking pause in the player shooting script

> **Important note**
>
> As usual, we have pursued the simplest way here, but there is a better approach. I challenge you to try to create `PauseManager` with a Boolean indicating whether the game is paused or not, changing `timeScale` in the process.

Now that we have a simple but effective way to pause the game, let's make the **Pause** menu visible to resume the game by doing the following:

1. Add a field of the `GameObject` type called `pauseMenu` in the `Pause` script. The idea is to drag the **Pause** menu here so that we have a reference to enable and disable it.

2. In `Awake`, add `pauseMenu.SetActive(false);` to disable the **Pause** menu at the beginning of the game. Even if we disabled the **Pause** menu in the editor, we add this just in case we re-enable it by mistake. It must always start disabled.

3. Using the same function but passing `true` as the first parameter, enable the **Pause** menu in the *Esc* key pressure check:

```csharp
public class Pause : MonoBehaviour
{
    public GameObject pauseMenu;

    void Awake()
    {
        pauseMenu.SetActive(false);
    }

    void Update()
    {
        if (Input.GetKeyDown(KeyCode.Escape))
        {
            pauseMenu.SetActive(true);
            Time.timeScale = 0;
        }
    }
}
```

Figure 18.25 – Enabling the Pause menu when pressing the Esc key

Now, we need to make the **Pause** menu buttons work. If you recall, in the previous chapter, we explored the concept of events, implementing them with `UnityEvents` and the `Button` script. Our **Pause** menu buttons use the same class to implement the `OnClick` event, which is an event that informs us that a specific button has been pressed. Let's resume the game when pressing those buttons by doing the following:

4. Create a field of the `Button` type in our `Pause` script called `resumeButton`, and drag `resumeButton` to it; this way, our `Pause` script has a reference to the button.

5. In `Awake`, add a listener function called `OnResumePressed` to the `onClick` event of `resumeButton`.

6. Make the `OnResumePressed` function set `timeScale` to 1 and disable the
    Pause menu, as we did in `Awake`:

```
public GameObject pauseMenu;
public Button resumeButton;

void Awake()
{
    pauseMenu.SetActive(false);
    resumeButton.onClick.AddListener(OnResumePressed);
}

void OnResumePressed()
{
    pauseMenu.SetActive(false);
    Time.timeScale = 1;
}
```

Figure 18.26 – Unpausing the game

If you save and test this, you will notice that you cannot click the **Resume** button because
we disabled the cursor at the beginning of the game, so make sure you re-enable it while
in `Pause` and disable it when you resume:

```
void OnResumePressed()
{
    pauseMenu.SetActive(false);
    Time.timeScale = 1;
    Cursor.visible = false;
    Cursor.lockState = CursorLockMode.Locked;
}

void Update()
{
    if (Input.GetKeyDown(KeyCode.Escape))
    {
        Cursor.visible = true;
        Cursor.lockState = CursorLockMode.None;
        pauseMenu.SetActive(true);
        Time.timeScale = 0;
    }
}
```

Figure 18.27 – Showing and hiding the cursor while in Pause

Regarding the Visual Scripting version of the Pause script, let's start discussing the pause mechanism:

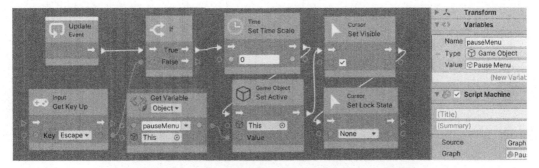

Figure 18.28 – Pausing when Escape is pressed

So far, nothing new. We detect that *Esc* is pressed, and then we call **Set Time Scale** and specify the 0 value. Then, we activate the Pause menu (having a reference through a **pauseMenu** variable in the **Variables** component), and finally, we enable the cursor.

Regarding the resume behavior, the nodes to add to the same Pause graph will look like this:

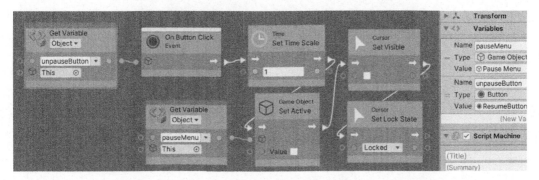

Figure 18.29 – Unpausing when the resume button is pressed

The only new element on this graph involves the use of the **On Button Click** node. As you might expect, that node is an event, and anything connected to it will execute under the pressure of a button. The way to specify which button we are referring to is by connecting the button reference variable to the input pin of **On Button Click**. You can see how we created a variable of the Button type called unpauseButton in the Variables component to do this.

Now that you know how to code buttons, I challenge you to code the `Exit` button's behavior. Again, remember to add `using UnityEngine.UI`. Also, you will need to call `Application.Quit();` to exit the game, but take into account that this will do nothing in the editor; we don't want to close the editor while creating the game. This function only works when you build the game. So, for now, just call it and if you want to print a message to be sure that the button is working properly, you can, and a solution is provided in the following screenshot:

```csharp
using UnityEngine;
using UnityEngine.UI;

public class QuitButton : MonoBehaviour
{
    Button button;

    void Awake()
    {
        button = GetComponent<Button>();
        button.onClick.AddListener(Quit);
    }

    void Quit()
    {
        print("Quitting");
        Application.Quit();
    }
}
```

Figure 18.30 – The Quit button script

This solution proposes that you add this script directly to the **Quit** button Game Object itself so that the script listens to the `onClick` event on its `Button` sibling component, and in that case, executes the `Quit` function. You could also add this behavior to the `Pause` script, and while that will work, remember that if a script can be split into two because it does two unrelated tasks, it is always best to split it so that separate behavior is unrelated. Here, the Pause behavior is not related to the **Quit** behavior.

Regarding the Visual Scripting version, the graph to add to the Quit button would look like this:

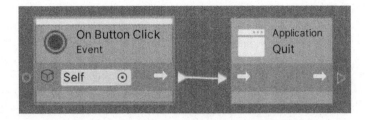

Figure 18.31 – The Quit button Visualscript

Simple, right? As we put this in the button itself, we don't even need to specify which button, as it automatically detects the fact that we are referring to ourselves.

Now that we have our **Pause** system set up using the UI and buttons, let's continue looking at other visual and auditive ways to make our player aware of what has happened.

Scripting feedback

We just used the UI to pass on data to the user so that they know what is happening, but sometimes that's not enough. We can reinforce game events using other types of feedback, such as sound and explosions, which we integrated into previous chapters.

In this section, we will explore the following feedback concepts:

- Scripting visual feedback
- Scripting audio feedback
- Scripting animations

We will start seeing how to make our gameplay have more feedback, with different visuals used in the right moments, such as audio and particle systems. Then, we are going to make the animations of our characters match these moments, for example, we will create the illusion that they are actually walking.

Scripting visual feedback

Visual feedback is the concept of using different VFX, such as particles and a VFX graph, to reinforce what is happening. For example, say right now we are shooting, and we know that this is happening because we can see the bullet. It doesn't exactly feel like shooting as a proper shooting simulation needs our gun to show the muzzle effect. Another example would be the enemy dying—it just despawns! That doesn't feel as satisfying as it should be. We can instead add a little explosion (considering they are robots).

Let's start making our enemies spawn an explosion when they die by doing the following:

1. Create an explosion effect or download one from the Asset Store. It shouldn't loop and it needs to be destroyed automatically when the explosion is over (ensure **Looping** is unchecked and **Stop Action** is set to `destroy` in the main module).

2. Some explosions in the Asset Store might use non-URP-compatible shaders. You can fix them by setting the **Edit | Render Pipeline | Univeral Render Pipeline | Upgrade Selected Materials** option to **UniveralRP Materials** while keeping the materials selected.

3. Manually upgrade the materials that didn't upgrade automatically.

4. Add a script to the `Enemy` prefab called `ExplosionOnDeath`. This will be responsible for spawning the particles prefab when the enemy dies.

5. Add a field of the `GameObject` type called `particlePrefab` and drag the explosion prefab to it.

> **Important note**
>
> You may be expecting to add the explosion spawning to the `Life` component. In that case, you are assuming that anything to do with life will spawn a particle when dying, but consider scenarios where characters die with a falling animation instead, or maybe an object that just despawns with no effect whatsoever. If a certain behavior is not used in most scenarios, it is better to code it in a separate optional script to allow us to mix and match different components and get the exact behavior we want.

6. Make the script access the `Life` component and subscribe to its `onDeath` event.

7. In the `listener` function, spawn the particle system in the same location:

```
public class ExplosionOnDeath : MonoBehaviour
{
    public GameObject particlePrefab;

    void Awake()
    {
        var life = GetComponent<Life>();
        life.onDeath.AddListener(OnDeath);
    }

    void OnDeath()
    {
        Instantiate(particlePrefab, transform.position, transform.rotation);
    }
}
```

Figure 18.32 – The explosion spawner script

The Visual Scripting version would look like this:

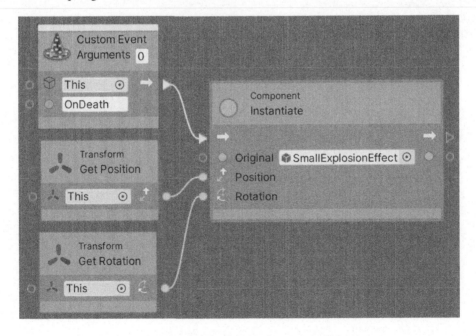

Figure 18.33 – The explosion spawner visual script

As you can see, we are just using the same concepts we learned about in previous chapters, but combining them in new ways. This is what programming is all about. Let's continue with the muzzle effect, which will also be a particle system, but we will take another approach this time:

1. Download a weapon model from the Asset Store and instantiate it so that it is the parent of the hand of the player. Remember that our character is rigged and has a hand bone, so you should put the weapon there:

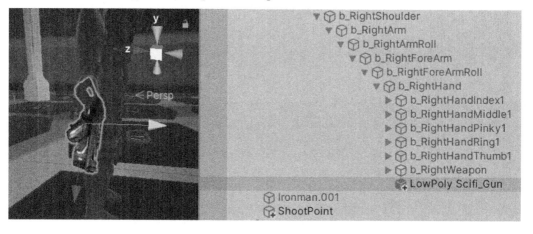

Figure 18.34 – Parenting a weapon in the hand bone

2. Create or get a muzzle particle system. In this case, my muzzle particle system was created as a short particle system that has a burst of particles and then automatically stops. Try to get one with that behavior because there are others out there that will loop instead, and the script to handle that scenario would be different.

3. Create an instance of the particle system prefab in the editor and parent it inside the weapon, locating it in front of the weapon, aligned with the cannon of the gun. Make sure the **Play On Awake** property of the main module of the particle system is unchecked; we don't want the muzzle to fire until we press the fire key:

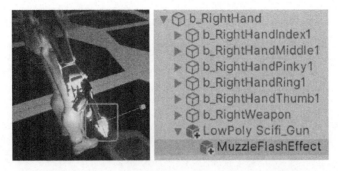

Figure 18.35 – The muzzle parented to the weapon

4. Create a field of the `ParticleSystem` type called `muzzleEffect` in `PlayerShooting` and drag the muzzle effect that is parented in the gun to it. Now, we have a reference to the `ParticleSystem` component of the muzzle to manage it.

5. Inside the `if` statement that checks whether we are shooting, execute `muzzleEffect.Play();` to play the particle system. It will automatically stop and is short enough to finish between key pressures:

```
public GameObject prefab;
public GameObject shootPoint;
public ParticleSystem muzzleEffect;
public int bulletsAmount;

void Update()
{
    if (Input.GetKeyDown(KeyCode.Mouse0) && bulletsAmount > 0 && Time.timeScale > 0)
    {
        bulletsAmount--;
        muzzleEffect.Play();

        GameObject clone = Instantiate(prefab);
        clone.transform.position = shootPoint.transform.position;
        clone.transform.rotation = shootPoint.transform.rotation;
    }
}
```

Figure 18.36 – The muzzle parented to the weapon

The Visual Scripting version additional nodes and variables would be the following:

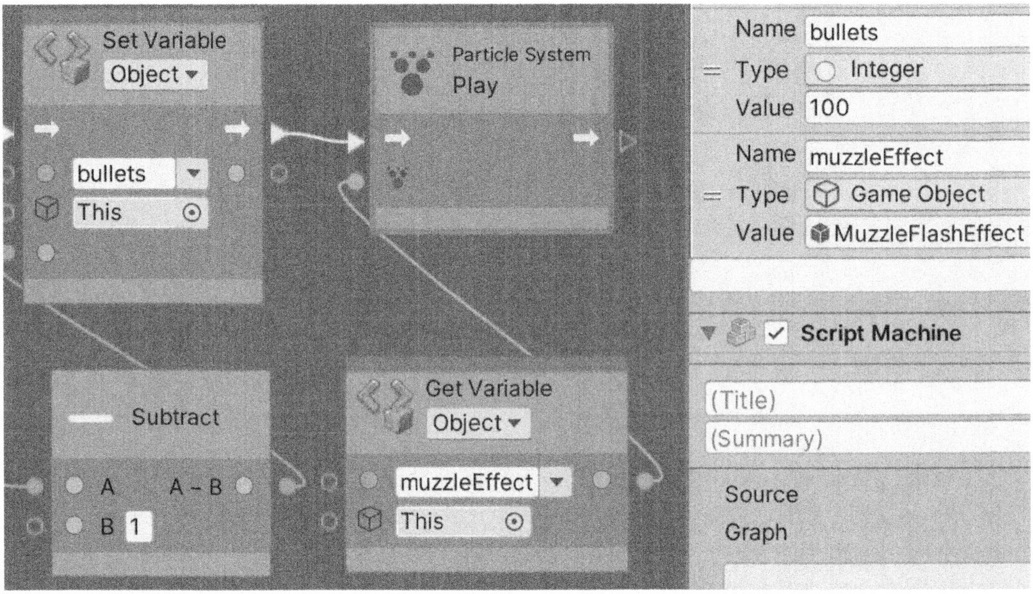

Figure 18.37 – The muzzle playing script

> **Important note**
>
> Here, we again have the same question: Will all the weapons have a muzzle
> when shooting? In this scenario, I would say yes due to the scope of our
> project, so I will keep the code as it is. However, in the future, you can create
> an onShoot event if you need other components to know whether this script
> is shooting. This way, they can extend the shooting behavior. Consider using
> events as a way of enabling plugins in your script.

Now that we have some VFX in place, let's add sound effects.

Scripting audio feedback

VFX added a good depth of immersion to what is happening in the game, but we can
improve this even further with sound. Let's start adding sound to the explosion effect by
doing the following:

1. Download an explosion sound effect.

2. Select the explosion prefab and add **Audio Source** to it.

3. Set the downloaded explosion's audio clip as the **AudioClip** property of the audio source.

4. Make sure **Play On Awake** is checked and that **Loop** is unchecked under **Audio Source**.

5. Set the **Spatial Blend** slider to **3D** and test the sound, configuring the **3D Sound** settings as needed:

Figure 18.38 – Adding sound to the explosion

As you can see here, we didn't need to use any script. As the sound is added to the prefab, it will be played automatically at the very moment the prefab is instantiated. Now, let's integrate the shooting sound by doing the following:

6. Download a shooting sound and add it through an audio source to the weapon of the player, this time unchecking the **Play On Awake** checkbox, and again setting **Spatial Blend** to **3D**.

7. In the PlayerShooting script, create a field of the AudioSource type called shootSound and drag the weapon to this property to connect the script with the AudioSource variable in the weapon.

8. In the `if` statement that checks whether we can shoot, add the `shootSound.Play();` line to execute the sound when shooting, using the same logic applied to the particle system:

```
public GameObject prefab;
public GameObject shootPoint;
public ParticleSystem muzzleEffect;
public AudioSource shootSound;
public int bulletsAmount;

void Update()
{
    if (Input.GetKeyDown(KeyCode.Mouse0) && bulletsAmount > 0 && Time.timeScale > 0)
    {
        bulletsAmount--;
        muzzleEffect.Play();
        shootSound.Play();
```

Figure 18.39 – Adding sound when shooting

The Visual Scripting additional nodes would look like this:

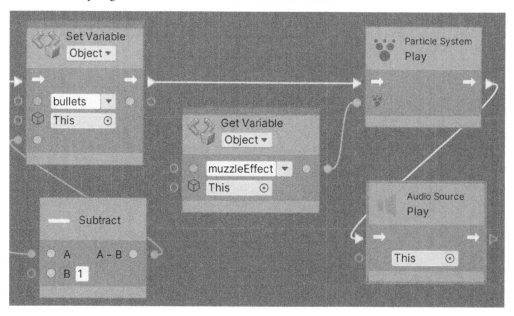

Figure 18.40 – Adding sound when shooting in Visual Scripting

The only thing to highlight here is that as **AudioSource**, which plays the shoot sound, is located in the Player, we just left the **AudioSource Play** node disconnected, referring to our own audio source. If we need to refer to an AudioSource in another GameObject, we would need to reference it via a variable, as we did with the particle system.

Another approach to this would be the same as the one we did with the explosion; just add the shooting sound to the bullet, but if the bullet collides with a wall, soon enough the sound will be cut off. Or, if, in the future, we want an automatic weapon sound, it will need to be implemented as a single looping sound that starts when we press the relevant key and stops when we release it. This way, we prevent too many sound instances from overlapping when we shoot too many bullets. Take into account those kinds of scenarios when choosing the approach to script your feedback.

Now that we have finished with our audio feedback, let's finish integrating our animation assets, which we prepared in *Chapter 13, Creating Animations with Animator, Cinemachine, and Timeline*.

Scripting animations

In *Chapter 13, Creating Animations with Animator, Cinemachine, and Timeline*, we created an animator controller as a way to integrate several animations, and we also added parameters to it to control when the transitions between animations should execute. Now, it is time to do some scripting to make these parameters be affected by the actual behavior of the player and match the player's current state by following these steps:

1. In the `PlayerShooting` script, add a reference to `Animator` using `GetComponent` in `Awake` and cache it in a field:

```
Animator animator;

void Awake()
{
    animator = GetComponent<Animator>();
}
```

Figure 18.41 – Caching the Animator reference

2. Call the `animator.SetBool("Shooting", true);` function in the `if` statement that checks whether we are shooting and add the same function, but pass `false` as a second argument in the `else` clause of the `if` statement. This function will modify the `"Shooting"` parameter of the animator controller:

```
void Update()
{
    if (Input.GetKeyDown(KeyCode.Mouse0) && bulletsAmount > 0 && Time.timeScale > 0)
    {
        animator.SetBool("Shooting", true);
        bulletsAmount--;
        muzzleEffect.Play();
        shootSound.Play();

        GameObject clone = Instantiate(prefab);
        clone.transform.position = shootPoint.transform.position;
        clone.transform.rotation = shootPoint.transform.rotation;
    }
    else
    {
        animator.SetBool("Shooting", false);
    }
}
```

Figure 18.42 – Setting the Shooting Boolean depending on whether we are shooting

If you test this, you may notice an error—the animation is not playing. If you check the script, you will notice that it will be `true` just for one frame as we are using `GetKeyDown`, so the Shooting Boolean will immediately be set to `false` in the next frame. One solution, among the several we could implement here, would be to make our shooting script repeat shootings while pressing the key instead of releasing and clicking again to shoot another bullet. Check the following screenshot for the solution and try to understand the logic:

```csharp
float lastShootTime;
public float fireRate;

void Update()
{
    if (Input.GetKey(KeyCode.Mouse0) && bulletsAmount > 0 && Time.timeScale > 0)
    {
        animator.SetBool("Shooting", true);

        var timeSinceLastShoot float = Time.time - lastShootTime;
        if(timeSinceLastShoot < fireRate)
            return;

        lastShootTime = Time.time;

        bulletsAmount--;
        muzzleEffect.Play();
        shootSound.Play();

        GameObject clone = Instantiate(prefab);
        clone.transform.position = shootPoint.transform.position;
        clone.transform.rotation = shootPoint.transform.rotation;
    }
    else
    {
        animator.SetBool("Shooting", false);
    }
}
```

Figure 18.43 – Repetitive shooting script

The added nodes in the Visual Scripting version would look like this:

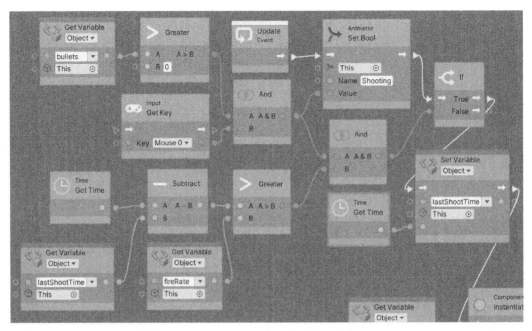

Figure 18.44 – Animating shooting in Visual Scripting

We essentially use the same condition we used in the If also in the **Animator Set Bool** node, as the condition is the same for both. We also changed the Get Key. Also, as you can see, our script now uses GetKey to keep shooting while keeping the shoot button pressed, and to prevent shooting in every frame, we compare the current time against the last shoot time to check how much time has passed since the last shot. We created the fireRate field to control the time between shots.

For the animator controller's Velocity parameter, we can detect the magnitude of the velocity vector of Rigidbody, the velocity in meters per second, and set that as the current value. This can be perfectly separated from the PlayerMovement script, so we can reuse this if necessary, in other scenarios. So, we need a script such as the following, which just connects the Rigidbody component's velocity to the animator's Velocity parameter:

```
using UnityEngine;

public class VelocityAnimator : MonoBehaviour
{
    Rigidbody rb;
    Animator animator;

    void Awake()
    {
        rb = GetComponent<Rigidbody>();
        animator = GetComponent<Animator>();
    }

    void Update()
    {
        animator.SetFloat("Velocity", rb.velocity.magnitude);
    }
}
```

Figure 18.45 – Setting Velocity Animator variables

And regarding the Visual Scripting version, this is what it would look like:

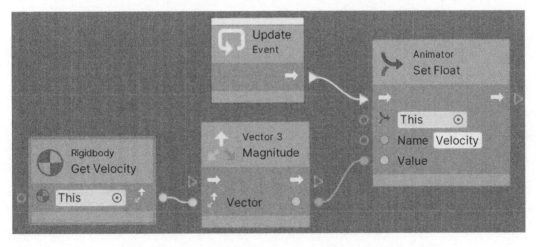

Figure 18.46 – Setting Velocity Animator variables in Visual Scripting

You may need to increase the `0.01` transitions threshold used so far slightly in the conditions of the transitions of the animator controller because `Rigidbody` keeps moving after releasing the keys. Using `1` worked perfectly for me. Another option would be to increase the drag and the velocity of the player to make the character stop faster. Pick whatever method works best for you.

As you can see, we can gather data about the actual movement and shooting action of our player to inform the animator controller of its state so that it can react accordingly.

Summary

Feedback is an important topic in video games. It gives valuable information to the player, such as the location of enemies if there is a 3D sound setup, distant shooting depicted by muzzles being shot in the background, life bars indicating that the player is about to die, and animations that react according to the player's movements. In this chapter, we saw different forms of feedback, sounds, VFX, animations, and the UI, which we created in part 2 of this book. Here, we learned how to use scripting to connect the UI to the game.

Now, you can script the UI, particle systems, and sounds to react to the game status, including changing the score text or the life bars of the UI or playing particle and sound effects when the character shoots. This improves the player's immersion experience in your game.

In the next chapter, we are going to discuss how to create a challenging AI for our enemies.

19

Implementing Game AI for Building Enemies

What is a game if not a great challenge to the player, who needs to use their character's abilities to tackle different scenarios? Each game imposes different kinds of obstacles on the Player, and the main one in our game is the enemies. Creating challenging and believable enemies can be complex; they need to behave like real characters and must be smart enough not to be easy to kill, but also easy enough that they are not impossible to kill either. We are going to use basic but good enough AI techniques to make an AI capable of sensing its surroundings and, based on that information, make decisions. These decisions will be executed using intelligent pathfinding.

In this chapter, we will cover the following topics:

- Gathering information with sensors
- Making decisions with FSM
- Executing FSM actions

By the end of the chapter, you will have a fully functional enemy capable of detecting the player and attacking him. So, let's start by learning how to make the sensor systems.

Gathering information with sensors

An AI works first by gathering information about its surroundings and then analyzing that data to choose an action. At this point, the chosen action is executed. As you already know, we cannot do anything without information, so let's start with that. There are several sources of information our AI can use, such as data about itself (life and bullets) or maybe some game state (winning condition or remaining enemies), which can easily be found with the code we've looked at so far. However, one important source of information is the AI's senses. Based on the needs of our game, we might need different senses such as sight and hearing, but in our case, sight will be enough, so let's learn how to code that.

In this section, we will examine the following sensor concepts:

- Creating Three-Filters sensors with C#
- Creating Three-Filters sensors with Visual Scripting
- Debugging with Gizmos

Let's start by learning how to create a sensor with the Three-Filters approach.

Creating Three-Filters sensors with C#

The most common way to code senses is by using a Three-Filters approach to discard enemies that are out of sight. The first filter is a distance filter, which will discard enemies too far away to be seen. Then, there's an angle check, which will check for enemies inside our viewing cone. Finally, there's a raycast check, which will discard enemies that are being occluded by obstacles such as walls. Before we start, a word of advice: we will be using Vector Mathematics here, and covering such topics in-depth is outside the scope of this book. If you don't understand something, feel free to just copy and paste the code from the Github repository provided and look for those concepts online. Let's start coding our sensors:

1. Create an empty GameObject called `AI` as a child of the **Enemy** Prefab. You need to open the Prefab first to be able to modify its children (double-click the Prefab). Remember to set the transform of this Object to **Position (0,1.75,0)**, **Rotation (0,0,0)**, and **Scale (1,1,1)** so that it will be aligned with the Enemy's eyes. We are doing this to benefit the future sight sensors we will create. Note that your Enemy prefab might have a different height for the eyes. While we can certainly just put all the AI scripts directly in **Enemy**, we did this just for separation and organization purposes:

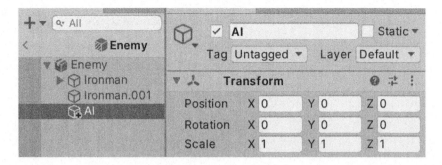

Figure 19.1 – AI script container

2. Create a script called `Sight` and add it to the **AI** child Object.

3. Create two fields of the `float` type called `distance` and `angle`, and another two of the `LayerMask` type called `obstaclesLayers` and `ObjectsLayers`. `distance` will be used as the vision distance, angle will determine the amplitude of the view cone, `ObstacleLayers` will be used by our obstacle check to determine which Objects are considered obstacles, and `ObjectsLayers` will be used to determine what types of Objects we want the sight to detect.

We just want the sight to see enemies; we are not interested in Objects such as walls or power-ups. `LayerMask` is a property type that allows us to select one or more layers to use inside code, so we will be filtering Objects by layer. In a moment, you will learn how to use it:

```
using UnityEngine;

public class Sight : MonoBehaviour
{
    public float distance;
    public float angle;
    public LayerMask objectsLayers;
    public LayerMask obstaclesLayers;
}
```

Figure 19.2 – Fields to parameterize our sight check

4. In `Update`, call `Physics.OverlapSphere`, as shown in the *Figure 19.3*.

    This function creates an imaginary sphere in the place specified by the first parameter (in our case, our position) and with a radius specified in the second parameter (the distance property) to detect Objects with the layers specified in the third parameter (`ObjectsLayers`). It will return an array containing all the Object Colliders that were found inside the sphere. These functions use Physics to do this check, so the Objects must have at least one collider. This is how we will be getting all the enemies inside our view distance, and we will be filtering them further in the following steps. Notice that we are passing our position to the first parameter, which is not actually the position of the Enemy, but the position of the **AI** child object, given our script is located there. This highlights the importance of the position of the `AI` object.

    > **Important Note**
    >
    > Another way of accomplishing the first check is to just check the distance to the Player, or, if you're looking for other kinds of Objects, to a Manager containing a list of them, but the way we chose here is more versatile and can be used in any kind of Object.
    >
    > Also, you might want to check the `Physics.OverlapSphereNonAlloc` version of this function, which does the same but is more performant by not allocating an array to return the results.

5. Iterate over the array of Objects returned by the function:

```
void Update()
{
    Collider[] colliders = Physics.OverlapSphere(transform.position, distance, objectsLayers);

    for (int i = 0; i < colliders.Length; i++)
    {
        Collider collider = colliders[i];
    }
}
```

Figure 19.3 – Getting all the Objects at a certain distance

6. To detect whether the Object falls inside the vision cone, we need to calculate the angle between our viewing direction and the direction to the Object itself. If the angle between those two directions is less than our cone angle, we consider that the Object falls inside our vision.

    We can start detecting the direction toward the Object, which is calculated by normalizing the difference between the Object position and ours, as shown in the following screenshot. Note that we used `bounds.center` instead of `transform.position`; this way, we can check the direction to the center of the Object instead of its pivot. Remember that the Player's pivot is in the ground and that the raycheck might collide with it before the Player does:

```
Vector3 directionToCollider = Vector3.Normalize(collider.bounds.center - transform.position);
```

Figure 19.4 – Calculating the direction from our position to the collider

7. We can use the `Vector3.Angle` function to calculate the angle between two directions. In our case, we can calculate the angle between the direction toward the Enemy and our forward vector to see the angle:

```
float angleToCollider = Vector3.Angle(transform.forward, directionToCollider);
```

Figure 19.5 – Calculating the angle between two directions

> **Important Note**
>
> If you want, you can use `Vector3.Dot` instead, which will execute a dot product. `Vector3.Angle` actually uses that one, but to convert the result of the dot product into an angle, it needs to use trigonometry, and this can be expensive to calculate. Anyway, our approach is simpler and fast as you don't have a big number of sensors (50+, depending on the target device), which we won't have.

8. Now, check whether the calculated angle is less than the one specified in the `angle` field. Consider that if we set an angle of 90, it will actually be 180, because if the `Vector3.Angle` function returns, for example, 30, it can be 30 to the left or the right. If our angle says 90, it can be both 90 to the left or the right, so it will detect Objects in a 180-degree arc.

9. Use the `Physics.Line` function to create an imaginary line between the first and the second parameter (our position and the collider's position) to detect Objects with the layers specified in the third parameter (the obstacles layers). Then, return a `boolean` indicating whether that ray hit something.

    The idea is to use the line to detect whether there are any obstacles between ourselves and the detected collider, and if there is no obstacle, this means that we have a direct line of sight toward the Object. Again, note that this function depends on the obstacle Objects having colliders, which in our case, they do (walls, floor, and so on):

```
if (angleToCollider < angle)
{
    if (!Physics.Linecast(transform.position, collider.bounds.center, obstaclesLayers))
    {

    }
}
```

Figure 19.6 – Using Linecast to check for obstacles between the sensor and the target Object

10. If the Object passes these three checks, this means that this is the Object we are currently seeing, so we can save it inside a field of the `Collider` type called `detectedObject`. By doing this, we can use this information later in the rest of the AI scripts.

    Consider using `break` to stop `for`, which is iterating the colliders, to prevent resources from being wasted by checking the other Objects. Also, set `detectedObject` to `null` before `for` to clear the result from the previous frame. So, in case, in this frame, we don't detect anything – it will keep the null value so that we can see there is nothing in the sensor:

```
public float distance;
public float angle;
public LayerMask objectsLayers;
public LayerMask obstaclesLayers;

public Collider detectedObject;

void Update()
{
    Collider[] colliders = Physics.OverlapSphere(transform.position, distance, objectsLayers);

    detectedObject = null;
    for (int i = 0; i < colliders.Length; i++)
    {
        Collider collider = colliders[i];

        Vector3 directionToCollider = Vector3.Normalize(collider.bounds.center - transform.position);

        float angleToCollider = Vector3.Angle(transform.forward, directionToCollider);

        if (angleToCollider < angle)
        {
            if (!Physics.Linecast(transform.position, collider.bounds.center, obstaclesLayers))
            {
                detectedObject = collider;
                break;
            }
        }
    }
}
```

Figure 19.7 – Full sensor script

Important Information

In our case, we are using the sensor just to look for the Player, the only Object the sensor is in charge of looking for. However, if you want to make the sensor more advanced, you can just keep a list of detected Objects, and then place every Object that passes the three tests inside it, instead of just the first one.

11. In the **Editor** window, configure the sensor as you desire. In this case, we will set `ObjectsLayer` to `Player` so that our sensor will focus its search on Objects within that layer, and `obstaclesLayer` to `Default`, which is the layer we used for walls and floors:

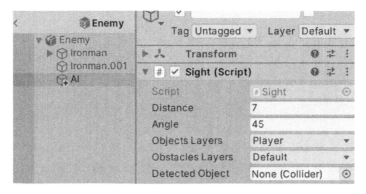

Figure 19.8 – Sensor settings

12. To test this, just place an Enemy with a movement speed of 0 in front of the Player, select its **AI** child Object, and then play the game to see how the property is set in the **Inspector** window. Also, try putting an obstacle between the two and check that the property says "None" (`null`). If you don't get the expected result, double-check your script, its configuration, and whether the Player has the `Player` layer and the obstacles have the `Default` layer. Also, you might need to raise the **AI** Object a little bit to prevent the ray from starting below the ground and hitting it:

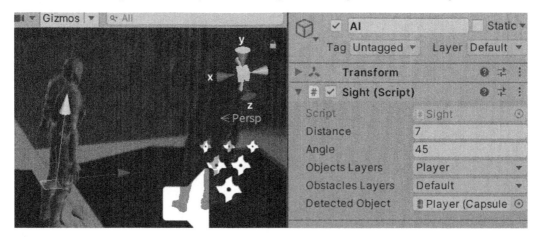

Figure 19.9 – The sensor capturing the Player

Given the size of the script, let's dedicate an entire section to the Visual Scripting version, given that it also introduces some new Visual Scripting concepts that are needed here.

Creating Three-Filters sensors with Visual Scripting

Regarding the Visual Scripting version, let's check it part by part, starting with **Overlap Sphere**:

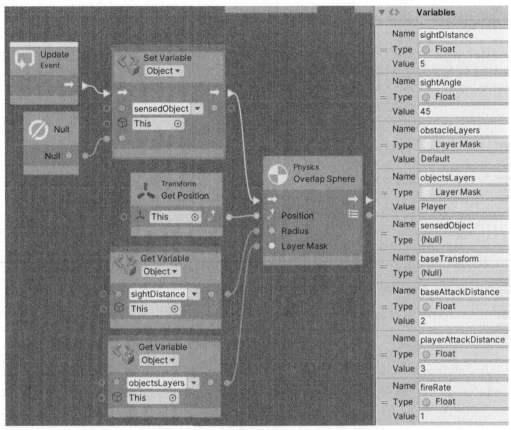

Figure 19.10 – Overlap Sphere in Visual Scripting

So far, we called **Overlap Sphere** after setting the sensedObject variable to null. Something to look for in the **Variables** component in the **Inspector** window is how the sensedObject variable doesn't have a type (a Null type is no type here). This isn't possible in C# as all variables must have a type, and while we could set the sensedObject variable to the proper type (**Collider**), we will keep the variable type to be set later via a script. Even if we set the type now, Visual Scripting tends to forget the type if no value is set, and we cannot set it until we actually detect something. Don't worry about this, though – when we set the variable through our script, it will acquire the proper type. Actually, all variables in Visual Scripting can switch types at runtime based on what we set for them, given how the **Variables** component works. Anyway, I don't recommend doing this – try to stick with the intended variable type.

> **Important Information**
>
> We just said that all the variables in C# must have a type, but that's not entirely true. There are ways to create dynamically typed variables, but it is not a good practice I recommend unless no other option is present (there are always other options).

Another thing to observe is how we set sensedObject to null at the beginning using the **Null** node, which effectively represents the null value.

Now, let's explore the **For Each Loop** part:

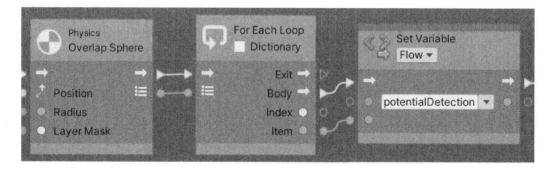

Figure 19.11 – Iterating collections in Visual Scripting

We can see that one of the output pins of **Overlap Sphere** is a little list that represents the **Collider** array that's returned by **Overlap Sphere**. We connect that pin to the **For Each Loop** node, which, as you might imagine, iterates over the elements of the provided collection (array, list, dictionary, and so on). The **Body** pin represents the nodes to execute in each iteration of the loop, and the **Item** output pin represents the item currently being iterated – in our case, one of the colliders that was detected in **Overlap Sphere**. Finally, we save that item in a Flow `potentialDetection` variable. Flow variables are the equivalent of Local Variables in C# functions. The idea here is that, given the size of the graph and the number of times we will be needing to query the currently iterated item, we don't want the line connecting the output **Item** pin to the other nodes to cross the entire graph. Instead, we will save that item in the `Flow` variable to reference it later, essentially naming that value so that it can be referenced later in the graph, as you will see shortly.

Now, let's explore the **Angle** check:

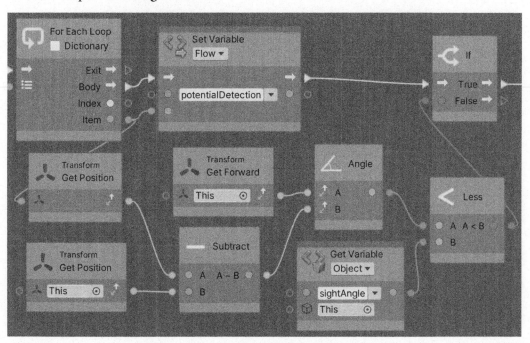

Figure 19.12 – Angle check in Visual Scripting

Here, you can see a direct translation of what we did in C# to detect the angle, so this should be pretty self-explanatory. The only thing here is given the proximity of the **Item** output pin to the **Get Position** node, where we query its position, we directly connected the node, but we will use the `potentialDetection` Flow variable later.

Now, let's explore the **Linecast** part:

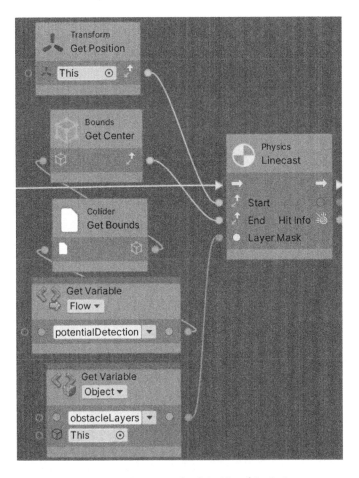

Figure 19.13 – Linecast check in Visual Scripting

Again, essentially, this is the same as we did previously in C#. The only thing to highlight here is the fact we used the `potentialDetection` Flow variable to get the position of the current item being iterated, instead of connecting the **Get Position** node to the Foreach **Item** output pin.

Now, let's explore the final part:

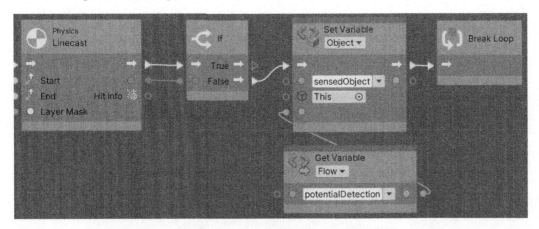

Figure 19.14 – Setting sensedObject

Again, this is pretty much self-explanatory: if **Linecast** returns false, we set potentialDetection (the currently iterated item) as sensedObject, which is the variable that will be accessed by other scripts later to query which object our AI can see right now. Something to consider here is the usage of the **Break Loop** node, which is the equivalent of the C# break keyword. Essentially, we are stopping the Foreach we are currently in.

Now, even though we have our sensor working, sometimes, checking whether it's working or configured properly requires some visual aids we can create using Gizmos.

Debugging with Gizmos

As we start creating our AI, we will begin to detect certain errors in edge cases, usually related to misconfigurations. You may think that the Player falls inside the sight of the Enemy, but maybe you cannot see that the line of sight is occluded by an Object, especially since the enemies move constantly. A good way to debug those kinds of scenarios is by using Editor-only visual aids known as Gizmos, which allow you to visualize invisible data such as the sight distance or the Linecasts that have been executed to detect obstacles.

Let's start by learning how to create `Gizmos` by drawing a sphere representing the sight distance:

1. In the `Sight` script, create an event function called `OnDrawGizmos`. This event is only executed in the **Editor** window (not in builds) and is where Unity asks us to draw `Gizmos`.

2. Using the `Gizmos.DrawWireSphere` function, pass our position as the first parameter and the distance as the second parameter. This will draw a sphere around our position that specifies the radius of our distance. You can check how the size of the Gizmo changes as you change the distance field:

Figure 19.15 – Sphere Gizmo

3. Optionally, you can change the color of the Gizmo by setting `Gizmos.color` before calling the drawing functions:

```
void OnDrawGizmos()
{
    Gizmos.color = Color.red;
    Gizmos.DrawWireSphere(transform.position, distance);
}
```

Figure 19.16 – Gizmos drawing code

> **Important Information**
>
> At this point, you are drawing `Gizmos` constantly. If you have lots of enemies, they can pollute the Scene view with too many `Gizmos`. In that case, try the `OnDrawGizmosSelected` event function instead, which draws `Gizmos` only if the object is selected.

4. We can draw the lines representing the cone using `Gizmos.DrawRay`, which receives the origin of the line to draw and the direction of the line. This can be multiplied by a certain value to specify the length of the line, as shown in the following screenshot:

```
Vector3 rightDirection = Quaternion.Euler(0, angle, 0) * transform.forward;
Gizmos.DrawRay(transform.position, rightDirection * distance);

Vector3 leftDirection = Quaternion.Euler(0, -angle, 0) * transform.forward;
Gizmos.DrawRay(transform.position, leftDirection * distance);
```

Figure 19.17 – Drawing rotated lines

5. Here, we used `Quaternion.Euler` to generate a quaternion based on the angles we want to rotate. If you multiply this quaternion by a direction, we will get the rotated direction. We are taking our forward vector and rotating it based on the angle field that will generate our cone vision lines. Also, we are multiplying this direction by the sight distance to draw the line as far as our sight can see; this way, the line matches the end of the sphere:

Figure 19.18 – Vision Angle lines

We can also draw the Line Casts, which check the obstacles, but since those depend on the current situation of the game, such as the Objects that pass the first two checks and their positions, we can use Debug.DrawLine instead, which can be executed in the Update method. This version of DrawLine is designed to be used at runtime only. The Gizmos we saw also execute in the **Editor** window. Let's try them out:

1. First, let's debug the scenario where LineCast didn't detect any obstacles. For this, we need to draw a line between our sensor and the Object. Here, we can call Debug.DrawLine in the if statement that calls LineCast, as shown in the following screenshot:

```
if (!Physics.Linecast(transform.position, collider.bounds.center, obstaclesLayers))
{
    Debug.DrawLine(transform.position, collider.bounds.center, Color.green);
    detectedObject = collider;
    break;
}
```

Figure 19.19 – Drawing a line in Update

2. The following screenshot shows DrawLine in action:

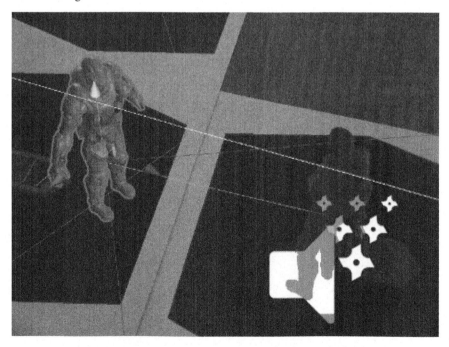

Figure 19.20 – Drawing a Line toward the detected Object

3. We also want to draw a line in red when the sight is occluded by an Object. In this case, we need to know where `Linecast` hit so that we can use an overloaded version of the function. This provides an `out` parameter that gives us more information about what the line collided with, such as the position of the hit and the normal and the collided Object, as shown in the following screenshot:

```
if (!Physics.Linecast(transform.position, collider.bounds.center, out RaycastHit hit, obstaclesLayers))
{
```

Figure 19.21 – Getting information about Linecast

> **Important Information**
>
> Note that `Linecast` doesn't always collide with the nearest obstacle but with the first Object it detects in the line, which can vary in order. If you need to detect the nearest obstacle, look for the `Physics.Raycast` version of the function.

4. We can use this information to draw the line from our position to the hit point in `else` of the `if` sentence when the line collides with something:

```
if (!Physics.Linecast(transform.position, collider.bounds.center, out RaycastHit hit, obstaclesLayers))
{
    Debug.DrawLine(transform.position, collider.bounds.center, Color.green);
    detectedObject = collider;
    break;
}
else
{
    Debug.DrawLine(transform.position, hit.point, Color.red);
}
```

Figure 19.22 – Drawing a line in case we have an obstacle

5. The following screenshot shows the results:

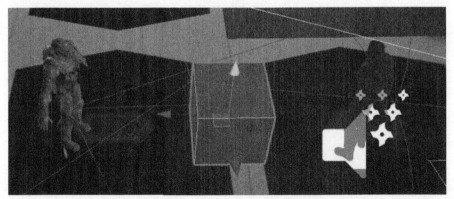

Figure 19.23 – Line when an obstacle occludes vision

Regarding the Visual Scripting version, the first part will look like this:

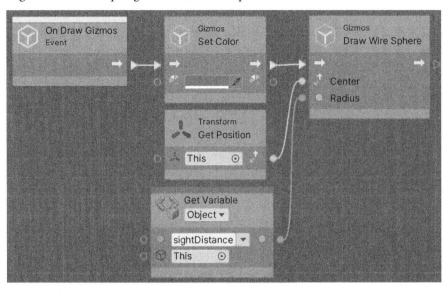

Figure 19.24 – Drawing Gizmos with Visual Scripting

Then, the angle lines look like this:

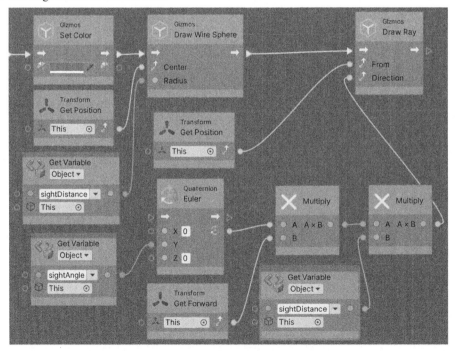

Figure 19.25 – Drawing Angle lines of sight in Visual Scripting

Here, we are only showing one, but the other is essentially the same except we multiply the angle by minus one. Finally, the red lines toward the detected object and obstacles will look like this:

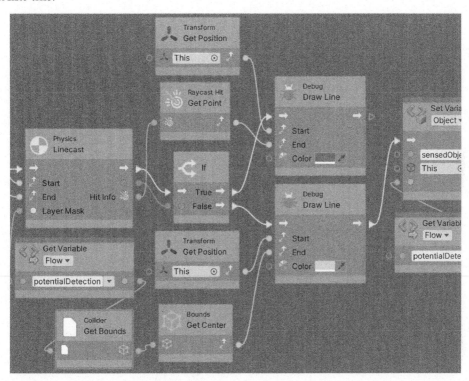

Figure 19.26 – Drawing lines toward obstacles or detected objects with Visual Scripting

Note that to accomplish this, we needed to change the previous **Linecast** node for the version that returns **RaycastHit** information at the end.

In this section, we created a sensors system that will give sight to our AI, as well as plenty of information about what to do next. Now that we have completed our sensors, let's use the information provided by them to make decisions with FSMs.

Making decisions with FSMs

We explored the concept of **Finite State Machines** (**FSMs**) when we used them in the Animator. We learned that an FSM is a collection of states, each one representing an action that an Object can be executing at a time, and a set of transitions that dictate how the states are switched. This concept is not only used in Animation but in a myriad of programming scenarios, and one of the most common ones is in AI. We can just replace the animations with AI code in the states to get an AI FSM.

In this section, we will examine the following AI FSM concepts:

- Creating the FSM in C#
- Creating transitions
- Creating the FSM in Visual Scripting

Let's start by creating our FSM skeleton.

Creating the FSM in C#

To create our FSM, we need to recap on some basic concepts. Remember that an FSM can have a state for each possible action it can execute and that only one can be executed at a time. In terms of AI, we can be Patrolling, Attacking, Fleeing, and so on. Also, remember that there are transitions between States that determine conditions that must be met to change from one state to the other. In terms of AI, this can be the user being near the Enemy to start attacking or their life being so low that they need to start fleeing. The following screenshot shows a simple example of the two possible states of a door:

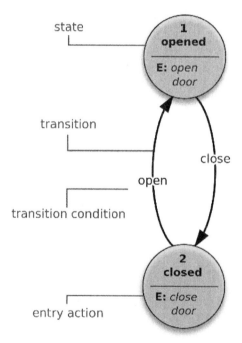

Figure 19.27 – FSM example

There are several ways to implement FSMs for AI; you can even use the Animator if you want to or download an FSM system from the Asset Store. In our case, we are going to take the simplest approach possible, a single script containing a set of `if` sentences, which can be basic but are still a good start for understanding the concept. Let's implement this:

1. Create a script called `EnemyFSM` in the **AI** child Object of the Enemy.

2. Create an `enum` called `EnemyState` with the `GoToBase`, `AttackBase`, `ChasePlayer`, and `AttackPlayer` values. We are going to have these states in our AI.

3. Create a field of the `EnemyState` type called `currentState`, which will hold the current state of our Enemy:

```csharp
public class EnemyFSM : MonoBehaviour
{
    public enum EnemyState { GoToBase, AttackBase, ChasePlayer, AttackPlayer }

    public EnemyState currentState;
```

Figure 19.28 – EnemyFSM state definition

4. Create three functions named after the states we defined.

5. Call those functions in `Update`, depending on the current state:

```csharp
void Update()
{
    if(currentState == EnemyState.GoToBase)
        GoToBase();
    else if(currentState == EnemyState.AttackBase)
        AttackBase();
    else if(currentState == EnemyState.ChasePlayer)
        ChasePlayer();
    else if(currentState == EnemyState.AttackPlayer)
        AttackPlayer();
}

void GoToBase() {print("GoToBase"); }
void AttackBase() { print("AttackBase"); }
void ChasePlayer() { print("ChasePlayer"); }
void AttackPlayer() { print("AttackPlayer"); }
```

Figure 19.29 – If-based FSM

> **Important Information**
>
> Yes, you can use a switch here, but I just prefer the regular `if` syntax.

6. In the **Editor** window, test how changing the `currentState` field will change which state is active while checking the messages being printed in the console:

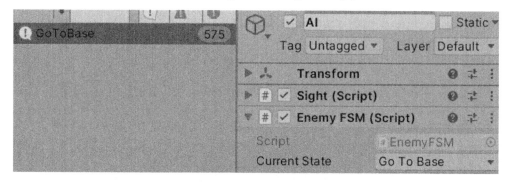

Figure 19.30 – State testing

As you can see, this is a pretty simple but functional approach, so let's continue with this FSM by creating transitions for it.

Creating transitions

If you remember the transitions we created in the Animator Controller, those were a collection of conditions that are checked if the state the transition belongs to is active. In our FSM approach, this translates into `if` sentences that detect conditions inside the states. Let's create the transitions between our proposed states, as follows:

1. Add a field of the `Sight` type called `sightSensor` to our FSM script, and drag the AI `GameObject` to that field to connect it to the `Sight` component there. Since the FSM component is in the same Object as `Sight`, we can also use `GetComponent` instead. However, in advanced AIs, you might have different sensors that detect different Objects, so I prefer to prepare my script for that scenario, but pick the approach you like the most.

2. In the `GoToBase` function, check whether the detected Object of the `Sight` component is not `null`, meaning that something is inside our line of vision. If our AI is going toward the base but detects an Object on the way there, we must switch to the `Chase` state to pursue the Player. This can be seen in the following screenshot:

```
public Sight sightSensor;
void GoToBase()
{
    if (sightSensor.detectedObject != null)
    {
        currentState = EnemyState.ChasePlayer;
    }
}
```

Figure 19.31 – Creating transitions

3. Also, we must change to `AttackBase` in case we are near enough to the Object that it must be damaged to decrease the base life. We can create a field of the `Transform` type called `baseTransform` and drag the Base Life Object there so that we can check the distance. Remember to add a float field called `baseAttackDistance` to make that distance configurable:

```
public Transform baseTransform;
public float baseAttackDistance;

void GoToBase()
{
    if (sightSensor.detectedObject != null)
        currentState = EnemyState.ChasePlayer;

    float distanceToBase = Vector3.Distance(transform.position, baseTransform.position);
    if (distanceToBase <= baseAttackDistance)
        currentState = EnemyState.AttackBase;
}
```

Figure 19.32 – GoToBase Transitions

4. In the case of `ChasePlayer`, we need to check whether the Player is out of sight so that we can switch back to the `GoToBase` state, or whether we are near enough to `Player` to start attacking it. We will need another distance field, which determines the distance for attacking the Player, and we might want different attacking distances for those two targets. Consider an early return in the transition to prevent getting `null` reference exceptions if we try to access the position of the sensor-detected Object when there isn't one:

```
void ChasePlayer()
{
    if (sightSensor.detectedObject == null)
    {
        currentState = EnemyState.GoToBase;
        return;
    }

    float distanceToPlayer = Vector3.Distance(transform.position, sightSensor.detectedObject.transform.position);
    if (distanceToPlayer <= playerAttackDistance)
        currentState = EnemyState.AttackPlayer;
}
```

Figure 19.33 – ChasePlayer Transitions

5. For `AttackPlayer`, we need to check whether `Player` is out of sight to go back to `GoToBase` or whether it is far enough to go back to chasing it. As you can see, we multiplied `PlayerAttackDistance` to make the stop-attacking distance a little bit larger than the start-attacking distance; this will prevent switching back and forth rapidly between attack and chase when the Player is near that distance. You can make it configurable instead of hardcoding `1.1`:

```
void AttackPlayer()
{
    if (sightSensor.detectedObject == null)
    {
        currentState = EnemyState.GoToBase;
        return;
    }

    float distanceToPlayer = Vector3.Distance(transform.position, sightSensor.detectedObject.transform.position);
    if (distanceToPlayer > playerAttackDistance * 1.1f)
        currentState = EnemyState.ChasePlayer;
}
```

Figure 19.34 – AttackPlayer Transitions

6. In our case, `AttackBase` won't have any transition. Once the Enemy is close enough to the base to attack it, it will stay like that, even if the Player starts shooting at it. Its only objective, once there, is to destroy the base.

7. Remember that you can use `Gizmos` to draw the distances:

```
void OnDrawGizmos()
{
    Gizmos.color = Color.blue;
    Gizmos.DrawWireSphere(transform.position, playerAttackDistance);

    Gizmos.color = Color.yellow;
    Gizmos.DrawWireSphere(transform.position, baseAttackDistance);
}
```

Figure 19.35 – FSM Gizmos

8. Test the script by selecting the **AI** object before hitting play and then move the Player around, checking how the states change in the **Inspector** window. You can also keep the original print messages in each state to see them change in the console. Remember to set the attack distances and the references to the Objects. The following screenshot shows the settings that we used:

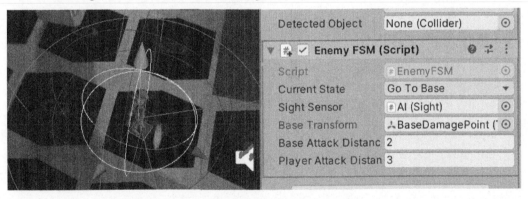

Figure 19.36 – Enemy FSM settings

A little problem that we have now is that the spawned enemies won't have the necessary references to make the distance calculations for **Base Transform**. You will notice that if you try to apply the changes for the Enemy of the scene to the Prefab (**Overrides -> Apply All**), **Base Transform** will say None. Remember that Prefabs cannot contain references to Objects in the scene, which complicates our work here. One alternative would be to create `BaseManager`, a singleton that holds a reference to the damage position, so that our `EnemyFSM` can access it. We could also make use of functions such as `GameObject.Find` to find our Object.

In this case, we will see the latter. Even though it may be less performant than the Manager version, I want to show you how to use it to expand your Unity toolset. In this case, just set the `baseTransform` field in `Awake` to the return of `GameObject.Find` while using `BaseDamagePoint` as the first parameter, which will look for an Object with that name, as shown in the following screenshot. Also, feel free to remove the private keyword from the `baseTransform` field; now that is set via code, it makes little sense to display it in the **Editor** window; we should debug it instead. You will see that now, our wave-spawned enemies will change states:

```
Transform baseTransform;
void Awake()
{
    baseTransform = GameObject.Find("BaseDamagePoint").transform;
}
```

Figure 19.37 – Searching for an Object in the scene by name

Now that our FSM states have been coded and transition properly, let's learn how to do the same in Visual Scripting. Feel free to skip the following section if you are only interested in the C# version.

Creating the FSM in Visual Scripting

So far, every script we created in Visual Scripting was mostly a mirror of the C# version, but with some differences in some nodes. With State Machines, we could do the same, but instead, we are going to use the State Machine system of Visual Scripting. The concept is the same in that you have states and can switch between them, but how the states are organized and when the transitions trigger is managed visually, in a similar way to what the Animator system does. So, let's learn how we can use the system to create our first State Machine Graph and some States. Follow these steps:

1. Add the **State Machine** component to our `Enemy`. Remember that it is called **State Machine** and not **Script Machine**, the latter being the component for regular Visual Scripts.

2. Click the **New** button in the component and select a place to save the **State Machine Graph** asset, in a similar way to what we've been doing so far for regular Visual Scripts. In my case, I called it `EnemyFSM`:

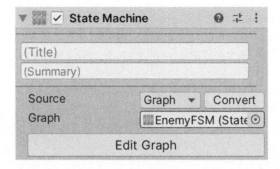

Figure 19.38 – Creating a Visual State Machine

3. Double-click the State Machine Graph to edit it as usual.

4. Right-click in an empty area of the **Graph** editor and select **Create Script State** to create our first state:

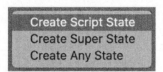

Figure 19.39 – Creating our first Visual State Machine State

5. Repeat *step 4* three more times to create the necessary states:

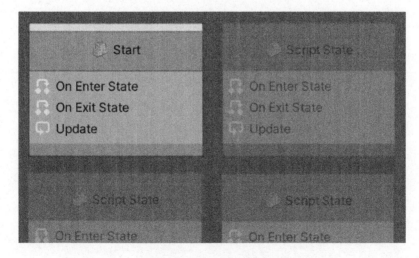

Figure 19.40 – Visual States

6. Select any of them. Then, in the **Info** panel on the left, fill in the **Title** field (the first one) with the name of any of the states we created previously (GoToBase, AttackBase, ChasePlayer, or AttackPlayer). If you don't see the **Info** panel, click the button with the "**i**" in the middle to display it:

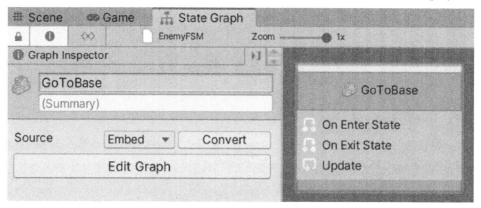

Figure 19.41 – Renaming a Visual State

7. Repeat this for the rest of the state nodes until you have each node named after each state we created in the C# section:

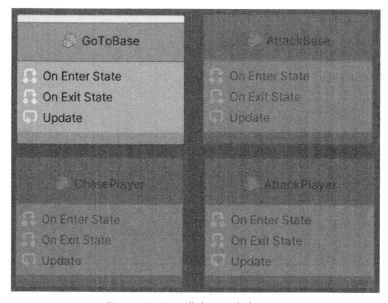

Figure 19.42 – All the needed states

8. Here, you can see that one of the states has a green bar at the top, which represents which node is supposed to be the first one. I renamed that initial state GoToBase as that's the one I prefer to be the first, but if you don't have that one as the starting one, right-click the node that currently has the green bar in your state machine and select **Toggle Start** to remove the green bar from it. Then, repeat this for the node that you want to be the first one (GoToBase, in our scenario), adding the green bar to that one.

> **Important Information**
>
> Something to consider is that you can have more than one Start State in Visual Scripting, which means you can have multiple states running at the same time and transitioning. Even if possible, I recommend that you avoid having more than one state active at a time to make things simple.

9. Double-click GoToBase to enter the logic edit mode for them. Connect a print message in the **Update** event node to print a message saying GoToBase:

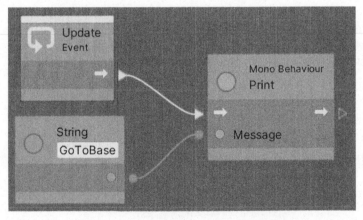

Figure 19.43 – Our first state machine logic

10. In the top bar, click the EnemyFSM label at the left of GoToBase to return to the whole **State Machine** view.

11. Feel free to delete the other event nodes if you are not planning to use them:

Figure 19.44 – Returning to the state machine's editor mode

12. Repeat *steps 9* to *11* for each state until all of them print their names.

With this, we have created the nodes representing the possible states of our AI. In the next section, we will be adding logic to them to make them meaningful, but before that, we need to create the transitions between the states and the conditions that need to be met to trigger them. To do so, follow these steps:

1. Create three variables in the **Variables** component of the Enemy called `baseTransform`, `baseAttackDistance`, and `playerAttackDistance`. We are going to need them to do the transitions.

2. Don't set any type to `baseTransform` as we will fill it later via code. However, regarding `baseAttackDistance`, make it a **Float** type with a value of 2. Finally, for `playerAttackDistance`, also make it a **Float** type with a value of 3. Feel free to change those values if you wish:

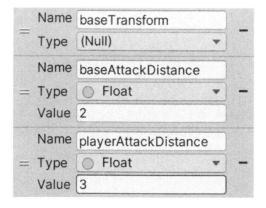

Figure 19.45 – Variables needed for our transitions

3. Right-click the **GoToBase** node and select the **Make Transition** option; then, click the **ChasePlayer** node. This will create a transition between the two states:

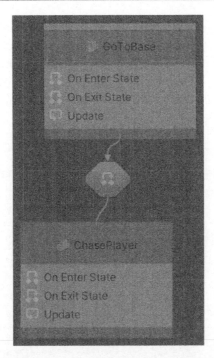

Figure 19.46 – A transition between two nodes

4. Repeat *step 9* for each transition we created in the C# version. It will need to look as follows:

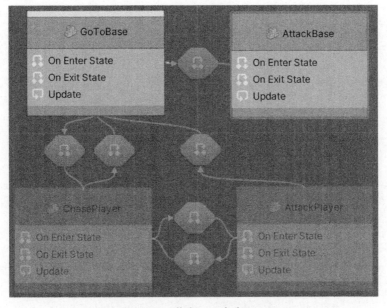

Figure 19.47 – All the needed transitions

5. Double-click the yellow shape in the middle of the transition between **GoToBase** and **Chase Player** to enter the **Transition** mode. Here, you will be able to specify the condition that will trigger that transition (instead of using an `if` statement during the state logic). Remember that you have two yellow shapes, one for each transition direction, so ensure that you are double-clicking the correct one based on the white arrows connecting them.

6. Modify the graph to check if the `sensedObject` variable is **Not Null**. It should look like this:

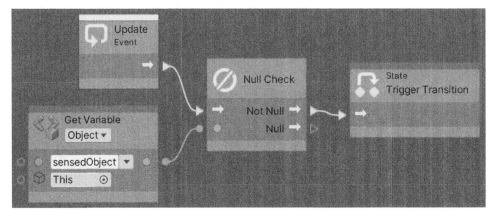

Figure 19.48 – Adding a transition condition

7. The transition between **GoToBase** and **AttackBase** should look like this:

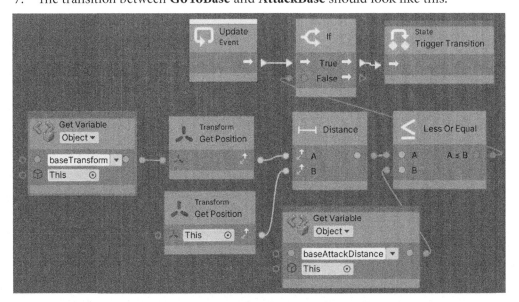

Figure 19.49 – GoToBase to AttackBase transition condition

8. Now, **ChasePlayer** to **GoToBase** should look as follows:

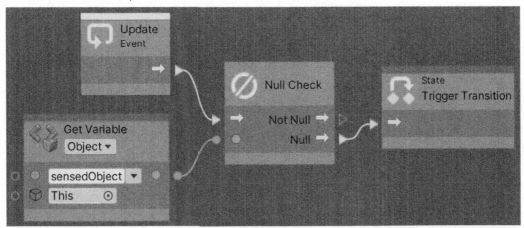

Figure 19.50 – ChasePlayer to GoToBase transition condition

9. **ChasePlayer** to **AttackPlayer** should look like this. Essentially, this is the same as **GoToBase** and **AttackBase** in that there's a distance check, but there's different targets here:

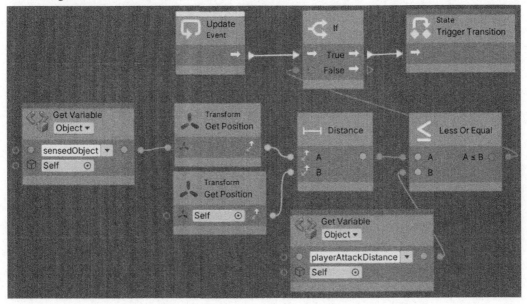

Figure 19.51 – ChasePlayer to AttackPlayer transition condition

10. **AttackPlayer** to **ChasePlayer** should look like this. This is another distance check but this one is checking whether the distance is greater and multiplying the distance by `1.1` (to prevent transition jittering, as we explained in the C# version):

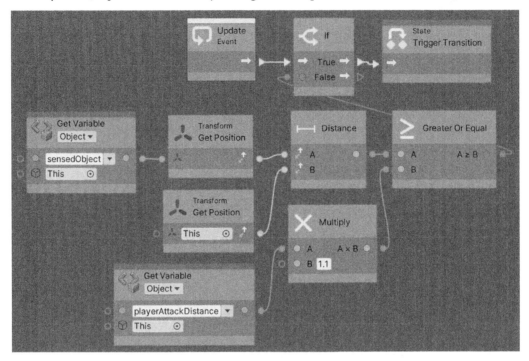

Figure 19.52 – AttackPlayer to ChasePlayer transition condition

11. Finally, for **AttackPlayer** to **GoToBase**, this is the expected graph:

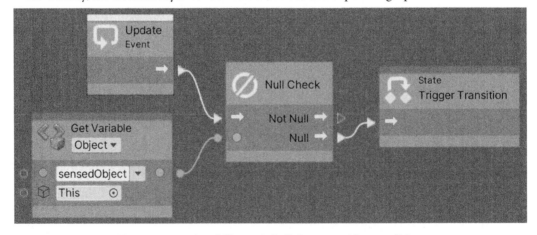

Figure 19.53 – AttackPlayer to GoToBase transition condition

Something we need to tackle before moving on is the fact that we still don't have any value set in the baseTransform variable. The idea is to fill it via code, as we did in the C# version. However, something to consider here is that we cannot add an **Awake** event node to the whole state machine, just to the states.

In this scenario, we could use the **OnEnterState** event, which is an exclusive event node for state machines. It will execute as soon as the state becomes active, which is useful for state initializations. We could add the logic to initialize the baseTransform variable in **OnEnterState** of the **GoToBase** state, given it is the first state we execute. This way, the **GoToBase** logic will look as follows. Remember to double-click the state node to edit it:

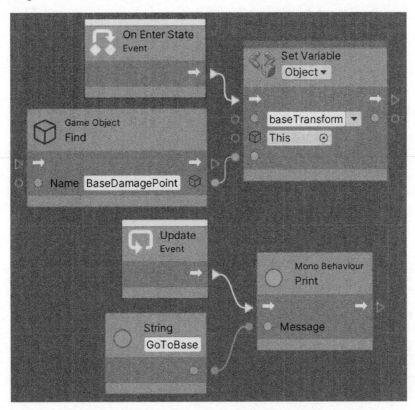

Figure 19.54 – GoToBase initialization logic

Notice how here, we just save the result of the **Find** node in the variable, instead of getting the transform and then saving it. While this is possible, it's not needed, given the **GetPosition** node also works with GameObjects directly, so there's no need to pass only **Transform** (as we've done so far). Also, consider that in this case, we will be executing the **Set Variable** node not only when the object initializes, but also each time **GoToBase** becomes the current state. If this results in unexpected behavior, other options could be to create a new **Initial State** that initializes everything and then transition to the rest of the states, or maybe create a classic Visual Script graph that initializes those variables in **Awake**.

With that, we have learned how to create a decision-making system for our AI through FSMs. It will make decisions based on the information that's gathered by sensors and other systems. Now that our FSM states have been coded and transition properly, let's make them do something.

Executing FSM actions

Now, we need to do the last step—make the FSM do something interesting. Here, we can do a lot of things, such as shoot the base or the Player and move the Enemy toward its target (the Player or the base). We will be handling movement with a Unity Pathfinding system called NavMesh, a tool that allows our AI to calculate and traverse paths between two points while avoiding obstacles, which needs some preparation to work properly.

In this section, we will examine the following FSM action concepts:

- Calculating our scene's Pathfinding
- Using Pathfinding
- Adding the final details

Let's start by preparing our scene for movement with Pathfinding.

Calculating our scene's Pathfinding

Pathfinding algorithms rely on simplified versions of the scene. Analyzing the full geometry of a complex scene is almost impossible to do in real time. There are several ways to represent Pathfinding information that's been extracted from a scene, such as by using Graphs and NavMesh geometries. Unity uses the latter – a simplified mesh similar to a 3D model that spans all the areas that Unity determines are walkable. The following screenshot shows an example of a NavMesh that's been generated in a scene; that is, the light blue geometry:

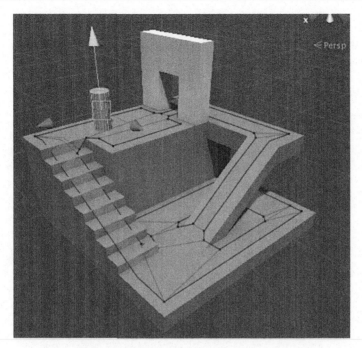

Figure 19.55 – NavMesh of the walkable areas in the scene

Generating a `NavMesh` can take seconds to minutes, depending on the size of the scene. That's why Unity's Pathfinding system calculates that once in the **Editor** window: so that when we distribute our game, the user will use the pre-generated `NavMesh`. Just like Lightmapping, `NavMesh` is baked into a file for later usage. Like Lightmapping, the main caveat here is that the `NavMesh` Objects cannot change at runtime. If you destroy or move a floor tile, the AI will still walk over that area. The NavMesh on top of that didn't notice the floor isn't there anymore, so you are not able to move or modify those Objects in any way. Luckily, in our case, we won't suffer from any modifications being made to the scene at runtime, but consider that there are components such as `NavMeshObstacle` that can help us in those scenarios.

To generate a `NavMesh` for our scene, do the following:

1. Select any walkable Object and the obstacles on top of it, such as floors, walls, and other obstacles, and mark them as **Static**. You might remember that the **Static** checkbox also affects Lightmapping, so if you want an Object not to be part of Lightmapping but contribute to generating `NavMesh`, you can click the arrow to the left of the static check and select **Navigation Static** only. Try to limit **Navigation Static** Objects to the ones that the enemies will traverse to increase the generation speed of `NavMesh`. Making the Terrain navigable, in our case, will increase the generation time a lot, and we will never play in that area.

2. Open the NavMesh panel in **Window | AI | Navigation**.

3. Select the **Bake** tab, click the **Bake** button at the bottom of the window, and check the generated NavMesh:

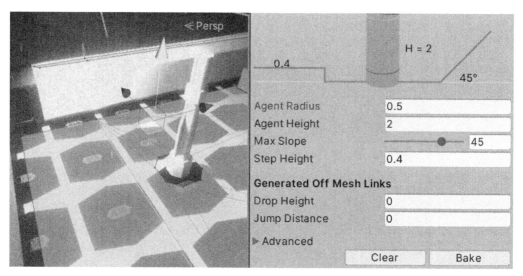

Figure 19.56 – Generating a NavMesh

And that's pretty much everything you need to do. Of course, there are lots of settings you can fiddle around with, such as **Max Slope**, which indicates the maximum angle of the slope the AI will be able to climb, and **Step Height**, which will determine whether the AI can climb stairs, connecting the floors between the steps in NavMesh. However, since we have a plain and simple scene, the default settings will suffice.

Now, let's make our AI move around NavMesh.

Using pathfinding

To make an AI Object that moves with NavMesh, Unity provides the NavMeshAgent component, which will make our AI stick to NavMesh, preventing the Object from going outside it. It will not only calculate the Path to a specified destination automatically but also move the Object through the path by using Steering Behavior Algorithms, which mimic the way a human would move through the path, slowing down on corners and turning with interpolations instead of instantaneously. Also, this component is capable of evading other NavMeshAgents running in the scene, preventing all the enemies from collapsing in the same position.

Let's use this powerful component by doing the following:

1. Select the **Enemy** Prefab and add the `NavMeshAgent` component to it. Add it to the root Object, the one called **Enemy**, not the **AI** child – we want the whole Object to move. You will see a cylinder around the Object representing the area the Object will occupy in `NavMesh`. Note that this isn't a collider, so it won't be used for physical collisions:

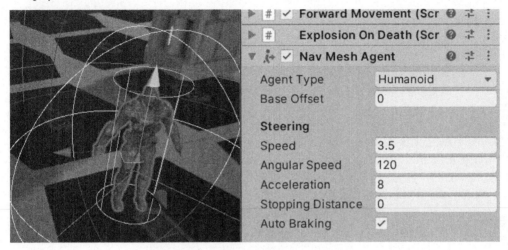

Figure 19.57 – The NavMeshAgent component

2. Remove the `ForwardMovement` component; from now on, we will drive the movement of our Enemy with `NavMeshAgent`.

3. In the `Awake` event function of the `EnemyFSM` script, use the `GetComponentInParent` function to cache the reference of `NavMeshAgent`. This will work similarly to `GetComponent` – it will look for a component in our `GameObject`, but if the component is not there, this version will try to look for that component in all the parents. Remember to add the `using UnityEngine.AI` line to use the `NavMeshAgent` class in this script:

```
NavMeshAgent agent;

void Awake()
{
    baseTransform = GameObject.Find("BaseDamagePoint").transform;
    agent = GetComponentInParent<NavMeshAgent>();
}
```

Figure 19.58 – Caching a parent component reference

> **Important Information**
>
> As you can imagine, there is `GetComponentInChildren`, which searches for components in `GameObject` first and then in all its children, if necessary.

4. In the `GoToBase` state function, call the `SetDestination` function of the `NavMeshAgent` reference, passing the position of the base Object as the target:

```
void GoToBase()
{
    agent.SetDestination(baseTransform.position);
```

Figure 19.59 – Setting the destination of our AI

5. Save the script and test this with a few enemies in the scene or with the enemies spawned in waves. You will see a problem where the enemies will never stop going toward the target position, entering inside the Object, if necessary, even if the current state of their FSMs changes when they are near enough. That's because we never told `NavMeshAgent` to stop, which we can do by setting the `isStopped` field of the agent to `true`. You might want to tweak the distance of `AttackBase` to make the enemy stop a little bit nearer or further:

```
void AttackBase()
{
    agent.isStopped = true;
}
```

Figure 19.60 – Stopping agent movement

6. We can do the same for `ChasePlayer` and `AttackPlayer`. In `ChasePlayer`, we can set the destination of the agent to the Player position, and in `AttackPlayer`, we can stop the movement. In this scenario, `AttackPlayer` can go back again to `GoToBase` or `ChasePlayer`, so you need to set the `isStopped` agent field to `false` in those states or before doing the transition. We will pick the former, as that version will cover other states that also stop the agent without extra code. We will start with the `GoToBase` state:

```
void GoToBase()
{
    agent.isStopped = false;
    agent.SetDestination(baseTransform.position);
}
```

Figure 19.61 – Reactivating the agent

7. Now, let's continue with ChasePlayer:

```
void ChasePlayer()
{
    agent.isStopped = false;

    if (sightSensor.detectedObject == null)
    {
        currentState = EnemyState.GoToBase;
        return;
    }

    agent.SetDestination(sightSensor.detectedObject.transform.position);
```

Figure 19.62 – Reactivating the agent and chasing the Player

8. Finally, let's alter AttackPlayer:

```
void AttackPlayer()
{
    agent.isStopped = true;
```

Figure 19.63 – Stopping the movement

9. You can tweak the Acceleration, Speed, and Angular Speed properties of NavMeshAgent to control how fast the Enemy will move. Also, remember to apply the changes to the Prefab for the spawned enemies to be affected.

Regarding the Visual Scripting versions, **GoToBase** will look as follows:

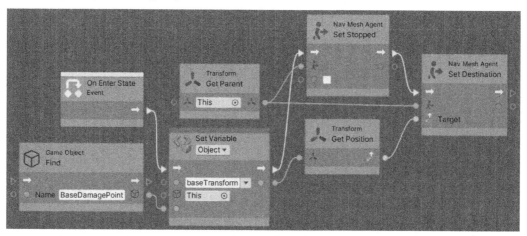

Figure 19.64 – Making our agent move

Note that we deleted **Update**, which is printing a message, as we don't need it anymore. Also, note that we call the **Set Destination** node after, also in the **OnEnterState** event, as we just need to do this once. We do this for every frame in the C# version for simplicity, but this isn't necessary, so we are taking advantage of the **OnEnterState** event. We can emulate this behavior in the C# version if we want, executing these actions when we change the state (inside the Ifs that check the transition conditions), instead of the update. Finally, notice how we needed to use the **GetParent** node to access the **NavMeshAgent** component in the Enemy's root object. This is needed because we are currently in the **AI** child object.

The **AttackBase** state will look like this:

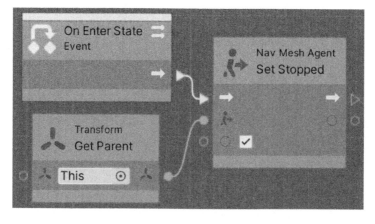

Figure 19.65 – Making our agent stop

The **ChasePlayer** state will look like this:

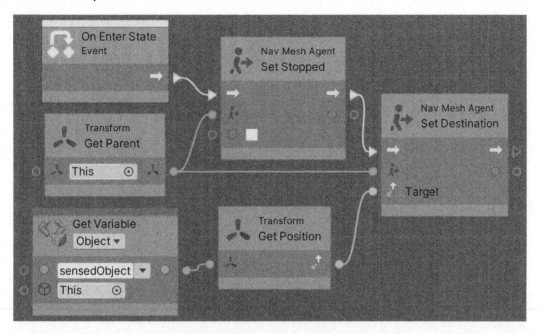

Figure 19.66 – ChasePlayer logic

Finally, **AttackPlayer** will look like this:

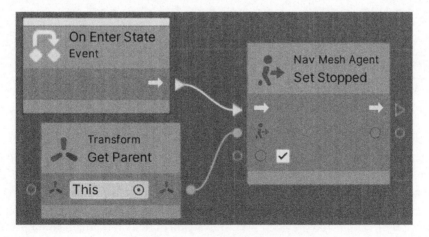

Figure 19.67 – AttackPlayer logic

Now that we have movement in our enemy, let's add the final details to our AI.

Adding the final details

Two things are missing here: the Enemy is not shooting any bullets and it doesn't have animations. Let's start by fixing the shooting issue:

1. Add a `bulletPrefab` field of the `GameObject` type to our `EnemyFSM` script and a float field called `fireRate`.

2. Create a function called `Shoot` and call it inside `AttackBase` and `AttackPlayer`:

```
void AttackPlayer()
{
    agent.isStopped = true;

    if (sightSensor.detectedObject == null)
    {
        currentState = EnemyState.GoToBase;
        return;
    }

    Shoot();

    float distanceToPlayer = Vector3.Distance(transform.position, sightSensor.detectedObject.transform.position);
    if (distanceToPlayer > playerAttackDistance * 1.1f)
        currentState = EnemyState.ChasePlayer;
}

void AttackBase()
{
    agent.isStopped = true;
    Shoot();
}

void Shoot()
{

}
```

Figure 19.68 – Shooting function calls

3. In the `Shoot` function, place code that's similar to the code we used in the `PlayerShooting` script to shoot bullets at a specific fire rate, as shown in the following screenshot. Remember to set the Enemy layer in your **Enemy** Prefab, in case you didn't previously, to prevent the bullet from damaging the Enemy itself. You may also want to raise the AI script a little bit to shoot bullets in another position or, better, add a `shootPoint` transform field and create an empty Object in the Enemy to use as the spawn position. If you do that, consider making the empty Object not rotated so that the Enemy rotation affects the direction of the bullet properly:

```
void Shoot()
{
    if (Time.timeScale > 0)
    {
        var timeSinceLastShoot float = Time.time - lastShootTime;
        if(timeSinceLastShoot < fireRate)
            return;

        lastShootTime = Time.time;
        Instantiate(bulletPrefab, transform.position, transform.rotation);
    }
}
```

Figure 19.69 – Shooting function code

> **Important Information**
>
> Here, you will find some duplicated shooting behavior between
> PlayerShooting and EnemyFSM. You can fix this by creating a Weapon
> behavior with a function called Shoot that instantiates bullets and takes into
> account the fire rate, before calling it inside both components to re-utilize it.

4. When the agent is stopped, not only does the movement stop but also the rotation.
    If the Player moves while the Enemy is attacked, we still need the Enemy to face
    it to shoot bullets in its direction. For this, we can create a LookTo function that
    receives the target position to look toward and call it in AttackPlayer and
    AttackBase, passing the target to shoot at:

```
    LookTo(sightSensor.detectedObject.transform.position);
    Shoot();

    float distanceToPlayer = Vector3.Distance(transform.position, sightSensor.detectedObject.transform.position);
    if (distanceToPlayer > playerAttackDistance * 1.1f)
        currentState = EnemyState.ChasePlayer;
}

void AttackBase()
{
    agent.isStopped = true;
    LookTo(baseTransform.position);
    Shoot();
}

void LookTo(Vector3 targetPosition)
{

}
```

Figure 19.70 – LookTo function calls

5. Complete the `LookTo` function by giving the direction of our parent to the target position. We can access our parent with `transform.parent` because we are the child AI Object. The Object that will move is our parent. Then, we must set the `Y` component of the direction to `0` to prevent the direction from pointing upward or downward – we don't want our enemy to rotate vertically. Finally, we must set the forward vector of our parent to that direction so that it will face the target position immediately. You can replace this with interpolation by using quaternions to get a smoother rotation if you want to, but let's keep things as simple as possible for now:

```
void LookTo(Vector3 targetPosition)
{
    Vector3 directionToPosition = Vector3.Normalize(targetPosition - transform.parent.position);
    directionToPosition.y = 0;
    transform.parent.forward = directionToPosition;
}
```

Figure 19.71 – Looking toward a target

Finally, we can add animations to the Enemy using the same Animator Controller we used in the Player and set the parameters with other scripts.

6. Add an `Animator` component to the Enemy, if it's not already there, and set the same Controller that we used in the Player; in our case, this is also called `Player`.

7. Create and add a script to the Enemy root Object called `NavMeshAnimator`, which will take the current velocity of `NavMeshAgent` and set it to the Animator Controller. This will work similar to the `VelocityAnimator` script and is in charge of updating the Animator Controller velocity parameter with the velocity of our Object. We didn't use that one here because `NavMeshAgent` doesn't use `Rigidbody` to move. It has its own velocity system. We can actually set `Rigidbody` to `kinematic` if we want because of this since it moves but not with Physics:

```
using UnityEngine;
using UnityEngine.AI;

public class NavMeshAnimator : MonoBehaviour
{

    Animator animator;
    NavMeshAgent agent;

    void Awake()
    {

        animator = GetComponent<Animator>();
        agent = GetComponent<NavMeshAgent>();
    }


    void Update()
    {
        animator.SetFloat("Velocity", agent.velocity.magnitude);
    }
}
```

Figure 19.72 – Connecting NavMeshAgent to our Animator Controller

8. Cache a reference to the parent Animator in the EnemyFSM script. Just do the same thing we did to access NavMeshAgent:

```
Animator animator;

void Awake()
{
    baseTransform = GameObject.Find("BaseDamagePoint").transform;
    agent = GetComponentInParent<NavMeshAgent>();
    animator = GetComponentInParent<Animator>();
}
```

Figure 19.73 – Accessing the parent's Animator reference

9. Turn on the `Shooting` animator parameter inside the `Shoot` function to make sure that every time we shoot, the parameter is set to `true` (checked):

```
void Shoot()
{
    animator.SetBool("Shooting", true);
```

Figure 19.74 – Turning on the shooting animation

10. Turn off `boolean` in all non-shooting states, such as `GoToBase` and `ChasePlayer`:

```
void GoToBase()
{
    animator.SetBool("Shooting", false);
    agent.isStopped = false;

    agent.SetDestination(baseTransform.position);

    if (sightSensor.detectedObject != null)
        currentState = EnemyState.ChasePlayer;

    float distanceToBase = Vector3.Distance(transform.position, baseTransform.position);
    if (distanceToBase <= baseAttackDistance)
        currentState = EnemyState.AttackBase;
}


void ChasePlayer()
{
    animator.SetBool("Shooting", false);
    agent.isStopped = false;
```

Figure 19.75 – Turning off the shooting animation

Regarding the Visual Scripting version, **GoToBase** will look like this:

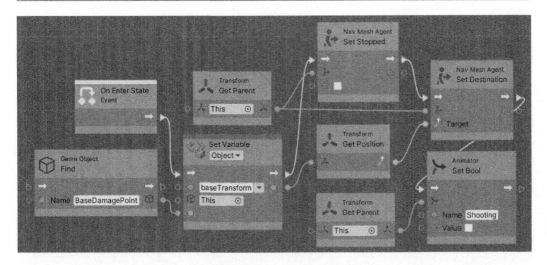

Figure 19.76 – GoToBase state

Notice that we needed the **GetParent** node to access the Enemy's root GameObject again, this time for **Animator**. The **ChasePlayer** state actions look like this:

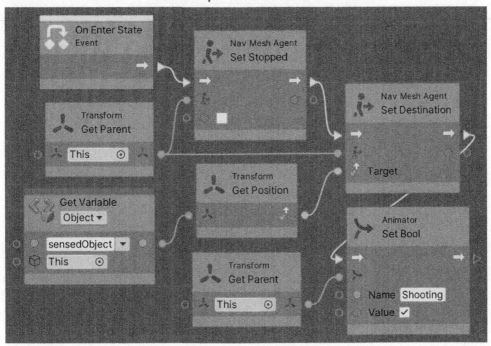

Figure 19.77 – ChasePlayer state

The **AttackBase** actions look like this:

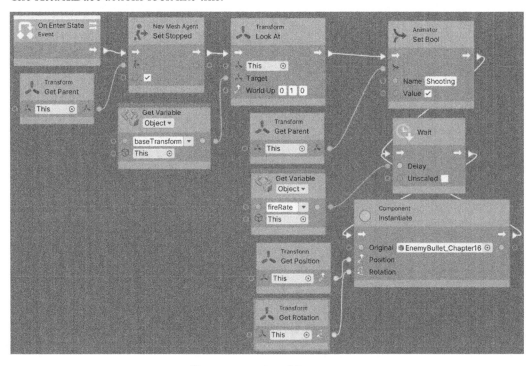

Figure 19.78 – AttackBase state

In this state, we have some things to highlight. First, we are using the **LookAt** node in the **OnEnterState** event node. As you might imagine, this does the same as we did with math in C#. We specify a target to look at (our base transform) and then we specify that **World Up** is a vector pointing upward (0,1,0). This will make our object look at the base but maintain its up vector pointing to the sky, meaning our object will not look at the floor if the target is lower than him. We can use this function in C# if we want to (`transform.LookAt`), but the idea was to show you all the available options. Also, consider that we only execute **LookAt** when the state becomes active. Since the base doesn't move, we don't need to constantly update our orientation.

The second thing to highlight is that we used coroutines to shoot, which is the same idea we used in **Enemy Spawner** to constantly spawn enemies. Essentially, we make an infinite loop between **Wait For Seconds** and **Instantiate**. We took this approach here because it was convenient, given it takes fewer nodes in Visual Scripting. Remember to select the **OnEnterState** node and check the **Coroutine** checkbox, as we did previously. Also, note that we need a new **Float** type variable called `fireRate` in the Enemy's **AI** child object:

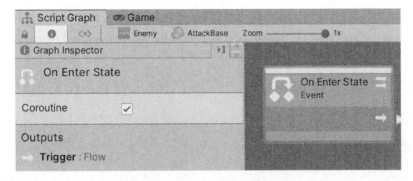

Figure 19.79 – Coroutines

Then **AttackPlayer** will look like this:

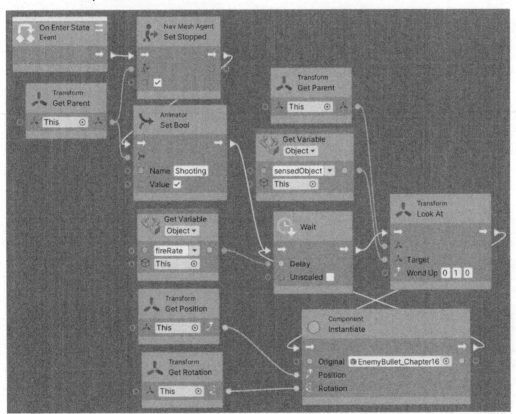

Figure 19.80 – AttackPlayer state

Essentially, this is the same as **AttackBase**, with the only difference that we do a **LookAt** at the root object before instantiating the bullet to make the bullet go toward the player. In **AttackBase**, state wasn't necessary because the base doesn't move.

Finally, we need to create a new Script Graph (regular, not a state graph) in the Enemy's root object to recreate the `NavMeshAnimator` component we did in C#. This will simply look like this:

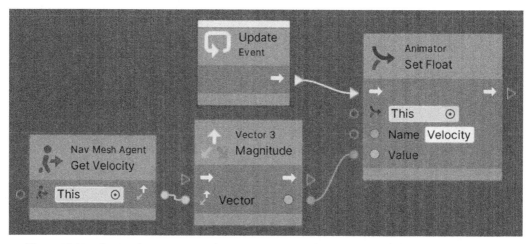

Figure 19.81 – Setting the Animator velocity parameter so that it's the same as our NavMeshAgent

Notice that we don't need the **GetParent** node, given that this graph is located at the Enemy's root object, along with **Animator** and **NavMeshAgent**. With that, we have finished all our AI behaviors. Of course, these scripts/graphs are big enough to deserve some rework and splitting in the future, and some actions such as stopping and resuming the animations and `NavMeshAgent` can be done in a better way. But with this, we have prototyped our AI, and we can test it until we are happy with it, and then we can improve this code.

Summary

I'm pretty sure AI is not what you imagined; you are not creating SkyNet here, but we have accomplished a simple but interesting AI for challenging our Player, which we can iterate and tweak so that it's tailored to our game's expected behavior. We learned how to gather our surrounding information through sensors to make decisions on what action to execute using FSMs, as well as using different Unity systems such as Pathfinding and Animator to make the AI execute those actions. We used those systems to diagram a State Machine that's capable of detecting the player, running to them, and attacking them, and if the Player's not there, just going to the base and accomplishing the task of destroying it.

With this, we have ended *Part 3* regarding C# scripting. In the next part, we are going to finish our game's final details. In this first chapter of the next part, we are going to learn how to optimize our game.

20
Scene Performance Optimization

Welcome to the third part of this book—I am glad you have reached this part as it means that you have almost completed a full game! In this chapter, we are going to discuss optimization techniques to review your game's performance and improve it, as having a good and constant frame rate is vital to any game. Performance is a broad topic that requires a deep understanding of several Unity systems and could span several books. We are going to look at how to measure performance and explore the effects of our changes to systems to learn how they work through testing.

In this chapter, we will examine the following performance concepts:

- Optimizing graphics
- Optimizing processing
- Optimizing memory

By the end of this chapter, you will be able to gather performance data on the three main pieces of hardware that run your game—the GPU, CPU, and RAM. You will be able to analyze that data to detect possible performance issues and understand how to solve the most common ones.

Optimizing graphics

The most common cause of performance issues is related to the misuse of assets, especially on the graphics side, due to not having enough knowledge of how Unity's graphic engines work. We are going to explore how a GPU works at a high level and how to improve its usage.

In this section, we will examine the following graphics optimization concepts:

- Introduction to graphic engines
- Using the Frame Debugger
- Using batching
- Other optimizations

We will start by looking at a high-level overview of how graphics are rendered to better understand the performance data that we will gather later in the Frame Debugger. Based on the debugger's results, we are going to identify the areas that we can apply batching to (which is a technique to combine the rendering process of several objects, reducing its cost), along with other common optimizations to keep in mind.

Introduction to graphic engines

Nowadays, every gaming device, whether it is a computer, a mobile device, or a console, has a video card—a set of hardware that specializes in graphics processing. It differs from a CPU in a subtle but important way. Graphics processing involves the processing of thousands of mesh vertices and the rendering of millions of pixels, so the GPU is designed to run short programs for a massive length of time, while the CPU can handle programs of any length but with limited parallelization capabilities. The reason for having those processing units is so that our program can use each one when needed.

The problem here is that graphics don't just rely on the GPU. The CPU is also involved in the process, making calculations and issuing commands to the GPU, so they must work together. For that to happen, both processing units need to communicate, and because they are (usually) physically separated, they need another piece of hardware to allow this—a bus, the most common type being the **Peripheral Component Interconnect Express (PCI Express)** bus.

PCI Express is a type of connection that allows massive amounts of data to be moved between the GPU and CPU, but the problem is that even though it's very fast, the communication time can be noticeable if you issue a lot of commands between both units. So, the key concept here is that graphics performance is improved mainly by reducing the communications between the GPU and CPU:

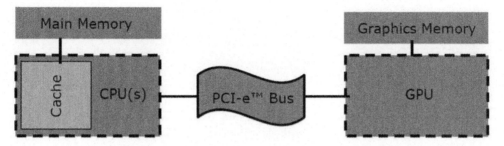

Figure 20.1 – CPU/GPU communication through a PCI Express bus

> **Important note**
>
> Nowadays, new hardware architecture allows the CPU and GPU to coexist in the same chipset, reducing communication time and even sharing memory. Sadly, that architecture doesn't allow the necessary processing power needed for video games. It is possible that we will only see it applied to high-end gaming, but not in the near future, or even ever.

The basic algorithm of a graphics engine is to determine which objects are visible using culling algorithms, sorting and grouping them according to their similarities, and then issuing drawing commands to the GPU to render those groups of objects, sometimes more than once (as in *Chapter 8, Lighting Using the Universal Render Pipeline*). Here, the main form of communication is those drawing commands, usually called **draw calls**, and our main task when optimizing graphics is to reduce them as much as we can. The problem is that there are several sources of draw calls that need to be considered, such as the lighting, the scale of objects to see whether they are static or not, and so on. Studying every single one of them would take a long time, and even so, new versions of Unity can introduce new graphic features with their own draw calls. Instead, we will explore a way to discover these draw calls using the Frame Debugger.

Using the Frame Debugger

The **Frame Debugger** is a tool that allows us to see a list of all the drawing commands or draw calls that the Unity rendering engine sends to the GPU. It not only lists them but also provides information about each draw call, including the data needed to detect optimization opportunities. By using the **Frame Debugger**, we can see how our changes modify the number of draw calls, giving us immediate feedback on our efforts.

> **Important Note**
>
> Note that reducing draw calls is sometimes not enough to improve performance, as each draw call can have different processing times; but usually, that difference is not big enough to consider. Also, in certain special rendering techniques, such as ray tracing or ray marching, a single draw call can drain all of our GPU power. This won't be the case in our game, so we won't take that into account right now.

Let's use the Frame Debugger to analyze the rendering process of our game by doing the following:

1. Open the Frame Debugger (**Window | Analysis | Frame Debugger**).

2. Play the game and if you want to analyze the performance, click the **Enable** button in the top-left corner of the window (press *Esc* to regain control of the mouse while playing):

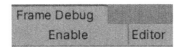

Figure 20.2 – Enabling the Frame Debugger

3. Click on the **Game** tab to open the **Game** view.

> **Important note:**
>
> Sometimes, it is useful to have both the **Scene** and **Game** panels in sight, which you can accomplish by dragging one of them to the bottom of Unity to have them separated and visible.

4. Drag the slider to the right of the **Disable** button slowly from left to right to see how the scene is rendered. Each step is a draw call that is executed in the CPU for that given game frame. You can also observe how the list in the left part of the window highlights the name of the executed draw call at that moment:

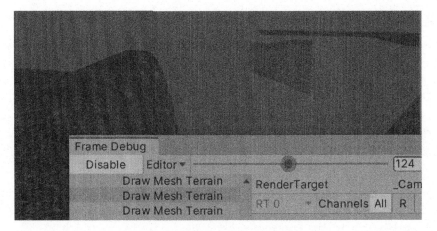

Figure 20.3 – Analyzing our frame's draw calls

5. Click on any draw call from the list and observe the details in the right part of the window.

    Most of them can be confusing to you if you are not used to code engines or shaders, but you can see that some of them have a human-readable part called **Why this draw call can't be batched with the previous one**, which tells you why two objects weren't drawn together in a single draw call. We will examine those reasons later:

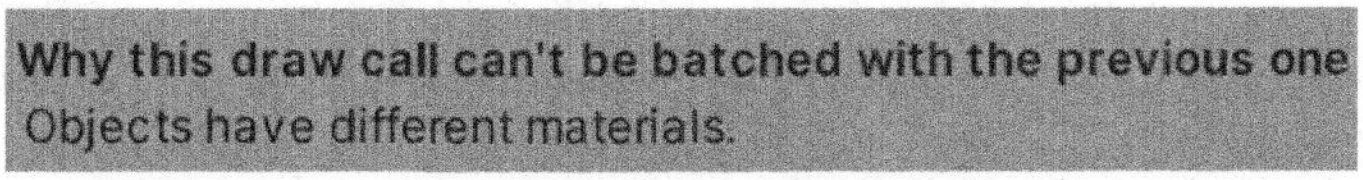

> **Why this draw call can't be batched with the previous one**
> Objects have different materials.

Figure 20.4 – The batching break reasons in the Frame Debugger

6. With the window open in **Play** mode, disable the terrain and see how the amount of draw calls changes immediately. Sometimes, just turning objects on and off can be enough to detect what is causing performance issues. Also, try disabling postprocessing and other graphics-related objects, such as particles.

Even if we are not fully aware of where each one of these draw calls came from, we can at least start by modifying the settings throughout Unity to see the impact of those changes. There's no better way of discovering how something as massive as Unity works than going through every toggle and seeing the impact of those changes through a measuring tool.

Now, let's discuss the basic techniques for reducing draw calls and see their effects in the Frame Debugger.

Using batching

We discussed several optimization techniques in previous chapters, with lighting being the most important one. If you measure the draw calls as you implement the techniques, you will notice the impact of those actions on the draw call count. However, in this section, we will focus on another graphics optimization technique, known as batching. Batching is the process of grouping several objects to draw them together in a single draw call. You may be wondering why we can't just draw everything in a single draw call, and while that is technically possible, there is a set of conditions that need to be met in order to combine two objects, the usual case being combining materials.

Remember that materials are assets that act as graphic profiles, specifying a **Material** mode or Shader and a set of parameters to customize the aspect of our objects, and remember that we can use the same material in several objects. If Unity has to draw an object with a different material than the previous one, a SetPass call needs to be called before issuing its draw call, which is another form of CPU/GPU communication used to set the **Material** properties in the GPU, such as its textures and colors. If two objects use the same materials, this step can be skipped. The SetPass call from the first object is reused by the second, and that opens the opportunity to batch the objects. If they share the same settings, Unity can combine the meshes into a single one in the CPU, and then send the combined mesh in a single draw call to the GPU.

There are several ways to reduce the number of materials, such as removing duplicates, but the most effective way is through a concept called texture atlasing. This means merging textures from different objects into a single one. This way, several objects can use the same material due to the fact that the texture used there can be applied to several objects and an object that has its own texture requires its own material. Sadly, there's no automatic system in Unity to combine the textures of three-dimensional objects, such as the **Texture Atlas** object we used in 2D. There are probably some systems in the Asset Store, but automatic systems can have several side effects. This work is usually done by an artist, so just keep this technique in mind when working with a dedicated 3D artist (or if you are your own artist):

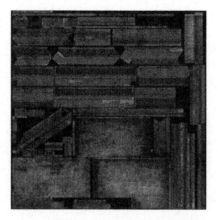

Figure 20.5 – Pieces of different metallic objects

Let's explore batching with Frame Debugger by doing the following:

1. Search for the **Render Pipeline** asset that we currently want to use (**Edit | Project Settings | Graphics | Scriptable Render Settings**):

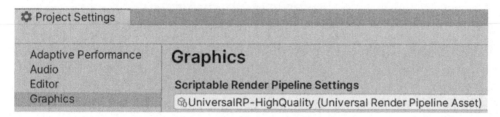

Figure 20.6 – Scriptable Render Pipeline settings

2. Uncheck **SRP Batcher** in the **Advanced** section and check **Dynamic Batching**. We will discuss this later:

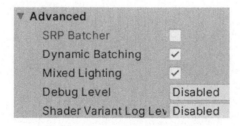

Figure 20.7 – Disabling SRP Batcher

3. Create a new empty scene for testing (**File | New Scene**).

4. Create two materials of different colors.

5. Create two cubes and put one material into the first and the other into the second.

6. Open the Frame Debugger and click **Enable** to see the call list for the draw calls of our cubes:

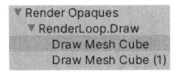

Figure 20.8 – The draw calls for the cubes

7. Select the second **Draw Mesh Cube** call and look at the batch-breaking reason. It should say that the objects have different materials.

8. Use one of the materials on both cubes and look at the list again. You will notice that now we just have one **Draw Mesh Cube** call. You might need to disable and enable the Frame Debugger again for it to refresh properly.

Now, I challenge you to try the same steps but to create spheres instead of cubes. If you do that, you will probably notice that even with the same materials, the spheres are not batched! Here is where we need to introduce the concept of dynamic batching.

Remember that GameObjects have a **Static** checkbox, which serves to notify several Unity systems that the object won't move so that they can apply several optimizations. Objects that don't have this checkbox checked are considered dynamic. So far, the cubes and spheres we used for our tests have been dynamic, so Unity needed to combine them in every frame because they can move and combining is not "free." Its cost is associated directly with the number of vertexes in the model. You can get the exact numbers and all the required considerations from the Unity manual, which will appear if you search `Unity Batching`. However, it is enough to say that if the number of vertexes of an object is big enough, that object won't be batched, and doing so would require more than issuing two draw calls. That's why our spheres weren't batched; a sphere has too many vertices.

Now, things are different if we have static objects because they use a second batching system—the static batcher. The concept of this is the same: merge objects to render them in one draw call, and again these objects need to share the same material. The main difference is that this batcher will batch more objects than the dynamic batcher because the merging is done once, at the time that the scene loads, and is then saved in memory to use in the next frames, costing memory but saving lots of processing time each frame. You can use the same approach we used to test the dynamic batcher to test the static version just by checking the **Static** checkbox of the spheres this time and seeing the result in **Play** mode; in **Edition** mode (when it is not playing), the static batcher won't work:

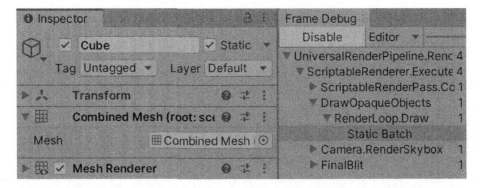

Figure 20.9 – A static sphere and its static batch

Before moving on, let's discuss why we disabled SRP Batcher and how that changes what we just discussed. In its 2020 edition, Unity introduced the **URP** (**Universal Render Pipeline**), a new Render Pipeline. Along with several improvements, one that is relevant right now is SRP Batcher, a new batcher that works on dynamic objects with no vertex or material limits (but with other limits). Instead of relying on sharing the same material with batch objects, SRP Batcher can have a batch of objects with materials that use the same Shader, meaning we can have, for example, 100 objects with 100 different materials for each one, and they will be batched regardless of the number of vertexes, as long as the materials use the same Shader and Variant:

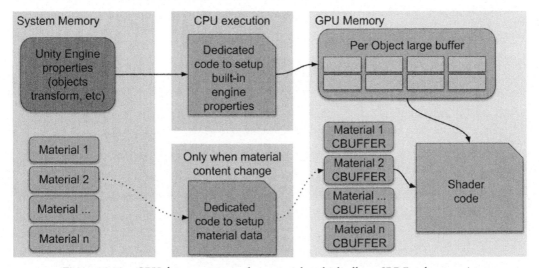

Figure 20.10 – GPU data persistence for materials, which allows SRP Batcher to exist

One Shader can have several versions or Variants, and the selected Variant is chosen based on the settings. We can have a Shader that doesn't use normal mapping and a Variant that doesn't calculate normals will be used, so that can affect SRP Batcher. So, there's basically no drawback to using SRP Batcher, so go ahead and turn it on again. Try creating lots of spheres with as many materials as you can and check the number of batches it will generate in the Frame Debugger. Just consider that if you need to work on a project done in a pre-URP era, this won't be available, so you will need to know the proper batching strategy to use.

Other optimizations

As mentioned before, there are lots of possible graphics optimizations, so let's discuss briefly the basic ones, starting with **Level of Detail (LOD)**. LOD is the process of changing the mesh of an object based on its distance from the camera. This can reduce draw calls if you replace, for example, a house with several parts and pieces with a single combined mesh with reduced detail when the house is far away. Another benefit of using LOD is that you reduce the cost of a draw call because of the reduction in the vertex count.

To use this feature, do the following:

1. Create an empty object and parent the two versions of the model. You need to use models that have several versions with different levels of detail, but for now, we are just going to test this feature using a cube and a sphere:

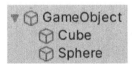

Figure 20.11 – A single object with two LOD meshes

2. Add an LOD group component to the parent.

3. The default LOD group is prepared to support three LOD mesh groups, but as we only have two, right-click on one and click **Delete**. You can also select **Insert Before** to add more LOD groups:

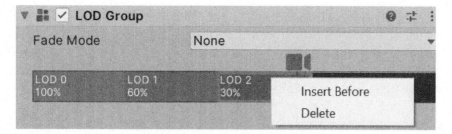

Figure 20.12 – Removing an LOD group

4. Select **LOD 0**, the highest-detail LOD group, and click on the **Add** button in the **Renderers** list below this to add the sphere to that group. You can add as many mesh renderers as you want.

5. Select **LOD 1** and add the cube:

Figure 20.13 – Adding renderers to LOD groups

6. Drag the line between the two groups to control the distance range that each group will occupy. As you drag it, you will see a preview of how far the camera needs to be to switch groups. Also, you have the culled group, which is the distance from where the camera will not render any group.

7. Just move the camera around in **Edit** mode to see how the meshes are swapped.

8. Something to consider here is that the colliders of the objects won't be disabled, so just have the renderers in the LOD sub-objects. Put the collider with the shape of the LOD 0 in the parent object, or just remove the colliders from the LOD group objects, except group 0.

Another optimization to consider is frustum culling. By default, Unity will render any object that falls into the view area or frustum of the camera, skipping the ones that don't. The algorithm is cheap enough to always use, and there's no way to disable it. However, it does have a flaw. If we have a wall hiding all the objects behind it, even if they are occluded, they fall inside the frustum, so they will be rendered anyway. Detecting whether every pixel of a mesh occludes every pixel of the other mesh is almost impossible to do in real time, but luckily, we have a workaround: occlusion culling.

Occlusion culling is a process that analyzes a scene and determines which objects can be seen in different parts of the scene, dividing them into sectors and analyzing each one. As this process can take quite a long time, it is done in the editor, as is done with lightmapping. As you can imagine, it only works on static objects. To use it, do the following:

1. Mark the objects that shouldn't move as static, or if you only want this object to be considered static for the occlusion culling system, check the **Occluder Static** and **Ocludee Static** checkboxes of the arrow to the right of the **Static** checkbox.

2. Open the **Occlusion Culling** window (**Window | Rendering | Occlusion Culling**).

3. Save the scene and hit the **Bake** button at the bottom of the window, and then wait for the baking process. If you don't save the scene before the baking process, it won't be executed.

4. Select the **Visualization** tab in the **Occlusion Culling** window.

5. With the **Occlusion Culling** window visible, select the camera and drag it around, seeing how objects are occluded as the camera moves:

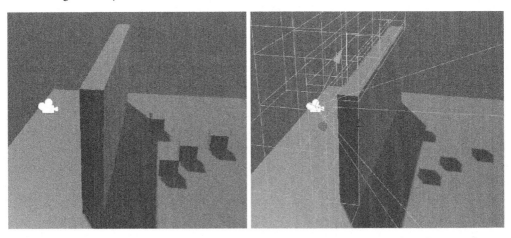

Figure 20.14 – On the left is the normal scene and on the right is the scene with occlusion culling

Take into account that if you move the camera outside the calculated area, the process won't take place, and Unity will only calculate areas near the static objects. You can extend the calculation area by creating an empty object and adding an **Occlusion Area** component, setting its position and size to cover the area that the camera will reach, and finally, rebaking the culling. Try to be sensible with the size of the cube. The larger the area to calculate, the larger the space needed in your disk to store the generated data. You can use several of these areas to be more precise—for example, in an L-shaped scene, you can use two of them:

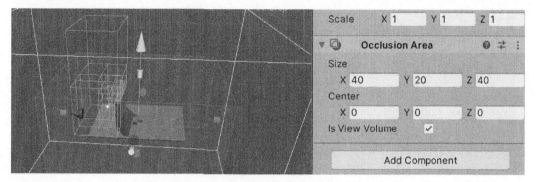

Figure 20.15 – Occlusion Area

If you see that the objects are not being occluded, it could be that the occluder object (the wall in this case) is not big enough to be considered. You can increase the size of the object or reduce the **Smallest Occluder** setting in the **Bake** tab of the window. Doing that will subdivide the scene further to detect small occluders, but that will take more space in the disk to store more data. So again, be sensible with this setting.

There are still some more techniques that we can apply to our game, but the ones we have discussed are enough for our game. So, in this section, we learned about the process of rendering graphics in a video card, the concept of batch, how to profile them to know exactly how many of them we have and what they are doing, and finally, how to reduce them as much as we can. Now, let's start discussing other optimization areas, such as the processing area.

Optimizing processing

While graphics usually take up most of the time that a frame needs to be generated, we should never underestimate the cost of badly optimized code and scenes. There are several parts of the game that are still calculated in the CPU, including part of the graphics process (such as the batching calculations), Unity Physics, audio, and our code. Here, we have a lot more causes of performance issues than on the graphics side, so again, instead of discussing every optimization, let's learn how to discover them.

In this section, we will examine the following CPU optimization concepts:

- Detecting CPU- and GPU-bound
- Using the CPU Usage Profiler
- General CPU optimization techniques

We will start by discussing the concepts of CPU and GPU bound, which focus on the optimization process, determining whether a problem is GPU or CPU related. Later, as with the GPU optimization process, we will look at how to gather the performance data of the CPU and interpret it to detect possible optimization techniques to be applied.

Detecting CPU- and GPU-bound

As with the Frame Debugger, the Unity Profiler allows us to gather data about the performance of our game through a series of Profiler modules, each one designed to gather data about different Unity systems per frame, such as Physics, audio, and most importantly, CPU usage. This last module allows us to see every single function that Unity called to process the frame—that is, from our script's executed functions to other systems, such as Physics and graphics.

Before exploring the CPU usage, one important bit of data that we can gather in this module is whether we are CPU or GPU bound. As explained before, a frame is processed using both the CPU and GPU, and those pieces of hardware can work in parallel. While the GPU is executing drawing commands, the CPU can execute Physics and our scripts in a very efficient way. But now, let's say that the CPU finishes its work while the GPU is still working. Can the CPU start to work on the next frame? The answer is no. This would lead to de-synchronization, so in this scenario, the CPU would need to wait. This is known as being CPU bound, and we have also the opposite case, GPU bound, when the GPU finishes earlier than the CPU.

Important note:

It is worth mentioning that on mobile devices, it is sometimes preferable to reduce the framerate of our game to reduce battery consumption, making the game idle for a moment between frames, but that could lead to a slower response in our commands and input. To solve that, Unity has created a package that adds the ability to skip the rendering process after a configurable number of frames, which keeps the processing working but skips rendering. So, naturally, those frames will be CPU bound only.

It is important to concentrate our optimization efforts, so if we detect that our game is GPU bound, we will focus on GPU graphics optimization, and if it is CPU bound, then we will focus on the rest of the systems and the CPU side of graphics processing. To detect whether our game is one or the other, do the following:

1. Open **Profiler** (**Window | Analysis | Profiler**).

2. In the **Profiler Modules** dropdown in the top-left corner, check **GPU Usage** to enable the GPU profiler:

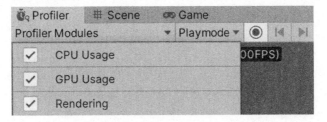

Figure 20.16 – Enabling the GPU profiler

3. Play the game and select the **CPU Usage** profiler, clicking on its name in the left part of the **Profiler** window.

4. Click the **Last Frame** button – the one with the double arrow pointing to the right, to always display the info of the last frame being rendered:

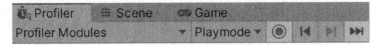

Figure 20.17 – The last frame button (double arrow to the right)

5. Also click the **Live** button to enable the Live mode, which allows you to see the results of profiling in real time. This can have an impact on performance, so you can disable it later:

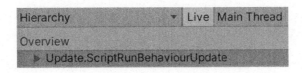

Figure 20.18 – Enabling Live mode

6. Observe the bar with the **CPU** and **GPU** labels in the middle of the window. It should say how many milliseconds are being consumed by the CPU and GPU. The one with the higher number will be the one that is limiting our framerate and will determine whether we are GPU or CPU bound:

CPU:4.07ms GPU:0.87ms
Self
Calls
GC Alloc
Time ms

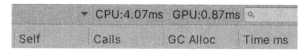

Figure 20.19 – Determining whether we are CPU or GPU bound

7. There is a chance that when you try to open the GPU profiler, you will see a not supported message, and this can happen in certain cases (such as on Mac devices that use the Metal graphics API). In that scenario, another way to see whether we are GPU bound is by searching `waitforpresent` in the search bar right next to the CPU/GPU labels while selecting the **CPU Usage** profiler:

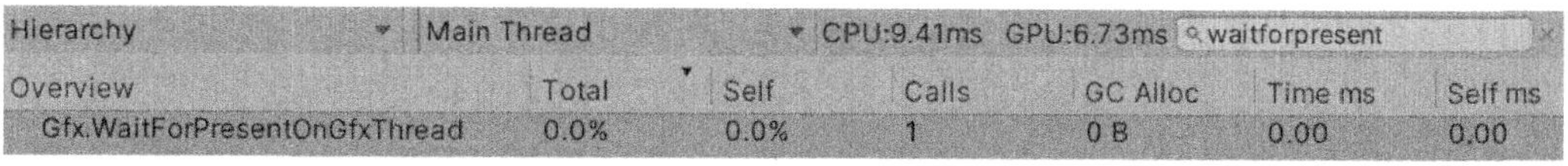

Hierarchy
Main Thread
CPU:9.41ms GPU:6.73ms
waitforpresent
Overview
Total
Self
Calls
GC Alloc
Time ms
Self ms
Gfx.WaitForPresentOnGfxThread
0.0%
0.0%
1
0 B
0.00
0.00

Figure 20.20 – Searching waitforpresent

8. Here, you can see how long the CPU has been waiting for the GPU. Check the **Time ms** column to get the number. If you see **0.00**, it is because the CPU is not waiting for the GPU, meaning we are not GPU bound. In the preceding screenshot, you can see that my screen displays **0.00** while the CPU is taking **9.41ms** and the GPU is taking **6.73ms**. So, my device is CPU bound, but consider that your device and project might give different results.

Now that we can detect whether we are CPU or GPU bound, we can focus our optimization efforts. So far, we have discussed how to profile and optimize part of the GPU process. Now, if we detect that we are CPU bound, let's see how to profile the CPU.

Using the CPU Usage Profiler

Profiling the CPU is done in a similar way to profiling the GPU. We need to get a list of actions the CPU executes and try to reduce them, and here is where the CPU Usage Profiler module comes in—a tool that allows us to see all the instructions that the CPU executed in one frame. The main difference is that the GPU mostly executes draw calls, and we have a few types of them, while the CPU can have hundreds of different instructions to execute, and sometimes some of them cannot be deleted, such as a Physics Update or audio processing. In these scenarios, we are looking to reduce the cost of these functions if they are consuming too much time. So, again, an important note here is to detect which function is taking too much time and then reduce its cost or remove it, which requires a deeper understanding of the underlying system. Let's start detecting the function first.

When you play the game with the **Profiler** tab opened, you will see a series of graphics showing the performance of our game, and in the CPU Usage Profiler, you will see that the graphic is split into different colors, each one referring to different parts of frame processing. You can check the information to the left of the **Profiler** to see what each color means, but let's discuss the most important ones. In the following screenshot, you can see how the graphic should look:

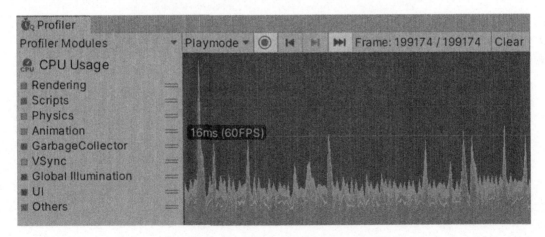

Figure 20.21 – Analyzing the CPU Usage graph

If you check the graphic, you will probably assume that the dark-green part of the graph is taking up most of the performance time, and while that is true, you can also see from the legend that dark green means **Others**, and that's because we are profiling the game in the editor. The editor won't behave exactly like the final game. In order for it to run, it has to do lots of extra processing that won't be executed in the game, so the best you can do is profile directly in the build of the game. There, you will gather more accurate data. We are going to discuss how to do builds in the next chapter, so for now, we can ignore that area. What we can do now is simply click on the colored square to the left of the **Others** label to disable that measurement from the graph in order to clean it up a little bit. If you also see a large section of yellow, it is referring to VSync, which is basically the time spent waiting for our processing to match the monitor's refresh rate. This is also something that we can ignore, so you should also disable it. In the next screenshot, you can check the graphic color categories and disable them:

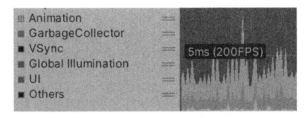

Figure 20.22 – Disabling VSync and Others from the Profiler

Now that we have cleaned up the graph, we can get a good idea of our game's potential framerate by looking at the line with the **ms** label (in our case, **5ms (200 FPS)**), which indicates that frames below that line have more than 200 FPS, and frames above that line have less. In my case, I have excellent performance, but remember, I am testing this on a powerful machine. The best way to profile is not only in the build of the game (as an executable) but also in the target device, which should be the lowest spec hardware we intend our game to run on. Our target device depends a lot on the target audience of the game. If we are making a casual game, we are probably targeting mobile devices, so we should test the game on the lowest spec phone we can, but if we are targeting hardcore gamers, they will probably have a powerful machine to run our game on.

> **Important note:**
> If you are targeting hardcore gamers, of course, this doesn't mean that we can just make a very unoptimized game because of that, but it will give us enough processing space to add more detail. Anyway, I strongly recommend you avoid those kinds of games if you are a beginner as they are more difficult to develop, which you will probably realize. Stick to simple games to begin with.

Looking at the graphics colors, you can observe the cost on the CPU side of rendering in light green, which the graph shows is taking up a significant portion of the processing time, which is actually normal. Then, in blue, we can see the cost of our scripts' execution, which is also taking up a significant portion, but again, this is quite normal. Also, we can observe a little bit of orange, which is Physics, and also a little bit of light blue, which is Animation. Remember to check the colored labels in the Profiler to remember which color refers to what.

Now, those colored bars represent a group of operations, so if we consider the **Rendering** bar to be representing 10 operations, how do we know which operations that includes? Also, how do we know which of these operations is taking up the most performance time? Out of those 10 operations, a single one could be causing these issues. Here is where the bottom part of the profiler is useful. It shows a list of all the functions being called in the frame. To use it, do the following:

1. Clear the search bar we used earlier. It will filter function calls by name, and we want to see them all.

2. Click on the **Time ms** column until you see an arrow pointing downward. This will order the calls by cost in descending order.

3. Click on a frame that is catching your attention in the graph—probably one of the ones with the highest height that consumes more processing time. This will make the Profiler stop the game straight away and show you information about that frame.

> **Important Note**
> There are two things to consider when looking at the graph. If you see peaks that are significantly higher than the rest of the frames, that can cause a hiccup in your game—a very brief moment where the game is frozen—which can break the performance. Also, you can look for a long series of frames with higher time consumption. Try to reduce them as well. Even if this is only temporary, the impact of it will easily be perceived by the player.

4. **PlayerLoop** will probably appear as the most time-consuming frame, but that's not very informative. You can explore it further by expanding it by clicking on the arrow to its left.

5. Click on each function to highlight it in the graph. Functions with higher processing times will be highlighted with thicker bars, and those are the ones we will focus on:

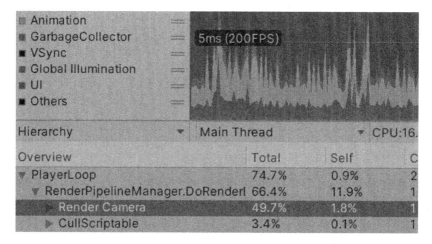

Figure 20.23 – The Render Camera function highlighted in the graph

6. You can keep clicking on the arrows to further explore the functions until you hit a limit. If you want to go deeper, enable the **Deep Profiler** mode in the top bar of the Profiler. This will give you more details but take into account that this process is expensive and will make the game go slower, altering the time shown in the graph, making it appear much greater than the real time. Here, ignore the numbers and look at how much of the process a function is taking up based on the graph. You will need to stop, enable **Deep Profile**, and play it again to make it work:

Figure 20.24 – Enabling Deep Profile

With this knowledge, we can start improving our game's performance (if it's below the target framerate), but each function is called by the CPU and will need to be improved in its own unique way, which requires a greater knowledge about Unity's internal workings. That could span several books, and anyway, the internals change on a version-to-version basis. Instead, you could study how each function works by looking up data about that specific system on the internet, or again, by just disabling and enabling objects or parts of our code to explore the impact of our actions, as we did with the Frame Debugger. Profiling requires creativity and inference to interpret and react accordingly to the data obtained, so you will need some patience here.

Now that we have discussed how to get profiling data relating to the CPU, let's discuss some common ways to reduce CPU usage.

General CPU optimization techniques

In terms of CPU optimizations, there are lots of possible causes of high performance, including the abuse of Unity's features, a large number of Physics or audio objects, improper asset/object configurations, and so on. Our scripts can also be coded in an unoptimized way, abusing or misusing expensive Unity API functions. So far, we have discussed several good practices for using Unity Systems, such as audio configurations, texture sizes, batching, and finding functions such as `GameObject.Find` and replacing them with managers. So, let's discuss some specific details about common cases.

Let's start by seeing how a large amount of objects impacts our performance. Here, you can just create lots of objects with `Rigidbody` configured in **Dynamic Profile**, and observe the results in the Profiler. You will notice, in the following screenshot, how the orange part of the profiler just got bigger and that the `Physics.Processing` function is responsible for this increase:

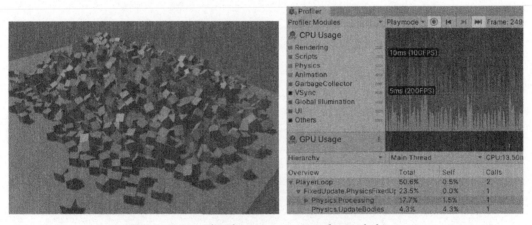

Figure 20.25 – The Physics processing of several objects

Another test to see the impact of several objects could be creating lots of audio sources. In the following screenshot, you can see that we needed to re-enable **Others** because audio processing comes under that category. We mentioned earlier that **Others** belongs to the editor, but it can encompass other processes as well, so keep that in mind:

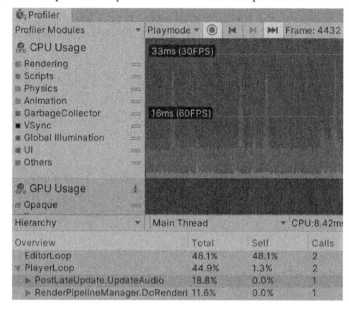

Figure 20.26 – The Physics processing of several objects

So, to discover these kinds of problems, you can just start disabling and enabling objects and see whether they increase the time or not. A final test is on particles. Create a system that spawns a big enough number of particles to affect our framerate and check the Profiler. In the following screenshot, you can check how the particle processing function is highlighted in the graph, showing that it takes a large amount of time:

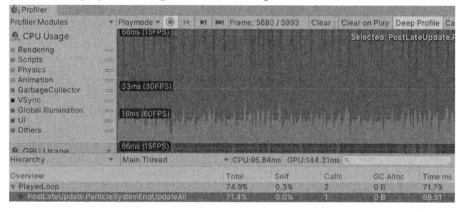

Figure 20.27 – Particle processing

Then, on the scripting side, we have other kinds of things to consider, some of which are common to all programming languages and platforms, such as iterating long lists of objects, the misuse of data structures, and deep recursion. However, in this section, I will mainly be discussing Unity-specific APIs, starting with `print` or `Debug.Log`.

This function is useful to get debugging information in the console, but it can also be costly because all logs are written onto the disk immediately to avoid losing valuable information if our game crashes. Of course, we want to keep those valuable logs in the game, but we don't want it to affect the performance, so what can we do?

One possible approach is to keep those messages but disable the non-essential ones in the final build, such as informative messages, keeping the error-reporting function active. One way to do this is through compiler directives, such as the ones used in the following screenshot. Remember that this kind of `if` statement is executed by the compiler and can exclude entire portions of code when compiling if its conditions are not met:

```
#if UNITY_EDITOR || DEVELOPMENT_BUILD
print("Informative Message");
#endif
```

Figure 20.28 – Disabling code

In the preceding screenshot, you can see how we are asking whether this code is being compiled by the editor or for a development build, which is a special kind of build intended to be used for testing (more on that in the next chapter). You can also create your own kind of logging system with functions with the compiler directives, so you don't need to use them in every log that you want to exclude.

In this section, we learned about the tasks a CPU faces when processing a video game, how to profile them to see which ones are not necessary, and how to reduce the impact of those processes. There are a few other script aspects that can affect performance not only on the processing side but also on the memory side, so let's discuss them in the next section.

Optimizing memory

We discussed how to profile and optimize two pieces of hardware—the CPU and GPU—but there is another piece of hardware that plays a key role in our game—RAM. This is the place where we put all of our game's data. Games can be memory-intensive applications, and unlike several other applications, they are constantly executing code, so we need to be especially careful about that.

In this section, we will examine the following memory optimization concepts:

- Memory allocation and the garbage collector
- Using the Memory Profiler

Let's start by discussing how memory allocation works and what role garbage collection plays here.

Memory allocation and the garbage collector

Each time we instantiate an object, we are allocating memory in RAM, and in a game, we will be allocating memory constantly. In other programming languages, aside from allocating memory, you need to manually deallocate it, but C# has a garbage collector, which is a system that tracks unused memory and cleans it. This system works with a reference counter, which tracks how many references to an object exist, and when that counter reaches 0, it means all references have become null and the object can be deallocated. This deallocation process can be triggered in several situations, the most common situation being when we reach the maximum assigned memory and we want to allocate a new object. In that scenario, we can release enough memory to allocate our object, and if that is not possible, the memory is expanded.

In any game, you will probably be allocating and deallocating memory constantly, which can lead to memory fragmentation, meaning there are small spaces between alive object memory blocks that are mostly useless because they aren't big enough to allocate an object, or maybe the sum of the spaces is big enough but we need continuous memory space to allocate our objects. In the following diagram, you can see a classic example of trying to fit a big chunk of memory into the little gaps generated by fragmentation:

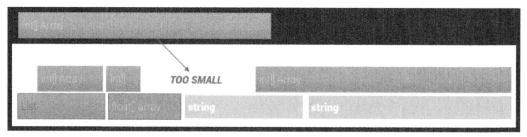

Figure 20.29 – Trying to instantiate an object in fragmented memory space

Some types of garbage collection systems, such as the one in regular C#, are generational, meaning memory is split into generation buckets according to the "age" of the memory. Newer memory will be placed in the first bucket, and this memory tends to be allocated and deallocated frequently. Because this bucket is small, working within it is fast. The second bucket has the memory that survived a previous deallocation sweep process in the first bucket. That memory is moved to the second bucket to prevent it from being checked constantly if it survived the process, and it is possible that that memory will last the length of our program's lifetime. The third bucket is just another layer of bucket two. The idea is that most of the time, the allocation and deallocation system will be working in bucket one, and as it is small enough, it is quick to allocate, deallocate, and compact memory in a continuous fashion.

The problem here is that Unity uses its own version of the garbage collection system, and that version is non-generational and non-compacting, meaning memory is not split into buckets and memory won't be moved to fill the gaps. This suggests that allocating and deallocating memory in Unity will still result in the fragmentation problem, and if you don't regulate your memory allocation, you might end up with an expensive garbage collection system being executed very often, producing hiccups in our game, which you can see in the Profiler CPU Usage module as a pale-yellow color.

One way to deal with this is by preventing memory allocation as much as you can, avoiding it when is not necessary. There are a few tweaks here and there that you can do to prevent memory allocation, but before looking at those, again, it is important to first get data about the problem before starting to fix things that may not be an issue. This advice applies to any type of optimization process. Here, we can still use the CPU Usage Profiler to see how much memory is allocated to each function call that the CPU executes in each frame, and that is simply done by looking at the **GC Alloc** column, which indicates the amount of memory that the function allocated:

Overview	Total	Self	Calls	GC Alloc
▼ Update.ScriptRunBehaviourUpdate	6.4%	0.0%	1	2.3 KB
▼ BehaviourUpdate	6.4%	1.2%	1	2.3 KB
Sight.Update()	2.0%	0.5%	69	2.2 KB
Physics.OverlapSphere	1.4%	1.4%	69	0 B
GC.Alloc	0.0%	0.0%	69	2.2 KB
Physics.Raycast	0.0%	0.0%	1	0 B

Figure 20.30 – The memory allocation of the Update event function of Sight

In the preceding screenshot, we can see how our function is allocating too much memory, which is produced because there are many enemies in the scene. But that's no excuse; we are allocating that much RAM at every frame, so we need to improve this. There are several things that can contribute to our memory being claimed by allocations, so let's discuss the basic ones, starting with array-returning functions.

If we review the Sight code, we can see that the only moment where we are allocating memory is in the call to `Physics.OverlapSphere`, and that is evident because it is an array-returning function, which is a function that returns a varying amount of data. To do this, it needs to allocate an array and return that array to us. This needs to be done on the side that created the function, Unity, but in this case, Unity gives us two versions of the function—the one that we are using and the `NonAlloc` version. It is usually recommended to use the second version, but Unity uses the other one to make coding simpler for beginners. The `NonAlloc` version looks as in the following screenshot:

```
static Collider[] colliders = new Collider[100];

void Update()
{
    int detectedAmount= Physics.OverlapSphereNonAlloc(transform.position, distance, colliders, objectsLayers);

    detectedObject = null;
    for (int i = 0; i < detectedAmount; i++)
```

Figure 20.31 – Memory allocation of the Update event function of Sight

This version requires us to allocate an array with enough space to save the largest amount of colliders our `OverlapSphere` variable can find and pass it as the third parameter. This allows us to allocate the array just once and reuse it on every occasion that we need it. In the preceding screenshot, you can see how the array is static, which means it is shared between all the Sight variables as they won't execute in parallel (no `Update` function will). This will work fine. Keep in mind that the function will return the number of objects that were detected, so we just iterate on that count. The array can have previous results stored within it.

Now, check your Profiler and notice how the amount of memory allocated has been reduced greatly. There might be some remaining memory allocation within our function, but sometimes there is no way to keep it at 0. However, you can try to look at the reasons for this using deep profiling or by commenting some code and seeing which comment removes the allocation. I challenge you to try this. Also, `OverlapSphere` is not the only case where this could occur. You have others, such as the `GetComponents` function family, which, unlike `GetComponent`, finds all the components of a given type, not just the first one, so pay attention to any array-returning function of Unity and try to replace it with a non-allocating version, if there is one.

Another common source of memory allocation is string concatenation. Remember that strings are immutable, meaning they cannot change if you concatenate two strings. A third one needs to be generated with enough space to hold the first ones. If you need to concatenate a large number of times, consider using `string.Format` if you are just replacing placeholders in a template string, such as putting the name of the player and the score they got in a message or using `StringBuilder`, a class that just holds all the strings to be concatenated in a list and, when necessary, concatenates them together, instead of concatenating them one by one as the + operator does. Also, consider using the new string interpolation functionality of C#. You can see some examples in the following screenshot:

```csharp
string name = "John";
string score = "100";
string template = "{0} has won {1} points";

print(string.Format(template, name, score)); //John has won 100 points
print($"{name} has won {score} points."); //John has won 100 points


StringBuilder builder = new StringBuilder();
builder.Append("My ");
builder.Append("name ");
builder.Append("is ");
builder.Append("Neo.");
print(builder.ToString()); //My name is Neo.
```

Figure 20.32 – String management in C#

Finally, a classic technique to consider is object pooling, which is suitable in cases where you need to instantiate and destroy objects constantly, such as with bullets or effects. In that scenario, the use of regular `Instantiate` and `Destroy` functions will lead to memory fragmentation, but object pooling fixes that by allocating the maximum amount of required objects possible. It replaces `Instantiate` by taking one of the preallocated functions and it replaces `Destroy` by returning the object to the pool. A simple pool can be seen in the following screenshot:

```csharp
public class Pool : MonoBehaviour
{
    List<GameObject> storedObjects = new List<GameObject>();

    [SerializeField] GameObject prefab;

    public GameObject Get()
    {
        if (storedObjects.Count > 0)
        {
            var obj GameObject = storedObjects[0];
            storedObjects.RemoveAt(0);
            obj.SetActive(true);
            return obj;
        }
        else
        {
            return Instantiate(prefab);
        }
    }

    public void Return(GameObject obj)
    {
        obj.SetActive(false);
        storedObjects.Add(obj);
    }
}
```

Figure 20.33 – A simple object pool

There are several ways to improve this pool, but it is fine as it is for now. Note that objects need to be reinitialized when they are taken out of the pool, and you can do that with the `OnEnable` event function or by creating a custom function to inform the object to do so.

Now that we have explored some basic memory allocation reduction techniques, let's look at the new Memory Profiler tool, introduced in the latest version of Unity, to explore memory in greater detail.

Using the Memory Profiler

With this Profiler, we can detect memory allocated on a frame-by-frame basis, but it won't show the total memory allocated so far, which would be useful to study how we are using our memory. This is where the Memory Profiler can help us. This relatively new Unity package allows us to take memory snapshots of every single object allocated both on the native and managed side—native meaning the internal C++ Unity code and managed meaning anything that belongs to the C# side (that is, both our code and Unity's C# engine code). We can explore snapshots with a visual tool and rapidly see which type of object is consuming the most RAM and how they are referenced by other objects.

To start using the **Memory Profiler**, do the following:

1. Open **Package Manager** (**Window | Package Manager**) and enable preview packages (**Wheel Icon | Advanced Project Settings | Enable Pre-release Packages**):

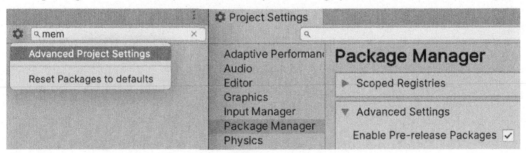

Figure 20.34 – Enabling preview packages

2. Click the Plus (+) button and select **Add package from git URL…**:

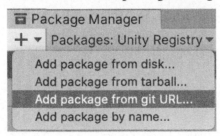

Figure 20.35 – Installing packages from git URLs

3. In the dialog box, enter `com.unity.memoryprofiler` and click **Add**. We need to add the package this way as it's still an experimental one:

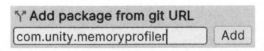

Figure 20.36 – Installing the Memory Profiler

4. Once installed, open the Memory Profiler in **Window | Analysis | Memory Profiler**.

5. Play the game and click on the **Capture** button in the **Memory Profiler** window:

Figure 20.37 – Capturing a snapshot

6. Click on the **Open** button next to the snapshot that was captured to open the tree view, where you can see the memory split into blocks by type. It can take a while so be patient:

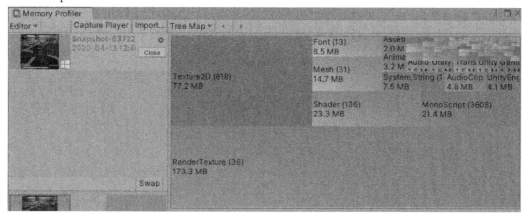

Figure 20.38 – Memory blocks

7. In our case, we can see that RenderTexture uses up the most memory, which belongs to the image that is displayed in the scene, as well as some textures used by postprocessing effects. Try to disable the PPVolume object and take another snapshot to detect the difference.

8. In my case, that dropped off 130 MB. There are other textures needed for other effects, such as HDR. If you want to explore where those remaining MBs came from, click on the block to subdivide it into its objects and take your own guesses based on the names of the textures:

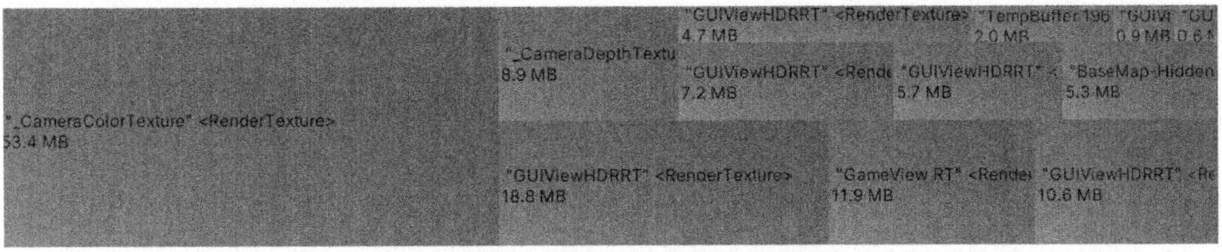

Figure 20.39 – Memory blocks in detail

9. You can repeat the same process in the `Texture2D` block type, which belongs to the textures used in the materials of our models. You can look at the biggest one and detect its usage—maybe it is a big texture that is never seen close enough to justify its size. Then, we can reduce its size using the Max Size of the **Texture import** settings.

> **Important note**
>
> As with any profiler, it is always useful to carry out the profiling directly in the build (more on that in the next chapter) because taking snapshots in the editor will capture lots of memory that is used by the editor and will not be used in the build. An example of this is the loading of unnecessary textures because the editor probably loaded them when you clicked them to see their previews in the **Inspector** window.

Take into account that due to the Memory Profiler being a package, its UI can change often, but its basic idea will remain. You can use this tool to detect whether you are using the memory in unexpected ways. Something useful to consider here is how Unity loads assets when loading a scene, which consists of loading all assets referenced in the scene at load time. This means that you can have, as an example, an array of prefabs that have references to materials that have references to textures, and even if you don't instantiate a single instance of them, the prefabs must be loaded in memory, causing them to occupy space. In this scenario, I recommend that you explore the use of addressables, which provide a way to load assets dynamically. But let's keep things simple for now.

You can do more with the Profiler, such as access a list view of all objects and observe every field of it and its references to see which objects are using it (from the main menu, go to **TreeMap | Table | All objects**), but for beginners, I found that view a little bit confusing. A good alternative to the Memory Profiler reference navigation system is using the **Memory** module of the **Profiler**. This is a basic version of the Memory Profiler that won't show you the memory with a nice tree view or in the amount of detail that the Memory Profiler can provide, but provides a simpler version of a reference navigator, which can be enough most of the time.

To use it, do the following:

1. Open the Profiler (**Window** | **Analysis** | **Profiler**).

2. While in play mode, scroll down through the list of Profiler modules and select **Memory**.

3. With the **Gather object references** toggle turned on, click on **Take Sample Playmode**.

4. Explore the list that pops up, open the categories, and select an asset. In the following screenshot, you can see that I have selected the texture and on the right panel, I can explore the references. This texture is used by a material named base color, which is referenced by a mesh renderer in a GameObject called `floor_1_LOD0`. You can even click on an item in the reference list to highlight the referencer object:

Detailed ▾	Take Sample Playmode	Gather object references	Memory usage in the Editor is not the same as it would be in a Player.		
Name		Memory	Ref count	Referenced By:	
▶ Other (431)		0.71 GB		▼ base color(Material)	
▼ Assets (4296)		116.6 MB		▼ floor_1_LOD0(MeshRenderer)	
▼ Texture2D (90)		61.4 MB		▶ floor_1_LOD0(GameObject)	
rocks		10.7 MB	1	Scene Object()	
base-color-normal		5.3 MB	1	▶ floor_1_LOD0(MeshRenderer)	
mud		2.7 MB	1	▶ floor_1_LOD0(MeshRenderer)	

Figure 20.40 – Memory Profiler module

As you can see, both the Memory Profiler and the **Memory** module in the Profiler do similar things. They can take snapshots of memory for you to analyze them. I believe that with time, Unity will unify those tools, but for now, use one or the other based on their strong and weak points, such as the ability of the Memory Profiler to compare two snapshots to analyze differences, or its ability to explore low-level data of the memory, such as seeing which managed object is using which native object (which is pretty advanced and most times unnecessary). You can use the **Memory** module to analyze references to see which object is using which texture and why.

Summary

Optimizing a game is not an easy task, especially if you are not familiar with the internals of how each Unity system works. Sadly, this is a titanic task, and no one knows every single system down to its finest details, but with the tools learned in this chapter, we have a way to explore how changes affect systems through exploration. We learned how to profile the CPU, GPU, and RAM and what the key hardware in any game is, and also covered some common good practices to avoid abusing them.

Now, you are able to diagnose performance issues in your game, gathering data about the performance of the three main pieces of hardware—the CPU, GPU, and RAM—and then use that data to focus your optimization efforts on applying the correct optimization technique. Performance is important as your game needs to run smoothly to give your users a pleasant experience.

In the next chapter, we are going to see how to create a build of our game to share with other people, without needing to install Unity. This is also very useful for profiling, given that profiling builds gives us more accurate data than profiling in an editor.

Section 4 – Releasing Your Game

Now that we have a prototype, it is time to show it to the world! We will be learning how to prepare our project for publishing by building it and polishing it sufficiently.

This section comprises the following chapters:

- *Chapter 21, Building the Project*
- *Chapter 22, Finishing Touches*
- *Chapter 23, Augmented Reality in Unity*

21
Building the Project

So, we have reached a point where the game is mature enough that we can test it with real people. The problem is that we can't pretend people will install Unity, open a project, and hit Play. They will want to receive a nice executable file to double-click and play right away. In this chapter, we are going to discuss how we can convert our project into an easy-to-share executable format. Then, we will learn how to apply the profiling and debugging techniques we learned about in *Chapter 20*, *Scene Performance Optimization*, but this time on the build. After reading this chapter, you will be able to detect potential performance bottlenecks and know how to tackle the most common ones, leading to an increase in your game's framerate.

In this chapter, we will cover the following Build concepts:

- Building a project
- Debugging the Build

Building a project

In software development (including video games), the result of taking the source files of our project and converting them into an executable format is called a Build. The generated executable files are optimized to get the maximum performance possible. We can't get performance while editing the game due to the ever-changing nature of a project. It would be time-consuming to prepare the assets so that they're in their final form while editing the game. Also, the generated files are in a difficult-to-read format. They won't have the textures, audios, and source code files just there for the user to look at. They will be formatted in custom file structures, so in a way, they are protected from users stealing them.

> **Important Note**
>
> Actually, there are several tools we can use to extract source files from video games, especially from a widely used engine such as Unity. You can extract assets such as textures and 3D models, and there are even programs that extract those assets directly from the VRAM, so we cannot guarantee that the assets won't be used outside the game. In the end, users have the data of those assets on their disks.

The Build process is pretty simple when you target desktop platforms such as PC, Mac, or Linux, but there are a few settings we need to keep in mind before building. The first configuration we are going to see is the scenes list. We have already discussed this, but now is a good time to remember that it is important to set the first element of this list to the scene that will be loaded first. Remember, you can do this by going to **File -> Build Settings** and dragging your desired starter scene to the top of the list. In our case, we defined the **Game** scene as the first scene, but in a real game, it would be ideal to create a **Main Menu** scene using the UI and some graphics:

Build Settings

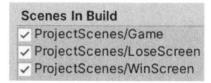

Figure 21.1 – The Scene's list order

Another setting you can change here is the target platform; that is, the target operating system that the build will be created for. Usually, this is set for the same operating system you are developing on, but in case you are, for example, developing on a Mac, and you want to build for Windows, just set the **Target Platform** setting to **Windows**. That way, the result will be exe instead of app. You may see Android and iOS as other target platforms, but making mobile games requires that we make other considerations that we are not going to discuss in this book:

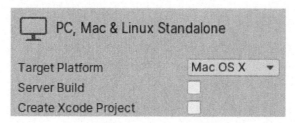

Figure 21.2 – Target Platform

In the same window, you can click the **Player Settings** button at the bottom left, or just open the **Edit | Project Settings** window and click on the **Player** category to access the rest of the Build Settings. Unity calls the generated executable files the game's "Player." Here, we have a set of configurations that will affect how the Build or Player behaves, and here is a list of the basic ones:

- **Product Name**: This is the name of the game in the window title bar and executable file.

- **Company Name**: This is the name of the company that developed the game, which is used by Unity to create certain file paths and will be included in the executable information.

- **Default Icon**: Here, you can select a texture to act as the executable icon.

- **Default Cursor**: You can set a texture to replace the regular system cursor. If you do that, remember to set the **Cursor Hotspot** property to the pixel of the image you want the cursor to do the clicks for.

- **Resolution and Presentation**: There are settings regarding how our game's resolution is going to be handled.

- **Resolution and Presentation | Default is Native Resolution**: With this checked and when the game is running in full-screen mode, the resolution that's currently being used by the system will be the one that's used by Unity. You can uncheck this and set your desired resolution.

- **Splash Image**: This provides settings about the splash image the game will show after loading for the first time.

- **Splash Image | Show Splash Screen**: This will enable a Unity splash screen that will display logos as an introduction to the game. If you have the Unity Pro License, you can uncheck this to create your custom splash screen, if you want to.

- **Splash Image | Logos List**: Here, you can add a set of images that Unity will display when launching the game. If you are using the free version of Unity, you are forced to have the Unity logo displayed in this list.

- **Splash Image | Draw Mode**: You can set this to **All Sequential** to show each logo, one after the other, or to **Unity logo Below** to show your custom introductory logos with the Unity logo always present below yours:

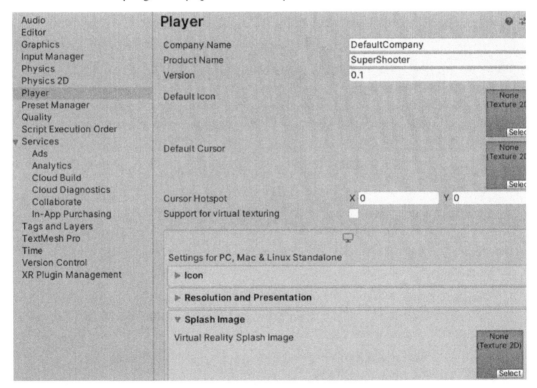

Figure 21.3 – Player settings

After configuring these settings as you wish, the next step is to do the actual Build, which can be accomplished by hitting the **Build** button in the **File | Build Settings** window. This will ask you to set where you want the Build files to be created. I recommend that you create an empty folder on your desktop so that you have easy access to the result. Be patient – this process can take a while based on the size of the project:

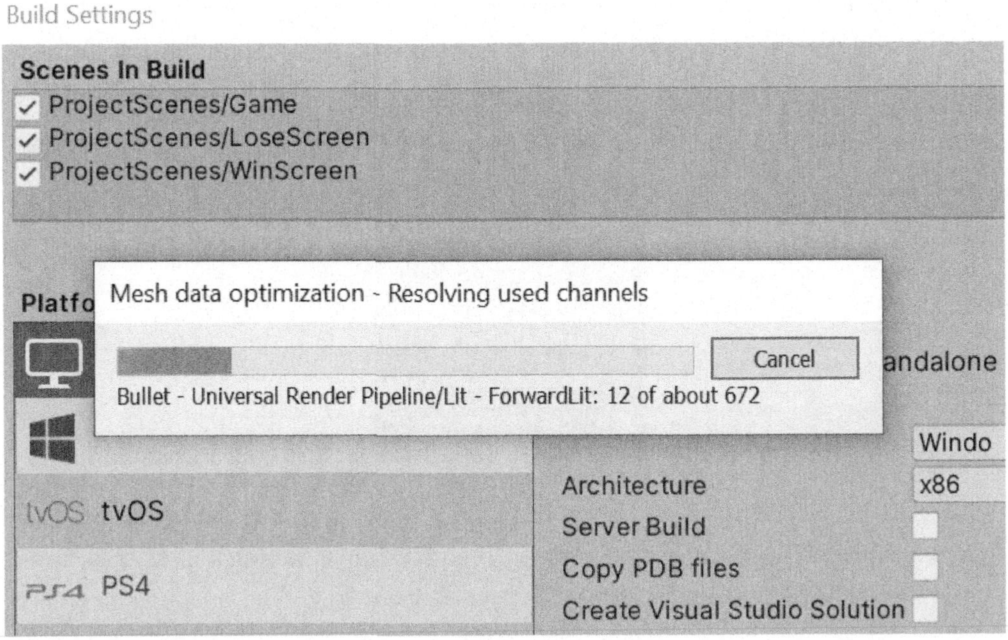

Build Settings

Scenes In Build
- ✓ ProjectScenes/Game
- ✓ ProjectScenes/LoseScreen
- ✓ ProjectScenes/WinScreen

Platfo

Mesh data optimization - Resolving used channels

[progress bar]   Cancel   andalone

Bullet - Universal Render Pipeline/Lit - ForwardLit: 12 of about 672

Windo

Architecture   x86

Server Build

Copy PDB files

Create Visual Studio Solution

tvOS tvOS

PS4 PS4

Figure 21.4 – Building the game

Something that can fail here is having non-build compatible scripts – scripts that are intended to be executed only in the **Editor** window, mostly Editor extensions. We haven't created any of those, so if you receive an error message in the console after building, similar to what's shown in the following screenshot, this can happen because of a script in an Asset Store package. In that case, just delete the files that are shown in the console before the Build Error message. If, by any chance, there is one of your scripts there, ensure you don't have the using UnityEditor; line in any of your scripts. This line will try to use the **Editor** namespace, the one that is not included in the Build compilation, to save space on the disk:

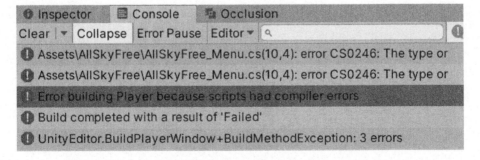

Figure 21.5 – Build errors

And that's pretty much everything you need to know. With that, you have generated your game! Something to take into account is that every file that was created in the folder that you specified when building must be shared, not just the executable file. The `Data` folder contains all the necessary assets and it is important to include when sharing the game in the case of Windows Builds. For Linux and Mac Builds, just one file is generated (`x86/x86_64` and `app packages`, respectively):

Figure 21.6 – A Windows-generated folder

Now that we have the build, you can test it by double-clicking the executable file. Now that you have tried your build, we will discuss how to use the same Debugging and Profiling tools we used in the Editor to test our build.

Debugging the Build

In an ideal world, the Editor and the build will behave the same, but sadly, that isn't true. The Editor is prepared to work in fast-iteration mode. Code and assets go through minimal processing before being used to make changes often and fast, so we can test our game easily. When the game is built, a series of optimizations and differences from the **Editor** project will be applied to ensure the best performance we can get, but those differences can cause certain parts of the game to behave differently, making the profiling data of the player differ from the Editor. That's why we are going to explore how we can debug and profile our game in the Build.

In this section, we will examine the following Build Debugging concepts:

- Debugging Code
- Profiling Performance

Let's start by discussing how to debug the code of a Build.

Debugging Code

As Player code is compiled differently, we can get errors in the Build that didn't happen in the Editor, and we need to debug them somehow. We have two main ways to debug – by printing messages and by using breakpoints. So, let's start with the first one, messages. If you ran your executable file, you may have noticed that there's no console available. It's just the **Game** view in full screen, which makes sense; we don't want to distract the user with annoying testing messages. Luckily, the messages are still being printed, but in a file, so we can just go to that file and look for them.

The location varies based on the operating system. In this list, you can find the possible locations of this file:

- **Linux**: `~/.config/unity3d/CompanyName/ProductName/Player.log`
- **Mac**: `~/Library/Logs/Company Name/Product Name/Player.log`
- **Windows**: `C:\Users\username\AppData\LocalLow\CompanyName\ProductName\Player.log`

In these paths, you must change `CompanyName` and `ProductName` and use the values of the properties in the `Player` settings we set previously, which have the same names; that is, Company and Product Name. In Windows, you must replace `username` with the name of the Windows account you are executing the game in. Consider that the folders might be hidden, so enable the option to show hidden files on your operating system:

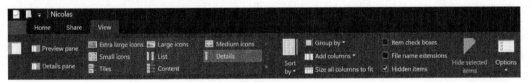

Figure 21.7 – Showing hidden files

Inside that folder, you will find a file called `Player`; you can open it with any text editor and look at the messages. In this case, I have used Windows, so the directory path looks like this:

Figure 21.8 – Debugging directory

Aside from downloading a custom package from the Asset Store, there is a way to see the messages of the console directly in the game -the error messages, at least – and that is by creating a development build. This is a special Build that provides extended debugging and profiling capabilities in exchange for not fully optimizing the code like the final Build does, but it will be enough for general debugging. You can create this kind of Build by just checking the **Development Build** checkbox in the **File | Build Settings** window:

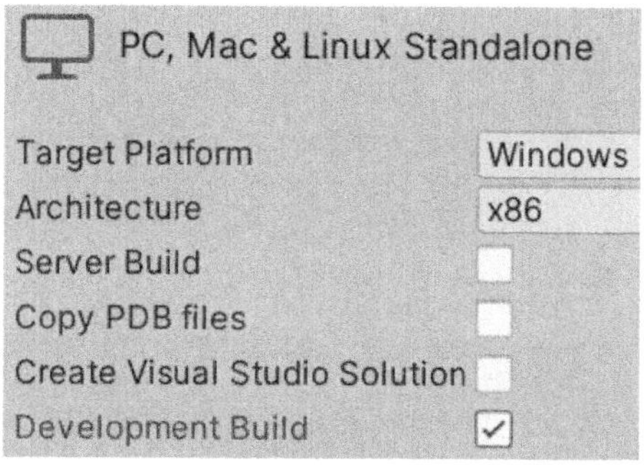

Figure 21.9 – The Development Build checkbox

Remember that just the error messages will be displayed here, so a little trick you can do is replace the `print` and `Debug.Log` function calls with `Debug.LogError`, which will also print the message in the console but with a red icon. Note that this is not a good practice, so limit the usage of this kind of message for temporal debugging. For permanent logging, use the log file or find a custom debugging console for runtime in the Asset Store.

One little trick we performed is that we enabled **Development Build** – pay attention to the **Script Build Only** checkbox in the **Build** window. If you only changed your code and want to test that change, check it and do the build. This will make the process go faster than a regular build. Just remember to uncheck this option if you have changed anything else in the Editor because those changes won't be included if you have it checked. Also, remember that this won't work for Release builds (non-development builds).

Remember that for **Development Build** to work, you need to build the game again; luckily, the first build is the one that takes the most time, and the next will be faster. This time, you can just click the **Build and Run** button to do the Build in the folder where you did the previous Build:

```
public class PlayerShooting : MonoBehaviour
{
    void Start()
    {
        Debug.LogError("Testing Player Shooting Start");
    }
```

Figure 21.10 – Debugging error messages

Something interesting regarding Development Builds is that, unlike regular builds, the error messages are displayed directly in the build, allowing you to properly debug your project. In the following screenshot, you can see the error message being displayed in the runtime:

Figure 21.11 – Error messages in a development Build

Note that aside from showing the error message, there's an **Open Log File** button on the right, allowing you to view the log file. This is a text file containing detailed information regarding all the messages and logs that occurred in this run of the game to pinpoint the issue. Essentially, this is the same information that the **Console** panel shows in the editor.

Also, you can use regular breakpoints in the same way as we explained in *Chapter 14, Introduction to C# and Visual Scripting*. Upon attaching the IDE to the Player, it will show up in the list of targets. But for that to work, you must not only check **Development Build** in the **Build** window but also **Script Debugging**. Here, you have an additional option that, when checked, allows you to pause the entire game until a debugger is attached. This is called **Wait for Managed Debugger**. This is useful if you want to test something that happens immediately at the beginning and doesn't give you enough time to attach the debugger:

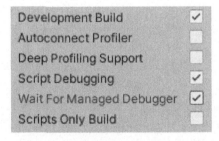

Figure 21.12 – Enabling script debugging

We have another way to view these messages, but that will require the Profiler to work, so let's use this as an excuse to also discuss how to profile the Editor.

Profiling performance

We are going to use the same tools we looked at in the previous chapter, but to profile the Player this time. Luckily, the difference is minimal. As we did in the previous section, you need to build the Player in **Development** mode by checking the **Development Build** checkbox in the **Build** window. Upon doing this, the profilers should automatically detect it.

Let's start using the Profiler on the Build by doing the following:

1. Play the game through the Build.

2. Switch to Unity using *Alt + Tab* (*Cmd + Tab* on Mac).

3. Open the Profiler.

4. Click the menu that says **Playmode** and select the item that contains **Player** in it. Because I have used Windows, it says **WindowsPlayer**:

Figure 21.13 – Profiling the Player

Notice that when you click a frame, the game won't stop like it does in the **Editor** window. If you want to focus your attention on the frames at a specific moment, you can click the record button (the red circle) to make the Profiler stop capturing data so that you can analyze the frames that have been captured so far.

Also, you can see that when the Profiler is attached to the Player, the console will also be attached, so you can see the logs directly in Unity. Note that this version requires Unity to be open, and we cannot expect our friends who are testing our game to have it. You might need to click on the **Player** button that appears in the **Console** window and check **Player Logging** for this to work:

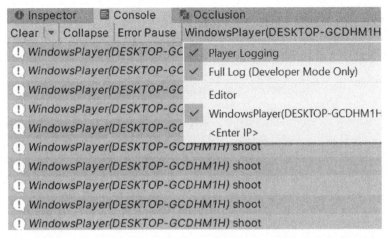

Figure 21.14 – Enabling Player Logging after attaching the Profiler

Frame Debugger must also be enabled to work with the Player. Here, you need to click the **Editor** button in **Frame Debugger**. Again, you will see the player in the list of possible debugging targets; after selecting it, hit **Enable** as usual. Consider that the preview of the Draw Calls won't be seen in the **Game** view but in the Build itself. If you are running the game in full-screen mode, you might need to switch back and forth between Unity and the Build:

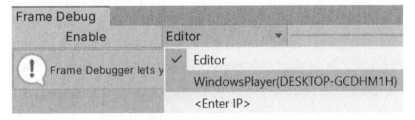

Figure 21.15 – Debugging the frames of our game's Player

You may also wish to run the game in Windowed mode, which you can do by setting the **Fullscreen Mode** property in the Player settings to **Windowed**, as well as establish a default resolution that is smaller than your desktop resolution to have both Unity and the Player visible:

▼ **Resolution and Presentation**

Resolution

Fullscreen Mode	Windowed
Default Screen Width	1024
Default Screen Height	768
Mac Retina Support	✓

Figure 21.16 – Enabling Windowed mode

Finally, **Memory Profiler** also supports profiling the Player. As you might have guessed, you can just select the Player from the list that is displayed when you click the first button shown in the top bar of the window, and then click **Capture Player**:

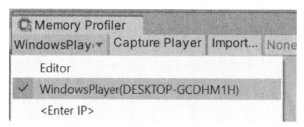

Figure 21.17 Taking memory snapshots of the Player

And that is it. As you can see, Unity Profilers are designed to be easily integrated with the Player. If you start to take data from them, you will see the difference compared to Editor profiling, especially in **Memory Profiler**.

Summary

In this chapter, we learned how to create an executable version of the game and configure it properly so that you can share it with not only your friends but potentially the world! We also discussed how to profile our Build; remember that doing that will give us more accurate data than profiling the Editor, so we can improve the performance of our game even more.

But before we do that, we must discuss some final details. These are not Unity-related details, but game-related ones – things you need to consider before and after showing your game to people other than yourself or any person that saw your game while it was being developed. In the next chapter, we will briefly discuss the non-technical aspects of game development, and what you should do before and after finishing your game.

22
Finishing Touches

Here we are! At this point, we have a fully developed game, so can we get some money now? Sadly not. A successful game relies on heavy refinement; the devil is in the details! Also, don't get too hyped about earning money yet; this is your first game and there are a lot of non-development-related tasks to accomplish. It's time to discuss what can we do now with what we have achieved so far. By the end of this chapter, you should be aware of the work you need to do to make your game reach its full potential, as well as the processes and challenges of releasing a game to the market.

In this chapter, we will cover the following topics:

- Iterating your game
- Releasing your game

Iterating your game

We are about to finish the first iteration of our game. We had an idea, we implemented it, and now it's time to test it. After this test, we will get feedback on the things that can be improved, so we will formulate ideas to improve them, implement them, test them, and then repeat this. This is what an iteration is.

In this section, we will examine the following iteration concepts:

- Testing and feedback
- Solving feedback

Let's start by discussing how to properly test the game on people.

Testing and feedback

Apart from a strong marketing strategy, the success of your game relies on the first 10 minutes of gameplay. If you can't grab the attention of the player in that time, you will certainly lose them. The first impression of your game is important. Those first 10 minutes must be flawless and sadly, our perception of the game is not relevant here. You have spent several hours playing it and you know every inch of the levels and how to properly control your character, as well as all the mechanics and dynamics of your game – it is YOUR game, after all. You love it as it is. It's a big accomplishment. However, someone who has never played the game won't feel the same way. That's why testing is so important.

The first time you make someone play your game, you will be shocked – believe me, I've been there. You will notice that the player probably won't understand the game. They won't understand how to control the player or how to win the game and will get stuck in parts of the level that you never imagined to be difficult. There will be bugs everywhere and it will be a total mess – and that is great! That is the purpose of testing your game: to get valuable information or feedback. This feedback is what will make your game better if you tackle it properly.

In a testing session, there are two main sources of feedback – observation and user feedback. Observation is the act of silently looking at the person who is playing the game and seeing how they play it – which keys they press first, their reaction when something happens, when they start getting frustrated in a non-expected way (some games rely on frustration, such as *Dark Souls*), and generally checking that the player is getting the exact experience you expected.

The silent part of the observation is crucial. You must *not* talk to the player, and especially not give them any hints nor help, at least not unless they are completely lost and the testing session can't progress without help – a situation that is also a form of useful feedback. You must observe the player in their natural state so that it's the same situation where they would be playing your game in their house. If not, the feedback that's gathered will be biased and won't be useful. When testing big games, they even carry out tests in Gesell chambers. These are rooms with a pane of glass that can be seen from one side only – like an interrogation room but less scary. This way, the player won't feel any kind of pressure about being observed:

Figure 22.1 – Gesell chamber

The second source is direct feedback, which is asking the tester about their impressions of the game after the session. Here, you can let the tester tell you their experience and provide any feedback that they have, if any, and then you can start asking questions related to that feedback or other questions related to the test. This could include questions such as, how did you find the controls? Which part of the game did you find most frustrating? Which part was the most rewarding? Would you pay for this game?

Something important to consider when taking feedback from the tester is who they are. Are they a friend, a relative, or a total stranger? When testing with people close to you, it's possible that the feedback won't be useful. They will try to water down the poor parts of the game as they might think that you asked them to play the game to receive compliments, but that cannot be farther from the truth. You want real, harsh, objective feedback – that's the only way you can really improve your game.

So, unless your friends are really honest with you, try to test your game on unknown people. This could be other students in your educative institution, or at your workplace, or random people in the streets. Try to go to game conventions with spaces to showcase indie games. Also, consider your target audience when testing. If your game is a casual mobile game, you shouldn't be taking it to a *Doom* meet-up as you will mostly receive unrelated feedback. Know your audience and look for them. Also, consider that you will probably need to test your game on at least 10 people. You will notice that maybe one person didn't like the game and the other nine did. As in statistics, your sample must be big enough to be considerable.

Also, even though we said that our perception doesn't count, if you apply common sense and be honest with yourself, you can get feedback from your own playtesting. But now that we have gathered feedback, what we can do with it?

Interpreting feedback

So, you've got what you wanted – lots of information about your game. But what do you do now? Well, that depends on the feedback. You have different types and different ways to solve them. The easiest feedback to tackle is errors – for example, the door didn't open when I put in the key, the enemy won't die no matter how many bullets I shoot at it, and so on. To solve these, you must carry out what the player did step by step so that you can reproduce the issue. Once you've reproduced it, debug your game to see the error – maybe it's caused by a null check or a misconfiguration in the scene.

Try to gather as much detail about the situation as possible, such as when the issue occurred and at what level, which gear the player had, the number of lives the player had left, or if the player was in the air or crouched down – any data that allows you to get to the same situation. Some bugs can be tricky and can sometimes happen in the strangest situations. You might think that strange bugs that happen 1% of the time can be ignored, but remember that if your game is successful, it will be played by hundreds, maybe thousands, of players – that 1% can really affect your player base.

Then, you have to balance the feedback. You could get feedback such as there weren't enough bullets, I had too many lives, the enemies are tough, the game is too easy, or the game is too hard. This must be considered alongside your objectives. Did you really want the player to be short on bullets or lives? Did you want the enemies to be hard to defeat? In this scenario, things that the player found difficult might be the exact experience you desired, and here is where you need to remember the target audience. Maybe the user that gave you that feedback is not who you expect to play the game (again, think of the example of *Dark Souls*, a game that is not for everyone). But if the player is the target audience, you might need to create a balance.

Balance is when you need to tweak the game numbers, the number of bullets, the number of waves, the enemies, the enemies' lives, the enemies' bullets, and so on. That's why we exposed lots of properties of our scripts – so that they can be easily changed. This can be an extensive process. Getting all those numbers to work together is difficult. If you increase a property too much, another one might need to be reduced. Your game is a big spreadsheet of calculations. Actually, most game designers master the use of spreadsheets to do exactly this – balance the game, make calculations, and see how changing one cell changes the other – and before testing it the hard way, play the game. In the following screenshot, you can see how we prepared our Player object to be easily configured in the **Editor** window:

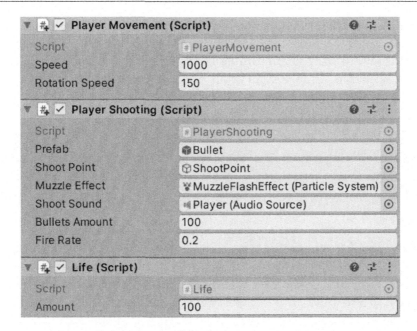

Figure 22.2 – Some of the properties that affect gameplay

You can also get some feedback such as "I don't understand why the player does what they do," "I don't understand the motives of the villains," and so on. This can be easy to underestimate, but remember that your game mechanics, aesthetics, and story (if any) must be in sync. If one of those elements fails, there is the risk of the rest of them also failing. If you have a futuristic history setting but your main weapon is a metal sword, you need to justify its existence somehow, perhaps with a story point. If your enemy wants to destroy the world but appears to be a kind person, you need to justify that somehow. These details are what make the game believable.

Finally, you have perception feedback, such as "the game didn't entertain me" or "I didn't enjoy the game." That feedback can be converted into other feedback if you ask the right questions, but sometimes, the tester doesn't know what the problem is; the game can just feel wrong in their eyes. This, of course, is not useful by itself, but don't underestimate it. It might be a hint that you need to do further testing.

In game development, when you think you are finished with the game, you will discover that you have just started to develop it. Testing will make you realize that the game is not finished until the players are happy with the game, and that can take even more time than preparing the first version, so prepare for having to iterate the game a lot.

Big game developers, where their first prototype could take years, carry out testing in the early stages of their game, sometimes with fake assets to hide sensitive information that can spoil the game or make the competitors aware of their plans. Some developers even release a mini-game based on the main game, with a different story and aesthetics, just to test an idea. Also, there is the soft launch, where the game is released but to a restricted audience – maybe to a specific country that will not be your main audience and source of income – to test and iterate the game before releasing it to the rest of the world.

So, have patience. Testing is where the real development of the game starts, but once all those extensive testing sessions have ended and the game is finished, what is the next step? Releasing it!

Releasing your game

We are here – the big moment! We have the gold build, which is the final version of the game. Do we just throw it at our target store (such as Steam, the Play store, the Apple App Store, and so on)? Well… no – actually, we still have lots of work to do, work that we should have started before getting to the gold build. So, let's explore what that extra work is and in which phase it should be carried out.

In this section, we will examine the following release phases:

- Pre-release
- Release
- Post-release

Let's start by discussing the pre-release phase.

Pre-release

One thing you should do before pre-release, and ideally before you start developing your game, is decide where you are going to sell your game. Nowadays, that means choosing a digital store – selling physical copies of games is not an option for newly starting independent developers. You have several options, but for PCs, the most common place for this is Steam, a well-known platform that allows you to upload your game to the platform for 100 USD. Once it has been reviewed, it can be published. On iOS, the only way to do this is by using the App Store, which charges 100 USD per year for you to publish on it. Finally, on Android, you have the Play store, which allows you to publish on it for a one-off payment of 25 USD. Consoles have harder requisites, so we are not going to mention them.

After picking a digital store, if you just release your game without any preparation, your game can be easily lost in the sea of releases that happen on the same day. Nowadays, the competition is strong, and dozens of games might be released on the same day as yours, so you must highlight your game somehow. There are lots of ways to do this, but it requires experience in digital marketing, which can be difficult. It requires skills other than regular developer ones. If you insist on doing it by yourself without hiring someone, here are some things you can do.

First, you can create a game community, such as a blog or group, where you can post information about your game regularly. This includes updates on its development, screenshots of new features, new concept art, and so on. Your job here is to capture the interest of players and keep them interested in your game, even if it's not been released yet, just to prepare them to buy your game as soon as it's released. Here, you need to be creative to keep their interest in the game – vary the content you post, maybe share some mini-games with your community with the opportunity to win prizes, or post questionnaires or giveaways; really, do anything that captures the attention of your audience.

Also, try to develop a community when you are not too near but not too far from the release date. That way, you won't lose the attention of the players due to long wait times and you can be honest about the expectations of your game. They will change a lot during development and the scope is likely to be reduced from its initial design. You will need to deal with the hype, which can be dangerous.

Of course, we need people to join the community, so you must publish it somewhere. You can pay for ads, but aside from the cost and difficulty of making them relevant, there are other free ways of doing this. You might send a free copy of your game to an influencer, such as a YouTuber or an Instagrammer, so that they can play your game and give a review to their audience. This can be difficult if the influencer doesn't like the game as they will be honest, and that can be bad for you. So, you really need to be sure to give them a polished version, but not necessarily a final version. There are also paid influencers that you can approach, but again, that requires money.

You have other free options, such as going onto forums or groups and posting information about your game, but be sensible here. Don't make your post feel like cheap advertising – know where you are publishing. Some groups don't like those kinds of posts and will reject them. Try to look for places that allow that kind of self-advertising. There are groups intended just for that, so just avoid being invasive in certain communities.

Finally, another option you have is to contact a publisher, a company that specializes in doing this kind of marketing. They will allocate money for publishing and will have people that work to manage your communities, which can be a big relief. You have more time to create your game, but this option also has some drawbacks. First, they will get a cut of your game revenue, and depending on the publisher, this can be high. However, you need to contrast that with the revenue you will get by doing your own marketing. Also, publishers will ask you to change your game to meet their criteria. Some will ask for your game to be localized (support several languages) or ask for your game to support certain controllers, have a certain way of doing tutorials, and so on. Finally, consider that certain publishers are associated with certain types of games, so if you are creating an intense action game, you wouldn't publish it with a casual games publisher. Find the right publisher for you:

Figure 22.3 – Some well-known publishers, some of which don't develop their own games, just publish them

Now that we have the foundations prepared for release, how do we release the game?

Release

Aside from all the setup and integrations your game might need to have for the selected digital store platform (which, again, depends on your audience), there are some things to consider when releasing it.

Some stores might have a review process, which consists of playing your game and seeing whether it meets the criteria of the store. As an example, at the time of writing this book, the Apple App Store requires every game they publish to have some kind of social sign-in option (such as Facebook, Google, and so on) and must also support Apple sign-in. They will simply not admit your game if you do not comply. Another example is PS Vita, which asks your game to support some kind of interaction with its front or rear touchpads. So, be aware of these requirements early on. They can influence the release of your game a lot if you don't take care of them.

Aside from these requirements, of course, there are other criteria to be met, such as whether there is adult or violent content. Consider a platform that supports the kind of game you have created. Some may even ask you to get ratings from the **Entertainment Software Rating Board** (**ESRB**) or similar rating boards. Another common requirement that you need to be aware of is that the game should not crash, at least not in the usual workflow of the game. Also, the game must perform well, can't have intense performance issues, and sometimes, your initial game download size can't exceed a specified maximum limit, which you can usually solve by downloading the content in the game itself (look for the **Addressables** Unity package for this). Again, all of these requirements vary, depending on the store.

Now, even if these requirements are met, the process of checking them can take time – days, weeks, or sometimes even months. So, keep this in mind when defining a release date. In big consoles where this process can take months, sometimes, the developers use that time to create the famous day-1 patch, a patch that fixes bugs, which won't stop the game from being released but helps with the overall game experience. It's a questionable but understandable practice.

Finally, remember that the first day of the release is critical. You will be in the **New Releases** section of the store, and this is where you will have the most exposure. After that, all exposure will mostly rely on your marketing and sales. Some stores allow you to be featured. You can talk directly with the representatives of the store and see how you can do this. If the store is interested in your game, they might feature you (or you might have to pay for it). The first day is important, so be prepared for that.

At this point, the game is out and in the hands of people. Have we finished our work? A few years ago, this might have been true, but not today. We still have the post-release work to do.

Post-release

Even if the game has been released, this is not an excuse to stop testing it. You can get even more feedback if your game is played by thousands of people. Sadly, you can't be there to observe them, but you can automate the information-gathering process. You can do this by making your code report analytics to a server, as the Unity Analytics package does. Even if this information is not as direct as in-person testing, a massive amount of data and statistics can be gathered this way, and you can improve the game on the fly thanks to updates, something that old games couldn't do as easily as they can today. No game is released perfect, and sometimes, due to time pressures, you might need to roll out an early release, so prepare your game to be updated regularly after release. There are some cases of games that had a bad launch but were resurrected from the grave. Don't underestimate that last resource. You have already spent too much to give up on your badly released game.

Also, if your monetization model relies on in-app purchases, which means people spend money on loot boxes or cosmetic items, you will need to have constant content updates. This will keep the players playing your game. The more they play the game, the more money will be spent on it. You might take advantage of the information you gather through analytics, not only to fix your game but also to decide which content is being consumed the most by your players, and then focus on that. You can also carry out A/B testing, which consists of releasing two versions of the update to different users and seeing which one is the most successful. This allows you to test ideas on a live game. As you can see, there is still plenty of work to do. Also, use metrics to track whether players are losing interest in your game, and if so, why – is there a difficult level? Is the game too easy? Pay attention to your player base. Ask them questions in the communities you created, or just look at the reviews – users are usually willing to tell you how they would like their favorite game to be improved.

Summary

Developing a game is just one part of the job; releasing it so that it's successful can be a huge task. Sometimes, it can cost more than the game itself. So, unless you are making a game for fun, if you want to make games for a living, you will need to learn how to manage releases or hire people that are capable of helping with the pre-release, release, and post-release phases of your games, which can be a smart move.

Of course, this chapter just provided a simple introduction to this big topic, so I would recommend that you read some extra material if you want to take this part of game development seriously. A very well-explained and bite-sized source of information on this topic is the *Extra Credits* YouTube channel, which provides short videos to convey valuable information. Also, there is a great book called *The Art of Game Design: A Book of Lenses*, which provides a thorough introduction to game design.

Congratulations, you have almost finished *part 3* of this book! You have gained some basic knowledge to kick-start your game development career and choose some of the several roles you can do in it. I recommend that you put this to practice before reading more books on this topic. Gaining information is important, but the only way to convert that information into knowledge is through experimentation. Just be sure to balance theory and practice.

In the next chapter of this book, we are going to explore some extra topics regarding augmented reality applications, by learning how to make a simple game that uses the device's camera to bring the real world into your game, and then extend it with virtual objects.

23
Augmented Reality in Unity

Nowadays, new technologies are expanding the fields of the application of Unity, from gaming to all kinds of software, such as simulations, training, apps, and more. In the latest versions of Unity, we saw lots of improvements in the field of **augmented reality** (**AR**), which allows us to add a layer of virtuality on top of our reality, thereby augmenting what our device can perceive to create games that rely on real-world data, such as the camera's image, our real-world position, and the current weather. This can also be applied to work environments, such as when viewing a building map or checking the electrical ducts inside a wall. Welcome to this extra section of this book, where we are going to discuss how to create AR applications using Unity's AR Foundation package.

In this chapter, we will examine the following AR Foundation concepts:

- Using AR Foundation
- Building for mobile devices
- Creating a simple AR game

By the end of this chapter, you will be able to create AR apps using AR Foundation and will have a fully functional game that uses AR Foundation's framework so that you can test its capabilities.

Let's start by exploring the AR Foundation framework.

Using AR Foundation

When it comes to AR, Unity has two main tools to create applications: Vuforia and AR Foundation. Vuforia is an AR framework that can work on almost any phone and contains all the features needed for basic AR apps; but with a paid subscription, we get more advanced features. On the other hand, the completely free AR Foundation framework supports the latest native AR features of our devices but is supported only on new devices. Your choice of one or the other depends a lot on the type of project you're going to build and the target audience. However, since this book aims to discuss the latest Unity features, we are going to explore how to use AR Foundation to create our first AR app for detecting the positions of images and surfaces in the real world. So, we'll start by exploring its API.

In this section, we will examine the following AR Foundation concepts:

- Creating an AR Foundation project
- Using tracking features

Let's start by discussing how to prepare our project so that it can run AR Foundation apps.

Creating an AR Foundation project

Something to consider when creating AR projects is that we will not only change the way we code our game, but also the way we design our game. AR apps have differences, especially in the way the user interacts, and also limitations, such as the user being in control of the camera all the time. We cannot simply port an existing game to AR without changing the very core experience of the game. That's why, in this chapter, we are going to work on a brand-new project; it would be too difficult to change the game we've created so far so that it works well in AR.

In our case, we are going to create a game where the user controls a player moving a "marker," a physical image you can print that will allow our app to recognize where the player is in the real world. We will be able to move the player while moving that image, and this virtual player will automatically shoot at the nearest Enemy. Those enemies will spawn from certain spawn points that the user will need to place in different parts of the home. As an example, we can put two spawn points on the walls and place our player marker on a table in the middle of the room so that the enemies will go toward them. In the following figure, you can see a preview of what the game will look like:

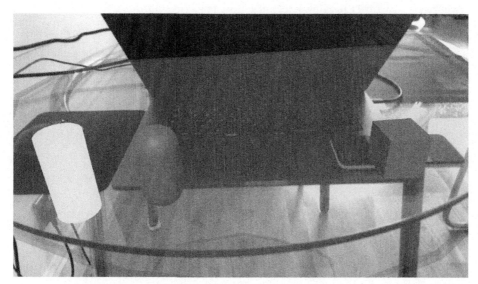

Figure 23.1 – Finished game. The Cylinder is an Enemy Spawner, the Capsule is the Enemy, and the Cube is the Player. These are positioned in a marker image displayed by the cellphone

We'll start creating a new URP-based project in the same way that we created one for our first game. Something to consider is that AR Foundation works with other pipelines, including built-in ones, in case you want to use it in already existing projects. If you don't remember how to create a project, please refer to *Chapter 2, Setting Up Unity*. Once you're in your new blank project, install the AR Foundation package from the Package Manager, just like we've installed other packages previously; that is, go to **Window | Package Manager**. Remember to set the Package Manager so that it shows all packages, not only the ones in the project (the **Packages** button at the top-left part of the window needs to be set to **Unity Registry**). At the time of writing this book, the latest release is 4.1.7, but if you find a newer version than mine, you can try using that one, but as usual, if something works differently to what we want, please install this specific version:

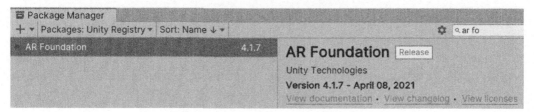

Figure 23.2 – Installing AR Foundation

Before we install any other needed packages, now is a good moment to discuss some core ideas of the AR Foundation framework. This package, by itself, does nothing; it defines a series of AR features that mobile devices offer, such as image tracking, cloud points, and object tracking, but the actual implementation of how to do that is contained in the **Provider** packages, such as **AR Kit** and **AR Core XR** plugins. This is designed like this because, depending on the target device you want to work with, the way those features are implemented changes. As an example, in iOS, Unity implements those features using AR Kit, while in Android, it uses AR Core; they are platform-specific frameworks.

Something to consider here is that not all iOS or Android devices support AR Foundation apps. You might find an updated list of supported devices when searching for AR Core- and AR Kit-supported devices on the internet. At the time of writing, the following links provide the supported device lists:

- **iOS**: `https://www.apple.com/lae/augmented-reality` (at the bottom of the page)

- **Android**: `https://developers.google.com/ar/devices`

Also, there isn't a PC Provider package, so the only way to test AR Foundation apps so far is directly on the device, but testing tools are going to be released soon. In my case, I will be creating an app for iOS, so aside from the **AR Foundation** package, I need to install the **ARKit XR** plugin. However, if you want to develop for Android, install the **ARCore XR** plugin instead (or both if you're targeting both platforms). Also, I will be using the 4.1.7 version of these packages. Usually, the versions of the **AR Foundation** and **Provider** packages match but apply the same logic as when you picked the **AR Foundation** version. In the following screenshot, you can see the **ARKit** package in **Package Manager**:

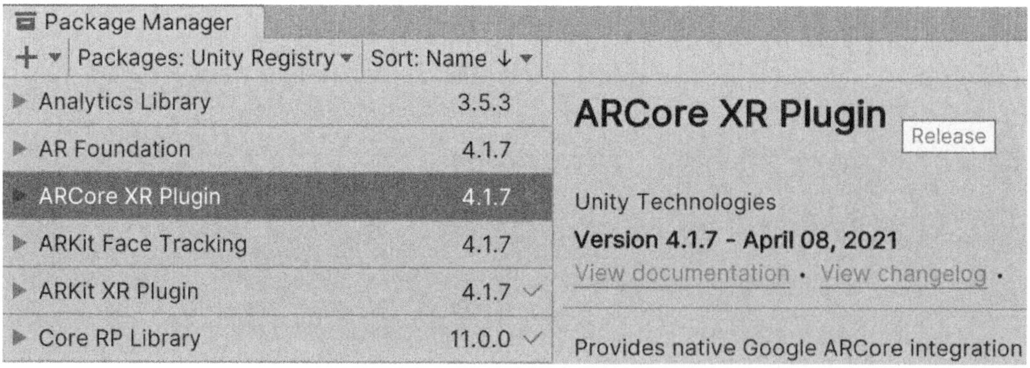

Figure 23.3 – Installing the platform-specific AR provider package

Now that we have the needed plugins, we need to prepare a scene for AR, as follows:

1. Create a new Scene in **File | New Scene** and select the **Basic** template.
2. Delete **Main Camera**; we are going to use a different one.
3. In the **GameObject | XR** menu, create an **AR Session** Object.
4. In the same menu, create an **AR Session Origin** Object that has a **Camera** object inside it:

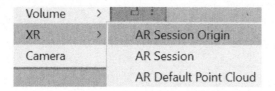

Figure 23.4 – Creating the Session objects

Your hierarchy should look as follows:

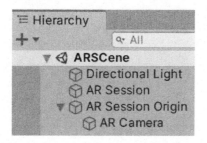

Figure 23.5 – Starter ARScene

The **AR Session** object will be responsible for initializing AR Framework and will handle all the update logic for the AR systems. The **AR Session Origin** object will allow the framework to locate tracked objects such as images and point clouds in a relative position to the scene. The devices inform the positions of tracked objects relative to what the device considers "the origin." This is usually the first area of your house you were pointing at when the app started detecting objects, so the AR Session Origin object will represent that point in your physical space. Finally, you can check the camera inside the origin, which contains some extra components, with the most important being **AR Pose Driver**, which will make your **Camera** object move along with your device. Since the device's position is relative to the Session Origin object's point, the camera needs to be inside the origin object.

One extra step if you are working on a URP project (as in our case) is that you need to set up the render pipeline so that it supports rendering the camera image in the app. To do that, go to the `Settings` folder that was generated when we created the project, look for the `Forward Renderer` file, and select it. In the **Renderer Features** list, click the **Add Renderer Feature** button and select **AR Background Renderer Feature**. In the following screenshot, you can see what the Forward Renderer asset should look like:

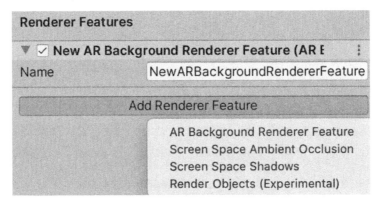

Figure 23.6 – Adding support for URP)

And that's all! We are ready to start exploring the AR Foundation components so that we can implement tracking features.

Using tracking features

For our project, we are going to need two of the most common tracking features in AR (but not the only ones): image recognition and plane detection. The first one consists of detecting the position in the real world of a specific image so that we can place digital objects on top of it, such as the player. The second one, plane detection, consists of recognizing real-life surfaces, such as floors, tables, and walls, so that we have a reference of where we can put objects such as the enemies' spawn points. Only horizontal and vertical surfaces are recognized (just vertical surfaces on some devices).

The first thing we need to do is tell our app which images it needs to detect, as follows:

1. Add an image to the project that you can print or display on a cellphone. Having a way to display the image in the real world is necessary to test this. In this case, I will use the following image:

Figure 23.7 – Image to track

> **Important Note**
>
> Try to get an image that contains as many features as you can. This means an image with lots of little details, such as contrasts, sharp corners, and so on. These are what our AR systems use to detect it; the more detail, the better the recognition. If your device has trouble detecting our current image, try other images (the classic QR code might help).

Consider that some devices might have trouble with certain images, such as the image suggested in this book. If this generates issues when testing, please try using another one. You will be testing this on your device in the upcoming sections of this chapter, so just keep this in mind.

2. Create a **Reference Image Library** asset, an asset containing all the images we wish our app to recognize, by clicking the + button in **Project Panel** and selecting **XR | Reference Image Library**:

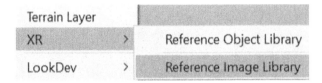

Figure 23.8 – Creating a Reference Image Library

3. Select the library asset and click the **Add Image** button to add a new image to the library.

4. Drag the texture to the texture slot (the one that says **None**).

5. Turn **Specify Size** on and set **Physical Size** to the size that your image will be in real life, in meters. Try to be accurate here; on some devices, not having this value right might result in the image not being tracked:

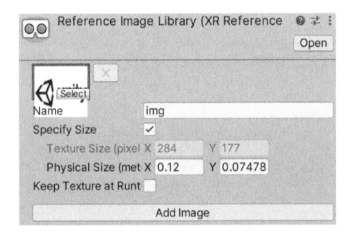

Figure 23.9 – Adding an image to be recognized

Now that we've specified the images to be detected, let's test this by placing a cube on top of the real-life image:

1. Create a prefab of a cube and add the **AR Tracked Image** component to it.

2. Add the **AR Tracked Image Manager** component to the **AR Session Origin** object. This will be responsible for detecting images and creating objects in its position.

3. Drag the **Image Library** asset to the **Serialized Library** property of the component to specify the images to be recognized.

4. Drag the **Cube** prefab to the **Tracked Image** prefab property of the component:

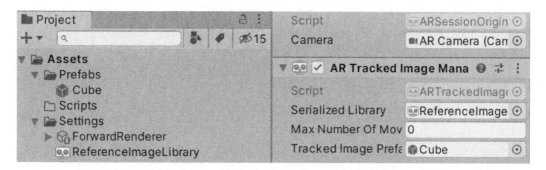

Figure 23.10 – Setting up the Tracked Image Manager

And that's all! We will see a cube spawning in the same position the image is located at in the real world. Remember that you need to test this in the device, which we will do in the next section, so for now, let's keep coding our test app:

Figure 23.11 – Cube located on top of the image being displayed by the cellphone

Let's also prepare our app so that it can detect and display the plane surfaces the camera has recognized. This is simply done by adding the **AR Plane Manager** component to the **AR Session Origin** object:

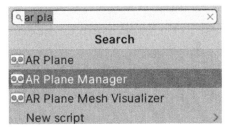

Figure 23.12 – Adding the AR Plane Manager component

This component will detect surface planes over our house as we move the camera over it. It can take a while to detect them, so it's important to visualize the detected areas to get feedback about this to ensure it's working properly. We can manually get information about the plane from a component reference to the AR Plane Manager, but luckily, Unity allows us to visualize planes easily. Let's take a look:

1. Create a prefab of a plane, first by creating the plane in **GameObject | 3D Object | Plane**.

2. Add a **Line Renderer** component to it. This will allow us to draw a line over the edges of the detected areas.

3. Set the **Width** property of the **Line Renderer** component to a small value such as 0.01, set the **Color** gradient property to black, and uncheck **Use World Space**:

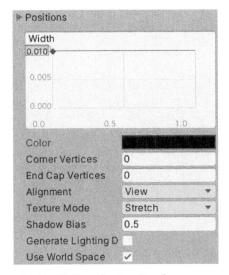

Figure 23.13 – Setting the Line Renderer component

4. Remember to create a material with the proper shader (**Universal Render Pipeline/ Unlit**) and set it as the material of the **Line Renderer** component under the **Materials** list property:

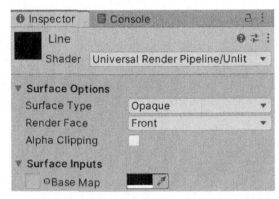

Figure 23.14 – Creating the Line Renderer Material

5. Also, create a transparent material and use it in the **MeshRenderer** plane. We want to see through it so that we can easily see the real surface beneath:

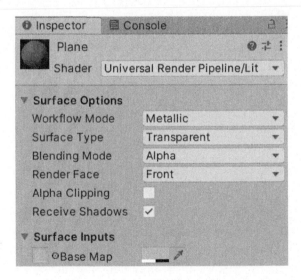

Figure 23.15 – Material for the detected plane

6. Add the **AR Plane** and **AR Plane Mesh Visualizer** components to the **Plane** prefab.

7. Drag the prefab to the **Plane Prefab** property of the **AR Plane Manager** component of the **AR Session Origin** object:

Figure 23.16 – Setting the plane visualization prefab

Now, we have a way to see the planes, but seeing them is not the only thing we can do (sometimes, we don't even want them to be visible). The real power of planes lies in placing virtual objects on top of real-life surfaces, tapping a specific plane area, and getting its real-life position. We can access the plane data using the AR Plane Manager or by accessing the AR Plane component of our visualization planes, but an easier way is to use the **AR Raycast Manager** component.

The **AR Raycast Manager** component provides us with the equivalent to the `Physics.Raycast` function of the Unity Physics system, which, as you may recall, is used to create imaginary rays that start from one position and go in a specified direction in order to make them hit surfaces and detect the exact hit point. The version provided by **AR Raycast Manager**, instead of colliding with Physics Colliders, collides with tracked objects, mostly Point Clouds (we are not using them) and the Planes we are tracking. We can test this feature by following these steps:

1. Add the **AR Raycast Manager** component to the **AR Session Origin** object.

2. Create a custom script called `InstanceOnPlane` in the **AR Session Origin** object.

3. In the **Awake** cache, add the reference to `ARRaycastManager`. You will need to add the `using UnityEngine.XR.ARFoundation;` line to the top of the script for this class to be usable in our script.

4. Create a private field of the `List<ARRaycastHit>` type and instantiate it; the Raycast is going to detect every plane our ray hit, not just the first one:

```
List<ARRaycastHit> hits = new List<ARRaycastHit>();
```

Figure 23.17 – List to store hits

5. Under **Update**, check if the Left Mouse Button (`KeyCode.Mouse0`) is being pressed. In AR apps, the mouse is emulated with the device's touch screen (you can also use the `Input.touches` array for multi-touch support).

6. Inside the `if` statement, add another condition for calling the `Raycast` function of **AR Raycast Manager**, passing the position of the mouse as the first parameter and the list of hits as the second.

7. This will throw a raycast toward the direction the player touches the screen and store the hits inside the list we provided. This will return `true` if something has been hit, and `false` if not:

```
if (Input.GetKeyDown(KeyCode.Mouse0) && raycastManager.Raycast(Input.mousePosition, hits))
{

}
```

Figure 23.18 – Throwing AR raycasts

8. Add a public field to specify the prefab to instantiate in the place we touched. You can just create a Sphere prefab to test this; there's no need to add any special component to the prefab here.

9. Instantiate the prefab in the **Position** and **Rotation** fields of the **Pose** property of the first hit stored in the list. The hits are sorted by distance, so the first hit is the closest one. Your final script should look as follows:

```
using System.Collections.Generic;
using UnityEngine;
using UnityEngine.XR.ARFoundation;

public class InstanceOnPlane : MonoBehaviour
{
    List<ARRaycastHit> hits = new List<ARRaycastHit>();
    ARRaycastManager raycastManager;
    public GameObject prefab;

    void Awake()
    {
        raycastManager = GetComponent<ARRaycastManager>();
    }

    void Update()
    {
        if (Input.GetKeyDown(KeyCode.Mouse0) && raycastManager.Raycast(Input.mousePosition, hits))
        {
            Instantiate(prefab, hits[0].pose.position, hits[0].pose.rotation);
        }
    }
}
```

Figure 23.19 – Raycaster component

In this section, we learned how to create a new AR project using AR Foundation. We discussed how to install and set up the framework, as well as how to detect real-life image positions and surfaces, and then how to place objects on top of them.

As you may have noticed, we never hit play to test this, and sadly at the time of writing this book, we cannot test this in the Editor. Instead, we need to test this directly on the device. Due to this, in the next section, we are going to learn how to do builds for mobile devices such as Android and iOS.

Building for mobile devices

Unity is a very powerful tool that solves the most common problems in game development very easily, and one of them is building the game for several target platforms. Now, the Unity part of building our project for such devices is easy to do, but each device has its non-Unity-related nuances for installing development builds. In order to test our AR app, we need to test it directly on the device. So, let's explore how we can make our app run on Android and iOS, the most common mobile platforms.

Before diving into this topic, it is worth mentioning that the following procedures change a lot over time, so you will need to find the latest instructions on the internet. The Unity Learn portal site (`https://learn.unity.com/tutorial/how-to-publish-to-android-2#5f95b4b7edbc2a00201965d4`) may be a good alternative in case the instructions in this book fail, but try the steps here first.

In this section, we will examine the following mobile building concepts:

- Building for Android
- Building for iOS

Let's start by discussing how to build our app so that it runs on Android phones.

Building for Android

Creating Android builds is relatively easy compared to other platforms, so we'll start with Android. Remember that you will need an Android device capable of running AR Foundation apps, so please refer to the link regarding Android-supported devices we mentioned in the first section of this chapter. The first thing we need to do is check whether we have installed Unity's Android support and configured our project to use that platform. To do that, follow these steps:

1. Close Unity and open **Unity Hub**.
2. Go to the **Installs** section and locate the Unity version you are working on.

3. Click the three dots button at the top-right corner of the Unity version and click **Add Modules**:

Add Modules

Show in Explorer

Uninstall

Figure 23.20 – Adding modules to the Unity version

4. Make sure **Android Build Support** and the sub-options that are displayed when you click the arrow on its left are checked. If not, check them and click the **Done** button at the bottom-right to install them:

∨ ☑ Android Build Support	Installed	1.1 GB
☑ Android SDK & NDK Tools	Installed	2.9 GB
☑ OpenJDK	Installed	70.5 MB

Figure 23.21 – Adding Android support to Unity

5. Open the AR project we created in this chapter.

6. Go to **Build Settings** (**File | Build Settings**).

7. Select the **Android** platform from the list and click the **Switch Platform** button in the bottom-right corner of the window:

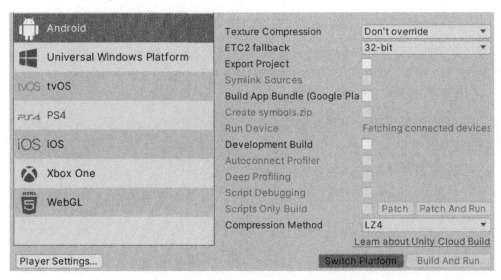

Figure 23.22 – Switching to Android builds

To build an app on Android, there are some requirements we need to meet, such as having the Java SDK (not the regular Java runtime) and Android SDK installed, but luckily, the new versions of Unity take care of that. Just to double-check that we have installed the needed dependencies, follow these steps:

1. Go to **Unity Preferences** (**Edit | Preferences** on Windows, **Unity | Preferences** on Mac).

2. Click **External Tools**.

3. Check that all the options that say …**Installed with Unity** on the Android section are checked. This means we will be using all the dependencies installed by Unity:

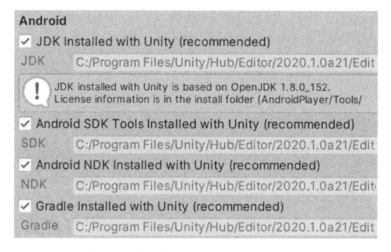

Figure 23.23 – Using installed dependencies

There are some additional Android AR Core-specific related settings to check that you can find at https://developers.google.com/ar/develop/unity-arf/ quickstart-android. These can change if you are using newer versions of AR Core. You can apply them by following these steps:

1. Go to **Player Settings** (**Edit | Project Settings | Player**).

2. Uncheck **Multithreaded Rendering** and **Auto Graphics API**.

3. Remove **Vulkan** from the **Graphics APIs** list.

4. Set **Minimum API Level** to **Android 7.0**:

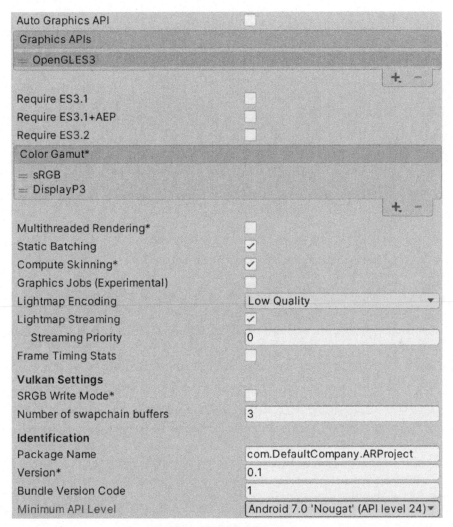

Figure 23.24 – AR Core settings

5. Go to **Edit | Project Settings** and select the **XR Plug-in Management** option.

6. Check **ARCore** under **Plug-in Providers** to make sure it will be enabled in our build; if not, we won't see anything:

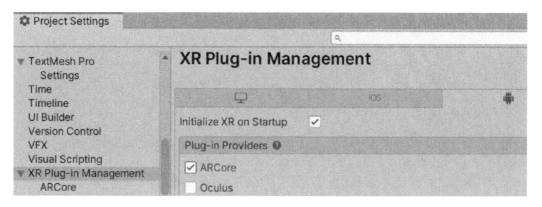

Figure 23.25 – ARCore plugin enabled

Now, you can finally build the app from **File | Build Settings** as usual, by using the **Build** button. This time, the output will be a single APK file that you can install by copying the file to your device and opening it. Remember that in order to install APKs that weren't downloaded from the Play Store, you need to set your device to allow **Install Unknown Apps**. The location for that option varies a lot depending on the Android version and the device you are using, but this option is usually located in the **Security** settings. Some Android versions prompt you to view these settings when installing the APK.

Now, we can copy and install the generated APK build file every time we want to create a build. However, we can let Unity do that for us using the **Build and Run** button. This option, after building the app, will look for the first Android device connected to your computer via USB and will automatically install the app. For this to work, we need to prepare our device and PC, as follows:

1. On your device, find the build number in the **Settings** section of the device, whose location, again, can change depending on the device. On my device, it is located in the **About Phone | Software Information** section:

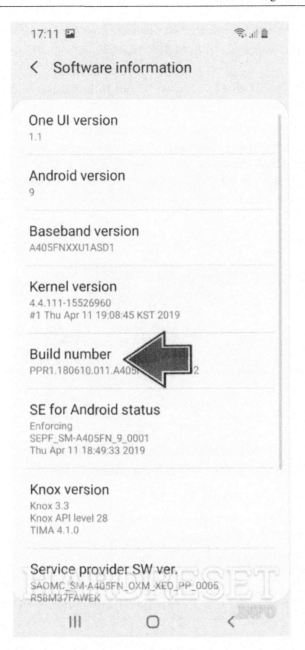

Figure 23.26 – Locating the build number

2. Tap it a few times until the device says you are now a programmer. This procedure enables the hidden developer option in the device, which you can now find in the settings.

3. Open the developer options and turn on **USB Debugging**, which allows your PC to have special permissions on your device. In this case, it allows you to install apps.

4. Install the USB drivers from your phone manufacturer's site onto your computer. For example, if you have a Samsung device, search for `Samsung USB Driver`. Also, if you can't find that, you can look for `Android USB Driver` to get the generic drivers, but that might not work if your device manufacturer has their own. On Mac, this step is usually not necessary.

5. Connect your device (or reconnect it if it's already connected). The **Allow USB Debugging** option will appear on the device. Check **Always Allow** and click **OK**:

Figure 23.27 – Allowing USB debugging

6. Accept the **Allow Data** prompt that appears.

7. If these options don't appear, check that the **USB Mode** setting of your device is set to **Debugging** and not anything else.

8. In Unity, build with the **Build and Run** button.

Please remember to try another image if you have trouble detecting the image where we instantiate the player (the Unity logo, in my case). This might vary a lot, according to your device's capabilities.

And that's all! Now that you have your app running on your device, let's learn how to do the same for the iOS platform.

Building for iOS

When developing on iOS, you will need to spend some money. You will need to run Xcode, a piece of software you can only run on OS X. Due to this, you'll need a device that can run it, such as a MacBook, a Mac mini, and so on. There may be ways to run OS X on PCs, but you will need to find this out and try it for yourself. Besides spending on a Mac and on an iOS device (iPhone, iPad, iPod, and so on), you'll need to pay for an Apple developer account, which costs 99 USD per year, even if you are not planning to release the application on the App Store (there may be alternatives, but, again, you will need to find them).

There are a few iOS-specific steps regarding AR Foundation, the following ones:

1. Go to **Edit | Project Settings** and select the **Player** option.

2. In **Other Settings**, set the **Camera Usage Description** property. This will be a message shown to the user to tell them why we need access to their camera:

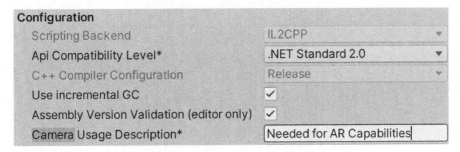

Figure 23.28 – Message regarding camera usage

3. Go to **Edit | Project Settings** and select the **XR Plug-in Management** option.

4. Check **ARKit** under **Plug-in Providers** to make sure it will be enabled in our build; if not, we won't see anything:

Figure 23.29 – ARKit plugin enabled

Now, to create an iOS build, you should do the following:

1. Get a Mac computer.

2. Get an iOS device.

3. Create an Apple developer account (at the time of writing this book, you can create one at `https://developer.apple.com/`).

4. Install the latest Xcode from the App Store onto your Mac.

5. Check whether you have iOS build support in Unity Install on the Unity Hub (please refer to the *Building on Android* section for more information about this step):

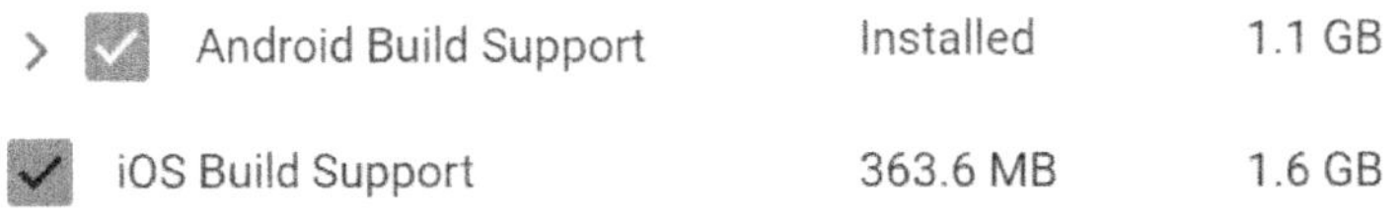

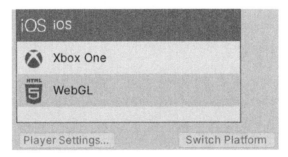

Figure 23.30 – Enabling iOS build support

6. Switch to the iOS platform under **Build Settings**, by selecting iOS and clicking the **Switch Platform** button:

Figure 23.31 – Switching to iOS build

7. Click the **Build** button in the **Build Settings** window and wait.

You will notice that the result of the build process will be a folder containing an Xcode project. Unity cannot create the build directly, so it generates a project you can open with the Xcode software we mentioned previously.

The steps you need to follow to create a build with the Xcode version being used in this book (12.4) are as follows:

1. Double-click the `.xcproject` file inside the generated folder:

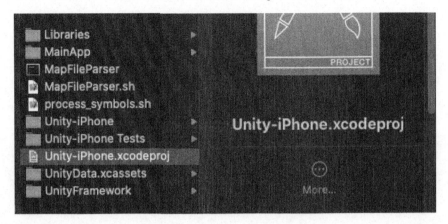

Figure 23.32 – Xcode project file

2. Go to **Xcode | Preferences**.

3. In the **Accounts** tab, hit the + button at the bottom-left part of the window and log in with your Apple developer account:

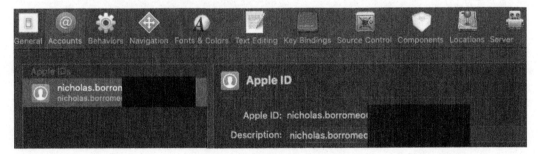

Figure 23.33 – Account settings

4. Connect your device and select it from the top-left part of the window, which should now show your iPhone's name or **Generic iOS device**:

Figure 23.34 – Selecting the device

5. Xcode might ask you to install certain updates to support your device, please install it if needed.

6. Your device might prompt you to trust your computer. Click **Trust** and enter your unlock code if requested.

7. In the left panel, click the folder icon and then the **Unity-iPhone** settings to display the project settings.

8. From the **TARGETS** list, select **Unity-iPhone** and click on the **Signing & Capabilities** tab.

9. In the **Team** settings, select the option that says **Personal Team**:

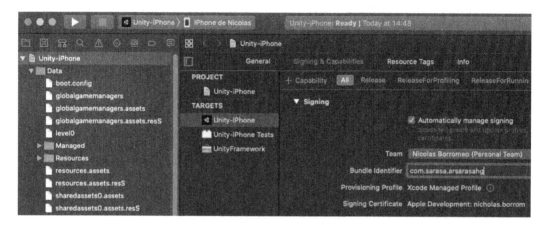

Figure 23.35 – Selecting a team

10. If you see a **Failed to register bundle identifier** error, just change the **Bundle Identifier** setting for another one, always respecting the format (com.XXXX. XXXX), and then click on **Try Again** until it is solved. Once you find one that works, set it in Unity (**Bundle Identifier** under **Player Settings**) to avoid needing to change it in every build.

11. Hit the **Play** button at the top-left part of the window and wait for the build to complete. You might be prompted to enter your password a couple of times in the process, so please do so.

12. When the build completes, remember to unlock the device. A prompt will ask you to do that. Note that the process won't continue unless you unlock the phone.

13. After completion, you may see an error saying that the app couldn't be launched but that it was installed anymore. If you try to open it, it will say you need to trust the developer of the app, which you can do by going to the settings of your device.

14. From there, go to **General | Profile & Device Management** and select the first developer in the list.

15. Click the blue **Trust ...** button and then **Trust**.

16. Open the app again.

17. Please remember to try another image if you're having trouble detecting the image where we instantiate the player (the Unity logo, in my case). This might vary a lot, depending on your device's capabilities.

In this section, we discussed how to build a Unity project that can run on iOS and Android, thus allowing us to create mobile apps – AR mobile apps, specifically. Like any build, there are methods we can follow to profile and debug, as we saw when we looked at PC builds, but we are not going to discuss that here. Now that we have created our first test project, we will convert it into a real game by adding some mechanics to it.

Creating a simple AR game

As we discussed previously, the idea is to create a simple game where we can move our player while moving a real-life image, and also put in some Enemy Spawners by just tapping where we want them to be, such as a wall, the floor, a table, and so on. Our player will automatically shoot at the nearest Enemy, and the enemies will shoot directly at the player, so our only task will be to move the Player so that they avoid bullets. We are going to implement these game mechanics using scripts very similar to the ones we used in this book's main project.

In this section, we will develop the following AR game features:

- Spawning the Player and Enemies
- Coding the Player and Enemy behavior

First, we are going to discuss how to make our Player and Enemies appear on the app, specifically in real-world positions, and then we will make them move and shoot each other to create the specified gameplay mechanics. Let's start with spawning.

Spawning the Player and Enemies

Let's start with the Player, since that's the easiest one to deal with: we will create a prefab with the graphics we want the player to have (in my case, just a cube), a `Rigidbody` with **Is Kinematic** checked (the Player will move), and an **AR Tracked Image** script. We will set that prefab as **Tracked Image Prefab** of the **AR Tracked Image Manager** component in the **AR Session Origin** object. This will put the Player on the tracked image. Remember to set the size of the Player in terms of real-life sizes. In my case, I scaled the Player to $(0.05, 0.05, 0.05)$. Since the original cube is 1 meter in size, this means that my player will be *5x5x5* centimeters. Your Player prefab should look as follows:

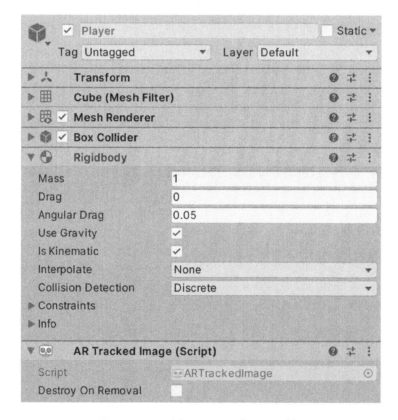

Figure 23.36 – The starting Player prefab

The enemies will require a little bit more work, as shown here:

1. Create a prefab called `Spawner` with the graphic you want your Spawner to have (in my case, a cylinder) and its real-life size.

2. Add a custom script that spawns a prefab every few seconds, such as the one shown in the following screenshot.

3. You will notice the usage of `Physics.IgnoreCollision` to prevent the Spawner from colliding with the `Spawner` object, getting the colliders of both objects and passing them to the function. You can also use the **Layer Collision Matrix** to prevent collisions, just like we did with this book's main project if you prefer to:

```csharp
using UnityEngine;

public class Spawner : MonoBehaviour
{
    public GameObject prefab;
    public float frequency;

    void Awake()
    {
        InvokeRepeating(methodName: "Spawn", time: frequency, repeatRate: frequency);
    }

    void Spawn()
    {
        var obj GameObject = Instantiate(prefab, transform.position, transform.rotation);

        var myCollider = GetComponentInChildren<Collider>();
        var spawnedCollider = obj.GetComponentInChildren<Collider>();

        //Check if both objects have collider
        if (myCollider != null && spawnedCollider != null)
        {
            Physics.IgnoreCollision(myCollider, spawnedCollider);
        }
    }
}
```

Figure 23.37 – Spawner script

4. Create an `Enemy` prefab with the desired graphic (a Capsule, in my case) and a `Rigidbody` component with the **Is Kinematic** checkbox checked. This way, the Enemy will move but not with physics. Remember to consider the real-life size of the Enemy.

5. Set the **Prefab** property of the Spawner so that it spawns the Enemy at your desired frequency:

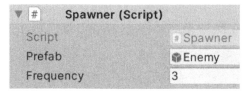

Figure 23.38 – Configuring the Spawner

6. Add a new `SpawnerPlacer` custom script to the **AR Session Origin** object that instantiates a prefab in the place the player tapped using the AR Raycast system, as shown in the following screenshot:

```csharp
using System.Collections.Generic;
using UnityEngine;
using UnityEngine.XR.ARFoundation;

public class SpawnerPlacer : MonoBehaviour
{
    List<ARRaycastHit> hits = new List<ARRaycastHit>();
    public GameObject spawnerPrefab;

    void Update()
    {
        if (Input.GetKeyDown(KeyCode.Mouse0) &&
            GetComponent<ARRaycastManager>().Raycast(Input.mousePosition, hits))
        {
            Instantiate(spawnerPrefab, hits[0].pose.position, hits[0].pose.rotation);
        }
    }
}
```

Figure 23.39 – Placing the Spawners

7. Set the prefab of `SpawnerPlacer` so that it spawns the **Spawner** prefab we created earlier.

And that's all for the first part. If you test the game now, you will be able to tap on the detected planes in the app and see how the Spawner starts creating enemies. You can also look at the target image and see our Cube Player appear.

Now that we have the objects in the scene, let's make them do something more interesting, starting with the Enemies.

Coding the Player and Enemy behavior

The Enemy must move toward the player in order to shoot at them, so it will need to have access to the player position. Since the Enemy is instantiated, we cannot drag the Player reference to the prefab. However, the Player has also been instantiated, so we can add a `PlayerManager` script to the player that uses the Singleton pattern (as we did with managers). To do that, follow these steps:

1. Create a `PlayerManager` script similar to the one shown in the following screenshot and add it to the Player:

```
using UnityEngine;

public class PlayerManager : MonoBehaviour
{
    public static PlayerManager instance;

    void Awake()
    {
        instance = this;
    }
}
```

Figure 23.40 – Creating the PlayerManager script

2. Now that the Enemy has a reference to the player, let's make them look at the player by adding a `LookAtPlayer` script, as shown here:

```
using UnityEngine;

public class LookAtPlayer : MonoBehaviour
{
    void Update()
    {
        if(PlayerManager.instance == null) return;

        transform.forward = PlayerManager.instance.transform.position - transform.position;
    }
}
```

Figure 23.41 – Creating the LookAtPlayer script

3. Also, add a simple `MoveForward` script like the one shown in the following screenshot to make the **Enemy** not only look at the player but also move toward them. Since the `LookAtPlayer` script is making the Enemy face the Player, this script moving along the *z* axis is just enough:

```
using UnityEngine;

public class MoveForward : MonoBehaviour
{
    public float speed;

    void Update()
    {
        transform.Translate(0, 0, speed * Time.deltaTime);
    }
}
```

Figure 23.42 – Creating the MoveForward script

Now, we will take care of the Player movement. Remember that our player is controlled through moving the image, so here, we are actually referring to the rotation, since the player will need to automatically look and shoot at the nearest Enemy. To do this, follow these steps:

1. Create an `Enemy` script and add it to the **Enemy** prefab.

2. Create an `EnemyManager` script like the one shown in the following screenshot and add it to an empty `EnemyManager` object in the scene:

```
using System.Collections.Generic;
using UnityEngine;

public class EnemyManager : MonoBehaviour
{
    public static EnemyManager instance;

    public List<Enemy> all = new List<Enemy>();

    void Awake()
    {
        instance = this;
    }
}
```

Figure 23.43 – Creating the EnemyManager script

3. In the Enemy script, make sure to register the object in the **all** list of EnemyManager, as we did previously with WavesManager in this book's main project:

```
using UnityEngine;

public class Enemy : MonoBehaviour
{
    void OnEnable()
    {
        EnemyManager.instance.all.Add(this);
    }

    void OnDisable()
    {
        EnemyManager.instance.all.Remove(this);
    }
}
```

Figure 23.44 – Creating the Enemy script

4. Create a LookAtNearestEnemy script like the one shown in the following screenshot and add it to the **Player** prefab to make it look at the nearest Enemy:

```
using UnityEngine;

public class LookAtNearestEnemy : MonoBehaviour
{
    void Update()
    {
        if(EnemyManager.instance.all.Count <= 0) return;

        var nearestEnemy = EnemyManager.instance.all[0];

        for (var i = 1; i < EnemyManager.instance.all.Count; i++)
        {
            var enemy = EnemyManager.instance.all[i];
            var distToNearest float = Vector3.Distance(nearestEnemy.transform.position, transform.position);
            var distToEnemy float = Vector3.Distance(enemy.transform.position, transform.position);

            if (distToEnemy < distToNearest)
                nearestEnemy = enemy;
        }

        if (nearestEnemy)
            transform.forward = nearestEnemy.transform.position - transform.position;
    }
}
```

Figure 23.45 – Looking at the nearest Enemy

Now that our objects are rotating and moving as expected, the only thing missing is shooting and damaging.

5. Create a `Life` script like the one shown in the following screenshot and add it to both the **Player** and **Enemy** components. Remember to set a value for the field for the amount of life. You will see this version of `Life` instead of needing to check whether the life amount has reached zero every frame. We have created a `Damage` function to check that damage is dealt (the `Damage` function is executed), but the other version of this book's project also works:

```csharp
using UnityEngine;

public class Life : MonoBehaviour
{
    public int amount;

    public void Damage(int damageAmount)
    {
        amount -= damageAmount;
        if(amount <= 0)
            Destroy(gameObject);
    }
}
```

Figure 23.46 – Creating a Life component

6. Create a `Bullet` prefab with the desired graphics, the collider with the **Is Trigger** checkbox on the collider checked, a `Rigidbody` component with **Is Kinematic** checked (a Kinematic Trigger Collider), and the proper real-life size.

7. Add the `MoveForward` script to the **Bullet** prefab to make it move. Remember to set the speed.

8. Add a `Spawner` script to both the **Player** and **Enemy** components and set the **Bullet** prefab as the prefab to spawn, as well as the desired spawn frequency.

9. Add a `Damager` script like the one shown in the following screenshot to the **Bullet** prefab to make bullets inflict damage on the objects they touch. Remember to set the damage:

```
using UnityEngine;

public class Damager : MonoBehaviour
{
    public int amount;

    void OnTriggerEnter(Collider other)
    {
        other.GetComponent<Life>()?.Damage(amount);
        Destroy(gameObject);
    }
}
```

Figure 23.47 – Creating a Damager script – part 1

10. Add an `AutoDestroy` script like the one shown in the following screenshot to the **Bullet** prefab to make it despawn after a while. Remember to set the destroy time:

```
using UnityEngine;

public class AutoDestroy : MonoBehaviour
{
    public float time;

    void Awake()
    {
        Destroy(gameObject, time);
    }
}
```

Figure 23.48 – Creating a Damager script – part 2

And that's all! As you can see, we basically created a new game using almost the same scripts we used in the main game, mostly because we designed them to be generic (and the game genres are almost the same). Of course, this project can be improved a lot, but we have a nice base project to create amazing AR apps.

Summary

In this chapter, we introduced the AR Foundation Unity framework and explored how to set it up and how to implement several tracking features so that we can position virtual objects on top of real-life objects. We also discussed how to build our project so that it can run on both iOS and Android platforms, which is the only way we can test our AR apps at the time of writing. Finally, we created a simple AR game based on the game we created in the main project but modified it so that it's suitable for use in AR scenarios.

With this new knowledge, you will be able to start your path as an AR app developer, creating apps that augment real objects with virtual objects by detecting the positions of the real objects. This can be applied to games, training apps, and simulations. You may even be able to find new fields of usage, so take advantage of this new technology and its new possibilities!

Well, this is the end of this journey into Unity 2021; I'm really glad you reached this point in the book. I hope this knowledge will help you to improve or start your Game Development career with one of the most versatile and powerful tools on the market, Unity. Hope to see your creations someday! See you on the road!

Packt›

Packt.com

Subscribe to our online digital library for full access to over 7,000 books and videos, as well as industry leading tools to help you plan your personal development and advance your career. For more information, please visit our website.

Why subscribe?

- Spend less time learning and more time coding with practical eBooks and Videos from over 4,000 industry professionals

- Improve your learning with Skill Plans built especially for you

- Get a free eBook or video every month

- Fully searchable for easy access to vital information

- Copy and paste, print, and bookmark content

Did you know that Packt offers eBook versions of every book published, with PDF and ePub files available? You can upgrade to the eBook version at packt.com and as a print book customer, you are entitled to a discount on the eBook copy. Get in touch with us at customercare@packtpub.com for more details.

At www.packt.com, you can also read a collection of free technical articles, sign up for a range of free newsletters, and receive exclusive discounts and offers on Packt books and eBooks.

Other Books You May Enjoy

If you enjoyed this book, you may be interested in these other books by Packt:

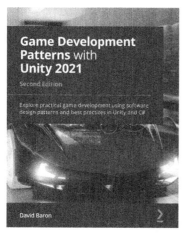

Game Development Patterns with Unity 2021 - Second Edition

David Baron

ISBN: 978-1-80020-081-4

- Structure professional Unity code using industry-standard development patterns

- Identify the right patterns for implementing specific game mechanics or features

- Develop configurable core game mechanics and ingredients that can be modified without writing a single line of code

- Review practical object-oriented programming (OOP) techniques and learn how they're used in the context of a Unity project

- Build unique game development systems such as a level editor
- Explore ways to adapt traditional design patterns for use with the Unity API

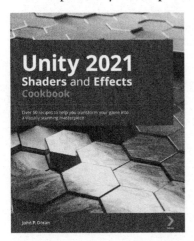

Unity 2021 Shaders and Effects Cookbook - Fourth Edition

John P. Doran

ISBN: 978-1-83921-733-3

- Understand physically based rendering to fit the aesthetic of your game
- Create eye-catching effects for your games by testing the limits of what shaders can do
- Apply advanced shaders techniques for your AAA-scale games
- Use Shader Graph to create 2D and 3D elements for your games without writing code
- Master the math and algorithms behind the most used lighting models
- Get to grips with the post-processing stack to tweak the appearance of your game effectively

Packt is searching for authors like you

If you're interested in becoming an author for Packt, please visit `authors.packtpub.com` and apply today. We have worked with thousands of developers and tech professionals, just like you, to help them share their insight with the global tech community. You can make a general application, apply for a specific hot topic that we are recruiting an author for, or submit your own idea.

Hi!

I am Nicolas Borromeo, author of Hands-on Unity 2021 Game Development Second Edition. I really hope you enjoyed reading this book and found it useful to enter the world of Game Development with Unity or improve your knowledge of it.

It would really help me (and other potential readers!) if you could leave a review on Amazon sharing your thoughts on Hands-on Unity 2021 Game Development Second Edition.

Your review will help me to understand what's worked well in this book, and what could be improved upon for future editions, so it really is appreciated.

Best Wishes,

Nicolas Borromeo

Index

Symbols

A

H

I

Printed in Great Britain
by Amazon

JEWELLERY
1789~1910
The International Era

Volume I 1789~1861

JEWELLERY
1789~1910
The International Era

Volume I 1789~1861

Shirley Bury

Antique Collectors' Club

Published for the Antique Collectors' Club
by the Antique Collectors' Club Ltd.

British Library CIP Data
Bury, Shirley
  Jewellery 1789-1910 — The International Era
  1. Jewellery, history
  I. Title
  739.2709

ISBN 1 85149 104 X (the set)
ISBN 1 85149 148 1 (Volume I)
ISBN 1 85149 149 X (Volume II)

Printed in England by the Antique Collectors' Club Ltd.,
Woodbridge, Suffolk, England

Publisher's Preface

Books of this nature are conceived, researched, written and produced over a number of years, in this
case more than a decade. As is often the case with standard works of reference, continuing research
threw up a great deal more new information than had been envisaged and so the book gradually
expanded in size.

At the same time economics of bookselling have changed so that fewer bookshops stock £100 books,
even on a key collecting subject such as nineteenth century jewellery.

It has therefore been decided to publish this book in two parts, available separately at a more
affordable price. There is logic in this approach because the book proceeds by date (inevitably some
topics stretch over the date division), and so one can choose to invest first in either the earlier or later
period according to one's preference.

*Frontispiece: Mrs Vaughan, painted by William Etty in about 1829 (see Plate 151). Reproduced by
permission of the Trustees of the National Museum of Wales.*

THE ANTIQUE COLLECTORS' CLUB

The Antique Collectors' Club was formed in 1966 and now has a five figure membership spread throughout the world. It publishes the only independently run monthly antiques magazine *Antique Collecting* which caters for those collectors who are interested in widening their knowledge of antiques, both by greater awareness of quality and by discussion of the factors which influence the price that is likely to be asked. The Antique Collectors' Club pioneered the provision of information on prices for collectors and the magazine still leads in the provision of detailed articles on a variety of subjects.

It was in response to the enormous demand for information on 'what to pay' that the price guide series was introduced in 1968 with the first edition of *The Price Guide to Antique Furniture* (completely revised, 1978 and 1989), a book which broke new ground by illustrating the more common types of antique furniture, the sort that collectors could buy in shops and at auctions rather than the rare museum pieces which had previously been used (and still to a large extent are used) to make up the limited amount of illustrations in books published by commercial publishers. Many other price guides have followed, all copiously illustrated, and greatly appreciated by collectors for the valuable information they contain, quite apart from prices. The Antique Collectors' Club also publishes other books on antiques, including horology and art reference works, and a full book list is available.

Club membership, which is open to all collectors, costs £17.50 per annum. Members receive free of charge *Antique Collecting,* the Club's magazine (published ten times a year), which contains well-illustrated articles dealing with the practical aspects of collecting not normally dealt with by magazines. Prices, features of value, investment potential, fakes and forgeries are all given prominence in the magazine.

Among other facilities available to members are private buying and selling facilities, the longest list of 'For Sales' of any antiques magazine, an annual ceramics conference and the opportunity to meet other collectors at their local antique collectors' clubs. There are over eighty in Britain and more than a dozen overseas. Members may also buy the Club's publications at special pre-publication prices.

As its motto implies, the Club is an amateur organisation designed to help collectors get the most out of their hobby: it is informal and friendly and gives enormous enjoyment to all concerned.

For Collectors — By Collectors — About Collecting

The Antique Collectors' Club, 5 Church Street, Woodbridge, Suffolk

For Morley

Contents

Preface and Acknowledgements

This study had its genesis in the Exhibition of Victorian and Edwardian Art staged in commemoration of the centenary of the Victoria and Albert Museum in 1952. The late Peter Floud, CBE, the Keeper of Circulation, lined up his four young and hopeful research assistants and allocated various areas to them; mine included jewellery and silver. Afterwards only one, John Lowry, changed course and ended up in the Indian Department. The others, Barbara Morris, the late Elizabeth Aslin and myself, were hooked for life. So this is a salute to a fruitful association.

The jewellery in the 1952 exhibition, aside from pieces by Pugin, was almost wholly the product of the Arts and Crafts Movement. Arts and Crafts work figures in Margaret Flower's pioneering *Victorian Jewellery*, which appeared in 1951, with illustrations of fashion plates and photographs as well as a high percentage of goldsmith's or secondary jewellery in gold or silver set with comparatively modest stones. The unprecedented expansion of the middle market in the nineteenth century seemed to invite further investigation into its causes and its connection with the production of expensive jewellery lavishly adorned with precious stones on the one hand and with imitation or costume trinkets on the other. The discovery of huge new sources of minerals was plainly a decisive factor, as was the advance of technology, modified by revolutions, wars and politics.

Changes in fashion invariably stemmed from the leading firms in Paris, followed at some distance by those in London, Rome, Vienna and elsewhere (including, later, New York), where designers and designer-jewellers played a dominant role. These concerns accommodated themselves to the predilections of their most important clients, as Nitot undoubtedly did to the Empress Josephine. George IV, one of the greatest English royal patrons, even when young and impecunious, was similarly served by Rundell's and other firms, as were Queen Victoria and Prince Albert later by Garrard's. I have been fortunate in being able to investigate the relationship between the royals and their jewellers.

I must express my great gratitude at receiving the gracious permission of Her Majesty the Queen to use the Royal Archives at Windsor, to quote from them and to reproduce paintings, photographs and drawings in the Royal Collection, the Royal Archives and the Royal Library. I gratefully acknowledge the help of two successive Royal Librarians, Sir Robin Mackworth-Young, KCVO and Mr Oliver Everett, LVO, of three Registrars of the Royal Archives, Miss Jane Langton, CVO, Miss Elizabeth Cuthbert, LVO and Lady de Bellaigue, MVO, of the Hon. Mrs Jane Roberts, CVO, Curator of the Print Room, the Royal Library, Miss Frances Dimond, MVO, Curator of the Photographic Archives, the Royal Archives and of Sir Oliver Millar, KCVO, FBA, FSA, now Surveyor Emeritus of the Queen's Pictures. Sir Geoffrey de Bellaigue, KCVO, FSA, Director of the Royal Collection and Mr Marcus Bishop, MVO, the Registrar, have both been immensely kind over this project and another, initiated by Sir

Geoffrey, of preparing a catalogue raisonné of the Crown Jewels in the Tower of London, from my own part in which I have learned an immense amount.

The first drafts of this study date to the 1970s and two at least were read by Mrs Elaine Barr, FSA. This act of generosity was compounded more recently when she read and commented on the galley proofs, for which she has my lasting gratitude. There were plans afoot for the Museum to publish the study before I retired in 1985 but disaster struck when a colleague was the unwitting cause of the loss of over a hundred key transparencies and black and white photographs. The Chief Administrative Officer, Mr J.W. Close, managed to replace some of them but many which I had specially commissioned were irreplaceable. The shock was the worse because it was clear that parts of the text would have to be entirely re-written. I temporarily abandoned the project.

The reaction of friends and colleagues over the next few years was heart-warming. Pursuing all possible leads — even to the extent of borrowing pieces from fellow-students at an evening class — they jointly and severally came up with a more comprehensive sampling of jewellery than I could have hoped to have achieved on my own. Alas that such kindness cannot be acknowledged, for they have all requested anonymity. But friends and acquaintances in the antique trade, who have been generous with photographs and transparencies, can however be thanked.

There was ample cause here to return to the text again, but I had meanwhile retired and was immersed in the regalia. In December 1988 my section of the catalogue entries was handed over to the editor, Mr Claude Blair, FSA and I was forcibly impelled back to the book. The Court of the Worshipful Company of Goldsmiths had generously given me a grant towards publication when Mr C.P. de B. Jenkins MBE, MC was Clerk. Naturally I was immensely grateful. This was subsequently commuted into a loan to my new publisher, Mr John Steel of the Antique Collectors' Club. The new Clerk, Mr R.D. Buchanan-Dunlop, CBE and Mr Steel proved an irresistible joint force. Between December 1988 and June 1989 (appropriately approaching the bi-centenary of the French Revolution with which the book opens) the new sections were written and in a sustained fit of enthusiasm twenty-seven chapters were 'lop't and crop't' into seventeen (including the Introduction). 80,000 words were jettisoned, including innumerable footnotes, though a great many still remain to enable statements to be verified and indicate areas of further research.

In the long period of the book's gestation, I was fortunate in having congenial colleagues in all three Museum departments in which I served. To Claude Blair, my predecessor as Keeper of Metalwork, I owe an incalculable debt. He has always been generous in imparting the results of his research and generous, too, with encouragement. The following, who have all been most helpful, are listed without regard to department. Some have retired, a few have died and several have taken their talents elsewhere. To use the (unfamiliar) formal mode, they are Miss Elizabeth Aslin; Dr Charles Avery, FSA; Mrs Elizabeth Bonython, FRSA; Mrs Frances Bryant; Mr Anthony Burton; Mr Martin Chapman; Mr Robert Charleston, FSA; Mr David Coachworth; Miss Anna Somers Cocks, FSA; Mrs

F.B. de B. Crichton, who patiently worked through the jewellery holdings with me in the course of rearranging the collection in the Jewellery Gallery; Dr Richard Edgcumbe; Mrs Philippa Glanville, FSA; Mrs Patricia Griffiths (Wardle); Mr John Harthan, FLA; Mr Carol Hogben; Mr Simon Jervis, FSA; Miss Vera Kaden; Professor C.M. Kauffmann, FMA; Mr Robert Kenedy; Ms Julie Laird; Miss Susan Lambert; Mr Lionel Lambourne; Mr Ronald Lightbown, FSA, FRAS; Mr John Mallet, FSA, FRSA; Mrs Barbara Morris; Mr A.R.E. North, FSA; Miss Deirdre O'Day; Mrs Estelle O'Dwyer; Mrs Felicity Oldham; Mr Charles Oman, FSA; Dr John Physick, FSA; Miss Natalie Rothstein; Mrs Jean Schofield; Mr Michael Snodin, FSA; Mrs Jane Stancliffe; Mr Peter Thornton, FSA; Mr Charles Truman, FSA; Mr Eric Turner and Mrs Alexandra Wedgwood, FSA.

The following must also be thanked for their help in the course of researching for this book: Mrs Pamela Ansell; Miss Felicity Ashbee; the Hon. Mrs I.A. Astor; the Duke of Atholl; Mr David Beasley, Librarian, Goldsmiths' Company; Mr Brian Beaumont-Nesbitt, FRSA; Miss Vivienne Becker; Mrs Phyllis Benedikz, Librarian, Assay Office, Birmingham; Mr David Bennett and his colleagues at Sotheby's, Miss Alexandra Rhodes, Dr Daniela Mascetti, Miss Claire Parker and Mr Jonathan Condrup; Mrs Rhoda Bickerdike; Mrs Joan Blair; Dr John Blair; Mrs Georgiana Blakiston; Mr Alf Bøe; Mrs Janet Boyd-Brent; Mr John Brandon-Jones, FRIBA, FSA; Mrs Ursula Brock; Mademoiselle Yvonne Brunhammer, Musée des Arts Décoratifs, Paris; Mr Edmund Bulmer, MP; Mr David Callaghan, Hancocks & Co.; Mrs Joscelyne V. Charlewood-Turner; Mr John Christian; Miss Hilary Clarke; Miss Julia Clarke, Sotheby's; Mr Alan Crawford; Mrs Elaine Dee, formerly of the Cooper-Hewitt Museum; Madame Marie-Noël de Gary and Madame Monique Kenedy, Musée des Arts Décoratifs, Paris; Mr Edward Donohoe; Miss Lyn Ehrhard; Dr Fritz Falk, Pforzheim Museum; Miss Susan Farmer, Diamond Information Centre; Miss Mary Feilden, Christie's; Mrs Ferguson; Dr Maria Teresa Gomes Ferreira, the Calouste Gulbenkian Museum, Lisbon; Mrs Margaret Flower; Mrs O. Fossard; Mrs Charlotte Gere, National Art-Collections Fund; Mrs Halina Graham, Cecil Higgins Art Gallery, Bedford; Mr Keith Grant-Peterkin; Miss Rosamund Griffin, the Waddesdon Bequest; Mr Arthur Grimwade, FSA, formerly of Christie's; Dr Yvonne Hackenbroch, FSA, formerly of the Metropolitan Museum, New York; Mrs Raizel Halpin; Viscount Hampden; the late Mr and Mrs Charles Handley-Read; Dr Roger Harding, Gem-testing Laboratory of Great Britain; Miss Susan Hare, FSA, formerly Librarian, Goldsmiths' Hall; Mrs Amanda Herries, Museum of London; Mr Bevis Hillier; Mr Peter Hinks; Mr Graham Hughes, FSA; Mrs Colta Ives, Print Room, Metropolitan Museum of Art; Mrs Dora Jane Janson; Mr John Jesse; Mr E. Allan Jobbins, formerly of the Geological Museum; Mr Eric Kelly, Bank of England archives; Mr Landsberg; Miss Irina Laski; Mr Donald P. McClelland, SITES, Washington; Mr David Revere McFadden, the Cooper-Hewitt Museum; Dr Stephan Tschudi Madsen; Mr A. Kenneth Snowman, Mr Geoffrey Munn, Mr Stephen Dale and Mr Robert Parsons, of Wartski's; Mr Brian Norman, Harvey & Gore; the Norton family of S.J. Phillips; Mr Jack Ogden, FSA; Mr Andrew McIntosh Patrick and Mr Peyton Skipwith, the Fine Art Society; Miss Mary

Peerless; Miss Orrea Pernel; Miss Madeleine Popper; Professor Michael Port, FSA; Miss Rosemary Ransome-Wallis, Goldsmiths' Hall; Miss Judy Rudoe, British Museum; Mr and Mrs Joseph Sataloff; Mrs Diana Scarisbrick, FSA; Professor Phoebe Stanton; Mrs Virginia Surtees; Mr Hugh Tait, British Museum; Mrs Gulderen Tekvar; Mr Mark Turner, Silver Studio Collection; Mrs Jane Vickers; Mrs Jane Wainwright, House of Commons Library; Mr A. Weisberg; the Duke of Wellington; Mr A.H. Westwood; Miss Glennys Wild, Birmingham City Museum and Art Gallery; Mrs Joan Wilson; Mr Paul Wood, Sotheby's.

Warm gratitude is due to Miss Primrose Elliott, my editor at the Antique Collectors' Club, who with calm competence steered me through the complex operations of correcting and cross-referencing. Mrs Diana Steel kindly found time from her usual responsibilities to take additional photographs; I also owe thanks to Mr Andrew Winton, the designer and Mrs Sandra Pond, the typesetter.

My debt to Mr John Culme of Sotheby's, ever willing to share information (among other things, he introduced me to the lawsuit over the Pigot diamond which is discussed in the text) has been made the greater by his organisation of the index. Rowland and Betty Elzea of the Delaware Art Museum have nobly kept me in touch with exhibitions in the United States of America; Mrs Audrey Procter has turned many a palimpsest into type; and my husband Morley has sustained my spirits even in adversity. The book is dedicated to him.

Thanks are also due to the many organisations and institutions, public and private, whose possessions are illustrated.

Finally I must acknowledge with gratitude the kindness of the following firms in furnishing photographs and transparencies: Maurice Asprey Ltd.; The Clarendon Gallery Ltd.; Collingwood of Bond Street, Ltd.; Scott Cooper Ltd., Cheltenham; Donohoe; Hancocks & Co. (Jewellers) Ltd.; Harvey & Gore; John Jesse; Nigel Milne Ltd.; S.J. Phillips Ltd.; Silver; Wartski; and Whitfield & Hughes.

Photographers include Stanley Eost and Peter MacDonald, Sally Chappell, A. & C. Cooper, Mike Kitcatt, Christine Smith, Ben O'Dwyer, Philip de Bay.

As a rider, I should point out that slips in the text spotted after the book had gone to press have been corrected as far as possible in the next footnote and in the index. Some errors however need remarking: (p. 229) for Alexis read Lucien Falize; (p. 237) for Antonio Calvi, read Carli; (p. 278) for Sir Edward Landseer, read Sir Edwin; (p. 396) of course the bracelet bought by Queen Victoria was intended for female wear, though as a result of a misapplied correction it now appears in doubt; (p. 485) for North America, read Africa; (p.652) for Edward read Eugène Colonna; for *japonoiserie* read *japonaiserie*.

Shirley Bury
1991

Unless otherwise stated, all objects are illustrated approximately actual size.

INTRODUCTION
Setting the Scene

Parisian fashions in dress and jewellery had captured the imagination of women all over Europe and beyond long before the French Revolution broke out in 1789. Thereafter curiosity had either to be reconciled to patriotism or suppressed. England, the most consistent of her enemies, was at war with France from 1793 until 1815 with two intermissions, the first during the Peace of Amiens of 1802-03 and the second from Napoleon's first abdication in April 1814 until his escape from Elba in February 1815. The almost unseemly haste with which prominent Englishmen and women rushed to Paris on the first occasion to see for themselves and if possible to meet the legendary Napoleon and Josephine, and the equal celerity with which they came again, especially after the final defeat of Napoleon at Waterloo in June 1815, was loudly deplored by some of their patriotic contemporaries. Such disapproval was disregarded by the Englishwomen who found themselves in France. For years they had had perforce to content themselves with often unreliable reports of French modes in English magazines. At last they had the opportunity of observing and judging fashions at first hand, even if some of them concluded that they were perhaps too advanced for home consumption.

It was not only that Paris had a reputation for innovation, creativity and luxury. The French trades and their patrons were credited with the power of making or breaking external fashions that came their way. Though many English manufactures were excluded by Imperial decree from the Austrian Empire from November 1784, the Anglomania which swept Europe before the Revolution had been accorded the imprimatur of Paris, a far more important consideration. The American envoy Gouverneur Morris (his first name was his mother's surname), writing from Paris to George Washington on 3 March 1789, declared: 'Every Thing is *à l'Anglois* and a Desire to imitate the English prevails alike in the Cut of a Coat and the Form of a Constitution.'[1] Tom Paine aside, it was a profitable time for English manufacturers and exporters, among whom was Matthew Boulton, whose cut steel trinkets (see Colour Plate 1C) prompted the French to start up their own manufactories. In the course of the nineteenth century Paris was to invoke the same power, usually with considerable success. The magic failed in a very few instances, most notably in the international vogue for archaeological jewellery in the classical mode which was dominated by the productions of the firm of Castellani of Rome from the 1830s to the 1870s and beyond (Colour Plates 105 and 141). Parisian jewellers produced elegant variations on the style without denting the pre-eminence of Castellani.

The leading British jewellery firms all had contacts with Paris and other parts of the Continent. Though more than a hundred years had elapsed since the arrival of the Huguenots, French was still the common language of jewellery workshops in London, especially in Soho, to where many subsequent immigrants found their

Colour Plate 1. A. An aigrette set with brilliants, an emerald, turquoises and other coloured stones, about 1810; some of the coloured stones were added in the 1820s or '30s.
B. A pendant with a carnelian (an alternative term for cornelian) intaglio of Jupiter and Venus with Cupid, set in enamelled gold. Probably by the gem-engraver Luigi Pichler (1773-1854) and acquired as an antique by Prince Stanislaus Poniatowski (1754-1833) for his collection of engraved gems which were discovered after his death to be largely fakes.
C. Cut steel fob, probably by Boulton's Soho Manufactory, set with a jasper medallion and hung with a jasper vinaigrette by Wedgwood. On one side is a profile portrait of George Prince of Wales, modelled by John Lochée, who worked for Wedgwood's 1774-88; the Prince of Wales' feathers are on the reverse. Boulton started mounting Wedgwood jasper medallions in 1773; the fob probably dates to about 1785.

VICTORIA AND ALBERT MUSEUM

Colour Plate 2. George Prince of Wales in 1792, a miniature by Richard Cosway, RA, which depicts him in a Cavalier dress and a lace collar modified by an eighteenth century cravat. The Garter cloak with Star is draped across his shoulders and the George hangs from a ribbon around his neck. The romantic impression is reinforced by powdered hair. The miniature is set in a hinged gold fausse-montre *with his arms on the front and his cipher and motto on the back, which also contains a plait of brown hair.*

NATIONAL PORTRAIT GALLERY

way. Some firms had been founded by immigrants. François Jean Duval, born in Geneva, came to London before 1748; by 1753 his brother Louis David Duval had followed him. Within a few years Louis David was off to St Petersburg, where he worked in association with Jéremé Pauzie. Duval was still in Russia in 1801; in 1816 his workshop had passed to his son Jean François André Duval. Meanwhile François Jean (John) Duval[2] (associated with Peter Duval) was appointed jeweller to George III (Plate 1), who had succeeded to the throne in 1760 and married Princess Charlotte of Mecklenburg-Strelitz in 1761 (Plates 2-4). Years later, Queen Charlotte had descriptive plates attached to her jewel boxes, one of which read: 'This box contains the great pearls which the King calls Family pearls, and were given to me at my arrival in England in 1761; they were by the King's leave, and the recommendation of Mr Duval, the then King's jeweller, afterwards re-set, and consist of a necklace of forty-one pearls . . .; a pair of single-drop ear-rings, set round with diamonds; three bows, set round with brilliants, the drops make the centre of the bows.'[3] The fate of these pieces, documented in consequence of the Hanoverian Claim to the Crown Jewels, is considered in Chapters V, VII and Appendix II.

Rundell & Bridge, successors to Pickett & Rundell and later styled Rundell, Bridge & Rundell before reverting to Rundell, Bridge & Company, were among the most international of the London firms. From their principal premises in Ludgate Hill in the City of London they conducted a flourishing trade as dealers in stones and finished jewellery on the Continent and in South America. Catherine the Great of Russia was said to have been 'an excellent Customer' before her death in 1796.[4] In 1804 they were appointed the principal royal goldsmiths to George III, possibly at the behest of the Prince of Wales,[5] though like all the Hanoverian monarchs and their heirs neither was usually inclined to take the other's advice. The King and Queen, now the parents of a large and sometimes resentful family, were not renowned for their devotion to current vogues, though they remained fully alive to the importance of jewellery in reinforcing the image of majesty.

The firm's principal patron was the Prince of Wales (Colour Plates 1C and 2), amateur antiquary and connoisseur of fashions which he indulged with an

Plate 1. King George III in his coronation costume of 1761, by Allan Ramsay, 1762. His tunic and breeches are cloth-of-gold, his robes of red velvet, lined with ermine. He wears the Collar of the Garter over his shoulders, the Garter just below his knee and a pair of shoe-buckles set with diamonds from the Hanoverian Crown Jewels which were later claimed by Queen Victoria's uncle, the King of Hanover (see Appendix II).   ROYAL COLLECTION

Plate 2. Charlotte of Mecklenburg-Strelitz, Queen of George III, wearing part of her marriage jewellery of 1761, including the 'family pearls'. Drawn from life and engraved by Frye; published on 24 May 1762.

uninhibited extravagance regardless of whether he had the money to spend. As the war went on, Britain's isolation from the Continent drove her to a greater dependence on her own agriculture; landowners and farmers prospered in consequence. Some of the enhanced riches found their way into Rundell's coffers as the Prince's admirers decided to buy plate and jewellery, not only for themselves, but for their wives and mistresses. Rundell's executed many jewelled orders, the most showy of male jewels, which in the course of the war were increasingly massed on the chests of royalties, courtiers, diplomats, politicians and military and naval heroes.

The fortunes of war accelerated the arrival of Continental craftsmen and others in England. Rundell's chief diamond-setter and jeweller designer Philippe (Philip) Liebart,[6] a native of Liège, seems to have joined them as a result of the French invasion of the Low Countries in 1793; as the French moved on to Holland, members of the Hope family, the bankers, merchants and diamond dealers, also transferred to London.[7] Henry Hope's celebrated collection of diamonds, partly

Colour Plate 3. A. Padlock pendant of garnets set in gold cut-down collets; in the centre is a curl of hair decorated with gold wire and covered by rock crystal (quartz). B. Padlock locket set with seed pearls and blue glass paste also embellished with pearls and hung with a gold heart and key. These two sentimental tokens are English, c.1800.

VICTORIA AND ALBERT MUSEUM

dispersed in 1839, included the eponymous blue diamond exhibited at the Great Exhibition of 1851. It is now in the collection of the Smithsonian Institution, Washington.

Liebart was greatly trusted by the senior partner in the Ludgate Hill firm. Philip Rundell despatched him secretly to Paris in 1804 with a selection of jewellery and the great Pigot diamond, in which the firm had a share, with instructions to try to sell them to Napoleon, who was known to be acquiring jewels on a large scale for his Coronation in December. The mission was extremely delicate, as Britain and France were again at war, and though negotiations were conducted through an intermediary, Napoleon got wind of the source of the articles and Liebart had to beat a hasty retreat leaving the jewellery behind him. The story is recounted in more detail in Chapter II; it is mentioned here to demonstrate that Rundell's were confident that their jewellery was in the French taste. This was probably due to Liebart, who might well have had previous experience of working in Paris. It was also helped by the presence of French aristocratic refugees in England who had been forced to realise their portable wealth in order to support themselves in exile. The diamond market all over Europe outside France was glutted with the jewels sold by emigrés and prices dropped sharply in consequence. Given the unsettled times, most jewellers were reluctant to buy. Rundell's stepped in boldly and later made a profit of between two and three hundred per cent on their investment.[8]

The Prince of Wales, but for the accident of war, would undoubtedly have bought extensively from Paris. Comparatively few of his bills dating to before the Revolution of 1789 have survived, but they include an account running from 1784 to 1786 with one John Gregson of Paris, who supplied an enamelled and gem-set watch among other items through an agent, Robert Fogg of New Bond Street. The Prince is known also to have patronised the Parisian watchmaker Lépine.[9] The London firms were to become an acceptable substitute for Parisian concerns, though it must be said that the Prince spread his custom over a wide field of at least forty-four goldsmiths, jewellers and watchmakers, on the evidence of the bills which have been preserved.[10]

In 1784, the Sub-Governor to the royal princes, Lieutenant-Colonel George Hotham, wrote to the twenty-two year old Prince to reproach him for being

Plate 3. Queen Charlotte in robes of state, wearing a jewelled sprig in her hair, a diamond necklace tight around her throat, her great diamond stomacher (made in three sections to allow a little flexibility) and pearls on her wrists, all part of her marriage jewellery of 1761, which was presented to her by George III on her arrival in England. The Queen's left hand touches her Crown, also included in her wedding jewellery. Studio of Allan Ramsay, c.1762.
NATIONAL PORTRAIT GALLERY

Plate 4. This portrait of Queen Charlotte by Sir Thomas Lawrence, painted in 1789, did not find favour with the King and Queen, who gave very few sittings. Her assistant dresser, Mrs Papendiek, was deputed to pose to the artist wearing the Queen's bracelets, the gift of her husband. One was set with a portrait miniature of King George III and the other with his cipher in hair.
NATIONAL GALLERY

already at the mercy of his builder, upholsterer, jeweller and tailor.[11] The Prince's passion for building and decorating in a variety of historic styles is now commemorated only by the Oriental fantasy of Brighton Pavilion and Wyatville's later gothicisation of Windsor Castle. Enormous sums were also poured into the extension, decoration and furnishing of Carlton House, the great mansion which is commemorated only in the portico of the National Gallery and the street known as Carlton House Terrace, built on its site. But all the stylistic experimentation that went into the architecture eventually found expression in jewellery, for the artists and designers working for the trade were willing and able to try their hand at reproducing historic manners (Plates 91A-C).

The Prince of Wales, self-centred but good natured and fond of his numerous brothers and sisters, did his best to help them in difficult circumstances. His younger brothers had been despatched to Germany by their father, anxious to protect them from his profligate example. His sisters were kept in attendance on their mother and those who eventually managed to marry did so with difficulty.

Plate 5. Mrs Fitzherbert, a detail engraved by Roffe from a full length portrait by Richard Cosway of her in a sylvan setting. The original must date to shortly after she and the Prince of Wales went through a marriage ceremony in December 1785, though the portrait medallion she wears is too crude to be identified as depicting the Prince. Her long Roman nose is, however, clearly delineated.

The Prince of Wales had also to provide jewels for his unacknowledged wife, Mrs Maria Fitzherbert (Plate 5), already twice widowed before she married the Prince at a secret ceremony in 1785,[12] and for a variety of mistresses as well as for his cousin Princess Caroline of Brunswick,[13] whom he took as his legal wife in 1795 in an attempt to secure Parliamentary agreement to clear his debts.[14] The marriage produced a child, Princess Charlotte of Wales,[15] who was born in January 1796. A few months later the Prince effactually parted from his wife.

Immured on the Continent until George III was forced to recall them for fear of their being taken hostage by the French, the Prince's brothers importuned him with requests for jewels to which he usually, though belatedly, responded. In the 1780s their demands were modest. On 9 February 1781 Prince Frederick (later the Duke of York)[16] wrote to say that if 'there is anything new in London in the buckle way I should be glad to have it.' With remarkable swiftness the Prince of Wales replied on 30 March, promising the buckles and alluding to a sword decorated with 'a mixture of gold and steel beads', one of two weapons which Gray (probably Thomas Gray of Sackville Street) was making for his brother. On 10 April the Prince of Wales reported that both swords were ready and he was about to send them with the buckles and 'a watch & chain wh. I hope you will like & wear for my sake. Ye hair in ye chain is mine...'[17] Quantities of buckles were despatched from London to the royal siblings in the course of the next few years, and hair was frequently set in jewellery exchanged with his family, a practice which found widespread favour with others of lesser birth (Colour Plate 3A).

In 1791 the Duke of York made a match with Princess Frederica of Prussia.[18] Rumours of the impending marriage came to the ears of Nathaniel Jefferys,[19] goldsmith to Queen Charlotte and goldsmith and jeweller to the Prince of Wales and the Duke of York. He promptly went to see the Prince and asked for a letter which would give him access to the Duke in Berlin. He got it; the Prince was already in debt to him. The Prince's covering note to his brother from London, dated 29 July, shows something of English trade practice before the outbreak of war in 1793. Jefferys, he said, 'always took a tour abroad every summer [together,

19

Colour Plate 4. The Duchess of Devonshire, a miniature by Richard Cosway set in a diamond surround; c.1785. CHRISTIE'S

clearly, with a selection of his stock]...he meant at first merely to have gone to Bruxelles, but...having heard a report...he intended on every account to push on to Berlin,' and had reminded the Prince of 'his devotion & attachment both to you & me...' Jefferys' efforts were rewarded and the Duke wrote on 5 September, 'I have taken the spray and a pair of earrings which I think are very handsome, and have chosen some designs for the necklace & earrings, but have referred him totally to you as you are in every respect a much better judge than myself; and besides, you will be able to know whether the King has already given orders about the diamonds or not. I think it will be impossible for me to go to a less expence than between fifteen and twenty thousand pounds for the diamonds, as I remember that those of the Dutchess of Devonshire cost ten thousand and do not make a great shew...'[20] The Duchess, one of the celebrated beauties of the age (Colour Plate 4), was a close friend of the Prince of Wales.

The Prince of Wales duly dealt with Jefferys, who must have raised his prices. The Duke complained bitterly that Jefferys 'does not now stick to what he at first said'. The Duke's horses were probably sacrificed to help meet the revised demands after the marriage. The wedding took place in Berlin on 29 September, but the re-marriage in England, essential under the Royal Marriage Act, occurred only on 23 November, the bride wearing in her headdress three brilliant pins presented by King George III. At an extra Drawing-room held in her honour at St James's Palace the following day, the Duchess, dressed in white and silver, wore at the top of her bodice 'a very large bow of brilliants, with a splendid lacing of the same...' and on her head 'a very large double sprig of brilliants of uncommon lustre,' together with a brilliant bandeau and George III's three pins, which were reported to be star-shaped. She was also garnished with diamond earrings given her by the Queen 'and a number of other rich ornaments of brilliants, which sparkled with uncommon lustre.'[21]

Nathaniel Jefferys, after his triumphant pre-emptive strike, received the even grander commission to make Princess Caroline of Brunswick's marriage jewellery in 1795. The Prince of Wales' bride necessarily had to have a suite of jewellery of surpassing importance and Jefferys set about garnering the best available diamonds from the trade. Buoyed up by his profits on the French jewels he had acquired so cheaply, according to his former shopman, George Fox, Philip

Colour Plate 5. A diamond-framed pre-Revolutionary miniature of Henrietta-Lucy Dillon (Madame de la Tour du Pin) wearing large pearl drop earrings. The daughter of one of Marie-Antoinette's ladies, she was married before the Revolution, from which she managed to escape with her husband and family. For a time they farmed in the United States of America, where Talleyrand visited them, restoring to its rightful owner a portrait cameo of the French Queen which had been impounded. Returning during the First Empire, Madame de la Tour du Pin wrote the first part of her Memoirs, dating them 1 January 1820, a few months before her husband was created a Marquis and appointed Ambassador in Turin. They fell from grace in 1831 when their son supported the Duchesse de Berri in the insurrection in the Vendée. She wrote the second part of her memoirs after her husband's death in 1835, while residing in Italy.
SOTHEBY'S

Rundell decided to speculate on supplying some of the diamonds needed by Jefferys. The set of jewellery was duly made and delivered to the Prince; the necklace alone, wrote Fox, 'being of the value of Thirty five Thousand Pounds and the rest of the suit in proportion...'[22]

The Prince of Wales' marriage was unhappily a financial as well as a personal disaster. His debts, settled by Parliament in 1787 on condition that he managed his finances better in future, subsequently grew again to alarming proportions. All the royal brothers were in financial difficulties, blaming their father for keeping them on a tighter rein than they felt they merited, but the Prince of Wales' debts were on an heroic scale. The brothers engineered loans at home and on the Continent; the money disappeared almost as soon as they got it.

By 1795 the Prince's debts had accumulated to some £630,000[23] and a body of Commissioners was appointed to deal with his affairs. His creditors were requested to submit statements of their claims but the Commission subjected them to close scrutiny, challenging them when the amounts seemed excessive. Jefferys was among those affected. He had claimed a total of £85,028.19s.6d., of which the marriage jewels for the Princess of Wales cost £54,685. The Commissioners proposed to deduct £14,000 from the overall sum, but Jefferys asked leave to appeal and won his case. The Commissioners then requested an abatement of ten per cent. After consulting his political friends and his lawyers and under threat from his creditors, Jefferys agreed.[24] He confided in 1797 to Joseph Farington, the artist and diarist, that he had gone to see the Prime Minister, William Pitt, who took off thirty per cent and told him that he would have to resort to law again if he wished to challenge the decision.[25] Jefferys declared himself ruined, gave up his shop and briefly became a property agent. George Fox, probably exaggerating in the interests of dramatic effect, held that Rundell's lost about £30,000 in the transaction.[26] Jefferys continued to air his grievances, culminating in the publication of a pamphlet in 1806, *A Review of the conduct of...the Prince of Wales in his various transactions with Mr J...* Farington first heard of it from an acquaintance on 17 June and the following day purchased a copy at Jefferys' premises in Pall Mall.[27] What had been formerly the subject of gossip became an open scandal and the Prince's reputation was further diminished. His discarded wife had long since proclaimed her wrongs to her intimates, alleging that the Prince had reclaimed bracelets from her and given them to his mistress, Lady Jersey.[28]

The Prince of Wales never enjoyed the same popularity as his father, even when he was made Regent in 1811 after the onset of George III's final and lasting attack of madness. But his excesses, though loudly deplored, failed seriously to affect the standing of the monarchy, despite fears to the contrary. It was otherwise in France, where the luxuriousness of the Court of Versailles was increasingly resented and Queen Marie Antoinette was unwittingly embroiled in a scandal over a costly diamond necklace.

The necklace, reputedly made as a speculation by the court jewellers Böhmer et Baszanger in 1774 in the hope that it would be acquired by Louis XV for his favourite, Madame du Barry, had not been finished when the King died and Louis XVI succeeded him. A confidence trickster of noble birth, Jeanne de la Rémy (Madame La Motte), pretending to act on the instructions of Marie Antoinette, persuaded Cardinal de Rohan in January 1785 to purchase the necklace on behalf of the Queen, who would reimburse him afterwards. The Cardinal, who was out of favour with the Queen, leapt at the chance of ingratiating himself with her. He accordingly negotiated with the jewellers over their asking price of 1,600,000 livres (some £91,400).[29] It was agreed that the money was to be paid in quarterly instalments. The following month he took possession of the necklace and handed it over to Jeanne de la Rémy to convey to the Queen; instead, it was taken to London and broken up. The Queen did not learn of the fraud until July. Jeanne de la Rémy was tried and sentenced in 1786; the Cardinal was acquitted.

The affair of the necklace haunted Marie Antoinette. The revolutionary idealists of 1789 nursed principles inimical to the possession of jewellery, which symbolised to them all that was undesirable in the monarchy. On 7 September, Madame Moitte, the sculptor's wife,[30] led a group of like-minded women into the Assembly at Versailles and offered up their jewels to the cause of the Revolution. Their action, said to have been inspired by the virtuous matrons of the Roman Republic who made a similar sacrifice, was effective enough to provoke a gesture from the male members of the Assembly. On 26 September, under the sceptical gaze of the American envoy, Gouverneur Morris, the gentlemen divested themselves of their gold fobs, diamond buckles and other items of masculine finery. Morris confided to his diary that these 'Gifts of Patriotism' might more properly be deemed 'Sacrifices to Vanity'.[31] But as a new aspirant to the amatory favours of Madame de Flahaut,[32] whose husband held a post at Court, he perhaps looked more kindly on the French monarchy than he might have done, and more derisively on the Revolutionaries.

Madame Moitte's action had repercussions in and outside France. Ironically, Prussian women exchanged their gold wedding rings for iron ones to help maintain their armies in the field during the war of liberation against France in 1813,[33] and France re-adopted the idea after her humiliating defeat in the Franco-Prussian war of 1870-71. French jewellers then produced black jewellery mourning the lost French territories in Alsace and Lorraine (Plate 293A-C).

Gouverneur Morris devised one of the many plans for the escape of Louis XVI and Marie Antoinette with their children from Paris. Many members of their court had already departed (Colour Plate 5). The King, in a constant state of vacillation, made only one attempt, in June 1791, but he and his family were recognised and carried back to Paris. The Terror, signalised by the massacre of several hundred royalists and the Declaration of the Republic in September 1792, made incidents such as the theft of the French Crown Jewels from the Garde-Meuble insignificant by comparison. It was clear that the King was to die, and after a summary trial in December he was guillotined in January 1793; Marie Antoinette was executed nine months later. With churches turned into Temples of Reason, the end of the old order was brutally emphasised by the execution of royalists and their sympathisers. The process continued until July 1794.

In the hysterical atmosphere of the Terror the possession of even a pair of silver shoe buckles might identify their owner as a candidate for the guillotine. Jewellers, who had already seen their Corporation temporarily abolished in March 1791 (though it was resuscitated until 1797), felt themselves redundant. Those formerly patronised by monarchists practised discretion, either closing their premises or hurriedly changing sides. Some sort of a living was to be had from making souvenir jewellery from stones taken from the Bastille, stormed by the people on 14 July 1789 and still a potent symbol of the start of the Revolution. Other cheap trinkets exploited different patriotic associations. It has been claimed that ornaments were made in the form of miniature guillotines, aimed at the least squeamish; a pair of guillotine earrings in the Musée Carnavalet, Paris, are however dated to about 1805.[34]

The men who came to power at the ending of the Terror failed to halt either the corruption or the rampant inflation which enriched a few and impoverished the majority. Henri Meister, a friend of Louis XVI's last Controller-General, Jacques Necker, visited Paris in 1795 and remarked that the inhabitants had in general lost much of their revolutionary fervour in the struggle to keep alive. Food was short, whole areas of the city deserted, and the confiscated houses of the aristocracy, stripped of their contents, up for sale. Church treasures as well as secular items were hawked on the streets. But for those with money pleasures and luxuries were available at dance-halls, restaurants, bordellos and jewellers' shops.[35]

The precarious prosperity of France was increasingly shored up by military conquests. Napoleon Bonaparte[36] had this objective in mind when he embarked on his brilliant campaign against Austrian possessions in Italy in 1796. His victories forced the Peace of Campo Formio in 1797, under which most of Northern Italy and the Rhineland were added to the territories administered directly or indirectly by the French. Among other major concessions, Austria recognised France's annexation of the Austrian Netherlands. Napoleon in his turn offered German lands to Austria. All the vanquished territories were required to pay taxes and levies to France. Napoleon made similar exactions as he swept through Europe, not exempting those countries in which he installed members of his family as rulers.

The vassal states were likewise a useful source of art and artefacts. Treasures flowed into Paris from the conquered territories, some given (probably in expectation of favours), others confiscated to the regret of their owners who hoped,

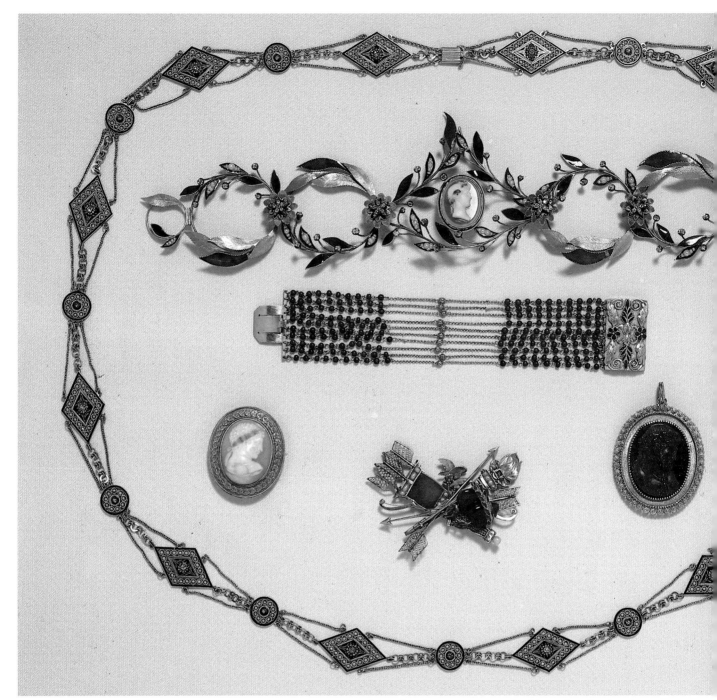

Colour Plate 6. A. A long gold sautoir, designed to be worn over one shoulder and under the other, enamelled and set with seed pearls and small diamonds, said to have been inspired by French military costume in the 1790s. Probably made in France in about 1795 and then taken out of the country, returning in the second half of the nineteenth century; struck with French import marks for 1864-93.
B. Wreath tiara of enamelled gold leaves ornamented with diamonds, pearls and a paste cameo of a classical head; c.1810. The diamond-set rosettes conceal hinges which allow the piece to be laid flat.
C. Bracelet with a chased and enamelled coloured gold clasp and chain band threaded with beads, c.1815.
D. Brooch in coloured gold, set with a shell cameo of a classical male head, c.1810.
E. A trophy of love, an openwork gold brooch set with seed pearls, carnelians and small emeralds and decorated with enamel, in the form of a bow and arrow, a quiverful of arrows, a flaming torch, a pair of turtle doves and two flaming hearts bound by an enamelled wreath, c.1800.
F. Pendant set with a bloodstone cameo of Christ (on the reverse, the Virgin Mary), in a gold frame with cannetille. Paris warranty mark for 1840 onwards.
All the pieces are French or in the French manner.   VICTORIA AND ALBERT MUSEUM

Colour Plate 7. A pair of French bracelets in coloured gold decorated with cannetille *and* grainti *and set with forget-me-nots in turquoises with* cannetille *centres, mounted over bosses formed of flowers and buds; the intervening links decorated with flowers and leaves. The spring clasps are attached to lengths of interlocking spiralling chains. The lozenge-shaped maker's marks are indecipherable except for the letter B; c.1815.*

HARVEY AND GORE

sometimes in vain, for their return after the eventual defeat of Napoleon. The Duke of Wellington, in Paris on behalf of the Allied Powers in 1815, was blamed by the French for having insisted that many things be sent back.[37] Meanwhile, Parisian jewellers were able to study antique examples of metalwork from a variety of sources, an invaluable opportunity when design was dominated by antiquarian principles. Though their trade had begun to rally when the Terror was ended, they had to contend with a shortage of money and materials for several years until Napoleon's campaigns brought new supplies. Adroitly, they made a virtue of necessity and, inspired by regional or peasant jewellery, worked their gold into thin strips of filigree decorated with seed pearls, modest stones and, exceptionally, small diamonds (Plate 6 and Colour Plate 6).

During the First Empire this work was further developed. Some tiny components were stamped out in hand presses. The wire openwork was also decorated in the manner of medieval filigree with pellets (*grainti*) and wire spirals or squabs (*cannetille*) (Colour Plate 7). This technique spread from France to many other countries, but English jewellers practised it less enthusiastically than their counterparts on the Continent. Their clients preferred substantial areas of solid gold, and they had necessarily to comply, though several Birmingham makers produced some remarkable cast imitations of French filigree in silver (Plate 73).

The hostilities brought celebrity and honours to heroes such as Nelson (Colour Plate 8), but also effected the usual involuntary redistribution of wealth. During the Terror, the revolutionary armies of France were accused of deflecting their attention from patriotic duties to embrace the charms of incidental looting. In Bailleul, Cassel and Dunkirk soldiers were said to have 'forcibly removed gold and silver jewellery and gold crosses from the women,'[38] a charge which, though indignantly denied, has a ring of truth about it. Ornaments such as rings, chains, watches and lockets set with the hair or portraits of loved ones changed hands inadvertently on the field of battle. Sir Herbert Taylor,[39] later private secretary to George III, Queen Charlotte and William IV, served in the campaign in the Low Countries in 1793. He remarked that the Hessians and the Hanoverian infantry were great plunderers, but so, he was forced to admit, were the English. The cavalry regiments were in general better disciplined, in Taylor's view. Worst of all were 'the women who followed the English and Irish regiments', who had no compunction about stripping the dead and wounded of their valuables and even raiding houses in the vicinity of battle.[40] When the British and German armies returned years later and fought the French troops at Waterloo the battlefield was afterwards pillaged. An English soldier's wife was reported to have found two great diamonds in the pocket of a dead Prussian. She took them to a jeweller in Brussels, asking two Napoleons (about 40 francs) for them. Lord Anglesey's niece, who was then living with her parents in Brussels, went to inspect the diamonds and wrote to her grandmother in England that the jeweller, with great honesty, had told the finder they were worth 'at least 6000*l* being two of the finest stones ever seen and supposed to have belonged to the Queen of Westphalia who had been robbed...; the woman's fortune is made and the Diamonds bought by an Englishman yesterday.'[41] The stones thus re-cycled were probably given to the Queen by

Plate 6. Necklace of enamelled gold filigree; the three oval units enclosing flowers are joined by two festoons of chains with stamped details. The Maltese cross pendant inside, with inserted leaf-shapes radiating from the central rosette, is entirely of gold. Both pieces are probably French, dating to c.1800.

THE NECKLACE, VICTORIA AND ALBERT MUSEUM, THE CROSS, PRIVATE COLLECTION

Colour Plate 9. The Empress Josephine painted by Robert Lefèvre in 1806. She is wearing a Spartan diadem with arched front, a fillet behind and a comb at the back of her head, all set with diamonds and other stones. The red gems in the fillet are possibly carnelian intaglios. WELLINGTON MUSEUM, APSLEY HOUSE

Colour Plate 8. Horatio, Viscount Nelson, posed to Sir William Beechey in 1800 for this portrait commissioned by the Corporation of Norwich. Nelson's hat is embellished with the diamond chelengk *presented by the Sultan of Turkey after the British Admiral's decisive victory over the French at the Battle of Aboukir (Abu Qir) off Alexandria in 1798. The Sultan, who numbered Egypt among his vassal states, was gratified at this setback to Napoleon's extraordinary force in the country.*

NORFOLK MUSEUMS SERVICE (NORWICH CASTLE MUSEUM)

Napoleon or his brother Jérôme, who had been created King of Westphalia in 1807.[42]

Similar occurrences were recorded in the Iberian Peninsula. At Corunna the future General Charles Napier was clubbed insensible. On coming round he found that his watch and purse had gone, 'and a little locket of hair which hung round my neck' was being torn from him.[43] The looters were an Italian and a French soldier, but the temptation to pillage affected the highest ranks.

Two spectacular diamonds adorning the ears of Madame Soult, the wife of one of Napoleon's Marshals,[44] at Parisian functions in 1814 were rumoured to have been removed from the statue of the Virgin in the treasury of the Virgin of the Pillar in Saragossa Cathedral.[45]

Shortly after Napoleon became First Consul in 1799, he and his wife Josephine[46] (whose first husband had perished by the guillotine) were already acting as monarchs. Their Court was recognised by some of the returning French emigrés as well as by foreigners. Lady Bessborough, in Paris during the short-lived Peace of Amiens, had no qualms about launching her seventeen-year-old daughter Caroline Ponsonby[47] into French society. In January 1803 Lady Bessborough

Colour Plate 10. A. A brilliant aigrette bound by a shuttle-shaped device probably dating to the 1770s, a later variant of an example with flaring spines worn by Queen Charlotte in a painting of 1764 by Zoffany (Queen Charlotte at her Dressing-Table, in the Royal Collection).
B. A rose-cut diamond flower brooch probably made in the mid-eighteenth century; pieces of similar type were still worn in the coiffure some forty years later (see Plate 20). S.J. PHILLIPS

wrote a long account of a reception staged for the Bonapartes at the Ministry of Marine in a letter to her lover, Lord Granville Leveson Gower.[48] 'Mad. B. [was] quite enthron'd,' she declared, on a 'rich Embroider'd chair a little rais'd. Behind her stood two Ladies of Honour, the Préfets du Palais, Genl. Caffarelli in full uniform, and the Master of the House all over embroidery....Mad. B. was magnificently dress'd; it look'd exactly (barring hoops) like a court ball at St. James's.'

Lady Bessborough had put her finger exactly on the essential differences between the new French regime and the established Court in England. Josephine, she implied, though gracious, was all too plainly still an apprentice royal: 'she seems embarrass'd and as if she did not know exactly what to do...'[49] But she and Napoleon had already begun to establish a distinctive style, classical in inspiration but opulent in its interpretation. The dress of Josephine and her attendants, simple in profile, fell from a high waist. Queen Charlotte had the advantage of birth and long experience, but she was old-fashioned and at Court clung tenaciously to the wide spreading hooped skirts of her youth. These were still the required costume at Drawing-rooms and other receptions at St. James's Palace (Plate 7).

Published as the Act directs, July 1.1798, by N. Heideloff, at the Gallery of Fashion Office, N.° 90 Wardour Street.

Plate 7. Plate showing a lady wearing hooped Court dress, from Heideloff's Gallery of Fashion, *1 July 1798. The jewelled aigrette on her coiffure has the same kind of truncated elegance as the ornament on the left of Colour Plate 10.*

The title of Emperor of the French was formally decreed to Napoleon by the obedient Senate on 18 May 1804. The Coronation ceremony took place the following December in the presence of Pope Pius VII, in token of the reconciliation of Church and State (Plate 8). Thanks to the new Emperor and the Empress (Colour Plate 9), the Parisian jewellery trade had reasserted its traditional hegemony and even the diamond dealers, particularly afflicted in the previous decade, had begun to look on their growing profits with considerable satisfaction. This remarkable improvement was undoubtedly partly due to the need to replace the jewellery removed from France after the Revolution, much of which was broken up and re-set for the new owners. Napoleon, Josephine and the Bonaparte and Beauharnais clans all demanded jewellery and with Josephine it was a veritable passion which was satisfied by the trade with gratitude and alacrity. New craftsmen were attracted to Paris to replace those dispersed during the 1790s and the traditional, slower, cycle of movement of jewellers in and out of Paris resumed.

The Court style of Empire jewellery is best exemplified by large suites or parures comprised of two or even four head ornaments, a necklace, earrings, a pair of bracelets and perhaps also a bodice ornament (Colour Plate 20), belt clasp or jewelled girdle. Their bold neo-classical forms, described by coloured step-cut stones in diamond or pearl borders, derive from the more delicate shapes current in the last decades of the eighteenth century. A great many eighteenth century shapes were simply magnified. Shallow tiaras rising to a point, fashionable in the 1790s and early 1800s (Plate 9) were elevated and extended into what the English called Spartan diadems (Colour Plate 9). Aigrettes (Colour Plate 10A), stylised representations of the feather head ornaments which had been in vogue on and off since the late sixteenth century, were mainly executed in diamonds from the 1760s but after 1800 were reinterpreted with coloured stones (Colour Plate 1A). The Oriental crescents (Plate 10) popular from the mid-eighteenth century were revivified by Napoleon's invasion of Egypt in 1798 while French army costume is credited with the revival of the seventeenth century practice of wearing long chains slung over one shoulder and under the other. These chains, looking most unmilitary, were known as sautoirs (Colour Plate 6A). The constant ability of the trade to seek out and re-work old motifs in a modern guise has remained one of its strongest features, as has its internationalism. Long sautoirs, worn round the neck, were popular in the early 1900s, while the treatment of natural forms in jewellery ranged from the conventionalised in the late eighteenth century (Colour Plate 10) to the organic between 1810 and 1855 (Plate 11) and then to the highly stylised forms of Art Nouveau (Colour Plate 11).

French was the lingua franca of workshops in many countries, providing the terminology which became accepted, or at least understood, by craftsmen and their clients. Sadly the English language, usually so rich and flexible, defines all ornaments made for personal wear as jewellery regardless of the materials employed in their manufacture. The French, on the other hand, distinguish between *joaillerie*, in which precious stones predominate, and *bijouterie*, in which goldsmith's work is more important than any stones employed. The latter term also embraces small objects such as gold boxes, desk seals and the like which fall into the English category of 'toys' (small fancy articles). The most satisfactory English equivalents of *joaillerie* and *bijouterie*, fine or primary jewellery for the first and secondary jewellery for the second, are modern art historical terms and nothing to do with trade usage. It has to be added that the precision of the French language sometimes gives way to the requirements of brevity. Henri Vever's standard work, *La Bijouterie française au XIXe Siècle* (1906-1908) covers both categories of precious jewellery and deals to some extent with a third class, ornaments made of imitation or substitute materials. Much of this imitation (or

Colour Plate 11. A design for a pendant in wash and bodycolour by the great French Art Nouveau jeweller René Lalique. It was reproduced (with another, signed, drawing) in the Magazine of Art *in 1902 (see Colour Plate 179).*

costume) jewellery falls within the English category of toys on grounds of size.

Technically, the fine diamond jewellery produced towards the end of the eighteenth century was constructed mainly with brilliant-cut diamonds, with the older rose-cut frequently playing a subsidiary role. The brilliants were given a greater depth and sparkle by being mounted in open-backed collets which allowed the light to reflect and refract through the stones. Open or 'transparent' settings were not a new invention (and almost certainly not English). The sharp-eyed rattle Celia Fiennes had noticed that as Queen Anne was carried in procession to her coronation in 1702 she wore a circlet set with diamonds and further garnished with 'a sprig of diamond drops transparent'.[50] A monde and cross, 'all Set Transparent,' adorned the top of George II's coronation Crown in 1727,[51] as was the cross on George III's Crown in 1761.[52] The diamond drops on Queen Anne's

Plate 8. The Coronation of Napoleon on 4 December 1804, by Jacques-Louis David, Revolutionary turned Bonapartist, 1808. MUSEE DU LOUVRE

circlet were probably drilled and capped, but the large stones surmounting the crowns of 1727 and 1761 were secured in collets and it was a matter of time before transparent settings were taken up by the trade. Though made of silver to consort with the diamonds, the backs were lined with gold, a sensible device to prevent tarnished silver from discolouring the skin. The first London jeweller to adopt the technique as a 'new improvement' was 'Mr. Cox' (probably the celebrated goldsmith, jeweller and toy-maker James Cox)[53] who used it in making 'a very costly neck or breast ornament of diamonds' for the wedding jewellery of Frederica Wilhelmina, affianced to William V, the Stadholder of Holland.[54] Sylas Neville, who had a sight of the jewel in 1767, recorded in his diary that the principal stone was valued at £3,000 and the whole piece £7,000, but 'as it must pass through several hands ere it gets to the Prince of Orange, [it] may cost him £10,000 or £15,000.' Neville was intrigued by Cox himself, 'an extraordinary person', he wrote, who had 'acquired his great knowledge of precious stones etc by mere force of uncommon natural genius. He cannot even keep his own accounts.'[55]

Secondary jewellery supplied two markets in England. The first comprised the rich women who wore a profusion of diamonds on certain well-defined occasions, namely, at Court, formal receptions, balls, grand dinner-parties and the like. At other times they had strings of pearls looped round their necks, threaded through their hair, arranged on their bodices and round their wrists, sometimes with a modicum of secondary jewellery. Thus embellished, they posed to portraitists, if not always in the open air, then often with a segment of sky in the background.

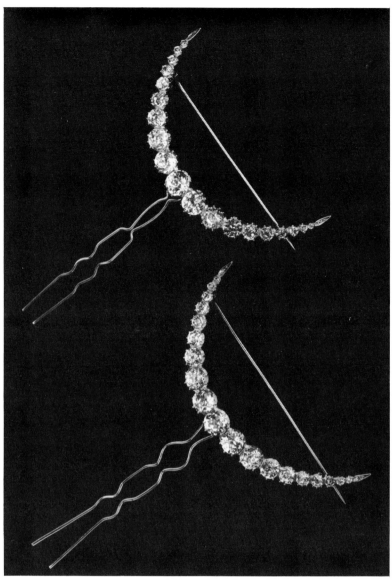

Plate 9. 'London fashionable full dress'; from the Lady's Magazine, *1805. The lady wears a shallow arched tiara, too small to qualify as a Spartan diadem, and a necklace with pendent cross.*

Plate 10. A pair of large early nineteenth century crescent head ornaments set with pastes in foiled and cut-down silver settings; the fittings are silver-gilt. The swivelling hair pins are removable to permit the crescents to be pinned to a cap or bodice. The pins and clasps are permanent fixtures, acting as safety fastenings when the ornaments decorated the hair. (Shown smaller than actual size.) HARVEY AND GORE

The great diamond suites were thus seldom recorded in paintings. The ladies who adhered to the rules were contemptuous of those who did not. One noblewoman who on a visit to Norfolk in 1794 encountered the wife of the famous agriculturalist 'Tom' Coke, the future Earl of Leicester, was '*shocked* at Mrs Coke's *vulgarity* in wearing her diamonds in the country every evening at Holkham during the hunting season.'[56] That the Coke's house was one of the grandest in the country did not excuse such a breach of good manners.

Much of the secondary jewellery owned by these women was sentimental in nature. A well-connected Norfolk woman, Jane Burrough, cited her jewellery in a will drawn up on 10 May 1790 and proved on 2 January 1799. She specified that she be given a frugal burial in Wisbech church, and her jewels demonstrate that she lived on a comfortable but not a lavish scale. Her most ambitious pieces were a 'Diamond Knot' (a bodice ornament in the shape of a bow), a pair of diamond earrings, 'my best Diamond Ring' and a 'Rose Diamond Ring', indicating that the best one was set with brilliants. For the rest, she had 'a pair of Moco [moss agate] Studs set in gold with Garnets,' two family miniatures, one set with diamonds, two lockets, one containing her father's and the other her mother's hair, a slide with her sister's hair and three further rings, one of onyx and diamonds, one an amethyst with her grandfather's hair and one of garnets. The jewellery was divided between her son, two daughters and her brother.[57]

Costume or imitation jewellery also spanned many levels of society. The best paste jewellery was made of lead glass cut and polished like the diamonds it imitated and carefully set in closed and foiled silver collets. The idea of using this glass,[58] an improvement on an old formula, is credited to Georges Frédéric Stras, a pastor's son from the vicinity of Strasbourg, where he was trained as a jeweller from 1714 to 1719. In the early 1730s Stras became celebrated for his paste articles and was appointed Jeweller to the French King in 1734, by which time he had premises in Paris. He lent his name to glass paste in France (strass) and inevitably had many rivals and imitators at home and abroad.[59] Their skill was still in demand in the early years of the nineteenth century (Plate 10).

The pre-Revolutionary trade in false jewellery was recognised by the foundation in about 1767 of a corporation of *bijoutiers-faussetiers* in Paris. Marcasite, gilt metal, artificial pearls and other materials were used in the production of trinkets. French imitation pearls were held in particular regard. Though the corporation did not long survive the Revolution, the manufacture of costume jewellery remained an important aspect of the French trade.

English makers could boast of no comparable organisation, however short-lived. They were distributed throughout the country but principally concentrated in London (where Clerkenwell was of traditional importance) and in Birmingham, which was rapidly capturing trade from towns like Derby and Wolverhampton. Cut steel toys, including buckles, were made in Clerkenwell, Woodstock, Wolverhampton, Birmingham and sundry other places. Steel trinkets from Matthew Boulton's manufactory at Soho on the outskirts of Birmingham were popular in France and elsewhere on the Continent during the pre-Revolutionary years when Anglomania raged. Cut steel was first produced in imitation of the Soho work in the Low Countries, inspiring a French manufacturer named Dauffe to produce it in his turn in about 1776. Dauffe's monopoly in France enabled him to charge high prices for his trinkets, according to the *Journal de Paris* of 18 July 1787.[60] But he too soon had rivals among his fellow-countrymen. By the second decade of the nineteenth century new industrial techniques evolved by French manufacturers had begun to kill off a large part of the cut steel trade in Birmingham and make production elsewhere in England little more than a cottage industry.[61] Though a few Birmingham manufacturers like the Heeleys survived and even contributed to international exhibitions in the second half of the nineteenth century they had lost the technical initiative which even in the late seventeenth century had resulted in steel wares which one traveller at least thought were better and cheaper than those of Milan,[62] a renowned centre of iron and steel production.

The English toymakers who used gold and silver for the whole or part of their output benefited from the exemptions from the legal requirement to have their wares assayed and hallmarked. The articles so exempted in 1738 included jewellers' work set with stones (and presumably by extension, pastes), jointed night-earrings of gold (these were ornaments to be worn in the evening, not at night), rings (except for mourning rings, which had to be hallmarked), chains, necklace beads, lockets, jointed stock or garter clasps, filigree work, small work set with amber, and wrought and gem-set seals. Nor did the makers of such objects need a licence entitling them both to manufacture and sell, as did goldsmiths in general from 1758.[63]

The exemption from licensing, granted in 1759, applied to those selling gold wares not exceeding 2 dwts. and silver goods not exceeding 5 dwts. a piece, aside from articles already expressly omitted on grounds of their liability to be damaged in the process of assaying and hallmarking.

Matthew Boulton, whose Soho Manufactory turned out domestic and church silverwork in considerable quantities in addition to toys and other wares, positively welcomed hallmarking. He was one of the prime movers in the successful campaign to get a bill through Parliament establishing assay offices in Birmingham and Sheffield. When the Birmingham assay office opened on 31 August 1773 Boulton submitted over 840 oz. of silver, mostly plate but including thirty pairs of buckle frames.[64] Since Boulton supplied a number of London retailers with goods (as did other Birmingham workshops), it is conceivable that a pair of silver buckles bought by the great lexicographer and wit Dr Samuel Johnson in London emanated from Soho. According to Johnson's biographer Boswell, in 1778 he drove with Johnson to 'Wirgman's, the well-known *toy-shop,* in St. James's Street' (this was Peter Wirgman, a leading London jeweller patronised by the Prince of Wales). Boswell waited in the coach and Johnson went inside, but after a while he was summoned to advise on the purchase of a pair of silver buckles. 'Sir,' said Johnson, 'I will not have the ridiculous large ones now in fashion; and I will give no more than a guinea for a pair.'[65]

Buckle-makers were recruited and trained in large numbers to meet the demand, and in 1790 some 20,000 were engaged in the trade in Birmingham alone. But already the vogue had reached its apogee and business thereafter fell away leaving many unemployed.

Boulton was at first exceptional in his large manufactory and in some of the advanced technical aids he employed. His partnership with James Watt brought the benefits of steam power to Soho, and years later one of Watts' steam-engines powered the diamond-cutting machine bought by Rundell's.[66] But in general, at the close of the eighteenth century, Birmingham resembled London in having a number of workshops, some very small and specialising in single techniques such as gem-setting. Such craftsmen could only operate in the near vicinity of other specialists, who between them were able to create finished articles. The craftsmen were dependent on their suppliers; dealers in stones who were almost exclusively Jewish,[67] traders in precious and base metals, the rolling mills which produced metals to the required gauge in quantity for the larger workshops, though the jewellers usually relied on their own small hand-operated machines, and sellers of pastes and quartzes such as 'Bristol diamonds', tortoiseshell, ivory and other materials, including hair and marcasite.[68]

The system promoted both independence and a sense of community and it is scarcely surprising that immigrant craftsmen preferred to join their own kind, mainly in Soho but also in the City and in Clerkenwell. Birmingham was likewise a target for Huguenot and Jewish craftsmen and dealers as well as jewellers and designers of other nationalities, all contributing to the growth of the trade and leavening the core of native nonconformists who had also found comfort in gathering together. Not everything they produced went to London or abroad. Thomas Richards, the son of a jeweller who went to Birmingham from Sussex in the middle of the eighteenth century and later took his own son Theophilus into partnership, ran a shop in the High Street which in 1808 was described as 'the toyshop of Birmingham', almost unrivalled 'for the elegance of its appearance and the multiplicity of its valuable articles.'[69] Six years earlier it had been graced by a visit from Nelson and Sir William and Lady Hamilton.

The cheaper end of the trade in London still used pinchbeck, the most famous of the zinc copper alloys, the precise proportions of which were never revealed. The invention is credited to the Fleet Street watchmaker, Christopher Pinchbeck, who died in 1732. His business was continued by his son, who advertised against makers pirating the alloy, to no avail. Workshops also gilded and plated base metals by various means. Copper was usually gilt; brass might be left unimproved, to judge by the pathetic collection of tokens left by mothers depositing their babies at the Foundling Hospital founded by Thomas Coram. In the days before receipts were issued, these tokens were used to identify the children if their mothers were ever in a position to claim them. Most of the surviving specimens date to between 1741 and 1760, with a few running up to the early years of the nineteenth century. The most valuable item is a modest mid-eighteenth century seal set with a carnelian. Of several hearts, a mother-of-pearl example with the initials EL and another, very tiny one set with three pastes in metal, both dating to the 1740s and '50s, stand out from a motley collection of pieces in bone, fake pearls and glass beads, spangled trimmings, a base metal pendant dated 1757, a broken brass cross, a hairpin of the same material, coins, plaques, religious pendants and medallions cheap enough to have been bought at a fair.[70]

The poverty of these ornaments clearly reflected special circumstances, for most of the children admitted to the Foundling Hospital were illegitimate and the mothers likely to have been in desperate need. The price of trinkets was relatively high and it is remarkable that the women found anything at all to leave with their children unless, as is perfectly feasible, they were in service and had access to the cast-offs of their employers.

The days of mass-production were however already at hand. On 7 March 1769 a London toymaker called John Pickering patented 'a new method of performing that kind of work called chasing, for gold, silver, brass, tin, and other metals' used in the manufacture of coffin furniture and fittings for coaches, cabinets, chests and similar domestic articles. On 7 August 1769 Richard Ford of Birmingham adapted the invention, consisting of two upright rods guiding a falling hammer to which was attached a 'force' or convex die. This was allowed to drop on to metal placed over an intaglio or concave die. The metal was forced to assume the shape engraved in the lower die or stamp. Ford used the stamp to shape scales, sauce and warming pans and the like, but in 1777 it reached the toy trade in the town. John Marston, a brassfounder and Samuel Bellamy, a die sinker or engraver, patented the stamping of rolled gilt and plated metals into hat and cloak pins and other ornaments as well as furniture and lock fittings. Some of these articles were pierced and coloured foils were set behind the openings; others were given coats of coloured lacquer.[71]

Curiously, though Marston was associated with one of the staple trades of Birmingham, his patent makes no reference to stamped brass. The brass watch or guard chains made by one or two workshops in the town towards the end of the century were not stamped but put together from wire in a single, uniform, pattern. The chains were either left in their natural colour or were silvered or gilt.[72] Chains such as these were favoured by farmers and small businessmen. Silver guard chains were not made in Birmingham until about 1806.

Several of the large London workshops were able to afford the services of designers, as were Matthew Boulton and his pupil Sir Edward Thomason in Birmingham.[73] Most workshops put together their own designs from pattern-books and other sources which reflected the current modes. Thus, despite the paucity of documentation, it is possible to assign a date to some of the items in the collection of the Thomas Coram Foundation already described. Itinerant craftsmen also brought news of fashions in other countries and wherever possible the heads of large firms travelled abroad to see for themselves and pick up ideas. But the introduction of fashion plates in magazines and almanacs in the mid-eighteenth century ensured a wider audience for innovatory modes. At first the circulation of these publications was nominally very small, but the prints were passed from hand to hand.

Parisian publications such as the *Galerie des Modes et des Costumes Françoises* (1778-1787) inspired an English periodical, Heideloff's *Gallery of Fashion,* which was launched in London in 1794 (Plate 12). Niklaus von Heideloff, a miniaturist from Leipzig, worked in Paris from 1784 until 1789[74] and the grace and urbanity of his draughtsmanship transformed English fashion plates. His wittiness and powers of observation are demonstrated by the appearance in several plates of the distinctive long, aquiline nose of Mrs Fitzherbert (Plate 5).[75]

The artist's hand-coloured aquatints were heightened by a liberal use of gold and silver to show up the jewellery and trimmings which, like Mrs Fitzherbert's nose, were studied from existing models. Virtually every piece illustrated in the first volume of the *Gallery,* for instance, can be paralleled by items listed in a contemporary Workmen's Ledger of Garrard's of London. A head ornament in the *Gallery* corresponds to the ledger description of a pearl article supplied on 30 October 1795 by Miss Leaf, an outworker to Garrard's; diamond pins for the hair to some made for the firm by Clinton & Coles and entered on 22 April 1794; and pendants in the form of anchors, emblematic of fidelity, to one executed by another outworker by the name of Hitchman and recorded in the ledger on 21 April 1795. Heideloff's later illustrations and framed portrait miniatures, usually called medallions and worn on ribbons round the neck or on the body (Plate 12), are

Plate 11. A brilliant flower spray with needle-shaped drops; c.1850. The spray has a brooch fitting and was probably worn as a bodice ornament.
HARVEY AND GORE

comparable to one furnished by Clinton & Coles on 4 February 1796.[76]

Heideloff's first subscribers, who are listed at the back of the volume of 1794, included the three eldest daughters of George III, the Princess Royal (Plate 20) and the Princesses Augusta and Elizabeth, together with their sister-in-law the Duchess of York.[77] The Landgravine of Hesse Darmstadt, the Dowager Duchess and a Princess of Württemberg, the Russian Ambassador to London (Count Woronzow) and the Secretary to the Embassy of the Grand Sultan of Turkey appear with other royalties, a sprinkling of English and Continental aristocrats, 'a lady in Philadelphia,' a few booksellers and several females, including 'Miss Jones, Turnham Green', who were probably modistes or dressmakers. Among later subscribers were, somewhat surprisingly, Queen Charlotte herself, the painter Zoffany and, demonstrating a preference for English over French fashions in the 1790s, further German royalties, members of the Spanish and Portuguese royal families and two more Americans, one of whom lived in Charleston, Carolina.

Perversely, some English men and women (including designers and manufacturers of jewellery) still hankered for information about the new French fashions. The Parisian *Journal des Dames et des Modes* (1797-1837) was a useful source. A German version of the *Journal,* started in Frankfurt in 1799, ended only in 1848. Before Germany was overrun by Napoleon in 1806, the Frankfurt version of the periodical was apparently ransacked by English fashion correspondents for the delectation of their readers. John Bell, who in 1806 launched the *Belle Assemblée* (which was English despite its title), acknowledged that he drew on the French *Journal* without however admitting to resorting to the Frankfurt offshoot.[78] Another English periodical to carry news of French fashions was Rudolph Ackermann's *Repository of Arts, Literature, Manufactures, Fashion and Politics*

(1809-1828), dedicated initially to the Prince of Wales. Ackermann, born in Stuttgart, trained as an engraver and worked in Paris as a designer of carriages before arriving in London.

French magazines illustrated first with engravings, then with lithographed plates and finally with photo-engravings, continued to be trawled for information throughout the nineteenth century and beyond. Travelling through Italy in 1823 with her husband and their companion, Count d'Orsay (Plate 230),[79] Lady Blessington[80] remarked on 'the celerity with which *Le Petit Courrier des Dames* voyages, and enables the female aristocracy of Lucca who cannot visit that emporium of fashion, Paris, to look somewhat like its fair denizens — albeit three months out of date.'[81] The ladies of Lucca probably wanted the right kind of jewellery too, forcing manufacturers to adjust their sights and change their patterns. One of the Italian concerns which actually came into existence for the express purpose of making jewellery in the French and English manners was Castellani of Rome, founded in 1814-15 and afterwards celebrated for its classical designs.

Steam was to speed up the transmission of fashion news, both in terms of transport (railways and steamships) and in the production of periodicals. Koenig's steam cylinder printing press, adopted by *The Times* in 1814, opened the way for the mass circulation of the Victorian age, 'the paper circulation of knowledge', as it was picturesquely termed in a report of 1836.[82] In 1842 another technological innovation was exploited in a new periodical, the *Illustrated London News*. Sketches made by artists were engraved on wood, and from this stereotypes or metal relief plates were taken. When the stereotypes wore out, more were made from the wood blocks which were thus capable of indefinite reduplication. Like many of its later rivals, the *Illustrated London News* reported on fashions in dress and, though less frequently, on jewellery.

Before, during and after the Napoleonic wars, the somewhat garbled accounts of the latest fashions which appeared in some English periodicals strongly suggest that the original French was mistranslated or misunderstood by a male member of the editorial staff. The information was usually conveyed in the form of a so-called letter signed by a female. The *Belle Assemblée* invented a young lady called Eliza, while the imaginary correspondent of Ackermann's *Repository* was Belinda, whose exhausting social life in London was assiduously catalogued in letters to her rural sister (or her friend: the editorial staff vacillated over the relationship). At the end of hostilities Gallic signatures adorned the fashion pages of many English magazines, implying that the correspondents concerned were writing from Paris. Their reports were so self-consciously larded with French phrases, carefully chosen so as not to tax the comprehension of their readers, that it is fair to conclude that these were further products of the fertile editorial mind.

Periodicals, for all the drawbacks enumerated above, remain an invaluable source of information about trends in nineteenth century jewellery. They complement manuscript sources as well as the innumerable reports, manuals, encyclopedias and books of exegesis which were published in vast quantities commensurate with the remarkable growth in the population of Europe, America

Plate 12. Plate showing three ladies in a box at the theatre, from Heideloff's Gallery of Fashion,
1 June 1796. The woman on the right is wearing a large medallion suspended from a three-row necklace.

and the colonial countries following European modes. Jewellery was an essential
ingredient of dress, so much so that its absence occasioned comment. It was worn
to such an extent and in such quantity it is scarcely remarkable that a great deal
has survived.

In subsequent chapters, the various styles of jewellery, nearly all revived or
continued under the umbrella of the Antiquarian movement, are considered in the
light of rulers and the ruled, technical developments and expanding markets.
Chapter I further pursues the jewellery of the 1790s, a vital period in which the
ideas developed after the Revolution were launched upon the approaching century.
Thereafter the chapters are arranged in triplets, covering roughly two decades at

a time, the dates being adjusted to the accession of Queen Victoria and the death of the Prince Consort. The first part of each triplet covers events, personages and current styles, the second deals with materials and their treatment in both general and special categories and the third with the forms and types of fashionable jewellery. The emphasis is laid on English work and the Continental (and, later, American) designs and techniques which so often inspired it, though the influence was reciprocal.

The internationalism of the trade exacerbates the problem of identifying the provenance of jewellery. Often, though a style was common to much of Europe and to many other countries, it was interpreted in such a way as to make the country of origin instantly recognisable. Other types of jewellery were peculiar to a particular nation or group of nations. Some at least of the rest is ambiguous, and attribution is made no easier because so little of it was marked. France, where compulsory hallmarking was reintroduced in 1798, was the only country which persistently applied the law. Other Continental countries instituted compulsory hallmarking from time to time, but none so persistently as the French. The English hallmarking laws, rigidly applied in respect of plate, virtually excluded jewellery, as noted above, until the Birmingham assay office began to call in small silver trinkets in the last thirty years or so of the century. An abuse of the legal gold standards was the inevitable consequence of the absence of legal control.

The vexed question of fakes must be confronted, if only in passing, though resumed in the Epilogue. In an age so firmly committed to historicist design, research into defunct or obsolescent techniques was regarded as an essential preliminary to the correct interpretation of revived styles. Few designers and manufacturers considered that the machine imposed its own aesthetic[83] but accepted that historic styles, passing down the trade from the primary or secondary levels, should merely be interpreted in the most economic way for mass-production. This attitude was shared by those who purchased such trinkets, for they liked to feel they were in the fashion.

In the nineteenth century, the classical, medieval and Renaissance styles were particularly popular with makers of secondary jewellery who became skilled exponents of old techniques. Their productions were acts of homage to the past, made with no intent to deceive. But the great collectors of the age, some of whom had begun to acquire ecclesiastical artefacts released on to the French market in consequence of the post-Revolutionary secularisation of churches, created a demand for antique pieces which could not always be met. There were always living craftsmen only too happy to remedy the deficiency, ranging from the late eighteenth century and early nineteenth century Neapolitan goldsmiths, precursors of the Castellani firm, who from openly producing jewellery inspired by antique pieces excavated locally also turned to restoring the originals and then to making outright fakes,[84] to the Aachen goldsmith Reinhold Vasters and others like him in the last half of the nineteenth century, whose forgeries were often commissioned by dealers.[85]

Lefournier of Paris, who supplied the jeweller Charles Duron with enamelled *bijouterie* in the Renaissance taste in the 1860s and 1870s, probably had no idea beyond that of copying articles in the Louvre and elsewhere to the best of his ability, but his virtuosity drew dealers and collectors alike to Duron's shop.[86] The goods were acknowledged as modern, but who can tell whether such honesty was maintained in later dealings?

Gem-engravers, practising an art which in technique as well as in subject matter had changed little over the centuries, were frequently exploited by unscrupulous dealers and sometimes also lent themselves to fraud. A well-known instance of unwitting deception on the part of the artist was the cameo of Flora engraved in Rome by Benedetto Pistrucci[87] in about 1808. It was acquired by the dealer Bonelli, who sold it as an antique specimen to the English collector Richard Payne Knight.[88] The sale of the Poniatowski gems after the Prince's death in 1833 precipitated a scandal which affected the demand for antique specimens on the part of collectors. Jewellers continued to mount gems in their own productions for a small number of clients, but shell cameos were employed in vast quantities as cheaper alternatives to the hardstone examples.

The occasional references in subsequent chapters to this substratum of the jewellery trade which, by its very nature, was usually kept secret, must be recognised as no more than indicative of widespread and lucrative activities.

CHAPTER I
From the Revolution to the early years of the War with France

In June 1789, with a fine disregard of the disturbances in France, the Duke and Duchess of Devonshire, travelling with Lady Elizabeth Foster and the Duke's natural daughter, arrived in Paris. The Duchess (Colour Plate 4), known to have spent prodigally in the past, was besieged by mantua makers and jewellers. On this occasion she bought very little, being deeply in debt. Nevertheless she accompanied her husband to the Court at Versailles, though procrastinating on grounds of the general unrest about presenting the daughters of Thomas Coutts the banker, to whom she owed large sums of money. As the troubles increased, the Devonshires and Lady Elizabeth withdrew from Paris before the storming of the Bastille. They returned in time for the birth of a son and heir in May 1790.[1] The Duchess proudly showed him to Marie Antoinette; it was the last time she saw the Queen.

It was some years before English families wholly relinquished their customary trips to Europe, and young Englishmen abandoned all idea of making the traditional Grand Tour. Cosmopolitan families, such as that of Richard Wynne and his French wife, drifted through Europe just ahead of the French armies, their life recorded in the diaries of two of the Wynne children, the sharp-eyed Betsey and her sister Eugenia. These illuminating records show, incidentally, that the two girls occasionally bought trinkets for their servants at fairs, traditional sources of personal ornaments. Early in 1790 they visited a fair in Switzerland, where Betsey purchased a handkerchief pin for their maid, Mary Edmonds. Eugenia would have liked to have got something for her also, but had been instructed by her mother to buy a pin for the cook.[2]

The hostilities bore hardly on Britain. By 1796 ports were closed to English ships from the Elbe to the Adriatic, except for those of Portugal, Elba and Naples. Even Genoa and Leghorn (Livorno) were reported to have excluded English goods, breaking a connection which had existed for centuries.[3] But the ban was often disregarded. English wares were infiltrated into Europe from Heligoland, for instance, and even found their way to France. Late in the same year, when Pitt introduced the Budget for 1797, the expenses of the war (including subsidies paid to the Austrian Emperor to ensure his support), were estimated at nearly £28,000,000. Some two-thirds of the money were to be met by raising a public loan.[4] The cost of running the war precipitated a financial crisis and the country came off the gold standard in 1797; in April 1798 further revenues were raised by the introduction of income tax.

Mercantile difficulties, married to the expenditure on the war, inevitably had an effect on the civilian population. The high price of meat was already bewailed by Lord Sheffield's daughter, Maria Josepha Holroyd, in 1793.[5] By March 1800 a West Country clergyman, William Holland, commented that with wheat costing

15 shillings a bushel, the poor could rarely afford to eat it and had to resort to oats.[6] Disastrous weather ruined the crops in the same year and the price of a quarter of wheat (eight bushels) rose to a dizzying 120 shillings and more,[7] forcing many people to turn to potatoes, potato flour and even rice, which had to be imported. Hunger occasioned civil disturbances. Parson Holland distributed 'boiling pease' to the poor of his parish at Christmas.[8]

The distress in the towns and the countryside, sympathetically observed by many at the time, was not reflected in fashion magazines and reports. Fashion was something which concerned only the comfortably off, some of whom, accustomed to French modes and manners before the Revolution, were unable to break the habit. Lady Bessborough,[9] whose lover Lord Granville Leveson Gower went to Paris in 1796 as a member of Lord Malmesbury's abortive peace mission, was one such. When Leveson Gower mentioned in a letter to her that the ('cropped') wigs worn by most Frenchwomen were so becoming that, had he no reservations on grounds of hygiene he would 'try to get them introduced in London', Lady Bessborough, the Duchess of Devonshire's sister, ignored this quibble and asked him to procure one for her. 'I should like to have it' she wrote, 'even if I do not wear it, and it would be remarkably convenient just now, for I have cut off all my hair.' She had her wish; Leveson Gower went to the finest *perruquier* in Paris,[10] patronised by at least one of the celebrated beauties of the Directory, Madame Tallien,[11] who despite the war blithely had fabrics for her clothes sent from London.

The French wigs were carefully created to produce an effect less formal than the coiffures prevailing in England. For several years after its first appearance in 1794, Heideloff's *Gallery* depicted English elegants wearing clothes which, while not possessing the fluidity of contemporary French chemise dresses, had high waists and full graceful skirts; heads were piled high with sausage curls and ringlets cascaded over the shoulders and down the back of the bodice (Plates 7 and 12). It is clear enough that nature was invariably assisted by artificial aids, if not by full wigs then by toupees and hair pieces.[12] Further embellishment on ceremonial occasions was provided by bandeaux, strings of pearls or stones, aigrettes and jewelled pins in various combinations. The ensemble of hair, real and false, feathers and ornaments constituted the coiffure or 'head'.

The rush of decoration to the head, though somewhat less extreme in the early 1790s than in the preceding decade, was still formidable, but in the closing years of the century English hair styles were less rigidly composed. Powdered hair was on the way out, encouraged in England by the imposition of the war-time tax on hair powder. The new French mode of wearing wigs which were cropped short in front and curled round the face in calculated disarray, though initially resisted by women less cosmopolitan than Lady Bessborough, soon caught on. By 1798 it was represented in the fashion plates of a new periodical, the *Lady's Monthly Museum*.[13] The overall size of the coiffure was considerably reduced and remained so for nearly two decades, but the passion for head ornaments scarcely abated.

The peculiar problem experienced by Frenchwomen during the Terror of 1793-94, when it was positively dangerous to be seen wearing jewellery, struck few sympathetic chords abroad. Women in other countries did not cease wearing their diamonds and pearls because of what was happening in France, nor did their menfolk refrain from ordering them. There were naturally occasions when men and women alike were driven by gaming or improvidence to sell or pawn their jewels, a traditional resort which had been naïvely remarked by Mrs Hardcastle in Goldsmith's play, *She Stoops to Conquer*, first performed in 1771. A countrywoman, modelling her costume and coiffure on fashion plates, Mrs Hardcastle was under the impression that the neighbours who went to London with their diamonds, returning with marcasites and paste ornaments, did so in the interests of the mode alone.[14]

In May 1791 George Prince of Wales, owing above £25,000 to the bankers Ransome, Morley & Hammersley of Pall Mall and apparently in the expectation of further advances, deposited with them as security a casket containing a diamond epaulette, a diamond George, Star and Garter, and various other diamond 'trinkets and ornaments belonging to his Royal Highness and also a diamond hilted sword'. The Prince undertook to repay the loan, together with five per cent interest, on 10 December, in which case the jewels were to be returned to him; if not, after giving three months' notice, the bankers were empowered to sell them and hand over to the Prince any surplus over what they were owed.[15]

The great suite of diamond jewellery commissioned from Nathaniel Jefferys by the Prince of Wales in 1795 for his bride, his cousin Princess Caroline of Brunswick (see page 20), has long since disappeared, but the necklace at least was recorded by Gainsborough Dupont in a portrait of the Princess in her marriage robes (Plate 13).[16] It appears to be a rivière (a string of graduated stones) with drops. The Crown worn by the Princess bears a strong resemblance to Queen Charlotte's (Plate 14) and may indeed have been lent by her. Low on the bride's bodice is a medallion set with a miniature of the Prince of Wales, supplied by Jefferys for £2,625.

Shortly after the birth of Princess Charlotte of Wales in January 1796 Princess Caroline was informed by one of the King's officers that her husband was no longer prepared to live with her. The Princess claimed that the message was reinforced by the removal of much of the furniture in her apartments. She had already lost her pearl bracelets to the Prince's current mistress, Lady Jersey.[17] The Princess eventually removed to the environs of Blackheath, where her indiscreet behaviour was soon the subject of gossip. Regarding her allowance from the Prince as inadequate, she treated her jewellery as portable wealth to be realised as necessity dictated. In about 1810 the Princess took up with a family of Italian singers named Sapio who battened on her. She asked her lady-in-waiting, Lady Charlotte Campbell (later Lady Charlotte Bury) to try and sell 'two enormous diamonds' for her. Lady Charlotte reluctantly took them to several jewellers, one of whom, she wrote, 'by referring to his books, declared that they were jewels belonging to the Crown'.[18] The jeweller may have been Philip Rundell, recognising two of the stones he had supplied to Jefferys for the Princess's marriage jewellery. One man offered a mere £150 for both diamonds; Lady Charlotte, aware that this was derisory, brought them back to the Princess in some

Plate 13. *Princess Caroline of Brunswick in her wedding costume, by Thomas Gainsborough's nephew, Gainsborough Dupont. The Princess, daughter of George III's sister, married George Prince of Wales on 8 April 1795. The Prince, a fastidious man, was repelled by her habits and broke with her soon after the birth of their only child, Princess Charlotte of Wales, in January 1796. The King had been sanguine about the success of the marriage and commissioned the portrait which was started by Dupont in June 1795. He depicted the Princess wearing a Crown (perhaps lent by Queen Charlotte — see Plate 14) and the diamond necklace from the great suite of marriage jewellery valued at over £54,000, for which the jeweller Nathaniel Jefferys received only partial payment. The portrait medallion with a miniature of the Prince of Wales is an ironical ornament in view of the rapid breakdown of the union.*

ROYAL COLLECTION

Plate 14. *Queen Charlotte's brilliant Crown, part of the new marriage jewellery given to her by King George III on her arrival in England for their wedding on 8 September 1761. She bequeathed this jewellery to Hanover, and when in 1837 Queen Victoria succeeded to the English throne and her uncle the Duke of Cumberland to that of Hanover, the new King determined to lay claim to the jewels. For various reasons, the claim was only settled in December 1857. The verdict favoured Hanover and the Queen thus lost her grandmother's Crown in addition to other pieces.*

PHOTOGRAPH FROM: TWINING COLLECTION, WORSHIPFUL COMPANY OF GOLDSMITHS

embarrassment. She had no idea of the subsequent fate of the stones, which were probably sold. A letter from the Princess, published in Lady Charlotte's memoirs, confirms that other gifts from her royal relatives were treated with equal contempt. '— I found a pair of old earrings which the *d —* of a *Q —* once gifted me with. I truly believe that the sapphires are *false* as her *heart* and soul is, but the diamonds are *good,* and £50 or £80 would be very acceptable for them indeed. . . .'[19]

The diamonds imported into London were then priced in their rough or uncut state according to their quality. Those brought from India, often by Jewish merchants who sent out in exchange coral purchased from dealers in Leghorn, were already classified in five grades, the best of which were determined by considerations of size and purity. Some were cut in London, but the majority went to Amsterdam. The small and cheapest stones were usually consigned to Antwerp to be made into mixed-cuts or small roses. These neat arrangements were always vulnerable to the outbreak of war. An even bigger threat to the traditional trade with India was posed in the second half of the eighteenth century by the increasing import of Brazilian diamonds and the rapid exhaustion of the old Indian mines. By the early 1800s South American stones predominated.

The uneasy times of 1793-94 and the consequent glut of diamonds on the European market were reflected in the quantity of stones brought from India. The overall value of the Indian diamonds imported in 1793 was £78,000. In 1795 it was £4,800, too large and rapid a fall to be attributed to the dwindling output of the Indian mines alone. The demand from England had itself diminished, albeit temporarily. By 1796 the value of rough stones imported from India rose to £22,000.[20]

Large and medium-sized diamonds, usually cut as brilliants, were increasingly set 'transparent' in unbacked collets or mounts from the mid-1790s. Wakelin & Garrard of Panton Street, Haymarket (later better known as Garrard & Company, the Crown Jewellers to Queen Victoria and her successors), often sold jewellery set in this fashion. In the late eighteenth century they were best known as goldsmiths and silversmiths and already held warrants as suppliers to various members of the royal family, though they ranked below the principal Royal Goldsmiths Jefferys & Jones of Cockspur Street (of whom Nathaniel Jefferys was a family connection) and the fast-rising firm of Rundell & Bridge in Ludgate Hill. Garrard's (as they are hereinafter termed for the sake of brevity and consistency) had their own silversmithing workshop but farmed out all or most of their jewellery commissions to outside concerns; some were jewellers and retailers, others specialised in working for the trade in general. They probably did not bother to set up a jewellery workshop of any size until they succeeded Rundell's as the principal goldsmiths and jewellers to the Crown in 1842.

The jewellery commissions passed on by Garrard's were respectable rather than sumptuous, with a few exceptions, and apparently frequently involved re-setting stones broken out of old family jewellery. This was a traditional custom; jewels were often re-set for the bride of an eldest son or on the marriage of a daughter. The information regarding Garrard's patrons and their outworkers is derived from an incomplete series of ledgers largely preserved in the Victoria and Albert Museum.[21] The series includes one of the original two Workmen's Ledgers of 1793-1800 as well as Gentlemen's Ledgers which record the purchases made by clients of both sexes. So many craftsmen are recorded in the Workmen's Ledger that it is impossible to cite them all, and the same must be said of the firm's patrons. One of the latter, named Grigg, had the honour of acquiring one of the first examples of transparent-set brilliants to be sold by Garrard's in February 1796. Employing diamonds supplied to them, Clinton & Coles of 16 Salisbury Street, Strand, set them open-backed in a cross, charging Garrard's £1.11s.6d. for their work. Instances of diamonds supplied by Garrard's or the craftsmen being comparatively rare, it is difficult to determine the price of stones on the partial recovery of the trade in 1796. In this year, however, William Watson, perhaps the William Watson with premises in the Strand from about 1784-96, was credited with supplying Garrard's with fourteen small brilliants weighing 7 grains (some 1¾ carats) priced at £7 per carat, making a total of £12.5s. Clinton & Coles charged £8 per carat for another group of modest diamonds. Larger diamonds, then as now, were proportionately far more expensive, their price rising steeply with each carat. Entries in the Workmen's Ledger of 1793-1800 relating to work performed by Benjamin Levy, a diamond cutter, of 5 Gray's Inn Terrace, shows that he re-cut six roses into brilliants weighing 4½ carats in 1795 for £3.3s. No reference is made to the final cost to the client. The question of price is further pursued in Chapter III.

Transparent settings for coloured stones were adopted shortly before or after 1800. The *Belle Assemblée,* illustrating a 'full' (formal) Parisian robe in 1807, commented that the necklace and earrings depicted with it were 'of rubies, set transparent'.[22] All but very small stones were mounted in individual cup-shaped collets, which lost part of their undersides in transparent settings. The tops, the part holding the stones on the front, conformed to two established types. In the cut-down variety, the most recent, the metal (silver in the case of diamonds, gold for coloured stones) was carefully worked up over the widest part of the stone (the girdle) and gathered at intervals into ribs, as described in Chapter III. Viewed from the front, in plan, the ribs cluster like granules around the edges of the stones. Cut-down settings outnumbered the older, rubbed-over type, in which the stone was secured without ribs; however the latter was still employed for some coloured stones. A variety of rubbed-over mounting comprised a gold strip worked up from a central groove or depression in the border to hold the stone. Traditionally used for engraved gems, a collective term for cameos, which are carved in relief, and intaglios, which are cut into the surface of the hardstone or other material, these mounts are still known as Roman settings (Plate 33).

Opaque stones were still mounted in closed cup-shaped collets. Pastes also continued to be set in closed-back mounts lined with foil to enhance their sparkle (Plate 15). Filigree borders in the French taste might be set with pearls held in conjoined gold rings (Plate 16A). It was more usual in England to make borders of half-pearls or small stones inserted in hollows cut in a continuous closed setting and secured with grains of metal teased up with a tool from the ground (Plate 16 B and C). The 'thread and grain' technique was also used to hold stones at the inner edges of borders, where ribs would have looked clumsy. This comparatively recent innovation permitted pavé (pavement) mounting, in which the stones were packed densely over the surface of an article (Colour Plate 12).

Pearls were an essential component of much jewellery. They ranged from large specimens used in work of primary quality to tiny ones aptly called seed pearls which might be strung in ropes, threaded with horsehair on to a frame cut from mother-of-pearl (Plates 67 and 68), split in two and used in borders, as mentioned above, or as garnishes in hairwork (Colour Plate 13A). The pearl stringers were

Plate 15. A white paste necklace set in silver, backed with gold. Essentially a rivière of graduated stones, it is garnished with leaf and bud drops, simplified versions of those on more costly works set with precious stones. The pastes are brilliant-cut and finely mounted in cut-down settings. The necklace is probably French, but might have been executed elsewhere by a craftsman trained in France; it dates to about 1790-1805. VICTORIA AND ALBERT MUSEUM

invariably women, working either on their own account in a cottage industry, or employed in a workshop, sometimes under male management. The one extant late eighteenth century Garrard Workmen's Ledger shows that the firm patronised several specialist pearl and bead stringers. Martha Taylor appears to have been especially favoured by Garrard's, who also passed commissions to Flower & Son and a Miss Leaf. Concerns of this kind strung not only pearls and conventional beads, but dried seeds and berries, some coming from India. Carnegy & Co (probably the workshop listed in Holden's *Directory* for 1805-07 as Carnegy & Kinnear of 51 Berwick Street, Soho) were prepared on occasion to drill berries for stringing, although they were jewellers by trade. Other workshops called upon by Garrard's to string items include Bilger (presumably Bilger & Son of 45 Piccadilly). There may well have been even more in the second Workmen's Ledger of the period which no longer survives. The Piccadilly business, though clearly employing a stringer or stringers, also supplied Garrard's with trinkets such as a pair of enamelled earrings at a charge of £1.5s. in 1795 and two steel chains commissioned in the same year. One with a hook cost Garrard's £1.4s. and was entered in the ledger on 4 May. The other, interestingly, suggests that Bilger's had access to a local maker of steel chains and toys, for their bill transcribed in the Workmen's Ledger on 17 September, runs, 'making a steel Chain with addition'; this was charged at 6s.

On 17 November 1797 Bilger's furnished Garrard's with mourning jewellery comprising 'a Black Necklace' (priced at 5s.) and a matching pair of earrings (9s.). The name of the client set against the entry in the Workmen's Ledger is Weatherstone. This must be Mrs Watherstone of the contemporary Gentlemen's Ledger, who on 18 November acquired a black bead necklace for 7s.6d. and earrings for 12s., the difference in price representing Garrard's profit. Martha Taylor undertook the stringing of several pieces for a clergyman, Mr D'Oyley (probably D'Oyly)[23] in the same year. One of the items, entered in the Workmen's Ledger on 18 March, 'By Stringing a p^r. Tassels & gold pieces', was charged at 5s. This appears to correspond with an entry dated 17 March in the Gentlemen's Ledger, 'To Stringing a pair of Pearl Tassel Earrings and furnish^g Gold Loops', for which work D'Oyly paid 8s. In this case the difference of 3s. included the provision of a small amount of gold; the pearls, as was frequently the case, were provided by the client.

Martha Taylor, though principally concerned with pearls, also strung stones, including in 1796 'a pair of double loop Garnet Earrings' for D'Oyly together with 'a 6 row'd Garnet necklace [with] Silver gilt rings', the latter either links or the traditional loops for tying the necklace at the back. Again, the components were supplied by Garrard's and Martha Taylor charged 1s.6d. for stringing the former and 5s.6d. for the latter.[24]

Many of Garrard's customers without family pearls for re-stringing and reluctant to buy the genuine article resorted to 'patent' or artificial pearls. The firm sold nine rows of 'fine patent pearl' priced at 5s. a row in July 1797; if this, as appears likely, was a necklace, it can be compared with a two-row specimen of real pearls acquired by another client a few months earlier for £2.12s.6d., that is, £1.6s.3d. per string. At approximately one-fifth of the price of true pearls, 'patent pearls' were undoubtedly cheap, but compared with the mass-produced specimens on sale a century later, too expensive for the great mass of the population. Beads and seeds, which cost very little, were often used to set off gold components, which again put them out of reach of the poor.

The surviving Garrard Ledgers, taken together with fashion reports, demonstrate that though diamonds and pearls remained of primary importance, coloured stones, whether precious, semi-precious or pastes, grew steadily in importance from about the mid-1790s. On 17 May 1797 the eccentric Lady Mary Coke, known as 'the White Cat' because of her uncannily pale skin and 'the fierceness of her eyes', unshaded by eyebrows,[25] took possession of a disappointingly conventional 'Brilliant and Emerald Handkerchief pin' set with eleven small brilliant-cut diamonds and three emeralds. Lady Mary, who supplied the stones, paid Garrard's £4.4s. for the piece. Handkerchief pins were in fact small brooches of the type known in the late nineteenth century as 'lace pins'. They owed their original name to their function of fastening the 'handkerchief', the scarf or drapery worn around the neck or shoulders to conceal or emphasise the decolletage, according to preference.

Clinton & Coles, listed in *The General London Guide* of 1794 at 16 Salisbury Street, Strand, were much used by Garrard's. According to the Garrard Day Book of March 1797 to May 1799, in April 1798 these jewellers set 'a Sapphire round with fine pearls and Gold back for the Centre of a Necklace'. This was part of an order placed by Lady Macclesfield,[26] who furnished the sapphire in an old setting, the value of which was credited to Clinton & Coles. The necklace centre, to which was attached fine gold chains, pearls, stones or beads to encircle the throat, was exactly what the term implies: a single large unit, often fitted with a spring clasp, placed in the front of the necklace and worn above or below the collar bone. Occasionally such a centre was flanked by two or more smaller units, linked by festoons of chains. Lady Macclesfield's necklace centre had a pearl border. Coloured stones framed in diamonds or pearls constituted one of the most characteristic devices of the early nineteenth century (Colour Plates 22 and 23).

Convention dictating that fine jewels were appropriate only to grand occasions (interpreted by aristocrats as referring to the primacy of the London Season), secondary jewellery was widely worn. Pieces set with amethysts, genuine and imitation, garnets, mocho stone (or moss agate, a chalcedony with moss-like markings), jasper, aquamarines, opals and (rock) crystals all occur and recur in the ledgers, as do carnelian and topaz, for which a positive rage developed as the new century drew close. This passion, like so many others, probably derived from France. Carnelian was also a favourite stone of gem-engravers and specimens of their work crop up in the Garrard Ledgers, but the firm's counterparts in France used engraved gems to a far larger extent than in England. 'Antiques', the contemporary term for engraved gems, which looked classical even when modern, were mainly set in rings for Garrard's clients. One of the few exceptions, entered in the Workmen's Ledger on 27 July 1798, shows that Clinton & Coles removed an engraved gem from a ring and set it in a pearl border to form the centre of a necklace, for which they charged a total of £3.8s.

Paste of various kinds, as well as 'beads', some at least of which must have been made of glass, are frequently mentioned in the Garrard Ledgers. Plaques of opaline paste and vitreous dark blue composition were often employed as backgrounds to arrangements of hair, pearls and small stones in many sentimental

Plate 16. Three sentimental pieces in gold and pearls.
A. The heart-shaped gold pendant once contained hair under crystal and is bordered by pearls in continuous ring collets; the construction is revealed where two pearls are missing. It is possibly English in the French taste, late eighteenth century.
B and C. The shuttle-shaped brooch on the lower left is set with half-pearls in a solid border surrounding a hair plait under a crystal cover, while the shaped oval one on the right, which also once contained hair under crystal, is encircled by a serpent formed of graduated half-pearls; ruby eye. English, they are slightly later than the pendant and probably date to the early nineteenth century. VICTORIA AND ALBERT MUSEUM

lockets and medallions (Colour Plate 13A, C and D). Pieces of this kind were a minor speciality of William Duncan, another of Garrard's outworkers. By 12 September 1795 he had completed the task of 'Setting a large miniature with Comp[n] hair Braid & Colour'd Gold Cypher on Opal', for which he charged £3.13s.6d., the miniature having been supplied. A large case for it cost a further 3s.6d. Perhaps it was too large to wear, though the size of portrait medallions was usually no deterrent. Duncan frequently incorporated human hair in his work. In some instances it was his principal material. On 16 December 1797 he supplied 'a Hair Cord Necklace wth 4 Gold joinings & Bracelet', the latter presumably having a band formed of separate strings of hair set in gold joints and attached to a gold spring clasp. The two articles cost £1.1s. T. & H. Davies, described in Holden's *Directory* for 1805 as goldsmiths and jewellers of 39 Brewer Street, Soho, furnished Garrard's with three hair braid necklaces and a braided neckchain and ring in 1799.

Coral, though frequently mentioned by fashion writers and admired in England as well as on the Continent, makes only occasional appearances in the Garrard Ledgers. One of their clients, Thomas Hodgkins, purchased 'a large Coral Necklace with gold clasp' in December 1800. This plainly had no connection with the tiny necklaces and bracelets worn by infants (Plate 17). Though English ships still had access to Naples, where most coral was worked, it is probable that the English navy monopolised the facilities, leaving little room for merchant ships. The same difficulties do not seem to have prevented goldsmiths and jewellers in England from obtaining small quantities of Italian mosaics, either of the Roman variety comprising slices of glass rods arranged in compositions frequently representing Roman buildings, or the Florentine type (*pietra dura*), a hardstone marquetry depicting flowers and other devices (see Colour Plate 52). Miniature versions of these mosaics suitable for jewellery were eagerly acquired by the Empress Josephine and, largely through her example, were admired everywhere from the early years of the nineteenth century.

Plate 17. Two solemn infants, both dressed in white and wearing coral necklaces, gaze from this miniature by Andrew Plimer (1763-1837) which is set in a portrait medallion of silver-gilt; the reverse has locks of hair mounted on opalescent paste. SOTHEBY'S

The Garrard Ledgers probably give a misleading impression of the popularity of cut steel, which was more widespread than might be gathered from the commissions transmitted by the firm to their outworkers. Martha Taylor strung a pair of 'fancy pearl and steel bracelets' in May 1797, the steel element plainly comprising beads, probably faceted. The beads might have been purchased in bulk from Birmingham. Bilger's steel chains have already been cited: another jeweller, William Potter (who in 1805 was at 10 Gough Square, Fleet Street), supplied a pair of blue steel shoe buckles costing 10s.6d. on 10 March 1797, but his principal speciality was mourning buckles set with 'jet' (usually black pastes)[27] mainly intended to fasten breeches at the knee and to adorn shoes. Garrard's also dealt occasionally with the Boulton & Smiths partnership at Soho which turned out shoe latches in silver, steel and plated metals. These are discussed presently.

Matthew Boulton, whose steel toys enjoyed wide popularity in Europe (Plates 18 and 19), was a member of the Birmingham Lunar Society; its members congregated together when a full moon made travelling easier and discussed matters philosophical and scientific. The potter Josiah Wedgwood,[28] another member, left some of his tiny ceramic reliefs with Boulton to be set as buttons, writing on 14 June 1786 that he would 'be glad to increase our connection in this way, as well as selling you cameos for your own trade, as in having them mounted by you for mine, both in gilt metal and steel, or in any other better way which your inventive genius may strike out.'[29] Boulton did indeed strike out. Some of the designs for cut steel trinkets in the Soho pattern book adumbrate areas labelled 'I W — d camios' while others were designed to incorporate paste or small enamel plaques. Wedgwood himself collaborated with other firms in the Midlands in addition, namely Hazlewood & Vernon and Green & Vale, so that it is far from true that all Wedgwood cameos set in cut steel derive from Soho.

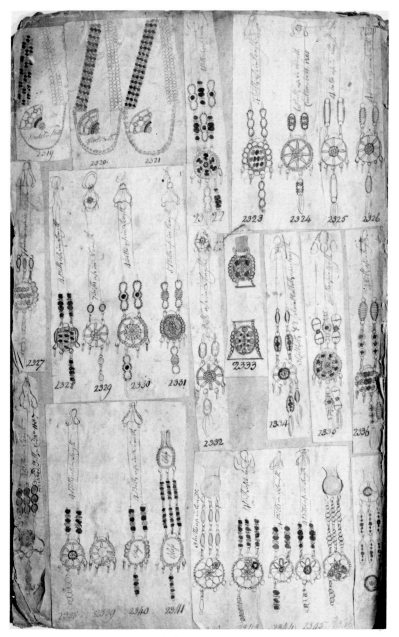

Plate 18. Detail of a page in Volume B of the Boulton Pattern Books, showing designs for cut-steel chatelaines with hook plates. Nos. 2340 and 2341 have oval plaques marked 'Glass', perhaps a reference to Tassie pastes. BIRMINGHAM COLLECTION, REFERENCE LIBRARY, BIRMINGHAM

It is unclear whether Garrard's sold much jewellery set with glass paste cameos and intaglios by James Tassie, whose business in Leicester Fields passed on his death in 1799 to his nephew William.[30] But both Tassie and Wedgwood 'gems' were set in seals, probably for male wear. There is little evidence of marcasite jewellery in the ledgers. Made of iron pyrites, it had largely gone out of fashion and was probably produced only in small quantities in England at this time. It is also possible that retailers had formerly depended to a great extent on imported wares and now did little to promote it. The records of one firm cannot be expected accurately to reflect every nuance of fashion, but the Garrard Ledgers afford much information otherwise impossible to obtain, such as the popularity of morocco leather for use as earrings, bracelet bands or even on occasion as necklaces.

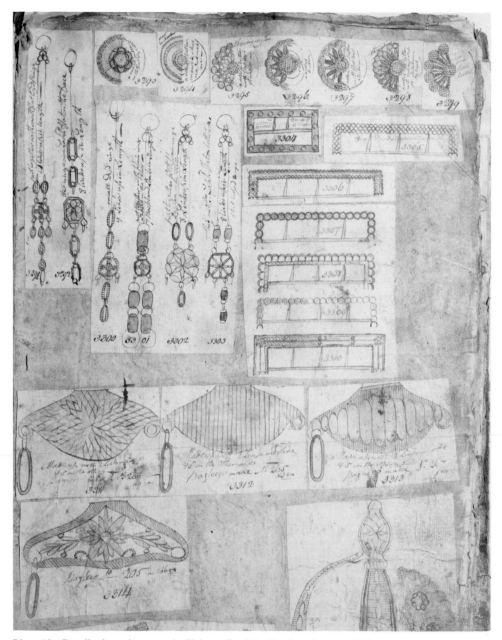

Plate 19. Detail of another page in Volume B of the Boulton Pattern Books.

Spangled trinkets, figuring in several entries, were far more expensive than the frippery remnants at the Thomas Coram Foundation and were clearly quite different in type. Thomas & Henry Davies of Brewer Street[31] supplied three pairs of 'Oval Spangle Earrings' costing £1.16s. a pair, which were entered in the Workman's Ledger on 17 May 1793. A pair of morocco earrings furnished by the same firm on 29 May cost Garrard's £1. They also set a conch shell in gold for a necklace on 4 July 1797.

Gold, unadorned by stones, was much in demand, to judge by the references to trinkets of this type in Heideloff's *Gallery*. Jewellers had their methods of treating gold to improve its colour which were especially useful when they worked with heavily alloyed metal. On the whole, however, the gold used immediately before and after 1800 in England was of a higher quality than was employed in mass-produced wares in the second half of the nineteenth century. It lent itself to elaborate contrasting effects. Once the shortages arising from the mismanagement of the French economy before, during and after the Terror had been overcome, Parisian jewellers often combined up to four different kinds of gold in one article, a technique manifested earlier in the decoration of pre-Revolutionary snuff boxes. There is some evidence that English jewellers were doing much the same thing, probably however using fewer colours. In 1796, according to the Garrard Ledger, James Hyde gilded 'a Chas'd Coral' (a combined rattle and teething implement for a baby) in two colours. If the craftsman could gild in two colours, he might work gold in similar fashion. On 2 January 1800 T. & H. Davies supplied Garrard's with 'a coloured Neck Chain' costing £2.2s. This may simply have been gold with its surface chemically treated[32] to remove the alloy; on the other hand, it might have been composed of differently coloured golds. The surviving account book of another London jeweller, N. Goetze, which covers the years 1809 to 1814, shows that he used coloured golds and he cannot have been exceptional.

Simple contrasts of texture were achieved by polishing part of a gold article and matting other areas with tools. Symmetrical patterns were produced with the aid of lathes. William Duncan furnished 'A pair of Gold Bracelets [with] Engine turn'd tops' on 28 April 1795 at a cost of £1.11s.6d. On 12 April the following year Clinton & Coles were credited in the Workmen's Ledger with setting 'a large B^t Bracelet' with fifteen brilliants weighing over 6 carats in all and fitted with a clasp decorated with engine-turning. The brilliants, priced at £8 a carat, were in this instance supplied by the makers, who charged £50.10s. for them. They costed their workmanship at £5.15s.6d. Other outworkers patronised by Garrard's also executed engine-turned patterns on a small scale to decorate jewellery. They were likewise accomplished engravers, though they used the technique sparingly and only rarely added chased ornament. Much goldwork was left plain, but there are occasional references to milled edges and friezed gold (see Plate 56).

The larger workshops probably had already begun to buy their gold ready flatted to the required gauge. When they wanted to stamp out small components they used a fairly thin gauge. To judge by entries in the Garrard Ledgers, some of these tiny stamped motifs were used in the construction or embellishment of elaborate chains, as in France (Plate 6). The jeweller Peter Delauney of 17 Crown Street, Soho[33] furnished Garrard's on 23 March 1799 with 'a Stamp Chain & topaz snap' (clasp) at a cost of £2.4s. A full yard of this pattern, supplied with other varieties on 19 October following, was priced at £3.3s. The other types, also in yard lengths, were 'single bent' (£2.14s), 'double bent' (£3.13s.6d.), 'Oak leaf', a likely candidate for stamped details (£4) and 'Strong Maltese' (£4.4s.). At other times the same jeweller made a twenty-nine inch long 'flatt Maltese Chain', for which he charged £3.7s., and another piece simply described as 'a Maltese neck Chain' costing £3.13s.6d. In 1798 his namesake A. Delauney added six inches of 'fillagree Bent Chain' to an existing ornament, colouring it and mending it; this was plainly a complicated job, as he charged Garrard's £9.9s. for it.

Several items in gold or silver filigree were supplied to Garrard's between about 1794 and 1798. One craftsman, identified in the Workmen's Ledger only by his surname, Harris, provided a pair of 'large filagree Slides' for 5s. which were entered on 5 March 1798. They were probably intended to be worn on velvet ribbons or morocco bands as bracelets. A pair of filigree earrings costing £1.16s. was supplied by Peter Delauney in May of the same year. Though the metal used was rarely cited it is plain enough that the traditional art of filigree which had flourished in England in the seventeenth century had not died out in London, as is often thought, but was still conducted on a small scale. The filigree jewellery cited in English periodicals (the *Lady's Magazine* for June 1790 provides one such instance)[34] was clearly based on reality. Birmingham was a well-known centre for the manufacture of filigree before and after 1800, but most of the articles turned out there were silver toys such as caddy spoons and nutmeg graters.[35] Henry Adcock's ingenious cast versions of silver filigree jewellery dating to 1807 and later were not however unique (Plate 73).

Specialist filigree-makers were not numerous in England, even in Birmingham. The tradition was stronger on the Continent, especially in areas where the technique was used in the production of regional or peasant jewellery which made no pretence of conforming to current modes. Parisian jewellers, forced by the shortage of materials to turn to filigree in the 1790s, were able to study the work of living craftsmen in the countryside. It is more likely, however, that they derived their technical information from medieval artefacts.

Enamelwork was especially favoured for sentimental jewellery. Two techniques were employed: *champlevé,* comprising opaque enamel fired into designs hollowed out in the metal ground, and *basse-taille,* a more sophisticated variety in which the ground, textured or patterned with a tool, is visible through the translucent enamel. It is possible that a pair of enamelled gold earrings bought by Sir Edward Warrington from Garrard's for £2.2s. on 6 February 1793 bore the colours of mourning (white or white and blue for an unmarried girl or woman, white for a bachelor and black for all married persons).[36] No hint of the colour or nature of the enamel appears in this entry nor in several others of an equally ambiguous nature. Occasionally colours are mentioned in the description of pieces of a recognisably sentimental nature. According to an entry dated 1 March 1796 Clinton & Coles executed 'a large blue & white' enamelled locket set with seventy-eight brilliants, blue 'composition' and opal paste at the back. The diamonds were obviously supplied by Garrard's, since Clinton & Coles charged only £11.11s. for a complicated piece of work.

This locket was perhaps set with a portrait, though it is not mentioned in the entry. A later specimen supplied by the same firm and entered in the ledger on 31 December in the same year was constructed around a miniature: 'By setting a picture in a locket flat-edge blue comp^n wth medallion & hair on opal.' It cost Garrard's £3.8s. A 'round Locket' with an enamelled gold border and motto (inscription) was purchased by Thomas Tryon from Garrard's on 16 January 1796; it may have been either a memorial piece with a commemorative inscription or a love token bearing an amatory message. Enamelled 'motto' rings frequently crop up in the Garrard Ledgers. These were mainly mourning rings and the mottos again commemorative.

The guiding principle in design for most of the decade was the delicacy, both real and illusory, characteristic of much neo-classical art in the 1770s and 1780s. The effect was often achieved by a trick of construction: lockets were sometimes made with a convex centre tapering down to a thin or flat edge (see Colour Plate 13A). The locket supplied by Clinton & Coles late in 1796 and described above might well have been of this type.

A corresponding taste for fine detail on a small scale is exemplified by the continued popularity of miniature compositions painted on ivory and by the more esoteric ivory reliefs which were widespread on the Continent, especially in France, Switzerland, the Low Countries and Germany.[37] Betsey Wynne bought ivory articles when her family were in Geislingen in November 1789. Unfortunately she acquired only a pencil and a thimble but her mama purchased 'all sorts of Knicnacs'. A few days afterwards the Wynnes arrived in another German town, Pforzheim, which was known, wrote Betsey, for its 'ivory and steel manufacture'. Four years later, when the family had temporarily settled in Switzerland, Betsey noted a visit to a craftsman named Perigo at Ouchy near Lausanne who 'works very well in Ivory Hair and pearls.'[38] This combination of materials strongly suggests that he made sepia miniatures on ivory, set off with hair and pearls as in Colour Plate 13F. But Perigo may have carved tiny reliefs in ivory, setting them in jewellery with hair curls and pearls mounted under crystal or glass on the reverse. The best-known practitioners of this craft in England (indeed the diarist Mrs Philip Lybbe Powys proclaimed them the only ones) were G. Stephany & J. Dresch of Bath and London. They must have been immigrants: their miniature carvings are reminiscent of articles made in Schwäbisch-Gmünd and elsewhere in Germany at the time.

Mrs Lybbe Powys inspected a display of Stephany & Dresch's work at Bath in 1798. As an amateur carver of cherry stones she was impressed by its quality. Portraits of King George III and Queen Charlotte were 'astonishing well done', while the carved devices for 'lockets, bracelets, rings, or toothpick cases [were] in as small pieces as I did the cherry-stone baskets, . . . done with something like the same knives, and must be equally trying to the eyes.'[39] Mrs Lybbe Powys made no mention of any settings; perhaps Stephany & Dresch patronised outworkers or simply supplied specimens of their work on request to jewellers for mounting.

Sentimental jewellery of this kind was customarily set in gold. Garrard's sold comparatively few articles in gilt metal. Some, including twelve gilt chains at 3s.6d. apiece, supplied in 1799, and a gilt locket costing 1s.9d. furnished in 1800, came from Perchard & Co., afterwards Perchard & Brooks, small workers in gold and metal and also 'gilt and water gilders', of 12 Charles Street, Hatton Garden. Given the general level of Garrard's clientele, it is likely that these were bought as gifts to servants. The water gilding process is synonymous with mercury or fire-gilding; a solution of nitrate of mercury was applied to the metal objects to be gilded. This prepared the surface for an amalgam of gold and mercury. When the object so treated was set over a fire, the mercury evaporated with the heat, leaving a gold-covered surface. The technique was effective but dangerous: gilders tended to die of mercury poison before the age of forty. The thicker the application of the mercury amalgam, the more expensive the finished object. In the case of very cheap articles the amalgam was thin. An even more exiguous coating was probably achieved by dipping in a solution of gold, but this practice was largely unacknowledged. The traditional close-plating technique, in which silver or gold was applied with flux to a base metal ground and fixed by heat, was tricky to execute. Many makers of cheap trinkets preferred to create the illusion of gold by using pinchbeck for their articles.

The shape of jewellery reflected the current concern with purity of form. Many devices were geometric ovals, rectangles (sometimes described in the Garrard ledgers as long squares) which were either left plain or had their corners clipped. There were also 'oval squares', in which the two forms were overlaid to produce a square or rectangle with generously rounded sides, octagons, circles and crescents, the latter turning up in almost every material and in all types of jewellery from head ornaments to earrings, necklace centres, lockets, pins and bracelet snaps (clasps). A. Delauney made a pair of textured gold bracelet clasps in June 1797 which were entered in the Workmen's Ledger as 'Matted Crescent snaps'.

Slight national differences are discernible in the neo-classical repertory of devices. As the new century approached, the long chains known as sautoirs appear in French fashion plates (and in copies made and published elsewhere) with massive oval, rectangular, circular or lozenge-shaped links far bolder than those obtaining in chains in other countries (Plate 78). Moreover lozenges found more favour in France than in England. Square-shaped medallions and oblong specimens worn horizontally were more Continental than English. Goya's portrait of the Condesa de Fernan Nunez (1803) in the Prado, Madrid, depicts her wearing a pendent miniature in a rectangular frame.

Neo-classical principles were gently stretched to accommodate naturalistic devices pre-dating the Revolution, though it is evident that the floral pieces still occasionally made in England were less tolerated in France. Among the flower motifs inherited from earlier decades were 'jessamine' (jasmine) and roses. Garrard's received a number of old naturalistic pieces for repair, indicating that such jewels were still acceptable in fashionable circles. Their craftsmen were also asked to execute a number of new diamond sprays with stalks and leaves; known as sprigs, they were usually worn in the coiffure. In April 1794 Clinton & Coles set a pair of brilliant earrings for £7.7s., furnishing a case for an additional 5s., following these with a 'Jessamine pin wth 417 B[t] in do', charged at £10.10s. and a case at 5s. The name of the same client (Taylor) appears in both entries. The diamonds probably came from this source, though they may have been supplied by Garrard's.

Bodice ornaments in the form of jewelled nosegays larger than sprigs were out of favour. On the other hand, the practice of decorating the head continued. George III's eldest daughter Charlotte, the Princess Royal,[40] was sketched by P.W. Tomkins wearing an elaborate coiffure (Plate 20) in which a jewelled peacock feather rises vertically from a rosette on the front of her turban, apparently resting against a cluster of the ostrich feathers mandatory in Court dress.[41] The combination of the small imitation feather and the towering group of real ones is

Plate 20. Charlotte Augusta Matilda, Princess Royal, the eldest daughter of King George III and Queen Charlotte, in a study made by P.W. Tomkins in 1797. She is shown wearing a diamond peacock feather aigrette rising from a rosette in front of ostrich feathers, a jewelled flower pin and a string of stones or pearls in her coiffure, earrings, two rows of pearls and a cross, and a portrait medallion. Charlotte chafed at her unmarried state and in 1797, already in her early thirties, she was happy to become the second wife of Frederick, the immensely fat Hereditary Prince of Württemberg. Endowed with a managing disposition and lacking living progeny of her own, she cheerfully undertook his existing family and showered the Prince of Wales with letters of advice regarding the upbringing of his daughter, Princess Charlotte of Wales. The Princess Royal, like her younger sisters, accumulated a great deal of diamond jewellery in her childhood and possessed far more than was recorded by Tomkins.
BRITISH MUSEUM, DEPARTMENT OF PRINTS AND DRAWINGS

Plate 21. Detail from a portrait by an unknown artist of William Cecil, Lord Burghley (1520-1598), Lord High Treasurer and chief minister to Queen Elizabeth I. According to the inscription, it was painted in 1586 and clearly shows the jewel on the front of his hat clasping a spray of feather spines.
SOTHEBY'S

a strikingly effective visual pun. Aigrettes of this kind were not new; Clinton & Coles fitted a stalk and a screw to an existing diamond feather in May 1797. Ears of wheat were an acceptable alternative to feathers. The stylised treatment of aigrettes, already noted in the Introduction, had historic precedents (Plate 21).

Decorations to the head also included ornaments known as sultanas. Queen Charlotte herself had had a 'sultana feather' made from diamonds 'set by myself'.[42] On 23 December 1796 Clinton & Coles set 'a B^t Sultana (500 Bts in D^o)' for a client of Garrard's charging £21 for their work. The wording of an entry dated 29 March 1798, 'By Frame & String^g a Sultana', indicates that Martha Taylor threaded seed pearls on a carcass cut from mother-of-pearl, for which she charged £3.16s. For the same client, she strung a pair of earrings and a necklace with a fall, making a matching suite or parure. On 11 November Lord Seaford bought a 'pearl Sultana & Crescent' from Garrard's, together with other items including a pearl necklace with a fall and tassels. The Sultana cost him £3.3s.; if it were a feather like the specimen made for Queen Charlotte, the crescent presumably occupied the place of the rosette in the Princess Royal's aigrette. An early nineteenth century French variation on the theme, with splayed spines surmounted by pearls and star-shaped devices rising from a rosette, is illustrated in Fontenay, *Les Bijoux Anciens et Modernes* (1887).[43] But the term was probably extended to embrace other types of aigrette worn on the turbans which were still in vogue as the most recognisable component of the Turkish costume popularised by Lady Mary Wortley Montagu, whose *Letters from the East* were published after her death in 1762.[44] Maria Josepha Holroyd, writing to Miss Anne Firth about current fashions in 1794, declared that gowns were 'mostly Turkish and seem so loose from the Body, I expect if a foot is set upon a Train, to see the Ladies disrobed'.[45]

Pins of all kinds, including some with flower or butterfly heads (Colour Plate 14), further graced the coiffure, together with the traditional strings of pearls or stones. Tiaras were rare, though they existed, usually taking the form of small fronts rising to a peak over a curved band.

Necklaces fell into two main categories, and were increasingly fastened with metal spring clasps, instead of being tied at the back with ribbons threaded through metal loops. In the first were rivières of stones in individual collets, with or without drops and their counterparts formed of units or clusters of more modest stones, often having a small linking device of a different pattern between. The second (the commonest) type of necklace comprised a necklace centre which also acted as a clasp in front, with or without smaller units of the same design, connected by multiple festoons of fine gold chains, beads or stones (Plate 22). These festoons might be brought down to create a tracery over the ample decolletage admired at the time. Sometimes further chains, interspersed with smaller units echoing the shape of the necklace centre, were suspended perpendicularly from the main necklace. These created the fall already cited in some of the entries in the Garrard Workmen's Ledger. A handsome specimen of a cut steel and cameo necklace and fall, probably dating to about 1790, is illustrated in Clifford Smith's *Jewellery* (1908).[46] Martha Taylor also strung pearl necklaces with tassels; tassel earrings and bodice bows with similar pendants were also popular, to judge by the entries in her name in the same ledger. In April 1799 she also strung a row of diamonds; she only charged 1s. for this work, so that it was scarcely long enough for a necklace, unless it had been intended for a child.

Martha Taylor had not been asked to thread the stones themselves, but to re-string existing collets, each set with a diamond. From the late seventeenth century into the eighteenth, closed collets were often furnished on the underside with two parallel tubes through which threads (usually silk) were passed. The stones were thus secured by a double row of threads: if one broke, the other held the necklace together. There is some contemporary evidence that necklaces of diamond strings

Plate 22. Plate from Heideloff's Gallery of Fashion *for November 1794, showing a lady wearing a black-and-white afternoon dress with a watch suspended from her belt. She is in half-mourning, the second stage of mourning following the initial period when nothing but black might be worn for a length of time governed by the degree of her relationship to the deceased. The black trinkets sold by Garrard's were intended for full mourning. These seem to have been set aside for the second stage, for the caption describes her as wearing a gold necklace (festoon) and earrings though not, of course, coloured stones.*

were still fashionable in the late eighteenth century: an example is shown with a Court dress in Heideloff's *Gallery* in 1795, accompanied by diamond earrings, a silver girdle and, decorating the coiffure, a silver crape bandeau crossed with silver laurel and diamond ornaments in addition.[47] But most contemporary strings of brilliants were probably not threaded at all, the collets being connected by metal links or rings.

Pastes, if in closed-back settings, might still be strung. Coloured stones such as garnets were sometimes pierced to form beads and then threaded. The six rows of garnets strung by Martha Taylor in 1796 as a necklace for Garrard's client, Mr D'Oyly, were trumped by a plate in Heideloff's *Gallery* the following year depicting a lady in morning dress wearing no fewer than eight such strings.[48] An effect of equal complexity was easily created by sporting a combination of necklaces. Often a single string was contrasted with the festoon type, worn one above the other. Among the instances of this practice illustrated in the *Gallery* is one of 1795 in which a lady has a diamond necklace clasped high around her throat and another below it consisting of two chains with a medallion between.[49] A variation in the form of a triple tier of necklaces and medallions appeared in the German *Journal des Luxus und der Moden* in 1801.[50]

Simple earrings comprised a unit to the back of which was fastened a hook. The unit was often called a 'top'. When furnished with a pendant, the two together were known as 'top and drop', as in the filigree earrings in Plate 23. The combined ornament might be moderately long or wide, but in any case rarely approached the size of Spanish earrings, which were huge. Complex types included a 'knot' (bow), which was usually neither a top nor a drop but was interposed between the two, the 'drop' comprising three or more tear-shaped units. This traditional design (the girandole) had its origins in the baroque and was now on the way to revival. Girandole earrings were sometimes so heavy that they were uncomfortable to wear. Some of the devices to which women resorted to enable them to endure the

Plate 23. A pair of gold filigree top and drop earrings in the French manner, decorated with enamels and hung with pearls. Unmarked, it dates to the late 1790s and is comparable to the sautoir illustrated in Colour Plate 6A.

VICTORIA AND ALBERT MUSEUM

weight were to be advocated when earrings again became heavy in the late 1820s and 1830s. The side-effects of over-indulgence in weighty earrings were never eradicated. Queen Victoria, who loved them in her youth and during her married life, suffered from stretched ear-lobes which are evident in photographs of her in old age (Plate 324).

The solid drops hitherto in use were to develop into open silhouettes with a line of stones describing the shape and the centre filled with another motif of varying degrees of complexity which fell independently from the top. A later example of this construction can be seen in the emerald and diamond earrings in Colour Plate 25; the reverse, shown in Plate 62, demonstrates the extent to which open-backed collets lightened the weight of the setting which, like the old closed-back variety, was still lined with gold.

The earrings cited in the Garrard Ledgers, aside from those already noted such as crescents and tassels, are not always named. Those given some form of appellation include 'acorn', 'fluted', 'small melon', 'bar', 'loop', 'double loop', 'fancy loop', 'crown', 'fancy', 'lily drop' and (presumably different from the loops), 'pierc'd oval', 'round', 'circular' and 'ring'. Some earrings were fitted with fine chains not described as tassels; they were probably used to connect the top to the drop. Loops (hoops) were the most popular; ephemeral fashions included the Egyptian earrings supplied by Peter Delauney on 23 March 1799, the year after Nelson's victory in the Battle of the Nile. It is not clear what form they took and it is worth noting that certain stones associated with Egypt included a banded jasper. The earrings were to be followed by many other jewels celebrating English victors and victories: the French had already exploited the same patriotic market and other nations did exactly the same.

Matching necklaces and earrings were widespread. In 1796 A. Delauney supplied Garrard's with an unusual set in which the necklace had '3 Enamel'd hearts'; the earrings must have had heart-shaped drops. Two years later Peter Delauney produced 'a Bow Necklace wth Topaz' and earrings to suit. Fashion plates demonstrate that other sets comprised pendants and earrings. Two examples consist of an anchor pendant with matching earrings and a cross with corresponding ear-drops.[51]

Many fashionable women in the 1790s owned sets of no more than two to four matching pieces and expected to harmonise these ornaments with others. Diversity, particularly in secondary jewellery, was perfectly acceptable. The jewellery worn with a costume illustrated by Heideloff in 1800 comprised a pearl necklace, gold earrings and sleeve clasps made from 'Wedgwood's medallions'.[52] Medallions, with or without portraits, were rarely themselves included in sets of jewellery, though the chains from which they were often suspended might match

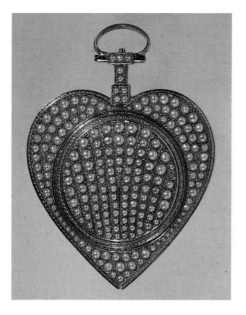

Colour Plate 12. A heart-shaped gold watch of about 1800, the movement signed Breguet à Paris, the face concealed by a hinged cover; the outside covered with pavé-set half-pearls. Several French watches changed hands at Garrard's in the 1790s. They were probably second-hand, but the war with France did not stop English people from regarding Parisian work as superior to London productions. There is no evidence, however, that this watch was ever in England. CHRISTIE'S GENEVA

other items in the owner's possession. Some of the medallions made by Garrard's outworkers have already been cited. The hair which was frequently set in the back under crystal or glass was a permanent installation, unlike the curls inserted in a recessed 'box' in lockets and covered by a crystal in a hinged gold frame which gave access to the contents.

On the whole, lockets were smaller than medallions and were either mourning or love tokens. Few were as extravagant as two ordered by George Prince of Wales after his unofficial marriage to Mrs Fitzherbert in 1785. The first was set with a miniature of himself in a diamond frame and the second with one of his wife, each covered by one half of a large diamond sawn in two. He gave the first locket to Mrs Fitzherbert and kept the second. Though they finally parted long before he succeeded to the throne as George IV, the Duke of Wellington was touched to discover the locket with Mrs Fitzherbert's portrait hung round the neck of the dead King and hidden by his shirt as he lay in his open coffin in 1830.[53]

Another surviving pre-Revolutionary pendant, the *fausse-montre,* was probably originally so-called because it replicated the shape of a watch. As time went by it became oval rather than round, but retained the distinctive swivel-ring. Sometimes it had a painted watch-face, though this was unusual. It was likely to be set, inside or outside, with a miniature or miniatures and sometimes further embellished with hair, blue paste and enamel in emulation of medallions. In 1789 a Gloucestershire client acquired from the goldsmith, jeweller and sword cutter William Nodes of 126 New Bond Street 'A Fause Montre Ena[d] plate and Dia[ds] strung round with fine pearls'. Costing £60, it had a secret spring, indicating that a miniature lurked under a hinged cover.[54] In contrast, T. & H. Davies charged Garrard's only £17.17s. in October 1793 for a 'plain Stand[d] Gold Faus[e] Montre'. The specimen

Colour Plate 13. Gold jewellery decorated with pearls and hairwork.
A. The crystal-covered reverse of a gold medallion which is set in front with a miniature of a woman. In the centre is a wheatsheaf worked in hair with gold wire ears of corn and a binding of wire and half-pearls, mounted on an opalescent vitreous ('composition') ground touched with gold. The border is of plaited hair within tapering gold edges. It is uninscribed, but is a standard sentimental piece probably made for the mother or another female relative of the sitter, though it is just conceivable that it was worn by a man. English, 1790s.

B. *The gold lyre-shaped pendent watch surmounted by a mask in a sunburst is probably Swiss; its openwork gold border, set with pearls in conjoined rings with flat enamelled gold edges, follows the French fashion like so much work produced in Switzerland in the late eighteenth century and later.*

C. *A gold medallion, the centre set under a crystal cover with a delicate composition in tiny pearls representing turtle doves at a fountain on a blue composition ground. The openwork gold border is set with pearls and edged with enamelled gold like the Swiss watch in B. But this piece is undoubtedly French, for the suspension ring is struck with a cock's head, the restricted warranty mark for gold in use in France from 1798 until 1819.*

D. *A pendent miniature case which might have been worn suspended on a neck-chain or attached to a fob at the waist. The gold neo-classical urn in the centre is decorated with applied scrolling filigree and half-pearls in addition to white champlevé enamel. The figures, romantic rather than neo-classical, are multi-coloured against a sky of dark blue translucent enamel, a hectic combination demonstrating its Swiss origin. It probably dates to about 1800.*

E. *A small gold pendant set with a mother-of-pearl, pearl and gold urn with flowers, over a dark blue composition ground. The rectangular gold frame has clipped corners and is decorated with white champlevé enamel. The carved mother-of-pearl suggests a Continental craftsman working in the late eighteenth century.*

F. *A gold mourning pendant with a standard miniature painted in sepia on ivory depicting a white-robed female figure contemplating an urn executed in hair and gold wire, mounted in gold chased with toothed ornament. A characteristic late eighteenth century English piece.*

G. *A pair of mourning slides, probably to be worn on ribbons, one with a wheatsheaf in hair, gold and half-pearls, the smaller version of 13A, and the other with a single curl, both mounted on ivory with gum in the usual manner. These are, however, Dutch, dating to the late eighteenth century. As Holland was under French domination from the mid-1790s, Dutch jewellers also became skilled at working in the French manner.*

VICTORIA AND ALBERT MUSEUM

Plate 24. A fausse-montre *in gold, the hinged cover opening to reveal a portrait of Lady Fanny Chambers by the miniaturist John Smart (1742/3-1811), dated 1792. The daughter of the sculptor Joseph Wilton, Lady Fanny was married at the age of sixteen to Sir Robert Chambers (1737-1803) just before he took up his appointment as a judge of the supreme court of Bengal in 1774. The portrait was thus executed in India, where John Smart practised from 1785-95. It may have been set by one of the many English goldsmiths working in India, or mounted later, when Sir Robert returned home with his wife.* SOTHEBY'S

in Plate 24 is also plain; it contains a portrait of Lady Fanny Chambers painted by John Smart in 1792.[55] These mock watches were still popular at the turn of the new century: Bisset's *Magnificent Directory* of 1800 carries an advertisement by Matthew Boulton's former pupil Edward Thomason, later the first Knight of the Birmingham trades, listing items available for export (presumably mainly outside Europe): 'Buttons, Watch Chains, Ear rings, Necklaces, Seals, Keys, faux Montres, *And all such kind of Toys'* (Plate 25).

One of the most original contributions to sentimental jewellery was the 'eye' portrait, another pre-Revolutionary innovation. Lady Eleanor Butler, one of the celebrated 'Ladies of Llangollen',[56] noted in her diary on 6 December 1785 that two brothers had called. The elder, fresh from the Grand Tour, was anxious to display his souvenirs which included 'An Eye, done at Paris and Set in a Ring. A true French Idea,' wrote Lady Eleanor, 'and a delightful Idea, which I admire more than I confess for its singular Beauty and Originality'. The Prince of Wales, early off the mark, sent a miniature of his eye with a letter proposing marriage to Mrs Fitzherbert dated 3 November 1785.[57] Lockets, brooches, pendants and clasps as well as rings were set with portraits of a single eye of a loved one or friend under a crystal cover. They had the advantage of baffling the inquisitive, it being difficult to identify the sitter on the evidence of one eye alone (Colour Plate 31). Several leading miniaturists executed eye portraits on occasion. Richard Cosway, who styled himself principal painter to the Prince of Wales from 1785 at least, listed an eye priced at £5.5s. as the second item in his statement of claims submitted to the Commissioners appointed to deal with the debts accumulated by the Prince of Wales between 1787 and 1795.[58]

The sentimental message of eye jewellery was often reinforced by curls or plaits of hair such as were housed in a variety of other pieces. The practice of incorporating associated sentimental emblems in a single item found widespread popularity. Not only were there padlock-shaped lockets, but others of more conventional form were sometimes supplied with their own miniature padlocks and keys to represent the locking away of the heart's secrets. Hearts were likewise fashionable. T. & H. Davies made one of carnelian counterset with a diamond cipher in 1797.

Mourning pendants, lockets and rings, the counterparts of the miniature ivory carvings already mentioned, had been produced in England since the 1760s (and later on the Continent). These were set with miniature paintings of funereal themes executed in sepia on ivory or vellum. Snippets of hair were sometimes mixed in with the paint and the results adorned with seed pearls, gold wire and, less frequently, with devices cut from mother-of-pearl, all glued into position and covered as usual with crystal or glass. The mass-produced paintings were largely the work of women, who interminably copied compositions assembled from a standard repertory of motifs including weeping willows shading urns bearing the name or initials of the deceased, raptly contemplated by classically-garbed females in white (Colour Plate 13F) and cherubs bearing consolatory tags hovering solicitously about. Obelisks, broken columns, flaming hearts, anchors and other devices signifying grief and fidelity were often incorporated. Many of these motifs, such as hearts and cherubs, together with urns dedicated to love and friendship instead of mourning, reappear in similar jewellery celebrating worldly attachments.[59] Both types were often fitted with boxes for hair at the back. Though these small trinkets went out of fashion in the early years of the nineteenth century many of the themes were adopted by the hairworking trade.

Traditional crosses, anchors, symbols of hope ('the anchor of the Soul'), hearts (Colour Plate 15), Cupid's bow and arrows and similar motifs were later to be assembled, with appropriate mottoes, in Knight's *Gems and Device Book* (1836), one of the last of a long line of emblem and device books going back to the sixteenth century.[60] All these motifs were in vogue in the 1790s, the anchor among those finding royal favour. George III's second daughter, Princess Augusta, wore an enamelled anchor pendant to her necklace when she sat to Sir William Beechey for a three-quarter length portrait exhibited at the Royal Academy in 1797 (Plate 26).[61] The dual nature of the device was invariably revealed in its treatment: made of gold or stones with a hair locket and an amatory inscription, the anchor was an appropriate gift from a lover. Enamelled in black, set with dark-coloured stones or jet, it became a mourning jewel. Very occasionally indeed, it symbolised professional concerns (Plate 27). The contemporary prevalence of crosses generally had as much to do with politics and fashion as religion. A gold Maltese cross presented by the Emperor of Russia to Nelson's mistress Lady Hamilton, whose husband was the English minister to Naples, encouraged a vogue for this type of cross in 1800 (Plate 40). Bows and arrows, favourite betrothal and marriage gifts (Colour Plate 6E) were naturally not used in mourning jewellery.

The crosses, arrows and hearts worn by the ladies depicted in Heideloff's *Gallery* were usually suspended from ribbons or gold chains.[62] Serpents with their tails in their mouths to symbolise eternity had already begun to wrap themselves around lockets and other articles. They spawned with remarkable rapidity from 1805 owing to the French passion for them. The butterfly, an emblem of the soul in neo-classical art, had fluttered into jewellery even earlier, staying for several decades.

Colour Plate 14. A late eighteenth century diamond flower brooch/ pin, a more elaborate version of the piece worn by the Princess Royal on her coiffure.
SOTHEBY'S

Though not greatly in evidence in the 1790s it reappeared in the new century.

Sentimental devices as well as hair were often incorporated in bracelets, which were mainly made and worn in pairs, one on each wrist. The bands were usually, though not invariably, formed of multiple strings of stones, pearls, beads or chains of various kinds. The decorated snaps of clasps, an important element of the design, might have a border pierced with a row of holes on one side for the attachment of one end of the strings; on the other side was a slitted edge made to receive an independent spring clip to which was fastened the other end of the strings. In this way it was possible to fasten and unfasten the bracelet. This system was also frequently used for necklace centres. Some centres, with apertures on both sides, were completely independent of the strings and might therefore be transferred from a bracelet to a necklace and vice versa. The Garrard Ledgers contain entries for independent clasps; in one such, dated August 1797, Sir Yelveton Peyton had a 'large Paste' set in 'Gold for a bracelet' (clasp). Some clasps had locket backs. Clinton & Coles inserted 'hair platts' under crystal in a pair of bracelets in September 1794. They charged only 5s. for the work which must also have included the hairworkers' fee.

Clasps were sometimes large enough to display portrait miniatures on the front. Queen Charlotte had a portrait of George III in a bracelet-setting (Plate 4)[63] and the custom persisted. Her granddaughter Queen Victoria was rarely without one of her four or so bracelets mounted with miniatures of Prince Albert (Plate 110).

Armlets or armbands, worn on the bare arm above the elbow, were in this respect a post-Revolutionary development dependent on the fashion for short sleeves which can be confidently ascribed to France.[64] Nevertheless they probably derived in part from the narrow pearl or stone-set bands worn by women over their sleeves in the 1780s. Gainsborough's group portrait of the three eldest daughters of George III, completed in 1784, shows Princess Charlotte wearing several of these bands one above the other, the stuff of the sleeves pulled through them to make puffs.[65] Some of the centres sold by Garrard's in the 1790s may well have had strings long enough for use as armlets.

Brooches do not figure much in the Garrard Ledgers, partly due to the custom of describing the tiny specimens used to fasten neckerchiefs as 'pins', a term which is still used for brooches of all types and sizes in America. Large bodice brooches

Colour Plate 15. A gold heart pendant decorated with pearls and filigree and bearing the enamelled motto, Il mest fidel *(il m'est fidèle); preserved in a velvet-lined case. It is set with the gold initials and hair of Georgiana Duchess of Devonshire, her lover Charles Grey and their illegitimate daughter (named 'Eliza Courtney'), born in France on 20 February 1792. The Duchess had been temporarily banished there by the Duke. The provenance of the piece is a mystery. Though executed in the French manner of the 1790s, the spelling of the motto rules out a native French-speaking craftsman. It was probably made in London. Eliza Courtney was brought up by Grey's mother, the wife of the first Earl Grey. In 1807, the year after Georgiana's death (see Colour Plate 31E), Grey (1764-1845) succeeded to the Earldom and as Prime Minister in the Whig administration carried the Reform Bill of 1832. Eliza Courtney married General Robert Ellice and one of her daughters, also Eliza, became the wife of Sir Henry Brand (1814-1892), Speaker of the House of Commons, 1872-1884, who was created Viscount Hampden in 1884.* VISCOUNT HAMPDEN

were thin on the ground, their place being usurped by pendants of various kinds, but old preferences died hard. Clinton & Coles charged Garrard's £2.15s. for setting a brilliant bow for Lady Mary Coke in February 1796. It contained 109 brilliants weighing 13.10 grains supplied by Lady Mary and a larger specimen furnished by Garrard's for the centre of the bow. She paid £3.13s.6d. for the setting and a further £4.4s. for the additional brilliant. At the age of nearly sixty-nine Lady Mary cannot have been expected to be an enthusiastic follower of advanced fashion and her ornament was probably similar to the sets of bows decorating stomacher fronts in mid-century.[66]

Sets of brooches (sometimes graduated in size), often known as clasps, were used on the shoulders and sleeves of gowns. A traditional form of ornament, such pieces remained popular. A set of clasps decorated the Empress Josephine's sleeve in 1806 (Colour Plate 9) and similar brooches were still in use in the 1840s and later (Plate 220A).

Jewelled girdles with clasps occur only rarely in the Garrard Ledgers. One of the few clients to order one was Lady Mary Coke in 1800; a Garrard Gentlemen's Ledger includes the item: 'To Setting her Roses for a Girdle with a Snake [the clasp] friezed Circles', for which she was charged £5.15s.6d. Peter Delauney had executed the piece for £4.14s.6d. so that Garrard's profit was £1.1s. Despite the reluctance of Garrard's clients to buy jewelled belts, to which the term cestus was often applied in pre-Revolutionary days, they survived in fashionable circles on the

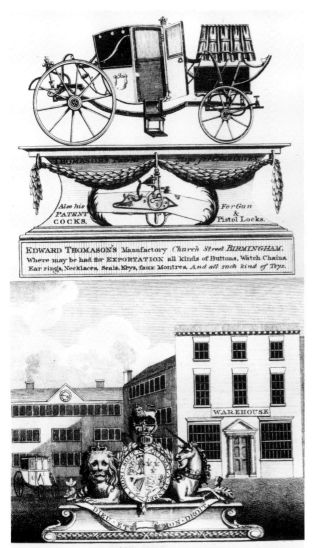

Plate 26. This portrait of Princess Augusta, the second daughter of King George III and Queen Charlotte, was one of a set of paintings of the 'Sisterhood' commissioned by their brother George Prince of Wales, later George IV, from Sir William Beechey (1753-1839). Exhibited at the Royal Academy in 1797, Beechey's portrait shows the Princess holding a sketchbook and wearing an enamelled anchor suspended from a necklace. Admired by Fanny Burney (Madame D'Arblay) for her friendliness and lack of vanity, the Princess never married.   ROYAL COLLECTION

Plate 25. An advertisement by Edward Thomason (1769-1849), for the trinkets produced in his Church Street factory, published in Bisset's Magnificent Directory in 1800. Among the articles are faux Montres. The son of a buckle-maker who at the height of his success produced about 6,000 buckles in 'white metal' (with a small quantity which were plated) every week until he retired. Thomason succeeded to his father's premises in 1793. He began by making gilt and plated buttons and then proceeded to jewellery in the same materials before expanding into a variety of different fields. He was knighted by William IV in 1832.

Continent and enjoyed a renaissance during the French Empire. At Ratisbon (Regensburg) in 1795 Betsey Wynne described a charade at which a royal participant was embellished with a diamond girdle.[67] Amateur theatricals in England often attracted spectacular jewellery, some of it borrowed.

Rings occur frequently in the Garrard Ledgers without distinction as to the sex of the wearer. The jewelled examples with cluster heads were plainly intended for female wear. One made for Garrard's by William Duncan in April 1799 was set with a ruby, an opal and thirty-two brilliants. Jewelled and pearl-set hoops and half-hoops were often made as engagement or keeper rings. Duncan had charged £1.16s. for setting the cluster ring; a brilliant hoop ring by Clinton & Coles which had been supplied to Garrard six years earlier at a cost of 14s. reflected the simpler

Plate 27. A combined commemorative and mourning medallion commissioned by Lady Hamilton (1765-1815), the wife of the collector and antiquary Sir William Hamilton, Minister to the Court of Naples (1730-1803). Her husband's position did not deter Emma Hamilton from becoming Nelson's mistress and acting as go-between in the arrangements for the secret flight of the royal family from Naples to Sicily after the failure of the campaign against the French in Rome.

The front commemorates Nelson's victory over the French fleet at Aboukir Bay (the Battle of the Nile); a trophy incorporating a trident and anchor is framed by a lock of Nelson's hair worked into curls, and an enamelled plaque carries the date, 1 August 1798. On the reverse is a mourning composition with four locks of hair and an inscription recording the death of the six year old Prince Carlo Alberto, who suffered from convulsions and died in Emma's arms during the sea passage on the Vanguard *on 25 December 1798.*

It is probable that Lady Hamilton had the medallion made up when she returned to England with Sir William and Nelson in November 1800.   VICTORY MUSEUM, PORTSMOUTH

nature of their task. Often the head or decorative top was set with a vitreous composition ornamented with diamonds (Plate 28).

Portrait rings were mainly set with painted miniatures, silhouettes or cameos. Men were more likely to wear 'antiques' or engraved gems in the classical taste. Like these, Wedgwood cameos and Tassie pastes were invariably put in the settings which were occasionally described by Garrard's clerk as 'Roman borders' (Plate 29). The hoops or shanks ranged from narrow to broad, occasionally with an undulating profile ('bent' in the ledgers), sometimes with branched shoulders. Shanks might also consist of multiple chains like a bracelet band. There were few signet rings as such. When every well-dressed man and many fashionable women carried on fob-chains at least one seal with their arms, crest or cipher, there was no need for them to use a signet ring to seal their letters.

Motto rings, mainly commemorative, were in constant demand; the 'motto' was the inscription, often carried on the hoops, the letters reserved on a ground of champlevé enamel. If it were specially made, the inscription might comprise the name and dates of the deceased. This information was alternatively placed on the head, as in the case of the mourning ring of Gabriel Wirgman who died at the age of fifty-three in 1791. In the centre of the head is an urn on a plinth over hair, the composition secured under crystal (Colour Plate 16) according to the instructions in Wirgman's will.[68] Wirgman was following a long tradition, like many of his contemporaries. One of Garrard's clients, Miss Ward, took possession in March 1797 of '6 broad Enamel Motto Rings' costing £1.4s. apiece, together with two more with the motto engraved under the head, which was ornamented with gold ciphers. The money for such articles was usually left specifically for the purpose

Colour Plate 16. A mourning ring made to commemorate a jeweller, Gabriel Wirgman, and as elaborate as a craftsman could make it. The urn and plinth in the middle of the head are of enamelled gold set over hair. The inscription is reserved on dark blue translucent enamel within white enamelled edges: GAB[L] WIRGMAN. DIED 12. SEP: 1791. AGED. 53. On the underside of the head is a further inscription commemorating Thomas Garle, who died aged sixty-seven in September 1789. Wirgman had been in partnership with the goldsmith and enameller James Morisset in Denmark Street, Soho, until 1778.

VICTORIA AND ALBERT MUSEUM

in the deceased's will. In some instances, however, Garrard's experienced difficulty in obtaining the moneys due for mourning orders. On the death in 1794 of the second Duke of Newcastle, the Cofferer of the Royal Household, the firm supplied fourteen pairs of black shoe buckles with straps at 4s. a pair (£2.16s.), the same number of knee buckles at 1s. (14s.) and sleeve buttons at 6d. (7s.), an additional buckle (2s.6d.) and '22 Broad Black Enamel'd Motto Rings w[h] white edges' each costing £1.5s. The overall total (which excluded the accoutrements ordered by the new Duke) was £32.10s.6d., a modest enough sum for the obsequies of a nobleman of such standing, but Garrard's had to resort to a solicitor to swear the debt in Chancery.[69]

While many rings, including motto rings, were simply hoops, others were dominated by heads of various forms. Some were large enough to hold funereal miniatures on ivory. Another popular variety comprised the hair of the deceased person framed by enamelled gold, half-pearls or melanite (a black garnet found in Russia, Saxony and Italy). Diamond, pearl and cameo urn heads[70] grace both commemorative (Colour Plate 16) and sentimental motto rings. In the latter instance the inscriptions expressed sentiments of love and friendship, usually in French, the international language of affection. Gold filigree rings and others buckled like garters must also be noted.

Other jewellery was common to both sexes. Chatelaines might be a female accessory but some of the appendages such as watches, watch-chains and seals (Plate 22) were variants of articles made for male consumption. A 'Green Enamell'd Ladys watch Chain' acquired from Garrard's by Mr Trefusis for £11.11s. in February 1793 was almost certainly intended to be displayed with a watch on the costume in the manner depicted by Heideloff the following year. In the first volume of his *Gallery* he showed women wearing watches depending from a belt.[71] By 1796, if Maria Josepha Holroyd is to be believed, the fashion had changed. Betrothed to John Stanley (later Lord Stanley of Alderley), she amused herself by alleging that he was approaching ruin by giving her so many things. 'My Watch is beautiful and the Chain the most elegant I have seen', she wrote to a friend. 'Neither of them [is] ornamented with Diamonds; but as handsome as possible without, and as it is not the fashion to show Watch or Chain, I like it much better than if it were finer.'[72]

Women wore fobs, like men, but in their case as an alternative to chatelaines. They had neck-chains, as did men, often attaching spy-glasses and other trinkets to them. Frenchmen and Italian males were also observed wearing earrings. Richard Twiss noticed the phenomenon in Paris in 1792, while Mrs Lybbe Powys remarked among the French emigrants in Bath five years later 'one with large gold

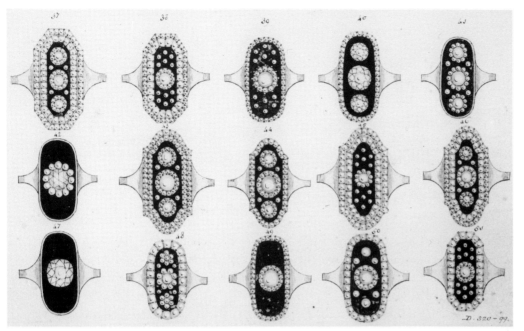

Plate 28. *A page of rings from a late-eighteenth century design book in the Victoria and Albert Museum. Though thought to be Portuguese, the international character of jewellery design is clearly demonstrated in these drawings, which include examples of 'oval squares' and rectangles with clipped corners. The stones indicated are brilliants and roses, together with pearls, probably set over vitreous paste in the manner of the 1770s and '80s.* VICTORIA AND ALBERT MUSEUM, PRINT ROOM

Plate 29. *A paste cameo portrait of Frederick Augustus, Duke of York, the second son of George III and Queen Charlotte, produced by James Tassie after an intaglio by Edward Burch, RA, and mounted in a Roman setting as the head of a gold ring. The paste portrait was first made in 1787 but remained in production.*
BRITISH MUSEUM,
HULL GRUNDY GIFT

earrings; to us in England [it] appear'd extraordinary, but is, I believe, common in France'.[73] Twiss had seen officers as well as ordinary working men with earrings; in Italy in 1798 the Wynne family were equally astonished to find their postilions hired at Verona adorned not only with gold chains but 'rings in their ears'.[74]

Seals came in two types, free-standing examples for writing desks and small specimens for men and women. Fashionable gentlemen usually wore more than one seal suspended from a fob at the waist. Barnes & Co. (a concern which later, as Halfhide, Barnes & Co., worked for the Prince of Wales) engraved a number of seals for Garrard's. Barnes often worked with carnelian, but Mr Trefusis ordered an octagonal rock crystal seal from Garrard's in 1793; mounted in gold, it cost him £4.4s.

Women were becoming less interested in buckles, though men found them indispensible. Stock buckles held high cravats off-centre at the back of the neck (Plate 30) and small buckles fastened shirts and also knee-breeches. A hopeful man of fashion, the Prince of Wales sported a buckle on his hat. Despite the introduction of laces many men still wore shoe-buckles. The trade was kept going by a mixture of conservatism and innovation, the former fuelled on the part of the privileged by the need for buckles in ceremonial and Court dress[75] and the latter by inventions and novelties. The London silversmith and buckle-maker William Eley patented an improvement in 1784 in which the hinged frames might be raised out of the way while the working parts (spring fasteners instead of the usual tongue and loop fittings, known collectively as the chape) were attached to the shoes. Leather inserts filled the area within the frame.[76] In 1792 James Smith, describing himself as a buckle-maker of Birmingham, obtained a patent for a further development in which a springy or 'elastic' steel plate covered with leather was furnished on the underside with claws to grip the shoe.[77] He brought his

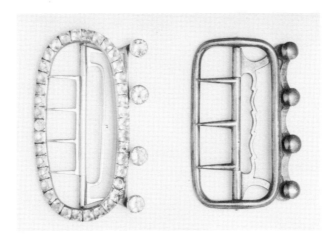

Plate 30. Two silver stock buckles, the left-hand one set with pastes, dating to 1780-95. Stock buckles, in use from about 1720 to the late eighteenth century (and perhaps later) were furnished with studs which were passed through holes made at one end of the stock or cravat. The other end was wound round the neck and then fastened with the prongs of the buckle. VICTORIA AND ALBERT MUSEUM

brother Benjamin, an 'Ingenious Chaser' already working in the silver department at Soho, into sub-partnership with Matthew Boulton for the purpose of manufacturing his 'shoe-latchets'. Their workshop was filled with various relatives and friends of whom Boulton became suspicious. Benjamin walked out in 1801 to join Digby Scott in managing Rundell's first silver workshop in Lime Kiln Lane, Greenwich, in 1802.[78] James followed him there after the expiry of the patent.

Meanwhile the sub-partnership of Boulton and Smiths enjoyed a degree of prosperity and Garrard's acquired a number of specimens, paying 7s. for a pair with silver frames in 1795, 3s. for two 'Black Latchets', perhaps of lacquered steel or base metal; others were made of Sheffield plate, that is, copper with a fused plating of silver on the top and underside (Plate 31). It is doubtful whether the Smith concern used the old and laborious technique of close-plating steel and other base metals by dipping the article concerned first in sal ammoniac and then in melted tin. Thin silver or gold foil, laid on top, was fused to the metal below by passing a soldering iron over it.[79]

There may have been some delay in getting word about Smith's invention to London, on the admittedly indirect evidence of Lady Stafford. Writing to her son Granville Leveson Gower on 16 February 1794 to tell him that a courier was leaving London for Rome to bring him and his party back from their Italian tour, she added later, 'I have been puzzling my Brain to think of a Present for you, but there is not a Thing new in the fine Men's Dress. It is the same as last Year, except a particular kind of Buckle, which they wear over or without Shoe-Strings; they are thought neat and pretty. I think them shabby to go so far, but I will send one Pair for you, and another for Lord Boringdon. I believe Lady Carlisle sends a Pair for Lord Morpeth, or I should.'[80]

Buckles were no different from other types of jewellery in that black examples were required for mourning. Garrard's outworker William Potter supplied 'Black Buckles' usually costing 6s.6d. a pair, 'Jet Knee Buckles' (4s.6d.) and 'Jet Shoe Buckles' (16s.). He also blacked a set of buckles for 9d. Some black buckles were made of japanned tin; others of darkened brass.

Fine, rich and privileged gentlemen wore not only diamond-set shoe buckles worth several thousand pounds but also diamond loops and buttons to fasten the upturned brims of their hats as well as rings, lockets and other small items. When their chests were to blaze with the Orders of Chivalry it was to Rundell's, not to Garrard's, that they increasingly turned for these great jewels.[81] A few heroes like Nelson were also able to sport testimonials from the rulers of other nations; Nelson,

Plate 31. A pair of Boulton & Smiths patent shoe buckles with a Sheffield plate frame, made according to James Smith's patent of 1792.
BIRMINGHAM ASSAY OFFICE

like Admiral Lord Keith after him, owned a diamond *chelengk* or plume presented by the Sultan of Turkey (Colour Plate 8).[82]

Children were introduced to jewellery at a very early age. Still regarded as miniature adults, infants were adorned with tiny gold, pearl or coral necklaces and bracelets (Plate 17); some were even given buckles.[83] Little girls often had to be bribed with promises of earrings to undergo the ordeal of having their ears pierced. The diarist Mrs Delany found that earrings and even the presence of a royal jeweller, Dutens, was insufficient to persuade her young niece Mary to consent to piercing in March 1756; it was two months before she assented.[84] The Prince of Wales' only legitimate child, Princess Charlotte of Wales, received a respectable collection of jewellery on her first birthday in January 1797, though earrings were not yet included in the gifts. Queen Charlotte sent a cross to be tied round the child's neck; the Princess Royal a necklace and Princess Augusta a pair of bracelets. The other offerings from the 'Sisterhood' were a doll, a silver rattle and a china toy.[85] Earrings and, doubtless, watches and rings were eventually to follow. Princess Charlotte was by no means unusual except in the quantity of jewellery she accumulated. Betsey Wynne, then aged twelve, and her sister Eugenia, a year younger, were each given 'little gold rings' by a friend of their parents in 1791. The following year their mother gave them watches and chains.[86] Once they had discarded the petticoats and the occasional necklaces of their infancy boys received scaled-down versions of adult male jewellery.

The Garrard Ledgers, so informative in respect of clients and outworkers and the jewellery ordered by the former and made by the latter, also demonstrate the inevitable consequences of wearing delicate objects. Numerous entries relate to the repair and re-stringing of necklaces and bracelets and the replacement as well as the re-cutting of stones, the furnishing of new clasps and pins, the replacement of enamels and the like. Lady's-maids were traditionally in charge of their mistress's jewellery and but for their care and vigilance the damage might have been even greater. Even so, the repairs executed by Garrard's craftsmen leave the impression that comparatively little jewellery survived in a pristine condition. When the re-making of pieces on grounds of fashion is also taken into consideration the number of jewels surviving intact is even lower.

CHAPTER II

Hanoverians,
Bonapartes and Bourbons, 1801-1820

The Parliamentary Commissioners appointed in 1795 to regulate the financial affairs of George Prince of Wales were singularly unsuccessful. In 1811, when he became Regent (Plate 32), he entertained renewed hopes that Parliament would settle his debts which had risen to a total of £552,000. The government refused to recommend anything of the kind and the Regent had to be satisfied with the Cabinet's offer of £100,000 in recognition of his new responsibilities. Unfortunately Carlton House, the subject of continual architectural work, was as yet unfinished and ate up money (he had recently added a gothic conservatory). But the Regent's fascination with jewellery persisted, as is plain even from the admittedly incomplete series of bills in the Royal Archives. His expenditure on jewels, though certainly somewhat abated between 1795 and 1811, was still governed less by prudence and more by an instinctive response to quality or novelty, characteristics shared with the Empress Josephine who was equally prodigal in her purchases.

The bills, running from 1783 until his death as George IV in 1830, record some at least of his transactions in the course of his purchasing career. Many of his acquisitions reflect his attachment to his family (though not to his father, from whom he was frequently estranged), his antiquarianism matched by a lively appreciation of fashion, his passion for engraved gems, old and new, his friendships and amours and, finally, his loyalty to certain firms. This last was probably governed as much by indebtedness as sentiment. Rundell's for instance, according to their shopman George Fox, were happy to allow his bills to run because, as a leader of fashion, he brought others in his train to their premises in Ludgate Hill.[1] But an element of loyalty is discernible. Thomas Gray[2] of 41 Sackville Street was regularly patronised by the Prince, who ordered goods to the value of £21,201.11s.2d. between 1786 and 1789 alone. Gray's successors, Joseph Delafons & Sons (formerly among Garrard's outworkers),[3] themselves supplied the Regent in 1819.[4] In 1799 Gray was briefly in partnership with William Constable, whose nephew Joseph Kitching was apprenticed to the firm. Kitching, who set up on his own account in Dover Street in 1817, immediately securing the Regent's patronage, proudly announced his connection with Gray and his relationship to Constable in a billhead sent to the Regent in 1817. The items supplied, which included 'A Turkois Diamd Padlock wh Heart & Key', were

Colour Plate 17. Shown in the centre of the sapphire and diamond necklace and earrings, c.1810, is a large gold medallion with a relief portrait in gold of the Prince Regent wearing a laurel wreath. It is signed with the Latin title of Rundell's and the name of the artist who cast the relief, J. Barber. The head is mounted on dark blue paste and bordered by palm and laurel branches, the whole covered by glass. The victor's wreath worn by the Prince Regent is in ironic contrast to the one made for Napoleon's coronation in December 1804 (Plate 36). VICTORIA AND ALBERT MUSEUM

copied into his firm's earliest surviving ledger, which runs from 1817 to 1821.[5] J. Laurière of 13 St James's Street,[6] who claimed to have formerly worked for Thomas Gray, was also patronised by the Regent.

As a young man, the Prince turned to George III's jewellers John Duval, Sons & Co., buying quantities of 'Antiques' from them between 1783 and 1785. These included rings with heads set with Minerva, Caesar and other classical subjects. Nathaniel Jefferys, then describing himself as goldsmith to Queen Charlotte and goldsmith and jeweller to the Prince of Wales and the Duke of York, supplied the Prince in 1793 with a number of items including a pair of 'motto Earrings' costing £4.4s. and another of 'Enamel'd Constitutional Earrings' at £5.5s.[7] The business of the Princess of Wales' jewellery in 1795 inevitably ruptured the Prince's relations with Jefferys and by 1799, if not before, Rundell's had begun to move into the position of primary supplier.[8] Appointed the Royal Goldsmiths to George III and the Royal Family in 1804, their principal patron remained the Prince of Wales. Using the services of such distinguished sculptors as William Theed and John Flaxman, both Royal Academicians, the French artist J.J. Boileau, who came to England in about 1787, the painter Thomas Stothard and the architect C.R. Cockerell, Rundell's were able to produce impressive silverwork in a variety of styles from neo-classical and Egyptian to the gothic and Renaissance as well as experimenting with naturalism.[9] Their jewellery designers are less well documented, aside from the diamond-setter Philip Liebart and the enamelist, Charles Muss,[10] who experimented with Holbeinesque floriated letter forms for a pendant to a chain (Plate 91A) in about 1820-24.

The Prince's passion for engraved gems led him to supplement his purchases from Duval's with others from Thomas Martyn of 16 Great Marlborough Street.[11] On 13 September 1785 the Prince characteristically combined antiquarianism with sentiment in acquiring 'A Curious & Matchless Ring, of Sardonyx. Elegantly Engrav'd, in the Natural Colours, with the Striking likeness of the Bust of the Right Honble Charles James Fox[12] Neatly Mounted in Gold, & sett Round with fine Large Brilliants of the first Water.' The supplier was Benjamin Laver, a working silversmith and jeweller then of Bruton Street, whose specialities included 'Mourning Rings & Devices in Hair neatly executed'. Laver, who had clearly passed on the commission for the engraved portrait to an outworker, charged £105 for the mounted ring.[13] The price was high enough to testify to the strength of the Prince's regard for Fox, a shrewd Whig politician with a taste for gambling and dissipation. The friendship was temporarily interrupted by Fox's attempts to dissuade the Prince from marrying Mrs Fitzherbert on 15 December.

Family sentiment probably accounts for the Prince's purchase of seven cameo heads of Frederick Duke of York from the gem-engraver Joachim Smith for a total of £7.7s. in 1792.[14] Several engraved gems portrayed the Prince himself. Rundell's furnished a 'fine sardonyx medallion in gold with cameo of His Royal Highness' for £21 in 1802.[15] The Royal Goldsmiths set an intaglio portrait executed in carnelian in April 1811 as a signet ring and among other examples a sardonyx cameo, also as a ring, in 1819.[16] Other purchases represent the Prince's

Plate 32. *The Prince Regent; a miniature on ivory by Paul Fischer, after a portrait executed by Sir Thomas Lawrence for Lord Londonderry in 1814-15. Around his neck he wears the Order of the Golden Fleece bestowed by the Emperor of Austria following the defeat of Napoleon. Fischer, born in Hanover, came to England in 1810; he probably saw Lawrence's portrait at the Royal Academy in 1815. He was not the only artist to copy it; other miniaturists also produced versions.*

Plate 33. *An onyx cameo portrait ring of King George IV in a gold Roman setting, tentatively ascribed by the British Museum to Benedetto Pistrucci. The cameo is inscribed on the reverse: GEORGIUS IV D.G. BRIT. REX MDCCCXXI. Possibly commissioned in 1820 when the King had already determined to postpone his coronation to 19 July 1821. An entry dated 31 July 1820 in a bill submitted to the King by Rundell's includes an entry for 'A Ring, Cameo Head of His Majesty,' costing £9.9s. If it refers to this piece, the price rules out Pistrucci, who commanded high sums for his work.*

interest in historic royal figures; in 1800 he bought from Rundell & Bridge a ring set with a cameo of Queen Elizabeth I[17] and many similar instances occur in the accounts. The Prince was always conscious of the traditional royal practice of giving jewels set with his image to relatives, attendants, diplomats and the like. After his accession as George IV in January 1820 and before his coronation, which had originally been planned for the following August but was postponed until July 1821, he ordered quantities of ornaments set with his portrait as souvenirs of the ceremony. The ring in Plate 33 is probably one of these. It appears to be itemised in one of the bills submitted by Rundell's in the hectic months after the King's accession.[18] A larger bill from the Royal Goldsmiths running from October 1820 to March 1821 contains several further items of this kind, including seven (possibly eight) rings bearing cameo portraits of the King, one executed in onyx but mounted with diamonds and turquoises; the rest were in carnelian and sardonyx. The charges ranged from £8.18s.6d. to £146, the highest price reflecting the profuse use of diamonds in the setting. Four intaglio portrait rings in the same bill, two in bloodstone and two in carnelian, were priced from £6.16s.6d. to £13.13s. Four gold medallion portrait rings, one at £4.4s. and three at £2.2s., also figured in the bill; medallion rings, favoured by both the Revolutionaries and by Napoleon, perhaps inspired these coronation souvenirs. Pistrucci might have modelled them.

A Tassie paste cameo of George IV was mounted in a ring costing £2.12s.6d; the next two items are a Tassie brooch and locket, probably *en suite* with the ring. Another locket was set with an onyx cameo of the King and adorned with brilliants, the whole costing £33. Two diamond-set medallions costing £395 apiece and two smaller ones at £234 each were set with portrait miniatures of George IV by Henry Bone, who received £147 for all four. A large gold medallion portrait of the King, mounted on a ground of lapis lazuli, cost £18.18s.6d; twelve assorted medallions of gold, each described as 'A large Medallion Cameo of The King in Gold setting', were priced, probably according to size, between £2.12s.6d. and £16.16s.[19] Further variations appear in another bill from Rundell's covering the months leading up to the coronation on 19 July 1821.

The brief description of the twelve gold medallions furnished by Rundell's in one of their coronation accounts demonstrates that they were of much the same type as the piece in Colour Plate 17, which was presented to George Purefoy Jervaise of Herriard Park, Basingstoke. Jervaise served in the Privy Purse Office. The gold portrait relief in his medallion is signed on the truncation: *Rundell, Bridge et Rundell, J. Barber F.* (J. Barber made it)[20] and is bordered by palm and laurel branches. The head clearly derives from a portrait of the Regent on a medal executed by Barber in association with Thomas Wyon of the Royal Mint to celebrate (prematurely, as it turned out) the Pacification of Europe in 1814. The portrait is similar to one adorning the lid of a gold box presented by the Prince Regent in 1815 to John Watier, his chef, who had founded a well-known gaming club in 1807. The relief on this box is signed: *ROUW CER. EF^T/BARBER FEC^T* (Rouw modelled it in wax, Barber made it.)[21] Peter Rouw, a wax-modeller of Flemish origin, was appointed Sculptor and Modeller of Gems to the Prince of Wales in 1807. It seems likely that Barber used Rouw's wax models of his royal patron in other medallions made for presentation purposes, including the piece given to Jervaise. The inclusion of the attributes of peace and victory in the design and the marked absence of any regal insignia such as a crown and cipher on the Jervaise medallion points to a date of 1814 or 1815.[22] Nevertheless it is in a long and honourable tradition of royal medallic jewellery which was to inspire Alfred Gilbert later in the century (see Plate 337).

On many occasions engraved gems were set in jewellery for the same royal patron. Whether Prince of Wales, Regent or King, George IV was always prepared to extend the boundaries of English taste, as was another great collector and patron, William Beckford,[23] though Beckford's stylistic experiments rarely encompassed jewellery. Unhappily the abbreviated entries in most of the bills in the Royal Archives afford only occasional hints of George IV's readiness to embrace French design or to adopt historicist manners. In 1800 he acquired from Rundell's 'a fine gold Tiara with Antique Cameo's' (*sic*) and a pair of matching armbands at a total cost of £126. The tiara must have been made sufficiently deep to allow the cameos to be set on it, which suggests that it was inspired by the shape of a larger head ornament currently in vogue in Paris. A French fashion plate of about 1800, depicting a woman dressed for a ball with necklace, armlets and an arched tiara decorated with three crescent-shaped motifs is illustrated in Vever's

Plate 34. A lady in court costume, said to be the Empress Josephine, wearing a Spartan diadem with rounded arch, attributed to Robert Lefèvre, c.1806. The portrait was acquired by the first Duke of Wellington (1769-1852) as one of Josephine, though the full lips and heavy jaw are unlike the Empress's features (see Colour Plate 9), which are characterised by an oval face and narrow mouth. The robe is only sketched in, but the right sleeve is fastened with clasps, as is Josephine's left one in Colour Plate 9. WELLINGTON MUSEUM, APSLEY HOUSE

La Bijouterie française au XIXᵉ siècle.[24] The tiara is already wrapped around the head as far as the ears and probably beyond, but its general form appears to be a greatly enlarged version of a small ornament with a rounded arch worn on the top of her head by Queen Maria Carolina of Naples[25] with her royal robes in a miniature executed by Heinrich Friedrich Füger in 1790.[26] The Queen, who was Marie-Antoinette's sister, cannot have been pleased by the thought that tiaras like hers were to develop into the Spartan diadem form of the Consulate and the French Empire.

Lefèvre's portrait of a lady in the costume of the French Court (Plate 34), believed by the first Duke of Wellington[27] to represent Josephine, shows her wearing a Spartan diadem with a rounded arch and beaded edge. The construction of her robe is so similar to the dress worn by Josephine in Lefèvre's portrait of 1806 (Colour Plate 9) that the same date is likely. Pointed fronts were far more popular than rounded arches. Details of settings were constantly changed at the Parisian Court, though the essential silhouette, comprising a circlet or near-circlet flaring upwards and outwards from the base, persisted for over three decades. As soon as he began to plan his coronation shortly after his accession, King George IV had a circlet made to a shape echoing the head ornaments of the First Empire. It was executed by Rundell's in 1820 with a broad crest of patriotic motifs (four sprays each of a rose, thistle and shamrock) alternating with crosses pattée, all set with diamonds, and was worn by the King as a magnificent hatband as he processed in traditional fashion from Westminster Hall to his coronation in the Abbey on 19 July 1821[28] (Plate 35). His estranged wife had a specimen of similar form (Plate 71) and other Courts likewise followed the mode,[29] wearing faithful copies or inventive variations of French work.

Plate 35. *George IV's diamond and pearl circlet, made by Rundell's in 1820 for his coronation, and worn by the King over a large plumed hat as he processed to Westminster Abbey. Set transparent with brilliants valued at over £8,000 and hired out for the occasion by Rundell's, it was remounted permanently at a later date. It has since been worn by Queens regnant and consort, from Queen Adelaide, consort of William IV, to Queen Elizabeth II, and never by a King.*

The original band was higher (see Plate 113) and was altered for Queen Alexandra in 1902. The sprays of roses, shamrocks and thistles alternating with crosses-pattée on the crest reflect the union with Ireland which came into effect on 1 January 1801. The emblems of England, Ireland and Scotland only were used; Wales, being a principality and not a kingdom, was not represented. George IV was so enthusiastic about these motifs he wanted them on his Crowns but this was vetoed by the College of Heralds.

ROYAL COLLECTION

In the early years of the century, Englishwomen preferred flat bandeaux to tiaras. A plate in Heideloff's *Gallery*, dated August 1801, illustrates a diamond bandeau worn with matching earrings and a pearl necklace and fall with an afternoon dress (dinner was often at three or four p.m.). Heideloff's drawing demonstrates that the bandeau was placed flat across the head behind the front curls, disappearing behind the ears beneath the back hair.[30] Among the bandeaux in Garrard's Ledgers, one was set 'transparent with gold back' for Mr Langham in February 1802, the client apparently furnishing the 291 brilliants used, for Garrard's charged only £20 for the work. A similar piece containing 236 diamonds was supplied to Miss Burdett for £18.18s. a month later. She seems to have been dissatisfied with the result, for an ambiguous entry follows a few weeks later referring to 'Setting 8 double leaves & colletts & altering Brilliant Bandeau', for which the firm supplied 134 brilliants totalling 7 carats 2 grains in weight, charging £8.8s. a carat. Miss Burdett paid £73.10s., but as she appears to have had two lockets mended for £10.10s, the cost of which was included in her bill, she must

Plate 36. Gérard's painting of Napoleon in coronation robes, wearing the laurel wreath of golden leaves each representing a victory, made for him by Biennais. It has disappeared, except for two of the six leaves which were removed by the goldsmith a few weeks before the ceremony on 2 December 1804 because the Emperor found the wreath too heavy. The six surplus leaves were later given to the goldsmith's six daughters as souvenirs but despite their association four have gone from sight. The Prince Regent, as already remarked (see Colour Plate 17), metaphorically purloined the Emperor's wreath for a medallic portrait commemorating the Peace of 1814. MUSEE DU LOUVRE

Plate 37. A page from the sketchbook of J.-L. David showing Napoleon placing the crown on Josephine's head, a pencil study for his great painting of the coronation (Plate 8). His wreath appears to be tied with ribbons in the nape of the neck, as is the Prince Regent's wreath in Colour Plate 17, though the latter was the invention of the artist, while Napoleon's was real.

GRENVILLE L. WINTHROP BEQUEST, FOGG ART MUSEUM, HARVARD UNIVERSITY

have paid very little for having the diamonds set. The inclusion of leaves suggests a wreath, and the addition of a leaf to a bandeau repaired for another client, William Hanbury, in 1802, supports the hypothesis.

English wreath bandeaux were probably shallower than the classical wreath of golden laurel leaves designed by the miniaturist Jean-Baptiste Isabey for Napoleon and made by the goldsmith Biennais for 8,000 francs. Each leaf represented one of Napoleon's victories, but when he tried it on a few weeks before he was to wear it at his coronation on 2 December 1804 he found it too heavy for comfort and six leaves were removed.[31] It was in Napoleon's interests to buttress his regime by this visual reference to the laurel wreaths crowning Roman heroes as they processed into their city to celebrate their victories (Plates 36 and 37); inevitably the theme was plagiarised for female fashions. J.-L. David's great commemorative painting of the coronation ceremony (Plate 8) depicted Josephine wearing a modish diadem based on a wreath and one of her ladies a variant on the same theme.

The Prince of Wales bought comparatively few tiaras, preferring such pieces as 'A very elegant brilliant Caducis [caduceus, an ancient herald's wand, as carried by the messenger-god Hermes] for the hair with fine cameo of Jupiter Serapis' and 'a fine brilliant & sapphire Arrow for hair', both acquired from Rundell's in 1803 for £115 and £268 respectively, together with a 'very elegant saphire Comb set with brilliants' costing £118 and a gold comb, also denominated 'very elegant', priced at a mere £19.19s.[32] He had already seized the chance of acquiring from Rundell's in 1802 'A cameo french Necklace with 2 gold chains & chas'd enamel'd centre' costing £21 and probably bought in Paris during the brief Peace of Amiens of 1802-3. His discriminating eye for new techniques and novelties is evident in two more pieces dating to 1802. The first involved open-backed settings for coloured stones and comprised a 'pair fine transparent topaz bracelet Bands set in gold for Her Royal Highness The Princess Augusta.' Supplied by Rundell's,[33] the bracelets cost £41, considerably less than a similar pair sold by Garrard's in June 1808 to Miss Shuckburgh Evelyn for £52.10s. Princess Augusta was nevertheless delighted by her present. She sent her brother an enthusiastic letter on 8 November, her birthday: 'I return you many thanks for the beautifull *bracelets* little Sophy put into my hand this morning, saying, "they come from some lady [*sic*] who don't *love you & who you* don't love *neither"*, so I directly guessed they came from you!'[34] From Rundell's also came 'A small gold enamel'd Watch for the neck in form of a flower' costing £16.16s. with a further 7s. for a gold key. The flower was probably a pansy, as the watch was entered in Rundell's bill against the date 1 November 1802, and two days later the Prince's sister Sophia sent him a letter declaring: 'I am in extacies with my *lovely pensée*. . .'[35] For his youngest sister Amelia, who died in 1810, the Prince acquired in August 1804 a head ornament described by Rundell's in their bill as 'An elegant brilliant Butterfly for the hair, for Her Royal Highness The Princess Amelia'.[36] Priced at £142.15s., it was the second most expensive item in the bill. The most costly, for which Rundell's again deployed their favourite adjective, was 'An elegant brilliant Tiara with large amethyst & brill^t Broach in centre' at £280; the brooch itself cost an additional £59, demonstrating that it might be removed at will for use elsewhere on the person. It was not necessarily fitted with a pin, but probably had spring clips to enable it to serve as a necklace or bracelet centre on occasion, a form of economy which found widespread favour.

Hair souvenirs figured prominently in gifts exchanged between the Prince and his family and friends. His younger brother William (later Duke of Clarence and King William IV)[37] wrote to him from Portsmouth on 25 November 1785 requesting 'a lockit for my shirt with your hair and a pair of buckles'.[38] In 1799, having long since sickened of his wife and disposed of a mistress, Mrs Crouch, the Prince again laid siege to Mrs Fitzherbert. They were reconciled before the end of the year, the Prince sending her in token of his sincerity a copy of his will drawn up after the birth of Princess Charlotte in January 1796, in which he left his property, jewels, furniture and other possessions to his unofficial wife. This was reinforced by various presents including a gold bracelet with a locket set with another painting of his right eye said to be by Cosway, while the bracelet itself was engraved with the motto, *rejoindre ou mourir*.[39]

Three items dated 15 November 1799 in a bill submitted by Thomas Gray[40] may also have been ordered for Mrs Fitzherbert: 'A Cross with hair' cost £3.13s.6s., 'An Hair Necklace with hasp' £2.6s., while a charge of 3s. was made for engraving a heart on a cross. In 1804 the Prince bought from Thomas Gray 'An Hair Serpent Bracelet with Diam^d Head' for £45.[41] The hair, like that used for earlier items, was almost certainly his own, but what he gave away was more than offset by the many tokens accumulated from his lady-loves. According to the diarist Charles Greville, the Duke of Wellington, going through George IV's effects as his Executor in 1830-31, found a 'prodigious quantity of hair — women's hair — of all colours and lengths, some locks with the powder and pomatum still sticking to them.'[42]

The serpent device was a favourite with the Prince, whose acquisitions from Rundell's in 1799 included a 'neat gold Talisman Ring with device of Serpents hearts & cyphers on Onyx Ring & Emerald' costing £5.15s.6d., followed in 1800 by a 'Gold Serpent elastic Necklace' at £13.18s. with a pair of matching bracelets at £9.9s. and earrings at £2.12s.6d.[43] The first bill totalled £1,123.14s.8d. and the second £593.17s.5d. The Gray account of 1804 which included the serpent bracelet of hair (and also an 'Elk's Claw & Gold Chain' for £4 and a malachite snuff-box costing £42) amounted to £782.12s.6d. The Prince received other bills from the two firms in 1799 and 1804, but it is clear that he was making some effort at restraint, certainly enough to turn down the offer undoubtedly made him by Rundell's to sell him the Pigot diamond, in which they had an interest.

The diamond had belonged to Sir George Pigot,[44] who was created an Irish baron in 1766 after his first term of office as governor of Madras. After spending some years in England he was again appointed governor in 1775, but died in confinement two years later, having been arrested at the instigation of dissident members of his council. The House of Commons subsequently ordered their prosecution, but rumours that he had been guilty of taking bribes were never dispelled. He owned at least two diamonds which had probably been given him by the Nawab of Arcot from whom he actually admitted receiving certain trifling presents. If, as seems likely, they included a stone weighing, according to Liebart's drawing (Plate 38), 189½ grains (about 47⅔ old carats), one trifle at least was considerably more valuable than Pigot cared to acknowledge.

Pigot bequeathed the eponymous stone to his two brothers and his sister. Attempts to dispose of it in England were fruitless on account of its size and expense. In 1800 his surviving brother, the widow of the other and his sister promoted a private bill in Parliament to enable them to sell the diamond by lottery.[45] The bill, duly enacted, specified that no more than 11,428 tickets at two guineas (£2.2s.) each be sold. The issue attracted widespread attention. Mary

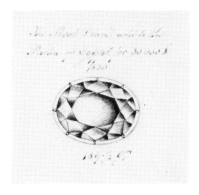

Plate 38. The Pigot diamond, from a drawing executed in about 1830-1835 by Philip Liebart of Rundell's, whose repeated attempts to dispose of the stone for nearly twenty years finally met with success in 1820. Inscribed: The Pigot Diam^d sold to the Pasha of Egypt for 30,000£/1820 *with the weight in grains below.*

Heber, the wife of the Rector of Malpas, Cheshire, wrote to her sister-in-law Elizabeth in London on 8 October to say: 'I beg the favour of you to get me a ticket in the Lottery for the Piggott Diamond and send it in the next letter. Wish me good luck and let this be a great secret from all but Papa. It is but 11427 to one — and what is that if a woman has luck!'[46] The odds were even shorter for fewer than the permitted number of tickets were sold, denying Pigot's relatives the agreed maximum return of £23,998.16s.

The winner of the lottery was a consortium which had purchased quantities of tickets and consigned the stone to Christie's for sale on 12 May 1802. It was knocked down for 9,500 guineas to one Parker (the goldsmith William Parker, in partnership with William Birkett at Prince's Street). After turning down applications from other firms for an interest in the stone, the weight of which they recorded as 189⅛ grains[47], Parker & Birkett offered a moiety to Rundell's. On 24 September all the interested parties met at Rundell's shop on Ludgate Hill. Philip Rundell proposed paying 5,000 guineas but offered to bet £500 on their still having the stone on their hands in three years' time. Parker declined but mentioned Bonaparte as a possible purchaser in the knowledge that the Emperor was acquiring stones for his coronation.

Philip Rundell, who like his senior partner John Bridge was a jeweller by training[48], was anxious to set the stone in a piece of jewellery but Parker and his partner refused to incur any more expense. Rundell at this stage must have decided to take the initiative which led to his firm being sued by Parker, William Birkett and James Birkett the following year. The depositions made by the plaintiffs and defendants afford a detailed account of a remarkable enterprise and incidentally amplify what is known of Philip Liebart, the chief protagonist. According to the complaint made by Parker & Birkett on 25 April 1805, they had learned from Rundell's that Liebart, then of Craven Buildings, was well known to Peregeaux of Paris, probably a clearing house which had entrusted considerable property of its own to him. If this refers to a pre-Revolutionary connection and not to dealings conducted in 1802 or 1804, Liebart probably had worked in Paris.[49] An affidavit signed by Philip Rundell, John Bridge and Rundell's nephew Edmond Waller Rundell on 28 June justified their action in despatching Liebart secretly to France with the diamond and other jewellery to offer to Napoleon and indignantly refuted the suggestion that he was untrustworthy by pointing out that he had come to them on the recommendation of the Royal jeweller, John Duval.

The sequence of complaints and answers demonstrates that Parker & Birkett were probably correct in assuming that Philip Rundell had not fully consulted them before Liebart left London on his mission on 30 September, the diamond concealed in the strap of his breeches and various articles of jewellery sewn on to his smallclothes. Rundell sent round a note to Parker and his partners in the morning, but they were not at the shop and only saw it after Liebart's departure. Travelling by way of Rotterdam and Liège, his native town, Liebart entered France with the assistance of his brother, a priest,[50] unaware that as a result of strong representations from Parker & Birkett Rundell's had despatched another member of staff to Gravesend on 2 October with instructions to retrieve the stone and bring it back to London. The second man was too late to catch Liebart, who had already sailed.

On arriving at Paris, Liebart deposited the jewellery and the Pigot diamond with the agents recommended to Rundell's by Thellusson & Company of London.[51] These French agents managed to arrange for Napoleon to be shown the pieces; he is said to have displayed interest until he somehow got wind of their source. Liebart fled from Paris, leaving the jewels in the care of the French firm and returned to London. Parker & Birkett's suit against Rundell's in 1805 was probably settled out of court, but E.W. Rundell had to go to law twice in Paris, the first time after the Peace of 1814 and again following the final defeat of Napoleon in 1815, before he finally retrieved the articles. In 1820 Rundell's at last managed to achieve the price they had wanted from Napoleon (£30,000) when they sold the Pigot to the Pasha of Egypt, although their expenses in the interim had been considerable. The diamond has since disappeared.

The enterprise demonstrates more clearly than anything else the limited nature of the hostilities. Rundell's, the Royal Goldsmiths, attracted little or no opprobrium for sending Liebart to Paris to deal with the enemy. Though they might have tried to suppress the story they cannot have been wholly successful in view of the lawsuit. Admittedly they exposed Liebart to great danger, as the Prince Regent was later to do when in 1811 he sent the expatriate Italian merchant Angiolo Bonelli to Italy to recover the Stuart papers.[52] The Regent's justification was that the French were anxious to get hold of the documents, and Rundell's, as they explained in 1806, that they were 'great dealers and exclusively concerned in the buying and selling of Jewels particularly in the foreign markets and having better means or opportunities of disposing of the Jewel [the Pigot Diamond] of such magnitude and value as the said Diamond than almost any other person in this Country.'[53]

A large part of Rundell's trade abroad was with precious stones brought to Europe from India and elsewhere, but they also exported finished articles of jewellery. They showed supreme confidence in sending examples of the latter to Paris, the fountainhead of fashion, in 1804, but it is clear from their sale of a French necklace to the Prince of Wales in 1802 that they had taken advantage of the brief suspension of hostilities to explore new developments in design in the city. It is very likely that they despatched Liebart on this mission.

An inventory of the jewellery which Rundell's hoped to sell to Napoleon appears in the firm's 'joint and several answer' of 28 June 1805 to Parker & Birkett's complaint. It comprised 'A large Pearl Necklace of thirty-three capital Pearls a

Plate 39. A miniature of the Empress Josephine, probably by Daniel Saint, c.1807-09, showing her wearing a pearl parure with a Spartan diadem, huge top and drop pearl earrings and two large necklaces, one with pear-shaped pearl drops. A row of pearls outlines the top of her skirt. Josephine adored pearls and was frequently painted wearing the necklace with drops, adding more pearls to lengthen the row to comply with the fashion of bigger necklaces in the second decade of the century (see Plate 47). SOTHEBY'S

large drop to ditto' (the Empress Josephine owned a pearl necklace with numerous drops — Plate 39), 'a pink Brilliant for clasp a pair of very large single drop pearl Earrings with Brilliant tops and an emerod and Brilliant Broach a very large pearl drop to ditto a very capital Brilliant Necklace a pair of capital Brilliant drop Earrings a pair Brilliant Bracelet Bands a fine large India polished Saphire a fine single small brilliant Necklace a pair of fine brilliant drop earrings a very long and capital Brilliant...', the unset diamonds being sealed up in a separate packet.[54] Unfortunately the valuation was not supplied: it was undoubtedly very high.

In the months leading up to Liebart's perilous adventure in Paris the Prince of Wales, still practising his version of economy, acquired from Rundell's jewellery including a transparent-set parure comprising an amethyst and diamond necklace, drop earrings, bracelet, bracelet bands, locket, 'Brilliant amethyst Crescent Comb' and, finally perhaps, the 'elegant brilliant Tiara with large amethyst & brill' Broach in centre'. The complete set cost £587.2s. and might have been designed to match 'A remarkable large & fine transparent Amethyst Cross' acquired in May 1800 for £42, though the gap of four years probably indicates otherwise. As always, however, the Prince had chosen one of the most fashionable (and expensive) coloured stones of the decade for the parure.

The following year Rundell's began to essay organic naturalism for the Prince in the form of 'An elegant gold Tiara for back of the head with chas'd gold vine leaves & garnet bunches of grapes' costing £26.5s. and 'A brilliant Fly with emerald back' at £9.9s. Presaging the full-blown naturalism of later decades (Plate 181), which became one of the most charming styles of the early Victoria era, articles such as these show the most innovative aspect of the Prince as patron. Since innovation can often be equated with antiquarianism at this time it is equally significant that the Prince bought from Rundell's in 1807 a gold George (the badge of the Order of the Garter) with 'gold Garter & Motto both sides', the work of the

Plate 40. Maltese cross in gold and enamel presented to Emma Hamilton by the Tsar of Russia. Emma Hamilton, the former Emma Hart, had achieved respectability as the second wife of Sir William Hamilton, the antiquary and collector who was also the English Minister to the Court of Naples. Queen Maria Carolina appointed Emma her deputy in receiving Maltese petitions for aid, as the island, taken by the French (later driven out by the English), suffered distress. She wrote to her former lover Charles Greville on 25 February 1800: 'I have had a letter from the Emperor of Russia, with the Cross of Malta; Sir William has sent his Imperial Majesty's letter to Lord Grenville, to get me permission to wear it. I have rendered some service to the poor Maltese. I got them ten thousand pounds, and sent them corn when they were in distress. . . The Queen is having the order set in diamonds for me, but the one the Emperor sent is gold.' The cross was given in indirect compliment to Nelson, who was infatuated with Lady Hamilton. Emma received permission to wear the cross and did so, setting an international fashion.

ROYAL NAVAL MUSEUM, PORTSMOUTH

celebrated master of the rococo style, the chaser G.M. Moser.[55] Rundell's exercises in revived rococo were extremely influential, as was their work in the gothic manner, though the first sign of the latter in the Prince's accounts is a snuffbox bearing miniatures of his parents and decorated with 'Gothic Ornaments in raised gold to Drawings received' in 1811.[56] On this evidence, the Prince was pre-empted by both the Empress Josephine and the Queen of Prussia in 1807, as appears presently.

The Prince of Wales responded readily to feats of heroism. Nelson's death at the Battle of Trafalgar in October 1805 prompted the Prince to acquire two 'Nelson Pyramid' brooches at £1.16s. and a locket at £2.2s. On 8 January following Rundell's sold him 'A gold enamel'd medallion with motto in honor of Lord Nelson' costing £9.9s., more than they charged later for some of George IV's coronation medallions discussed above. In May 1811 Rundell's supplied 'A gold Broach. chased Eagle & motto. Victory of Barossa' [Barrosa] for £4.14s.6d.,[57] commemorating the desperate action fought on 6 March by a British force of 4,000 with some support from the Spanish to relieve Cadiz which was besieged by about 20,000 French troops.

Nelson's mistress Lady Hamilton, whom he bequeathed to an ungrateful nation, still managed to spark off a rage for Maltese crosses in Britain as well as in Naples and elsewhere by reason of the piece presented to her by the Tsar of Russia (Plate 40). The Prince of Wales gave an example in brilliants, supplied by Rundell's for £185, as a present to his youngest sister Amelia in 1806. The following year, when the *Belle Assemblée* illustrated several Spartan diadems in its fashion plates,[58] the Princess was the recipient of one of the Prince's standard gifts, a 'large Brilliant Tiara to transpose & receive different Ornaments in the Centre', executed by Rundell's with diamonds supplied to them and an additional thirty-nine brilliants whose cost was included in the charge of £48.18s. The firm followed this with 'A fine brilliant Broach to place in the centre' (of the tiara) costing £118. Three years later they were commissioned by the Prince to make fifty-two enamelled gold mourning rings after her death (Colour Plate 18).[59] Costing £151.13s., the rings were distributed among members of the family and the Royal Household. Princess Elizabeth wrote to him on 12 December, mentioning, 'I have had a thousand grateful expressions from Lady George Murray & Mrs Fielding about the rings; it is impossible to say too much for them, for they are thoroughly sensible of your goodness.[60]

Princess Amelia's death, coming after years of ill health, is said to have tipped George III over into his final attack of madness. Suffering from tuberculosis since 1798, her misery was compounded by her hopeless love for General Fitzroy, the second son of Lord Southampton and himself a descendant of Charles II.[61] Her chief consolations were her sister Mary[62] and the Prince of Wales, to both of whom she was devoted, and who returned her affection.

The Prince of Wales was more ambivalent in his attitude towards his daughter Princess Charlotte of Wales (Plate 41). Her chief drawback was to be the child of an uncongenial marriage. She was an uncomfortably tomboyish girl who looked like her grandfather George III and had a mind of her own, strong enough to resent being used as a pawn by her parents. She was fond of her father, but frequently found him remote, especially after he became Prince Regent. Anxious to marry her off, he seized on the government's suggestion and pressed her to accept the hand of the Hereditary Prince of Holland, who had been educated in England. The brief engagement, commenced in December 1813, was soon terminated by the Princess, to her father's fury. The government had granted her £15,000 for her marriage jewellery which she never received and she got herself seriously in debt by buying pearls, a 'fine emerald cross and broach to it', diamonds and other items which were apparently returned to Rundell's when Charlotte decided against the marriage.[63]

She already had accumulated a collection of jewellery, some of it given to her by her father, so that the loss of her marriage jewels did not leave her entirely bereft. 'A fine brilliant & Ruby Maltese Cross for Her Royal Highness The Princess Charlotte' costing £155 appeared in a bill from Rundell's on 1 January 1811. It must have been a present from her father on her fifteenth birthday on 7 January. On 27 January 1812 the Royal Goldsmiths entered the cost of 'A large brilliant furnished & setting it in Diamond Arrow on top of Comb for Her Royal Highness The Princess Charlotte' at £12.12s.[64] Arrow-headed combs were a popular French conceit, while arrow-shaped hairpins were popular in Spain,[65] England and elsewhere. A vine armband followed from the Regent in 1813.

The gathering of the Allied Sovereigns brought another young man to England in the wake of the Tsar of Russia. Prince Leopold of Saxe-Coburg[66] had served with the Russian army and now had to find a new avocation. In May 1816 he achieved it in marrying Princess Charlotte. The government, informed of the betrothal, granted the Princess only £10,000 on this occasion for her jewellery, doubtless with the earlier fiasco in mind, though the necessitous times following the Peace would have made it difficult to give a larger sum. However the funds were made available and the Princess's aunt Elizabeth promised to buy back the emerald cross of 1814 as her marriage gift, while Charlotte intended to re-purchase the pearls if she could. She particularly wanted a pearl necklace, she told her friend Margaret Mercer Elphinstone[67] in a letter of 9 February 1816. 'A fine large Pearl Necklace, containing 54 Pieces, with a single stone Brilliant Clasp' costing £861 and annotated 'Princess Charlotte' appears in a bill from Rundell's to the Prince Regent; the entry is dated 1 April 1816, and two days later a set of chrysolite (olivine) jewellery was noted for one of the ladies attending her at her marriage.[68]

Plate 41. Princess Charlotte of Wales painted in 1817 by George Dawe. Married to Prince Leopold of Saxe-Coburg-Saalfeld the previous year, she wears a ruby ring and wedding ring on her left hand, pearls threaded through her hair and three pearl clasps fastening each sleeve; an emerald and diamond handkerchief pin, and, below, a tripartite serpent belt clasp of the same materials; the Star of St Catherine of Russia on her left breast completes her jewellery. This portrait is said to be the first of a group of the Princess painted by Dawe from life and remained in the painter's possession until his death.

NATIONAL PORTRAIT GALLERY

Plate 42. A portrait miniature of Princess Charlotte of Wales by Charlotte Jones, miniature painter to the Princess, executed in 1817. The Princess is wearing her pearl necklace, mentioned in her letter to Margaret Mercer Elphinstone of 9 February 1816, pearl top and drop earrings '& the 2 strings of perls for perl bracelets' ordered with her friend. Green and red stones ornament her hat and green stones (probably emeralds) are placed at intervals at the edge of her bodice and sleeves. The striped scarf is draped to disguise her pregnancy.

BONHAM & SONS

In a miniature by Charlotte Jones (Plate 42) the Princess is seen wearing her pearl necklace together with bracelets, earrings and a jewelled hat-band.

For a time Princess Charlotte feared that her father would again give her the massive diamond necklace he ordered in 1814 and then returned to Rundell's. The Regent, with his reputation as a leader of fashion to maintain, had necessarily embraced the current trend to greater size and assertiveness in jewellery design. This development, endorsed by Thomas Hope in his *Household Furniture and Interior Decoration* (1807), applied internationally to the decorative arts in general. Nevertheless, the Princess, who is known to have designed at least one item of jewellery, not only disliked the necklace of 1814 but balked at the expense for though nominally a present from the Regent she knew that its cost would be debited to her account. Fortunately her grandmother Queen Charlotte intervened and the Princess was able to report to her friend Miss Elphinstone on 17 March that a new 'Diamond necklace is done, & very handsome for 3,000 pound', adding that she was 'also to have the diamond belt & 2 head ornaments *we ordered together,* & the 2 strings of perls for perl bracelets...' These, she thought, would be sufficient, leaving her money to spare for plate and furnishings.[69]

One of the head ornaments may have been the sprig supplied by Rundell's to the Regent in April 1816 and described in their bill as 'An elegant Brilliant Bouquet for the Hair in form of a Rose' costing £900. On 26 June the firm furnished 'A large Brilliant Medallion to hang, with Brilliant Crown over', set with the Regent's portrait and priced at £1,243.[70] It is possible that this was a wedding gift to his sister Mary, who married their cousin the Duke of Gloucester in July, though it may equally have been presented to her bridegroom.[71] The Prince was greatly attached to this sister, whose portrait in Plate 43, a replica of a painting by Lawrence which was exhibited in 1817, shows her wearing a handsome sautoir, brooch and pearls.

Princess Charlotte and her husband, determined to live within their income, retired to Claremont Park in Surrey where on 6 November 1817 the Princess died a few hours after giving birth to a stillborn son. Once again Rundell's were commanded to produce mourning jewellery, and on 21 November they furnished 'A Chased Gold Broach' set with a miniature of the Princess and 'Celestial Crown, Rose bud etc.' costing £14.14s. and a ring with a serpent encircling a miniature and an enamelled gold shank at £9.9s.[72]

The pendant in Colour Plate 31C was probably made at Leopold's behest; set with a miniature of the Princess after Charlotte Jones, the royal arms are enamelled on the reverse. Other mourning jewels were undoubtedly produced as speculations by jewellers aware of the Princess's popularity with the nation. The Prince Regent, though temporarily prostrated by his daughter's death, later demanded that her widower return the 'Stuart Sapphire', said to have adorned the mitre of Cardinal Henry of York, the younger brother of Prince Charles Edward and the last of the titular Stuart Kings. This great stone, purchased for the Regent in Leipzig in 1811 or 1812 and delivered to him in 1813, was almost immediately given in a fit of generosity to his daughter at a dinner party at Carlton House.[73] Leopold was reluctant to hand it back to his father-in-law, but did so when informed that it was a Crown Jewel. A few months after his accession as George IV, however, the new King had the stone set as the detachable clasp in an armlet of diamonds and pearls from a set of stomacher bows which had belonged to his mother, Queen Charlotte, who died in November 1818. The stone was eventually returned to royal ownership and was set in the front of Queen Victoria's Crown in 1838 (Colour Plate 19 and Plate 44).[74]

Princess Charlotte's death precipitated three marriages in the royal family. The Regent was still legally married to Princess Caroline and his second brother the Duke of York was childless. Three of their younger brothers now concluded that it was their duty to marry and provide an heir to the throne. They all chose German brides; the Duke of Clarence secured Princess Adelaide of Saxe-Coburg Meiningen (Plate 96),[75] the Duke of Kent chose Leopold's widowed sister Victoria, Princess of Leiningen[76] and the Duke of Cambridge attached himself to Princess Augusta of Hesse.[77] The first two couples, married in Germany, went

Plate 43. Princess Mary, Duchess of Gloucester, dressed in white and wearing pearl top and drop earrings, a pearl necklace with a stone-set clasp in front, and a jewelled sautoir passed under a bodice ornament with a pearl drop. The Princess gave the original of this portrait by Sir Thomas Lawrence, which was exhibited at the Royal Academy in 1817, to her lady-in-waiting, Miss Adams. The replica was executed in Lawrence's studio, but not by his hand. Nevertheless, the Princess's gentleness is still apparent in her expression. ROYAL COLLECTION

Plate 44. Queen Victoria in her coronation robes, wearing her new Crown with the Stuart Sapphire in front of the band, below the Black Prince's Ruby in the cross above, by Sir J. Hayter, 1838.
NATIONAL PORTRAIT GALLERY

through a second ceremony in the presence of Queen Charlotte at Kew in July 1818. A bill to the Regent from Rundell's contains an entry dated 8 July 1818 which is annotated 'Princess [*sic*] on marriage' but refers to 'An elegant Brilliant Sprig for the Hair' priced at £700 and another costing £570.[78] It is tempting to see these pieces as carefully modulated marriage presents to the wives of the senior and junior brothers.[79]

The new Duchess of Clarence was subsequently to bear children who died in infancy, but before his unexpected death in January 1820 the Duke of Kent fathered a healthy daughter, who was born on 24 May 1819. Christened Alexandrina Victoria, she succeeded to the throne as Queen Victoria in June 1837 and always retained a lively interest in the life and character of the cousin to whose demise she owed her own existence.

George IV tried to establish grounds for divorcing his wife in 1820 ('the Trial of Queen Caroline')[80] and failing, basked in the comfortable presence of Lady Conyngham, his antiquarian experiments in architecture and the decorative arts and his collections. Rundell's happily cross-fertilised historic styles from plate to jewellery. Their essays in revived rococo, first demonstrated in their plate in the opening decade of the century, began to be manifested in scroll-and-flower borders

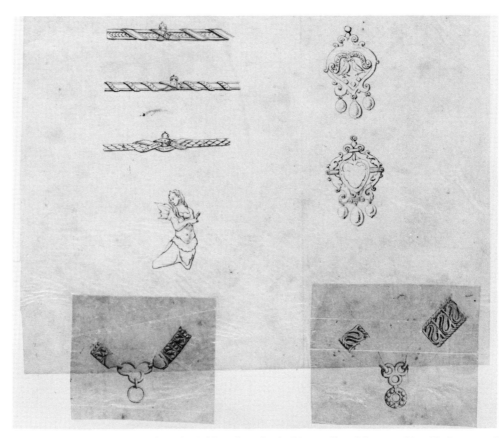

Plate 45. A sheet of drawings from the Bridge album in the Metropolitan Museum, New York, executed on tracing paper. The three details of bands on the top left are variations on the Garter: the lowest one bears the Prince of Wales' motto in reverse. The two heart pendants on the right are mid-eighteenth century in inspiration, the winged figure might be baroque and the two lowest drawings are details of livery Collars of SS. METROPOLITAN MUSEUM OF ART, HARRIS BRISBANE DICK FUND, PRINT ROOM ALBUM, FO. 9

on rings, lockets and the like in the second decade. The gothic revival, well established in English architecture by the mid-eighteenth century, affected only a modicum of plate and scarcely touched jewellery at the time. In the early years of the new century it probably took the additional stimulus of Continental interest for the firm to appreciate the possibilities of gothic motifs in jewellery. The Renaissance style, used in plate executed for Beckford in 1814, spread to jewellery by the mid-1820s. Exotic styles such as the Chinese were also part of Rundell's repertory.

The complicated process of visual research, absorption and re-creation is demonstrated in the album once in the possession of John Bridge's nephew John Gawler Bridge, who appears to have had a great deal to do with the firm's designers.[81] It contains sketches of details of the traditional collars of SS such as were made for Clarenceux and Norroy Kings of Arms in 1820 as part of their coronation perquisites.[82] On the same page is a reinterpretation of a mid-eighteenth heart pendant with turtle doves (Plate 45). Copies of Holbein's drawings of jewellery in the Print Room of the British Museum (Plate 90), including floriated letter pendants, clearly inspired the design for a monogram pendant with a gothic chain illustrated in Chapter V (Plate 91B). Two versions of this design were executed for King George IV in 1825, at a time when he was obsessed with the medievalising of Windsor Castle. The blithe mixing of gothic

Colour Plate 18. A mourning ring for Princess Amelia, George III's youngest daughter. Executed by Rundell's in enamelled gold with a crowned A on a black ground and a white border signifying her unmarried status poignantly inscribed: REMEMBER ME. *The hoop bears a further inscription:* Pss AMELIA. DIED 2 NOV : 1810 AGED 27. *The Princess's death was widely believed to have precipitated George III's final attack of insanity.* VICTORIA AND ALBERT MUSEUM

and Renaissance motifs, characteristic of the time, should not obscure the fact that the designer responsible (probably the enameller Charles Muss, whose obituary notice is mounted between two designs for bracelets in the Bridge album)[83] treated them in an antiquarian spirit. As an admirer of the poems and novels of Sir Walter Scott,[84] George IV must have found these designs congenial.

Muss died in June 1825, aged about forty-three. The fact that he was entrusted with producing jewellery designs for the firm's greatest royal patron indicates that he had experience in the genre. J.G. Bridge was later to take up A.W.N. Pugin when the latter was barely fifteen years old, but it is worth noting that the designs made in 1827 by the prodigy for a set of church plate for the Chapel Royal, Windsor, were never executed.

It is clear from essays in the manner of the Parisian jeweller and designer Simon Petiteau[85] which are mounted in the Bridge album (one of these is illustrated in Chapter V, Plate 91B) that Rundell's were well aware of current French fashions. Petiteau was a skilled exponent of the elaborate filigree work with *grainti* and *cannetille* which began to emerge during the First Empire and flourished for at least two decades after the Restoration of 1814/15 (Colour Plate 7). It was far more popular in France and in other European countries than in England, where jewellers were perfectly capable however of employing this form of filigree and did so on occasion (see page 192). Though news of French fashions reached England after the resumption of the war in 1803, designers of secondary jewellery in Paris and London developed their work on somewhat different lines thereafter.

During the Peace of Amiens English curiosity about the new regime in Paris drove many to visit France. Among them were Lord and Lady Holland and the former's uncle, Charles James Fox. Both men admired Napoleon. Lady Holland, although sympathetic, could not help casting a critical eye over the persons of Napoleon and his wife. Josephine fared worst: 'her figure and *tournure* are perfect', Lady Holland wrote afterwards, 'her taste in dress exquisite, but her face! ghastly, deep furrows on each side of her mouth, fallen-in cheeks... a worn-out hag, prematurely gone, as she is not above 40 years old!'[86] Josephine may indeed have appeared haggard in contrast to the opulent beauties of the English Court, though painters like Robert Lefèvre might be relied upon to improve nature (Colour Plate 9). She grew plumper later but never lost her reputation for elegance, expensively maintained.

Lord Holland, struck with the ostentation of those within the Bonaparte circle, declared that it was as well that the ladies in London were ignorant of it.[87] Josephine naturally patronised the leading jewellers in Paris, including Nitot, Biennais, Foncier and the latter's successor, Marguerite. She also encouraged others less firmly established, among them two concerns run by members of the same family, Italians who had settled in Paris in the sixteenth century. The representative of one branch, François Mellerio, had himself only arrived in France in 1784 and joined the French army as a means of removing himself from Paris during the Terror. He afterwards worked for Manini of Milan before returning to set up in business in the Rue du Coq-Saint-Honoré in 1801. Josephine made modest purchases from him, probably as gifts to her attendants. Jean-Baptiste Mellerio of the other branch had been patronised in a small way by the Bourbon Court and left Paris with most of the Italian community in 1793 to go to Lombardy, the home of his ancestors. When Napoleon's campaign in Italy brought Lombardy under French rule J.-B. Mellerio returned to Paris to establish a shop in the Rue Vivienne under the sign of the Iron Crown of Lombardy. At about the time that Napoleon was crowned King of Italy with the Iron Crown itself in 1805, the Empress Josephine, attracted by Mellerio's sign, bought a magnificent pearl necklace from him.[88] Among the specialist suppliers to the Empress were Capparone (cameos) and Oliva & Scotto (corals).

Josephine's insatiable craving for jewels was deplored by the Bonaparte family. Napoleon's uncle Joseph Fesch (a priest, later a Cardinal, who was also an army contractor) wrote to Joachim Murat in March 1801 to warn him against Josephine's continual requests for 'necklaces, statues etc.' from the conquered territories.[89] During her marriage to Napoleon, she invariably exceeded her annual allowance and he usually settled her debts, though she became an increasingly costly burden. But, like the Prince Regent, her extravagance had a creative side, enabling her by sheer weight of acquisition to influence the direction of design far beyond her immediate circle. In both instances, their standing reinforced their enlightened patronage and jewellers on all levels sought to produce work which suggested, if it could not replicate, ornaments current in the French and English Courts.

The French Empress's continual desire for change, inseparable from a dedicated pursuit of fashion, is manifested in a collection of papers relating to her dealings with Nitot et fils in 1809. Josephine adored coral (Plate 46). A list of red and pink coral jewellery sent by the firm on 29 April includes quantities of necklaces, bracelets, earrings and buttons as well as a bandeau. On 10 July the firm wrote announcing the despatch of a coral parure mounted by command of the Empress, together with a gold belt set with cameos and another of diamonds belonging to Josephine's daughter Hortense,[90] Queen of Holland (Plate 70).

Josephine had to purchase a considerable number of pieces for presentation purposes. These were often modest by comparison with the Empress's own jewels, some of which were designed by the painter Prud'hon.[91] The difference is demonstrated by two lists prepared by Nitot when Josephine was in Strasbourg while Napoleon directed his forces against Austria at Wagram. The first is an inventory of the jewels taken to Strasbourg for her use. The articles appear in categories, commencing with diamonds, a necklace composed of twenty-seven brilliants in collets, a comb topped with brilliants arranged in trefoils, a belt with

Plate 46. A suite of diamond-cut coral and gold, said to have been presented by the Empress Josephine to the bride of Alexandre Macdonald, Duc de Tarante and Marshal of France; c.1805.   WARTSKI

Colour Plate 19. Queen Victoria's Crown set with the Stuart Sapphire in the front of the band, from a print of 1838. Purchased for George IV when Regent in about 1812, it was presented by him to his daughter Charlotte of Wales. After Princess Charlotte's death he retrieved the stone and in 1820 had it mounted as a gift to Lady Conyngham. Returned to the Royal Collection in about 1838, it is now set at the back of the Imperial State Crown.

large rose diamonds and a pair of earrings with briolette drops, all probably in her possession between 1802 and 1804. She also had in 1809 a pair of girandole earrings, another pair with three drops, a fourth circular with brilliant borders and finally a brilliant cross. The next, pearls, equally lavish, comprised three necklaces, one of a single row of thirty-three pearls, the second with three strings of forty-nine, fifty-seven and eighty pearls respectively and thirteen pear-shaped drops attached to one row, the third of a row of 131 pearls, a pair of large pear-shaped pearl drop earrings and another, smaller pair, a rich comb with pear-shaped pearls and a lesser one, a pearl and cameo parure consisting of a bandeau, necklace, comb and earrings and finally a belt with three plaques decorated with pear-shaped pearls and bordered with 197 others. The third category, devoted to articles made from coloured stones, mainly with brilliant borders, is too long for more than a brief summary to be given. Beginning with a necklace centre composed of an apricot-coloured ruby in a diamond surround suspended from forty-three pearls, it lists parures and demi-parures composed of emeralds (a necklace with cross, earrings and bracelets open-set without diamonds), opals, aquamarines, amethysts, rubies, garnets, topazes, emeralds and pearls, turquoises, chrysolites and coral. Some were adorned with carnelian, sardonyx and malachite cameos. There were also mosaic earrings and chains and sautoirs and, among other items, a hair necklace with a pendent cross of blue pearls and a crystal heart set with turquoises. None of these items is valued, and only a few included bandeaux, let alone the fillets which appear in earlier portraits (Colour Plate 9) and in the parure in Colour Plate 32.

The second list, dated 26 May, consists of articles sent on approval to the Empress, apparently intended for distribution in Strasbourg. Some items, including a silver watch on an enamelled necklace (250 francs or about £11.8s.), a gold chain (72 francs), a gold seal and key (78 francs) and a simple gold watch (280 francs) seem to have been given to servants or minor functionaries. Queen Hortense took possession of an opal ring with a brilliant border (360

Colour Plate 20. A spray of laurel, formed of brilliants and rubies set transparent in silver and gold; probably designed to be worn as a bodice ornament. It was made for the Empress Josephine and the original fitted case survives, its lid stamped in gold with her initial J below the Imperial Crown. A torn label on the underside bears the names of Ouizille et Lemoine of Rue Duphot, Paris, to whom Josephine's daughter presumably took the piece for attention some time after she had inherited her mother's jewellery in 1814. It was probably this firm which converted the piece so that it could be divided into two parts.

PRIVATE COLLECTION, LENT TO THE VICTORIA AND ALBERT MUSEUM THROUGH WARTSKI

francs), her mother of two more set with violet-coloured rubies (1,500 and 4,000 francs), while four others, two emerald, one ruby and an opal (800, 750, 1,500 and 500 francs) were given away. Josephine also bought a number of unmounted stones, some of which she presented; one was a brilliant of 4 carats costing 3,500 francs. Three pairs of brilliant earrings ranging in price from 900 to 2,500 francs were not taken up. Nor were a parure of Florentine mosaics (1,200 francs), one of gold pavé-set with turquoises (600 francs), another of peridots and pearls (2,400 francs) and others. The overall value of the objects listed was 58,330 francs (about £2,673).[92]

The Empress Josephine adored colour. The clasps of some of her necklaces were made brighter with enamels, as well some of her neckchains. Her well-known passion for cameos, which prompted Napoleon to remove eighty-two engraved gems from the old royal collections for her use, was also reputedly indulged by the Queen of Naples with the gift of a large enamelled gold parure adorned with cameos and intaglios in the classical taste (Colour Plates 32 and 33). The donor is unlikely to have been the Bourbon Queen, who hated the French for executing her sister Marie Antoinette, but Napoleon's sister Caroline Murat, whose husband Joachim, created King of Naples by Napoleon in 1808, is known to have sent Josephine a necklace of cameos and intaglios on his own account.[93] It is also worth noting that some years earlier, when Napoleon was still First Consul, Ferdinand IV had included jewellery excavated from Herculaneum among his diplomatic gifts to Bonaparte and that this had passed to Josephine.

The engraved gems given to the Empress by the Queen of Naples were set in Paris; the smaller of the two diadems bears the restricted warranty mark in use between 1798 and 1809 and an undecipherable maker's mark. It is not beyond the bounds of possibility that Caroline Murat herself paid for the setting.

It is difficult to determine the identity of the jeweller who made the ruby and diamond spray in Colour Plate 20, which still has its fitted case stamped in gold with the crowned cipher of the Empress. Stuck to the underside of the case is the paper label of Ouizille & Lemoine, who entered into partnership only in 1818, four years after Josephine's death, though the firm in the Rue Duphot had been run by Ouizille's father from 1789. Perhaps Josephine's daughter Hortense, who with her brother Eugène de Beauharnais[94] shared their mother's estate, took the spray back to the original suppliers for repair and the label was added at this stage. It has certainly been adapted to form two separate ornaments when required, though it was originally probably worn diagonally across the bodice (see also Colour Plate 34).

Josephine, divorced by Napoleon late in 1809, died at Malmaison on 29 May 1814, just after Napoleon had arrived at Elba, his first place of exile. Ferdinand Quaglia's portrait of the ex-Empress, painted in the year of her death (Plate 47) shows her stouter than heretofore but still wearing her necklace with pearls with huge pear-shaped drops owned since about 1799 and missing at her death, top and drop earrings, a Spartan diadem with a crest of cameos and a smaller piece behind, perhaps a tiara-comb. Josephine had apparently added to the necklace since she wore it at the marriage in 1807 of Jérôme Bonaparte, King of Westphalia. The

Plate 47. A miniature of the Empress Josephine by Ferdinand Quaglia, painted in 1814, the year of her death. Still elegant but plump (though she is said to have lost weight immediately before she died on 29 May), Josephine is wearing pearls, a favourite necklace with drops arranged in a near-perfect circle around her neck (quite unrealistically), top and drop earrings, an elaborate diadem with pearl trefoils alternating with cameos and a comb or tiara-comb behind. A large pearl drop is set at the centre of her bodice, and her belt is clasped with two pearl plaques. The diadem is missing from the inventory made of Josephine's jewellery after her death. WALLACE COLLECTION

ceremony was recorded by J.-B. Regnault,[95] who depicts Josephine resplendent in her pearl necklace with drops, bracelets, belt, long pearl earrings and an arcaded diadem of pearls with a comb behind. This was the suite in its original state, and she appears with the same necklace and diadem in the miniature by Daniel Saint set in a gold box by Blerzy (Colour Plate 21). The earrings may be her smaller pair, but there is no question that the diadem is the same; with the points of the pyramidical arcade topped with pearl trefoils, it manages to suggest the gothic without departing from classical simplicity. Another miniature portrays Josephine wearing a pearl tiara with an anthemion device in front (Plate 39). These magnificent pieces lend some force to the comment made by the *Belle Assemblée* in 1815 to the effect that in France women preferred pearls to diamonds, whereas the reverse applied to England. Like all such aphorisms, it is open to challenge. The rage for pearls was universal and it would have been difficult to find a European Court in which they did not figure prominently.

Josephine's purchases of jewellery during her years as Empress were made from a fund known as the *Toilette.* From 1804 to her divorce in 1809 it stood at 360,000 francs a year, from which she had to buy her clothes, contribute to charity and cover other personal expenditure. Since she had already accumulated large debts during the Consulate and invariably over-spent her current allowance Napoleon was called upon to authorise additional payments totalling 3,200,000 francs between 1805 and 1810. It is probable, however, that despite her other fund, the *Cassette,* which gave her another 120,000 francs a year, Josephine still contrived to spend over a million francs a year and left about three million owing at her death.

The posthumous inventory of her jewellery, published by Serge Grandjean in 1964, comprises 139 articles valued by B.A. Marguerite at only 1,923,263 francs which, at the volatile exchange rate of 1814, amounted to some £87,000-£113,000.

Colour Plate 21. A miniature of the Empress Josephine by Daniel Saint, showing her wearing her pearl necklace with drops and matching earrings, together with the arcaded gothic diadem in which she appeared at the marriage of her brother-in-law Jérôme Bonaparte, King of Westphalia, in 1807. The miniature, in a rose diamond frame, is set in an enamelled box by Blerzy, Paris, c.1803-09.

Marguerite's estimates were probably about half the true value, but the total was still remarkably low in view not only of the former Empress's expenditure but also in terms of the gifts she had received as Napoleon's consort. In 1802 a sapphire parure valued at 100,000 francs was presented to her by an Italian anxious to procure a government post. Napoleon is said to have commanded her to return it but she might have managed to evade parting with it. In 1809 Napoleon, probably consumed by guilt as he planned to divorce Josephine, sanctioned the acquisition of a ruby and diamond suite augmented by a bouquet and garlands. It cost nearly 101,100 francs despite the fact that she herself furnished Nitot et fils with most of the rubies and some of the diamonds used, which were probably removed from a parure in her possession at the outset of her reign.

The jewels listed by Marguerite at Malmaison were personal or private ornaments. On her divorce Josephine was required to return pieces designated as Crown Jewels. An inventory of the Crown Diamonds compiled in 1811 produced an overall total of some 12,500,000 francs, of which the Emperor's share amounted to 7,500,000 francs and that of his new Empress, Marie-Louise, to about 4,000,000 francs. The remainder, worth about 1,000,000, apparently largely consisted of jewels bought by Josephine. The inventories of the diamonds, pearls and precious stones belonging to the Crown made in 1811, 1812 and 1813 valued them at a total of 14,393,881 francs.[96]

Napoleon must have expected that more jewellery would be found at Malmaison after Josephine's death than proved to be the case. To allay suspicion of malpractice, Josephine's ladies were asked to testify that nothing had been concealed. They complied without making difficulties, from which it may be inferred that the former Empress had either sold jewels during her latter years or, more likely, had given away pieces to her children and her friends. Diamonds were particularly lacking at Malmaison, though one piece, a necklace of twenty-seven

Colour Plate 22. The Comtesse Daru, painted by J.-L. David in 1810, her head wreathed in flowers shaped like a Spartan diadem. Her necklace and earrings, of milky green stones set in borders of diamonds, are remarkably similar to the peridot and diamond pieces in Colour Plate 23, though the latter are linked with diamond rosettes, while the intermediate links on Madame Daru's necklace are set with small green stones. FRICK COLLECTION, NEW YORK

brilliants, probably came from the great parure given to her by Napoleon in 1802 or thereabouts and taken to Strasbourg in 1809. With a pair of pear-shaped drops and two buttons or studs, it was assessed by Marguerite at 541,200 francs. Another item, an incomplete diamond diadem, was probably the head ornament added to the suite in 1804; it was valued at 108,000 francs.

The other major items mainly consisted of suites of coloured stones in brilliant borders. A bandeau, necklace, earrings, comb and belt clasp survived from the great ruby parure of 1810, and were assessed at 156,000 francs; the bouquet and garlands were missing. An emerald suite with a jewelled belt was valued at 162,000 francs; an opal set, likewise having a belt, at 204,000; a sapphire parure comprising bandeau, necklace and two pairs of earrings, 84,000 francs; one of 'Brazilian rubies' (pink topaz), which had two bandeaux, one smaller than the other, a necklace, comb and earrings, at 72,000 francs and a turquoise set comprising a bandeau, necklace, comb and earrings, at 30,000. Sets known to have been in Josephine's possession had disappeared, though a packet of 220 amethysts valued at 6,000 francs probably represented the remains of one of these.

Marguerite described all the surviving head ornaments as bandeaux, which was probably his preferred term rather than a literal description of their shape. Most suites lacked bracelets. Josephine had taken to long sleeves, to judge by Quaglia's portrait (Plate 47), which perhaps explains their absence. She might not have cared to wear bracelets over wristbands, but single bracelets do figure in Marguerite's inventory.

The pearl diadem set with cameos which was worn by the ex-Empress when she sat to Quaglia in 1814 is missing from the inventory, though she had several pearl necklaces in her possession at the time of her death, including one of thirty-five pearls valued at 48,000 francs and thirty pear-shaped pearls which with two ovoid specimens and a pair of pearl buttons were assessed at 90,000 francs.

The lesser suites owned by Josephine included one of mosaics and pearls, valued at 3,600 francs. Another of corals and pearls, comprising a bandeau, necklace, earrings, comb, belt and bracelets assessed at 12,000 francs was probably among Josephine's older sets, as was an agate and pearl parure in which bracelets likewise figured. A set of balas rubies (spinels) at 3,000 francs, another of cameos with ruby and pearl borders at 7,200 francs, a jet parure (with one bracelet) at 480 francs, two steel sets at 240 francs apiece and two more coral suites with raspberry motifs, a pink one at 640 francs and the other strawberry-coloured with the same valuation, were accompanied by other parures and quantities of singletons or pairs of articles.[97]

Josephine's unexpected death at the age of fifty gave her no opportunity to compound with her creditors, among whom were the jewellers Nitot, Frieze, Pitaux, Grancher and Lebrun, the first-named alone being owed 73,722 francs for articles purchased in 1812. Fortunately at least for her daughter Hortense, in 1829 the Tsar of Russia purchased the necklace of twenty-seven brilliants without its accessories for 700,000 francs, an impressive increase on the valuation of 1814.

The Emperor Napoleon was in the habit of buying stones, as Rundell's were well aware. Some must have been supplied by the jewellers commissioned to set articles for him. More than 2,000 diamonds valued at nearly 900,000 francs were assembled for setting in Josephine's diadem, Crown and belt for the coronation in 1804, the setting being charged at 15,000 francs. Seventeen years later, George IV too was resplendent in a Crown set with diamonds valued at over £65,000, while the hat he wore in processing to his coronation was garnished with the brilliant circlet already cited (Plate 35). But the diamonds set in both ornaments were hired.[98]

Napoleon, wooing the Archduchess Maria Luisa (Marie-Louise) of Austria[99] through intermediaries in 1810, felt it necessary to accelerate the rate of his acquisitions. Between 1810 and 1812 he spent some 6,000,000 francs on stones. Where the Emperor led, others followed. An anonymous article on the fluctuating value of diamonds appearing in the *Belle Assemblée* in 1811 attributed the current sharp increase in prices to the difficulties experienced by Continental dealers in getting stones from South America past the British blockade.[100] However small diamonds could be made to go a long way when set as borders around large coloured stones, enabling the privileged still to make an impressive show of jewels. Madame Daru (Colour Plate 22), the wife of Napoleon's Secretary-at-War, was painted by J.-L. David as a surprise for her husband in 1810; her massive necklace and earrings are virtual counterparts of the set of peridots and brilliants in Colour Plate 23.

The Emperor sent a casket filled with jewellery to his unseen bride in Vienna in 1810.[101] Marie-Louise, though shy and awkward, as an Archduchess by birth fully appreciated the importance of looking like an Empress. In a letter written to her husband on 26 September 1811 she took the opportunity of informing him that she had ordered a new gown adorned with diamonds as she knew he liked her to be well dressed.[102] She was shrewd enough to know that she might spend as she liked, having recently given the Emperor the son he so ardently desired.[103] Since their marriage in 1810 Napoleon showered her with Crown jewels, including a diamond parure and others set with coloured stones. On the birth of her son, the King of Rome, in 1811, Napoleon gave her a diamond necklace executed by the Nitot firm; it was valued at 376,275 francs in June 1811. She was painted in 1812 wearing the necklace, which as it formed part of her personal jewellery has survived;[104] her other ornaments in the portrait were the diadem, earrings and girdle from the state parure of diamonds, dating to 1810-1812 (Plate 48).

Another piece still in existence is a girdle front of 1813, a delicate specimen of gold openwork decorated with pearls and with a central cameo (Plate 83); a long pendant falls from it, the inner border of the lower edge ornamented with a gothic arcade. Firmly confined within their classical frames, the gothic motifs are small subordinate details,[105] less striking though more archaeological than the pointed arcades on Josephine's pearl diadem (Colour Plate 21). But romantic medievalism had already been proudly manifested in a large German circlet of arching classical form with a crest of gothic trefoils which was worn by Queen Luisa of Prussia at Tilsit in 1807,[106] when Napoleon, in temporary alliance with the Tsar of Russia, connived to deprive her country of half its territories.

A pair of bracelets from Marie-Louise's ruby and diamond parure, adapted for the use of the Duchesse d'Angoulême in 1816, was presented to the Louvre in 1973.[107] Most of the Crown Jewels of the First Empire were dismantled and re-set for the restored Bourbons, but Marie-Louise, like Josephine, retained personal pieces. G.B. Borghesi portrayed her in later years as Duchess of Parma wearing a jewelled bandeau and tiara front, her huge necklace of 1811 and earrings to match, together with a belt.[108]

The marriages arranged by the Emperor cost him a great deal by way of jewellery. With the aim of promoting the Confederation of the Rhine in 1806 Napoleon adopted the sixteen-year-old Stéphanie de Beauharnais,[109] a relative by

marriage of the Empress Josephine, then married her off to the heir of the Grand Duke of Baden. Gérard painted the young bride wearing Napoleon's wedding gift, a full parure of emeralds and diamonds in the standard Empire manner, comprising a diadem, comb, necklace with festoons and drops, earrings and a pair of bracelets (Plate 61). The necklace and earrings, set transparent (Colour Plate 25 and Plate 62), are in the collection of the Victoria and Albert Museum. The marriage was not happy, but Stéphanie survived to be admired for her elegance and her diamonds by Queen Victoria.[110]

Emerald and diamond parures were standard wedding presents in the Bonaparte circle. On the marriage in 1808 of Napoleon's favourite aide-de-camp, General Bertrand, to Fanny Dillon, Josephine, the bride's aunt, gave her niece a suite of emeralds and diamonds. Napoleon saw it, thought it inadequate and ordered Josephine's daughter Hortense to augment it with items from her own set. Fanny's half-sister, Henrietta-Lucy de la Tour du Pin (Colour Plate 5), as a former member of Marie-Antoinette's Household was not enamoured of the Bonaparte clan and was amused by the sight of Hortense sulking at the wedding reception.[111]

The Marquise de la Tour du Pin and her family had suffered hardship in exile before returning to France. She welcomed the return of the old order in 1814, as did many of the inhabitants of Napoleon's vassal states who had had their lives disrupted by war. Lord and Lady Holland, arriving in Spain on a self-appointed diplomatic mission in 1809, went to Seville and found shelter in a house abandoned by the Marquesa de Ariza who, fearing that the French would soon occupy the city, had fled precipitately, leaving her plate and much of her jewellery behind.[112] But Napoleon's disastrous campaign in Russia had resulted in few spoils by way of jewellery and the huge stones favoured by royals and nobles were displayed to

Colour Plate 23. A necklace and top-and-drop earrings of step-cut peridots set transparent in gold with clawed edges, with shaped borders of brilliants in silver cut-down settings. The units of the necklace are unevenly graduated and might have been assembled from components taken from other articles of jewellery which for some reason were broken up, perhaps at the request of the owner who wanted a fashionable necklace in about 1810.

VICTORIA AND ALBERT MUSEUM

109

Plate 49. Marie-Thérèse de Bourbon, Duchesse d'Angoulême (Madame Royale), the daughter of King Louis XVI and Queen Marie Antoinette. She had been imprisoned in the Temple during the Terror and only released to the protection of the Emperor of Austria in 1795, in exchange for French prisoners-of-war. During the first months of the Restoration ladies desisted from wearing jewels and other ornaments in deference to the known inclinations of the Duchesse, except on occasions of ceremony. Then the Duchesse herself appeared in jewellery of considerable splendour. The diadem in this print was re-made in 1814 as was, probably, the upper necklace, which was her own and apparently set with diamonds from Marie-Antoinette's own jewellery. The print, freely adapted from a portrait by Baron Gros in the Château de Versailles, credits the necklace with more drops than are depicted in the original painting, which shows only three.

great effect on the persons of the Tsar and members of his suite during the peace celebrations.

On 6 April 1814 Napoleon signed an Act of Abdication and two weeks later quit Paris on his way to exile on Elba. In England, the new Bourbon King prepared to take up the throne. Louis XVI's brother, known as Louis XVIII in deference to the Dauphin who had died in captivity after the Terror, left the house in Buckinghamshire where he and his family had lived in exile for some years and, gallantly escorted by the Prince Regent, came to London on the first stage of his journey. In a gesture of gratitude, the French King took the Order of the Saint-Esprit from his own shoulders and placed it around the Regent's neck. The Regent invested the King with the Order of the Garter at Dover, and having bid him farewell with his inimitable grace, returned to London to await the arrival of the Allied Sovereigns.

The restored Bourbons inevitably tried to put the clock back, even to the extent of re-making the Crown Jewels returned to the Chief Treasurer to the Crown by Napoleon and his Empress after he had signed the instrument of abdication in April 1814. Louis XVIII's Court comprised an odd mixture of Bonapartists turned royalists, who were accustomed to the advanced modes of the First Empire, and aristocratic survivors of the Revolution who frequently had to resort to wearing remnants of their old costumes garnished with the few jewels which they had managed to preserve. The King's niece, the Duchesse d'Angoulême, a melancholy and pious figure marked by her years of incarceration, was not fond of display, though said to have 'grown quite pretty' since the Restoration.[113] Nevertheless on occasion she cut an impressive figure, regally bedecked in jewels. The Duchesse

Plate 50. A ruby and diamond diadem from a suite designed by J.-E. Bapst himself and remounted by Bapst-Ménière from the Crown Jewels of the First Empire in 1816. The small rubies flanking some of the flower motifs on the lower stage are set in collets with strongly-marked ribs all round their faces, a development of the grouped ribs on the collets holding the ruby and diamond berries on the Empress Josephine's laurel spray (Colour Plate 20). The suite was offered in separate lots at the sale of the French Crown Jewels in 1887. The diadem sold at 160,000 francs. SOTHEBY'S

had the use of some of the reconstructed suites, including a diadem made from the Empress Marie-Louise's diamonds. She also had a number of pieces of her own, among them a new necklace comprising a rivière furnished with drops which was probably set with diamonds from a piece belonging to her mother, Queen Marie-Antoinette.[114] In 1824 the Duchesse's diamond diadem was re-set for her with new stones purchased by Louis XVIII, who allowed her to regard the piece as her own. The engraving in Plate 49, inspired by a painting by Baron Gros, shows her resplendent in the diadem and other pieces of her personal jewellery, including the necklace with drops.

The Duchesse's more habitual austerity made her unpopular with Parisian shopkeepers, who were kept going by the English flooding into Paris in 1814. The re-emergence of Napoleon in 1815 prompted the King's flight to Ghent with the Crown Jewels which he brought back with him after Wellington's victory at Waterloo in June. The following year the arrival of the Duchesse d'Angoulême's younger and far more frivolous sister-in-law, the bride of the King's nephew the Duc de Berri, signalled hope for the Parisian trade. She proved only too happy to set the mode.[115]

There were new royal jewellers at the Restoration. The younger Nitot retired. The task of adapting and re-making the Crown Jewels of the First Empire fell to the firm of P.-N. Ménière, who was Jeweller to King Louis XVI just before the Revolution. Ménière was associated with his son-in-law J.-E. Bapst, who came of a family whose long and distinguished record of service to the Bourbon monarchy stemmed from the appointment of G.F. Stras[116] as Jeweller to the King of France in 1734, for on Stras's retirement from business in 1752 his nephew G.M. Bapst took over the firm. His descendant J.-E. Bapst of Bapst-Ménière was closely concerned in orchestrating the conversion of the First Empire jewellery, aided by the firm's artist, Seiffert and by C.-F. Bapst, who oversaw the execution of the new work.

Marie-Louise's diamond suite and another of her parures which was set with coloured stones were the first to be partially dismantled and re-made in 1814. Work was resumed after Napoleon's final defeat at Waterloo and completed in 1820[117] (Plate 50 and Colour Plate 35). The new pieces, though graceful, lacked the forcefulness and simplicity of the jewellery made for the Empress Josephine. Yet the Restoration jewellery was not innovative: it represents a continuation of stylistic developments already apparent in the closing stages of Napoleon's regime. A softened profile and more complex detailing characterise Marie-Louise's diadem in Plate 48.

There is, however, little evidence of a serious and concerned attempt to revive pre-Revolutionary design in the new Bourbon pieces. Vever illustrated a brilliant bouquet made by Bapst for presentation to the Duchesse de Berri on the birth of her son in 1820 (Plate 182) stating that it reinterpreted a diamond spray executed by the same firm for Marie-Antoinette in 1788.[118] The nineteenth century piece was, however, several decades later than he thought, representing the apogee of the organic treatment of nature already noticeable during the First Empire in France, England and elsewhere. The naturalistic style swept over Europe during the first half of the century.

The transition from war to peace had been difficult for goldsmiths and jewellers to ride. The value of precious metals fell dramatically. Owing to the shortage during the war gold had sometimes approached £10 per oz.; now it dropped to £3.17s.10½d. and silver fell from about 7s. per oz. to 5s.2d., according to George Fox.[119] Jewellers like Rundell's who had large stocks on their hands suffered immediately. Moreover the agricultural depression inevitably affected the luxury trades. Setting in after Waterloo, the depression persisted for some twenty years and materially contributed to the transformation of England from a primarily agricultural nation to one dominated by industry. Some landowners benefited from industrial development, others, indirectly, from trade. The rich were augmented in number by industrial magnates and the best jewellers eventually managed to recover a large part of their business.

The new manufacturing towns housed a high percentage of the population which was to grow from some eighteen and a half millions in 1811 to about forty millions in 1891. Though this growth exceeded that of other European countries Germany ran England a close second and the population everywhere would have been higher but for the mass emigration to the New World and to various colonies and dependencies. In the course of the century some forty million people left Europe, carrying to their new homes their cultural habits and traditions which made them a ready market for the familiar goods of their natal countries. To meet the hugely-increased demand at home and abroad the production of much secondary and virtually all tertiary jewellery was industrialised and the search for new sources of the raw materials of jewellery was intensified.

CHAPTER III
On Stones

1. The Commerce in Stones

The decree issued by Napoleon from Berlin on 21 November 1806 barring Continental ports (even those of neutral countries) against British ships added to the difficulties experienced by dealers in France and the vassal states in obtaining stones from South America. The British compounded the problem by extending their existing blockade of European ports. English maritime supremacy enabled the diamond-dealers in London and elsewhere to find new contacts in Portuguese Brazil, for the French invasion of Portugal in 1809 had disrupted their normal channels of trade. Since the 1720s, when diamonds were found in the state of Minas Gerais in Brazil, about three hundred and fifty miles north of Rio de Janeiro, the trade with England had been largely in the hands of members of the Jewish community whose forebears had left Portugal to settle in London during the last years of the Commonwealth.[1] Their connections in Portugal enabled them to buy diamonds imported from the Portuguese colony and bring them to England in exchange for wool and other goods. Their dealings interlocked with those of other merchants who had come to England via Holland, where they had built up connections with the diamond-cutters of Amsterdam. These merchants imported rough diamonds from India, paying duties to the East India Company and often sending the stones to Amsterdam for processing. Among the items they exported to India were South American emeralds and coral from the Mediterranean.[2]

Rundell's, as working jewellers, obtained their stones in return for articles of a complexity and magnificence especially designed for Eastern consumption. They found a ready market in Constantinople (Istanbul), Alexandria, Smyrna, Baghdad, Calcutta, Madras, Bombay and elsewhere, and 'the Proceeds were remitted...in Bulses [sealed parcels] of Rough Diamonds, in considerable quantities of fine Pearls or in Rubies Emeralds Sapphires and other precious stones by which large sums were made.'[3] Philip Rundell, a skilled judge of quality, also bought from London dealers, driving a very hard bargain in the process, as he did when private persons in need of immediate relief tried to dispose of their jewellery to him. He was normally courteous to customers,[4] but perhaps it was fortunate that Jane Austen was acquainted with Thomas Gray's of Sackville Street rather than Rundell's. She sent Elinor Dashwood, the heroine of *Sense and Sensibility* (1811), 'upstairs to the first floor showroom of Gray's to negotiate the exchange of a few old-fashioned jewels of her mother'.[5] Miss Dashwood, the incarnation of sense, plainly regarded the destruction and re-making of family pieces as a commonplace matter, as indeed it was.

A slave-driver to his staff, according to George Fox, who was employed as a shopman (that is, a shop-assistant) in the firm, Philip Rundell kept a watchful eye on the stock of precious stones. He was particularly careful of the diamonds and, Fox wrote, 'he would not suffer any of them [to] be set up in either any Articles for Sale or in those already [ordered] by Customers without his being present when they were looked out from the papers by the workmen who after selecting whatever was needful had to take them home and arranged [sic] them very carefully on wax and then they were brought for his Inspection previously to their being set up and when the piece of Jewellery was finished he would examine it with great attention and if he had failed to observe any of the diamonds that were defective either in shape, cutting or color when he saw them arranged, his sharp eyes would be sure to detect them now that they were mounted, and he would invariably insist on their removal and have better ones put in their stead.' The resulting jewellery, as Fox acknowledged, was unsurpassed.[6]

There is nothing surprising in the careful tally kept of the stones nor in the trial setting in wax which was customarily also shown to the customer for approval (Princess Charlotte of Wales saw some of her jewellery set in this way). It is however remarkable that Rundell's anxiety to get the most out of his craftsmen overruled any uneasiness about the stones being removed from his custody and taken home. But he combined meanness with the recklessness of a gambler to an extraordinary degree. Even during the war, when he had arranged to send a consignment of jewellery to Rio de Janeiro by diplomatic bag, he grudgingly agreed under strong pressure from his partners to insure it with Lloyds but only to half the valuation of £16,000. Unhappily the whole collection was jettisoned when the English ship was chased off Cape St Vincent by a French privateer and threatened with capture. Confidential despatches and letters for Rio de Janeiro were dropped overboard to prevent the French reading them: weighted with shot, they must have sunk like a stone. Down went the jewellery with them in the same bag. In the event, the English ship got away. Philip Rundell, only slightly daunted, despatched replacement jewellery by the same method and insured it fully. It actually reached Rio de Janeiro.[7]

The shortage of stones on the Continent, exacerbated by the incessant demands of agents employed in every major city to make purchases for the extended Bonaparte family, led to the price rise reported in the *Belle Assemblée* in 1811: 'A letter from Frankfort, of a recent date, quotes of the finest water [a term indicating purity and brilliance in diamonds], at more than 12*l.* sterling per carat.' These stones were, it was said, eagerly acquired for the Courts of France and Germany; inferior specimens found their way to Constantinople,[8] an interesting sidelight on Fox's description of the articles supplied by Rundell's to the Turkish market.

The 'fine yellow Diamond' costing £136.10s. which was bought from Garrard's by Georgiana's son the sixth Duke of Devonshire in 1812 might be computed as weighing between three and four carats, to judge by the pricing system in current use in the trade, set out by the mineralogist and dealer John Mawe[9] in his *Treatise on Diamonds* (1813). But the fact that it was coloured enhanced the value per carat. Even dealers found it a complex business to calculate prices, for the carat was not standard. In modern terms, the carat was estimated in England at 205.3 milligrams; in Amsterdam it was 205.7 milligrams and in Paris 205.5.[10] But this basic difficulty was not allowed to impede the international conduct of the trade. There were four grains to the carat; but weights were also expressed as fractions of 64 parts. An international metric standard of 200 milligrams was agreed in the early twentieth century.

The value of a diamond was reckoned to increase with the square of the weight in carats. This partly reflected the loss of weight in cutting: a rough diamond weighing 2 carats might emerge from cutting as a brilliant of 1 carat, though it was often less. If a fine cut brilliant free from flaws and absolutely colourless or, rather, blue-white ('a diamond of the first water') weighing 1 carat cost £10, a 2 carat stone of the same quality would be worth about four (2 x 2) times £10, that is, £40, and one of 3 carats nine times £10, or £90. This was a rule of thumb rather than a consistent guide.

A later edition of Mawe's book came out in 1823 during the post-war depression when the price of diamonds had dropped. He now assessed the value of a good brilliant weighing 1 carat at between £9.9s. and £10, valued one of twice the weight at £35 maximum, and an example of 3 carats at between £70 and £80.[11] Coloured diamonds were still worth more. In about 1825 a Viennese jeweller working in London, Charles Winter, referred in his *Pattern-book for Jewellers, Goldsmiths and Ornamentmakers* to having mounted in Vienna a blue diamond of 3½ carats worth £100.[12]

Mawe, like Philip Rundell, recognised that the old diamond mines of the sub-continent of India were incapable of producing large yields by the 1820s. Mawe cited the case of a company, largely funded by English capital, which tried to exploit one of these mines with the approval of the local ruler; it failed after three years, despite, possibly, the existence of other coloured stones which were also frequently recovered from the diamond-bearing areas.[13] Diamonds were nevertheless still mined in India, Borneo and elsewhere in South-east Asia, though not in sufficient quantities to make a noticeable impact on the European market. South-east Asia, however, continued to furnish Europe with a wide variety of coloured stones, including rubies and sapphires from Burma and Ceylon. Decades later, deposits of rubies and sapphires were exploited in Siam (Thailand). New finds of sapphires were also made in Kashmir, in Montana, Colorado and in Australia.

It had taken a long time for Brazilian diamonds to be accepted in Europe. The Portuguese government imposed restrictions on the diamonds exported from its colony and merchants holding stocks of Indian diamonds feared that the arrival of Brazilian stones would adversely affect their business. Some dealers assiduously spread rumours that the South American diamonds were inferior to the Indian or alternatively denied that the former were local, alleging that the refuse of Indian mines had been planted in Brazil. More far-sighted merchants executed the trick in reverse, shipping Brazilian diamonds to India where they were parcelled up with local stones in bulses and taken to Europe. No one, apparently, spotted the difference. By the early 1820s there was no question as to the ascendancy of South American diamonds. The government exercised a monopoly over the mines and exported some 25,000-30,000 carats of rough diamonds annually to Europe. Surprisingly, these converted into brilliants weighing only 8,000-9,000 carats.[14]

In about 1843 or 1844 another large deposit of diamonds began to be worked in Brazil in the region of Bahia, north of Minas Gerais. Mawe's former pupil James Tennant, Professor of Geological Mineralogy at King's College, London, discussed the find in a paper given at the Society of Arts in 1852. Tennant had not visited the site but had obtained his information from a dealer called Maiden, who informed him that nearly 600,000 carats of diamonds had been extracted from the Sincora mine in the first two years. Most had gone to Europe in their rough state. Inevitably the market was glutted and the trade price of rough diamonds fell 'from 38s. and 40s. [per carat] to 18s. and 20s.'; eight months afterwards prices 'went down as low as 12s. and 14s.'

Discouraged by their poor rewards, many miners left the site and by 1852 annual production had dropped to about 130,000 carats. This reduction was moderated by the discovery a few years earlier of another deposit in Minas Gerais which must have been better regulated, for following a noticeable lack of demand in 1848, the year of Revolution in Europe, prices began to pick up once more. In 1852, according to Tennant, a brilliant of 1 carat cost £8.[15] It is clear that there was still some way to go before the prices quoted by Mawe were equalled, and longer still before the £12 per carat obtaining in Frankfurt in 1811 was matched. However, according to the London jeweller, dealer and writer, E.W. Streeter, the value of diamonds increased at an approximate rate of five per cent a year until, with the ending of the American Civil War in 1865, such was the demand, prices rose by twenty-five per cent. In 1867, a brilliant of 1 carat had reached £17.[16] Another, smaller, increase followed the conclusion of the Franco-Prussian war of 1870-71. By this time South African diamonds had begun to pour on to the market, precipitating a dramatic fall in prices in the following decade.

The discovery of diamonds in South Africa in 1867 effected profound changes in the trade. When Brazil became independent of Portugal in 1825 most of the diamond mines were operated by concessionnaires. Only one Englishman figured among them in 1852, but British capital was invested in the two companies working mines in Minas Gerais and Bahia towards the end of the century. English dealers, like their Continental counterparts, maintained agents in Brazil whose task it was to secure rough diamonds and also many varieties of coloured stones including amethyst, topaz, agate and rock crystal.

This cosmopolitan form of dealing was to be replaced by one in which British interests were paramount. The South African find, according to James Tennant, had been predicted by Mawe in 1812,[17] but it was not until the spring of 1867 that Dr Atherstone of Grahamstown, who had a local reputation as a mineralogist, identified as a diamond of over 22 carats a stone which had been sent to him from the Hopetown district of the Cape Colony, just south of the Orange River. Shortly afterwards the diamond was shown at the Paris Universal Exhibition of 1867 and was subsequently sold for £500 to Sir Philip Wodehouse, the governor of the colony. One of the two people concerned in the initial find, Schalk van Niekerk, then turned up with another diamond of 83½ carats which he had purchased from its finder, a Griqua boy. This stone was acquired for some £11,200 by the Lilienfeld brothers, diamond merchants of Hopetown (later also of Hatton Garden) and named the 'Star of South Africa' (Plate 51).[18] It passed into the collection of Lord Dudley, whose second wife was famous for her jewellery (Plate 338).

The jewellery trade at first greeted the news of these finds with a coolness amounting to incredulity. Rumours abounded that they were Brazilian diamonds planted as a hoax, familiar echoes of the past. But one well-known London jeweller and gemmologist, Harry Emanuel,[19] then of New Bond Street and a celebrated participant in the 1862 (Plate 52) and 1867 exhibitions, took the precaution of commissioning an English mineralogist, J.R. Gregory, to go to South Africa and survey the site where the stones were alleged to have been discovered. Gregory reported that the terrain was quite unlike other diamond-bearing terrains and the finds could therefore be discounted. Emanuel professed to believe him and in a letter published in the *Journal* of the Society of Arts in 1868 not only endorsed Gregory's negative report on the diamondiferous areas but added for good measure the mineralogist's belief that rumours of gold fields were 'as equally a myth as the "diamond mines" '.[20] Though challenged, Emanuel stuck to his guns in another letter appearing early in 1869. He finally retracted in May, declaring that he was 'very anxious to state that there no longer exists any doubt in my mind as to the Cape Colony being a "diamond-producing country" '.[21] Some sort of apology was due from Emanuel, the author of the much-respected *Diamonds and Precious Stones* (1865) but his was generously expressed.

While the controversy was at its height in London, the hunt had shifted to the Vaal river, the banks of which were crowded with prospectors. But even those lucky enough to discover large specimens in the course of the next few years found prices already beginning to fall. A diamond found by the river in 1872, weighing 288½ carats, brought the owner only a little more than half the sum paid for the much smaller 'Star of South Africa'. But with all the new arrivals the South African economy, hitherto depressed, wonderfully improved and English tool manufacturers and suppliers did well out of the demand for picks, shovels and wheelbarrows.

In 1870 some prospectors moved about twenty-four miles away from the river to a farm called Du Toit's Pan (or Dutoitspan), there to begin 'dry diggings' (so-called because there was no water on the site). The following year the place was a township and two nearby farms, Bultfontein and Vooruitzigt, the latter owned by the De Beers family, were also worked for diamonds. In July came the spectacular discovery of diamond pipes a mile from the De Beers' estate. These became the Big Hole of Kimberley, a huge quarry mined by open-cast methods until the first shaft was sunk in the 1880s (Plates 53, 54 and 55). Britain achieved effective control of the area in 1871, ratified by a formal agreement with the Orange Free State five years later. The whole territory of Griqualand West, in which the diamond fields lay, annexed to the Cape Colony,[22] was to be bitterly disputed during the Boer War of 1899-1902, when most of the mines were closed.[23]

117

Plate 51. The (first) 'Star of South Africa' mounted as a pendant. This great diamond (not to be confused with the Cullinan Diamond which was cut in 1908 into stones given much the same name) weighed 83½ carats when discovered on the banks of the Orange river and bought from the finder by a local farmer, Schalk van Niekerk. The find effectively banished all doubts about the presence of diamonds in South Africa. Lilienfeld Brothers, who purchased the diamond from van Niekerk, were forced to establish their right to it in the law courts under challenge from a company granted the concession to prospect for minerals north of the river. Winning the case in 1869, Lilienfeld's had it cut in Amsterdam into a pear-shape of 47.69 (metric) carats. The diamond was eventually sold to the first Earl of Dudley, a compulsive jewellery collector whose second wife (see Plate 338) is said to have worn it as a hair ornament. Its whereabouts were unknown for several decades until it was sold by Christie's Geneva in 1974 to a private collector. CHRISTIE'S GENEVA

The licensees operating the mines were mainly concerned with rapid returns. The *Journal* of the Society of Arts declared in 1887 that from 1883-36 exports amounted to a total of 10,250,000 carats valued at £11,500,000; two years later the same periodical assessed the yield of the Kimberley mine alone from 1871 to the end of 1885 at 17,500,000 carats valued at £26,000,000 and representing some 3½ tons of stones.[24] Though other authorities came up with differing estimates of yields there was no question but that in terms of sheer quantity South African diamonds were unparalleled. Their quality was a different matter. They were widely regarded as less hard and, often having a slight yellow tinge, less brilliant than Indian or South American diamonds. Nevertheless, less than two decades after their discovery South African stones constituted between ninety and ninety-

Plate 52. A much reduced page from the Official Catalogue *of the London 1862 Exhibition, which included several chromolithographed plates of Harry Emanuel's jewellery. The pearls in the necklace were of 'stupendous size,' as Emanuel claimed, but the diamond, emerald and pearl brooch in the centre is even more striking. The step-cut emerald once formed part of the Braganza jewels, the princely house of Portugal, and weighed 160 carats; the pearl drop falling from the diamond bow came from the booty seized by the French from the Summer Palace at Pekin. According to the* Illustrated London News, *which published an allegedly life-size engraving of the brooch in May 1862 (page 542), the pearl drop was 'somewhat wanting in orient tint and brilliancy'. The writer had to acknowledge the overall splendour of the brooch, which was priced by Emanuel at £10,000, but clearly regretted the English taste for 'as much intrinsic value as can well be put into the space' in the form of 'immense masses of precious stones'. Harry Emanuel only received an Hon. Mention for his trouble. The emerald, unmounted, was sold at Sotheby's in June 1965.*

five per cent of the diamonds cut in Europe, if the production of the Jagersfontein mine in the Orange Free State (first worked in 1870 but fully exploited from 1878) were included.

In the early 1880s the market was plainly glutted. The price per carat of rough Cape diamonds in 1881 and 1882 ranged from about 30s. (Kimberley and De Beers), to 32s. (Bultfontein) and 45s. (Dutoitspan). Three years later prices had virtually halved. A partial recovery was achieved by 1889; stones from Kimberley and De Beers reached 28s. per carat, Bultfontein 30s. and Dutoitspan 40s.[25] The shortage of rough stones from Kimberley in consequence of the Boer War drove up their price between June 1901 to June 1902 to 35s.6d. per carat.[26]

Plate 53. A view of the Kimberley mine in about 1872, showing the early roads used by the diggers to transport loads of excavated 'ground' to the edge of the mine to be broken up, screened and sorted. The sides of the roads were soon undermined by the diggings (like the one in the foreground) and the roads were abandoned by 1874.   PHOTOGRAPH BY DE BEERS CONSOLIDATED MINES

Plate 54. The same mine photographed in 1877. On the top right can be seen part of the staging erected all round the edge of the mine after the disappearance of the roads. Endless ropes connected the pulleys on the claims to others on the staging, enabling the diggers to haul up the ground in buckets. The ropes are so numerous that they look like rain driving over the moonscape of the Great Hole.

PHOTOGRAPH BY DE BEERS CONSOLIDATED MINES

Plate 55. A later stage in the diggings, when the ropes had been replaced by iron or steel cables and the buckets by bin-shaped trolleys.   PHOTOGRAPH BY DE BEERS CONSOLIDATED MINES

The fall in the 1880s was exacerbated by the world-wide trade depression, the most serious of the century. But enough purchasers of means remained to encourage jewellers in the lavish use of diamonds. Extravagant articles which in the past had been largely confined to Courts were now commonplace among the rich. Some two dozen firms between them contributed diamonds worth about £7,000,000 or £8,000,000 to the Paris 1889 Exhibition. A model of the Eiffel Tower, some 3½ ft. (over 1m) tall and destined for an American client, glittered with diamonds. Lottery tickets costing one franc apiece were available to visitors to the exhibition; the grand prize was a diamond parure valued at £8,000.[27]

The colonial administrator and politician, Cecil Rhodes,[28] who had been concerned with establishing the De Beers' Mining Company in 1880, set himself the task of stabilising diamond prices. After a prolonged struggle with Barney Barnato, which contributed to the fall in prices in the mid-1880s, Rhodes' Company acquired the Kimberley mine in 1888 and re-formed itself under the style of De Beers Consolidated Mines. The overall output of the mines run by the Company was limited to about 2,000,000 or 2,500,000 annually, though it could not prevent rogue sales from other sources. When this happened, as in 1901, the trade panicked. In the course of time, the De Beers group, by acquiring more mines (including new ones) and controlling the release of the stones, effectually dominated the market, as it has continued to do. Its success is demonstrated by the fact that in the first half of 1913 prices were 125 per cent higher than in 1889.[29]

The early achievements of the group were celebrated at the South African and International Exhibition at Kimberley in 1892. Diamonds from the Jagersfontein mine, also owned by the group, were included; though not numerous, they were held to be superior to those of Kimberley, for they lacked the yellowish tinge so often remarked in the latter.

Emanuel's former manager, E.W. Streeter,[30] who set up in business on his own account in Conduit Street in 1867/8, moved to premises vacated by his old employer in 1873, when he advertised that he stocked South African diamonds. Streeter, author, diamond-dealer, goldsmith and jeweller, had some of Philip Rundell's aggressive relish in the pursuit of stones and markets. He despatched one Professor Tobin to Kimberley, who found a few stones before striking barren rock and selling off the concession to an Australian. Nothing daunted, Streeter took up a concession with J.W. Benson in 1889 to mine sapphires and rubies in Siam,[31] ten years after the first rush of prospectors to the country. Again in 1889 Streeter was finally able to confirm the provisional rights granted to his syndicate in 1886 to exploit the ruby mines of Burma[32] more or less contemporaneously with the annexation of the upper area of the country by Britain.

Coloured stones from South America and Ceylon, much prized by jewellers, were supplemented by specimens from South Africa, Australia and, to a lesser extent, from the United States of America, which tended to consume its own products and bring in others. From South Africa came such stones as red and green garnets, chalcedony, jasper, 'cairngorm', amethyst and crocidolite or tiger's eye, a fibrous quartz of golden-yellow colour which vied with cymophane or cat's eye quartz from Ceylon. Many of these stones duplicated those emanating from Brazil. South American 'cairngorms' (a brownish-yellow quartz) had already replaced the native Scottish variety in much so-called 'Scottish' jewellery mass-produced in Birmingham and the South African stones formed a useful supplement. The red (pyrope) garnets of South Africa, a by-product of the diamond mines falsely styled 'Cape rubies', virtually supplanted the diminishing supply of garnets from north-east Bohemia.

Diamonds were discovered in Australia in 1851 and again in 1867, 1872 and later. The total output was small in relation to that of South Africa. In an attempt to create a market for diamonds from New South Wales, Ford & Wright of Clerkenwell were commissioned to cut and polish specimens which were shown at the Colonial and Indian Exhibition in London in 1886.

The most popular of all Australian stones at the end of the nineteenth century were opals, the 'misfortune's stone' of Sir Walter Scott's *Anne of Geierstein* (1829), though the eponymous heroine ascribed its allegedly unlucky qualities to a legend. The English royal family sturdily disregarded the myth for decades. Prince Albert preferred opals to most other stones, but Queen Alexandra took particular pains to avoid wearing them (Plate 172). Others shared her views and the price of opals suffered in consequence.

Traditionally, opals were mined at Czernewitza in Hungary and an orange-red variety known as fire opals in Mexico, together with the commoner milky type. The Hungarian mines were becoming less productive than formerly, according to Streeter, when opals were found in Queensland, followed in 1889 by black opals in New South Wales. Streeter, while admitting the beauty of Australian opals, held that they were less dense than the Hungarian specimens, which reduced their resistance to wear. In his view, Mexican opals, for all their attractiveness, were so porous that they soon became colourless when exposed to water,[33] a phenomenon incorporated by Scott in his description of the seemingly magical opal in his novel of 1829.

Next to opals, Australian sapphires had pride of place at the end of the nineteenth century, though they were generally darker than the 'Oriental sapphires' from Kashmir, Siam, Ceylon and Burma. Turquoises, zircons, topazes, garnets, rubies, amethysts, tourmalines and beryls were also mined in Australia. The best turquoises still came from the famous mines of Nishapur in Persia (Iran); the stone also existed in some quantity in Mexico. Other sources were smaller.

An attempt to start an emerald mine in New South Wales in 1890 was abandoned because of difficulties of extraction. Demand for the stone had not been satisfied by the discovery of emeralds in the Urals in 1830. The celebrated mines of Muzo in Columbia were found to be worth reopening in 1844 after a period of quiescence and remained the principal world source of the stone. Muzo emeralds came in all colours, ranging from a deep velvety green (the most admired hue) to light green, yellow, white and even red. Covetous eyes were often cast on the Columbian concessions. In 1888 a company was formed in London on the basis of a lease purchased from a member of the Mateus family of Bogota; it ended in voluntary dissolution several years later.[34] Clearly expectations of dramatic yields were not realised. But the scarcity of emeralds led to high prices. At the beginning of the twentieth century, good emeralds of more than 5 carats frequently fetched from two to ten times the price of diamonds of equivalent weight.

The United States of America, with a massively expanding population, was a net importer of precious stones. The limited quantities of diamonds mined within its territories were insufficient to meet the demand. In 1873 the country imported rough diamonds to the value of $176,426. In 1882 the figure had risen to $449,515. It dropped in 1886 to a little over $300,000 but this probably reflected sharply-reduced prices rather than a diminution in the number of stones imported.

Sapphires and rubies were found by gold-miners in Montana in 1865 and specimen stones eventually came into the possession of Tiffany's of New York.[35] Garnets and peridots occurred in Arizona and New Mexico and turquoise in Arizona, Nevada and California, though even Navajo Indians made occasional use of Persian stones in their silver jewellery.[36]

Stones such as amethysts, in high fashion in the late eighteenth and early nineteenth centuries, were expensive on account of the relative sparseness of the traditional supplies from India and elsewhere. Once a prolific source of the stone was found in Minas Gerais prices fell and amethysts slipped down the social scale. Likewise, the discovery of sapphires in Kashmir and Siam halved their value.[37] Lapis lazuli (Plate 56), used in jewellery made for the Empress Josephine and the Prince Regent,[38] was rare outside royal and aristocratic circles in Western Europe[39] until the last twenty years of the century, though the major source of supply in Siberia was supplemented by another in South America. But it was much imitated (Colour Plate 108A). The colour, dark and saturated, was so dominant that jewellers had to treat the stone with great respect. The same is true of malachite from the Urals and elsewhere. It too was strong enough to register in the neo-classical designs of the early nineteenth century. The stone survived into the Victorian period, though again on a limited scale.

The fluctuating palette of fashion was determined by several considerations. In the early nineteenth century, when topazes were greatly favoured, they came in a variety of hues and shades,[40] in obedience to the latest whim of royalty. Demonstrating that neither Napoleon's Berlin Decree nor the British blockade were entirely successful, Brazilian topazes turned up among the jewellery owned by the Empress Josephine at her death (see page 106). But the 'Oriental topaz' also listed by Nitot was not topaz at all but corundum of the appropriate colour. The same adjective was also applied to the green corundum or spinel ('Oriental emerald') and violet corundum ('Oriental amethyst'). Scarcity and cost invariably underlaid the emergence of stones in vogue, even when the influence of these factors was exercised in a negative manner. For much of the nineteenth century, diamonds and pearls were the prime favourites of the rich. After the discovery of diamonds in South Africa, which made them accessible to a far greater range of people, those who could afford them in the past often reacted with distaste and refused to buy them. The Arts and Crafts Movement in England, and its counterparts on the Continent and in America, were floated to success on a protest vote by men and women who had decided that minor and often imperfect stones such as chrysoprase and moonstones[41] possessed a greater charm than the geometric precision of brilliants (Colour Plates 167 and 170).

2. The Cutting and Processing of Diamonds

During the prolonged war between England and France, when leading jewellers in London were profiting from the isolation of their rich customers from the attractions of Parisian shops, Rundell's used their enhanced revenues to invest in machinery. In 1812 Philip Rundell began negotiating with Boulton and his

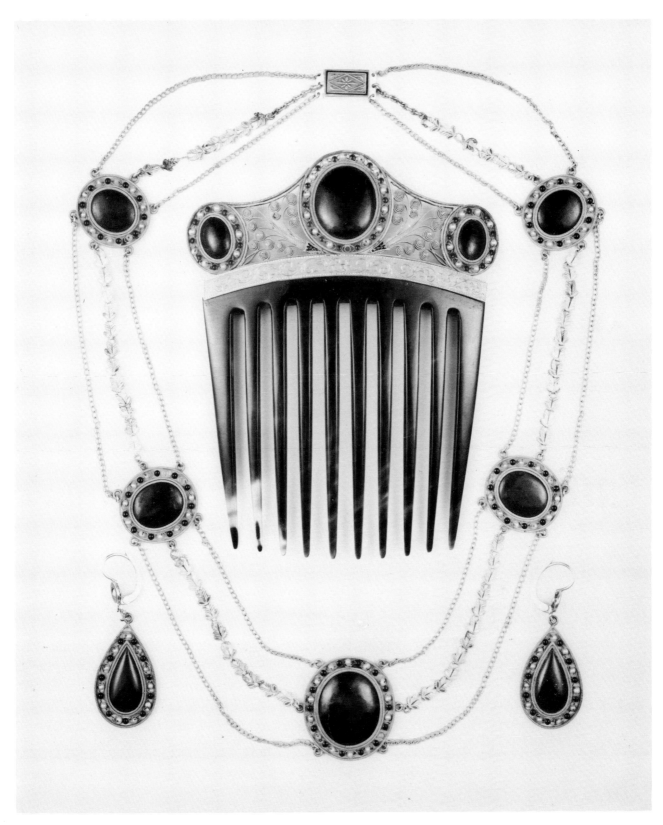

Plate 56. *A French parure of about 1810, made of gold and set with lapis lazuli cabochons secured in openwork borders with milled edges enclosing small blue-enamelled details alternating with tiny pearls. The central chain of the necklace is composed of stamped husks and the two outer ones are both of the loop-in-loop type. The top (or head) of the tortoiseshell comb is further embellished with trails of gold wire spirals known as cannetille. Beautifully and precisely executed, this parure is a fine example of French Empire* bijouterie.

partner, the engineer and inventor James Watt, for a steam engine which was delivered and fitted up the following year. The machine may have been used to drive rolling mills for flatting the silver required in the production of plate in their second manufactory in Dean Street, Soho, which was then under the direction of Paul Storr. On 25 February 1822 the firm took out an insurance policy with the Sun Fire Office which shows them using the engine, or another like it, to process diamonds. The policy reads: 'Messrs. Rundell & Co. of Ludgate Hill, jewellers. On a house and manufactory communicating Situate in Brick Lane Spitalfields in tenure of a diamond cutter — £500. Steam engine and machinery therein — £500.'[42] As Rundell's paid the insurance it is clear that the unnamed diamond-cutter was in their employ.

It was a characteristically bold stroke on Rundell's part to install a steam engine to process diamonds decades before steam-power was introduced into the diamond-cutting workshops of Amsterdam and Antwerp. George Fox loyally maintained in his history of Rundell's that English diamond-cutters excelled the Dutch.[43] Nevertheless most of the business carried on in London during the eighteenth century was lost in the course of the nineteenth to two leading Continental centres, Amsterdam and Antwerp. Before 1830, about 10,000 carats of diamonds were processed in Antwerp, which was largely dependent on Amsterdam for supplies of rough stones and for furnishing a market for its finished specimens. The revolution of 1830 which led to Belgium becoming independent of Holland temporarily disrupted trading relations between Amsterdam and Antwerp. Several cutters in Amsterdam seized the opportunity to adopt the Brabant cut, a rose-cut speciality of Antwerp. But a rich Antwerp merchant, J.-J. Bovie, recruited skilled workmen who trained apprentices in the usual way. This staff was employed in mills powered by steam-engines from 1841. Bovie substantially contributed to the subsequent increase in the processing of diamonds in Antwerp. Annual production rose to 50,000 carats by 1860 but fell back subsequently for lack of demand. Matters began to improve in 1867 when about 30,000 carats were produced.[44]

London and Paris made several attempts to regain their share of the diamond cutting trade[45] but lost to New York in the late nineteenth century. London jewellers often used Dutch craftsmen. Hunt & Roskell of New Bond Street, then styled Mortimer & Hunt,[46] brought over J.B. de Yungh to re-cut a great triangular stone known as the Nassak diamond in 1841. Seized as part of the 'Deccan Booty', the diamond was handed over to Warren Hastings, who passed it to the East India Company which sold it to Rundell's. It was eventually acquired at auction in 1837 by the first Marquis of Westminster, who must have asked the Bond Street firm to re-cut it. Weighing well over 89 carats 2 grains, the stone was expertly re-worked with minimal loss of weight (to 85 carats) by de Yungh who remained in London for some time at the head of Hunt & Roskell's new diamond-cutting department. On his return to Amsterdam he was succeeded by Levi Moses Auerhaan.[47] De Yungh tendered to re-cut the Koh-i-Nûr diamond for Queen Victoria in 1852 but lost the commission to Coster's of Amsterdam. Guillaume Coster brought over two trusted craftsmen, Fedder and Voorzanger, to process the stone at Garrard's (Plate 57).[48]

Most rough diamonds are irregular crystals; only occasionally is a perfect cube, octahedron or dodecahedron encountered. The process of shaping the diamond began with the craftsman called a cleaver or splitter, who from long practice was able to identify the direction of the grain (the natural grain of the crystal) along which the stone might be split while excluding as many flaws as possible. He first attached the diamond to a wooden rod (a 'cement stick'), using a mixture of shellac and resin, and studied it before making an incision by means of another diamond similarly mounted. The cleaver introduced a sharp instrument into the nick and tapped it sharply with a mallet to split it. This operation was repeated until the diamond was blocked out.

The stone then went to the cutter or bruter. He took two diamonds mounted on cement sticks and ground them together to shape the facets, the action of 'diamond cut diamond' requiring vigorous effort from the craftsman, who worked over a box to catch the chips and dust (Colour Plate 24). A skilled bruter could deal with about 2 carats' worth of stones a day, according to Mawe.

The illustration in Mawe of the final cutting and polishing shows that several diamonds at a time were embedded in soft metal and mounted in a holder called a tang. This rode on a pivot over a horizontal grinding wheel in the form of a flat cast-iron disc or lap known as a scaife ('skive') which was driven by a large fly-wheel (Plate 58) and lubricated with oil and diamond dust. As the stones were brought into contact with the scaife the facets were given their final definition and were also polished, one by one, the stones being rotated until their entire surface had been treated. Mawe held that the fly-wheel, then operated by hand, was capable of two hundred revolutions a minute, by which means a workman would complete an average of 1 carat of stones a day. Mawe was probably already out of touch with recent developments. According to Eric Bruton, *Diamonds* (1970), horse-power was in fairly general use in the first quarter of the nineteenth century, to be followed by steam.[49] This ignores Rundell's engine, but it is nevertheless the case that steam was widespread by mid-century. The diamond-cutting display mounted by Hunt & Roskell at the London 1862 Exhibition included a scaife revolving between two and three thousand times a minute.[50] This remarkable improvement could only have been effected by steam. A steam-engine was certainly part of a similar demonstration by Coster of Amsterdam at the Paris Exhibition of 1867.[51]

In 1867 Coster's, the largest factory in Amsterdam, housed some 425 workers and apprentices, including some eighty-eight bruters, twenty-one cleavers and an unspecified number of women recently recruited by the head of the firm. Their total weekly earnings amounted to between £1,000 and £1,200.[52] Twenty years later, when it was estimated that there were no fewer than six thousand and possibly as many as eight thousand diamond mills in the city, the number of women workers had increased. In one unnamed factory women and girls processing rose-cut diamonds (roses) earned between about £1.5s. and £1.15s. a week. Cutters (probably all male) received from £1.15s. to £3.15s., cleavers £2.10s. to £6.10s. and polishers £2 to £6. They all worked a twelve-hour day, probably for six days a week. These wages were earned by piece-work, recently

Plate 57. The Duke of Wellington placing the Koh-i-Nûr diamond on the scaife for the cutting of the first facet in the course of converting the stone from a rose into a brilliant, 16 July 1852. This engraving from the Illustrated London News *depicts the Duke at the huge steam-powered polishing machine hired by Garrard's and installed in their Panton Street premises. On the left are Guillaume Coster with his two Dutch workmen, Voorzanger, the chief cutter at the Amsterdam factory, and Fedder.*

The Koh-i-Nûr (the 'Mountain of Light') from the Treasury at Lahore came into the possession of the East India Company in 1849 and was presented to Queen Victoria the following year. As a huge rose-cut diamond of a little over 186 carats it was shown at the Great Exhibition of 1851. The Queen was delighted to lend it, for her beloved husband, Prince Albert, was President of the 1851 Commission and she regarded the whole organisation of the exhibition as uniquely his. The public flocked to see the stone but many were disappointed by its lack of brilliance. After consulting Professor Tennant and other authorities, the Prince persuaded Queen Victoria to have the diamond re-cut as a brilliant. The work was finished before the middle of September and the workmen left for Amsterdam, after reducing the stone to 108.93 metric carats. The results were not completely successful, but Queen Victoria often wore the Koh-i-Nûr as a brooch (Plate 174) or alternatively, in a circlet (Plate 173).

The Koh-i-Nûr is now set in the front of Queen Elizabeth the Queen Mother's Crown of 1937 in the Jewel House at the Tower of London.

introduced by the larger factories to replace the old practice whereby craftsmen rented factory space, light and machinery at a fixed rate. The change may have been brought about through the influence of dealers in Paris and London who had invested in the mills.[53]

Antwerp, where there were only about twenty or thirty craftsmen working during the post-war depression of the 1820s, grew in importance. Local cutters were said to command as much as £40 to £48 weekly when they were deluged with South African diamonds to process. This was probably an exaggeration, for skilled hands in Amsterdam were reported to earn £20 in 1873.[54] But earnings on this level may well have induced some English dealers to switch their rough diamonds to cutters at Hanau in Germany. In the ensuing depression, when prices dropped, so did the income of the diamond-cutters. In 1905, average wages in Antwerp were well below £3 a week.[55] There were probably too many craftsmen on the market. The outworkers in particular suffered grievously when work was short. In her

Colour Plate 24. The bruter or cutter at work, from a later edition of John Mawe's Treatise on Diamonds *(1823). A cement stick mounted with a diamond in each hand, the bruter works over a box to receive the diamond dust and chips as one diamond cuts and shapes the other, and vice versa. The charcoal brazier in front of the window softens the cement.*

autobiographical novel *Deborah* (1936/46), Isaac Bashevis Singer's sister Esther Kreitman, the wife of a diamond-cutter in Antwerp dependent on casual work, describes her eponymous heroine and her husband literally starving during the year leading up to the outbreak of the First World War in 1914.[56] He was particularly unfortunate since he depended on another outworker for the few jobs he received. It is clear from the novel that both men were survivors from a pre-industrial age, for their benches were kept in their rooms.

The pressure to develop new powered machinery for processing diamonds was the more intense because of the prospect of rich financial rewards. Sophisticated machines came slowly at first and far more rapidly towards and immediately after 1900. A specimen was patented in England on behalf of C.M. Field on 10 July 1873.[57] According to Bruton, in 1891 D. Rodrigues took out an English patent for a power-driven bruting machine, the prototype of those later adopted by the trade.[58] Machines introduced in America and on the Continent increasingly blurred the distinction between the old techniques of splitting, cutting and polishing. Even in the mid-nineteenth century large diamonds such as the Koh-i-Nûr went straight from the cleaver to the polishing machine without being touched by the cutter.[59] A report on the diamond industry in Antwerp, summarised in the *Journal* of the Society of Arts in 1905, referred to a cleaving machine comprising a small powered circular saw made of copper, the cutting edge embedded with diamond dust. The stone, fixed in an arm overhanging the saw, was pressed gently against the blade, sometimes for as long as two weeks, before the operation was complete. The saw was said to have been invented by a Belgian working in America. A bruting machine also in use retained the old practice of employing one

Plate 58. A polishing bench, from Mawe's Treatise (1823). A weighted tang is pressed against the horizontal scaife on the left and another is held by the craftsman while he inspects the progress of the polishing. On the far left, at the front of the bench, is a pestle and mortar for grinding diamond chips into powder and next to it, containers for the powder and for oil.

diamond to cut another and was even fitted with a box to catch the diamond dust produced when one stone, fixed in the centre of a rotary unit, met with the second which was pressed down against it.[60] This machine was clearly associated with the one patented by Rodrigues in 1891. It had also been put to use in Amsterdam.[61]

The use of machines was not, however, uniform. Among the sixty concerns in Amsterdam in the early twentieth century was an unnamed factory founded in 1843, which started recruiting women in 1875 and therefore might be identified as the Coster firm. It was described in the *Journal* of the Society of Arts in 1907. The factory employed between three hundred and five hundred men (clearly some were outworkers) and twenty women, engaged in diamond-cutting. About twelve splitters or cleavers worked entirely by hand, dividing a rough diamond of about 10 carats into several stones in about fifteen minutes. Most of the bruting was performed by the female employees by hand, 'difficult' stones being cut by men with the aid of machinery. The final stage of finishing and polishing was always executed by machine. Since ninety per cent of all the rough diamonds received in Amsterdam for processing came from South Africa, principally from Kimberley, it is fair to conclude that the 400,000,000 finished stones turned out in one year by this factory came largely from this source.[62]

The number of facets cut on a diamond was governed by the size of the stone, the type of cut and the date when it was executed, for the well-known cuts were reinterpreted from time to time. Most cuts were derived from India but refined and perfected in Europe. The table cut, used for many diamonds gracing sixteenth and seventeenth century jewellery, was afterwards embellished with facets surrounding the flat table. This variant cut, having between four and sixteen facets, excluding the table and the little facet in the centre of the underside (the culet), was still occasionally employed in the nineteenth century. By and large it was confined to diamonds too shallow for the elaborate brilliant or rose cuts, but as the step cut it was widely used for coloured stones (Plate 52).

Rose-cut diamonds (roses) usually have a rounded base when viewed on plan, but other shapes, including ovals, also occur. The underside is flat or hollowed (unless it is a double rose) and the front or upper side is domed and faceted. The main Dutch or Holland rose-cut (the *rose couronné*), as evolved in Amsterdam and still practised there in the nineteenth century, was more pointed than others (figure 1); its triangular facets, arranged in groups of six, amounted to twenty-four in all. The *rose Brabant* or *rose d'Anvers,* already cited as the victim of Belgium's assertion of independence in 1830, was less complicated than the Dutch cut and particularly suitable for small stones. It accommodated eighteen, fifteen, twelve, six or even three facets. The base was excluded from the count, as it was in the case of the *rose couronné.* In 1865 Harry Emanuel asserted that the better kind of rose diamonds had recently enjoyed a renewed popularity, 'as the same amount of display' might be obtained 'at less than half the cost of the brilliant'. But the Antwerp rose did not come into this favoured category, being 'only used for the commoner kind of work.'[63] In about 1900 a modified rose-cut was patented in America under the name of twentieth century cutting.[64] It was presumably developed in New York.

The brilliant cut, a development of the table and rose cuts, advanced on several fronts in the eighteenth and nineteenth centuries. However each variant retained the essential form of the natural diamond crystal in having two truncated pyramids, one rising and the other, inverted, descending from their common base (the girdle), which forms the widest part of the stone. The upper pyramid, known as the crown or bezel, always had a table at the top and the lower pyramid (the pavilion or culasse) the small facet called the culet or collet. The old single-cut brilliant had an octagonal girdle and was favoured in India; it might have sixteen or more facets exclusive of the table and culet. The English star cut had sixteen facets on the crown and eight on the pavilion. European cutters usually preferred a cushion-shaped girdle. According to Emanuel, the cut might be elaborated into as many as thirty-eight facets. The double cut was more complex still, giving rise to variants which co-existed in the latter part of the eighteenth century and into the nineteenth. One persisted into the early twentieth century and survived in modified form thereafter. Another appears to have died off towards 1900. They went under a variety of names and it appears uncertain whether they should be called double-cut (as Emanuel held in 1865) or triple cut (Bruton's version of 1970).[65] Their popular names have been superseded by a single term, the old mine cut, but this disguises important differences (figure 2). Most had a table and thirty-two facets on the crown (the Lisbon cut had thirty-eight).[66] The size and disposition of the facets varied, though theoretically at least they were cut with geometric precision. But commercial considerations had already obtruded by 1823. Mawe complained that 'the old rules for proportioning the dimensions are now nearly obsolete: the diamond-cutters have almost discarded the use of

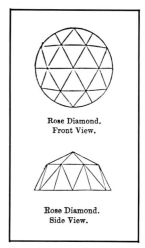

Figure 1. The Dutch or Holland rose-cut, front and side views, from Harry Emanuel, Diamonds and Precious Stones, *1865. Small stones rose-cut with fewer facets were known as Antwerp roses.*

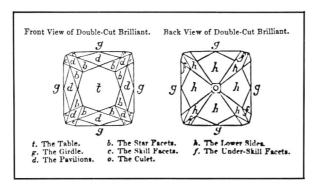

Figure 2. The double-cut brilliant, which according to Harry Emanuel was 'the most common form at the present day' (1865). The views of the upper part (the crown) and underside (the pavilion) clearly show the cushion-shaped plan (the girdle) of the stone, unchanged until towards the end of the century.

measures, and, in forming the facets, trust wholly to the eye... At present it is the practice in cutting a diamond almost exclusively to consider which form the rough stone is best calculated to produce, without any regard to scientific accuracy.'[67]

Ideally, when the brilliant was viewed in elevation, the crown comprised one-third of the whole and the pavilion two-thirds. The number of facets on the pavilion, excluding the culet, was either thirty-two or twenty-four. In the first case, the diamond had a total of sixty-four facets on crown and pavilion, and in the second, fifty-eight. By the mid-nineteenth century, sixty-four facets were the most favoured, being cited both by Emanuel (figure 2) and the French jeweller Charles Barbot in his *Guide Pratique du Joaillier* (1858), though the latter inconsistently chose to illustrate a diagram of a brilliant with a pavilion of twenty-four facets.[68] A far more famous Parisian jeweller, Oscar Massin, again mentioned the standard brilliant with sixty-four facets in his report on the jewellery shown at the Paris 1889 Exhibition.[69] It was not a French phenomenon, for the notice of Hunt & Roskell's diamond-cutting display at the London 1862 Exhibition mentions double-cut brilliants with sixty-two facets, that is, thirty-three on the crown (which is accurate if the table is counted in) and a mysterious twenty-nine facets on the pavilion (the odd number presumably being the culet).[70] The description was probably written by someone with no knowledge of diamond cuts, but it may have been an intermediate cut. In 1892, to judge by the fifth edition of Streeter's *Precious Stones and Gems,* the standard brilliant had fifty-eight facets.[71] In 1907 the American Consul in Amsterdam confirmed that the brilliant was cut with fifty-eight facets: a few years earlier, he reported, it had sixty-four or more, 'for there are fashions in diamond cutting.'[72]

Barbot complained in 1858 that the conservatism of the Amsterdam cutters prevented them from adopting his suggestions for new cuts; he had hopes of Philippe the elder, who had returned to Paris in 1852 after fifteen years in Amsterdam and set up new mills. Later the trade also spread to the Jura. The greater rapidity of change before and after 1900 was, however, in large part due to the emergence of New York as a diamond-cutting centre, greatly aided by the tariff imposed on the importation of processed diamonds in the mid-1890s. Though not high enough to halt the trade in diamonds cut in Europe (diamonds valued at £2,400,000 arrived in America from Amsterdam alone in 1907),[73] the

Colour Plate 25. An emerald and diamond necklace with matching earrings which formed part of the marriage parure of Stéphanie de Beauharnais, a relative of the Empress Josephine, who was married in 1806 to the heir of the Grand Duke of Baden.

Standard wedding presents among the Bonaparte clan and their relatives, the parures, on the evidence of these pieces, were mounted open-backed in cut-down settings of great delicacy, the diamonds set in silver, lined with gold, and the emeralds in gold. Nitot et fils, the royal jewellers, probably made most of them. The parure was broken up after the Second World War and the necklace and earrings were acquired by Count Tagliavia, whose widow, Countess Margharita Tagliavia, presented them to the Victoria and Albert Museum in memory of her son.　VICTORIA AND ALBERT MUSEUM

tariff was sufficient to protect the cutters while they were establishing themselves. Many of them were emigrants from Amsterdam, Antwerp and Hanau, who evolved a new rose-cut with twenty facets.

The part played by American diamond-cutters in the development of a brilliant with a rounded girdle and flatter crown to replace the old cushion-shaped double-cut brilliant was obliquely acknowledged in 1903.[74] This presaged the appearance in 1914 of a theoretical treatise on diamond-cutting by Marcel Tolkonsky, which gave rise to a further revised brilliant, much shallower than the old type, in which the angles of the crown and the pavilion were both reduced to increase the brilliance of the stone. This has been later modified.[75] In 1892 Streeter declared that English cutters made the girdle rather sharp while the Dutch made it broader. It is unlikely that national distinctions of this kind survived the establishment of the new diamond-cutting centres in the twentieth century.

The only other type of European cut mentioned by Streeter is the briolette, which he described as pear-shaped or oval, covered all over with triangular facets and frequently pierced for suspension, but it must be added that mixed cuts of all kinds were widespread. They include the marquise, an oval pointed at both ends like a vesica. Engraved diamonds were rare indeed and were guaranteed to excite curiosity when exhibited, as they were in Paris in 1867, 1878, 1889 and 1900. The chief exhibitor was C. Bordinckx of Antwerp, whose work was shown by Boucheron of Paris on the last two occasions.[76]

3. The cutting and processing of other stones

All cities where jewellers were grouped in numbers had their lapidaries. When huge consignments of South African diamonds flooded into London in the 1870s and it was decided to re-establish the diamond-cutting trade in Clerkenwell, Dutch workmen were recruited to work from Monday morning until Friday evening at a wage of £10 a week. They struck several times for more money, which was granted, but when they demanded £18 weekly they were discharged and English lapidaries brought in to learn the trade. Unused to the hardness of diamonds, they each managed only about one diamond a month but with persistence reduced the time to four days. Baroness Burdett Coutts[77] and her husband, both members of the Worshipful Company of Turners, were among the benefactors funding prizes for diamond-cutting, in which English workmen successfully competed against the Dutch.[78] When times were hard, the new diamond-cutters were able to fall back on their old trade.

The rough material of the lapidary's trade was usually cut to shape or sawn on a lathe with a vertically rotating metal disc. This was charged with oil and diamond or emery powder and worked by hand, water or, later, other forms of power. The faceting and polishing were done at another bench, the lapidary holding the stone on a cement stick against a grindstone.

Increasingly, many stones used by jewellers were not cut locally, but were imported already processed. The great German cutting and polishing mills at Idar, Oberstein and Birkenfeld had originally been set up to treat agates quarried in the

Plate 59. The agate workers of Oberstein, from a photograph reproduced in the Journal *of the Society of Arts in 1904, still prone before their sandstone grindstones in traditional fashion while they polished stones.*

neighbourhood. The mills survived when the supply of agates began to run out by treating stones of all kinds from South America, the East Indies and elsewhere. C.A. Collini noted twenty-six mills in the region in 1776; a hundred years later there were about one hundred and eighty establishments, half of which dated to 1850-70. Collini's illustrated account of the cutting equipment at Oberstein in his *Journal d'un Voyage. . . .* shows a method of working which was to persist for virtually the whole of the nineteenth century. At the end of a hut built over a water-race worked by a great wheel was a revolving cylinder with a belt leading to a splitting bench. Nearer the water-wheel were four huge grindstones in a row, partly immersed in water. A wooden bench about 18in. (45cm) high, shaped to the contours of the workman's prone body, was placed in front of each wheel on a wooden floor. The workman lay on this, facing the grindstone, with his feet braced against a foot-rest. This position enabled him to exert considerable pressure as he held the stone against the revolving grindstone, which threw up enough water to lubricate itself. The workman, literally nose to grindstone, could not help but be drenched as he laboured. He usually contracted tuberculosis and died young. A report published in 1900 remarked the continued survival of water-powered mills 'which bear evidence to the lives sacrificed to this industry'. Replacements were easily found, for earnings (ranging between £3 and £5 a week in 1900), 'were comparatively high'.[79]

The cutters and polishers were independent workers. Many invested some £20 in their own grindstone; others, unable to afford the full price, paid for a half-share. They then contracted to work on rough stones supplied to them by dealers and manufacturing jewellers at a fixed price per gram. Towards the end of the nineteenth century steam-powered works began first to outnumber and then to replace the old mills. Electricity was introduced after 1900. A photograph of the interior of one of the new factories, published in the *Journal* of the Society of Arts in 1904, shows the workmen still lying face down on the traditional benches, but no longer sprayed with water (Plate 59).[80]

The traditional trade of the Oberstein area was extended to embrace the staining of stones. Agate, carnelian and chrysoprase, major varieties of chalcedony, are all sufficiently porous to take colour. Black-banded agate and red sardonyx occasionally occur naturally but their colours are often enhanced. Banded agates,

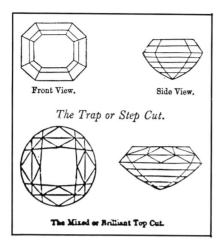

Figure 3. The step or trap cut and the mixed or brilliant top-cut. Harry Emanuel held that the step-cut, the less complex cut, was most usually employed for emeralds and other coloured stones. The size of the table, the central facet and the number of steps on the pavilion was governed by the size and depth of the stone. The mixed top-cut, also used for coloured stones, was shaped as a brilliant above the girdle and a trap cut below.

popular with nineteenth century gem-engravers as well as with jewellers, were immersed in a heated solution of sugar and honey for several days before being washed and soaked in sulphuric acid which converted the sugar absorbed by their bands into carbon, thus staining them black. Chalcedony was converted into sardonyx by soaking in iron nitrate heated to turn into ferric oxide. In its natural state chrysoprase is a chalcedony stained apple-green by nickel. Passable imitations of this and other stones were achieved with the aid of metallic oxides in the course of the nineteenth century.

The colouring of agates and other stones continued as a staple of the Idar and Oberstein area. The local cutting mills also processed a wide range of stones, mainly those formerly denominated semi-precious, though costly specimens, including diamonds, were cut and polished in the usual fashion in workshops in the vicinity. Pearls were also polished, drilled and cut in the neighbourhood.

Idar and Oberstein largely flourished on the backs of the manufacturing trade, if the needs of the gem-engravers are excluded. The makers of fine jewellery in the great cities preferred to trust to the services of local lapidaries for their coloured stones. This became a matter of honour to the French after their crushing defeat in the Franco-Prussian War.[81]

Lapidaries everywhere often employed the step (emerald, or trap) cut for coloured stones such as rubies, emeralds, sapphires and peridots (Plate 52). The mixed or brilliant cut for stones other than diamonds, virtually unknown in the early nineteenth century, was occasionally used later. Stones cut in this way were fashioned as brilliants above the girdle but stepped below (figure 3). Translucent or opaque stones such as opals and turquoises were mainly cut and polished *en cabochon*. This cut, derived from the Middle Ages, is characterised by a plain domed and polished top; its flat base, either oval or circular in plan, was sometimes embellished with facets on the edge and underside. Double cabochons were made with a smaller dome below and a larger above. Ordinary cabochons were sometimes hollowed inside to increase whatever transparency the stone possessed. Variant cuts of all kinds abounded and some are mentioned elsewhere.

4. Setting

As remarked elsewhere (see pages 63 and 64), the practice of stringing diamonds and other stones persisted in the late eighteenth century. A diamond necklace was strung for a client of Garrard's in November 1804. The Frankfurt edition of the

Colour Plate 26. A group of turquoise pavé-set jewellery.
A. A gold scarf-pin with a plumed bust of St George, made by John Whenman of Clerkenwell, 1864.
B and C. A serpent armlet and necklace in gold and silver, set with pearls, rubies and brilliants in addition to turquoises; c.1835-40.
D. A convolvulus brooch, the stamens of pearls; c.1845-50. VICTORIA AND ALBERT MUSEUM

Plate 60. The Crown frame made by Rundell's in 1831 for Queen Adelaide, the consort of William IV, which was set with stones temporarily removed from Queen Charlotte's stomacher. The ribs on the cut-down settings are particularly apparent in the front cross.

EX AMHERST COLLECTION

Journal des Dames reported three years afterwards that silk or gold thread was employed to string necklaces and earrings comprising undrilled diamonds set in light collets. Other stones used for the purpose, such as agate, amethyst and carnelian, were unmounted and therefore presumably consisted of pierced beads.[82]

The principal settings in use in the late eighteenth and early nineteenth centuries have already been noticed (pages 49 and 50). They consisted of the established 'cut-down' variety, in which metal was worked up and over the girdle of the stone and reinforced by vertical ridges which were very marked until the 1840s (Plate 60), and rubbed-over settings, including the 'Roman' type. The metal was usually silver, lined with gold, in the case of diamonds, and gold for coloured stones. Collets were increasingly made unbacked for coloured stones as well as for diamonds (Colour Plate 25 and Plates 61 and 62). Pavé settings, often using half-pearls or small stones such as turquoises (Colour Plate 26A), required the setter to raise small 'grains' from the surface of the metal ground to secure the stones. This technique was (probably later) termed 'thread and grain'.

The metallic foils placed inside the collets of traditional closed-back settings were usually made of copper or tin coated with silver and, if necessary, coloured by means of stains mixed with oils or varnish. They increased the sparkle of colourless pastes and, when tinted, corrected or enhanced the colour of genuine but poor stones or lent depth and lustre to vitreous imitations.

Claw or coronet settings, which last enjoyed marked favour in the Middle Ages, again became the mode in about 1830. From about 1830 to 1850 settings were sometimes built up to create the illusion that the stones they contained were larger than was the case.[83] The custom appears to have been international. English craftsmen were certainly not averse to similar practices; manufacturers of modest jewellery in the second half of the century often countersunk stones in the centre of a star incised in the surface of a solid metal setting so that the eye took in not

Plate 61. Stéphanie de Beauharnais wearing her emerald and diamond marriage parure in a portrait by François Gérard, painted in 1806, the year of her marriage to Charles, Prince of Baden, who succeeded his father as Grand Duke.

The marriage was a dynastic one, part of a complex ploy by Napoleon to cement new alliances. First, he arranged the wedding of the Empress Josephine's son by her first marriage, Eugène de Beauharnais, and Augusta Amelia, eldest daughter of the new King of Bavaria. She had been betrothed to Charles of Baden, whose father had been recently elevated to a Grand Dukedom by Napoleon. Stéphanie was his substitute bride.

PHOTOGRAPH PRESENTED TO THE
VICTORIA AND ALBERT MUSEUM BY
THE COUNTESS MARGHARITA TAGLIAVIA

only the stone but the extended arms of the star. This type of mount, known as the gypsy setting, was especially popular with the manufacturers of rings but was also used in other kinds of jewellery (Plate 291).

An early form of prefabricated mount was evolved in Vienna, brought to Paris by the jeweller Viennot in about 1840 and may well have been carried to England by Charles Winter and other peripatetic jewellers. It consisted of a carcass constructed from wires soldered together. From this rose wire supports for devices set with stones.[84] Sometimes wire spirals ('tremblers'), which first embellished jewellery in the late seventeenth or early eighteenth century, were substituted for the stalks so that the devices moved with the wearer. Tremblers became popular in the mid-nineteenth century (Colour Plate 95).

The great drawback to the Viennese mount was its instability, though Massin thought it superior to the French method of cutting out the support from a sheet of silver which was then lined with gold. Massin was contemptuous of French jewellers' work in the reign of Louis Philippe, regarding the output of his own later generation as infinitely superior in delicacy matched by strength.[85] One of the factors contributing to this improvement was the deployment of platinum in settings. The metal, known and worked in an unrefined state in South America for centuries, was taken up and used by one or two French goldsmiths and jewellers in the latter part of the eighteenth century, following Lavoisier's success in melting the metal in 1782. M.E. Janety or Jeannety, Royal Goldsmith to Louis XVI, was awarded a prize for a group of platinum jewellery and medical vessels at the second French national exhibition of 1802.[86] Extremely intractable, platinum was little used by his contemporaries except for making equipment used in scientific experiments. The apparent exception, a diadem of diamonds set in platinum which is said to have been made for the Empress Josephine, passing to her daughter Hortense and to the latter's son Napoleon III, is unlikely on stylistic grounds to

Colour Plate 27. A pair of gold bracelet clasps set with diamonds and blue vitreous plaques, one ornamented with the initials of Marie Antoinette (1755-1793) and the other with turtle doves and hymeneal torches signifying her marriage to the Dauphin (later Louis XVI) in 1770. The gold edges of the open borders are textured.

VICTORIA AND ALBERT MUSEUM

Plate 62. The back of the emerald and diamond necklace and earrings (see Colour Plate 25 and Plate 61), showing all the stones, except for the capped drops, in open-backed collets. The two upper drops, hooked on to links, are later replacements and may have been intended for occasional use as earrings.

VICTORIA AND ALBERT MUSEUM

140

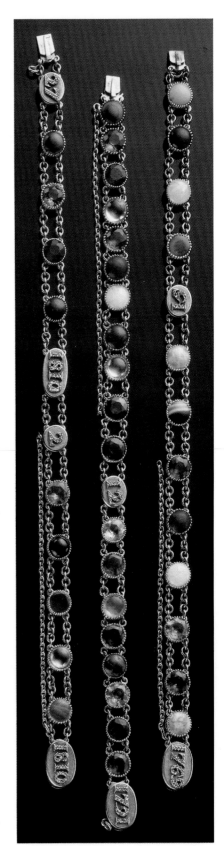

Colour Plate 28. Three gold and gem-set bracelets employing the language of stones, with dates in rose diamonds, arranged by the Empress Marie-Louise in 1812. The first, set with natrolite, amethyst, peridot, opal, lapis lazuli, emerald, onyx, natrolite; agate, opal, uranium, turquoise, spells Napoleon 15 Août *and the date* 1769 *(next to the commencement of his name); this was the Emperor's date of birth. The second, with malachite, amethyst, ruby, iris, emerald; diamond, emerald, chrysoprase, emerald, malachite, beryl, ruby, emerald, runs:* Marie [Louise] 12 Decembre 1791 *(her birthday) and the third, with malachite, amethyst, ruby, serpentine; amethyst, vermeil (coral), ruby, iris, labradorite,* 27 Mars 1810 2 Avril 1810, *the dates of their first meeting at Compiègne and their wedding in Paris. The Empress is said to have amused herself by organising these bracelets during Napoleon's absence on campaign.* SOTHEBY'S

be earlier than 1830.[87] It is possible that Napoleon III's consort Eugénie had it re-mounted in the late 1850s. The first piece in which platinum was allegedly employed for setting some of the diamond components was a head ornament of 1855, designed by Fontenay in the form of sprays of wild blackberries.[88]

The metal crept into English jewellery with the name of platina not long before 1820, though English scientists had carried out valuable investigations into its properties in the middle of the previous century.[89] Platina was mainly used in the production of chains. Rundell's and Garrard's both sold examples. Though subsequently used to a limited extent by a few London jewellers (a platinum bracelet set with an assortment of stones was included in a sale of Streeter's stock in 1884),[90] it cannot be claimed that the metal was employed on any scale by diamond-setters until towards the end of the Edwardian era. Several Parisian jewellers, on the other hand, were said to have adopted it wholesale for the fine diamond jewellery shown at the Paris 1900 Exhibition, though one, eccentrically, used aluminium instead.[91]

A switch from massiveness to delicacy, if not quite as evident in English work as in French from the late 1850s onwards, nevertheless occurred. The change was aesthetic and the ideal was to reveal as little of the setting as possible when it was viewed from the front. To this end the French dropped their new passion for setting rose diamonds in gold, much remarked in the jewellery shown at the Paris 1867 Exhibition, reverting to silver by 1878[92] and finally moving on to platinum. Knife-edge settings, in which widely-spaced stones were clasped by claws and connected by thin strips of metal laid on the edge, were probably evolved in consequence of the fashion, widespread from the 1850s to the 1870s, for attaching drops or swinging fringes to jewellery (Colour Plates 95 and 101). Long claws holding the stones high from invisible collets or bezels, customary components of the invisible setting, were adopted internationally. Sometimes the tips of the claws were reinforced with platinum to provide additional strength. Perversely, after all these attempts at concealment, those edges of settings still revealed were frequently textured with a graining tool towards 1900, a reinterpretation of a technique (*millegriffe* or *millegrain*)

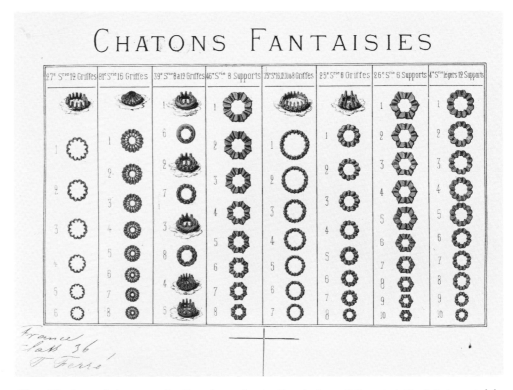

CHATONS FANTAISIES

Plate 63. Some of the stamped collets shown by the French firm of Bouret et Ferré (represented by T. Ferré) at the Paris 1867 Exhibition. No. 5 in the third row from the left is pierced with circular openings, forming a primitive gallery.   VICTORIA AND ALBERT MUSEUM ARCHIVES

dating back to pre-Revolutionary days and still in evidence in the form of plain milled edges in the early years of the nineteenth century (Colour Plate 27 and Plate 56). The revival persisted to the art deco period.

It can be argued that the trend towards light, elegant settings received a further impetus from the development of prefabricated collets for stones. Massin attributed the invention of a machine for manufacturing these components to one Belletête (or Beltête) when working for Fester in 1852. Officially, the invention was credited to two Parisians, Jean-Louis-Antoine-Marie Bouret and Charles Théophile Ferré, who described themselves as stampers and engravers when taking out an English patent in 1860. The specification of the invention cites the production of 'solid claw bezils or settings for mounting stones' in earrings, breast pins, brooches and other items of jewellery by cutting, stamping and shaping pieces of metal 'in an ordinary stamping press'.[93] Examples of their stamped settings attracted much attention at the London 1862 Exhibition. The French jeweller Fossin raved about the savings in material, the great precision of form, the obviation of solder and the economies in cost; he estimated that the stamped settings were sixty to eighty per cent cheaper than specimens made by hand in the traditional way. The official English report, while not venturing into financial calculations, was equally enthusiastic.[94]

The partners gained a medal in 1862. Five years later, when the next international exhibition was staged in France, T. Ferré alone represented the firm. The stamped settings (Plate 63) again elicited praise, an English observer remarking that they were used by many Parisian jewellers.[95] But there was already a French rival on the scene with an improved version of the process.[96]

Pierced galleries were soon in widespread use, as often as not completely detached from the stone which was grasped by the claws alone. This made it even easier for jewellers to use prefabricated settings, for there was no longer any need to match them precisely to the dimensions of the stone. The claws, the operative part, had merely to be opened to receive the stone and then carefully eased down round it.

Variations and improvements in stamped settings were made in other countries. Following the first flush of novelty, the makers of fine jewellery often reverted to hand work, but machine-produced settings passed into the staple repertory of the manufacturers of cheaper wares. The technical ingenuity of firms such as T. & J. Bragg of Birmingham was also directed at cut-down and other settings. They demonstrated a 'mechanical process, by which the thinly-cut edges of the gold itself are pressed over the edges of the gem, to secure it,' at the London Exhibition of 1872.[97] Nine years earlier A.T.N. Goll, using an address in the Caledonian Road, then in Middlesex, obtained provisional protection for die-stamped thread-and-grain settings finished by hand.[98] Cast and electrotyped mounts were also known in the trade, the first dating to the 1820s and the second to the 1840s. For the latter, the mount was modelled and a negative mould made in copper. When this was attached to the negative pole in a plating bath the copper dissolved in the electrotype or plating solution was deposited into the mould, eventually building up into a thickness enabling it to be removed and, after being plated or gilded, used as a support for imitation stones. Stamped settings were, however, far more general.

5. Legends, Superstitions and the Language of Sentiment

Centuries of superstitions attached to stones were too powerful an accretion to be dissipated in the Age of Englightenment. Even in the nineteenth century, as already noted, a novel by Scott deterred some people from buying and wearing opals. The remnants of the magical powers attached to stones, by then both ambiguous and conflicting, had become a matter of antiquarian research. Madame de Barrera attempted to reconcile some of these attributes in *Gems and Jewels* (1860). To cite one instance, the emerald was said to put evil spirits to flight and to preserve chastity. When its powers were unable to prevent inconstancy, it crumbled into fragments. It was also an ill omen when it fell out of its setting. On the other hand, it brought the owner foresight, eloquence and increased wealth.[99]

Faced with a plethora of traditions and interpretations, Cyril Davenport made his own selection of what he termed 'the most universal' meanings for one of his Cantor lectures at the Society of Arts in 1902, from which this sample is taken:

Emerald — For ensuring purity of thought.
Sapphire — Cooling; used for priests' rings, to show their coolness for wordly pleasures.[100]
Carbuncle — [usually an almandine garnet cut *en cabochon*]. For preserving health and rejecting luxury.
Turquoise — Indicates the presence of poison or illness by changing colour....

Colour Plate 29. Two English gold pendants exemplifying the language of stones, c.1830.
A. A curving bar with four heart pendants set with a lapis lazuli, opal, garnet and emerald. These spell
LOVE if another old name for a garnet (vermeil) is used, a typical example of the resourcefulness of
jewellers.
B. A heart-shaped locket in chased coloured golds, set with a forget-me-not in turquoises (an instance
of the language of flowers), surrounded by a ruby, emerald, garnet, amethyst, ruby and diamond, spelling
REGARD.
VICTORIA AND ALBERT MUSEUM

Semaine stones (for the days of the week), much promoted by jewellers with an eye to custom, were given by Davenport as follows:

Sunday —	Gold or yellow topaz
Monday —	Pearls or white topaz
Tuesday —	Ruby or garnet
Wednesday —	Sapphire or turquoise
Thursday —	Amethyst
Friday —	Emerald
Saturday —	Diamond.

For *birthstones,* Davenport offered the following, with the attributes they signified:

January —	Garnet	(Constancy)
February —	Amethyst	(Sincerity)
March —	Bloodstone	(Courage)
April —	Diamond	(Innocence)
May —	Emerald	(Success in Love)
June —	Agate	(Health)
July —	Carnelian	(Content)
August —	Sardonyx	(Conjugal felicity)
September —	Chrysolite	(Sanity of mind)
October —	Opal	(Hope)
November —	Topaz	(Fidelity)
December —	Turquoise	(Truth).[101]

The language of stones, which engrossed both Napoleon and his second Empress, Marie-Louise (see Colour Plate 28), was reported 'in high favour' by the *Belle Assemblée* in 1817, which explained only that the initials of the stones 'form devices or sentimental words'.[102] The sentiment usually expressed was affection. A popular word, which gave its name retrospectively to the genre, was 'Regard', represented by:

Ruby
Emerald
Garnet
Amethyst
Ruby
Diamond

as in Colour Plate 29B.

The name of a loved one was a favourite, not only in royal circles. Here Sophia, spelled in stones, shows that jewellers frequently had to hunt around to find a stone with a suitable initial letter:

Sapphire
Opal
Peridot
Hyalite [a clear colourless opal]
Iolite [a silicate of aluminium and magnesium with water]
Amethyst.[103]

The game, played in several different languages but mainly in French, spawned quantities of jewellery in the 1820s and 1830s. It was revived in the 1880s and was still current in the Edwardian era.

Plate 64. A necklace and earrings of garnets set in gold. The stones are all mounted in close-backed foiled collets, a common practice to enhance the colour of the dark garnets. The full-face flowers of the necklace are linked by oval stones; the clasp at the back, set with a row of three stones punctuated by pellets in the spandrels, is attached by chains. The necklace may have been reduced in length and the earrings were originally furnished with gold hooks. Garnet jewellery was popular in the late eighteenth and early nineteenth centuries: these pieces are probably English, dating to about 1820.

PRIVATE COLLECTION, ON LOAN TO THE VICTORIA AND ALBERT MUSEUM

CHAPTER IV
A Typology of Fashion, 1801-1820

The fashionable woman, for all the hazards of war, was usually able to command a wide range of stones for her jewellery. Diamonds and pearls, essential on formal occasions, were followed by (and frequently combined with) coloured stones such as emeralds, rubies and sapphires (Colour Plates 20 and 25). Amethysts and topazes were so highly valued that they were sometimes also associated with diamonds, as were chrysoprases (the Prince Regent acquired a cross and earrings in diamonds and chrysoprase from Edmund Smith's of Maddox Street in 1819),[1] and garnets (Plate 64), peridots (Colour Plate 23) and other stones. Opals, mocho stones, turquoise, agates, aquamarines, malachite and lapis lazuli (Plate 56), carnelians, bloodstone and labradorite were joined by 'Scotch' and other pebbles. Pastes were sometimes used in preference to topaz when, for instance, a particularly intense colour, impossible to achieve even in a dyed stone, was required, and were still employed in sentimental jewellery. Their use was naturally essential in imitation or costume jewellery. Real or false, coloured stones were often combined in polychromatic effect. Miss Catherine Boyd bought an opal brooch bordered by rubies and pearls from Garrard's in 1803.[2] A 'rainbow coronet formed of diverse precious stones' was reported to have been worn by an unnamed marchioness at a function in 1807.[3]

Natural materials such as coral, ivory, jet and hair were popular. Gold and silver were used, separately or together, in all fine jewellery and the overwhelming majority of secondary articles, though Janety in France, himself a considerable scientist, persisted in the production of platinum wares. His display at the Paris Exhibition of 1802 was followed in 1819 by platinum jewellery and other wares displayed by Janety fils & Châtenay.[4] Steel trinkets were still produced in Birmingham and also in Germany and elsewhere. Berlin ironwork was almost unknown in England in 1813, when Princess Charlotte of Wales informed her friend Margaret Mercer Elphinstone that Lord Castlereagh, then Foreign Secretary, had offered 'to get me from Berlin if *possible* (for they are very difficult to be procured) one of the iron rings the ladies wear there now instead of gold wedding ones and diamond hasps...'[5] Berlin ironwork was to become an important export (see pages 698 to 702).

Varieties of pinchbeck were often used in the manufacture of cheap jewellery. One, described in Lardner's *Cabinet Cyclopaedia* of 1833 as mosaic gold or Parker's metal, was defined as 'a fine yellow composition metal, consisting of copper and zinc in about equal proportions'. The term 'mosaic' is problematic; a gold tiara supplied by Rundell's to the Prince of Wales in 1806 was decorated 'with dead roses in mosaic',[6] which cannot refer to Parker's metal. The term may either refer to a method of tooling the surface, possibly in a pattern of roundels and squares reminiscent of a mosaic floor, to the contrasting effects produced by

Plate 65. *The figure of Fame on the right is wearing some of the productions of the toymaker and silversmith Joseph Taylor in this advertisement engraved by Francis Egerton for Bisset's* Magnificent Directory of Birmingham, 1800. *Taylor was an important figure in the town; appointed a Guardian of the Assay Office in 1813, he died in 1827.*   BIRMINGHAM ASSAY OFFICE

matted and polished areas or to the use of differently coloured golds. Unless the design literally depicted fading roses (as in the sentimental piece in Colour Plate 36), the tiara is unlikely to have been set with *pietre dure* or Florentine mosaic plaques or with stone or vitreous tesserae (Roman mosaics), though these were growing in popularity.

Birmingham manufacturers started making silver watch-chains in about 1806, though steel and base metal trinkets continued to be made in the town. The silversmith, jeweller and toymaker Joseph Taylor of Newhall Street advertised 'Gilt & General' toys or trinkets in 1800 (Plate 65). Interestingly, he showed the arms of the Worshipful Company of Goldsmiths at the head of the advertisement; less surprisingly, he already had a London address, probably a small warehouse with showroom, which nevertheless indicates that he supplied goods to London shops. The ship on the right must signify an export trade, while the figure of Fame, trumpet laid ready on the ground, is bedizened with a pendant on a chain, bracelet and armlet.

Imitation gold trinkets were advertised by A. Mesure of 420 Strand in April 1812. Mesure, who described himself as an inventor and sole proprietor of 'Petit-Or', which was probably a version of pinchbeck, acknowledged that it tarnished more easily than gold but asserted that it readily responded to polish. Watch-chains for men and women cost between £1 and £4.4s; seals were about half the price of gold ones; neck-chains ranged from £2 to £3.3s., bracelets from £2 to £4, combs from £2 to £3 and rings from 5s. to 15s. Such prices could only be afforded by fairly substantial citizens. A fortunate housemaid in an aristocratic household might well be able to command annual wages of over £5 plus, of course, her keep; Lady Bessborough computed them together to amount to about £39.0s.6d. a year in 1804. But it would take a reckless servant to devote a large part of her disposable income to such trinkets.[7]

The tradition of regional or peasant jewellery, non-existent in England, survived even the French Revolution. Fanny Burney, Madame D'Arblay, was fascinated on arriving at Calais in 1802 to see women in peasant costume wearing long gold drop earrings, necklaces, chains and crosses, but, she noted, earrings were also worn by 'even the maids who were scrubbing or sweeping. . .'[8] Evidently this was unknown in England. Away from the small towns and the countryside, however, there was sufficient demand for imitation gold in French cities to encourage the development of a product called *chrysocale,* an alloy which possessed the same drawback as Mr Mesure's imitation gold, for it had a marked tendency to discolour on exposure to the air. Once plated, it gained greater acceptance, garnering a considerable export trade with the encouragement of the restored Bourbons.

One of the novelties current in the second decade of the century was the coquilla nut. *Ackermann's Repository* reported that it was derived from Portuguese possessions in Africa; a glossy mottled red-brown nut (according to the *Oxford English Dictionary* however it was the fruit of the Brazilian palm tree), it had recently begun to be re-imported into England after a hiatus of over sixty years and was made into trinkets and articles of jewellery. A coquilla nut rosary and cross, worn with a promenade dress, appeared in a fashion plate in the *Repository* in 1812. A rage for 'petrified palm' (said to be a translucent, durable substance) had swept Paris in 1807, naturally involving the Empress Josephine, who had a belt ornament made from it with a pearl surround.[9] The fashion is unlikely to have crossed the Channel. Ireland was already furnishing an alternative in the form of bog oak (see pages 532 to 537).

The standard neo-classical repertory of anthemion (honeysuckle) ornament, palmettes, water leaves, rosettes, stylised vines and other devices such as lion-masks, serpents (Plate 66) and lyres dominated design, though the natural forms began to assume the characteristics of organic growth by 1810. Geometric shapes were much as in the late eighteenth century, with some changes of emphasis. The popularity of squares and rectangles with rounded sides ('blunt squares') is exemplified by two gold brooches of about 1805-10 with silhouette portraits by John Miers (Colour Plate 30). Such shapes were echoed in miniature by the cushion-shaped girdles of contemporary brilliants. The hieratic scroll settings in which these stones were mounted in the first decade of the century were somewhat relaxed in the second, when they were often supplied with comma-like terminals and sprouted flowers and foliage (Plates 49 and 50 and Colour Plate 35).

Crescents, stars and other souvenirs of the East persisted, as well as the devices of sentiment, popular or specific to individuals (Colour Plate 31, A, C, D-F). The revival of rococo motifs was marked by the reappearance of double scrolls, birds, insects, shell forms (Plates 67 and 68)[10] and also real shells. The influence of medievalism was largely manifested in running patterns of trefoils similar to those later adopted by A.W.N. Pugin in the 1830s and '40s (Colour Plates 83 and 100).

While Wellington was campaigning against the French in the Peninsula from 1808 until 1813 English periodicals, while still borrowing from Parisian publications, attempted to reduce or disguise references to French fashions. But

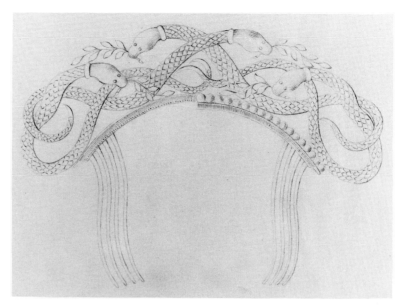

Plate 66. An Italian design for a tiara-comb with a head of interlacing collared serpents bearing olive branches in their jaws. The design, probably dating to about 1815-20, is a working drawing offering alternative patterns for the band holding the teeth. It is gadrooned on the left, and crested with large pellets on the right. The artist has not bothered to draw all the teeth, which must have been pivoted to the band, allowing the head of the comb to stand upright like a tiara.

COOPER-HEWITT MUSEUM, THE SMITHSONIAN INSTITUTION'S MUSEUM OF DESIGN

from time to time a few articles crept in, among which were a French watch, chain and seals decoratively displayed on the bodice of a carriage or promenade costume illustrated in 1810.[11] The following year the *Belle Assemblée* could not forbear to publish a report on French modes by 'a lady just returned from France'.[12]

The Lisbon chain of 1811 and Spanish filigree buttons, cited in 1812,[13] were manifest tributes to Wellington and lilies were to bloom in jewellery in 1814 on the restoration of the Bourbons. In that year, until Napoleon turned up again, and after the Battle of Waterloo, Paris was crowded with English military and civilians. For the edification of Englishwomen unable to join the throng, the London periodicals could scarcely have enough of French fashions. The hegemony of Paris was reasserted with the willing co-operation of women everywhere.

In the early years of the nineteenth century parures (or suites or sets, in the parlance of contemporary English jewellers) were larger and more comprehensive than before. For most women ownership of a parure set with precious stones was an unattainable ideal, yet they still wanted to read about them. Even those with means often had to be satisfied with part-sets or single items. The Garrard Ledgers show that the firm sold more articles as pairs and singletons than anything else, though they certainly provided suites on occasion. On the evidence of a single surviving account book, N. Goetze, a working jeweller in London, made no sets at all during the years 1809-15, though he supplied several leading retailers.[14]

Suites were nevertheless available for women with modest resources. A seed-pearl parure by J.H. Barlow (Plate 67), published in *Ackermann's Repository* in 1811, was made with them in mind. According to the accompanying caption, the set comprised 'a necklace, sprig, bracelets, tops and drops [earrings], and three broaches, two of which can be worn as a pair of [belt] clasps.'[15] 'The sprig is so contrived as to fix on a comb, and the centers play on springs,' it added, establishing that it was not only diamonds which were mounted on tremblers. The

Plate 67. An engraving of a parure of seed pearl jewellery designed and executed by a London pearl-worker, J.H. Barlow, and published in Ackermann's Repository *in 1811. The five scallop shell motifs of the necklace were cut out of mother-of-pearl and fretted to leave solid areas for the attachment of the pearls. Each pearl was pierced and threaded on horsehair or silk which was secured through holes drilled in the mother-of-pearl frame. The linking festoons were strung without backings. The bracelets were similarly constructed. The sprig, designed to be worn on the bodice or coiffure, was probably solid-backed, as were the shell devices of the earrings and brooches. The clasps were gold, bordered by pearls.*

dual function of the sprig and the two smaller brooches is characteristic of much jewellery design; as noted earlier (see page 86), the Prince of Wales acquired convertible items from time to time. With his fashionable scallop shell motifs Barlow, whose premises were at 1 Grange Court, Carey Street, Lincoln's Inn Fields, should have met with more success than apparently came his way. The illustration was almost certainly an editorial advertisement for which he had paid. By March 1812 he had turned to the *Belle Assemblée* to announce price reductions: 'Several complete suits of Pearls, new Patterns, in Morocco Cases...' with the constituents enumerated above cost between £20 and £30. Bandeaux cost from £10.10s., sprigs from £4.4s. and 'Pearl Necklaces any Pattern' from £5.15s.6d.[16] In May Barlow was back again, correcting any impression that his prices indicated the employment of 'patent pearls'. He used 'Orient Pearl from the fisheries of Ceylon and Persia, which, being manufactured by the real workman, are offered to the public much under their usual charges.'[17]

A full parure had no standard number of components, though a necklace and earrings were usually a staple. A demi-parure, on the other hand, might comprise the necklace and earrings or a brooch and earrings by themselves. Married women or single women of standing in society were the chief wearers of full parures. Young girls were required to wear modest clothes and jewellery. Generally speaking, provided the owner was sufficiently rich, the grander the function, the larger the parure. A complete suite of jewellery set with precious stones would be in order at Court, at balls and at other full-dress functions. But a woman out riding or paying and receiving morning calls might be merely adorned with a watch, earrings and gold chain. In between these extremes were a number of afternoon and evening occasions at which a parure of lesser value was considered appropriate.

The large sets made for the Empress Josephine in the first decade of the nineteenth century usually comprised one or two diadems, a fillet or small bandeau, comb, necklace, earrings, brooches for the bodice or sleeves, bracelets and perhaps an armlet as well as a girdle or belt clasp. Though many of Josephine's parures were conventionally set with precious stones, the French presence in Italy undoubtedly encouraged the inclusion of mosaics and modern engraved gems from Rome and elsewhere in some of her jewellery (Colour Plates 32 and 33).

George IV, when Prince of Wales and Regent, bought several suites, though none was on a scale comparable to the great parures affected by Josephine and the Bonaparte clan. The English royals tended to build up sets over a period of years. The Regent's sister Princess Mary, at last permitted to marry her cousin the Duke of Gloucester in 1816, wore pearl earrings with her diamond jewellery at the ceremony. A wreath of roses set with brilliants was placed in front of another head ornament, a diamond coronet of crescents supporting floral devices. She also wore a sprig on her bodice, a pair of bracelets and a girdle made to match her wreath.[18] The wreath, sprig and girdle, manifestation of the growing obsession with naturalism, were probably new.

Princess Amelia's death in 1810 prompted *Ackermann's Repository* to publish in December a plate of a 'Mourning Evening Dress trimmed with black bugles and steel' (beads). The ornaments were described as 'a neck-chain and convent cross of jet, with earrings and bracelets to correspond.'[19] One of Garrard's clients, Miss Nugent, ordered a set of 'jet' jewellery which, according to a ledger entry dated 21 January 1811, comprised a pair of bracelets, necklace, bandeau, clasp and two pairs of earrings costing £13.13s. in all. Enamelled gold would have been dearer, black beads cheaper. The fashionable world, formally bound to observe the decreed periods of mourning, usually had appropriate jewellery in reserve.

Head ornaments were large and, aside from rarities such as openwork gem-set helmets, the largest of all were circlets or near-circlets which encompassed the

Plate 68. *A seed pearl necklace of about 1810 with three shell motifs which are slightly more elaborate than those in the engraving of J.H. Barlow's parure in Plate 67. The clasp, like that of the Barlow necklace, is placed at the back; in the form of a gold parallelogram, it contains hair set under glass with a border of seed pearls and a spring catch on the right.*

The pendant in the centre dates to about 1815 and is part of a set of which a necklace, brooch and hair pin survive. It is decorated with a plaque and drop of moonstones and peridots set in gold with grainti ornament. VICTORIA AND ALBERT MUSEUM

Plate 69. Maria Laetitia Ramolino Bonaparte (Madame Mère), Napoleon's mother, painted by Gérard between 1802 and 1804, the bust of her most illustrious offspring, then still First Consul, a powerful presence in the right-hand side of the picture. Her diadem, rising to a peak in front, shows that one of the most characteristic types of the Court of the French Empire was already in existence. Its form is similar to that of the piece worn by Josephine's daughter Hortense de Beauharnais when Queen of Holland (Plate 70). NATIONAL GALLERY OF SCOTLAND

Plate 70. Baron François Gérard, the pupil of J.-L. David, painted Hortense, Queen of Holland with her son Louis in about 1806. The Queen wears a head ornament with the same arched front as that worn by Madame Mère in Plate 69, together with top and drop earrings and a necklace in coloured stones and diamonds. The portrait was among a group of paintings removed from the Palais de Saint-Cloud by Field-Marshal Blücher von Wahlstatt after Napoleon's defeat at Waterloo. SOTHEBY'S

head, securing the short curls framing the face and passing under the long back hair drawn up to the crown of the head. They went under several names, being variously called tiaras,[20] diadems,[21] bandeaux[22] and coronets. Lady Cholmondeley was described as wearing examples of the two latter with her Court dress in 1808,[23] though the engraving of her in costume (Colour Plate 34), depicts only the coronet, which has an arched front of the type soon to be adopted in England as the large Spartan diadem. The bandeau was probably in this case a narrow flexible fillet passed over the hair behind the diadem. A specimen of such a fillet, mounted with agate cameos alternating with sardonyx intaglios, is shown in Colour Plate 33 with items in a parure said to have belonged to the Empress Josephine.

The basic shape of the Spartan diadem is discernible in a series of large jewelled head ornaments usually with a crest of motifs rising to a peak in front, as in the portrait of Madame Mère, Napoleon's mother, executed by Gérard between 1802 and 1804 (Plate 69). The same artist later painted Josephine's daughter Hortense de Beauharnais, Queen of Holland, wearing a similar ornament (Plate 70).

Plate 71. An oil sketch on wood, one of several studies made by Sir George Hayter in 1820 of George IV's estranged Queen attending the enquiry in the House of Lords into allegations of her adulterous behaviour on her travels abroad. For his finished picture, The Trial of Queen Caroline, *completed in 1823, Hayter omitted the circlet, though it appears in other drawings. Popular support for the Queen was so vociferous that the government did not dare test the proceedings in the Commons.*

Plate 72. Pauline Bonaparte, Princess Borghese, a celebrated beauty, sat for her portrait to Lefèvre in 1806 wearing a semi-transparent white gown and a headdress fastened by two gold tissue bands passing over her hair and under her chin, partially concealing a jewelled bandeau worn forward on the brow. Opal clasps gather the folds of her sleeves at the shoulders; it is clear that she had no qualms about the unlucky qualities later attributed to the stone.

Josephine herself owned diadems of this kind, as well as others which departed from the norm in matters of detail (Colour Plate 32). One was her pearl diadem with pointed arches and trefoils and another set with pearls and cameos (Plates 39 and 47), but they were all essentially high circlets or near-circlets. The flaring form and arching crest of this type survived Bapst's gently diffused reinterpretations of the Empire style for Louis XVIII: the emerald and brilliant diadem in Colour Plate 35 dates to 1819-1820.[24] The influence of the tall encircling constructions of the French Empire on English design is apparent in fashion plates issued in London from about 1807 onwards.[25] Its continuance is demonstrated in Sir George Hayter's sketch of Queen Caroline seated in the House of Lords in 1820 during her so-called 'Trial', the hearing of the Bill of Pains and Penalties by which George IV hoped to divorce her. Her head ornament may not have been composed of precious materials, but despite its lack of an arched front it is comparable to Josephine's pearl diadem with pointed arches (Plates 39 and 71). George IV's coronation circlet (Plate 35), which followed the same flaring shape, has survived as one of the most celebrated pieces of Crown jewellery.

The equally ambiguous bandeau, worn with a semblance of decorum under a headdress of gold bands by Napoleon's far from demure sister Pauline, Princess

Borghese,[26] in Lefèvre's portrait of 1806 (Plate 72), was often an oblong band, flexible, hinged or made rigid to the shape of the head. It too was subject to elaboration while remaining, essentially, a band. Current in England at the turn of the century, bandeaux were sufficiently prominent to attract the satirical eye of Jane Austen, who in a letter written to her sister Cassandra on 20 November 1800 referred to an acquaintance, the star of a recent ball, who 'appeared exactly as she did in September, with the same broad face, diamond bandeau, white shoes, pink husband, and fat neck.'[27] Unfortunately in England diadems and tiaras were also called bandeaux, which further complicates the matter. Englishwomen adopted the French style of wearing such head ornaments in about 1805, bringing them forward on the hairline or dropping them further down on the forehead.

Napoleon's coronation wreath of gold laurel leaves (Plate 36) was not in itself a new idea; it was an antiquarian exercise. Fashionable jewelled interpretations of the classical wreath were worn by several ladies at the ceremony of 1804, some crossed with bandeaux (Plate 8). But Napoleon's head ornament probably gave a fillip to the vogue. Alas for consistency, however, Princess Amelia was reported to have attended a Drawing-Room in 1807 in a patriotic bandeau (not a wreath) composed of diamond oak-leaves.[28] Bandeaux were said to be replacing tiaras at the time and perhaps the fashion correspondent got carried away by constant repetition of the word.[29] Perhaps the Princess's ornament was the 'large Brilliant Tiara' given her by the Prince of Wales in the same year (page 91).

Wreaths and demi-wreaths of flowers were noted between about 1807 and 1812,[30] some of metal and some be-jewelled. Madame Daru may have worn a headdress of real flowers for her portrait (Colour Plate 22) but she would not have risked it wilting in hot ball-rooms and receptions. Though milliners were ready with artificial flowers, jewelled alternatives inevitably found favour with the rich. In 1818 the fashion correspondent of *Ackermann's Repository* wrote in glowing terms of a Parisian wreath of wild berries executed in coral and emeralds, 'made strictly to imitate nature',[31] a refrain much heard in the ensuing three decades.

Ephemera such as Persian head ornaments and a curious Chinese diadem with finger-like struts waft in and out of fashion reports.[32] Oriental influences were however more usually apparent in the appellation than in the design.

Combs were much worn. In the early years of the century they were usually pushed through the hair at the back of the head, near the crown or to one side of it, so that the ornamental tops (or heads) projected at an angle in line with the teeth. The latter were either made of metal (Colour Plate 33), horn or tortoiseshell; in April 1802 Garrard's charged a Mr Langham 7s.6d. for a tortoiseshell comb on which they set an existing diamond ornament. In a new development, probably introduced in France towards 1810, the heads of some combs were pivoted so that they stood upright like a tiara while the teeth were pushed through the hair at right angles. In 1809 the *Journal des Dames* mentioned that the teeth went through the hair horizontally,[33] so that unless the decorated tops were laid flat on the head, a great waste of workmanship, pivots must have already existed.

Early comb heads were often made in France in the form of a simple arch or with a concave curve like the back-rail of an Empire chair. Trellised heads,[34] reminiscent of contemporary silver dessert or bread baskets, were fashionable from about 1807 to 1812, especially in Paris.[35] Combs forming part of a parure were naturally decorated to harmonise with the rest of the set, so that they incarnated the standard motifs of the time. Metal teeth were probably more common than tortoiseshell and horn in France, whereas the reverse was true in England. The two silver combs of Henry Adcock of Birmingham (Plates 73 and 74) have teeth cut from silver sheets (fully hallmarked for 1808-9) and stapled to heads of great refinement in which fashionable shell motifs predominate. Both heads are cast, one solid, the other open, in imitation of cut steel work, but they manage at the same time to evoke French *cannetille* decoration. Adcock or his contemporaries seem to have turned out quantities of silver jewellery by the same technique. The *Belle Assemblée* reported with an uncharacteristic lack of enthusiasm in 1808: 'silver filigree ornaments are now very generally adopted. We see them not only forming decorations for the hair, but composing also the neck-chains, bracelets, brooches, and ear-rings. They have rather a poor, insipid, and tin-like effect. Their extreme neatness may, however, render them an acceptable change, and softening ornament for coloured dresses.' But silver filigree articles outlasted their bad reception and were cited by a fashion correspondent in 1811.[36]

Garrard's furnished the Marchioness of Exeter with 'a fine Garnet Head Ornament' with gilt teeth in 1810. The following year Miss Burdett paid 1s.6d. to have horn teeth fitted to a 'Gilt Mounting'. But tortoiseshell combs predominate in the Ledgers. The employment of pivots, so useful in small combs, made possible the development in about 1810-14 of the tiara-comb, a combination article which became popular as a substitute for a full set of head ornaments on informal occasions (Plates 66 and 75). Almost certainly French in origin, it is difficult to discover whether this useful ornament was as fully appreciated in England as on the Continent. The heads of both combs and tiara-combs were frequently adorned with a crest of stones, pearls and coral. In the 1820s the newly burgeoning French trade in imitation jewellery exported large quantities of tiara-combs in gilt metal, adorned with paste crestings. The pivoted combs worn in England were often smaller than French examples. Tall rigid specimens continued to support the hair at the back of the head.

Aigrettes remained popular and the traditional feather type found favour (Colour Plate 10A). Bouquets and sprigs were often supplied with (removable) brooch fittings, enabling them to be transferred from the bodice to the coiffure (Plate 140). Pins with elaborate heads, some with flowers mounted on tremblers to match those on the sprigs, adorned hair ribbons and caps. Other favourite devices for pins included ears of wheat, butterflies (such as the one given by the Prince of Wales to his sister Amelia in 1804),[37] crescents, stars, comets (in response to sightings in France in March 1811 and in England in August),[38] clusters and arrrows.[39]

Decorative hat clasps known as loops, provided with or without a matching button, were worn by both sexes. Women placed jewelled specimens on their evening turbans and caps and men on the upturned brims of their headgear on ceremonial occasions. Napoleon had a splendid example in diamonds in 1805.

Plate 73. Front and back views of a silver comb with a cast filigree head by Henry Adcock of Birmingham, fully hallmarked for Birmingham, 1808. The comb is rigid; the head is riveted to the band at the top of the teeth.

Plate 74. Adcock's cast silver comb with whelk shells and a lion mask evokes cut steel ornaments and cannetille. Birmingham, 1908.

Rundell's set 'a very large & rich brilliant Military button & loop for the Hat. with scrolls & knots. large brilliant Star in the centre. a fine brilliant Button added with large Brilliant in centre' for the Prince Regent in 1811, using diamonds partly obtained from an Indian sword and a stud, some of which they re-cut and polished. Their total bill for the item was £124.[40] The Regent wore the ornament at his great fête at Carlton House in 1811, which was attended by the 'Comte de Lille' (Louis XVIII), the Duchesse d'Angoulême and other members of the exiled French royal family.[41]

There were exceptions to the rule that necklaces were essential to the parure. One of Garrard's customers, Mrs Hawkins Browne, acquired a set in 1801 which consisted only of a pair of diamond earrings, a bandeau and a cross. The cross was presumably intended to be suspended from a chain in lieu of a necklace, though she might well have already possessed a suitable necklace. Mrs Browne must have supplied her own diamonds for the new pieces, for she was charged only for the cost of setting, which amounted to £34.14s.

Single and multiple strings of stones, pearls and beads of various materials, with and without drops (Plate 75), were popular. Festooned necklaces were still in

vogue; a specimen with a triple row of pearls and a ruby clasp in front was
illustrated in *Ackermann's Repository* in 1812.[42] A necklace centre made from an
emerald set 'in colour'd gold and pearls,' was supplied by Garrard's to their client
Miss Catherine Boyd in 1803. It came without chains, which probably means that
it was intended as a convertible ornament, to be used variously as a necklace and
bracelet clasp. The number of units additional to the front one in festooned
necklaces increased; a festoon necklace of about 1805 in the Victoria and Albert
Museum (Plate 118), has six plaques of Florentine mosaics connected by triple gold
chains and another suspended in front as a pendant. Roman mosaics were often
mounted in the same way.

Necklaces of this kind might also be set with engraved gems or the cheaper shell
cameos, usually depicting classical subjects. The Frankfurt edition of the *Journal
des Dames* claimed in 1805 that the latest cameo necklaces comprised a complete set
of the Roman Emperors from Caesar to Nero, and from the latter to
Constantine.[43] In 1815 Garrard's sold a necklace and earrings of shell cameos in
'coloured beaded' settings strung with Maltese chains to a member of the Bagot
family; the set cost £12.8s.6d. Five years later the sculptor Richard Westmacott[44]
commissioned a necklace of twelve 'Amelekites' set in gold linked by chains from
Garrard's, supplying his own design for the piece. 'Amelekite' or 'amalakite' was
malachite.

In 1813, when natural forms had already begun to make inroads into the
geometric motifs of current jewellery design, *Ackermann's Repository* drew attention
to necklaces and bracelets made of 'coloured enamel, to represent small natural
flowers'.[45] The flower units presented full-face in the garnet necklace in Plate 64
remain formal, while conveying the idea of naturalism.

The 'conqueror's necklace' with twenty heart-shaped pendants of carnelian, palm wood, sardonyx, malachite, garnet and lapis lazuli was first produced in Paris in 1806-07 in homage to Napoleon after his triumphant campaign in Germany. After a discreet interval of two years, during which time the connection with Bonaparte might be conveniently overlooked in England, Belinda of *Ackermann's Repository* came up with a reference to a currently-fashionable 'neck-chain of divers-coloured hearts'.[46]

In 1811 the *Belle Assemblée* attempted to put some order into the complex nature of necklace fashions by classifying them in two types, the first comparatively short but lying loosely around the throat and the second long, with pendants of various kinds.[47] The latter was termed the 'pilgrim style' necklace, though it was more usually known as a negligé. The analysis, though over-simplified (many short necklaces had pendants), at least demonstrates that all necklaces were growing longer. The increasing size of the Empress Josephine's pearl necklace has already been noted (Plates 39, 47 and Colour Plate 21).

Pendants were added to chains as well as necklaces, and were probably often interchangeable. The Maltese cross predominated, largely thanks to Lady Hamilton (Plate 40). Betsey Fremantle's sister Eugenia Wynne was given a Maltese cross of amethysts and diamonds as a wedding present in 1806.[48] A year later the Prince of Wales' wife Caroline wore a similar cross at a Drawing-room, the first she had attended after surviving an enquiry into her conduct by a Commission appointed to make the 'Delicate Investigation'.[49]

Jane Austen's sailor brother Charles, in receipt of £30 in prize money from the capture of a French privateer, and expecting another £10, celebrated by 'buying gold chains & Topaze Crosses' for his two sisters. Jane Austen wrote with mock ruefulness to her sister from Bath in May 1801 to give her the news and declare that Charles 'must be well scolded'.[50] The two crosses in Plate 76 are said to be the very ones concerned. They are however different and one may well be earlier than the other. Unfortunately Jane Austen never described the pieces nor mentioned their shape.

Carmelite crosses were cited in fashion reports without being defined, but the convent cross of jet which appears in a fashion plate after Princess Amelia's death in 1810 appears to be straight-sided with a long lower limb like the right-hand specimen in Plate 76. A cross of similar shape, suspended from a rosary of gold and amber, adorns a walking dress illustrated in the *Repository* in 1809.[51] The use of religious terminology reflects the secularisation of the churches in France after the Revolution. Though Napoleon ensured that the Church and State were reconciled there were no qualms about appropriating types and forms of religious artefacts and reproducing them as fashionable jewellery, especially after Pope Pius VII gave rosaries to the ladies of the French Court when he came to Paris for Napoleon's coronation in 1804.

'Egyptian amulets', hearts, baskets of flowers, lyres, padlocks and keys, medallions and lockets of all kinds, often encircled by serpents, were all in demand (Plate 78 and Colour Plates 31D and 36). *Fausses-montres* survived into the new century and then disappeared. Goetze frequently made lockets in coloured gold,

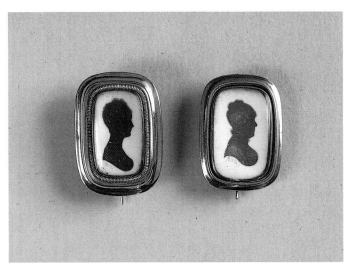

Colour Plate 30. Two small gold brooches with silhouette portraits of unidentified ladies by John Miers, both mounted under glass. One of the brooches, which may have begun their existence as slides for chains or ribbons, has a box for hair at the back. The brooch on the left has an inner milled border reminiscent of the mounts on the French parure in Plate 56, but these two pieces are English, c.1805-10.

Colour Plate 31. A. An eye locket of c.1800-10; the miniature of a lady's eye, painted on ivory, is set under glass in a gold mount with a milled inner border like the one on the left in Colour Plate 30. The outer border is composed of graduated half-pearls; on the reverse is a glass-fronted fitting with hair and pearls. The suspension loop is plain gold.

B. An enamelled gold Swiss chatelaine of the 1770s-80s, of a type revived in the 1870s. The hook-plate is decorated with an applied pointed oval plaque with a garlanded urn on a plinth over a monochrome landscape with further urns and plinths. The enamelled watch-key and seal are flanked by tassels, a device which survived into the early nineteenth century.

C. An enamelled mourning pendant for Princess Charlotte of Wales, who died in November 1817. The miniature of the Princess, set in a shield-shaped frame, is a virtual duplicate of one executed in 1814 by Charlotte Jones and probably shown at the Royal Academy two years afterwards. Charlotte Jones held the appointment of Miniature Painter to the Princess of Wales and was probably responsible for this copy, which depicts the Princess in a white dress and red and gold jewellery, her left arm resting on a robe lined with ermine. Her crown is just visible behind her left elbow. The urn-shaped pendant below is set with the Prince of Wales' feathers executed in hair with a diamond label and PC/ 1817 is engraved on its back. The reverse of the miniature is enamelled with the Royal Arms. The miniature and the use of hair shows that this piece was made for a member of the royal family, probably for her widower, Prince Leopold of Saxe-Coburg (who had locks of his wife's hair), shortly after the Princess's death (see Frampton, Journal, page 300).

D. A gold pendant in the form of a padlock with a graduated border of half pearls and a suspension loop set with pearls. The inner border is milled and the centre filled with a domed vitreous composition counterset with small pearls to represent a keyhole. A tiny gold heart and a key are suspended from gold chains, one on each side of the padlock; c.1805.

E. Made as a bracelet clasp and subsequently converted into a brooch, this piece was commissioned as a mourning jewel for the celebrated Duchess of Devonshire, the friend of the Prince of Wales and of Charles James Fox. She died in 1806; her name, abbreviated to Georgiana D, is engraved on grey onyx below a ducal coronet, with the date of her death below. The intaglio is in the original Roman setting: only the back has been altered.

F. An octagonal brooch/pendant with a milled inner border enclosing two curls of different colours adorned with pearls and gold wire mounted on opalescent glass under a glass cover. Inscriptions engraved on the back commemorate four deaths, the first in 1804 and the last in 1831, but the piece probably dates to about 1810.

---

sometimes set with bloodstone, and furnished with compartments for hair. Among the items commissioned by 'Mr Wirgman' in 1809 was 'a Green Gold leaf Locket Bloodstone front Polish'd Back to open for Hair'.[52] It cost Goetze £2.17s. to make and he charged Wirgman £4.14s.6d. for it. Two further lockets with bloodstone fronts were edged with serpents; the engine-turned backs opened to reveal a box for hair.

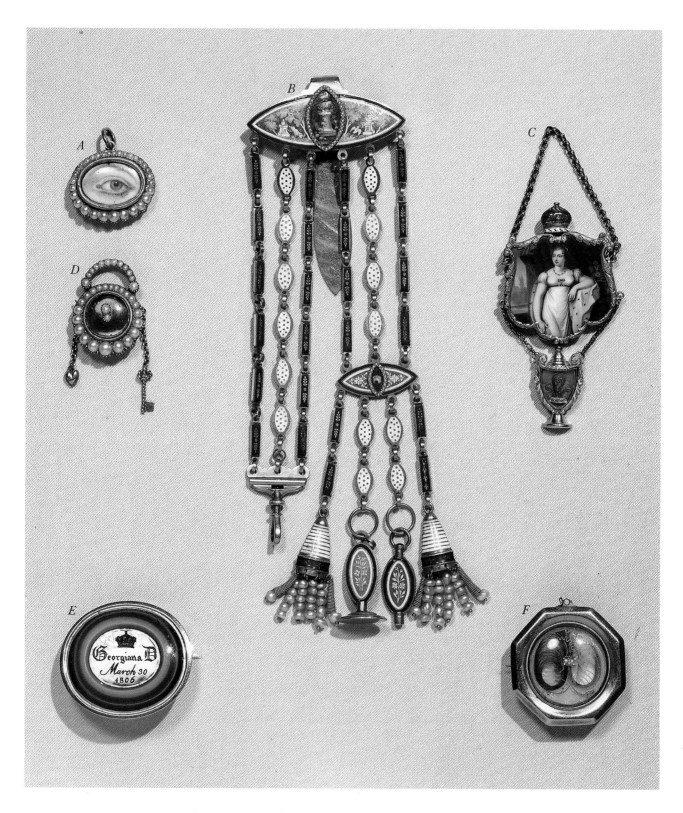

The range of pendants can be indefinitely extended to include articles normally suspended from long chains rather than necklaces. Prominent among these are watches, seals, charms and novelties (Plate 79) as well as eye-glasses (often called 'sights'). The chains themselves ranged from delicate varieties which went under several names such as Maltese, Venetian or *jaseron,* Trichinopoly (which is known to have been of the loop-in-loop type) and Damascus, to more substantial forms

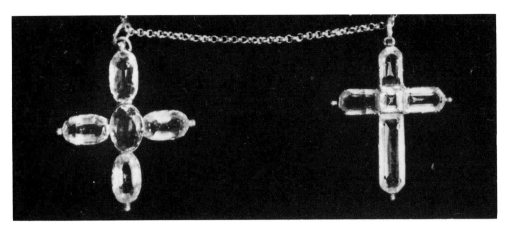

Plate 76. Two topaz and gold crosses said to have been given by Lieutenant Charles Austen, the sixth son of the Reverend Francis Austen, to his sisters Jane and Cassandra in 1801. Purchased with his share of the prize money earned by the capture by the Endymion, *on which he was serving, of the French ship, the* Scipio, *in a heavy gale, the crosses and the accompanying chains were a delight to his sisters. As Jane Austen wrote to Cassandra: 'We shall be unbearably fine'. She drew on the gift later in her novel,* Mansfield Park *(1814), making Fanny Price's sailor brother William give her an amber cross though, unlike Charles Austen, he was unable to afford a gold chain to go with it. Charles Austen rose to the rank of Rear-Admiral in 1846 and died in 1852.*

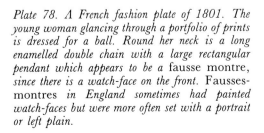

Plate 77. An emblem and motto from Knight's Gems and Device Book *(1836) showing a butterfly about to settle on a rose in full bloom. The tag is given in both English and French, the latter being the international language of sentiment.*

Plate 78. A French fashion plate of 1801. The young woman glancing through a portfolio of prints is dressed for a ball. Round her neck is a long enamelled double chain with a large rectangular pendant which appears to be a fausse montre, *since there is a watch-face on the front. Fausses-montres in England sometimes had painted watch-faces but were more often set with a portrait or left plain.*

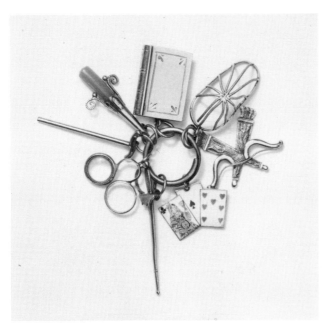

Plate 79. A collection of eight charms in gold, some enamelled, symbolising the Ages of Man, all mounted on a split ring. Struck with the Paris warranty mark for 1809-19, there is no doubt that the charms are French, but the majority of the symbols correspond with Shakespeare's Seven Ages of Man in As You Like It, *Act II, sc. vii, which is the probable source of inspiration. Infancy is signified not only by a cradle but a coral as well, childhood and education (the boy 'creeping unwillingly to school') by a book, quarrelsome and reckless young manhood by the sword and cards; love by Cupid's accoutrements of bow, quivers and arrows and old age ('sans eyes, sans teeth, sans every thing') by the eye-glasses and stick.* VICTORIA AND ALBERT MUSEUM

which might occasionally be gem-set or enamelled. Aside from the loop-in-loop type (Plate 56), the most popular patterns were curb, cable, fetter and woven,[53] as far as can be judged. The Garrard Ledgers are not helpful on this point, the clerk often being content to describe chains merely as 'strong gold' or 'rich gold'. Pearl chains, others strung with carnelian or amber beads[54] or made from human hair, woven or plaited and fitted with gold joints and clasps, were current everywhere. When Ingres painted Madame Devauçay in 1807 she wore a long hair chain jointed with gold, wound round her neck several times.[55]

Princess Mary, Duchess of Gloucester, owned a sautoir which was certainly substantial (Plate 43). It was probably too long for a clasp to be necessary, but some chains and all necklaces were fitted with 'snaps'. The old fashioned front fastening was already beginning to disappear in the first decade of the century and clasps were increasingly relegated to the back of the neck (Plates 67 and 68). Some were set with stones or pearls and had hair inserted in tiny boxes on the underside. Cameo-set snaps were high fashion: Princess Sophia Matilda of Gloucester[56] ordered an example from Garrard's in 1816. Other clasps, often slightly convex, were decorated with enamel or engine-turning. Many were fitted with V-shaped spring catches (a 'new spring ketch to gold neckchain' was entered in one of the Garrard ledgers in 1816).

'Patent snaps' were mentioned by the *Belle Assemblée* in 1807. They were possibly barrel snaps, cited in the same periodical in the following year.[57] These consisted of an elongated barrel-shaped cylinder with a spring clasp or made in the traditional manner with a screw fitting.[58] The loop and ribbon fastening was virtually obsolete, but a derivative, composed of a ring and bar, was still in existence in 1802, to judge by entries in a Garrard Ledger.

Earrings were only occasionally out of favour. They began to lengthen in about 1797 and in the first decade of the century they were sometimes fairly long. They then slowly diminished in size (with some exceptions), lengthening again in the 1820s to achieve the remarkable size of the 1830s (Colour Plate 68A and Plate 134). Top and drop earrings were supreme. The drops were either solid or constructed with a frame enclosing an independent centre (Colour Plate 25). Tops

Colour Plate 32. Two diadems from an incomplete parure made in Paris and said to have belonged to the Empress Josephine. Their openwork gold ribbon construction follows the arched form of the Spartan diadem, though they are not full circlets, having gold loops at the back for ribbon ties. The ribbons were concealed when the back hair was drawn up to the top of the head.

Decorated with opaque blue champlevé enamel, their great glory is a collection of engraved gems in Roman settings, small sardonyx intaglios in the larger ornament above and large cameo heads in the smaller one below.

The parure, by tradition, was owned by the Queen of Naples and passed from her to the Empress Josephine. If it was a gift, the donor must have been Napoleon's sister Caroline Murat rather than her predecessor Queen Maria Carolina of Naples, who as Marie Antoinette's sister execrated the French. Queen Caroline, whose husband Joachim Murat was made King of Naples by Napoleon in 1808, paid several extended visits to France and may have had the gems, acquired from artists working in Rome, set in the parure by a Parisian jeweller. But she might equally have sent the gems to Josephine for setting. One of the other surviving items in the parure (see Colour Plate 33) is struck with Paris marks for 1798-1809.

Colour Plate 33. The comb, earrings, belt and bracelet clasp from the Empress Josephine's parure (see Colour Plate 32). Below these, a fillet (or bandeau) enamelled in a darker blue and set with nine cameos and ten intaglios, mounted on black velvet ribbon, is of the same date but a different design. It and the necklace, which is hung with cameos and intaglios, probably do not belong to the parure.

PRIVATE COLLECTION, ON LOAN TO THE VICTORIA AND ALBERT MUSEUM

167

and drops alone were frequently worn informally. Tassel earrings, though still made, were less popular than formerly. Earrings were made in the form of squares, rectangles, octagons, zig-zags, melons, hearts, hoops, and clusters (the latter a favourite of the Duchesse d'Angoulême);[59] twisted patterns also found favour. Serpents too wound their way into earrings, as they did into every other category of jewellery.

The naturalistic devices current in Paris in 1805 included apples and pears,[60] stylised butterflies, shells (Plates 67 and 68), birds and related motifs. An especially elaborate French design, described in 1810, comprised a bird holding three chains in its beak, with a lamp or balance suspended from them.[61]

In 1807 earrings went briefly out of fashion ('exploded' in contemporary parlance), but a fashion writer was soon at hand to explain that their disappearance as an essential constituent of morning costume was an exaggeration and that females 'of a correct taste' still wore huge ring or octagonal earrings.[62] In 1816 Princess Charlotte of Wales declared that she did not wear earrings,[63] presumably neither in the morning nor the evening. Ear ornaments undoubtedly went through another period in which they were diminished in size and importance. In 1817 *Ackermann's Repository* reported that earrings and bracelets were 'not very general' in London,[64] but women soon resumed them. One of Garrard's clients, Mrs Clark, bought a 'pair fine Gold filigree top and drop Earrings' in 1819.

Brooches occur with increasing frequency in the ledgers and bills of the first two decades of the century, but they remain ambiguous in form and function. They might be an adaptable unit serving to decorate the bodice, or be set in a tiara (see page 86) or double as a bracelet clasp. Made in sets, often graduated in size, they were worn on sleeves (Plate 34). An odd number indicates that one was designed for the bodice and the rest for the sleeves or shoulders. In 1808 Miss Julia Shuckburgh Evelyn went to Garrard's for two parures, one of pink topazes, the other of diamonds; both included three brooches, a head ornament (the diamond one had a shell motif), a necklace and two bracelets. There were no earrings in the topaz set. The diamond suite was larger and had in addition to the items cited a comb, armlet, a Maltese cross and (possibly) a pair of bracelet snaps in addition to the bracelets. The coloured set cost £156.15s. Miss Shuckburgh Evelyn supplied her own diamonds for the second, so that Garrard's charge of £157.19s.6d. represented the cost of the setting and their own profit on the commission. It took two years for Belinda of *Ackermann's Repository* to spot the trend and claim to have acquired a parure with three brooches.[65]

Garrard's, already in possession of a royal warrant as jewellers to George III's daughters, made a 'Square Brilliant Broach' for Princess Mary in December 1806; it cost £12.12s. A squared oval example appears in Raeburn's portrait of Mrs Lumsden, who appears also to be wearing a seal hanging from her belt (Plate 80). Goetze made two versions of 'a blunt square Color'd Broach with Green chas'd Border & Glass for Hair' for the City jewellers Kentish & Haynes in 1811, charging £1.8s. for the first and £1.10s. for the second, making a profit of 6s. on each.[66] Other brooches conformed to the usual repertory of neo-classical motifs or reflected the rising vogue for naturalism. The language of flowers was expressed

Plate 80. Mrs Lumsden, painted by Sir Henry Raeburn in about 1814, wears a large brooch in the centre of her bodice, a coloured stone set in a border of pearls. Sketched in more indistinctly is a seal (possibly two seals) suspended from her belt, counterbalanced by an oval form, probably a watch.
HUNTERIAN ART GALLERY, UNIVERSITY OF GLASGOW, HEPBURN COLLECTION

by flowers such as the forget-me-not and heart's-ease. Birds and flies were fashionable and the Napoleonic emblem of the bee was purloined for the benefit of an English heiress, Miss Catherine Tylney-Long, the bride of Wellington's nephew William Wellesley-Pole. Her bee brooch was set with precious stones 'in the most natural manner; the wings of the bee are extended, and upon touching a spring they open,' it was reported in the *Belle Assemblée* in 1813, 'and discover one of the smallest watches that has perhaps ever been seen.'[67] It must have been sumptuous: her marriage jewels in 1812 included a necklace reputedly worth £26,250.[68]

The small 'pins' (brooches) made to fasten drapery or handkerchiefs at the neck were occasionally purely decorative but were more often sentimental, set with hair in a border of pearls or black stones and often inscribed. These too frequently had 'blunt square' borders, but occasionally appeared in other forms such as highly schematised comets (Colour Plate 37B).

Bracelets, still generally made in pairs, were an invariable constituent of the parure for much of the first decade of the century. In 1808 the *Belle Assemblée* noted a departure from the custom of wearing identical bracelets: it was now fashionable to have two bracelets, one of 'elastic [i.e. flexible] hair, with variegated stud; the other of Scotch pebbles, or mocho stone, set in gold.'[69] Three years later, the custom of wearing bracelets at all was apparently in abeyance, for the same periodical announced their imminent revival owing to the prevalence of short sleeves.[70] This was possibly premature, since the Empress Josephine, an arbiter of fashion until her death in 1814, dropped bracelets from many of her parures in her last years. But though Josephine is without them in Colour Plate 9, when she posed in long sleeves, others, similarly dressed, were happy to wear them over their cuffs (Plate 75).

Colour Plate 34. Lady Cholmondeley's Court Dress, illustrated and described in the Belle Assemblée *in July 1808. The bodice of her robe is adorned 'with the most splendid diamond wreath' to represent the oak leaf and fruit, placed obliquely across the front of her bust, and her pannier skirt is festooned with diamond chains. Her arched diadem (merely a front on a band) is described as a 'rich coronet' worn with a 'diamond bandeau', a single row of stones.*

The rest of her jewellery, likewise of diamonds, consists of oval earrings, necklace, bracelets and cestus *or belt. Not mentioned, but clearly shown in the engraving, is the portrait medallion pendent from Lady Cholmondeley's necklace.*

Colour Plate 35. This emerald and diamond diadem, completed on 25 July 1820, was one of the last of the new pieces to be made by Bapst-Ménière, Jewellers to King Louis XVIII. The fourteen largest emeralds in the piece came from a group of stones unmounted since the beginning of the First Empire; the remaining twenty-six were supplied by the jewellers. The flowing brilliant scrolls in the diadem reflect the fluent shapes of neo-classical design characteristic of the Bourbon Restoration. 1,031 diamonds were set in the diadem, which fetched 45,900 francs at the sale of the French Crown Jewels in 1887. The retrospective catalogue of 1888 gives the weight of the brilliants as 176 carats and that of the emeralds as 77 carats (amended by Morel, The French Crown Jewels, *1988, to over 79 carats).*

PRIVATE COLLECTION, PHOTOGRAPH COURTESY OF WARTSKI

The traditional type of bracelet composed of a solid clasp with side plates pierced for the attachment of strings of stones, pearls, beads or chains, was still made in quantity. In the early 1800s two or three rows were general, though the number of strings was often as much a matter of personal taste and finances as fashion. In April 1810 Goetze made a bracelet clasp for Wirgman in the form of a chased gold serpent with 'Bloodstone front to open for Hair' and a diamond eye, fitted for the attachment of nine rows of chain. This demonstrates the tendency for the number of rows to increase, resulting in a wider bracelet. In 1817 Garrard's furnished pearls for an additional two rows to an existing bracelet, but in the same year, with a healthy independence, Lady Willoughby de Eresby[71] had a garnet and turquoise necklace altered to serve 'as a 3 row'd bracelet occasionally.' Clasps continued to be made independent of strings: an intaglio commemorating the Duchess of Devonshire, now mounted as a brooch (Colour Plate 31E) began life as a bracelet clasp in 1806.

The reference in the *Belle Assemblée* to 'elastic' hair in 1808 betokened the arrival of solid bands instead of multiple strings. For a time a compromise was made by making some of the motifs on the strings larger to give the impression of solidity. The fashionably-minded, however, turned to gold mesh bracelet bands towards 1820.

Pre-Revolutionary armlets worn over the sleeves on the upper arms were transmogrified afterwards into independent ornaments constructed like large bracelets but still worn above the elbow. Fashion reports often cite pairs of armlets.

The mythical Belinda of *Ackermann's Repository* wrote in 1809 that she intended to wear with her new ballgown 'a *bandeau* of pearl, of a somewhat new construction, being a little arched in front [a belated recognition of the Spartan diadem]: my earrings of the melon-drop form — a necklace and armlets to correspond.'[72] The Prince Regent however gave his daughter Charlotte a single 'beautiful diamond armlet' in late December 1813. This was probably the brilliant vine and grape armband to which Rundell's made an addition for £79.13s., presumably an enlargement so that it fitted the Princess's upper arm.[73] The Garrard Ledgers show that single armlets were often made, sometimes as part of a suite of jewellery, at other times as an independent item.

Belt or girdle clasps were common (Plates 81 and 82), far outnumbering complete jewelled girdles, though the Empress Marie-Louise owned one with a fall which has survived (Plate 83) and Napoleon's sister Queen Caroline of Naples was painted by Gérard wearing an elaborate example.[74] Some Englishwomen, royal and otherwise, owned specimens, but the Regent's sister Princess Elizabeth was reported as having only a diamond clasp, admittedly 'superb', at the waist of her wedding dress in 1818.[75] Clasps were usually made in two parts joined by a hook and loop, and ranged from neo-classical lion masks to snakes.[76]

Buckles were still occasionally worn by women, according to the fashion correspondents. A plate of a walking dress illustrated in *Ackermann's Repository* in 1809 was described as having a deep amber brooch or a 'gold filigree buckle, confining the dress at the throat and waist, with bracelets *en suite*.'[77] The buckle-makers, anxious to recoup the trade lost with the virtual disappearance of their product on shoes, must have hoped that the female fashion for rather masculine-looking buckled hats towards 1820 might benefit them. Unfortunately the buckles were usually made of non-metallic materials such as mother-of-pearl.

Watches and seals remained important accessories of female as well as male costume. They were both worn depending from the waist or from a chain slung

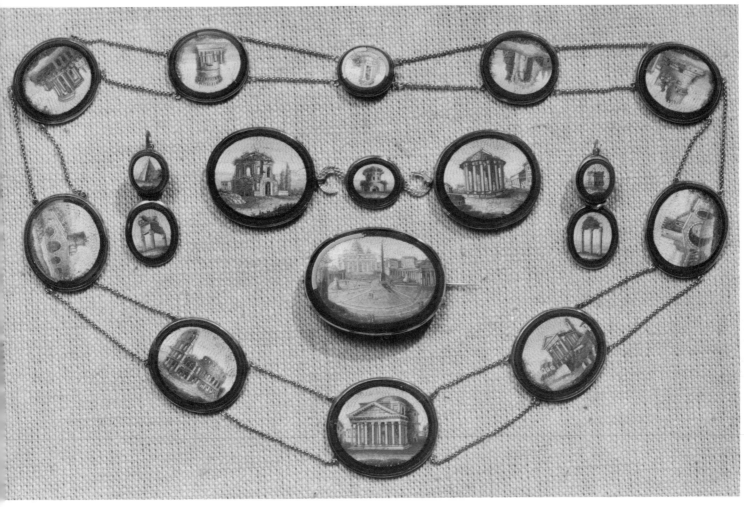

Plate 82. A Roman mosaic parure comprising a necklace of units linked by gold chains, top and drop earrings, brooch and belt clasp with two hooks as fastenings. The micromosaics, all set in dark blue glass, represent architectural antiquities and views in and around Rome. St. Peter's Square decorates the brooch; the largest unit in the necklace shows the Pantheon without 'Bernini's donkey ears' which were only demolished in the early 1880s, demonstrating that the mosaicist used an engraving pre-dating Bernini's seventeenth century additions. The parure dates to about 1800-10 and the construction of the belt clasp relates to the piece worn by Lady Maria Hamilton in Plate 81. PRIVATE COLLECTION

round the neck and across the bodice.[78] The fashion correspondent of the *Belle Assemblée* gave a detailed description of a toilette seen at a reception in 1807 which included a gold watch, with a delicate matted and polished gold chain, 'finished at the swivel with an oval cornelian; from whence is suspended six most elegant small seals of the same, variously shaded, with a curious key of wrought gold, finished with a brilliant in the centre. The devices engraved on these seals render this an ornament of much interest; they are entitled: ''Cupid's Progress''!' The interest, it was explained, derived from their authorship. The designs had been made by Princess Elizabeth 'some time since'.[79]

Chatelaines went out of fashion soon after 1800 and the example in Colour Plate 31B, which is probably Swiss, commemorates the passing of the vogue which was inevitably resuscitated decades later.

Many late-eighteenth century patterns for rings continued into the new century, to judge by the Garrard Ledgers. The short entries nevertheless make it difficult to chart the introduction and spread of heavier forms and decorative details such

Colour Plate 36. A. A gold locket encircled by a serpent grasping its tail in its mouth to symbolise eternity. In the centre is a composition in enamelled gold set on a plaited hair ground representing a drooping rose bush abandoned by a butterfly, surrounded by two inscriptions reserved on white enamel: LA. ROSE. FLETRIE. LE. PAPILLON. S' ENVOLE, *which exactly describes the composition, and* NAPPED. IT. FELL. TO. THE. GROUND. *Is this the expression of a misfortune in love or of mourning for, say, a child? The theme reverses a current sentimental theme recorded in Knight's* Gems and Device Book *(1836): see Plate 77. The back of the locket is engraved:* And such I exclaim'd is the pitiless part, Some art by the delicate Mind, Regardless of Wringing and Breaking a Heart, Already to sorrow resigned. *There are no accompanying details in the form of a name or a date, but the locket was probably made in about 1815-20.*
B. An enamelled gold mourning locket, the blue border inside the frame bears the inscription: LOUISA. BOHUN. OB. 14 APR: 1816. AET: 18. *The miniature of a girl in Elizabethan costume is probably of the dead girl. On the reverse an inscription records another member of the family to die young:* FRANCES: BOHUN: OB. 1 AUG: 1816: AET: 15. *The locket must have been made shortly after the death of the latter.* VICTORIA AND ALBERT MUSEUM

as chased rococo borders, which appear to have caught on between 1810 and 1820. Gothic lettering spread into commemorative inscriptions after 1800. A black-enamelled mourning ring in the Royal Collection has a large serpentine bezel cut with the initials of the celebrated Duchess of Devonshire in gothic letters below a ducal coronet.[80] The date of her death in 1806 is rendered in italic script much as in the commemorative piece in Colour Plate 31E which differs from the ring in giving her first name, Georgiana, in full.

Mourning rings with urn-shaped heads or other appropriate devices, suitably inscribed on the instructions of the client, were still the norm for private orders. Others commemorating well-known figures were often made as speculations for general sale, a practice of some antiquity. William Tassie, the nephew of James, mentioned in a letter to Alexander Wilson at Glasgow which was written towards the end of 1805 that he and his staff had been busy turning out small cameo heads of Nelson. The heads had been ordered by jewellers anxious to set them in rings

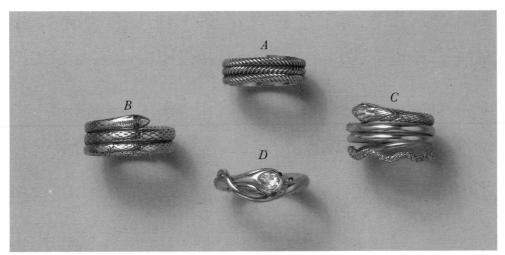

Colour Plate 37. A. A carnation spray brooch with a carved shell blossom, gold stamens and garnet centre on a gold stem and leaves, an early Victorian manifestation of the passion for naturalism which began to burgeon in the early years of the nineteenth century; c.1840.

B. A gold handkerchief brooch inspired by the comet appearing in 1811; decorated with chased scrolls, the head is set with a garnet and the tail with a tiny emerald. This specimen probably dates to about 1811-20, but comet pins remained in fashion into the 1830s and probably beyond (see Plate 104).

C. A tiny gold heart set with a miniature of King Louis XVIII under rock crystal; on the reverse, the legend fidelité *painted within a wreath, also under crystal. It might have been worn secretly by a legitimist during the First Empire or openly, perhaps as a pendant to a bracelet or as one of a group of charms, after the restoration of the Bourbon monarchy in 1814.*

D. A handkerchief brooch ('pin') of gold and foil-set garnets bordering a rock-crystal panel mounted over hair, edged by half-pearls; the stones are in cut-down closed settings; c.1805.

PRIVATE COLLECTION

Colour Plate 38. Four gold serpent rings.

A. A ring with three chased coils but no snake head. It is possibly English work of the early nineteenth century.

B. This is said to have been a favourite ring of King George IV, who might have been wearing it when he was painted, seated on a sofa, by Sir Thomas Lawrence in 1822. The portrait is now in the Wallace Collection. The ring has three coils and the serpent head is set with ruby eyes.

C. A ring with four turns, based more closely than the others on classical prototypes. It was in fact purchased by the South Kensington Museum from the sale of Alessandro Castellani's effects in 1884 as an antique Roman ring, but it now appears more likely that it was made in Rome by his family firm in the mid-nineteenth century.

D. A single coiled ring with ruby eyes and a diamond set in the top of the head; it is probably English, mid-nineteenth century.

VICTORIA AND ALBERT MUSEUM

and brooches as souvenirs of the dead hero. Nelson's discarded wife herself acquired from Tassie 'three of the small heads on cornelian for brooches'.[81]

'Magic pattern' rings are noted in the Garrard Ledgers with no amplifying details, but Goetze's account book contains entries for 'magic rings' in coloured gold with between two and four 'turns', sometimes with the addition of knurled decoration, occasionally with a snake head fitted to contain hair. They were made between 1810 and 1813. Goetze also produced other serpent rings, including 'a double Snake Ring Color'd with Glass for Hair' executed for Wirgman in July

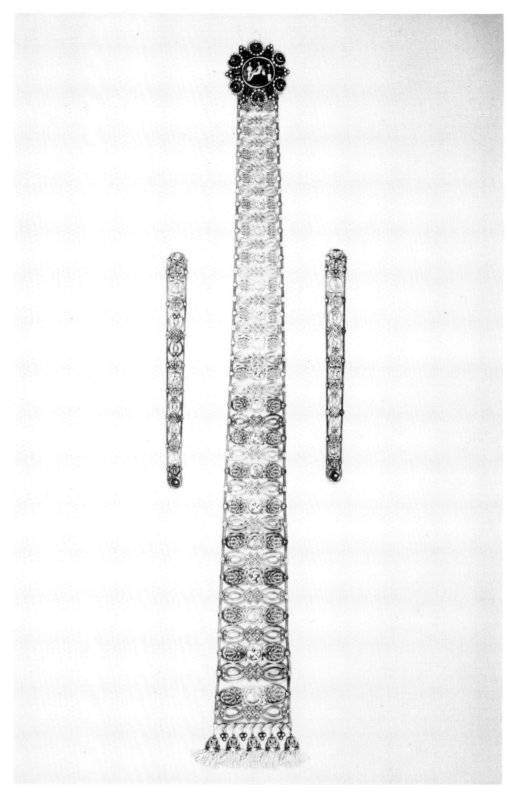

Plate 83. Marie-Louise's gothic girdle ornament in gold openwork decorated with pearls and with a rosette set with an antique onyx cameo depicting Apollo and his mother Leto in a frame of sardonyx and pearls; it cost 10,540.07 francs. The goldwork bears the maker's mark L beneath a laurel spray; the fitted case is stamped: M.E. NITOT ET FILS A PARIS; 1813. *The gothic element largely consists of a running pattern of inverted trefoils at the bottom of the girdle fall; the Napoleonic bee appears at intervals along its length. The ornament was bequeathed by the Empress Marie-Louise in 1847 to the wife of the 11th Earl of Westmorland, a friend who lived at Parma and Florence from 1815 to 1830. 32 ¾ in. (83cm) long.*

PHOTOGRAPH: CHRISTIE'S

1809. It cost 16s.6d. to make and the charge to Wirgman was £1.11s.6d. The Prince of Wales, Wirgman's principal patron, was fond of serpent rings and an example in Colour Plate 38B is said to have belonged to him.

Goetze turned out other types of ring. Motto rings figure in his account book, as do chased leaf rings with polished edges to match lockets and brooches similarly decorated, so they must have been intended for female use. 'Dom'd rings' are also cited and more rarely, 'hand in hand rings', tokens of affection dating back to Roman times. Antique examples were designated *fede* rings (*mani in fede*, hands clasped in faith).[82] Some were garnished by Goetze with double hearts and secret compartments for hair; the combined hands and heart motif appear in medieval rings. He also made cable cord and 'fall down' rings and, exceptionally, 'a small Heart & Padlock' to hang on a ring.

Some categories of ring were worn by men and women alike, differing only in their dimensions. Others were specifically designed for one sex. On the evidence of the Garrard Ledgers, diamond hoops and half-hoops were the most popular gifts from a bridegroom to his bride. In 1816 one client bought a diamond ring for £58, a ruby one for £18.18s., an emerald specimen for £23.2s. and a 'plain Gold Hoop Ring' for 11s. Bridal and otherwise, gem-set half-hoop rings generally had a head of rectangular (or shaped rectangular) outline joined by solid or split shoulders to a shank sometimes decorated with a few neo-classical details such as consoles. Gem-set clusters were executed for females and probably also examples with heads in the form of crosses or flowers. Cameos and intaglios in Roman settings were common to both sexes, as were probably 'Union', 'puzzle' and buckle rings. In June 1812 the Prince Regent acquired from Rundell's two rings, four brooches and two lockets set with ivory cameos. The subjects are not described in the bill but they might have been portraits of the Regent himself; the firm set an ivory cameo likeness of the Prince in a gold frame a fortnight later. The two rings were mounted for a total charge of £9.9s., but the ivory cameos were probably excluded from the cost.[83] Rings with engraved gems were still widespread.

In January 1816 Lord Mornington had a small medal set by Garrard's craftsmen in a diamond ring. This device was probably inspired by a set of rings mounted with medallion portraits of Napoleon which had been made in France two years earlier to commemorate his escape from Elba. Different loyalties found analogous expression. The French legitimists, for instance, wore rings and lockets (Colour Plate 37C) bearing the likeness of Louis XVIII or a loyalist motto.[84]

Following the dictates of fashion, women varied the number of decorative rings they wore. In 1808 the *Belle Assemblée* reported that three or four rings were worn on the little finger. 'They consist of a simple gold hoop, with a small stone in the centre of each, of the diamond, ruby, emerald and amethyst. The rainbow hoop-ring, formed in similar variety, takes place of the diamond, by way of guard to the wedding ring.'[85] It is clear that the gem-set ring was the guard and not the wedding ring itself; Queen Charlotte's diamond hoop was also denominated a guard ring.[86]

Madame de Senonnes, painted by J.-A.-D. Ingres in 1814-16, was the incarnation of current French fashion, wearing about thirteen rings distributed over the first and third fingers of both hands, with one on the middle finger of the left hand.[87] Inevitably a reaction set in; the fashion correspondent of *Ackermann's Repository* declared in 1817 that rings, which had been 'little worn' for some time past, 'begin to be in request'.[88]

The range of male jewellery was in a state of flux during the first two decades of the century. The production of shoe buckles further diminished, as did that of breeches buckles when long trousers began to replace breeches except in formal and sporting costume. But some manufacturers still found a market for their wares. A pair of silver shoe buckles from Edward Thomason's factory dates to about 1806 (Plate 84). A silver stock buckle cost one of Garrard's clients 12s. in December 1815 and a pair of knee buckles, which were much smaller, went to another purchaser in 1802 for 5s. Garrard's sold many similar specimens, some in gold, but probably not on quite the same scale as before. Stock or cravat pins, on the other hand, were in the ascendant.

Gentlemen still suspended seals in clusters or singletons on chains from their waists. The mounts of seals, heavily gadrooned in the neo-classical manner or deeply chased in the second decade of the century with the scrolls and flowers of the revived rococo, might also be as fanciful as those affected by ladies and have bows or handles in the form of animals and birds. Lord Fitzroy Somerset bought a 'chased gold squirrel seal' with the head of Raleigh engraved in bloodstone from Garrard's in 1814; it cost £4. A contemporary piece, a carnelian seal engraved with a head after Botticelli, is in the Victoria and Albert Museum; its bloodstone handle is carved in the form of a parrot.[89] The museum piece was designed for a desk, but other animal seals were fitted with loops for attachment to a chain. Lyre and stirrup handles were, however, more general. One of Garrard's clients bought a bright chased gold seal in July 1817 and had the motto *Pensez à Moi* engraved on it, so it was probably intended as a present to a lady. The Ledgers naturally do not enter into domestic details of this kind. The fact that men wore lockets and portrait medallions has already been mentioned. Byron, after a violent but abortive flirtation with Lady Frances Webster, was left in October 1813 with 'foolish trophies (foolish indeed without victory), such as epistles, and lockets...'[90] An unhappy lady in Brussels, who had given her portrait in a medallion or locket to her admirer, a young Englishman killed at Waterloo, was said to have had it returned 'almost shivered to pieces', for he had worn it round his neck in battle.[91]

Watch-chains in gold, silver, steel and brass came in various patterns. A clerical client of Garrard's took possession in 1809 of a 'very strong fetter link' specimen but curb chains were also popular. The long chains slung around the neck, to which were attached watches or eye-glasses, were somewhat slighter. The watches were sometimes pocketed, the eye-glasses often left dangling. Thackeray's partly autobiographical novel, *Pendennis* (1848-50), contains a description of the eponymous hero's uncle, the Major, whose taste was formed during the Regency, looking over his letters 'through his gold double eye-glass'.[92] At his age, he probably resorted to the eye-glass out of necessity, but both men and women were accused of affecting it as a costume accessory. For this purpose, yards of chain were consumed.

Plate 84. A pair of silver shoe buckles of about 1806 from the factory of Edward Thomason in Church Street, Birmingham. The open frames are decorated with beading and applied pellets. They have no chapes, and it is possible that they were originally supplied with inserts with their own fastenings. Thomason, the son of a buckle-maker, was apprenticed to Matthew Boulton. A colourful character, he nurtured ambitions to rival Rundell's once he had started to run his own business but never succeeded in attracting all the royal commissions he would have liked. However he prospered and became the first Knight of the Birmingham trades, an honour bestowed by William IV in 1832. Retiring from business in 1844, he published his Memoirs during Half a Century *the following year.*

In 1819, the Garrard Ledgers record Colonel Hanbury's purchase of '2 Color^d Gold Pins with a chain to them' for £1.4s. If these were intended to fasten a cravat, they are an early example of a type still fashionable in the late 1830s. Many cravat or stock pins were set with stones. But, however glittering, they were easily outshone by the insignia of the orders of chivalry and other decorations. The recipients of civil honours were occasionally tempted to commission badges of great splendour, more costly than they could well afford, to enable them to compete with the great military and naval figures on formal occasions. In 1811 the diarist Joseph Farington recorded that Lord Wellesley, the eldest brother of the future Duke of Wellington, was in trouble over a diamond-set Badge of the Garter which he had commissioned from Rundell's without actually being able to pay for it. The firm refused to hand it over until they had received £2,000. George Fox of Rundell's held that Wellesley had commissioned a full set of insignia together with a diamond epaulette. He supplied most of the stones himself from articles presented to him in India, but Rundell's were at some expense in adding extra gems.[93]

Young bucks in England sported more jewels of a personal nature than some of their contemporaries. Byron, encountering Lord Blessington in Italy in 1823, found him much changed from the young man he remembered from some ten years earlier, 'in all the glory of gems and snuff-boxes...'[94] Even the most showy of Englishmen was easily outshone by his contemporaries on the Continent. Earrings went irrevocably down the social scale and were mainly confined to male servants and peasants.[95] Necklaces were another matter. Lady Shelley, who found the Hungarian noblemen at the Viennese Court a dazzling sight in 1816, observed Count Palffy wearing a turquoise and diamond necklace which he had flaunted in Paris the year before; it had struck her then as 'extremely ridiculous in a man', but she had never seen turquoises so large. The Count told her that he had spent a lifetime amassing the stones. She learned afterwards that he had been almost ruined by speculating in the theatre. Metternich and other friends paid his debts and kept the necklace as security, permitting the Count to borrow it on special occasions.[96]

Palffy was in turn overshadowed by Prince Pál Esterházy,[97] who had taken up his post as Ambassador to the Court of St. James in 1815 and, back in Vienna for his Emperor's marriage,[98] impressed Lady Shelley with his costume of an officer in the Hungarian *Garde-noble*. His uniform was of scarlet cloth, embroidered from head to foot with pearls. 'The tops of his yellow boots, and his spurs, were set with diamonds. His cloak, lined with the finest fur, was fastened with a magnificent cluster of diamonds, so also were the belt, sword-knot, the handle and scabbard of his sword. A heron's feather and aigrette of diamonds rose from his fur cap, whose loops, like his sabre-tache, were of pearls and diamonds. He and others told me that his dress that day was worth more than one million pounds sterling, and yet he had not on his person more than a quarter of the family diamonds, which have been collecting for centuries. The head of the family is obliged to lay out a certain sum every year on jewels.'[99]

Children's jewellery is frequently cited in diaries and letters and very occasionally appears in the Garrard Ledgers, most notably in the form of a 'fancy Gold Neckchain for a Child' costing £10.10s., which was supplied to Mr T. Parker in 1817. No further information is vouchsafed in the Ledger, but this is true of most references to children's jewellery. It was probably still a mixture of scaled-down versions of fashionable adult jewellery designed to be worn by the child, such as coral necklaces, and full-size pieces intended to be kept for adulthood. Betsey Fremantle recorded on 14 May, 1805 that her children Tom and Emma, summoned to the Queen's House by Princess Sophia,[100] were exhibited to the Queen before departing with presents from the Princess which included a necklace for Emma. A fortnight later they returned and saw the King, the Queen, the Princesses and Princess Charlotte of Wales.[101] 'The Queen,' wrote Mrs Fremantle, 'gave Emma an Acqua Marine Broach.' Boys normally received watches. The country parson William Holland, dining with one Mr Mathew, who took in pupils, noted that some of the parents were very prosperous and that one of them had presented Mathew's son with 'an excellent Silver Watch worth eight guineas' [£8.8s.].[102]

Small girls still had to be bribed to undergo the ordeal of having their ears pierced, an operation sensitively recorded by Sir David Wilkie (Plate 155). In old age, Lady Login described her experiences to her daughter. Her father, who had married in Edinburgh in 1804, insisted that his daughters wear earrings. He bore off the future Lady Login, then aged three, and her five year old sister to a jeweller in Perth named Browne. They submitted to Browne's ministrations on the promise of simple pearl earrings.[103] In 1816, Ellen Brown, the nine year old daughter of an Englishman who had flourished in India, appeared at her parents' parties in finery which included a gold chain and heart, trinkets which might equally have graced a grown woman.[104] There was however no need for her to have elaborate ornaments for the coiffure such as were given to Princess Charlotte of Wales.

The examples of jewellery culled from the Garrard Ledgers were often set with stones furnished by the customer in traditional manner. This usually meant that old items of jewellery were dismantled for the purpose, the melt value of the discarded settings being set against the cost of re-mounting. Mr Philip Howard, for instance, had his bill for two carnelians mounted as brooches and for repairs to other jewellery abated by 6s. in 1804 on account of 'old Settings'. Jane Austen, an acute observer of contemporary customs, was exactly right in sending her heroine Miss Dashwood to Gray's with a similar purpose in mind (see page 113).

Plate 85. A detail from George IV's coronation circlet of 1820 by Rundell's, showing one of the sprays of patriotic motifs representing the United Kingdom.
ROYAL COLLECTION

CHAPTER V
The Impact of Regal Splendour, 1821-1836

George IV had waited a long time to succeed to the throne, and during his father's declining years he had ample opportunity to consider the celebration of his own coronation. He hated black and as soon as possible after his accession in January 1820 he cut short the period of mourning for his father on the grounds of its harmful repercussions on trade.[1] The date of the coronation was at first fixed for August 1820. Rundell's completed the first part of the work on the ornaments required by the new monarch in May, little more than three months after George III's death. The firm's bill, dated 6 May, itemises an 'elaborate Brilliant Sword of State', the hilt and scabbard set with diamonds and coloured stones and a belt clasp to correspond, three diamond heron's feathers for the King's Cap of State, the diamond and pearl circlet already mentioned (Plate 35), and a diamond loop, which was presumably a more elaborate version of the one acquired from the Royal Goldsmiths in 1811. The circlet and loop together cost £8,216, the King being charged £7,126; of the balance of £1,090, which was debited to the 'Public Account', £290 represented the cost of setting and £800 the charge made for the loan of diamonds, it being customary for stones to be hired for decorating the regalia at each coronation.[2]

The coronation was postponed after the King's wife, Queen Caroline, returned to England in June 1820 from a long stay on the Continent, where her scandalous behaviour persuaded the King that he might at last be able to divorce her. The 'Trial of Queen Caroline' evoked widespread demonstrations of support for her[3] which were inspired less by belief in her innocence than by dislike of the King and his Tory government. His government's decision to abandon the proceedings was a grievous blow to George IV, who was haunted thereafter by the fear that his wife would try to take part in the coronation ceremony, now scheduled for 19 July 1821. He nevertheless made no change in the elaborate and costly arrangements for his coronation day, which was to start with the traditional walking procession from Westminster Hall to the Abbey.

The jewels listed in Rundell's bill of 6 May were designed to be worn by the King at various stages during the day. The jewelled feathers, traditional aigrettes, clasped plumes of real feathers on a black Spanish hat and the loop decorated its front. The most elaborate piece, the circlet, was placed over the hat as a particularly splendid hatband. The aigrettes and loop have disappeared; only the circlet has been preserved in a recognisable state. Permanently set with brilliants, its cresting of crosses pattée alternating with sprays of a rose, thistle and shamrock (Plate 85), patriotic motifs emblematic of the United Kingdom (Wales, as a principality, was not represented)[4] made it a favourite head ornament of queens regnant and consort.

Plate 86. George IV in his coronation robes, wearing the collars of the Golden Fleece, the Guelphic Order, the Bath and the Garter. The portrait was painted by Sir Thomas Lawrence for the King, apparently towards the end of 1821. George IV's right hand touches the table on which rests his new Crown. July 19 1821, the coronation day, was extremely hot and the King was exhausted by the heat and the weight of his apparel. ROYAL COLLECTION

George Fox of Rundell's held that George IV had had the circlet made in order that his new favourite, Lady Conyngham, might wear it after the coronation.[5] Though he was probably retailing a rumour current at the time, there was a tradition, probably originated by William III in 1689, of a male sovereign processing to his coronation in a circlet. It is, however, indisputable that circlets of the shape made by Rundell's for the King were fashionable female wear in England in 1820.

Clad in his finery and jewels and wearing an elaborate wig under his Spanish hat, George IV made a stunning entrance in Westminster Hall on his coronation day. The painter B.R. Haydon, there to watch the pageantry, declared that the monarch in his splendour 'showed like some gorgeous bird of the east' as he gracefully acknowledged the presence of the nobles and dignitaries present.[6] While the procession was forming, Sir Walter Scott, one of George IV's favourite poets and novelists,[7] awaited the King's arrival in the Abbey. Scott charged himself with the task of justifying the immense cost of the whole occasion. In his description of the ceremony, first published by a newspaper owned by his associate, Ballantyne, Scott argued that the 'expense, so far as it is national, has gone directly and instantly to the encouragement of the British manufacturer and mechanic'.[8]

The chief beneficiaries in terms of jewellery and ornaments were of course the Royal Goldsmiths, whose principal, Philip Rundell, left a fortune of almost

Plate 87. The frame of George IV's new crown, designed by Philip Liebart and set at Rundell's in 1820, mainly with diamonds hired out by the firm, supplemented by stones which had belonged to the King's mother Queen Charlotte. The stones, which may have included the Arcot diamonds, were finally broken out of the frame in 1823. EX-COLLECTION OF LORD AMHERST OF HACKNEY

Plate 87A. Detail of the silver setting, showing the open-backed cut-down collets of silver lined with gold and the concave gold edges of the band on which pearls were threaded.
EX-COLLECTION OF LORD AMHERST OF HACKNEY

£1,500,000 on his death six years later. The costumes of the major participants in the pageantry, specially designed in the Elizabethan mode and including blue and white satin outfits with puffed trunks for certain Privy Councillors, had filled some people with foreboding. Yet on the day the men wearing them 'seemed not at all ludicrous, but blended perfectly into the corporate magnificence', Sir Walter Scott was relieved to note.[9] The King was crowned with a new crown designed by Liebart of Rundell's. The first Crown in the English regalia fully to be set transparent (Plates 86 and 87), it contained some of his mother's personal stones (Plate 88) as well as hired diamonds which were retained, with the government's grudging assent, until 1823.[10]

Critical observers at George IV's coronation, including the Duke of Wellington's friend, Mrs Arbuthnot, saw the King ogling Lady Conyngham throughout the ceremony. Once, noted Mrs Arbuthnot censoriously, he 'took a diamond brooch from his breast &, looking at her, kissed it, on which she took off her glove & kissed a ring she had on!!!'[11] Lady Cowper, who observed that Lady Conyngham was flaunting the Stuart Sapphire given her in May 1820 by her royal admirer (see Colour Plate 19),[12] claimed to be seated in the line of fire between her monarch and his beloved. As he exchanged glances with Lady Conyngham, she wrote, the King kissed his coronation ring. Lady Cowper conjectured that he meant to give the ring to his favourite to keep company with the sapphire;[13] in fact, the ring appears in a list of George IV's jewellery compiled after his death

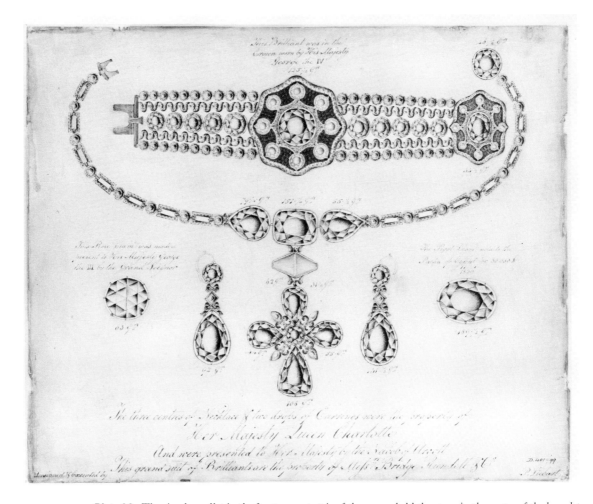

Plate 88. *The circular collet in the front cross-pattée of the crown held the stone in the centre of the bracelet forming part of a 'Grand suit of Brilliants' designed by Liebart in about 1831 as a vehicle for the seven Arcot diamonds and other stones once owned by Queen Charlotte. They were all her 'personals', that is, jewels which she regarded her own rather than Crown Jewels, and on her death in 1818 she left instructions that they be sold for the benefit of several of her daughters. As George IV appropriated all his mother's jewellery, the provisions of her will were only executed after his death in 1830. No customers were forthcoming for the jewels although approaches were made to the principal European Courts. John Bridge the elder then bought the important stones, the minor ones being either distributed among the beneficiaries or sold by auction at their direction. Rundell's chose the latter method to dispose of the Arcot diamonds in 1837. Liebart's suite may never have been made up, his drawing only being shown to prospective customers. This is a copy by another member of the firm, who added two stones, an oval rose-cut diamond presented to George III by the Sultan of Turkey and the notorious Pigot diamond which Rundell's had attempted to sell to Napoleon in 1804.* VICTORIA AND ALBERT MUSEUM, PRINT ROOM

in 1830. Prince Esterházy, perhaps out of consideration for the King, wore only some £80,000 worth of jewellery at the ceremony.[14] The Duchess of Wellington resolutely refused to add to the general glitter: she chose carnelian ornaments instead of diamonds because of the distressed state of the country at large.[15]

The King's fears that his wife Caroline might try to force her way into Westminster Hall or the Abbey on his coronation day were borne out by the event: she made the attempt, but was refused admission, as Farington noted.[16] Caroline died the following month. Scandal followed her even in death; Thomas Creevey reported that she had proposed leaving her diamonds to the eldest daughter of her Italian Chamberlain, Pergami, the man widely believed to have been her lover.[17] The bequest is unlikely to have been honoured, for the Duke of York told Greville

Plate 89. Lady Elizabeth Conyngham with her harp, painted by Sir Thomas Lawrence in 1824. Dressed simply in white, Lady Elizabeth seems an open, eager young girl. Her jewellery is not on the whole ostentatious, consisting of a single row of pearls with a jewelled clasp in front, a bow brooch with a pearl drop, two gold bracelets with gem-set clasps and two rings on her right hand. But her large belt-buckle is adorned with diamonds. Lady Elizabeth became the Marchioness of Huntly.

CALOUSTE GULBENKIAN FOUNDATION MUSEUM, LISBON

in January 1823 that his brother had appropriated to his own use all the jewellery left by his parents and his wife.[18]

George IV made no effort to remarry and Lady Conyngham reigned supreme for the rest of his life. Her husband, raised to the marquisate in 1816, was appointed Lord Steward of the Household in 1821 and Constable of Windsor Castle in 1829.[19] The King was generous to all the Conyngham family, lavishing quantities of jewellery on Lady Conyngham and her daughters. In August 1822 Creevey informed his step-daughter, Miss Ord, that the Privy Purse 'was exhausted by paying for diamonds for Lady Conyngham'.[20] The rivière of cushion-shaped brilliants in Colour Plate 39 is traditionally held by the Conyngham family to have been one such gift. In May 1821, observing that Lady Conyngham protected her reputation by never permitting her daughter, Elizabeth, to leave her side in the King's Pavilion at Brighton, Greville commented that the daughter, as well as the mother, had received 'magnificent presents' (see Plate 89), but that the pearls given to the older woman were particularly valuable.

Greville had been told by the Princess Lieven,[21] the uncomfortably acute wife of the Russian Ambassador, that 'she had seen the pearls of the Grand Duchesses [of Russia] and the Prussian Princesses, but had never seen any nearly so fine as Lady Conyngham's'.[22] The pearls must indeed have been striking, for in 1814 Lady Shelley cast a fascinated eye over the pearls worn to a London party by Tsar Alexander I's sister, the Grand Duchess of Oldenburg, and noted in her diary that they were 'the most magnificent...I ever saw — scattered all over her head in large bunches and drops. She wore a necklace of egg-shaped pearls of enormous size'.[23] Lady Cowper commented in May 1821 that the 'family pearls' of which Lady Conyngham had talked the previous year had increased remarkably.[24]

The splendour of Lady Conyngham's 'family pearls' was due to their having been removed by the King's command from his mother's jewellery. Even so, George IV bought further specimens from the Royal Goldsmiths, some of which were probably destined for her. In March 1820, Rundell's supplied the King with goods including a 'very fine large single row pearl necklace' containing forty-seven pearls and a diamond-set clasp for £780.5s. Each pearl, weighing eighteen and three-quarter grains, cost £15.15s. and the clasp £40, so that no extra charge was made for the workmanship. This necklace exceeded in price an emerald and diamond necklace and matching earrings costing £680.10s. which appear in the same bill; however the King almost certainly furnished some of the stones used.[25] The high price of superlative pearls at the time is demonstrated by an entry dated 26 April 1820 in another bill from Rundell's, for a 'fine and very large pearl drop undrill'd' costing £472.10s. and a pair of 'very fine pearl single drop earrings, with brilliant tops' priced at £577.10s.[26]

Orders for pearl jewellery continued to be executed at Rundell's for the King. 'A very capital and superb pearl Necklace consisting of 37 remarkably large Oriental Pearls' cost £3,534 including a brilliant clasp at £384.[27] Even excluding the clasp, each pearl would have been priced at under £100; if, however, the necklace was as superb as Rundell's maintained it must be assumed that the King supplied some of the pearls.

The Stuart Sapphire was set by Rundell's in May 1820 in the centre of an armlet which was described in their bill as a 'very large Brilliant and Sapphire Armlet to open at back, with rows of Brilliant collets round the Arm, and large scroll pattern Centre, one Sapphire and 2 Emerald drops added to the centre Broach & small Brilliants, Extra springs, etc'. The firm charged £183 for it, a modest sum considering that the Royal Goldsmiths had to dismantle Queen Charlotte's diamond and pearl bows to obtain the stones. The Stuart Sapphire was mounted in a border of sixteen diamonds as a detachable unit with springs (and probably) screw fittings. Also ambitious enough for a royal favourite was an opal and diamond suite acquired by the King from Rundell's in May 1821. Comprising a necklace costing £1,567.14s.6d., earrings at £236 and two combs, one for the back of the head at £612 and the other, larger (presumably a tiara-comb), 'to suit for front of the Head', priced at £1,014, the set cost £3,429.14s.6d. in all; a pair of bracelets and subsequent enlargements were charged at £534.[28]

It cannot be claimed that everything purchased by the King found its way on to the ample form of Lady Conyngham or the slighter figures of her daughters. George IV did not neglect his obligations to relatives and to members of his household; these, together with the normal diplomatic exchanges of gifts, naturally required a steady supply of articles from his jewellers. A bill of 4 June 1821 from Thomas Hamlet of Leicester Square, a goldsmith and jeweller whose Shakespearean name conceals the fact that he was a natural son of the notorious Sir John Dashwood,[29] is marked 'His Majesty for the Coronation'. It includes several items with national or royal connotations, such as an 'Enamell Garter Ring' with the initials GR and a crown of diamonds, costing £18.18s., a 'Rich Diamond Garter Broch' at £52, and a 'Gold Enamell British Badge' at £6.16s.6d. and matching ring at £4.4s., two 'Chas'd Gold and Enamell Harp' brooches, one

Plate 90. Photographs of studies of jewellery by Hans Holbein the younger (1497/8-1543), Court painter to Henry VIII, in the Print Room of the British Museum. The drawings were repeatedly pillaged for ideas by nineteenth century jewellery designers and Holbein's name was borrowed in the 1850s and later for a range of work in the Renaissance style (see Colour Plate 107B).

at £3.13s.6d. and the other costing £3.16s., 'Diamond Crown', which at £19.19s. can only have been a small trinket, and 'a Ring with Diamond Crown' costing £26.5s.[30] These were plainly intended as gifts to mark the occasion, as were sets of 'Coronation Ornaments' with 'globe' (Orb) devices, two of which included chains with necklaces 'representing the Collar of the Garter'. Usually comprising a necklace, earrings and brooch set with diamonds, pearls and a variety of coloured stones, four of these sets were supplied by Rundell's in the coronation year.[31] The duplication of types, especially of rings, pendants, brooches and lockets set with the King's likeness in engraved gems, enamel miniatures or in medallion form indicates a large number of recipients.

Outside this range George IV's lively interest in the fashionable and unusual was for a time allowed full play. In 1820, Rundell's made him three armlets, a necklace, and a bracelet on the theme of Shakespeare's Seven Ages of Man;[32] the tiny cluster of French pendants in Plate 79 is an earlier version of the same subject. Rundell's experiments in the gothic style are exemplified by items such as 'an elegant diamond and Ruby Ring, William of Wykham's pattern' (presumably based on the fourteenth century piece in New College, Oxford), acquired by the King for £19.19s. in 1821. In 1825 the firm executed two versions in jewelled gold of a pendant hung with George IV's cipher treated in the manner of Holbein (see Plate 90), as the Muss drawings in the Bridge album in the Metropolitan Museum, New York, make plain (Plate 91A and B). Both were given enamelled gothic chains. Late in 1824 the firm possibly also made a bracelet to Muss's design (Plate 91C), though the description in Rundell's bill is too cursory for the identification to be more than conjectural.[33]

A 'globe' brooch inspired by the Sovereign's Orb of 1661.

189

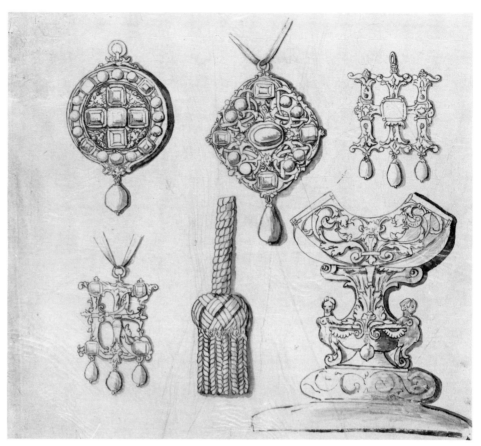

Plate 91A. A page from an album formerly owned by John Gawler Bridge, the nephew of John Bridge and himself a partner in the firm of Rundell, Bridge & Rundell. J.G. Bridge is known to have used the British Museum Print Room as a source of ideas and he clearly sent his staff artists there. This sheet of tracing paper is covered with ink and wash drawings (including floriated letters) after Holbein, probably made by Charles Muss between about 1820 and 1824.

George IV was infatuated with medievalism and bought other pieces in the style from Rundell's and other jewellers. Rundell's supplied him with 'A Ruby and Brilliant Gothic pattern' necklace with broad gold chain in September 1823 for £98.10s., with a matching bracelet at £69.6s.[34] The following year the firm sold him 'a gold enamelled gothic Cross' for £24.3s.[35] This pre-dates Pugin's enamelled medieval parure by more than twenty years (Colour Plate 83). In 1825, the King purchased from J. Benois of Paris (who is not mentioned by Vever in *La Bijouterie Française*) a bracelet 'au Corouzonne [sic] Gothique', decorated with unspecified medallions; it cost £10.[36] George IV had acquired in 1821 an elaborate gold chain and gem set medallion with a cross costing £204.15s. and described by Rundell's as 'pattern of Joan of Navarre'.[37] This may either refer to the late thirteenth century Queen of France and Navarre or to Henri IV's mother, who in 1569 dedicated her son to the Huguenot cause. The piece was thus either gothic or Renaissance in design, a matter of little concern in the first half of the nineteenth century when the medieval period was regarded as ending only in the early 1600s. But stylistic distinctions were already made. Thus in 1829 a client of Garrard's commissioned three figurative pieces built round a large pearl in the Renaissance manner.

George IV witnessed the beginnings of sporting jewellery; in 1822 he purchased from Rundell's a 'Dog's head shirt pin', an early documented example of the

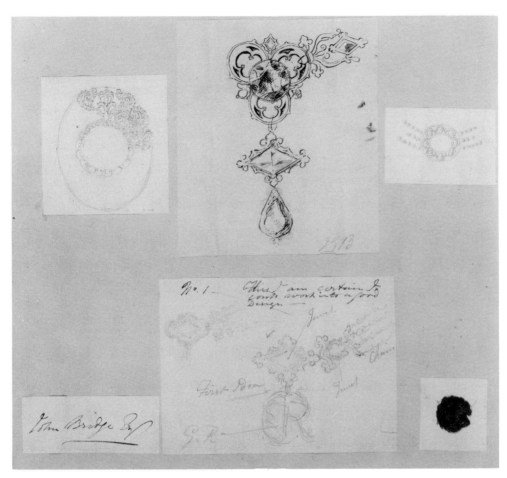

Plate 91B. Another page from Bridge's album. The pencil sketch marked No. 1, for a pendant with chain and drop formed of the cipher GR (for George IV) is annotated. 'This I am certain I could work into a good Design'. The drawing is also marked 'First Idea' and two settings for stones are noted. The pen drawing above, countersigned with the initials of J.G. Bridge, is probably another version. Bridge often signed the designs approved for production. The piece was certainly intended for presentation by the King but it appears only to have been executed in 1825. A bill submitted to the King by Rundell's includes an entry dated 28 April for 'an elegant chased gold Cypher G.R. as Medallion for the neck, set with Brilliants & Rubies, with Ruby & Pearl Drop', costing £245 and an enamelled gold chain for it, £54.1s. The same design was repeated in brilliants and rubies for £314, and an identical gold chain provided for the same price. The oval drawing on the left is in the manner of Petiteau.

genre costing £2.4s.[38] Further novelties came from other jewellers patronised by the King. E. & W. Smith of Maddox Street sold him in 1824 a chased gold bracelet with enamels representing the Swiss Cantons[39] which clearly had been imported (see a comparable article in Plate 207). Other pieces supplied by Smith include an enamelled Garter bracelet, demonstrating that bracelets (as well as rings and brooches) inspired by the Order of the Garter were very fashionable. The King, who might be termed a visual antiquarian, was little concerned with techniques. He bought platina chains but did nothing to encourage the further application of platinum to jewellery. He was, however, the recipient of the first chain to be made of a related material, palladium, which was presented to him by the metallurgist Percival Norton Johnson in 1826 (Plate 92).[40] However, George IV's visit to Ireland in 1821, followed by his appearance in Edinburgh resplendent in Scottish dress and accoutrements (Colour Plate 128), did much to promote the burgeoning production of Celtic revival jewellery which became an industry during the reign of his niece Victoria.

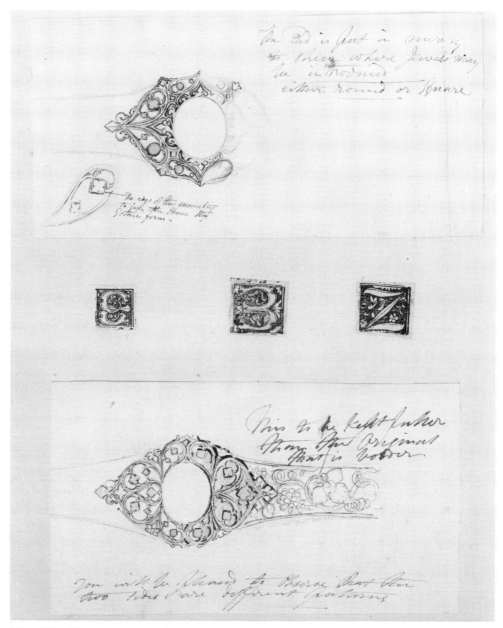

Plate 91C. Two more sketches from the Bridge album. Probably by Charles Muss, and executed in pencil, ink and red colour, they are variations of a bracelet centre or clasp in the gothic style. In the top drawing, the artist has been at pains to draw an enlarged detail of one of the mouchettes, *curved dagger-shaped motifs with gothic tracery, annotating it: 'The edge of the mounting to give the Stone the Gothic form'. The main drawing is annotated: 'The Red is put in merely to shew where Jewels may be introduced* either round or Square'. *The lower design affords two variations, as is pointed out at the bottom of the sheet, the left side of the bracelet centre being different from the right. A vigorous hand on the top right of this drawing has written: 'This is to be kept [?] darker than the Original that is bolder', a line from the inscription running to the band, which is decorated with scrolling vines perhaps copied from a medieval wood or stone carving. It may appear in the same bill from Rundell's against the date 24 November 1824, as 'a chased gold Bracelet with gold gothic Clasp set with Turquoise & Brilliants', costing £39.18s.*

METROPOLITAN MUSEUM OF ART, HARRIS BRISBANE DICK FUND, 1923 (23.68.1), *BRIDGE ALBUM, ff. 2, 29, 30.*

In 1822 Montague Levyson of Pall Mall sold the King a 'fine Gold filigree Waist clasp studded with Aquamarines'[41], perhaps an example of delicate *cannetille* and *grainti* imported from France. English jewellers were, however, perfectly capable of executing this work. Rundell's lengthened a 'Cantille' chain on another occasion for George IV. On the whole, however, they preferred bolder effects, exemplified by the cross in Plate 93; the amethysts mounted in gold openwork with shell and *grainti* decoration resemble the setting of the stones in the Durer Cup made by Rundell's for the King in 1827 (Plate 94).[42] Joseph Laurière furnished the King with a pair of 'long fillagree Gold Earrings set with Turcoises' at £1.11s.6d. in February 1821. Other articles purchased from Laurière in the same year included an 'Elastic pattern' chain bracelet, a sentimental piece costing £14.14s. in which the word 'Regard' was spelled in the usual fashion (see page 145).[43] In 1824 Hamlet sold the King another bracelet for £42; this was enamelled with the word 'Souvenir'.[44]

Some of George IV's acquisitions of sentimental jewellery probably went to Lady Conyngham, who by virtue of her husband's Irish origins may also have been the recipient of one of the harp brooches and rings acquired by the King in 1820 and 1821.[45] She must certainly have had the 'gold Giraffe Bracelet', for which no account survives but which was repaired by the Royal Goldsmiths in January 1830.[46] To the gratification of caricaturists the King and Lady Conyngham often visited the giraffe presented by the Pasha of Egypt which ailed its life away at Windsor from 1827 to 1829.[47]

The true extent of the jewellery given by the King to Lady Conyngham can only be hazarded, despite what is now known of his use of the Crown Jewels for her benefit. Sir Benjamin Bloomfield, the King's Private Secretary and Keeper of the Privy Purse from 1817 to 1822, whose handling of the Royal finances was believed by some of his contemporaries to be not above reproach, held that George IV expended about £1,000,000 on her jewellery.[48] A statement of the King's purchases from Rundell's alone between January 1821 and January 1829 amounts to £105,618.10s.4d. with an additional £5,732.17s.9d. for expenditure incurred in January 1830,[49] and though this sum includes plate as well as jewels it must be remembered that the jewellery set with the family stones was intrinsically far more valuable than the amount entered in the accounts. The King's cavalier redeployment of stones from his mother's jewellery created appalling problems for his successors, for Queen Charlotte left quite specific instructions about her jewels which had eventually to be implemented. Nevertheless, his last Private Secretary, in all but name, Sir William Knighton, was at pains to settle the King's bills.[50]

In 1830, when it became clear that the King would not live much longer, Lady Conyngham was popularly believed to have sent from Windsor two waggon-loads of plate and jewellery: 'First she packed, and then she prayed; and then she packed again'.[51] William Heath was responsible for the topical caricature in Colour Plate 40, 'The new Master of the Crown Inn discharging Betty the head Chamber maid' (in other words, William IV at Windsor seeing off Lady Conyngham, who clutches a casket under each arm, both spilling out with jewels). But she behaved better than her detractors were prepared to believe possible. She initially refused George IV's offer of a legacy of all his plate and jewels, made early in June when he learned he was dying. After he died (intestate), the Duke of Wellington, one of the King's executors, represented to Lady Conyngham that her royal admirer had given her pieces set with stones taken from the Crown Jewels. She relinquished

Plate 92. A massive ceremonial chain in palladium presented to King George IV by Percival Norton Johnson in 1826 and still preserved at Windsor Castle. It was offered through an intermediary, the King's surgeon Sir Astley Cooper, who was connected to Johnson by marriage. Cooper wrote on 25 June to Sir William Knighton, Keeper of the Privy Purse: 'Mr Johnson who is a great Metallurgist has a Chain of Palladium which is the only one which has ever been made, and which he wishes to present to our beloved Monarch'. Cooper added, 'From his taste and talent I believe his Majesty would be pleased to accept it — '. This proved to be the case. George IV was remarkably well-informed about modern developments when he chose to turn his mind to them, but he was disinclined to apply his knowledge to the furtherance of industry in the way that Prince Albert was to do later. ROYAL COLLECTION

Plate 93. *A pendent cross of gold wire filigree with shells and* grainti *ornament, set with amethysts. The setting is so similar to that in Plate 94 that it must be by Rundell's, c.1825-30.* VICTORIA AND ALBERT MUSEUM

Plate 94A. *A detail of the Durer cup in Plate 94, showing the setting of the stones. As in contemporary jewellery, the surface of the cup has polished areas contrasting with matting.* ROYAL COLLECTION

Plate 94. *This 'elegant chased silver gilt Cup after Albert Durer enriched with colored stones' was made by Rundell's for King George IV in 1827 and entered in a bill on 11 September; it cost £150. The artist responsible for sketching the original Durer drawing in the Print Room of the British Museum was A.W.N. Pugin, a youthful prodigy who had been spotted at his task by J.G. Bridge of Rundell's. Though startlingly precocious, Pugin had no technical knowledge then of either goldsmithing or gemsetting and it is probable that the decorative surround of the collets, executed in a bold filigree with* grainti *and shell terminals, was a standard setting used by the firm in other articles of jewellery. It is very like the goldwork of the cross in Plate 93. Note also the resemblance to the decoration of the shoulders of a bracelet in another illustration from Knight, reproduced in Chapter VII (Plate 129).* ROYAL COLLECTION

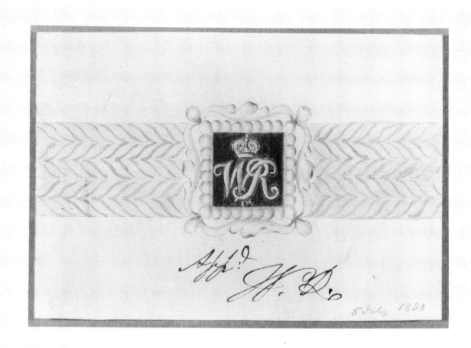

Plate 95. A design for a presentation bracelet submitted to William IV by John Bridge of Rundell's. It has a woven band and a centre bearing the crowned cipher of the King. Endorsed by the King, it must have been intended to mark his accession. But variations on the theme were produced by Rundell's for several years, often with different bands, as gifts from the King. A pair with solid bands went to Mrs Fitzherbert, for as William IV had established that she had gone through a marriage ceremony with his brother he gave her considerable sympathy and support. WORSHIPFUL COMPANY OF GOLDSMITHS

them, writing to the Duke in November 1830: 'I have reason to believe that I have in my possession some jewels presented me at different times upon Birth Days and the Coronation by the Late King, which it appears doubtful whether his Late Majesty ought to have given away...'. Lady Conyngham accordingly sent back the armlet, a pair of pearl earrings and other items six days later. Though William IV insisted on the Stuart Sapphire being returned to her,[52] it found its way back into Royal hands by 1838 (Colour Plate 19).[53]

William IV, while not a connoisseur of jewellery like his brother, patronised the Royal Goldsmiths to a greater extent than might have been expected of such a bluff, unpretentious man, and bought intermittently from several other concerns, some of which had held warrants from George IV. Among these were Joseph Kitching & Company, from whom William IV acquired a gold chain in 1834.[54] His Privy Purse accounts also show that he made regular provision for his brother's unacknowledged first wife, Mrs Fitzherbert.

The jewellery made for William IV and Queen Adelaide for presentation purposes largely conformed to conventional royal types, including portrait bracelets (Colour Plates 41 and 42). John Gawler Bridge of Rundell's was always at hand with special designs by the firm's artists. One, for a bracelet with the crowned cipher 'WR', was produced for the King shortly after his accession (Plate 95 and Colour Plate 43); the list of recipients accompanying the drawing includes the Duchess of Kent and her daughter, the future Queen Victoria, as well as William's surviving sisters and another sister-in-law. Variations of the original design were made on subsequent occasions.[55]

Plate 96. Sir David Wilkie's portrait of Queen Adelaide in coronation robes, painted in 1833. The Queen is depicted wearing her 'Grand Brilliant Diadem' with a crest of alternating crosses-pattée and fleurs-de-lis, mounted with diamonds from Queen Charlotte's stomacher, and three rows of the family pearls. One of her bracelets probably bears a miniature of King William IV. The Crown adumbrated on the table beside her had already been dismantled of the family stones set in it for the coronation. These may have included some or all of the Arcot diamonds.

ASHMOLEAN MUSEUM, DEPARTMENT OF WESTERN ART

Queen Adelaide bedecked herself with Crown Jewellery when occasion demanded, though she was not normally addicted to great personal displays of finery. The few new pieces made for her by the Royal Goldsmiths were mainly adorned with stones broken out of Queen Charlotte's jewellery. Diamonds from Charlotte's stomacher (Plate 3), and perhaps the Arcot diamonds, were temporarily set in Adelaide's crown in 1831 before being used for a new brilliant circlet with a crest of alternating crosses-pattée and fleurs-de-lis (the Grand or Regal diadem). With her Crown frame on a table beside her, the Queen posed in her coronation robes and new circlet to Sir David Wilkie in 1833 (Plate 96). The Queen also had a fringe necklace mounted in 1830 'with diamonds formerly the property of George III'[56]; convertible with stays into a ray tiara (Plate 156), it was much worn by Queen Victoria in the early years of her reign (Plates 157 and 180).

While George IV was still on the throne, his flair for fashion was rivalled by that of the Duchesse de Berri in Paris. In old age, to judge by the bills preserved in the Royal Archives, the King was no longer greatly interested in widening his circle of suppliers. He seems to have bought nothing, for instance, from Storr & Mortimer of New Bond Street, a concern which owed its existence to Paul Storr breaking his connection with Rundell's in 1819. Over the years, George IV had accumulated considerable debts to Rundell's, especially for plate. Though these were gradually settled by Knighton the King meanwhile was probably reluctant to offend the Royal Goldsmiths by patronising the new firm.

Plate 97. A gold brooch set with an emerald, turquoises and topazes; in the form of a basket of flowers. A naturalistic exercise in the revived Louis Quatorze (rococo) style, it was made in Paris in about 1830 and is struck with an unidentified maker's mark and the Paris warranty mark for 1819-1838.

VICTORIA AND ALBERT MUSEUM

The Duchesse de Berri had had less time to develop obligations to her principal goldsmiths. Following her husband's assassination in 1820 and the posthumous birth of her son (which was marked by the gift of a great spray of jewelled flowers[57]), the Duchesse devoted herself for the better part of ten years to consolidating her role as a leader of taste until she was forced from France by the Revolution of 1830. One of the new craftsmen to be patronised by the Duchesse was Fauconnier, the silversmith; his experiments in the revived Renaissance style were intended as a corrective to the prevailing French fashion for naturalism (Plate 97), a vogue which was partly blamed on English influence.[58] But whatever prompted Fauconnier to experiment with the Renaissance manner, the revival was in prospect ever since Schiller's drama, *Maria Stuart,* completed in 1800, captured popular imagination to the extent of influencing fashionable costume. It only needed the spark of antiquarian interest to bring the revival into being, and this was struck in several countries. In Schiller's native Germany the Renaissance style was a symbol of national identity during and after the Napoleonic Wars.

In 1814, when William Beckford was commissioning silverwork in the Renaissance style in England,[59] in Germany the Duchess Amalie August von Leuchtenberg was portrayed by Joseph Stieler in sixteenth century costume with an appropriate cross and chain round her neck.[60] Fourteen years later Lady Londonderry held a costume ball, at which she appeared as Queen Elizabeth I. In 1830 the *Belle Assemblée* published an engraving of her in costume, the contemporary lady clearly discernible behind the antiquarian facade. Her two necklaces and her earrings were modern in style, but the cartouche-shaped jewels embroidered or sewn on her bodice are a gesture to Renaissance design, a fashion for which, promoted by Rundell's, Garrard's and, probably, by other firms, had burgeoned during the 1820s.[61] The Mary Stuart quadrille organised by the Duchesse de Berri in January 1829 gave her the opportunity to have Crown Jewellery valued at over three million francs reset by Bapst for the occasion. A painting of the duchess by Dubois-Drahonnet shows her wearing a huge gem-set girdle with a long fall decorated in a style more reminiscent of the seventeenth than the sixteenth century, though it must be part of the jewellery mounted by Bapst.[62] The duchess's girdle, a clear development of the Bonaparte model, was none the less taken up and popularised as gothic, inspiring a host of cheaper versions.

Despite sheltering under the umbrella of medievalism Renaissance themes inspired several fantasies ordered by a client from Garrard's in 1829, in which two birds and a fish were each constructed around a baroque pearl. The ferronnière, a popular head ornament (Plate 98) introduced slightly before 1830, was inspired by the fillet worn by the so-called 'Belle Ferronnière' in the Louvre, a painting attributed to Leonardo. Renaissance inspiration is also evident in the moresques engraved on standard items of jewellery in the latter part of the 1830s and early seventeenth century influence in the widespread use of the lozenge, already extant in neo-classical design.

One of the jewellers patronised by the Duchesse de Berri was Franchet of Rue Vivienne, who was possibly only a retailer. He is said to have spent six months fitting up his shop to his satisfaction before opening his doors in about 1820[63] and was noted both for his courtesy and the elegance of his stock. Bernauda of the Quai des Orfèvres also supplied the duchess. He specialised in platinum, and platinum alloy jewellery with gold detailing, contributing specimens to the Paris National Exhibitions of 1823, 1827, 1834 and later. Many firms, including Rundell's and Garrard's, dealt in platinum jewellery to a small extent, but Bernauda was among the few who concentrated on these wares; in 1844 he even embellished some specimens with damascening.[64]

In late July 1830, little more than a month after the accession of William IV in England, revolution broke out in France after Charles X and his government revoked the Constitution granted by Louis XVIII in 1815. The King was forced to flee to England with his family. The liberal-minded Duc d'Orléans was elected King of the French on 9 August under the style of Louis-Philippe.[65] The new King and his Queen, Marie-Amélie conducted themselves in a manner more acceptable to the bourgeoisie than had Charles X, just as William IV and Queen Adelaide lived on a far more modest scale than George IV. Neither Louis-Philippe nor his wife wore the Crown Jewels. In 1832 their eldest daughter, Louise,[66] became the second wife of Princess Charlotte of Wales' widower, Prince Leopold of Saxe-Coburg, who had accepted the crown of Belgium the previous year.

The railway age had begun; a greater prosperity seemed in prospect. In England the passing of the Reform Bill in 1832 brought more representatives of the manufacturing and mercantile classes into the House of Commons to express their support for free trade. They were naturally anxious to gain as large a share as possible of world markets. But, though firmly convinced of English technological superiority, they were still anxious about the strong challenge offered by French manufacturers in particular. A number of influential Englishmen came to the conclusion that the general high quality of French design was largely due to the state-aided training schools which had been set up in France under the Directory with the encouragement of theorists and politicians led by Quatremère de Quincy.[67]

It appeared to many interested observers in England, who knew the French schools and similar institutions in Germany and elsewhere, that government aid

Plate 98. A sheet of engraved coiffures, c.1828-32. Six of the ladies are wearing ferronnières, one appears to have a tiara-comb and another comb behind, and one has a Spartan diadem or tiara-comb with leafage sprays issuing from a loop of hair, while the female in the middle of the lowest group has four gigantic pins stuck through her looped hair. The real hair must have been supplemented with gummed or lacquered false hair loops for these coiffures.

should be enlisted for this purpose in their own country. They were well aware that English manufacturers purchased or copied French designs, while those who could afford to do so enticed Continental artists and craftsmen to work for them. Some of the more articulate critics of contemporary English design voiced their views to the Select Committee on Arts and Manufactures which was appointed in 1835 on the motion of William Ewart, a man of radical and humanitarian views who represented a Liverpool constituency in Parliament.[68]

The Committee's brief was to 'inquire into the best means of extending a knowledge of the Arts and of the Principles of Design among the People (especially the Manufacturing Population) of the Country; also to enquire into the Constitution, Management and Effects of Institutions connected with the Arts...'. Evidence from manufacturers, retailers, architects, artists, designers, government officials and educationalists was taken in the 1835 session and again in 1836. The astonishing unanimity of opinion displayed by the majority of witnesses was probably a tribute to the care with which they had been selected. Almost to a man, they subscribed to the entrenched historicist approach to design, in some instances also conceding the value of natural forms as an alternative source of inspiration. Holding principles first enunciated in the Age of Reason, they asserted that good design was moral and bad immoral, attributing to the former 'purity of taste'[69], which can be construed as a scholarly appreciation of historic styles. 'Impure' or inaccurate styles were the outcome of bad training or ignorance.

Robert Butt, a manager of Howell & James of Regent Street, a general store with a jewellery department,[70] was the sole witness to discuss jewellery. He excepted plate, jewellery and ironwork from his general view that 'in metallic manufactures the French are vastly superior to us in matters of design'.[71] Butt admitted, however, that cheap French trinkets were flooding into England. He failed to point out that many well connected Englishwomen scarcely felt themselves married without going to Paris for their wedding clothes and jewellery. In 1836, when the Committee on Arts and Manufactures was preparing its final report, Lady Jersey[72] was put to the trouble of 'cancelling the orders for diamonds and chiffons' in Paris after the postponement of the marriage of her daughter Sarah and Prince Nicholas Esterházy.[73]

The Committee had only completed its first session when Parliament voted for the establishment in London of a Normal School of Design on the lines of existing Continental institutions. In its final report the Committee advocated that similar schools be founded in the provinces to serve local industries. Many regional schools were set up during the following decade with the support of local manufacturers, aided by government grants. The London and Birmingham schools, in particular, turned out a number of designers who were later employed in the jewellery trade.

The Committee endorsed the suggestion, made by several witnesses, that the protection of copyright be extended to manufactured goods.[74] The first Designs Act was passed in 1839 after another Select Committee had considered the question in detail. A further Act of 1842 replaced the serial numbers on copyright wares with lozenge-shaped Registry marks which remained in force until 1884,

Plate 99. A group of designs for jewellery from Knight's Fancy Ornaments *of 1834-5. Most reflect the influence of the baroque, bordering on rococo, with occasional touches of neo-classicism, but gothic quatrefoils are introduced into the brooch in the centre of the top row and into the two earrings on the right-hand side.*

when serial numbers were reintroduced (see Appendix I). The volumes of registered designs in the Public Record Office show that copyright facilities were mainly used by manufacturers of mass-produced jewellery. With a few exceptions, the great firms ignored the provisions. Among other recommendations, the Committee of Arts and Manufactures was concerned that the general standard of public taste, as well as that of designers and manufacturers, should be raised by the establishment of museums.

Witnesses to the Committee were obsessed by the need to bring a sense of order to the existing medley of revived styles. Viewed through their moral screen, rococo came off badly. As the architect J.B. Papworth explained in evidence in 1835, even the name ('Louis XIV') by which it was generally known, was erroneous: it was in fact the 'debased manner' of Louis XV, 'in which grotesque varieties are substituted for classic design'.[75] It was decades before the trade acknowledged any distinction between the baroque and rococo styles and began to assign them to the correct monarch.

Attacks of this kind had little immediate effect on the jewellery trade. Rococo designs figure prominently in a series of pattern books issued by the enterprising engraver, Frederick Knight, between 1825 and 1838. All were claimed to draw on

Plate 100. A pair of gold and chrysoprase earrings with a matching brooch. The shaped profiles of the earring drops, with their ogee arches and scallops below, bear some resemblance to the earring on the upper right-hand side of the plate in Knight (Plate 99). The moulded edges are polished and the ground bordering the stones matted; the tops are decorated with applied pellets and the drops with fleurets or conventional flower heads (see those in the brooch in the top row in Knight). The brooch, a quatrefoil set at an angle, is ornamented with alternating applied leaves and pellets. The set is probably English, dating to about 1828-30, when earrings had already started to lengthen.   S.J. PHILLIPS

international sources, but though some designs are reminiscent of French filigree,[76] suggesting that Rundell's and other great London firms were not long in essaying the techniques, there is a strong English flavour about most of the plates in Knight's *Scroll Ornaments* of about 1825, his *Unique Fancy Ornaments* of 1834-5 and his *Gems and Device Book* of 1828 (new edition 1836).

The first two publications contain designs ranging from gothic to neo-classical, taking in, besides rococo, the baroque and naturalistic styles (Plates 99 and 102). Neither pattern book is innovatory, and only rarely measures up to the high standard of antiquarian fidelity demanded by the Select Committee on Arts and Manufactures. The mixture of neo-classical with vigorous acanthus, rococo scrolls and gothic quatrefoils in Plate 99 bears comparison with pieces in Plate 100. The

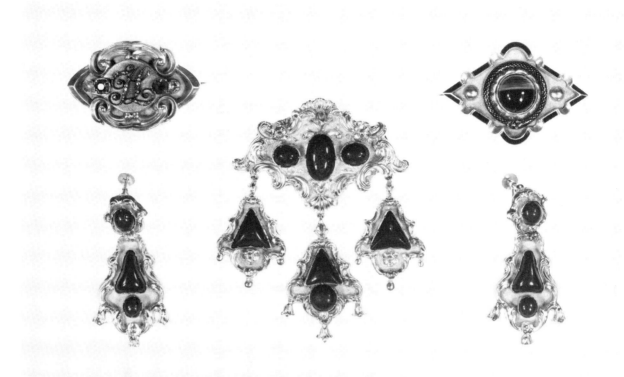

Plate 101. A bodice ornament and matching earrings in gold and porphyry, together with two mourning brooches. The brooch on the left, bearing the initials TL in diamonds, flanked by two diamonds and emeralds, commemorates T. Leyson, who died on 8 February 1838; an inscription on the back records another death, that of F. Lewes in 1795. That on the right, lozenge-shaped with a black enamelled edge and a cat's eye (a cabochon showing evidence of chatoyancy) in the centre, edged by the serpent of eternity, commemorates Mr N.W. Rothschild, who died on 28 July 1836; it appears to be one of six made by Garrard's for a total of £30. The set of bodice ornament and earrings is bordered by foliated scrolls of polished gold and the drops of the bodice brooch are also decorated with fleurets on a matted ground. The earrings have had screw fittings substituted for the original hooks. MUSEUM OF LONDON

curious twisted foliated terminals in the design for a pendant and cross in Plate 102 are echoed in the diamond specimen in Plate 103. The four narrow brooches or pins with tails flanking the pendant cross are comet brooches, possibly introduced in expectation of the reappearance of Halley's Comet in 1835-36 (an example is illustrated in Plate 104). Some of the plates are signed with the names of James Johnson, W. Donald and J. Page, but they may simply have been draughtsmen or engravers.

Knight's *Gems and Device Book,* a compilation of motifs, rebuses and inscriptions appropriate to the makers of sentimental jewellery, owes much to earlier authors and publishers including Samuel Fletcher, a seal engraver whose *Emblematical Devices* appeared in 1810.[77] The fanciful gothic in Knight's publications was anathema to antiquarians, and most particularly to A.W.N. Pugin,[78] the architect and designer, who by taking the Middle Ages seriously persuaded others to do likewise. He assailed the metalworkers of Birmingham and Sheffield ('those iniquitous mines of bad taste') for producing so-called gothic wares whose only connection with the style was 'a quatrefoil or acute arch' introduced haphazardly into the design.[79]

Many of Rundell's jewellery designers were probably recruited by J.G. Bridge. Muss has already been mentioned, but it is likely that a few of the firm's celebrated designers of silverwork also turned their hands to jewellery. The

Plate 102. Another page from Knight's Fancy Ornaments *of 1834-5, some of the designs adapted to stones on the left and to goldsmith's work on the right. The two tiny objects in the top row are probably ring heads; there are more below the head ornament. The four brooches with tails were inspired by comets (see Plate 104). The twisted foliated scroll ends of the cross are echoed by the example in Plate 103, while the earrings in Plate 101 share the complex structure of the two specimens in Knight.*

painter, Thomas Stothard, is said to have done so.[80] Pugin was discovered by J.G. Bridge copying old drawings and prints in the British Museum early in 1827 when he was only in his fifteenth year and was promptly engaged to design for Rundell's. Pugin's first executed effort was the Durer Cup adapted from a design he had copied in the museum. He cannot have been responsible for the settings of the stones on the cup nor for the amethyst pendant (Plates 93 and 94), for they are far from gothic.

In 1826 Rundell's former silversmith, Paul Storr, introduced a nephew by marriage, John Samuel Hunt, into his Bond Street firm. The concern was known as Mortimer & Hunt after Storr's retirement in 1838 until 1843, when Mortimer also retired.[81] Mortimer seems to have made periodic forays to Paris to survey the scene and pick up new ideas. Princess Lieven, now living in Paris, wrote to her friend Lady Cowper in 1838, complaining of poverty and declaring that she would have to sell her diamonds. She thought Storr & Mortimer worth approaching, as

Plate 104. A paste comet brooch, mounted in silver, lined with gold. Like the designs in Knight's Fancy Ornaments, *it may have been inspired by the sightings of a comet by Sir James South at Kensington and John Herapath at Cranford, Middlesex from 7-26 January 1831 which were reported in* The Times *on 15, 19, 20, 25 and 26 January or by the reappearance of Halley's comet in the mid-1830s.*

PRIVATE COLLECTION

Plate 103. A pendant-cross set mainly with brilliants with a few roses. Based on the Maltese cross or cross-pattée, the arms are widest at their terminals, the scrolls twisting at their ends into leaf forms which give the design a sense of nervous energy, as in the cross in Plate 102. CHRISTIE'S

'they always send one of their representatives to Paris every winter'.[82] One of these visits may have resulted in the recruitment of Joseph Julien Billois, who was responsible for setting up the firm's jewellery department. Billois, installed in 8 Queen Street, Soho in the 1820s, moved to Frith Street early in the following decade. The date of his retirement seems to be unknown though he was apparently succeeded by Adolphe Devin in the late 1830s. As an 'artist-jeweller of great skill and long experience', Billois was awarded a First-Class Medal as a collaborator by the jury of the Paris 1855 Exhibition.[83] Devin also had returned to Paris, there to design a head ornament for the Empress Eugénie.

English jewellery designers were largely anonymous. The fashionable portrait painter E.T. Parris received an early training in enamel-painting and metal-chasing with the Regency goldsmiths Ray & Montague of London.[84] Possibly Parris also designed jewellery, which he certainly depicted with an informed eye in his paintings (Plates 105 and 106). George Foggo, an historical painter, is another possible candidate: he gave evidence to the Select Committee of 1835-36 on the grounds of his long experience of designing for the decorative arts.[85] Foggo was only one of many English artists and aspiring students who were forced to eke out a living by designing for manufacturers who were by no means anxious to acknowledge their work.

Many manufacturers in England and on the Continent made no attempt to use the services of artists, but continued to derive their patterns from architectural detailing, paintings and sculptures as well as from published material, old and new, usually supplemented by a close study of the work of their rivals. One of the pattern books currently available to them had the advantage of having been prepared and published by a working jeweller, Charles Winter. Winter was employed in London, probably in the 1820s, but earlier had had experience of the jewellery trade in Vienna and Paris. His undated *Pattern-Book for Jewellers, Goldsmiths and other Ornament Makers,* published with titles and text in German and

Plate 105. The Lily, *a painting by E.T. Parris executed in 1832 with a pendant,* The Rose. *Parris' early training in the goldsmith's trade shows in his treatment of the jewellery depicted in the painting. The girl on the left has a heavy jewelled chain or necklace round her neck and long drop earrings hooked through the ears. The young woman in the centre wears a jewelled fillet, gold hoop earrings and a long chain, the infant a twisted necklace and the girl on the right a jewelled brooch and gold bracelet.*

VICTORIA AND ALBERT MUSEUM

Plate 106. A pair of white chalcedony top and drop earrings with sprays of forget-me-nots in gold and turquoises, long enough to have been worn by the girl on the left of Parris' painting. They might have been made any time between about 1828-37.

SOTHEBY'S

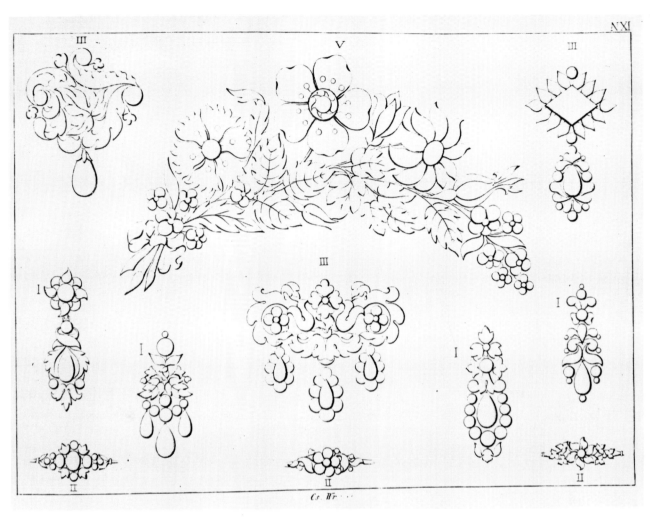

Plate 107. A plate of engraved designs from a work by Charles Winter, probably a Viennese by birth and certainly by training. Winter also worked in Paris before arriving in London and issuing his designs, probably in the 1820s. The bodice ornament (III) is decorated with everted scrolling foliage, echoing that in Plate 101.

English, contains twenty-four plates representative of the prevailing taste of the three capital cities in which he had worked (Plate 107).

The periodic exhibitions of French manufactures held in Paris did much to persuade Parisian jewellers of the value of their artists, and consequently they were more prepared to acknowledge their assistance than their English counterparts. Charles (formerly Carl) Wagner, a German, who entered into association with the French goldsmith Mention on arriving in Paris in 1830, employed sculptors such as A.V. Geoffroy de Chaume.[86] Geoffroy is mainly associated with large items of plate executed in the 1830s and later, but he also designed and modelled small items of goldwork for Wagner's successor, F.J. Rudolphi.

The heads of many Parisian firms possessed a practical knowledge of jewellery manufacture. Several, including Simon Petiteau, also acted as their own designer. Their talent was celebrated in France, especially in the case of the goldsmith-jewellers, whereas in England similar abilities went unremarked. The goldsmith-jeweller, Benoît Marrel, who had trained and worked as a chaser, went into business with his brother in the early 1830s, also assuming responsibility for the design side of the new concern.[87] J.-B.-M. Barnard,[88] employed by the firm of

Colour Plate 39. A rivière of large cushion-shaped brilliants set transparent in cut-down collets, formerly in the possession of the Conyngham family and believed to have been given by King George IV to Lady Conyngham, who provided him with the domesticity he had largely lacked since his parting from Mrs Fitzherbert. The King first singled out Lady Conyngham in about 1819-20, having tired of his current mistress Lady Hertford. Her fair opulent beauty was greatly to his taste and though by the mid-1820s gossips held that the first fine rapture had worn off and the King was well aware of the 'Vice-Queen's' acquisitiveness he had become habituated to her and her family.

Gibert from 1812, rising to be sole director, had begun to engrave gems in the late eighteenth century. He was patronised by the Bourbons of the senior and cadet branches both before and after the Revolution of 1830. J.-B. Fossin (who took over the Nitot workshop in 1815), was another skilled draughtsman, capable of conjuring up a design before the marvelling eyes of a client. He had three workshops and his firm executed most of the marriage jewellery given to his bride by the Duc d'Orléans, the eldest son of Louis-Philippe.[89]

The tradition of royal and aristocratic concern with jewellery design was continued on what was virtually a professional basis in Italy by Michelangelo Caetani, Duca di Sermoneta, who entered into a long association with the Castellani firm in Rome in 1828,[90] some fourteen years after the concern had come into existence, making jewellery in the French and English manners. At first the Duke merely procured for the Castellanis access to archaeological excavations, thus enabling them to make detailed examinations of all the classical jewellery brought to light. Later he made detailed suggestions for designs.

The Revolution of 1830 immediately disrupted the luxury trades in Paris. On 12 September, Mrs Arbuthnot, primed by the Duke of Wellington, wrote in her

Plate 108. A pair of adjustable silver-gilt bracelets by Ledsam, Vale & Wheeler, hallmarked for Birmingham, 1830. An early attempt to produce bracelets suitable for wearers from the slender to the plump. The eagles are cast and riveted on.

journal: 'The destruction & ruin & flight of the old Court & the departure of most of the English, it is calculated, will diminish the consumption of luxuries in Paris to the amount of 140 millions. The consequence is, all trade is at an end and the workmen all discharged & the streets of Paris are full of a disorderly crowd, who break the machinery of the different establishments and refuse to let those work who are willing to work, saying that they caused the revolution and ought to benefit by it'.[91] Rioters attempted to break into the premises of Bapst, where the Crown Jewels were kept, but were turned away empty-handed by Charles and Constant Bapst, who managed to convince them that the jewellery had already been removed. The next day it was spirited off to the Louvre, where it lay in store for twenty years.[92]

In London, happily untouched by revolution, the leading jewellers stood to benefit by the chaos in Paris. But nothing could insulate them from the consequences of bad management, as was to happen to Rundell's who were driven into dissolution in 1842 as a result of some unfortunate speculations, among which was a scheme for pearl fishing off the coast of Central America with the aid of a diving bell. Thomas Hamlet preceded the Royal Goldsmiths into bankruptcy. Hamlet too speculated unsuccessfully in pearl fisheries and (like Count Palffy in Vienna) in the theatre. A sale of stock was held on behalf of his creditors in 1834. The catalogue of the first part of the sale, conducted by Foster & Son at Hamlet's own premises in Princess Street from 25 August to 2 September, includes a substantial number of jewellery items. Among them were 'A large single-stone Brilliant Comet Brooch , with guard, pin and chain', 'A Cross, formed of five Peridots of Rare Lustre, *richly ornamented with* Brilliants of the Purest Water with a pair of matching earrings', and 'A Magnificent Head Ornament, formed of Brilliants of the Purest Water, expensively set in the shape of a Sprig of Effusia [fuschia], surmounted by a Bird of Paradise and Butterflies'.[93]

The fact that two of the examples cited were probably made in the 1820s did not make them less fashionable, for they were types that continued into the following decade. The head ornament is characteristic of the florid taste of the period. It is regrettable that so few of these costly extravaganzas have survived subsequent changes of fashion, for the modest versions which have been preserved, scaled down in size and usually set with semi-precious stones, fail to convey the almost bizarre splendour of the expensive pieces.

The Hamlet sale catalogue and other contemporary material compensates to an extent for the scarcity of Garrard Ledgers at this time. Only three survive for the period 1821-46, and all the subsequent Gentlemen's or Workmen's Ledgers of the nineteenth century have been destroyed. The Royal Ledger for Queen Victoria remains, together with two others containing the accounts of her children and other royalties.

The manufacturers of imitation or costume jewellery, probably even more vulnerable to the effects of war and revolution than their grander contemporaries, as their profit margins were so small, nevertheless made considerable advances during this time. Some of the larger Birmingham concerns, employing steam-power to stamp out parts of vessels, soon realised that the technique might be applied to the production of trinkets. The introduction of gas-fed blowpipes in the town in 1817 speeded up the processes of soldering and annealing metals, opening up further prospects of mass-production. But all jewellers, however modest, benefited from the blowpipe, including Benjamin Coley, a goldsmith and jeweller of Caroline Street. He was the grandfather of the painter, Sir Edward Coley Burne-Jones, who himself designed jewellery (Colour Plate 122E and Plate 253). Henry Adcock, the maker of the cast filigree combs in Plate 73, was another, as was James Heeley of Great Charles Street, a manufacturer of steel toys whose firm was among the few to survive French competition.[94] Ledsam, Vale & Wheeler of Newhall Street turned their attention to adjustable jewellery which would suit the maximum number of clients, to judge by the pair of silver-gilt bracelets of 1830 in Plate 108. One end of the plain curved band is pierced with slots to receive the hook. The bracelet centre, no longer the clasp, is decorated with a cast eagle attached by rivets.

While the Birmingham trade was directing its attention to the mass-production of stamped wares in precious and plated materials, certain categories of manufacture in the West Midlands, not only steel but pastes and some lapidary work, diminished under intense competition from France and Germany. The battle for world markets was now fairly launched.

Colour Plate 40. The new MASTER of the CROWN INN discharging BETTY the head Chamber maid, *a cartoon by H. Heath, published by S.W. Fores, Piccadilly, 1830. William IV, dressed plainly in a black coat and grey trousers, wearing the Garter Star and a single seal, holds a scroll in his right hand reading, 'No Gambling will be allowed in my House, nor in the Tap or Stables'. As he bids Lady Conyngham and her 'Crew' to depart he remarks that her boxes ought to be searched as they were much fuller than when she arrived at the Inn. Heath makes them so full, in fact, that the lids could not be closed. The cartoon is at variance with the new King's gallantry over the Stuart Sapphire. Lady Conyngham was more popular with the Royals than might be imagined. Even Queen Victoria, who met her in childhood, had fond memories of her.*

VICTORIA AND ALBERT MUSEUM, PRINT ROOM

Colour Plate 41. A gold bracelet with an enamelled miniature of King William IV with the Garter Star and ribbon, set under crystal in a frame shaped like a Tudor rose, a device used for several years by Rundell's. The frame is detachable, being fitted with a spring catch on each side. The tapering band has a polished moulded edge and an applied trail of enamelled forget-me-nots and leaves decorates its matted surface. The bracelet may have been a Christmas or birthday present from the King. SOTHEBY'S

Colour Plate 42. A gold bracelet set with an enamelled miniature under crystal of Queen Adelaide by William Essex, miniature painter to the King and Queen. The miniature, signed and dated 1834 on the reverse, is bordered by a bevelled frame decorated with bold wire filigree scrolls and fitted on both sides with a spring catch as in the bracelet with the miniature of the King. The tapering matted band is adorned with four cushion-cut brilliants, two turquoises and two pearls linked by applied foliated scrolls.

The original fitted case for this bracelet has survived. Inside is Rundell's paper label. The bracelet was probably a standard gift of the Queen to her ladies-in-waiting.   PRIVATE COLLECTION

Colour Plate 43. A bracelet centre which closely follows the form of the drawing in Plate 95 except that the King's crowned cipher is placed so low, touching the brilliant border, that there is no space for the tiny 'IV' provided for in the drawing. The ground is enamelled blue except for the area behind the crown which is red.   S.J. PHILLIPS

CHAPTER VI

Artistry
and Craftsmanship in the Service of the Trade

1. Cameos

The parure said to have been made for the Empress Josephine in the first decade of the century (Colour Plates 32 and 33) was set with both hardstone cameos and intaglios. At this time, the gem-set cabinets of sovereigns and nobles, full of antique, renaissance and more recent specimens were revered, visited and described. But the cult of gem-collecting was in decline and received a near-mortal blow when John Tyrrell, who had acquired part of Prince Poniatowski's collection (see Colour Plate 1B), put it up for sale at Christie's in April 1839. In consequence, persistent rumours that the Poniatowski gems were fakes blew up into a public scandal.[1] Henceforward fewer engraved gems found their way into cabinets and more were insinuated into jewellery.

Women showed a marked preference for cameos over intaglios in their jewellery. The latter were largely confined to seal or signet rings and even these declined in number after the introduction of envelopes in the 1840s, when only the conservative clung to the habit of sealing their letters. There were no intaglios cut on shells, which constituted the bulk of the trade. The technical description below is, therefore, confined to cameos in both hardstone and shell. A variety of stones was used, including amethysts, sapphires, garnets, malachite, chalcedony, opals and rock crystals (quartzes); emeralds and diamonds, rarely employed, were usually engraved in intaglio. Onyx, sardonyx, carnelian and bloodstone were the most popular. A complex subject might take several weeks, even months, to engrave on hardstone; shell carving was much quicker and the material far cheaper.

A. Gem-engraving

The gem-engraver first produced his design, then made a relief model in wax the exact size of the stone, adapting his work to the peculiarities of the strata. Once this was accomplished, the outline of the shape was traced on the surface of the stone, usually with a pointed brass tool. The next stage, of engraving the gem, was either performed with a diamond point tool, a method already old-fashioned in the eighteenth century, or on an engraving lathe. Until the end of the century, when electric power came into use for cheap work, a lathe of this kind (often known as a seal-engraver's engine) was usually operated by a treadle. The tools were made of soft iron in various shapes suitable for the different cutting operations. Most were small wheels, with heads usually no larger than 1/6 in. (.4cm) in diameter. The principal exception was a circular saw which was used to cut away the parts outside the perimeter of the bas-relief when a cameo was being made. Cuts were first made horizontally around the area of the design down to the table or ground stratum; the unwanted top layers were then sliced away horizontally with the saw.

*Colour Plate 44. A Bull's Mouth shell (*Cassis Rufa*) carved with a double personification of Night and her attributes, with stars and a new moon, an eagle and an owl. Probably Italian, c.1880. The red ('sardonyx') ground of the cameo is much deeper towards the lip of the shell on the right-hand side.*

The tools were inserted as needed in a spindle at the top of the arm of the lathe and lubricated with oil and pulverised bort (diamond fragments). The stone, cemented with wax and resin to a stick, was held against the tool which, rotating at speed, abraded it with the diamond dust and thus cut the design. Work on such a small scale usually necessitated the use of a powerful magnifying glass, though Pistrucci never needed one.

When engraving was completed and (if necessary) the stone re-stained to sharpen the colour, the gem was polished, first being smoothed with copper instruments shaped like cutting-tools and charged with oil and fine diamond powder, then with boxwood implements, aided by oil and an even finer powder, and finally with copper tools, rottenstone and water.

B. The Trade in Shells

The favourite shells of nineteenth century cameo carvers were those of gastropod molluscs with three layers, the central one lying at right angles to the outer two,

Colour Plate 45. A process set by James Ronca, illustrating the carving of a shell cameo portrait of the painter Sir John Everett Millais.
1. The prepared blank cut from a Cassis Rufa *shell, with the outer layer partially stripped off.*
2. The profile cleared to the ground and a little of the top layer retained on the head.
3. The halfway stage in the carving, with the principal features cut.
4. The finished result, detailed even to the wispy curls at the top of the head, silhouetted against the dark ground. The remnants of the upper layer have been used to add colour and tone to the side-whiskers and the hair at the temples.
Ronca, credited in the Art Journal *in 1898 with having studied under Pistrucci's brother (actually he was taught engraving in London by an Italian called Celli), exhibited at the Royal Academy between 1865 and 1871. He presented this set to the Museum.*   BETHNAL GREEN MUSEUM

which permitted the craftsman to use the inner layer for his ground, the middle (white) stratum for his subject, and the top for additional colour and relief.

Allowing for the hazards of war, shells were probably imported during the Napoleonic Wars by established English merchants such as John Turner of Wellclose Square, Whitechapel, who may even have contrived to forward some to Italy. From about 1830 Turner increasingly switched the shells to France. According to a paper given to the Society of Arts in 1847 by J.E. Gray, who acknowledged Turner's help in compiling it, comparatively few shells were consumed in the early years of the century. At the end of the Napoleonic Wars only about three hundred specimens were used annually by the carvers in Rome, who paid the equivalent of 30s. apiece for them.[2]

The most popular shell was the Black Helmet (*Cassis (L.) Madagascariensis*) which has a black inner layer known in the trade as onyx. Despite their classification these shells were fished near Jamaica, Nassau and New Providence. Each shell yielded about five cameos of various sizes large enough for brooches besides providing materials for studs and other small trinkets.

The Bull's Mouth (*Cassis (L.) Rufa*), which has an attractive sardonyx ground, was also used. The shells came from Madagascar and Ceylon. In the early decades of the century, when only about a hundred specimens a year were available, the best specimens fetched 10s. apiece in Rome, a high price when it is appreciated that the colour shaded rapidly from red at the mouth to pink further down (Colour Plates 44 and 45) and yielded fewer cameos than the Black Helmet.

The rapid expansion of the shell cameo trade in the 1830s brought other shells into commission. The chief of these was the Horned Helmet (*Cassis (L.) Cornuta*), which is distinguished by a yellow or orange ground, and the Queen Conch (*Strombus (L.) Gigas*), by a pink ground. Both had drawbacks: the upper layers of the first were apt to separate from the ground and the pink of the second (which yielded only one good piece) was fugitive when exposed to the light (Colour Plate 46). The vast quantities of Queen Conches used by carvers suggests that the latter difficulty was overcome by a little judicious staining. Cowries, small and very cheap, were sometimes carved in Naples (where large shells were also processed) and elsewhere. Other shells were also employed for cameos, including mother-of-pearl.

C. The Carving of Shell Cameos

The cameo blanks were either cut from the shells with a hacksaw lubricated with emery powder or with a slitting-mill fed with diamond powder and oil. Each blank was then ground down to the desired thickness and the edges bevelled. Most of the outer layer was stripped, leaving enough to be used for contrasting details. Lathes were employed for this purpose by 1840 or earlier and were probably also used to clear the area around the design, though traditional methods were retained in many workshops. If the natural protuberances of the shell could not be avoided in cutting the blanks, the carver had to incorporate them in the design rather than abrade them away, for the white stratum followed the contours of the projections. The head in the foreground of the Bull's Mouth shell with a cameo in Colour Plate 44 is modelled over a projection, as are the two emblematic birds.

The stages in the production of a shell cameo are made clear by James Ronca's process set in Colour Plate 45. It needs only a brief commentary. The blank would have been mounted on a block of wood and the outlines of the design marked out with a pencil or a sharp pointed tool. Three main types of tool, all small, were usually employed in the carving, one flat-faced, one rounded and one three-cornered, together with lengths of tempered steel wire, cut and ground at one end at an angle of about forty-five degrees. The ground of the finished cameo was worked over with chisels to ensure a smooth surface, which was then polished with pumice stone, wooden tools and powdered pumice and oil, or with a mixture of vitriol and putty powder, washed off with soap and water.

D. The Development of the Trade

Rome, the great magnet for artists, both Italian and foreign, attracted a goldsmith and engraver from the Tyrol, Antonio (Johann Anton) Pichler. His two best-known sons, Giovanni and Luigi,[3] were half-brothers. Luigi, the younger, trained as a painter before studying modelling and gem-engraving under his brother. His experience of the fine arts was by no means unusual, for gem-engravers were still regarded as sculptors in miniature and the talented ones remunerated accordingly. Luigi Pichler left Rome for Vienna after his brother's death in 1791, returning later in the decade. In 1818 he was invited to take up the post of Professor of Engraving at the Vienna Academy. He retired in 1850 to Rome, having survived the Poniatowski scandal in which he and his brother were among the gem-engravers implicated.[4]

The ranks of the foreign artists in Rome were swelled by the English gem-engraver Nathaniel Marchant, who arrived in 1772 and remained for sixteen years[5] and the Danish sculptor, Bertel Thorvaldsen, who lived and worked there from 1797 until 1838, except for a short visit to his native Copenhagen in 1819-20.[6] Thorvaldsen's work was much copied in miniature by gem-engravers and cameo-cutters; casts of the gems already made after the artist's sculptures were issued in Rome in about 1830. Another sculptor whose productions were seized upon by gem-engravers was John Gibson. On coming to Rome in 1817[7] Gibson was welcomed into the studio of the Italian artist, Antonio Canova,[8] whose own work was accorded the compliment of being copied extensively in miniature. Gibson rarely visited England and died in Rome in 1866. His patrons, however, were almost exclusively English.

The gem-engraver Benedetto Pistrucci made the journey in reverse, following the example of Luigi Isler and others by working in England. While still in Rome, his small cameo of Flora (executed in under a week) was acquired for less than £5 by the dealer Angiolo Bonelli, who took it to London. The antiquary Richard Payne Knight bought it from Bonelli in about 1808 for a sum variously represented as between £100 and £500.[9]

Pistrucci came to London at the suggestion of Bonelli, who left his London establishment for Rome to retrieve the Stuart Papers for the Prince Regent in about 1812, and bought the Sapphire *en route*.[10] The gem-engraver accompanied Bonelli on his return journey as far as Paris and remained for a time to execute commissions, leaving for England on the downfall of Napoleon in 1814. He was offered the post of Chief-Engraver to the Royal Mint in 1817; his St George and the Dragon appeared on the reverse of new coinage in the same year (see Colour Plate 85G) It is therefore conceivable, to put it no higher, that Pistrucci modelled the medallic portrait of George IV for rings made by Rundell's in 1821.[11]

Pistrucci was fortunate in obtaining commissions from English connoisseurs still anxious for examples of contemporary work, for which they were prepared to pay highly. He received 350 guineas (£367.10s.) from Lord Lauderdale for a sardonyx badge of the Order of St Andrew and 500 guineas (£525) from another patron for a large cameo of Minerva. But it is significant that his two daughters, Elena and Maria Elisa, whom he trained, returned to Rome and devoted themselves largely to cutting shell cameos for jewellery.[12]

In 1821 Rome was still the focus of gem-engravers, though they often had to transmute themselves into shell cameo-carvers or at best practise both techniques.

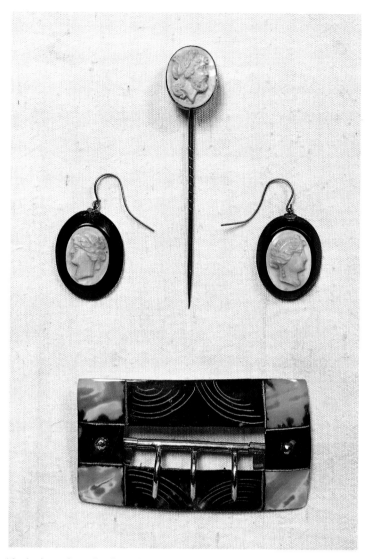

Colour Plate 46. A pin and a pair of tortoiseshell earrings set with cameo heads in pink shell and below, a buckle (from a set of six) of mother-of-pearl with incised decoration. These are all cheap items designed for mass consumption. The pink shell pieces were purchased in 1874 from P.L. Simmonds, the author of a series of articles, 'Marine Contributions to Art', published in the Art Journal *in 1871-74.*

An anonymous young Englishman visiting Rome in that year bought a shell cameo from Giovanni (Johann) Dies,[13] who was among those to supply gems to Poniatowski. The Englishman was pleased with his acquisition, but lamented the high price both of shell cameos and Roman mosaics.[14] In his survey of jewellery production up to and including the Great Exhibition of 1851, the Duc de Luynes named Dies as one of the two outstanding executants of shell cameos who, in his day, had had an annual turnover of 22,000-25,000 scudi per annum. Since De Luynes furnished rates of exchange, it appears that this amounted to about £5,000. It is, therefore, likely that Dies had assistants who copied his work endlessly. De Luynes remarked in general terms that the mechanical aids already in use had resulted in a deterioration of quality.

De Luynes classed the medallist and gem-engraver Pestrini[15] as the equal of Dies, noting particularly his work after Thorvaldsen, including the Triumph of Alexander. He also cited a former pupil of Dies, Luigi Rosi, who, like his master,

Colour Plate 47. A. This brooch in enamelled gold and diamonds was designed by Prince Albert as a gift to Queen Victoria on his birthday in 1851 and commemorates his guiding role in the Great Exhibition of the Works of Industry of all Nations held in Hyde Park in that year. Characteristically, the design is full of allusions. The diamond-set letter A recalls the same letter in a pendant made for the Electress Anna of Saxony, 1576-1580, in the Grünes Gewölbe, Dresden. The palm branch thrust through the A signifies his dream of international trade and friendship and the laurel wreath the huge success of the Exhibition. The ribbon bears the enamelled inscription: EXHIB/ITION/MAY 1/1851. *It is also inscribed on the back:* From Albert — 26 Augt. 185(1).
B. Badge of the Royal Order of Victoria and Albert, the double portrait engraved on sardonyx by Tommaso Saulini and signed T. SAULINI F. *(T. Saulini made it). The badge was set by Garrard's with diamonds and some small rubies in the crown above, which is also enamelled in red to simulate the cap. At some stage the large diamonds on the frame were replaced by pastes, before the Badge passed into its present ownership. Since Tommaso Saulini died in June 1864 the cameo at least cannot be later than this date.*

A. PRIVATE COLLECTION; B, VICTORIA AND ALBERT MUSEUM

catered for the jewellery trade.[16] De Luynes admitted that since about 1845 times had becomes hard for the Roman craftsmen and their export trade was now exiguous. One of the few practitioners to receive commissions, he acknowledged, was Tommaso Saulini, whose considerable talent had largely to be devoted to engraving portraits.[17] Saulini, who had studied in Thorvaldsen's studio, never indulged in the exaggerated reliefs popular with some of his contemporaries. He trained his son Luigi,[18] whose style was more vigorous and perhaps less subtle than that of Tommaso. Luigi nevertheless proved a faithful pupil and assistant, copying his father's work whenever necessary. Hardstone cameos were frequently reproduced several times over and also translated into shell.

Tommaso contributed to the Great Exhibition of 1851. The English compositors working on the official catalogue, however, made a sad hash of foreign names and turned him into Thomas Savalini.[19]

Tommaso Saulini showed two hardstone cameos in 1851, one of Jupiter Fulminator, the other a portrait of an English clergyman, Dr Townsend. Of the twelve shell cameos in his display, five (each of the Four Seasons, and Cupid and Hymen) were after Thorvaldsen and another five after Gibson (the Birth of Venus, the Hours bringing the horses to the Chariot of the Sun, the Marriage of Cupid and Psyche, Bellerophon receiving Pegasus from Minerva, and Celestial and Terrestrial Love contending for the soul). The other two were Mount Roveto, after a fresco by Raphael, and Young Bacchus attended by Fauns, from an antique relief in the Campana Collection, Rome. Saulini decided to participate in subsequent international shows, sending work to the Dublin 1853 Exhibition for which he gained an Honourable Mention, and later contributing to the London 1862 Exhibition, at which he won a Medal.[20] Meanwhile, he received a commission from Queen Victoria, probably at the suggestion of Gibson, who numbered the Queen and her husband among his patrons.

Plate 109. A daguerrotype taken on 25 January 1858 of Queen Victoria, Prince Albert (now the Prince Consort) and their eldest daughter Victoria, the Princess Royal, in her bridal gown, wearing her Order on a white moiré ribbon on her left shoulder, before they left Buckingham Palace for the Chapel Royal, St James's Palace, where the Princess was married to Prince Frederick William of Prussia. 'I trembled so', wrote the Queen in her Journal, 'that it has come out indistinct'. ROYAL ARCHIVES

Plate 110. Queen Victoria in widowhood, after a painting of 1875 by Heinrich von Angeli in the Royal Collection. This copy, executed in watercolour in 1883 by Lady Julia Abercromby, one of the Ladies of the Bedchamber, shows the Queen in her customary black dress and widow's cap with veil, wearing the Garter Star and, pinned to her shoulder, her Badge of the Royal Order of Victoria and Albert, with the Prince Consort's head uppermost. On her left wrist is one of several bracelets set with a miniature of the Prince. NATIONAL PORTRAIT GALLERY

The Queen determined on an unofficial family Order in 1856 or earlier, for which she required Tommaso Saulini to engrave double cameo portraits of her and the Prince (Colour Plate 47B). These were to be based on the obverse of the Great Exhibition Medal with its profile head of the Queen placed over that of her consort, the President of the 1851 Commissioners (Colour Plate 48). Prince Albert was interested in Orders, official and unofficial (Plate 178) and as a designer himself (Colour Plate 47A) was probably concerned with the Badges on which the cameos were to be set. Garrard's mounted the first Badge in diamonds and cabochon rubies at a cost of £235[21] for presentation to the Princess Royal on her confirmation in 1856.[22] It can be descried suspended from a white moiré silk bow on her shoulder, in a daguerrotype taken on her wedding day in January 1858 (Plate 109).[23]

Queen Victoria decided to make the Order official in homage to her husband shortly after his unexpected death in December 1861. Instituted as the Royal Order of Victoria and Albert on 10 February 1862, her own wedding anniversary,[24] it was exclusively for females, and at first limited to members of her immediate family. The Queen commissioned a variant of the cameo for her own Badge in which the paired profiles were reversed. She wore it at the marriage of her son, Albert Edward, Prince of Wales[25] and Princess Alexandra of Denmark[26] on 10 March 1863, probably for the first time, for she wrote in her Journal on the same day: 'I have had dearest Albert's head put above mine.'[27] This Badge appears in virtually all subsequent portraits of the Queen (see Plate 110).

The first cameos for the Order were all engraved on hardstone. These were intended for the First Class Badges, but the Queen wanted shell cameos for the Second Class ones, which had pearl instead of diamond borders. She had a change of heart over the size of the lesser Badges. A letter to Gibson (who acted as go-between) from one of the Queen's ladies, written on 22 September 1863, asked him to order two more shell cameos smaller than the others. She wanted Saulini to submit 'a slight sketch' for the Queen's approval before he started work.

Tommaso died in June 1864 before completing all the royal commissions, and Sir C.B. Phipps wrote at the Queen's behest to Gibson, tactfully urging completion of the outstanding order. Gibson replied saying that two shell cameos would soon be ready and presumably Luigi 'will with the help of a clever workman finish the others. . .'[28] In late December 1864, the *Journal* of the Society of Arts reported the arrival of specimens which brought the total so far executed to six onyx and four shell cameos, with five more of the latter still to come. The hardstone cameos, it added, had each taken between three and four months to engrave, which makes it unlikely that Luigi had had time to execute more than one of these, at most, after his father's death.[29] He may, however, have gone on to engrave further examples for the Queen, though she also extended her patronage to a gem-engraver and cameo cutter in London, probably at Henry Cole's suggestion. This was James Ronca, a Royal Academy exhibitor whose process set is shown in Colour Plate 45. Ronca sold the Queen two shell cameos 'from the Exhibition Medal of 1851', for which he received £6.6s. apiece by a cheque dated 28 March 1865.[30] They were probably the pieces executed the previous year for a Society of Arts competition for Art-Workmanship which offered prizes of £10 and £5 for double cameo portraits of the Queen and Prince Albert based on the 1851 Medal.[31] Four of his shell cameos, including two commissioned by the Art Union of London, were shown at the London 1871 Exhibition.[32]

Most cameo portraits were now executed from photographs, which obviated the need for the customary preliminary drawings. In 1873 Mr and Mrs Dearman Birchall of Gloucestershire, in Rome on their honeymoon trip, had their photographs taken in April 'for Sanlini's [*sic*] cameos, then to Sanlini to arrange for them to be carved on one shell mentioning that we should want four.'[33] Cameo portraits, however, were more usually mounted in jewellery.

Two years before his death Tommaso sent a selection of work to the London 1862 Exhibition. This included a process set which must have been similar to Ronca's in Colour Plate 45. He showed, in addition, Day and Night after Thorvalden's reliefs of 1815, Cupid and Psyche after Gibson and several other

Colour Plate 48. A set of Great Exhibition Medals, the obverse of the Council, Prize and Jurors' Medals bearing the double portraits of Queen Victoria and Prince Albert which Saulini was requested to copy in his cameos for the Badges of the Royal Order of Victoria and Albert. This set of medals belonged to Henry Cole, who was active on the Executive Committee of the Great Exhibition of 1851.

Plate 111. An onyx cameo of Medusa signed: T. SAULINI. F., *the central one of three onyx cameos set in a gold bracelet. The two flanking cameos, possibly representing Apollo and Diana, are unsigned but are attributed to Saulini. The setting is Italian, c.1850. The Medusa was copied in shell for the Castellani brooch in Colour Plate 49A.*   BRITISH MUSEUM, HULL GRUNDY GIFT

pieces, some described as original. They were all shell cameos. His onyx cameos were Rome, personified by a head of Minerva, Aurora (shell versions of both are in the Hull Grundy collection in the British Museum),[34] Antinous, Hercules and a Nymph, and, perhaps, a portrait cameo of Cardinal Wiseman.[35] The Jury, in awarding Saulini a Medal, cited a stone cameo 'chariot' (identifiable as Aurora), the Rome/Minerva piece and shell cameo heads of Britannia and Ossian, apparently all original compositions.[36] Saulini's onyx cameo of Medusa[37] (Plate 111), was not included in the display; it was clearly the model for the unsigned shell cameo in Colour Plate 49A, which was probably cut in his workshop.

Luigi in his turn contributed one mosaic and eighteen shell cameos to the Dublin 1865 Exhibition.[38] One of his most celebrated works dates to about this time; a head ornament, the fruit of a tripartite collaboration between Gibson, Luigi and the Castellani firm (Plate 112), it is in the Metropolitan Museum, New York, together with a necklace and brooch set by Castellani with further engraved gems signed by Luigi.

A sardonyx bust of a young girl, executed by Luigi, probably in the 1860s (Colour Plate 50A), is taken from a marble bust, 'Clytie', an ambiguous work, perhaps Roman embellished in the eighteenth century. Formerly in the Townley collection and in the British Museum since 1805, Nathaniel Marchant had engraved an intaglio of it while in Rome, using a plaster cast taken of the bust before it left Italy for England. Marchant's intaglio was included in a collection of cast copies of his work issued with a catalogue in 1792. Luigi used the same viewpoint: can he have seen Marchant's catalogue? (Most of the engravings of Clytie published in the mid-nineteenth century, when the bust was also reproduced by Copeland's in parian, were full-face.) Another piece, the portrait cameo of a bearded man in Colour Plate 50B signed: *L. SAULINI F.,* is clearly an autograph work and not a studio production.[39]

Further gem-engravers to have work shown at international exhibitions included Pietro Girometti, the son of Giuseppe Girometti, another contributor to the Poniatowski collection, and Calandrelli, a known forger of antique gems, who died in 1852. Both were represented at the Paris 1855 Exhibition, four years before the younger Girometti's death.[40]

The great bulk of craftsmen had perforce to be represented anonymously at international exhibitions only in the displays of dealers, importers and jewellers. The gem dealer, Bonelli, had many successors whose own names were public property as a result of their participation in the exhibition round, but the engravers they patronised, however talented, went unacknowledged. Among the most celebrated of these firms were Francati and Santamaria of 65 Hatton Garden, London, importers of cameos (mainly in shell), Italian mosaics, coral, goldwork and almost every other material relating to their trade. They showed in London

in 1862, 1871 and 1872, in Dublin in 1865 and in Paris in 1867 and 1878, at the Italian Exhibition in London in 1888, in Melbourne in 1888-1869 and probably on other occasions as well.[41]

The prices of the goods in which they and similar firms specialised were not high. According to an article by P.L. Simmonds in the *Art Journal* of 1854, hardstone cameos were available between £12 and £20.[42] Giuseppe Laudicina of Naples, already an 1862 exhibitor and, therefore, far from anonymous, priced his shell cameos in the Dublin 1865 Exhibition at between £1.12s. and £4. One of these, personifications of Night and Day costing £3,[43] had nothing to do with Thorvaldsen but was a pattern widespread in the trade (see Colour Plate 44). The subjects were often also personified by single heads with the same attributes of moons, suns and birds.

Dickens, who had lived in Italy for a while, evoked one of these in *Great Expectations* (1861), describing Miss Skiffens wearing a 'classic brooch..., representing the profile of an undesirable female with a very straight nose and a very new moon...'.[44] Not the least interesting point to emerge is that Miss Skiffens, a member of the aspiring lower middle class, was now able to sport such a brooch. A loose sheet of annotated sketches in an album in the Victoria and Albert Museum from the London firm of John Brogden of Henrietta Street, Covent Garden, includes a Night and Day cameo, set in gold with two snakes, priced at £7.15s. complete.[45] But jewellery manufacturers in Birmingham could mount such cameos in base metal, stamped and gilt, for much less.

Shell cameos, mass-produced to stereotyped patterns, were made more cheaply in France than in Italy. Napoleon, anxious to promote the glyptic art in Paris, had extended the Prix de Rome to gem-engravers in 1805. He also fostered a school of gem-engravers under the direction of Roman-Vincent Jeuffroy of the Paris Mint,[46] who had executed a cameo portrait of the Emperor as First Consul in 1801. The school was short-lived, but the experiment prompted later ventures. Charles Laboulaye claimed in 1856 that craftsmen had been brought to France from Rome, Florence, Venice and Naples, by implication in the 1830s. He might have added Genoa, where both coral and shell cameos were produced.[47] Some were employed by the Parisian firm of Blanchet, the recipient of a Silver Medal at the Paris 1844 Exhibition for shell cameos cut on the lathe. Italian shell carvers were also employed in Marseilles; some worked at the coral factories set up by Barbaroux de Mégy and Bertoux in the 1830s.[48]

The English shell dealer, Turner, furnished Gray with the following statistics relating to the shells imported by France in 1846:

80,000 Bull's Mouths — average price 2 francs (approximately 1s.8d.)
 8,000 Black Helmets — average price 6 francs (5s.)
   500 Horned Helmets — average price 3 francs (2s.6d.)
12,000 Queen Conch — average price 1½ francs (1s.2½d.)

The approximate total cost of the shells was £9,105. The value of the finished cameos was £40,000. Large cameos, worth about 5 francs each, amounted to about £32,000 of this sum, while the rest consisted of small specimens.

In the mid-1840s more shell cameos were produced in France than in Rome, according to Gray, who declared that some 'three hundred persons are now employed in Paris in this branch of trade, earning wages which vary from three to twenty-five francs per day, according to their talent and skill'. A punitive English import duty of twenty per cent levied on the finished work had deterred English jewellers from bringing over more than a modicum of specimens, but Gray believed that much was smuggled in. The duty had been recently reduced to five per cent and imports officially quadrupled. A substantial proportion went to Birmingham jewellers who mounted them and exported many of the finished articles to America and the British Colonies.[49] Some of the French cameos were taken up in London, but the 'beautiful cameo of Jupiter and Juno', given to John Ruskin's young wife Effie by her father-in-law as a birthday present, was probably Italian. Ruskin senior recorded in his account book that he gave £3.15s.6d. for it. The Ruskins lived on the edge of London and Effie's husband, a redoubtable critic of jewellers in general, promised to have it set for her.[50] He probably took it to Hunt & Roskell, for all his scorn of the trade.

The cameo-workers in France, who increasingly consisted of native-born craftsmen, were perfectly happy to churn out copies of standard Italian designs. But the best of them experimented with revived techniques under the umbrella of the antiquarian movement. The French sculptor and gem-engraver, Paul Victor Lebas, was a frequent exhibitor at the Paris Salon between 1852 and 1876, where he showed a few classical subjects and also portraits in hardstone and shell.[51] But in 1851 he supplied the large French firm of Félix Dafrique of the Rue Jean-Jacques Rousseau, Paris, with at least one *commesso* made of carved shell,

Plate 113. An engraving by C.E. Wagstaff, published in 1839, of Sully's portrait of Queen Victoria, painted in 1838, in the Wallace Collection. The print depicts George IV's circlet and the Queen's elaborate girandole earrings (which had belonged to Queen Charlotte) and indicates her gem-set necklace. Lebas, in cutting his commesso, ignored the earrings, while the necklace is represented merely by the length of the twisted wire. VICTORIA AND ALBERT MUSEUM

enamelled gold and tiny precious stones, which was inspired by sixteenth century compositions in hardstone, enamelled gold and jewels produced in the court workshops of Henri II of France.[52] Lebas' piece was a portrait of the young Queen Victoria, a reversed detail taken from an engraving of Thomas Sully's 1838 painting (Colour Plate 51 and Plate 113). Lebas probably made more specimens of this kind, using other themes. Dafrique's display at the Great Exhibition of 1851 included a number of mounted *commessi* in addition to large chains which the jeweller, when a young designer, had introduced to a trade bored with the delicate specimens hitherto in use. The Jury singled out the 'polychromic cameos' in awarding Dafrique a Prize Medal.[53] A related revival, the *camée habillé* (or a cameo head dressed with jewels), appears also to have been introduced in France.

Napoleon III, emulating his distinguished uncle the first Napoleon, encouraged gem-engraving largely as a cabinet art. The more modest work of such craftsmen as Michelini, born in Rome but a naturalised Frenchman, was of greater importance to jewellers.[54] L. Michelini was awarded a First Class Medal at the Paris Exhibition of 1855 for a fine collection of cameos executed for the trade, while the firm of Titus Albitès, who showed engraved gems and shell cameos, gained a Second Class Medal.[55] L. Purper, one of the French contingent at the London 1862 Exhibition, gained a Medal for excellence of design and workmanship in cameos also made to 'supply the requirements of commerce'. This somewhat condescending approval was echoed by the Parisian jeweller, Jules Fossin, who nevertheless thought Purper would do better to derive his models from museums and the great collections of antique specimens. Fossin levelled the same criticism

Plate 114. An onyx cameo signed: G. BISSINGER, *representing Bianca Capello inspired by a marble bust of 1863 by 'Marcello' (Adèle d'Affry, Duchesse de Castiglione-Colonna). Mounted as a pendant with diamonds variously set in gold and in silver lined with gold, and with two pearls, probably in France; c.1875.*
GARRARD & COMPANY

at C.J. Jouanin, a gem-engraver and medallist who went on to exhibit cameo portraits and other subjects at the Paris Salon between 1863 and 1886.[56]

Georges Bissinger, a gem-engraver of German origin who settled in Paris, showed work at the Paris 1867 Exhibition, was awarded a Silver Medal and had an international success.[57] An English owner lent a Bissinger cameo of Prudence and Love set in diamonds as a brooch, with earrings *en suite,* to the loan exhibition of jewellery staged at the South Kensington Museum in 1872.[58] Carlo Giuliano of London mounted Bissinger cameos, including one of Marie de Médicis (Colour Plate 125C).[59] Bissinger exhibited at Vienna in 1873, Philadelphia in 1876 and again in Paris in 1878.[60] The Parisian designer and jeweller Alexis Falize, reporting on Bissinger's work at Philadelphia, remarked the prodigious technical effects obtained by the artist with the aid of a lathe, citing lace collars on busts (as in the Marie de Médicis cameo). In his view, Bissinger was squandering his talent,[61] but the artist was sometimes more restrained (Plate 114).

The French gem-engravers showing at the Paris 1889 Exhibition included Alphonse Lechevrel, allegedly a former pupil of the Swedish-born artist, Salmson, who was held in high repute in France. The last years of the century saw a great burgeoning of the gem-engraver's and medallist's art in jewellery, from the work of Auguste Burdy and Edmond Becker,[62] who supplied Boucheron, to Lalique. Glyptics were transformed in Lalique's jewellery; glass cameos, gold medallions, figures and reliefs carved in stones, horn, ivory and rock crystal were melted into his richly deliquescent designs (Plate 377).

The French shell cameo trade fared less prosperously in the last three decades of the century. One writer declared in 1897 that it had been annihilated by the Franco-Prussian war of 1870-1871, when the siege of Paris effectively prevented the flow of goods into and out of the capital.[63] The trade indeed suffered badly but recovered somewhat, though cameos had gone out of fashion. According to P.L. Simmonds in 1874, the annual value of imported French cameos recorded by the British Customs had dropped to about half the pre-war average of £8,000-£10,000. He still held to the view that French production outstripped Italian, assessing the current annual value of all the cameos produced in Rome at about £8,000.[64]

It cannot be claimed that many significant developments in gem-engraving and shell cameo carving occurred in England. The English were mainly consumers of imported goods, though a few artists and craftsmen practised in London, Birmingham and elsewhere. Pistrucci and a few others who had worked for George IV lingered on for a while. George Brown, seal-engraver to George IV, had taken on as pupil, and then partner, the Irish modeller and gem-engraver, John De Veaux, who succeeded to the business. De Veaux received a royal appointment to William IV in 1831 and then to his niece, Victoria.[65] Later, John Nicholson of

Plate 115. A gold bracelet adorned with shell cameos of a man and two young children by John Nicholson of Dorking. Its fitted case bears the label: Turner's, Jewellers etc. to the Queen and Royal Family, 58 & 59 New Bond St, London; *c.1845. Nicholson exhibited at the Royal Academy in 1848 and 1850 and in 1848 also contributed to one of the exhibitions of Art Manufactures organised by Henry Cole at the Society of Arts.*   CHRISTIE'S

Dorking, 'Cameo Engraver in Ordinary to Her Majesty Queen Victoria and H.R.H. The Duchess of Kent', demonstrated his competence in three unidentified shell cameo portraits of, presumably, a father and two children, which were mounted in a bracelet in about 1845 (Plate 115).[66] The conscientious efforts to promote the craft made by the Society of Arts certainly focused attention on Ronca from 1864 to 1866 and again in 1871. He gave his cameo of Psyche carrying the vase of Stygian water to Venus, entered in 1871, to the Bethnal Green Museum in 1874.

Ronca's rivals in the 1864-1865 Society of Arts competition were three London craftsmen, E.H. Renton, A. Warner and John Wilson, but none had the same impact as Ronca. The Society's *Journal,* commenting on the continuing neglect of ivory and cameo carving in 1871, remarked that both offered 'a field for artistic industry to female as well as male art-workers',[67] as indeed the two Pistrucci daughters had shown. The suggestion took root: Miss Alice Scholfield contributed cameos to Arts and Crafts Exhibitions in 1889 and 1890.[68] But she and others like her were overshadowed by the German-born sculptor and gem-engraver, Wilhelm Schmidt of Hatton Garden, who studied in Paris before arriving in London. Several of his opal cameos were mounted as pendants by Child & Child of South Kensington.[69] A. Lyndhurst Pocock worked in London for Fabergé, and the son of a seal-engraver, Cecil Thomas, who gave a paper to the Society of Arts on gem-engraving in 1912, himself practised the art briefly before turning to large-scale sculpture after the 1914-18 War.[70]

E. Reverse Intaglios

The display of the London firm of Lambert and Rawlings[71] at the 1862 Exhibition included a novelty remarked by the *Illustrated London News,* 'some

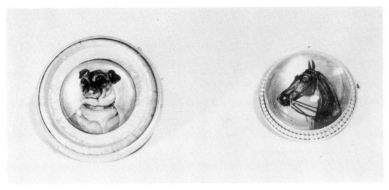

Plate 116. Two reverse intaglios of a pug dog and a horse, both set in gold frames as brooches. English, late nineteenth century. These examples are coloured, like the first examples to attract attention at the International Exhibition held in London in 1862. The exhibitors were Lambert & Rawlings, but a variant, painted with white enamel alone, was shown at the Paris 1878 Exhibition by Marshall's of Edinburgh. This was a short-lived vogue: the polychromatic specimens were much preferred everywhere.

MUSEUM OF LONDON

Plate 117. A particularly elaborate reverse intaglio with a robin inspired by William Wier's colour print, The Christmas Carol Singer, published in 1858; set as a pendant in gold with a locket fitting containing a tinted photograph of a man on the reverse, c.1860. BRITISH MUSEUM, HULL GRUNDY GIFT

crystal cameos engraved by Mr Charles Cook, and afterwards coloured to the life, which have a very curious effect, and which are certainly pretty objects of jewellery, either as lockets, brooches, or solitaires'. The French jeweller Fontenay acknowledged that they were an English invention, but only in the restricted sense that pigment was introduced into the traditional art of engraving reverse intaglios.[72] Cook cut his subjects into the underside of flat-backed rock crystals with domed tops which slightly magnified the finished work. Sporting and animal subjects were popular (Plates 116 and 117).

The attribution of the invention to Charles Cook has been disputed and assigned instead to a Clerkenwell seal-engraver, Thomas Cook, who taught the craft to his apprentice, Thomas Bean. The latter founded a small family business which was continued by his son Edmund and grandson Edgar, supplying goods to Hancock's and Harvey & Gore until Edgar's death in 1954. Ernest William Pradier, the son of a French-born diamond-setter and jeweller settled in England with an English wife, began to specialise in the craft in the late 1870s. Much of his early work was taken to Paris by his father and sold to the fashionable jewellers there. His own son, Ernest Marius, was brought up in the trade. Ernest William and Ernest Marius Pradier worked together until the former's death, upon which the latter moved to Dunstable and thence to Luton. E.M. Pradier furnished specimens to America, presumably to Tiffany's, and also to Longman & Strong-i-th'arm of Albemarle Street, London, continuing a connection originating with his father. He died soon after Edgar Bean.[73] Reverse intaglios were also sold by Wilson & Gill of Regent Street and other firms in the 1890s and later.

F. Other Cameos

Stone cameos were sometimes fabricated in two parts, the subject being carved separately and glued to a support. Among imitations, Tassie cameos have been cited; sulphide cameos patented by the glassmaker, Apsley Pellatt, in 1819 and styled 'Crystallo-Ceramie' were popular for several decades and were highly

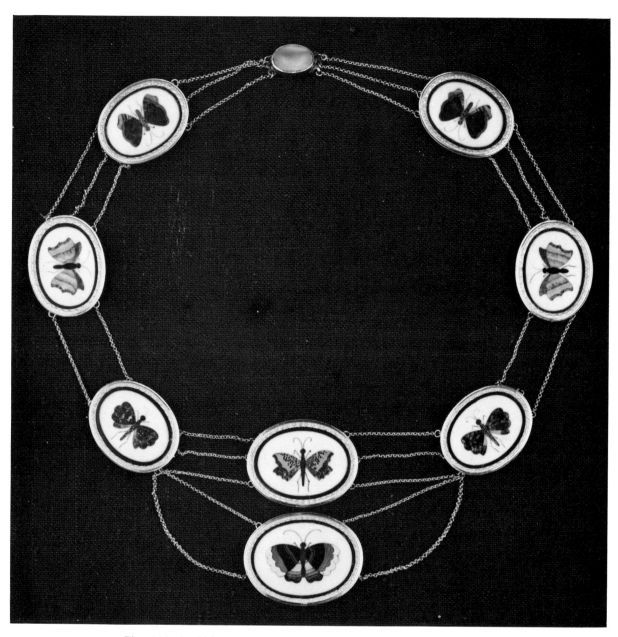

Plate 118. A gold festoon necklace with chased foliated decoration in the French style, set with Florentine mosaics (pietre dure) *representing varieties of moth, inlaid on a white ground. The clasp is set with mother-of-pearl; c.1805.*

praised by the *Art Journal* as late as 1854.[74] Cameos were also carved from 'lava' (in fact limestone from the region around Vesuvius), coral, ivory and jet, and moulded in horn and tortoiseshell.

2. Italian Mosaics

A. Florentine Mosaics

These mosaics derived from the traditional *commessi di pietre dure* (literally, 'placing together of hard stones'). The technique was practised at the *Opificio delle Pietre Dure* founded by the Medici in the sixteenth century, which specialised in the production of large stone marquetry panels and roundels for furniture and architectural decoration. Work of this kind was also produced in Lombardy and at the *Laboratorio delle Pietre Dure* established in Naples in 1738, which survived until 1860. A small cottage industry in Florentine mosaic jewellery was carried on in Derbyshire in the second half of the nineteenth century as the offshoot of the manufacture of larger works in Ashford and Bakewell, which enjoyed the patronage of the Duke of Devonshire. It was also practised in Paris, in St Petersburg at works founded by immigrant Italian craftsmen in 1840 as well as in other European countries. Germany had its own tradition of stone marquetry.

The stones used by the craftsmen included amethyst, lapis lazuli, rock crystal, jasper, sardonyx, chalcedony, agate, porphyry, jade, marble, saussurite (a green stone found near Lake Geneva and in several places in Italy and Corsica), flint, limestone and labradorite, together with coral. Some stones must have been imported. It is unlikely that the lapis lazuli employed was the so-called German or Swiss lapis (stained jasper) so that it was probably brought from Afghanistan, Siberia or Iran. Some stones however came from the locality: various coloured limestone pebbles from the Arno were popular.

Miniature plaques were produced in small quantities in the eighteenth century, but their wholesale production for jewellers only began after 1800. A gold parure in the Gilbert Collection, Los Angeles County Museum, is an early example. Set with twenty-four *pietre dure* plaques representing shells and pearls deriving from late eighteenth century designs made for the *Opificio,* it is said to have belonged to Napoleon's sister, Queen Caroline of Naples. The festoon necklace of mosaic moths in Plate 118, mounted in a gold setting chased in a similar manner, is of approximately the same date.

A brief retrospective survey of the Florentine trade by the British Consul General in Florence, Sir Dominic Colnaghi, published in 1889, showed that from the mid-1820s the jewellery plaques turned out by workshops independent of the *Opificio* were simplified versions of the old *pietre dure.* Wherever possible, materials more easily worked were substituted for the old hardstones. These included petrified wood and fossils (classed with marble as *pietre tenere* or soft stones). Shells were employed for red and white tints, and coral was also used for red. Black agate, or marble, supplemented from about 1850 by its Derbyshire equivalent, was often used for the support or ground of mosaics (Colour Plate 52); white was more unusual, as were other colours.

According to Colnaghi, the maker of miniature mosaics required only a few pieces of equipment. 'With a small table, a basin of water, a brazier, a vice, some copper and iron blades to be used as files, a bow strung with iron wire [the traditional bow-drill], a little emery powder, and a few stones already cut into slices..., his equipment is complete.' As the stones were shaped to a template before slicing, the craftsman had a supply of ready cut pieces enabling him to replicate a design, though the fitting still required considerable time and labour.

The stones and other materials were sawn very thin: the maximum thickness for miniature mosaics was 2.5mm to 3mm. The edges were bevelled to enable them to fit more easily into the design, which was usually one of a standard series of compositions of insects, flowers and the like, probably originally deriving from herbals and flower prints. The gradated shading of a turned leaf or petal was

Plate 119. A Florentine mosaic floral pendant in red, green and white on a black ground, mounted in a gold locket decorated with applied vine leaves, wire tendrils and shells, terminating top and bottom with the 'flat band' scrolls apparent in the three brooches by Montelatici in Plate 120. By Torini/Torrini of Florence; c.1865, but mounts of this type existed in the early 1850s. The pendant has a fitted case with a trade label: FABBRICA DI MOSAICI/G.TORINI/FIRENZE/6 LUNG' ARNO NUOVO/BORGO OGNISSANTI 3.

represented by separate slivers of stone. Since the components were of varying degrees of hardness each had to be individually polished with lead and emery powder and scored on the underside before being heated and put in position over a cement made of mastic and wax laid on the hollowed ground. The bonding cement was afterwards used to seal the composition. Colnaghi did not introduce the subject of dyed stones, though they may have formed part of the palette.[75]

Popular though costly tourist souvenirs, and long since imported by jewellers abroad, Florentine mosaics found a wider stage at the London 1851 Exhibition, where mosaic furniture, decorative panels and other items were on view. Whether or not jewellery was included in the displays is not recorded, but G. Bianchini, who contributed a table, may also have shown trinkets.[76] The Italian catalogue of the London 1862 Exhibition is little more specific, referring, however, in general terms to 'the art of mosaic in *Pietre Dure,* called Florence mosaic [which] has acquired great importance in certain shops, where necklaces and other ornaments set in gold are specially made'. It lists only imitations of Florentine mosaic jewellery in scagliola, a coloured gesso, which were exhibited by Pietro della Valle of Leghorn (Livorno).[77]

G. Torroni and C. Vecchi of Florence, however, appear in the official English catalogue of the 1862 Exhibition, credited with showing brooches and small wares in mosaic. Given the typographical errors in the 1851 catalogue, the first name may be construed as G. Torrini or Torini of 6 Lung' Arno Nuovo, who was cited among the leading practitioners in Murray's *Handbook* of 1867 and took part in the Dublin 1865 Exhibition and the International Workmen's Exhibition in London in 1870.[78] Torini executed the pendant in Plate 119, which was bought in Florence. The prominent paired scrolls on its border are echoed by the mounts of three brooches contributed by Montelatici of Florence to the Paris 1867 Exhibition (Plate 120). This local style of mount was apparently still in use at the Paris 1878 Exhibition, when an English craftsman commented on the 'flat band scrolls' on the settings of some Italian mosaics.[79]

A well-known maker, Enrico Bosi, who was later honoured by the patronage of the King of Italy, won a Bronze Medal at the New York 1853 Exhibition for

Plate 120. Three Florentine mosaics shown by Montelatici of Florence at the Paris 1867 Exhibition, engraved for the Art Journal Illustrated Catalogue, *1867-8.*

Florentine mosaic brooches and bracelets. Among later exhibitors, Pietro Bazzante (or Bazzanti) & Son, who contributed a mosaic table to the Dublin 1865 Exhibition, were probably merchants. They sent mosaic jewellery and other items by B. Berchietti and by Martelli & Guagui to the London 1871 Exhibition, at prices ranging from £18.10s. to £30. In 1872, when they again figured in an exhibition catalogue, the art establishment began to voice doubts about their contribution, declaring that some pieces were good, but some bizarre.[80] The vulgarity of some expensive Italian mosaic jewellery at the Paris 1878 Exhibition irritated Alessandro Castellani.[81] By this date, the mosaic industry, which had seen a great expansion from 1863 to 1873, when Florence was the capital of the newly-united Italy, had gone into sharp reverse.

B. Roman Mosaics

Deriving from the *opus tesselatum* and *opus vermiculatum* of classical Rome, Roman mosaics were composed of stone or glass tesserae. The late sixteenth century project for decorating St Peter's Rome with mosaics was linked to the *Fabbrica di S. Pietro,* from which the *Studio Vaticano del Mosaico* sprang in 1727. Miniature mosaics (recently denominated micromosaics) were produced in the seventeenth century but were turned out on a larger scale in the eighteenth by craftsmen who combined working in the *Studio* with free-lance activities. The occupation of Rome by the French in 1798 brought the mosaicists to a state of near-destitution, soon forcing them to concentrate on producing miniature mosaics of secular subjects for gold boxes and jewellery, using slivers of hardstone or glass. The former were gradually abandoned after about 1830. One of the most popular was Pliny's Doves, after a mosaic of birds perched on a basin which was so called on the grounds that it had been mentioned as a marvel of execution by Pliny himself. Also in demand were views of Roman monuments, landscapes, flowers, animals and birds (Colour Plate 53). The mosaics in a parure set in Paris in about 1825 (Colour Plate 54) constitute a guided tour to the great buildings of Rome, largely by way of prints by Piranesi and others. Pistrucci, Chairman of one of the 1851 Juries, acidly observed that he 'was not aware that any mosaicist has ever worked from his own original design'. He might have added that many gem-engravers too were primarily copyists.[82]

The *smalti* used by mosaicists working on a large scale were glass cakes produced in Rome and Murano, the former rendered opaque by the addition of tin oxide and the second shiny and translucent, sometimes enclosing gold and silver leaf. The craftsman fashioned his tesserae by striking the glass with a hammer and then cutting the fragments into the required shape. The maker of micromosaics used

Plate 121. A Roman mosaic basket of flowers dating to about 1838 and loosely based on an antique example in the Vatican. It is perhaps by Antonio Roccheggiani. Purchased by an Englishman in Rome as a present to his niece, this brooch passed to her daughter, Helen Savory, who twice had it repaired in Rome in the 1860s or 1870s. The coloured gold brooch frame may be English, or perhaps executed in the English manner by Castellani of Rome.

MUSEUM OF LONDON

a simplified technique, employing glass rods (*smalti filati*), 'varying in thickness from that of a piece of string to the finest cotton thread'. *Smalti filati,* already known in the early eighteenth century, may have been first employed in micromosaics by Giacomo Raffaelli, a Vatican worker; he certainly exhibited specimens in his workshop in Rome in 1775.[83] Several of his contemporaries, including Cesare Aguatti, began to use the technique at the same time. For some time the filaments were each made in a single colour; later several colours were combined in one piece; a brooch by Gioacchino Barberi in the Hull Grundy collection in the British Museum is constructed with parti-coloured filaments which subtly turn the forms of the fruits depicted.[84] Antonio Aguatti, who trained many of the mosaicists of the mid-nineteenth century, was himself responsible for improvements in the vari-coloured *smalti.* Giuseppe Mattia, active in the first half of the nineteenth century, succeeded under the direction of Michelangelo Barberi in producing colours clearer and more brilliant than heretofore (*tinte di soffio*), using a blowpipe fed by bellows.

To make his mosaic, the craftsman used a support, traditionally copper but, for jewellery, of stone or glass with side walls and a shallow central depression. This was partially filled with plaster, into which went mastic or cement to secure the tesserae, inserted with the aid of pointed tweezers. When the mosaic was completed, the spaces between the tesserae were filled with coloured wax, then the surface was smoothed and polished.[85]

Giacomo Raffaelli's workshop was in the Piazza di Spagna, where many other craftsmen were to be found. It was the haunt of tourists and of temporary foreign residents. John Keats died in a house on the Spanish Steps in 1821. The Duc de Luynes named Aguatti, also of the Piazza di Spagna, as the most celebrated mosaicist, Michelangelo Barberi as having the most complete workshop, and Mattia as among the most important mosaicists working in Rome in 1810, later followed by Domenico Moglia and his son Luigi, Gioacchino Barberi and Giuseppe Dies. By the 1820s, some twenty mosaicists were turning out small work suitable for jewellery. De Luynes estimated the turnover of the trade in Rome in mid-century at 30,000 to 35,000 scudi.[86] There were also workshops elsewhere in Italy and in Paris (from the late eighteenth century).

Michelangelo Barberi, Luigi Moglia and Dies sent work to the London 1851 Exhibition, but it was limited to large pieces, according to the official catalogue. They also contributed to subsequent exhibitions.[87] Another 1851 exhibitor was Antonio Roccheggiani, who showed a mosaic of the Temples of Paestum in the sunset. The trade card of his grandson, Cesare, citing Medals from the 1851

Exhibition, Chile in 1875, Philadelphia in 1876, and Paris in 1855 and 1878, is preserved with a brooch in the Museum of London (Plate 121). The Jury award of a Second Class Medal to Roccheggiani as a *coopérateur* at the Paris 1855 Exhibition describes him as a very clever workman employed by Galand of Rome;[88] this must have been Luigi Gallandt of the Piazza di Spagna. Later, when the name of Roccheggiani of the Via Condotti figured again in exhibitions, it was Cesare who was commended by the Jury at the Philadelphia Exhibition for 'the very careful and artistic execution of landscape subjects familiarized by the Roman workers in mosaics'.[89]

The Roccheggiani brooch, given to her mother in about 1838 by a relative, Lord Kingsdown, was the subject of an undated letter from Helen Savory of Buckhurst Park, Ascot, to a nephew about to leave for Rome, probably in the 1870s. She asked him to deliver the piece to Cesare for attention, saying that some two years since, when her father had taken it to Roccheggiani to have the cracked red ground repaired, the mosaicist expressed great admiration 'and said he was sure it was the work of his grandfather'. He had duly repaired or replaced the support and the brooch was brought back to its owner, but while she was wearing it one day the gold slip frame sprang apart, without warning, releasing the whole of the mosaic, which fell out and was smashed on a stone staircase. Roccheggiani once again restored it and the brooch, with its handsome outer frame of roses executed in coloured gold, shows little sign of its chequered history.[90]

The price of mosaics is difficult to establish, but Biagio Barzotti, who contributed to the Dublin 1865 Exhibition, included in his display small oval mosaics of the Roman Forum and the Temple of Vesta, costing £8 apiece.[91] Though many mosaics were exported unset to Birmingham and elsewhere, those mounted in Rome in mid-century were often given characteristic borders incorporating a row of pellets (Colour Plate 55). The archaeological influence of the Castellani firm popularised rope mouldings and wire filigree borders in Rome and elsewhere (Colour Plate 56). The pieces in Colour Plate 57 are later; the mosaic work is carried close to the edge of the setting, a reversion to early nineteenth century practice, and the mounts are more insistently archaeological.

The Castellanis (who had their own mosaic workshop) and others mounted pieces drawn from early Christian and Byzantine mosaics in churches. The more restrained Castellani compositions were often outlined in gold strips or cloisons. The Holy Lamb figures prominently in the parure in Colour Plate 57, which bears the applied mark, CALVI, denoting the goldsmith Antonio Calvi of Rome. The mosaics themselves are more characteristic of work of the 1860s and 1870s, which made use of filaments of increasingly varied sections, often with the aim of creating a naturalistic effect. The fleece of the Lamb in Calvi's set is composed of sickle-shaped tesserae simulating the appearance of the wool.

The vogue for Roman mosaics had waned before the mid-1870s.

3. Amber

A translucent or transparent fossil resin, usually occurring in hues ranging from white to brown (Colour Plate 58), some specimens contained insects. Most of the amber used in the jewellery trade in the nineteenth century was obtained from the traditional source, the Baltic coast in East Prussia, between Danzig (Gdansk) and Konigsberg (Kaliningrad) and Memel (Klaypeda). In 1873, P.L. Simmonds reported that some 80,000-90,000 lb. (36,000-41,000kg.) of amber was dredged annually off Memel. Four steam-powered and a large number of hand-operated dredgers, working shifts round the clock, brought quantities of sand to the shore, where it was sifted for amber. The substance was also mined in blue clay about a hundred feet deep under sandhills. It was found in other countries, including Denmark, Sweden, France, Austria, Switzerland and Russia. An exotic variety, exhibiting colours ranging from bright red to reddish yellow and a bluish tinge, emanated from the banks of the Simeto, a river in Sicily; specimens carved into forty-three beads strung as a necklace were lent to the Dublin 1865 Exhibition by J.G. Jeans, the English Vice-Consul at Catania. Simmonds also referred to amber washed up on the Suffolk coast below Aldeburgh during winter gales, which was worked into crosses, bracelets and other ornaments by a family at Trimley near Felixstowe.[92]

Classified according to size and quality, the amber was sold both in its rough state or processed into beads and other articles at Danzig, the chief centre of the trade, though Simmonds mentioned rival amber-working establishments recently established near Memel and at Konigsberg, Moscow and New York. From Danzig, amber was exported to Vienna, London, Paris, Moscow and New York. Agents held stocks in all these cities.

Bright yellow transparent amber was the cheapest variety; a lemon colour was more highly regarded. Drawing on official returns, Simmonds estimated the approximate price of amber beads in the trade in the early 1870s as £3 for thirty large specimens weighing 1lb. (approximately 470 grams), £18 for the same weight of sixty smaller pieces and £12 for one hundred. Several specialist German and Austrian firms contributed to the international exhibitions, mainly displaying beads and carved work, which might have included cameos as well as mouthpieces for pipes and the like. G.E. Jantzen of Stolp (Slupsk), not far from Danzig, showed a necklace, brooches and other articles of lemon amber mounted in gold in 1851, for which he received an Honourable Mention.[93] Among those who contributed to other exhibitions, not always international, was H.L. Perlbach of Danzig, whose 1862 display included beads made for the African market; his London agent was Meyer Levin of South Street, Finsbury.[94]

Amber came into prominence among the beads favoured by ladies of the Aesthetic Movement in the 1870s and 1880s. It was itself capable of being moulded, but for plastic imitations, see Chapter IX.

4. Coral

Coral, the opaque calcareous skeleton of tribes of marine polyps, was fished by dragnets from about April to July in the seas around Capri, Corsica, Sardinia and off the Bay of Naples. It was also found in the Red Sea and the Persian Gulf. Local coral was traditionally worked at Trapani in Sicily and on the mainland in and about Naples. The royal coral factory was at Portici; many other workshops, some large, were at Torre del Greco. Genoa and Leghorn (Livorno) were also important centres of coral-working. The sources of supply off the Italian coast and the French shores, which were fished from Nice to Marseilles, were supplemented by coral from Tunisia and Algeria, the latter conquered by the French in 1830. Quantities of Algerian coral were processed in the factories set up at Marseilles by Barbaroux de Mégy, Boeuf et Garaudy and others. Before the end of the nineteenth century, Japanese coral had to be imported in increasing quantities by Italian coral-workers, due to over-fishing and pollution in the Mediterranean.

The coral worked by the jewellery trade came in several colours. The commonest and cheapest was red; variations, ranging from deep crimson to pale pink and clear white, were rarer and more expensive. The pale pink was the most costly. Black (found in quantity off Jeddah) was fashioned into beads, mainly for non-European consumption. Dull white coral, which did not take a good polish, was used only for cheap work.

The rough coral fished by Italian boats was sold in the markets of Naples, Genoa and Leghorn, the price varying according to availability and to size. The smallest pieces, according to the catalogue of the Italian contribution to the London 1862 Exhibition, fetched between 9d. and 10d. per kilogram, and the largest, according to origin, £4.4s. and £4.12s.6d. for the same amount. But Robert Hunt claimed the rare pink variety cost £20.15s.5d. per (English) oz.[95] Once processed, it was naturally more expensive. It is clear from several writers that prices also fluctuated wildly according to supply and demand; the discovery of a major reef off Sciacca, Sicily, in 1880 had a depressive effect for a while. It was exhausted fairly quickly. A report published in the *Journal* of the Society of Arts in 1894 quoted the current price of rough coral as ranging from about 9d. to £8 per kilogram.[96] In 1911 the commoner kinds of coral fetched between about 2s. and £11 per lb., a vast increase, and the rarer sorts £1 to £100 for the same weight.[97]

The coral-working factories, which employed men, women and children, were complemented by a cottage industry largely specialising in the production of beads. In Genoa, once coral branches had received their first polishing, they were sawn up into pieces, which were then graduated by being passed through sieves. Most of the workers engaged on these operations were women. The pieces were then assigned to different villages in the Val de Bisogno, each of which specialised mainly in beads of a set size and shape, often spherical or ovoid, plain or faceted. The work of piercing (with a primitive bow drill), shaping and polishing the beads on a rough grindstone, was often carried out by women, though men were employed in faceting the beads and also in carving cameos of standardised design (Plate 122). Small pieces were shaped into thin leaves and flower petals and from the early 1830s the tips of coral branches were simply polished and sold to jewellers who mounted them on metal, interspersing them with beads, to form wreaths (Colour Plate 59A). The beads were shaped into compressed spheres or made into ovals or full globes. The final polishing was accomplished with pumice and water, followed by hartshorn and water.

A proportion of the processed coral was sold to Italian jewellers, but much was exported, the beads being strung on silk and sold by weight. *Negligés* and other rows made from the tiny pieces otherwise known as seed corals were also available. The

Plate 122. A group of coral jewellery mainly dating to about 1840-65. The earrings and brooch are composed of separate components wired together; the links are carved with figure motifs (the right-hand pair is upside-down). These were intended for the European market and might have been executed in Italy. The articulated bracelet with its dragon-head was probably made for the South Indian market, where corals were much in demand. VICTORIA AND ALBERT MUSEUM

official figures of coral imported into England were considered useless by P.L. Simmonds, who held that they did not apply to the coral used by jewellers. He believed that quantities were brought into the country in the personal baggage of travellers and merchants; in 1873 he assessed the value of these unofficial imports as exceeding £100,000 annually. Jewellers elsewhere in Europe (especially in Russia) took a share of Italian coral, but the greatest part went elsewhere, to America, the West Indies, Morocco, India, China, Africa and Japan. Processed coral to the value of £600,000 was exported from Europe in 1862.[98] By 1895, Italy alone exported rough and worked coral worth more than £1,000,000, some sixty per cent of it destined for India.[99]

In the early 1880s, the factories at Torre del Greco, numbering forty in all, employed 3,200 people, of whom 2,800 were women. Some 2,600 workers were engaged in the trade elsewhere in Italy. The men earned between 10d. and 3s.6d. a day and the women and children from 8d. to 1s.8d.[100] Towards the end of the century, the Neapolitan factories were overhauled by those of Leghorn, though for years they had been sustained by the patronage of leading jewellers. Prominent among these was Robert Phillips of the firm of Phillips Brothers of Cockspur Street, whose contribution to the trade in Naples was recognised by the award of the Order of the Crown of Italy in 1870.

Garrard's sold Miss Julia Shuckburgh Evelyn sixty-three beads costing £2.10s. for bracelet strings in March 1806. The firm themselves purchased 15 dwt. of coral at the rate of £1.15s. per (troy) lb. from their fellow goldsmith and jeweller, Thomas Hamlet, in 1808. This was clearly of a better quality than the coral used in the '4 Small Coral Necklaces' sold by Garrard's for £1 apiece to Mrs Halsey, who must have bought them as gifts to infants. The set of 'seed coral', comprising a necklace, earrings and brooch mounted in gold, acquired by the Prince Regent from Rundell's in 1811, was far more expensive, costing £22.14s.[101]

The Duchesse d'Angoulême bestowed her patronage on a new coral-working factory in the rue de Grammont, Paris, shortly after the Restoration. The firm contributed to the French National Exhibition of 1819.[102] The factories which followed later in Marseilles were very successful, sending work destined for export to the Paris Exhibition of 1839. Barbaroux, who had already built up an export trade amounting to 700,000 francs, then employed 250 carvers, engravers, chasers, lapidaries and polishers, while Boeuf et Garaudy had a workforce of one hundred. Barbaroux was awarded a Silver Medal and his rivals a Bronze. At the 1844 Exhibition, when Barbaroux had his award renewed, his firm's exports to Africa, the East Indies and South America were said to have increased. Barbaroux had mechanised some of the processes of working and added shell cameos to his repertory, which already included coral cameos. Though the 1848 Revolution forced him to reduce his workforce and output, Barbaroux managed to make a favourable impression at the 1849 Exhibition. He had established an agency in Paris by 1844[103] and it is conceivable, given French pride in their native industry, that the coral cameos used by the Parisian jeweller Froment-Meurice in a pendant and paired brooches in about 1855 were carved in Paris or Marseilles (Plate 220A).

The Duc de Luynes, writing in the early 1850s, noted that the trade in Naples too had diminished. It was still enough, however, to provide stock for the Italian firm of importers, Paravagua & Casella, based in Brabant Court in the City of London, who contributed coral beads and jewellery to the Great Exhibition. Phillips Brothers also exhibited in 1851; their display included a coral inkstand imported from Gagliardi of Naples,[104] demonstrating that their connection with the Neapolitan trade was already established. Robert Phillips later exhibited under his own name and not that of his firm. Coral constituted a minor element in his

Colour Plate 49. A. This shell cameo brooch, a close copy of the signed Medusa in the bracelet in Plate 111, must have been copied in Saulini's workshop by assistants; the heavy corded gold frame is by Castellani of Rome; c.1855.
B. Shell cameo brooch representing Summer or Abundance, set in gold. The cameo is Italian, the setting indeterminate, c.1845-50.
C. A shell cameo head of Christ crowned with thorns, carved in Rome and set in a simple slip frame. Roman, 1840-60. BETHNAL GREEN MUSEUM

display at the Dublin 1853 Exhibition and probably (though it is not mentioned) at the Paris 1855 Exhibition. In 1862, it was altogether a more prominent feature, as the *Illustrated London News* made plain, citing Phillips' 'ornaments made of pink and fancy coral, some almost white, other specimens variegated, others of a kind of flesh colour, and all very excellent and beautiful of its kind. . . . the price which fine pink coral has now attained is enormous'.[105] A bracelet of gold and coral, part of a parure executed for the wife of Sir Thomas Fairbairn, was illustrated in the *Official Catalogue* (Plates 235 and 236). Hunt's *Handbook* spoke of Phillips' 'remarkable collection of corals' and 'extraordinary displays of workmanship' expressed in such pieces as a chain carved from a single piece of coral.[106] In later exhibitions, Phillips was equally distinguished for his archaeological jewellery.

There were few London firms to rival Phillips at Dublin in 1865, but Aubert & Linton of Regent Street showed a remarkable large pink coral parure comprising a floral tiara, comb, bodice ornament and necklace with earrings, bracelets and other items. Valued at £1,000, it was designed and carved by one Signor Gismondi, who spent twenty years assembling the materials.[107]

Colour Plate 50. A. A sardonyx cameo of Clytie, signed: L. SAULINI. F., *set in a silver-gilt brooch with corded wire borders and wirework ovals decorated with blue enamel; c.1865, the setting possibly English.*
B. An onyx cameo portrait of an unidentified bearded man, signed: L. SAULINI. F., *set in a gold slip frame within a tubular surround decorated with corded wires, scrolls and pelleted decoration in the archaeological classic style. The pendant loop is ornamented with applied wire scrolls and pellets. Italian, c.1850-70.* PHOTOGRAPH BY COURTESY OF ARES RARE, NEW YORK AND CAMEO CORNER, LONDON.
BOTH PIECES ARE NOW IN THE BRITISH MUSEUM, HULL GRUNDY GIFT

Colour Plate 51. Commesso *brooch of Queen Victoria, after a reversed detail of Wagstaff's engraving of Thomas Sully's portrait of the Queen in Robes of State, wearing George IV's circlet. The furred robes are represented in enamelled gold, the circlet in gold, diamond chips and emeralds. The bust was cut on a Bull's Mouth shell, which is signed on the back:* Paul Lebas/Graveur/1851/Paris; *the gold frame, decorated with enamelled roses of Lancaster and York, bears the maker's mark of Félix Dafrique of Paris and a French export mark for 1840 onwards. The piece was clearly part of Dafrique's display at the Great Exhibition of 1851 and the theme perhaps chosen to arrest the Queen's attention. Unfortunately she failed to remark on it in her Journal.* VICTORIA AND ALBERT MUSEUM

The principal Neapolitan exhibitors at the great international fairs included F. Avolio (Paris 1855 and 1867 and London 1862 and 1871).[108] In 1862 Avolio & Sons of Naples showed examples of so-called lava jewellery, carved from coloured limestones (see Colour Plate 59D). It is not surprising that the coral carvers, suffering from time to time from the whims of fashion, should turn their hand to making lava cameos and other ornaments. Vincenzo Castaldi showed lava and coral cameos priced at £1 apiece at the Dublin 1865 Exhibition, as Giuseppe Fusco had done in London in 1862.[109]

L. Gagliardi, presumably the maker patronised by Phillips, contributed coral and lava items to the Paris 1867 Exhibition.[110] The awards at the Naples Maritime Exhibition of 1872 included a Gold Medal to Giuseppe Mazza of Torre del Greco and another to Casalta and Morabito of Naples for suites of carved coral and other works.[111] Carlo Guida from Trapani showed coral and shell cameos ranging in price from £4 to £12 at the London 1862 Exhibition and Leonardo Guida a similar mixture of articles costing between £3.3s. and £9 at the Dublin 1865 Exhibition.[112] Among others, T.D. Oneto of Genoa sent coral trinkets to the Paris 1867 Exhibition. P. Raffaelli & Son of Leghorn contributed coral jewellery to the New York 1853 Exhibition after showing in London in 1851.[113]

Scagliola was also made to simulate coral; alabaster and ivory were dyed and processed to look like the material. Imitation amber and coral were shown at the Paris 1867 Exhibition by J. Belladina of Marseilles. The latter was probably coraline (or coralline), much in evidence in the cheap shops in the Palais Royale, Paris, but various kinds of imitation were in widespread use (see Chapter IX).

5. Ivory

Elephant ivory was the principal material used in nineteenth century jewellery, though for a time at least some French carvers used the canine teeth of the hippopotamus (known in the trade as sea-horse). Elephant tusks from India, Ceylon (Sri Lanka), South-East Asia and Africa were exported in rapidly increasing quantities until the last decade of the nineteenth century. Towards 1800, some 192 cwt. (9,754 kg) of ivory was brought into England. From London, the principal European market, considerable quantities were re-exported to other countries in Europe and elsewhere. In 1827, imports had grown to some 3,000 cwt. (152,407 kg); in 1850, to 9,396 cwt. (477,338 kg); in 1860, to 10,854 cwt. (551,408 kg); in 1870, to 59,423 cwt. (3,018,825 kg); in 1880, to 62,484 cwt. (3,174,331 kg) The wholesale slaughter of elephants caused supplies to diminish. The comparable figure in 1890 was 14,349 cwt. (728,962 kg) but by this time ivory from the Belgian Congo had begun surging through Antwerp.

Fossil ivory had been obtained from the bodies of mammoths from Siberia to China (and later also from Alaska) for some two hundred years; often partially rotten, it was cheaper than the elephant variety. Several tons annually passed through the London market, though whether or not it was used to any great extent in the European jewellery trade is unknown.

The so-called sea-horse ivory was complemented by walrus tusks. Between 1870 and 1880 some 400,000 lb. (181,440 kg) was obtained from about 100,000 animals in the Bering Sea, but such wholesale slaughter drastically reduced the number of tusks available thereafter. These tusks were coarser and less dense than hippopotamus teeth and, therefore, less satisfactory for detailed work. Bone, likewise much coarser than elephant ivory, was used in the cheaper kinds of jewellery.[114]

Ivory was usually seasoned and either turned or carved with chisels and gouges and smoothed with files, polished with very fine glass or emery paper and finished with whiting and water. It took stain easily.[115] Most ivory was consumed in the production of billiard balls, piano keys, knife handles, small statuary, combs and trinkets. Ivory was worked to an extent in London, Birmingham and elsewhere, but though Rundell's set ivory portrait plaques in work for George IV, English jewellers did not make extensive use of the material. The resourceful Harry Emanuel obtained a provisional patent on 15 March 1862 for metal jewellery decorated with ivory plaques counterset with stones, and went on to show these 'perfectly novel' specimens at the 1862 Exhibition shortly afterwards (Plate 123).[116] The Emanuel display in 1862 also included a statuette of a female slave dressed only in jewels, carved (except for her arms) from a single block of ivory (Plate 234). The reviewer of the *Illustrated London News* cast a lacklustre eye over Emanuel's exhibit, noting that the ivory, gold and gem-set jewellery was effective, 'combining cheapness, softness, and a certain adaptability of colour...; but as such ornaments were made in the time of the first Napoleon, and as very similar ones can be bought abroad and are even exhibited here, we think Mr. Emanuel's caution as to pirating should be needless...',[117] a clear reference to the provisional patent, which was intended to deter copyists. Hennig Brothers of St Giles's High Street, London, who proclaimed themselves 'Manufacturers of every description of ivory jewellery' in the *Business Directory of London* (1878), probably had German connections.

The chief centres of ivory-working in France were Paris, Méru, south of Beauvais, Dieppe (where brooches were cited among the offerings of local carvers in 1851), Chamonix in Haute-Savoie and the Jura. Some French carvers employed in the jewellery trade were reported in 1874 to use sea-horse ivory in preference to elephant ivory for articles in which 'great delicacy is required...especially in the manufacture of fine brooches'.[118] A Parisian jeweller, Bender, showed a brooch with an ivory cameo of Minerva mounted on a lapis ground at the London 1862 Exhibition. The type of ivory was not mentioned.[119] However, Richard Barter of Frederick Street, Dublin, contributed brooches with intaglios carved in sea-horse ivory mounted on carnelian to the Dublin 1853 Exhibition.[120]

Italian ivory carvers in Naples, Lucca and elsewhere sent work to successive international exhibitions; unfortunately the catalogue entries are not detailed enough to show whether they executed pieces small enough to be incorporated in jewellery. The brooch in Colour Plate 60, which combines lava and ivory, is possibly Neapolitan.

The ivory carvers of Erbach in Odenwald, where a school and workshop were established under the patronage of Count Franz von Erbach-Erbach in 1781, fostered the popularity of hunting scenes, or rather of rural idylls, with browsing

Colour Plate 52. Three specimens of Florentine mosaic on black marble grounds.
A. A mock locket with a silver loop; the mosaic depicts convolvulus and forget-me-not; c.1875.
B. A brooch with a mosaic of a pink rose and rose-buds in a scrolling gold frame; c.1840.
C. A circular brooch with a mosaic of jasmine and forget-me-not; the moulded frame is decorated with corded wire; c.1850.

stags (Plate 124). These were a speciality of Ernst Kehrer and his son Eduard; three brooches of about 1840 are illustrated in Brigitte Marquardt's *Schmuck* (1983).[121] The Kehrers probably had many assistants, though brooches of similar type were produced in other towns (Plate 125). In the second half of the nineteenth century Friedrich Hartmann specialised in floral compositions: he was responsible for designing the 'Erbacher Rosen', rose sprays tied with ribbons and hands holding roses. Philipp Willmann and Franz Wilhelm Wegel, also of Erbach, specialised in flower carvings; their fellow townsman, J. Michel, charged between 1s.8d. (his cheapest pendant) to £1.10s (his costliest brooch) for floral jewellery shown at the London 1862 Exhibition.[122]

L. Geismar & Co. of Wiesbaden were awarded a Prize Medal at the London 1851 Exhibition for 'Brooches and lids for boxes, carved in ivory, with subjects of the chase.'[123] Meiningen was another important centre of the craft, while Friedrich Schmidt of Geislingen, where Betsey Wynne's mother had purchased ivory 'Knicnacs' in 1797, sent brooches and other small wares in ivory and bone to the 1851 Exhibition.[124] In the ninth edition of Murray's *Handbook for Travellers in Southern Germany* (1863) those intending to visit Geislingen by train were warned that on arrival they would be 'beset by a crowd of girls and old women offering for sale toys in bone, wood, and ivory, which are manufactured on the spot...'

J.H. Sieber of Zurich sent brooches and other ivory trinkets to the London 1862 Exhibition;[125] they probably depicted Swiss flora and fauna. Similar work was reputedly executed in Thün and Brienz in Bern, though the naturalistic specimens in Colour Plates 61 and 62 were probably carved in Germany or Austria. Pieces of this type were imported by Waldemar Lund & Company of Chandos Street, near Charing Cross.[126] The wheat cross is very similar to one illustrated in a catalogue of about 1889 issued by the wholesale firm of Silber & Fleming of Wood Street, in the City of London. Any retailer who bought it would have paid 4s.6d. A hand and flower brooch in the same catalogue also cost 4s.6d. while a rosebud

Colour Plate 53. A parure of Roman mosaics of fruit, flowers and birds on a lapis lazuli ground, mounted in gold frames adorned with shells and scrolls in the 'Louis Quatorze' style; the longer of the two brooches may have been designed as a belt buckle. Possibly set in Italy; c.1830.

Plate 123. A chromolithographed page from the Official Illustrated Catalogue *of the International Exhibition held in London in 1862, showing Harry Emanuel's patented ivory, gold and gem-set jewellery. Some of the designs, including the disc brooches with petal centres, appear to have been inspired by Castellani.*

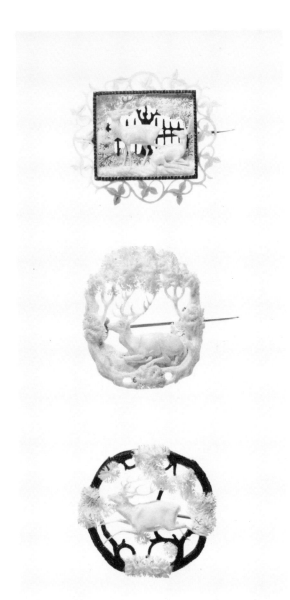

Plate 125. This intricate brooch of deer in a landscape, in a textured and stained ivory frame mounted on a mother-of-pearl backplate, was shown at the International Exhibition of 1862 and purchased from the exhibitor, L. Wagner or Wagener of the Hanseatic Department, by the Science and Art Department for £3.10s. and allocated to the Museum in Edinburgh.

NATIONAL MUSEUMS OF SCOTLAND

Plate 124. Three carved ivory brooches, perhaps from Erbach in South Germany. The frames are an integral part of the design and in two instances have been stained. Brooches of this kind were immensely attractive tourist souvenirs and were also imported by many countries.

MUSEUM OF LONDON

was priced at 3s. The firm's catalogues (mainly dating to the 1880s) which are preserved in the National Art Library at the Victoria and Albert Museum, demonstrate their immense range of goods of all kinds. Jewellery is represented by imported as well as British-made goods. Novelties are present, but many designs offered by Silber & Fleming in 1889 were distinctly old-fashioned.

In the early 1890s King Leopold II lent his support to a scheme for turning some of the ivory pouring into Belgium from the Congo to better artistic account. This bore fruit in work shown by the sculptor and jeweller Philippe Wolfers at the Antwerp 1894 Exhibition.[127] Taken up by Lalique and others in France and elsewhere, ivory figured prominently in Art Nouveau jewellery.

Carved alligator teeth were reported to be set in American jewellery in 1891; twenty years earlier, P.L. Simmonds wrote of 'glittering insects, or the teeth and claws of animals mounted in gold'[128] (see Plate 267). The English royals were particularly fond of deers' teeth jewellery (Colour Plate 131).

Corozo nuts, the fruit of South American trees allied to palms, were imported in quantity into Europe and, under the name of vegetable ivory, were carved and

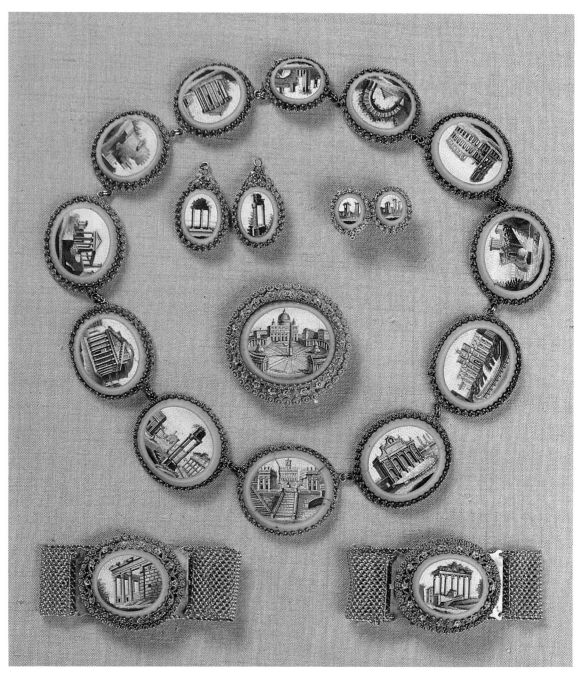

Colour Plate 54. A parure of Roman mosaics set in gold with cannetille *decoration, comprising a necklace, a pair of mesh bracelets with mosaic-set clasps, earrings, a brooch and small double belt-clasp. The mosaics, set in a light blue glass, illustrate most of the major sights of Rome. Those on the necklace include the Temple of Vesta, the Tomb of Cecilia Metella, the Temple of Hercules at Cora, the Pantheon, the Forum, the Capitol, the Fontana Paola, the Fontana di Trevi, the Temple of the Sybil at Tivoli and the Colosseum. On the bracelets are the Temple of Antoninus and Faustina and the Temple of Saturn. The Piazza of St Peter's is set in the brooch and the earrings bear the Temple of Vespasian and the Temple of Castor and Pollux. The mosaics on the clasp appear to be details of larger views in other items. The setting is Parisian and bears gold warranty marks for 1819-1838; it probably dates to about 1825.*

GILBERT COLLECTION, LOS ANGELES COUNTY MUSEUM OF ART

turned into buttons and trinkets in Birmingham as a cheap substitute for ivory.[129] They turned yellow in time but might also be dyed. The trade was largely lost to Germany by the 1880s. The first plastics were also coloured to resemble ivory, as mentioned in Chapter IX.

Colour Plate 55. A Roman mosaic brooch and earrings, representing mixed bunches of flowers, including roses, tulips and violets, on a black ground with purple glass support. Lush and somewhat seventeenth century in feeling (though not, of course, in date), the mosaics were probably mounted in Rome, c.1850.
BETHNAL GREEN MUSEUM

Colour Plate 56. A Roman mosaic brooch with fruit and curling vine leaves of a similar kind to the flower subject in Colour Plate 55. The archaeological gold frame with corded wire ornament was inspired by Castellani, but the type was in such widespread use that it is impossible to attribute it to Italy; c.1855.
BETHNAL GREEN MUSEUM

6. Marcasite

Marcasite (faceted crystals of iron pyrites), chiefly worked into jewellery in the Jura, was a popular substitute for diamonds in the latter half of the eighteenth century. Set in silver with rubbed-over collets, surviving specimens were brought out again as fashionable wear by Aesthetic ladies a hundred years later. Those unable to procure Georgian examples were able to purchase pieces newly made in France and elsewhere in central Europe (Plate 406D). In the cheapest types of work the crystals were glued on to pre-formed mounts.

251

One of the Dublin firms of Goggin used marcasite in some of their jewellery (Plate 126), though it is unclear whether this was intended as a substitute for the so-called 'Irish diamonds' (in fact, quartz crystals from the Wicklow Hills), which figured prominently in revived Celtic jewellery shown at international exhibitions.

7. Mother-of-pearl

All molluscs yielding pearls have a similar nacreous lining inside their shells and dealings in mother-of-pearl shells were conducted as a subsidiary of the pearl trade. The shells were often given names which signified the localities from which they had traditionally been shipped, though in some cases the original port of departure had lost the business to another. Lingeh shells from the Persian Gulf were so-called because they had formerly been handled at the port of that name. Bombay shells came from the east coast of Arabia but were shipped from the Indian port. Egyptian or Alexandria shells derived from the Red Sea.[130] For some time these latter were forwarded by way of Trieste to Vienna, where they were worked for the American market until the United States looked to local supplies. Panama shells from the coasts of Mexico, Costa Rica, Panama and California were plentiful. A proportion of the Red Sea shells were thereafter sent to Liverpool and London. Others went to Bethlehem, where they were carved with the aid of a graver, etching point and nitric acid. Shells from Western Australia were an important additional source of supply from the mid-1860s (see under Pearls).

Huge quantities of shells were consumed by Birmingham button-makers in the early years of the nineteenth century until fashion turned against them (it revived later). Lingeh shells, the smallest, were also the cheapest. Prices for the best shells ranged from 10s. to 20s. per cwt. (50.8 kg.) in the 1870s.

The shells were difficult to work. Circular saws, drills and files, sulphuric and nitric acids were used to process them.[131] The finished pieces were polished with calcined sulphate of lime. Widely used for cheap jewellery, fitted with base metal pins and attachments (Plate 127),[132] mother-of-pearl also found its way into work of a better kind. Harry Emanuel, who showed gold and pink shell at the London 1862 Exhibition, sent some mother-of-pearl ornaments worked on the lathe to a smaller international exhibition held in London ten years later.[133]

Green ear shells from New Zealand (*Haliotis splendens*) were employed in the manufacture of fancy buttons, studs, sleeve-links and earrings. The Turk's cap (*Turbo sarmaticus*), among other shells, was also used to decorate ornaments such as brooches.

Plate 126. A marcasite parure by Goggin of Dublin, with shamrock links and two harps of Brian Boru, one pendent from the necklace and the other from the brooch. There were several members of the Goggin family in the trade; Cornelius Goggin of Nassau Street and J. Goggin of Grafton Street were enthusiastic participants in international exhibitions. This set probably dates to the late nineteenth century. A bracelet in the same style, also set with marcasites, is in the Ulster Museum, Belfast.
BIRMINGHAM CITY MUSEUM AND ART GALLERY, HULL GRUNDY GIFT

Colour Plate 57. A Roman mosaic parure, comprising a necklace, brooch and earrings with devices taken from early Christian and Byzantine sources. The Lamb of God appears on the largest pendant on the necklace and in the centre of the brooch. The Chi-Rho for Christ, the Dove, emblem of the Holy Spirit, and the Evangelists figure among the other motifs. The archaeological gold setting bears the Roman hallmark and the applied mark of Antonio Carli (1830-1870), who closed down his business in the Piazza San Silvestro in 1866. This parure probably dates to 1860-66. GARRARD & COMPANY

8. Pearls

A. Marine and Freshwater Pearls

The great bulk of the pearls used by jewellers in the nineteenth century was obtained from the salt-water mollusc *Pinctada vulgaris*. The chief sources were the Persian Gulf and the Gulf of Manaar in Ceylon (Sri Lanka). Pearl-bearing molluscs were also fished in many other localities, including the Red Sea, the Californian coast, the Gulf of Mexico, Panama, Venezuela, Ecuador, the Pacific Islands and Malay Archipelago, the Dutch East Indies, Japan and (from about 1865) Western Australia, where E.W. Streeter had a boat. The shells from which a large proportion of the pearls derived had a separate commercial value (see under Mother-of-Pearl).

Colour Plate 58. Three varieties of amber, opaque, cloudy and transparent, are used with moonstones in a long pendant and chain. The opaque pendant, carved roughly in the shape of a fist and embellished with a ring-like cluster of silver granules, is capped with a cluster of silver leaves and pellets decorated with moonstones and transparent amber. Cloudy amber and moonstones are set in the chain. A late piece of Arts and Crafts design, the pendant and chain may be the work of Sybil Dunlop, who set up in business in London in 1919.

PRIVATE COLLECTION

Plate 127. A group of costume jewellery with a mother-of-pearl butterfly hairpin, a glass and metal fly made to a design registered by Elijah Atkins of Birmingham in 1869, a gilt metal leaf brooch with a fly and a shell butterfly, all dating to the second half of the nineteenth century.

The fine 'orient' of the best pearls is the optical effect created by the nacreous plates composing the inner layer, which reflect a soft sheen. Their weight was expressed in carats and grains (four grains to the carat). By 1865 a fine white pearl of thirty grains was worth £80-£100, and a drop pearl much more.

Freshwater pearls are formed in one of the mussels of the genus *Unio,* found in rivers; their lustre is less evident. The river Conwy in North Wales was a traditional source of supply, but of little or no importance in the nineteenth century. The Scottish rivers, however, still yielded pearls, and the dealer Moritz Unger, who travelled around the country buying specimens from the finders in 1865, estimated that the total value of Scottish river pearls in the same year amounted to some £12,000. At that time, Scottish pearls averaged £2.6s. to £2.10s. apiece, but prices rose subsequently and Queen Victoria, a keen collector, was said to have expended £42 on a particularly fine example.[134] This was in line with prices of between £40 and £50 for river pearls found in the river Strule at Omagh, County Tyrone in Ireland. River pearls were also obtained in Bavaria,[135] Saxony (where seed pearls weighing less than half a grain, as well as larger varieties, were found), Sweden, Lapland and elsewhere, and (from the late 1880s) the Mississippi Valley in the United States of America.[136]

Colour Plate 59. A. A branch coral wreath with applied coral berries, mounted on gold; c.1830-1850.
B. A coral cameo of the infant Bacchus, set as a brooch in a gold slip frame; c.1840-60.
C. A cherub carved in malachite, set like the Bacchus and probably the same date.
D. A carved lava cameo of Flora, set in gold as a brooch with a toothed border. The cameo is probably
Neapolitan; c.1860-70.   VICTORIA AND ALBERT MUSEUM

The pearling season in the Persian Gulf, centred on Bahrain, ran from June to October. Most of the pearls fished by divers were either white or yellowish, with a few pink, bluish, grey and (even rarer) black specimens. Black pearls were not popular until the Empress Eugénie took them up and others followed her. Black pearls were often obtained in Panama and Mexico, but any deficiency was made up by soaking ordinary pearls in silver nitrate and exposing them to sunlight, which gave them a lustrous black hue. An exceptional brown pearl, valued at £16,000, was shown at the Naples 1872 Exhibition by the royal jeweller Marchesini of Rome and Florence.[137]

The Arab divers at Bahrain used a bone or horn nose clip and worked with an attendant. The diver went over the side of the boat with a rope and a stone heavy enough to take him straight to the bottom, together with a basket. He rapidly shovelled the shells into his basket and shook the rope to indicate that he should be hauled up. The rising value of the yield from 1893 onwards was partly occasioned by the vast increase in the price of pearls, which soared past that of diamonds, still unhappily affected by the glut of the previous decade. Pearls in their turn were brought down sharply by the development by Mikimoto of Japan of the completely spherical cultured pearl in the first decade of the twentieth century.

Most of the pearls went to Indian dealers, many of whom helped to finance the fishery, and the rest to Baghdad. Consignments of pearls were remitted from Bombay to clients in Europe and America.

The pearl fishery in the Gulf of Manaar in Ceylon yielded more intermittently. The Dutch allowed no fishery from 1768 to 1796; the British, on taking over the island, leased the rights to a merchant of the East India Company, who sublet them. Later, the government assumed the administration of the fishery. No pearling was permitted in the years when stocks were reduced, but the fishery was in a flourishing state in the early 1900s.

Leonard Woolf, the grandson of a Jewish diamond merchant from Holland who had settled in London, was in the British Colonial Service in Ceylon for some years before returning to England and marrying the future novelist Virginia Stephen. From 20 February to 3 April 1906, Woolf helped to supervise the fishery in the Gulf of Manaar from Marichchukaddi, a normally deserted township which only came alive with the arrival of about 20,000 to 30,000 people during the season. They included Tamil and Arab divers (the latter from the Persian Gulf), jewellers, dealers, traders and criminals. If conditions were favourable, wrote Woolf, a gun was fired at 2 or 3 a.m., signalling the launching of some 473 boats. A maroon sounded for their return in the afternoon, but not all obeyed.

Each boat-load was divided into three heaps in an official enclosure, two of which were chosen by Woolf as the government's share and auctioned off every evening. The remaining heap was removed by the fishermen and sold separately. The purchased molluscs were put into dugouts and the flesh left to putrefy for several days in the heat. Finally, the decayed matter was swilled out with sea-water and the shells searched for pearls. Up to two million molluscs were landed each day; Woolf wrote feelingly of the vile stench permeating the township, attracting myriads of flies.[138]

The introduction of more sophisticated diving apparatus in about 1880 increased the catches in many areas for a while. A French company purchased a concession to fish for pearls with apparatus off the Venezuelan island of Margarita, a traditional source of supply which in 1901 yielded pearls to the value of about £120,000, most of which were consigned to Paris. The French firm clearly hoped to improve on this figure, but instead helped to exhaust the fishery.

Pearls never went out of fashion until the introduction of the spherical cultured pearl. Round pearls, pear-shaped pearls (favoured for earrings), baroque or misshapen pearls and the blister variety which grew on the inner surface of the mollusc, as well as tiny seed-pearls, were all used by jewellers to a greater or lesser extent. By 1862 Hunt & Roskell exhibited a necklace comprising a single row of thirty-two pearls, with a brilliant and black pearl pendant. Priced at £8,000,[139] it represented a modest peak of High Victorian luxury. But even the Empress Josephine would have been impressed by the be-coroneted and swagged magnificence of Mrs Gould, the wife of an American millionaire, at the turn of the century (Plate 375).

It is possible to rectify damage to a pearl by stripping off the outer layer, but this operation is not always successful.

B. Cultured Pearls

For centuries the Chinese had practised pearl culture by introducing irritants into freshwater molluscs. Sometimes consisting of baked earth pellets and sometimes fragile cast metal images, they were removed when they had received a nacreous coating. Widespread commercial development of the technique was made possible by Kokichi Mikimoto of Japan, who after extensive experimentation inserted seed pearls into pearl oysters placed on mechanically-rolling racks in a shallow bay and managed to obtain spherical pearls shortly after 1900.[140] It took several years for the full implication of cultured pearls to dawn on dealers and the public, but by the 1920s the price of natural pearls had come down very considerably.

The long history of imitation pearls is discussed in Chapter IX.

9. Tortoiseshell and Horn

The tortoiseshell in the trade derived from the hawksbill and caret turtles, which have thicker and stronger plates than other types. The thirteen plates on the carapace were known as 'the head', four on each side and five on the back. The two middle side plates were regarded as the most valuable. In addition, the animal has twenty-four marginal plates. The yellowish scales of the plastron, or under-shield, were employed for many objects which would otherwise be made from horn. Together with the 'hoofs', the plates on the back of the carapace and the margins, they were also often used in the production of semi-transparent combs. In 1862, when they contributed tortoiseshell specimens to the London 1862 Exhibition, Stewart's of Aberdeen were said to be the largest comb factory in the world.

In the 1840s, when ornamental combs were still sought after, the price of tortoiseshell reached as much as £4.4s. per lb. (.455 kg.). In 1873, after a period

Colour Plate 60. A lava cameo, possibly Flora or a personification of Summer, set in the centre of a carved floral ivory frame, stained a yellowish-brown, and mounted in a gold slip surround as a brooch. This may have been carved in Naples; c.1880. PRIVATE COLLECTION

Colour Plate 61. An ivory cross of oak leaves and acorns with matching earrings; c.1880. Fitted with a gilt metal pin and hooks, the pieces were mass-produced in Germany, probably with the aid of a powered tool. The artful naturalism is heightened by a few empty acorn cups. PRIVATE COLLECTION

of depressed prices, good mottled shells from Zanzibar, Bombay and Singapore were sold wholesale at 28s. to 29s.6d. per lb. and West Indian specimens from 31s. to 41s. per lb. Ox and buffalo horn was much cheaper. Buffalo horn from Sierra Leone sold at 25s. to 30s. per cwt. (50.8 kg.) in mid-century. One million buffalo horns were shipped from Madras alone in 1856. Rhinoceros horn was little used in Europe until the end of the century; ram's horn was more usually employed in the manufacture of snuff boxes and other items associated with Scotland. Stag's horn was a popular type of cheap jewellery in Nuremberg and elsewhere in Germany. In 1856 Bing of Frankfurt, manufacturers of stag's horn jewellery and other items, advertised in Murray's *Handbook for Travellers in North Italy* that their productions were sold by J. & R. McCracken of 7 Old Jewry in the City of London, who also imported Florentine mosaics by Bianchini and Genoese filigree by G. Loleo. A Nuremberg horn brooch found its way into Charlotte Yonge's *Clever Woman* (1865, Chapter IV).

The materials were worked in a very similar fashion once cut into sections. Softened in boiling salted water, they might be pressed or moulded in heated dies, though horn required greater heat than tortoiseshell. The latter tended to blacken when over-heated. The materials might also be worked on the lathe. Any shreds left over were sufficiently plastic to be melded together and shaped into objects in a brass mould immersed in a boiler. Large combs were cut with drills and fine saws; from about 1828 a machine invented by a Mr Lynn enabled two small side combs to be cut at Stewart's from a single plate. In 1862 these machine-made combs were offered retail at 1d. per pair,[141] a reduction of about 1,600 per cent on the prices of twenty years earlier.

Colour Plate 62. An ivory cross formed of ears of wheat such as was imported and sold at the trade price of 4s.6d. by Silber & Fleming in the City of London. The turned ivory chain was an extra; c.1889.

Horn was made to imitate tortoiseshell by brushing it over with a paste, described in 1873 as comprising two parts of lime, one part litharge (lead monoxide) 'and a little soda-lye', which was allowed to dry. This mixture formed sulphuret of lead, with the sulphur in the albumen of the horn, producing a dark mottled effect.[142] Towards the end of the century, when a pale colour was wanted by Art Nouveau jewellers, horn was bleached with hydrogen peroxide (Colour Plate 207).

The materials might also be pierced with drills and fine saws, and engraved with patterns. Like ivory, it was often ornamented with inlays of gold and silver, a technique known as piqué and much employed by makers of small boxes and, in the nineteenth century, of jewellery (Plate 128).

A Parisian manufacturer named Philip showed tortoiseshell jewellery at the London 1851 Exhibition, to which E. Nash of Clerkenwell contributed tortoiseshell piqué boxes.[143] S. Corbeels of Paris was the sole French exhibitor of piqué jewellery at the London 1862 Exhibition; F. Labriola of Naples, another exhibitor, contributed articles similarly inlaid.[144] A decade later, the technique was taken up

in Birmingham. The display of piqué trinkets by Charles Lyster & Son of Spencer Street, Birmingham, at the London 1872 Exhibition, was considered by the Jury to have 'the merit of prettiness at least...unpretending as to general tone, but their geometric treatment is good, though capable of much further development and enrichment'. George Wallis commented in the *Art Journal* catalogue of 1872: 'This branch of the trinket trade has long been confined almost exclusively to Paris, and Messrs. Lyster have been the first to manufacture this inlaid work at Birmingham....Some of the crosses are especially interesting for the excellence of their form and workmanship....Geometric in character, the details cover the ground of tortoiseshell in an effective and perfectly legitimate manner, producing a pleasing and brilliant result. The *ultra-naturalesque* details so much in vogue for the decoration of these tortoiseshell trinkets, are chiefly the result of a vulgar want of taste in the middle-man who buys for the market...'. In fact, Lyster may already have been using a machine to inlay the work, for which purpose running patterns were much more suitable than naturalistic details (Plate 370D).[145] Four years later Wallis added, in another essay, that the piqué trinkets made in Birmingham consisted not only of tortoiseshell (and, by implication, horn), decorated with gold and silver, but an imitation of the former. This was 'produced by running gelatine mixed with metallic salts, into moulds, [creating] the effect of the markings of tortoiseshell by the staining with hydro-sulphate of ammonia.' It was inlaid with gilt metal.[146]

Plate 128. Tortoiseshell piqué jewellery, mainly dating to the second half of the nineteenth century. Most of the naturalistic decoration in gold and silver is earlier than the more geometric type, which was strongly endorsed by members of the British cultural establishment. VICTORIA AND ALBERT MUSEUM

Colour Plate 63. A. A bracelet formed of gold cable links which are solid and pierced, rather than open, fastened by a heart-shaped padlock inscribed GRATITUDE *in gothic script. Dating to about 1835, the bracelet is believed to have been given by King William IV to Queen Adelaide as a gesture of thanks for her kindness to him during an illness. The padlock has a tiny gold key.*

B. In contrast to the simple piece above, this unmarked bracelet is in the French manner and virtually identical to one illustrated by Vever (I, opposite page 106). It is constructed of oval units with jointed diavolo-shaped links between, the latter decorated with chased acanthus leaves in green gold and set with stones bordered by grainti *and the former with amethyst cabochons surrounded by other coloured stones over filigree openwork interspersed with* cannetille *and* grainti. *Boxes for hair are set behind the main stones. In the attempt to create the desired polychromatic effect, the jeweller has amplified the genuine stones with pastes. It probably dates to 1825-30.* VICTORIA AND ALBERT MUSEUM

CHAPTER VII
A Typology of Fashion, 1821-1836

*A*ckermann's Repository, surveying current French fashions in 1820, reported that rubies now ranked next to diamonds in 'full-dress' jewellery, that pearls were not quite so much in favour, though still worn a great deal, while the 'perfect rage' for coral which had developed a few seasons ago, when it ranked so high in estimation as to be used in conjunction with diamonds in full-dress, had abated to such an extent that it was now 'confined, very properly, to half dress'.[1] A pair of coral top and drop earrings acquired by Mrs Garrard from the family firm in December 1821 was almost certainly wanted for informal occasions.

In 1823 diamonds, normally the essential ingredient in the jewels of the rich, were more in evidence in London than in Paris, according to a fashion writer who noted a lady resplendent in a parure worth some £240,000[2] at a recent ball given by the Duke of Devonshire. But early in 1825 it was announced that diamonds had returned to high fashion in Paris,[3] the forthcoming coronation of Charles X presumably having enticed the stones out of hiding.

During the 1820s coloured stones were still frequently used in conjunction with diamonds in primary jewellery; even so, a tendency to revert to diamonds alone is discernible. Rundell's made 'a very fine Ruby & Brilliant Fuschia pattern Head Ornament' priced at £560 for George IV in 1828.[4] Pearls replaced diamonds in other ornaments in which coloured stones were prominent.

In secondary jewellery stones were crowded together in an almost unlimited series of polychromatic combinations (Colour Plate 63B) or counterset to create the saturated effect currently much admired (Colour Plate 64A). Sometimes a dozen or so stones of different colours were set together in one piece. Among the more modest arrangements, taken from items in George IV's accounts, were rubies and turquoises with diamonds (1820)[5]; rubies, emeralds, pearls and diamonds (1821) and coral and malachite (1821).[6]

In 1828 the fashion correspondent of *Ackermann's Repository*, referring to the popularity of multi-coloured jewellery in France, stated that the latest necklaces comprised lozenge or oval units decorated with three or four different stones. A variation mentioned by the writer was a 'necklace composed of one kind of gems only, and ...suspended from it a cross, in which are four different coloured stones'. These also adorned matching earrings.[7]

The most popular stones, real and fake, in all types of jewellery, included rubies, sapphires, emeralds, amethysts, garnets, opals (despite Sir Walter Scott), jacinths, peridots, topazes, chrysolites, aquamarines, carnelians, onyx, sardonyx and bloodstone, the last four also continuing popular with gem-engravers. These coloured stones were not always used to polychromatic effect, nor were others which appear more sporadically in royal and other bills, ledgers and fashion reports of the time. Chrysoprase, little known in London until towards 1820, was much admired thereafter. George IV was among the first to adopt the Parisian vogue for the stone when it reached London. His purchase of a diamond and chrysoprase cross and earrings from the Royal Goldsmiths in December 1819 was followed in 1820 by a 'pair of fine Crisopaz Earrings' costing £30, also supplied by Rundell's.[8] The King, who had earlier developed a liking for lapis lazuli, bought a 'Lapis-Lazuli cross mounted in fine gold gothic pattern necklace' for £14.14s. in 1824.[9]

Three specimens of engraved Oriental stones mounted in jewellery figured in Thomas Hamlet's sale of 1834, reflecting a continuing taste for the exotic. Other items in the sale were set with cameos and Italian mosaics. Amber from the Baltic[10] was mildly popular; jet flourished in both fashionable and mourning wear, and the demand for coral increased. There was, as noted elsewhere, a restricted market for ivory articles. Aside from jewellery made from Scottish stones, pebbles of all kinds, picked up on beaches or in the countryside, were frequently set in trinkets, a practice which had already developed into a tourist industry on the Continent, especially in Switzerland.[11] In 1829, Garrard's made a pair of 'Bognor Stone Braceletts in Gold with Gold Chain between 4 Stones each' for their client, Colonel Todd, charging him £28; these articles were subsequently returned to the firm to be shortened.

The most noticeable change in the appearance of diamond settings resulted from the gradual shedding of the prominent ribs crowding the profiles of complex articles. When small stones were grouped together, they were secured by grains within smooth walled mounts (Colour Plate 65). Ribbed cut-down collets continued to be employed for larger stones and claw settings also appear, but these were in the minority (Colour Plate 66). Shaped borders of diamonds in cut-down settings were still made. In the 1830s the collets in which coloured stones were set were sometimes scalloped or indented at the junction with the stones. The English retained their preference for large stones packed together as closely as possible. In Paris, except in royal circles, smaller stones were more general, but this was probably less a matter of taste than of economic necessity.

Gold, still cheaper than during the Napoleonic wars, was much in evidence on all but the most ceremonial occasions, plain and matted, coloured, embossed, cast and chased, enamelled or made into filigree (Colour Plate 64). The consumption of gold greatly increased from 1815 to the 1820s and later, but the quality of the metal was variable. Only in France, where all articles of jewellery were legally required to be hallmarked, was there any real control over the fineness of the gold employed in the trade. The two English standards currently in force, of 22 and 18 carats, were ignored by most jewellers on the false grounds that the many exemptions allowed to their work under the hallmarking laws effectively placed everything they made outside the legal system. As the mass-production of gold trinkets was expanded, it was to become customary for manufacturers to use what was tactfully described in Dionysus Lardner's *Cabinet Cyclopaedia* (1849) as 'gold alloyed in various degrees'.[12] The more alloy was added, the more the fineness of the gold departed from the legal standards.

The popularity of gold unadorned by stones was perhaps due to its effectiveness as a foil to the exuberant cacophony of many gem-set and enamelled pieces (Colour Plates 63B and 64). In 1831, catching on to a rage for mouse jewellery launched in Paris about seven years earlier, the Duchess of Gloucester bought from Garrard's 'A Gold Bracelet with Mouse' costing £4.10s. Thomas Creevey reported in the same year to his step-daughter, Miss Ord, that he had attended a dinner-party at which Lady Cecilia Underwood (the morganatic wife of the Duke of Sussex)[13] sported 'such a profusion of gold bijouterie in all parts that nothing was wanting but something hanging from her nose'.[14] Mesh was widely used for necklaces, bracelet bands and the like (Colour Plate 64). Filigree with *cannetille* and *grainti,* backed and unbacked (Colour Plates 63B, 64, etc.,) was still produced in quantity in France, the Low Countries,[15] Germany, Switzerland, Italy and elsewhere on the Continent and to a lesser extent in England. French inspiration is apparent in all the work of this kind, whether made in London or Vienna.[16] Jewellers liked it because they could make a little gold go a long way in the creation of elaborate effects, but it is possible to speculate that it was admired by many of their female clients, practitioners of the amateur art of quilling, or decorating boxes and the like with patterns formed of scrolled paper,[17] who could appreciate the intricacy of the work.

It is difficult to determine the extent to which the technique was practised in England outside the restricted circle of the leading firms, many of which employed craftsmen born or trained on the Continent. Some of these concerns also imported French-made articles. On the whole, however, it was probably less costly to have the filigree-work executed locally, using as models a few specimens purchased in Paris. In the first part of the Hamlet sale of 1834 there were some 260 lots of jewellery (including watches), many comprising groups or sets rather than single articles. Twenty-two of these lots were made in whole or in part of filigree, a small enough proportion but still substantial. A further two had a 'grain setting',[18] clearly a reference to *grainti.* None was given a French provenance in the catalogue, though it would undoubtedly have appealed to prospective purchasers. Two imported French clocks were, however, cited which increases the chance that the jewellery was made in England. Three years before the Hamlet sale the Duchess of Gloucester acquired from Garrard's 'An Aquamarine Sevigné & Ear rings in filigree Gold'. Complete with a case, this demi-parure of earrings and a bodice ornament (usually bow-shaped but see Colour Plate 67 and Plate 129) cost her £24. Unfortunately no contemporary Workmen's Ledger survives to establish the actual maker.

Some of the best work in the intricate late neo-classical style of the 1820s was made of cast and coloured gold, as in the previous decade. The contrasting effects produced by the juxtaposition of matted and polished surfaces were also exploited internationally by jewellers. Rococo borders, popular with makers of mourning rings, spread to larger items (Colour Plate 68C) and scroll edges were sharply ridged. Engraved decoration began to be used extensively in the 1830s. English and Continental tastes were most fully reconciled, however, in the strongly-defined die-stamped components which emerged from presses in higher relief and larger than heretofore (Colour Plate 68A). Sometimes the units were backed with a flat plate of gold. The solder used in this operation by some French jewellers was below standard, putting them at odds with the law. But the swelling forms were often left

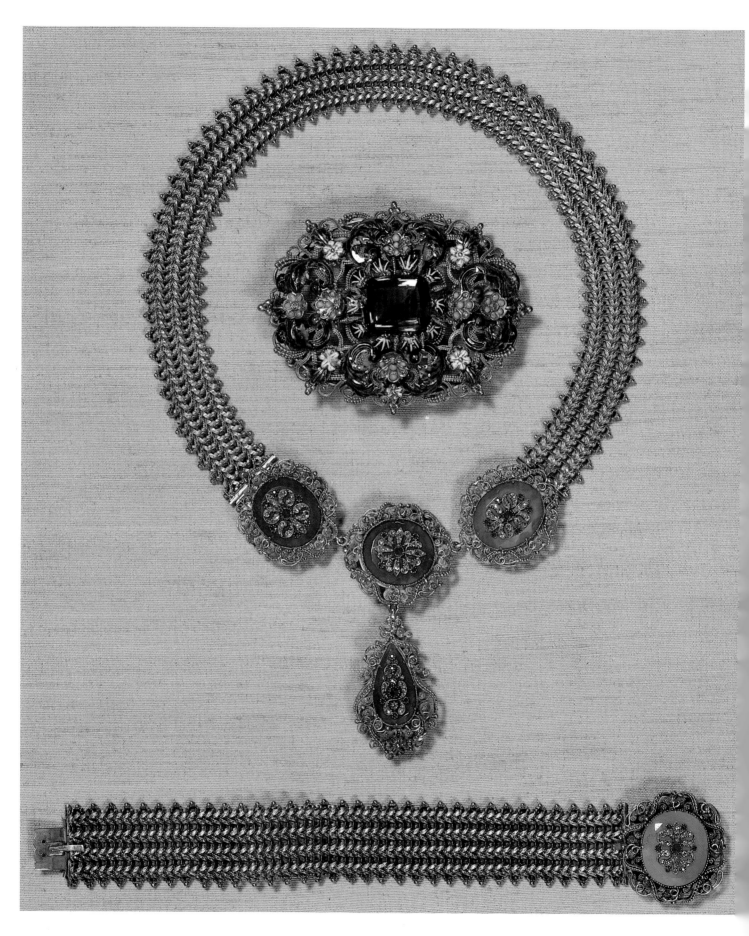

Colour Plate 66. Another spray, of mixed flowers (including a daisy), the stalks gathered together to form a shape reminiscent of the Bourbon lily. Made of coloured gold, it is embellished with brilliants held in open scalloped collets punctuated by claws which hold the stones. It is almost certainly Continental, c.1825.
VICTORIA AND ALBERT MUSEUM

Colour Plate 65. A diamond fuschia spray brooch, a favourite theme of jewellers in the 1820s and 1830s. The lowest blossom droops abruptly, returning to the stem. A liking for sharply turning forms is also noticeable in the Maltese cross in Plate 40. The walled gold settings enclose brilliants and roses secured by grains. It probably dates to about 1830-1835. VICTORIA AND ALBERT MUSEUM

unbacked, especially those intended for earrings, which began to lengthen in the late 1820s to the extent that weight became an important consideration. Engine-turning was used in a fairly limited way.

Gold or copper were the usual supports for most enamels. Pictorial enamelists such as Henry Bone and William Essex rarely produced original studies for setting in jewellery: they mainly worked from existing paintings (including portraits), scaling them down to an appropriate size. They were regarded, however, as artists and remunerated accordingly.[19] The King, who had never visited Switzerland, was indebted to E. & W. Smith in February 1824 for furnishing a specimen of a popular tourist souvenir (see Colour Plate 68B), a bracelet with enamelled views of the Swiss Cantons.[20] The ultimate recipient of the bracelet found that it did not fit, for within a month Smith's were required to add another piece (a view of the Canton of Bern) to the article. Had it been intended for Lady Conyngham's plump wrist? Swiss enamellers, like their counterparts elsewhere, worked in a range of styles for their clients. The painted enamel flowers on the cover of a watch set in the clasp of a bracelet by Bautte et Moynier of Geneva in about 1825 has a fashionable seventeenth century flavour (Plate 130). The dark background is an admirable foil for the brightly-coloured flowers. The enamelled decoration of its baluster band, however, is characteristic of Swiss and North Italian work of the 1830s.

Colour Plate 64. A. A gold mesh necklace and bracelet; the three linked units and the single pendant at the front of the necklace, together with the bracelet clasp, are adorned with chrysoprases counterset with small brilliants and rubies in a scrolling design. They are all bordered by filigree openwork with cannetille *and* grainti. *In the French style, the pieces date to about 1825.*
B. A brooch large enough to be used as an impressive bodice ornament, in gold filigree with cannetille *and* grainti *and applied enamel decoration, set with a large amethyst and small turquoise forget-me-nots with diamond centres and shells. Another example of work in the French style, the piece was probably made in about 1825-30.* VICTORIA AND ALBERT MUSEUM

Plate 129. A plate from Knight's Fancy Ornaments, *1834, demonstrating the eclecticism of the time. The panel on the left has scrolling foliage interspersed with gothic quatrefoils and that on the right has the interlaced angular ornament characterising the Duchess of Kent's pendant in Colour Plate 71. The large bodice ornament in the middle (which, though not bow-shaped, might have been called a sévigné) mixes elements of the baroque and rococo with, in the larger pendants, suggestions of the gothic rather in the manner of the pendant and earrings in Plate 132. The bracelet below has a baroque cartouche as a centre, but shares leafage and scrolls with the bodice ornament. Aspects of both are reflected in Colour Plate 67.*

The Swiss bracelet band is decorated with champlevé enamel, in which the ground was hollowed out, as already described in the Introduction, to receive the different enamel colours. These were made of ground glass formed into a paste. The colours, revitrified by firing in a muffle furnace, were opaque; the variant known as *basse-taille* showed translucent over a textured ground (see page 59). The most fashionable hues of the period were strong to hectic.

Platinum and silver alloy was used in France as a ground for enamels, according to the Duc de Luynes.[21] Its largely humble role at the time was emphasised by a report in the *Belle Assemblée* in 1830, which gave details of an imitation gold alloy much employed by German jewellers. It consisted of sixteen parts of platinum, seven of copper and one of zinc.[22] By this time the French had already developed a different substitute for gold in *'Or doublé'* or *'Doublé d'or'*, inspired by Sheffield plate. Instead of fusing plates of silver to the top and underside of a copper ingot and rolling the combined result into the required gauge they used gold for the outer coating but kept the copper core.[23] The technique (later known in England as 'rolled gold') was so successful that it was copied in Birmingham using either copper or brass, but perhaps not to the same extent as in France. English manufacturers were soon to adopt electro-gilding, introduced in about 1838.

Platinum jewellery by Bernauda, who embellished his products with coloured gold, was said to be so popular in France in 1823 that the cost of the pieces almost rivalled that of gold wares, another instance of hyperbole on the part of fashion writers.[24] The London price of platinum in 1831 was 25s. per oz., about 3s. cheaper than its cost in Russia, a curious situation since the metal was mined in the Urals from about 1825. But it was used by the Imperial Mint of Russia for coinage, which kept the price up. The American mineralogist, James Dickson, visited Russia in 1831 and was impressed by the yield and price of what he called 'platina',[25] further evidence that the platina chains sold in London were not a mixture of platinum and gold but consisted chiefly of the first metal with a small amount of alloy. Thus, the 'platina and gold chain' purchased by George IV from E. & W. Smith in 1824 must have been made of platinum decorated with gold on its surface, like the Bernauda trinkets.

Silver acquired a new prestige, partly owing to the work of Charles Wagner, a German-born goldsmith who settled in France in about 1830 and experimented with enamelling on platinum alloy. While in Berlin, Wagner had studied specimens of Russian silverwork decorated with niello, a dark grey mixture of silver, lead, copper and sulphur which was inlaid in depressions engraved in the surface of the metal. It was sometimes fired at a low temperature, sometimes simply allowed to dry. The technique had died out in Western Europe after the Middle Ages, and Wagner's work in reviving it after his arrival in Paris created a considerable stir, enhanced by his reputation as a protagonist of the gothic and Renaissance styles.[26] However, niello was not widely adopted in the jewellery trade. It was largely left to the artist-craftsmen of the late nineteenth century to realise its decorative potential. Much the same may be said of damascening (the technique of decorating one metal such as steel with inlays of gold or silver). Practised on a small scale in Paris in the 1830s and 1840s, it dwindled away until revived there in the 1870s. Damascened jewellery was however produced throughout this time and afterwards in Spain (Plate 293D). More significant, as far as jewellery was concerned, was the introduction in Paris of oxidisation, a technique for darkening and shading metal which was to be much used in the figurative silver jewellery made in Paris in the 1840s and 1850s by Wagner's former pupil F.J. Rudolphi and others (Colour Plate 96).

Berlin ironwork, manufactured in Paris from 1827 (see Colour Plate 69 and Plate 131) as well as in several areas in Germany and Austria, was still largely

Colour Plate 67. A gold and turquoise bodice brooch with sharp polished scrolls, foliage and lobed ornament derived from the gothic, which must be contemporaneous with the Knight pattern. Though bow-shaped sévignés were traditional, objects like this bodice brooch seem to have been given the same name.

GARRARD & COMPANY

Colour Plate 68. A. An English bodice brooch and matching earrings of about 1835 in stamped gold set with carbuncles (almandine garnets cut en cabochon). Light and cheap to make, the gold components were shaped, polished and set before being fitted together. The stones are mounted in closed and foiled collets with flat claws. The articles are unbacked, but the brooch has an applied locket fitting behind the central stone.
B. An enamelled Swiss scenic brooch, set in an openwork scrolling frame which is decorated with many of the motifs appearing in Knight but deployed in a different fashion. The thin open scrolls are not characteristic of English work, but it appears likely that English jewellers imported complete articles as well as enamelled plaques; c.1830.
C. The amethyst in this brooch has been set in the same fashion as the carbuncles in the bodice brooch and earrings above. The matted border is edged with polished scrolls.

A AND C, VICTORIA AND ALBERT MUSEUM, B PRIVATE COLLECTION

unknown in England. In 1825, ornaments from the Berlin foundry were sent to King George IV by the British Minister in the city. Sir William Knighton, Keeper of the Privy Purse, received two pairs of bracelets from the same source.[27] Among other materials hair (Colour Plate 70) and horsehair (Colour Plate 193) were fashionable, and morocco survived in use for bracelet bands.[28]

The geometrical shapes current in the 1820s and 1830s were dominated by lozenges (transmuted into a running pattern in Colour Plate 71), ovals and rectangles, their outline frequently interrupted with scrolls or naturalistic devices as in Plate 132. Many of the standard decorative motifs of the time, including those of gothic inspiration (Plates 129 and 132) were encapsulated by Knight, though his books, while claiming to survey the riotous eclecticism of international styles, were modified for English tastes. For instance, several designs in Knight's publications are naturalistic or contain naturalistic elements, but it takes the remarks of a French wit, reported in *Ackermann's Repository* in 1824, to bring to imaginative life a lady in full fashionable fig. Her jewellery represented a menagerie, he declared, her bracelet and necklace composed of serpents, her earrings of doves, her ring of a mouse, while a butterfly clasp adorned her girdle and a Bird of Paradise perched on her head.[29] He did not greatly exaggerate. Not only did a similiar head ornament figure in the Hamlet sale[30] but all the other objects can be paralleled in English records from the Duchess of Gloucester's mouse bracelet to the butterfly ornaments acquired by her brother, George IV. The King developed a positive passion for butterflies after his accession, purchasing an onyx butterfly ring from Hamlet in 1821, together with another in amethyst, while a butterfly ornament was included in a suite of pink topazes, brilliants and emeralds set in chased gold which was supplied to him by Rundell's in the same year at a cost of £465.[31]

Parures were still much worn, especially on grand occasions. A large order executed by Garrard's craftsmen for Lord Montagu[32] in 1829 included a half-set comprising a brilliant necklace composed of '4 Star Brooches, clusters, Springs & Scrolls' set with 656 stones, a pair of earrings with 404 brilliants and a drop furnished by the firm, and a snap or clasp with thirty-four brilliants and nine rose diamonds. At the same time Lord Montagu acquired two pairs of diamond and pearl earrings, one set with 154 brilliants and eight pearls, the other with 124 brilliants and ten pearls, and a sévigné with ninety-three roses, 157 brilliants and six pearls (eight brilliants and nine roses only being supplied by Garrard's). The last items in the order are a pair of pearl tops and (entered on the next line) pearl drops, which were presumably designed to be united on occasion as top and drop earrings. Garrard's overall charge for resetting what were clearly family diamonds was £252.17s., including the extra stones and the unspecified cost of a new fitted case and relining another.[33] The full cost of expensive parures for which the jeweller supplied the stones is evident in the firm's account with another, very rich, patron who was married in 1829. He was charged £27,266.17s.6d. in all for a brilliant parure complete with head ornament and armlet, one of emeralds and diamonds, a third of pearls and a fourth, a modest set of turquoises and diamonds, together with seven jewelled rings and a plain gold hoop.

Clients unwilling to purchase large parures often had recourse to hiring them for

Plate 130. A watch bracelet by Bautte et Moynier of Geneva. The watch is detachable from the bracelet band and the front cover is enamelled with flowers. The baluster-shaped components of the band are decorated with conventional rosette, anthemion and scroll motifs. The watch key is also enamelled with the boldness characterising Swiss and North Italian work of the 1820s and 1830s.   SOTHEBY'S

Plate 131. A 'Berlin ironwork' cross and chain remarkably similar to those worn by Mademoiselle de la Boutraye (Colour Plate 69), though the long links of her chain are not connected by rosettes and the lobed terminals of her cross are simpler than in the piece shown here. But the surface of the cross and chain, a very dark grey rather than a lustrous black, may indicate French manufacture; c.1830.

VICTORIA AND ALBERT MUSEUM

special functions. Garrard's, in common with other jewellers, were always prepared to lend pieces in this way. Henry Drummond, for instance, paid £41.10s. in 1832 to hire two parures, one of diamonds which included a head ornament, and another of diamonds and pearls. The overall value was £8,300 but the service was apparently profitable for the firm, even if the expense of insurance is taken into account.

Plate 132. A bodice brooch and earrings in stamped gold and peridots, an eclectic design which manages to suggest gothic inspiration with its angular framework though it is conventionally adorned with foliated scrolls; English, c.1825.

VICTORIA AND ALBERT MUSEUM

Mixed jewellery was permitted — even encouraged — especially in informal dress. Madame Marcotte de Sainte-Marie sat to Ingres for her portrait in 1826 wearing a day dress, a long cut steel chain (to which was attached a steel-rimmed lorgnette) and a gold buckle and other trinkets decorating her waist; on her left arm, one above the other, was a pair of gold mesh bracelets with amethyst clasps. Only a year earlier *Ackermann's Repository* reported a new fashion for wearing two matching bracelets on one arm and a third, of a different design, on the other.[34] Some Englishwomen took note of a Paris fad for massing different bracelets on the arms; Lady Peel had evidently joined their ranks when she was painted in 1827 (see the engraving in Plate 133). But A.E. Chalon's watercolour portrait of Lady Owen, signed and dated 1830, depicts a self-assured woman wearing a demi-parure of immensely long earrings and two bracelets (worn one on each arm) which might or might not be a pair (Plate 134). Another Englishwoman, painted by Thomas Wyatt in 1828, has no bracelets visible over the ribbon bands trimming her gauze sleeves, but exemplifies the wearing of mixed jewellery even with a costume intended for a dinner party, to judge by her gown and enormous feathered hat. She dangles her lorgnette on a long gold chain looped through her left hand (Plate 135), while her brilliant necklace and long earrings are confidently married to a brooch with a coloured stone set in a border of small diamonds (see Plate 136).

Coiffures were elaborate to the point of fantasy in the evenings. Mature ladies like Wyatt's sitter wore towering turbans and huge hats which were suitably embellished with jewelled loops, chains, cameos, aigrettes of conventional or naturalistic design (Plate 137) and a variety of brooches or pins. Younger women often dispensed with headgear, mingling flowers with their jewels, which often included pins with dangerously long stalks[35] (Plate 98). The extraordinary constructions shown in fashion plates are extreme expressions of the current mode, but the evidence of surviving ornaments, coupled with jewellers' bills and other records, demonstrates that the illustrations were not wholly imaginary but merely exaggerated reality. Naturally, however, many women demanded more modest ornaments such as the dignified bandeau in Plate 138, discussed below.

Plate 133. (Above left.) Lady Peel, a mezzotint of 1905 after Lawrence's portrait, which was exhibited at the Royal Academy in 1827 and is now in the Frick Collection, New York. A print by S. Cousins was first published in 1832; this much later version follows it closely. In the original picture Lawrence clearly depicts gold bracelets with a blue cabochon and pearls on the upper one and possibly also on the one nearest her hand; the great stone in the centre of the middle bracelet is as dark as the mezzotint suggests. Sir Robert Peel commissioned the portrait of his wife as a pair to the Rubens portrait of Susanna Fourment (the Chapeau de Paille) which hung in his room and is now in the National Gallery.

Plate 134. (Left.) Mary Frances, Lady Owen of Taynton House, Gloucestershire, wears huge gold and green stone top and drop earrings and a bracelet of the same materials on each wrist in a watercolour by A.E. Chalon, signed and dated 1830. The decoration of her buckle is difficult to decipher, but it does not match the other jewellery. FINE ART SOCIETY, EDINBURGH

Plate 135. (Above right.) A portrait of a lady, thought to be a member of the Vansittart family, in a yellow silk dress and black be-feathered hat and white lace, by Thomas Wyatt, 1828. Her lavish diamond earrings and necklace are matched to an oval brooch of a coloured stone in a diamond surround. Her lace chin-strap was a popular device among women of a certain age. CHRISTIE'S

Plate 136. A sapphire and diamond brooch of the same type as the one in Wyatt's painting; the brilliants are set in cut-down collets, creating a scalloped edge on which the ribs are visible. COLLINGWOOD'S

Plate 137. Two of a set of three gold and turquoise peacock feather aigrettes, fashionable articles for the coiffure (or bodice); articulated, they are furnished with pins; c.1830. MUSEUM OF LONDON

Circlets and diadems, when worn, attained their maximum size in England in about 1821,[36] exemplified by George IV's circlet (Plate 35), diminishing by degrees thereafter into less dominating articles. Tiara fronts mounted on narrow bands (Colour Plate 72A) were virtually universal. Usually given crested or heavily indented profiles, they rose high over the forehead but extended no further than the temples, a change partly necessitated by the vogue for ringlets *à la Vandyke*[37], which were worn in luxuriant clusters on each side of the face in emulation of seventeenth century beauties (Plate 147). Small coronets confining a knot of hair at the back of the head, of a type favoured by Charles I's Queen, Henrietta Maria, two centuries earlier (Plate 168) enjoyed a revival for a decade or so. The fashion reporter of the *Ladies' Cabinet,* searching for words to describe these pieces in 1835, called them 'a jewelled bracelet' encircling the hind hair.[38] Queen Victoria owned an example set with sapphires which was probably designed for her by Prince Albert in 1842 (Plate 169).

Bandeaux composed of multiple strings of pearls or stones appeared in about 1825 and persisted into the following decade. Deriving from the seventeenth and eighteenth century practice of threading pearls through the hair, the new bandeaux were passed over the forehead at a jaunty angle and wound through the hair at the back of the head (Plates 138 and 148).[39] The lines of strings were so disciplined that they must have been sewn on to ribbons or supported from behind with

Plate 139. This pen-and-ink cartoon by Sir Edward Landseer is believed to depict General Phipps and Lord Alvanley with Mrs Norton at the theatre. General Phipps died in 1837, and the fashion of Mrs Norton's costume, her long earrings and double serpent headdress support a date of about 1835. Mrs Norton, Sheridan's granddaughter, poet, society wit and beauty, married the Hon. G.C. Norton in 1827, but allegations that she was Melbourne's mistress forced her husband to bring an unsuccessful court case against the statesman. A later portrait of her wearing a brooch in the archaeological taste is illustrated in Plate 213.

Plate 138. A fashion plate from Ackermann's Repository *of 1825; the lady in evening dress wears an armlet, bracelet, necklace and pendant, together with a pair of earrings. Her coiffure is threaded with a flexible bandeau.*

transverse metal stays. The supports were evidently flexible, for otherwise they could not have been threaded over and through the coiffure.

Other fashionable head ornaments of the 1820s and 1830s ranged over a variety of shapes and styles. Neo-classical devices such as serpents (Plate 139) co-existed with motifs drawn from the baroque and rococo; suites of snake jewellery were denominated *parures à la Cléopâtre* in France in 1823.[40] The gothic manner, the darling of devotees of the Romantic Movement everywhere, also subsumed Renaissance design, as already mentioned. Nominally gothic, therefore, was the ubiquitous ferronnière which flourished towards 1830 and into the 1840s, despite a small hiatus in 1834. Women determined to possess an example often had old pieces of jewellery altered for the purpose. In 1831 Garrard's converted for one of their customers 'an onyx Centre [presumably from a bracelet or necklace] into a Ferronier' with the addition of a twenty-inch chain. A variant of the ferronnière in which the usual central device was upright instead of pendent enjoyed a mild

popularity, though it was far from challenging the true ferronnière with its pendant, which was held to be particularly becoming. An American writer, Nathaniel Parker Willis, who visited England in 1834, was enchanted by the sight of Lady Blessington wearing 'a rich ferronier of turquoise' on 'a head with which it would be difficult to find a fault'.[41] The young Princess Victoria owned several of these head ornaments. She received no fewer than three specimens on her fourteenth birthday in 1833,[42] one of pink topazes and a second of turquoises, both gifts from her mother, the Duchess of Kent. The third, of pearls, was a joint present from two aunts, the Duchess of Gloucester and Princess Sophia, and an uncle, the Duke of Sussex.[43]

The ferronnière, for all its success, never completely ousted the sprig (Plates 140 and 141) which, with its flower-heads often mounted on tremblers, was regarded as a particularly suitable head ornament for young women and girls. Daisy sprigs were popular in the late 1820s,[44] but roses and other flowers were always in favour. The costly gem-set versions were usually the prerogative of married women. A sprig described as 'a *bouquet* of lilies, the flowers of pearls, the foliage emeralds' formed the head ornament in a parure cited in a fashion report of 1823. The other items noted were a necklace of 'three rows of pearls attached by emeralds, placed at short distances', a fair description of a festoon necklace, and matching bracelets and armlets, together with earrings with emerald drops bordered by pearls.[45]

The passion for naturalism guaranteed the survival of floral and foliated wreaths, though many, on account of the new hair-styles, were made as demi-

Plate 141. A seed pearl sprig, threaded on fretted mother-of-pearl frames and fitted with a large hook at the back. Probably English, 1820-25.

VICTORIA AND ALBERT MUSEUM

wreaths. Laurel, roses, daisies and convolvulus were all popular; snowberries were an innovation. An English fashion report of 1823 cites a wreath of 'British oak' interpreted in seed-pearls, with acorns of large pearls which must have been artificial, as the article, obtainable at 'Mr. Hill's Parisian Depot' in Regent Street,[46] was a piece of dressmaker's or costume jewellery. Vine wreaths were still in vogue[47] and others of branched coral (Colour Plate 59) were pronounced fashionable in 1832.[48] Some wreaths and other head ornaments were colonised by butterflies and birds, but probably few were as lavish as the brilliant head ornament in the Hamlet sale, which was 'expensively set in the shape of a sprig of Effusia [fuschia], surmounted by a Bird of Paradise and Butterflies'.[49]

Pins and brooches for the coiffure in the form of single flowers were in demand[50] and floral aigrettes vied with feathers, a few of which were attached to particularly sumptuous diadems. Possibly the 'very elegant Peacock's Tail Head Ornament' set with amethysts, rubies, turquoises and emeralds which George IV acquired from Rundell's in 1821 for £157.10s.[51] was a combination piece. If not it was an aigrette. Three gold specimens set with turquoises in the collection of the Museum of London (see Plate 137) attest to their popularity. The 'chased gold Peacock head ornament, set with rubies' in the Hamlet sale of 1834[52] was presumably a complete bird.

Arrows resurged in the mid-1820s,[53] but the newest device for pins was an ear of wheat, a motif which also embellished wreaths and coronets. The vogue originated in Paris, where *coiffures à la Cérès*, decked with ears of corn, were first remarked in about 1821[54] and lasted until the late 1830s. The Duchesse de Berri lent her approval to the mode by wearing diamond ears of wheat to a ball in Paris in 1829, an event chronicled in England.[55] Oats were an alternative motif; corn of one kind or another was often combined with the flowers of the field (Plate 142). As an alternative to gem-set examples, ears of wheat pins were available in plain gold and silver[56]; the latter, regarded as white or colourless, were recommended as a useful alternative to jet ornaments for mourning purposes after George IV's death in 1830.[57]

Pins were made with heads of bows, insects such as butterflies, animals and reptiles; clowns and other human figures in costume vied with sober cameos and

Plate 142. The flowers and fruits of the field form the crest of this tiara front made in gold with stamped details, the colours simulated by coloured stones such as garnets, carnelians, turquoises, pearls, aquamarines and amethysts; c.1835, a fine example of the passion for naturalism. MUSEUM OF LONDON

huge 'Swiss bodkins'. A novelty introduced in Paris in the early 1820s had a shaped or spherical top, frequently set on a trembler.[58] Known as the Glauvina pin, it must have been a souvenir of Glorvina, the heroine of Sydney Owenson's novel, *The Wild Irish Girl* (1806); as Lady Morgan, the author was much fêted on her first visit to Paris in 1816.[59]

Combs and tiara-combs were often overpowered by pins and other coiffure ornaments, though they did not entirely disappear (Plate 98). Garrard's made Mrs Arbuthnot a tiara-comb with a detachable head in 1821. Side combs were sometimes used to hold the ringlets in place. These occasionally formed part of a parure but were also made separately. Lady Jodrell bought a pair of diamond side combs costing £115 from Garrard's in June 1836; a few weeks later she acquired a diadem centre for a bandeau which might well have been designed to match the first two pieces.

The exuberant French coiffures of 1827 were derided in England as thickets 'of flowers, and gold and silver oats',[60] but English versions were not very different. Thackeray's eponymous hero of *Pendennis* (1848-50) was a young man in the late 1820s and early 1830s. At a ball held during this time Pendennis was greatly struck by one lady who 'seemed to have a bird's nest in her head; another had six pounds of grapes in her hair, beside her false pearls'.[61] A return to greater simplicity was already under way. Before 1830 some women at least disposed their front hair in two flat bands curving from a centre parting and carried flat over the ears to the back of the head, or achieved the same effect with plaited loops, a vaguely late fifteenth century fashion peculiarly sympathetic to the ferronnière.

The design of necklaces followed a similar pattern to that of head ornaments, reaching a peak of complexity in the late 1820s and very early 1830s, followed by signs of recognition that the most effective ornaments were not necessarily either large or complex. The traditional type of necklace centre was still made, often connected to other large units, but pendent drops were now usually confined to the front. Linking chains, though sometimes still festooned, were often shorter than heretofore. The units were usually based on the old geometric forms, with lozenges in the ascendant, but the profiles were interrupted by scrolls and other devices. Rosettes were also fashionable.[62] In 1830 the *Belle Assemblée* illustrated a necklace worn with an evening dress, describing it as consisting either of pink topazes or Ceylon rubies set *à l'Antique* in gold filigree. The fashion plate shows the units placed close together with three large pendants grouped in front.[63] Variations are shown in Plates 29 and 148. The same periodical, discussing a formal evening costume in its section on Parisian fashions in September 1830, declared that the necklace was composed of diamond stars (a motif already used by Garrard's in four brooches for Lord Montagu). The illustration demonstrates that the lady was bedizened with jewellery, wearing a Spartan diadem with a comb behind, diamond earrings, a necklace above the one mentioned and below that rows of gold chain. These were accompanied by gold bracelets set with rubies.[64]

The negligés still in demand in the early 1820s were often made of tasselled pearls[65] or artificial pearls. Lord Suffield bought a mock pearl negligé with a gold snap (clasp) for £3 from Garrard's in March 1821, acquiring another row for it at a cost of 10s. a week later. In 1823 it was reported that pearl negligés had been superseded by specimens strung with flower-shaped units set with precious stones.[66] But a negligé made of 'rock coral' (presumably seed coral), fairly long and furnished with a large tassel in front, was illustrated and described as an accessory to a morning dress in *Ackermann's Repository* in 1828.[67] Twisted ropes of pearls, stones and beads, some further embellished with small festoons, did not always meet with critical approval. A '*rouleau* of fine pearls, closely twisted, with pearl ear-rings', designed to be worn with evening dress, was dismissed by the *Belle Assemblée* in 1823 as 'more costly than beautiful'.[68] A short-lived fashion for dog-collar necklaces in the late 1820s is of interest principally because of the revival of the type later in the nineteenth century, just as the negligé with tassel was to return as the popular sautoir of the Edwardian era.

An innovation also described as a negligé on making its début was the necklace *à la Jeannette,* which derived from French regional jewellery. It often had a heart motif, probably borrowed from Huguenot christening jewellery. Filigree versions were said to be current in Paris by 1823,[69] whence they spread to other countries. The necklace consisted of a black ribbon of silk or velvet caught at the neck by a gold slide to which the heart device was applied; the two ends of the ribbon then descended together to terminate in a gold cross, solid or filigree. The adapted version worn by the wife of the Dutch Ambassador to Vienna has a shell or perhaps an anthemion slide (Plate 143). The cross and slide were also produced in other materials, including pearls, but gold was more general and specimens of the latter were still cited in the *Ladies' Cabinet* in 1836.[70]

Plate 143. A miniature by Moritz Michael Daffinger of the Baroness Amélie Stuers, wife of the Dutch Ambassador to Vienna, painted in about 1836 (or perhaps later). Clad in white with a vermilion shawl draped over her left arm, she wears a gold cross à la Jeannette on a black ribbon which is gathered together at her neck by a flared slide, not a heart, as was usually the case with French items of this kind.

SOTHEBY'S

Plate 144. Baroness Anselm de Rothschild by Ary Scheffer, a portrait painted in 1827, the year after her marriage. Her long gold chain is coloured red, blue and green; it was probably gem-set, not enamelled. Her over-sleeves are caught with clasps; two bracelets are indicated on her left arm, but a third, which is depicted in more detail on her right wrist, is remarkably similar to the clasp of the French bracelet shown in Plate 145C. Baroness Anselm was Charlotte, the daughter of Nathan Mayer de Rothschild, and married her cousin.

NATIONAL TRUST, WADDESDON MANOR

Detachable necklace units, already cited, were put to a variety of uses, but a diamond necklace centre supplied by Garrard's in April 1830 to Miss Caroline Fox, Lord Holland's sister,[71] was made specifically to double as a sévigné; 272 pearls were strung to it and she was charged £48.5s. for the work.

Vines, still popular, entwined themselves convincingly around necks. Other plant motifs in the naturalistic mode flourished; an enamelled strawberry necklace and cross appeared in the Hamlet sale of 1834.[72] Aside from the shell devices already discussed, some motifs had marine themes. The repertory of novelties, partly drawn from animal, insect, avian and reptilian life, included the inevitable serpent necklaces and inanimate bagatelles like bells with clappers strung on chains.[73]

The practice of wearing two necklaces, one above the other, was revived in the 1820s, as already noted. An evening gown depicted in *Ackermann's Repository* in 1828 was shown with two necklaces. The upper one was said to consist of a row of garnets set in gold, fastened in front 'with a handsome medallion snap'; the lower was a wreath necklace of embossed gold leaves.[74] The latter was extremely long, slung wide over the shoulders and across the collar bones in front, a seeming

Plate 145. A. A gold cross, seen from the reverse in order to show the enamelled rosettes, which compare with the roundels on the French bracelet in C. The front is set with pearls and emeralds; c.1830. B. A pair of gold filigree earrings with cannetille *decoration, set with small turquoises; c.1830. C. A coloured gold bracelet with a panelled band decorated with enamels; the clasp is set with an amethyst in an elaborate cast and chased acanthus border with* grainti *ornament. Struck with the Paris warranty mark for 1819-38, the resemblance of the clasp to that on Baroness Anselm de Rothschild's bracelet (Plate 144) makes it likely that this piece dates to about 1825.* VICTORIA AND ALBERT MUSEUM

impossibility. Unless it was pinned or sewn, as seems likely, such a piece would probably have either slipped off the shoulders or fallen forwards over the bodice. But virtually all long necklaces were elaborate chains which ideally were worn wide over the shoulders, in the manner demonstrated by Baroness Anselm de Rothschild in a portrait by Ary Scheffer in 1827 (Plate 144).[75] It is also worth noting that some women continued to wear jewelled sautoirs over one shoulder, though they probably acquired them earlier in the century.

The decoration of clasps usually reflected the style of the necklace, with a few exceptions which increasingly include hand fastenings. Tiny modelled hands appeared everywhere, clasping necklaces and bracelets alike. A gold curb neckchain acquired by George IV for £16.16s. in 1821 had a 'Turcois hand in hand Snap with Pearls'.[76]

Plate 146. A Maltese cross in chalcedony and coloured gold, with a square centre set with an emerald in a square border of pearls; there is a box for hair at the back. The coloured gold, finely chased, is decorated with roses, leaves and four-petalled flowers. The points between the arms and the suspension loops have a row of pellets; c.1825.

BRITISH MUSEUM, HULL GRUNDY GIFT

Crosses were still among the most fashionable pendants. The once dominant Maltese variety (Plate 146) was gradually overtaken by others such as the cross *à la Jeannette* and convent, apostolic and Greek crosses, as well as many loosely termed gothic (Plate 145A). The 'gold enamelled gothic cross' costing £24.3s. in 1824 was only one of the many medievalising pieces to be supplied to George IV by Rundell's in the mid-1820s (see Plate 91C).[77] The French had their Saint Louis crosses (which were naturally borrowed by the English)[78] but these were surpassed in popularity by crosses *à la Marie Stuart,* a manifestation of the long-lived vogue for costumes and ornaments inspired by the unhappy Queen of Scots.

Some French crosses owed nothing to medievalism (*'le style Troubadour'* or *cathédrale*) or to the Renaissance. These were occasionally set with watches or an eye-glass;[79] others consisted of the omnipresent serpents, their bodies curved into the required shape and their open mouths each biting an apple.[80] Hands were now frequently substituted for the usual suspension loops, a practice which was widespread.[81]

Lockets were also very general. In the Hamlet sale of 1834 there were several with floral motifs, one described as a 'richly chased gold Peacock locket', two with canine devices and another in the form of a Spanish guitar. Heart-shaped lockets remained very popular[82] (Plate 147), but women who persisted in wearing lockets with eye portraits branded themselves as irredeemably old-fashioned (though Queen Victoria was later to join their ranks). In the early days of Master Dombey in *Dombey and Son* (1848), Dickens introduced Miss Tox, an archetypal genteel spinster in straitened circumstances. When 'full-dressed, she wore round her neck the barrenest of lockets, representing a fishy old eye...'.[83] It transpires later in the novel that the eye was that of her uncle.

Most of the other devices for pendants current in the Regency remained in favour: there are references in fashion reports to padlocks (which were also, of course, used as clasps), keys, watches, seals, and scent bottles, often of crystal, mounted in gold. Many were often attached to long chains which were caught at the belt (Plate 148). Lyres, so popular in the early years of the century, were less in evidence. With his habitual sensitivity to the nuances of fashion, George IV had stones taken out of two lyre ornaments, one of diamonds and the other of emeralds, and set against the cost of a large brilliant added to a necklace centre in 1824. The King acquired many pendants with naturalistic themes, ranging from a 'Locket with a Mosaic of a Dog' (an emblem of fidelity) set in two-colour gold, bought from Laurière in 1821,[84] and 'an Agate Ornament for the Neck in form of an Apple with chased gold leaves, etc.' costing £7.7s., which was supplied together with a long chain at £6.6s. by Rundell's in 1823. Somewhat surprisingly, since such ornaments had ceased to be mentioned in fashion reports, the same bill included a 'gold engine turned Fausse Montre with secret spring to receive picture'.[85]

Neckchains, with some exceptions, grew steadily larger during the 1820s. Mesh work and traditional fine chains of the Maltese, jaseron and Trichinopoly varieties were still worn, but a 'Gold Elastic pattern round Chain' acquired by George IV in 1821 suggests that Brazilian or snake chains (Colour Plate 91) might be in production. In 1823 the *Belle Assemblée* noted another innovation, 'a gold chain, of an entire new pattern, with long links'.[86] Four years later the same periodical reported that the latest French chains were made of oblong links;[87] the portrait of Baroness Anselm de Rothschild (Plate 144) shows that links formed of lozenges were also current. Gem-set and enamelled chains, worn in the 1820s, continued in vogue at least until the mid-1830s.[88] Others were plainer. 'A long Gold link & rosette Chain in Stan^d [standard] Gold' costing £35 was purchased by the Earl of Harborough from Garrard's in 1830. The reference to rosettes makes it likely that it was intended for female use.

Earrings continued in high fashion and usually (though not invariably) matched necklaces. Their overriding characteristic was their length (Colour Plate 68A, Plates 135 and 145B). Even fashion writers acknowledged that they were exceedingly uncomfortable to wear. The popularity of girandole earrings reintroduced (under their old name) in the 1820s[89] added width to elongation. Top and drop earrings (Plate 128) were often extended by the insertion of a separate element or of a pendant below the drop.

In 1829 these ornaments were so large and the gem-set ones so heavy that the *World of Fashion* felt obliged to instruct its readers in various ways of alleviating the weight. Parisians, it declared, carried their earrings with them to parties or the theatre and put them on before making their entrance. Once on, a small piece of silk placed behind the ear provided a support for the hook, an old method in use in the eighteenth century.[90] Even so, ear-lobes were invariably distended, never to recover. Queen Victoria, who adored long earrings in her youth, still showed the effects of their weight in old age (Plate 324). There were other drawbacks. The *Ladies' Museum* reported with relish in 1832 the death of an innkeeper's wife who, in 'correcting' (that is, whipping) a servant, slipped and fell, breaking one of her long earrings which penetrated the jugular vein. The unfortunate woman bled to death.[91]

Crosses, hearts and serpents were still among popular devices for earrings. A pair of 'pure gold serpent and scroll earrings' was included in the Hamlet sale of 1834.[92] A variant of an old type, 'Turkish' earrings in the shape of crescents, with pendent spheres and feathers added, was reported in current use in 1829.[93]

Plate 147. The young girl in A.E. Chalon's miniature of about 1835 wears a gold heart-shaped locket on a thick flexible chain and a panelled bracelet. Her ringlets probably fall from side-combs, but these are not visible.   SOTHEBY'S

Plate 148. Queen Adelaide is elegantly embellished with a bandeau looped through her hair in this portrait of about 1831 by Sir William Beechey, a version of a full-length painting of the Queen in evening dress at Trinity House. The Queen also wears a fashionable (bow-shaped) sévigné with three drops, long matching top and drop earrings with tiny terminals and a long fetter-link chain with a watch hooked over her belt. The diarist Charles Greville thought the Queen's complexion poor; if so, it was tactfully corrected by Beechey.   NATIONAL PORTRAIT GALLERY

Complex earrings of various kinds were general. George IV bought a pair with sixteen gold spheres for £5.5s. from J. Laurière in 1821;[94] examples in the form of sévignés and miniature pagodas, the latter an instance of chinoiserie fostered by the rococo revival, were included in the Hamlet sale of 1834.[95] Naturalistic devices included the inevitable vines and flowers: a pair of forget-me-not earrings of coral and coloured gold was sold to George IV in 1821,[96] while ears of wheat, coiled into hoops, figured in the Hamlet sale.[97]

Armlets were resuscitated to control huge sleeves towards the end of the 1820s. Bracelets were still often produced in pairs; in the mid-1820s, as already noted, the pair was worn on one arm. But this was modest. As early as 1822 it was reported that fashionable Parisians were sporting no fewer than five bracelets, all different and all with large clasps. Large bracelets were widespread but not always admired: Lady William Russell[98] wrote to Lady Holland from Paris in 1823 deriding the latest fashions which included 'Bracelets the size of knight errants shields on skinny arms'.[99] Two years later the *Belle Assemblée* described a party dress worn with 'splendid bracelets up to the elbow'.[100] In the engraving of Sir Robert Peel's wife (Plate 133) her left wrist is adorned with three large bracelets which gather in the stuff of her long sleeve.[101] For good measure she wears tiers of gem-set rings above her wedding ring, including a fine half-hoop.

Plate 149. A. A brooch with a shell cameo of Ariel on a bat's back in a narrow gold border of matted gold edges with scrolls. The cameo is probably Italian; the treatment of the subject, taken from Shakespeare, The Tempest *(Act V, sc.i), closely resembles a painting of 1826 by Joseph Severn in the Victoria and Albert Museum Print Room. Severn, a friend of John Keats, spent many years in Rome. The setting might have been made in several European countries, but the donor stated (in 1976) that the brooch had been purchased in Rome. Can it have been set by the Castellani firm, established in 1814/15 to make jewellery in the French and English styles and only later turning to archaeological design?*
B. A stamped gold openwork brooch set with foiled crystals; it has a small pendant and another, larger one, suspended from two lengths of Brazilian or snake chain; 1830s.
C. A variation of the amethyst and gold brooch in Colour Plate 68C, the border is executed in stamped gold, matted and edged with indented polished gold; c.1835.   VICTORIA AND ALBERT MUSEUM

Solid band bracelets rapidly gained acceptance during the 1820s and 1830s and were usually either hinged or jointed (Plates 144 and 145C). Some bands were so solid as to be described as bangles; Hamlet sold an enamelled and chased example to George IV in September 1824.[102] The adoption of solid bands confirmed a development which had already occurred in the construction of bracelet clasps. The illustration of Barlow's seed pearl bracelets of 1811 (Plate 67) shows that small spring catches fastened the solid bands on the underside of the wrist and the centres were purely decorative. The process of change was neither rapid nor comprehensive. The old type of bracelets with central clasps continued to be made in the 1830s.

In general terms, the new solid bands were usually of equal width throughout their length until the early 1830s, when they increasingly (though, again, not invariably) tapered from the centre to the clasp. The edges of the bands were occasionally scalloped or, in consequence of the growing popularity of medievalism, gabled and crested at the top and bottom, as the *Belle Assemblée* reported in 1826.[103] The introduction of figurative elements in jewellery was always more limited in England than in France, where knights and medieval damsels adorned items such as bracelet centres from the mid-1830s. Rundell's

were among the few English jewellers to incorporate the human figure in jewellery, though not necessarily in the round.[104]

In the 1820s bracelets were frequently worn over gloves. The reaction came in 1828, when elegant Parisians, it was said, found 'the fashion too common' and gave up the practice.[105] A diminishing French interest in bracelets in general was said to have been revived in 1829 by the latest serpent examples, which were large enough for the heads to descend over the back of the hand while the tails wound up the arm,[106] prefiguring the snake bracelet made much later by Fouquet for Sarah Bernhardt (Plates 407 and 408). When the serpent bodies were made of gold, enamelled or otherwise, they had to be jointed: those executed in hair were elastic enough not to need hinges. 'A Hair Serpent Bracelet w^h antique fine gold head' was sold to George IV by Joseph Kitching in 1825.[107] An enterprising French jeweller and designer, Edouard Marchand, who set up business in Paris shortly after 1835, had an early success with a gold snake bracelet, inspired by an antique statue of Ariadne in the Vatican; its body was tooled in imitation of scales and then covered with translucent rose-coloured enamel.[108]

In the early 1830s, narrower bracelets became general and for a time the old chain bands were restored to high favour (Colour Plate 63A).[109] Dog-collar bracelets also came into fashion, the clasp or centre set with a cameo or coloured stones, with an attached chain bearing a ring at the other end to put on the finger.[110] Many bracelets carried sentimental inscriptions and often had pendants of various kinds, including charms, padlocks and lockets. The Hamlet sale of 1834 included a 'lapped band bracelet, surmounted with quiver and arrows and padlock heart suspended', and another with devices taken from the collars of the Orders of the Garter and the Bath.[111] Not for the first time does an object shadow George IV's taste; some of the articles in Hamlet's sale seem either to have been left on

Colour Plate 69. *The young French girl in this portrait of 1834 by Eugène Delacroix, Mademoiselle Julie de la Boutraye, is probably in half-mourning and wears a long black chain terminating in a cross which is tucked into her belt while a dark comb is silhouetted above her modest bows of hair. A further comb holds back the front hair above her curls; it was almost certainly one of a pair. She appears also to be wearing substantial earrings. Mademoiselle de la Boutraye (later the Comtesse Raymond de Tillet) may be wearing French specimens of 'Berlin ironwork'.* CLEVELAND MUSEUM OF ART

Colour Plate 70. *A hair band bracelet with gold fittings, the clasp set with a shell cameo representing Mars and Venus and a genius with torch and arrow. The plaited ropes of hair are held by two fittings decorated with* cannetille *and* grainti; *the border of the clasp is edged with small stamped units mingled with scrolling wires and* cannetille. *The goldwork is unmarked, suggesting that it was made outside France, though there must have been jewellers within that country willing to evade the law on occasion;* c.1825. VICTORIA AND ALBERT MUSEUM

the jeweller's hands after supplying his sovereign or were sold back to him by the recipients of the King's generosity.

Hair bracelet bands (Colour Plate 70) usually had a sentimental significance. On the eve of her eighteenth birthday in 1832 Mrs Fitzherbert's niece, Georgina Smythe, temporarily exchanged hair bracelets with Louisa Craven. Louisa's was the gift of her brother, Augustus, who immediately on discovering the exchange gallantly requested Miss Smythe to keep the bracelet as a birthday present. Convention forced her to return it to her friend, though she wrote in her Journal

Colour Plate 71. An enamelled gold bodice brooch set with garnets; many of its decorative motifs, including the fretted tracery, can be associated with illustrations in Knight's Fancy Ornaments *(see Plate 129). This piece was owned by the Duchess of Kent, who on her death in 1861 was found to have left her jewellery to her daughter Queen Victoria. The Queen gave some articles to relatives and the Duchess's ladies as mementoes and put others aside to use later as presents. The brooch, which dates to about 1830, was among the latter, for when the Queen gave it to her daughter Helena, Princess Christian of Schleswig-Holstein, as a twenty-fourth birthday present in 1870, she had it inscribed on the reverse:* Belonged to dear Grandmama V. [Victoire, Duchess of Kent] From Mama V.R. to Helena 25th May 1870.

PRIVATE COLLECTION

of her wish that 'there were not so many *prudish* rules in this Country, as abroad there is not half the consequence attached to a *Cadeau d'Amitié'*. She need not have worried, for she married Augustus Craven.[112]

Lady Jersey, capitalising on the vogue for horse hair jewellery (Colour Plate 193), tried in vain to persuade the Duke of Wellington to give her hair for a bracelet from the tail of his famous charger, Copenhagen, which had carried him to victory in Spain and at Waterloo. Unabashed, Lady Jersey resorted to bribing the Duke's groom in about 1833, to the great indignation of Wellington's friend Lady Salisbury.[113]

In 1829 the *World of Fashion* noted a new Paris vogue: bracelets of tortoiseshell inlaid with what was called gold, 'stamped in relief', possibly a reference to the traditional technique of piqué work. These tortoiseshell bracelets were said to be further adorned with cameos, paintings on porcelain and ivory.[114]

The giraffe presented in 1827 by the Pasha of Egypt to Charles X of France inspired a great deal of souvenir jewellery of the type favoured by the jewellers of the Palais Royal in Paris; one example has the giraffe and its attendant enamelled on the clasp.[115] But the giraffe bracelet acquired by George IV was almost certainly specially designed for him, for there is little record of similar pieces in England.

The Hamlet sale included a few examples of bracelets with a dual function. The cameo snap of one piece clearly had a hinged cover which concealed 'a watch movement of a superior description'.[116] Miniatures set in bracelet clasps or centres were sometimes provided with a jewelled or chased cover which might be removed at will. Garter bracelets first came into favour during the reign of George IV. The King himself bought 'an enamelled Garter Bracelet' for £28.7s. from

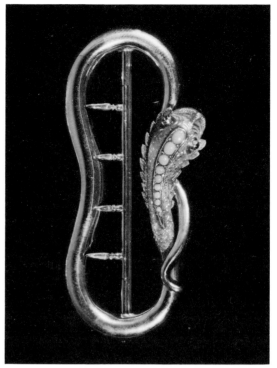

E. & W. Smith in 1824.[117] A later specimen, set with the coronation medal of William IV and Queen Adelaide, was probably made as a royal gift in 1831.

Bodice brooches were back in high favour. Sprigs which might be worn on the bodice or in the hair remained popular (Plates 140 and 141). Brooches with multiple pendants were hailed as an innovation in the *Belle Assemblée* in 1826.[118] These were probably the sévignés of fashion reports. A related type, with a single pendant suspended from a chain attached to each side of the brooch (Plate 149B), was also introduced in the 1820s.[119] Handkerchief pins were once again in favour. One specimen, cited in 1824, took the form of an enamelled gold or steel Gordian knot, currently a popular motif.[120]

George IV's purchase from Laurière in 1822 of a 'Pearl & Turcois Dove Shap'd Broach with a small Ruby & Pearl Heart pendant' at £8.8s. reflected the fascination with naturalistic jewellery which led him to acquire a profusion of butterfly designs. The Hamlet sale included 'An ivy leaf brooch with a hovering Fly' and 'a sprig of barberry set as a brooch'.[121] A fashion correspondent noted sleeve clasps in the form of single flowers at a Parisian ball in 1830.[122] Sleeve clasps of all kinds were made, some *en suite* with bodice brooches. Fittingly for a great heiress, Lady Londonderry wore two pairs of enormous sleeve brooches, a pair on each arm, when she was painted by Sir Thomas Lawrence in about 1827. Each had a large stone set in an elaborate diamond surround.[123] Heart, snake and sévigné brooches were much in demand: some made in the traditional form (Colour Plate 72B). Garrard's set brilliants belonging to their client Mrs Higgins in a 'bow ornament w^h tassels' in March 1837, three months before Queen Victoria acceded to the throne.

Many brooches, like lockets, bracelets and rings, were adorned with stones carrying a sentimental message or device, like the forget-me-not pieces in Plate 150. These trinkets were often still fitted in traditional fashion with small glass-covered recesses for hair. Some were set with miniatures. The newer varieties of miniature brooch were furnished with covers, as were bracelets, but fashions of this kind were often disregarded. An innovation consisted of two brooches connected by a single or double chain, which followed the line of the bodice from one shoulder to the centre front. This complex ornament, the precursor of the French Léontine watch-chain, had a watch concealed in one of the brooches. One of these articles was worn in about 1829 by Mrs Vaughan when she sat to Etty for her portrait (Plate 151).[124] Her gold buckle, smothered in plant forms, is a fine example of the naturalistic genre. Waist clasps were still produced, including some with the hand in hand device, but buckles were by far the most popular form of belt fastening despite being reported out of fashion from time to time.[125] Clasps continued to be made in the form of serpents (Plate 152).

Seals, watches and scent bottles still hung from the waist; the Duke of Wellington gave Mrs Arbuthnot a *pensée* (pansy) to attach her seal to her waist in 1823.[126] The rebuses used for fancy seals, to judge by Knight's *Gems and Device Book,* were not demanding. 'You shall hear from me' was represented by a yew tree, the word 'shall' followed by a human ear, with 'from me' below.[127]

Watches were slighter than before. French specimens were prized by men and women everywhere. In 1823 the Duke of Bedford told Lord William Russell that he was anxious to acquire from Falon of Paris a lady's watch 'as a *cadeau* to the Duchess [his second wife] on her wedding [anniversary] day. I gave her one some time after my marriage, but it is a *warming* pan as compared with the present fashion...'.[128]

The revived mode for chatelaines was reported to have spread from France to England in 1829; some were in the gothic style, with trefoil links.[129]

While men took to wearing signet rings, which spelled the death of the vogue for portable seals, women were reported in 1822 to be sporting on their watch-chains seals set on spokes.[130] But armorial rings the size of papal ones were also worn. The *Journal des Dames* asserted in 1826 that an assortment of rings, including a wide band of hair with a gold buckle, was distributed over four fingers of each hand.[131] Chain rings fastened by small pendent hearts, gem-set hoops and half-hoops, flower and love rings which were inscribed in hieroglyphics or Hebrew characters to baffle the curious and rings with tiny scent flasks attached, are among the types mentioned in periodicals. George IV was a great acquirer of rings. Some of his purchases have already been cited. They ranged from specimens acquired for presentation to sentimental and other pieces with devices of forget-me-nots,

Colour Plate 72. A. A stamped copper-gilt tiara front with indented scrolls and floral, foliated, cannetille *and* grainti *ornament; set with chrysoprases. The intricate energy of the design is characteristic of the early and mid-1830s.*
B. A sévigné with tassel pendants and a pair of top and drop earrings with an intermediate motif, in gold filigree with cannetille *and* grainti *decoration, set with turquoises and pearls. In the French manner and dating to about 1825, this half-set may have been executed anywhere in western Europe, including London.*
C. A necklace and earrings in gold filigree with cannetille *and* grainti *ornament, set with emeralds, citrines, sapphires, garnets, rubies, aquamarines, peridots and pearls. These pieces, harmonising ovals and lozenges, are unmarked, but they have a strong French feeling about them; c.1825. (Shown smaller than actual size.)*
                                                                         VICTORIA AND ALBERT MUSEUM

Colour Plate 73. A fine parure of amethysts set in filigree with cannetille *and* grainti, *in the French manner. Comprising a necklace with chains confined to the back, top and drop earrings (which may once have had tiny stones pendent from rings which can still be seen), cross and brooch, it also includes a finger ring, the amethyst head bordered by a row of large and small pellets. Similar pellets run up the upper sides of the earring drops. The suite probably dates to about 1825, when amethysts were still much prized and relatively expensive.*
                                                                                          WARTSKI

294

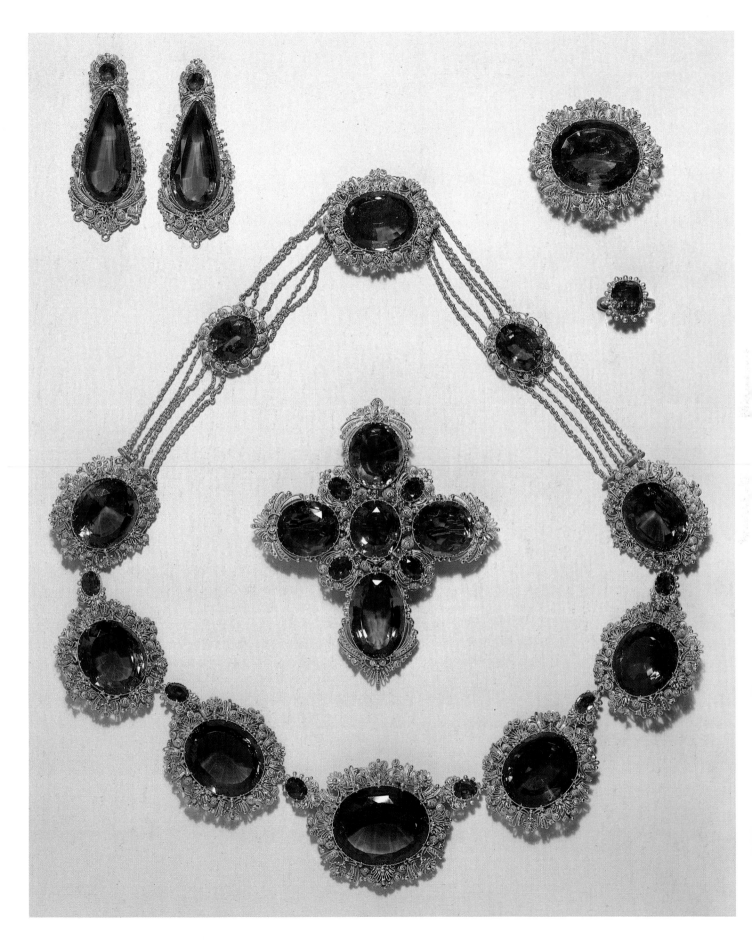

A YOUNG POODLE, but not one of the Sagacious Breed!!

Plate 153. Henry Heath's cartoon of a dandy, published by S.W. Fores on 12 August 1827 with the title A YOUNG POODLE, but not one of the *Sagacious Breed!!* Thomas Carlyle's wife Jane was later to be scathing about the Count d'Orsay's innumerable gold chains, so that Heath's cartoon was not completely exaggerated.

VICTORIA AND ALBERT MUSEUM, PRINT ROOM

double hearts and snakes, double knots and hearts, birds and insects, gordian knots, hands and hearts (*fede*), serpents (one example was called an eternity ring), shamrocks, harps and 'union' pattern rings, among others. In addition he bought conventional clusters, hoops and single-stone rings, enamelled Garter rings (from Rundell's)[132] and from Laurière a 'Gold Lozenge Shaped Ring with an enamel fly'.[133] Neapolitan lava jewellery was rarely mentioned in fashion reports. The lava ring given by Byron to the Count d'Orsay in Genoa in 1823 was accompanied by a barbed allusion to its appropriateness to the recipient's 'fire of...years and character'.[134] The Count was a famous dandy completely uninterested in combustible qualities.

Buckles, of lessened importance in male jewellery, were still employed to fasten cravats as well as the breeches and shoes of Court and official costume. Though seals began to drift into near-obsolescence, stock, cravat or shirt-pins remained fashionable. The double-headed form suitable for anchoring a wide cravat was regarded as particularly desirable by the smart. In 1823 the statesman Lord John Russell acquired an unexpected reputation as *un élégant* in Paris and wore 'a cherry coloured underwaistcoat and two sardonyx pins'.[135] Watch-chains were often splendid, looped round the neck, the two ends caught by a slide before disappearing with the watch into a bag or waistcoat pocket. By way of contrast, Plate 153 shows Heath satirising extreme male fashions in 1827 while Plate 154 is a sober representation of Lord George Bentinck[136] wearing an altogether more modest chain and a jewelled stock-pin.

Plate 154. Lord George Cavendish Bentinck, a copy by Samuel Lane of his earlier portrait of the statesman, painted in 1834. Bentinck, resting his hand authoritatively on a pile of papers, wears a jewelled stock-pin and a gold chain caught by a slide, the ends carrying his watch to his waistcoat pocket and emerging with a watch-key and, perhaps, a seal.   NATIONAL PORTRAIT GALLERY

Plate 155. Sir David Wilkie's chalk, watercolour and gouache study for his painting, The First Earring, *which was exhibited at the Royal Academy in 1835. A second version of the painting was shown at the Academy in 1836 with the tag, 'Il faut souffrir pour être belle,' a lesson which is being early learnt by the wary infant in this preliminary study, one of several made by the artist from 1833-35.*   YALE CENTER FOR BRITISH ART, NEW HAVEN

Thackeray's hero *Pendennis,* up at the university in about 1830, was transformed into a dandy rumoured to wear rings over his gloves. His old schoolfriend Foker was metamorphosed into a sporting gentleman. Foker had 'a bulldog between his legs, and in his scarlet shawl neckcloth...a pin representing another bulldog in gold'.[137] Foker, like his monarch, was a devotee of the new genre of sporting jewellery, acknowledged to be an English invention. Among the shirt-pins in the Hamlet sale was one with the head of a fighting cock.[138]

Children's jewellery continued to replicate most adult types, sometimes in costly materials, sometimes in cheaper substitutes, though it was still beyond the reach of the great mass of the population. Wilkie's study of a little girl submitting to having her ears pierced (Plate 155) documents the price exacted for a first pair of earrings. Coral necklaces were still worn in infancy, but to judge by Parris' painting (Plate 105) pearls and stones were also acceptable. The young Princess Victoria received many gifts of valuable jewellery, mingled with the hair brooches, bracelets and other sentimental items from relatives. Boys, who were normally given watches, might now also sport stock-pins.

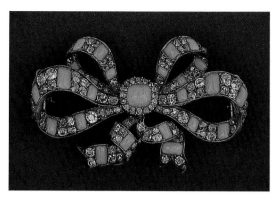

Colour Plate 74. The day after King Leopold I of the Belgians sailed into Ramsgate harbour on 29 September 1835 on a visit to the Duchess of Kent and her daughter Victoria, the young Princess was entranced to receive two turquoise and diamond sévignés, one of which is shown here. Victoria's ecstasies were increased when Queen Louise raided her own wardrobe for further gifts such as ribbons and a cap.

Colour Plate 75. A.E. Chalon's watercolour of the Queen in robes of state, standing and looking towards her right, in the Royal Collection of Belgium, was painted in 1838 and head-and-shoulders copies were soon produced for mounting in jewellery. The Queen's head was also reproduced on postage stamps, including the penny black. The copyists probably used the engraving by S. Cousins which was published by F. Moon in 1838. The enamel version here shows George IV's coronet, Queen Charlotte's girandole earrings and probably also one of her necklaces of diamond collets. The frame is closed-set with pearls in gold and the outer edge with brilliants in open-backed silver settings, lined with gold.

Queen Victoria may have had this pendant made for presentation between 1838 and 1841. In the latter year, when she began to keep her private accounts, she recorded the gift of a bracelet with 'My Portrait by Chalon, set in Diamonds' to Princess Marie d'Orléans on her marriage to the Queen's cousin, Prince Alexander of Württemberg. The Princess was Louis-Philippe's daughter.

CHAPTER VIII

Queen Victoria
and the Cultural Establishment, 1837-1861

Queen Victoria succeeded to the throne in June 1837 when she was barely eighteen years old. Industry was then fast expanding. The jewellery sector in Birmingham was on the verge of developing a number of highly mechanised workshops, one of which in 1859 took up an American invention, a chain-making machine, reputedly the first of its kind. But the growth of international trade on which Britain, in common with all manufacturing nations, increasingly relied, was far from uninterrupted. Severe economic crises occurred in 1838-39 and again in 1846-47 and the British jewellery trade suffered from a depression which started in 1840 and persisted for several years. The social distress endured by the working population at such times fuelled the growth of the Chartist movement, which aimed to make Parliament subject to the will of the people. Jewellers' shops, which so blatantly represented riches, were inevitably a target when distress erupted in riots. On 5 May 1848, the year of revolutions in Europe, a crowd of about five thousand men attacked the principal shops of Glasgow, including those belonging to gunsmiths and jewellers.[1]

In general, the men and women engaged in the trade in Britain held themselves aloof from political agitation, for their pay and conditions were better than average. When the Birmingham jewellers wished to draw attention to the bad state of business in 1845, they did so by the genteel method of despatching a delegation to Buckingham Palace bearing gifts for the Queen and her husband, Prince Albert. For Victoria, there was an enamelled brooch and bracelet variously set with

Colour Plate 76. A. The enamel miniature of Queen Victoria by William Essex, set as the head of a pin, is taken from F.X. Winterhalter's portrait of the Queen in Garter Robes, standing, executed in 1843 and in the Royal Collection at Windsor. The painting was engraved by T.L. Atkinson and published by F.G. Moon, 1847. The Queen wears the familiar combination of George IV's circlet and the rosette necklace with long earrings.
B. A gold ribbon brooch set with opals, emeralds and rubies; c.1845.
C. A gold Garter brooch, engraved and set with garnets; a fashionable conceit and nothing to do with the Order; c.1835.
A, VICTORIA AND ALBERT MUSEUM,
B AND C, PRIVATE COLLECTION

diamonds, pearls and rubies by Thomas Aston of Regent Place,[2] together with a pair of earrings; a buckle for the Queen by John Balleny of St. Paul's Square,[3] was accompanied by a watch-chain, seal and key, presented to Albert. The Prince received the deputation, and one of the delegates, who represented Birmingham in the House of Commons, read a memorial appealing to the Queen and the Prince 'to set the example of wearing British jewellery on such occasions and to such an extent as may meet the Royal approval', an action which would be bound to benefit trade in Birmingham and 'in different parts of the British Empire'. The Prince tactfully expressed his surprise 'that fashion could perversely persist in going abroad for articles of *bijouterie* when it could command so admirable and exquisite a manufacture of them at home'.[4]

The Prince's action in receiving the Birmingham deputation on his wife's behalf was symptomatic of a trust which the Queen had not bestowed lightly. Growing up in seclusion in Kensington Palace with her mother, the Duchess of Kent, and the latter's domineering and ambitious Comptroller, Sir John Conroy,[5] the young Princess had been subjected to intense and continuing pressure before her succession, first to agree to a prolongation of a Regency, should William IV die before she came of age at eighteen and then to make him her private secretary. There was little escape: she even slept in her mother's room. Sustained by her beloved governess, Baroness Lehzen, Victoria held out.[6] On the day of her accession, the young Queen moved out of her mother's room and denied her admittance to her consultations with ministers and officials. Conroy was induced to retire from the Duchess's service in 1839.

The Queen's experiences reinforced a naturally strong will but failed to destroy her directness and honesty. She found in her Prime Minister, Lord Melbourne, a new source of instruction and friendship.[7] Eager to learn, her Journals of the time are full of his advice and enlightening gossip. But in matters unconnected with the State, she found it hard to shake off habits and tastes inculcated in Kensington Palace.

The elaborate ceremony of exchanging gifts at birthdays and at Christmas, so marked a feature of her subsequent life with her own family, stemmed from her childhood, when small decorated fir trees adorned the tables on which the presents were laid out on Christmas Eve. The Queen's love of sentimental jewellery, her practice of giving, as well as receiving, presents on her birthday and other anniversaries, were also learned at Kensington. On her fourteenth birthday in 1833, for instance, she received 'a very pretty enamel watch-chain' from Conroy's children, and from Victoire Conroy a pair of enamel earrings. Victoria gave her in return, as she noted in her Journal, 'a portrait of Isabel, her horse. . .'.[8] The recorded enthusiasm for the watch-chain was a gesture to the Duchess, who read her daughter's diary. The young princess disliked the Conroy girls.

Victoria's surviving paternal relatives were generous in their gifts to her. One of the most splendid of her early acquisitions, a diamond-set miniature presented by George IV in 1826,[9] was more than matched by subsequent gifts from William IV and Queen Adelaide. Their offerings on her fourteenth birthday were, from the Queen, a bow brooch of turquoises and gold, and from the King, a pair of diamond earrings. On 24 May 1835, King William sent 'a beautiful pair of sapphire and diamond earrings' to mark her sixteenth birthday. After the Princess's confirmation ceremony two months later, the King gave her 'a very handsome set of emeralds, and the Queen a head-piece of the same kind'. Her mother's contribution was 'a very pretty bracelet with her hair in it' (fastened by the *fede* device of two clasped hands) and a set of turquoises.[10]

A few of the Duchess's gifts of jewellery to her daughter are preserved in a private family collection assembled by Queen Mary. They include a gold serpent brooch dating to 1832 and a pair of gold earrings in a mixed gothic style, set with garnets and turquoises, probably made a year or so later and comparable with those in Plate 132. Among other items from her mother noted in the Princess's Journal were an opal brooch and earrings, a Christmas present in 1832. At Christmas 1836 her gifts included 'a beautiful massive gold buckle in the shape of two serpents'.[11] Like many of her elders and contemporaries the Queen owned a number of serpent trinkets, some jewelled, others set with, or consisting entirely of, hair.

Over the years her uncle Leopold, now King of the Belgians, and his second wife Louise, Louis-Philippe's eldest daughter, presented Victoria with a nicely-judged mixture of fashionable and sentimental jewellery. In 1835, Queen Louise delighted the Princess with the gift of a handsome pair of diamond and turquoise pavé-set sévignés (Colour Plate 74).[12]

The royal jewels passed by Queen Adelaide to her husband's niece on her accession included Queen Charlotte's nuptial Crown (Plate 14), George IV's circlet (Plate 35), Adelaide's Grand, Regal or Royal diadem or circlet and her ray necklace-tiara, both set for her in 1830-1831 with diamonds removed from Queen Charlotte's stomacher (Plate 3). The new Queen wore them all, never suspecting that her uncle the King of Hanover's claim to these jewels, based on his knowledge that part had been left to Hanover by George II in 1760 and the rest bequeathed to the same country by Queen Charlotte in 1818, might eventually be upheld (see Appendix II).

Rundell's proceeded to compound the problem by altering and reconstructing further specimens of the family jewellery for Queen Victoria's use. They made a simple enamelled Garter armlet for her in August 1837 and followed it in November with a more elaborate one, also enamelled, set with some diamonds taken from George III's Garter. The following April, they removed brilliants from George IV's Garter and tassel to make a necklace and head ornament for the Queen and, in May, set five diamonds from the 'Old Garter' in a half-hoop ring and another four, together with an emerald, in another ring. In July, the firm put unidentified brilliants belonging to the Queen 'in a pair of large single stone Earring Tops' for £3.3s. and made 'a Ruby and Brilliant William of Wykeham Ring' for £19.19s. and another in diamonds and emeralds costing £16.16s. The sources of the diamonds set by Rundell's in 1838 in 'a handsome flower pattern Bracelet' and a bracelet of four strings are also unknown, but 'Brilliants from buckles, etc.' were used for a pair of large 'Knotts' (bows) and a matching smaller bow which constituted a stomacher of three separate items. The process of reconstruction continued into 1839.

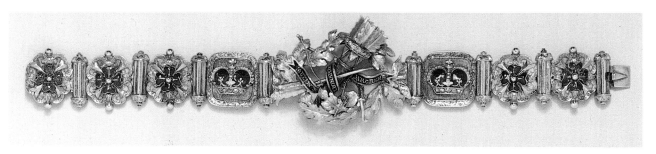

Colour Plate 77. A royal archery prize in the form of a gold bracelet with enamelled crowns and roses, the centre a trophy of a bow, arrow and quiver bordered by oak leaves and bound by an enamelled ribbon commemorating its presentation by Queen Victoria to the archers of St. Leonards-on-Sea, 1839. The Queen was a keen toxophilite and she had a soft spot for St. Leonards-on-Sea. While staying there with her mother in 1834 they had an accident in their carriage, but a clergyman, Mr Gould, and Mr Peckham Micklethwaite came to the rescue and held the horses' heads. VICTORIA AND ALBERT MUSEUM

The fringe necklace handed over by Queen Adelaide was more usually worn by Victoria as a ray diadem, presumably converted by the addition of stays (Plates 156 and 157). The Queen also had another fringe necklace, restrung for her by Rundell's in April 1838,[13] and among others, a row of large diamonds in single collets which had probably been Queen Charlotte's and was worn with or without her long girandole or chandelier earrings (Plates 157 and 158).

Portraits of the young Queen by Hayter,[14] A.E. Chalon[15] and others were copied by her miniaturists for setting in jewellery (Colour Plate 75). William Essex[16] executed a head and shoulders after Hayter for a brooch presented by the Queen to Lady Lyttelton[17] in 1838. In 1842, Essex received £26.5s. for each of two enamels of the Queen's head[18] after Hayter's painting of her marriage (Plate 159), for setting in bracelets to be presented to her ladies. Essex substituted George IV's circlet for the Queen's marriage wreath. H.P. Bone was paid the same amount for two similar miniatures. Another of the same type was mounted in a bracelet given by Queen Victoria to Lady Douro in 1843 (Plate 160). The Queen's Maids of Honour received brooches set with the royal portrait.

Jewels given by Sultan Mahmud of Turkey to the Queen in 1838 furnished the diamonds for a 'Grand Necklace, composed of three rich clusters, and three rows in the centre, and two rows at each side...', which was set by Rundell's for £78.15s. in April 1839.[19] This went with 'tassel pattern' earrings costing £36.15s. The necklace was enlarged by the addition of twelve brilliants in November.[20] The Queen loved this set and chose to wear it at her marriage in 1840 (Plate 159). Fourteen years afterwards Roger Fenton[21] photographed the Queen in Court dress and the same jewellery (Plate 161). The necklace also appears in Henrietta Ward's drawing[22] in the Royal Library, Windsor (Plate 162) and in further paintings, most notably in Winterhalter's[23] full-length portrait of the Queen in Garter Robes in the Royal Collection, executed in 1843 and likewise much copied by miniaturists (Colour Plate 76A).

Victoria wore Queen Adelaide's Grand circlet (Plate 96) to her coronation at Westminster Abbey on 28 June 1838,[24] removing it before attiring herself in St Edward's Chapel for the crowning. She recorded in her Journal that her eight train-bearers were 'all dressed alike and beautifully in white satin and a silver tissue and wreaths of silver corn-ears in front, and a small one of pink roses' encircling their back hair (Plate 163).[25] Though corn was currently a more fashionable motif than laurel leaves, the classical derivation of the wreaths is evident. The Queen gave rings to her train-bearers as souvenirs (Plate 164A).

Colour Plate 78. A set of white porcelain orange blossoms mounted in matted gold, given by Prince Albert to Queen Victoria by instalments from 1839 to 1846. The first of the two brooches was despatched to the Queen by the Prince from Germany and she afterwards had a plaque attached to its fitted case, inscribed: Sent to me by dear Albert from Wiesbaden Novr 1839. *The brooch and earrings were a Christmas present in 1845 and the wreath completed the set on their wedding anniversary on 10 February 1846. The Queen wrote in her Journal: 'My beloved one gave me such a lovely unexpected present, a wreath, going right round the head, made to match the brooch and earrings. . . It is entirely his own design, & beautifully carried out. The leaves are of frosted gold, the orange blossoms of white porcelaine & 4 little green enamel oranges, meant to represent our 4 Children.' She wore the parure that evening at dinner and usually on subsequent wedding anniversaries during the Prince's lifetime.*

ROYAL COLLECTION

In the final phase of their conversion of the royal jewellery for the young Queen, Rundell's used her diamonds and supplied sixteen emeralds for a pair of emerald and diamond earrings and a matching sévigné in September 1839, for which they charged a total of £208. At the same time they set for £8 the two brilliant loops to secure the Garter ribbon to her shoulder[26] which appear repeatedly in her portraits (see Plate 170). With these and other items, Queen Victoria was by now well equipped with fine jewels for all occasions. Her strong sense of family history ensured that she also collected sentimental and commemorative jewellery

Plate 156. The fringe necklace set by Rundell's for Queen Adelaide with family diamonds in 1830-1 and worn by Queen Victoria as a diadem. Though subsequently altered, the general shape of the piece is evident in Wagstaff's print in Plate 157 and in the Queen's own sketch of 1851 (Plate 180).

ROYAL COLLECTION

Plate 157. E.T. Parris sketched the Queen in the Royal Box at Drury Lane theatre shortly after her accession in 1837 and worked up a painting from it which was engraved by C.E. Wagstaff and published by Hodgson & Graves in 1838. The engraving clearly depicts the ray diadem adapted from Queen Adelaide's fringe necklace and Queen Charlotte's girandole earrings. The diadem was one of the Queen's favourite head ornaments; she wore it, with Queen Charlotte's Crown, at the opening of the Great Exhibition on 1 May 1851 (Colour Plate 81 and Plate 180).

VICTORIA AND ALBERT MUSEUM

associated with her ancestors. Aware of her passion, King Leopold gave Victoria, on her birthday in 1848, a bracelet designed by his first wife, Princess Charlotte of Wales, which the Queen in her turn left to the Crown.[27] For all her concern with family pieces, Queen Victoria never ignored her obligation to commission jewellery for presentation purposes, including the bracelet in Colour Plate 77.

On 10 October 1839 the Queen's cousins Ernest and Albert of Saxe-Coburg-Gotha came to England to visit her for the second time. The sight of Albert, grown stunningly handsome at twenty, prompted the Queen to propose marriage to him on 15 October. Albert, always intended by King Leopold as Victoria's consort, gracefully acquiesced. Some five weeks afterwards, the Queen acquired the first of a series of some four or five bracelets set with the Prince's miniature (see an example in Plate 165), describing it in her Journal on 22 November. Its most important constituent, 'Albert's picture beautifully done by Miss Ross' (after a miniature by Sir William Ross) was already in her possession. It was 'Albert's present (bracelet and picture) and is to be set in a very pretty bracelet making at Paris; but I have meanwhile had it put in another bracelet, in order to wear it, and wore it this night for the 1st time'.[28] The next day, the Queen wore it again and, she wrote, 'it seemed to give me courage at the [Privy] Council' at which she announced her forthcoming marriage. According to Charles Greville, 'the Queen came in, attired in a plain morning-gown, but wearing a bracelet containing Prince Albert's picture. She read the declaration in a clear, sonorous, sweet-toned voice, but her hands trembled so excessively that I wonder she was able to hold the paper which she held.'[29] Albert himself was not happy with the likeness, and on 25 January sent the Queen, from Germany, another miniature of himself which

305

Plate 159. The marriage of Queen Victoria with Prince Albert of Saxe-Coburg-Gotha, 10 February 1840, in the Chapel Royal, St James's Palace. The artist, Sir George Hayter, is seen sketching on the right, hidden by the majestically-plumed figure of Princess Sophia Matilda. King Leopold I, tall and commanding, stands next to the Queen-Dowager, Adelaide, facing the Archbishop of Canterbury. On Queen Victoria's left is her uncle the Duke of Sussex in a black skull cap and on his left the Duchess of Kent, generously plumed. The child in the foreground is Princess Mary of Cambridge, the mother of Queen Mary. 'My jewels,' wrote the Queen in her Journal after the wedding, 'were my Turkish diamond necklace & earrings & dear Albert's beautiful sapphire brooch' (his wedding gift to her).

ROYAL COLLECTION

Plate 160. A gold presentation bracelet set with an enamel by H.P. Bone, signed and dated 1843, based on Hayter's painting of the Queen at her marriage (Plate 159) but substituting George IV's circlet for her bridal wreath. The double strings of the Queen's diamond rosette necklace, together with her girandole earrings, are also depicted. The reverse of the bracelet centre is engraved: To/The Marchioness of Douro/from her sincere friend Victoria R/1843. *A Christmas present in 1843, the Queen paid £23 for the bracelet, exclusive of the enamel; it was made by Kitching's. The Marchioness was Lady Elizabeth Hay (d.1904), daughter of the 8th Marquis of Tweeddale, and married the 1st Duke of Wellington's son and heir, 18 April 1839. She was Bedchamber Woman to Queen Victoria, 1843-58, and Mistress of the Robes, 1861-8 and 1874.*

SOTHEBY'S

Plate 161. *Queen Victoria in Court dress, photographed by Roger Fenton on 11 May 1854. The Queen and Prince Albert had just returned from a Drawing-room at St. James's Palace and posed to Fenton, separately and together, in Buckingham Palace, 'I hope successfully', wrote the Queen in her Journal. The photograph is clear enough to show the rosette necklace with its two strings and the tasselled earrings made by Rundell's from the diamonds given by Sultan Mahmud.* ROYAL ARCHIVES, WINDSOR CASTLE

Plate 162. *A sheet of sketches by Henrietta Ward, probably executed in the mid-1850s. The Queen's rosette necklace is clearly shown, though her earrings, barely adumbrated, are not the long tassels made to accompany the necklace in 1838. Mrs Ward also carefully delineates the Grand or Regal diadem originally executed for Queen Adelaide in 1831 and re-made by Garrard's in 1853 with detachable crosses and fleurs-de-lis to enable the Queen to substitute another cresting including a lozenge-shaped device to hold the Koh-i-Nûr diamond. Details of the circlet appear on the left and on the right, together with a section of the Garter Collar and George. Pencil, heightened with white.* ROYAL LIBRARY, WINDSOR CASTLE

was put into a bracelet with a mesh band (Plate 166C). Victoria, however, continued to prefer the one by Ross' sister Magdalena.

On 21 November, the Prince despatched from Wiesbaden 'a trifle which came to me here and appealed to me on account of its sentiment'. The Queen, on receiving it a week later, declared it 'a lovely broach, — an orange flower . . .'.[30] From it sprang a whole suite of orange flower jewellery in porcelain and gold (Colour Plate 78). This pledge from her affianced husband was also, as it happened, a thematic variation on two existing diamond orange flower ornaments which Rundell's had converted for the Queen in April 1838,[31] for what reason is unclear. Before the Privy Council meeting on 23 November the Duchess of Kent gave her daughter 'a very pretty bracelet' of flat tapering gold links and two hearts cut from a single amethyst (Plate 166A). Albert's Christmas present of a bracelet set with diamonds and an emerald (Plate 166B) was probably more welcome to the Queen.

Victoria and Albert exchanged presents on the day before their marriage on 10 February 1840.[32] Albert's principal gift to his bride was a brooch, a fine large

Plate 163. The Duchess of Sutherland, the Mistress of the Robes, and some of the Queen's train-bearers wearing their corn-ear wreaths, a detail from the engraving by S. Cousins after C.R. Leslie's painting, Queen Victoria receiving the Sacrament at her Coronation, *1838. The Duchess is wearing a bracelet with a portrait of the Queen in George IV's circlet. The engraving was published by F.G. Moon, 1843.*
VICTORIA AND ALBERT MUSEUM, PRINT ROOM

sapphire in a border of diamonds (Plate 167) which Victoria wore with the 'Turkish diamond necklace and earrings' at her wedding and repeatedly thereafter (Plates 159 and 161), finally bequeathing it to the Crown.[33] Hers to him were the insignia of the Garter. After the marriage service, the Queen gave the Prince his wedding ring, while each of her twelve young train-bearers received 'as a souvenir, a small eagle brooch in turquoises' (Plate 164C).[34] Her wedding presents included a bracelet set with a large emerald and diamonds, the joint gift of the four surviving daughters of George III. The Queen also left this piece to the Crown.[35]

Queen Victoria had several jewels besides bracelets adorned with Albert's miniature. A brooch with his likeness in a diamond surround dated to 1840.[36] But the bracelets are more familiar from portraits of the Queen. One example was set in about 1840 with the Prince's profile after Ross in a diamond border; the band seems to have consisted of diamond strings supplied by Rundell's in 1838. Another, also dating to 1840, was decorated with diamonds and turquoises and a third had a pearl surround with matching strings (Plate 165). Lord Monkswell, in attendance at Windsor as a Lord in Waiting in 1894, noticed the pearl bracelet on the Queen's wrist at dinner.[37] One further example must be mentioned. This bore an enamel portrait of the Prince in armour after a miniature executed by Robert Thorburn in 1843. Prince Albert, who gave it to his wife at Christmas 1844, designed the bracelet with an enamelled miniature Collar of the Garter.[38]

The Prince came to his new country eager to help the Queen with state business. At first unwilling to accept his assistance, she capitulated shortly after the birth, in November 1840, of their first child Victoria (Vicky), the Princess Royal.

Plate 164. A. A ring given by Queen Victoria to a train-bearer at her Coronation, its head set with a sapphire flanked by two diamonds. The inside of the gold hoop is inscribed: 28 June 1838 and engraved with the Queen's crowned cipher with her hair in a glass box between.

B. A serpent brooch in blue-enamelled gold with a ruby eye and four moonstones set between its coils. The gift of Louis-Philippe's youngest daughter, Princess Clementine d'Orléans, it must be French; the reverse is inscribed: C/10th June/1840. The Queen was fond of Princess Clementine, who was two years her senior. In 1843 the Princess was married to Prince Augustus of Saxe-Coburg whom even Queen Victoria, with her devotion to her husband's family, found 'odd and inanimate'.

C. A gold eagle brooch with wings displayed, clasping a pearl in each of its claws, pavé-set with turquoises, with a cabochon eye and diamonds in its beak and claws. The Queen gave one of these brooches to each of the twelve train-bearers at her marriage on 10 February 1840; this example probably came from the collection of her grand-daughter Princess Marie-Louise. Lady Lansdowne called the brooches Coburg eagles (Frampton, page 412).

ROYAL COLLECTION

Plate 165. The Princess Royal as an infant, clasping her mother's pearl-set bracelet with a miniature of Prince Albert, in a stipple engraving by James Thomson after a painting by John Lucas; c.1844. The Queen is depicted with the same bracelet in Plate 177.

NATIONAL PORTRAIT GALLERY ARCHIVES

Plate 166. A. A gold bracelet with a tapering band of hinged links, engraved with foliated scrolls and the centre formed of two hearts carved from a single amethyst. A gift to the Queen from the Duchess of Kent, who was anxious to appease her daughter after their estrangement over Sir John Conroy, it is inscribed on the back: 23 Nov 1839, *the day on which Victoria announced her engagement to the Privy Council.*

B. A delicate gold bracelet engraved with hearts and true-lovers' knots, the centre set with an emerald flanked by two diamonds, with another diamond in the padlock pendant. A Christmas present from Prince Albert to the Queen, it is inscribed on the back: From Albert/Decr 24 1839. *The Queen probably had the inscription added herself; she consistently followed this practice.*

C. A gold bracelet with a broad mesh band, the centre set with a miniature of Prince Albert which he sent to the Queen from Germany early in 1840. Inside the cover, which is chased with flowers and shells on a matted ground, is the inscription: ALBERT/1840. *The shell-shaped pendent locket contains a coloured photograph of the Princess Royal and is inscribed:* from Victoria/1st Feb. 1858. *It was presumably added just after the Princess Royal's marriage.*   ROYAL COLLECTION

Henceforth, he was her principal adviser. The Prince had strong scientific, antiquarian and artistic interests, the last of which he shared with his wife. Both were talented amateur artists, but Victoria was far less concerned than he with the niceties of historical styles in the fine and decorative arts, nor did she fully appreciate the new technological developments in industry which so excited her husband, though for his sake she laboured to learn and comprehend.

Prince Albert became President of the Society of Arts in succession to the Queen's uncle the Duke of Sussex in 1843. He was thus, in his twenty-fourth year,

Plate 167. A sapphire brooch in a border of twelve brilliants in open-backed collets, Prince Albert's principal present to Queen Victoria on the day before their marriage. She wrote in her Journal on 9 February: 'Dearest Albert gave me a splendid Brooch, a large sapphire set round with diamonds, which is really quite beautiful'. It also reveals the Prince's admiration of early nineteenth century design. The Queen wore the brooch at her wedding and many times thereafter. It appears in the Winterhalter painting of 1842 (Plate 169). She left it to the Crown. ROYAL COLLECTION

the head of an increasingly influential cultural establishment. He revived one of the Society's original aims, the encouragement of manufactures, and eventually set in train the Great Exhibition of 1851. The Prince's manifold public responsibilities were offset by more personal concerns. Designing and supervising the design of others was, like his sporting activities, a means of recreation. Nothing escaped his attention. He influenced his wife's choice of clothes and late in 1840, if not before, began on her jewellery. Badly advised by her Ministers, the Queen and the Prince behaved as if the Crown Jewels claim was non-existent.

As a designer and patron of the arts, Prince Albert was sensitive, conscientious and knowledgeable. Without precisely possessing George IV's infallible flair for scenting new trends, he nevertheless felt his way towards one of the main developments of mid-century design, the revival, or rather the reinterpretation, of First Empire and Regency forms, while his interest in new technologies persuaded his wife that photographs were an acceptable substitute for painted miniatures in jewellery. The Prince also admired the Renaissance, which inspired some of his designs[39] and alerted him to the decorative potential of enamelling. Though he essayed Oriental motifs and was very fond of naturalism, fashions pre-dating his own birth in 1819 are most frequently recalled in the jewellery made at his behest for the Queen.

The Prince's earliest documented designs were sentimental in character, but his most ambitious work was undoubtedly the re-ordering of his wife's jewellery, resulting in parures constructed on the First Empire model of a single coloured stone set off by diamonds. His first attempts in the genre probably included a turquoise and diamond bracelet set with his miniature and matching head ornament, the latter a present to his wife on her twenty-second birthday in 1841.[40] The process was probably well under way when, in late February 1843, the Queen noted in her Journal: 'We were very busy looking over various pieces of old jewelry of mine, settling to have some reset, in order to add to my fine "parures". Albert has such taste, and arranges everything for me about my jewels.'[41]

The Prince's efforts gave Queen Victoria enormous pleasure, expressed in her Journal with characteristic immediacy and directness. By 17 November, the Queen was able to write in her Journal: 'Wore for the 1st time my new Turquoise Parure, all designed & arranged according to my precious Albert's directives & excellent taste. All the Turquoises come from St Petersburg, where L^y Stuart[42]

311

got them for me, to go with some I had before.' The somewhat fraught letters about the turquoises written to Lady Stuart de Rothesay, the wife of the British Ambassador Extraordinary, by her daughter Lady Canning (Colour Plate 79), the Queen's Lady of the Bedchamber, were published by Virginia Surtees in her biography of Lady Canning. Lady Stuart eventually sent forty-two turquoises costing 3,500 roubles for which the Keeper of the Privy Purse disbursed £175. Then she discovered she had overcharged and despatched four more stones to make up the difference, too late, apparently, for them to be incorporated in the parure,[43] which was largely made by Joseph Kitching.

Fortunately some records relating to Queen Victoria's purchases of jewellery have been preserved, though they are far from complete. The most important of these, the Garrard Royal Ledger for the Queen, is of no help before 1844. Part of the gap is bridged by her private account books which were started in 1841. Under the heading, '*1843, For Jewelry for Myself*', the Queen struggled nobly to summarise the contents of several complex bills. She noted a turquoise and diamond necklace purchased for £98 from Turner's of 58 and 59 New Bond Street, who held several royal warrants. Below this Kitching's name appears, credited with mending or altering various articles including a turquoise and diamond head ornament (probably the ferronnière given by her mother in 1833) which was converted into a bracelet. Then come the turquoises bought from Lady Stuart de Rothesay. Finally, Kitching is credited with setting eight brooches with drops, supplying 796 roses and other diamonds (presumably brilliants) and mounting them with turquoises in a head ornament. All this, together with some complicated work on Orders for the Prince, cost £445.2s., largely offset by a diamond and gold miniature frame, 'a diamond band' and two drops from an unspecified turquoise ornament which were credited to the jeweller and reduced the bill to £40.2s.[44]

A second turquoise parure was made in 1859. As in the case of other suites of jewellery belonging to this decade, it probably owed its existence to two factors. One was the judgement in the Crown Jewels case late in 1857, which was based on the discovery of two wills of George III, empowering Queen Charlotte to leave her jewels as she thought fit. The Queen therefore lost her grandmother's Crown and part or the whole of other articles which were set with stones belonging to Queen Charlotte.[45] This left Victoria requiring further sets of jewellery. The second was an entirely unexpected bequest in September 1852 from a miserly old barrister, John Camden Nield, who, having no dependents, left a handsome fortune to his sovereign[46] and made the frugality of the previous decade unnecessary.

The Queen noted in her Journal on 24 February 1859: 'Busy with Garrard, arranging a set of turquoises' (Prince Albert's presence must be understood). This parure, entered in the Garrard Royal Ledger on 9 August, comprised a head ornament, necklace with pendant, earrings and brooch (the last piece was probably converted to a locket in April 1861).[47] Queen Victoria supplied all the turquoises and some of the diamonds used in the set, perhaps taken from ornaments belonging to the singer Castellane, which the Queen purchased in 1848.[48] The firm added 1,461 brilliants, charging a total of £1,093.15s. for the stones and workmanship. Like the other coloured parures, the set would be better known from portraits and photographs had not the Prince Consort's premature death on 14 December 1861 sent the Queen into perpetual mourning. On 4 July 1866, the day before the marriage of her third daughter, Helena,[49] the Queen remarked in her Journal that she had intended bequeathing the turquoises to her but decided to give them instead, 'as I shall never wear those coloured stones, which dearest Albert had arranged'.

The word 'arranged' was absolutely accurate, as it is likely that Prince Albert often outlined his ideas to the jeweller, who then made up a traditional wax model with stones affixed to it. The Prince had only to transpose a few stones or correct the profile of the model. This is different from producing an original design, as he occasionally did. The Queen sometimes distinguished between the two operations, though she did not always document the progress of remaking her jewellery in her Journals. But it is possible to detect the Prince's hand in a set of sapphire and diamond jewels comprising a 'Small Coronet' costing £415, a pair of earrings, a brooch and a bracelet, the two latter priced together at £360. The Queen listed the items in her private account book in 1842,[50] though she cited no maker.

The small coronet, with its band of alternating sapphires and diamonds and a trefoil crest, is reminiscent both of a head ornament owned by Queen Henrietta Maria (Plate 168), as well as of the crown adorning the Badge of the Order of the Saxon Rauten Krone,[51] which points to Prince Albert as the author. Queen Victoria's coronet is well known from Winterhalter's first portrait of her, executed in 1842 (Plate 169). Besides Albert's brooch, the artist also depicted the tiny diamond-set heart pendant, an engagement gift from Queen Louise of Belgium in November 1839, into which the Prince put the lock of his hair which Victoria had already worn 'night and day' in a glass heart for several weeks.[52]

Circlets might be made to expand with the insertion of additional sections, the kind of ingenious refinement calculated to appeal to the Prince. The small coronet of 1842, enlarged in this fashion, may have been worn by the Queen when she posed to the miniaturist Robert Thorburn in 1844 with her eldest son Albert Edward, Prince of Wales.[53]

On 24 December 1842, Queen Victoria wrote in her Journal: 'Splendid indeed were the presents my beloved one gave me, amongst them the rearrangement of some of my jewels, to be worn in different ways, a complete antique Parure...' But her statement is ambiguous. The antique parure (now in the Museum of London) was distinct from the rearranged jewels and was largely concocted from seventeenth and eighteenth century components supplemented by a fake Renaissance mermaid which was evidently passed off on the Prince as original (Colour Plate 80).[54] The rearranged jewellery might be the sapphire and diamond set. Though the Queen's account book shows that she bore half the cost of the earrings (£280) — the other £280 presumably contributed by Prince Albert — she would have thought it perfectly reasonable to pay towards a present to herself. She always required her daughters to furnish the whole or a considerable part of the cost of the jewellery which she gave them to mark their confirmation.[55] A greater objection is that the coronet would have had to be given to Queen Victoria earlier

Plate 168. Queen Henrietta Maria, a portrait after Van Dyck, attributed to H. Van Steenwyck; c.1632-1635. The Queen's pearl jewellery includes a small crested coronet worn over her back hair, a fashion which inspired the Prince Consort.   NATIONAL PORTRAIT GALLERY

Plate 169. Queen Victoria in 1842, by Winterhalter. Wearing white and holding a rose, her chignon encircled by a small sapphire and diamond coronet with a trefoil cresting, a locket around her neck and the Prince's marriage gift, the sapphire and diamond brooch, on her fichu, the Queen stands against a darkening sky. Even Sir George Hayter thought the likeness good and the Queen herself described it as 'perfect'.   ROYAL COLLECTION

in the year for her to have worn it for the Winterhalter portrait, but even this can be answered. The Prince often presented his wife with matching jewellery by instalments, thus ensuring that he was adequately provided with gifts on the many anniversaries celebrated during their life together.

The Prince gave his wife a sapphire and diamond brooch for her birthday in 1845, a smaller version, as the Queen described it, of his wedding present to her.[56] He also appears to have been responsible for another head ornament with a crest of large tear-shaped sapphires and a band of the same stones. This was worn by the Queen with diamond and sapphire girandole earrings and a stomacher of three lozenge-shaped brooches, each with three sapphire drops, when she posed with the Prince and their four eldest children for a family group by Winterhalter in 1846 (Plate 170).

In July 1838, Victoria had purchased from Rundell's 'an Emerald and Brilliant Elizabethan Locket with large Pearl Drop'[57] for £66.3s and the following year the

Plate 170. Queen Victoria, Prince Albert and their five elder children, painted by Winterhalter in 1846. The Queen wears a sapphire and diamond coronet with a cresting of large cabochon-cut stones, sapphire girandole earrings and a stomacher of three diamond and sapphire brooches with sapphire drops, in addition to the Garter Star, her little heart pendant and the diamond loops securing the Garter ribbon to her shoulder. Her right arm encircles Albert Edward, Prince of Wales and her eldest child, Victoria, Princess Royal, is on the right, cradling the head of the last born, Princess Helena, with Princess Alice leaning over the baby. The small boy in skirts toddling towards them is Prince Alfred, later Duke of Edinburgh and Coburg. ROYAL COLLECTION

sévigné with an emerald drop and the pair of matching earrings already cited. She and the Prince jointly gave a set of emeralds and diamonds to Princess Alexandrine of Baden on her marriage to Albert's elder brother Ernest[58] on 3 May 1842. The jewellery, comprising a ferronnière, bracelet, cross and heart, brooch and pair of earrings, cost the donors £1,000.[59]

In 1843, two entries in the Queen's private account book show that a new emerald and diamond parure was well under way for herself, and that the Kitching concern was once more responsible for at least part of it. Queen Victoria noted that some of the jeweller's charges for supplying emeralds and setting two brooches were offset by other emeralds and diamonds from a ferronnière and drops. A less ambiguous entry, for a 'Chain Necklace' containing 168 diamonds and fourteen emeralds, was a straightforward purchase at £600.[60] Among the Queen's Christmas presents from her husband in the same year, recorded in her Journal on 24 December, was a bracelet enamelled in white with emeralds in the centre, though it is doubtful whether this formed part of the set. In 1844, a further addition to the parure was obtained from Kitching's in the form of 'a pair of fine solid drop emerald earrings' priced at £245.1s.6d. An existing pair of earrings was partially dismantled at the same time and the spare stones credited to the jewellers.[61] These were presumably elements in a parure for which Kitching's executed an

315

Plate 171. A detail from a watercolour by the French artist Eugène Lami of Queen Victoria at the christening of Prince Arthur on 22 June 1850, at which she wore her emerald and diamond parure with the Spartan diadem designed by Prince Albert.

ROYAL LIBRARY, WINDSOR

emerald and diamond diadem costing £1,150 in 1845.[62] The Queen, describing a state ball, wrote in her Journal on 25 April 1845: 'I was "coiffée" before dinner, with a lovely Diadem of diamonds and emeralds, designed by my beloved Albert....'

In tribute to the Prince, the Queen wore the complete parure in July 1847 at a banquet at Trinity College, Cambridge, celebrating Albert's installation as Chancellor of the University.[63] Lami's watercolour of the Queen wearing it at the christening of her third son, Prince Arthur[64] (Plate 171), demonstrates that the head ornament was a Spartan diadem.

For their first few years as Crown Jewellers, Garrard's appear to have had little to do with the Queen's new parures. She purchased a pair of emerald and diamond twin pins from the firm for £50 in February 1844, followed by other items, including a ribbon pattern bracelet set with emeralds and diamonds costing £18.10s., but it is unlikely that they formed part of the suite planned by her husband. The Queen paid £52.10s. for an emerald and diamond heart locket in 1848, in which year she acquired a 'Large Emerald and Diamond Necklace' for £1,200. In 1850 the firm made her a 'Large Emerald and Diamond Brooch' for £450 and a pair of matching earrings for £330.[65]

Garrard's executed further ornaments for the Queen in 1852 as part of an important series of commissions following the East India Company's presentation, first of an armlet set with the Koh-i-Nûr diamond in 1850[66] and second, after they had been lent to the Great Exhibition, of other jewels from the Treasury of Lahore which had fallen to the British on the annexation of the Punjab in 1849.[67] The new pieces, set with emeralds, diamonds and pearls, were completed by 1 November. The total charge for the workmanship was £107.15s. The Crown Jewellers mounted fifteen ornaments set with lask (or lasque) diamonds (a thin, flat cut, much used by Indian jewellers) as an 'Indian circlet' or tiara with fifteen 'betweens' of the same diamonds: pearls and emeralds were also incorporated into the design, thirty emeralds being cut (in fact re-cut) into drops for the purpose. The firm added a row of diamonds for £7.18s. on 27 November and enlarged the piece in 1853, furnishing eight additional emeralds and a number of small brilliants for £148. The ledger entry for 1 November 1852 also includes a stomacher adorned with twenty-seven re-cut emeralds and lask diamonds removed from an undescribed necklace with pendants. Fourteen lask diamond ornaments and fourteen re-cut emeralds were set in a pair of bracelets at the same time.[68]

Arrayed in a white dress with coloured ribbons and the emerald and diamond parure, the Queen attended the Paris Opera on 21 August 1855 during the State visit made by her and Prince Albert to France at the height of the Crimean War. She was quite unperturbed to find the Empress Eugénie[69] and Princess Mathilde,[70] whose jewels were legendary, also wearing emeralds and diamonds.[71] In January 1858, shortly before the marriage of her eldest daughter Victoria to Prince Frederick William (Fritz) of Prussia,[72] the Queen appeared at a State dinner resplendent in a rose pink dress trimmed with Honiton lace and the same parure.[73]

Garrard's references to lask diamonds and re-cut emeralds all point to the East India Company's gift as the probable source of the materials. A list of the articles presented to the Queen by the Company is inserted in her Journal before the entry of 23 October 1851, but once the famous stones are excluded the rest are described so cursorily that it is impossible to arrive at any useful conclusion. In one respect at least the list is misleading. A ruby armlet appears in it, but the Queen noted in her Journal that the great Timur ruby and the three rubies accompanying it had already been unset.

The Queen's ruby and diamond jewellery followed much the same course as the other suites. In 1842 she acquired a pair of ruby and white enamel earrings and a matching brooch costing £42.10s. in all and another brooch at £36.10s. These probably had nothing to do with any parure. Two years later, however, Kitching's altered two existing ruby and diamond brooches, furnishing additional rubies and charging a total of £52, supplying also a ruby and diamond bandeau for £590.[74] Prince Albert's birthday presents to his wife in the same year included 'a splendid single ruby brooch set round with diamonds'. He followed this with another brooch with a ruby and pearl drop for their wedding anniversary in 1848 and for her birthday in May 1849 gave her a ruby locket.[75]

Another suite was probably commenced in 1848 when Garrard's mounted eight large rubies in diamond surrounds as a necklace for the Queen at a cost of £285. This was apparently reset in April 1849, the Crown Jewellers supplying eleven additional rubies, all bordered with diamonds, charging £413.15s. Shortly afterwards Garrard's added further diamonds to the necklace and made a brooch and earrings at an overall cost of £1,400.[76] The Queen enthused in her Journal on 30 July 1849: 'Much pleased with a beautiful necklace, earrings & a brooch of rubies & diamonds, which dearest Albert had arranged for me, out of stones of my own, with the addition of new ones I purchased with money inherited from Aunt

Plate 172. A circlet or tiara of 'Oriental design' made by Garrard's in 1853 and set with opals and diamonds. The lotus motifs and lobed frames suggest that Prince Albert had something to do with the design. Altered in 1858 in satisfaction of the award in the Hanoverian claim to the crown jewels, the ornament was simplified for Queen Alexandra in 1902. Unlike Queen Victoria and the Prince Consort, she must have had a phobia about opals and had them replaced by Indian rubies which had been presented to her mother-in-law in 1876. ROYAL COLLECTION

Augusta and Aunt Sophia.[77] The parure is really beautiful, & Albert has such wonderful taste....'

In 1853 Garrard's made a further ruby and diamond necklace, using the Indian stones and providing fittings to receive either the Timur ruby or the Koh-i-Nûr.[78] Though slightly altered, it has survived. Queen Victoria wore her 'very large Indian rubies' and a diamond diadem during the visit of Napoleon III and Eugénie to England in April 1855.[79]

Kitching's ruby and diamond bandeau appears to have been remodelled in 1860, to judge by an entry in the Garrard Royal Ledger for Queen Victoria: 'Remounting Ruby and Diamond and head Ornament, addition of Strawberry leaves, scrolls and Ruby between'. For this the Crown Jewellers supplied two additional large brilliants, 727 smaller ones, forty-six rose diamonds, seven large rubies and thirty smaller specimens, charging £1,115 for the whole.[80] It can be reasonably inferred that Albert was responsible for 'arranging' this tiara to match the set of 1849. The Queen, who regarded it as his design, treated it as integral to the parure. Ten years after her husband's death, she once more put on coloured

318

jewellery for the marriage on 21 March 1871 of her fourth daughter Louise[81] to the Marquis of Lorne, the eldest son of the Duke of Argyll, noting in her Journal the same day: 'I wore a black satin dress, trimmed with jet, on my head, over my veil, my ruby and diamond Tiara and my Parure to match'. She gave the set to her youngest daughter Beatrice[82] as a wedding present in 1885.[83]

The Queen and Prince Albert were fond of opals and she believed them to be his favourite stone.[84] Opals were set by Garrard's in a circlet of 'Oriental design' with alternative crestings in 1853, for which the firm supplied seventeen opals, 328 of the 1,348 brilliants and 1,102 of the 1,330 roses used in the piece, charging £861.10s.6d. in all.[85] Early in 1858, when most of the brilliants and roses contributed by the Queen had to be broken out of the front of the tiara in satisfaction of the Hanoverian claim, it was re-made. The piece was altered and simplified in 1902, the opals being replaced with Indian rubies which had been presented to the Queen by Sir Jung Bahadur in 1876, while the seventeen ogee arches and 'betweens' were each reduced to eleven[86] (Plate 172).

In 1854, Garrard's followed the tiara with a 'very fine Opal & Brilliant Necklace' with twelve clusters, each with an opal in the centre, for which the firm furnished ten opals and 'fine selected brilliants' and a large opal drop as a pendant for an existing brooch, the whole costing the Queen £2,242.[87] The Prince had designed the necklace and the brooch, together with a pair of earrings which were apparently made by another firm, unless they were entered under a separate account with Garrard's, which does not survive. Queen Victoria wore her opal parure with a yellow gown during the visit of the Emperor Napoleon III and the Empress Eugénie to Windsor in 1855 and again with a pink dress when she and the Prince went to Paris a few months later.[88] The Queen left the parure to the Crown, together with a small opal stud or slide which she had given to her husband in 1840. The opals in the entire set were replaced by rubies, some to the order of Queen Alexandra in 1902, the rest for Queen Mary in 1926.

An opal and diamond parure, presumably executed to the Prince's requirements by Turner, figured among the wedding presents from Queen Victoria and her husband to their eldest daughter, the Princess Royal, in 1858.[89] Prince Albert went on to design similar suites for his second daughter Alice[90] and his son Albert Edward's future bride. Both were made by the Queen's command after her husband's death in December 1861. Thereafter, all the royal daughters received opal and diamond parures on their marriages, with the apparent exception of Princess Beatrice in 1885.

Queen Charlotte's magnificent pearls came to Victoria on her accession and she was permitted to retain most of them in 1858 through the generosity of her cousin, who had succeeded his father as King of Hanover. In 1844, almost certainly at Prince Albert's behest, Kitching's mounted a diamond and pearl brooch for the Queen. All the materials, apart from one pearl, came from family jewels.[91] The Prince returned to the theme in 1847, when his presents to his wife on Christmas Eve, as she recorded in her Journal, included 'a fine large brooch of one single pearl set round with diamonds' which she wore that same evening. It may well appear in Lady Abercromby's painting in Plate 110, in which case it was the

Plate 173. The frame of the Grand or Regal circlet re-made for Queen Victoria by Garrard's in 1858, in a fitted case provided by the Crown Jewellers when they altered it for Queen Alexandra in 1902. The velvet-covered tray at the back once held the anthemion fitments which formed the alternative crest to the crosses and fleurs-de-lis; the lozenge-shaped depression in the centre was designed for the Koh-i-Nûr in its fitting (see Winterhalter's painting in Plate 174). (Shown half actual size.) MUSEUM OF LONDON

prototype of the circular units in the pearl and diamond necklace given by the Prince of Wales to his bride in 1863 (Plate 263). Prince Albert probably also concerned himself with a coral suite incorporating material bought in Naples for the Queen in 1845 by Sir A.C. Murray, formerly Master of her Household. These pieces were remounted by Garrard's in 1855.[92]

The Queen lent the Indian armlet with the Koh-i-Nûr and two flanking stones to the Great Exhibition. The stones had already been broken out of it and were shown separately. Jane Welsh Carlyle, who inspected the great rose-cut diamond at the exhibition, informed a young relative that 'the big diamond — unset — looked precisely like a bit of crystal the size and shape of the first joint of your thumb!'[93]

The diamond, recut as a brilliant in 1852 (see Plate 57), was then mounted in a surround of small roses. The diamond and its border was capable of slotting when required into the centre of a large anthemion brooch reputedly designed by Nicholas Chevalier. The same brooch was also adapted to receive a smaller alternative stone, the Cumberland Diamond.

In 1853, Queen Adelaide's Grand or Regal circlet was reconstructed by Garrard's, its crest of alternating crosses and fleurs-de-lis made detachable to allow for the insertion of the anthemion brooch and smaller matching devices (Plate 173). The whole piece with its alternative fittings contained 2,203 brilliants and 662 roses (322 brilliants and 515 roses being supplied by Garrard's who charged the Queen £693.10s. for mounting them).[94] Though Queen Victoria wore the Koh-i-Nûr in her new circlet and could also insert it in the Indian ruby necklace, she probably used it chiefly as a bodice brooch (Plate 174). After the judgement in the Hanoverian case late in 1857, which necessitated diamonds being broken out of the circlet, it was reconstructed with diamonds again partly provided by Garrard's, others coming from unwanted royal jewellery. The replacement piece, charged at £8,044, contained a substitute stone for the Cumberland Diamond which was presumably ceded to Hanover. It came from one of the jewels which had been presented to the Queen by the Sultan of Turkey to mark the successful conclusion of the Crimean War in 1856.[95] The circlet of 1858 was finally dismantled to furnish the stones for Queen Elizabeth the Queen Mother's Crown in 1937.

Other items re-made or partly replaced by Garrard's after the Hanoverian judgement included a rivière of twenty-eight diamond collets mainly taken from a Garter Badge and a jewelled sword hilt, earring tops with drops borrowed when necessary from those on the Indian ruby necklace (Plate 175) and two large and one small diamond brooches for use as a stomacher. By and large clusters of smaller royal diamonds had to be substituted for larger stones relinquished to Hanover. The necklace cost £65, the earrings £23.10s. and the bow brooches £71.10s. (Plate 176). All the work of remounting and remaking the Queen's jewellery affected by the judgement was charged at £8,851.1s. (£8,777 net). She wore her new necklace and earrings for Winterhalter's portrait of 1859 (Plate 177).

Prince Albert's minor offerings of jewellery to his wife included a brooch representing Vicky in her cradle, a present to her on their first wedding anniversary, which was also the day on which the Princess Royal was christened. The Queen was enraptured by the piece — 'the quaintest thing', she wrote in her Journal on 10 February 1841, 'I ever saw & so pretty'. The birth of the Prince of Wales on 9 November following was commemorated by 'a beautiful brooch in the shape of our Boy's crest, in enamel, jewelled'.[96] In December Prince Albert gave his wife an enamel of the Princess Royal after a miniature by Sir William Ross, 'mounted as a brooch with diamond wings', a cross set with rubies and diamonds suspended from the child's hands. Albert, she recorded in her Journal on 24 December, 'was so pleased at my delight over it, it having been entirely his own idea & taste'. Years afterwards, when the Princess Royal was married and living in Prussia, Queen Victoria wrote to her daughter to describe the confirmation ceremony of the Prince of Wales adding, 'I wore the brooch of you as a little angel'.[97]

Plate 174. Queen Victoria painted by Winterhalter in 1856 wearing her new Regal circlet with detachable cresting which had been made for her by Garrard's in 1853, following the general form of Queen Adelaide's Grand circlet of 1831. She has chosen here to wear the Koh-i-Nûr diamond as a bodice brooch. Her rivière of diamonds belonged to Queen Charlotte. Less than two years later the necklace and many of the stones in the circlet had to be relinquished to Hanover, so that Winterhalter's portrait is an important record of the Queen's jewellery in the mid-1850s before the judgement on the Hanoverian claim upheld her grandmother's right to bequeath her jewels as she wished. ROYAL COLLECTION

The Prince naturally fell in with the family custom of giving what the Queen invariably called 'trifles' or 'souvenirs' to his nearest and dearest on his own birthday. A bracelet he presented to her on 26 August 1842, his twenty-third birthday, is illustrated in Colour Plate 94A. Their accumulation of hair jewellery, their love of trinkets set with pebbles picked up in favourite localities, their patronage of Scottish and Irish jewellers and their admiration of deer's teeth transmogrified into thistle tops, acorns, plants and flowers when set in enamelled gold (Colour Plate 131) are discussed in Chapters XII and XV. Prince Albert's other designs include a brooch given by the Queen to Florence Nightingale for her work in the Crimea which looks like an unofficial Badge of an Order (Plate 178).

Plate 175. *The Crown Jewellers, Garrard's, required to mount a new rivière of large diamonds for Queen Victoria in April 1858 to replace Queen Charlotte's necklace, broke out twenty-eight brilliants from a Badge and a jewelled sword hilt for the purpose. The diamond pendant and the two earring drops were removed when required from the necklace of Indian rubies. The necklace was reduced in size in 1937 for Queen Elizabeth the Queen Mother, who also had the diamond pendant (the 'Lahore diamond') recut and temporarily set in her new Crown.*

ROYAL COLLECTION

323

Plate 176. Queen Victoria lost her grandmother's bow brooches to Hanover, and Garrard's made three new diamond ones in May 1858, two large and one small, using 497 (possibly 516) diamonds supplied by the Queen. These are two of them. ROYAL COLLECTION

In December 1855, Garrard's made two Crimean brooches in enamelled gold as an 'Order of Mercy' and another in plain gold for presentation to Miss Nightingale's assistants.[98]

The Crimean War, the only major conflict between European powers in which Britain was involved during the Prince's lifetime, was fought in alliance with France and Turkey against Russia from 1854 to 1856. But it had been preceded by considerable unrest in Europe, which reached a peak in 1848. The great Chartist demonstration in England fizzled out, but a series of revolutions erupted on the Continent, beginning in Sicily and spreading to Italy, France, Germany, the Austrian Empire and elsewhere. Though the revolts were mainly suppressed, lasting effects were felt in some countries. King Louis Philippe, who had come to the throne in France on the Revolution of 1830, lost it in consequence of the

Plate 177. The last painting of Queen Victoria in robes of state, wearing George IV's circlet and the collet necklace and earrings re-made by Garrard's in 1858 (see Plate 175), one of her portrait bracelets of Prince Albert and a fringed corsage ornament; the portrait was painted by Winterhalter in 1859.

ROYAL COLLECTION

Plate 178. The Nightingale Jewel, presented by Queen Victoria to Florence Nightingale in 1855 in gratitude for her work in the Crimea. The Illustrated London News, *publishing an engraving of it early in 1856, declared: 'The design is said to be from the pencil of the Prince Consort', who had it executed by Garrard's. The enamelled cross in the middle, bearing the Queen's crowned cipher in diamonds, is set against rays implying 'Heavenly sympathy', reinforced by the motto on the frame and the diamond stars above. The palm branches in gold and green enamel signify friendship and peace and on the label below,* CRIMEA *is reserved on light blue enamel similar to that on the Crimea Medal. The inscription on the reverse runs:* To Miss FLORENCE NIGHTINGALE, as a mark of esteem and gratitude for her devotion towards the Queen's brave soldiers. From VICTORIA R., 1855.

NATIONAL ARMY MUSEUM

Revolution of 1848 and fled with his family to England, spending the rest of his life at Claremont.

Queen Victoria, though naturally distressed by this turn of events, nevertheless could not resist recording a side-effect of the troubles in France in her Journal on 5 July: 'There is no end', she wrote, 'to the jewellers & artists arriving from Paris, half ruined, and with beautiful & tempting things, some of which one cannot resist buying'. She probably had in mind the designers and craftsmen who came to England with the Parisian goldsmith and jeweller Jean-Valentin Morel. The latter, who entered into partnership with E.-J. de Bommeville, established himself at 7 New Burlington Street.[99] Morel, patronised in France by Louis Philippe, was taken up by the Queen and the Prince, who bought several articles from him. The head of Morel's workshop was Edouard Marchand, whose innovations included, besides his own variety of serpent bracelet, gold brooches in the form of cartouches bordered by scrolling straps (called *cuirs roulés*), introduced in about 1838, and gold tubes twisted into knots inspired by Algerian gimp or cord embroidery, which followed shortly afterwards.[100] By the time he came to London Marchand had begun to interest himself in naturalistic jewellery with enamelled decoration: specimens of his work were illustrated in the *Art Journal* in 1850.[101]

The Parisian trade began to recover after Louis Napoleon, the nephew of the Emperor Napoleon I, was elected President of France in December 1848. The French were seriously considering turning their next national exhibition of manufactures after 1849 into an international exhibition, when they found themselves pre-empted by the English. Inspired by the French, the Society of Arts had staged a series of small exhibitions devoted to English manufactures from 1847 to 1849. These were organised by an ambitious civil servant from the Public Record Office, Henry Cole,[102] who gave generous space to wares produced under his own scheme, conducted under his pseudonym of Felix Summerly and exemplifying an alliance of artists and manufacturers. The shows met with sufficient success to encourage the Prince, as President of the Society, to take up the cause of the first international exhibition. Formally named the Great Exhibition of the Works of Industry of all Nations, it was intended to celebrate the remarkable industrial expansion made possible by contemporary inventions and technology.

Henry Cole, appointed to the executive committee of the Exhibition, bustled about to some purpose, publicising it and allocating space to exhibitors. He already knew some of the English contributors, for they had participated in his Summerly Art Manufactures, launched in 1847 with characteristically bold claims. Citing great Renaissance artists who were then regarded as working in the Middle Ages, Cole asserted: 'there was scarcely a mediaeval Artist, when Art was really Catholic, who did not essay to decorate the objects of everyday life. . . . So it still ought to be, and we will say, shall be again.'[103] In fact Cole favoured naturalism over Renaissance design and instructed his artists to take their decorative details from nature.

The venture gave rise only to a small amount of jewellery. The sculptor John Bell[104] designed brooches to be set with miniature versions of his statuary,

Plate 179. Daniel Maclise's design for a bracelet for Henry Cole's Summerly Art Manufactures, executed in March 1848 and purchased by Gass of Regent Street at the end of the year. The first of the projected series of bracelets was only made in time for the firm to show it at the Great Exhibition of 1851. Maclise was deeply disappointed by the mechanical engraving, which was designed to be filled with niello, and there is no indication that the planned edition was ever completed. As an essay in art and industry it was a failure. The design is a conceit within a conceit. It represents, in vignettes framed by rustic interlacing, three stages in the ordering and making of the bracelet: 'In the first, the lover measuring his mistress's arm; in the second, giving the order to the jeweller; and in the third, fixing the bracelet,' wrote Cole.   VICTORIA AND ALBERT MUSEUM, PRINT ROOM

probably scaled down by Benjamin Cheverton's pantograph and cast in parian, an early Victorian development of biscuit porcelain. These were made at Herbert Minton's potteries in Stoke-on-Trent. Minton, a friend of Cole, was credited by the latter with inventing parian jewellery when he showed specimens at the Society of Arts in 1847. Minton was soon rivalled by Mrs Mary Brougham of Burslem whose 'elegant Parian brooches, bracelets, etc.' were said to have attracted the patronage of the Queen. Her wares were probably naturalistic, the English equivalent of the German orange-blossom brooch sent by the Prince to the Queen in 1839. Cole illustrated a floral brooch in parian in his *Journal of Design* in 1850, stating that it was produced by both Minton and Mrs Brougham;[105] the design was conceivably a Summerly one. Later on, Cole had second thoughts about naturalism. Mrs Brougham was then advised by the *Journal* to extend the use of parian 'beyond mere floral ornaments', as her pieces were not only fragile but might be regarded as nothing more than imitations of ivory carvings.[106] But parian trinkets continued to be turned out in a naturalistic manner (Plate 224).

The painter Daniel Maclise[107] designed a bracelet in March 1848 for Summerly (Plate 179) in pursuance of Cole's idea that its decoration might be '*reproduced mechanically* at a moderate price' by the same method as was employed in the printing of banknotes and postage stamps. It would gain in prestige, Cole considered, if the engraved lines were then filled with niello, thus marrying industrial production with a medieval technique. Cole, who never neglected an opportunity of demonstrating his active concern for manufactures to Prince Albert, showed him Maclise's design (for which the artist asked £30) on 4 July.[108]

Cole may have attempted to interest the Crown Jeweller, Sebastian Garrard, in Maclise's design but, if so, met with no success. On 23 November he tried Kitching's with the same result and went on to Gass's of 166 Regent Street.[109] Gass's took the design in November and Cole drafted a brochure advertising the

Plate 180. Queen Victoria's sketch of her coiffure at the opening of the Great Exhibition, in profile and full face, and a profile of the Princess Royal, from her Journal. 'I forgot to mention,' she wrote in her Journal, 'that I wore a dress of pink & silver, with a diamond ray Diadem & little crown at the back with two feathers, all the rest of my jewels being diamonds.' The ray diadem was Queen Adelaide's (see also Plates 156 and 157) and the little Crown Queen Charlotte's (Plate 158).

ROYAL ARCHIVES, WINDSOR CASTLE

first edition of the piece in different materials and prices. John Crewe was credited with executing the engraving and Felix Summerly, Cole's *alter ego,* with suggesting the method of reproduction.

It is doubtful whether more than one or two of these promised bracelets were ever executed. One specimen was shown by the Gass firm at the Great Exhibition; Maclise, who saw it in the making on 7 January 1851, was desperately worried about the blotchiness of the engraving.[110] In the event, the Jury of the goldsmithing and jewellery section of the Great Exhibition ignored the bracelet in awarding the Prize Medal to Gass's, though another Jury (for sculpture and plastic art), redeemed the situation and gave the firm an Honourable Mention for the piece.[111] Gass's were probably exclusively retailers and the bracelet may have been executed for them by Chapman & Son, manufacturing jewellers in Soho. Cole illustrated one of Chapman's standard bracelets in the *Journal of Design* in 1849, stating that it was supplied to Hunt & Roskell, Gass and others.[112] Gass's had sufficient confidence in the niello technique to exhibit another piece in 1851, a bracelet set with a reversed image of Thorburn's miniature of the Queen and the Prince of Wales engraved by Crewe.

The Great Exhibition was a great triumph for Prince Albert and the Queen was ecstatic. On 1 May, after gracing the opening ceremony in a pink and silver dress, Queen Adelaide's ray diadem and Queen Charlotte's Crown, which she sketched in her Journal (Colour Plate 81 and Plate 180), Victoria recorded proudly: 'This day is one of the greatest & most glorious days in our lives, with which, to my pride & joy the name of my dearly beloved Albert is forever associated!'. The Queen constantly returned to the exhibition, commenting on the great improvement in the British wares, 'for the greater part of which they [the manufacturers and the

Plate 181. A great diamond bouquet tied with a bow, by Hunt & Roskell of New Bond Street, engraved for the Official Illustrated Catalogue *of the* Great Exhibition *of 1851. The flowers were probably set on tremblers, like those in Colour Plate 104. Valued at some £9,000, it was cited by the Jury in awarding a Council Medal to the firm. See also Plate 240.*

public] have to thank my beloved Husband. The taste of some of the plate & jewelry is beautiful.' But the two jewellers named in the Queen's Journal were Parisian. They were G. Lemonnier of the Place Vendôme,[113] whose graceful naturalistic jewellery for the Queen of Spain evidently met with Victoria's approval, and François-Désiré Froment-Meurice of the rue St Honoré,[114] one of the most celebrated exponents of gothic and Renaissance design, or often a mixture of the two which was regarded as perfectly acceptable by antiquarians.

The Queen and her husband purchased items from Froment-Meurice's display on 20 May and again on 13 October. Given his interest in modern technology, it is likely that the Prince bought an enamelled platinum brooch by Froment-Meurice representing St George and the Dragon in a chased gothic setting which the Queen is said to have possessed.[115] Examples of Froment-Meurice's work were also purchased for the founding collections of the new Museum of Manufactures, the ancestor of the Victoria and Albert Museum, under the direction of Henry Cole (Colour Plate 82E).

The British exhibits, ranging from large pieces of cast iron and furniture to small items of jewellery, were alike suffused with naturalism. The jewellery was charming, from Hunt & Roskell's costly bouquet of nearly six thousand diamonds (Plate 181), much in the manner of Fester's larger (and later) bouquet for the Empress Eugénie (Plate 182), to the more modest pieces shown by Watherston & Brogden of Henrietta Street, Covent Garden (Plate 183A-C). Similar work was shown by Continental firms such as J.F. Backes of Hanau[116] but most such concerns also nodded in the direction of the antiquarian styles favoured by critics. Cole and his chief ally, the painter Richard Redgrave,[117] who were faced after the

Plate 182. A huge diamond bouquet or corsage spray held by a bow, set with 2,637 brilliants (computed to weigh 136 carats) and 860 small roses. Executed in 1855 by Théodore Fester of rue Vivienne, Paris, for the French Crown Jewels, the bouquet was catalogued in 1887 as an ornament presented by the City of Paris to the Duchesse de Berri to mark the birth of her son in 1820.

Exhibition with the task of training the students at the Schools of Design which had been founded from 1837 onwards, reacted strongly against naturalism in favour of the archaeological classical, gothic and Renaissance styles.

Everyone united in admiration of Froment-Meurice, for whom the title of 'Orfèvre-Joaillier de la Ville de Paris', which had lapsed since the Revolution of

Plate 183A and B. Watherston & Brogden of Henrietta Street, Covent Garden were manufacturers to the trade of a superior kind, for they employed designers. A design book belonging to John Brogden and now in the Victoria and Albert Museum contains drawings for a number of pieces contributed to international exhibitions, including these two for brooches exhibited in 1851.   SOTHEBY'S

1789, was revived. From the time he began to contribute to the French national exhibitions in 1839, Froment-Meurice employed sculptors such as J. Pradier, Jean-Jacques Feuchères and P.J. Cavelier to model the figures for his pieces, scaling down their work to the size of an umbrella head or a pin like the Amazon in Colour Plate 82C. His work was not expensive; the enamelled gold and oxidised silver bracelet in the same illustration cost £18. Aside from Bell's parian trinkets and the fox heads and other items popular in sporting trinkets, sculptural jewellery was comparatively rare in England. Perhaps the little gold pin of a knight on horseback given by Queen Victoria to her husband in 1842 had been procured for her in France.[118]

The chief protagonist of the gothic in England was Augustus Welby Northmore Pugin, the son of A.C. Pugin, allegedly an aristocratic refugee from the French Revolution of 1789 and himself an architectural draughtsman of distinction. Since A.W.N. Pugin had been taken up by Rundell's as a youth he had retained his interest in metalwork, though it is unlikely that he designed for the Royal Goldsmiths after 1827. Converted to Roman Catholicism in the mid-1830s, he dedicated himself thereafter to propagating his doctrine that the only true Christian style was gothic, dismissing classical design as pagan. Pugin mounted the

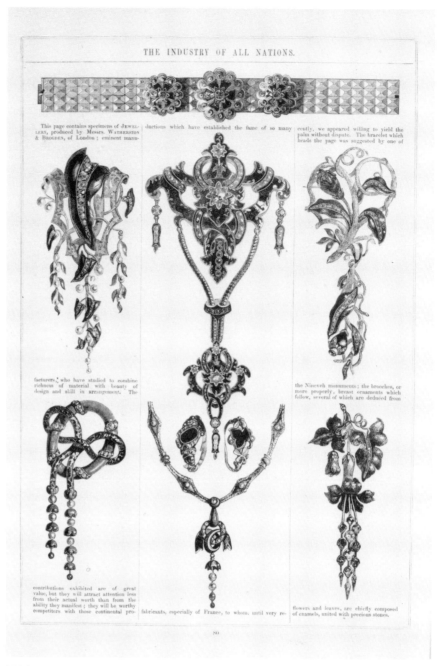

Plate 183C. The two brooches illustrated in A and B appear reversed in the Art Journal Illustrated Catalogue *of the Great Exhibition. Some of the designs were provided by F.R.P. Bööcke of Leviny & Bööcke (see page 462).*

Mediaeval Court at the Great Exhibition, filling it largely with work of his own design. This included a large gothic parure (Colour Plate 83),[119] nominally executed for him by his friend and fellow Catholic, the button-maker and metalworker John Hardman the younger of Birmingham. In fact, Hardman probably subcontracted to Thomas Aston, one of the deputation of Birmingham jewellers to be received by Prince Albert in 1845.

Twice-widowed, Pugin designed the parure late in 1847 and early in 1848 as a marriage gift to his intended third wife, an Anglican girl named Helen Lumsden. While it was being made, Miss Lumsden's family forcibly intervened and broke

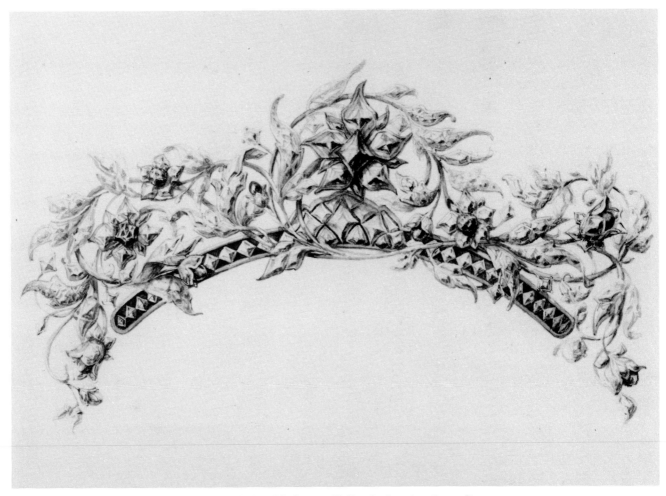

Plate 184. The floral head ornament was credited to Watherston & Brogden's artist, James Brown, in the Art Journal *of 1852, which published several of his designs, including figurative and decorative pendants in the Renaissance style.*   SOTHEBY'S

off the marriage in March 1848. Pugin riposted by writing and publishing a pamphlet retailing his ill-usage and privately circulated it among his friends and patrons. His sense of grievance was also focused on the quality of the parure. Hardman had duly seen to it that the stones, aside from the diamonds in the headband, were cut and polished *en cabochon* in medieval fashion, but the treatment of the pearls appalled Pugin. The jeweller had split them and set them in the borders as if he were making mourning jewellery, whereas Pugin had wanted whole pearls standing proud of the edges in true medieval fashion. 'I think the half pearls execrable I won't have it it is too horrid. . .,' he wrote vehemently to Hardman after he had seen one of the brooches, but little was done to rectify matters. Only the earrings, which are in private possession, showed that Hardman had heeded Pugin's words. Pugin also had vehement views on the gold: 'the colour of the gold is as bad as possible. . . I want gold like my old ring yellow gold rich looking gold precious looking gold like all the old work. . . I believe your jeweller is a humbug. . . .'

The parure was finished none the less, and together with a casket fitted to hold the pieces Pugin was charged £255.9s.6d.[120] He had found himself a new bride in the person of Jane Knill, a Roman Catholic and a cousin of one of his principal patrons, Sir Stuart Knill. They were married in August 1848 and she happily wore

the jewellery (Plate 185), lending it to the Mediaeval Court where, according to Pugin's first biographer, Benjamin Ferrey, the Queen saw and admired it.[121] Knill must have liked it also, for he commissioned a modest set of ornaments for his own bride, whom he married in 1850. This jewellery, completed in January 1850, comprised a wedding ring embellished with a cross on an enamelled shield, a gold headband bearing the initials MR and set with pearls and turquoises, a rosary ring decorated with enamel and turquoises, a small brooch with the enamelled initial M, like the brooch in Jane Pugin's set, which was based on the William of Wykeham brooch in New College, Oxford. With a fitted case, the set cost only £15.[122]

Two more important brooches were executed for another patron, John Sutton, who paid for the restoration and embellishment of the Chapel of Jesus College, Cambridge. The first, 'with Drops', was made of gold set with a ruby, sapphire, diamonds, pearls, garnets and a turquoise and cost £42.10s., according to the Hardman day book entry for June 1848. It was probably a wedding present for Sutton's sister. The second, entered in April 1849, was 'a Rich gold Cross Brooch, set with Pearls, Stones, etc., & enameled & Engraved...'; this was charged at £25.[123] Both were more expensive than other jewellery, secular and ecclesiastical, executed to Pugin's design. Pugin's silver crosses usually sold for between 7s.6d. and 10s. (or 10s.6d. if they were decorated) to Roman Catholics and Tractarians alike. Enamelled and with a figure of Christ, they cost £1.12s. Cheap brass versions, charged by Hardman's at 4d. each, were sold in London by James Burns, founder of the publishing firm of Burns Oates and himself a convert. Gilt and enamelled morses or clasps for copes were priced between £5 and £7.10s., while a richly gilt pectoral cross, enamelled and gem-set, cost £10.7s.6d. in 1848.[124]

Garrard's showed their sympathy with the antiquarian movement by exhibiting in 1851 a gothic bracelet with two angels, 'the design by Mr Smith', a pendant in the Renaissance style, 'with figures in gold, rubies, brilliants and pearls, upon green and red enamels, of fine workmanship' and a bracelet inspired by Layard's excavations of Assyrian antiquities at Nineveh.[125] Garrard's joined Hunt & Roskell, Morel, Froment-Meurice, Rudolphi and others in receiving a Council Medal, the highest award bestowed by the Jury.

The fascination with old techniques, obsolete and obsolescent, was fed by publications such as the treatises of Theophilus, usually identified as the Benedictine monk Roger of Helmershausen, who appears to have written the original work betwen 1100 and 1140. A French edition of his three manuscripts (the Arts of the Painter, the Worker in Glass and the Metalworker) was published in 1843 with the Latin text and a French translation by Comte Charles de L'Escalopier as *Theophile prêtre et moine. Essai sur divers Arts.* Robert Hendrie used this for the first full English translation which appeared in 1847, amplified by reference to a thirteenth century manuscript copy of the treatise in the British Museum. Cole was among those who called for an English translation of Cellini's treatises on sculpture and metalworking, though this was not forthcoming until C.R. Ashbee undertook the task, publishing his version in 1898.

Cole intervened in concerns properly thought to be the exclusive property of the antiquarians in the Mediaeval Movement, who looked kindly upon Pugin's demands that his gothic designs be realised by old techniques, while Ruskin was in the offing, trumpeting his hatred of industry. Cole's brief as Superintendent of the Department of Practical Art at South Kensington from 1852 onwards was to train designers to raise the standard of English manufactures but, like Prince

*Plate 187. Two gold pendants in the form of Roman lamps, both decorated with the Chi-Rho monogram.
The larger one on the right bears the mark of the Castellani firm and is engraved on the reverse:* From
Albert Edward P.W/June 1859. *A gift to his mother from the Prince of Wales on his first visit to
Rome, the pendant was later set with a photograph of the Queen's second daughter, Princess Alice, Grand
Duchess of Hesse, who died in 1878. The example on the left is inscribed:* From Albert Edward
P.W/4 Dec[r] 1862.   ROYAL COLLECTION

Albert, he could not help but prefer quality and craftsmanship. Retaining an active
role in the organisation of subsequent international exhibitions, Cole's expertise
as a publicist was often directed at articles which were feats of craftsmanship far
removed from industrial production.

Antiquarian interests hovered over the Great Exhibition. Castellani's of
Rome[126] did not participate, but their work was already held to represent the
quintessence of archaeological design. Patronised by the Princesse de Broglie, who
wore with elegance an Etruscan *bulla,* almost certainly by the Castellani firm, with
a blue silk gown for her portrait in 1853 (Plate 186), their productions were
probably also acquired by Englishwomen such as Mrs Norton, who was adorned
with an archaeological brooch when she sat to Etty for her portrait in the 1840s
(Plate 213). Cole himself appears to have acquired specimens of their work for his
museum on a visit to Rome in 1858 and the young Prince of Wales, travelling in
1859 to visit his elder sister at Berlin, went from thence to Rome, where he bought
a small piece of Castellani jewellery as a souvenir for his mother, adding another
on a return trip in 1862 (Plate 187).

Antiquarianism of one sort or another should have swept the board, since the
powerful weight of the leading figures of the cultural establishment were dedicated
to historicist design. That it did not do so immediately after the Great Exhibition
was largely due to women who found naturalistic jewellery becoming and
sympathetic to their costume. Even the Empress Eugénie,[127] who wore ornaments
in a variety of styles (Plate 188), adored naturalistic jewellery. The French Crown
Jewels, brought out of store, were dedicated to her use. Adolphe Devin, who had
succeeded J.J. Billois as head of Hunt & Roskell's jewellery workshop,[128] left
them to return to Paris in the wake of Louis Napoleon and became Inspector of
the Crown Jewels in France. He suggested that some jewels be re-set for the
Empress to wear at functions celebrating the opening of the Paris Universal
Exhibition of 1855. Devin's own design for a tiara incorporating the famous
Regent diamond did not find favour even when modified by Massin. Eugénie wore
it on the opening day of the Exhibition but considered its design of flame-like
scrolls more appropriate to the Devil than to her. It was dismantled the following

Colour Plate 80. The mermaid pendant from the 'antique parure', a Christmas present from Prince Albert in 1842; c. 1840.

MUSEUM OF LONDON

Colour Plate 79. Lady Canning, painted by Winterhalter at Queen Victoria's command in 1849, was one of the Queen's Ladies from 1842 until 1855, when she left for India, where her husband had been appointed Governor-General. She never returned but died there of a fever in 1861. A statuesque beauty in her early thirties when Winterhalter painted her, she demonstrated her antiquarian interests by wearing a late Renaissance ornament (or a skilled copy of one) in her hair. The portrait was given by King George V to his brother-in-law the 6th Earl of Harewood.

THE EARL OF HAREWOOD

Colour Plate 81. The official painting of the opening of the Great Exhibition on 1 May 1851, by H. C. Selous. In the centre stands the Queen with Prince Albert on her left and the Prince of Wales in a kilt on her right, next to the Princess Royal. The Duchess of Kent is behind the two children. Third from the left in the second row of officials in the foreground, stepping slightly forward, is Henry Cole.

VICTORIA AND ALBERT MUSEUM

Plate 188. The Empress Eugénie, an engraving by Francis Holl after a photograph. She wears an
emerald and diamond circlet made by Eugène Fontenay in 1858 with a pearl necklace and earrings.

year and replaced by the first of three sucessive versions of a Greek fret tiara. But
a naturalistic design for a parure including a garland of sixteen clusters of currant
leaves and fruits (one of the elements is shown in Plate 189), once thought to be
by Devin and now reassigned to Alfred Bapst, was much loved by the Empress.
The garland alone was set with 2,315 brilliants weighing over 540 carats, together
with 353 rose diamonds. Divided into eight lots, the head ornament fetched
241,600 francs at the sale of the French Crown Jewels in 1887, excluding a large
brilliant from the centre of the garland which reached 16,100 francs.[129]

Jewellery simulating organic growth was still evident at the International
Exhibition of 1862, but the cultural establishment succeeded in making it a
comparatively minor presence. Queen Victoria, prostrated with grief at the Prince
Consort's death on 14 December 1861, was no longer personally interested in the
preparations. She trusted Henry Cole, who had so ably supported the Prince in
the past, and Cole ensured that classicising design was well represented. The rigid
formalism described and illustrated in Owen Jones' Grammar of Ornament (1856),
the manual most used in the schools under Cole's management, meant that all
styles, even naturalism, were subjected to a geometric discipline. All forms of
classicism were thus given a natural advantage.

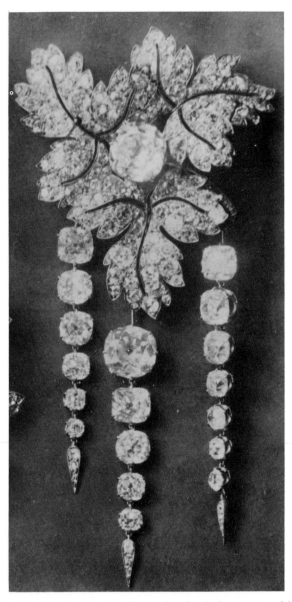

Plate 189. One of the sixteen components of a diamond garland of currants and leaves designed for the French Crown Jewels by Alfred Bapst and delivered in July 1855 by Bapst et neveu. Dismantled for the sale of the Crown Jewels in 1887, the components went to different purchasers, including the makers themselves, Tiffany's of New York and Garrard's of London, so that the Empress Eugénie, an exile in England, had the consolation of knowing that no one else would wear it.

PHOTOGRAPH FROM THE TWINING COLLECTION, GOLDSMITHS' HALL

Colour Plate 82. A group of French antiquarian pieces by Froment-Meurice and Rudolphi of Paris, c.1844-1855.
A. An oval brooch with an enamelled silver frame with a gabled niche and a cast female figure playing a viol da gamba. Made in the workshops of F.D. Froment-Meurice and signed with the name of the firm; c.1844-8.
B and C. St George and the Dragon, a brooch-pin, and an Amazon and panther pin, both in cast and enamelled gold. Made in Froment-Meurice's workshops and acquired for the Museum by Henry Cole from the Paris Universal Exhibition of 1855.
D. Silver brooch of an angel with a scroll, cast and probably once oxidised. A miniature version of the stone and wood corbels often decorating churches and cathedrals in the Middle Ages, the piece was probably made in the workshops of F.J. Rudolphi, Wagner's pupil and successor.
E. A bracelet in silver, parcel-gilt, with cast figures of cherubs alternating with openwork foliage. This was purchased for the Museum from Froment-Meurice's display at the Great Exhibition of 1851, but may have been made by an outworker. In his standard work on nineteenth century French jewellery, Henri Vever illustrated a very similar bracelet, ascribing it to Rudolphi. VICTORIA AND ALBERT MUSEUM

Colour Plate 83. The gothic parure designed by A.W.N. Pugin and shown in his Mediaeval Court at the Great Exhibition of 1851. It was drawn by W.H. Millais, one of the artists engaged in compiling a record of the principal exhibits for Matthew Digby Wyatt's great commemorative work, The Industrial Arts of the Nineteenth Century, *illustrated with chromolithographs and published in three volumes, 1851-3. Three pieces from the parure are in the Victoria and Albert Museum (see Colour Plate 100).*

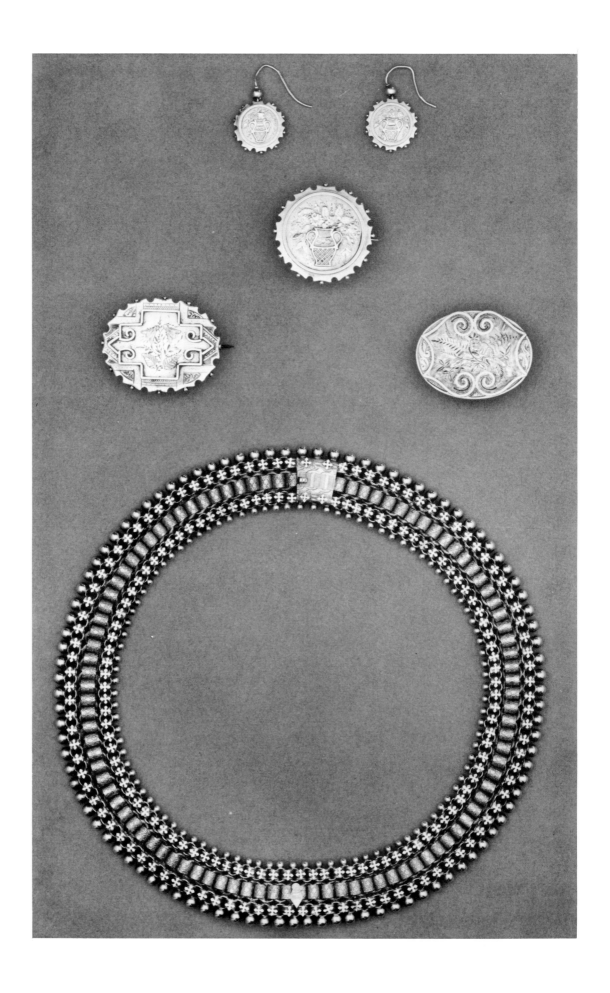

CHAPTER IX

Ingenuity and Inventiveness

1. Metals and Alloys

Gold occurs in many countries in the world but the principal deposits until the mid-nineteenth century were sited in Asiatic Russia, in the Urals and the Altai Mountains, and to a lesser extent in South America. Supplies were vastly augmented by the finding of gold in California in 1848. An Australian named Hargraves, who had joined the Californian gold-rush, returned to his native country and made his first discovery of gold in New South Wales in 1851, setting off a hunt which met with particular success in the new State of Victoria. Strikes were also made in Queensland, Western Australia and in New Zealand, while back in the United States the Comstock Lode was exploited for gold and silver from about 1859. Further mines were opened up in Colorado, Dakota and elsewhere before a major strike was eventually made in Alaska. The existence of South African gold was known decades before a major vein was discovered in the Transvaal in the 1880s. In about 1886 this was eclipsed in importance by the Main Reef of Witwatersrand.

Much of the gold obtained from 1850 onwards required increasingly sophisticated powered equipment to extract and refine it. The technology was forthcoming and jewellers were no longer forced to rely in large part on gold recovered from articles consigned for melting. But old habits died hard and as late as 1866 Birmingham manufacturers still purchased old gold coin from the Bank of England at £3.17s.10½d. per ounce.[1] Legal sanctions in France obliged jewellers to observe the 18 carat standard, that is, to use metal composed of eighteen parts of gold to six parts of alloy, pure gold being reckoned as 24 carats. In many other European countries hallmarking laws were either non-existent or

Plate 190. Machine-made jewellery.
A. The design of the circular brooch and earrings in silver with applied flowers and leaves in yellow and red gold was registered by Frederick Banks of 149 Warstone Lane, Birmingham, on 22 October 1881 and hallmarked in Chester, 1881-2. The brooch has a locket back. Birmingham manufacturers often turned to Chester when the Birmingham Assay Office was busy. The use of coloured golds was inspired less by early nineteenth century practice than by the rage for japonoiserie. *The English hallmarking laws prohibited the soldering of base metals on to gold or silver, so that once silver jewellery was submitted for assay, an alternative had to be found to the copper encrustations on specimens imported from Japan (Colour Plate 124). Coloured gold was the only solution acceptable to the Assay Offices.*
B. An oval silver brooch stamped and knurled; the leaves of the spray in the centre and the two bees hovering over it are in coloured gold, surrounded by an angular cartouche of applied wire. Birmingham hallmarks for 1885-6; maker's mark largely obliterated.
C. This brooch is unmarked but the coloured gold flower and leaves applied over stamped decoration, together with the strip cartouche, indicate Birmingham manufacture; c.1885.
D. A flexible silver necklace registered under the Designs Acts on 25 March 1882 by W. Musgrave, who had flatting mills in Gloucester Street, Clerkenwell. The diamond-shaped Registry Mark is applied to the centre front as a decorative device. The border links, machine-made, are decorated with applied crosses; the flexible tubular devices in the middle are cut, stamped and shaped by machine. There is an attachment for a pendant, now missing.
(Shown 25% smaller than actual size.) PRIVATE COLLECTIONS

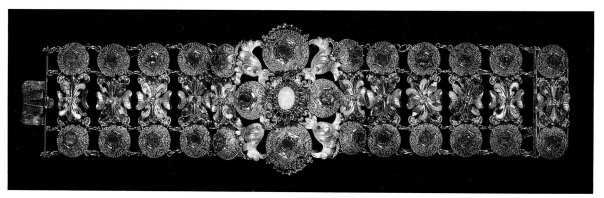

Colour Plate 84. A bracelet in coloured gold ornamented with cannetille *and* grainti, *enamelled and set with an opal in a diamond surround, rubies and emeralds. Reputedly associated with the Saxe-Coburg family, the fitted case is lettered: V: No.1. It may have belonged to Victoire of Saxe-Coburg who married the Duke of Kent as her second husband in 1818 and became the mother of Queen Victoria. French or in the French style, it might even have been a wedding present.*

PRIVATE COLLECTION, U.S.A.

Colour Plate 85. Popular jewellery in gold, silver and base metals.
A. This silver horseshoe brooch (which might be worn either way up) was stamped in one piece complete with hunting horns and spur and then backed with a flat plate. Birmingham hallmarks for 1882; maker's mark, B & C.
B. A silver name brooch with a stamped fret in which LIZZIE *appears amongst birds and flowers with additional knurled decoration. The outer edge of the indented border is decorated with applied pellets or beads. Stamped on the reverse* REAL/SILVER; *c.1890.*
C. A double heart brooch in silver with pelleted edges and applied gold motifs. On the left, MIZPAH *(Genesis 31, 49: 'And Mizpah; for he said, The Lord watch between me and thee, when we are absent one from another'), a flower and a leaf; on the right an anchor, Christian symbol of hope. Chester hallmarks, but the date letter and maker's mark are obscured by the pin fittings; c.1895.*
D. A red gold bar brooch with applied details in green and red gold; knurled decoration and applied pellets and a central rosette with a pink tourmaline and half pearls in a gypsy setting. Chester hallmarks for 9 carat gold, 1896; maker's mark illegible. Like C above, this is probably a Birmingham piece hallmarked for convenience at Chester.
E. An oval name brooch with MOTHER *stamped in red on a scalloped green gold surround; the back plate is made of gilt metal. Unmarked, c.1905.*
F. A silver scarf or cravat pin (the stem is invisible). An engraved flower and butterfly heightened with white within an applied gold fan-shaped strip is off-centre to a chequered ground with polished crosses alternating with textured squares. Influenced by the rage for japonoiserie, *it probably dates to about 1880.*
G. A silver crown of 1821 with Pistrucci's St George and the Dragon enamelled in seven colours in Birmingham in the mid-1880s or thereabouts and mounted as a brooch (see page 219).
H. An imitation Pistrucci coin brooch enamelled in dark blue only and fitted with a locket back. Even the milled edge is bogus; it is probably German, early 20th century.
I. An enamelled £5 brooch executed on plated copper. An example of the cheap Austrian-made money brooches peddled on the streets of London and elsewhere, to the fury of the Bank of England which held that such productions were illegal; c.1885.
J. A solitaire constructed as I above, but with part of the front page of the Daily Telegraph *forming the decoration. Stamped on the reverse,* DÉPOSÉ *(signifying patent protection, a term often employed by German makers) and the initials·* HH.

PRIVATE COLLECTIONS

interpreted in a fairly lax fashion, allowing jewellers a free hand. German jewellers, however, usually employed 14 carat gold, a quality adopted elsewhere, including the United States of America.

The legal position in the British Isles was ambiguous. On the one hand, an Act in 1798 established two distinct standards of 22 and 18 carats, supplemented in 1854 by three lower standards of 15, 12 and 9 carats. On the other, much gold jewellery (except for mourning rings on which duty was then payable) and some silver articles had been legally exempted from hallmarking in 1738 on grounds of size or liability to incur damage in the process of assaying and marking. The list

was extended by later Acts. Jewellers were happy to assume that all their work was outside legal control. The Worshipful Company of Goldsmiths, the traditional guardian of legal standards, subscribed to the same view. Refuting any suggestion that a uniform 18 carat standard might be imposed on the trade, the Clerk of the Company declared before the Select Committee on Hallmarking in 1879 that jewellery was 'expressly exempt' from hallmarking by Act of Parliament. 'We have no more to do with jewellery than we have to do with tin-pots and kettles,' he concluded.[2] He ignored mourning rings and also gold wedding rings which, by an Act of 1855, were made liable to hallmarking.

The Duc de Luynes observed in his report on the Great Exhibition that the gold employed in the manufacture of English jewellery was usually of a lower quality than 18 carats. The best firms adhered to a standard of between 16 and 14 carats, but ordinary jewellery and work made for export was between 12 and 10 carats.[3] In 1892, the Birmingham jeweller and chainmaker, George Gee, revealed details of what he called the 'Old fashioned bright gold alloy of thirty years ago [which] was then extensively used for all kinds of jewellery,' but especially for chains. A mixture of equal parts of gold and silver, with slightly smaller quantities of copper and a mineral composition, it 'was about 7½ carats, and the lowest alloy worked by respectable manufacturers'.[4]

The coloured golds popular in the first four decades of the nineteenth century and again towards the end of the Victorian era were obtained by varying the alloys employed (Colour Plates 84 and 85D and Plate 190A-C). The constituents were the same for every standard, except that as the quantity of gold diminished the amount of alloy (mainly fine silver with an admixture of copper) was increased. The metal used to form the alloy with gold naturally affected its colour. The more copper was added to the alloy, the redder it became, while other metals produced different tints. Yellow gold was obtained by alloying with zinc or zinc and silver. Greyish yellow gold was effected by the addition of charcoal iron, green gold by silver in the proportion of three parts of gold to one of silver (later silver and cadmium); white gold was produced by mixing equal parts of gold and silver (or platinum and later, nickel). There were other recipes.

Victorian jewellers, while conforming to the earlier fashion of coloured golds, were happy to cater for the English taste for plain, pure gold — in appearance, if not always in reality. A favourite method of creating this opulent effect was to 'pickle' or 'bloom' an article in a heated solution of common salt, saltpetre (potassium nitrate) and alum which dissolved out the copper alloy from its surface, allowing it, as was claimed in 1853, 'to develope [sic] its full colour';[5] the piece was then cleaned by dipping it into nitric acid. This process, though involving immersion, was known as dry colouring and held to be suitable for 22, 20, 19, 18 and 17 carat gold. There was not enough gold in the lower qualities to produce a good surface appearance.

The English remained so attached to their yellow gold that the French still referred to 'la couleur Anglaise' as late as 1873.[6] Most jewellers had their own formulas which they kept to themselves. But the cessation from business of one of the 'most eminent Manufacturing Goldsmiths and Jewellers in this country' enabled James Collins to publish their concoctions in 1871. For dry-colouring, he cited equal quantities of alum and salt, with twice the amount of saltpetre in a boiled solution. Gee varied the formula a little for 'Etruscan gold'.[7] Muriatic (hydrochloric) acid was included in the solution for a second process, termed wet-colouring, which was employed for alloys containing a higher proportion of copper. The objects were immersed in the heated solution for several minutes at a time, the process being repeated twice. The longer the period of immersion, the deader the finish; a brighter surface resulted from an abbreviated exposure to the mixture. The articles were finished by scratch brushing on a lathe, a brass wire brush running on a mixture of ale and water, or by burnishing with steel or agate tools.

The acid used in wet-colouring dissolved away so much of the surface of the articles that their weight was noticeably lessened. The precious metals were reclaimed and the process persisted in use because wet-colouring was effective on low-quality gold, producing good results on gold of a fineness of between 15 and 12 carats. In 1892 Gee complained that, in recent years, wet-coloured articles, 'burnished so as to produce a smooth, mirror-looking surface' had 'been pushed

Plate 191. Machine-made jewellery.
A. A silver-plated brooch stamped with a bird and butterfly device; c.1885. The front was made in one piece and shaped and largely decorated in the die.
B. A silver brooch stamped in two parts with applied pelleted edge. The spray decoration was die-stamped at the same time. Birmingham hallmarks for 1884; maker's mark L.S. & Co.
C. Stamped silver or silver-plated brooch, unmarked, with an applied lobed strip cartouche and scrolling framing a panel with a flower and leaves with a knurled background. The piece has a locket back and pellets around the edge. Probably Birmingham, c.1885.   PRIVATE COLLECTION

on to the market as goods bearing the dry-coloured surface upon them', the difference only being detectable by the 'diminished lustre' of the inferior goods.[8] An alternative method of colouring low quality gold was to dip the articles in a bath of mercury and sulphuric acid, and then immerse them in a boiling solution containing gold chloride.

Silver was, like gold, distributed over Europe. But the European silver mines together contributed only a fraction of the output of the Americas. The principal silver-producing countries were Mexico, Peru, Chile and Bolivia. The United States of America joined their ranks towards 1860. The Comstock Lode of Nevada alone, extending over 250 miles, had yielded about $325,000,000 worth of bullion by 1 January 1880, although from 1876 this tremendous output had already begun to decline. Despite the diminution of supplies, the availability and cheapness of silver from the Comstock Lode stimulated the manufacture of vast quantities of silver jewellery in Britain from the 1860s into the Edwardian era (Plates 190 and 191) and prompted the Birmingham Assay Office, at a time when the plate trade was depressed, to call them in for marking. This move had a salutary effect on those manufacturers who had previously been tempted to adopt a standard lower than sterling (925 parts of silver to 75 of alloy).

Platinum, both chemically and in natural occurrence, is closely related to palladium, rhodium, iridium, rutherium and osmium. Traces of platinum are found in almost all native gold. Worked by the pre-Colombian Indians of Ecuador and Columbia, the New World was to become the principal source of supply, supplemented in the early nineteenth century by platinum from the Urals.

Colour Plate 86. An early example of aluminium jewellery, made in France when the metal had been recently refined and so costly that it was classed as precious. The cast cherubs are reminiscent of those in the Rudolphi bracelet in Colour Plate 96, but they share a common source of inspiration in sixteenth and seventeenth century design. Because it was impossible to solder the cast aluminium sections, they are riveted to a gold carcass and a feature made of the rivet heads. Parisian; c.1856-58, probably chased by Honoré Bourdoncle.   PRIVATE COLLECTIONS

The Spanish colonisers of South America probably noticed the presence of this heavy and (then) infusible metal in the gold ore of the mines of New Granada at an early date. Their goldsmiths occasionally made use of it in small wares but the Spanish Government forbade its exportation. In the mid-eighteenth century, however, platinum became an object of scientific interest in Europe. Its chemical qualities determined, it was refined by forming a fusible alloy of platinum and arsenic.

The first articles made from platinum produced by the arsenic process in 1786 were the work of the Parisian goldsmith Marc Etienne Janety (or Jeannety).[9] He also dealt in the metal, offering it in London in 1789 at 26s. per ounce. But, as Royal Goldsmith to Louis XVI, he discreetly withdrew to Marseilles after the King's execution, returning in better times. Janety's Silver Medal at the French National Exhibition of 1802 was awarded for his contribution to the new metallurgical process. With his son and successor, F.-J.-M. Janety, he was honoured with a Silver Medal from the Société d'Encouragement pour l'Industrie Nationale in 1818. The younger Janety and his new partner Châtenay,[10] Silver Medallists at the French National Exhibition of 1819, were soon faced with competition from Bernauda of the quai des Orfèvres, patronised by the Duchesse de Berri, whose platinum jewellery was on view at the French exhibitions from 1823 to 1844.[11]

The great English chemist, William Hyde Wollaston, the first to refine the metal on a commercial scale, had supplied platinum through an associate at an average

Colour Plate 87. A. A buckle in doublé d'or *or rolled gold, the frame stamped in two parts and soldered together. The double scrolls and foliated terminals are a gesture to medievalism. The chape is steel; probably a French export piece, c.1840.*

B. A die-stamped brooch in copper-gilt set with a black glass plaque secured by a flower-headed rivet with a mock opal in the centre, and backed by a plate. The depth and sharpness of the asymmetrical frame are similar to the set on the upper right-hand side of the card with costume jewellery by Morgenstern of Leipzig (Colour Plate 88). Probably German, c.1865-70.

C. A brooch of machine-chased aluminium in a gilt metal frame; c.1870.

D. The silver setting of this horseshoe brooch grasps opaline pastes in high claws. They might be intended to represent opals or moonstones but they are certainly artificial; c.1905.

E. Inspired by the vogue for jewellery made from old watch-cocks in the mid-1880s, the brooch appears to have been cast from genuine examples in base metal, then gilded and set with pastes; c.1890.

F and G. Two hinged book lockets in base metal gilt with enamelled covers, both c.1900-05. F, inscribed Souvenir, *contains illustrations of Oxford, taken from photographs. G, inscribed* EDWARD VII/ALEXANDRA/1902, *is a coronation souvenir with portraits of the new King and Queen and their family.*   PRIVATE COLLECTION

price of 16s. per ounce to several London goldsmiths and another in Birmingham before ceasing to deal in it in 1820. It was at about this time that Rundell's sold a platina [i.e. platinum] and gold chain to George IV and similar articles were purchased from Garrard's by clients such as the Duke of Wellington who bought a 'Platina Chain…& Swivel' for £14.6s. in July 1833. Though the metal was still largely employed in the manufacture of vessels for medical, scientific and industrial use, it is evident that there were craftsmen in London capable of working it for decorative purposes. Wollaston's retirement from the field left it clear to Percival Norton Johnson,[12] the founder of Johnson Matthey, who had set up in business as a refiner and fabricator in 1817. His enthusiasm may perhaps have encouraged a manufacturing goldsmith to try his hand at making platinum chains in the French manner.

In 1829, the manufacture of jewellery in gold and silver or gold and platinum or a combination of all three was officially sanctioned in France, indicating that Bernauda had jumped the legal gun. A bronzed platinum bracelet and another in oxidised platinum were among the fashionable trinkets reported to be on sale in Paris in 1846, but the Duc de Luynes was hard put to find many jewellers of distinction currently working the metal when he compiled his report on the 1851 Exhibition. He declared, however, that Wagner, Rudolphi's predecessor, had used platinum in conjunction with silver as a base for his enamels[13] (a story also told, with variations, of Froment-Meurice).

Platinum remained cheaper than gold, though its price was governed by new methods of refining as well as by demand. Unlike silver, it was virtually untarnishable, but its hardness made it difficult to work and it took polish less easily than either gold or silver. Its slightly dead bluish-grey colour was also considered a drawback, but it none the less continued to be used by jewellers in the production of secondary jewellery. In 1871, Collins cited its employment as an alternative to silver when grey or white floral devices were required as applied ornaments on articles.[14] Vever's assertion that Fontenay had resorted to platinum for some of his settings for the diamond head ornament in the Paris 1855 Exhibition is conceivably mistaken, but diamonds were often set in platinum mounts towards 1870 and ornamented an enamelled gold bracelet shown by the Parisian firm, Teterger, at the 1878 Exhibition.[15] By then its strength was already being exploited in high claw settings for diamonds. Platinum was in such widespread use among French jewellers by 1900 that its price rose.[16]

The increased cost of the metal reflected its enhanced prestige. Alloys discussed by Gee in 1892 included one of silver and platinum and another of silver and gold 'reproduced from the old formula formerly used in diamond set work' and now being made 'as a cheap substitute for platinum, to be used alternately with red 9-carat gold for chain links, crosses, bracelets, and numerous other wares manufactured by the jeweller.' Both alloys were claimed to possess 'spark-like brightness' and to be untarnishable, though Collins disagreed. The alloy of gold and silver or platinum (sometimes varied by nickel) was white gold, much used by English jewellers in preference to platinum in the early years of the twentieth century.

Several other alloys quoted by Gee contained platinum, sometimes combined with precious but more often (as earlier in the century) with base metals. One formula consisted of pure copper, fine gold, pure platinum and tungsten. Named 'Aphthit' (unchangeable), the alloy looked like 18 carat gold but cost the equivalent of 5 carat gold to produce. Another, known as 'false gold' or 'mystery gold', passed for 15 or 12 carat gold, although less malleable to work; it was compounded of copper wire, platinum scrap and pure bar tin.[17]

The traditional English substitute for gold, Christopher Pinchbeck's eponymous alloy of copper and zinc in the proportion of about eighty-three parts of the former to seventeen of the latter, continued to survive in a series of variations probably designed to minimise its chief drawbacks, its dark colour and proneness to tarnish. One of these, an alloy of sixty-six parts of copper to thirty-four of zinc, was used in the manufacture of a chain discussed in a paper given in 1872 by W.G. Larkins, who edited the *Journal* of the Society of Arts. Larkins claimed that this alloy had provided the closest approximation to gold until the discovery of aluminium.[18]

Sir Humphrey Davy had first postulated the existence of this metal in the oxide, alumina, in the early years of the nineteenth century, but he was unable to reduce it. The Danish chemist, Hans Christian Oersted, isolated a few particles in 1825 and molten aluminium was obtained two years later by Friedrich Wöhler, in Berlin. The first commercially successful reduction process was developed in Paris by Henri Sainte Claire Deville. He had received funds from Napoleon III enabling him to cheapen the production of sodium which he then used to reduce aluminium chloride. Deville published his results in 1854 and a few aluminium articles, including a rattle made for the Prince Imperial, caused a sensation at the Paris Exhibition of 1855. Deville then turned his attention to the platinum metals, in 1857 devising a furnace with Jules Debray which for the first time made it possible to melt the metal and its alloys on a large scale.

Deville's aluminium process was worked by F.W. Gerhard in Battersea from 1859 to 1863 and by Bell Brothers of Newcastle-on-Tyne from about 1859 to 1874. Bell's hollow-wares attracted a great deal of attention at the international exhibitions held in London in 1862 and Dublin in 1865.[19] Two works were set up in the 1880s near Birmingham. Johnson Matthey & Company, already selling agents for the metal, were associated with a factory at Patricroft, near Manchester, from 1890 to 1894. The last important British works were those of the British Aluminium Company at Foyers, Scotland. The electrolytic reduction process patented in 1886 to 1887 by Charles Martin Hall in America and Paul Héroult in France and England were used at both Patricroft and Foyers. This process was operated by the Neuhausen Aluminium Company in Germany, Austria and Switzerland from 1887 and afterwards at Froges in France. The Pittsburgh Aluminium (later Aluminum) Company was formed to operate Hall's process in about 1888-9.

Aluminium, though deriving from clay, was classed as a precious metal for several years. The first kilogram made by Deville in 1854 was priced at 3,000 francs. Thereafter, the cost fell dramatically. In 1856, the same quantity cost 1,500 francs, but in 1859 was only 400 francs. In 1864, it had fallen to 100 francs, in 1889, to 80. In 1891, in consequence of the Hall-Héroult process, it had dropped to 20 francs. By 1899 it was a mere 3.5 francs per kilogram and went on falling.[20]

The metal, extremely light, took to casting but was resistant to soldering. The first items of jewellery, probably produced shortly after the Paris 1855 Exhibition, used gold as a carcass on to which the aluminium was riveted. An example chased by Honoré Bourdoncle is in the Musée des Arts Décoratifs, Paris; the piece in Colour Plate 86 must be contemporary. A decade or so later, when aluminium came down the scale, it was mounted in gilt metal (Colour Plate 87C and Plate 192A). E. Schmoll of Paris and A.J. Hoffstädt of Altona, Prussia, showed

CHR. MORGENSTERN & C.º IN LEIPZIG

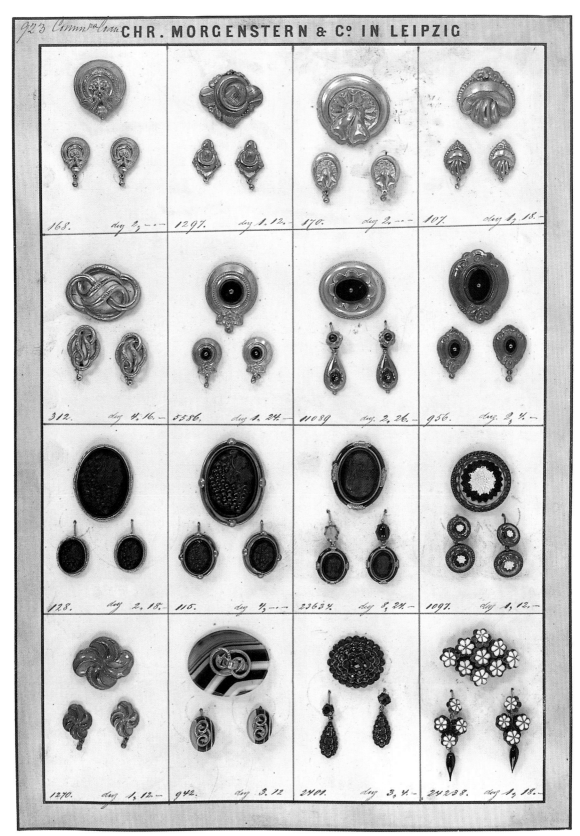

168.   deg 2, -. -   1297.   deg 1. 12.   170.   deg 2, -. -   107.   deg 1, 18. -

312.   deg 4, 16. -   5586.   deg 1. 24. -   11089   deg 2, 26. -   956.   deg 2, 4. -

128.   deg 2, 18. -   115.   deg 4, -. -   23634.   deg 8, 24. -   1097.   deg 1, 12. -

1270.   deg 1, 12. -   942.   deg 3. 12   2401.   deg 3, 4. -   24238   deg 1, 18. -

*Colour Plate 88. A display card of imitation or costume jewellery by C. Morgenstern & Co., Leipzig,
mounted with articles in stamped and tubular metal, gilt and set with pastes. The pieces show a keen
awareness of patterns on view at the 1855 and more recent 1862 Exhibitions, with an inclination
towards classical design. They were probably acquired at an international exhibition; c.1865-70.
(Shown 25% smaller than actual size.)* 1851 COMMISSIONERS, ON LOAN TO THE VICTORIA AND ALBERT MUSEUM

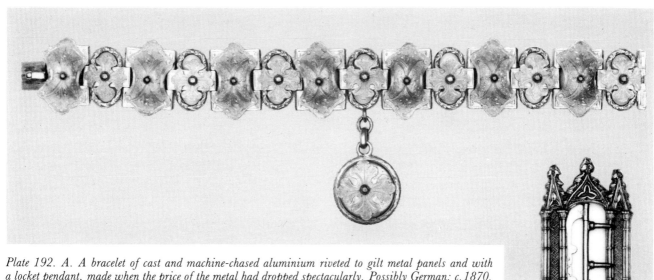

Plate 192. A. A bracelet of cast and machine-chased aluminium riveted to gilt metal panels and with a locket pendant, made when the price of the metal had dropped spectacularly. Possibly German; c.1870. B. A gilt metal buckle in the romantic French gothic (troubadour or cathédrale) style of the 1830s; bright and frosted, it was probably made in France for export. It is a skilled though slightly coarse interpretation of a type of a design also made in gold and silver; c.1840. MANCHESTER CITY ART GALLERIES

specimens of aluminium jewellery at the Paris 1867 Exhibition.[21] American aluminium goods imported by Louis Leakey of Farringdon Road, London in 1897 included hair pins with ornamental heads as well as buckles, but it took Lalique to transform the metal, with the aid of carved ivory and garnets, into an imaginative stage tiara for the French actress, Julia Bartet, two years later.[22]

The English seem mainly to have used aluminium in alloys. The new alloy cited by Larkins in 1872, developed by the metallurgist, Dr John Percy, in about 1856-1857, was known variously as aluminium bronze, mosaic gold[23] or 'Abyssinian Gold', the last a trade name used by the retail firm of Lionel and Alfred Pyke, who ran a chain of shops in the City and the West End. One of the Pykes lent a selection of goods for display at Larkins' lecture. Aluminium comprised only five per cent of the alloy, the other ninety-five per cent consisting of copper. But its presence, according to Larkins, imparted a hardness to the copper, 'rendering it capable of being polished to a high degree, but without destroying its malleability'. Nor was it 'sensibly tarnished by exposure to air'.[24] To judge by an advertisement for 'Abyssinian gold' jewellery in 1883, the metal was valued highly enough to warrant setting with tiny pearls and corals in a bracelet costing £1.5s. or with ruby, sapphire or emerald doublets in another priced at £3.10s. Pastes were used in the remaining items.[25]

Another alloy employing aluminium was described by Gee. 'Aluminium silver' composed of copper, nickel and aluminium, was 'said to receive a high lustre and polish, and in many respects to imitate real silver of good quality'. A further 'alloy in imitation of sterling silver' consisted of charcoal iron, pure nickel, tungsten, aluminium and copper, the mixture costing about as much as the nickel alloy then known as German silver.

Gee's receipt for a 'deep gold-like alloy' required no aluminium but specified Swedish copper wire, spelter (zinc), charcoal iron and lead. This alloy possessed the advantage of resembling 20 carat gold and of being resistant to oxidisation, but Gee warned that it was 'rather more difficult to solder than the ordinary copper zinc alloys', showing that the modified shades of Pinchbeck still walked in 1892.[26]

2. Plating and Gilding

The traditional methods of aping gold and silver with articles made of base metal coated with precious metal were much used by manufacturers in the nineteenth century. The most lasting form of gilding, in which articles were covered with a gold amalgam, the mercury being then volatised by heat, was extremely dangerous. Gilders were liable to die of mercury poisoning before they reached the age of forty. For this reason the introduction of electrogilding in the late 1830s was much acclaimed, though the thin covering of gold deposited by electrical action proved to be far less satisfactory in appearance and in wear. But it had the advantage of being much cheaper than mercury gilding.

George Richards Elkington and his cousin Henry experimented with methods of gilding in Birmingham, taking out three patents independently between 24 June 1836 and 24 July 1838, the last of which hints at electro-deposition. Their joint patent for electroplating with silver, granted on 25 March 1840, owed much to the development in about 1800 of the electric pile by Alessandro Volta, Professor of Physics at the University of Pavia, who was in turn inspired by the work of his distinguished fellow-countryman Luigi Galvani. Between 1800 and 1840 many scientists attempted (in some cases successfully) to plate metals by the action of the electric pile. The trouble was that the plating often failed to adhere. Elkington's specification was partly worked out by their metallurgist Alexander Parkes. But the effectiveness of the coating was determined by the formula for the electrolyte, the solution of metallic salts, through which the current passed, precipitating the plating metal in the form of ions, on the object to be plated, which was attached to the negative pole. The chemical composition of this electrolyte was developed by a local surgeon, Dr John Wright, from whom G.R. Elkington purchased the formula.[27]

Strictly speaking, though electrogilding was carried out by the same process as electroplating, the difference consisting only of the exclusive use of gold in the plating solution, it was not covered by the Elkington patent of 1840. Nor was the related technique of electrotyping. But the existence of the decisive patent, reinforced by later ones protected internationally, gave the Elkington concern an importance beyond its own sphere, the manufacturing of plated and silver hollow-ware and flatware. Jewellery manufacturers often used electro-deposition.

Mercury gilding nevertheless continued in workshop use. Gee also referred to other gilding formulas, some of which contained gold chloride. In discussing methods of producing a bright (shiny) or frosted (matt) finish on articles (Plate 192B), Gee held that, while gold might be advantageously frosted by acids, silver should be scratch-brushed.[28] In the 1820s and '30s matted grounds had been more laboriously achieved with the aid of a tool. By the 1880s the new technique of sand-blasting was in widespread use.

The French development of *doublé d'or* (Colour Plate 87A), the equivalent in gold of fused or Sheffield plate, resulted in a flourishing industry recognised in the square mark introduced by the Paris Mint in 1829. By mid-century, according to the Duc de Luynes, fifteen firms in Paris employed on average 1,300 journeymen, polishers and apprentices in the trade. Six hundred of these were men, five hundred were women and the apprentices numbered some two hundred. The men did the work of die-stamping, enamelling, chasing, gilding and the like, working eleven and a half hours and earning about 5 francs (about 4s.) daily. The women received 2 francs 50 centimes. The annual total sale of goods amounted to about 3,000,000 francs, from which 1,840,000 was reserved for wages, 750,000 for gold, silver and copper and 400,000 for expenses and profits.

De Luynes, drawing on the report of the Jury of the Paris National Exhibition of 1839, held that *double d'or* owed its origin to the Parisian firm of Poiret, but this and other concerns such as that of Lelong and Houdaille, who in the mid-1830s had received a Medal from the Société d'Encouragement for improvements and the manufacture of imitation jewellery, were outclassed in mid-century by François Auguste Savard, who set up in business in 1829, turning out military equipment in gilt copper and using gold, silver and *chrysocale* (see page 149). In 1844, Savard devoted himself exclusively to *doublé d'or,* the plated ingots being rolled into workable sheets in his workshops. The articles were die-stamped in two or more parts and soldered together. Savard (whose trinkets were later known as *Bijoux Fix*) was able to imitate coloured gold jewellery and also added enamelling to his repertoire. In 1840, he had one hundred employees; by mid-century the number had increased to over three hundred, including outworkers. He won a Prize Medal in 1851 for work which he exported to America, Spain, Germany and Belgium; his productions were excluded from Austria, Lombardy and Naples. Three years later, having put his furnaces and rolling mills at the disposal of Deville, who had turned his attention to platinum, Savard achieved platinum-plated copper, brass and silver.[29]

De Luynes acknowledged that some Birmingham manufacturers used *doublé d'or* (rolled gold). Ironically, they had probably been inspired by the success of the French firms rather than by their eighteenth century predecessors in the plating trade. The equipment in the Paris workshops derived from machinery developed by the Sheffield platers. English jewellery manufacturers used similar machinery, which was so effective that few patents were taken out by jewellers in the early years of the century. Thereafter patents flowed in an endless stream as production became more sophisticated.

3. Craftsmanship and Machine-production

The full implication of machinery is perhaps best appreciated by comparison with the traditional techniques practised in the trade. Casting, for instance, requires a model from which a mould is made, into which molten metal is poured. Lost wax casting, in which the wax is melted out from a mould by the hot metal, was a favourite method of producing delicate work. Embossed or repoussé work involves beating up a design from the back with hammers and punches, while chasing, executed with somewhat similar tools, produces a pattern of lower relief from the front. Engraving is linear ornament cut into the flat metal with fine tools. A worker might have several dozen such tools, some of them shaped by himself to suit his own needs.

Plate 193. Two process sets of 1875 by T. & J. Bragg of Birmingham illustrating:
I. the making by hand of a 15 carat gold pendant set with pearls and diamonds, a-l in the top two rows;
II. the manufacture of a machine or die-stamped brooch, also in 15 carat gold, a-j in the two lower rows.
The description supplied by the manufacturers from whom the sets were commissioned forms the basis of the following:

I. a.   The back cut from a sheet of gold and hammered into shape.
*   b.   The rim of the pendant which is soldered on the edge of c.*
*   c.   This is cut from a sheet of gold and hammered into shape, forming the cupped front of the pendant.*
*   d.   The inner rims.*
*   e.   Details of the wire filigree on the frill.*
*   f.   The frill ornament formed by filing out the shape and then soldering.*
*   g.   The thick beaten-up or embossed centre, showing where the engraver has outlined the ornament.*
*   h.   The frill added to the embossed centre.*
*   i.   The border and suspension loop.*
*   j.   The finished article with the stones added.*
*   k.   The rim of the 'box' or receptacle for hair or a photograph at the back.*
*   l.   The suspension loop before insertion.*

II. a.   The front of the brooch produced from a single die.
*   b.   The back of the brooch cut from thin sheet gold.*
*   c.   The stamped 'straps' to carry the leaves.*
*   d.   The leaves, also stamped.*
e and f.   The die-stamped parts of the domical centre.
*   g.   c, d and part of e soldered to the brooch.*
h and i.   The pin, hinge and clasp.
*   j.   The completed brooch.*
(Shown two-thirds of actual size.)   VICTORIA AND ALBERT MUSEUM

Most of the techniques either used or developed during the Industrial Revolution by the manufacturers of fused plate are described in Frederick Bradbury's *History of Old Sheffield Plate* (1912). A few of the processes relevant to jewellery have already been touched on, including the rolling of metal by machinery into sheets of a uniform gauge, and die-stamping. Many small workshops also possessed a traditonal drawplate for the purpose of making, lengthening and shaping wire to various patterns and sizes. This consisted of a steel plate or gauge held in a vice and pierced with several rows of holes of diminishing diameter, through which, in succession, strips of metal were drawn by pincers in order to round them, then reduce their size or change their form. If the holes were themselves shaped in section, the profile was transferred to the wire. As the century progressed, jewellers tended to buy ready-made wires from specialist workshops.

The process of wire-drawing has been described, not only because wires were much employed in the manufacture of jewellery (Plate 193), but also because it was used to make 'joint wire'. This is a hollow wire employed for hinges and was made from a strip of metal shaped into a hemispherical section and tapered at one end. Before being pulled through the drawplate a wire was inserted in the strip. The act of drawing forced the metal to assume the form of a tube, the wire lining being afterwards removed. With the aid of a mandril, a cylindrical tool, hollow tubes of larger bore might also be drawn. It is worth noting that hollow wire might also be made by hammering the metal in a grooved block of wood or metal, a simple and effective process which was, however, time-consuming.[30]

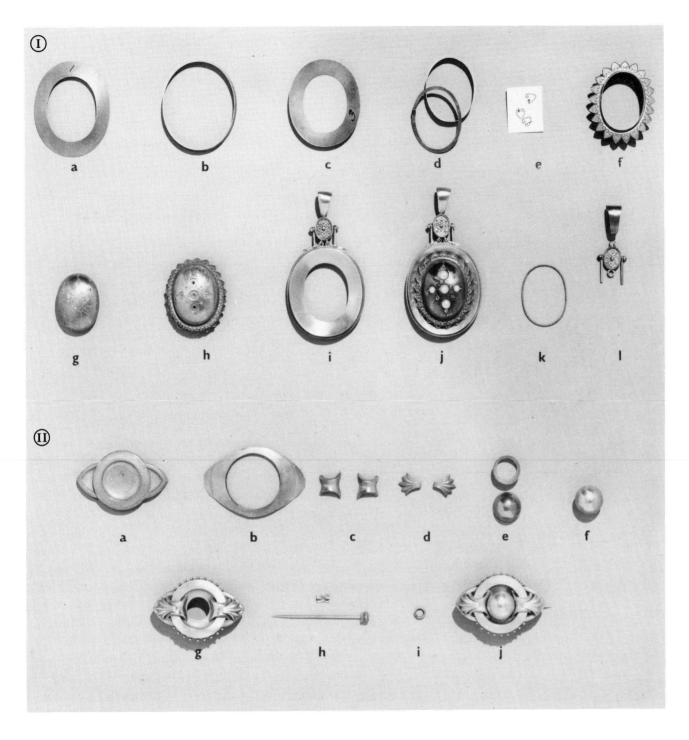

An invention patented by Daniel Winwood, a buckle chape maker, on 28 May 1781, was the first to specify the use of joint wire hinges,[31] though this does not mean that the process was not in use earlier.

Hollow wires and tubes were useful to jewellers for other purposes; a hollow tube, twisted or knotted into shape, formed a fashionable ornament in itself (Colour Plate 88). Bracelet links and chains were also usually made hollow in the interests of both the manufacturer and the wearer. The latter was more comfortable while the manufacturer saved metal.

The need to achieve an appearance of substance with the minimum expenditure of material encouraged the use of dies. The die-sinkers, the aristocrats of the trade,

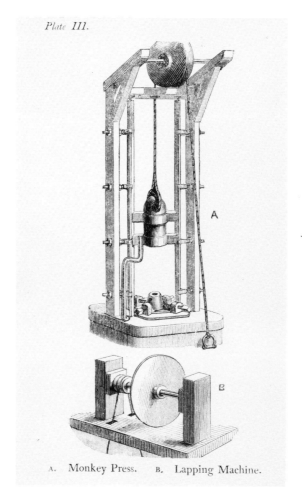

Plate III.

Plate 194. In his booklet, Hints to Purchasers of Jewellery, *which appears to have gone into eight editions by 1867, E.W. Streeter expounds two of his favourite themes, the desirability of a single gold standard of 18 carats, for which he campaigned with E.J. Watherston and others, and the advantageous price of machine-made jewellery. In the cause of the latter he illustrated and explained the equipment used by the jeweller. The 'Monkey Press' or stamping machine is not steam-driven but operated by a stirrup pedal. The die is clamped in position on the base and the great drop hammer carrying the 'force' is raised above it. The lapping machine was used for polishing.*

A.   Monkey Press.   B.   Lapping Machine.

often possessed considerable artistic ability. Some were employed by manufacturers; others were members of independent workshops, accepting commissions as they came. Using small hardened chisels they cut out the required design in steel, working into the surface of the metal to create an intaglio or concave design. The steel was hardened after the pattern had been cut.

The goldsmith or jeweller might, however, choose to shape his metal blank, cut from a rolled sheet of precious metal, by hand (Plate 193, I). Alternatively, he could work it into a die or dies, with or without the aid of a press. The metal emerged from the concave die in convex form (Plate 193, II).

Stamping or 'Monkey' presses (Plate 194) were much in evidence in the manufacturing trade. Each press had a heavy drop hammer (the 'force') attached to a pulley which was either operated by foot pedal or by steam power. The die was securely fixed below the force and a lead impression from it was attached to the hammer head. The head struck the blank placed over the die, forcing it to assume the required shape. As with all processes involving stretching and shaping metal, the stamped blank had to be heated, or annealed, to prevent it from becoming too brittle.

J.S. Wright, writing on the Birmingham gilt toy trade in 1865, remarked that the 'fine Etruscan style, which is now so current in gold work, is imitated in a die, and stamped up to bear a close resemblance. The beautiful hinges and snaps, made by the goldsmith with the most delicate tools, are effectually imitated by bending, or making an indentation, by a screw press, in a simple piece of metal.' He instanced a locket, worth about 15s. to 30s. in gold, which could be produced in gilt metal for 1d. Another example, a book locket with hinges and clasp and portraits of the Prince and Princess of Wales (presumably a marriage souvenir of 1863), was sold wholesale for about ½d. (later versions are shown in Colour Plate 87 F and G). The 'force of cheapness cannot much further go!', Wright wrote in punning reference to the stamping press, adding that there was no reason 'why the factory girl should not display her gilt buckle and brooch of the same design as the golden one worn by the lady of the villa'.[32] By 1876, George Wallis was able to assert that in Birmingham even 'elegant designs for enamelled work, as well as imitations of engraved and engine-turned surface decorations are now produced by "stamping" all the details at the same time, and by the same blow which gives the contour to the metal.'[33] The mechanisation of the English trade had by then enabled it to overtake the French in the field of exports.

A lathe for polishing (Streeter called it a lapping machine) was an invaluable adjunct in the workshop (Plate 194). A knurling machine, a kind of powered roulette tool which produced shaky linear flicks and zigzags in imitation of engraved work,[34] was used in many large concerns: the brooches in Plates 190B and 191C were embellished in this fashion.

A British workman, commissioned to report on the jewellery shown at the Paris 1867 Exhibition, commented on the widespread use of machinery, 'with or without steam power', in factories making jewellery for export in Birmingham and Paris, as well as in Hanau and other German towns.[35] Not everything left the countries concerned. Considerable quantities of mass-produced articles from Birmingham, for instance, were sold by retailers all over Britain. In 1850, the Germans exported about half their total output of jewellery and the proportion increased thereafter, but never to the extent of denying local demand. In France, where the manufacture of articles for export was almost a distinct trade, some of the production of firms such as Payen and Savard were reserved for sale within the country. But all the important centres of jewellery manufacture had an export trade. M.H.N.S. Maskelyne held that Geneva, Stuttgart, Schwabisch-Gmünd, Vienna and Brussels all exported part of their output.[36]

Maskelyne was reporting on the situation in 1867 before the last and greatest trade depression of the century struck in the mid-1870s and dislocated the trade. In the mid-1860s, Wright estimated that some 20,000 people were employed in the Birmingham jewellery trade, most in workshops with between five and fifty operatives. He cited their earnings without making any distinction as to whether they worked in the top or bottom end of the market. The least able, he declared, earned £1.5s. weekly. The average wage ranged between £1.10s. and £2.10s. Enamellers might get from £3 to £5. Boy apprentices received 4s. a week until they were twenty-one, when their wages rose to 10s. or 11s., for which they worked (almost certainly for six days a week) eleven hours a day, less an hour and three-quarters for meals. He did not mention women's earnings.[37] It is difficult to compare these figures with Duckworth's investigations into London wages, published in 1895 and 1903, which distinguish between various branches of the trade. His statistics are given in Chapter XIV

Plate 195. A silver whelk locket brooch and earrings, the design registered on 20 October 1878 by G.C. Haseler & Co. of 19 Vittoria Street, Birmingham. The brooch was stamped in two parts; the glazed box on the underside is not hinged but its silver edge is shaped to allow for easy insertion and removal. The earrings are cast and the shell openings gilt. The brooch is illustrated in a Silber & Fleming catalogue of about 1889.   PRIVATE COLLECTION

4. Patents

In common with all workers in the decorative arts, jewellers strongly objected to having their designs pirated. The Acts of 1839 and 1842 afforded protection, usually for three years, to designs registered with what became the Patent Office Designs Registry (see Appendix I). In practice, the provisions were mostly taken up by manufacturers to the trade (Plates 195 and 196B). The protection applied only to the United Kingdom and there was no remedy for external piracy, which was perhaps just as well, considering the extent to which English jewellers pillaged French and other Continental designs. Manifesting a mixture of complacency and irritation, J.S. Wright remarked that agents in Birmingham, acting for German firms, regularly retailed information about new designs to their employers.[38] There was, however, a means of protecting inventions and 'improvements' in manufacturing processes under the Patent Acts.

The intense competition to sell in markets both in Europe and outside it prompted firms owning patent rights to new processes to protect their inventions internationally. Elkington's, the patentees of electroplating, obtained patents in Europe and America. Conversely, foreign firms availed themselves of English patenting facilities. J.M. Payen took out a provisional English patent in 1854 for making hollow gold jewellery on a cylindrical iron rod known as a mandril, dissolving out the base metal afterwards with acid.[39] Lucien Falize, the son of the Parisian jeweller and designer Alexis Falize (Plate 254), applied for a patent in 1879 for a method of laminating two metals such as silver topped with gold, and then cutting away (or dissolving in acid) parts of the upper layer to form a fretted pattern. The resulting depressions might be oxidised, that is, darkened with acid or a sulphide solution, decorated with niello or enamelled.[40] One of the motives for Falize's application for an English patent is indicated by an entry in the catalogue of the International Exhibition held in London in 1871. This includes jewellery (apparently by Falize) which was shown by Le Roy & fils of Regent Street (Colour Plate 112B).[41] As Le Roy's were associated with Martz of Paris, who habitually stocked Falize's work, there was good reason for protecting a new process which might come under the covetous eye of English manufacturers.

The Falize family specialised in comparatively expensive bijouterie, but jewellers like them did not disdain the opportunity of cutting a few corners in the

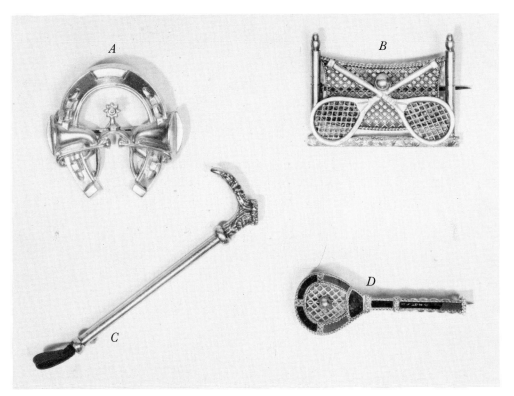

Plate 196. This group of jewellery with sporting devices probably comes mainly from Birmingham, though only two pieces are hallmarked; the whip may be German.
A. Horseshoe and hunting horn brooch in stamped and assembled silver. Birmingham hallmarks for 1882; maker's mark of Borton & Co.
B. A tennis net brooch in electroplate, the design registered on 11 September 1880; stamped J.T.SvD; probably by James Thornton of Birmingham.
C. A gilt metal whip brooch, the heel scumbled with brown stain in imitation of bark, the thong of leather; c.1890.
D. Tennis racquet brooch in silver set with pebbles in imitation of Scottish jewellery; possibly by William Manton of Birmingham; c.1865-70.   PRIVATE COLLECTIONS

process of manufacture. Carlo Giuliano, then of Frith Street (Colour Plates 108C and 109), was granted provisional protection in 1865 for 'improvements in the manufacture of chains, bracelets, necklaces, and other analogous articles' made from 'two semi-tubular' or 'trough-shaped' bands of metal which, when wound round a mandril, 'interlock and form a flexible or elastic structure, capable of bearing considerable tensile strain'.[42] His improvement appears to have been adapted from a spiral chain patented a year earlier by Jean Baptiste Buffoni, omitting only the wires which Buffoni had specified should be placed in the grooves of the shaped metal strips.[43]

O.W. Barratt patented methods of colouring ivory and bone on 7 October 1856.[44] Harry Emanuel's incursion into ivory jewellery has already been mentioned (Plate 123). In 1865, Emanuel followed his first invention with another employing feathers and plumage in jewellery, the feathers being glued with shellac to a prepared mount (see Colour Plate 89).[45] But even he did not go as far as to use complete heads and breasts of humming birds in earrings (Colour Plate 90). They do not bear comparison with the beetle and gold parure in Colour Plate 113, which is a masterly example of the goldsmith's art.

A patent granted in 1861 to W.H. Haseler of Birmingham specified a hinge for use on lockets and other items of jewellery. This was formed of two rings, one

STERLING SILVER LOCKETS.

No. 1717. Locket, silver, metal edge, engraved, 3/6 each.

No. 1712. Locket, raised flower centre, hall-marked, 8.9 each.

No. 1034. Locket, hall marked, richly engraved, 10/6 each.

No. 1674. Locket, engraved flower centre, burnished border, 8/6 each.

No. 1706. Locket, hall-marked sterling silver, engraved flower centre, lapped border, and shotted edge, 8/3 each.

DRAWN
FULL
SIZE.

No. 1690. Locket, hall-marked, frosted ground, ornamented with fine gold leaves, &c., in various colours, and shotted border, 18/6 each.

No. 1703. Locket, hall-marked sterling silver, lapped centre, and shotted edge, 12/ each.

No. 1692. Gold ornamented Locket, with raised stork, &c., in various colours, 18/6 each.

No. 1677. Locket, hall-marked, with coloured gold leaves, and raised gold stork, 18/6 each.

TRADE MARK.

No. 1691. Locket, hall-marked, frosted ground, ornamented with fine gold leaves, &c., in various colours, and shotted border, 18/6 each.

No. 1931. Locket, silver, metal edge, shotted border, 8/9 each.

No. 1930. Locket, silver, metal edge, 5/6 each.

No. 1668. Locket, sterling silver, gold ornamented, 16/6 each.

SILBER & FLEMING, WOOD STREET, LONDON.

Plate 197. A page of sterling silver lockets from the trade catalogue of Silber & Fleming, City of London wholesalers, dating to about 1889. Die-stamped complete with ornament, sometimes influenced by the rage for japonoiserie, the prices are those asked of retail firms resorting to Silber & Fleming for their stock. Even allowing for their profit, several items would have been sold for under £1 and two, priced at 3s. 6d. and 5s. 6d. respectively, would probably have cost the customer under 10s., a sum within the range of some artisans and working girls. For the first time, the combination of cheap silver and sophisticated methods of production brought articles made of precious metal to a huge market previously only able to afford base metal wares (see Plate 198). VICTORIA AND ALBERT MUSEUM, NATIONAL ART LIBRARY

Plate 198. A Lancashire
Wench, *by John Faed,
inscribed and dated 1884 on
the stretcher of the painting.
The artist has lovingly
delineated her silver locket,
proudly worn on a chain over
her best frock.*

SOTHEBY'S

soldered to the front and the other to the back of the locket, the two being united by a tubular rivet to which a suspension loop was attached.[46] Two years later, Alfred Antill and William Wilkinson were granted a patent for casting or drawing a joint in one piece and then cutting out space for a tongue or pin.[47]

The persistent vogue for lockets, at its peak from the 1860s to the 1880s (Plates 197 and 198), gave rise to a long series of patents. George Carter Haseler of Birmingham was responsible for several, the first of which dates from 1861 and covers various aspects of the manufacture of lockets, including the making of 'book lockets with double fastenings'. The following year he patented further 'improvements' to locket manufacture, one of which was for a detachable glazed frame for the inside which facilitated the insertion and removal of a photograph or miniature; another involved replacing the glass itself with parkesine, the earliest form of plastic. In 1865 he and his partner, John Bush Haseler, obtained a joint patent, the first part of which related to memorial or sentimental brooches. The body of each piece was made 'without seam, from one piece of metal' by raising it from a flat blank and curling the edges to form 'a frame or recess for the reception of an ordinary box or glass'. If very thin sheet gold was employed for the brooch, it was lined with a base metal to prevent it 'from becoming uneven in the part curled in'; the lining, if desired, might then be dissolved out by immersion in acid, the gold, of course, being immune.[48]

Lockets die-stamped from a single blank were patented by another partnership in 1870[49] and there were subsequent inventions of the same nature. The second section of the Haselers' specification of 1865 dealt with the manufacture of revolving or pivoting centres to brooches, a device (see the later example in Plate 199A) which was 'improved' rather than introduced by them. A provisional patent

Plate 199. A. A shell cameo, possibly representing one of the Three Graces, set in a gilt metal tubular frame with pivots above and below and stays on each side. It has a locket back; c.1870-80.
B. A gilt metal tubular bar brooch which doubles as a needle case; the end unscrews to allow access to the needles. The front is set with a roundel of artificial aventurine between two fleur-de-lis devices; c.1890.

for swivelling jewellery had been obtained by Richard Henry Jones and John Abrahall in 1863.[50]

George Perry patented calendar lockets in 1866.[51] Patents for variants were granted in 1876 to J. Fisslthaler, who gave an address in Clerkenwell[52] and by others thereafter. The electric lockets patented in 1874 by T. Welton had plainly been inspired by voltaic cell jewellery shown by a French jeweller named Picard at the Paris Exhibition of 1867.[53] Later versions implied a medicinal application by references to the current passing through the body from the jewel.

Many inventions played a more significant part in nineteenth century jewellery. Screw earrings, patented in October 1866 by a goldsmith named George Elliott Searle of 23 Bedford Street, Plymouth, were advertised in the *Illustrated London News* in 1868.[54] In 1867 H. Oakes obtained a provisional patent for earrings with spring jaws and clips, a year before Louis Baucheron of Paris patented spring clip earrings in France.[55]

Fastenings, especially those with some form of safety catch, were the subject of many patents. On 21 October 1847 Henry Ellis & Son of Exeter registered a safety fastening in the form of a sheathed pin under the Utility Design section of the Designs Acts, which was recognised as a cheap way of obtaining patent protection (see Plate 221). Five specimens were purchased by Queen Victoria as gifts for £28.10s. in 1848.[56] The pin and sheath fastening was capable of infinite variation. The stamper and piercer, Charles Rowley of Newhall Street, Birmingham, was granted a patent in November 1850 for 'improvements' in the manufacture of dress pins and other ornaments with a sliding sheath in the form of a tube,[57] a safety device which is often now regarded as a speciality of Continental jewellers. Rowley was an assiduous inventor, and made use of the Designs Acts in addition, registering several novelties. Other people, however, returned to the sheathed pin after him, introducing springs and increasingly complex refinements. Safety fasteners made of screws were another popular subject for inventors. An early form of the travelling screw for cravat and other pins was patented by C. Payne and P. Steel in 1876.[58]

The production of delicate loop-in-loop chains, variously known as jaseron, Trichinopoly and Venetian, fabricated from minute gold filaments, often flat on one side and convex on the other, required patience and craftsmanship of a high order. Venice had a reputation for such chains, but they were made in many places and were inevitably far too expensive for use in mass-produced jewellery. Cost and fashion combined to favour larger chains in the 1820s and afterwards. The next step was mechanisation. Outside the jewellery trade, manufacturers of steel chains and cables for industrial use began to bypass hand work. By the 1850s machines for making and joining wire links were already the subject of 'improvements', some of which had a bearing on the manufacture of jewellery. But the major advance came from America, in the form of a machine invented by E.H. Perry of Rhode Island and patented in 1857 by George Haseltine, formerly of Washington but then of London.[59] The machine was acquired by 'Mr Goode', who must have been John T. Goode, the principal of the chain-makers John Goode & Sons, of Regent Place, Birmingham.

W.G. Larkins showed a sample length of machine-made chain at his lecture at the Society of Arts in 1872, the secret of whose manufacture, he said, 'is possessed by Mr Holland'. Haseltine subsequently wrote to Larkins, explaining that the 'first machine ever employed in this kingdom for the purpose of manufacturing small ornamental chains, was introduced by me.... The machine was invented and chiefly constructed in America, but was completed for me by Mr Holland... and was sold to Mr Goode, a chain manufacturer of Birmingham. In 1869 [sic, in fact 1859], I patented another machine for making chains of a different pattern, and the patent for this invention was purchased by the same manufacturer. The first machine, which cost less than fifty pounds, performed the work of seventy operatives, and the chain was more perfect. The chain is constructed entirely by the machine complete for the finishers. Several of these machines have been employed by Mr Goode, and an immense number of these ''snake chains'', of which the example you exhibited to the members is a modification, have been sold, and a fortune realised from this new branch of manufacture, the origin of which I claim for America, and introduction of which into the kingdom is due solely to the patent laws.'[60] As a patent agent himself, Haseltine was well acquainted with the laws relating to inventions.

Haseltine's patent of 1857 specified links cut from strips of sheet metal by the machine; each stamped link took the form of a blank with radial arms which were forced upwards and made to interlock with the blank above without any need of soldering. The finished product was the flexible, articulated chain, alternatively termed 'snake' or 'Brazilian' like the traditional hand-made versions (Colour Plate 91 and Plate 200).

A spate of English inventions influenced by the 1857 patent followed. James Lancelott introduced an 'improvement' in 1860;[61] in 1865 came one from Edwin Wolverson, a Birmingham 'machinist' and another from John, Edward Richard and Thomas Hollands of London, whose joint patent specified a particularly elaborate Brazilian chain with outer and inner links.[62] John Hollands, perhaps significantly, was a lathe and tool manufacturer of Clerkenwell Green, but Haseltine's machine might well have been finished in Birmingham.

There were improvements yet to come, including one patented in February 1866 by Thomas Jenks, a Birmingham jeweller, and another in October 1870, by his fellow townsmen W. Bancroft and J. Wood, which specified a machine for making fancy watch, neck and other ornamental chains of various shapes in transverse section cut and pierced from thin metal.[63] A further patent was granted in 1874 to the Birmingham chain-makers J.G. Rollason and J. Wood, who advertised their machine-made chains in 1875.[64] Wires were substituted for metal strips in several inventions, including one patented in England by a German manufacturer of Pforzheim in 1871.[65]

P.A. Rasmussen, a British workman who reported on the gold and silver work at the Paris Exhibition of 1867, was clearly aware of English productions. He commented on the widespread use of machinery in the manufacture of gold chains on the Continent, especially in Germany and France,[66] and it seems clear that the American invention had sparked off many imitations.

Auguste Lion, a resourceful French jeweller and chain-maker, took out several patents in England. The first was a method of meshing wire by winding it on to a flat coil for use as bracelets and necklaces in 1867. In 1878, he obtained a patent for corrugating metal strips by passing them through rollers and using them in jewellery and the following year patented several ingenious methods of producing scale-patterned trinkets from stamped and shaped strips of metal with tongues which were bent over to lock them into position.[67] Wire and strip construction was soon used in England (Plate 190D); Lion's use of wire mesh had been anticipated in another form by Christofle (Plate 209) and by Richard Ford Sturges of Birmingham who in 1852 patented a method of transferring a pattern to metal by passing it through engraved rollers. Patents often represented adaptations rather than true innovations.

Ingenuity is the distinguishing quality of most patents. In 1886, F.S. Banks of Birmingham (see Plate 190A) patented brooches and lockets fitted with needle cases;[69] his specifications provided for a sliding or swivelling compartment at the back of his pieces. One end of the later brooch in Plate 199B unscrews to allow access to needles stored in the tubular bar. A patent was granted to J. Totton in March 1887, the year of Queen Victoria's Golden Jubilee, for brooches, earrings, studs, or breast pins made in the form of musical instruments with metallic tongues to emit sound when set in motion. The idea of tiny trumpets sounding off on Jubilee Day was a splendid one: Totton was probably unaware that his sovereign had purchased two Jubilee trumpet brooches with enamelled banners from Garrard's five weeks earlier.[70]

The fashion for coin jewellery in the 1880s and 1890s (Plate 201D) led to several patents concerned with ways of mounting the coins simply and economically.[71] A large number of patents relate to the fastening of studs, sleeve links, buckles and clasps. One of the most prolific patentees in this field was John Reading, a jeweller of Spencer Street, Birmingham, whose trade mark was an acorn. He took out patents in France and the United States as well as in England.[72]

Several jewellers contributed work to the Inventions Exhibition held in London in 1885. Carlo Giuliano showed 'open Arabesque work in gold and enamel' and demonstrated the cutting of stones in the natural crystal form. William West of Caroline Street, Birmingham, exhibited a collection of 'improvements' in dress, solitaire and bracelet fastenings, scarf rings and sleeve links, while F. Cox of Southampton Row, London, contributed jewellery made from old watch-cocks,[73] a current rage which gave rise to copies (Colour Plate 87E).

5. Pastes

Jewellery made with the pastes invented by G.F. Stras was turned out all over Europe until well into the nineteenth century. The high lead content of Stras' products was emulated in the pastes manufactured in Birmingham until it was discovered at the end of the Napoleonic Wars that it was cheaper to import them from Paris and Coblenz.

The leading Parisian manufacturers of imitation stones in the 1820s and 1830s cited by De Luynes in his report included Douault-Wieland, a prize-winner in a competition held by the Société d'Encouragement, Lançon, awarded the Gold Medal in the same competition, Bourguignon, whose artificial chrysoprases, exhibited in 1823, were favourably noticed by the Jury, and Bourguignon's former associate Bon, whose own successors were the 1851 exhibitors Savary et Mosbach. Some of these firms were held the equal or superior of German manufacturers. It was reported in 1876, however, that most French paste was currently made by men, women and children in the Jura and sent to Paris for cutting and mounting.[74] The area around Gablonz (Jablonec), then in Austria, now in Czechoslovakia, was also an important centre for the manufacture of coloured pastes.

A great deal of effort was expended on finding ways of improving the quality of strass, as it was still termed. Charles Barbot's formulas of 1858[75] include one for basic strass consisting of litharge (monoxide of lead), white sand and potash, and several for variants constituted with rock crystal, minium (lead), potash, arsenic and borax, the last an ingredient which, added to ordinary strass, was held to be an improvement on the eighteenth century formula. Artificial emerald was usually made of strass coloured with oxides of copper and chromium, although verdigris was used for the purpose in a receipt published in 1873.[76] Sapphire was coloured with the aid of oxide of cobalt while other oxides were used to produce different colours. The ingredients were usually powdered and fused in a crucible, after which the resulting mass was cooled very slowly before cutting. The slowness for cooling was designed to minimise the incidence of air bubbles, which, however, can usually be discerned in paste. Bon, who had the benefit of advice from Constant Valès, the well-known manufacturer of false pearls, achieved great success from the 1839 Exhibition onwards with his imitation opal, which was made of glass treated with acid. Savary et Mosbach, who won a Prize Medal for their paste jewellery at the Great Exhibition, were thought by De Luynes to have striven too hard after verisimilitude. Their attempts to reproduce the natural flaws of the emerald had simply resulted in obtrusive air bubbles.[77] At the other end of the scale, manufacturers of cheap costume jewellery bought coarse pastes and simply coated the backs with gold paint to enhance their colour.

In 1883, the *Queen* recorded a recent development: 'the old paste or strass. . . consisted of 38 parts of silica, 53 parts of red oxide of lead, 8 parts of calcined potash, and traces of calcined borax, alumina and arsenious acid. This receipt still holds good, but lately a much greater power of reflecting light has been imparted to the ordinary paste by adding thallium. . . [a metal discovered by Sir William Crookes in 1861]. This explains the great superiority of the latest imitations of brilliants. . . In the art of skilfully setting imitation diamonds Paris still retains the lead, but is run very close by Vienna.' Thallium oxide, replacing the alkaline content of white paste, raised the refractive index and thus increased its brilliancy, but it also rendered it soft and liable to surface corrosion (Colour Plate 198A). The Parisian Diamond Company of New Bond Street and Arthur Faulkner of Regent Street were among the English firms to meet with conspicuous success with their new paste jewellery, which was advertised aggressively.[78]

Pietro Bigaglia of Venice was awarded a Prize Medal at the 1851 Exhibition for 'his sparkling glass, called Artificial Aventurine; which is a silicate of oxide of

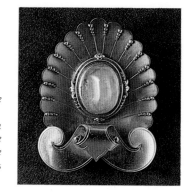

Colour Plate 89. A gold brooch with a scalloped shell or palmette rising from a scrolling strap and set with a cabochon emerald. Harry Emanuel's initials and the patent no. 1779 are struck on the reverse but there is no trace of the subject of the patent — the decorating of jewellery with feathers. Either the piece is incomplete or feathers were once glued to areas of the gold; c.1865. CHRISTIE'S

copper, wherein part of the oxide of copper has been reduced to the metallic state by processes which are kept secret. The reduced copper exists in the form of minute crystals.'[79] The copper flakes, octahedral in form, were enclosed in a readily fusible glass which was usually coloured brown (Plate 199B), although a blue, unknown in nature, was also made. Another type of decorated glass, also known as aventurine, which had been made by Venetian glass-blowers in the eighteenth century, was resuscitated in the nineteenth century (Plate 202B). Glass was coated with gold foil and then reworked, so that the foil, in the course of being dragged inside the glass body, crumbled into fragments, producing a crackled effect. Gold aventurine glass was made in several workshops, including those of the Venetian lawyer, Salviati, the friend of A.H. Layard, Henry Cole, Robert Phillips of Cockspur Street and many others. It was mainly used for decorative vessels, but also for 'jewellery, when it is cut and polished.'[80]

6. Laboratory Stones

In the search for improved substitute stones, some attention was paid to the traditional doublets and triplets, the former often composed of a sliver of precious stone, cut as a crown and cemented over a stone of lesser value such as quartz or a piece of glass which acted as the pavilion. Triplets were a sandwich. If the appearance of a coloured stone was desired, a slice of stone or coloured substance of appropriate hue was inserted at the girdle. A patent of 1872 cited a fairly classic instance of one of these simulated stones; spirit varnish and a mastic made the sandwich at the girdle.[81]

A patent of 1863 specified the use of poor-quality stones, pulverised and reconstituted.[82] An early nineteenth century invention, the oxyhydrogen blowpipe, a powerful version of the apparatus used by jewellers, enabled scientists to try fusing solid stones. A contemporary experiment was successful in fusing two rubies placed side by side on a charcoal bed.[83] Later attempts were also made to manufacture rubies from the chemical constituents of corundum exposed to great heat. Though crystals were achieved they were too microscopic for use. In the 1870s, however, Dr Edmond Frémy, head of the chemistry laboratory in the Musée d'Histoire Naturelle in Paris, and his assistant, C. Feil, reproduced rubies and sapphires by heating alumina and red lead in a fireclay crucible with a high acid content producing vitreous silicate of lead (the silica being derived from the crucible) and white crystallized alumina, which was coloured by the addition of metal chromates. An account of their work, which was conducted partly in the glass-furnaces of the Company of Saint-Gobain, was first published in December 1877.[84]

Plate 201. A group of jewellery dominated by a plastic comb of about 1870-1875.
A. Combs of this shape were fashionable accessories from the 1870s and were usually provided with similar bold crests whether in tortoiseshell or ivory. The plastic version has been moulded in one piece.
B. A gold locket with an applied monogram composed of the intertwined letters E I H on a bloomed ground; English, c.1870.
C. A stamped circular brooch with corded wire edging and a primrose enamelled on the front. Unmarked, it is probably an unofficial badge sported by supporters of the Primrose League, a Tory organisation founded in 1884 in memory of Benjamin Disraeli, Lord Beaconsfield; c.1885. Flora Thompson (Lark Rise to Candleford, 1945, Chapter 35), described how the League's social activities were an attractive recreation in small rural communities.
D. A George IV shilling of 1825, gilt and set in a silver frame with a pelleted edge. Chester hallmarks for 1900-1; maker's mark largely obliterated. The maker was almost certainly a Birmingham concern.

A AND B, VICTORIA AND ALBERT MUSEUM
C AND D, PRIVATE COLLECTION

Plate 202. A group of pieces with a gilt metal comb and tortoiseshell teeth, surrounded by items variously embellished with insects, and, in one case, a cross.

A. The head of the comb, which is probably French and dating to the late 1860s, is decorated with the neo-classical devices of a lyre and laurel wreaths, presumably in homage to the First Empire. The decoration is applied and embellished with a plentiful use of wire.

B and C. Two small Roman mosaic brooches in very thin gold mounts embellished with wire in the archaeological style. The beetle is made of filati *incorporating gold flakes in the Venetian manner; the cross is composed of standard Roman* filati, *c.1875.*

D. A gold and garnet bee brooch with naturalistically treated legs; c.1905.

E. A metal-gilt brooch set with artificial onyx with a butterfly in gilt perching on it; c.1880.

F. A lacewing or moth in gilt metal and red 'Vauxhall' glass made to a design registered by Elijah Atkins of Birmingham on 17 July 1869 and mass-produced in different sizes. The obsession with insects partly reflects French fashions, but also derived from renewed interest in sentimental jewellery, which led jewellers back to Knight's Gems and Device Book *(1836) and similar publications (see Plate 205).*

A, VICTORIA AND ALBERT MUSEUM, THE REST PRIVATE COLLECTION

Colour Plate 90. A pair of humming birds mounted on base metal as earrings, which may have come from the International Exhibition held in London in 1872. Two firms contributed bird and beetle jewellery, which was currently internationally fashionable. One was Ward & Co. and the other A. Boucard or Bouchard. The birds and beetles were native to South America, but the firms might have bought articles already mounted, perhaps in the United States which participated in the vogue. The official exhibition Report said of Boucard: 'Birds and insects have been utilised and treated as personal ornaments, by A. Boucard. As specimens of beautiful colour, one could scarcely hope to see anything better than these. . . ', but it is evident that the writer had reservations about the beetles. However the handsome suite of gold and beetles mounted by Phillips Brothers in Colour Plate 113 is lent formal grandeur by its Egyptian design. BETHNAL GREEN MUSEUM

Colour Plate 91. Three serpent jewels. The two lower pieces date to about 1845. The upper of the two is a necklace; its head and heart-shaped locket are decorated with dark blue basse-taille enamel, counter-set with cushion-shaped brilliants and a rose diamond; its eyes are rubies. Below it is a bracelet with a Brazilian or snake chain body, a blue-enamelled and diamond-set head and a (later) diamond tongue. The necklace at the top has a Brazilian chain and terminals only distantly related to two snake heads, enamelled with moresques and connected to a suspension loop holding an enamelled heart-shaped pendant set with a pearl and diamonds; c.1865. SOTHEBY'S (THE JOHN SHELDON COLLECTION)

Frémy, meanwhile, had taken on as his personal assistant A.V.L. Verneuil, a former pupil whose own contribution to the subject, an apparatus incorporating the blowpipe, was to become the decisive factor in the launching of a large and prosperous industry in the chemical manufacture of corundum. Together the two men made a series of advances which resulted in small crystals of ruby good enough to be faceted and mounted in jewellery by Taub of Paris. In about 1885 small rubies appeared on the market under the name of 'Geneva rubies' and remained available until 1905 or thereabouts. These rubies came from an unknown source and realised the price of genuine stones. It is now suspected that they were chemically fabricated.[85]

Synthetic rubies made by Verneuil's flame-fusion apparatus were shown at the Paris 1900 Exhibition, two years before he first published an account of his invention. Verneuil's last major contribution to the manufacture of corundum was

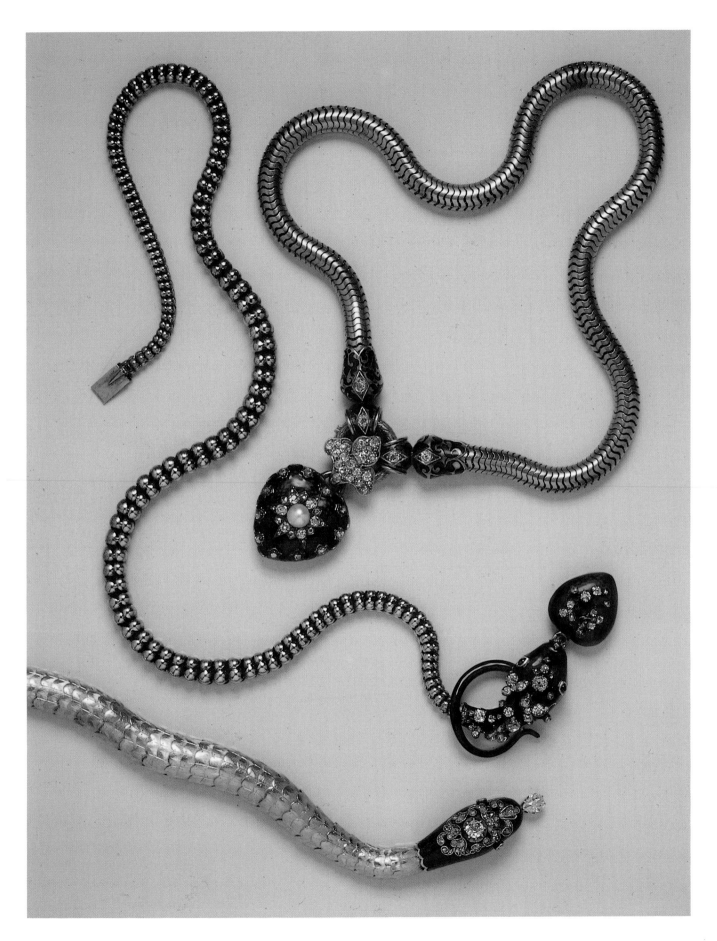

Plate 203. A cast and gilt metal bar brooch, with mock onyx beads secured by pins within the collets; a fly perches between the stones; c.1885. PRIVATE COLLECTION

a sapphire coloured with titanium oxides and iron; the process, evolved for the New York firm of Lazarus Heller & Son, was patented in America in 1910 and 1911.[86]

Experiments in the manufacture of diamonds met with less success than those in the production of corundum.[87] Spinel is said to have been manufactured with greater success, as was turquoise, earlier imitated by coloured ceramic or odontolite, fossil ivory stained green or blue by phosphate of iron.

7. Cutting

In general, the cutting of imitation, artificial and synthetic stones was originally performed by a lapidary and then by machine. Both shape and cut conformed to current fashions.

8. Setting.

Synthetic stones were naturally set as genuine stones. Open mounts were often used for pastes, though closed settings, which allowed for the insertion of metallic foil, remained popular throughout the nineteenth century. From about 1840 an alternative method to foiling colourless pastes was used, the glass itself being 'silvered' by immersion in various solutions.[88] The settings of good imitation pieces were often lined with gold. Real cut-down collets or imitations cast complete with ridges and claw, millegrain and knife-edged settings, hand-made or stamped or cast were all used at various times. The base metal setting in Plate 203 is cast and represents the cheapest kind of costume jewellery. Electro-metallurgy was also employed: the magazine *Industrial Art* reported in 1877 that some French jewellery manufacturers had begun to set stones in a prepared model, immersing the whole in a plating bath so that gold or silver was precipitated round the stones in the form of collets. One workman was able to set between 1,500 and 2,000 stones a day by this method, but only fifty when working by hand.[89] It is unlikely that real stones were set in this way and the technique must have been used for pastes.

9. Glass Beads.

Murano was an important centre of the bead trade, rivalled chiefly by Bavaria and Bohemia, though when Venice and Bohemia were part of the Austrian Empire there was a great deal of cooperation between manufacturers. The prosperity of bead-makers in the locality of Venice largely depended on overseas demand.

The first essential in a bead manufactory was a rope-walk which, as the making of beads was usually a side-line of a glass works, was not far from the furnaces.

The rope-walk was a narrow straight gallery about 150ft. (45m) long. A large wedge of molten glass ('metal') was gathered from the furnace and then rolled into a cylinder on an iron plate. The cylinder was pierced with an iron tool and then passed to two workmen who gradually stretched it out along the rope-walk into a long thin swinging tube. After being laid aside to cool, the tube was chipped into fragments of uniform size. These small pieces were picked up by boys and placed in a container filled with sand and ashes which entered the hollow centres of the glass. In this state, the fragments were either stirred over a very hot fire or revolved in a heated drum. The heat melted the ragged edges left from cutting and smoothed the beads, the sand and ashes ensuring that they retained their pierced centres. Cooled again, and the sand shaken out of them, the beads were sorted according to size, counted and threaded by boys and girls, who tied the strings into bundles.

Pressed glass beads were produced in moulds. These were cheaper. In Venice, Bohemia and Bavaria patterned beads were made with the aid of pointed implements to scratch out the design, which was then burnt in by a blowpipe. Acid was frequently used in Venice to deaden the surface but sand was more generally employed for the purpose in Bavaria.[90]

Venetian beads were frequently shown at international exhibitions. Their ornate decoration, even in the specimens contributed by Salviati's Venice and Murano Mosaic Company, did not always meet with unqualified approval.[91]

10. Glass

Reference has been made elsewhere to the paste cameos produced by the Tassie firm. Variations were widespread. The mirror portrait in Plate 204 is a rare survival of a technique introduced in the late seventeenth century by Bernard Perrot of Orléans.[92] The more orthodox cameos manufactured by Apsley Pellatt (see page 231) were highly praised by the *Art Journal* in 1854.[93] 'Vauxhall' (mirrored) glass, plain or coloured, was used in the production of cheap jewellery. The lacewing or moth brooch in Plate 202F is a specimen of mass-production from a design registered by Elijah Atkins of Birmingham in 1869; it is in the company of other pieces exemplifying a passion for small creatures and flowers which led designers and manufacturers back to the old emblem books (Plate 205).

11. Artificial Pearls

The simplest way of faking pearls from natural materials was to cut and shape them from the iridescent lining of shells. Seed pearls, dissolved in acid and formed into a paste, might be moulded into imitations of oriental pearls, and coral was occasionally employed to make simulated pink pearls. The oldest surviving process of manufacturing imitation pearls is said to have been invented (or adapted from Venetian practice) by the Parisian rosary maker Jaquin, who patented it in 1686. Jaquin applied an essence compounded of varnish and scales from the bleak, a fish found in the Seine, to the inside of blown glass globules. The cavities were afterwards filled with wax.[94]

Colour Plate 92. Two vulcanite crosses, one with a chain; c.1875. Both crosses are decorated with an anchor, symbolising the anchoring of the soul in Christian faith; the smaller also has a heart in the centre of a cross with trefoil ends. Primarily intended as mourning ornaments, the pieces are still black on the underside but on top have faded to a rich brown. PRIVATE COLLECTION

The bleak was virtually peculiar to the Seine and manufacturers elsewhere tried other fishes. It was claimed in 1853 that whitebait scales had been found superior to those of the bleak, and that roach and dace had been employed in the manufacture of imitation pearls of an inferior kind,[95] but the bleak remained supreme in Paris.

Colour Plate 93. Black vulcanite and composition trinkets; c.1875-1885. The upper four pieces, all brooches, are variants of popular themes; horseshoes and a whip, and female hands, one holding a closed fan and another with an open fan, while a third has a bat. The hand with the open fan bears a diamond-shaped Registry Mark on the reverse. The date letter for the year (see Appendix I) is partly obliterated, though enough remains to indicate that the design was registered in Class IV on 18 May 1880. This reading is unfortunately not supported by the surviving records in the Public Record Office. The brooches, with the rose pendant on the lower left, all in vulcanite, have faded from black to dark brown on the front. The piece on the lower right, which has the monogram AEI ('for ever') in gilt metal on the front, is still a glossy black. The surface is slightly uneven, as is the back, which has a box for hair inserted over an armature, recalling a method of construction used by Turnbull Brothers and Woodin of Whitby, Birmingham and London (see Chapter XV), though the material used is a composition, not jet.

PRIVATE COLLECTIONS

The Duc de Luynes held that jewellers in Russia, Germany, England, Spain and the East preferred the artificial pearls produced by the Jaquin process to anything manufactured in Rome or Venice.[96] German imitation pearls, which were made of exceedingly thin glass, were not highly regarded. They were known in the trade as German fish pearls, as a means of distinguishing them from the French versions. Nevertheless pearl essence prepared at Eberbach on the Neckar was purchased by Parisian and Swiss manufacturers.

The Parisian manufacturer, Bourguignon, won a Bronze Medal for a vitreous imitation of pearls at the French National Exhibition of 1827. Constant Valès, who started his firm in Paris in about 1834, showed imitation opals and artificial pearls

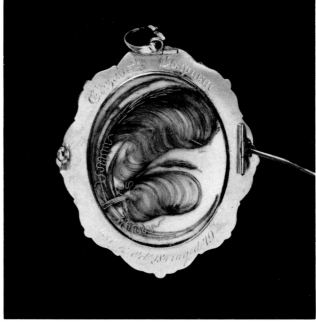

Plate 204. A gold brooch with a silhouette on a mirror ground, signed: Augt C Douart fecit 1837. *The fitted locket back contains two plumes of hair in a glass-fronted box and is inscribed:* Elizabeth Chapman/died 12 Octr 1847 aged 79. *She was therefore sixty-nine years old when her portrait was made.*

SCOTT COOPER, CHELTENHAM

simulating several natural varieties at the French 1839 Exhibition, winning a Silver Medal for the latter. In 1844 he received the same award when he and his current associate, Lelong, exhibited pearls filled with the aid of a blowpipe, which were said to last much longer than usual. Valès repeated his success in 1849 and gained a Prize Medal at the Great Exhibition of 1851. His greatest rival was E. Truchy, a descendant of Jaquin, who first exhibited in 1844, won a Silver Medal in 1849 and a Prize Medal in 1851. Valès outstripped Truchy by gaining a First Class Medal at the Paris Exhibition of 1855. Two strings of imitation pearls exhibited by Valès in 1862 cost £2; a row of real pearls shown with them was valued at £60.[97]

The artificial pearls made in Italy, often known as Roman pearls (though also a speciality of Naples), were held to be convincing imitations. Alabaster beads coated with wax were dipped into an essence of fish scales, a process claimed to have been taken from the Chinese, who had covered spheres of vitreous material with a paste composed of fish scales mixed with glue or with a cement made with pulverised mother-of-pearl. Pozzi of the Via Pasquino, Rome, was recommended for the quality of his stock in 1829.[98]

The fragility of the French blown glass globules with their filling of fish scales and wax prompted a continuous search for further improvements or alternatives. Opaline glass with a nacreous lustre imparted by hydrofluoric acid, introduced in 1834, was stronger than the traditional blown glass pearls, for as the colouring came from the outside, not the inside, the glass might be thicker. From the mid-1860s, the preparation of fish scales (known as 'essence d'Orient') was sometimes combined with parkesine, the first plastic (see page 380).

Enthusiastic press notices were cited in advertisements for the Parisian Diamond Company's new 'Orient' pearls in the 1890s. The colour, skin, shape and lustre

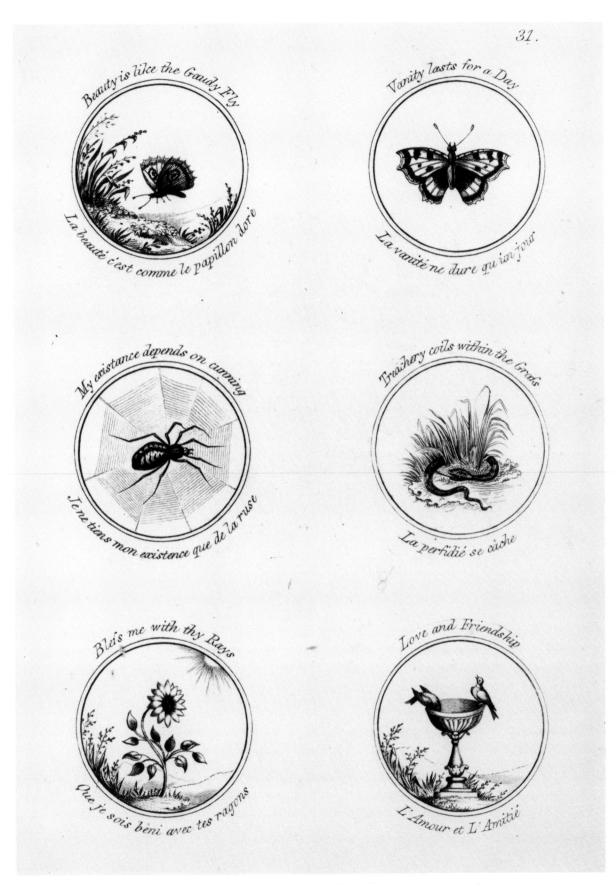

Plate 205. A plate from F. Knight, Gems and Device Book *(1836), illustrating some of the insect and floral devices still pillaged by jewellers in the 1880s and afterwards.*

were declared 'absolutely perfect. . . The Company's prices are moderate in the extreme; necklaces, for instance, ranging from one guinea upwards.'[99] But whether these pearls were made by Jaquin's method or were the product of one of the new techniques involving the use of silica[100] it is impossible to say.

12. Imitation Coral

Coral, like pearls, was a valuable commodity and a subject of many imitations. Ivory beads were sometimes dyed a coral colour. Samuel Isaacs of Newman Street, off Oxford Street, obtained a patent in 1855 for 'improvements in the manufacture of "artificial coral" ', employing alabaster treated with sulphuric acid, grease and colouring matter; two years later, provisional protection was obtained for an imitation made of vegetable ivory boiled in a solution of tin, lac and cochineal.[101] Several inventions made use of gutta percha, the sap of a tree growing mainly in the Malay archipelago.

It is difficult to believe that Isaacs was ignorant of coraline or coralline, a French invention made of alabaster mined at Volterra and coloured by undisclosed means. It was worked at a factory at Pomaia in the vicinity of Volterra and at another in the French Jura. Though a convincing looking imitation, it could be cut with a knife, unlike coral. P.L. Simmonds declared in 1873 that it was formerly available in France in the 'galleries of the Palais Royal, Paris, and other shops where cheap jewellery is sold.'[102] Staight Brothers of Hatton Garden, importers and dealers in ivory and other articles, showed 'Patent Coralline' at the London 1862 and Paris 1867 Exhibitions, optimistically asserting on the first occasion that it superseded coral.[103]

'American corals', described in an English periodical in 1877 as 'a new article of manufacture, used for articles of finery and ornament', were produced by Kingman & Hodges of Mansfield, Massachusetts. Made by a process which 'is still a secret', using milk obtained from the cheese-making factories of New York, it was clearly commercial casein, an early form of plastic which was often coloured to resemble horn, ivory, ebony and marble as well as coral. The casein was moulded into the desired forms and hardened by a long soaking in formaldehyde.[104] Gutta percha and india rubber imitations were patented in 1859 and 1866 (see page 382).

13. Plastics

The first plastic was not casein but parkesine. It owed its name to its inventor, Alexander Parkes, the chief chemist and metallurgist at Elkington's of Birmingham, who had been concerned with formulating the specification of their first electro-plating patent in 1840. During his years with Elkington's, Parkes developed or improved a wide variety of techniques and materials. In the early 1840s he began to cogitate a 'new material' and eventually succeeded in producing a substance 'partaking in a large degree of the properties of ivory, tortoise-shell, horn, hard wood, india rubber, gutta percha, etc. . .' He obtained his first patent for parkesine in October 1855, specifying the use of pyroxilin (nitro-cellulose), a 'less explosive' variant of gun cotton, which was made from vegetable fibres treated with nitric or sulphuric acid. The other principal ingredient was oil, which gave the product flexibility. Parkes added camphor and gelatine to facilitate its manufacture in sheet form. His new material, inspired by the collodion used in printing photographs, was still too costly and impracticable for manufacturing purposes in 1855. Parkes eventually brought down the cost of manufacture from £6.10s. to less than 1s. per pound, though it was not yet so cheap when samples of the material in its rough and manufactured state were shown at the 1862 Exhibition and won Parkes a Medal.[105] Parkesine was made not only in sheet form but in blocks or tubes, bulked out with cork or wood-dust. It was capable of being moulded or shaped in a die, turned on a lathe, cut, sawn, engraved, carved, inlaid with metals and polished. It might be hard or flexible and variegated or uniform in colour. Ivory was at first difficult to imitate but amber and malachite were produced with aniline dyes and other pigments.

Parkes took out further patents for 'improvements' achieved at a cost of 'many thousand pounds'.[106] According to the *Art Journal,* he imparted texture to his material by laminating alternate sheets of pigmented and uncoloured parkesine together, 'working in geometric forms so as to give a pleasing figure or grain where the built-up mass is cut.'[107] This was the subject of a further patent which also covered imitation pearl, produced by combining fish scales and dyes with parkesine in its liquid state, after which the material was either moulded or shaped by other means, or rolled into sheets on heated rollers coated with platinum to prevent any chemical reaction from soiling it.[108] Parkesine was again exhibited by its inventor at Paris in 1867; he was awarded a Medal.[109]

The inventor's monopoly, exercised by the Parkesine Company at Hackney Wick, failed to bring him adequate financial returns, though in 1868 it was reported to employ agents in Scotland and abroad.[110] Daniel Spill took over the firm in the same year, using the trade names of Xylonite and Ivoride for his products, which included costume jewellery. But Spill, like his predecessor, had no lasting commercial success and the initiative passed to America (see Plate 201A).

The cellulose nitrate compound made by the American brothers James and Isaiah Hyatt was known as Celluloid. This trade name became so famous from the early 1870s onwards that it was adopted as the generic term for the material. The Celluloid Manufacturing Company obtained a patent in 1878 through an English agent for a method of making celluloid chains by extruding them from what was endearingly called a stuffing-machine on to a removable mandril.[111]

Parkes experimented in vulcanizing india rubber, but chose gutta percha for the electrotyping moulds developed for Elkington's. India rubber, then usually known as caoutchouc, is the coagulated milky juice of a tree growing in a wide belt of countries round the equator, especially in Central and South America, Africa and Asia. Naturally more elastic than gutta percha, caoutchouc was hardened or vulcanized by being combined with sulphur; and when a large amount of sulphur was used and the material put into prepared moulds and subjected to heat for several hours, a hard, horn-like product known as ebonite or vulcanite ensued.

The sulphur process was perfected by Charles Goodyear, an American, who had acquired the idea of combining it with india rubber from a former associate, and then, in the course of subsequent experiments, hit upon the heating method by accident. Goodyear's first American patent was granted in 1844; he then had to embark on extensive litigation to protect his invention from piracy. Among his competitors, a Londoner named Thomas Hancock claimed to have discovered the process of vulcanization independently and took out several patents[112] but the Jury reports on the Great Exhibition make it plain that Goodyear's invention anticipated Hancock's work.

Goodyear was awarded a Council Medal in 1851[113] and the *Grande Médaille d'Honneur* in Paris in 1855. Two years later he mounted a Vulcanite Court in the Crystal Palace at Sydenham. The *Illustrated London News,* in its review of the Court, made particular reference to articles imitating ivory, buckhorn and bone, which indicates that white and near-white work was prominent. The 'unexceptionable' jewellery in the display was not otherwise described.[114]

After Goodyear's death, the Scottish Vulcanite Company of Edinburgh contributed specimens of 'patent vulcanite' made of gutta percha as well as of india rubber to the 1862 Exhibition. The manufacturers were especially at pains to state that it supplanted 'all the appliances of whalebone', being 'infinitely more durable, and susceptible to a higher finish', and furthermore capable of 'receiving impressions as clear and sharp as the finest carved ivory'.[115] It is plain that moulded white vulcanite was still popular. Cheap coloured cameos were also made from vulcanite. The more familiar black vulcanite jewellery with a fine polish in imitation of jet (Colour Plates 92 and 93) was probably a slightly later phenomenon, but once launched, it remained in demand for the rest of the century (see Chapter XV). According to W.G. Larkins, in 1872 'a large number of persons in the east-end of London gain a livelihood by the manufacture of vulcanite ornaments', women and children as well as men.[116] It took decades before its principal drawback became apparent: the black gradually faded to dark brown on exposure to light.

Gutta percha, used by the Scottish Vulcanite Company, was first introduced into England in the early seventeenth century as a curiosity known as 'mazerwood'.[117] Much later it was brought to the country again partly through the interest of Dr W. Montgomerie, who in 1844 was awarded a Medal for his researches by the Society of Arts.[118] The Gutta Percha Company of London showed a wide variety of articles at the Great Exhibition, was rewarded with a Council Medal[119] and exhibited again in 1862, but there is no evidence that jewellery formed part of the highly catholic display on either occasion.

An English patent was obtained in 1859 by C.S. Rostaing, an American citizen residing in Germany, for 'improvements' in combining and mixing gutta percha with mineral and vegetable substances to produce imitation coral as well as ivory.[120] In 1866, another American, Frank Marquand of New Jersey, took out an English patent for a method of 'treating india rubber, gutta percha and similar gums' by bleaching them with ammonium chloride and other agents and afterwards colouring the results to simulate ivory, pearl, coral, enamel and porcelain.[121]

Papier-mâché, a moulded product made either from pulp or sheets of paper, was introduced in the sixteenth century. The process was brought to Birmingham in the mid-eighteenth century and there made the subject of many improvements, including several patented by Davenport & Cole of Birmingham, specialists in mourning jewellery (see page 679).[122]

Gelatine was an essential ingredient of certain other fabricated materials. George Wallis alluded in 1876 to the use of gelatine in the manufacture of imitation tortoiseshell in France.[123] In 1881, the *Artist* carried a note of the recent invention of compressed mother-of-pearl, made of pulverised shell solidified with gelatine.[124] Like tortoiseshell raspings which could be melted down and moulded (Colour Plate 186J) and even like parkesine, of which its inventor had proudly claimed that, cheap as it was to make, 'every particle, scrap or dust can be reworked', the use of scrap or pulverised material was infinitely attractive to manufacturers, for it prevented all possibility of waste. There were many inventions of a type similar to one patented by a Londoner named H.W. Patrick in 1859 as 'a new substance or material to be used in lieu of ivory and other like substances' for buttons, medallions and jewellery. In Patrick's process, pulverised amber was combined with an extraordinary range of materials including pulped paper, powdered pumice stone, asbestos, india rubber and potato flour.[125] Jet, a valuable substance, was treated in a similar manner by other inventors (see pages 679 and 680).

Colour Plate 94. A. Prince Albert gave Queen Victoria the gold band bracelet chased with foliated scrolls, and an applied enamelled spider in pursuit of an enamelled and gem-set fly. It was one of the 'trifles' or 'souvenirs' given on his birthday on 26 August 1842 in return for the presents he received, a custom which the Queen and all the royal family observed on their own birthdays. The Prince may even have designed the bracelet, though there is no evidence of it. After the Prince's unexpected death on 14 December 1861, Queen Victoria, who had already had the inside of the bracelet engraved: From Albert/26th Augt 1842, *wore it conscientiously on anniversaries, as she did with all the jewellery he had given her, presumably rotating the articles. Garrard's repaired it from time to time and also let in a piece to enlarge the band as the Queen grew plumper in old age; this required part of the inscription to be re-engraved. B. A turquoise enamelled gold bracelet, linked by gold rings set with pearls. The centre, a stylised flower, is adorned with a diamond fly with ruby eyes, made separately and applied, like the spider and fly in the royal bracelet above; c.1850.*   A. PRIVATE COLLECTION. B. GARRARD & COMPANY

CHAPTER X
A Typology of Fashion, 1837-1861

News of developments in design and manufacture were now easily dissemina-ted by publications which often owed their inception to steam-powered printing presses. One such, the *Illustrated London News,* which made its début in May 1842, occasionally engraved the jewels of distinguished personages and firms. The *Art Journal* (then the *Art-Union Journal*), which started in 1839, also intermittently discussed jewellery and jewellers. Henry Cole's *Journal of Design,* launched to publicise his Summerly Art-Manufactures and the Great Exhibition, was not produced for mass-consumption and its influence, though genuine, was more limited.

Cole's besetting sin, his instinctive preference for traditional craftsmanship, made it difficult for him to accept much industrial production, for all his efforts to do so. Once he began running the Schools of Design (which he re-named Art Schools) in association with the Museum of Manufactures in 1852, his curriculum was theoretical, not practical. The students were instructed in aesthetics with the aid of Redgrave's 'Supplementary Report on Design' at the Great Exhibition, which annihilated the naturalistic style with the panache and inside knowledge of a former devotee. This was augmented by publications such as L. Gruner's *Specimens of Ornamental Art* (1853) and R.N. Wornum's *Analysis of Ornament* (1856), but the chief source of the conventionalised historical design promoted by Cole and his cohorts was Owen Jones' *Grammar of Ornament* (1856). Envious eyes being cast on French design, pattern books brought over from Paris included L. Feuchère's *Art Industriel* (1839-48) and E. Julienne's *Ornemaniste des Arts Industriels* (1840). Both were available to Cole's students.

Adherents of the Mediaeval Movement had access to an international network of authoritative publications. In England, the *Archaeological Journal,* launched in 1845, carried articles on medieval enamelling (1846 and 1851) and niello decoration (1862). The results to date of international research into the first technique were summarised by De Laborde in his *Notice des Emaux. . .exposés dans les Galeries du Musée du Louvre* (1852-3). The discoveries had already filtered into the more prosperous branches of the jewellery trade (Colour Plate 100), while mass-manufacturers tried to imitate the processes by cheaper means.

The popularity of diamonds and pearls was attested in fashion reports and in such manuscript sources as survive. The last of the Garrard Gentlemen's Ledgers to have been preserved[1] (the Victorian ones post-dating 1846 have all been lost) demonstrates that coloured stones were still much in demand. Two ferronnières adapted by the firm in 1838 (one for Mrs de Rothschild) were set respectively with diamonds and emeralds and diamonds and pearls. In 1841 Queen Victoria's uncle, the Duke of Sussex, commissioned Garrard's to make a gold bracelet adorned with a sapphire and brilliants, supplying some of the stones and purchasing the rest. He was charged £56.

Plate 206. The enamelled portrait miniatures of Mr and Mrs Pandeli Ralli are mounted in identical double quatrefoil ribbon frames enamelled in dark blue and decorated with diamonds in bud-shaped collets. The Parisian maker (whose mark is JC with a bird) added attachments to enable either to be worn as a brooch or a bracelet centre. Here Mrs Ralli figures in the brooch and her husband in the centre of the chased gold bracelet band; c.1850. VICTORIA AND ALBERT MUSEUM

Sir Francis Shuckburgh was one of several clients to order a pair of pins connected by a length of chain, an ornament popular with both men and women. With opal and diamond heads and an enamelled chain, the pins made for Sir Francis cost him £20.10s. Another patron was Mr P. Ralli (Plate 206), who acquired a diamond head ornament for £200 and a matching bracelet for £45 early in 1838 and followed these with a pair of pink topaz and chrysolite earrings which together with a brooch and ring were priced (overall) at £15.2s. A labradorite stud in the form of a monkey's head with diamond eyes went to Mrs Henry Torre for £1.10s. in 1843. Popular stones such as turquoises appear regularly in entries and rarer ones like lapis lazuli intermittently. Imported coral and carved shell cameos figure in many orders. The firm supplied Miss E. Stanley with a cameo in 1840 and mounted it for her 'in fine gold as Brooch' for £3.16s. in all; perhaps the purchaser was Maria Josepha Stanley's daughter Emmeline, who married the antiquary Albert Way in 1844. Florentine mosaics were set for a few clients, one of whom also purchased 'A Berlin Necklace' (an example of Berlin ironwork) for £1 in 1838.

Garrard's sold fewer items demonstrating the rage for polychromy so dominant in the 1820s and early 1830s. The 1840s were altogether more sober, though multicoloured effects were still observed in naturalistic jewellery and these survived into the next decade. A marriage parure made in Paris for the Duchesse de Malakoff in 1858 comprised a wreath and a bodice bouquet set with diamonds, topazes, pearls and emeralds 'mounted in the form of daisies.'[2]

The *Illustrated London News,* using the Great Exhibition as a peg for a discussion of the fluctuating popularity of precious stones, declared that the aquamarine, formerly 'a stone of considerable value,' had recently glutted the market owing to new sources of supply and was now disdained by the trade and the public. The rich olive-green peridot, much admired in the early years of the century, was exceedingly rare and still difficult to obtain. Specimens of a lighter hue were currently plentiful enough and were chiefly employed in bracelets and sévignés. Garrard's had indeed sold a client[3] a bracelet set with peridots in engraved gold for £15 in 1837. Chrysoprase, favoured in the 1820s and 1830s, was dismissed as 'a poor stone, of comparatively little value' and topaz, once so prized, had fallen from favour; the red variety, the most uncommon, fetched the highest price. White topazes, 'familiarly known as the mina nova', presumably cost less.[4] A magnificent group of precious stones, part of the collection formed by the late Henry Philip Hope and exhibited by his nephew Henry Thomas Hope[5] in 1851, aroused enormous interest. Queen Victoria, who had inspected the collection a year earlier, was particularly impressed by Hope's diamonds, which ranged in colour from blue to yellow. The stones, she noted in her Journal on 19 April 1850, were mainly set as rings. H.T. Hope himself contributed a short piece on diamonds to the 1851 catalogue[6] and Hunt & Roskell included in their own display other stones purchased from the H.P. Hope collection.

The ring settings of the stones in the Hope collection cannot be taken to mean that they were intended to be worn. Another collection, partly based on stones formerly owned by H.P. Hope, was put together by the Rev. Chauncey Hare Townshend who had his acquisitions similarly mounted, presumably to facilitate storage and handling; Townshend bequeathed his rings to the South Kensington Museum in 1868. Stones as fine as these were not usually dedicated to female use, except in the case of royalty. Many people genuinely preferred stones of lesser quality, which were not only cheaper but easier to obtain.

A catalogue of 1851 exhibits contributed by the Liverpool concern of Joseph Mayer, which was respectable rather than avant-garde, lists items in diamonds, pearls and coloured stones often combined with enamel, including a pearl necklace with diamond pendants at £42, a sévigné in purple enamel and brilliants, also costing £42, a blue enamel and diamond brooch at £84 and a turquoise enamel and diamond brooch at £112. Among other articles of jewellery shown by the firm were a gold bracelet set with carbuncles in the form of grapes which cost £13.13s., and, the most expensive piece, an opal and diamond bracelet, valued at £350.[7] Marcasite, cited in a fashion report in 1848,[8] was probably too cheap to figure in Mayer's display.

Garrard's exhibited a brooch in onyx and brilliants, a pendant in turquoise and brilliants and several items set with three or more different stones, among them an emerald, sapphire, opal and brilliant fly brooch, a popular motif exemplified by the two bracelets in Colour Plate 94, one of them a gift from Prince Albert to

Queen Victoria. J.V. Morel, an honorary but temporary Englishman by reason of his New Burlington Street address, contributed a large bouquet representing a rose, a tulip and a convolvulus flower 'composed of Rubies and Diamonds, which can be converted into a Stomacher, Head Ornament, or separate brooches'. This agreeably adaptable piece cost £15,000 and was cited by the Jury in their award of a Council Medal to the firm.[9]

The catalogue entries of foreign exhibitors are less detailed, though some of the omissions are rectified by the Jury which noted, for instance, scent-bottles in lapis lazuli, Venetian aventurine and jasper in the display of Marrel frères of Paris,[10] on whom another Council Medal was bestowed. Kämmerer & Zeftigen of St Petersburg were also recipients of a Council Medal, on account of the perfection of their settings. They showed a dress ornament in the form of bouquets of currants, the stems and foliage set with diamonds and the fruit with polished uncut rubies; among other exhibits was a spray of convolvulus in diamonds and fine turquoises.[11]

In his *Essai sur l'Art Industriel* (1856), inspired by the 1851 and 1855 Exhibitions, Charles Laboulaye furnished a list of stones popular in France, citing diamonds, yellow, green and white sapphires as well as the more familiar blue sapphires, rubies, emeralds, aquamarines, topaz, amethysts, opals and pearls.[12] The list had an international relevance to the world of high fashion. But there were also many displays of local materials and crafts at the Great Exhibition. Bohemian garnets were exhibited by the Prince von Lobkowitz, who owned mines at Bilin. The sizes of the stones are tabulated in his prospectus, together with the prices.[13] The coral contributed by Paravagua and Casella included diamond-cut items and a series of beads of various colours and sizes.[14] Red seed coral was already cheap enough to be bought by factory girls, as Disraeli's eponymous hero in his novel *Coningsby* (1844) observed on a visit to a Manchester cotton mill.[15]

The well-known gem-engravers represented in 1851 were augmented by the less celebrated George Brett, a seal engraver of Tysoe Street, Spitalfields, who is said to have exhibited 'fine onyx cameos of elaborate workmanship'.[16] According to Vever, Tixier-Deschamps of the Palais-Royal had a great success from about 1850 to 1868 with *camées habillées* representing negresses' heads adorned with tiny rose diamonds.[17] But the retail firm concerned did not exhibit in 1851. China plaques painted with local views for setting in trinkets of a kind purchased by Prince Albert for the Queen on visits to Germany[18] were represented at the Great Exhibition by the work of Gustav Walther of Dresden.[19] Such wares were the equivalent of enamelled Swiss topographical brooches (Plate 207).[20]

The Viennese system of constructing settings from trellises of wires was much despised in retrospect by the Parisian jeweller Oscar Massin, who had been forced to use it when he started his career in the workshops of Théodore Fester in 1851. Fester, the successor of Viennot, who had introduced the Viennese method into France, interminably combined round flowers with pointed leaves or pointed flowers with round leaves, all set as economically as possible. Some of these pieces were striking enough, but Massin alleged that 100,000 francs' worth of diamonds might be set as a simple rivière or necklace of forty collets at a cost of no more than

30 francs. The collets were gilded to save the expense of laminating them with gold. But despite his contempt for Fester's stereotyped productions, Massin began to see the practical point of reducing the weight of settings. Vever credited him with cutting out an average of 3 milligrams per individual collet by 1867.

Massin averred that English settings were renowned for their conscientious execution, in consequence of which some French people bought their marriage jewellery in England.[21] But the Duc de Luynes, enraptured by the 'incomparable beauty' of Russian settings in 1851, trusted that French, English and German jewellers alike would learn from them. In his view, all three Western European countries produced mounts so heavy that they competed with the diamonds set in them.[22] Peter Hinks has pointed out that the Russian settings were particularly luxurious, each large stone often being held in place by a row or rows of tiny rose diamonds,[23] a technique which inspired the frame of the re-cut Koh-i-Nûr in 1852.

Early in the 1840s, articulated rains of stones, terminating in needle-like drops, were introduced into French floral jewellery. Known as *pampilles,* they were another expression of the craze for jewellery in constant movement (see Colour Plate 95), flowers and fruits already being set high on stalks as mobile as technology could contrive. Massin, when experimenting with flexible mounts much later, discovered that he had been anticipated by Fontenay, who, for his remarkable jewelled bramble head ornament shown at the Paris Exhibition not only used platinum in some of the small settings but also developed for others a laminate of iron and gold, turned on a mandril, which he patented.

Gold, in more plentiful supply in the 1850s following the discoveries in California and Australia, was much used in colour combinations in naturalistic jewellery and often chased, matted or enamelled in simulation of nature (Plate 208B and C), a practice which usually provoked accusations of artistic heresy from Redgrave after 1851. Engraving and chasing were employed in the decoration of gothic and Renaissance-inspired articles, which were often also enamelled (Colour Plate 82). The components of these jewels were either stamped or embossed, but the figurative work was cast. Though costly to produce, the use of cast miniature figures by Froment-Meurice, one of the pioneers of the genre in the 1830s, secured him an international reputation.

When Queen Victoria came to the throne the English had a penchant for polished red gold; elsewhere in Europe yellow gold was preferred. Some filigree

items were still made and sold in Britain in the late 1830s and early 1840s. In 1838 Garrard's mounted a cameo with the addition of coloured stones 'in filigree gold as Brooch' for the son of the former Home Secretary, Lord Sidmouth, charging him £2.2s.[24] French jewellers continued to experiment with filigree into the 1850s, though the leading firms gradually abandoned the type decorated with *cannetille* and *grainti,* turning instead to other models. The Duc de Luynes cited a new type of filigree by Charles Christofle of Paris, who from 1842 had operated Elkington's electroplating process under licence in France. Christofle's filigree, a kind of metallic tissue or mesh, was exported in large quantities to South America, together with more conventional jewellery. Examples of Christofle's work, illustrated by Burat in his survey of the French National Exhibition of 1844 (Plate

Plate 209. An illustration of jewellery shown by Charles Christofle et Compagnie at the French national exhibition of 1844 in Paris, from Burat, L'Exposition de l'Industrie française, II, 1844. *The ribbon brooch on the lower left is made of tissue. The rest is entirely naturalistic, with pendants à pampilles. Christofle had inherited from his brother-in-law, Calmette, a considerable trade with South America and the Antilles, which he expanded still further. The delicacy of his gold, silver and gem-set jewellery, according to Burat, was dictated by the demand for light and comfortable ornaments in the countries to which they were exported. A Gold Medallist in 1839 and 1844, Christofle handed over the jewellery side of his business to Léon Rouvenat, who exhibited under his own name in 1849.*

209)[25] are also represented in the firm's Design Books (see Plates 210 and also 211). By 1849 Christofle had handed over the jewellery side of his business to his former apprentice, Léon Rouvenat, leaving himself free to concentrate on producing hollow-wares in silver and electroplate.[26]

The English public on the whole clung to its gold jewellery, though even Queen Victoria owned trinkets made of silver. The silver filigree articles largely produced in Genoa (exemplified by the pin in Plate 292A) and similar work in gold and silver turned out in Malta were regarded as a special category of regional jewellery and completely different from the silver jewellery made by the French. The latter was particularly admired for its artistry. Froment-Meurice exhibited several silver items in 1851.[27] Rudolphi, who showed a silver angel brooch very similar to the example in Colour Plate 82D at the French National Exhibition of 1844, sent work in a similar vein to the Great Exhibition. A bracelet shown in 1851, made in oxidised silver with three cast figures of cherubs disputing over a bird, designed and modelled by Rudolphi's pupil Leroy, is illustrated in Vever.[28] The silver and emerald specimen in Colour Plate 96 is probably closer to another 1851 exhibit designed for Rudolphi by Masson which was mentioned by the Jury;[29] representing 'two Cupids playing among the stalks of a vine', it was adorned however with a sapphire, not emeralds.

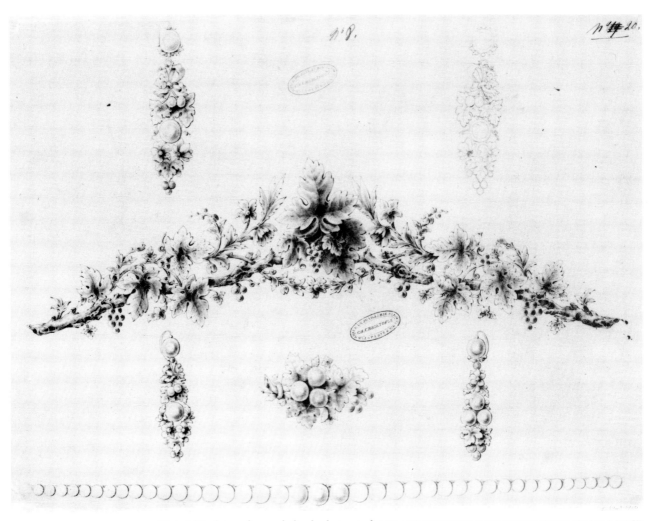

Plate 210. *A page from a design book stamped:* CH. CHRISTOFLE/FABRIQUE DE JOAILLERIE BIJOUTERIE. PARIS. *The vine parure with large and slightly smaller earrings, drawn in pen, ink and wash, was clearly intended to be realised in gold and large pearls augmented by seed pearls rather in the manner of the necklace and brooch in Plate 211; c.1840-45.*

In previous decades jewellers had been primarily dependent on coloured stones when they wanted intense hues. The effect was now increasingly provided by champlevé and basse-taille enamels. Dark blue was the commonest colour in the late 1830s and early 1840s, and remained in use thereafter, though light blue or turquoise was also in demand. In 1843 Queen Victoria gave a light blue enamel brooch costing £18.18s. to her cousin Victoire, Duchesse de Nemours, daughter-in-law of King Louis Philippe.[30] A necklet with a pendant enamelled in turquoise and set with diamonds which came under attack in the *Journal of Design* in 1849 on the grounds that it had been designed without due thought,[31] typified another common practice of the time, the use of small rose diamonds and other stones countersunk in settings embedded in enamel (Colour Plate 97).

Experiments were conducted in the 1850s in the use of *cloisonné* enamel, in which wire strips or *cloisons*, attached to a back plate, were used to contain and separate the colours. Mollard, a French jeweller, following Cellini's recipes, actually managed to revive the most difficult variety of *cloisonné*, *plique-à-jour* or translucent enamel, in which the enamel was either built up by degrees between the *cloisons*

Plate 211. A vine brooch and a necklace in coloured gold and pearls threaded on to a gold grid instead of a pierced mother-of-pearl frame as used by English makers of seed pearl jewellery during the Regency and later (see Plate 67). Tiny snails cling to some of the tendrils on the inner edges of the necklace and the rusticated frame of the brooch echoes that of the Christofle head ornament in Plate 210. These pieces are probably French, dating to about 1837-45, but Mrs Samuel Wilson's sleeve ornaments of 1838 (Plate 218) demonstrate that work of this kind was current in London. (Shown slightly smaller than actual size.) A, PRIVATE COLLECTION, B, VICTORIA AND ALBERT MUSEUM

or fired over a temporary back plate which was afterwards removed.[32] The technique was not much employed in jewellery until later in the century.

The manufacture of platinum was illustrated at the Great Exhibition by Percival Norton Johnson's firm, Johnson & Matthey,[33] but English jewellers do not appear to have been inspired as yet to depart from the conventional platina chains. The French continued to explore the possibilities of the metal, even deciding it was more acceptable when coloured, as it was in jewellery in bronzed platinum and gold which was reported to be on sale in 1846 at the retail jewellers, Gillion of 9 Boulevard des Italiens, Paris.[34]

Berlin ironwork, available in London not only at Garrard's but in 'great variety' from 1839 at a firm of importers, Muller's, was exhibited by several German manufacturers in 1851. Some of the Berlin ironwork jewellery bought for the founding collection of the Museum of Manufactures in 1852 had almost certainly been shown in the Exhibition (Plate 373). Steel wares were exhibited by a few English and a host of French manufacturers. Aluminium made its début at the Paris Universal Exhibition of 1855, though the first trinkets were made shortly afterwards.

The conservatism of the trade ensured that many popular motifs of earlier decades, such as hands, either single or double, were retained with comparatively little alteration. Rococo scrolls, which persisted mainly in mass-produced jewellery, lost some sharpness of definition but were otherwise much the same. Other devices were now treated in a somewhat different manner. Shells increasingly assumed an independent existence. Shedding the last remnants of formality, the forms of floral jewellery aped those of the flowers themselves, like Fester's bouquet for the elegant Empress Eugénie (Plate 182), which was tied with a jewelled bow. An almost agitated sense of movement was imparted to other naturalistic jewels by *pampilles* (Colour Plate 95). Even serpents, one of the most enduring of the neo-classical survivals (Colour Plate 98) were sometimes caught up in vegetation, textured in the imitative manner anathema to the Cole circle (Plate 208B and C).

Butterflies and insects of various kinds, combined with flowers or treated independently, remained in vogue; the modelled flies already remarked were a recent addition to the canon (Colour Plate 94). After 1851 more restrained forms of naturalism were very gradually introduced, except in headdress ornaments which, as before, were influenced by the milliner's art (Colour Plate 99 and Plate 212). The growing popularity of archaeological jewellery based on Greek and Graeco-Roman prototypes, the antithesis of organic naturalism, prompted a return to sharply-defined geometric forms (Plate 213) and reintroduced motifs such as rams' heads which had been last seen in quantity on neo-classical silverwork in the late eighteenth century.

The uneasy co-existence of styles led to some cross-fertilisation, but as historic purity was the order of the day, informed designers did their best to avoid it. Pugin and his fellow medievalists in England distinguished between gothic and Renaissance design and would have no dealings with the latter. They studied surviving examples of medieval jewellery and endeavoured to reproduce their forms, though Pugin, always hard-pressed for time, invariably resorted to his standard ornamental repertory of running trefoil patterns, quatrefoils and the like which he used in virtually all his designs for the decorative arts (Colour Plate 100). The Romantic elements in much French medievalising jewellery were gradually dropped in response to antiquarian research; Froment-Meurice and his colleagues increasingly concentrated on the Renaissance. Cartouches, balusters and strapwork, enamelled or engraved, were widespread. Marchand's *cuir roulé* brooches (so called because they imitated scrolled leatherwork) were closely related to and probably inspired the cartouche forms with rolled terminals used by other jewellers (Plates 207 and 208A). His engraved bows, a development of the sévigné but with the ribbon ends twisted or folded as if in movement, also became general

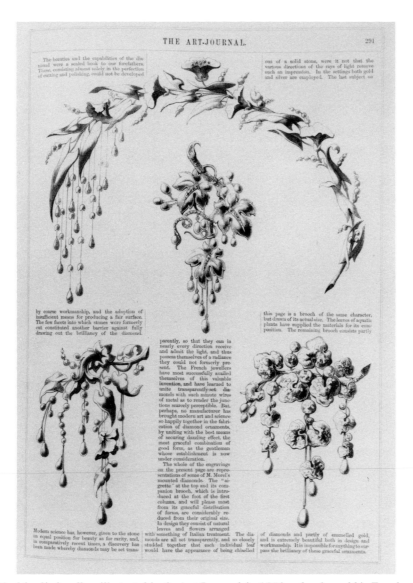

Plate 212. Morel's jewellery illustrated in the Art Journal *in 1850, when he and his French assistants were in New Burlington Street. The head ornament at the top, described, curiously, as an aigrette, and its matching convolvulus branch on the left, were said to be transparent-set with diamonds. The brooch on the lower right was partly set with diamonds and partly enamelled. The patronage of Queen Victoria and Prince Albert ensured Morel's acceptance by the cultural establishment in England.*

(Colour Plate 101). Two more talented French designer-jewellers, Eugène Petiteau[35] and Alexis Falize,[36] introduced jewels of oriental character, probably in the 1850s.[37] The earrings in Plate 214 may reflect their influence. Some of their pieces also had vase- or needle-shaped drops suspended from chains, a motif which became a cliché, so widely was it taken up.

The shaped rectangles which had flourished in the 1830s continued into the next decade. With the spread of classical designs, forms became more rounded, sometimes set off by stars. Intersecting circles and scallops were popular, as also were domical shapes comprising a gem-set border and a convex centre formed of a cabochon or, alternatively, an enamelled boss counterset with small stones, a reinterpretation of neo-classical motifs. For her portrait completed by Ingres in the mid-1850s, Madame Moitessier wore a bracelet composed of motifs of this kind, a splendid Renaissance brooch and a ring with a dark-coloured enamel or paste

head decorated with diamonds (Colour Plate 102 and Plate 215). Henry Cole, in his new role as a protagonist of classicism, could scarcely have influenced the style of her jewellery, which attests that the views of his circle were in line with general thinking. On the other hand, sporting proclivities rather than aesthetic attitudes fostered devices such as the horseshoe, which spread from masculine to feminine jewellery during this period. Perhaps the gold and turquoise horseshoe bracelet costing £30.10s. which was a Christmas present purchased by Queen Victoria from Garrard's in 1853[38] was intended for female wear.

In the decade leading up to the Great Exhibition suites for women underwent a series of changes in their nature and composition. The ferronnière, indispensable in the 1830s and early 1840s, fell dramatically from favour thereafter. Just before this occurred, Queen Victoria ordered a specimen in rubies and diamonds, accompanied by a pair of earrings and a brooch, as a wedding present to her cousin Princess Augusta of Cambridge,[39] who married the heir to the Grand Duke of Mecklenburg-Strelitz in 1843. Kitching's executed the set, which was completed by a bracelet given by Prince Albert.[40]

Garrard's craftsmen made a set comprising a pair of earrings, a sévigné and brooch, a necklace and bracelet (the last possibly convertible into a bandeau) for Sir Richard Simeon in October 1840, the client furnishing most of the diamonds for the work. A modest demi-parure for morning wear executed by Garrard's for another client comprised a pair of turquoise earrings, a brooch and a bracelet. A single bracelet was common to both sets, reflecting the newest fashion, though pairs of bracelets were still made and worn. The hostess of a French soirée in 1857 was reported to have worn shoulder fastenings of gold spangles and coral, a bandeau of the same materials, fastened by gold and coral pins, and coral necklet and bracelets.[41] Phillips Brothers showed an unusual parure by Goldschmidt & Son of Frankfurt at the 1851 exhibition, comprising a single gold and emerald

Plate 214. A pair of gold top and drop earrings finely fretted with foliated scrolls and with crescents attached to the drops. Set with chrysoprase, they perhaps date to about 1845-46, when 'Turkish earrings' were reported fashionable in Paris, or to 1850-60.

Plate 215. A detail from the portrait of Madame Moitessier (Colour Plate 102), showing her upper bracelet or bracelets of narrow hoops with a diamond-set heart and a large bracelet and ring.

bracelet, a brooch, watch-hook (or chatelaine), earrings and chains.[42]

One of the most comprehensive suites was designed in 1856 by the sculptor H.H. Armstead for C.F. Hancock of Bruton Street, for whom he worked on occasion as a designer, modeller and chaser of silverwork (Plate 216). Armstead was a favourite with the Cole circle because he had briefly studied at the London School of Design before moving on to the Royal Academy Schools. He was therefore requested by one of Cole's colleagues, George Wallis, to send him a list of the works shown at the 1862 Exhibition for which he had been responsible. Most were silver articles, some of which were cited by the Jury in awarding Armstead a Medal. The parure was included as a rider in the survey of past and present students' work at the 1862 Exhibition which was compiled by Wallis for publication in the 10th *Report* of Cole's Science and Art Department in 1863.[43] But for Armstead, Wallis' list would have appeared pretty thin.

The parure (Plate 216) was commissioned (on the recommendation of Sir Joseph Paxton) by Georgiana's son, the sixth Duke of Devonshire, and set with historic gems from the collection started by William, the second Earl of Devonshire, who had been born in Charles II's reign. The circumstances of the commission, the design and the components of the suite are all worth remarking. The Duke's nephew, the second Earl Granville, was appointed by Queen Victoria as Ambassador Extraordinary to represent her at the coronation of Tsar Alexander II in the summer of 1856. The Duke, who had performed a similar office for George IV some thirty years earlier came to his nephew's aid with funds, augmented by a loan of plate and the parure, which was made especially for Lord Granville's wife Marie to wear in Russia.

Hancock, who never acknowledged Armstead's part in the design, either to the Duke or anyone else, claimed himself to have had the idea of incorporating the engraved gems in the parure and of using diamonds to lighten the settings enamelled in the late sixteenth century manner. The suite comprises a diadem and a circlet, reminiscent of the head ornaments made for the Bonaparte family (Plates 69 and 70), as are the elaborate comb, bandeau and necklace with pendants. But the bracelet is a singleton, more characteristic of the mid-century than of 1810 or thereabouts. The triangular stomacher may have been intended to evoke the Elizabethan period, since two cameos of the Virgin Queen are set elsewhere in the parure (see Colour Plate 103), but it is not dissimilar in shape to Queen Charlotte's bodice ornament of 1761 (Plate 3).

The enamelled settings were perhaps inspired by work produced in the French royal workshops in the 1560s, but may well have been copied from antique English pieces such as the Gresley Jewel.[44] The enamelled fleurets on the Devonshire parure spawned the 'Holbein' jewellery popular in England for about three decades (Colour Plate 107B). Conveniently for English jewellers, this tribute to the fashionable Renaissance mode required no figurative work, most pieces being set with simple cabochons instead of engraved gems. It is evident from his surviving design book that John Brogden of Henrietta Street, Covent Garden, made a series of variations on the Holbein theme, presumably for several London retailers (Colour Plate 110).

Plate 216. The Devonshire parure, designed by Henry Hugh Armstead and made by C.F. Hancock in 1856, from a chromolithograph in J.B. Waring, Masterpieces of Industrial Art and Sculpture at the International Exhibition of 1862, *at which the jewellery was shown. Commissioned by the 6th Duke of Devonshire and set with historic engraved gems from his family collection, it was designed to impress, for it was to be worn by his nephew's wife Lady Granville at the elaborate festivities accompanying the coronation of the Tsar Alexander II in 1856. The Crimean War was over and English politicians were well aware that the French were investing heavily in their representation at the coronation in the hope of re-opening trade with Russia. When Lord Granville was appointed Ambassador Extraordinary by Queen Victoria that he might represent her in Russia, he informed his wife Marie of the honour. She 'danced a hornpipe and lamented that it would be necessary to buy twenty gowns and have her diamonds reset'. They were fortunately assisted by the immensely rich bachelor Duke. In 1857 the* Illustrated London News, *probably prompted by Hancock, declared that the parure 'has been valued at upwards of £20,000'.*

The Devonshire parure was mislaid on its way to Russia, though retrieved in time for Lady Granville to wear it at the Ambassador's state ball at Moscow.[45] It was subsequently exhibited at Manchester early in 1857, worn again by Lady Granville at a state ball given by Queen Victoria at Buckingham Palace in the same year, shown at the Archaeological Institute in London in 1861 and at the International Exhibition held in London the following year.[46] Hence its inclusion in Wallis' report. Though far from a beauty, Lady Granville (Plate 217), must have looked spectacular when she wore the suite in full fig. The combination of sixteenth and early nineteenth century themes distanced the set from the historicist exercises in neo-classical design made for the Empress Eugénie.

Lord & Lady Granville.

Plate 217. Granville Leveson Gower, 2nd Earl Granville and his wife Marie Louise, the only child of Emeric Joseph, Duc de Dalberg and widow of Sir Richard Acton; they were married in 1840, when he was twenty-five. She wore the Devonshire parure at the coronation festitivities in Russia.

BY COURTESY OF MRS ELIZABETH BONYTHON

Plate 218. Mrs Samuel Wilson, the wife of the Lord Mayor of London in 1838. In formal dress, she is shown wearing a narrow tiara front with a shaped crest, long earrings, a necklace with cross, a bracelet, rings and a large stomacher with flowers and foliage and vine armlets. MANSION HOUSE

Designers with antiquarian inclinations appear to have been responsible for comparatively few parures. Pugin designed only two suites of jewellery, the most important being the one shown at the Great Exhibition (Colour Plates 83 and 100). Froment-Meurice, Rudolphi and Jules Wièse,[47] formerly the head of Froment-Meurice's workshop, the brothers Fannière[48] and other goldsmith-jewellers working in Paris displayed many single items at exhibitions though naturally making suites for patrons.

Outside antiquarian circles women, at least on informal occasions, happily broke with the old conventions respecting the wearing of jewellery. Jane Welsh Carlyle accompanied friends when they paid a morning call in August 1842 on Lady Agnes Byng at Livermere in Suffolk. They found her ruralising under a beech tree in her garden, wearing 'a white-flowered muslin pelisse, over pale blue satin; a black lace scarf fastened against her heart with a little gold horse-shoe; her white neck tolerably revealed, and set off with a brooch of diamonds; immense gold bracelets, an immense gold chain...'[49]

In 1838, the year of Queen Victoria's coronation, many women still wore their hair in ringlets clustered high about their temples like Mrs Samuel Wilson, the wife

Colour Plate 95. A spray brooch set with brilliant-cut pastes in silver cut-down collets. The articulated pendants à pampilles *are similarly set and were intended to sway as the wearer moved. Probably French; c.1850.*

VICTORIA AND ALBERT MUSEUM

of the Lord Mayor of London (Plate 218). On account of her ringlets, Mrs Wilson has a narrow tiara front with a shaped top of a type introduced a few years earlier (see Colour Plate 72); her armlets appear to represent vines.

The newer smooth coiffures with bands drawn over the ears permitted the resumption of wider tiaras and even full wreaths, whether of leaves or, more usually, of foliage and flowers. Bapst et neveu admittedly made more conventional head ornaments for their royal patrons. The firm executed a ray diadem for the Empress Eugénie in 1863; though closely resembling Queen Victoria's, the French example was known as a Russian diadem, as it had been copied from one worn by a Russian Grand-Duchess at a ball given in her honour at Compiègne. This was followed in 1856 by their first version of a Greek diadem, again for Eugénie, its profile pierced with a fret.[50] But pieces such as these were few in comparison with naturalistic or near naturalistic wreaths. It is often difficult to discover from contemporary reports which of these were milliners' ornaments and which jewellers' work. Queen Victoria wore diamonds with a wreath of white roses at the christening of her daughter Helena on 25 July 1846. Her roses were possibly real, but in most instances artificial or imitation flowers were used. On a visit to Louis-Philippe and his family in France in 1843, the Queen was so impressed by the 'wreath of china asters' sported by one of the King's daughters-in-law, the Princesse de Joinville, that she sketched it in her Journal.[51]

Another perceptive observer, Effie Ruskin, described the appearance of a fashionable Frenchwoman who had apparently invited her, her husband and others to a concert by Offenbach in Paris in April 1850. A quantity of green-enamelled gold leaves decorated the lady's sleeves and the front of her cloak. Her bracelets and brooch were of 'splendid emeralds and diamonds', while her elaborate coiffure was embellished with 'scarlet silk ribbon in bows and green leaves immensely large on each side' threaded through with loops of white pearls and lace hanging down behind.[52] This mixture of precious materials, ribbons, and flowers, real and artificial, was characteristic of headdresses during the 1840s and much of the 1850s. Even after the ferronnière disappeared this formidable combination of ornaments was further embellished with jewellery, including high-galleried combs of tortoiseshell and metal,[53] the latter often set with coral or stones. The ferronnière was replaced by a bandeau or perhaps with diamond stars, a fashionable revival of a popular neo-classical device. Mounted on bands or on stalks as pins, they were greatly favoured. An Englishwoman at the Paris Opera in 1847 was seen to have decorated her back hair with stars. The same device decorated three velvet bands in another coiffure observed in Paris in 1851; the bands were joined on each side by a ribbon rosette with a diamond daisy in its centre and diamond fringes on trailing ribbons.[54]

The Parisian jewellers Marret et Baugrand were awarded a *Médaille d'Honneur* in 1855 for a collection of jewellery which included a garland of cornflowers so delicately mounted that the slightest breath set the flowers trembling.[55] Probably, in the manner of the 1850s, the garland passed across the top of the head to form a cluster on each side, from which foliage or flowers, sometimes with butterflies hovering over them, trailed down towards the shoulders. Though sprigs might still be worn in the hair they were almost eclipsed by garlands (Plate 212).

Ephemeral fashions were inspired by literature, operas and dramas. Among the most notable instances, La Motte Fouqué's romance of the sea nymph, *Undine*, first published in German in 1814 but afterwards translated into several languages, had infiltrated French fashions by 1848, when the Undine coiffure of seaweed 'mixed with light clusters of diamond grains' was reported to be as fashionable as Ceres wreaths.[56] Alexandre Soumet's drama *Norma* inspired the '*couronne Norma*, of oak leaves intermixed with small golden acorns'.[57] Ten years later the same motifs turned up in the guise of the *couronne Ristori* in honour of the great actress who had recently performed in *Medea*.[58]

Side combs were still produced in the 1840s and later, but figure only occasionally in fashion reports. Pins remained popular, often retaining their large and elaborate heads on diminished stalks. Flower heads imitating nature were varied by others which were shaped or spherical, made of solid gold and silver or in filigree, plain, enamelled or adorned with cameos, pearls and stones, and often hung with pendants on chains. Effie Ruskin was greatly struck by the pins with huge pear-shaped pearl heads surmounted by little diamond coronets which secured Princess Esterházy's gold lace headdress at a ball in Verona in 1852.[59] Arrow-headed pins were remarked, as were daggers worn by devotees of Romantic medievalism.[60] Double pins connected by chains were worn in the coiffure as well as on bodices. Sometimes their heads matched, but they were also made in contrasting shapes and materials.

Necklaces fell into two main categories, those comprising massed units with shaped outlines linked together and others inspired by late eighteenth and early

Plate 219. An opal and brilliant suite, a wood-engraved illustration of jewellery contributed by Hunt & Roskell to the Great Exhibition of 1851, from the Official Illustrated Catalogue. *The different units at the back of the festooned necklace, two floral and one bow-shaped, exemplify the current fashion for asymmetry. In contrast to the naturalism of the other pieces, the ribbon-bound brooch in the centre anticipates a greater formality in design.*

nineteenth century festooned types. A free interpretation of the latter with a naturalistic diamond device in front and opal bead festoons at the back was among several similar pieces shown by Hunt & Roskell at the Great Exhibition (Plate 219).

Queen Victoria's Turkish diamond necklace of 1838 was festooned (Plate 162), reflecting a taste which was also apparent in France. In the same year the *Court Magazine* noted the French demand for necklaces in which coral cameos were linked by fine chains.[61] Presumably the cameos came from the coral-working factories in Paris and Marseilles. More modest evidence of nostalgia were velvet necklaces (and bracelets) fastened with a 'brooch or pin of brilliants or marcasite,' cited in 1851.

Necklets, interpreted as elaborate pendants depending from integral chains, were current by the late 1840s. An example consisting of a brilliant bird suspended from a star, with a carbuncle heart in its beak, was presented in 1856 to Mademoiselle Piccolomini by Benjamin Lumley, the operatic impresario and manager of Her Majesty's Theatre in Haymarket. The singer's success in *Don Pasquale* was symbolised in the 'bird which seizes upon all hearts... a star in the ascendant.'[62]

Colour Plate 96. A fitted case stamped in gold: RUDOLPHI./BD des CAPUCINES, 23/PARIS *contains an oxidised silver bracelet with two cast cherubs nestling among vines and rococo foam ornament above an open quatrefoil setting with a cabochon emerald; further emeralds in gold slip settings decorate each side. Perhaps designed by Masson; c.1851.* Victoria and Albert Museum

Detachable pendants continued to be made; heart shapes, ovals and circles were popular. Crosses occurred in diminishing numbers. Some pendants doubled as brooches and were supplied for the purpose with dual fittings. Among these is a set of about 1854 by Froment-Meurice (Plate 220A). Nominally comprising a gold pendant and two brooches in the Renaissance style, set with coral cameos of Bacchus, Apollo and Venus, the pieces were all originally furnished with alternative fittings, though the brooch pin is now missing from the pendant and

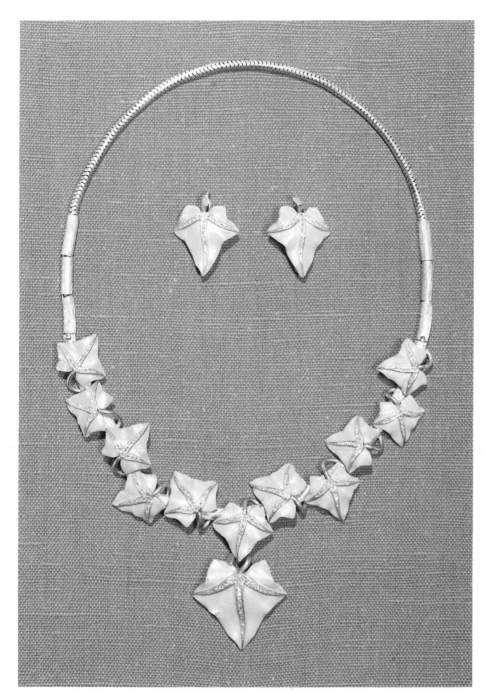

only the hinge and catch remain. The two brooches must have been designed primarily as sleeve clasps.

Lockets, usually comprising two parts hinged together with glazed recesses for mementoes, were increasingly fashionable, but pendants were still often fitted at the back with gold-rimmed, glass-fronted boxes. From the late 1840s and early 1850s both lockets and pendant lockets sheltered photographs more frequently than painted miniatures, though the traditional curls of hair remained popular. Enamelled pendants of all kinds were much in vogue; some were counterset with stones, often representing flowers, emblematic or otherwise. The forget-me-not motif persisted, but geometric devices were again fashionable.

A locket adorned with three interlacing lozenges and set with rubies, diamonds and pearls was among the jewellery commissioned in 1858 from Harry Emanuel for presentation to the Comtesse de Persigny, the wife of the retiring French Ambassador.[63] In the same year Queen Victoria purchased a 'Colored Stone Alhambra Locket' from Garrard's.[64] Six years earlier the firm had made a great table centre with a kiosk on the Prince Consort's instructions, its enamelled decoration based on Jones and Goury's *Plans, Elevations, Sections and Details of the Alhambra* (1842-5). It is now in Kensington Palace.

The neck-chains worn by women were no longer so conspicuous an article of dress (Colour Plate 102). Lord de Ros acquired a 'small Gold jazroon Neck Chain' for his wife in 1839 for £2.12s; Mrs de Rothschild purchased a 'very solid Gold Guard Chain with Slide' for £20 in the same year, perhaps intended as a present for a male relative. Fontenay held that the heavy stamped links introduced in the 1820s began to give way after 1830 to more supple articles known as *chaînes-sautoirs*, worn round the neck and supplied with a gem-set slide and the usual appendages such as watches. However Dafrique, who popularised substantial chains, exhibited specimens in 1851, establishing that there was still a market for them.

The Brazilian or snake variety (Colour Plate 91) presented a smooth outer surface to the slides, which were moved up and down to draw the chains together. A 'gold secret link Neck chain' sold by Garrard's at a cost of £6.6s. in 1843 may be a specimen of the type, which was already in widespread circulation when produced by machine from the late 1850s. Hair chains were still much worn.

Fastenings were much as before with a few innovations; S-shaped hooks on necklaces came in with archaeological jewellery. The Exeter firm of Henry Ellis & Son showed specimens of their patented brooches in 1851, their long pins sheathed by separate units linked by chains, and produced innumerable variations on the device for decades afterwards (Plate 221).[65]

Most earring types current in the early 1830s persisted into the early years of Queen Victoria's reign. Garrard's sold a pair of filigree top and drop earrings to

Plate 220. A. A demi-parure by Froment-Meurice in gold set with coral cameos of Apollo, Bacchus and Venus and hung with pearls. The winged figures on the frames, terminating in fish tails on the pendant and in foliated consoles on the brooches, typify the jeweller's interest in Renaissance design. Dating to about 1854, when he was at the height of his fame, the brooches are stamped F. MEURICE and struck with Paris warranty marks for 1838 onwards, but the pendant bears an illegible maker's mark which may not be that of Froment-Meurice, which seems to confirm contemporary allegations that he frequently resorted to outworkers. This was in fact normal trade practice. The set came to the Victoria and Albert Museum in a case bearing the Froment-Meurice label. The pieces were originally supplied with fittings which allowed them all to double as brooches or pendants.
B. A sévigné and pendent heart in gold decorated in dark blue basse-taille enamel, with brilliant sprays in and around the bow and another sprig of a single flower and two leaves applied to the heart; 1840-60.
C. An enamelled gold and diamond bodice ornament designed to be worn with one brooch pinned to the shoulder and the other to the centre of the bodice (see the portrait of Mrs Vaughan, Plate 151). A watch by David Soret of Geneva (d.1780) is set under a hinged cover in the circular brooch on the left, which has a diamond star countersunk in the blue enamel and a ribbon border not dissimilar to that of the opal and diamond brooch shown by Hunt & Roskell in 1851 (Plate 219). The whole piece probably dates to mid-century, which argues that an old watch was used in the circular brooch, perhaps for sentimental reasons.
D. The diamonds in this blue-enamelled bracelet are set in cut-down collets with pronounced ribs, like those adorning the right-hand brooch in C above; c.1845. VICTORIA AND ALBERT MUSEUM

Colour Plate 99. A brilliant and ruby floral ornament composed of a series of sprigs riveted to a gold frame and wearable either as a wreath or a necklace; the independent necklace clasp (not shown) is a later replacement. Presumably designed for the smoothly-dressed coiffure fashionable from the mid-1830s until the 1860s, most ornaments of this type have been dismantled into the component sprays and disposed of separately. VICTORIA AND ALBERT MUSEUM

Lord de Ros in 1840, while supplying other clients with drops alone. Bow and girandole, tassel and butterfly earrings were current at the same time, when earrings were still very large. In 1840 the firm lengthened a pair of gold earrings 'by addition of balls and pieces between'. Alas for this client, earrings began to shrink in size and importance in about 1843. The familiar patterns often survived by being made shorter or reduced overall in scale. To compensate for the loss of length, tops without drops were expanded into large convex buttons in the

Colour Plate 100. Three items from Pugin's parure illustrated in Colour Plate 83, demonstrating his intensive use of trefoils and fleurs-de-lis. Generously decorated with champlevé enamel and set variously with carbuncles and turquoises, all unfaceted in medieval fashion, the headband (not a bracelet) is embellished with a diamond at each end and inscribed: Christi crux est mea lux *(Christ's Cross is my [guiding] light). The half-pearls so despised by Pugin are everywhere; he undoubtedly lost that battle with his manufacturer John Hardman; 1848.*

VICTORIA AND ALBERT MUSEUM

Plate 221. A design by Henry FitzCook, one of a series of drawings for safety-chain brooches sold by Henry Ellis & Son of Exeter, published in the Art Journal *in 1854. Their peculiar two-part construction, the smaller unit acting as a sheath for a long pin, was invented by Henry Samuel Ellis, the son of the firm's founder, and allowed infinite variation. Many of these brooches were said to have been made from silver mined at Coombe Martin and some were set with pebbles from the sea-shore. Queen Victoria bought five specimens depicting Kingswear Castle and the fort and Church of St Petroc on the river Dart; some designs represented birds and floral devices, while others were made as mourning jewellery. The actual production was entrusted largely to Birmingham makers, who operated under licence. This practice was analogous to that of the retailers of 'Scottish' jewellery who bought their stocks from Birmingham manufacturers. These wares were sometimes set with 'cairngorms' from South America. The Birmingham firm of Hilliard & Thomason, formerly associated with Pugin's manufacturer John Hardman, were making Ellis safety chain brooches in the late 1840s. A fellow townsman, J.H. Williams, registered designs of the same type on 2 October 1850.*

mid-1840s. Naturalism, still popular, is exemplified by the earrings in Plates 209 and 210.

In 1851 earrings were pronounced 'almost wholly out of date...except...on "state occasions".'[66] The claim, though too sweeping, nevertheless shows that these articles were no longer the subject of innovation. One of the few exceptions was provided by Hunt & Roskell, whose 1851 display included earrings in emeralds, diamonds and carbuncles adapted from the ear ornaments represented in the great Assyrian sculptures from Nimrud and Nineveh which were excavated by Layard and Rassam between 1845 and 1855.[67] No artist was credited with the idea, though Hunt & Roskell spent generously on design and the Duc de Luynes was particularly impressed by their jewellery, which, he asserted, was produced by between six and seven hundred craftsmen in the employ of the firm, the best earning between £3 and £4 a week. This was far too generous an estimate of the work-force and the firm's outworkers must have been aggregated with their own jewellers.[68] Queen Victoria, who loved earrings and continued to wear even her huge tasselled specimens at Drawing-rooms (Plate 161), bought a pair of enamelled and gold serpent earrings costing £12 in 1855, probably as a Christmas present.[69] The opal and diamond parure given by her parents to the Princess Royal on her marriage in 1858 included a pair of top and drop earrings with an intermediate motif of two large diamonds.[70] By this time, moderately long earrings were on the way back. A gold pair with fringes (Colour Plate 107A) was registered under the Designs Act on 2 March 1857 by a firm of manufacturing jewellers, Sparrow Brothers of New North Street, Red Lion Square, London. Sparrow's followed this design with another of hoops and serpents in 1859. A more orthodox hoop motif made of gold tubes enclosing coral beads was employed in 1860 by a Parisian jeweller, Felix Duval, in a set of earrings, pendant and bracelet.[71] A decade earlier the coral would have been faceted; now it was smooth and polished.

At the time of Queen Victoria's accession in 1837 brooches were so well established that small sets of jewellery were as likely, perhaps even more likely, to include a brooch or brooches as a bracelet. The established type of bodice ornament with one to three pendants was still fashionable (Plate 222). Later such appendages were often transmuted into *pampilles,* especially if the brooch itself was naturalistic. Sleeve brooches were in widespread use in the evening. A dinner or evening dress illustrated and described in the *Court Magazine* of 1839 was adorned with a gold bodice clasp, a similar clasp looping the skirt on the right side and cameos on the sleeves and shoulders.[72] In the late 1850s a new French fashion for 'epaulets' was reported, consisting of 'a costly brooch of diamonds or other jewels, fixed on one shoulder, and on the other...a bow of velvet, with flowing ends, furnished with jewelled aiguillettes [or aglets, tags with pointed terminals]. The brooch frequently represents a flower, formed of jewels of various colours.'[73]

Queen Victoria was far from being the only possessor of a stomacher composed of a set of bodice brooches (Plates 170 and 176), but single brooches predominated. Phillips Brothers showed a Garter brooch of diamonds set over blue enamel surrounding a cameo at the Great Exhibition. Priced at £220, it was illustrated in the *Art Journal* catalogue of the exhibition.[74] The great naturalistic bouquet exhibited by Hunt & Roskell (Plate 181) took apart into seven brooches and was pronounced by the Jury to be 'as rich as it was elegant' and 'but for its weight would defy criticism'.[75] The huge diamond piece in the Victoria and Albert Museum (Colour Plate 104) probably dates substantially to the late 1840s or the early 1850s. The so-called sévigné in Plate 223, made to match the Empress Eugénie's currant garland and other pieces in 1855,[76] exemplifies the continuance of organic naturalism which permeated every level of production (Plates 189, 224 and 225). Smaller naturalistic brooches representing plant and insect life were contributed by many jewellers to the Great Exhibition. The *pampilles* and other articulated pendants adorning jewelled specimens reached a peak of complexity in the mid-1850s, gradually being simplified thereafter.

Colour Plate 101. A design for an enamelled and gem-set gold brooch of ribbons interlaced with tubular components, with a fringe and looped chains. From the Brogden Design Book, its asymmetrical construction and sense of movement date it to mid-century.

VICTORIA AND ALBERT MUSEUM, PRINT ROOM
(PHOTOGRAPH, SOTHEBY'S)

C. Rowlands & Son of 146 Regent Street, a retail firm erroneously described in the *Art Journal* catalogue of the 1851 Exhibition as manufacturers, contributed a cartouche brooch of triangular construction prefiguring Armstead's design for the stomacher in the Devonshire parure.[77] Simpler pieces with strapwork and other motifs evoked the Renaissance in generalised terms.

C.F. Hancock himself sent a diamond stomacher of foliated scrolls valued at £20,000 to the Paris 1855 Exhibition. Taking a leaf out of Cole's book, Hancock ensured that his major exhibits were shown to the Queen before being despatched to Paris. The jewels, remarkable enough also to be engraved for the *Illustrated London News,* included a girdle set with the Hope Blue Diamond (now in the Smithsonian Institution) and two magnificent rubies, the whole piece said to be worth £50,000. A necklace estimated at £10,500 and an openwork tiara hung with emerald drops at £5,000 were bagatelles by comparison.[78]

The Castellani firm had yet to contribute to an international exhibition and their impact was probably the greater when they finally did so in 1862. But, like Mrs Norton (Plate 213) and others, Queen Victoria acquired an archaeological classical piece before that date (Plate 187). Garrard's also sold her a gold 'Ram's head Brooch' in 1854.[79] But this did not dampen her enthusiasm for sentimental trinkets such as eye brooches and lockets. Sir William Ross appears to have received £6.6s. for eye miniatures of the Queen's half-sister, Feodora, Princess Hohenlohe, and her cousin Victoire de Nemours in 1843. After the latter's death

Colour Plate 102. Inès Moitessier was twenty-three years old when Ingres was asked to paint her in 1844. He had immense difficulties with the painting, abandoned it in 1849 and eventually began another of Madame Moitessier standing which is in the National Gallery of Art, Washington. The artist changed his mind about the lady's headdress and jewellery in the second portrait, asking her to replace her brooch as it was too dated. The painting was completed in 1851. The following year Ingres returned to the first portrait, twice changing his mind about the sitter's dress until settling on a chintz gown spread over one of the new crinolines. The jewellery too is in the latest mode, from her cartouche-shaped enamel brooch in the Renaissance style with a cabochon in the centre to the lower bracelet on her left hand which together with her ring demonstrate the influence of neo-classical design. A delicate neck-chain disappears into her bodice. 1856.

NATIONAL GALLERY

Plate 222. A French bridal costume, from the Petit Courrier des Dames of 31 May 1840. The bride wears long earrings with trefoil-shaped drops, a necklace of units linked by chain and a bodice ornament with a trefoil shaped motif and three drops.

Plate 223. The Empress Eugénie's bodice ornament, then described as a sévigné though it is certainly not bow-shaped, was part of her parure inspired by the homely currant bush (see Plate 189). Like the rest of the suite, this piece was designed by Alfred Bapst and executed by Bapst et neveu for 1,850 francs in 1855. The ornament, set with 321 brilliants weighing in all 173 metric carats, was bought by Tiffany's of New York for 120,100 francs at the sale of the French Crown Jewels in 1887. The large stone in the rosette at the top had decorated the comb in the diamond parure made for the Empress Marie-Louise in 1810. The diamond chains were costume accessories and could be taken apart and reconstituted as the Empress desired. (Shown smaller than actual size.)   PHOTOGRAPH FROM THE TWINING COLLECTION, GOLDSMITHS' HALL

in 1857 the Queen commissioned a replica of the eye miniature of Victoire which she gave to the Duc de Nemours.[80]

Bracelets were made and worn in profusion while armlets waned in importance. Mesh bands continued to be worn, as did bracelet strings, but many were old pieces, retained perhaps for sentimental reasons (Plate 226). However detachable clasps were still produced, which confirms that the old method of bracelet construction was obsolescent rather than obsolete.

The most fashionable bracelets at the outset of this period had an integral gem-set centre and narrow tapering jointed bands with engraved or chased scrolling ornament and, as an optional extra, one or more pendants. Considerable ingenuity went into the construction of hinged bands. The spider and fly bracelet given by Prince Albert to Victoria in 1842 (Colour Plate 94A) is closer to a bangle, as the band consists of two parts with a single hinge and a spring fastening. A naturalistic specimen decorated with pearls, brilliant flowers and green enamelled

Plate 224. A. A porcelain rose wreath brooch similar to the naturalistic pieces produced in parian from the late 1840s by Minton's and Mrs Brougham.
B and C. Two parian brooches, probably made for bridal gifts; c.1870.   PRIVATE COLLECTION

leaves and costing some £35 was shown by Phillips Brothers at the Great Exhibition; the same firm also contributed a ribbon bracelet enamelled with musical quotations.[81]

The construction of hinged bands was further varied by Marchand, who attached a trellis of struts to the backs of stamped components which allowed the stamped units to be extended as the bracelet was slipped over the hand.[82] Most bracelets were constructed of components hinged or linked by smaller devices or rings. Woven hair bands, which possessed a natural elasticity, remained fashionable throughout the period.

Several bracelets of differing designs were worn on the same arm, often placed over gloves, as in earlier decades. The serpent variety was still in vogue, even infiltrating mass-produced work, in which snakes were often suggested by looping tubes of metal without any attempt to represent a head. Effie Ruskin, intent on changing a bracelet chosen for her by her husband at Bautte et Compagnie of Geneva in May 1849, returned with him later in the year and emerged from the shop the proud possessor of a serpent 'with an opal head crawling in a flower made of a single opal with green enamel leaves'. They also bought a matching brooch.[83]

Colour Plate 103. An onyx cameo of Queen Elizabeth I, engraved in the sixteenth century and mounted as a locket set with diamonds and enamelled with fleurets in the so-called Holbein manner. It ornaments the diadem seen in the top left of the chromolithograph in Plate 216.

Colour Plate 104. A large bodice bouquet of brilliants and a few rose-cut diamonds set in silver laminated with gold. It was originally made in about 1850 to dismantle into smaller sprigs which might be distributed about the person, though it is likely that the three leaf and berry sprays date to the 1830s and were added subsequently. The lustre of the bouquet was enhanced in wear, as the largest blossoms were mounted on tremblers. The last owner, Lady Cory, who bequeathed her extensive collection of eighteenth and nineteenth century jewellery to the Victoria and Albert Museum in 1951, is said to have appeared resplendent in the bouquet and other items on first nights at Covent Garden before the Second World War. The range of flowers, including roses, a carnation, a chrysanthemum and a fuschia, are comparable with those in the bouquet shown by Hunt & Roskell at the Great Exhibition (Plate 181).

Plate 225. An orange blossom brooch in porcelain and enamelled gold in its original fitted case with the label of Hunt & Roskell; c.1845. This piece is directly comparable with Queen Victoria's orange blossom jewellery (Colour Plate 78), but the Queen herself claimed no exclusive right to the design and, indeed, purchased an opal and enamel brooch with the same motif from Garrard's as an archery prize in 1847. Another firm patronised by the Queen and Prince Albert, Turner's of New Bond Street, supplied Miss Anne Anson, daughter of General Sir William Anson and a cousin of George Anson, the Prince's private secretary, with six orange blossom pins in enamelled gold on 14 February 1846. Five days later, when she married the Rev William Thornton, Vicar of Dodford, she distributed the pins among her bridesmaids. BRITISH MUSEUM, HULL GRUNDY COLLECTION

An article in the English edition of *Le Follet* dilated at length on bracelets in 1850 citing, amongst other patterns, dark blue enamelled ribbons with bow fastenings and fringes or buckles, some comprising large links with traditional engraved padlocks and various pendants; Plate 227 shows a jewelled variety. Snake bracelets

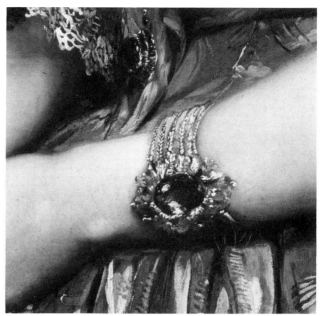

Plate 226A. A detail of Miss Laing's arm, showing the bracelet with a large clasp and plaited chain band.

FITZWILLIAM MUSEUM, CAMBRIDGE

Plate 226. Miss Laing, painted by Leighton against the clarity of an Italian sky in 1854, wearing a bracelet analogous to the one owned by Baroness Anselm de Rothschild in 1827 (Plate 144). It had perhaps belonged to her mother or another member of her family.

now encircled the arm up to three times (Plate 228): 'Those made of gold and silver mixed, forming scales, with emerald eyes and ruby tongue, are extremely beautiful.'[84]

Bracelets in every current style figured at the Great Exhibition. A fine naturalistic example by Hunt & Roskell was engraved for the *Illustrated London News.* Filigree interpretations were shown by A. Payen of Boulevard Saint Denis, Paris, a manufacturer specialising in goods for export.[85] The use of photographs in bracelets came a little later. Garrard's set many photographs for the Queen and the Prince, some in lockets to hang from bracelets, others in the bracelet band itself. An unrecorded number was put in an oxidised silver bracelet ornamented with carbuncles made for the Queen in 1857 while twelve were mounted for her in 1860 in another of the same metal, without stones.[86]

A French fashion for *manchette* or cuff bracelets, which rose to a peak in the late 1850s and early 1860s (Plate 229B), may have influenced the design of a 'double ruffle Gold Bracelet' purchased by the Queen from Garrard's for £13.5s. in 1859.[87] She certainly owned a specimen in 1861. In a letter to her daughter, the Princess Frederick William of Prussia, describing how she had spent her wedding anniversary on 10 February 1861, the Queen remarked 'Dear Papa gave me a beautiful bracelet which he got at Coburg — from Gotha — a large elastic gold bracelet like a cuff — and so pretty.'[88]

Chatelaines were back in fashion and Rudolphi offered a selection of silver specimens at the Great Exhibition. Chatelaines carrying a watch and key 'and a thousand other fancies' were an essential part of indoor costume by 1852,

Plate 227. A diamond-set curb chain bracelet fastened by a heart-shaped padlock furnished with a gold key attached by a chain. This dates to c.1840-50, but the sentimental conceit of the padlock persisted for decades, gaining a new lease of life at the end of the nineteenth century. WARTSKI

Plate 228. A serpent bracelet decorated with dark blue basse-taille *enamel, the eyes, head and hinges marked by brilliants set in silver. Two of the hinged sections are visible inside the coils. French gold warranty marks, c.1840.* GARRARD & COMPANY

according to a fashion report.[89] Buckles were however pronounced out of fashion in morning dress in 1837.[90] Though they regained lost ground to some extent thereafter they were never much discussed by fashion correspondents, whose interest had shifted to such items as studs, jewelled buttons and pins which variously fastened wristbands, collars, girdles and other parts of the clothing.

Rings were sturdier than in earlier decades, often having elaborate hoops, though many of the types popular before Victoria's accession were still worn. Garter and buckle rings were popular. Serpents, suitably enamelled, served their turn as decorative or mourning rings. Queen Victoria purchased a gold union ring as late as 1857. A '5 stem brilliant Wykeham Ring' was among the gifts taken by the Queen on her State visit to France in 1855, while a 'Sapphire & Diamond Cross' ring was included in the presents she distributed in Germany in 1860.[91] Jewelled half hoops were still much in demand. One of Garrard's clients bought a solitaire ring in 1838 as well as a ring with a hair braid and a diamond head; an example with a gold filigree ball suspended from a chain was sold to another customer the same year.

In 1838 Garrard's supplied a client with two enamelled mourning rings set with diamonds at £8.8s. apiece and a similar but smaller specimen at £6.6s.; a fourth, enamelled only, cost £4.4s. The charge for engraving these was 9s. in all. Pugin's

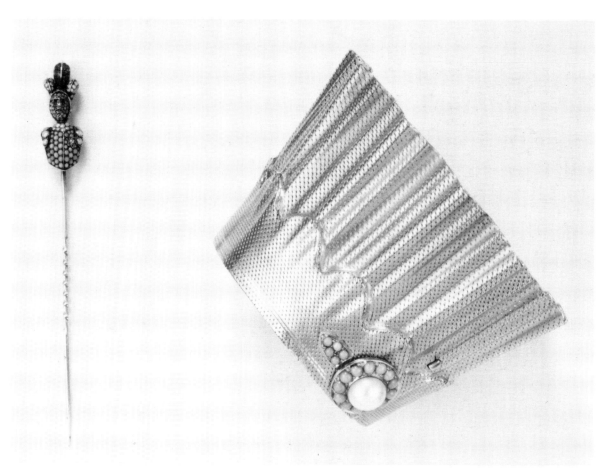

Plate 229. A. A gold stock or scarf pin with a helmeted bust of St George with roses, rubies, pearls and pavé-set turquoises. Made by John Whenman of Clerkenwell and shown at the North London Working Classes Industrial Exhibition of 1864, at which he received 'a first prize certificate'.
B. A gold manchette or cuff bracelet, textured in imitation of cloth, with a button and buttonhole represented by a large pearl and turquoises. Possibly English, c.1860. VICTORIA AND ALBERT MUSEUM

hated half pearls still decorated many standard mourning rings. Signet rings were popular; armorials, ciphers or crests were mainly engraved on carnelian or onyx, or on gold shields or cartouches.

Scalloped or shaped ring heads were set with miniatures or, later, with photographs. Specimens set with cameos were still in demand. Other examples were made in the current mood of nostalgia, evoking the late eighteenth century practice of setting diamonds over dark blue paste. Vever remarked that the Parisian manufacturing jeweller Frédéric Phillipi, born in Hanover, had made a speciality of rings having oval heads with diamond borders surrounding glass paste counterset with diamond sprigs. He turned them out in quantity from 1860.[92]

The growing popularity of jewellery studs and buttons in male as well as female costume led to the emergence of modest parures for gentlemen, functional and usually discreet, in keeping with the new mood of sobriety in men's clothing. At Christmas 1843 Queen Victoria gave a Lord in Waiting a set of blue enamel studs decorated with diamond flies, bought from Turner's.[93] Larger suites might comprise waistcoat and sleeve buttons and studs. Cravat or stock pins, double and single, were general; though clusters of seals suspended from the waist were outmoded, a single charm, seal or small locket was frequently attached to the watch-chain.

Plate 230. Count d'Orsay, artist and gentleman of fashion, painted by Sir George Hayter in 1839, the year in which Thomas Carlyle's wife was amused by his blue and cream outfit and jewellery in which several gold chains figured prominently. He has the posture of the dandy in this portrait, but Hayter has suppressed or subdued the watch-chains, only two of which appear to run across to his waistcoat pocket on his left and another two disappear to his right. NATIONAL PORTRAIT GALLERY

Plate 231. In 1846, when Sir William Newton painted this miniature of the Right Honourable Fox Maule, the latter became Secretary of State for War at the age of about forty-five. Wearing a pink rosebud in his buttonhole and a neck-chain which disappears inside the waistcoat and emerges as two ends carried to his pocket, the future Lord Panmure and Earl of Dalhousie also has a signet ring, presumably engraved with his arms, on the little finger of his left hand. SOTHEBY'S

Long chains, looped round the neck, were still (just) admissible. Jane Welsh Carlyle was amused in 1839 by the sight of the dandy, Count d'Orsay (Plate 230), clad in blue and cream, with 'two glorious breast-pins attached by a chain, and length enough of gold watch-guard to have hanged himself in'. But D'Orsay soon caught the new mood of understatement and some five years later hove into her view in black and brown garments, wearing a single cravat pin of pearl and diamonds and 'only one fold of gold chain round his neck, tucked together right on the centre of his spacious breast with one magnificent turquoise'.[94] Fox Maule, painted by Newton in 1846 (Plate 231), sported a chain but hid the slide beneath his waistcoat. In *Dombey and Son* (1846-8), Dickens made much of Mr Dombey's consequence by constantly referring to the heavy gold watch-chain which he jingled at critical moments in the story, a feature picked up by his illustrator Hablôt Browne ('Phiz').[95]

Cheaper and shorter watch-chains were introduced in mid-century which instead of being looped round the neck were slotted into a button-hole in the waistcoat with a hook or bar at one end; the other end, bearing the watch, was carried across to a pocket. Sometimes double chains extended from the buttonhole to waistcoat pockets on each side; a single chain was naturally carried to one pocket only. This new type of chain was known in England as the Albert in homage to the Prince. A design for a section of an elaborate French watch-chain incorporating a tiny huntsman, hounds and a wild boar, by Nevillé, a designer associated with Morel, is illustrated in Vever.[96]

The pins offered for sale by Phillips Brothers at the Great Exhibition were single, not double. It is uncertain whether they were for male or female use, though the firm's chased gold brooch with a stag and dogs indicate a certain feminine interest in the portrayal of sporting pursuits. Gold pins with heads in the form of falcons, moorhens, cocks, dead game, and a sporting trophy comprising an enamelled cap, whip, fox's brush and spurs, contrasted with another topped with a bust of Shakespeare, were offered at prices upwards of £2.[97] In the same spirit, the Pre-Raphaelite painter John Everett Millais (Colour Plate 45), who was to marry Effie Ruskin in 1855, designed two gold cravat pins in 1853, one with a wild duck for his brother William and the other with a goose for himself. They were made up by Hunt & Roskell.[98] The ablest modeller and chaser of animal pins and charms in France was Hubert Obry,[99] the son of a former huntsman to the Duc de Berri. One of Obry's associates was Honoré Bourdoncle, who worked on some of the first and best aluminium jewellery (see Colour Plate 86).

Children's jewellery changed very little. Little girls wore earrings and infants of both sexes were still adorned with gold and coral necklaces. While in Venice in 1849 Effie Ruskin had wanted to buy 'some of the pretty gold & coral necklaces with charms hanging at the end' for her little sisters and a cousin but desisted when she discovered that they cost rather more than £3 each. The following month she visited Murano and went over a factory making glass beads, acquiring 'an immense bunch' of small beads for 2s.6d. and ordering more expensive red ones. She hoped to get 'pretty clasps for them at Genoa where they work gold so beautifully'.[100]

Queen Victoria's Journal is a useful source of information about the jewellery given to her children. Some gifts, of course, were not intended to be worn until the recipients had attained a suitable age. Prince Albert's father, for instance, sent 'a fine diamond brooch' as a christening present to Victoria, the Princess Royal, in February 1841. The Duchess of Kent gave the child her miniature set in a small wreath of diamonds, with a row of pearls, and King Leopold of the Belgians 'a splendid diamond & turquoise Cross'.[101] On her first birthday, the infant Princess received from her great-aunts, the Duchess of Gloucester and Princess Sophia, a pearl necklace and bracelets which had belonged to Queen Charlotte, but the Duchess of Kent gave her granddaughter 'a little necklace of coral & gold', clearly for immediate use.[102] As the Princess grew older, she received gifts of money with which to buy pearls; later still, when she was fourteen years old, the Queen purchased from Hunt & Roskell six fine oriental pearls and four smaller ones, the cost of which was partly met from Vicky's own income.[103] The pearls went to the making of a necklace which had been begun earlier, in accordance with a practice which the Queen adopted for all her daughters and later (though increasingly reluctantly in view of the numbers involved) for her granddaughters.

In 1855, now almost grown up, the young Princess Royal was enchanted by the elegance of the Empress Eugénie who paid a state visit to England with the Emperor Napoleon III. The Empress generously gave the Princess her own 'beautiful watch of rubies and diamonds, and a beautiful little chain, seal and watch-key to it. It was so kind of her', wrote the Queen, 'Vicky was in ecstasies'.[104]

The jewellery of the royal sons is less well documented, but an entry in the Queen's Journal is worth noting. Prince Alfred, her second son, joined the Navy at the age of fourteen. On the eve of his departure in 1858 the Queen described in her Journal the parting gifts from herself and Albert to their son: 'We gave the dear Boy a small bronze cross on which was engraved tomorrow's date & the words: "Do right & fear God", on the one side & on the other "God [be] with you"...a small locket with our photographs, & of course his Chest, & outfit.'[105] The locket was presumably to be attached to his watch-chain. All boys coming from families with means owned watch-chains and the most fortunate had jewelled cravat pins. Charles Dickens' second son Walter came out 'on birthdays in a blaze of shirt pin', thanks to the generosity of the boy's godfather, Walter Savage Landor.[106]

Footnotes to Volume I

INTRODUCTION

1. Morris, *Diary,* I, p.xxxviii; in December 1789 Morris (1752-1816) took Madame de Flahaut from the Paris Opera 'to the store of Mr. Sykes where a great Number of Things are exhibited, the Manufacture of England and abominably dear.' (id., p. 354). Several English merchants set up in business in Paris, encouraged by the trade agreement of 1786.

2. Heal, p. 145; Coke, II, p. 387; Thieme Becker.

3. Charlotte Sophia of Mecklenburg-Strelitz (1744-1818) married George III (1738-1820) in London on 8 September 1761; crowned, 22 September. RA C 58/61.

4. Fox MS, ff. 52-3. Catherine II (1729-1796) ascended the throne of Russia in 1762 by the dethronement of her husband Tsar Peter III and the exclusion of her son.

5. George Prince of Wales (1762-1830); in consequence of his father's fourth and last attack of insanity Prince Regent, 1811-1820, until succeeding to the throne as George IV.

6. Liebart was recommended to Rundell's by Duval, the royal jeweller to George III (PRO C 13/69 23; Fox MS, fo. 20). Liebart designed and also set George IV's Coronation Crown in 1820; he was still with Rundell's in the 1830s (Bury, 1988, pl. 4).

7. The extended Hope family came to England in 1794 (Farington, *Diary,* 27 January 1795).

8. Fox MS, ff. 17-8.

9. RA 25643. Gouverneur Morris bought a watch from the same maker on 16 October 1789 (Morris, *Diary,* I, p. 260).

10. An incomplete set of bills for personal purchases is in the Royal Archives, Windsor Castle; other statements submitted to the Commission appointed in 1795 to manage the Prince's financial affairs are contained within the Expired Commissions, Various (H.O.73, P.R.O., Kew: see Millar, 1986, pp. 586-591).

11. George Prince of Wales, *Correspondence,* I, p. 164, letter dated 27 October 1784.

12. Maria Anne Fitzherbert (1756-1837), elder daughter of Walter Smythe; married first Edward Weld of Lulworth Castle, 1775, second Thomas Fitzherbert of Swynnerton, 1778. Her marriage to the Prince of Wales at her house in December 1785 offended against the Royal Marriage Act and the Act of Settlement on two grounds: she was a Roman Catholic and he had not sought his father's consent to the match.

13. Caroline Amelia Elizabeth of Brunswick-Wolfenbüttel (1768-1821), the daughter of Duke Charles and of Augusta, George III's sister. King George III favoured the match with his eldest son, but Queen Charlotte had heard reports of the Princess's unseemly conduct with men (George Prince of Wales, *Correspondence,* III, p. 9, letter from the Queen to the Duke of Mecklenburg-Strelitz, August 1794).

14. Princess Caroline and the Prince of Wales were married at St James's Palace on 8 April 1795, but he was immediately repelled by her disregard for cleanliness. Moreover, the Commission appointed by Parliament continued to manage his financial affairs.

15. Charlotte Augusta of Wales (1796-1817) married Prince Leopold of Saxe-Coburg in 1816 and died in childbirth the following year.

16. Frederick Augustus, Duke of York and Albany (1763-1827), the second son of George III and Queen Charlotte; he commanded the English army in Flanders, 1793-95.

17. George Prince of Wales, *Correspondence,* I, pp. 48, 56-8, 64, 91; Thomas Gray of 41 Sackville Street took William Constable into partnership briefly in the late 1790s. For his bills to the Prince of Wales: see RA 25650 and 2, 25661, 3-4, 25663-9, 25671, 25673, 25677-8 and others subsequently. The Prince also patronised Robert, then William, Gray of 13 New Bond Street (RA 25646); *passim.*

18. Frederica of Prussia (1767-1820), eldest daughter of King Frederick William II of Prussia.

19. Nathaniel Jefferys, of 70/71 Piccadilly and later of Pall Mall and a family connection of Jefferys & Jones, the royal goldsmiths; M.P. for Coventry, 1796-1803. Appointed jeweller to the Prince of Wales, 1790, he once advanced £1,600 to his royal patron to settle a pressing debt of Mrs Fitzherbert and was repaid (Wilkins, II, pp. 87-8; further information kindly supplied by Mrs Jane Wainwright).

20. George Prince of Wales, *Correspondence,* II, pp. 178, 180, 183-4, 190, 315.

21. Watkins, pp. 170-2, 177-8.

22. Fox MS, fo. 18.

23. Millar, 1986, p. 586.

24. George Prince of Wales, *Correspondence,* IV, pp. 243-4, 268-9.

25. Farington, *Diary,* 9 March 1797, 17, 27 June, 11, 24 July 1806; Wilkins suggested that Jefferys had overcharged to cover his personal extravagance and in fact had made a profit of £15,000 (Wilkins, II, p. 89). Jefferys however was bankrupted in 1797 and 1806.

26. Fox MS, fo. 18.

27. Noted by Farington in his *Diary,* 27 June 1806.

28. Lady C. Bury, I, p. 23.

29. The price appears to range from 1,600,000 to 1,800,000 livres (roughly equivalent to the franc), the difference perhaps explained by the suggestion that the Cardinal de Rohan (1734-1803) had negotiated a reduction with the jewellers (see also *Memoire* and Morel, I, 1988 pp. 205, 208). Marie Antoinette (1755-1793), Archduchess of Austria, married the future Louis XVI in 1770.

30. Madame Moitte was the wife of J.G. Moitte (1746-1810), sculptor and designer (Le Neo-classicisme, Dessins français de 1750-1825, Musée du Louvre, 1972, cat. no. 114). I am indebted to Michael Snodin for this reference; see also Schama, pp. 439-40.

31. Morris, *Diary* I, p. 231.

32. Adelaide de Filleul, adventuress and novelist; her husband, the Comte de Flahaut, was guillotined. His widow, author of *Adèle de Senanges,* etc., later married the Marquis de Souza-Botelbol, the Portuguese Ambassador to France. Her son Auguste-Charles de Flahaut (1785-1870), reputedly fathered by Talleyrand, was himself the lover of Josephine's daughter, Hortense de Beauharnais.

33. Schmidt, p. 194.

34. Vever, I, p. 13; 1989-90, New York, Age of Napoleon exhibition. A pair of guillotine earrings shown are later.

35. Herold, pp. 151-2.

36. Napoleon Bonaparte (1769-1821), born of Italian stock in Corsica, began his career as a lieutenant in a French artillery regiment, 1785.

37. Capel, *Letters,* p. 151.

38. Cobb, p. 485; see also Morris, *Diary,* II, p. 542.

39. Lieutenant-General Sir Herbert Taylor (1775-1839).

40. Taylor *Papers,* p. 30.

41. Capel, *Letters,* p. 124.

42. Jérôme Bonaparte (1784-1860); Napoleon arranged his dynastic marriage to the daughter of Frederick, King of Württemberg, in 1807.

43. Lawrence, pp. 34-5.

44. Nicolas (Jean de Dieu) Soult (1769-1851), Duc de Dalmatie, commanded the French army in Spain from 1808 to 1811 and again in 1814.

45. Madame de la Tour du Pin, p. 338.

46. Josephine Tascher de la Pagerie (1763-1814), born in Martinique; married the Vicomte Alexandre de Beauharnais (guillotined 1794), by whom she had two children, Eugène and Hortense-Eugénie. She married Napoleon in 1796; he divorced her in 1809/10.

47. Lady Caroline Ponsonby (1785-1828), only daughter of the 3rd Earl of Bessborough and his wife Henrietta Frances, married William Lamb (1774-1848), afterwards 2nd Viscount Melbourne, in 1805 and later conducted a notorious affair with Byron.

48. Lord Granville Leveson Gower, 1st Earl Granville (1773-1846).
49. Lord Granville Leveson Gower, *Private Correspondence,* I, pp. 407-8.
50. Fiennes, p. 300.
51. Twining, 1960, pl. 56b.
52. Ibid., pl. 56c.
53. Le Corbeiller, 1970, pp. 351-8.
54. The Stadholder was the son of George II's eldest daughter, the Princess Royal.
55. Sylas Neville, *Diary,* p. 24.
56. Fitzgerald, p. 215.
57. Norwich Consistory Court Wills 1799, no. 1, Norfolk Record Office.
58. Lewis, p. 38, remarks that lead glass was first commercially exploited in England, but for vessels, not jewellery.
59. Lewis, p. 39.
60. Cited in Fontenay, p. 364.
61. The trade seems to have died out in Wolverhampton before the end of the nineteenth century but was continued in a small way in Woodstock.
62. Westwood, p. 6; the traveller was H. Misson de Valbourg.
63. The exemptions were introduced in the act of 1738 (12 George II, c.26).
64. Westwood, p. 11.
65. Ibid., p. 8.
66. Culme, 1977, pp.47-8.
67. Yogev, pp. 41, 82-180; *passim.*
68. The seventeenth century traveller Celia Fiennes noted 'Bristol Diamonds' in the collection of St John's College, Oxford, and acquired a specimen of 'Cornish Diamond' on a visit to Cornwall (Fiennes, pp. 35, 258).
69. Westwood, pp. 17-18.
70. In the collection of the Thomas Coram Foundation, Brunswick Square.
71. Timmins, 1866, Aitken, p. 292.
72. Timmins, Wright, p. 460.
73. Sir Edward Thomason, apprenticed to Matthew Boulton, set up in business in Church Street, Birmingham, in 1793. At first making plated and gilt buttons, he extended into other branches of manufacture including plate, metals and toys. Author of *Memoirs during Half a Century* (1845).
74. Niklaus von Heideloff (1761-c.1839), was patronised by Rudolph Ackermann, another immigrant.

75. Harriet Wynne encountered her in 1804 and wrote: 'I cannot reckon Mrs. Fitzherbert handsome, her nose is certainly too long.' (Wynne, *Diaries,* III, 1804, p. 109).
76. *G,* I, 1794, fig. XIV: GWL 1793-1800, id., fig. XV: GWL; id., figs. XVI-XVIII; *G,* II, fig. LVII.
77. King George III and Queen Charlotte had nine sons and six daughters. The three eldest daughters were Charlotte Augusta Matilda, Princess Royal (1766-1828), the second wife of the Hereditary Prince of Württemberg, 1797; Augusta Sophia (1768-1840), died unmarried; and Elizabeth (1770-1840), who married the Hereditary Prince of Hesse-Homberg, 1818.
78. *BA,* ns III, 1811, p. 158.
79. Alfred de Grimaud, Count d'Orsay (1801-1852), dandy and skilled amateur artist; made a marriage of convenience with Lady Harriet Gardner, the daughter of Charles, 1st Earl of Blessington (1782-1829).
80. Margaret (or Marguerite), Countess of Blessington (1789-1849), beauty, adventuress and author, born in Ireland. After the failure of her first marriage she placed herself under the protection of two gentlemen, the second of whom, the 1st Earl of Blessington, later married her. The Blessingtons lived in a notorious ménage-à-trois with d'Orsay and Lady Harriet (see fn. 79 above) was an irrelevance.
81. Sadleir, p. 88.
82. *The Select Committee on Arts and Manufactures* (henceforward SCAM) report, 1836.
83. Ibid., minutes of evidence. The engineer James Nasmyth (1808-1890) was an exception.
84. Munn, 1984, p. 14. The leading jeweller was named Sarno.
85. Truman, 1979, pp. 154-161; Hackenbroch, 1986, pp. 163-268.
86. Philadelphia 1876 exhibition, Falize report, p. 12; Fontenay, p. 369.
87. Benedetto Pistrucci (1784-1855), gem-engraver, medallist and coin engraver, born and trained in Rome. From 1817 worked at the Royal Mint, London; Chief Medallist, 1828.
88. Forrer, IV, pp. 582-620.

CHAPTER I

1. Georgiana Spencer (1757-1806), eldest child of John, 1st Earl Spencer; married William, 5th Duke of Devonshire (1748-1810), 1774. Her only son William George Spencer Cavendish, Lord Hartington (1790-1858), succeeded his father as the 6th Duke. See Bessborough, pp. 149-151, two letters to Thomas Coutts dated Paris 27 June 1789 and one received by him on 9 July, revealing that the royal jeweller Duval was among her numerous creditors.
2. Wynne, *Diaries,* I, p. 30. Elizabeth (Betsey) Wynne (b.1779), the second daughter of Richard Wynne, himself of mixed English and Italian parentage, and his French wife; married, 1797, Captain (later Vice-Admiral) Thomas Fremantle (1765-1819).
3. *Annual Register,* 1797, pp. 260-2.
4. The loan of £18,000,000 was said to be oversubscribed within three days of its launching (Cholmondeley, *Heber Letters,* p. 102); William Pitt (1759-1806), Prime Minister.
5. Adeane, pp. 212-3. Maria Josepha Holroyd (1771-1863), daughter of the 1st Earl of Sheffield, married, 1796, Sir John Thomas Stanley (1776-1850), created 1st Baron Stanley of Alderley, 1839.
6. Holland, 6 March 1800.
7. D'Arblay, *Diary and Letters,* III, p. 192. Frances (Fanny) Burney, Madame D'Arblay (1752-1840), novelist and, for a short time, Second Keeper of Queen Charlotte's robes.
8. Holland, 20, 24 December 1800.
9. Henrietta (Harriet) Frances Spencer (1761-1839), younger daughter of the 1st Earl Spencer; married, 1780, Lord Duncannon, who succeeded his father as the 3rd Earl of Bessborough, 1793.
10. Lord Granville Leveson Gower was created the 1st Earl Granville, 1833. See Introduction, fn. 48.
11. Lord Granville Leveson Gower, *Private Correspondence,* pp. 134-8; the lady concerned was Marie J. Thérèse Cabarrus (1773-1835), 'Nôtre Dame de Thermidor'; married, first, 1788, J.J. Devin, Marquis de Fontenay. Divorced, 1793, she married J.L. Tallien, 26 December 1794; he divorced her in 1802.

In 1796 Barras was one of her most prominent admirers. She was said to have ingratiated herself with Tallien, whom she abhorred, to save a friend from probable execution, and she subsequently interceded on behalf of many others similarly threatened.
12. *G,* IV, 1797, fig. CLVIII.
13. *L.M.M.,* 1, 1798, p. 228; *passim.*
14. Oliver Goldsmith, *She Stoops to Conquer,* Act III, sc. 1.
15. George Prince of Wales, *Correspondence,* II, pp. 151-2; the indenture is dated 10 May 1791.
16. Millar, 1969, cat. no. 768, pl. 106. George III had originally intended commissioning Hoppner, but changed his mind. Dupont started the portrait in June 1795.
17. Frances Twysden (1753-1821), daughter of the Rev. Philip Twysden and wife of the 4th Earl of Jersey (d.1805). Lady Jersey had been cynically sent by the Prince to escort his bride from Greenwich to London. The Prince, having given his wife the bracelets, took them back and gave them to Lady Jersey.
18. Lady C. Bury, I, pp. 23, 160.
19. Ibid., p. 43, 106; II, p. 380, no. VIb.
20. Yogev, Appendix I.
21. The first of two Gentlemen's Ledgers are still with Garrard & Company of Regent Street. The (incomplete) series of Garrard ledgers passed to the Victoria and Albert Museum includes the Workmen's Ledger of 1793-1800 listing outworkers and the commissions executed by them. A contemporary Workmen's Ledger has not survived, but the accounts are continued in another volume 1799-1808. The Gentlemen's Ledgers cited in this chapter are 1784/7-92, 1792-99 and 1800-6 etc.; a Day Book, 1797-99, has also been used.
22. *BA,* II, 1807, p. 273.
23. He was probably related to Sir John H. D'Oyly of Calcutta and D'Oyly Park, Hampshire (1754-1818), a friend of Warren Hastings and MP for Ipswich, 1790-96.
24. Martha Taylor strung four 'long rows' of garnets in June 1799, for which she charged 3s. The client was M. Packe (? a relative of C.J. Packe, see Farington, *Diaries,* 14 September 1805).

25. Mary (1726/7-1811), daughter of the 2nd Duke of Argyll and divorced wife of Edward Coke, styled Viscount Coke. Common gossip had it that Lady Mary had married George III's brother, the Duke of York but this is improbable (*Complete Peerage*, VII, 561; Noble, p. 34).

26. Mary (1761-1823), wife of George Parker, who succeeded as Earl of Macclesfield, 1795. She was Lady of the Bedchamber to Queen Charlotte, 1811-18.

27. See Swann, pl. 32, for a black japanned shoe buckle set with black pastes.

28. Matthew Boulton (1728-1809); Josiah Wedgwood (1730-1795), potter.

29. Boulton Letter Books, Birmingham Assay Office.

30. James Tassie (1735-1799), modeller, born in Glasgow. In collaboration with Dr Quin in Dublin, developed the vitreous glass which he used for casting from antique gems and also from wax portrait medallions modelled from life. Arrived in London 1766; three years later was invited by Wedgwood to furnish him with cameos and intaglios. R.E. Raspe compiled a *Descriptive Catalogue* of Tassie's gems in 1791. William Tassie (1777-1860) issued an enlarged edition in 1816.

31. Heal, p. 137; noted as in Brewer Street in 1796.

32. A solution of salt, alum and saltpetre was favoured in the nineteenth century (and probably before). It was heated and the article immersed in it. The alloy was dissolved off the surface which was cleaned by dipping it in nitric acid.

33. Holden's *Triennial Directory* for 1805-07. Neither of the two Delauneys employed occasionally by Garrard's appear in Heal's *London Goldsmiths, 1200-1800*.

34. Cited in Evans, 1970, p. 171.

35. Westwood, p. 44; Birmingham Gold and Silver 1773-1973, Birmingham City Museum and Art Gallery, 1973, B 33, 82, *passim*.

36. Oman, 1974, p. 73 and fn. 10.

37. Zick, pl. 12; *passim*.

38. Wynne, *Diaries*, I, pp. 17, 219.

39. Lybbe Powys, p. 294; cf. Marquardt, p. 257, cat. no. 411. Stephany & Dresch exhibited work at the Royal Academy in 1791 and 1793 (see Tait, I, 1984, cat. nos.

187-8, 191, 193).

40. Introduction, fn. 77.

41. Tait, 1984, I, cat. no. 12; II, fig. 3.

42. RA Add. C.58.61, fo. 39.

43. Fontenay, p. 421, and emerald and diamond star and crescent ornament in the Sotheby jewellery sale of 3 October 1974 (lot 256).

44. Lady Mary Wortley Montagu (1689-1762); spent 1716-18 in Constantinople with her husband, the Ambassador Edward Wortley Montagu. On her return to England, she introduced the practice of inoculation for small-pox.

45. Adeane, p. 283.

46. Clifford Smith, pl. XLVII.

47. G, II, 1795, fig. LIX.

48. Ibid., IV, 1797, fig. CLIX.

49. Ibid., II, 1795, fig. LIII.

50. Marquardt, 1983, fig. 26.

51. G, IV, 1797, fig. CLXI; II, 1795, fig. L.

52. Ibid., VII, 1800, fig. CCLXV.

53. Wilkins, II, pp. 222-3.

54. Blathwayt Papers, D.1799. Gloucester Record Office.

55. Lady Fanny Chambers was about thirty-four years old when she sat to Smart.

56. Lady Eleanor Butler (c.1740/45-1829), sister of the 17th Earl of Ormonde, fled from Ireland with Miss Sarah Ponsonby; they set up house together in the vale of Llangollen, Wales.

57. Leslie, 1939, Appendix I; *Hamwood Papers*, p. 65. The brothers were the sons of John, 3rd Earl of Darnley.

58. Millar, 1986, p. 587.

59. Often expressed in French.

60. S. Bury, 1985; endpaper.

61. Millar, 1969, I, cat. no. 666.

62. G, I, 1794, figs. XVI-XVIII.

63. Millar, 1969, I, p. 22, pl. X; the King and Queen disliked Lawrence's portrait.

64. Vever, I, p. 63 (*ill.*).

65. Millar, 1969, I, cat. no. 798.

66. Two of a set of three bodice bows set with diamonds are illustrated in Evans, 1970, pl. 154; mistakenly described as English, c.1770, the set (part of the Cory Bequest in the Victoria and Albert Museum) came from the Russian Crown Jewels and may have been the work of Louis Duval of St Petersburg, court jeweller.

67. Wynne, *Diaries*, II, p. 56. Ratisbon was the seat of the

Imperial Diet of Germany, 1663-1806. Its large Roman Catholic community was sympathetic to the French royalist cause.

68. Bury, 1984, pl. 42A.

69. Note in Garrard Ledger.

70. Oman, 1974, pl. 84B etc.

71. Mr Trefusis was a member of a well-known Cornish family; G, I, 1794, figs. XXVII, XLIII.

72. Adeane, p. 389, letter to Miss Ann Firth, 30 May 1796.

73. Twiss, quoted by Thompson, p. 165; many men, Twiss noted, wore plain gold earrings, but officers and other gentlemen displayed specimens 'as large as a half-crown piece.' Lybbe Powys, p. 294. Joachim Murat also wore earrings.

74. Wynne, *Diaries*, II, entry dated '10th Tuesday,' 1798.

75. Swann (Introduction); a deputation of unemployed bucklemakers from Birmingham, Walsall and Wolverhampton petitioned the Prince of Wales in 1791 and their London counterparts Queen Charlotte in 1792, resulting in buckles being formally required in Court dress.

76. Patent no. 1427, 17 April 1784. Five years later Samuel Hand patented another form of fastening using double S loops (Swann, '1760's-1790's').

77. Patent no. 1908, 1792.

78. I am indebted to Mrs Jane Vickers and Mr A.H. Westwood for their help in elucidating the genealogy of the Smith family and the connection with Boulton. The jeweller John Lander, inventor of another 'Elastic Shoe Latchet', joined them in 1794 (see also Grimwade, 1976, p. 661).

79. Bradbury, pp. 4-7, 22-3.

80. Lord Granville Leveson Gower, *Private Correspondence*, I, p. 83.

81. Garrard's furnished a few Orders and Stars to their clients, but these were modest.

82. Lady Hamilton exhibition, Iveagh Bequest, Kenwood, 1972, cat. no. 85, pl. IV, portrait of Nelson with the jewel in his hat by Leonardo Guzzardi, 1799, from the Museo di San Martino, Naples. In a portrait by Sir William Beechey, 1800-1 (Leggatt Trustees) the *chelengk* appears on Nelson's chest.

83. LeFanu, p. 183. Hoppner's portrait of the Sackville children, 1797, in the Metropolitan Museum, New

York, shows Lady Mary Sackville (1792-1864) wearing a coral necklace.

84. Mrs Delany, *Autobiography and Correspondence*, III, p. 412.

85. George Prince of Wales, *Correspondence*, III, p. 309. The 'dear Sisterhood' were the Prince of Wales' unmarried sisters, kept in attendance on their mother.

86. Wynne, *Diaries*, I, pp. 54, 134.

CHAPTER II

1. Fox MS, p. 13.

2. Thomas Gray is said to have been a Streatham innkeeper whose cockfighting mains attracted the Prince of Wales. Impressed by Gray's knowledge of jewellery, the Prince suggested he open a shop in London. See brochure issued by Messrs. Collingwood of Conduit Street; Culme, I, pp. 89-90.

3. The Delafons firm appears in the Garrard Workmen's Ledger, 1793-1800. They probably continued to work for Garrard's and other firms in addition to selling direct to private clients.

4. RA 25954, Delafons & Sons, 'Successors to Mr. Thos. Gray,' of 11 Sackville Street.

5. RA 25925, 'J. Kitching. From Mr. T. Gray, Sackville Street, & Nephew to the late Mr. Constable'. The ledger is owned by Kitching's successors, Messrs. Collingwood.

6. RA 25956, 25965.

7. RA 25686; entries dated 12 January, 15 March 1793; the latter earrings may refer to the bitter opposition expressed by leading Whigs to Pitt's declaration of war against France in February 1793.

8. RA 25960; Culme, I, p.398. Rundell's absorbed Duval's.

9. Bury, 1987, pp. 158-9.

10. Charles Muss (1779-1824), artist in stained glass and enamelist.

11. Probably the designer of a medal engraved by T. Wyon commemorating the centenary of the Union of England and Scotland, 1807; Forrer, III, p. 599. RA 25657; Martyn's bill in 1784 amounted to £1412.7s.6d.

12. RA 25648. Charles James Fox (1749-1806), Whig politician, friend and adviser of the Prince of Wales, was later to claim for him the inherent right to the Regency during George III's bout of insanity, 1788-89.

13. RA 25648; Heal, p. 192.
14. RA 25687. Joachim Smith, modeller in wax and gem-engraver, worked for Wedgwood & Bentley; executed a portrait of Mrs Fitzherbert; Forrer, V, p. 553, VIII, p. 209.
15. RA 26272.
16. RA 26256; RA 25979.
17. RA 25698.
18. RA 25996; Tait, 1984, Gere, cat. no. 899. But another ring in the Hull Grundy Collection (op. cit., cat. no. 845), firmly assigned to Pistrucci, probably appears against the date 26 April 1821 in Rundell's bill (RA 26021): 'A fine Cornelian Ring with Intaglio of His Majesty, polished inside, with Brilliant & Turquoise on the shoulders', costing £31.10s.
19. RA 26003.
20. For J. Barber, see Forrer, I, p. 122.
21. Tait, 1984, I, Gere, cat. no. 389.
22. Bury, 1982, Case 17, Board E, 10 (erroneously dated 1821).
23. William Beckford (1759-1844), author of *Vathek;* notable patron and collector and occasional Member of Parliament; his gothic revival mansion, Fonthill, housed much of his collection. His daughter Susan Euphemia (b.1786) married the Marquis of Douglas (1767-1852), later 10th Duke of Hamilton. Her son, afterwards the 11th Duke, married Princess Marie of Baden (1818-1888), 1843.
24. RA 25698; Vever, I, p. 11.
25. Maria Carolina (1752-1814), Archduchess of Austria, married, 1768, Ferdinand IV of Naples and III of Sicily (1751-1825). She had seventeen children. Though friendly towards Sir William and Lady Hamilton, she disliked the English as well as the French.
26. Keil, 1977, cat. no. 131 and colour plate, p. 23.
27. Arthur Wellesley (1769-1852), 1st Duke of Wellington, Field-Marshal and statesman; victor of the Peninsular campaign, 1809-1813; finally defeated Napoleon at Waterloo, 1815. Kauffmann, 1982, cat. no. 96.
28. Nayler, pl. 4; the King is depicted seated in Westminster Hall before the procession assembled, wearing a large hat with upturned brim decorated with jewels, aigrettes and plumes. The circlet is just visible.

29. Marquardt, 1983, pp. 106-7, pl. 82-4, portraits of royal ladies.
30. *G,* VIII, 1801-3, fig. CCCX.
31. Grandjean, 1976, p. 276; Vever, I, opp. p. 39. Jean-Baptiste Isabey (1767-1855), painter and lithographer, recorded the principals at the coronation for the *Livre du Sacre* (Musée du Louvre).
32. RA 27271. Rundell & Bridge's billhead refers to them as 'Jewellers & Goldsmiths to Their Majesties'. The following year they became the Royal Goldsmiths, that is, the principal goldsmiths to the King.
33. RA 26264; RA 26272.
34. George Prince of Wales, *Correspondence,* IV, p. 319, 1687. The writer was Princess Augusta Sophia (1768-1840), George III's second daughter; 'little Sophy' was Princess Sophia (1777-1848), his fifth daughter. Both died unmarried.
35. RA 26272; George Prince of Wales, *Correspondence,* IV, p. 317, 1685.
36. RA 26261; Princess Amelia (1783-1810), George III's youngest child.
37. Prince William (1765-1837), George III's third son; served in the navy; created Duke of Clarence, 1789. Married, 1818, Princess Adelaide of Saxe-Coburg Meiningen; their children died in infancy. By the actress Dorothea Jordan he had a large brood of illegitimate children, the Fitz-Clarences, before he severed the connection in 1811.
38. George Prince of Wales, *Correspondence,* I, p. 203, 150; see also p. 332, 265; *passim.*
39. Ibid., III, pp. 133-9, will dated 10 January 1796, IV, p. 39. Mrs Fitzherbert rejoined him in January 1800 (Leslie, 1939, p.380). See also South Kensington loan exhibition, 1872, p. 62, cat. nos. 662-4.
40. RA 25694, billhead of Thos. Gray & Constable (the latter's name scored through), 1799.
41. RA 25694; 25755.
42. Greville, *Memoirs,* 8 September 1831.
43. RA 25690; RA 25697.
44. George Pigot (1719-1777), 1st baronet, 1764; baron, 1766.
45. Balfour, pp. 81-3.
46. Cholmondeley, *Heber Letters,* pp. 124-5.

47. PRO, Chancery Proceedings, Division I, C 13/69/23, Complaint by William Parker, William Birkett and James Birkett, 25 April 1805. Rundell's put the weight of the diamond at 189^{1}/$_{6}$ grains in their affidavit of 28 June 1805.
48. Philip Rundell (1743-1827) served his apprenticeship with William Rogers, a jeweller in Bath; arriving in London about 1767, joined Theed & Pickett; partner, 1772; sole owner, 1785. Took John Bridge (1755-1834) into partnership, 1788 and nephew E.W. Rundell, about 1804. Miserly in habits, Rundell left a fortune of about £1,500,000, most of it to his nephew Joseph Neeld; Grimwade, p. 648; Culme, I, p. 398.
49. See Introduction, fn.6.
50. Fox MS, fo. 13.
51. According to the Chancery Proceedings, Rundell's dealt with G.W. Thelluson. Peter Thelluson (1737-1797), who founded the London concern, was a Huguenot merchant of Parisian origins who became a naturalised Englishman, 1762.
52. A. & H. Tayler, *Stuart Papers,* Introduction, pp. 15-18; letter of Angiolo Bonelli to Sir John Coxe Hippisley, 23 April 1813, transcribed from RA SP M 66/36.
53. PRO C 13/69 23; 'The joint and several Answer' of Philip Rundell, John Bridge and Edmond Waller Rundell, 31 May 1806.
54. Id., 28 June 1805.
55. RA 26261 (1804); 25757 (1805); 25780 (1807). George Michael Moser (1704-1783), chaser and enameller; born at Schaffhausen, Switzerland; came to England and was drawing-master to George III; founder-member and first Keeper of the Royal Academy.
56. RA 25824.
57. RA 25771; 25776 (also 25778, 25779); 26256; George Prince of Wales, *Correspondence,* VII, p. 294, 2954.
58. *BA,* II, 1807, pp. 105, 161.
59. RA 25815; fifty-one rings cost £2.18s. apiece; one surrounded by a serpent, £3.15s. The Duke of Cumberland paid half the bill.
60. George Prince of Wales, *Correspondence,* VII, pp. 98-9, 2777.
61. Ibid., pp. 2-3.
62. Princess Mary (1776-1857), George III's

fourth daughter; married her cousin William Frederick (1776-1834), Duke of Gloucester, 1816.
63. Princess Charlotte, *Letters,* p. 220. Princess Charlotte Augusta of Wales (1796-1817); William (1792-1849), Hereditary Prince of Orange, later William II, King of the Netherlands.
64. RA 25820; 25831.
65. See Goya's painting of Charles IV of Spain and his family, 1800-01; Museo del Prado, Madrid.
66. Prince Leopold of Saxe-Coburg-Saalfeld (1790-1865), later King of the Belgians.
67. Princess Charlotte, *Letters,* p. 220. Margaret Mercer Elphinstone (1788-1867), daughter and heiress of Admiral Lord Keith (1726-1823); married, 1817, the Comte de Flahaut (1785-1870), the reputed son of Talleyrand.
68. RA 25911; Frampton, pp. 280-1. The recipient was either Miss Charlotte or Miss Lucy Cotes.
69. Princess Charlotte, *Letters,* p. 233.
70. RA 25886.
71. The Duke of Gloucester was popularly known as 'Silly Billy'.
72. RA 25920.
73. Knight, I, p. 227.
74. Bury, 1988, p. 11.
75. Princess Adelaide (1792-1849), eldest daughter of George, Duke of Saxe-Coburg Meiningen and Queen of William IV. Pious and plain, she was a good wife who tolerated the Fitz-Clarences with composure.
76. Prince Edward Augustus (1767-1820), Duke of Kent, George III's fourth son; pursued a military career, 1786-1803, in which he showed himself a disciplinarian. Parted regretfully from Madame de Saint-Laurent, his mistress of some twenty-seven years' standing, to marry Leopold's widowed sister (1786-1861). She had two children by her first husband, the Prince of Leiningen.
77. Adolphus Frederick (1774-1850), Duke of Cambridge, George III's seventh son, also a soldier; married Princess Augusta of Hesse-Cassel (1797-1889). They were the grandparents of Princess Mary of Teck, who married the future King George V in 1893.

78. RA 25938.

79. Princess Elizabeth had married the Hereditary Prince of Hesse-Homburg on 7 April, though it is most unlikely that the Regent would have given her two sprigs.

80. A bill (of Pains and Penalties) for divorcing the Queen was introduced in the House of Lords, July 1820, but was abandoned in November after public hearings at which Queen Caroline insisted on being present.

81. Print Room, Metropolitan Museum of Art, New York, 23.68.1. Album annotated in pencil, 'from the collection of John Bridge (Court Jeweller to Geo. III & Geo. IV)'. The owner is likely to have been John Gawler Bridge, the elder Bridge's nephew.

82. PRO LC2-50, Rundell's last bill for work on George IV's coronation, dated 1 April 1822, fo. 124v. Eight silver-gilt collars of SS were also made for the Heralds and eight more for the Serjeants at Arms. See also LC2-53, ff. 5-6.

83. Bridge album, fo. 28v; these two designs are not the ones illustrated in Plate 91C but are clearly by the same hand. Charles Muss, patronised by the royal family, executed in 1824 a copy of John Jackson's portrait of the Duke of York (Walker, I, p. 582).

84. Sir Walter Scott (1771-1832), novelist, poet and lawyer; studied German and published a translation of Burger's *Lenore* and other ballads, 1799. Scott's *Border Minstrelsy* (1802-03), followed by the *Lay of the Last Minstrel*, 1805 (greatly admired by the Prince of Wales), were the first of a long series of works presenting a characteristic antiquarian and romantic view of the past.

85. Vever, I, p. 229.

86. Keppel, p. 120. Henry Richard Fox (1773-1840), 3rd Lord Holland, married, 1797, Elizabeth Vassall, formerly Lady Webster (1771-1845), following her divorce from her first husband. At Holland House in Kensington Lady Holland presided over a brilliant Salon of Whig politicians, writers, wits and artists.

87. Id.

88. Vever, I, pp. 231-44.

89. Bear, p. 35. Joachim Murat (1767-1815), Marshal of France, 1804; King of Naples, 1808; married Napoleon's sister Caroline (1782-1839), 1800. Arrested and shot in trying to recover his kingdom, 1815.

90. Hortense de Beauharnais (1783-1837), Josephine's daughter by her first marriage, married Napoleon's brother Louis, King of Holland.

91. Grandjean, 1976, p. 276. Pierre Prud'hon (1758-1823).

92. Josephine, original documents in the V & A library, 'État des Bijoux emportés pour le service de Sa Majesté...pendant son voyage' ('à Strasbourg' added later), dated Paris 14 April 1809 by Nitot et fils; 'État des Merchandises envoyées conditionellement à Sa Majesté l'Imperatrice Reine par E. Nitot et fils ses joailliers..., 26 May 1809.' Other lists are included in the collection. See also Morel, 1988, pp. 258, 260-2.

93. Cameo tiara formed of one piece of shell, Musée Massena, Nice (*Apollo,* July 1977, p. 8).

94. Eugène de Beauharnais (1781-1824), Josephine's son by her first marriage; Viceroy of Italy, 1805-14.

95. Vever, I, opp. p. 46.

96. Knapton, p. 264; Grandjean, 1976, p. 276. According to Grandjean, the 'Inventaire général des Diamans, Perles et Pierres Précieuses de la Couronne, années 1811, 1812, 1813' excluded twenty-four historic cameos in the collections of the Bibliothèque Impériale. The Regent diamond alone was valued at 6,000,000 francs.

97. Grandjean, 1964, pp. 34, 54-61.

98. Knapton, p. 223; PRO LC2-50, fo. 40.

99. Archduchess Maria Luisa (1791-1847), daughter of the Emperor Francis I of Austria, married Napoleon, 1810. She was prevented from seeing her husband on his return from Elba; her father gave her the title of Duchess of Parma and despatched her to Italy with General Count von Neipperg, her *Chevalier d'Honneur*. (See Shelley, *Diary,* 18 February 1817, pp. 383-4.)

100. *BA,* ns III, 1811, p. 45.

101. Vever, I, pp. 53-4; Morel, pp. 282-3.

102. Masson, p. 134.

103. François Charles Joseph Napoleon Bonaparte (1811-1832), designated by his father King of Rome; later the Duke of Reichstadt.

104. The necklace now has additional drops and has lost two other stones (Morel, pp. 285-6); it was given by Mrs Marjorie Merriweather Post to the Smithsonian Institution, Washington in 1962. A diadem (also altered) which had belonged to the Empress is in the same collection (Desautels, 1979, p. 63).

105. Christie's sale, Napoleon, Nelson and their Times (the Calvin Bullock Collection), 8 May 1985, cat. no. 24, now in the Al-Tajir collection; Morel, p. 286.

106. Marquardt, pl. 35; painting by Nicholas Gosse of the meeting at Tilsit, Musée National du Château de Versailles. Queen Luisa of Prussia was the consort of King Friedrich Wilhelm III (1797-1840).

107. Grandjean, 1976, colour pl. C, p. 280.

108. Painting in the Galleria Nazionale, Parma.

109. Stéphanie-Louise-Adrienne de Beauharnais (1789-1860), daughter of Claude, Comte de Beauharnais, married Karl Ludwig Friedrich, heir to the Grand Duke of Baden, April 1806. Her youngest daughter Marie (1818-1888) married William, Marquis of Douglas (1811-1863), later 11th Duke of Hamilton.

110. RA Queen Victoria's Journal, 26 February, 25 April 1845, 31 January 1850; *passim.*

111. Madame de la Tour du Pin, pp. 303-6. Fanny Dillon's mother was the Empress Josephine's sister. Fanny's half sister, the Marquise de la Tour du Pin (1770-1853), the daughter of one of the Queen's ladies, was close to the Court.

112. Keppel, p. 165.

113. Shelley, *Diary,* p. 54. After her release from imprisonment in 1795, Marie-Thérèse de Bourbon (1778-1851) married her cousin, the Duc d'Angoulême (1775-1844).

114. Morel, 1988, p. 298.

115. Shelley, *Diary,* pp. 108-9; Knight, II, pp. 106-7. Princess Carolina of Naples (1798-1870) was the second wife of the Duc de Berri (1778-1820), who had contracted a marriage with an Englishwoman while in exile. He was assassinated in Paris in 1820. His father, Charles X, was overthrown in 1830, but his widow instigated an unsuccessful rising in the Vendée in 1832 and was imprisoned. She had already re-married, to Count Lucchesi-Palli of an old Sicilian family; on release from prison, lived with her family in Italy, 1833-1870.

116. See p.367.

117. Vever, I, pp. 121-3.

118. Ibid., pp. 121, 125.

119. Fox MS, fo. 145.

CHAPTER III

1. Yogev, p. 27.

2. Ibid., pp. 82-5.

3. Fox MS, fo. 27.

4. Ibid., ff. 10, 33, 39-41.

5. Austen, *Sense and Sensibility,* Chapter 33.

6. Fox MS, ff. 34-5.

7. Ibid., fo. 52.

8. *BA,* ns III, 1811, p. 45.

9. John Mawe (1764-1829), mineralogist; visited the diamond mines of Minas Gerais in Brazil, 1809-10. Returning to London, he opened a shop for minerals and general goods at 149 Strand.

10. Bruton, p. 246. Venice also had a variant carat weight.

11. Mawe, 1823, pp. 9-13.

12. Winter, 'A concise but exact account of the diamond', in his *Pattern-book.*

13. Mawe, 1823, pp. 54, 56.

14. Ibid., pp 52-4, 61.

15. Tennant, 'Gems and precious stones', London 1851 exhibition, *Lectures,* 2s, pp. 89, 96-7. The mineralogist James Tennant was apprenticed to Mawe and later took on his business. Appointed teacher (later Professor) of mineralogy, King's College, London, 1838.

16. Streeter, 1892, p. 43; see also Paris 1867 exhibition. English *Reports,* II, Maskelyne, p. 601.

17. SA *J,* XXIV, 1876, pp. 379-80.

18. Ibid., XXIX, 1881, pp. 370-2; Balfour, pp. 132-8, cites a figure of £11,100.

19. Culme, III, pp. 145-8. Harry Emanuel (c.1830-1898) succeeded to his father's business at Hanover Square, 1855 and retired in 1873 to France.

20. SA *J,* XVI, 1868, p. 849. Gregory, of 15 Russell Street, Covent Garden showed precious stones at the Paris 1867 exhibition (Class 21, British section, 10).

21. Ibid., pp. 854-5; id., XVII, 1869, pp. 46, 517. Balfour, pp. 132-8, suggests that Gregory's purpose was to protect Emanuel's large stocks of diamonds until they were unloaded; in other words, the negative report was a delaying tactic.
22. Ibid., XXIX, 1881, pp. 370-2.
23. Pakenham, Chapter 27.
24. SA *J*, XXV, 1887, pp. 992-3; ibid., XXXVII, 1889, pp. 846-7.
25. Ibid., XXXVII, 1889, pp. 846-7.
26. Ibid., LII, 1904, p. 171.
27. Ibid., XXXVII, 1889, pp. 846-7.
28. Cecil Rhodes (1853-1902), made a fortune at Kimberley in its early years. Prime Minister of the Cape Colony at the age of thirty-seven, he resigned after the notorious Jameson raid in 1896.
29. Wagner, p. 137.
30. Culme, I, pp. 437-8; E.W. Streeter (1834-1923) was, like Harry Emanuel, a dealer in stones as well as a retail jeweller and author. His buccaneering ventures in mines and a pearl fishery are mentioned by Culme.
31. PRO, BT 31/4835, file no. 32064, Sapphires and Rubies of Siam Ltd. The Company was wound up in 1896. For the stone rush see SA *J*, XXVIII, 1880, pp. 770-1.
32. SA *J*, XXXVII, 1889, pp. 266-75; Streeter, 1892, pp. 179-88; PRO BT 31/31142, file no. 28334.
33. Streeter, 1892, pp. 236-7.
34. SA *J*, LIV, 1906, pp. 200-1; PRO BT 31/4104, file no. 26344. Standard Mining Company Ltd., 17 April 1888 (title changed August 1888 to Emerald Mines of Columbia Ltd.).
35. SA *J*, XXXIX, 1891, p. 821.
36. Streeter, 1892, p. 253.
37. SA *J*, XXXV, 1887, p. 994.
38. RA 25781, TG. Gray, 1807. 'A large Mosaic & Lapis Lazuli Broach,' £12.12s.
39. As Lord Fitzroy Somerset, Lord Raglan (1788-1855), Wellington's aide-de-camp, asked Garrard's to alter a lapis lazuli necklace and bracelets in 1814.
40. *BA*, ns I, 1810, p. 42; *AR*, VI, 1811, p. 236.
41. SA *J*, XXIX, 1881, p. 448.
42. Culme, 1977, p. 48, citing Sun Registers, Guildhall Library, MS 11936/492.

43. Fox MS, fo. 29.
44. Paris 1867 exhibition. Belgian reports, II, Class 36, pp. 341-2.
45. London 1862 exhibition, Hunt's *Handbook*, II, p. 113; SA *J*, XXXV, 1888, p. 50; Paris 1889 exhibition, French reports, Massin, p. 33.
46. Culme, I, pp. 245-6.
47. Ibid., see also *ILN*, 40, 1862, p. 584. The Marquis lent the Nassak and Arcot diamonds to Hunt & Roskell for display at the London 1862 exhibition.
48. RA Add. T/54-61. Voorzanger, described as the chief diamond-cutter at Coster's, was awarded a 1st class medal as a *coopérateur* at the Paris 1855 exhibition (French reports, II, Fossin, p. 924).
49. Bruton, p. 152.
50. London 1862 exhibition, Hunt's *Handbook*, II, pp. 112-3; English *Reports*, Class 33, p. 8.
51. Paris 1867 exhibition, English *Reports*, Maskelyne, p. 599.
52. Ibid., p. 601.
53. SA *J*, XXXV, 1887, p. 992.
54. Ibid., XXI, 1873, p. 175.
55. Ibid., LIII, 1905, p. 942.
56. Kreitman, Chapter 15.
57. F. Curtis for C.M. Field, 10 July 1873, patent no. 2389.
58. Bruton, p. 154.
59. London 1862 exhibition, English *Reports*, Class 33, p. 8.
60. SA *J*, LIII, 1905, p. 941.
61. Ibid., LI, 1903, pp. 300-1.
62. Ibid., LV, 1907, p. 1047; summary of a report by the American Consul in Amsterdam.
63. Emanuel, pp. 76-7.
64. SA *J*, 1904, p. 167.
65. Bruton, p. 162.
66. Ibid., p. 169, fig. 10.4.
67. Mawe, 1823, p. 69.
68. Barbot, p. 287 and 'Tableau des Diamants les plus remarquables bruts et taillés.'
69. Paris 1889 exhibition, French reports, Massin, p. 37. Oscar Massin born in 1829 in Liège, studied at the Academy there as a designer, went to Paris and worked for Fester, successor of Viennot; in 1854 he joined Rouvenat as head of his workshop, then worked for Viette on a diadem for the Empress Eugénie, 1855; went to London for a year and a half. Returned to Paris; set up on his own account in the Rue des Moulins, 1863.
70. London 1862 exhibition, English *Reports*, Class 33, p. 8;

see also Hunt's *Handbook*, II, p. 113.
71. Streeter, 1892, p. 30.
72. SA *J*, LV, 1907, p. 1048.
73. Ibid., LVI, 1908, p. 210.
74. Ibid., LII, 1904, p. 167.
75. Bruton, p. 163, fig. 10.4.
76. Paris 1867 exhibition. Catalogue, Belgium, Class 36, no. 1, Bordinck (*sic*); Paris 1889 exhibition, French reports, Massin, p. 40. See also Vever, III, p. 420.
77. Angela Burdett-Coutts (1814-1906), philanthropist; granddaughter of the banker Thomas Coutts. Married W.L. Ashmead-Bartlett, 1881.
78. SA *J*, XXXVI, 1888, p. 50.
79. SA, *J*, XLVIII, 1900, pp. 789-90.
80. Ibid., LII, 1904, p. 176.
81. Dècle, p. 25. See also Paris 1900 exhibition, French reports, Class 94, p. 269.
82. *JD*, July-October 1807, p. 142.
83. London 1851 exhibition, French reports, De Luynes, Class 23, pp. 204-5.
84. Fontenay, p. 370.
85. Paris 1889 exhibition, French reports, Massin, pp. 66-7.
86. Vever, I, pp. 119-20; Antoine Laurent Lavoisier (1743-1794), used Priestley's discovery of oxygen to melt small quantities of platinum.
87. Desautels, p. 214; Morel, p. 267.
88. Vever, II, p 164; for Massin's part in the change to platinum, see ibid., III, p. 472.
89. McDonald and Hunt, pp. 30-4, 37-40.
90. Culme, I, p. 437.
91. Paris 1900 exhibition, French reports, Class 95, p. 379; see also Saunier, p. 229. The experimentally-minded jeweller was Coulon.
92. Paris 1878 exhibition, Belgian reports, Class 39, pp. 540-1.
93. Paris 1889 exhibition, French reports, Massin, p. 23; see also Vever, II, p. 231, fn. 1. The patent was taken out by the agent William Clark on behalf of Bouret and Ferré, 20 October 1860. The firm's address in 1867 was the Rue du Perche, Paris.
94. London 1862 exhibition, French reports, VI, Fossin, Class 33, p. 452; English *Reports*, Class 33, p. 5.
95. Paris 1867 exhibition, Birmingham Artisans' *Reports*, Introduction, p. 37.
96. Paris 1867 exhibition, English *Reports*, Class 36,

Maskelyne, p. 616.
97. London 1872 exhibition, *AJIC*, p. 40.
98. A.T.N. Goll, provisional patent, 20 June 1863, no. 1554.
99. De Barrera, pp.245-6.
100. Cf. Oman, 1974, pp. 46-7. Sapphires were often used for medieval pontifical rings; Oman, however, does not discuss the powers attributed to the stone.
101. SA *J*, L, 1902, p. 788. Davenport slightly adapted the lists for his *Jewellery* (1905).
102. *BA*, ns XV, 1817, p. 135; Bury, 1985, pp. 28, 32.
103. Kunz, 1917/1973, p. 227.

CHAPTER IV

1. RA 25963; the cross cost £84, the earrings £42 and a gold chain £16.16s.
2. The Garrard Ledgers consulted for this chapter are SL 1795-1814; WL 1799-1808; SL 1800-6; GL 1800-7; GL 1802-11; WL 1800-16; GL 1804-11; SL 1805-19; GL 1806-14; SL 1811-18; GL 1814-18; DB 1815-16; SL 1811-18; GL 1818-27.
3. *BA*, II, 1807, p. 219.
4. Vever, I, p. 120.
5. Princess Charlotte, *Letters*, p. 90. In the published version of the letter Berlin is rendered as Russia, which is a nonsense. The letters belong to the Earl of Shelburne and his archivist at Bowood House now prefers the reading Berlin. I am grateful for this help.
6. RA 25776.
7. *BA*, ns, 1812, 'The Universal Advertising Sheet…', April, p. 23; Lord Granville Leveson Gower, *Private Correspondence*, I, p. 453.
8. D'Arblay, *Diary and Letters*, III, p. 213.
9. *AR, VIII*, 1812, pp. 45, 111. *JD*, January-March 1807, p. 27; Grandjean, 1964, no. 99, valued at 300 francs.
10. The passion for shells was inherited from the eighteenth century (see *The Autobiography and Correspondence of Mrs Delany* (ed. Lady Llanover), 6 vols., 1861-2. Current models were provided by Mary Gartside, *Ornamental Groups*, 1808, Group V.)
11. *AR*, III, 1810, p. 45, pl. 5.
12. *BA*, ns IV, 1811, p. 89.
13. Id., p. 213; *AR*, VIII, 1812, p. 45.
14. N. Goetze's Account Book, 1809-15, Victoria and Albert Museum Library.

15. *AR,* V, 1811 p. 237.
16. *BA,* ns V, 1812, 'The Universal Advertising Sheet', April, p. 23.
17. Ibid., May, p. 31.
18. *BA,* ns XIV, 1816, pp. 3-4.
19. *AR,* IV, 1810, p. 365.
20. Ibid., II, 1809, p. 262.
21. *BA,* II, 1807, p. 105.
22. *BA,* II, 1807, p. 217.
23. Ibid., IV, 1808, p. 285. Georgiana Charlotte (1764-1838), daughter of the 3rd Duke of Ancaster and Kesteven and a considerable heiress; married, 1791, George (1749-1827), 4th Earl of Cholmondeley, created Marquis, 1819. He was Lord Chamberlain to the Prince of Wales, 1795-1800, and Lord Steward of the Household, 1812-21.
24. Vever, I, p. 123. Morel, pp. 316, 318.
25. *BA,* II, 1807, p. 47, a 'Grecian Diadem'.
26. Pauline Bonaparte (1780-1825), married firstly General Charles Leclerc (1772-1802) and secondly Prince Borghese, but soon separated from him.
27. W. and R.A. Austen-Leigh, p. 151.
28. *BA,* II, 1807, pp. 200-1; cf. RA 25780.
29. *BA,* II, 1807, p. 164.
30. Id., p. 162; *AR,* VII, 1812, p. 49.
31. *AR,* ns V, 1818, p. 299.
32. *BA,* III, 1807, p. 223.
33. *JD,* September-December 1809, p. 25; see also Vever, I, p. 19.
34. Ibid., January-March 1807, p. 151.
35. Grandjean, 1976, p. 280, colour pl. B; Morel p. 295.
36. *BA,* IV, 1808, p. 286; *LMM,* ns X, 1811, p. 342.
37. RA 26261.
38. Knight, *Autobiography,* I, p. 180.
39. *BA,* II, 1807, p. 55.
40. Vever, I, p. 17; Morel, pp. 259-60; RA 26256.
41. *BA,* ns III, 1811, pp. 321-4. See also Romilly, *Memoirs,* II, p. 211.
42. *AR,* VIII, 1812, p. 355.
43. *JD,* April-June, 1805, p. 142.
44. Sir Richard Westmacott (1775-1856) or his son Richard (1799-1872); both were sculptors, but probably the elder Westmacott was the client.
45. *AR,* X, 1813, p. 54.
46. *JD,* January-March 1807, p. 154; *AR,* II, 1809, p. 262.
47. *BA,* ns IV, 1811, p. 48.

48. Wynne, *Diaries,* III, pp. 291-2.
49. *BA,* II, 1807, p. 329. The Commissioners acquitted the Princess of the charges of adultery laid against her but held that her conduct was open to misinterpretation.
50. W. and R.A. Austen-Leigh, p. 171.
51. *BA,* III, 1807, p. 171; *AR,* II, 1809, p. 402.
52. The client was probably Thomas Wirgman, jeweller and goldsmith of 67 St. James's Street, who was patronised by the Prince of Wales.
53. *BA,* II, 1807, p. 50.
54. *AR,* X, 1813, p. 116.
55. Gaudibert, p. 37, pl. 15.
56. Princess Sophia Matilda of Gloucester (1773-1844), sister-in-law of Princess Mary, Duchess of Gloucester.
57. *BA,* II, 1807, p. 163; ibid., IV, 1808, p. 95.
58. Fontenay, p. 240.
59. *AR,* ns I, 1816, p. 59.
60. *JD,* April-June 1805, p. 41.
61. *BA,* ns I, 1810, p. 42.
62. Ibid., II, 1807, pp. 49-50.
63. Princess Charlotte of Wales, *Letters,* p. 237.
64. *AR,* ns III, 1817, p. 303.
65. Julia Shuckburgh Evelyn was the daughter and heiress of Sir George Shuckburgh Evelyn (1751-1804), a distinguished mathematician and scientist; *AR,* IV, 1810, p. 113.
66. Kentish & Haynes had premises at 18 Cornhill; like Rundell's, they had refused to join the general trek of goldsmiths and jewellers from the City to the West End.
67. *BA,* ns VII, 1813, p. 167. Mrs Wellesley-Pole died in 1825 and her graceless husband, who had succeeded as 4th Earl of Mornington, in 1857.
68. Ibid., ns V, 1812, pp. 164-5.
69. *BA,* IV, 1808, p. 283.
70. Ibid., ns IV, 1811, p. 157.
71. The sister of Lady Cholmondeley; see Shelley, *Diary,* p. 41.
72. *AR,* II, 1809, p. 195.
73. Princess Charlotte of Wales, *Letters,* p. 96; RA 25858.
74. The Empress Marie-Louise bequeathed her girdle by Nitot to Lady Westmorland (wife of the eleventh Earl). See Christie's London, 8 May 1985 (the Calvin Bullock collection), lot no. 24. The painting, a group portrait of

Queen Caroline with her children, is at Malmaison (Morel, 1988, p. 291).
75. *AR,* ns V, 1818, p. 296.
76. Ibid., III, 1810, p. 392.
77. Ibid., II, 1809, p. 258.
78. Ibid., III, 1810, p. 45, pl. 5.
79. *BA,* II, 1807, p. 164. All George III's daughters were amateur artists; drawing and painting were regarded as desirable accomplishments for ladies.
80. Taylor and Scarisbrick, cat. no. 904.
81. Thomson, 1972, p. 219.
82. Oman, 1974, p. 38.
83. RA 26258.
84. *AR,* ns III, 1817, p. 182.
85. *BA,* IV, 1808, p. 284.
86. The guard ring was bequeathed to Queen Victoria by her aunt Charlotte Augusta, Princess Royal and Queen of Württemberg, who died in 1828.
87. In the Musée des Beaux-Arts, Nantes.
88. *AR,* ns III, 1817, p. 303.
89. Bury, 1982, Case 2, Board K, 76.
90. Byron, *Letters,* to Lady Melbourne [11], 21 October 1813.
91. Capel, *Letters,* p. 131.
92. Thackeray, *Pendennis,* Chapter I.
93. Farington, *Diary,* 15 June 1811; Fox MS, ff. 84-5. Richard Colley Wellesley (1760-1842), created Marquis in the Irish peerage, 1799; governor-general of India, 1797-1805.
94. Sadleir, p. 72; Byron's letter to Thomas Moore, 2 April 1823. John Charles Gardiner, 1st Earl of Blessington, married, 1818 Marguerite (1789-1849), authoress and second party in the notorious menage-à-trois with Alfred, Count d'Orsay.
95. Ibid., p. 97; Stuart, p. 216.
96. Shelley, *Diary,* pp. 304-5.
97. Prince Pál Anton von Esterházy von Galanthe (1786-1866), diplomatist. Served as the Austrian Ambassador at London, 1815-38. His jewels were sold in London by Christie's, 29 March 1867.
98. The Emperor Francis I of Austria (1768-1835), the father of the Empress Marie-Louise, re-married, 1816. His bride was Princess Caroline Augusta, daughter of King Maximilian of Bavaria.
99. Shelley, *Diary,* pp. 304-5.
100. Princess Sophia (1777-1848), 5th daughter of George III.

101. Wynne, *Diaries,* III, pp. 166-7.
102. Holland, 1 February 1810.
103. Login, *Recollections,* pp. 8-9.
104. Carola Oman, *Ayot Rectory,* pp. 68-9.

CHAPTER V

1. PRO LC 5/199; *AR* ns IX, 1820. Mourning for George III, twice adjusted, ended on 30 April 1820. See also Lieven-Palmerston, p. 7, letter dated 25 December 1828.
2. RA 25994; PRO LC2/51.
3. Creevey, I, pp. 318, 320 and 334.
4. George IV was particularly fond of the national emblems of the United Kingdom.
5. Fox MS, fo. 136. Elizabeth Denison (1769-1861) married the then Viscount Conyngham in 1794.
6. Haydon, II, 19 July 1821.
7. Walter Scott brought to light the Scottish Crown Jewels in Edinburgh Castle, 1818, and was created a baronet by George IV in March 1820.
8. Quoted in Nayler, p. 131.
9. Penzer, p. 77, Nayler, p. 131.
10. The diamonds were hired at ten per cent of valuation.
11. Arbuthnot, I, p. 108; Mrs Arbuthnot, the second wife of The Right Honorable Charles Arbuthnot, MP, died of cholera at the age of forty, 1834.
12. RA 25995, item dated 27 May 1820 in a bill from Rundell's. It was enlarged (Lady Conyngham was on the ample side) on 7 June 1821 (RA 26021). Lady Cowper was Emily Mary (1787-1869), sister of Lord Melbourne, who as a widow married in 1838 her lover, Henry John Temple (1784-1865), 3rd Viscount Palmerston, the statesman.
13. Lady Palmerston, *Letters,* p. 86; Wellington archives, Stratfieldsaye.
14. Hibbert, *George IV,* chapter 35; Nayler, p. 133.
15. Longford, *Wellington,* II, Chapter V.
16. Farington *Diary,* VIII, p. 291, 19 July 1821.
17. Creevey, II, pp. 23-24. Bartolommeo Bergami (d.1841), or Pergami, as he preferred to be called, rose from *valet de place* to become Chamberlain in the Princess's household.

431

18. Greville *Memoirs;* the entry itself is undated but written before 25 January 1823.

19. Henry Conyngham (1766-1832), Baron Conyngham of Mount Charles; Viscount 1789; Earl 1797; Viscount Slane, Earl of Mount Charles and Marquis Conyngham, 1816.

20. Creevey, II, p.43. The rivière was sold at Sotheby's on 23 May 1985 (lot 427). It may have been cut down from a larger piece (see RA 26054).

21. Dorothea de Benckendorff (1785-1857), daughter of General de Benckendorff, married 1800, Count (later Prince) de Lieven, who became Russian Minister (later Ambassador) in London, 1812-1834. Princess Lieven was the mistress of, among others, Metternich and (at the end of her life) Guizot, and the confidential correspondent of several leading statesmen. Shortly after Palmerston secured the return of the Lievens to St Petersburg, the Princess left her husband and spent most of her remaining years in Paris.

22. Greville *Memoirs,* 2 May 1821.

23. Catherine, Grand Duchess of Oldenburg (1788-1819), was widowed shortly before her arrival in London. Fully conscious of her standing as the Tsar's sister, she was both clever and meddlesome by nature. There was no love lost between her and the Prince Regent. Shelley, *Diary,* p. 61, 11 June 1814.

24. Lady Palmerston, *Letters,* p. 79.

25. RA 25997.

26. RA 25995.

27. RA 26161, entry dated 19 September 1821.

28. RA 25995 (armlet); 26021, 26022.

29. Chaffers, pp. 95-60.

30. RA 25990.

31. RA 26026.

32. RA 26001.

33. RA 26028; cf. Oman, 1974, frontispiece, A; RA 26161; RA 26306 (Rundell's bill in which the gothic items of 1824-25 appear).

34. RA 26066.

35. RA 26306.

36. RA 26107.

37. RA 26161.

38. RA 26032.

39. RA 26098.

40. RA 26296.

41. RA 26037; the waist clasp, together with a gold necklace and cameo pendant of Apollo, cost £50.

42. Bury, Wedgwood and Snodin, 1979, pp. 343-353.

43. RA 26017; RA 26011.

44. RA 26093.

45. RA 26003, Rundell, Bridge & Rundell; RA 25990, Thomas Hamlet.

46. RA 26200. Another giraffe was given to Charles X and giraffe bracelets were the rage in Paris in 1827 (Vever I, pp. 98-100).

47. Hibbert, *The Court at Windsor,* p. 147 (*ill.*); Lambourne, 1965, pp. 1498-1502.

48. Arbuthnot, I, 38.

49. RA 26318.

50. Sir William Knighton (1776-1836), officially Keeper of the Privy Purse from 1822-30, was a surgeon and physician.

51. Wilkins, II, p. 210; cf. Greville *Memoirs,* 31 July 1831.

52. Arbuthnot, II, p. 362 and Appendix C, letter from the Duke of Wellington to Lady Conyngham, 7 June 1830; Appendix A, letter from Lady Conyngham to the Duke, 21 November 1830, etc; Wellington archives.

53. Bury, 1988, p. 13.

54. RA 36281; with discount, the chain cost £20.17s.6d.

55. Hinks, 1975, pl. 20; Gere, 1975, pl. 6; a pair of bracelets given to Mrs Fitzherbert.

56. Garrard, MS, inventory of the Crown Jewels, 1861, (Messrs Garrard). The shadowy crown in Wilkie's painting had long lost its stones.

57. Vever, I, p. 125, reproduces a piece of 1855 (see Plate 183), dating it to 1820.

58. Vever, I, pp. 110-111.

59. Silver-gilt dish in the Renaissance manner made for Beckford by Burwash and Bateman, 1814, Victoria and Albert Museum.

60. Marquardt, 1983, p. 89, fig. 65.

61. *BA,* 3s XI, 1830, p. 257. Frances Anne Emily (1800-1865), daughter and heir of Sir Henry Vane-Tempest, married the 3rd Marquess of Londonderry as his second wife, 1819. She was for many years a leader of fashion in London society. It is also worth noting that Mrs Arbuthnot was costumed as Mary Queen of Scots for a ball held at Covent Garden on 12 May 1826 for the relief of the Spitalfields silk weavers (Arbuthnot, II, p. 26).

62. Vever, I, p. 102, opp. p. 126 (*ill.*).

63. Id., pp. 116. (*ill.*), 118; *AR,* 3s, III, 1824, p. 43.

64. London 1851 exhibition, French reports, VI, De Luynes, Class XXIII, p. 148; Paris 1844 exhibition, Burat, II, p. 36; Vever, I, p. 119.

65. Louis Philippe, Duc d'Orléans (1773-1850), the son of Philippe-Egalité, was descended from a younger brother of Louis XIV; married 1804, Princess Marie-Amélie (1782-1866); daughter of Ferdinand I, King of Naples and his Queen, Maria Carolina.

66. Louise-Marie-Thérèse-Charlotte-Isabelle (1812-1850), eldest and favourite daughter of Louis-Philippe.

67. Antoine Chrysostome Quatremère de Quincy (1755-1849), politician, archaeologist and architectural and art historian.

68. William Ewart, MP (1798-1869) lawyer, politician, free trader.

69. SCAM, *Report,* pp. i-vi.

70. *CM & BA,* VII, 1835, pp. 99-101.

71. SCAM, Minutes of Evidence, paras. 544, 552.

72. Sarah Sophia (1785-1867) eldest daughter of the 10th Earl of Westmorland and heiress of Robert Child the banker; married the 5th Earl of Jersey, 1804. She was the model for Lady St. Julians in Disraeli's *Coningsby,* 1844.

73. Lieven-Palmerston, p. 125. The marriage finally took place in 1842.

74. SCAM, *Report,* p. vii.

75. Id., p. iii.

76. Knight's *Scroll Ornaments,* pl. 45 (cf. a bracelet by Simon Petiteau of Paris, c.1820, *ill.* Fontenay, p. 295, Vever, I, p. 229).

77. Bury, 1985, p. 9.

78. Augustus Welby Northmore Pugin (1812-1852), architect, designer, writer, converted to Roman Catholicism 1835; from 1838 associated with John Hardman, junior, a member of a Birmingham button-making firm, in the manufacture of Pugin's metalwork, jewellery, embroidery, glass, etc.

79. Pugin, *True Principles,* p. 24.

80. *At,* XV, 1894, p. 45.

81. Culme, I, pp. 245-247. Mortimer had been the assistant of William Gray of New Bond Street.

82. Lieven-Palmerston, p. 159.

83. Paris 1855 exhibition, English reports, II, 1856, Redgrave, p. 365; French reports, II, 1856, p. 921.

84. Edmund Thomas Parris (1798-1873) served an apprenticeship to Ray & Montagu before entering the Royal Academy Schools, 1816. He certainly designed plate (*ILN,* 22, 1853, p. 480; 34, 1859, p. 624).

85. George Foggo entered the Royal Academy Schools in 1820 at the age of twenty-seven; won a Silver Medal, 1821.

86. A.V. Geoffroy de Chaume (1816-1892), studied at the Ecole des Beaux-Arts; worked with David d'Angers.

87. Vever, I, p. 196, fn. 1.

88. Jean-Benoît-Martial Barnard (1784-1846); Vever, I, pp. 209-212.

89. Vever, I, p. 221; Ferdinand-Philippe, Duc d'Orléans (1810-1842), married Hélène (1814-1858), daughter of Frederick-Ludwig of Mecklenburg-Schwerin, 1837.

90. Gere, 1975, p. 160.

91. Arbuthnot, II, p. 384.

92. Vever, I, pp. 198-9.

93. Hamlet sale cat., Part I, lot nos. 374, 371, 375.

94. Heeley advertised in Wrightson's Birmingham directory, 1829-30, and his firm contributed to international exhibitions from 1851 to 1867 and later.

CHAPTER VI

1. *Polytechnic Journal,* VI, 1842, pp. 100-1; nos. 344-7; Tait, 1984, Gere, cat. no. 836.

2. Gray, in SA *Transactions,* Supplement, 1852, pp. 138-141.

3. Forrer, IV, pp. 509-21, Giovanni Pichler (1734-1790/1); pp. 522-30, Luigi Pichler (1773-1854).

4. Tait, 1984, Gere, cat. no. 836.

5. Forrer, III, pp. 560-5; Nathaniel Marchant (1739-1816), Apprentice Engraver to the Mint, 1797, rising to Assistant Engraver; Seidmann, 1985, pp. 59-63.

6. Forrer, VI, pp. 84-6; Bertel Thorvaldsen (1770-1844), presented his works and collections to the City of Copenhagen. The Thorvaldsen Museum opened in 1848.

7. John Gibson (1790-1866) was offered a place in Canova's studio; on the latter's death he transferred to Thorvaldsen. Gibson bequeathed his effects to the Royal Academy.

8. Antonio Canova (1757-1822); born at Possagno, settled in Rome, 1780.

9. Forrer, IV, pp. 582-620, Benedetto Pistrucci — his Flora is illustrated on p. 585; ibid., VIII, p. 137.

10. RA (Stuart Papers), M66, fo. 36, letter from Bonelli describes his hazardous journey.

11. RA 26004; see also page 81.

12. Forrer, IV, pp. 620-1, Elena Pistrucci (1822-1886), Signora Poggioli, and Maria Elisa Pistrucci (1824-1881), Signora Marsuzi.

13. Forrer, I, p. 587; VII, p. 223. Giovanni (Johann) Dies (1796-1839).

14. Lightbown, 1985, p. 180, citing Anon., *A Classical and Historical Tour Through France, Switzerland, and Italy in the Years 1821 and 1822,* II, pp. 208-9.

15. London 1851 exhibition, French reports, VI, De Luynes, p. 188; Forrer, IV, p. 461.

16. De Luynes, pp. 188-9; Tait, 1984, Gere cat. no. 907.

17. De Luynes, pp. 187-9; Carr in *Connoisseur,* 1975, pp. 171-181; Bulgari, II, p. 381. Tommaso Saulini (1793-1864).

18. Carr op. cit. Luigi Saulini (1819-1883).

19. London 1851 exhibition, catalogue, III, pp. 1286-7.

20. Dublin 1853 exhibition, detailed catalogue, p. 686; London 1862 exhibition, *Reports,* Class 33, p. 8, no. 2702, Saulini, Cav. T.; 1862, French reports, VI, Fossin, p. 470.

21. Medal obverse by W. Wyon. GRLV, fo. 48, 25 June 1856, presumably a post-dated entry.

22. RA Queen Victoria's Journal, 20 March 1856. Victoria (1840-1901), Princess Royal, the eldest child of Queen Victoria and Prince Albert, married Prince Frederick William of Prussia (1831-1888), who died in his first year as German Emperor.

23. See also Martin, *Prince Consort,* V, opp. p. 145, *ill.,* H.R.H. Victoria, The Princess Royal, 1856, engraved by Francis Holl after a sketch by Winterhalter.

24. Fulford, 1964, p. 27 and fn. 4.

25. Albert Edward (1841-1910), Prince of Wales, the eldest son of Queen Victoria and Prince Albert; succeeded his mother as King Edward VII, 1901.

26. Princess Alexandra of Denmark (1844-1925), daughter of Prince Christian of Schleswig-Holstein-Sonderburg-Glucksburg, who succeeded to the Danish throne in November 1863.

27. RA Queen Victoria's Journal, 10 March 1863.

28. Carr, *Connoisseur,* 1976, pp. 175-77; the Hon. Sir Charles Beaumont Phipps had been Keeper of the Privy Purse to the Prince Consort.

29. SA *J,* XIII, 1865, p. 99, 23 December 1864.

30. RA 8459; Ronca's invoice, 27 March 1865, record of cheque issued the next day; the artist's receipt, 30 March 1865.

31. SA *J,* XII, 1864, pp. 264-5; ibid., XIII, 1865, pp. 117-8, 163-5, 359-61; ibid., XIX, 1871, pp. 227-30. Ronca was awarded the second prize of £5 for the double cameo portrait in 1865 and won a prize of £2 for cameos of Psyche and Clytie, together with an ivory carving in 1871 (see also *AJ,* 1873, p. 320; SA *J,* XXXV, 1887, pp. 148-50).

32. London 1871 exhibition, catalogue, Division I, Class II, p. 158, nos. 3145-6. For one, St George and the Dragon, see Sotheby's, Fine Jewels, 5 October 1989, lot no. 20. See also Forrer, VIII, p. 171.

33. Birchall, p. 59.

34. Tait, 1984, Gere, cat. nos. 912, 917 (attributed).

35. London 1862 exhibition, catalogue, III, Class 39, Sculpture, Foreign Division, Rome, p. 267, no. 2702.

36. London 1862 exhibition, *Reports,* Class 33, p. 8; French reports, VI, Fossin, p. 470.

37. Tait, 1984, Gere, cat. no. 913.

38. Dublin 1865 exhibition, *Reports,* p. 89, no. 16. Tommaso is cited, but the Medal appears to have gone to Luigi.

39. Tait, 1984, Gere, cat. nos. 919, 918.

40. Forrer, II, pp. 273-4, VII, pp. 367-8; Bulgari, II, p. 552; Giuseppe Girometti (1780-1851), Pietro Girometti (1811-1859). Forrer, I, pp. 327-8; Giovanni Calandrelli (d. 1852); see also London 1851 exhibition, French reports, De Luynes, VI, pp. 81, 187. Babelon, p. 229; Paris 1867 exhibition, catalogue, English version, p. 440, Rome, Class 36, nos. 3, 4.

41. Compiled partly from exhibition catalogues and reports, including the catalogue of the British Section, Philadelphia 1876 exhibition, which lists the exhibitions in which the firm had participated to date and the *Official Record* of the Melbourne 1888-89 exhibition, Class 37, p. 739. They also used English talent: William King was among the gem-engravers to work for them (SA *J,* XXXV, 1887, p. 150).

42. *AJ,* 1854, pp. 20-2.

43. London 1862 exhibition, catalogue, III, Italy, Class 33, p. 85, Laodicini (*sic*), no. 2373; Dublin 1865 exhibition, Italian catalogue, p. 51; *Reports and Awards,* p. 89, no. 432, Hon. Mention.

44. Dickens, *Great Expectations,* Chapter 37.

45. The example cited was no. 359; no. 362, also with two serpents, is noted as 50s. (presumably the cost of the cameo) and £6.15s.

46. Vever, I, p. 68.

47. Laboulaye, 1856, p. 178; cf. *AJ,* 1874, p. 52.

48. London 1851 exhibition, French reports, VI, De Luynes, pp. 168-9, 188.

49. Gray, in SA *Transactions,* Supplement, 1852, pp. 139-142.

50. Lutyens, 1965, p. 112.

51. Forrer, III, pp. 352-3; Tait, 1984, Gere, cat. nos. 904-5.

52. Hackenbroch, 1979, pp. 87-93, plates 221-2; *passim.*

53. London 1851 exhibition, French reports, VI, De Luynes, p. 153; *Reports,* Class 23, p. 518.

54. Ibid.; see De Luynes, p. 172, citing 205 workers in the Parisian cameo trade (not all by any means actual carvers) in 1847, reducing to about 86 after the 1848 Revolution.

55. Paris 1855 exhibition, French reports, II, Class 17, p. 915, Michelini; ibid., p. 916, Albitès, France. Albitès may have come from Rome. The elder Girometti married Maria Albitès.

56. London 1862 exhibition, *Reports,* Class 33, pp. 6-7; French reports, VI, Fossin, pp. 469-70.

57. Paris 1867 exhibition, French reports, p. 110, Silver Medal, *coopérateur.* Georges Bissinger was born in Hanau (Vever, II, pp. 227, 296).

58. SKM loan exhibition, 1872, p. 63, nos. 692-3.

59. Cf. Tait, 1984, Gere and Rudoe, cat. no. 927.

60. Babelon, 1902, pp. 235-7.

61. Philadelphia 1876 exhibition, French reports, Lucien (not Alexis) Falize, pp. 18-19.

62. Vever, III, pp. 434, 460; Forrer, III, pp. 357-62; V, pp. 317-8.

63. *AJ,* 1897, pp. 267-70.

64. Ibid., 1874, pp. 53-4.

65. Forrer, VII, pp. 220-1; see also Christie jewellery sale, 8 June 1982, paste cameo of the Duchess of Northumberland in box with trade label describing De Veaux as holding royal appointments to Queen Victoria and the Duke of Sussex; Tait, 1984, Gere, cat. no. 847.

66. Forrer, VIII, p. 95; SA exhibition, 1848, p. 45, no. 258.

67. SA *J,* XIX, 1871, p. 227.

68. A & C E catalogues, 1889, no. 604, 1890, no. 89; Seidmann, *Apollo,* July 1988, pp.12-6.

69. Sotheby's jewellery sale, 11 July 1985, no. 86.

70. SA *J,* LX, 1912, pp. 360-371.

71. Culme, I, pp. 281-3.

72. *ILN,* 40, 1862, p. 585; Hunt's *Handbook,* II, pp. 119-20; Fontenay, p. 375.

73. W. Davenport, *CL,* 1978, pp. 1662-4.

74. *AJ,* 1874, pp. 20-2; B. Morris, 1978, p. 41.

75. Gonzalez-Palacios, cat. no. 32; SA *J,* XXXVII, 1889, pp. 884-5.

76. London 1851 exhibition, catalogue, III, p. 1299, no. 119.

77. London 1862 exhibition, Italian catalogue, Class 33, p. 352.

78. Ibid., catalogue, III, Italy, Class 33, p. 85, no. 2368; Dublin 1865 exhibition, Italian catalogue, p. 55, no. 477, described as Giocondo Torrini & Co., manufacturers, Florence; *AJ,* 1870, p. 316.

79. Paris 1878 exhibition, Artisans' *Reports,* Kirchoff, p. 469.

80. London 1871 exhibition, catalogue, p. 157, Division I, Class II, no. 3134; *AJIC,* 1872, p. 55.

81. Paris 1878 exhibition, Italian reports, Castellani, Class 39, p. 35.

82. London 1851 exhibition, *Reports,* Class 27, p. 577.

83. Petochi, 1981, Branchetti, pp. 65, 94; Gonzalez-Palacios, Röttgen, pp. 32-33.

84. Tait, 1984, Rudoe, cat. no. 933; Petochi, pp. 44-6, 61.

85. A far fuller description appears in Petochi, 1981, Alfieri, pp. 85-92. Judy Rudoe's recent research into the evolving shape and disposition of tesserae is an important development in dating mosaics.

86. London 1851 exhibition, French reports, VI, De Luynes, p. 187; see also biographies in Petochi.

87. Ibid., *Reports,* Rome, Barberi, 15, Council Medal; Dublin 1865 exhibition, *Reports,* p. 90, Hon. Mention. London 1851 exhibition, catalogue, III, Rome, p. 1286, L. Moglia, 20, E. (*sic*) Dies, 34-9. Dies also showed in 1862 and 1865, etc.

88. Paris 1855 exhibition, French reports, II, p. 926.

89. Philadelphia 1876 exhibition, reports and awards, p. 54.

90. The letter is preserved with the brooch and trade card in the Museum of London. 54. 67/11.

91. Dublin 1865 exhibition, Italian catalogue, Biagio Barzotti, p. 86, no. 431.

92. Rice, p. 202. *AJ,* 1873, p. 297.

93. London 1851 catalogue, III, Prussia, p. 1059, no. 205; id., 41, C.L. Tessler, Stolp, showed yellow and milk-white amber jewellery.

94. London 1862 catalogue, III, Prussia, 2197 (and also Paris 1867 catalogue, English version, p. 438, Prussia, Class 36, no. 8).

95. Ibid., Italian catalogue, Class 33, p. 355; Hunt's *Handbook,* II, pp. 121-2.

96. SA *J,* XLII, 1894, pp. 742-3.

97. Ibid., LX, 1912, p. 939.

98. *AJ,* 1873, pp. 229-231; London 1862 exhibition, Italian catalogue, Class 33, p. 355.

99. SA *J,* XLV, 1897, p. 478.

100. Ibid., XXXII, 1884, p. 681.

101. RA 26256.

102. French national exhibition, 1819, cat. no. 1224.

103. London 1851 exhibition, French reports, VI, De Luynes, p. 167.

104. Ibid., catalogue, II, Class 23, p. 683, no. 84, Paravagua & Casella; p. 684, no. 87, Phillips Brothers.

105. *ILN,* 40, 1862, p. 585.

106. London 1862 exhibition, Hunt's *Handbook,* II, p. 123.

107. Dublin 1865 exhibition, catalogue, p. 287 no. 661; *ILN,* 19 August 1865, supplement, p. 165 (*ill.*).

108. Paris 1855 exhibition, French reports, II, Class 17, p. 917, no. 17; London 1862 exhibition, Italian catalogue, p. 353, Class 33, no. 2246, etc.; Paris 1867 exhibition, catalogue, Class 36, Italy, p. 210, no. 23; London 1871 exhibition, catalogue, Division I, Class II, p. 158, no. 3150.

109. Dublin 1865 exhibition, catalogue, p. 437, Castaldi; *ILN,* 40, 1862, p. 584.

110. Paris 1867 exhibition, catalogue, English version, p. 440, Class 36, no. 26.

111. *AJ,* 1873, p. 230.

112. London 1862 exhibition, Italian catalogue, Class 33, p. 356, no. 1997 (Hon. Mention); Dublin 1865 exhibition, catalogue, p. 437, no. 430.

113. Paris 1867 exhibition, catalogue, English version, p. 440 (Oneto); New York 1853 exhibition, Wallis, *Report,* p. 42 (Raffaelli, Bronze Medal); London 1851 exhibition, catalogue, III, p. 1297, no. 84.

114. *AJ,* 1874, pp. 121-4. SA *J,* XXX, 1882, pp. 1018-9; ibid., LIV, 1906, pp. 1127-42, 1175-83.

115. London 1851 exhibition, foreign states, catalogue, p. 1526, no. 811, L.W. Schultz (technical footnote).

116. H. Emanuel, provisional patent no. 713 for improvements in personal wear, 15 March 1862; London 1862 exhibition, catalogue, II, Class 33, no. 6622, pp. 24-7.

117. *ILN,* 40, 1862, p. 585.

118. *AJ,* 1874, pp. 123-4.

119. London 1862 exhibition, French reports, VI, Fossin, p. 456.

120. *AJ,* 1874, p. 124.

121. Marquardt, 1983, nos. 379-81; I am grateful to Dr. Marquardt for supplementary information.

122. London 1862 exhibition, catalogue, III, Hesse, p. 36, Class IV, no. 499.

123. London 1851 exhibition, *Reports,* Class 23, p. 520, Nassau, 13, Hon. Mention (Prize Medal in Class 28).

124. Wynne, *Diaries,* I, p. 17; London 1851 exhibition, catalogue, III, Württemberg, p. 1119, no. 83 (A. Wittich, Kemmel & Co., no. 82, also showed ivory jewellery). Kauzmann Brothers showed ivory and hartshorn trinkets at the 1862 exhibition.

125. London 1862 exhibition, catalogue, III, Class IV, p. 87, Switzerland, no. 86.

126. Paris 1867 exhibition, catalogue, English version, p. 442, no. 18; the Lund firm contributed to many other exhibitions.

127. *S,* 4, 1894-5, p. 150.

128. *AJ,* 1871, p.218.

129. Ibid., 1874, p. 124; Timmins, 1866, p. 438; *Handbook to Birmingham,* 1886, p. 181.

130. SA *J,* XXXV, 1887, p. 609.

131. *AJ,* 1873, pp. 70-2; Kunz, p. 99.

132. Paris 1878 exhibition, English *Reports,* II, p. 225, Class 39.

133. SA *J,* XX, 1872, p. 289.

134. *LP,* XV, 1888, p. 78; *AJ,* 1873, pp. 110-111, 145-6.

135. Shelley, *Diary,* p. 281.

136. Kunz and Stevenson, p. 30; *passim.*

137. *AJ,* 1873, p. 110.

138. Woolf, *Autobiography,* I, Growing, Jaffna.

139. *ILN,* 40, 1862, p. 584.

140. Kunz and Stevenson, p. 288; *Sp,* LXXV, 21 May 1921, pp. 180-1. I am indebted to Claude Blair for the second reference.

141. London 1862 exhibition, catalogue, I, Class IV, p. 5; Stewart, Rowell-Stewart & Co., no. 1015.

142. *AJ,* 1873, pp. 5-6.

143. London 1851 exhibition, catalogue, III, p. 1211, no. 680, Philip, Passage Choiseul, Paris, manufacturer; *Reports,* Class 23, p. 520, E. Nash, Hon. Mention.

144. London 1862 exhibition, catalogue, III, France, p. 149, Class 33, no. 3244, Corbeels; p. 85, Italy, Class 33, nos. 2275-1998, Labriola.

145. London 1872 exhibition, *Reports,* p. 25; *AJIC,* 1872, Wallis, pp. 34, 38.

146. Wallis in Beavan, 1876, p. 40; see also a French invention using tortoiseshell waste, gelatine and metallic salts (SA *J,* XX, 1872, p. 289).

CHAPTER VII

1. *AR,* ns IX, 1820, p. 112.

2. *JD,* July-December, 1823, p. 177. The value of the diamonds was given as £240,000 or five million francs.

3. *BA,* 3s I, 1825, p. 77.

4. RA 26326.

5. RA 26002.

6. RA 26161; RA 26024.

7. *AR,* 3s XII, 1828, p. 181.

8. RA 25996.

9. RA 26306.

10. Then in German hands.

11. Byron's *Letters,* V, p. 91, 8 September 1816, to Augusta Leigh.

12. Lardner, 133 vols, 1830-49.

13. Cecilia ('Cis'), daughter of the Earl of Arran and widow of Sir George Buggin, married George III's sixth son, Augustus Frederick, Duke of Sussex, as his second unofficial wife shortly after the death in 1830 of the first, Lady Augusta Murray. Lady Cecilia reverted to her maiden name of Underwood until Queen Victoria recognised the marriage and created her Duchess of Inverness in 1840.

14. Creevey, II, pp.230-1.

15. Gertie van Berge, Rijksmuseum *Bulletin,* 1975, no. 2, p. 67.

16. Marquardt, 1983, cat. nos. 77-8, 152-3; *passim.*

17. Jane Austen, *Sense and Sensibility,* Chapter 23.

18. Hamlet sale catalogue, 1834, lot nos. 582, 587.

19. RA 26026; see also Farington, *Diary,* 22 December 1810; *passim.* Henry Bone, RA (1755-1832), turned from painting on ivory to enamel in 1780.

20. RA 26098.

21. London 1851 exhibition, French reports, VI, De Luynes, Class 23, pp. 179, 256. Charles Wagner exhibited specimens in 1839.

22. *BA,* 3s XI, 1830, p. 182.

23. London 1851 exhibition, French reports, VI, De Luynes, p. 198.

24. *JD,* July-December, 1823, p. 19; cf. De Luynes, p. 148.

25. McDonald and Hunt, p. 243.

26. Vever, I, pp. 163-6.

27. George IV, *Letters,* III, 108.

28. *BA,* ns XXVII, 1823, p. 329.

29. *AR,* 3s III, 1824, p. 59.

30. Hamlet sale catalogue, 1834, lot no. 1376.

31. RA 26073; 26027.

32. Henry Montagu-Scott (1776-1845), Baron Montagu of Brighton.

33. The Garrard Ledgers consulted include GL 1818-27, GL 1827-36.

34. Gaudibert, nos. 45-47 (the painting is in the Louvre).

35. *AR,* 3s VI, 1825, p. 362.

36. Ibid., ns XI, 1821, pp. 62, 121.

37. Ibid., 3s I, 1823, p. 242.

38. *LC,* VII, 1835, p. 271.

39. *AR,* 3s VII, 1826, p. 305.

40. *JD,* July-December 1823, p. 570.

41. Dudley Ward, p. 208.

42. Queen Victoria, *Girlhood,* I, p. 75; RA Queen Victoria's Journal, p. 31, 24 May 1833.
43. The Duke of Sussex's first morganatic wife (1793) was Lady Augusta Murray, the mother of his son and daughter (who took the name of d'Este). The marriage was declared void under the Royal Marriage Act in 1794.
44. *BA,* 3s VII, 1828, pp. 122, 214; id., 3s X, 1829, p. 29.
45. *AR,* 3s I, 1823, p. 183.
46. *BA,* ns XXVII, 1823, p. 41.
47. Ibid., 3s VII, 1828, p. 122.
48. *LM,* ns III, 1832, p. 144.
49. *JD,* July-December, 1823, p. 221; Hamlet sale catalogue, 1834, lot no. 376.
50. *WF,* VI, 1829, p. 105, pl.3.
51. RA 26027.
52. Hamlet sale catalogue, 1834, lot no. 482.
53. *BA,* 3s VII, 1828, p. 216.
54. *AR,* ns XI, 1821, p. 185.
55. *WF,* VI, 1829, p. 60; Vever, I, p. 135 (*ill.*).
56. *BA,* ns XXVII, 1823, p. 336; ibid., 3s I, 1825, p. 169.
57. *BA* 3s XII, 1830, p. 74.
58. *BA,* ns XXVII, 1823, p. 265; ibid., 3s I, 1825, p. 123.
59. Sydney Owenson (1776-1859), daughter of the Irish actor Robert Owenson; author, married, 1812, Sir Thomas Charles Morgan (see Mary Campbell, *Lady Morgan,* 1988).
60. *BA,* 3s V, 1827, p. 225.
61. Thackeray, *Pendennis,* Chapter 26.
62. *AR,* ns XIII, 1822, p. 232.
63. *BA,* 3s XI, 1830, p. 26.
64. Ibid., 3s XII, 1830, p. 119.
65. *AR,* ns XI, 1821, p. 301; ibid., ns XII, 1821, p. 236.
66. Ibid., 3s I, 1823, p. 121.
67. Ibid., 3s XII, 1828, p. 179.
68. *BA,* ns XXVII, 1823, p. 180.
69. *JD,* July-December, 1823, p. 14.
70. *LC, IX,* 1836, p. 68.
71. The 3rd Baron Holland was the nephew of Charles James Fox. Lord Holland's sister Caroline died in 1845.
72. Hamlet sale catalogue, 1834, lot no. 515.
73. *BA,* 3s VII, 1828, p. 169.
74. *AR,* 3s XII, 1828, p. 245.
75. Baroness Anselm de Rothschild (1807-1859), the mother of Baron Ferdinand, who built Waddesdon Manor, Buckinghamshire.

76. RA 26013; the vendor was Laurière.
77. RA 26306.
78. *AR,* 3s III, 1824, p.242.
79. *JD,* January-June, 1822, p. 617.
80. Ibid., July-December, 1823, p. 304.
81. Vever, I, p. 117.
82. Hamlet sale catalogue, 1834, lot nos. 578, 553, 590, 593.
83. Dickens, *Dombey and Son,* Chapter 1.
84. RA 26053; 26013.
85. RA 26054.
86. RA 26011 (Laurière); *BA,* ns XXVII, 1823, p. 222.
87. Ibid., 3s V, 1827, p. 123.
88. *CM & BA,* VIII, 1836, February, p. v.
89. *BA,* 3s VII, 1828, p. 70.
90. *WF,* VI, 1829, p. 252.
91. *LM,* ns III, 1832, p. 96.
92. *BA,* 3s XI, 1830, p. 27; Hamlet sale catalogue, 1834, lot no. 565.
93. *WF,* VI, 1829, p. 12.
94. RA 26017.
95. Hamlet sale catalogue, 1834, lot nos. 572, 564.
96. RA 26017.
97. Hamlet sale catalogue, 1834, lot no. 560.
98. Elizabeth ('Bessy') Rawdon (1793-1874), niece to the Earl of Moira, was born in England but brought up on the Continent; married, 1817, Lord William Russell (1790-1846), soldier and diplomat, second son of John, sixth Duke of Bedford.
99. Blakiston, p. 95.
100. *BA,* 3s I, 1825, p. 75.
101. Julia, daughter of General Sir John Floyd; married, 1820, Sir Robert Peel (1788-1850), statesman.
102. RA 26095.
103. *BA,* 3s III, 1826, p. 264.
104. RA 26162; an opal and diamond heart brooch 'with Psyche at top', acquired by George IV from Rundell's in 1822 at a cost of £73.10s.
105. *BA,* 3s VII, 1828, p. 169.
106. *WF,* VI, 1829, pp. 132, 204.
107. CL 1817-25; fo. 4; it cost £7.17s.6d.
108. Fontenay, p. 298. Marchand, of 43 rue Coquillière, Paris, came to London with J.V. Morel, 1848/9 (see page 326). He died in about 1867 aged seventy-six.
109. *BA,* 3s XII, 1830, p. 215.
110. *CM & BA,* VII, 1835, September, p. xi.
111. Hamlet sale catalogue, 1834, lot nos. 534-5.

112. Buckle, pp. 96, 211. (Charlotte) Georgina Smythe married the Hon. (George) Augustus Craven (1810-1836), 1833.
113. Carola Oman, *Gascoyne Heiress,* p. 109.
114. *WF,* VI, 1829, p. 155.
115. Bracelet in case with label, 'Dieu, Bijoutier, Palais Royal No.45', seen at Messrs Armytage Clark, London, 1979.
116. Hamlet sale catalogue, 1834, lot no. 531.
117. RA 26098.
118. *BA,* 3s III, 1826, p. 170.
119. Ibid., 3s VII, 1828, p. 139, visible in a miniature of Lady Forester by Miss E. Kendrick.
120. *LMM,* XIX, 1824, p. 293.
121. RA 26047; Hamlet sale catalogue, 1834, in lot no. 583.
122. *BA,* 3s XI, 1830, p. 210.
123. Sir Thomas Lawrence exhibition, National Portrait Gallery, 1979-80, cat. no. 48.
124. Fontenay, p. 245. The Vaughans were a Roman Catholic family. Mrs Vaughan, born Louisa Rolls, was a Catholic convert. Six of her eight sons entered the priesthood; Herbert (1823-1903) became the Cardinal-Archbishop of Westminster and two others were bishops.
125. *BA,* 3s III, 1826, p. 77.
126. Arbuthnot, *Journal,* I, p. 256.
127. Knight's *Gems and Device Book,* 2nd edn., 1836.
128. Blakiston, p. 97. Lady Georgiana Gordon (1781-1853) married John, 6th Duke of Bedford as his second wife, 1803.
129. *WF,* VI, 1829, pp. 57-8.
130. *JD,* January-June, 1822, p. 617.
131. Ibid., January-June, 1826, p. 698.
132. RA 26028; 26304; 26043, etc.
133. RA 26030; it cost £1.11s.6d. in 1822.
134. Sadleir, p. 81.
135. Blakiston, p. 111.
136. Lord George Cavendish Bentinck (1802-1848), statesman.
137. Thackeray, *Pendennis,* Chapter 3.
138. Hamlet sale catalogue, 1834, lot no. 592.

CHAPTER VIII

1. Roche, 1927, pp. 21-22; Martin, II, p. 28.
2. Thomas Aston, jeweller and silversmith; registered a mark at the Birmingham Assay Office, 7 April 1840; outworker for John Hardman; in partnership with his son William, 1857; 1862 exhibitor.
3. John Balleny, goldsmith and jeweller; registered a mark, 21 August 1844; 1862 exhibitor; additional premises at 74 Hatton Garden.
4. *ILN,* VI, 1845, p. 352 (*ill.*).
5. Sir John Conroy, Bart. (1786-1854), had been the Duke of Kent's military equerry and was thus inherited by the Duchess on her husband's death.
6. Woodham-Smith, 1972, pp. 136-7. Louise Lehzen (1784-1870), the daughter of a Lutheran clergyman in Hanover, had been appointed governess to the Duchess of Kent's elder daughter, Feodora (1807-1872), Princess of Leiningen, 1819 and then to Princess Victoria, 1824. Created a Hanoverian baroness by George IV, 1827, she stayed with the Queen until 1842.
7. William Lamb (1779-1848), 2nd Viscount Melbourne and husband of the notorious Lady Caroline Lamb; statesman, Prime Minister 1835-41.
8. Queen Victoria, *Girlhood,* I, p. 76.
9. Queen Victoria, *Letters,* 2s I, p. 11. The Queen did not leave the miniature to the Crown, but another bequeathed to her in 1829 by her aunt, the Queen of Württemberg (Twining, 1960, p. 193).
10. Queen Victoria, *Girlhood,* I, pp. 76, 116-7 and 124-6.
11. Ibid., pp. 62, 75 and 179-80.
12. RA Princess Victoria's Journal, 30 September 1835; Woodham-Smith, 1972, p. 104.
13. RA Add. T 10/15/16/ 19, Rundell's bills, 1838; Rundell, 'Particulars'.
14. Sir George Hayter (1792-1871), portrait and historical painter to the Queen, 1837, painter in ordinary, 1841; knighted, 1842. One of his celebrated portraits of the Queen shows her seated, in Robes of State, wearing George IV's circlet; it is in the Guildhall Art Gallery (Lorne, p. 105; Ormond, p. 480).
15. A.E Chalon (1780-1860), born in Geneva.

16. William Essex (d.1869, aged eighty-five) was enamel-painter to the Queen and Prince Albert.

17. Sarah (1787-1870), daughter of the 2nd Earl Spencer; married William Henry, afterwards 3rd Lord Lyttelton, 1813. Lady-in-waiting to Queen Victoria, 1838-42, then governess to the royal children. A similar miniature of the Queen, set in a bracelet, was presented to Lady Normanby (Lorne, p. 98).

18. RA Add. T/231, fo. 17; the recipients of the bracelets with the Essex miniatures were Lady Canning and the Duchess of Buccleuch.

19. Rundell, 'Particulars'; RA Add. T/21. Sultan Mahmud II (1808-1839), though of a martial character, presided over the virtual dissolution of the Turkish Empire; he was supported by England in an effort to diminish the growing Russian influence in the Levant.

20. Rundell, 'Particulars'.

21. Roger Fenton (1819-1869), the great photographer of the Crimean War.

22. Henrietta Ward (b.1832), artist, married the painter E.M. Ward and was the mother of the cartoonist, Sir Leslie Ward ('Spy').

23. Franz Xaver Winterhalter (1805-1873), the most successful Court painter of the Victorian era (Ormond and Blackett-Ord, 1987-8).

24. The circlet is depicted in the Queen's sketch of herself in the Abbey (Warner, p. 84).

25. Queen Victoria, Girlhood, I, p. 121.

26. Rundell, 'Particulars'.

27. Twining, 1960, p. 196.

28. RA Queen Victoria's Journal, 22 and 23 November 1839. All subsequent dated references to the Queen's Journals must be understood as coming from the Journals in the Royal Archives.

29. Greville, Memoirs, 23 November 1839.

30. Jagow, p. 28; RA Queen Victoria's Journal, 28 November 1839. The Queen dated Prince Albert's letter to 23 November.

31. RA Add. T/15.

32. RA Queen Victoria's Journal, 9 February 1840.

33. Twining, 1960, p. 193.

34. RA Queen Victoria's Journal, 10 February 1863; ibid., 10 February 1840; Princess Marie Louise, p. 152.

35. Twining, 1960, p. 193.

36. RA Queen Victoria's Journal, 10 March 1863, when the Queen noted that she had worn the brooch since 1840.

37. Collier, p. 258; Robert Collier (1845-1909), 2nd Lord Monkswell.

38. Ormond, Early Victorian Portraits, pl. 15: RA Queen Victoria's Journal, 24 December 1844. Bequeathed by Queen Victoria to Edward VII for eventual addition to the Crown Jewels (Twining, p. 195).

39. A large table centre made by Garrard's to a Renaissance design suggested by the Prince in 1842 and now in Kensington Palace was shown at the Society of Arts in 1849 and at the Great Exhibition of 1851.

40. RA Queen Victoria's Journal, 24 May 1841.

41. Ibid., 22 and 23 February 1843.

42. Elizabeth Margaret (1789-1867), the wife of Charles Stuart (1779-1845), created Lord Stuart de Rothesay, 1828. He was Ambassador Extraordinary and Minister Plenipotentiary to the Court of St Petersburg, 1841-44.

43. Surtees, 1975, pp. 76-7, 80-3, and 121-5. Charlotte (1817-1861), the wife of Charles John Canning (1812-1862), created an Earl in 1859, died intestate in India. Her husband died the following year and Queen Victoria bought two rings of Lady Canning's from the sale of his effects and gave them to Lady Stuart de Rothesay, as a souvenir of her daughter.

44. RA Add. T/231, fo. 45.

45. See Appendix II.

46. Martin, II, p. 462.

47. GRLV, ff. 70, 83.

48. RA Add. T/231, fo. 148. The Queen had heard the singer in Donizetti's L'Elisir d'Amore on 22 April 1847.

49. Princess Helena Augusta Victoria (1846-1923), married Prince Christian of Schleswig-Holstein and was the mother of Princess Marie Louise, whose reminiscences are cited in this and later chapters.

50. RA Add. T/231, fo. 19.

51. Werlich, Orders and Decorations, p. 136. Princess Mathilde had a similar ornament (Gere, 1972, pl. 34).

52. RA Queen Victoria's Journal, 12 November 1839.

53. A 'young Scotchman of great talent, who studied for 2 winters in Italy' (RA Queen Victoria's Journal, 23 February 1844).

54. The parure was bequeathed by the Queen to her grand-daughter, Princess Louis of Hesse, who gave it to the Museum of London in 1920 (Princely Magnificence, Victoria and Albert Museum, 1980-1981, cat. no. H.1.).

55. Fulford, 1964, pp. 184-5. Princess Beatrice's Trustees paid £3,887.19s.6d. into the Queen's account with Garrard's on 11 February 1874, a month after her confirmation.

56. RA Queen Victoria's Journal, 24 May 1845.

57. RA Add. T/19: Rundell's bill; Rundell, 'Particulars'.

58. Ernest of Saxe-Coburg-Gotha (1818-1893); succeeded his father as Duke, 1844; notoriously dissolute, his marriage was childless.

59. RA Add. T/231, ff. 26-7.

60. Ibid., fo. 52.

61. RA Add. T/231, ff. 69-70.

62. Ibid., ff. 99.

63. RA Queen Victoria's Journal, 6 July 1847.

64. Ibid., 22 June 1850; Prince Arthur (1850-1942), Duke of Connaught and Strathearn.

65. GRLV, ff. 3, 4, 8 February, 29 April 1844; fo. 13; 5 May, 16 August 1848; fo. 19, 1 April 1850.

66. RA Queen Victoria's Journal, 25 May 1849; 3 July 1850. The diamond was presented on behalf of the Company by Byron's old friend, Sir John Cam Hobhouse.

67. Ibid., 23 October 1851.

68. GRLV, ff. 25 and 33, 1, 5, 26, 27 November 1853.

69. Eugénie, Comtesse de Montijo (1826-1919); educated Paris; married Napoleon III, 1853.

70. Princess Mathilde (1820-1904), daughter of Jérôme Bonaparte; married Prince Anatole Demidov (1813-1870) but they soon separated. See also fn. 51.

71. Queen Victoria, Leaves from a Journal, 1961, p. 95. 21 August 1855.

72. Victoria Adelaide Mary Louise (1840-1901), Princess Royal. Her husband Frederick William (1831-1888) succeeded his father as Emperor of Germany, 1888, dying of cancer of the throat a few months after his accession.

73. RA Queen Victoria's Journal, 16 January 1858.

74. RA Add. T/231, ff. 19, 70.

75. RA Queen Victoria's

Journal, 24 May 1845, 10 February 1848, 24 May 1849.

76. GRLV, ff. 14, 19 July 1848, 16, 4 April, 27 June 1849.

77. George III's daughters; RA Queen Victoria's Journal, 30 July 1849.

78. Twining, 1960, p. 187, pl. 73a.

79. Queen Victoria, Leaves from a Journal, 1961, p. 52. 19 April 1855.

80. GRLV, fo. 77, 16 April for 1 July 1860.

81. Princess Louise (1848-1939), the most artistically talented of the Queen's daughters and a Royal Academy exhibitor; married John, Marquis of Lorne (1845-1914), later 9th Duke of Argyll.

82. Princess Beatrice (1857-1944), ninth and youngest child of Queen Victoria and Prince Albert. Queen Victoria clung to her 'Baby', but eventually allowed her to marry in 1885 Prince Henry of Battenberg (1858-1896), the third son of Prince Alexander of Hesse by his morganatic marriage with the Polish Countess Hauke.

83. RA Queen Victoria's Journal, 21 July 1885.

84. Ibid., 4 July 1866.

85. GRLV, fo. 29, 1 April 1853.

86. Twining, 1960, p. 190 and pl. 72a, describes it as an Indian tiara.

87. GRLV, fo. 38, 30 March 1854.

88. Queen Victoria, Leaves from a Journal, 1961, pp. 32, 88; 16 April (Windsor), 20 August (Paris) 1855.

89. RA Queen Victoria's Journal, 24 January 1858; ILN, 32, 1858, p. 132.

90. Princess Alice (1843-1878), married Prince Ludwig ('Louis') of Hesse (1837-1892), later Grand Duke, 1 July 1862, and died on 14 December 1878, the anniversary of the Prince Consort's death, after contracting diphtheria from her children.

91. RA Add. T/231, fo. 70.

92. The Hon. Sir Charles A. Murray (1806-1895), then Secretary of the Legation at Naples; GRLV, fo. 40, 5, 13 March, 2 April 1855.

93. Bliss, p. 221.

94. GRLV, fo. 28, 1 April 1853.

95. RA Queen Victoria's Journal, 8 May 1856; RA PP 12/30/9119.

96. RA Queen Victoria's Journal, 9 November, 2 December 1841.

97. Fulford, 1964, p. 83, letter dated 1 April 1858.

98. *ILN,* 28, 1856, p. 109; GRLV, ff. 44-5 (the enamelled brooches cost £30 apiece, the gold one £11). There is no reference to Miss Nightingale's brooch in Garrard's Royal Ledger, except to the cost of engraving the inscription (16s.).

99. Culme, I, pp. 331-2; Jean-Valentin Morel (1794-1860) operated in London between 1849 and 1852; Dussieux, 1876, pp. 301-6; RA Add. O, fo. 43, 1849.

100. Fontenay, pp. 367-8.

101. *AJ,* 1850, pp. 289-92.

102. Henry Cole (1808-1882); knighted, 1875; see Bonython, *King Cole* (1982).

103. Summerly Art Manufactures catalogues, Cole collection, Victoria and Albert Museum Library.

104. John Bell, R.A. (1812-1895), was so busy about Summerly articles he set up a studio for the purpose.

105. Society of Arts 1847 exhibition, cat. nos. 48-9; *J of D,* III, 1850, p. 53.

106. *J of D,* IV, 1850-1, p. 46.

107. Daniel Maclise, R.A. (1806-1871), studied at the Cork Academy before coming to London.

108. Cole Miscellanies 8, fo. 53, Victoria and Albert Museum Library; Cole, 1884, II, p. 189.

109. Culme, I, pp. 175-6; the firm was styled S.H. & D. Gass at the time of the 1851 exhibition but existed under various styles from about 1808 until after 1916.

110. Maclise's letter to Cole, 7 January 1851; Cole Collection, Victoria and Albert Museum Library.

111. London 1851 exhibition, *Reports,* Class 23, p. 516, Class 30, p. 687.

112. *J of D,* I, 1849, p. 10.

113. London 1851 exhibition, catalogue, III, France, G. Lemonnier, no. 304; he was awarded a Council Medal; *AJIC,* 1851, p. 323. In 1855 Lemonnier exhibited French Crown Jewels (Paris 1855 exhibition, *Visite,* p. 634).

114. F.-D. Froment-Meurice (1802-1855), the darling of antiquarians and connoisseurs such as the Duc de Luynes,

exhibited in London in 1849 with Rouvenat, Rudolphi and others (*ILN,* 15, 1849, p. 357); Vever, I, p. 173. London 1851 exhibition, catalogue, III, p. 1258, no. 1720; *Reports,* Class 23, p. 514, Council Medal.

115. Dussieux, 1876, p. 291.

116. London 1851 exhibition, catalogue, III, Prussia, no. 411, J.F. Backes & Co., pl. 124, 153, 173. The firm registered designs in England in the Assyrian style in 1872 (e.g. 263988-93).

117. Richard Redgrave, RA (1804-1888), painter, writer and teacher; Surveyor of the Crown Pictures.

118. RA Add. T/231, fo. 23; it cost £4.

119. London 1851 exhibition, Digby Wyatt, II, pl. 82. The drawings from which the illustration was made are in the Victoria and Albert Museum Print Room (D 2152, 3-1885).

120. Bury, 1969, pp. 85-6; the letters were transcribed by Professor Phoebe Stanton.

121. Ferrey, 1861, p. 224.

122. Hardman Day Book, 1849-54, fo. 77, 16 January 1850; Sir Stuart Knill, wharfinger (1824-1898); Lord Mayor 1893.

123. Sir John Sutton (c.1820-1873), later a Roman Catholic convert; Hardman Day Book, 1845-9, 30 June 1848; id., 11 April 1849.

124. Hardman Day Books, 1845-9, 1849-54, 9 December 1848, 9 January, 15 March 1849, 26 April, 20 December 1850; *passim.* Day Books in the Birmingham Reference Library.

125. London 1851 exhibition, *Reports,* Class 23, p. 512.

126. Fortunato Pio Castellani (1793-1865) and his sons (Munn, 1984, pp. 23-38).

127. Eugénie de Montijo married Louis Napoleon in January 1853, after he became the Emperor Napoleon III in consequence of a *coup d'état* in 1851.

128. Devin is recorded at 3 Frith Street, Soho, c.1839-1851; see also Paris 1855 exhibition, English *Reports,* II, p. 365; Culme, I, pp. 245-6.

129. Bloche, 1888, pp. 44-5; Morel, pp. 339, 341-2, 377.

CHAPTER IX

1. Timmins, 1866, Wright, p 458.

2. Select Committee on Hallmarking, *Report,* 1879, Minutes of Evidence, p. 30, para. 422.

3. London 1851 exhibition, French reports, VI, De Luynes, pp. 20-5.

4. Gee, 1892, p. 192. Gee registered a mark at the Birmingham Assay Office in 1878 which lapsed in 1918.

5. Dublin 1853 exhibition, detailed catalogue, p. 376.

6. Vienna 1873 exhibition, French reports, II, Rouvenat and Fontenay, p. 385.

7. Collins, 1871, pp. 23-5; Gee, 1892, p. 45.

8. Gee, 1892, p. 42-3.

9. Vever, I, 119-20.

10. McDonald and Hunt, 1982, Chapters 1-10.

11. London 1851 exhibition, French reports, VI, De Luynes, p. 148; Paris national exhibition, 1827, Blanqui, p. 193. Vever, I, p. 119, mentions only the 1823 exhibition.

12. McDonald and Hunt, 1982, Chapter 11.

13. London 1851 exhibition, French reports, VI, De Luynes, pp. 179, 256.

14. Manuels-Roret, I, p. 190; Collins, 1871, p. 31.

15. Paris 1878 exhibition, Bergerat, II, p. 190.

16. Paris 1900 exhibition, French reports, Class 95, pp. 383-4.

17. Gee, 1892, pp. 127-8, 133, 136-7.

18. SA *J,* XX, 1872, p. 288.

19. McDonald and Hunt, pp. 277-8; London 1862 exhibition, *Reports,* Class I, p. 34; 33, p. 2; Dublin 1865 exhibition, *Reports,* no. 655.

20. SA *J,* XLVIII, 1900, pp. 484-5; ibid., L, 1902, p. 60. Vever, II, p. 286, prints statistics slightly different from those in the preceding two references.

21. Paris 1867 exhibition, English catalogue, Class 36, France, p. 437, E. Schmoll, no. 115; Prussia, no. 5, A.J. Hoffstädt, no. 5.

22. *Journal of Acetylene Gas Lighting,* December 1897, p. 124. I am indebted to Jack M. Ogden for this reference. The Lalique 'Berenice' tiara, after the Racine tragedy, is in the Musée Lambinet, Versailles (Vever III, p. 721, Barten, cat. no. 14.1).

23. The difficulty about accepting any terminology as definitive is demonstrated by a reference to mosaic gold as a cheap bronze powder.

24. SA *J,* XX, 1872, p. 288.

25. *Myra's Threepenny Journal,* 1 October 1883, p. 295 (*ill.*).

26. Gee, 1892, pp. 148, 141, 133.

27. Bury, 1971, pp. 8-10.

28. Gee, 1892, pp. 98-111.

29. London 1851 exhibition, French reports, VI, De Luynes, pp. 195-8; McDonald and Hunt, pp. 278-80.

30. Bradbury, p. 107; Maryon, 3 edn. 1954, pp. 41-2, 45.

31. Prosser, p. 50, no. 1293.

32. Wright in Timmins, 1866, pp. 452-62.

33. Wallis in Beavan, 1876, p. 16.

34. See patent granted to A.E. Morley, J.R. Ellis and J.G. Rollason, no. 1182 (provisional protection only), 3 May 1871.

35. Paris 1867 exhibition, Workmen's *Reports,* Rasmussen, p. 38.

36. Paris 1867 exhibition, English *Reports,* II, Maskelyne, pp. 617-8.

37. Timmins, 1866, Wright, p. 453; *Handbook to Birmingham,* 1886, p.188.

38. Wright, p. 455.

39. See London 1851 exhibition, French reports, VI, De Luynes, p. 161. The Payen firm was in business from 1839; provisional English patent, 10 March 1854, no. 587.

40. W.R. Lake for L. Falize, 20 March 1879, no. 1117 (see also Gueyton of Paris, provisional patent, 1859, no. 1554).

41. Le Roy et fils of 211 Regent Street were the London agents of Martz of Paris (*AJ,* 1869, p. 114; Martz advertisement in *The American Traveller's Guide to Paris,* London, 1869, p. xlv.) Le Roy et fils passed into the hands of T.G. Hall, who patented an improvement to watch bracelets in 1890, no. 4313.

42. Carlo Giuliano, 28 September 1865, no. 2497; SA *J,* XX, 1872, p. 290. Giuliano also registered designs (eg. 213513-6, 11 November 1867).

43. J.B. Buffoni, 13 August 1864, no. 2021.

44. O.W. Barratt, 7 October 1856, no. 2340.

45. Harry Emanuel, 5 July 1865, no. 1779. An emerald and gold brooch (sans feathers) stamped HE and the patent number was sold by Christie's on 4 October 1989, lot no. 35.

46. W.H. Haseler, 5 March 1861, no. 557. Haseler entered a mark at the Birmingham Assay Office from 73½ Caroline Street on 9 May 1850.
47. A. Antill and William Wilkinson, 7 December 1863, no. 3067.
48. G.C. Haseler, 13 September 1861, no. 2277; G.C. Haseler, 10 May 1862, no. 1400; G.C. Haseler and J.B. Haseler, 11 February 1865, no. 385. The two Haselers registered a joint mark at the Birmingham Assay Office from 19 Vittoria Street on 26 July 1860.
49. J. Craddock and C.F. Richards, 29 July 1870, no. 2129.
50. R.H. Jones and J. Abrahall, 3 March 1863, no. 591.
51. G. Perry, 12 November 1866, no. 2951.
52. J. Fisslthaler, 27 January 1876, no. 334.
53. T. Welton, 28 July 1874, no. 2628; Paris 1867 exhibition, English *Reports*, II, Maskelyne, p. 607.
54. G.E. Searle, 4 October 1866, no. 2554; *ILN*, 52, 1868, p. 39.
55. H. Oakes, 29 May 1867, no. 1601; Vever, III, p. 527.
56. *ILN*, 12, 1848, p. 52. Queen Victoria's Privy Purse Ledger for 1837-49; entry dated 19 January 1849. I am grateful to Sir Geoffrey de Bellaigue for this reference.
57. C. Rowley, 30 November 1850, no. 13,371.
58. C. Payne and P. Steel, 14 October 1876, no. 3973.
59. G. Haseltine (a communication), 14 November 1857, no. 2863.
60. SA *J*, XX, pp. 290, 319. Haseltine's second patent was obtained on 26 March 1859, no. 761.
61. J. Lancelott, 4 August 1860, no. 1894. The patent specification gives an address in Essex, but according to the *Jeweller* (I, 1868, p. 86), Lancelott worked in Birmingham.
62. E. Wolverson, 25 March 1865, no. 843; J., E.R. and T. Hollands, 30 November 1865, no. 3076.
63. Thomas Jenks, 1 February 1866, no. 317; W. Bancroft and J. Wood, 20 October 1870, no. 2766. Bancroft was a press tool maker and Wood a machinist.
64. J. Rollason and J. Wood, 4 March 1874, no. 784; *Kelly's*

Post Office Directory for Birmingham, 1875, p. 442.
65. H. Witzenmann, 2 December 1871, no. 3266.
66. Paris 1867 exhibition, workmen's *Reports*, Rasmussen, p. 38.
67. A. Lion, 13 June 1867, no. 1731; ibid., 18 November 1878, no. 4674; ibid., 25 September 1879, no. 3863. Lion (1830-1895) was a well-known Paris manufacturer (Vever, II, pp. 318-322), who registered several designs under the Designs Acts (nos. 323437-42).
68. R.F. Sturges, 24 January 1852, no. 13,914.
69. F.S. Banks, 30 January 1886, no. 1403.
70. J. Totton, 22 March 1887, no. 4286; GRLV, fo. 185, 12 February 1887.
71. e.g., H. Barrett, 8 November 1887, no. 15,223.
72. J. Reading, 1 March 1856, no. 528; J. Reading, 16 January 1861, no. 125; J., S.A., G.E. and F. Reading, 16 October 1865: 25 June 1866, no. 1690.
73. London Inventions Exhibition, 1885, catalogue, Group 19, p. 207, Giuliano, no. 1643; Cox, no. 1644; West, no. 1648. West's most recent patents dated to 11 February 1881, no. 601; 5 January 1884, no. 802.
74. Lewis, 1970, pp. 36-8; London 1851 exhibition, French reports, VI, De Luynes, pp. 216-220; Wallis in Beavan, 1876, pp. 23-5; SA *J*, XXVII, 1879, pp. 786-7.
75. Barbot, pp. 533-5.
76. First noted by Allen, 1843.
77. London 1851 exhibition, French reports, VI, De Luynes, pp. 217-22.
78. *Q*, 73, 1883, p. 604; see also SA *J*, XXVIII, 1880, pp. 105, 188, 289. Becker, 1988, p. 85.
79. London 1851 exhibition, *Reports*, Class 24, pp. 536, 675. I am grateful to Robert Charleston and Barbara Morris for their advice.
80. SA *J*, XXXVII, 1889, pp. 630-1.
81. A. Nourick and W.C. Wild, 3 January 1872, no. 22; see also S. Grossford, 1898, no. 18,689.
82. A. Boubée, 21 January 1863, no. 184.
83. SA *J*, LIX, 1911, p. 579, citing E.D. Clarke, *The Gas Blowpipe*, 1819.
84. SA *J*, XXVI, 1878, pp. 304-5. A specimen of ruby flakes produced by Frémy and

Feil is in the Natural History Museum, London.
85. Nassau, *Lapidary Journal*, 1971, pp. 1284-96, 1442-7, 1524-32.
86. Nassau and Crowningshield, *Lapidary Journal*, 1969, pp. 114-9; *passim*.
87. SA *J*, XXVII, 1880, p. 105.
88. Lewis, 1970, p. 64.
89. *IA*, 1877, p. 91.
90. SA *J*, XXI, 1873, p. 315; ibid., XLIV, 1896, pp. 145-6.
91. London 1872 exhibition, *Reports*, p. 27.
92. *Connaissance des Arts*, September 1976, p. 17.
93. *AJ*, 1854, p. 22; see Morris, 1978, p. 41.
94. Lister, 1699, p. 142.
95. Dublin 1853 exhibition, detailed catalogue, p. 388.
96. London 1851 exhibition, French reports, VI, De Luynes, p. 220-1.
97. Ibid., pp. 221-4; Paris 1855 exhibition, French reports, II, Class 17, p. 918; *JG & WM MM*, 1862, p. 117.
98. Lightbown, 1985, p. 180.
99. *Q*, 91(1), 1892, advertisement, 2 January.
100. E.g., J.B.F. Frédereau, 31 May 1886, no. 7285.
101. S. Isaacs, 19 January 1855, no. 145, etc..
102. *AJ*, 1873, p. 231.
103. Patent no. 235, 1855. London 1862 exhibition, catalogue, I, Class 4, p. 89. Staight Brothers, no. 1014.
104. *IA*, 1877, p. 58.
105. London 1862 exhibition, catalogue, I, p. 103. Class 4, A. Parkes, no. 1112; *Reports*, Class 4, Section C, p. 46. Alexander Parkes (1813-1890), chemist, metallurgist and inventor, was the son of a Birmingham lock manufacturer.
106. SA *J*, XIV, 1865, pp. 81-6.
107. *AJ*, 1866, p. 224.
108. A. Parkes, 19 October 1866, no. 2709.
109. Parkes *Memoir*, p. 7.
110. *AJ*, 1868, p. 37.
111. W.R. Lake for the Celluloid Manufacturing Company, 4 March 1878, no. 878.
112. Brockedon and Hancock, November 1846, no. 11,455. This patent refers to earlier ones granted to Hancock and Parkes. See also SA *J*, XXVIII, 1880, p. 773.
113. London 1851 exhibition, *Reports*, p. 595, Charles Goodyear, United States, no. 378.

114. *ILN*, 30, 1857, p. 444.
115. London 1862 exhibition, catalogue, I, Class 4, p. 104, Scottish Vulcanite Company Ltd., Edinburgh, no. 1121.
116. SA *J*, XX, 1872, p. 289.
117. London 1851 exhibition, reports, p. 597.
118. SA, *Abstract of Proceedings* (etc.), 1845, p. 27.
119. London 1851 exhibition, *Reports*, p. 598. The American India-Rubber Works, Mannheim (Baden) however exhibited trinkets at Paris in 1867 (catalogue, English version, p. 439, Class 36, no. 1).
120. C.S. Rostaing, 28 December 1859, no. 2962.
121. W.R. Lake, communication from Frank Marquand, 31 January 1866, no. 300.
122. T.W. Davenport and S. Cole took out three patents between 1857 and 1863.
123. Wallis in Beavan, 1876, pp. 41-2; SA *J*, XX, 1872, p. 288 (the inventor was called Pinson).
124. *At*, II, 1881, p. 55.
125. H.W. Patrick, 26 May 1859, no. 1300.

CHAPTER X

1. GL 1835-46.
2. *ILN*, 33, 1858, pp. 405-6; her husband had commanded the French forces in the Crimea.
3. The Hon. C.C. Cavendish.
4. *ILN*, 19, 1851, pp. 242-3.
5. H.T. Hope (1808-1862), son of Thomas Hope; Vice-President of the Society of Arts. He and his two brothers were the heirs of their uncle, Henry Philip Hope (d. 1839), whose collection of precious stones was catalogued by B. Hertz in 1839. A copy now in the National Art Library, Victoria and Albert Museum, was annotated by Hunt & Roskell with the names of purchasers and prices.
6. London 1851 exhibition, catalogue, II, Class 23, p. 682, 73. The famous blue diamond is now in the Smithsonian Institution, Washington.
7. Joseph Mayer, Lord Street, Liverpool, collector, silversmith and jeweller; London 1851 exhibition, manufacturers' prospectuses, Science Museum Library.

8. *F* ((English version) 2 September 1848, p. 2.

9. London 1851 exhibition; manufacturers' prospectuses, J.V. Morel; catalogue, IV, Supplement, pl. 344; *Reports,* Class 23, p. 520; *ILN,* 19, 1851, p. 128.

10. The firm founded by Benoit Marrel and his brother in Paris in the 1830s. Gold Medal, Paris 1839 exhibition.

11. London 1851 exhibition, French reports, VI, De Luynes, pp. 212-3; *Reports,* Class 23, p. 515.

12. Laboulaye, 1856, p. 155.

13. London 1851 exhibition, manufacturers' prospectuses.

14. Ibid., catalogue, II, Class 23, p. 683, 84, *Reports,* Class IV, p. 164 (Hon. Mention).

15. Disraeli, *Coningsby,* Book IV, Chapter II.

16. *AJ,* 1854, p. 20.

17. Vever, III, p.397.

18. Martin, I, p. 209.

19. London 1851 exhibition, catalogue, III, Saxony, p. 112, 177.

20. Hinks, p.34.

21. Paris 1889 exhibition, French reports, Massin, pp. 66-8; Vever, II, p. 164, III, p. 472.

22. London 1851 exhibition, French reports, VI, De Luynes, pp. 212-3.

23. Hinks, p. 33.

24. Rev. William Addington (1794-1864), 2nd Viscount Sidmouth.

25. Paris 1844 exhibition, Burat, II, pp. 35-7.

26. Charles Christofle (1805-1863), worked for the Parisian jeweller Calmette from 1825 and succeeded to the business, 1831. Gold Medals, Paris 1839 and 1844 exhibitions. Rouvenat repeated the Gold Medal, 1849.

27. London 1851 exhibition, French reports, VI, De Luynes, p. 151.

28. Vever, I, p. 191.

29. London 1851 exhibition, *Reports,* Class 23, pp. 513-4.

30. RA Add. T/231, fo. 53. Victoire of Saxe-Coburg (1822-1857) married Duc de Nemours (1814-1896) in 1840.

31. *J of D,* II, 1849-50, p. 24.

32. Vever, III, p. 418.

33. London 1851 exhibition, *Reports,* Class I, p. 10, Prize Medal.

34. *F,* VII, 30 May 1846, p. 317.

35. Eugène Petiteau junior, innovatory jeweller and designer, succeeded to the business of his father Simon, c.1845.

36. Alexis Falize (1811-1892), designer and jeweller, born Liège. Entered Mellerio/Meller frères, 1833; head of Janisset's workshop 1835-38. Set up in business as a manufacturing jeweller, 1838; Bronze Medal as *coopérateur,* Paris 1867 exhibition; Vever, II, pp. 61-87.

37. Fontenay, pp. 372-3.

38. GRLV, fo. 33, 4 November 1853.

39. Augusta Caroline (1822-1916) elder daughter of the Duke of Cambridge and his wife Augusta; married, 28 June 1843, Frederick William (1819-1904), later Grand Duke of Mecklenburg-Strelitz.

40. RA Add. T/231, ff. 28, 57.

41. *F* (English version), XI, February 1857, pp. 1-2.

42. London 1851 exhibition, manufacturers' prospectuses, Phillips Brothers, p. 12, no. 178.

43. Science & Art Department, *10th Report,* 1863, Appendix, p. 157.

44. Princely Magnificence, Victoria and Albert Museum, 1980-1, cat. no. 46; altered.

45. Gere and Munn, 1989, p. 104.

46. *ILN,* 30, 1857, pp. 441-2; Scarisbrick, 1986, pp. 239-54 (in which all the gems are catalogued by Mrs Scarisbrick).

47. Jules Wièse (1818-1893), chaser and jeweller, pupil of Hossauer, Berlin goldsmith; worked in Paris for Morel and then for Froment-Meurice before setting up in business on his own account. Medallist 1849, 1855, 1862. Succeeded by his son Louis, 1880 (Vever, II, pp. 208-11).

48. Auguste Fannière (1819-1901), sculptor, designer; Joseph Fannière (1820-1897), chaser, craftsman. Medallists 1855, 1862, 1867, 1878, 1889 (Vever, II, p. 198-207).

49. Bliss, p. 103.

50. Bloche, 1888, nos. 32, 33; Morel, p. 342-3.

51. RA Queen Victoria's Journal, 3 September 1843; known to the family as 'Chica', the Princess was married to François, the King's third son (1818-1900).

52. Lutyens, 1965, pp. 162-3.

53. *F,* (English version), I, November 1846, p. 14.

54. Ibid., March 1847, p. 62; *ILN,* 18, 1851, p. 80.

55. Paris 1855 exhibition, French reports, II, class 17, p. 916, no. 5101; Vever, III, p. 362.

56. *LC,* 2s X, 1848 (2), p. 60.

57. Or Bellini? Id. V, 1846, p. 206.

58. *ILN,* 28, 1856, p. 486.

59. Lutyens, 1965, p. 257; Marie Thérèse, daughter of Prince Charles Alexander of Tour and Taxis, married, 1812, Prince Pál Anton von Esterházy.

60. *BLM,* VI, 1839, p. 248.

61. *CM,* ns IV, 1838, p. 147.

62. *ILN,* 18, 1851, pp. 180-1; 29, 1856, p. 117.

63. *ILN,* 32, 1858, p. 500; The Duc de Persigny (1808-1872), French Ambassador to London, 1855-58 and 1859-60. His wife was Marshal Ney's daughter.

64. GRLV, fo. 58; the locket cost £15 and an engraved inscription 4s.6d.

65. Scarisbrick, 1985, pp. 55-7.

66. *AJIC,* 1851, p. 127.

67. *ILN,* 17, 1850, pp. 332, 484.

68. London 1851 exhibition, French reports, VI, De Luynes, p. 92; cf. Culme, I, pp. 245-7.

69. GRLV, fo. 45, 10 December 1855.

70. *ILN,* 32, 1858, p. 132.

71. Vever, II, p. 264.

72. *CM,* ns IV, 1839, p. 707, no. 804.

73. *ILN,* 32, 1858, p. 450.

74. London 1851 exhibition, manufacturers' prospectuses, Phillips Brothers, no. 94 (described as blue enamel); *AJIC,* p. 326.

75. London 1851 exhibition, *Reports,* Class 23, p. 513.

76. Bloche, 1888, no. 43; Morel, p. 342.

77. London 1851 exhibition, *AJIC* p. 127; Culme, I, p. 396.

78. *ILN,* 27, 1855, pp. 51-2; the Hope diamond was presented to the Smithsonian in 1958 by Harry Winston, the jeweller (Balfour, pp. 102-12).

79. GRLV, fo. 38, 14 September 1854.

80. RA Add. T/231, fo. 41; Queen Victoria's Journal, 20 November 1857.

81. London 1851 exhibition, manufacturers' prospectuses, Phillips Brothers, pp. 7, 10; *AJIC,* 1851, p. 326.

82. Fontenay, p. 299.

83. Lutyens, 1972, pp. 190-1; Ruskin alludes to the firm in *Praeterita,* p. 325.

84. *F* (English version), IV, August 1850; Fontenay, p. 302.

85. London 1851 exhibition; Payen was awarded a Prize Medal (*Reports,* Class 23, p. 519).

86. GRLV, ff. 53, 79.

87. Ibid., fo. 73.

88. Fulford, 1964, p. 307.

89. *ILN,* 20, 1852, pp. 97-8.

90. *LC,* XII, 1837, p. 269.

91. GRLV, ff. 42, 78; *passim.*

92. Vever, II, p. 196.

93. RA Add. O, fo. 18.

94. J.W. Carlyle, I, pp. 299-300; Bliss, p. 83.

95. Dickens, *Dombey and Son,* Chapter 1; see also Forster, Book 6, Chapter II.

96. Vever, I, p. 276.

97. London 1851 exhibition, manufacturers' prospectuses, Phillips Brothers, pp. 1-3.

98. Gere, 1972, p. 152.

99. Hubert Obry (1808-1853); Vever, I, pp. 313-32.

100. Lutyens, 1965, pp. 69, 79.

101. RA Queen Victoria's Journal, 8, 10, 11 February 1841.

102. Ibid., 21 November 1841; Duchess of Kent's Journal.

103. RA PP. 2/6/4396. Six oriental pearls at £12.12s. each and four at £8 apiece, amounting to £107. The Princess Royal contributed £40.

104. Queen Victoria, *Leaves from a Journal,* 1961, p. 52. 19 April 1855.

105. RA Queen Victoria's Journal, 26-7 October 1858; Prince Alfred (1844-1900), later Duke of Edinburgh and Duke of Saxe-Coburg Gotha.

106. Forster, Book 8, Chapter VII. Walter Dickens died in Calcutta in 1863.

Abbreviated Bibliography for Volume I

(The full bibliography may be found at the end of Volume II)

Unless otherwise stated, the published titles originated in London

ORIGINAL SOURCES

Blathwayt Papers, Gloucester County Record Office.

Boulton Papers, including letters and memoranda, incomplete, Birmingham Assay Office.

Boulton Pattern Book B (one of eight surviving volumes), Birmingham Reference Library.

Bridge Album (apparently the property of John Gawler Bridge of Rundell's). Lettered on binding, H. Holbein's Jewellery. Metropolitan Museum of Art Print Room, New York.

Brogden Design Book or Album. Designs for jewellery etc., 1848-1884, from the workshop of Watherston & Brogden/John Brogden. Victoria and Albert Museum Print Room.

Christofle, Charles, *Design Book* or *Album*, stamped: CH. CHRISTOFLE/FABRIQUE DE JOAILLERIE BIJOUTERIE. PARIS, containing original designs, mainly naturalistic, c.1840-45.

CL. Joseph Kitching, Ledger 1817-25, Collingwood of Bond Street, Ltd.

Cole Collection. The papers of Sir Henry Cole, including diaries, miscellanies, correspondence, Summerly Art Manufactures catalogues, etc. Victoria and Albert Museum Library.

Fox MS. (An account of) the firm of Rundell, Bridge & Co...., c.1843-6. Baker Library, Harvard School of Business Administration, Harvard University; photostat and typescript copy in the Victoria and Albert Museum Library.

GL, WL, DB, GRLV etc. Garrard Gentlemen's Ledgers, Workmen's Ledgers, Day Books [Stock Books]; Garrard Royal Ledger for Queen Victoria. (The Royal Ledger for Queen Victoria and other royal and official ledgers and inventories are closed to access.) The other ledgers (which terminate in 1846, subsequent volumes having disappeared) are in the Victoria and Albert Museum Archives.

Goetze Account Book. Descriptions of regimental badges, and N. Goetze's account book, 1809-1815. Victoria and Albert Museum Library.

Hardman Day Books, 1845-49, 1849-54, from the records of John Hardman & Co. of Birmingham. Birmingham Reference Library. (The Pugin letters to Hardman cited in the text were transcribed by Professor Phoebe Stanton from originals then in the possession of the late Sebastian Pugin Powell.)

Josephine, original documents (see Nitot et fils).

London 1851 drawings. Coloured drawings of exhibits made for reproduction in M. Digby Wyatt, *Industrial Arts of the XIX Century* (see below).

Nitot et fils. MSS. Inventory of jewellery for the Empress Josephine at Strasbourg, Paris 14 April 1809; list of jewellery sent to the Empress on approval, 26 May 1809, etc. Victoria and Albert Museum Library.

Norwich Consistory Court Wills, Norfolk County Record Office.

PRO prefix. (Public Record Office) Chancery Lane, London.

Chancery Proceedings (Equity Suits), Series III, 1800-42, c 13/69 23. Case brought by the partners of Parker and Birkett against the principal directors of Rundell's over the Pigot diamond, 1805-6.

LC prefix. Lord Chamberlain's Department.

LC2-50, 51, accounts and expenses of George IV's coronation.

PRO prefix. Kew.

Company Registrations (BT 31 etc.).

Expired Commissions, H.O.73 (see Millar, 1986).

Registered Designs (BT 42-53; see Volume II, Appendix I).

RA prefix. Royal Archives, Windsor Castle (in chronological order).

The Stuart Papers.

King George IV. Private accounts with goldsmiths and jewellers.

King William IV. Privy Purse Accounts, 1833-6.

Queen Adelaide. Diary, January 1830 to December 1831 (copy of an English translation by Georgina Masson of the original in private ownership).

The Duchess of Kent's Journal, 1837-59, edited and translated by the Duchess, with commentary.

Hanoverian Claim to the Crown Jewels (see Volume II, Appendix II).

Ronca's invoice, receipt etc. (8459).

Princess Victoria's Journal, 1832-9. Typescript of transcription by Lord Esher (see published version under Queen Victoria, *Girlhood*).

Queen Victoria's Journals, 1840-1901, transcribed and edited from the originals by Princess Beatrice (Princess Henry of Battenberg), before destroying them.

Add. O. Christmas Presents, 1841-61.

Add. T. Jewellery and Pictures. Accounts, etc. 1837-1906.

Queen Victoria. Privy Purse Ledger, 1837-49. Also records of payment of individual bills (PP 2/6/4396, PP 12/30/9119).

Royal Library, Windsor, drawing by Henrietta Ward.

Rundell, 'Particulars', extracted from a royal ledger by the firm's successors, Garrard's. The original volume was then apparently destroyed.

Wellington Archives, Stratfieldsaye. The Papers of the 1st Duke of Wellington. Folder dated 1830, marked 'Papers from Mr Bridge' but also containing correspondence with Lady Conyngham and William IV.

PRINTED SOURCES

Adeane, J.H., ed., *The Girlhood of Maria Josepha Holroyd* [*Lady Stanley of Alderley*], 1896.

Aitken, W.C., 'Brass and Brass Manufactures' and 'The Revived Art of Metal-working...on Mediaeval, or True Principles', Timmins, 1866, pp. 225-79, 536-60.

Alexander, Michael and Anand, Sushila, *Queen Victoria's Maharajah, Duleep Singh, 1838-93*, 1980.

Allen, C., *The Young Mechanic's Instructor*, 1843.

Ames, Winslow, *Prince Albert and Victorian Taste*, 1968.

Arbuthnot. Bamford, Francis and the Duke of Wellington, eds., *The Journal of Mrs Arbuthnot, 1820-1832*, 2 vols., 1950.

Austen-Leigh, W. and R.A., *Jane Austen. Her Life and Letters. A Family Record*, 1913.

Babelon, Ernest, *Histoire de la Gravure sur Gemmes en France*, Paris, 1902.

Balfour, Ian, *Famous Diamonds*, 1987.

Barbot, Charles, *Guide Pratique du Joaillier*, Paris, 1858.

Barten, Sigrid, *René Lalique, Schmuck und Objets d'Art, 1890-1910*,

Munich, 1977.

Bear, Joan, *Caroline Murat, a Biography*, 1972.

Beavan, G. Phillips, ed., *British Manufacturing Industries*, 1876; Wallis, G., 'Jewellery'.

Becker, 1988. Becker, Vivienne, *Fabulous Fakes. The History of Fantasy and Fashion Jewellery*, 1988.

Bell, Quentin, *The Schools of Design*, 1963.

Bellier, Auvray. Bellier de la Chavignerie, E. and Auvray, L., *Dictionnaire général des Artistes de l'Ecole française*, 3 vols., Paris, 1882-87.

Bénézit, E., *Dictionnaire critique et documentaire des Peintres, Sculpteurs, Dessinateurs et Graveurs*, 10 vols., Paris, 1976.

Bennett, Daphne, *King without a Crown. Albert, Prince Consort of England, 1819-1861*, 1977.

Bessborough, the Earl of, ed., *Georgiana. Extracts from the Correspondence of Georgiana, Duchess of Devonshire*, 1955.

Billing, A., *The Science of Gems, Jewels, Coins, and Medals, ancient and modern*, 1875.

Birchall. *The Diary of a Victorian Squire. Extracts from the Diaries and Letters of Dearman & Emily Birchall, chosen and introduced* by David Verey, Gloucester, 1983.

Blakiston, Georgiana, *Lord William Russell and his Wife, 1815-1846*, 1972.

Bliss, Trudy, *Jane Welsh Carlyle, a New Selection of her Letters*, 1949.

Bloche, Arthur, *La Vente des Diamants de la Couronne..., avec le Catalogue raisonné des Joyaux*, Paris, 1888.

Bonython, Elizabeth, *King Cole. A Picture Portrait of Sir Henry Cole, K.C.B., 1808-1882*, 1982.

Booth, Charles, *Life and Labour of the People of London*, 2 series, 1903, VI, Part I, Precious Metals, etc., by G.H. Duckworth.

Bradbury, Frederick, *History of Old Sheffield Plate* (1 ed., 1912), reprinted Sheffield, 1968.

Bruton, Eric, *Diamonds*, 1970.

Buckle, Richard, ed., *The Prettiest Girl in England. The Love Story of Mrs Fitzherbert's Niece, from Journals*, 1958.

Bulgari, C.G., *Argentieri, Gemmari e Orafe d'Italia*, 4 vols., Rome, 1958-69.

Bury, Lady C. A. Francis Steuart, ed., *The Diary of a Lady in Waiting by Lady Charlotte Bury: Being the Diary Illustrative of the Times of George the Fourth*, 4 vols., 1838, 1839.

Bury, 1969. Bury, Shirley, 'Pugin's Marriage Jewellery', Victoria and Albert Museum *Year Book*, I, 1969, pp. 85-96.

Bury, 1971. Bury, Shirley, *Victorian Electroplate*, 1971.

Bury, 1982. Bury, Shirley, *Jewellery Gallery Summary Catalogue, Victoria and Albert Museum*, 1982.

Bury, 1984. Bury, Shirley, *An Introduction to Rings*, Victoria and Albert Museum, 1984.

Bury, 1985. Bury, Shirley, *An Introduction to Sentimental Jewellery*, Victoria and Albert Museum, 1985.

Bury, 1987. Bury, Shirley, 'The Nineteenth and Early Twentieth Centuries', Claude Blair, gen. ed., *The History of Silver*, 1987, pp. 157-95.

Bury, 1988. Bury, Shirley, 'Queen Victoria and the Hanoverian Claim to the Crown Jewels', Handbook to The International Silver and Jewellery Fair and Seminar, 29 January-1 February, 1988, The Dorchester, Park Lane, London.

Bury, Wedgwood and Snodin, 1979. Bury, Shirley, Wedgwood, Alexandra and Snodin, Michael, 'The Antiquarian Plate of George IV', *Burlington* Magazine, CXXI, 1979, pp. 343-53.

Byron, Letters. Leslie A. Marchand, ed., *Byron's Letters and Journals*, complete edition, London and Cambridge, Mass., 1973-1981.

Campbell, Mary, *Lady Morgan, the life and times of Sydney Owenson*, 1988.

Capel, *Letters*. The Marquess of Anglesey, ed., *The Capel Letters, being the Correspondence of Lady Caroline Capel and her daughters with the Dowager Countess of Uxbridge from Brussels and Switzerland, 1814-1817*, 1955.

Carlyle, J.W. Froude, J.A., ed., *Letters and Memorials* of Jane Welsh Carlyle, 3 vols., 1883.

Carr, *Connoisseur*, 1975. Carr, Malcolm Stuart, 'Tommaso and Luigi Saulini', *Connoisseur*, vol. 190, November 1975, pp. 171-81.

Chaffers, William, *Gilda Aurifabrorum*, 1883, new ed., 1899.

Charlotte, Princess, *Letters*. Aspinall, A., ed., *Letters of the Princess Charlotte 1811-1817*, 1949.

Cholmondeley, *Heber Letters*. Cholmondeley, R.H., *The Heber Letters, 1783-1832*, 1950.

Cobb, Richard, *The People's Armies (Les Armées Révolutionnaires*, 2 vols., Paris 1961 and 1963), translated by Marianne Elliott, New Haven and London, 1987.

Coke. *The Letters and Journals of Lady Mary Coke, 1756-1774*, 4 vols., 1889-1896; reprinted Bath, 1970.

Cole, 1884. Cole, Sir Henry, *Fifty Years of Public Work*, 2 vols., London, 1884.

Collier, Hon. E.C.F., *A Victorian Diarist, extracts from the Journals of Mary, Lady Monkswell, 1873-1895*, 1944.

Collingwood the Jeweller, brochure by Madeleine Masson, c.1978.

Collini, C.A., 'Manière de travailler les agates à Oberstein', *Journal d'un Voyage...*, 1776 (photocopy in the Victoria and Albert Museum Library).

Collins, 1871. Collins, James E., *The Private Book of Useful Alloys & Memoranda for Goldsmiths, Jewellers, etc.*, n.d. (preface dated July 1871).

Complete Peerage. Cokayne, George Edward, *Complete Peerage*, revised and enlarged by the Hon Vicary Gibbs, etc. 12 vols., 1910-1959.

Creevey. Maxwell, Sir Herbert, ed., *The Creevey Papers. A Selection from the Correspondence & Diaries of the late Thomas Creevey, M.P., born 1768 - died 1838*, 2 vols., 1903, 2 ed., 1904.

Culme, 1977. Culme, John, 'Beauty and the Beast', *Connoisseur*, 196, 1977, pp. 44-53.

Culme, I. Culme, John, *The Directory of Gold & Silversmiths, Jewellers & Allied Traders, 1838-1914. From the London Assay Office Registers*, 2 vols., Woodbridge, 1987.

D'Arblay, *Diary and Letters. The Diary and Letters of Madame D'Arblay (Frances Burney)*. With notes by W.C. Ward, etc. 3 vols., 1890.

Davenport, *Jewellery*. Davenport, Cyril, *Jewellery*, 1905.

Davenport, W., CL 1978. Davenport, Winifred M., 'Jewellery for Victorian Sportsmen', *Country Life*, 8 June 1978, pp. 1662-4.

De Barrera, Madame A., *Gems and Jewels*, 1860.

Dècle, A., *Historique de la Bijouterie française*, Paris, 1889.

Delany. Llanover, Lady, ed., *The Autobiography and Correspondence of Mary Granville, Mrs Delany*, 6 vols., Series I, 1861 and Series II, 1862.

Desautels, 1979. Desautels, Paul E., *Treasures in the Smithsonian. The Gem Collection*, Washington D.C., 1979.

Dussieux, 1876. Dussieux, L., *Les Artistes français à l'Etranger...*, Paris, 1856, 3 ed., 1876.

Emanuel, Harry, *Diamonds and Precious Stones: their History, Value, and Distinguishing Characteristics*, 1865.

Ernest Augustus, King of Hanover, *Letters of the King of Hanover to Viscount Strangford, K.C.B.*, 1925.

Evans, 1970. Evans, Joan, *A History of Jewellery 1100-1870*, 1953, 2 ed., revised and reset, 1970.

Farington, *Diary*. Greig, James, etc., eds., *The Farington Diary* by Joseph Farington, R.A., 8 vols., 1922-28.

Ferrey, 1861. Ferrey, Benjamin, *Recollections of A.N. Welby Pugin, and his father, Augustus Pugin*, 1861.

Fiennes. Morris, Christopher, ed., *The Journeys of Celia Fiennes*, 1949.

Fitzgerald, Brian, *Emily, Duchess of Leinster, 1731-1784. A Study of her Life and Times*, 1949.

Fontenay, Eugène, *Les Bijoux Anciens et Modernes*, Paris 1887, reprinted Florence, 1986.

Forrer, L., *Biographical Dictionary of Medallists*, 8 vols., 1904-1930, reprinted 1980.

Forster, John, *The Life of Charles Dickens*, 2 vols., first published 1872-1874 (single-volume ed., n.d.).

Frampton. Mundy, Harriot Georgiana, ed., *The Journal of Mary Frampton, from the year 1779 until the year 1846*, 3 ed., 1886.

Fulford, 1964. Fulford, Roger, ed., *Dearest Child, Letters between Queen Victoria and the Princess Royal, 1858-1861*, 1964.

Gartside, Mary, *Ornamental Groups, Descriptive Flowers, Birds, Shells, Fruit, Insects* [etc.], 1808.

Gaudibert, P., *Ingres*, Paris, 1970.

Gee, 1892. Gee, George E., *The Jeweller's Assistant in the Art of Working in Gold*, 1892.

George Prince of Wales, *Correspondence*. A. Aspinall, ed., *The Correspondence of George, Prince of Wales, 1770-1812*. 8 vols., 1963-71.

George IV, *Letters*. A. Aspinall, ed., *The Letters of King George IV, 1812-1830*, 3 vols., 1938.

Gere. (See Tait, 1984.)

Gere, 1972. Gere, Charlotte, *Victorian Jewellery Design*, 1972.

Gere, 1975. Gere, Charlotte, *European & American Jewellery*, 1975.

Gere and Munn, 1989. Gere, Charlotte and Munn, Geoffrey C., *Artists' Jewellery, Pre-Raphaelite to Arts and Crafts*, Woodbridge, 1989.

Goad, Thomas William, 'Gold and Silver Mining in the Rocky Mountains of Colorado', Society of Arts *Journal*, XXXVII, 1889, pp. 173-80.

Gonzalez-Palacios, Alvar; Röttgen, Steffi and others, *The Art of Mosaics, Selections from the Gilbert Collection*, catalogue and essays, revised ed., Los Angeles, 1982.

Grandjean, 1964. Grandjean, Serge, *Inventaire après décès de l'Impératrice Joséphine à Malmaison*, Paris, 1964.

Grandjean, 1976. Grandjean, Serge, 'Jewellery under the French Empire', *Connoisseur*, CXCIII, December 1976, pp. 275-81.

Graves, A., *The Royal Academy of Arts: A Complete Dictionary of Contributors and their Work 1769-1904*, 1905-6.

Gray, J.E., 'On the Manufacture of Shell Cameos', *Transactions of the Society of Arts, Manufactures and Commerce*, supplemental vol., 1852, pp. 138-41.

Gray, John M., *James and William Tassie, a Biographical and Critical Sketch with a Catalogue of their Portrait Medallions of Modern Personages*, Edinburgh, 1894, reprinted 1975.

Greville, *Memoirs*. Reeve, Henry, ed., *The Greville Memoirs. A Journal of the Reigns of King George IV and King William IV. By the late Charles C.F. Greville, Esq.*, 3 vols., 5 ed., 1875. *The Greville Memoirs (Second Part). A Journal of the Reign of Queen Victoria from 1837 to 1852...*, 3 vols., 1885.

Grey, Lieut.-General the Hon. Charles, *The Early Years of His Royal Highness The Prince Consort, compiled, under the direction of Her Majesty the Queen*, 2 ed., 1867.

Grimwade, 1976. Grimwade, Arthur G., *London Goldsmiths 1697-1837, their Marks and Lives, from the Original Registers at Goldsmiths' Hall and Other Sources*, 1976.

Gruner, L., *Specimens of Ornamental Art*, 1853.

Hackenbroch, 1979. Hackenbroch, Yvonne, *Renaissance Jewellery*, London, Munich and New York, 1979.

Hackenbroch, 1986. Hackenbroch, Yvonne, 'Reinhold Vasters, Goldsmith', *Metropolitan Museum Journal* 19/20, Metropolitan Museum of Art, New York, pp. 163-268.

Hamwood Papers. Bell, Mrs G.H. (John Travers), ed., *The Hamwood Papers of the Ladies of Llangollen and Caroline Hamilton*, 1930.

Hauser-Köchert, Irmgard, *Köchert Jewellery Designs, 1810-1940*, Florence, 1990.

Haydon. Taylor, Tom, ed., *The Life of Benjamin Robert Haydon, Historical Painter, from his Autobiography and Journals*, 2 ed., 3 vols., 1853.

Heal, Sir Ambrose, *The London Goldsmiths 1200-1800, a Record of the Names and Addresses of the Craftsmen, their Shop-signs and Trade-cards*, 1935, reprinted Newton Abbot, 1972.

Healey, Edna, *Lady Unknown. The Life of Angela Burdett-Coutts*, 1978.

Herold, J. Christopher, *Mistress to an Age. A Life of Madame de Staël*, 1959.

Hertz, B. *A Catalogue of the Collection of Pearls and Precious Stones formed by Henry Philip Hope, Esq.*, 1839.

Hibbert, Christopher, *The Court at Windsor*, 1964.

Hibbert, Christopher, *George IV*, single-vol. paperback, 1976, first published in 2 vols. as *George IV: Prince of Wales*, 1972, and *George IV, Regent and King*, 1973.

Hinks, Peter, *Nineteenth Century Jewellery*, 1975.

Holland. Ayres, Jack, ed., *Paupers and Pig Killers. The Diary of William Holland, a Somerset Parson, 1799-1818*, Gloucester, 1984.

Hope, Thomas, *Household Furniture and Interior Decoration*, 1807.

Howarth, Stephen, *The Koh-i-Noor Diamond. The History and the Legend*, London, Melbourne, New York, 1980.

Jagow, Kurt, ed., *Letters of the Prince Consort 1831-1861*, translated by E.T.S. Dugdale, 1938.

Jefferys, Nathaniel, *A Review of the Conduct of... the Prince of Wales in his Various Transactions with Mr. J;... containing a detail of many circumstances relative to... the Prince and Princess of Wales, Mrs. Fitzherbert, etc.*, 1806.

Kauffmann, 1982. Kauffmann, C.M., *Catalogue of Paintings in the Wellington Museum*, Victoria and Albert Museum, 1982.

Keil, 1977. Keil, Nora, *Die Miniaturen der Albertina in Wien*, Vienna, Albertina Collection, 1977.

Keppel, Sonia, *The Sovereign Lady. A Life of Elizabeth Vassall, third Lady Holland, with her family*, 1974.

King, C.W., *Handbook of Engraved Gems*, 1885.

Knapton, Ernest John, *Empress Josephine*, Cambridge, Mass. and London, 1964.

Knight. Kaye, Sir J.W. and Hulton, J., eds., *Autobiography of Miss Cornelia Knight, Lady Companion to the Princess Charlotte of Wales, with Extracts from her Journals and Anecdote Books*, 4 ed., 2 vols., 1861.

Kris, E., *Catalogue of Postclassical Cameos in the Milton Weil Collection*, Vienna, 1932.

Kunz and Stevenson. Kunz, G.F. and Stevenson, C.H., *The Book of the Pearl*, 1908.

Kunz 1917/1973. Kunz, G.F., *Rings for the Finger*, New York 1917, Dover ed. New York, 1973.

Labarte, Jules, *Handbook of the Arts of the Middle Ages and Renaissance*, translated from Labarte's Introduction to his catalogue of the Debruge-Duménil collection, Paris 1847-8, 1855.

Lambourne, 1965. Lambourne, Lionel, 'A Giraffe for George IV', *Country Life*, CXXXVIII, 2 December 1965.

Lardner, Dr Dionysus, *Cabinet Cyclopaedia*, 133 vols. (including Metal II), 1830-49.

La Tour du Pin. Harcourt, Félice, ed. and trans., *Escape from the Terror. The Journal of Madame de la Tour du Pin*, London, 1979.

Lawrence, Rosamund, Lady, *Charles Napier, Friend and Fighter, 1782-1853*, 1952.

Layard, Sir A.M., *Nineveh and its Remains*, 1849 (actually about Nimrud).

Leconfield, Maud Lady and Gore, John, *Three Howard Sisters. Selections from the Writings of Lady Caroline Lascelles, Lady Dover and Countess Gower, 1825 to 1833*, 1955.

Le Corbeiller, 1970. Le Corbeiller, Clare, 'James Cox, a biographical review', *Burlington* magazine, CXII, June 1970, pp. 351-58.

LeFanu, William, ed., *Betsy Sheridan's Journal. Letters from Sheridan's sister, 1784-1786 and 1788-1790*, 1960.

Leslie, 1939. Leslie, Shane, *The Life and Letters of Mrs. Fitzherbert*, 2 vols., I, 1939, II, 1940.

Leveson Gower, the Hon. F., *Letters of Harriet Countess Granville, 1810-1845*, 2 vols., 1894.

Lord Granville Leveson Gower, *Private Correspondence*. Granville, Castalia Countess, ed., *Lord Granville Leveson Gower (first Earl Granville), Private Correspondence, 1781-1821*, 2 vols., 1916.

Leveson Gower, Iris, *The Face without a Frown. Georgiana Duchess of Devonshire*, 1944, 4 ed., 1945.

Lewis, M.D.S., *Antique Paste Jewellery*, 1970.

Lieven-Palmerston. Sudley, Lord, trans. and ed., *The Lieven-Palmerston Correspondence, 1828-1856*, 1943.

Lightbown, 1985. Lightbown, R.W., 'Souvenirs of Italy (for Nineteenth-century Travellers)', Victoria and Albert Museum *Album* 4, ed. Anna Somers Cocks, 1985, pp. 178-86.

Lister, 1699. Lister, Dr Martin, *A Journey to Paris in the Year 1698*, 1699.

Lockhart, J.G., *Narrative of the Life of Sir Walter Scott, Bart.*, begun by himself and continued by J.G. Lockhart, 2 vols., Edinburgh, 1837, new ed., 1849.

Login, *Recollections*. Login, E. Dalhousie, *Lady Login's Recollections, Court Life and Camp Life, 1820-1904*, 1916.

London: House of Commons. Parliamentary Papers, SCAM (The Select Committee on Arts and Manufactures), properly the Select Committee on Arts and Principles of Design and their Connexion with Manufactures, 1835-6. *Second Report, Minutes of Evidence, Appendix and Index*, 1836.

London: House of Commons. Parliamentary Papers, Select Committee on Hallmarking, *Report from the Select Committee on Hall Marking (Gold and Silver); together with the Proceedings of the Committee, Minutes of Evidence, Appendix and Index*, 1879.

London [Victoria and Albert Museum]. *Department of Practical Art. A catalogue of the Articles of Ornamental Art, for the use of Students and Manufacturers, and the Consultation of the Public*, 2 ed., 1852.

London [Victoria and Albert Museum]. Science & Art Department. South Kensington Museum. *Catalogue of the Collection of Commercial Products of the Animal Kingdom*, 2 ed., 1860.

London [Victoria and Albert Museum]. Science & Art Department, *10th Report*, 1863. *Science and Art Department of the Committee of Council on Education, Tenth Report*, Appendix N1, George Wallis, 'Report on the employment of students of Schools of Art in the production of various works of ornamental manufactures...exhibited...in the International Exhibition, 1862', 1863, pp. 146-76.

Longford, Elizabeth, Lady, *Victoria R.I.*, 1964.

Longford, *Wellington*. Longford, Elizabeth, Lady, *Wellington: the Years of the Sword*, 1969 (paperback 1971).

Longford, Elizabeth Lady, *Wellington: Pillar of State*, 1972 (paperback 1975).

Lorne, the Marquis of, now his Grace the Duke of Argyll, *V.R.I., Her Life and Empire*, [1902].

Lutyens, 1965. Lutyens, Mary, ed., *Effie in Venice. Unpublished Letters of Mrs. John Ruskin written from Venice between 1849-1852*, 1965.

Lutyens, 1972. Lutyens, Mary, *The Ruskins and the Grays*, 1972.

McDonald and Hunt. McDonald, Donald and Hunt, Leslie B., *A History of Platinum and its Allied Metals*, 1982.

Manuels-Roret, I. *Nouvueau Manuel Complet du Bijoutier, du Joaillier, de l'Orfèvre...*, new ed., revised by Malepeyre, I, 1855.

Marie Louise, Princess. Her Highness Princess Marie Louise, *My Memories of Six Reigns*, 1956.

Marquardt, Brigitte, *Schmuck, Klassismus und Biedermeier, 1780-1850. Deutschland, Österreich, Schweiz*, Munich, 1983.

Martin, *Prince Consort*. Martin, Theodore, *The Life of His Royal Highness The Prince Consort*, 5 vols., 1875-1880.

Maryon, 3 edn., 1954. Maryon, Herbert, *Metalwork and Enamelling*, 3 ed., 1954.

Masson. *The Private Diaries of the Empress Marie-Louise, Wife of Napoleon I*, with introduction and commentary by Frédéric Masson, 1922.

Masters, Brian, *Georgiana Duchess of Devonshire*, 1981.

Mawe, 1823. Mawe, John, *A Treatise on Diamonds and Precious Stones; including their history — natural and commercial, to which are added the best methods of cutting and polishing*, new ed., 1823.

Mémoire. *Mémoire pour la demoiselle Le Guay d'Oliva, fille mineure, emancipé d'âge, accusée; contre M. Le Procureur-Général, accusateur; en présence de M. le Cardinal-Prince de Rohan, de la Dame de La Motte-Valois, du Sieur de Cagliostro, & autres; tous co-accusés*, Paris, 1786.

Millar, 1969. Millar, Sir Oliver, *The Later Georgian Pictures in the Collection of Her Majesty The Queen*, 2 vols., 1969.

Millar, 1986. Millar, Sir Oliver, 'Documents for the History of Collecting: 2. George IV when Prince of Wales: his debts to artists and craftsmen', *Burlington* magazine, CXXVIII, August 1986, pp. 586-92.

Montagu, Lady Mary Wortley. Wharncliffe, Lord, ed., *The Letters and Works of Lady Mary Wortley Montagu*, standard edition, 2 vols., 1893.

Morel, Bernard, *The French Crown Jewels. The Objects of the Coronations of the Kings and Queens of France followed by a History of the French Crown Jewels from François I up to the Present Time*, trans. Elsie Callander, Margaret Curran, Agnes Hall, Antwerp, 1988.

B. Morris, 1978. Morris, Barbara, *Victorian Table Glass & Ornaments*, 1978.

Morris, *Diary*. Davenport, Beatrix Carey, ed., *A Diary of the*

French Revolution, by Gouverneur Morris, 1752-1816, Minister to France during the Terror, 2 vols., 1939.

Munn, 1984. Munn, Geoffrey C., *Castellani and Giuliano, Revivalist Jewellers of the Nineteenth Century*, 1984.

Nassau, K. and Crowningshield. Nassau, K. and J. [on Verneuil and synthetic stones]. See *Lapidary Journal*, 1969, pp. 114-9; 1971, pp. 1284-96, 1442-7; 1524-32.

Nayler, Sir George, Garter Principal King at Arms, etc., *The Coronation of His Most Sacred Majesty King George the Fourth, solemnized in the Collegiate Church of Saint Peter Westminster upon the nineteenth day of July 1821*, 1839.

Neville, Sylas, *Diary*. Cozens-Hardy, Basil, *The Diary of Sylas Neville, 1767-1788*, 1950.

Noble, Percy, *Anne Seymour Damer, A Woman of Art and Fashion, 1748-1828*, 1908.

Oman, Carola, *Ayot Rectory*, 1965.

Oman, Carola, *The Gascoyne Heiress. The Life and Diaries of Frances Mary Gascoyne-Cecil, 1802-39*, 1968.

Oman, 1974. Oman, Charles, *British Rings, 800-1914*, 1974.

Ormond, Richard, *Early Victorian Portraits*, National Portrait Gallery, 1973.

Ormond and Blackett-Ord. See Exhibitions, 1987-8, Winterhalter.

Lady Palmerston, *Letters*. Lever, Sir Tresham, *The Letters of Lady Palmerston*, 1957.

Papendiek, Mrs Charlotte Louisa Henrietta. Broughton, Mrs V. Delves, ed., *Court & Private Life in the Time of Queen Charlotte: being the journals of Mrs. Papendiek, reader etc. to Her Majesty*, 2 vols., 1887.

Paris, Musée du Louvre, De Laborde or Delaborde, Comte, *Notice des emaux, bijoux et objets divers exposes dans les galeries . . .*, 1852-3.

Parkes *Memoir. A Short Memoir of Alexander Parkes (1813-1890), Chemist and Inventor*, n.d. (copy in Science Museum Library).

Penzer, N.M., *Paul Storr, 1771-1844, Silversmith and Goldsmith*, 1954, new ed., 1971.

Petochi, 1981. Petochi, Domenico; Alfieri, Massimo; Branchetti, Maria Grazia, *I Mosaici Minuti Romani dei secoli XVIII e XIX*, Rome, 1981.

Piacenti, K.A., 'The Neoclassical Cameo', *Antiquità Viva*, Florence, 1972.

Planché, J.R., *Souvenir of the Bal Costumé given by Her Most Gracious Majesty Queen Victoria at Buckingham Palace, May 12th, 1842*, 1843.

Poniatowski, Prince Stanislas. *Catalogue des Pierres Gravées Antiques de S.A. le Prince Poniatowski*, Florence, 1832-3.

Lybbe Powys. Climenson, E.J., ed., *Passages from the Diaries of Mrs Philip Lybbe Powys of Hardwick House, Oxon, A.D. 1756 to 1808*, 1899.

Prendeville, James and Maginn, Dr, Photographic Facsimiles of the Antique Gems formerly possessed by the late Prince Poniatowski . . . 2 vols., 1859.

Prosser, R.B., 'Birmingham Inventions and Inventors'. Newspaper cuttings from the *Birmingham Weekly Post*, 1880, with manuscript notes by the author and manuscript correspondence relating to the work, 1880-83. Birmingham Reference Library (50 copies privately printed under the same title, Birmingham, 1881).

Pugin, *True Principles*. Pugin, Augustus Welby Northmore, *True Principles of Pointed or Christian Architecture*, 1841.

Pugin, A.W.N., *Glossary of Ecclesiastical Ornament and Costume,*

compiled and illustrated from antient authorities and examples. Faithfully translated by the Rev. Bernard Smith, 1844.

Raspe, R.E., *A Descriptive Catalogue of Ancient and Modern Engraved Gems*, 2 vols., 1791.

Rice, Patty C., *Amber, the Golden Gem of the Ages*, New York and Toronto, 1980.

Righetti, R., *Incisori di Gemme e Cammei in Roma del Rinascimento all' Ottocento*, Rome, 1952.

Righetti, R., *Gemme e Cammei delle collezioni communale, Cataloghi dei Musei Communali di Roma*, IV, Rome, 1955.

Riisøen, Thale and Bøe, Alf, *Om Filigran/Filigree, its Technique and history*, Oslo, 1959.

Roche, J.C., *The History, Development and Organisation of the Birmingham Jewellery and Allied Trades*, Birmingham [1927].

Romilly, *Memoirs. Memoirs of the Life of Sir Samuel Romilly, written by himself*, edited by his sons, 3 vols., 2 ed., 1840.

Rudoe. (See Tait, 1984.)

Ruskin. Cook, E.T., and Wedderburn, Alexander, eds., *The Works of John Ruskin*, Library Edition, 39 vols., 1903-12.

Sadleir, Michael, *Blessington-D'Orsay, A Masquerade*, 1933.

SCAM. (See London: House of Commons Parliamentary Papers.)

Scarisbrick, 1985. Scarisbrick, Diana, 'Henry Ellis, Exeter Goldsmith', *Antique Dealer & Collectors' Guide*, 38, July 1985, pp. 55-7.

Scarisbrick, 1986. Scarisbrick, Diana, 'The Devonshire Parure', *Archeologia*, 108, 1986, pp. 239-54.

Scarisbrick, Diana, *Ancestral Jewels*, 1989.

Schama, Simon, *Citizens, A Chronicle of the French Revolution*, 1989.

Schmidt, Eva, *Der Preussische Eisenkunstguss*, Berlin, 1981.

Seaby, Wilfrid A. and Hetherington, R.J., 'The Matthew Boulton Pattern Books', *Apollo*, 51, 1950, pp. 48-50 and 78-80.

Seaby, Wilfrid A., 'A Letter Book of Boulton and Fothergill, 1773', Parts I & II, *Apollo*, September 1951, pp. 83-6, 113-6.

Seidmann, 1985. Seidmann, Gertrud, 'An English gem-engraver's life: Nathaniel Merchant (1739-1816)', Society of Jewellery Historians, *Jewellery Studies*, 2, 1985, pp. 59-63.

Shaw, Henry, *The Encyclopaedia of Ornament*, 1842.

Shaw, Henry, *Dresses and Decorations of the Middle Ages from the Seventh to the Seventeenth Centuries*, 2 vols., 1843.

Shelley, *Diary*. Edgcumbe, Richard, ed., *The Diary of Frances Lady Shelley, 1787-1817*, 1912, reprinted 1913.

Smith, H. Clifford, *Jewellery*, 1908, reprinted East Ardsley, Wakefield, Yorkshire, 1973.

Spon, Ernest, *Workshop Receipts, for the use of manufacturers, mechanics, and scientific amateurs*, Series I, 1873, reissued 1875, 1890, etc., Series 2, by R. Haldane, Series 3, 4, by C.G.W. Lock.

Steingräber, Erich, *Alter Schmuck*, Munich, 1956. English version, *Antique Jewellery: its History in Europe from 800 to 1900*, 1957.

Streeter, Edwin W., *Pearls and the Pearling Life*, 1886.

Streeter, 1892. Streeter, Edwin W., *Precious Stones and Gems*, 5 ed., 1892.

Streeter, E.W., *Hints to Purchasers of Jewellery*, 8 ed., 1867.

Streeter, G. Skelton, 'The Ruby Mines of Burma', Society of Arts *Journal*, XXXVII, 1889, pp. 266-75.

Stuart, Dorothy Margaret, *Dearest Bess. The Life and Times of Lady Elizabeth Foster, afterwards Duchess of Devonshire*, 1955.

Surtees, 1975. Surtees, Virginia, *Charlotte Canning*, 1975.

Swann. *Catalogue of Shoe and other Buckles in Northampton Museum*, by June Swann, Northampton Borough Council Museums and Art Gallery, 1981.

Tait, I, 1984. Tait, Hugh, ed., *The Art of the Jeweller. A Catalogue of the Hull Grundy Gift to the British Museum: Jewellery, Engraved Gems and Goldsmiths' Work*, by Charlotte Gere, Judy Rudoe, Hugh Tait, Timothy Wilson, 2 vols., 1984.

A. & H. Tayler, *Stuart Papers*. Tayler, A. and H., *The Stuart Papers at Windsor*, 1939.

Taylor *Papers*. Taylor, Lieut.-Gen. Sir Herbert, *The Taylor Papers*, arranged by Ernest Taylor, 1913.

Taylor and Scarisbrick. (See Exhibitions, Oxford, Ashmolean Museum, 1978.)

Tescione, Giovanni, *Il Corallo nella storia e nell arte*, Naples, 1965.

Tescione, Giovanni, *The Italians and their Coral Fishing*, Naples, 1973.

Théophile prêtre et moine, *Essai sur Divers Arts*, publié par Comte Charles de l'Escalopier, Paris, 1843.

Theophilus, called also Rugerus, Priest and Monk, *An Essay upon Various Arts...* translated, with notes, by Robert Hendrie, 1847.

Theophilus, *De diversis artibus. The Various Arts*. Translated from the Latin with introduction and notes by C.R. Dodwell, 1961.

Thieme Becker. Thieme, U. and Becker, F., *Allgemeines Lexikon der Bildenden Künstler*, 37 vols., Leipzig, 1907-50.

Thomas, Cecil, 'Gem Engraving', Society of Arts *Journal*, LX, 1912, pp. 360-70.

Thomason, Sir Edward, *Memoirs during Half a Century*, 2 vols., 1845.

Thompson, Flora, *Lark Rise to Candleford*, 1845.

Thompson, J.M., ed., *English Witnesses of the French Revolution*, Oxford, 1938.

Timmins. 1866. See also Aitken; Wright. Timmins, Samuel, ed., *The Resources, Products, and Industrial History of Birmingham and the Midland Hardware District. A Series of Reports, collected by the Local Industries Committee of the British Association at Birmingham, in 1865*, 1866.

Truman, 1979. Truman, Charles, 'Reinhold Vasters — "the Last of the Goldsmiths?" ', *Connoisseur*, 200, 1979, pp. 154-61.

Twain, Mark, *The Innocents Abroad*, Hartford, Connecticut, 1869, reprinted Ontario, 1966.

Twining, 1960. Twining, Lord, *A History of the Crown Jewels of Europe*, 1960.

Tyas, the Rev. Robert, *The Sentiment of Flowers; or language of Flora*, [an adaptation of the *Langage des fleurs* of C. de la Tour], 1833, 2 ed., London/Edinburgh, 1837.

Vever, Henri, *La Bijouterie française au XIXe Siècle*, 3 vols., Paris, 1906-8 (reprinted Florence, n.d.).

Victoria, Queen, *Girlhood*, I. Esher, Viscount, ed., *The Girlhood of Queen Victoria. A Selection from Her Majesty's Diaries between the Years 1832 and 1840*, 2 vols., 1912.

Victoria, Queen, *Leaves from a Journal, 1855*, 1961.

Victoria, Queen, *Letters*. Benson, A.C. and Esher, Viscount, eds., *The Letters of Queen Victoria, A Selection from Her Majesty's Correspondence*, First Series, 1837-61, 1907. (See also Fulford, 1964.)

Wagner, P.A., *The Diamond Fields of Southern Africa*, Cape Town, 1971.

Walker, Richard, *Regency Portraits*, National Portrait Gallery, London, 2 vols., 1985.

Wallis in Beavan, 1876. (See Beavan.)

Ward, C.H. Dudley, *A Romance of the Nineteenth Century*, compiled from the Letters and Family Papers of Baliol, Viscount Esher, 1923.

Waring, J.B., ed., *Examples of Metal-work and Jewellery, selected from the Royal and other Collections*, 1857.

Warner, Marina, *Queen Victoria's Sketchbook*, 1979.

Watkins, John, *A Biographical Memoir of his late Royal Highness Frederick, Duke of York and Albany*, 1827.

Wedgwood, Alexandra, *A.W.N. Pugin and the Pugin Family*, one of the series, *Catalogues of Architectural Drawings in the Victoria and Albert Museum*, 1985.

Werlich, Robert, *Orders and Decorations*, Washington, 1965.

Westwood, Arthur (Assay Master, Birmingham), 'The Manufacture of Wrought Plate in Birmingham', a paper read to the Birmingham Archaeological Society, March 18th, 1904, reprinted...from the *Transactions* of the Society, Birmingham, 1904.

Wilkins, W.H., *Mrs. Fitzherbert and George IV*, 2 vols., 1905.

Woodforde, James, *The Diary of a Country Parson, 1758-1802*, 1 ed., 5 vols., 1924-31, single-vol. eds., 1935-1986.

Woodham-Smith, 1972. Woodham-Smith, Cecil, *Queen Victoria - Her Life and Times, I, 1819-1861*, 1972.

Woolf, *Autobiography*. Woolf, Leonard, *An Autobiography, I, 1880-1911*, paperback, 1980 (two vols. first published as *Sowing*, 1960 and *Growing*, 1961.

Wornum, R.N., *Analysis of Ornament*, 1856.

Wright, J.S., 'The Jewellery and Gilt Toy Trades'. (See Timmins, 1866, pp. 452-76.)

Wyatt, Matthew Digby, *Metalwork and its Artistic Design*, 1852. (See also London 1851 exhibition.)

Wynne, *Diaries*. Fremantle, Anne, ed., *The Wynne Diaries, 1789-1820*, 3 vols., 1935, 1937 and 1940.

Yogev, Gedalia, *Diamonds and Coral. Anglo-Dutch Jews and Eighteenth-century Trade*, Leicester, 1978.

Zick, Gisela, *Gedenke mein*, Dortmund, 1980.

EXHIBITIONS

Paris 1819 exhibition

Catalogue. *Catalogue indiquant le Nom des Fabricants, celui de leur Domicile et Département, avec la désignation sommaire des produits de leur Industrie*, 3 ed., Paris, 1819. *Exposition Publique des Produits de l'Industrie française au Palais du Louvre*, Année 1819, Paris, 1819.

Paris 1827 exhibition

Blanqui, Adolphe, *Histoire de L'Exposition des Produits de l'Industrie française en 1827*, Paris, 1827.

Paris 1844 exhibition

Burat, Jules, *Exposition de l'Industrie française année 1844. Description Méthodique*, 2 vols., Paris, 1844.

London, Society of Arts, 1847-9 exhibitions

A Catalogue of Select Specimens of British Manufactures and Decorative Art, exhibited at the Society of Arts, London, 1847. *A Catalogue of Specimens of Recent British Manufactures and Decorative Art...1848. A Catalogue of Specimens of Recent British Manufactures and Decorative Art...1849*.

London 1851 exhibition

Catalogue. *Great Exhibition of the Works of Industry of all Nations, 1851. Official Descriptive and Illustrated Catalogue*, 3 vols. + Supplementary Volume, 1851.

Manufacturers' prospectuses, Morel, Phillips Brothers, etc. Exhibition of the Works of Industry of All Nations, 1851. Prospectuses of Exhibitors, Vol. XV, Manufactures, Classes XXIII-XXVI. Collected under the authority of the Royal

Commissioners. Science Museum Library. Incomplete set, Victoria and Albert Museum Library.

Great Exhibition, 1851. Class 23. No. 97 *Catalogue of Articles exhibited by Hunt & Roskell (late Storr and Mortimer)*, 1851.

Reports. Exhibition of the Works of Industry of All Nations, 1851. Reports by the Juries, single vol. ed., 1852. Redgrave, Richard, 'Supplementary Report on Design', in *Reports*, pp. 708-49 (also published separately).

AJIC. The Industry of all Nations, 1851. The Art-Journal Illustrated Catalogue, published separately, 1851.

John Cassell's *Illustrated Exhibitor and Magazine of Art*, 2 vols., 1852.

Lectures. Tennant, Professor James, 'Gems and Precious Stones', *Lectures on the Results of the Great Exhibition of 1851*, Second Series, 1853, pp. 73-104.

Digby Wyatt. Wyatt, Matthew Digby, *The Industrial Arts of the XIX Century*, 2 vols., 1853.

French reports, VI, De Luynes. *Exposition Universelle de 1851. Travaux de la Commission Française sur l'Industrie des Nations*, VI, 1854, Classe 23, D'Albert, Duc de Luynes, 'Industrie des Métaux Précieux', pp. 1-262.

Dublin 1853 exhibition
Detailed catalogue. Sproule, John, ed., *The Irish Industrial Exhibition of 1853: A Detailed Catalogue of its Contents*, Dublin, 1854.

Reports. Reports by the Juries, Dublin, 1853.

AJIC. Art Journal illustrated catalogue, in *AJ*, 1853.

New York 1853 exhibition
Official Catalogue of the New York Exhibition of the Industry of All Nations, first revised ed., New York, 1853.

Wallis, *Report.* New York Industrial Exhibition, George Wallis, *Special Report*, 1854.

Paris 1855 exhibition
French reports, II, Fossin. *L'Exposition Universelle de Paris, 1855. Rapports du Jury*, II, 1856, Classe 17, Fossin, Jules, p. 909; see also pp. 915-26.

Visite. Visite à l'Exposition Universelle de Paris, en 1855, publiée sous la direction de H. Tresca, Paris, 1855.

English *Reports*, II, 1856. *Reports on the Paris Universal Exhibition*, 3 parts, 1856, Redgrave, Richard, 'On the Present State of Design applied to Manufactures, as shown in the Paris Universal Exhibition', II, pp. 313-410.

AJIC. Art Journal illustrated catalogue, in *AJ*, 1855. Wallis, George, 'The Artistic, Industrial and Commercial Results of the Universal Exhibition of 1855', II, pp. I-XX.

London 1851 and Paris 1855 exhibitions
Laboulaye, Charles, *Essai sur l'Art Industriel, comprenant l'Etude des Produits les plus célèbres de l'Industrie à toutes les Epoques, et des Oeuvres les plus remarquées à l'Exposition Universelle de Londres en 1851, et à l'Exposition de Paris en 1855*, Paris, 1856.

London 1858 exhibition
London, Science and Art Department of the Committee of Council on Education. Catalogue of the Exhibition of Works of Art-Manufacture designed or executed by Students of the Schools of Art . . . with an Introduction by George Wallis, 1858.

London 1862 exhibition
Catalogue. *The International Exhibition, 1862. The Illustrated Catalogue of the Industrial Department*, 4 vols., 1862.

Reports. International Exhibition, 1862. Reports by the Juries, 1863.

Hunt's Handbook. Hunt, Robert, *Handbook to the Industrial Department of the International Exhibition, 1862*, 2 vols., 1862.

Waring, J.B., *Masterpieces of Industrial Art and Sculpture at the International Exhibition, 1862*, 3 vols., 1863.

AJIC. Art Journal illustrated catalogue, 2 parts, usually bound in with *AJ*, 1862 and 1863.

CIFE. Cassell's Illustrated Family [Paper] Exhibitor, 1862.

French reports, VI, Fossin. *Exposition Universelle de Londres de 1862.* Chevalier, Michel, ed., *Rapports*, 13 vols., Paris 1862-4. VI, Classe 33, Fossin, Jules, 'Joaillerie, Bijouterie et Orfèvrerie', pp. 409-79.

Italian catalogue. *International Exhibition, 1862. Kingdom of Italy, Official Descriptive Catalogue*, 1862.

London 1864 North London Working Classes Industrial Exhibition
Agricultural Hall, Islington. *Catalogue*, 1864.

Dublin 1865 exhibition
Catalogue. *Illustrated Guide*, Dublin, 1865. *Dublin International Exhibition of Arts and Manufactures, 1865. Official Catalogue*, 4ed., Dublin, 1865.

Parkinson, H. and Simmonds, P.L., eds., *The Illustrated Record and Descriptive Catalogue of the Dublin International Exhibition of 1865*, London, Dublin, 1866.

Reports. Dublin International Exhibition of Arts and Manufactures, 1865. Reports of the Juries . . ., 2ed., revised, Dublin, 1865.

Italian catalogue. *Dublin International Exhibition, 1865. Kingdom of Italy. Official Catalogue*, 1 ed., Turin (1865), 2 ed., 1865.

Paris 1867 exhibition
Catalogue, Belgium (see *Complete Official Catalogue*, English version).

English catalogue. *Paris Universal Exhibition, 1867. Complete Official Catalogue, including the British and all other sections. English version, translated from the French Catalogue*, 2 ed., London and Paris, 1867.

French reports. *Exposition Universelle de 1867 à Paris.* Chevalier, Michel, ed., *Rapports du Jury Internationale*, 13 vols., Paris, IV, Classe 36, Fossin, Jules and Baugrand, Gustave, 'Joaillerie et Bijouterie', 1868, pp. 409-36.

Belgian Reports. *Exposition Universelle de Paris en 1867. Documents et Rapports*, II, Brussels, 1868, Classe 36, Romberg, Edouard, 'Joaillerie, Bijouterie', pp. 339-48.

English *Reports*, II, Maskelyne. *Reports on the Paris Universal Exhibition*, II, 1868, Class 36. Maskelyne, M.H.N. Story, 'Report on Jewellery and Precious Stones', pp. 593-620.

Workmen's *Reports. Modern Industries: a series of Reports on Industry and Manufactures as represented in the Paris Exposition in 1867. By Twelve British Workmen, visiting Paris under the auspices of the Paris Excursion Committee*, 1868. Rasmussen, P.A., Barnsbury, 'Gold and Silver Work', pp. 22-40.

Birmingham Artisans' *Reports. Report presented to the Council of the Birmingham Chamber of Commerce, on Manufactures of a similar Kind to those of Birmingham, as represented in the International Exhibition, held at Paris, 1867*, I, Aitken, W.C., Introduction, pp. 1-88. II, Deeley, W.G., 'Jewellery, with Diamonds and Precious Stones', pp. 36-47. Plampin, James, 'Jewellery and Gilt Toys', pp. 48-53.

AJIC. Art Journal illustrated catalogue, 2 parts, usually bound in *AJ*, 1867 and 1868.

London 1871 exhibition
Catalogue. *London International Exhibition of 1871. Catalogue*, 1871, Division I, Class II.

AJIC. Art Journal illustrated catalogue, bound in with *AJ*, 1871.

London 1872 exhibition
Reports. Reports on the London International Exhibition of 1872, 1872.

AJIC, bound in with *AJ*, 1872; Wallis, George, 'The International Exhibition, 1872', pp. 37-61.

London 1872 South Kensington Loan exhibition
Science and Art Department. South Kensington Museum. Catalogue of the Loan Exhibition of Ancient and Modern Jewellery and Personal Ornaments, 1 ed., 1872.

Vienna 1873 exhibition
French reports, II, Rouvenat and Fontenay. *Exposition Universelle de Vienne en 1873*. France, *Rapports*, II, Paris, 1875, Group VII, Rouvenat, L. and Fontenay, E., 'Objets d'or et d'argent, joaillerie, orfèvrerie, bijouterie', pp. 373-92.

Philadelphia 1876 exhibition
Reports and awards. *United States Centennial Commission International Exhibition, 1876*.
Walker, Francis A., ed., *Reports and Awards*, V, Group XXVII, Class 253, Jewelry, Philadelphia, 1877; Washington, 1880.
Catalogue of British section. *Great Britain. Executive Commission, Philadelphia Exhibition, 1876. Philadelphia International Exhibition, 1876: Official Catalogue of the British Section*, I, 1876.
Falize report. Falize fils, L., *Les Bijoux, l'Orfèvrerie et la Joaillerie à l'Exposition de 1876. Rapport présenté au Jury de l'Union Centrale des Beaux-Arts appliqués à l'Industrie*, Paris, 1877.

Paris 1878 exhibition
Belgian reports. *Rapports des Membres des Jurys, des Délegués et des Ouvriers sur l'Exposition Universelle de Paris en 1878*. Brussels, 1879, Classe 39, 'Rapport de M. André Narcisse, ouvrier bijoutier, chef d'atelier chez M. Teldonck, Bruxelles', pp. 540-6.
Bergerat, II. Bergerat, E., *Les Chefs- d'Oeuvre d'Art à l'Exposition Universelle, 1878*, 2 vols., Paris, 1878.
English *Reports*. *Paris Universal Exhibition, 1878. Report of Her Majesty's Commissioners...*II, 1880, Class 39, 'Jewellery and Precious Stones', pp. 225-7; *passim*.
Artisan *Reports*. *The Society of Arts, Artisan Reports on the Paris Universal Exhibition of 1878*, 1879, Class 39, Kirchoff, Edward, 'Report on Jewelry', pp. 465-72.
Italian reports, Castellani. Castellani, Alessandro, *Degli Ori, Dei Gioielli nella Esposizione di Parigi, del DCCCLXXVIII*, Rome, 1879.

London Inventions exhibition 1885
Catalogue. *International Inventions Exhibition, 1885. Official Catalogue*, 3 ed., 1885, Group XIX, p. 207.

Melbourne 1888-9 exhibition
Official Record. Official Record of the Centennial International Exhibition, Melbourne, 1888-1889, Melbourne, 1890.

London Arts and Crafts Exhibition Society 1888-1916
A & CE catalogues, 1888-1916. Catalogues, London, 1888, 1889, 1890, 1893, 1896, 1899, 1903, 1906, 1910, 1916.

Paris 1889 exhibition
French reports, Massin. Massin, O., *Exposition Universelle de 1889. Classe 37. Etude et Rapport. Techniques sur la Joaillerie*, Paris, 1890.

Paris 1900 exhibition
French reports. *Ministère du Commerce, de l'Industrie des Postes et des Télegraphes. Exposition Universelle Internationale de 1900 à Paris. Rapports du Jury International*, Paris, 1902. Groupe XV, Classe 94 (Orfèvrerie); Classe 95, Soufflot, Paul, 'Joaillerie et bijouterie', pp. 357-401.
Saunier. Saunier, Charles, 'La Bijouterie et la Joaillerie à l'Exposition Universelle', *Revue des Arts Décoratifs (RAD)*, XXI, 1901, pp. 17-30, 73-97.

London 1952-3
Victoria and Albert Museum. *Exhibition of Victorian and Edwardian Decorative Arts Catalogue*, 1952.

London 1972
Iveagh Bequest, Kenwood. *Lady Hamilton in relation to the Art of her Time*, catalogue, Arts Council/Greater London Council exhibition at the Iveagh Bequest, Kenwood, July-October, 1972.

Paris 1972 exhibition
Musée du Louvre. *Le Neo-classicisme, Dessins français de 1750-1825*, catalogue, Paris, Musée du Louvre, 1972.

Birmingham 1973
Birmingham Gold and Silver, 1773-1973. An exhibition celebrating the Bicentenary of the Assay Office, catalogue, July-September 1973, City Museum and Art Gallery, Birmingham.

London and Oxford 1978
Finger Rings from Ancient Egypt to the Present Day. Catalogue by Gerald Taylor, introduction by Diana Scarisbrick. Goldsmiths' Hall, London and the Ashmolean Museum, Oxford. July-September, 1978.

London 1979-80
National Portrait Gallery. *Sir Thomas Lawrence, 1769-1830*, November 1979-March 1990. Catalogue by Michael Levey, 1979.

London 1980-1
Victoria and Albert Museum. *Princely Magnificence. Court Jewels of the Renaissance, 1500-1630*, Victoria and Albert Museum, October 1980-February 1981. Exhibition organised by A. Somers Cocks and catalogued by her and others.

London and Paris 1987-8
Franz Xaver Winterhalter and the Courts of Europe, 1830-70. Catalogue by Richard Ormond and Carol Blackett-Ord, etc. National Portrait Gallery, October 1987-January 1988 and at the Petit Palais, Paris, February-May 1988.

London 1989
Christie's. *The Glory of the Goldsmith, Magnificent Gold and Silver from the Al-Tajir Collection*, Christie's, 1989, catalogue by Charles Truman, Preface by Philippa Glanville.

New York 1989-90
Metropolitan Museum of Art. Le Bourhis, Katell, gen. ed., *The Age of Napoleon: Costume from Revolution to Empire, 1789-1815*, New York, 1989, published in conjunction, with the exhibition, December 1989-April 1990. Le Corbeiller, Clare, 'Jewels of the Empire', pp. 118-33.

NOVELS, DRAMA, OPERAS, etc.

Austen, Jane, *Sense and Sensibility*, 1811.
Austen, Jane, *Mansfield Park*, 1814.
Bellini, Vincenzo, *Norma*, 1831
Blessington, Lady, *The Belle of the Season: A Poem*, 1839.
Dickens, Charles, *Dombey and Son*, 1848.
Dickens, Charles, *Great Expectations*, 1860-1.
Disraeli, Benjamin, *Coningsby; or, the New Generation*, 1844.
Donizetti, Gaetano, *Don Pasquale*, c.1842.
Goldsmith, Oliver, *She Stoops to Conquer*, 1773.
Kreitman, Esther, *Deborah*, Warsaw, 1936, London, 1946.
La Motte-Fouqué, Friedrich, Baron von, *Undine*, 1814 + .
Owenson, Sydney, *The Wild Irish Girl*, 1806.
Schiller, Heinrich von, *Maria Stuart*, 1800.
Scott, Sir Walter, *Anne of Geierstein*, 1829.
Shakespeare, William, *As You Like It*, 1599 (first printed in the

folio of 1623).

Shakespeare, William, *The Tempest*, c.1611.

Thackeray, William Makepeace, *The History of Pendennis*, 1848-50.

Yonge, Charlotte, *The Clever Woman*, 1865.

PERIODICALS AND PATTERN-BOOKS

Magazines of social life and fashions, jewellers' trade journals and relevant publications and periodicals (single articles in other periodicals cited in the footnotes have been excluded).

AR. (Rudolph) *Ackermann's Repository of Arts, Literature, Commerce, Manufactures, Fashion and Politics*, 1809-29.

Annual Register, 1758-.

Apollo, 1925-.

Archaeological Journal, 1844-.

At. The *Artist*, 1897-1902, successor to *The Artist and Journal of Home Culture*, 1880-94 and *The Artist, Photographer and Decorator*, 1895-6.

AJ. See *AuJ.*

AuJ, AJ. Art-Union *Journal*, 1839-48, succeeded by *Art Journal*, 1849-1912.

BA. Belle Assemblée or *Bell's Court and Fashionable Magazine*, 1806-32, then the *Court Magazine and Belle Assemblée (and Monthly Critic)*, 1832-48. Then united with the *Lady's Magazine*, etc.

BLM, Blackwood's Lady's Magazine, 1836-60.

CL. Country Life, 1897-.

CM/CM & BA. Court Magazine. See *Belle Assemblée*.

Feuchère, Léon. *L'Art Industriel*, Paris and New York, 1839-48.

F. [*Le*] *Follet, Journal du Grand Monde, Fashion, Polite Literature, Beaux Arts* (etc.). Paris/London co-edition, 1846-July 1900.

Galerie des Modes et des Costumes Françoises, Paris, 1778-87 (extended sets of fashion plates, some republished in England).

G. Heideloff, Niklaus von, *Gallery of Fashion, 1794-1803.*

IA, 1877. *Industrial Art*, 1877-8.

ILN. Illustrated London News, May 1842-.

Jeweller, I, 1868. The *Jeweller*, 1868-9.

JG & WM MM. Jewellers, Goldsmiths, [Silversmiths] and Watchmakers Monthly Magazine, 1862-3.

Jones, Owen and Goury, Jules, *Plans, Elevations, Sections and Details of the Alhambra*, 1842-45.

Jones, Owen, *Grammar of Ornament*, 1856.

JD. Journal des Dames et des Modes (Paris 1797-1837), Frankfurt ed., 1798-1848.

Journal des Luxus und der Moden (*Journal der Moden*, Weimar 1786), 1787-1813 (continued as *Journal für Literatur, Kunst, Luxus und Mode*, 1814-26).

Journal of Acetylene Gas Lighting, 1897-1903.

J of D. Journal of Design and Manufactures, 1849-52.

Jullienne, Eugène, *L'Ornemaniste des Arts Industriels. Recueil complet de tous les styles d'ornements...*, Paris, 1840.

Knight's Scroll Ornaments. Designed for the use of Silversmiths, Chasers, Die-Sinkers, Modellers, etc. etc., F. Knight, c.1825-30.

Knight's Vases and Ornaments. Designed for the use of Architects, Silversmiths, Jewellers, Modellers, Chasers, Die-Sinkers, Founders, Carvers and All Ornamental Manufactures, F. Knight, vol. 2, 1833.

Knight's Unique Fancy Ornaments, F. Knight, 1834-5.

Knight's Gem and Device Book, F. Knight, new ed., 1836.

LC. Ladies' Cabinet of Fashion, Music, and Romance, ed. Margaret Beatrice de Courcy, etc., 1832-70. From July 1852 also issued as the *Ladies' Companion at home and abroad* and the *New Monthly Belle Assemblée*.

LM. See also the *Lady's Monthly Museum*. *Ladies' Museum*, 1829-32 (then united with the *Lady's Magazine and Museum of Belles Lettres*, 1832-7. Then with the *Court Magazine*, 1838-47.

LMM. Lady's Monthly Museum or, Polite Repository of Amusement and Instruction. By a Society of Ladies, 1798-1828. Continued as the *Ladies' Museum*, 1829-32.

London, Society of Jewellery Historians. *Jewellery Studies*, 1984-.

Myra's Threepenny Journal of Dress and Fashion, 1882-90.

Petit Courrier des Dames, Paris, 1822-8, subsequently revived.

Peyre, Jules, *Orfèvrerie, Bijouteries, Nielles, Armoiries, et Objets d'Art divers*, Paris, 1844.

Polytechnic Journal. A Monthly Magazine of Art, etc., 1839-45.

Q. The *Queen, the Lady's Newspaper*, 1861- (later absorbed by Harper's).

RAD. Revue des Arts Décoratifs, Paris, 1880-1902.

SA. Abstract of Proceedings, 1845. Society for the Encouragement of Arts, Manufactures, and Commerce, *Abstract of Proceedings and Transactions*, etc., 1845.

SA J. Society for the Encouragement of Arts, Manufactures and Commerce, *Journal*, 1852-.

SA Transactions, Supplement, 1852. *Transactions* of the Society for the Encouragement of Arts, Manufactures and Commerce, Supplemental volume, 1852.

Sp. Sphere, 1900-64.

S. The *Studio, An Illustrated Magazine of Fine and Applied Art*, 1893-1968 (later *Studio International*).

Winter, *Pattern-book.* Winter, Charles, *Pattern-Book for Jewellers, Goldsmiths and other Ornamentmakers*, c.1825-30.

WF. The *World of Fashion and Continental Feuilletons dedicated to High Life, Fashionables, Fashions, Polite Literature... of All Nations*, 1824-51. Then the *Ladies' Monthly Magazine*, 1852-79, then *Le Monde Elégant*, 1880-91.

SALE CATALOGUES, EARLY NINETEENTH CENTURY

(The Christie and Sotheby catalogues cited in footnotes are excluded here, as the dates given make them easily traceable.)

Hamlet Sale Catalogue, 1834. A Catalogue of the First Portion of Mr. Hamlet's Rare, Sumptuous, and Beautiful Jewels and Plate...which by Direction of Mr. Hamlet...Will be Sold by Auction by Messrs. E. Foster and Son...Princes Street,...On Monday, 25th of August, 1834...and Six following Days, Saturday and Sunday Excepted.

Poniatowski, 1839. A Catalogue of the Very Celebrated Collection of Antique Gems, of the Prince Poniatowski, Deceased. Christie & Manson, 29 April, 1839.

DIRECTORIES AND HANDBOOKS

The principal sources of the directories cited in the text and footnotes are the Guildhall Library (the most comprehensive holdings), the Victoria and Albert Museum Library, the Birmingham Central Reference Library and the Birmingham Assay Office. The publication cited below, the *Handbook to Birmingham*, 1886, is a worthy successor to Timmins.

Handbook to Birmingham, Birmingham 1886. Woodward, C.J., 'Manufacturing Industries', pp. 152-8. Bragg, John, 'The Jewellery Trade' [post 1865], pp. 187-91.

Index